Freemasonry & the Enlightenment

Architecture, Symbols, & Influences

By the same Author

Spas, Wells, & Pleasure-Gardens of London (London: Historical Publications Ltd., 2010)

Victorian Architecture: Diversity & Invention (Reading: Spire Books Ltd., 2007).

A Dictionary of Architecture and Landscape Architecture (Oxford: Oxford University Press, 2006).

The Egyptian Revival: Ancient Egypt as the Inspiration for Design Motifs in the West (London & New York: Routledge, Taylor & Francis Group, 2005).

Piety Proclaimed. An Introduction to Places of Worship in Victorian England (London: Historical Publications, Ltd., 2002).

Kensal Green Cemetery. The Origins & Development of the General Cemetery of All Souls, Kensal Green, London, 1824-2001 (Edited) (Chichester: Phillimore & Co. Ltd., 2001).

The Honourable The Irish Society 1608-2000 and the Plantation of Ulster. The City of London and the Colonisation of County Londonderry in the Province of Ulster in Ireland. A History and Critique (Chichester: Phillimore & Co. Ltd., 2000).

The Victorian Celebration of Death (Thrupp, Stroud: Sutton Publishing Ltd., 2000, 2004).

The Art and Architecture of Freemasonry. An Introductory Study (London: B. T. Batsford, Ltd., 1991, 2002, & Woodstock & New York: The Overlook Press, 1993, 2002 – Winner of the Sir Banister Fletcher Award for Best Book of the Year, 1992).

The Londonderry Plantation 1609-1914. The History, Architecture, and Planning of the Estates of the City of London and its Livery Companies in Ulster (Chichester: Phillimore & Co. Ltd., 1986).

The Life and Work of Henry Roberts (1803-76), Architect. The Evangelical Conscience and the Campaign for Model Housing and Healthy Nations (Chichester: Phillimore & Co. Ltd., 1983).

Freemasonry & the Enlightenment
Architecture, Symbols, & Influences

JAMES STEVENS CURL

with a Preface by Andrew Prescott

First published 2011

By Historical Publications Ltd
32 Ellington Street, London N7 8PL
(Tel: 020 7607 1628)
(website historicalpublications.co.uk)

© James Stevens Curl
The moral right of the author has been asserted
All rights reserved; unauthorised duplication contravenes applicable laws

ISBN 978-1-905286-45-4
British Library Cataloguing-in-Publication Data
A catalogue record for this book is available from the British Library

Designed and typeset by Two Plus George Ltd
25 Warren Way, Barnham, West Sussex PO22 0JX
(Tel: 01243 554444)

Printed in China by South China Printing Company

In Memoriam

JCWTSM

whose works illuminated many lives

'*Tod und Verzweiflung war sein Lohn.*'[1]

'The allegories that veil freemasonry, as also the symbols that illustrate it, are…
drawn from the lore of architecture and building.'
BERNARD EDWARD JONES (1879-1965):
Freemasons' Guide and Compendium (London: Harrap Ltd., 1956) 19.

---

1 Death and Despair were his Reward.

Contents

List of Subscribers	ix
List of Illustrations	xi
Preface (by Professor Andrew Prescott)	xv
Acknowledgements	xix
Introduction	xxiii

CHAPTER I
What is Freemasonry 1?   1
Introduction; Freemasons 1; Freemasons 2; Freemasons 3; Epilogue

CHAPTER II
What is Freemasonry 2? The Emergence of 'Non-Operative' or 'Speculative' Freemasonry   18
Introduction; Architecture, Geometry, and Masonry; Guilds, Fraternities, Chantries, and Religious Observance; The Scottish Dimension; Royal and other Connections

CHAPTER III
Hermeticism, Memory, Legends, and Syncretism   33
The Hermetic Tradition; Mnemonic Techniques; The Hiramic and Other Legends; Syncretism and Mysteries; Concluding Remarks

CHAPTER IV
Early Artefacts, Jacobites, and Hanoverians   55
Introduction; Visible Evidence of Early Freemasonry in Scotland; England, Scotland, Jacobites, and Hanoverians; The Two Pillars or Columns

CHAPTER V
The Great Prototype   71
Introduction: The Jewish Temple; The Decline and Destruction of Solomon's Temple; Zerubbabel's Temple; The Herodian Temple; Representations of the Temple; Fischer von Erlach; The Case of the Karlskirche; The Spiral Columns; Afterword: Into the Abyss

CHAPTER VI
Lodges, Designs, Architecture, and Symbols   97
Introduction; The Lodge; Tracing-Boards; Women and Freemasonry, Papal Disapproval, and Mopses; Certificates and Architectural Elements; Freemasons' Hall in London; Other Masonic Buildings; Epilogue

CHAPTER VII
Freemasonry, Neo-Classicism, Egyptian Rites, and Problems with the Enlightenment 141
Introduction; Freemasonry In Europe; Freemasonry and Neo-Classicism; Freemasonry and Egyptian Elements in Neo-Classical Architecture; Ledoux and Lequeu; Conclusion

CHAPTER VIII
Elysian Fields and Garden Transformations 175
Introduction; The Eighteenth-Century Landscape, Politics, and Meaning; The 'Graveyard Poets'; The International Significance of Night Thoughts; *Narcissa's Burial; The Arcadian Landscape and the Tomb; Burial and Commemoration in Gardens: The Emergence of the Cemetery; The Landscape Garden and Freemasonry; Fabriques; Hadrian's Villa at Tivoli; Some Other Significant Gardens*

CHAPTER IX
Landscapes, Allusions, and Meanings 204
Introduction; Wörlitz; Arkadia; The Garden of Allusions at Arkadia Considered; Schwetzingen; Conclusion

CHAPTER X
Mozart and Freemasonry 246
Introduction; Mozart's First Associations with the Craft; Later Developments; Die Zauberflöte, *Freemasonic Opera?; The Music and the Libretto; Stage-Sets and Egyptian Architecture; Epilogue*

CHAPTER XI
Conclusion 281
Monuments and Mausolea; Cemeteries; Opposition and Attacks; The Case of 'Greek' Thomson; Is there a Masonic Style?; Epilogue

Select Glossary of Terms 307
Select Bibliography 322
Index 347

List of Subscribers

E John T Acaster
Robert Adam
John-Adrian
Regina Akel
Frank Albo
Quentin Alder & Sarah Whittingham
Richard B Aldrich
Tom Allen RIBA
Nicholas Allen RIBA
Jan Anderson
Nigel Anderson
John F Ashby
John Ashdown
Professor Sir George Bain
Dr G M Barnes
Alex Barrow
Edward M Batley
Terence Bendixson
Glenn Benson
Mr and Mrs D Bigger
Philip Billingsley
J K Birksted
David Bjelajac
Ken Blackhurst
Roger Bowdler
J H Bowman
Sheilah Bradley
Geoff Brandwood
Timothy Brittain-Catlin
Alan C Brodrick
Rindert Brouwer
Cathie Bryan
Anthony Burrell
Anthony R Cartwright
Erik Cattermole
F Downs Cawley
Ernest Chaloner
Edward Chaney
Katy Cigno
David Clarke
Professor L A Clarkson
Colonial Williamsburg Foundation
Mr G C Cookson and Mr P Henry
Robert L D Cooper
The Lord Cormack FSA
Giovanna Lucia Costantini

Roger Cowles
Maxwell Craven
T Cribb and Sons
J Patricia Crichton (Mrs)
Stephen Croad
Andrew Crockart
Curt DiCamillo
Patricia Douglas
Henry Mansell Duckett
Ronald Dudley
Patrick Duerden
Sir James Dunbar-Nasmith
Viscount Dunluce
Dr K F Dunn
John Dyson
John Earl
Roland Easson
Edinburgh World Heritage
Lisbeth Ehlers
Lucas Elkin
Audrey Emerson
Avram Engel
Siegfried Engelmann
Sheila Fallon *née* Curl
Elizabeth Faulks
Dr and Mrs Ian Field
Robyn Hand Firth
John Fitzgerald
M H Ford
Dr Jenny Freeman
Robert Freidus
Dr Terry Friedman
Friends of Southampton Old Cemetery
Robert M Galea-Naudi
David Garnett
Dr A L Gibbs
Joscelyn Godwin
Roslyn Goldfarb
Grand Lodge of Scotland
Patrizia Granziera
Beau Greville
Brooke Greville
René Greville
Brendan Grimes
Leslie Grout
Dr Ivan Hall

Dr Gottfried Hamernik
Penelope Harris
Terence Haunch
Cedric Helsby-Proffit
George Henderson
Mrs Desmond Hill
Adrian J Hill
Desmond Hodges OBE and Margaret Hodges
Dan Holden
L J Holman
J St Brioc Hooper
Patrick, The Horsbrugh of Horsbrugh
Deborah Howard
Mark Phillip Howell
Professor William Hughes
A W Humphreys
Peter Hunter
Professor Brian Hurwitz and Dr Ruth Richardson
Eleanor and Peter Inch
Prof Dorota Iwaniec
Michael J S Jacobs
Mr and Mrs Richard Jay
Julian Jeffs
Hubert Charles Johnson
Ian Johnson
Mark Johnson-Watts
Ruth Johnston
Stephen Johnston
Stephen Jones
Gerald and Susan Kagan
E B Keeling
Josephine Marie Theodora Keller-Herder
Dr Georg Friedrich Kempter
Lorna Kennedy
John Knorr
Colin and Karen Latimer
John Law
Imre and Janet Leader
Professor Paul van der Lem
The Library and Museum of Freemasonry London
Dr Julian W S Litten
The London Library
Dr Lutz Luithlen

Neil and Jane McClure
Denis and Jill McCoy
John McDowell
John McGurk
David John McIntyre
Charles McKean
Harvey Macmillan
W Lawrence McMinn
David C Mander
Geoffrey Middleton
John Milbank
Margaret M Miles
Paul Millar RIBA
Stratton Mills
Clive R Moore
Jeffrey Morgan and Patricia Craig
Kathryn Morrison
Robert Moulder
Professor Timothy Mowl
Silvia Muschiol
Timothy Neville-Lee
Lord Northampton
Turlough O'Brien
Liam O'Connor
David Openshaw
Hippolyte O'Toole
William Pesson
Peterhouse, Cambridge
H Petter
David B Pettigrew
John L Phibbs
J Peter Phillips
John Physick CBE FSA
Denis Piggot

Prof Jack Pinkerton
Ricky C Pound
Robin Price
Godfrey Pringle
Maurice Regan
W N B Richardson DL
David Ridgeway
Derek Spencer Rogers
Pierre de la Ruffinière du Prey
Harriet Sandvall
Percival Scattergoode
Reinhard W Schmidt
Dr Brian G Scott
Professor Vincent and Mrs Karen Shacklock
David Shalit
David M V Short
Erica Simpson
John Simpson
Sir John Soane's Museum
Jan Smaczny
Ronnie Smartt
Barry S Smith
Brian Smith
Prof Dr J A M Snoek
Prof Georg Solms
Arthur Spencer
Emeritus Professor J Spencer
Bro Michael J Spencer
Gavin Stamp
Robert Stephenson
Mary McKinney Stevenson
Michael Stirton
C M Stoddart
T L Sudway FRICS

Professor Peter Swallow
Donald Henry Sykes
Michael Symes
Leanne Targett-Parker
Charles Taylor
Michael Taylor
Mr and Mrs Paul Teesdale
Peter Thomas
Mrs Joan Thompson
W E Thompson
Mary Thorp
Graham Tite MA Cantab MSc IHBC
Denis Tuohy
Eskdale Turner
Roger Turner
Cedric Unsworth
Henry Vivian-Neal
Professor Emeritus David M Walker
Julia Walton
Peter Walton
Professor David Watkin
Angus Gavin Watson
Trevor F Wellings
Mr and Mrs Adam Wilkinson
Christopher John Harries Williams
Martin Williams and Gillian Darby
Mr and Mrs Hal Wilson
Professor John Wilton-Ely
Ron Woollacott MBE FRSA
The Worshipful Company of Chartered Architects
David Wylde Architect
Rory Young
Count Adam Zamoyski

List of Illustrations

Sources are given in parentheses at the end of each caption, with the abbreviated form of the publication or collection indicated in either the caption or the source within the brackets. Abbreviations indicate the collection or collections from which the images derive, with the reference-number or shelf-mark after the abbreviation. Many illustrations are reproduced from Curl (1991d), but the original collections which supplied them are again acknowledged for the benefit of scholars. The key to abbreviations is given as follows:

AC	*Architecture Civile*	MC	© Martin Charles
AF	© Andreas Förderer	MNA	© *Muzeum w Nieborowie i Arkadii*
AFK	The late Anthony F. Kersting	MVP	© *Photothèques des Musées de la Ville de Paris*
BAL	© The Bridgeman Art Library	NB	Collections held in the Palace of Nieborów
BH	© Bernd Hausner	NGC	© National Gallery of Canada
BL	© British Library, London	NMR	Reproduced by Permission of English Heritage. National Monuments Record
BN	© *Bibliothèque Nationale*, Paris		
BO	© Bodleian Library, University of Oxford	PK	© Peter Kühn
CE	*Cabinet des Estampes, Bibliothèque Nationale*, Paris	RA	© Reinhard Alex, Wörlitz
		RCAHMS	© Royal Commission on the Ancient and Historical Monuments of Scotland
C-HM	Cooper-Hewitt Museum, the Smithsonian Institution's National Museum of Design		
CIA	© The Courtauld Institute of Art, London	RIBA	Reproduced by courtesy of the Royal Institute of British Architects Library Drawings Collection
CL	© Conway Library		
Collection JSC	Collection James Stevens Curl	RPS	*Regierungspräsidium*, Stuttgart
DO	Dumbarton Oaks	SAL	Society of Antiquaries of London
DT	*Deutsches Theatermuseum*, Munich, *Früher Clara Ziegler-Stiftung*	SGD	© *Staatliche Galerie*, Dessau
		SJSM	By courtesy of the Trustees of Sir John Soane's Museum, London
EH	© English Heritage. National Monuments Record		
GG	© Guy Gravett 1978	SMB	*Staatliche Museen zu Berlin*
GLCL	© Guildhall Library, City of London	Thiele	C. F. Thiele (1823): *Decoration auf den beiden Königlichen Theatern in Berlin* (Berlin: C. F. Thiele)
GLFI	© Image reproduced by permission of The Grand Lodge of Freemasons of Ireland		
		TMK	© *Theatermuseum des Instituts für Theaterwissenschaft der Universität Köln*
HU	© Trustees for Harvard University		
JSC	© James Stevens Curl	UGLE	By permission of the United Grand Lodge of England
KMH	© *Kurpfälzisches Museum*, Heidelberg	Wörlitz	*Staatliche Schlösser und Gärten Wörlitz*, Oranienbaum, Luisium, Anhalt-Dessau, Germany
KuSdZ	*Kupferstichkabinett und Sammlung der Zeichnungen*		
LAD	© *Landesamt für Denkmalpflege*	WP	Włodzimierz Piwkowski, or kindly supplied by him
LMA	City of London, London Metropolitan Archives		

LIST OF COLOUR PLATES

The Colour Plates are prefaced by **CPl.** (singular) or **CPls.** (plural), followed by the Chapter-number in Roman numerals, followed by the number of the Plate (also in Roman numerals) in each Chapter.

Int.I	Portrait of Sir John Soane in Masonic Regalia	xxv	VI.X	English Apron of *c*.1813	111
I.I	Building of the Tower of Babel with Masons and Lodge	14	VI.XI	Brooch made by French prisoners-of-war	111
			VI.XII	*Papier-mâché* snuff-box	111
I.II	Rebuilding of the Abbey at Vézelay with Masons and Lodge	15	VI.XIII	Meissen group with Pug	118
			VI.XIV	Female figure with Pug	118
I.III	Rebuilding of the Basilica of St Denis with Masons and Lodge	15	VI.XV	Pug-dog	118
			VI.XVI	Silver medal struck to commemorate the raising of subscriptions for Freemasons' Hall	123
III.I	Panorama of the *Hortus Palatinus* at Heidelberg	36			
V.I	Charney's Vision of the Temple	95	VI.XVII	*Freemasons' Tavern* as rebuilt 1786-9	124
VI.I	Board showing Masonic symbols	106	VI.XVIII	Gandy's Perspective of Soane's Council Chamber in daylight	126
VI.II	Plate with Masonic symbols	108			
VI.III	Plaque made by French prisoners-of-war	108	VI.XIX	Gandy's Perspective of Soane's Council Chamber in the evening	127
VI.IV	Masonic toast-rack	108			
VI.V	Ceremonial 'tools' of the First Degree	109	VI.XX	Egyptianising Chapter Room in Edinburgh	137
VI.VI	Ceremonial 'tools' of the Second Degree	109	VI.XXI	Royal Arch Chapter Room, Freemasons' Hall, Molesworth Street, Dublin	139
VI.VII	Ceremonial 'tools' of the Third Degree	109			
VI.VIII	Lewis suspended from tripod	109	VI.XXII	Exterior of Freemasons' Hall, Molesworth Street, Dublin	140
VI.IX	'A Free-Mason Form'd out of the Materials of his Lodge'	110	VII.I	The Trials by Fire, Water, and Air by Lequeu	165

VIII.I	Arcadian Shepherds by Nicolas Poussin	180
IX.I	Gothic House at Wörlitz	213
IX.II	Princess Helena Radziwiłłowa	214
IX.III	Plan of Arkadia	219
IX.IV	Loggia at The High Priest's Sanctuary, Arkadia	221
IX.V	Portico of the Temple of Diana at Arkadia	222
IX.VI	'Roman Aqueduct' at Arkadia	225
IX.VII	Design for Tomb of Illusions at Arkadia	226
IX.VIII	Remains of *spina* of Circus at Arkadia	227
IX.IX	Design for entrance to Circus at Arkadia	228
IX.X	Anna Karolina Orzelska with Pug	230
IX.XI	Plan of the Gardens at Schwetzingen	231
IX.XII	View of the Gardens at Schwetzingen	232
IX.XIII	View from the Bath-House at Schwetzingen	234
IX.XIV	Water-spouting birds at Schwetzingen	234
IX.XV	'End of the World' at Schwetzingen	234
IX.XVI	'Roman Water-Fort', Obelisk, and Aqueduct at Schwetzingen	235
IX.XVII	Temple of Apollo at Schwetzingen	236
IX.XVIII	Botanic Temple at Schwetzingen	236
IX.XIX	'Ruined' Temple of Mercury at Schwetzingen	238
IX.XX	'Mosque' at Schwetzingen	239
IX.XXI	Five-pointed star on the 'Mosque' at Schwetzingen	239
IX.XXII	Interior of 'Mosque' at Schwetzingen	240
IX.XXIII	Interior of cloister-walk around the 'Turkish Garden' at Schwetzingen	241
IX.XXIV	Corner-pavilion and part of the cloister at Schwetzingen	242
X.I	Viennese Lodge, probably *Zur gekrönten Hoffnung*, with Mozart present	261
X.II	Inauguration of Robert Burns as Poet Laureate of the Lodge Canongate Kilwinning	262
X.III	Schinkel's design for Act I, Scene 1, of *Die Zauberflöte*	269
X.IV	Schinkel's design for Act I, Scene 6, of *Die Zauberflöte*	270
X.V	Schinkel's design for Act I, Scene 15, of *Die Zauberflöte*	270
X.VI	Schinkel's design for Act II, Scene 1, of *Die Zauberflöte*	272
X.VII	Schinkel's design for Act II, Scene 8, of *Die Zauberflöte*	272
X.VIII	Schinkel's design for Act II, Scene 20, of *Die Zauberflöte*	273
X.IX	Schinkel's design for Act II, Scene 31, of *Die Zauberflöte*	273
X.X	Schinkel's design for the Closing Scene of *Die Zauberflöte*	274
X.XI	Schinkel's design for Act I, Scene 2, of *Olimpia*	275
X.XII	Schinkel's design for Act III, penultimate scene, of *Olimpia*	276
XI.I	Front cover of French pamphlet exposing the names of French Deputies and Senators who were Freemasons (1934)	294
XI.II	French anti-Masonic and anti-Semitic poster of 1941	295
XI.III	'Judéo-Ploutocratie et Bolchévisme' 1943	295
XI.IV-VI	Cast-iron capitals in St Vincent Street Church, Glasgow, perhaps alluding to 'Semitic Orders' and the Temple of Solomon	298
XI.VII	HRH the Prince of Wales as Grand Master	305

LIST OF PLATES

The Plates are prefaced by **Pl.** (singular) or **Pls.** (plural), followed by the Chapter-number in Roman numerals, followed by the number of the Plate (in Arabic numerals) in each Chapter.

I.1	Construction of the Abbey-Church of Schönau, with building-works and Lodge	13
II.1	Monument of William Schaw in Dunfermline Abbey	29
III.1	Title-page of *Hortus Palatinus*	37
III.2	Foundation of the Royal Order of the Free Masons in Palestine A.M. 4037	44
III.3	Labyrinth in Chartres Cathedral	50
III.4	Labyrinth in Rheims Cathedral	51
IV.1	Obelisk-sundial at Mount Stuart, Bute	57
IV.2	Obelisk-sundial at Tongue, Sutherland	57
IV.3	Lectern-sundials from Woodhouselee, Midlothian	58
IV.4	Lectern-sundials from Neidpath Castle, Peeblesshire	58
IV.5	Lectern-sundial from Lamancha House, Peeblesshire	58
IV.6	Multi-faceted sundial from Haddington, East Lothian	58
IV.7	Sundial from Newbattle Abbey, Midlothian	59
IV.8	Layout of a Lodge from *The Three Distinct Knocks*	67
IV.9	Jachin and Boaz, Würzburg	68
V.1	Moses Ben Maimon's plan of the Temple	77
V.2	Koberger's printed version of Nicolaus de Lyra's reconstruction of the Temple	78
V.3	Versions of Vatablus's Temple	79
V.4	Hafenreffer's version of the Temple	80
V.5	Villalpando's plan of the Temple and precincts from Lamy	81
V.6	Detail of Villalpando's plan of the Temple	82
V.7	Plan of Escorial and view from North	82
V.8	Plan of Temple by Constantinus l'Empereur	83
V.9	Inner courtyard of the Temple by Jan Lukyen	83
V.10	Merian's view of the Temple	84
V.11	Wood's plan of Solomon's Temple	84
V.12	Lamy's reconstruction of the Temple	85
V.13	Lamy's reconstruction of the Temple	85
V.14	Lamy's reconstruction of the Temple	85
V.15	Lamy's reconstruction of the Temple	86
V.16	Fischer von Erlach's version of Villalpando's Temple of Solomon	87
V.17	Plan of the *Karlskirche* in Vienna	88
V.18	West front of the *Karlskirche*	89
V.19	South façade of the *Karlskirche*	89
V.20	Section through the *Karlskirche*	89
V.21	The Temple by Heemskerck	89
V.22	Plan of the Temple by Perrault	90
V.23	Elevations of the Temple by Perrault	90
V.24	Ribart de Chamoust's French Order	91
V.25	Triple form of Ribart de Chamoust's French Order	91
V.26	French Masonic Certificate in the Egyptianising Taste	92
V.27	Lodge of Master Masons with Temple of Solomon	93
VI.1	Assembly of Freemasons for Reception of Apprentices	99
VI.2	Reception of Apprentice	99
VI.3	Lodge assembled for Reception of Master Masons	99
VI.4	Assembly of Freemasons for Reception of Master Masons	100
VI.5	Assembly of Freemasons for the Reception of members to the Degree of Master Mason	100
VI.6	The next stage of Initiation	100
VI.7	The Master raises the candidate from his symbolic Death	101
VI.8	Frontispiece of Larudan's 'Exposure': 'The Freemasons Ruined'	101

VI.9	Lodge for the Reception of an Apprentice	102
VI.10	Lodge layout for the Reception of a 'Compagnon'	102
VI.11	Lodge layout for the Reception of a Master Mason	102
VI.12	Frontispiece and title-page of Travenol's 'Exposure'	103
VI.13	Reception of Apprentices from Travenol	103
VI.14	Reception of 'Compagnons' from Travenol	104
VI.15	Reception of Master Masons from Travenol	104
VI.16	Dinner for Freemasons	104
VI.17	Plan of a Lodge of 'Apprentif-Compagnons'	105
VI.18	True Plan of a Lodge for the Reception of an 'Apprentif-Compagnon'	105
VI.19	English tracing-board associated with the First Degree	107
VI.20	English tracing-board associated with the Second Degree	107
VI.21	English tracing-board associated with the Third Degree	107
VI.22	Lodge layout from *Jachin and Boaz* (1776)	111
VI.23	Frontispiece of *Jachin and Boaz*	112
VI.24	Frontispiece and title-page of Pérau's 'Exposure'	112
VI.25	Plans of Lodges for the Reception of 'Apprentif-Compagnons' and Master Masons from Pérau	113
VI.26	Frontispiece and title-page of Pérau's *Les Secrets...*	114
VI.27	Plans for Lodges for the Reception of an Apprentice and of a Master from Pérau	114
VI.28	Frontispiece and title-page of Pérau's 'Exposure' of the Mopses	115
VI.29	The Female Freemason	115
VI.30	'The Free-Masons Surpriz'd'	116
VI.31	Papal condemnation	117
VI.32	Frontispiece of *The Constitutions of the Free-Masons*	119
VI.33	Masonic Summons	120
VI.34	Masonic Summons	121
VI.35	Masonic Summons	121
VI.36	*Goose and Gridiron*, London House Yard, London	122
VI.37	Freemasons' Hall by Sandby	123
VI.38	Elevation of the *Freemasons' Tavern*, 1783	123
VI.39	Allegorical vision of Sandby's Hall	125
VI.40	Soane's design for the Ark of the Masonic Covenant	125
VI.41	Soane's mausoleum in London	128
VI.42	F. P. Cockerell's new Hall, 1869	130
VI.43	Banqueting Hall by Cockerell, 1869	130
VI.44	Freemasons' Hall, London, 1900	131
VI.45	Masonic Peace Memorial, designed 1926	131
VI.46	Detail of façade of Masonic Peace Memorial, London	132
VI.47	Wilkins's Masonic Hall, Bath, 1817-19	133
VI.48	Freemasons' Hall, Boston, Lincolnshire, 1860-3	134
VI.49	*Le Droit Humain*, Paris, 1912	135
VI.50	Masonic Temple, Abercorn Rooms, Liverpool Street, London	138
VI.51	Detail of Masonic Temple, Liverpool Street, London	138
VI.52	Detail of Masonic Temple, Liverpool Street, London	138
VI.53	Furnishings at Barnstaple, Devon	140
VII.1	Lodge for the Reception of a Master Mason	149
VII.2	*Coup d'oeil du théâtre de Besançon*	151
VII.3	*Forge à Canons* by Ledoux	151
VII.4	*Barrière de la Villette*, Paris	152
VII.5	Cemetery at Chaux	152
VII.6	Elevation of Cemetery at Chaux	153
VII.7	Elevation of Cenotaph of Newton by Boullée	154
VII.8	Section through Cenotaph of Newton at night	154
VII.9	Section through Cenotaph of Newton during daylight	154
VII.10	Egyptian temple at Thebes by Gaitte	156
VII.11	Egyptian temple at Thebes by Gaitte	156
VII.12	Egyptianising Masonic certificate	157
VII.13	Egyptianising Masonic certificate	158
VII.14	Section through proposed Deist church at Chaux	161
VII.15	Temple of Memory by Ledoux	162
VII.16	Temple of Accomplished Virtue and School of Morals by Ledoux	162
VII.17	Temple of Sexual Instruction by Ledoux	163
VII.18	Detail from Lequeu's Initiation Route	164
VII.19	Trial by Fire by Lequeu	164
VII.20	Trial by Water by Lequeu	164
VII.21	Trial by Air by Lequeu	164
VII.22	Trials by Fire, Water, and Air for the Reception of Initiates at Memphis (1814)	166
VII.23	French Master Mason's apron showing Cambacérès, Joseph Bonaparte, and an Egyptian setting	167
VII.24	Cavern in the Gardens of Isis by Lequeu	168
VII.25	Temple of Silence by Lequeu	168
VII.26	Section through Temple of Silence by Lequeu	169
VII.27	Plan of Temple of Silence by Lequeu	170
VII.28	Small dwelling in the Egyptian style by Lequeu	171
VII.29	Temple of Ceres by Lequeu	171
VII.30	Temple of Divination or Prediction by Lequeu	172
VII.31	Temple of Wisdom and vestibule leading to Pluto's dwelling by Lequeu	172
VII.32	Temple of the Earth by Lequeu	173
VII.33	Monument for Victory Square by Lequeu	173
VII.34	Cool Room of a house in the Egyptian Taste by Lequeu	174
VIII.1	Mausoleum at Castle Howard, Yorkshire	176
VIII.2	Gothick Temple at Stowe, Buckinghamshire	176
VIII.3	Gothick Tower, Edgehill, Warwickshire	177
VIII.4	Gothic Temple at Shotover Park, Oxfordshire	179
VIII.5	Plan of the *Parc Monceau*, Paris	186
VIII.6	View of the *Bois des Tombeaux, Parc Monceau*, Paris	187
VIII.7	*Île des Peupliers* at Ermenonville with orginal tomb of Rousseau	187
VIII.8	*Île des Peupliers*, Ermenonville, with Hubert Robert's tomb of Rousseau	188
VIII.9	Detail of Rousseau's tomb at Ermenonville	188
VIII.10	Pantheon-temple at Franconville-la-Garenne	189
VIII.11	*Le Bosquet de l'Amitié* at Franconville-la-Garenne	189
VIII.12	*Le Rocher* at Franconville-la-Garenne	190
VIII.13	*La Piramide* at Franconville-la-Garenne	190
VIII.14	*Le Tombeau d'Haller* at Franconville-la-Garenne	191
VIII.15	*Tombeau de Court de Gébelin* at Franconville-la-Garenne	191
VIII.16	*Caverne d'Young* at Franconville-la-Garenne	192
VIII.17	'Ruined' pyramid and Coligny cenotaph at Maupertuis	193
VIII.18	Rostral column at Méréville	193
VIII.19	Cenotaph of Captain Cook at Méréville	193
VIII.20	Weymouth Pine and Tomb at Morfontaine	194
VIII.21	*Bosquet* at Morfontaine	194
VIII.22	*Grand Rocher* at Morfontaine	194
VIII.23	Tomb in the garden at Plessis-Chamand	195
VIII.24	View in the Paris Catacombs	196
VIII.25	View in the Paris Catacombs	196
VIII.26	Proposals for Père-Lachaise Cemetery, Paris, with Pyramid	197
VIII.27	Tombs of Molière and La Fontaine in Père-Lachaise Cemetery, Paris	197
VIII.28	*Rond-Point des Peupliers* in Père-Lachaise Cemetery, Paris	198
VIII.29	Tombs of Brongniart and Delille in Père-Lachaise Cemetery, Paris	198
IX.1	Prince Leopold III Friedrich Franz von Anhalt-Dessau	206

xiv / FREEMASONRY AND THE ENLIGHTENMENT

IX.2	Plan of the Garden at Wörlitz	206
IX.3	Iron Bridge at Wörlitz	207
IX.4	The 'First Iron Bridge' at Coalbrookdale, Shropshire	207
IX.5	Entrance to the Labyrinth at Wörlitz	208
IX.6	Detail of the inscription over the entrance to the Labyrinth at Wörlitz	208
IX.7	'Vesuvius' erupting at Wörlitz	208
IX.8	Stein at Wörlitz with 'Villa Hamilton'	209
IX.9	Rousseauinsel at Wörlitz	210
IX.10	Nymphaeum at Wörlitz	210
IX.11	View along the Elbewall towards the Synagogue at Wörlitz	211
IX.12	Distant view of the Temple of Venus, Wörlitz	212
IX.13	Gateway to the Cemetery at Dessau	213
IX.14	Temple of Memory at Puławy	215
IX.15	Hope feeding the Chimaera at Arkadia	220
IX.16	Arched niches at Arkadia	220
IX.17	Detail of the High Priest's Sanctuary at Arkadia	220
IX.18	Grotto of the Sybil and Gothic House at Arkadia	223
IX.19	View of the pteron of the Temple of Diana framed by the 'Greek' Arch at Arkadia	224
IX.20	Isle of Poplars with Neo-Classical Tomb at Arkadia	225
IX.21	Tomb on the Isle of Poplars, Arkadia	226
IX.22	'Margrave's House' and 'Greek Arch' at Arkadia	226
IX.23	Plan of a Lodge of Mopses from Pérau	229
X.1	Title-page of Der Maurerfreude	249
X.2	Kingdom of Death by Desprez	251
X.3	Decoration by Alberti for the Libretto of Die Zauberflöte	257
X.4	Design by Quaglio for Act II, Scene 20, of Die Zauberflöte	267
X.5	Design by Maurer for Die Zauberflöte	268
X.6	Design by Maurer for Act II, Scene 8, of Die Zauberflöte	268
X.7	Design by Maurer for Act II, Scene 31, of Die Zauberflöte	268
X.8	Fireplace design by Piranesi	269
X.9	Ceiling-fresco, Stiftskirche, Lindau-am-Bodensee	271
X.10	Title-page of a German Masonic Song-Book (1798)	271
X.11	Engraving from Le Régulateur du Maçon of 1801	271
X.12	Artemis/Diana of Ephesus	275
X.13	Simon Quaglio's design for Act I, Scene 13, of Die Zauberflöte	276
X.14	Simon Quaglio's design for Act I, Scene 2, of Die Zauberflöte	277
X.15	Simon Quaglio's design for Act I, Scene 20, of Die Zauberflöte	277
X.16	Etching by Bittner for Act I, Scene 13, of Die Zauberflöte	277
X.17	Etching by Bittner for Act II, Scene 20, of Die Zauberflöte	277
X.18	Beuther's design for Act I, Scene 13, of Die Zauberflöte	278
X.19	Beuther's design for Act II, Scene 8, of Die Zauberflöte	278
X.20	Hockney's design for an Egyptian Room in Die Zauberflöte	279
X.21	Hockney's design for the entrance to a pyramidal temple in Die Zauberflöte	279
XI.1	Statue of Gillespie in St Paul's Cathedral, London	282
XI.2	Monument to Gillespie in Comber, County Down	282
XI.3	Masonic symbols on the base of the Gillespie Monument	283
XI.4	The Wellington Testimonial, Dublin	284
XI.5	Ross obelisk at Rostrevor, County Down	284
XI.6	Colonne du Palmier, Place du Châtelet, Paris	285
XI.7	Design by Zocher for the monument to J. C. J. van Speijk	285
XI.8	Pyramid in Limehouse, London	286
XI.9	Illustration from Hypnerotomachia Poliphili	287
XI.10	Willson's design for a Pyramid-Cemetery in London	287
XI.11	Pyramid Mausoleum for President Garfield	287
XI.12	Henckel-Donnersmarck mausoleum	288
XI.13	Highgate Cemetery, London	290
XI.14	Front cover of a Nazi anti-Masonic booklet c. 1935	296
XI.15	Queen's Park Church, Glasgow	297
XI.16	Tau Cross in the tower of St Vincent Street Church, Glasgow	298
XI.17	St Vincent Street Church, Glasgow	299
XI.18	Egyptianising mausoleum of Monge in Père-Lachaise Cemetery	300
XI.19	Masonic time-pieces	301
XI.20	Eben Mausoleum, Berlin-Kreuzberg	301
XI.21	Crypt under the rotunda of the Capitol	302
XI.22	The R.I.B.A building in London	303
XI.23	Buildings in the Rue des Colonnes, Paris	303
XI.24	Pictorial cards published by Ackermann	304
XI.25	Coade Stone panel	306

LIST OF FIGURES

The Figures are prefaced by **Fig.** (singular) or **Figs.** (plural), followed by the Chapter-number in Roman numerals, followed by the number of the Figure (in Arabic numerals) in each Chapter. **Gl.**=Glossary.

III.1	Ptah with Was sceptre	48
III.2	Was and Ankh symbols	48
III.3	Djed column	48
V.1	Reconstruction of Plan of the Jewish Tabernacle	72
VII.1	Schematic layout of Lodge described by Beckford	150
IX.1	Plan of Zug's design for the Mniejszy Palace, Warsaw	217
IX.2	Possible route linking the Temple of Apollo to the Vision of the Paradise Garden at Schwetzingen	233
IX.3	Plan of the Temple of Mercury at Schwetzingen	238
IX.4	Plan of the 'Mosque' with cloisters around the 'Turkish Garden' at Schwetzingen	243
IX.5	Section through the 'Mosque' and 'Turkish Garden' at Schwetzingen	243
Gl.1	Composite capital	310
Gl.2.1	Greek Corinthian Order	311
Gl.2.2	Roman Corinthian Order	311
Gl.3	Various types of Cross	311
Gl.4.1	Greek Doric Order	312
Gl.4.2	Roman Doric Order	313
Gl.5	Hexalpha	314
Gl.6	Greek Ionic Order	315
Gl.7	Paestum Doric Order	317
Gl.8	Pentalpha	318
Gl.9	Types of portico	318
Gl.10	Ouroboros	319
Gl.11	Triple Tau	320
Gl.12	Tuscan Order	321

Preface

by Andrew Prescott

'The preface is the most important part of the book ... Even reviewers need a preface.'

PHILIP GUEDALLA (1889-1944): 'Conversation with a Caller' in *The Missing Muse: and Other Essays* (London: Hodder & Stoughton 1929) viii.

On 21 January 1788, Henry Holland, one of the leading English Georgian Architects best known for his remodelling (1783-96) of Carlton House, Pall Mall, London, for the Prince of Wales[1] and for the development (1777-c.1797) of Hans Town in Chelsea, was initiated as a Freemason in the Prince of Wales Lodge No. 259[2]. This Lodge had been established the previous year after the Prince himself had become a Freemason, and served a Lodge for his friends and members of his household. At the time of Holland's initiation, building work on Carlton House was well advanced, and it is perhaps no surprise to find the Architect adding this social bond to his business relationship with the Prince. However, as the late Dorothy Stroud pointed out, unlike John Nash (who does not seem to have been a Freemason), Holland did not take much part in the social activities of the Carlton House set[3]. Described by David Watkin as a man of 'a retiring disposition' who 'carefully avoided public notice'[4], Holland's involvement with Freemasonry seems out of character.

There may be other explanations for Holland's decision to become a Freemason. Dorothy Stroud noted an intriguing letter of 1767 in the Pakenham family archives relating to the development of Hans Town in which Lord Cadogan addressed Lancelot 'Capability' Brown, Holland's father-in-law, as 'Brother Brown'[5]. If this indeed indicates that Brown was a Freemason, it might help to explain Holland's interest in the Craft. Holland's father was Master (1772-3) of the Worshipful Company of Tylers and Bricklayers of the City of London, and the younger Holland was proud of his training as a builder. This may also have made the residual 'operative' connections of Freemasonry attractive.

---

1 George Augustus Frederick, Prince of Wales from 1762, later Prince Regent and King George IV (reigned 1820-30). The Prince was a close friend of Philippe 'Égalité', Duc de Chartres (later d'Orléans), Grand Master of the Grand Orient of France.
2 Fenn (1910) appendix.
3 Stroud (1966) 43 n.1.
4 Matthew & Harrison (*Eds.*) (2004): *ODNB* hereafter **xxvii** 664-9. See also Colvin (2008) 527, which makes the same point.
5 Stroud (1966) 43 n.1.

What ever prompted Holland to join the Prince's Masonic Lodge, he does not seem to have found Freemasonry to his taste, for he resigned his membership in 1792. Again, in explaining this move, it is tempting to look first at Holland's relations with his Royal Patron. By 1792, the escalating costs of the work on Carlton House had reached a crisis-point, and the Prince blamed Holland for making inaccurate estimates. However, despite these problems, Holland continued to work for the Prince, and was persuaded by him to purchase property in Devon in 1797 in order to secure the Parliamentary seat of Okehampton for his son, also called Henry. It was only in 1802, following an argument about the Prince's duplicity in this property transaction, that Holland finally withdrew from Royal Patronage.

It is possible, then, that Holland's resignation from the Lodge was not simply the consequence of deteriorating relations with the Prince. As somebody who was not particularly clubbable, Holland perhaps just wearied of the bonhomie of Lodge life. In October 1791, following a meeting at the *Thatched House Tavern* in St James's Street (the first meeting-place of the Prince of Wales Lodge and also the venue for meetings of the distinguished Lodge of the Nine Muses No. 235, whose members included the artists Francesco Bartolozzi and Giovanni Battista Cipriani), the Architects' Club was founded. Holland took a very active part in the activities of the new association, for example co-ordinating a pamphlet containing recommendations for the prevention of fire[6]. Holland may perhaps have decided to concentrate on the Architects' Club at the expense of his Masonic membership. Among the honorary members of the Club was Thomas Sandby, Architect of the first Freemasons' Hall built (1775-6) by the Premier Grand Lodge of England in Queen Street, Lincoln's Inn Fields[7]. Another member of the Architects' Club was John Soane, who on 29 March 1792 attended a meeting of the Club at the *Freemasons' Tavern* in London, which sought to define 'the profession and qualification of an architect'. It is intriguing to speculate how far Soane, who himself became a Freemason at the behest of the Duke of Sussex[8] in 1813, was encouraged to join the Craft by the knowledge that Holland (definitely) and Brown (possibly), who had employed Soane in 1772 as an architectural assistant for their work on Claremont House, near Esher, Surrey, had been Freemasons.

Holland's connection with Freemasonry, therefore, was brief and limited, so it is perhaps not all that surprising that Holland's membership of the Craft is not mentioned by Dorothy Stroud or reported in the *Oxford Dictionary of National Biography* entry on Holland. Nevertheless, Holland's membership of the Prince of Wales Lodge suggests many interesting further connections hinting at a forgotten Masonic culture within London architectural life: however, many of these possible links are speculative and uncertain. Holland never discussed or alluded to his experience as a Freemason, so we cannot say why he became one, whether he felt he derived any benefit from his membership, and what prompted him to resign. As a result, there is no direct evidence as to whether Holland's Architecture was influenced by Masonic myths and symbolism.

The roll-call of eighteenth- and early nineteenth-century Architects who were Freemasons is, as the present superb volume suggests, a lengthy and distinguished one. However, like Holland, they rarely explicitly discussed how Freemasonry affected their Architecture. In some cases, the Masonic influence is immediately evident; in many others, it is suitably veiled in allusion and symbolism. Such difficulties are particularly evident in the case of John Wood Senior, the Architect of many important developments in Bath. Wood was profoundly interested in Solomon's Temple as a hieroglyph of Jewish history. His remarkable volume, *The Origin of Building: or, the Plagiarism of the Heathens Detected*[9], shows an obsession with Masonic symbolism and ideas. Yet, because of the substantial gaps in English Masonic membership records between 1730 and 1760, we have no firm evidence that Wood himself was a Freemason, despite the published evidence that he was absorbed in esoteric matters, perhaps to the extent of being somewhat unbalanced.

It is easy to see how the study of these Masonic influences can foster speculation which is at best ill-disciplined and at worst unhinged. The dangers are vividly illustrated by the case of Washington DC, despite the work of such scholars as Stephen Bullock and others who have demonstrated the importance of Freemasonry in the political culture of the young American Republic[10], dramatically expressed by the various Masonic stone-laying ceremonies performed by George Washington and others for such major buildings as the Capitol and the White House. These ceremonies were remarkable events, but they have been interpreted and drawn upon to spin a web of speculation. Suggestions have been floated that the plan of the city incorporates allusions to the Zodiac and is replete with astrological and cosmological symbolism[11]. Unfortunately, little or no evidence that the planners of the city were themselves Freemasons[12] has been presented, and, moreover, heavy reliance seems to have been placed on a combination of coincidence and late nineteenth-century Masonic publications to arrive at conclusions that, at best, are unconvincing. It is perhaps regrettable that such speculations appear to have received encouragement from senior Freemasons: for example, in a Foreword to one

---

6 Stroud (1966) 134.

7 Reconstructed 1864-6, damaged by fire 1883, and demolished 1932: the fine interior was illustrated by Britton & Pugin **i** (1825) 321-3. The address is now Great Queen Street, and in the eighteenth century the site was regarded as part of Lincoln's Inn Fields.

8 Prince Augustus Frederick, Grand Master from 1811.

9 Wood (1741).

10 Bullock (1996).

11 *See* Ovason (1999). This work also appears under the title *The Secret Architecture of Our Nation's Capital: the Masons and the Building of Washington DC*.

12 For a lucid critique of such claims, *see* http://freemasonry.bcy.ca/anti-masonry/washington_dc/ovason.html.

book[13], the Sovereign Grand Commander of the Supreme Grand Council Ancient and Accepted Rite Southern Jurisdiction in the United States seems to have accepted uncritically the substance of the arguments presented[14]. Sensational fiction often draws on such publications, and this, too, is often accepted as fact, or as something like it: worse, such fictional publications seem to attract a vast readership which embraces popularist fantasies as facts.

In such hazardous territory, we need a sure guide, a man who has an encyclopaedic knowledge of eighteenth- and nineteenth-century Art and Architecture, who has an enormous range of aesthetic references and interests, who has steeped himself in Masonic and esoteric literature of the period, and who applies to the subject the most rigorous critical standards but is also capable of appreciating subtle and veiled symbolism and allusions. In the author of this volume, we are fortunate in having just such a guide. Curl is one of Britain's most distinguished architectural historians. He has produced in such publications as his *Classical Architecture*[15] and his *Dictionary of Architecture and Landscape Architecture*[16] concise and clear reference works which not only provide authoritative guidance to a highly technical field but are also at the same time entertaining and packed with pungent aphorisms. He has championed unfashionable architectural causes such as Victorian churches[17] and pubs, and in doing so has played a major part in fostering architectural conservation programmes in cities such as Oxford[18]. Above all, Curl has opened up completely new themes in the study of Architecture. His pioneering studies of the Egyptian Revival[19] paved the way for the present study. He has also opened our eyes to the rich material heritage associated with the commemoration of the dead and reminded us forcibly of the architectural wealth to be found in the great Victorian cemeteries[20].

In this new book, Curl introduces us to almost-forgotten esoteric undercurrents of the Enlightenment[21]. He shows us how Freemasonry fostered a fascination with a wealth of curious lore ranging from Solomon's Temple to Ancient Egypt which found expression in the buildings, art, gardens, and cemeteries of the period. Freemasonry can readily be seen as a neglected (and even slightly suspect) historical and cultural by-way, but Curl demonstrates how an understanding of the central rôle of Freemasonry in the world of the Enlightenment enables us to discern overarching themes which would otherwise elude us. Above all, Curl's investigations are grounded in the most rigorous and exacting research. He reminds us how scholarship of the highest calibre, wittily and lucidly presented, with a wealth of intellectual, aesthetic, and cultural allusion, can be consistently enthralling, entertaining, and exciting: such an achievement needs no embellishments. The Enlightenment is still often imagined as personified by dry periwigged *philosophes* exchanging aphorisms in elegant salons: Curl introduces us to that side of the Enlightenment which enthusiastically explored new tastes, values, and sensibilities in a way that makes much of the modern world seem timorous.

The vast quantity of sensationalist literature about Freemasonry published in recent years shows how the Craft is a subject which constantly titillates the public. Yet English-speaking scholars have been slow to take a serious interest in the subject. In 1969, the Oxford historian John Roberts published in the *English Historical Review* an article drawing a contrast between the academic studies of Freemasonry published in Continental Europe and work on the subject in England which at that time seemed dominated by conspiracy-theorists, Masonic apologists, and antiquarians[22]. A great deal has changed since then, however. British Freemasonry has been the subject of major studies by a series of scholars of international reputation, including not only Professor Curl himself but also Margaret Jacob[23], David Stevenson[24], and Peter Clark[25], among others. Young scholars such as Petri Mirala[26] and Jessica Harland-Jacobs[27] have also recently produced important monographs on the history of British Freemasonry. Some Masonic enthusiasts have begun to speak of the emergence of Freemasonry as a new academic discipline: such claims are perhaps somewhat precipitate, and some doubts must be felt as to whether it is appropriate or desirable to treat the history of Freemasonry as something separate from other disciplines. However, the various studies of Freemasonry published in the past twenty years have presented a fragmented view of the subject, so the need for a more synthetic view is evident. For this reason, it is particularly fortunate for those of us fascinated by the history of Freemasonry that Professor Curl has produced this completely rewritten, revised, and greatly enlarged version of his pioneering 1991 work[28]. By absorbing and drawing together in a masterly fashion the vast quantity of recent publications in this area, he provides a lucid, entertaining, and stimulating overview of recent scholarly advances in our understanding of Freemasonry as a cultural and social phenomenon which will remain an essential *vade mecum* for many years.

One of the reasons why Curl's overview is so valuable is that the history of Freemasonry is itself so closely bound up with the history of Architecture. The rituals of Freemasonry of course draw on myths and symbols derived from the craft of stonemasons. However,

---

13 Ovason (1999) vii-viii.
14 *Ibid.* vii.
15 Curl (2001*a*).
16 Curl (2006*a*).
17 Curl (2002*c*, 2007*a*).
18 *See*, for example, *The Erosion of Oxford* (Oxford: Oxford Illustrated Press, 1977).
19 Curl (2005).
20 Curl (1984*b*, 1987, 1994*a*, 2000*a*, 2001*b*, 2002*b*).
21 *See* also Curl (1986*b*, 1988, 1991*a*, 1991*d*, 1994*b*, 1995, 1996*a*, 1997, 2000*a*, 2000*b*, 2004, 2006*b*, 2006*c*, 2006*d*, 2007*b*).

22 Roberts (1969) 323-335.
23 Jacob (1981, 1991, 2006).
24 Stevenson (1984, 1988*a*, 1988*b*, 1997).
25 Clark (2001).
26 Mirala (2007).
27 Harland-Jacobs (2007).
28 Curl (1991*d*).

Freemasons who were not working stonemasons quickly sought to distance themselves from the manual origins of their preferred social diversion. Margaret Jacob notes how a Masonic preacher[29] at Colchester in 1777 sought to detach the 'Royal Art' from any association with working men. Freemasonry, he declared, 'is now advanced to a far higher degree of perfection than it could boast upon its first institution... Formerly it was only operative, confined to manual labor, and studied only the improvement of art'. Now, however, the vulgar working stonemasons had been displaced: as 'morals, learning, and religion advanced in the world, so Masonry then became speculative, and attended to the cultivation of the mind'. Indeed, as Jacob noted, the British Masonic 'imagination took flight. It became not just speculative but frequently utopian'[30].

Such high-flown claims make it easy to forget the strong architectural roots of Freemasonry in the early years after the formation of the first Grand Lodge in 1717. Among the books advertised in 1723 at the end of the first edition of the *Book of Constitutions* of the Freemasons were reprints of John Sturt's sumptuously illustrated editions of Claude Perrault's *Treatise of the Five Orders of Architecture*[31] translated by John James (himself a member of a Lodge in Greenwich) and Andrea Pozzo's *Rules and Examples of Perspective*[32]. John Senex, one of the publishers of the 1723 *Book of Constitutions*, had previously been involved in a reprint of John Slezer's 1693 *Theatrum Scotiae*[33], one of the precursors of *Vitruvius Britannicus*[34]. Indeed, James Anderson explicitly encouraged his readers to study that 'ingenious book', *Vitruvius Britannicus,* in order that Britain might become 'the MISTRESS of the earth for Designing, Drawing and Conducting and capable to instruct all other Nations in all things relating to the ROYAL ART'[35]. This thread of architectural propaganda in Anderson's *Constitutions* is also apparent in the songs at the end of the volume: several praise 'Wise Vitruvius[36], Master Prime of Architects'[37], while others refer to more recent Architects:

> 'The British mason sings:
> Till Roman style revived there
> And British crowns united were
> In learned James[38], a Mason King, who rais'd
> Fine heaps of Stones
> By Inigo Jones[39],
> That rivalled wise Palladio[40], justly praised

> In Italy and Britain too
> For Architecture firm and true...'[41]

At one level, Anderson's fabulous history of Freemasonry should be read as architectural propaganda. Insufficient attention has been paid to this aesthetic aspect of early literature on Freemasonry. An example is James Anderson's celebrated statement that the Lodges of Free-Masons in London 'dwindled' during the reign of James II and VII. This has usually been read as meaning that the numbers attending Lodges declined, but the beginning of this sentence reads in full: 'But in the reign of his Brother James II, though some Roman buildings were carried on, the Lodges of Free-Masons in London dwindled into ignorance...'[42]. The implication of Anderson's sentence is that the decline was as much one of understanding of Vitruvian principles of architecture as of numbers attending. This preoccupation with Architecture continues to be evident in Masonic literature throughout the eighteenth century – William Preston's influential *Illustrations of Masonry*[43] first published in 1772 and which ran to eight further editions before Preston's death, was as much concerned with Architecture and Building as with moral and esoteric lore[44]. In short, an understanding of Architecture is essential in considering the cultural and social impact of Freemasonry in the eighteenth century. Indeed, it is probably the key to a full appreciation of the significance of Freemasonry as a social movement. Professor Curl brings out, as nobody else has done before, the central aesthetic and architectural themes in the history of Freemasonry: he masterfully illustrates how these, so intimately connected with the cultural significance of the Art of Architecture, are central and indispensable for our understanding of Freemasonry in the age of Enlightenment. To begin to understand Freemasonry, we must be educated in Architecture: we are fortunate in having such an authoritative guide in Professor Curl to advance our Masonic knowledge.

Professor Andrew Prescott
Director of Research

Humanities Advanced Technology & Information Institute
University of Glasgow
April 2011.

---

29 The Reverend William Martin Leake. *See* his *A Sermon Preached at St Peter's Church in Colchester on June 24, 1777* (Colchester: W. Keymer 1778) 14-15.
30 Jacob (1991) 52.
31 Perrault (1708).
32 Pozzo (1707).
33 Slezer (1693).
34 Harris (1986) 341.
35 Anderson (*Ed.*) (1723) 48.
36 Marcus Vitruvius Pollio, Roman author.
37 Anderson (*Ed.*) (1723) 77.
38 That is, James VI of Scotland (reigned 1567-1625), and James I of England and Ireland (reigned 1603-25).
39 Inigo Jones, Architect.
40 Andrea Palladio, whose works had a profound effect on Architecture in the British Isles, especially during the eighteenth century.

41 Anderson (*Ed.*) (1723) 82.
42 *Ibid*. 41.
43 Preston (1772).
44 Indeed, a vast percentage of 'Masonic' literature avoids intelligent or informed discussion of architectural matters altogether, which is very peculiar given the importance of the Mistress of the Arts in Masonic Symbolism (JSC).

Acknowledgements

'La reconaissance de la plupart des hommes n'est qu'une secrète envie de recevoir de plus grands bienfaits.'[1]

FRANÇOIS VI, DUC DE LA ROCHEFOUCAULD, PRINCE DE MARCILLAC (1613-80): *Maximes* (1678), No. 298.

The author of a work such as this incurs many obligations, not least to his sources, without which his task would have been infinitely more onerous than has been the case. First of all, I gratefully acknowledge my debts to the works of the great German Freemasonic historians Georg Emil Wilhelm Begemann[2], Gottfried Joseph Gabriel Findel[3], and Georg Franz Burkhard Kloss[4]. In the United Kingdom the main published volumes have been by Robert Freke Gould[5], William J. Hughan[6], and Adolphus Frederick Arthur Woodford[7]. Douglas Knoop[8], Gwilym Peredur Jones[9], and Douglas Hamer[10] contributed an enormous amount to scholarly investigations since the 1930s, and their endeavours are especially useful when considering Mediaeval Freemasonry: their substantial works are mercifully free from any taint of the sensational or the half-baked. Among other studies relevant to an understanding of Freemasonry may be mentioned those of Frances A. Yates (whose delvings into previously obscure byways of Renaissance culture have served to illumine some of the stranger ideas prevalent in the sixteenth and seventeenth centuries)[11] and of Margaret C. Jacob[12], but many other books and papers are appearing in the twenty-first century, as scholars realise the huge wealth of material that has survived relating to a subject that has to be accorded more respect and attention than has been the case in the past. Joscelyn Godwin[13] has made several major contributions to an understanding of some of the more arcane aspects of Renaissance and Enlightenment culture,

---

1 The gratitude of the greatest part of mankind is only a secret wish to receive greater good turns.

2 Begemann (1906, 1909-10, 1911, and 1914).
3 Findel (1893).
4 Kloss (1844, 1845, 1848, 1852-3).
5 Gould (1884-7, 1903, 1911, 1931, 1951).
6 Hughan (1871-9, 1909).
7 Woodford (1871-9, 1872, 1874, 1878a, 1878b).
8 Knoop & Jones (1932, 1933, 1934, 1935, 1936a, 1936b, 1937a, 1937b, 1939, 1940, 1941, 1942a, 1942b, 1944, 1947, 1967).
9 *See* note 8.
10 Knoop, Jones, & Hamer (1938, 1945, 1963).
11 Yates (1947, 1964, 1966, 1972, 1975, 1979). Some of Yates's claims, about Rosicrucianism, for instance, have been overtaken by later scholarship.
12 Jacob (1981, 1991, 2006).
13 Godwin (1979a, 1979b, 1979c, 1981, 1999, 2009).

and he has remarked to me that we both seem to 'share the same delight in hunting down unfrequented paths and discovering a world of the Imagination'[14]: I record here my thanks to him for his generous encouragement of my own investigations. His support and criticism have been both helpful and beneficial[15].

Knoop and Jones were towering figures as historians of Freemasonry, and their work recognised the importance of Scotland in that history. Yet even before them, David Murray Lyon[16] and Begemann[17] (among others) had produced substantial studies that acknowledged the significance of Caledonian Masonic beginnings in the teeth of objections from south of the Border. More recently, David Stevenson has demonstrated that the contribution of Scotland to Freemasonry was truly immense, and his efforts have attempted to correct what he has claimed (with every justification) is an 'Anglocentric' tendency present in many supposedly 'historical' studies of Freemasonry. His important books[18] have been a huge influence on my own work, and I fully acknowledge my great debts to his scholarly exposition of so much interesting material. I am also grateful to Professor Stevenson for generously allowing me to quote from his sound and thorough publications. I salute a gentleman and a scholar who has become a friend. I know full well from experience how 'Anglocentric' attitudes can be patronising and based upon distortions and ignorance. That Freemasonic studies have suffered from more than a certain bias is really beyond dispute. As I have attempted to show here, however, Scotland's rôle, though undoubtedly important in the history of the Craft, was tempered by the move South of the Stuart Court, and by the immense influence of English custom, English legends, and changes in English governance, especially after 1689.

Bernard Edward Jones's works[19] are certainly of value in explaining much of the basic stuff of Freemasonry (although Jones could be unnecessarily and infuriatingly coy on far too many occasions), while Albert Gallatin Mackey[20] and Gould offer much food for thought, although their books must be treated with considerable caution and scepticism, requiring careful checks at all times. Of considerable value, however, is 'C. Lenning's' *Allgemeines Handbuch der Freimaurerei*[21], and many other scholarly German-language sources referred to in the Select Bibliography can be rewarding. 'Lenning's' work (probably by a German bookseller and Freemason who lived in Paris) was subsequently 'edited' by Friedrich Mossdorf, the real name, apparently, of 'Lenning'.

Anthony Vidler has considered[22] various aspects of eighteenth-century French architecture, and discussed building-types, including Freemasonic and other Lodges. I had the pleasure of reviewing[23] some of his works when they first came out, and paid tribute to the definitive flavour of a wide range of architectural preoccupations during a fecund period when the Western world erupted with phenomenal change. He and I inevitably covered similar ground in our considerations of the extraordinary veins of Freemasonic material and its manifestations in France during the *Ancien Régime* and the Revolutionary and Napoleonic periods. In some cases I have incorporated points made by Vidler which I think are pertinent to the present study, and thank him warmly for permission to quote from his *œuvre*.

In any study such as this it is inevitable that many ideas and much material are drawn from a huge range of sources, for the sheer mass of works consulted was enormous (and daunting and infuriating, for some volumes were more profitable than the majority), so distillation was a grave and thought-provoking problem. The Select Bibliography (I make no apology for its size, for it is only a small sample of what is available in terms of published material) and Footnotes give some indication of the cornucopia of works that exist, yet what I include is only a mere fraction of Freemasonic and related publications: there must be many ideas, thoughts, and images I have absorbed over some thirty years of considering the subject that have simply become part of my understanding, and which I can no longer differentiate as being anything other than part of the total impression I have formed in my mind. Once a subject begins to obsess a scholar whose interest is aroused, the mind and eye become open to all sorts of stimuli and connections that help to build up an overall impression: inevitably that conspectus contains elements from countless sources, and I acknowledge their invaluable contributions to the sum of ideas, facts, themes, and hypotheses that have helped to form the essence of this book. However, some specific acknowledgements other than those outlined above are necessary, and it is my pleasure and duty to thank many people who have helped me to assemble my material.

First of all, I am grateful to Terence O. Haunch, formerly Librarian and Curator of the Library and Museum of the United Grand Lodge of England, for first guiding me many years ago through the superb collections in Freemasons' Hall, London, when my interest in the subject was initially aroused, and this led to an article in *Country Life*[24] written at the request of Marcus Binney, prompted by the late Michael Wright (to whom I owe an enormous debt of gratitude for encouraging my early career as an author, and for publishing a considerable number of articles by me over many years)[25]. On 2 April 2008 Terence Haunch took the trouble to write me a long letter that was full of kind suggestions, advice, and mild but constructive

---

14 In a personal communication.
15 Though he is in no manner responsible for any of my views (or errors).
16 Lyon (1900).
17 Begemann (1906, 1909-10, 1911, 1914).
18 Especially Stevenson (1988*a*, 1988*b*).
19 Jones (1957, 1977) for example.
20 Mackey (1898-1906, 1919).
21 Lenning (1863-7, 1900, etc.).
22 Vidler (1976, 1987, 1990).

23 *The World of Interiors* (November 1987) 80; *The Architects' Journal* (23 January 1991) 60.
24 Curl (1986*b*).
25 See Bristoliensis **xxxiii** (July 2007) 62-4.

criticisms: I have incorporated virtually everything he mentioned, cut where appropriate, and honed the text accordingly. I acknowledge here T. O. Haunch's great generosity: any errors or clangers that survive are mine alone, and he is in no way responsible for them. Other persons connected with United Grand Lodge (including Messrs Ashby, Cherry, Meacham, and Page, and Mesdames Diane Clements and Katherine Jowett) dealt with my questions and requests with unfailing courtesy, and their help has been invaluable. I am also grateful to Peter Hamilton Currie, Carl I. Gibb of Atlanta, Georgia, Robert L. D. Cooper, Neville Barker Cryer, James Daniel, the late Malcolm Davies, Brent Elliott, Robert A. Gilbert, Ivor Grattan-Guinness, John Hamill, Arthur O. Hazel, R. J. C. Jamieson, Petra Maclot, John Milne, Andrew Pink, John A. Rice, Matthew Scanlan, Trevor Stewart, and Eugène Warmenbol, for useful suggestions and encouragement. Of especially liberal and speedy help was the infinitely generous Andrew Prescott (whose suggestions and thoughtfulness dispensed with such friendly charm went far beyond scholarly courtesies): Professor Prescott also wrote the elegant Preface to this book for which I am most grateful. Jan Snoek provided many insights and much bibliographical information, while Frank Albo, Andreas Förderer, Patrizia Granziera, Andréa Kroon, Cécile Révauger, Monika Scholl-Frey, Robert Jan van Pelt, Leon Zeldis, and many others interested in the Craft all helped in various ways: of particular assistance with gardens were Eva Eissmann[26], Andreas Förderer[27], Włodzimierz Piwkowski[28], and Ewa Święcka[29], to whom I shall always be indebted for many kindnesses.

In my London days I benefited greatly from the wisdom of Ralph Hyde, formerly Keeper of Prints and Maps at Guildhall Library, City of London: long after I left London, he kept me informed of new snippets of information, and a more generous-hearted fellow-scholar would be hard to find. John Fisher, Jeremy Smith[30], and their colleagues at Guildhall Library, Corporation of London, have also been of immense assistance. I have gratefully received enlightenment from the staff of the RIBA Library (especially Malcolm Green, Dawn Humm, Claudia Mernick, Richard Reed, and [in times past] Trevor Todd), the RIBA Library Drawings Collection (notably Jonathan Makepeace), Sir John Soane's Museum (particularly Tim Knox, Susan Palmer, Margaret Richardson, the late Peter Thornton, and others), the Statens Konstmuseer Stockholm, the Staatliche Museen Preussischer Kulturbesitz, the Deutsches Theatermuseum Munich, the Cologne Theatermuseum, the Matica Slovenská, the Cooper-Hewitt Museum, the Smithsonian Institute's National Museum of Design, the Rare Book and Manuscript Library of Columbia University in the City of New York, English Heritage National Monuments Record (in particular Ian Leith, Nigel Wilkins, and Robert Blow), the Royal Commission on the Ancient and Historical Monuments of Scotland, the Staatliche Schlösser und Gärten Wörlitz, Oranienenbaum, Luisium (Hartmut Ross and Reinhard Alex), the Germanisches Nationalmuseum Nürnberg, the Musée Carnavalet Paris, the Center for Studies in Landscape Architecture Dumbarton Oaks Washington DC, the Society of Antiquaries of London, the Bodleian Library University of Oxford, the British Library (especially Pam Taylor), the Bibliothèque Nationale Paris, the Bischöfliches Ordinariat Würzburg, the Museen der Stadt Wien, Archbishop Robinson's Library, Armagh (Armagh Public Libraries – where Lorraine Frazer was most helpful), the Science Library of The Queen's University of Belfast (particularly Karen Latimer and Dan Holden), the Bibliothèque Royale Albert Ier, Brussels, The Courtauld Institute of Art (notably Louisa Dare), the Library of Freemasons' Hall, Molesworth Street, Dublin (Rebecca Hayes most civilly aided my research), the Reference Department of Cambridge University Library (especially Lucas Elkin who has been extraordinarily kind), the Bridgeman Art Library (chiefly Joanne Hardy), the National Gallery of Canada (France Beauregard), the Kurpfälzisches Museum Heidelberg (Zeliha Devrim), and many other individuals, collections, and museums too numerous to list.

The material on gardens was drafted during a Visiting Fellowship at Peterhouse, University of Cambridge, in 2002: I record my thanks to the Master, Fellows, and Governing Body of that College, and express my appreciation of the many kindnesses of the Fellows who became friends (notably Professor E. J. Kenney) and of the College staff who made my period of residence so agreeable. In Poland, apart from the kindness of Pan Piwkowski and Pani Święcka, I received much help from Katarzyna Zachwatowicz-Jasieńska and that is gratefully acknowledged.

I also thank Geremy Butler, Martin Charles, Iona Cruickshank, and Rodney C. Roach for help with photography. Henri Bonnefoi, John Gamble, Michael Goldmark, Michael Holman, Peter Inch, Barry Ketchum, Jeremy Ridge, the late Meaburn Staniland, and many other friends helped to locate documents and books, for which I am most grateful.

Margaret Reed, of Starword, prepared my texts, notes, bibliography, and so on, and, as usual, has my thanks for her speed and efficiency. Auriol Griffith-Jones performed her customary miracles with the Index, a daunting task from which I am delighted she was able to relieve me. I owe much to Helen English, who advised, cajoled, threatened, and acted on my behalf with dazzling speed, rescuing me from much with zest and sparkling humour: for these things I thank her very much. Nicola Willmot, of Two Plus George Ltd., designed the book in conjunction with

---

26 Eva Eissmann first introduced me to the *Gartenreich* at Wörlitz.
27 At Schwetzingen: his help went beyond duty, and I am heavily in his debt.
28 For help with the Radziwiłł gardens at Arkadia, for which I am extremely grateful.
29 Ewa Święcka first showed me Arkadia and her work of conservation at the Temple of Diana: she was immensely helpful.
30 Jeremy Smith, in 2011, was at the London Metropolitan Archives Department of the Corporation of London, and provided valuable help and guidance.

the specifications agreed with my long-suffering and very helpful friend and publisher, John Richardson: it has been a pleasure to work with both of them on a project that took a great deal of time and effort to bring to fruition: without their very considerable input the book could never have appeared at all.

Finally, Adam Wilkinson kindly took an interest in my work: I thank him and Edinburgh World Heritage very much for invaluable practical support.

No Acknowledgements section would be complete without mention of my father, the late George Stevens Curl, who taught me so much about Mozart from the time I was very young, and who imparted an understanding of music and a love of literature that have remained with me since childhood: I owe his shade an immense debt of heartfelt gratitude.

If I have omitted anyone by name from these acknowledgements it is not for lack of appreciation: there have been so many that it would have been an immense task to individually name them all. I trust that this sincere expression of my indebtedness will suffice, for without the generous assistance of friends, colleagues past and present, and very many other people (including numerous fellow-academics), the task of writing this book would have been virtually impossible.

James Stevens Curl

Burley-on-the-Hill, Rutland; Peterhouse,
University of Cambridge; Schwetzingen;
and Holywood, County Down, 1986-2011.

Introduction

'…close as oak – an absolute free-mason for secrecy….'
GEORGE COLMAN THE ELDER (c.1732-94):
The Deuce is in Him: a Farce, in Two Acts (1763),
Act **ii** (London: printed for T. Becket,
P. A. De Hondt, & T. Davies, 1763) 29.

'Masonry is an art useful and extensive. In every art there is a mystery, which requires a progress of study and application to arrive at any degree of perfection… Masonry is wisely calculated to suit different ranks and degrees, as every one, according to his station and ability, may be employed, and class with his equal in every station. Founded upon the most generous principles, no disquietude appears among the professors of the art…; all unite in the same plan, to promote that endearing [sic] happiness which constitutes the essence of civil society.'
WILLIAM PRESTON (1742-1818):
Illustrations of Masonry
(London: G. & T. Wilkie, 1792) 29,31.

The Cambridge Don, John Saltmarsh, in a review of *An Introduction to Freemasonry* (1937)[1] by Douglas Knoop and Gwilym Peredur Jones, described the book as 'something rare in a department of history which is not only obscure and highly controversial, but by ill luck the happiest of all hunting-grounds for the light-headed, the fanciful, the altogether unscholarly and the lunatic fringe of the British Museum Reading Room'[2]. Saltmarsh went on to mention that only 'one section of Masonic historians has deserved the title of the "Authentic School"', but it was a 'weakness of this school that before the mystic year 1717 its historians had 'little to be authentic about'[3].

Knoop, Jones, and Douglas Hamer[4] might be described as the Trinity of genuine historians of Freemasonry: they had at their disposal the traditional corpus of Masonic lore, but they were also steeped in the histories of the Mediaeval Guilds and had an unsurpassed knowledge of the building-trades of the Middle Ages. They did not approach the problem of the origins of Freemasonry from an exposition of rituals, secrets, mysteries, and ceremonies, but from the fact that men who worked with stone were skilled artificers labouring in an industry which nevertheless had a highly developed Craft basis. Furthermore, Mediaeval masons were unlike other tradesmen who were members of local Guilds: masons, by the very nature of their work, were itinerant, bringing their skills to very wide geographical areas, as when they worked on parish-churches and the like. True, there were permanent centres of the Craft in the larger quarries, and on major building-projects, such as those involving the great cathedral-churches of Gothic Europe. Chapters I and II of the present work will enlarge upon the origins of Freemasonry.

Saltmarsh touched on a significant point, and that is that mainstream historians, on the whole, have avoided the history of Freemasonry, not least because much of the vast literature on the subject is nonsensical drivel, unworthy of the epithet 'history' at all. Having waded wearily (and

---
1 Knoop & Jones (1937).
2 Saltmarsh (1937) 103.
3 *Ibid.*
4 *See* Select Bibliography.

warily) through daunting piles of weird stuff in the pursuit of my researches, I can confirm that, although much serious scholarly work has been done (especially in the last few years when the Craft has at last been subjected to more and more scrutiny), tedious, barmy, entirely fanciful, and usually worthless material has appeared even since Saltmarsh's comments of over seventy years ago, and only serves to obscure and cloud issues that deserve careful attention and rigorous clarity of thought. Matters have not been helped by some Masonic historians, whose works have been written by Freemasons for Freemasons, and published (or publicised) only within a Freemasonic coterie, often exaggerating the importance of the Craft by making claims for it that are as inflated as they are absurd. Thus many Masonic historians have been ill-equipped to deal with what Professor Stevenson has called 'the wider knowledge of historical development which is necessary if what is happening is to be fully understood', and 'general historians remain unaware of a remarkable development' which took place in 'seventeenth-century Britain'[5]. Stevenson has paid tribute to Professors Knoop[6] and Jones[7], whose 'many works greatly enhanced the credibility of masonic history': he wrote that 'they argued with vigour that masonic history should not be studied in isolation from other aspects of historical development'[8]. However, even Knoop and Jones noted that 'whereas it has been customary to think of masonic history as something entirely apart from ordinary history, and as calling for, and justifying, special treatment, we think of it as *a branch of social history*[9], as the study of a particular social institution and of the ideas underlying that institution, to be investigated and written in exactly the same way as the history of other social institutions'[10]. Here one feels an eyebrow or two rising involuntarily: why on earth should 'masonic history' be thought of as 'a branch of social history', and not simply as a *branch of history*? Did not Knoop and Jones simply shift 'masonic history' from one 'ghetto' (as Stevenson[11] has termed it) to another? Besides, although Knoop and Jones 'thought of' 'masonic history' as being 'a branch of social history', a careful and patient re-reading of their very considerable *œuvre* reveals that their 'social history' more often than not actually meant *economic history*, with the catastrophic results that many other sides of the rich historical background to Freemasonry have been ignored or skipped over, including the aesthetic, cultural, intellectual, political, religious, *and even social* aspects[12]. As David Stevenson has written, what 'economic history in isolation' could reveal about Freemasonry 'turned out to be distinctly limited'[13]. Stevenson, very accurately, also identified a further problem with Knoop and Jones: their insistence that the duty of any historian is to 'hunt for facts and verify conclusions, and not to fill in gaps either by the dangerous argument of analogy… or by an equally dangerous exercise of the imagination'[14] certainly helped to raise standards of Masonic history, but inhibited many later commentators from sticking their necks out at all. When Knoop and Jones warned against filling gaps in the history of Freemasonry, 'not by the successful search for new facts, but by the use of the imagination,' they claimed such an approach would 'revert to the mythical or imaginative treatment of the subject'[15]. Any historian worth his salt knows how important is documentary evidence (or facts), but equally is aware that often the discovery of new or hitherto concealed facts can stimulate hypotheses which can then be tested: the excitement of finding a new lead is often given impetus *by imagination*, firing energies to explore new tacks. History based *entirely* on facts alone would be dull stuff indeed, and history written without fire, informed insights, or imagination would be deadly. Stevenson very charitably interprets Knoop and Jones's use of the word 'imagination' as actually signifying 'invention', for they abhorred (with reason) 'a tendency to invent convenient facts to fill gaps or add glory to freemasonry's past'[16]. Well, perhaps they *did* mean invention rather than imagination, but their work is in general very worthy but makes dull reading: dare one say lacking in imagination?

Many Masonic historians have or have had a proprietorial attitude to the history of the Craft, and deeply resent (it is not too strong a word) investigations by Cowans (persons who are not Freemasons), believing that such probers will either not understand Freemasonry or be hostile to it. It is true that ranters and irresponsible commentators have been responsible for sowing grave suspicions about the Craft, attributing to it improbable things, and their hostility has unquestionably created a reaction within and a closing of ranks among Freemasons. The most vociferous critics have included those of Leftist political persuasion (following the precedents set by the National Socialist German Workers' Party and the Stalinist régimes in the former Soviet Union); the Roman Catholic Church (notably in Ireland, but in many other countries as well, where there was vile talk of 'Judeo-Masonry' reminiscent of the most poisonous outpourings of Hitler, Goebbels, Streicher, and that disreputable crew[17]); assortments of fantasists, conspiracy-theorists, and paranoiacs of many types; and the more fanatical elements within other religions, whose effusions are not all that different when compared with those from other sources, some of which have been mentioned above. So Leftists, anti-Semites of many kinds, totalitarians, adherents of various religions, and capricious believers

---

5   Stevenson (1988*b*) xii.
6   A Freemason.
7   Not a Freemason.
8   Stevenson (1988*b*) xii
9   My italics.
10 Knoop & Jones (1947) v.
11 Stevenson (1988*b*) 2.
12 Stevenson (1988*b*) 2, also notes this fundamental point.
13 *Ibid*.

14 Knoop & Jones (1944) 9.
15 *Ibid*.
16 Stevenson (1988*b*), 3.
17 For a measured review of anti-Masonic and anti-Semitic matters *see* Gilbert (2006). Some of the nastier documents will be discussed in the final Chapter of this book.

To give but one obvious example of this curious reluctance on the part of historians to even mention Freemasonry, the great Architect Sir John Soane was not only a convinced Freemason (from 1813), designing the Council Chamber, Freemasons' Hall, London (1828 – regrettably demolished), but was benevolently liberal with donations, and even had his portrait painted (1828) by John Jackson, RA: this shows Soane wearing Freemasonic regalia as Grand Superintendent of the Works (a post he held until his death)[18] (**CPl.Int.I**). Yet very few conventional historians *even mention* Soane's Masonic affiliations, despite the fact that his portrait by Jackson hangs in Sir John Soane's Museum, London[19]. An exception is Professor Watkin[20], but others give the impression of being embarrassed by the merest whiff of the Craft[21].

The present study, therefore, is intended as a sober introduction to a subject that perhaps has generated wild, even hysterical, speculation, rather than cool appraisal and thorough scholarship, yet the importance of that subject must be obvious to anyone with an interest in European and American civilisation, especially during the eighteenth and early nineteenth centuries. There can be no doubt whatsoever that Freemasonry played a central rôle in the Enlightenment, so the fact that so many so-called 'academics' have avoided the issue is very peculiar, indicative of cowardice, dishonesty, or worse.

CPl. Int.I Portrait (1828) of Sir John Soane painted by John Jackson RA, now in Sir John Soane's Museum, London (*SJSM*).

in fanciful intrigues and sinister plots have demonstrated not merely enmity, but murderous hostility towards the Craft and its adherents. Freemasons themselves have often been guilty of fanning the flames of hatred by claiming for the Craft an antiquity that does not stand up to scrutiny, a history that is more legend and wishful thinking than fact, lists of Brethren about whom there is little or no evidence they were ever Freemasons, and an importance and significance in the shaping of great events for which there are only chimaerical tales and vaporous musings to give them dubious credence. Then there have been the attitudes and beliefs of conventional 'academic' historians, many of whom disapprove of the Craft and feel that the best way of dealing with what they regard as a distinctly dodgy subject is to ignore it: this in itself is a disreputable, even shameful stance, for if historians only bothered to investigate things of which they approved, history would be hopelessly distorted. This, however, is the case.

I first realised there was a book to be written on the topic when carrying out research for a work which became *The Egyptian Revival: An Introductory Study of a Recurring Theme in the History of Taste*[22], subsequently revised as *Egyptomania*[23] and re-written and hugely expanded as *The Egyptian Revival: Ancient Egypt as the Inspiration for Design Motifs in the West*[24], although it had gradually dawned on

18 Taylor (1982).
19 SM P 142
20 Watkin (1996) 41, 422-4.
21 Among them apparently Colvin (2008) 962-971, and Summerson (1952), but then Summerson clearly found Soane's personality and works uncongenial, which must have made his position as Curator of Sir John Soane's Museum uncomfortable at times. It is odd that in his paper 'Sir John Soane and the Furniture of Death' in *The Architectural Review* **clxiii**/973 (March 1978) 147-55, Summerson entirely avoided referring to Freemasonry in relation to Soane's work.
22 Curl (1982).
23 Curl (1994*b*).
24 Curl (2005).

me very much earlier that Egyptianising themes deserved investigation when I saw the marvellous designs for stage-sets for Mozart's *Singspiel*[25], *Die Zauberflöte*[26], by Karl Friedrich Schinkel in the composer's birthplace, Getreidegasse, Salzburg, in 1960. And although twenty-two years elapsed after that exhibition before my first book on *The Egyptian Revival*[27] was published, the enormous amount of material I had been through or acquired pointed to something I had only half-suspected when I first investigated seventeenth- and eighteenth-century Egyptianisms: the undoubted significance of and influence on design prompted by Freemasonry, especially during the European Enlightenment.

Now there is an obvious danger in seeing allusions to Freemasonry everywhere, and of ascribing to buildings and artefacts connotations that are, at best, tentative. That danger I have tried to avoid, proposing Freemasonic influences only where there are clear indications they are real and not figments of fancy. Some Freemasonic emblems and motifs[28] are shared by other societies and bodies, and some are simply part of an enormous range of images and elements that can be found within the rich language of Classical, pre-Classical, and Neo-Classical design. Two columns or a triangle, for example, are not necessarily indicative of Freemasonic allusions, but on the other hand they *might* be: I have attempted to differentiate where possible. Broken columns may indeed signify a life cut off, but they are not necessarily Freemasonic, yet they can be: they can also be the result of vandalism. All this sounds vague and difficult, and so it is, but there is no doubt in my mind that a careful study, as far as is possible, reveals interesting and relevant byways in the history of Architecture and Design that are closely connected with upheavals of organisation at the time of the Reformation, and that have clear links with certain esoteric themes linking Renaissance studies with the curious worlds of the Magus and of the Mysteries of Antiquity in the Graeco-Roman world.

Many personalities of the European Enlightenment were Freemasons, and some of the most familiar and celebrated works created in the eighteenth century had esoteric aspects, some of which could be regarded as having Masonic allusions, including, of course, *Die Zauberflöte*, by Wolfgang Amadeus Mozart, Emanuel Schikaneder, and (probably) Carl Ludwig Giesecke[29]: the *Singspiel* has baffled, delighted, infuriated, and irritated many commentators for more than two centuries, though its meanings were probably clearer to minds steeped in Enlightenment concerns than to those filled with other notions and layers of understanding (or lack of it) today. One must take seriously the fact that no less a person than Johann Wolfgang von Goethe (himself a Freemason) held *Die Zauberflöte* in the highest regard, and himself prepared a sketch for a sequel[30]. Most of us, however, have never seen or heard *Die Zauberflöte* given in full, and even so-called 'complete' recordings of the work omit a vast amount of the dialogue. If, say, about a third of a play were to be butchered (not adapted or abridged, but savagely cut, so that the story line became nonsensical), the work would not be highly regarded. Well, Mozart's wonderful creation nearly always is brutally mangled, as anyone who has studied the original libretto[31] will know. Now although the literary origins of *Die Zauberflöte* can be found among certain texts popular in the eighteenth century, the musical aspects of the *Singspiel* raise the story to a higher plane than most entertainments of the genre achieved, but if the text is not given in its entirety the work will puzzle and infuriate: furthermore, if the cultural climate of Vienna in 1790-91 is ignored (and that climate must include Freemasonry), *Die Zauberflöte* becomes a tedious and incoherent concoction of little consequence, albeit with some pretty music. With no Egyptianesque staging, no Freemasonic allusions on the visual level, and a total failure to connect with the cultural atmosphere of Vienna in the 1790s, *Die Zauberflöte* makes little sense, especially if its dialogue is so cut as to render its story meaningless. Some attempts to film the work or stage it in recent times (with references to Isis, Osiris, or Egypt wholly expunged, major mangling of the libretto, and ludicrous settings) have succeeded in removing any meaning from it, leaving it anchorless. It is quite simply absurd to attempt to 'up-date' eighteenth-century works and place them in a much later context (e.g. the 1914-18 War): we must try to judge them by the standards of their own time (so far as is possible today).

Similarly, the design of many late eighteenth-century buildings, gardens, and cemeteries, and the contents of some well-known Continental literary texts, can make sense only when allusions are understood and recognised. It is known that during the 1780s and 1790s in the Empire many musicians, architects, writers, theorists, philosophers, and even Churchmen (of many persuasions) joined Freemasonic Lodges in numbers, and there can be no doubt that Freemasonry not only offered many of the finest minds of the Enlightenment something not available in other organisations (including the Churches), but attracted the loyalty and interest of an astonishing number of significant historical figures, and unquestionably influenced aspects of endeavour in an age of fecund creativity. That Mozart and many of his associates were profoundly affected by the Craft is a fact beyond dispute, but there were countless other important personalities as well whose lives were more than touched by Freemasonry in many countries.

---

25 A series of musical numbers (arias, duets, ensembles, and choruses), linked by spoken dialogue rather than by recitative (as was used in *opera* of the period), so a *Singspiel* must be seen as something distinct from an *opera* (in which there is no, or very little, spoken dialogue).

26 *The Magic Flute*, K.620 (1791).

27 This book, and its two successors, include a considerable amount of Freemasonic material.

28 For a good range of symbols *see* Becker (1992).

29 Giesecke's involvement has been rejected by some scholars, but he himself claimed to have been responsible for some of the text (*see* Giesecke [n.d.] and *ODNB* **xxii** [2004] 114).

---

30 Goethe (1949).

31 *See* Berk (2004) 547-627; Curl (2007b); Giesecke (n.d.).

It is most regrettable that Freemasonic studies have been bedevilled by certain writings of a journalistic and sensational type. The 'secret' nature of much of Freemasonic ritual has, of course, encouraged speculation and a certain wild denunciation verging on the hysterical: it is not to the credit of many in public life today that exaggeration and condemnation have come so easily to them (but a cursory glance at their backgrounds and politico-religious affiliations explains much, and does nothing to instil confidence in their abilities to act free from prejudice). This is all the more peculiar since so much about Freemasonry is readily available in standard works of reference (although certain Freemasonic writers have not helped their cause by coyness and deliberate obfuscation). Persecutors of Freemasons have been many, and include repressive organisations terrified of open debate and dedicated to control. It is also nonsense to refer to Freemasonry as a 'secret' society: the Select Bibliography at the end of this book is a tiny trawl through the available literature, as any visitor to great Freemasonic Libraries in England, Ireland, Scotland, Germany, Austria, and the United States of America (to name but a few countries) will testify, and such literature is not kept under lock and key except in locations where totalitarianism and repression are dominant.

The conclusion is melancholy: it can only be assumed that the over-simplified messages emanating from an increasingly bigoted and idle class manipulating the media, from poltroons masquerading as politicians, and from those in public life (who ought to know better, but obviously do not) reflect a growing reluctance to read, to delve, to ascertain. The sensational, the 'controversial', the inaccurate, the disastrous, the sordid, and the 'newsworthy' are regarded as more important than the truth, because the effort of finding out seems to be beyond those who live by the vulgarities of popularist so-called 'culture'.

What is true of Mozart's *Singspiel* is also true of Architecture. Once a few points are understood, a considerable number of buildings will be shown to have aspects that allude in some way to Legends of the Craft. Yet this is hardly surprising, given the architectural context implicit in Freemasonry, while The Great Architect of the Universe is a Freemasonic metaphor that will need little elaboration. There are texts a-plenty dealing with Freemasonic ceremony, initiation, and ordeal, and these have been around for quite some time: I have used them freely, and they are readily available, so I make no apologies for exploiting them. So much for fantasies about 'secret' societies!

In an age where Death is regarded as a sensational disaster if it occurs to large numbers of people (as in an aircraft, train, ship, or terrorist attack), used as an excuse for 'entertainment', relegated to embarrassed shuffling when it occurs 'normally', or treated with horror if it happens as a result of disease, it is very odd that reflections about death, the ending of life, the question of individual existence, and the celebration of death are not given much consideration in Britain during recent times. We are too busy showing how 'caring' we are to face the harsh reality or to challenge the supposition that death and bereavement can be treated as antiseptically as rubbish disposal (and accorded even less significance). Death, in twenty-first-century Britain, Europe, and America, is part of a pornographic dystopia more frightening than ever, yet constantly being devalued.

Death, and facing death, however, are central to eighteenth-century Freemasonic texts, and involve the idea of a journey, trials, and rebirth. In Architecture and in the design of gardens, the themes of a route, a progression, of allusion, of metaphor, of mnemonics, of conjuring moods, cultures, or exotica, and of passing through to a climactic end are not unusual, and yet the esoteric content of such designs often escapes blinkered and prejudiced commentators. Freemasonic concepts of death, trial, and descent to the depths are clearly described in many books, and are implicit in the text of *Die Zauberflöte*, although obscured in the opera-houses of today where productions and designs strive after Post-Modern 'originality' and 'contemporary meaning' only to make nonsense of the work and display an abysmal ignorance of the essence of the piece as well as devaluing it and besmirching something beautiful.

This book draws on many sources, and attempts to explain the Freemasonic content in so many aspects of Western culture; it is necessarily only an introduction, for a detailed study would be very much longer than my publisher is prepared to allow me. The Select Bibliography, though fairly wide in scope (and offering the reader many enticing roads to explore), is by no means exhaustive: even the vast collection in Freemasons' Hall, London[32], if listed in a full Bibliography, would fill several volumes.

It therefore must be emphasised that the subject is an enormous one, daunting in its scope, and that there is no shortage of material, yet the odd thing is that, with several exceptions, most of those writing in English have tended to avoid any mention of Freemasonry when discussing Architecture or the design of gardens. This is most peculiar. The French and Belgians have not been so inhibited, and the Italians and Spaniards (despite the Pope) have gaily entered the fray. The Germans have touched upon these subjects, but more warily, which is not surprising, given the Freemason-bashing that went on during the ghastly Third Reich. The Scandinavians have made major contributions, as have the Dutch, and even the intrepid Poles (again despite the Pope) have not been slow to examine their own considerable Freemasonic history. Of course Continental Freemasonry has tended to be associated with political and cultural ideas alien to modern British Freemasonry (but not so alien in the seventeenth and eighteenth centuries when the British were less obsessed by the importance of politicians than they are today), and the anti-clerical (even anti-religious) and anti-establishment natures of many Continental Lodges (both before and after the French

---

32 Home of The United Grand Lodge of England.

Revolution) raise questions that, even today, are difficult with which to deal, for some of the literature in English that has attempted to discuss these tricky matters tends to be biased against Illuminism, Rosicrucianism, and their Freemasonic counterparts. American, Austrian, Belgian, Dutch, French, German, and Scandinavian writers have been more adventurous.

I have often been asked if I am a Freemason. I reply, with truth, that I am not a joiner, but such a remark prompts narrowed eyes, pursed lips, and an obvious certainty in my questioners that this denial must be an elliptical way of admitting adherence to the Craft[33]. The hostility is often overt, and it is obvious that the media have been successful in besmirching Freemasonry to the extent of giving it a wholly unwarranted Bad Name. That this campaign of vilification has succeeded is clear when one peruses the biographies of well-known personages (including Architects) who were prominent Freemasons (e.g. Soane): the authors of those works have avoided all mention of their subjects' Freemasonic connections (even though their affiliations are widely recognised, and, in some cases, where portraits exist, showing them wearing Freemasonic regalia, aprons, etc. [e.g. again Soane]). Such omissions are indicative, at best, of carelessness, or, at worst, of a desire to obfuscate by omitting or distorting the truth, which ill-serves history or scholarship, is unfair to those whose lives are the subjects of biographies, and is a shameful indictment of our times.

So to claim Freemasonic connections can call down the wrath of commentators. For example, suggestions that certain European gardens were kinds of social work-schemes have been offered by hostile critics[34] when those places were proposed as having mnemonic, educational, and Freemasonic elements in their designs: such a dreary, utilitarian, and unimaginative interpretation ignores the fact that in one of the gardens mentioned, the bridges over the waters offer many different *technical* and *stylistic* solutions to their design, clearly intended for *educational* and associated reasons to teach by example, allusion, and mnemonics[35]. Why bother, one might ask, if such gardens were only designed to give employment to out-of-work soldiers?[36] One is simply staggered by the poverty of learning and the banality of mind that cannot even *begin* to see beyond tedious materialist agendas.

Others (stuck with absurdly blinkered beliefs that *everything* began with the Old Testament) have offered niggling comments on aspects of Freemasonic words and symbols, entirely missing the whole picture, and failing to notice that there is more than one way in which those words and symbols can be used, because errors of interpretation yesterday can become 'truth' and 'orthodoxy' today. What has been truly upsetting is the vitriolic abuse[37], evidence of permanently closed minds (and shut eyes), and arrogant dismissal of things about which such pusillanimous critics have obviously never thought, and so may be motivated more by ignoble attitudes than by intellectual honesty (a commodity nowadays in short supply), to put it as kindly as possible.

This study will attempt to avoid excessive speculation, and will be concerned with Iconography, Architecture, Types, Gardens, Literature, Music, Stage-design, and much else. It will try to eschew the sensational, and will be based upon sound sources and on my own observations, although reasoned hypotheses are offered on more than one occasion, parallels are drawn, and comparisons are made on reasonable and logical bases. To the enquiring mind all subjects offer scope for investigation: the Architecture, Artefacts, Designs, Symbols, and Influences associated with Freemasonry are eminently respectable topics with which to be concerned. Unfortunately, some writers have tended to jeopardise Freemasonic studies by indulging in wild claims and sensationalism: like some recent investigations into the peculiar world of pre-Newtonian European culture, any study of Freemasonry is bedevilled by the existence of a vast 'literature' of worthless speculation and inaccurate outpourings from the loony fringe of Occultism. This does not mean that an attempt to study the relatively small percentage of what may be described as sound Freemasonic material should be avoided, for the Craft does have a serious, fascinating, and important history that is essential to approach and consider in any evaluation of certain aspects of architectural and cultural history – indeed, it would be irresponsible to ignore it. This book, therefore, is intended to offer a flavour of what may lie in wait for future historians sufficiently inquisitive, open-minded, and intellectually curious to delve further into fascinating realms, where sanity, not absurd speculation, prevails.

---

33 One of the reasons why I never wanted to become a Freemason is that I dislike meetings: as an academic I had to attend more time-wasting meetings than I care to remember, meetings revelled in by people who had nothing better to do, and who could never recall what was discussed at the last session. Pointless, fatuous meetings for the sake of having meetings are no way to use with profit one's brief time on earth.
34 Macpherson (1998).
35 Curl (2004).
36 As Macpherson (1998) would have us believe.

37 See Gilbert (*Ed.*) (1998*b*) 54-74.

CHAPTER I

What is Freemasonry 1?

Introduction; Freemasons 1; Freemasons 2; Freemasons 3; Epilogue

'The origin of Freemasonry is one of the most debated, and debatable, subjects in the whole realm of historical enquiry. One has to distinguish between the legendary history of Freemasonry and the problem of when it actually began as an organised institution. According to masonic legend, Freemasonry is as old as architecture itself…'

FRANCES AMELIA YATES (1899-1981):
The Rosicrucian Enlightenment
(London: Routledge & Kegan Paul, 1972) 209.

'In the world today there exists a great organization with a ritual and a code of conduct which entitle it to be called the direct descendant of the mysteries of later antiquity. Freemasonry justly claims to be a system of morality. Within it allegory and symbolism play an indispensable part…'

REGINALD ELDRED WITT (1903-80):
Isis in the Græco-Roman World
(London: Thames & Hudson, 1971) 157.

Introduction

The origins and meanings of the word 'Freemason' itself have been much disputed and have stirred up fierce passions. Four main views on the matter have been propounded:

1. that 'Freemason' stands for 'free-stone mason', a special grade of stonemasons specialising in the carving of *freestone*;
2. that Freemasons were 'free'[1] of a Guild[2];
3. that itinerant Masons were termed 'free' because they were exempt from the control of local Guilds of towns in which they temporarily settled in order to work, and that skilled artisans were emancipated in order to be able to travel and render their services where great stone buildings were being erected; and
4. that the word means a member of a Fraternity called, more fully, Free and Accepted Masons.

Let us examine the first three of these matters, starting with 1. Item 4 will be discussed in the following Chapter.

Freemasons 1

Freestone is any fine-grained limestone or sandstone that can be freely worked in any direction, sawn, or carved, and so can be used for fine work, undercutting, and sculpted decoration. A *Freemason*, therefore, in one sense, was one who worked with *freestone*, preparing it, carving it, and creating architectural enrichments from it: he should be contrasted with a Roughmason, Hard-Hewer, Layer, or Rowmason, the last four terms signifying those who roughly shaped stone using axes or scappling-hammers. Begemann and other scholars believed that the

---

[1] That is, invested with the rights or immunities of or admitted to the privileges of a Chartered Company, Corporation, City, Guild, or the like, e.g. free of one of the Livery Companies of the City of London.

[2] A Confraternity, Brotherhood, or Association formed for the material aid and protection of its members. Trade Guilds were associations of persons engaged in the same Craft, formed for the purpose of protecting and promoting their common interests, among them, before the Reformation, the maintenance of Chantry-chapels for frequent saying of Masses on behalf of the souls of departed Brethren.

Freemason, like the Marbler (who worked with marble) and the Alabasterer (who worked with alabaster, notably for funerary monuments, reredoses, etc.), was so named because he worked with freestone[3]. Now freestone, in the form of fine limestone (with which vast numbers of English Mediaeval buildings were constructed) can be found in a long belt from Dorset in south-west England to the Yorkshire coast, and was the favoured material for undercutting and elaborate decorative carving. Although sandstones occurred in several parts of the country (notably in Cheshire and Shropshire), and much finely carved work may be found of that material, the haunter of English ecclesiastical buildings will be fully aware that the most outstanding work is of limestone. It is probably significant that in Scotland, where freestone is not ubiquitous (and much of the stone is hard and intractable, like the granites of Aberdeenshire, although sandstone is found in places like Dumfriesshire), the word 'Freemason', as a trade-name, was rare or non-existent, although it does occur in the seventeenth century[4].

Freemasons seem to have been regarded as a cut above ordinary Masons, and the word apparently meant craftsmen who could hew and set freestone, whilst the term 'Mason' seems to have referred to all those who worked with stone. To confuse matters, the terms 'Freemason' and 'Mason' were sometimes synonymous[5], or at least interchangeable[6].

In Mediaeval work, therefore, freestone was used for tracery, carved capitals, canopies, images, crockets, finials, gargoyles, mouldings, and so on. The London Assize of Wages (1212)[7] refers to *sculptores lapidum liberorum*, meaning carvers of freestones, and the notion that a Freemason was a Mason who worked with freestone seems to derive from a reference to *mestre meson de franche peer* (master-mason of free stone) in 1350-1[8]. In 1391 a *Magister Lathomus Liberarum Petrarum* is mentioned in connection with building-works at Oxford[9], and the term 'Freestone Masons' may be found in connection with the building-accounts of Wadham College, Oxford, which would seem to clinch the case for 'Freemason' being a particular type of Mason[10]. Robert Grumbold[11] and other members of the Grumbold family associated with the quarrying villages of Raunds and Weldon in Northamptonshire were described as 'Freemasons', and the description 'Freestone Mason' also occurs in connection with Norwich building-accounts[12]. It is clear from many sources that a Freemason was not the same as a Hard-Hewer (who worked with the unattractive and very hard Kentish ragstone), Roughmason, or Rowmason[13], all of whom *only* worked with axes or scappling-hammers. Other terms included *cubitores* (cutters of stone into blocks) and *imaginatores* (carvers of images).

In Scotland and in the North of England are found references to Cowans, who appear to have been workers with stone who were equivalent to the Roughmasons of England. A Cowan was forbidden to work with lime-mortar, as was a dry-stone waller or *diker*: the term was also applied derogatorily to a labourer who worked with stone, but who had not been regularly apprenticed, so it was given to anybody who was uninitiated into the secrets of Freemasonry. The connection with men who *worked* with stone should be emphasised, contrasted with so-called 'Speculative' Freemasons. The Mother Kilwinning Lodge of Ayrshire described a Cowan as a Mason without the Word, and Freemasons were to guard the Lodge with drawn swords to protect it from all 'Cowens and Eves-Droppers'. Skilled masons had regulated wages, and were superior to Cowans, who were regarded with suspicion and hostility for trying to find out the secrets of the Craft which would enhance their position. Cowans, therefore, became defined as sneaks or prying persons, the uninitiated, the outsiders, the profane. So it is quite clear that Freemasons had an interest in maintaining their position as *craftsmen* of a superior type, and that their secret signs were a means of ensuring status, wealth, and the keeping of the untrained at bay. Thus a Freemason, in the Craft sense, would have been familiar with the trowel, but a Cowan would have had no use for such a tool, as he was forbidden to use lime at all. *Lime*, therefore, is of singular importance, in many senses, to the history of so-called 'Operative' and 'Speculative' Freemasonry (terms used here for convenience, but not universally approved).

The terms *Cementarius*, *Lathomos*, *Lathomus*, *Lapicida*, *Masonn*, *Masoun*, *Mazon* all occur in Mediaeval documents, so the Latin and Norman-French words were in common use then[14]. Some have claimed that 'Freemason' first occurs in English in the City of London *Letter-Book* H of 9 August 1376[15]. This was the year in which the composition of the Common Council of the City of London was changed under the mayoralty of John of Northampton, who determined to give the less wealthy citizens a greater say in the City's affairs by altering the means by which the members of that Council were elected. Until that time the merchant oligarchy[16] controlled London's government, and Northampton succeeded in obtaining agreement that members of Council should be nominated by the various Mysteries, or Guilds, or Livery Companies of the City rather than by Wards.

'Mystery', of course, is a corruption of the Latin *misterium* (an altered form of *ministerium*) as *mistera* or

---

3 Begemann (1909-10) *passim*. See also Knoop & Jones (1948) 14.
4 Stevenson (1988b) 11.
5 *See* Papworth (*Ed.*) (1852) **iii** 91-2.
6 Knoop & Jones (1948) 13,
7 BM. Add.MS.14252, fol. 133b to 134b.
8 25 Edw. III St. 2 c. 3.
9 Knoop & Jones (1948) 14, quoting Herbert Edward Salter's edited *Mediaeval Archives of the University of Oxford* (Oxford: Oxford Historical Society 1920-1) 22. See also Knoop & Jones (1967) esp. 198-9.
10 Knoop & Jones (1948) 14.
11 *See* Colvin (2008) 454-5.
12 *Ars Quatuor Coronatorum* (1930) **xliii** 223.

13 'Rowmasons' described layers of stone (or even bricklayers).
14 Knoop & Jones (1967) 82. *See* also City of London *Cal. Letter-Books* B 9 and other sources listed in Knoop & Jones (1967).
15 *Ars Quatuor Coronatorum* **li** (1938).
16 Prescott (2004) 64.

misterie, meaning a craft, skill, trade, occupation, art, service, profession, or calling, although there may also be a connection with *maistre*, an old form of *master* or *mastery*, indicating well-developed professional skills, related to the old French *mestier*, and its modern equivalent, *metier*, meaning trade or profession, or a person's 'line' in which he or she is specially skilled. An example of the use of the word 'mystery' can be found in the grandiose titles of some of the present-day Livery Companies of the City of London, such as 'The Master and Wardens and Brethren and Sisters of the Guild or Fraternity of the Blessed Virgin Mary of the Mystery of Drapers of the City of London'[17].

Following Northampton's intervention, the nominations made by the various Companies to the Common Council in 1376 were recorded in two of the City's official records: the *Plea and Memoranda Rolls* and the *London Letter-Books* (of which the relevant volume is that designated H). Four men (John Artelburgh, Robert Henwick, John Lesnes, and Thomas Wrek) were nominated as representatives of the stonemasons: in the *Plea and Memoranda Rolls* they were designated 'masons', but in the *Letter-Books* they were described as 'freemasons'[18], but the scribe scored this out, replacing it with 'masons'. Professor Prescott has suggested that, in the 'politically charged atmosphere of Northampton's mayoralty the change may have been more significant, perhaps suggesting that the representatives had originally been drawn from a particular group of stonemasons'[19]. Did this mean that the men were Roughmasons, or was 'Mason' substituted as a loose term to include 'Freemasons'? W. J. Williams, in his useful article on 'The Use of the Word "Freemason" before 1717'[20], points out that 'Freemason' (various spellings) recurs in documents, though 'Mason' is more usual. However, it is clear that four men were elected to represent the Mystery of Masons, which seems to have been of fourteenth-century date, probably established between 1356 and 1376. It has been claimed that 1376 was the earliest date when 'Freemason' was recorded, but this is not so. The Coroners' Rolls of the City of London contain an account of an escape from prison in 1325[21]. The Coroner and Sheriffs of the City held an inquiry, and it was found that ten prisoners had broken out of Newgate Gaol, and that they had been assisted in so doing by others, including one Nicholas le Freemason[22].

The metrical romance in Middle English *Floris*[23] and *Blancheflour*, which forms the basis of *Filocolo* by Giovanni Boccaccio, probably derives from a French original of *c*.1250-1300. In it is a description of a tower, finely made of limestone and marble, to which the hero gains access by pretending to be a Freemason[24], and emphasising the point by carrying a square and scale[25]. However, even manuscript versions of this poem vary: the so-called *Auchinleck MS*, dating from the 1330s, and now in the National Library of Scotland[26], refers to a 'masoun', but the *Egerton MS*[27], which belonged to George Granville Leveson-Gower, 2nd Duke of Sutherland (from 1833), and dates from the latter part of the fourteenth century, contains the term 'free mason'[28]. It would therefore appear that, by the fourteenth century, and especially the last quarter of that century, the word 'freemason' had probably come to mean a special type of mason. In 1396 'ffre maceons' are mentioned with regard to works at Maidstone in Kent, and in 1396-7 'fremason' is said to have been used in the Fabric Rolls of Exeter Cathedral, Devon[29]. In 1314, however, Sir John Bishopsden of Lapworth, Warwickshire, covenanted with two Masons for the erection of a convenient house of freestone (*de pere fraunche*) at his Manor there[30].

Knoop and Jones pointed out that in the fifteenth and sixteenth centuries the same men (e.g. a John Marwe of Norwich, a John Croxton of London, and a Gabriel Coldham of London) were described as both 'masons' and 'freemasons'[31]. The London organisation of the Craft was sometimes described as a Company of Masons and sometimes as a Company of Freemasons[32]. Later associations at Canterbury, Exeter, Kendal, Lincoln, Ludlow, Newcastle, and Norwich were called Companies of Masons, but those at Alnwick, Bristol, Durham, Gateshead, and Oxford were Companies of Freemasons[33]. We know that a Company of Masons existed in London in 1376, and it seems it was also called 'the company of ffreemasons of the City of London' until the middle of the seventeenth century[34]. Matters were drastically changed by the Great Fire of London in 1666, for the ancient monopoly of The Masons' Company was broken by the necessity of admitting 'foreigners' to assist with the rebuilding, but there was another factor that has been largely ignored by so-called 'masonic' historians: the Gothic style of Architecture largely survived, and was the *architectural language* familiar to members of The Masons' Company. Masons working under the direction of Christopher Wren had to work within the parameters of the Architecture of post-Renaissance Europe (that is, Architecture derived from Roman Classicism), not the principles of Gothic: the result was that nobody, after 1666, would have thought

---

17 See, for example, Curl (2000d) 38-40.
18 Actually 'free masons'
19 Prescott (2004) 65.
20 *Ars Quatuor Coronatorum* **xlviii** (1935).
21 Sharpe (Ed.) (1913) 130-1.
22 Prescott (2004) 65.
23 Also given as *Flores*.

24 This theme recurs, including in *Die Entführung aus dem Serail* (The Abduction from the Harem), a *Singspiel* in three Acts of 1782, with libretto by Christoph Friedrich Bretzner and Gottlieb Stephanie, and music by Mozart (K.384). The hero in this instance has become an Architect (*Baumeister*, often used instead of *Architekt*, but meaning a Master-Builder).
25 *Squyer and scantlon* in one version, and *squir and scantiloun* in another.
26 See Kooper (Ed.) (2006) and Taylor (Ed.) (1927).
27 British Library MS.2862, also known as the *Trentham MS*.
28 Prescott (2004) 64-7.
29 Papworth (Ed.) (1852) **iii** 91.
30 Parker (Ed.) (1853) **ii** 5-6.
31 Knoop & Jones (1948) 13.
32 See *Ars Quatuor Coronatorum* **xlv** (1932).
33 Knoop & Jones (1967) *passim*, and Knoop & Jones (1948) 13.
34 Jones (1986) 75.

of sending to London for Masons to build in Gothic, but in any part of the country where the Mason, rather than the Carpenter or Bricklayer, still dominated the building-trade, Gothic survived as a style, well into the eighteenth century[35].

The crisis caused by the need to rebuild London after the Fire led to it being made lawful for members of the building-trade who were *not* Freemen of the City to work there, and at the end of seven years such 'foreigners' earned the right to continue to work in London. According to Bernard E. Jones there 'is evidence of non-operative membership'[36] of The Masons' Company in 1663, even women being among the members. As early as 1630 *The Masons' Company* recorded Masons being 'Accepted', and in 1645-7 and 1649-50 there were 'Acception' dinners[37]. Some men who were already brethren of the Company by virtue of their being Operative Masons, were 'made' 'Accepted' Masons, which suggests that they were initiated into some special group within the Company[38], and 'Acception' can be traced back through documentary records to 1619-20[39]. However, 'Acception' or 'Accepted' Masons does not therefore mean that these terms were associated with men who did *not* work with stone, as has often been suggested, but that 'Acception' pointed to some kind of special category, perhaps connected with esoteric knowledge, or perhaps with rare or advanced skills.

It has been claimed that many of the records of the Company were lost during the Great Fire, but it would seem that this is not accurate, for, as Conder showed, a great deal of material survived, as late as 1722, including some dated prior to the Reformation[40]. In any case the Fire started far enough from the Company's Hall (situated between Basinghall and Coleman Streets) to enable all valuables to be rescued and taken to safety. It would appear from surviving material that some sort of highly elaborate ritual existed within the Craft of Masonry long before the Fire[41]. These matters will be discussed below. However, some further information has also survived. The Masons were thirtieth in order of precedence in 1616 and are so today. The Company was granted Arms[42] in 1472, although these are usually given inaccurately: the chevron is distinctly referred to as engrailed, yet it is often shown as a plain chevron. Under King Edward IV the Company was enfranchised in 1481, and called the 'Fellowship of Free Masons'[43].

Freemasons 2

The argument is that Freemasons were so-called because they were 'free' of a Guild. 'Free' in this usage, indicates status, as in a municipal organisation or in a Company or Guild (e.g. Freeman of the City of London or Freeman of a London Livery Company), where a person was invested with the rights and immunities of, or admitted to the privileges of, a Chartered Company, Corporation, City, or the like, *or* as an indication of freedom from some kind of obligation or serfdom. Yet, as Knoop and Jones pointed out[44], most Masons were not 'free' of a Company or Guild. It seems fairly clear from extant documents that Apprentices were not to be of servile status or birth, and that the peripatetic nature of domicile connected with the stonemason's trade made any binding to a Manor impossible, yet nevertheless an Apprentice could hardly be regarded as entirely free, and his status while an Apprentice resembled that of a servant[45], yet fifteenth-century 'Charges' were specific in stating Apprentices should not be of 'bond blood' (i.e. descended from serfs or base vassals)[46].

It is highly unlikely that such major works as London Bridge (begun 1176, completed some 30 years later) were carried on without some sort of organisation closely linked to the City. We know that in 1272 two Master Masons were chosen as City Viewers, with duties to inspect the walls and gates of the City at regular intervals[47]. They shared this task with two Master Carpenters. The Middle Ages are not mysteriously clouded (as is often assumed), for we know a great deal about English Mediaeval Masons (who were also designers of buildings, and therefore were Architects)[48]. Certainly the greatest of Master Masons were persons of considerable standing, such as Henry Yeveley (*or* Yevele), who has been called the 'Wren of the fourteenth century' and 'England's greatest architect'[49].

So the 'Mystery' of Masons had gained official recognition by at least the fourteenth century, although it seems the Company or Fellowship did not obtain its Livery until 1481. Before that, in 1463, it acquired ground and buildings from the Priory and Convent of Holy Trinity, Aldgate, in order to establish a Hall. In 1472, as we have seen, the Achievement of Arms was granted, and in 1481 a new set of ordinances was approved[50]. The property acquired in 1463 passed into private ownership after the Dissolution, but the Company re-acquired it in 1562. After the catastrophe of 1666 the Hall was rebuilt in 1670, but the site was sold in 1865, and the Company has since been without its own Hall.

In 1509-10 the 'hoole felliship of the craft mistere or science of Fremasons enfraunchesed within this Cittie' presented a petition to the Court of Aldermen relating to the quality of freestone, marble, and hard stone, and this

---

35 Colvin (1999) 222-3. *See* also Curl (2007a) Chapter I.
36 Jones (1986) 77-8.
37 Stevenson (1988b) 217.
38 *Ars Quatuor Coronatorum* **ix** (1896) 29-37.
39 Knoop & Jones (1948) 146-7.
40 Conder (1894) 188.
41 Conder (1894) 53-100.
42 *A feld of Sablys A Cheveron silver grailed thre Castellis of the same garnysshed w^t dores and wyndows of the feld in the Cheveron a Cumpas of Blak*. The Crest was also a Castle, as in the Arms, and the Motto was 'In the Lord is all our Trust'. This Motto, however, was not the original: that was 'God is our Guide'. *See* Conder (1894) 84-5.
43 London Companies MS. 108 **i** 38, quoted in Conder (1894) 97.

44 Knoop & Jones (1948) 15.
45 Knoop & Jones (1967) 108 and Knoop & Jones (1948) 15.
46 *Ibid*.
47 Smith (1989) 3.
48 *See*, for example, Harvey (1987) *passim*.
49 Harvey (1987) 366.
50 Smith (1989) 4-5.

appears to be the first surviving occasion on which the term 'Freemason' is applied to the Fellowship or Company as a whole (although it had earlier been used for individuals). In 1521 the 'mistere of Masons' petitioned for additions to their ordinances relating to the acceptance of Apprentices by indenture, to the number of Apprentices that could be taken on by the Wardens, Liverymen, and Fellowship, to the prohibitions on 'foreigners' from practising their Craft in the City, and to the necessity of making 'foreigners' pay quarterage to the Company, and to wages of Apprentices and regulations that Apprentices who had served four years should be presented to the Chamberlain of the City and the Wardens, then admitted to the Company. A further assize of 1580 refers to Purbeck stone and to 'Fremasons'. From 1607 records survive relating to the Master, Wardens, and organisation of the 'Company of Freemasons enfranchised within this City'[51]. Nobody was to be admitted to the Fellowship by redemption without first being examined and found proficient, and 'persons of the said craft mistery or science' were thenceforth once in every three years 'to be clad in one clothing convenient to their powers and degrees'[52].

By the early seventeenth century the Company consisted of a Master, two Wardens, a Court of Assistants, a Livery, and a body of Freemen or Yeomanry. Apprentices were bound for seven years, after which they were entitled to become Freemen of the Company on payment of a gratuity, a 'fine', and a fee. The 'fine' on promotion to the Livery was £3 plus a steward's 'fine' of £6, no small sums then. There were also 'fines' on election to the Court of Assistants, and Assistants could proceed to Renter Warden, then Upper Warden, then Master, so the organisation was similar to that of other Livery Companies. Admission to the Company could also be obtained by the sons of Freemen who were not necessarily Operative Masons: admissions by Patrimony cost the same amount an apprentice had to pay on becoming a Freeman.

Following the Restoration of the Monarchy in 1660, the Company determined to obtain a Royal Charter under the Great Seal, as it was experiencing difficulties in enforcing its regulations, and the Charter of The Carpenters' Company was used as the template. However, as has been explained above, the new, Continental architectural style and shortages of London Masons necessitated the employment of 'foreigners' to carry out work after the 1666 Fire, and Parliament passed an Act[53] permitting Masons and other craftsmen *not* Freemen of the City to work there during the rebuilding, and, furthermore, after seven years had passed, could have the same privileges as Freemen for the rest of their lives[54].

In 1677 the Charter was granted by which Masons Free of the City, and all others using the Art in London and Westminster, or within seven miles compass of the same, were incorporated in the name of The Master, Wardens, Assistants, and Commonalty of the Art and Mystery of Masons of the City of London. Rules and regulations were registered with the Court of Aldermen in 1678 in which year the Company acquired its Common Seal. The Charter was confirmed in 1683, renewed in 1688, and in 1702 a Charter of Exemplification of the original Charter of Charles II was obtained.

However, the Company was clearly severely weakened by its loss of influence to Architects and 'foreigners', and although it prayed (1694) for an Act of the Court of Common Council to lay it down that all Apprentices of Masons Free of other Companies should be bound and made Free of The Masons' Company, such enactments were largely ineffective, and by the beginning of the eighteenth century prevailing economic and cultural forces had proved to be too strong, and the traditional skills of Master Masons were usurped by Architects. Nevertheless, it was at Masons' Hall in 1682 that Elias Ashmole, Astrologer, Antiquary, Alchemist, and Founder of the Ashmolean Museum in Oxford, attended a Fellowship of Freemasons, after which they all dined at the 'Halfe Moone Tavern in Cheapside'. Of those present, several were members of The Masons Company (including the Master and Wardens)[55]. So it is clear from this and other evidence that so-called 'Speculative' Freemasonry and 'Operative' Freemasonry were closely connected in the seventeenth century, and that Masons in the upper echelons, called 'Accepted', were *essentially* craftsmen and *not* dilettanti, although certain worthy persons might be invited to events because of especial knowledge, interests, or intellectual attainments.

Thus 'Freemason' had, by the seventeenth century, acquired a new meaning. Although it still denoted an 'Operative' mason who cut or set freestone (as is clear from a letter of Daniel Finch [2nd Earl of Nottingham from 1682] which complained of a shortage of 'freemasons to prepare stone' for his great house at Burley-on-the-Hill, Rutland[56]), it also began to refer to a member of a Fraternity called 'Free and Accepted Masons'. Early in the seventeenth century, as has been mentioned, it appears that societies of Freemasons, or Guilds of Masons, began to admit honorary members who were not necessarily connected with the building-trades, but who might have achieved a certain eminence in Architecture and/or Antiquarian scholarship. Apparently those with interests in other aspects of esoteric knowledge were also admitted, and some of these were called 'Accepted Masons', although the name 'Freemasons' was often applied: they were given knowledge of secret signs, instructed in the legendary 'histories' of the Craft, and took part in convivial and social gatherings, but it should be emphasised that 'Accepted Masons' were *also* 'Operative' Masons (albeit in some sort of exalted category), so matters are by no means clear-cut.

---

51 Smith (1989) 6-7.
52 *Ibid.*.
53 18 & 19 Cha.II *c.*8.
54 *See* Conder (1894) 192-3.
55 Conder (1894) 204-5. Ashmole joined a Freemasonic Lodge in Warrington in 1646.
56 British Library Add. MS 29595 f.112. *See* Sir John Habbakuk (1990): 'Daniel Finch, 2nd Earl of Nottingham' in *Rutland Record. Journal of the Rutland Record Society* **x** 347-361.

It seems that the first 'histories' of Freemasonry date from the Middle Ages: in these documents Geometry is regarded as one of the Seven Liberal Arts, and Masonry (in the sense of the Craft of building with stone) was seen as equivalent to Geometry in significance. Given its importance, therefore, it is not surprising to find that the Greek mathematician, Euclid, was held to be a figure of great wisdom, and indeed began to be identified with the wisest of the Ancients, and was himself the keeper of mysteries and the deepest founts of knowledge[57]. John Lydgate, Prior of Hatfield Regis and poet, in his *Everything To His Semblable*, refers to the fact that

> 'By crafft of Ewclyde mason dothe his cure,
> To suwe heos mooldes ruyle, and his plumlyne…,'

and the equating of Architecture-with-Geometry-with-Freemasonry explains much of the legendary history as found in *MS. Constitutions of Masonry*, also known as the *Old Charges* ('Charges' being Orders for the conduct of the Craft or trade), of which the *Cooke MS* and *Regius Poem* are early versions, containing details of regulations, wages, and other matters concerning the 'Degrees' of Masters, Craftsmen, and Apprentices[58]. Knoop, Jones, and Hamer have edited *The Two Earliest Masonic MSS*, which appeared in 1938[59], but the reasons for the compilations of the manuscripts remain obscure: speculation as to why exactly these strange accounts developed would be profitless, but the documents are important as links between 'Operative' and 'Speculative' Freemasonry, for they stress the venerable nature of the connections of the Craft with myths, Antiquity, and a moral system of conduct.

The Reverend James Anderson published his *The New Book of the Constitutions of the Antient and Honourable Fraternity of Free and Accepted Masons* in London in 1738[60], a development of his earlier *The Constitution of the Free-Masons*[61], in which he collated, enlarged, and 'improved' the 'Gothic' Constitutions, transforming the Mediaeval Masonic texts into a weird amalgam of history and fairy-story in the process. Many of his claims do not stand up to serious examination: the Emperor Augustus as Grand Master of a Lodge in Imperial Rome, and similar promotion of King Nebuchadnezzar as a Masonic figure in Babylon, are only two ludicrous examples of spurious notions that gathered further accretions in the course of time, and only served to cloak real Masonic history in fictions, obfuscations, and fantasies, thereby ridiculing it in the eyes of sober professional historians.

The *Cooke MS* was shown at a meeting on 24 June 1721 during which John Montagu, 2nd Duke of Montagu from 1709, was elected Grand Master of the Grand Lodge of Freemasons in London: the meeting was described by the Antiquary William Stukeley, who had become a Freemason in 1720 when 'curiosity led him to be initiated into the mysteries of Masonry, suspecting it to be the remains of the mysterys of the antients'[62]. Stukeley noted that, during the meeting, Montagu's predecessor as Grand Master, George Payne, produced an 'old MS of the Constitutions which he got in the west of England 500 years old'[63]. Stukeley also made drawings of the MS[64] which show that the *Cooke MS*, now in the British Library[65], was indeed the document shown by Payne.

Now the document we know as the *Cooke MS* is in prose, written in Middle English: it contains a *legendary* history of the Craft of stonemasonry as well as regulations for stonemasons. Its appearance at Grand Lodge was the catalyst that prompted the following meeting of the Lodge to request James Anderson to prepare what was to become *The Constitutions…*, but the published work bears little resemblance to the *Cooke MS*, or indeed to any other 'Charges' that survived from before 1717[66]. Claims that Anderson had rescued the ancient texts from 'Gothic ignorance' of the 'dark illiterate ages' (as John Theophilus Desaguliers, who should have known better, described matters in the *Dedication* printed in 1723[67]), are both exaggerated and absurd, revealing woeful ignorance and lack of understanding of Mediaeval culture, further marred by dubious feelings of unwarranted moral and intellectual superiority. Transcripts of the MS were made by Grand Secretary William Reid in or around 1728[68], after which the *Cooke MS* passed into private hands (acquiring spurious additions in pseudo-Gothic script in the process) before being purchased by Sir Frederick Madden, Keeper of Manuscripts at the British Museum, in 1859[69]. The Freemason Matthew Cooke published a transcript with a fake facsimile (made with special type) in 1861[70].

Madden had noticed that what became known as the *Cooke MS* bore a strong resemblance to another MS in the British Museum[71], but this time the work is in verse, incorporating extracts from Middle English poems. It contains, like the *Cooke MS*, a legendary history of the Craft, with ordinances of stonemasons, and had been published[72] by James Orchard Halliwell[73] in his *Early History of Freemasonry in England*. Halliwell had realised the Masonic significance of the 'Poem of Moral Duties' in the Old Royal Library of the British Museum: it was entitled *Constitutiones Artis Geometrie Secundum Euclidem*[74] in the Catalogue

---

57 Knoop & Jones (1948) 1 and *passim*.
58 *Ibid.* 62.
59 Knoop, Jones, & Hamer (*Eds.*) (1938).
60 Anderson (*Ed.*) (1738).
61 Anderson (*Ed.*) (1723).
62 Lukis (*Ed.*) (1882-7) **i** 267. Stukeley had been constituted as Grand Master in 1721, and he was also a founder-member of the re-established Society of Antiquaries of London (1718).
63 See Haycock (2002) 176. See also Knoop, Jones, & Hamer (*Eds.*) (1938) 54-55.
64 Now among Stukeley's papers at the Bodleian Library, Oxford. See Knoop, Jones, & Hamer (*Eds.*) (1938) 55.
65 Add. MS23198.
66 Prescott (2005) 44.
67 Anderson (*Ed.*) (1723).
68 Now known as the *Woodford MS*. See Knoop, Jones, & Hamer (*Eds.*) (1938) 55ff.
69 *See* Prescott (2005) 44.
70 Cooke (*Ed.*) (1861).
71 Royal MS 17. A. I.
72 Halliwell (*Ed.*) (1844).
73 Later Halliwell-Phillipps.
74 *See* Knoop, Jones, & Hamer (*Eds.*) (1938) 53.

prepared in 1734 by David Casley, and Halliwell described his find in a paper he gave to the Society of Antiquaries of London in 1839, first published in 1840[75]. This manuscript had been owned by the antiquary John Theyer, after whose death it and several hundred manuscripts passed to his grandson, Charles Theyer, and then to the bookseller Robert Scott. William Beveridge (later [1704] Bishop of St Asaph) and William Jane prepared (1678) a partial catalogue of this material[76], 312 items from which were purchased by King Charles II. Among them was the poem, called by R. F. Gould the *Regius MS*: Gould seems to have been suspicious of anyone who was not a Freemason having anything to do with the Craft, so, unlike Cooke (who *was* a Freemason), *Royal MS* 17 A. I. was not named after Halliwell[77], and Gould's label stuck. The *Cooke* and *Regius MSS* are the only Mediaeval texts dealing with the legendary history of the stonemasons' craft and the ordinances for stonemasons that appear to have survived: they are known as the 'Old Charges' to distinguish them from later manuscripts.

Now these 'Old Charges' are very unusual documents. They seem concerned with the establishment of a sense of community and brotherhood[78] among stonemasons as well as the encouragement of pride in their works. Love of and loyalty to the Craft could be expressed through symbols and intellect, and the lines of demarcation between Masonry as a Craft skill and the social status accorded to those with the Mason's skills were blurred. The texts conferred legitimacy on the Craft by celebrating it and its legendary origins, and on its practitioners by providing frameworks and regulations within which they could carry out their work, and they provided craftsmen who had to travel great distances with texts that framed an intellectual and spiritual home[79].

Later versions of the 'Old Charges' have been regarded as indicative of Freemasonry in the 'Speculative' sense as having been in existence in the sixteenth century in England. However, just to take one example[80] of these, accepted by most 'Masonic' historians as being of *c.*1600 (probably because Sir Edward Augustus Bond, Keeper of Manuscripts at the British Museum [1866-78], opined that it was of that time), dating of texts was not always accurate. The Masonic writer, W. J. Hughan[81], true to form, reported that another Masonic scholar, A. F. A. Woodford, attempted to give the *Lansdowne MS* an even earlier date of *c.*1560. However, the script on the manuscript is certainly not Elizabethan, and would appear to be of the latter part of the seventeenth rather than the end of the sixteenth century. Indeed, it would seem to date from the period 1690-1700, and this dating is confirmed by other scholars.[82]

Similarly, the *Regius MS* has been dated *c.*1390[83] by numerous writers, who borrowed from Hughan, who, in turn, took his case from Casley. Now Casley, like many other early-eighteenth-century cataloguers, had only a rudimentary understanding of the problems of dating manuscripts, and was working long before scholarly methods of doing so evolved. Halliwell had dated the *Regius MS* as 'not later than the latter part of the 14th century'[84], but he cannot be regarded as an authority either, as he was working when methodical and scientific study of Mediaeval scripts was only beginning. Bond felt it dated from the middle of the fifteenth century, and that the *Cooke MS* dated from the middle or later part of that century[85], but subsequently thought that both dated from the first half of the fifteenth century[86]. Woodford could not accept these findings, and sought other opinions. If the *Regius MS* is to be dated by reference to its script, then it must date from the first half of the fifteenth century[87]. But it is unwise to rely on scripts alone: it was the great German scholar and philologist Begemann who drew attention to the *language* of the *Regius MS* which he identified as a dialect found in Herefordshire, northern Gloucestershire, and southern Worcestershire[88]. Hamer thought that both the *Regius* and *Cooke* MSS were written in the dialect spoken in the south-western Midlands of England during the latter part of the fourteenth century, but observed that the *Cooke MS* contained more southern forms, although the dialects of Gloucestershire and West Oxfordshire were detectable[89]. Further investigations were carried out on the *Regius MS* in *A Linguistic Atlas of Late Mediaeval English*[90], which placed it as having originated in Shropshire: the manuscript which most closely resembles the *Regius MS* is a version[91] of *Instructions for Parish Priests* by John Mirk (Augustinian Canon and later Prior of Lilleshall near present-day Telford in Shropshire), which has been dated to the second quarter of the fifteenth century[92]. Thus the *Regius MS* probably dates from some time between 1425 and 1450: indeed the last section of it includes just over one hundred lines on behaviour when attending Mass lifted from Mirk's *Instructions* (which seems to have been written in the 1380s[93]). The *Regius MS* also contains two

---

75 *Archaeologia* **xxviii** (1840) 444-7.
76 Now in the British Library Royal MSS Appendix 70.
77 Halliwell was regarded by Madden as a scoundrel who deserved transportation because he had apparently sold manuscripts from the Library of Trinity College Cambridge to the British Museum. *See* Bodleian Library Oxford MS. Eng. hist. C. 140-182.
78 *See*, for example, Cooper (2003).
79 *Ibid*. 23.
80 British Library Lansdowne MS 98 ff. 269-272.
81 Hughan (1895) 43-4.
82 *See* letter from Dr. Petrie (8 April 1960) in 'Old Charges – Various MSS' in the Library at Freemasons' Hall, London.
83 Knoop & Jones (1948) date it as *c.*1390.
84 Halliwell (1840) 7f.
85 Prescott (2005) 50-51.
86 *Masonic Magazine* **ii** (1874-5) 76ff.
87 Prescott (2005) 50-51.
88 Begemann (1902-10) **ii** 108-9. *See* also *Ars Quatuor Coronatorum* **vii** (1894) 34. Begemann was a truly remarkable scholar, and for a *German* to spot this geographical location says much about *English* native-born commentators.
89 Knoop, Jones, & Hamer (1938) 63, and *Ars Quatuor Coronatorum* **xciv** (1981) 166-9.
90 McIntosh, Samuels, & Benskin (*Eds.*) (1986) **i** 155, 233 ff., **ii** 424-38.
91 British Library Hand D, Cotton MS Claudius A.ii ff127r-152v.
92 *ODNB* **xxxviii** (2004) 368-9. *See* also Kristensson (*Ed.*) (1974) 13-15 and *passim*.
93 *See Notes & Queries* **ccxxvii** (1982) 487ff. and *ODNB* **xxxviii** (2004) 368-9.

other Middle English texts: one is a copy of *Urbanitatis*, a sort of manual of how to behave, especially with regard to eating and drinking[94], possibly associated with the reign of Edward IV, and a re-worked and shortened version of *Merita Missa*[95], a poem probably known in the mid-fifteenth century. Knoop, Jones, and Hamer reproduced parts of both the *Cooke* and *Regius* MSS[96], and a glance at their plates is sufficient to show that, although they are in different hands, they are contemporary. Bond's final view that they both date from the second quarter of the fifteenth century would appear to be not far off the mark. So what do these two documents contain?

The *Regius MS* starts with a description of how Euclid invented Geometry and called it Masonry, which created conditions for employment among the offspring of the Great and Good of Ancient Egypt. Euclid also ruled that although there were Masters among the Masons, yet all were equal, neither subjects nor servants (a remarkable notion which was to have an enormous resonance in the eighteenth century). The Craft was brought to England in the reign of King Æthelstan, who is supposed to have drawn up ordinances to regulate the Craft, and these are given in the poem: they include an emphasis on the importance of a general assembly of Masons (which all were expected to attend); the necessity of fair dealing, especially regarding payment for work done; the desirability of Masons treating with each other as equals, part of a Fellowship, members of which were obliged to assist each other in their tasks; the etiquette of table-manners, serving each other at table, and so on; and a very sensible warning against getting involved in litigation[97].

Now this mention of Æthelstan may not be as fanciful as it seems, for, arguably, he was the King of All England, and was noted for his piety: William of Malmesbury (Benedictine monk, historian, and man of letters), in his *Gesta Regum Anglorum*[98], states that there 'was scarcely any ancient house in all England that he (Æthelstan) did not adorn with buildings or ornaments, books, or estates', and the King's generosity as a donor of manuscripts and Relics was also remarked upon. Æthelstan's reign was also remarkable for the development of the monastic system[99]. With such a reputation, it is obvious that Architecture flourished in Æthelstan's time and that Architecture was practised by Master Masons, who also oversaw the building-works[100]. The *Regius MS* repeats that the ordinances relating to Masonry were established by King Æthelstan, then outlines the legend of the Four Crowned Martyrs (supposedly Christian stonemasons who were martyred during the reign of Emperor Diocletian) in 304, and were identified by Pope Melchiades [or Miltiades] as the *Quatuor Coronati*). Unfortunately, there appear to be two sets of Crowned Martyrs: one is a group of *five* Persian stonemasons, and the other four Roman soldiers. The Persians were named as Castorius, Claudius, Nicostratus, and Simpronian, but the fifth seems to have been dropped from popular accounts: Simpronian is supposed to have become a Christian because he thought the others' skills as stonemasons derived from their religion. They were killed for refusing to make a statue of Æsculapius and for refusing to sacrifice to the Roman deities. Their Relics were translated to the fine basilica of Santi Quattro Coronati on the Caelian Hill in Rome during the Pontificate of Leo IV. Another version of the legend makes the Martyrs four Roman soldiers, or four brothers, who were killed for not sacrificing to the god Æsculapius, and who were named SS. Carpophorus, Severianus, Severus, and Victorinus[101]. The Feast Day is 8 November: these Saints were popular in Mediaeval England, being recorded in numerous Benedictine calendars, and were especially the Patrons of Guilds of Stonemasons, the articles of which direct readers to read up about them in *The Golden Legend*[102], which also informed some of Mirk's effusions.

Regius MS then returns to the beginnings of stonemasonry, ascribing the destruction of the Tower of Babel to the pride of its creators. After this catastrophe, Euclid revived the Art of Masonry and divided all knowledge into the Seven Liberal Arts, consisting of the *Trivium* (Grammar, Logic [or Dialectic], and Rhetoric) and the *Quadrivium* (Arithmetic, Astronomy, Geometry, and Music)[103]. The poem ends with instructions for good living and appropriate behaviour drawn from Mirk, the *Merita Missa*, and *Urbanitatis* complete (including the necessity of being bare-headed in church, avoidance of spitting in certain company, and the unattractiveness of speaking with a full mouth).

The *Cooke MS* starts with a more expanded version of the history of stonemasonry, stressing the importance of God-given knowledge, such as that of Geometry, which was given supreme importance. All the world's crafts were founded by the sons of Lamech[104], with the eldest, Jabal, credited with the invention of Geometry. Lamech's sons inscribed their knowledge on two pillars of stone, and after the Flood Pythagoras found one of them and Hermes the other. Ham, son of Noah, Lamech's son, resurrected the Craft of Masonry and *his* son, Nimrod, sent trained Masons into Assyria and gave them Charges which, the

---

94 See Nicholls (1985) 69-74 and 194, and Myers (1959) 126f.
95 *See* Simmons (*Ed*.) (1879) 148-54 and *Cotton MS* Titus A xxvi ff.156-8.
96 Knoop, Jones, & Hamer (*Eds*.) (1938) 66ff.
97 Prescott (2005) 53. Clearly rapacious lawyers are nothing new.
98 Mynors, Thomson, & Winterbottom (*Eds. & Trs*.) (1998-9) 206-7.
99 *ODNB* **i** (2004) 428.
100 See Prescott, Andrew (2006): '"Kinge Athelston That Was a Worthy Kinge of England"' in Wilcox & Magennis (*Eds*.) 397-494. The fact that so little Anglo-Saxon Architecture survives does not mean it did not exist: the Normans, after all, did what they could to obliterate evidence of civilisation before 1066, even to demolishing the Minster at Winchester (which appears from excavations to have had close affinities with the great Churches of the Rhineland) and replacing it with a new Cathedral.

101 Baring-Gould **xiii** (1914) 185-6; Farmer (1992) 184-5; Kelly (1986) *passim*.
102 A Mediaeval manual of ecclesiastical lore, containing lives of Saints, homilies, commentaries on church services, etc. It was based on *Legenda Aurea* of Jacopo de' Varazze (Jacobus de Voragine), Archbishop of Genoa. See Jacobus de Voragine (1892).
103 The Seven Liberal Arts were thus identified by the fifth-century Carthaginian Martianus Minneus Capella, in his *De nuptiis Philologiae et Mercurii*, and given female personifications.
104 *Genesis* 5: 28-32.

Cooke MS held, survived, as did those given by Euclid. *Cooke* then repeats the Euclid story, but gives more Biblical references and information about Egypt, and goes on to mention Æthelstan, though it makes out that Æthelstan's son[105] became skilled in Masonry and gave ordinances to stonemasons, including the importance of holding an assembly at regular intervals when the Masons themselves thought that this was necessary, with severe penalties for those Masons who failed to attend. *Cooke* does not include material from Mirk, the *Merita Missa*, or *Urbanitatis*, but in taking the legendary history of stonemasonry back to *Genesis*, *Cooke* refers to Bede, Isidore of Seville, and others, but these supposed links are bogus[106].

Some commentators have assumed that both *Cooke* and *Regius* derive from some unknown original. *Cooke* appears to refer to an older set of Charges that credit Euclid with the origins of the Craft, and makes every effort to emphasise the Christian-Biblical connections by stretching the legends back beyond the time of Æthelstan to Saint Alban (third century of our era) who gave the stonemasons of England their first Charges. *Regius*, on the other hand, credits Æthelstan with the first English ordinances, and gives stonemasons an elevated status by stating the Craft was invented by high-class nobles in Ancient Egypt. It has also been suggested that these texts were written and composed by clerks, drawing on matter that had been transmitted orally by generations of stonemasons[107], but such a view can be challenged, for in the fifteenth century we know from records that senior stonemasons were anything but illiterate, and documentary evidence proves that Masons owned books[108]. Prescott has suggested that the possibility of a 'group of stonemasons based in Shropshire' commissioning 'a text such as *Regius* in the middle of the 15th century is not as remote' as some have held. If some peasants were literate[109], it is hardly likely that skilled craftsmen were not: besides, not only did literacy increase remarkably during the fifteenth century, but English became more widely used in documents, and we know that many City Companies required Apprentices to be literate[110].

Hugh of St Victor described[111] the Seven Liberal Arts, but also mentioned seven special sciences that were practical skills (e.g. Agriculture, Hunting, and Healing by means of medicines). His work appears to have influenced a fifteenth-century English treatise on the Several Liberal Arts which includes advice on their practical applications, such as how Geometry may be used to calculate areas of land, heights of buildings, depths of wells, etc.: furthermore, the importance of Geometry in the creation of buildings was discussed, and the abstractions were firmly linked with practicalities and the Crafts in Mediaeval society and the social structure of towns of the time[112]. This English text 'expresses a pride' in craft skills, in professionalism, and in trade[113].

There are other fifteenth-century texts that display pride in craftsmanship[114], including a comical debate between the tools of the Carpenter's trade, probably intended as entertainment during Guild Feasts. E. M. Müller produced a scholarly study of this Middle English text *in German* as his Thesis in 1899, given as *Der Streit der Zimmermannswerkzeuge: ein mittelenglisches Gedicht*, and more recently Edward[115] Wilson has examined the text[116], showing that the person or persons who composed the piece had gleaned much arcane knowledge of the Carpenter's Craft. Similarly, the author or authors of the Shipwrights' play concerning the building of Noah's Ark in the York Mystery Cycle demonstrates similar technical knowledge of the Shipwrights' Craft[117]. Given these and other exemplars that have survived from the fifteenth century, it is highly probable that both the *Cooke* and *Regius* MSS were either composed by stonemasons or informed by stonemasons' knowledge.

Many extant papers connected with Mediaeval Guilds deal with religious and charitable duties, including assistance for poor or incapacitated brethren, the maintenance of altars and altar-furnishings, and, most important of all, funerary rites and appropriate burial. Regrettably, many historians have seen Mediaeval fraternities associated with crafts as distinct from organised mysteries, but this over-eggs the facts, for trade- or craft-orientated organisations developed from fraternities that were established for purposes that included religious observations[118], especially those connected with prayers for the dead and funerals of the recently dead. This point cannot be over-stressed, for in the Mediaeval world the fate of the soul after death was of immense concern, and its welfare (sustained by prayers, Masses, and religious observances) did not come cheap: it was therefore important to band together in fraternities to keep an altar and pay priests to perform rituals. The magnificence of surviving palls in the possession of some Livery Companies is eloquent testimony of the imperative *need* to bury the dead with appropriate ceremony, and to maintain concerns for the dead by means of prayers and so on.

There is a possibility that both the *Cooke* and *Regius* MSS were concerned with the establishment of legitimacy: claims linking origins back to the time of Æthelstan may have been more than wishful thinking, more than legend,

---

105 There is no evidence that Æthelstan ever had a son.
106 Knoop, Jones, & Hamer (1938) 8ff.
107 *Ibid.* 1.
108 Prescott (2005) 58.
109 *Ibid.*
110 *See*, for example, Reynolds (1977) 169 and *passim*.
111 Hugh of St Victor (1991) *passim*.
112 Mooney (1993).
113 *Ibid.* 1036. I am indebted to Andrew Prescott for this and for other matters.
114 *See* Müller (1899), Prescott (2005) 59, and Wilson (1987). Müller is another remarkable instance of a fine German scholar getting to grips with an English text.
115 Given incorrectly as 'Edmund' in Prescott (2005) 59. The German title is 'The Dispute between the Carpenters' tools: a Middle English Poem'.
116 Bodleian Library MS Ashmole 61.
117 Wilson (1987) 453.
118 Veale (1991) 263.

giving assemblies of stonemasons a respectability through Royal patronage (and so, presumably, protecting the Craft from oppression by officialdom, Royal or otherwise). When fraternities claimed they had existed 'time out of mind' and that their assemblies had been authorised by persons such as Æthelstan, they were establishing a kind of legendary history and even genealogy. Gould and other Masonic historians have argued that *Cooke* and *Regius MSS* enshrined a very old oral tradition of stonemasonry, but it was a feature of the later Mediaeval and early Renaissance periods that spurious connections with Antiquity and even with legendary figures were made by numerous persons (including some Popes). In Italy, for example, Pope Paul II claimed descent from Ahenobarbus, the Massimi from Quintus Fabius Maximus Verrocosus; and the Cornaro from the Cornelii[119]. It appears that oligarchies began to gain power in the Guilds and Fraternities during the fourteenth century: were the *Cooke* and *Regius* MSS attempts to stop this trend by insisting that all Masons were equal, using the legendary history to show that the Craft had a noble, even Royal, origin, and that figures such as Euclid and Æthelstan had laid down the first principles? If so, did 'Edwin' (presumably Eadwine), supposedly the son of Æthelstan, hold stonemasons in even higher regard than did the King, and persuade his 'father' to grant a Charter permitting the stonemasons to convene an annual assembly in England? Although the essence of this story was recorded in the fifteenth century, it was further elaborated in documents prepared by stonemasons during the sixteenth century. According to these, the art of building had fallen into neglect, but was revived by Æthelstan: Eadwine was initiated into the secrets of Masonry, and called an assembly of stonemasons in York, where he created new Masons, taught the elements of polite behaviour, and provided them with ordinances regarding the practice of the Craft. This story was reiterated in copies of the 'Old Charges' produced during the seventeenth and eighteenth centuries, and is known as the York Legend[120]. However, Robert Plot, the Oxford Don, in 1686, pointed out that Æthelstan, as far as is known, had no son, let alone one called Eadwine: if there ever had been an Eadwine involved at all, it must have been Æthelstan's half-brother, the Ætheling[121] [122].

The need to claim historical and legal legitimacy for assemblies may have become urgent because, in 1425, the Commons complained that the Masons, in their chapters and assemblies were violating the Statutes of labourers, and in due course a Statute was enacted prohibiting such gatherings and imposing the threat of imprisonment[123]. Thus the *Cooke* and *Regius MSS* may have been attempts to legitimise the holding of assemblies or congregations despite legislation that made them illegal, and to halt the emergence of oligarchies within the Craft by stressing equality and origins in an organisation with Royal and noble associations. If this hypothesis is correct, then we have to view the Old Charges as a *response* to punitive and apparently arbitrary legislation: proof will only emerge after painstaking examination of the legal records dealing with the enforcement of legislation concerning labour[124]. It is a huge mistake to regard the 'Old Charges' as mere literature, as the gospel truth, or as fairy-stories: they may hold within them a smattering of a long tradition, and they may have been a considered response to draconian measures. The problem lies mostly in later accretions, interpretations, and fond imaginings.

Finally, it should be asked why, if 'Freemasons' means one 'free' of a Guild, there were not Freemercers, Freegrocers, Freefishmongers, or Freedrapers, to list but four possibilities? Nevertheless, the word 'Free' sometimes occurred in relation to other trades, though only as an adjective and not part of a compound noun. There were Free Butchers, Free Carmen, Free Scriveners, Free Sawyers, Free Vintners (the last free to sell wine in London, and who were exempt from certain financial liabilities), Free Waterman (or Lightermen), Free Fishers (free to catch or obtain fish, and free to sell it in their town), and Free Tylers. Yet of all the trades and crafts achieving freedom only one incorporated the word "Free" in a compound name – the Freemasons. It is unlikely that Masons became Freemasons only because they were Free of a Livery Company[125]. After all, the 'Company of ffree masons' became 'the Company of Masons' in 1655-6: this might suggest that if there existed within the Company some sort of esoteric society of Freemasons, then the Company itself might find it expedient to drop the 'ffree' with which it had styled its accounts until then[126]. Considering all the possibilities and what evidence survives, the word Freemason (though subjected to nuances of meaning and changes over the centuries) must refer in the operative sense to a mason who worked with *freestone*, and who was a highly skilled craftsman, capable of designing a building, carrying out carving, who was knowledgeable notably in Geometry, and who was literate. In this interpretation the present writer follows Begemann, Joseph Gwilt, Knoop, and Wyatt Angelicus van Sandau Papworth, among others.

One further point needs to be made, however: there may be a case for assuming that a stonemason, designated for two centuries or so as a Freemason, by the then almost forgotten truth of having worked with freestone, was *'maintained* in that designation by the fact' that Masons of the City of London 'found a new title to freedom in the membership' of a Company, 'and in so doing strengthened their hold of their former title. They were helped, no doubt, by a craft custom… of regarding' the Freemason as 'superior to the ordinary' Mason and 'allocating to him the parts of the work calling for the greater skill. So, although'

---
119 See Curl (2005) for these and other curious connections.
120 *See* Horne (1978). See also *Transactions of the Manchester Association for Masonic Research* **xc** (2000) 32-42.
121 Anglo-Saxon Prince of the Blood Royal, or the heir-apparent.
122 *ODNB* **i** (2004) 421.
123 Knoop & Jones (1967) 183; Prescott (2005) 64.

---
124 Prescott (2005) 66.
125 Jones (1986) 152-3.
126 *Ibid.*, 75, 89, 143.

Freedom of a Company 'would not in itself have produced the compound designation, it did apparently serve to help to strengthen its use'[127]. However, Jones reminds us that members of the Lodge of The Worshipful Company of Masons were themselves mostly Freemen of the Company and of the City of London, and their associates and friends would have been Freemen of other Compaines. Some commentators have held that the idea of forming the first Grand Lodge of Freemasons was to create an organisation based on that of a Company of the City of London[128].

So one cannot be dogmatic on this hoary topic: the word *may* owe its origins to more than one explanation.

Freemasons 3

This interpretation centres on stonemasons who travelled from place to place, finding employment where important buildings were being erected, and had a system of secret signs and passwords by which a craftsman could identify himself as possessing certain skills. Speth claimed that itinerant Masons were called 'Free' because they were *not* under the control of local Guilds of the towns and cities in which they settled on temporary bases in order to carry out specific works[129]. The migratory character of much of the stonemasons' trade meant that by the fourteenth century craftsmen could hardly be bound to the soil of a Manor[130].

It should be remembered that, in the Middle Ages, men who cultivated the land were, to a certain extent, self-governing, but in relation to the Lord of the Manor they were serfs, and were not permitted to leave their holdings unless they had express permission to do so. They were obliged to grind their corn at the Lord's mill, and they owed him field-service on certain days of the year, when they had to labour, not on their own lands, but on that of their Lord, under the orders of his Bailiff. Serfs could not enter into contracts, take an office of dignity, or give evidence without express permission. If a free man married a woman who was in bondage (i.e. in the position of a serf), he himself became a 'bond', and any children born of the union were of bond blood. Such persons who were serfs (or in bondage) could not apprentice their sons to any Trade or Craft, and it was virtually impossible for children to rise above the status of their parents, so acquiring an education was beyond the wildest dreams of any serf[131]. Clearly, it was in the interests of the upper echelons of society to keep the peasants stuck where they were from generation to generation, and the Commons, in 1391, sought to prevent any serf sending his children to school in order to better themselves, but the King, Richard II, very properly, rejected the plea. The Church, too, justified the condition of servitude, and indeed enforced it, for the monastic establishments controlled very large numbers of serfs, and there are many extant records of Wills in which serfs and their offspring were *bequeathed* to religious houses. Even pious writers justified serfdom. It is little wonder that there was so much feeling against the monasteries, so that when the Dissolution came in the sixteenth century, many rejoiced, and the matter was accomplished surprisingly easily.

During the fourteenth century English serfs began to make their demands to be free very clear: it also appears that there was great resentment against any serf who acquired his Freedom, and there was probably much of what today we would call snobbery in this. It was by escaping to a Chartered Town and living there for a year and a day that a serf could gain his Freedom, but he was obliged to be in 'scot and lot' i.e. pay taxes and perform the duties of a burgess, 'scot' being a tax ('scot-free' means without payment to this day).

Even so, townsmen were not exactly free either, for they were obliged to stay in the towns in which they were born, dress as required, and bring up their sons in their own calling: disobedience meant imprisonment, and those who were Masons were liable to be 'called up' by the King for works elsewhere (castles, fortifications, harbour-works, etc.). Some have suggested that the first Freemasons were stonemasons in the service of a Lord or religious house, who escaped to a town: however, other artisans escaped from servitude, and they were not termed Freecoopers or whatever. Given that town and city Craft Guilds insisted that *any* Apprentice taken on (no matter what the Craft was) had to be free-born and not the child of a serf or born 'in bondage', it is odd that the word seems only to have survived in relation to the Freemasons[132].

It is perhaps relevant that in early editions of the *Constitutions*[133] it is insisted that all candidates for acception as Freemasons should not only be free men, but free-born, and in 1813 candidates were required to declare they were 'free by birth', an apparent curiosity, but it should be remembered that in Great Britain a Bill for the gradual abolition of the Slave Trade was only passed into law in 1792[134], providing for the cessation of the Trade in 1796, but the supply of slaves to foreign settlements continued, and it was not until 1806 that the British Slave Trade was officially ended[135]. Even so, further legislation was passed in 1807 abolishing the Trade by preventing any vessel prepared for slaves leaving any port within British possessions after 1 May 1807, and that no slave could be landed in any British colony after 1 March 1808. This Act[136] was habitually violated, and it was not until an Act[137] was passed declaring traffic in slaves to be a felony punishable with Transportation that the Slave Trade came to an end so far as the British dominions were concerned. Clearly

---

127 Jones (1986) 153.
128 *Ibid.*
129 *OED* **iv** (1933) 527. *See* also Speth (1892).
130 Knoop & Jones (1948) 15.
131 For these matters, *see*, for example, Coulton (1918) and Trevelyan (2000).
132 Jones (1986) 152-8.
133 Anderson (*Ed.*) (1723, 1738).
134 32 Geo. III *c*.52
135 46 Geo. III *c*.119.
136 47 Geo. III. *c*.36.
137 51 Geo. III *c*.23.

the 'Old Charges' had been composed at a time when feudal serfdom existed, but in the eighteenth century Slavery still existed, and a kind of serfdom still survived *even at the end of that century*, for in certain coal- and salt-mines there were still hereditary bondsmen who were treated as chattels and were transferable with the mines on any change of ownership[138]. So the composers of the Old Charges in the Middle Ages and those responsible for editing and rearranging them for Freemasonic rituals in the eighteenth and nineteenth centuries were fully aware of the debasing nature of bondage, and made it quite clear that there was no place in Freemasonry for anyone who was not free from bondage of any kind.

As David Stevenson has pointed out[139], like other craftsmen, Mediaeval 'stonemasons had their own organisations, a mythical history' of their Craft 'stressing its antiquity and importance, and oaths of secrecy and initiation rites for new members…' Thus 'essentially the stonemasons were similar' to other Crafts, but had 'some distinctive characteristics. *Their mythical history was unusually elaborate and sweeping in its claims*'[140] for their Craft which was 'held to comprehend not merely manual labour but *the theoretical work of the architect*'[141]. Architecture was intimately connected with Geometry and the 'practical application' of Mathematics, so the 'traditional histories' of Freemasonry claimed the 'great Greek mathematician Euclid' as a Freemason, and indeed as one of the founders of the Craft. 'The central episodes in the development' of Freemasonry were set in Ancient Egypt (where Euclid made his appearance as an Egyptian, not a Greek) and in Jerusalem during the building of Solomon's Temple. Thus Mediaeval stonemasons 'proudly' associated their Craft with the science of Mathematics, and traced its origins to the oldest civilisation known to them[142] and to a major event recorded in the Bible[143]. In the fifteenth century these claims were enshrined in the 'Old Charges'.

It is not surprising that the stonemasons should have concocted a more elaborate mythology than that of other Crafts: after all, they had been responsible for creating stunning monuments that can still arouse admiration and awe today in all whose sensibilities have not been blunted or corrupted beyond redemption. The cathedrals, castles, monastic ruins, and the vast legacy of parish-churches remain as superb testaments to the skills and creativity of men who were sophisticated and intelligent: many of their names are known to us[144], and the greatest among them, including William de Ramsey, John Wastell, and Henry Yevele (mentioned earlier) were men of substance, men to be reckoned with[145]. A pilgrim visiting London or Canterbury Cathedrals (to name but two) could hardly fail to be impressed, even overwhelmed by the size, ingenuity displayed, and detail is such places: he would easily have been brought to his knees. The imagination and skill of the designers of vast structures were glowing testaments to their stature, providing overpowering evidence of their Craft above all other Mysteries.

Most Mediaeval craftsmen, as previously noted, worked within a town or a relatively small area, and were prevented from travelling far without special dispensations. Stonemasons differed from other Crafts in that they were much more mobile, for the very nature of their work obliged them to travel. A massive building-project such as a Cathedral needed many stonemasons to work on it for many years, and the craftsmen might be brought from widely spread locations. This mobility differed from the usual case with other Crafts, the organisation of the Guilds of which were inappropriate for the Craft of Masonry. Guilds were usually subordinate to the municipal authorities: they supervised entry to Crafts, regulated the working lives of Brethren, and protected the monopolies of members against non-members or interlopers (sometimes called 'foreigners') from outside the municipality.

However, Guilds, as they were intimately connected with towns (as in the City of London), could not really meet the needs of travelling stonemasons who, therefore, evolved their own Craft organisations. On building-sites stonemasons were provided with (or provided) shelters called Lodges, where work could be done during inclement weather, where materials and tools could be stored, and where craftsmen who did not live locally could sleep and eat. So a Lodge was originally a stonemasons' workshop, such as would be necessary for the construction of a major building, and the term seems to have been in use at least as early as 1278[146]. The word 'Lodge' was also used to denote a group of stonemasons working on any major project, or associated with any particular town or district (especially in Scotland). A Lodge could assign Marks, establish rules for terms and conditions of membership, settle disputes, and collect and distribute funds for the relief of distressed stonemasons and their families[147]. Such Lodges could exist for many years, and so developed their own customs and regulations, partly introduced by the stonemasons themselves, and partly imposed by Church or municipal authorities[148]. We know, for example, that the Lodge at York Minster had by-laws and ordinances imposed by the Dean and Chapter in 1352, 1370, and 1408-9, because the records survived[149].

The subject of Masons' Marks itself is enormous, and only a few words can be expended here on the subject.

---

138 Jones (1986) 157, and *see* also Trevelyan (2000) *passim*.
139 Stevenson (1988a, 2001 edn.) 1.
140 My italics.
141 *Ibid*.
142 But not in any detail, despite David Stevenson's claim, for Egypt was largely a closed book to Western Europeans after it was over-run after the collapse of the Roman Empire. *See* Curl (2005) *passim*.
143 This will be discussed below.
144 *See*, for example, Harvey (1987). There were, of course, great Master Masons on the Continent as well, whose names are recorded.
145 *See* Curl (2006a) *passim*. for short biographies of several mediaeval stonemasons.
146 Knoop & Jones (1948) 36.
147 Curl (1986b); Knoop & Jones (1948) 36-61; Stevenson (1988a) *passim*.
148 Stevenson (1988a) 2.
149 Knoop & Jones (1948) 37.

Marks of Operative Masons have been found on many buildings over a very long period, yet we can say for certain only that Marks were registered and properly organised in Germany and in Scotland, although it is highly unlikely that no such system existed elsewhere: we simply lack evidence. In England alone there are many thousands of examples of Marks cut into stone, and these were the Masons' equivalent of other Guild regulations of various trades which identified goods, makers, and quality. The Schaw Statutes in Scotland of the late sixteenth century indicate that Marks had to be recorded in Lodge minute-books, and these were, in effect, 'signatures' personal to individual Masons. Scots Operative Masons were obliged to register their Marks on entering the Fellow Craft from being apprentices[150], and Marks granted to or chosen by non-operative Masons were also registered in Mark-Books and minutes.

So a Lodge, in the sense of a temporary structure, was erected on site to provide protection from the weather and to store tools and materials. It was usually a timber shed, either free-standing or a lean-to structure built against the new permanent work (See **CPls.I.I, II, & III,** pp.14-15, and **Pl.I.1**). For very large and complex building-projects taking several years to complete, Lodges might be subdivided into several rooms, and might themselves have some architectural pretensions: it appears that the Lodges erected for the construction of the Cathedrals at Prague and Strasbourg[151] were built of stone[152]. A Lodge was a *Loge* or *Chantier* in French, a *Bauhütte* in German, and other versions included *Logia, Logge, Loygge, Luge,* and *Ludge.* Apart from their functions as workshops where stone was cut, carved, etc., it seems they were also establishments in which the craftsmen could eat, drink, and relax, as well as providing places where disputes could be ironed out and meetings held. A Lodge was both the place where feasting and convivial activities took place *and* the organising body which arranged such feasts for members.

Pl.I.1 The construction of the Abbey-Church of Schönau, dating from the sixteenth century. At the top left-hand is the quarry where stone is being extracted, blocks are being moved by means of crowbars, and transported by means of ox-carts to the site. In the foreground lime-mortar is being mixed and carried up the ladder to the area where dressed stone is being lowered into position by means of a primitive hoist. To the right is the Lodge, a lean-to structure, in which stone is being prepared by means of a pick-axe and a gavel, and within which the square and a template are prominently displayed. The figure in the foreground about to cross the river and carrying a rule and a square is presumably the Master-Mason; to the right one of the Brethren (who seem to be Lay-Brothers of the Abbey) is drinking from a flask, while the main supplies of drink are in large containers, one of which is cooling in the river. Two men are shifting a large undressed stone on the right by means of crowbars. Another point of interest is the flimsy cantilevered scaffold-platform just below the clerestory of the building on the right: construction work at high altitudes in the Mediaeval period must have been extremely dangerous and terrifying. For details see Legner (*Ed.*) (1978-80) 6 1ff.). (*Germanisches Nationalmuseum, Nürnberg. Hz. 196*).

In Scotland Lodges were territorial in the sense that they were associated with a town or an area[153].

The *Steinmetzen* of the German-speaking lands, like their colleagues elsewhere, had rules concerning behaviour: piety, charity, and the honour of the Craft (fornication and theft were to be avoided) were urged on members. Three Grades (those of Apprentice, Journeyman or Fellow, and Master) were settled by custom (Apprenticeships were

---

150 Stevenson (1988b) 35, 42, and *passim*.
151 Or Strassburg, as the building is German in character.
152 Svanberg (1983) 53.

153 Stevenson (1988*a* and *b*) go into these matters in detail, and are essential reading for any student of early-Renaissance Scotland.

CPl.I.I The Building of the Tower of Babel, showing Masons preparing stone, hoisting blocks into position, and working on the flimsy cantilevered scaffolding at the top. The Angels of Heaven are distorting the speech of the men so that they start fighting, fall to their deaths, and the Tower falls with them. On the left is the Lodge in which the Masons are preparing lime-mortar which is then carried on hods on the shoulders of the hod-carriers. A fifteenth-century illumination from the Duke of Bedford's *Book of Hours* (BL. Add. 18850, fol. 17v. Y850611).

normally five years[154], and there were precise rules about financial contributions and Masons' Marks (on which subjects the *Cooke* and *Regius MSS* are silent). The *Steinmetzen* also had special handshakes and forms of greeting, and were organised on regional bases with centres in each area. Other associations, Guilds, and trade Fraternities under the protection of Saints (the Parisian Masons had St Blaise as their Patron) existed on the Continent during the Middle Ages, and the *Steinmetzen* in particular appear to have had very sophisticated structured systems of organisation throughout the Holy Roman Empire of the German Nations, necessary because of the enormous geographical area and the host of Duchies, Principalities, Free Imperial Cities, Electorates, and the like that comprised what was to be called 'neither Holy, nor Roman, nor an Empire'[155].

---

154 Knoop & Jones (1948) 55.
155 François-Marie Arouet (Voltaire): *Essai sur l'histoire générale et sur les moeurs et l'esprit des nations* (1756) Ch. 70. *Ce corps qui s'appelait et qui s'appelle encore le saint empire romain n'était en aucune manière ni saint, ni romain, ni empire* (this commonalty which was called and still calls itself the Holy Roman Empire was neither Holy, nor Roman, nor an Empire).

In this respect the comparative compactness of England (and that Kingdom's relative political unity) seems to have made for different types of ordered arrangements.

Here again, however, we must beware of relying on 'Masonic' histories, for it was believed that Abbot William of Hirschau was responsible for training lay brethren as stonemasons and other artificers for the building and enrichment of the Abbey buildings and elsewhere[156]. These men, it was claimed, were made subject to rules, acquired secrets, and were grouped into Brotherhoods which were recognised by Papal Bulls and secular Charters[157]. Unfortunately, no such Bulls appear to have been produced (or at least have not surfaced). One of the sources for Abbot William's exploits was Johannes Trithemius (a writer, as Knoop & Jones wryly observed, 'by no means restrained in fancy')[158], and indeed it does not seem to be the case that the origins of the *Steinmetzen* were monastic at all, which is no surprise to students of the period.

Large buildings such as the Cathedrals of Strassburg (now Strasbourg) or Regensburg, of course, could never have been designed and built (*pace* romantic wishful thinkers and other dreamy fantasists) without *Bauhütten* of Masons, and it is likely that each Lodge attached to such major building-projects would have had individual rules, though many aspects of those rules would have been similar to each other, possibly carried from Lodge to Lodge by itinerant Masons who found work there[159]. We are fortunate in having information about an illustrious family of Master Masons called Roriczer or Roritzer which flourished in the fifteenth century and was active at the Cathedral of St Peter, Regensburg, among other places. Matthäus Roriczer was the author of a surviving tract on the design of Gothic finials[160], of a treatise on geometrical procedures[161], and of a tract on gables[162], all three of which are of considerable historical importance (unlike the work of Villard de Honnecourt mentioned elsewhere in this study).

The *Compagnonnages* of France seem to have developed from the groups of stonemasons working on the great French Cathedrals from the twelfth century[163], and they may have resembled a cross between a trade-union, a Livery Company (the *Compagnonnages* wore Liveries), and a Guild under the Patronage of a Saint[164]. As in England, French Masons travelling from place to place were given lodging by fellow-Masons, and helped with money to get them to the next Lodge. It would seem that itinerant stonemasons, be they French, English, German, or from any other language-group or country, were able to grant

---

156 Knoop & Jones (1948) 54.
157 *See* Heideloff (1844) and Janner (1876) for example.
158 Trithemius (1690).
159 Knoop & Jones (1948) 54.
160 *Das Büchlein von der Fialen Gerechtigkeit*, 1486. *See* the edn. edited by Geldner (1965).
161 *Geometria Deutsch* (1486-90).
162 c. 1488-9.
163 Saint-Léon (1901). *See* also Svanberg (1983) *passim* and Knoop & Jones (1948) 56.
164 *See* Curl (2000d) for a discussion of the Companies.

CPl.I.II The Duchesse de Roussillon visiting the building-site of the great Abbey of the Sainte-Madeleine in Vézelay and viewing the walls being built of dressed stone bedded in lime-mortar as depicted in a fifteenth-century French miniature in *L' Histoire de Charles Martel*. Note the trowels. The tops of unfinished walls are protected against the elements by means of temporary coverings of straw. The timber structure on the right is the Masons' Lodge, where stone is being prepared ready for carriage to the church, and in front of the Lodge is the Master-Mason with staff supervising the mixing of the mortar (© *Bibliothèque Royale Albert 1er, Bruxelles, MS 6 fol. 554 verso*).

CPl.I.III The rebuilding of the Basilica of Saint-Denis as shown in a fifteenth-century illuminated MS. To the left are the King and the Abbot (supposedly King Dagobert and the seventh-century Abbot; but, with the unmistakably Gothic form of the Basilica, the process of syncretism also identifies the figures with Kings Louis VI and VII and the famous Abbot Suger of the twelfth century). The Master-Mason is very dashing (the figure on the left with a feather in his cap). To the right is the Lodge where stone is being dressed, squared, and carved. Note the Masons' mallets, chisels, square, and the lime-mortar being carried (*BN. Ms. fr. 2609. fol. 60v*).

and receive benefits only when passwords and/or signs were given (and indeed it would have been imprudent for a Mason to bestow *largesse* on *any* traveller). Because the *Compagnons* had little chance of becoming Masters as the organisations became more oligarchic in character, they tended to band together against employers and Masters, so the motive for secrecy was increased. The necessity to protect the *Compagnonnages* from outside attack led the associations to evolve systems of enforced discipline to punish miscreants within the group[165]. *Compagnonnages* also evolved complex rituals for admission, arranged the funerals of members (as did the Guilds), and developed ceremonials for their feasts. Again, they built up legends to account for their beginnings, making them as impressive as possible[166].

These legends included a claim that the *Compagnonnages* had been founded by Hiram (Master Mason to King Solomon), who had been killed by three Apprentices; that they owed their origins to Maître Jacques, who had made the pillars embellished with pictures; and that they were the creations of Father Soubise (a Master Craftsman to Solomon), who fell out with Maître Jacques shortly after they had arrived in France[167]. The Soubise story throws up allusions to the Knights Templar (about which the hoary accretions have reached epidemic proportions in recent times), but M. Saint-Léon supposed that the tales of Hiram, Jacques, Soubise, and Solomon were only vaguely Biblicised memories of the building-works carried out by Masons at great Cathedrals as Temples of God[168]. Saint-Léon pointed out the close similarity between rituals of initiation in France and England, and suggested that English Freemasonic catechisms and rites of initiation were the models for the French *Compagnonnages*, although the last did not include Masters, but only Journeymen[169].

Knoop and Jones believed that Operative Masonry in England, France and Scotland once had common traditions (or parts of traditions), organisations, and objects[170]. English and Scots Operative Masonry, however, they thought, lost their rituals and organisations, and these had to be re-invented, elaborated, and developed by the Accepted and then by the Speculative Freemasons. It seems most likely that the reason for this was the break with so much tradition (including the Patronage of Saints, the formation of groups for the establishment and maintenance of Chantries and for seemly burial of the dead, and the religious and charitable aspects) caused by the upheavals of the Henrician Break with Rome, the subsequent nature of the Reformed Church, and the iconoclasm and violence of the Scottish Reformation[171].

Certainly the vehemence of Scottish Calvinism, and the destruction of Chantries and so many ancient Guilds in England (with the notable exception of the Livery Companies of the City of London) must have stripped much from Freemasonry in its Operative phase. This is borne out by the fact that the *Compagnonnages* held on to the rituals and secrecy, continuing as charitable bodies with a strong religious flavour throughout the nineteenth century: they also remained as groups of labour organisations, and kept aloof from French Speculative Freemasonry, which became first sceptical about religion and then violently anti-clerical.

Epilogue

Some of the interpretations of 'Freemason' have been outlined above, from which it will be seen that there was much more to organisations of stonemasons than can be explained by regarding organisations of tradesmen as sorts of proto-trades-unions: there were all sorts of ramifications over and above mere practicalities, involving attempted links with Antiquity and the Old Testament, beliefs in Purgatory and the need to care for the souls of the dead, complicated legends, and claims to hold secrets of Wisdom and Geometry in trust. That Mediaeval Masons created some extraordinary buildings is self-evident, but that their creations were steeped in symbolism and Platonic numerology is something that is less understood[172]. The Mason-Architects responsible for the great churches, abbeys, and cathedrals knew what they were doing: they were not barbarous 'Goths' (as some in the eighteenth century would have had it), but were sophisticated and literate artificers, steeped in Geometry and an understanding of measurement, and were men of substance. 'As early as the mid-thirteenth century, architects, painters, sculptors, and other artists, were ranked as esquires, and when accounts began to be kept in English in the fifteenth century they were often termed gentlemen… The chief craftsmen were often very much in the sovereign's confidence…'[173]. William of Wynford was portrayed as a dignified man in his robes in a window of c.1393 in Winchester College Chapel East Window, accompanied by Hugh Herland the Carpenter and Simon Membury, Clerk of Works. All three are recorded as having dined at Winchester College on 31 July 1393, and Henry Yevele is recorded as 'Mr.' in a record of a meal at Winchester House, Southwark, on 5 May 1393[174]. So artificers of the stature of Wynford or Yevele were not only handsomely turned out, but wore dignified clothes and robes, and dined with the Great and Good[175]. As Harvey noted, 'the master artisans of the highest level – masons, carpenters, carvers, painters, smiths – had a comparatively high position in society. *They were all, of necessity because of*

---

165 Knoop & Jones (1948) 57-8.
166 Saint-Léon (1901) *passim*.
167 *Ibid. See also* Knoop & Jones (1948) 58-9.
168 Saint-Léon (1901), 24.
169 Saint-Léon (1901), 24 and Knoop & Jones (1948) 59.
170 Knoop & Jones (1948) 59. I would agree with this view.
171 The upheavals of the sixteenth century in England and Scotland are often lumped together, but events were very different in the two countries, which were under separate Monarchs until 1603 and had separate Parliaments until the early eighteenth century.

172 For discussions of these questions *see* Hiscock (2000, 2003, 2007).
173 Harvey (1947) 22.
174 Harvey (1946) Plates 42-45 and 48 and *passim*.
175 *See* the magisterial Harvey (1987) *passim*.

the rules of their crafts, free men by blood and position[176]. More than that, they ranked, even in official tables of Court precedence, above yeomen and equal to or even just above "gentlemen" of minor degree'[177]. 'The dominant position of a William Ramsey[178], a Henry Yevele, or a Hugh Herland was comparable, *mutatis mutandis*, to that of a Wren, Vanbrugh[179] or Lutyens[180] in more recent times. It is a cardinal error to suppose' that English Mediaeval society 'was barbarous or unsophisticated, still more so to think it parochial. Communications were on the whole better than they were to be again until after 1790, when the canal and stage-coaches provided a false dawn of the railway age… In the Middle Ages vast numbers of men, skilled craftsmen by the score and labourers by the hundred, could be rapidly assembled for work on jobs a hundred miles or more from their places of origin'[181].

Stonemasons undoubtedly had professional standards of conduct, and had organisations of their own independent of municipal jurisdiction (made imperative because they had to move from place to place to carry out works). In this holding of Free Courts there are certainly parallels with other Crafts, but we know that the Masons' Lodge engaged on building at Strassburg Cathedral in 1275 assumed the 'freed Masonry after the English fashion', and had their Liberties confirmed in 1276 by the Emperor Rudolf I[182]. We also know that in 1459 there was a Congress of Master-Masons at Regensburg, attended by men from Strassburg, Basel, Bern, Passau, Salzburg, and Vienna, among other places in Central Europe, which must have helped to spread ideas and create a familiarity with new designs. In the course of the fifteenth century several assemblies of Masons were held in other German lands, and it is possible that something similar occurred in England, otherwise the rapidity with which types of tracery, mouldings, and plans moved across the country cannot be explained. Regional 'schools' of design suggest that there was some sort of design tradition in certain areas (e.g. the church-towers of Somerset and trefoiled cusping in tracery in main lights of windows in Gloucestershire, Warwickshire, and Worcestershire)[183].

So Mediaeval stonemasons enjoyed status and certain freedoms. Their claims and their demonstrable expertise gave them kudos, so much so that, as times changed and much of Mediaeval organisation altered beyond recognition, their legends and histories proved to have attractions for intellectuals searching for Wisdom and meaning in Antiquity and ancient texts. It is to a consideration of this complex phenomenon that we now turn.

---

176 My italics.
177 Harvey (1978) 42.
178 *fl.*1323-d.1349.
179 Sir John Vanbrugh.
180 Sir Edwin Landseer Lutyens.
181 Harvey (1978) 42.

182 *Ibid.* 38.
183 *Ibid.* 39.

CHAPTER II

What is Freemasonry 2? The Emergence of 'Non-Operative' or 'Speculative' Freemasonry

Introduction; Architecture, Geometry, and Masonry; Guilds, Fraternities, Chantries, and Religious Observance; The Scottish Dimension; Royal and other Connections

'The most satisfactory definition of freemasonry from the masonic historian's point of view would appear to be the organisation and practices which have from time to time prevailed upon mediaeval working masons and their "operative" and "speculative" successors, from the earliest date from which such organisation is traceable down to the present time.'

DOUGLAS KNOOP (1883-1948) &
GWILYM PEREDUR JONES (1892-1975):
The Genesis of Freemasonry (Manchester: Manchester University Press, 1948) 11.

'By "operative masonry" we understand the organisation and practices which from time to time prevailed among working masons in England and Scotland in the later Middle Ages and early modern times. Men who were not masons by trade but who joined such an organisation, as frequently happened in Scotland during the seventeenth century, we call "non-operative masons". In Scotland, such non-operative masons, or "non-operatives" for short, were known in the seventeenth century as "gentlemen masons"[1]... By "speculative masonry", or what Murray Lyon calls "symbolic masonry", we understand a peculiar system of morality, veiled in allegory and illustrated by symbols. In other words, we regard it as synonymous with "freemasonry" in its modern sense.'

Ibid. 129.

Introduction

The word 'speculatyf' occurs in Line 622 of the *Cooke MS*[2] in the sense of *theory* or *speculative* (contrasted with practical) *knowledge*, but Knoop and Jones ruled out that any question of morality or symbolism was implied in the fifteenth century, and suggested it may have been used in respect of persons interested in Geometry as one of the Seven Liberal Arts or possibly the mathematical or numerological sides of Architecture[3]: in other words it did not signify 'speculative mason' in the modern sense[4].

Speth proposed, however, that in the fifteenth and eighteenth centuries, Masonic documents used the word 'speculative' in 'precisely the same sense' and that the term had been handed down through oral use rather than re-introduced by Anderson and others[5]. Speth's interpretation was that 'speculative' was used in the eighteenth century to distinguish 'operative' or 'practical' Masonry. Chetwode Crawley[6] stated that Anderson[7] adopted 'speculative' in the Old Charges in 1723, but a perusal of Anderson shows that he described Masons associated with the newly-established Grand Lodge as 'free masons' and 'accepted free masons', which became 'free and accepted masons' in his later book[8]. In Anderson's 1723 work it is stated that 'the *Company of Masons,* being otherwise termed FREE MASONS of aunccient Staunding and good Reckoning, by means of affable and kind Meetings diverse Tymes, and as a *loving Brotherhood* should use to doe, did frequent this *mutual Assembly* in the Tyme of *King* HENRY IV. the 12th Year of his most gracious *Reign*[9]. And the said Record describing a *Coat of Arms,* much the same with *That* of The LONDON COMPANY of *Freemen* Masons, it is generally believ'd that the said *Company* is descended of the ancient

---

1 *See* Prichard (1730) and Knoop, Jones, & Hamer (*Eds.*) (1963).

---

2 Knoop, Jones, & Hamer (*Eds.*) (1938) 103.
3 Hiscock (2000, 2003, 2007).
4 Knoop & Jones (1948) 129-30.
5 Speth, G.W., in *Quatuor Coronatorum Antigrapha* **ii** (Masonic Reprints of the Quatuor Coronati Lodge No. 2076, London), pages not numbered.
6 Chetwode Crawley **i** (1895-1900) 6.
7 Anderson (*Ed.*) (1723). It must have been Anderson *and* Desaguliers.
8 Anderson (*Ed.*) (1738).
9 Reigned 1399-1413, so this probably refers to c.1411 or 1412. *See* Stow (1633). Conder (1894) 249 got this wrong, referring to Henry V (reigned 1413-22).

Fraternity; and that in former Times no Man was made *Free* of that *Company* [i.e. The Masons' Company of London] until he was install'd in some Lodge of *Free* and *Accepted Masons*, as a necessary Qualification…'[10] Now the curious thing is that Conder quotes this (not entirely accurately)[11], yet claimed that 'before a man could join the London Mason's Company he must be initiated into the mysteries of Speculative Masonry'[12], which, at best, is a very free rendering of what Anderson printed. But this idea did not begin with Anderson: it can be found in John Stow's *Survey of London*[13], and may have come down from even earlier sources. Stow, incidentally, was admitted to the Freedom of The Merchant Taylors' Company in 1547, but remained for some thirty years a Member of the Bachelors' or Yeoman Company, and was never admitted to the Livery or to any important Office[14].

Chetwode Crawley and Speth implied that Anderson adopted the word 'speculative', but there does not appear to be mention of 'speculative', nor, incidentally, does there seem to be use of the word 'initiated' in Anderson (though 'initiated' *was* used by the architect Edward Oakley in 1728[15]) in an important speech mainly concerned with Architecture[16] in which he set out the qualifications and duties of members of the Fraternity, laying stress on the dissemination of knowledge about Architecture and Building through talks and printed works: this lecture gained considerable authority among operatives in the building-trades after its publication in *The Ancient Constitutions of the Free and Accepted Masons* in the following year, brought out in a useful pocket-edition by Benjamin Cole[17].

The earliest use of the term 'speculative mason' seems to have been in 1757[18], and the earliest mention of 'speculative freemasonry' appears to have occurred in the second edition of *Illustrations of Masonry* by William Preston in 1775, where the statement 'Masonry passes and is understood under two denominations, it is operative and it is speculative' may be found[19].

In the 1720s, when Grand Lodge was formed, another publication appeared which specifically referred to The Worshipful Company of Masons of the City of London as having been 'call'd the Free Masons, a Fraternity of great Antiquity being Honoured by several KINGS & very many of ye Nobility & Gentry being of their Society'. This was *A Treatise of Architecture* by Sébastien Le Clerc with copper plates by John Sturt, translated from the French by Ephraim Chambers[20], of 1723-4, exactly the same period when Anderson's *Constitutions* came out[21] (of which more anon).

One of the common features of esoteric cults and secret societies[22] is a tendency to claim hidden knowledge not available to the outsider. Such claims are frequently enhanced (spuriously, more often than not) by associating knowledge or wisdom with lost civilisations, and especially with the great civilisations of Antiquity (Ancient Egypt [made even more enticing by its hieroglyphs which nobody could read until the nineteenth century], the Hellenistic cultures, and the Graeco-Roman World of the Mediterranean lands)[23]. The longing to recover what had been lost, the attempt to find again what was perfect, and the widespread tendency towards syncretism, or blending of legends, religions, cults, and ideas, are not recent phenomena, and have played no small part in Western European civilisation. The Garden of Eden, the Temple of Solomon, the Seven Wonders of the Ancient World[24], the glories of Greek and Roman Architecture, and the stories of Lost Continents and Lost Tribes were all potent examples of that sense of loss, and of a desire to rediscover something precious, essential, uplifting, noble, and powerful. The realms of magic, of Divine authority, of mystery, and of super-creativity are never far away. In this respect, the plentiful texts associated with Freemasonry are rarely exceptions, and some of their claims strain both credulity and patience to breaking-points.

More recently, the eloquent writings of the late John Hooper Harvey[25] have expressed another aspect of longing: that for the English Middle Ages, and the 'national culture' which produced the glories of Mediaeval Art and Architecture. Harvey's tone was elegiac and full of regrets, a fact perfectly understandable when we consider the great legacy of Mediaeval ecclesiastical Architecture and artefacts we still possess, and how much we might still have if iconoclasm, greed, misplaced fervour, philistinism, and ignorance had stayed the hands of Taleban-like destroyers.

Architecture, Geometry, and Masonry

The term 'Architecture' will be used throughout this book, as will 'Geometry', 'Masonry', and other labels, so it is well to remind ourselves what they mean. 'Architecture' implies

---

10 Anderson (*Ed.*) (1723) 82 (note).
11 Conder (1894) 249.
12 *Ars Quatuor Coronatorum* **ix** (1896) 38.
13 Stow (1633), first published 1598, then in an expanded edn. 1603, and in print ever since. *See* especially the 1971 reprint edited by C. L. Kingsford.
14 *ODNB* **lii** (2004) 983.
15 Knoop, Jones, & Hamer (*Eds.*) (1945) 6.
16 Oakley (1729). See also Colvin (2008) 755-6 and *Ars Quatuor Coronatorum* **xxvii** (1914) 145-7.
17 *ODNB* **xli** (2004) 323. *See* Oakley (1729).
18 *Ars Quatuor Coronatorum* **v** (1892) 110. But Anderson (*Ed.*) (1738) 221 refers to the Jews having a 'great regard' for 'this science' (meaning the Cabbala), and divided 'their Knowledge into Speculative and Operative', and this he apparently took from a pamphlet of 1730 entitled *A Defence of Masonry*, possibly the work of one Martin Clare.
19 Preston (1775) **vi** 17. *See* also Begemann (1914) 391n. Yet Prichard (1730) mentioned 'Operative Masons' as being the same as 'Accepted Masons', which would suggest that seventeenth-century 'Accepted Freemasons' were actually leading professional Stonemasons, but that other Tradesmen and persons who were not Stonemasons could join such Lodges of 'Accepted' Freemasons if they expressed wishes to do so, and possessed certain intellectual attainments.
20 Clerc (1723-4), dedication-page. Illustrated in Conder (1894) opposite 250.
21 Anderson (*Ed.*) (1723).
22 Although it is doubtful if Freemasonry can now be regarded as a 'secret' society at all. *See* Mackenzie (1967) 152-77 for a balanced synopsis.
23 *See* Curl (2005) *passim*.
24 The Pyramids at Giza, the Hanging Gardens and Walls of Babylon, the Temple of Artemis at Ephesus, the statue of Zeus at Olympia, the Mausoleum at Halicarnassus, the Colossus of Rhodes, and the Pharos at Alexandria.
25 *See*, for example, Harvey (1948) *passim*.

something much more than mere building: it signifies the art or science of constructing edifices (or making designs of such edifices) that have aesthetic pretensions; that have qualities on a higher plane than those of purely utilitarian structures; that have complexities, aspects capable of moving the beholder; and that possess evidence of an intellectual rigour that raises them to heights considerably loftier than those associated with a humdrum shed. Sir Henry Wotton famously identified the 'three conditions' for 'well building' as 'Commodity, Firmness, and Delight', a remark itself derived from Vitruvius[26], who insisted that Architecture derives from Order, Arrangement, Eurythmy (or Harmony of Proportion), Symmetry, Propriety, and Economy. Wren spoke of 'Beauty, Firmness, and Convenience'[27]. These definitions suggest that there is much in the built fabric of today that cannot be considered as Architecture at all. Architecture might be described as the art and science of designing buildings having qualities of Beauty, Geometry, emotional and spiritual power, intellectual content and complexity, soundness of construction, convenient planning, many virtues of different kinds, durable and pleasing materials, agreeable colouring and decorations, serenity and dynamism, good proportions and acceptable scale, and many mnemonic associations drawing on a great range of precedents. In the twenty-first century what passes for Architecture has been increasingly concerned with advertising, and the devaluation and utter ruin of architectural vocabulary, syntax, grammar, language, and symbols have led many to question the status of many buildings as Architecture. Modernism insisted that the man-made world should be free from the 'inhibiting restraints' of the past: in short, it jettisoned symbols, myths, the humane, harmony, respect for context, craftsmanship, feeling, and just about everything else of any worth. By devaluing Architecture it impoverished us all, and is still doing just that, for Architecture is the most public and visible of Arts. And, of course, Modernists insisted that they were on the side of 'progress', the 'future', and a spurious 'morality'. They also determined that one architectural style, one set of urban solutions, and one image of Modernity must be universally applied: there was more than a whiff of coercion about it. Meaning in Geometry was denied; numbers were only that, shorn of their associations; and Beauty was banished: it was a word that ceased to be used, for it had become meaningless, a victim of Relativism, that dragon with protean guises, representing, when one gets down to it, envy and spleen, something that becomes abundantly clear when dipping into the crabbed texts of Modernism

and the staccato sloganising of Corbusianity. Some of us have more telluric tastes[28].

An Architect used to be a master-builder, a skilled professor of the art or science of building, who prepared designs and supervised the realisation of his designs: he prepared the plans, elevations, and sections of the design of sophisticated buildings with an aesthetic content and supervised their construction in accordance with the drawings, specifications, and details. He was therefore a creator, even The Creator, because he created Order out of Chaos, or superimposed Order where there was none: such a definition would not hold water today, when persons calling themselves 'architects' create Chaos where before there was Order, eschew Beauty and Harmony, deny Meaning in Architecture, and are concerned only with image and making as much money as possible.

Geometry used to be an essential part of Architecture, for it is the science which investigates the properties and relationships of magnitudes in space, as lines, as surfaces, and as solids. In ancient texts Geometry was seen as a practical art for measuring and planning, and was indissolubly associated with Architecture. It was a necessary means of measuring ground, marking out plots, establishing areas, and imposing ordered subdivisions on territories, but an understanding of Geometry was also an essential skill of the stonemason, who created the most respected and highest form of Architecture, that of an Architecture of masonry. Henry Bradshaw, in his *The Holy Lyfe and History of Saynt Werburge: very frutefull for all Christen people to rede*[29], records 'masons... Counnynge in geometrie', and John Dee in 1570 considered that 'Geometrie is the Arte of Measuring sensible magnitudes, their just quantities and contentes'[30]. Architects, Masons, and Geometers, then, had close working knowledge of the art or science of Geometry, or that branch of Mathematics which treats of the description and properties of magnitudes in general. Deconstructivism has really finished off Geometry, despite its frantic and unnecessary convolutions, for it is intentional aggression on human senses, abuse of perceptive mechanisms in order to generate anxiety and discomfort, and rejection of all that went before. It can be seen as fundamentally destructive, failing to come up with any clear values that are not nihilistic[31].

A Mason, of course, is a builder and worker in stone, a person who dresses and lays stone in building: 'to mason' is to build of stone, to construct of masonry, to build up or strengthen with stone. To say that something was masoned means that it was built of stone. The essential elements of Masonic history are those primarily concerned with the Architecture-Geometry-Masonry links, and, as previously mentioned, these recur in the early manuscripts. Long before then, the seventh-century Bishop of Seville, St Isidore (whose attributes, interestingly enough, include

---

26 Marcus Vitruvius Pollio, the Roman Architect, Engineer, and Theorist, author of the only Antique treatise on Architecture to survive. Entitled *De Architectura* it was dedicated to Emperor Augustus, and although it was known and copied in manuscript form during the Middle Ages, from 1414, when Poggio Bracciolini publicised the existence of the fine manuscript in the Library of the Abbey of St Gallen, Switzerland, it began to be taken very seriously indeed, and was a major catalyst for the Renaissance in Architecture.

27 For definitions *see* Curl (2006a) *passim*.

28 *See* James Stevens Curl: *Journal of Urban Design* **iii**/3 (1998) 382-3.

29 *See* Bradshaw (1887).

30 Dee (1570): *Mathematical Preface* 16.

31 Salingaros *et al.* (2004) *passim*.

the hive of bees, a Masonic emblem), listed Geometry, comprehending the measures and dimensions of the Earth, as the sixth Liberal Art, but, by the time of the Mediaeval manuscripts referred to above, Geometry had become something more: it was the introductory source of *all* knowledge[32]. Thus, as early as the Middle Ages, Geometry had acquired an awesome status rather grander than we might suspect from the perspective of the twenty-first century, where the subject lies stripped of all its symbolisms and associational messages. In Antiquity Pythagoras held that everything had its origins in numbers, and Plato refused to allow anyone ignorant of Geometry to enter his Academy[33]. Plato believed that the Universe had been transformed from a state of Chaos into one of Order by a benign Creator, using mathematical laws, and resulting in Harmony because its various parts were made in proportion not only to each other, but to the whole. Platonic ideas were disseminated during the Middle Ages by several authors (e.g. Calcidius[34], Ambrosius Theodosius Marcobius[35], and Martianus Minneus Felix Capella[36], and given the *Imprimatur* of Christian writers such as St Augustine[37], Anicius Manlius Severinus Boethius[38], and Magnus Aurelius Cassiodorus[39]. Robert Grosseteste, Bishop of Lincoln, stated that measure led the understanding to the power that contains all things[40]. Hugh of St Victor explained that 'arithmetic' actually meant the 'power of number', and that the power of number lay in the fact that all things were formed in its likeness[41]. Even a passing acquaintance with Mediaeval texts influenced by Neoplatonism[42] should be sufficient to persuade the most sceptical of the pivotal rôle played by Geometry, Numerology, and Symbolism during the Middle Ages[43].

Although, historically, Geometry seems to have been primarily associated with the measurement of land, it became intimately connected, in an increasingly sophisticated form, with the art and science of Masonry. There can be no question but that the connection with exact measurements and with buildings of importance made of stone was a stimulus to accord Geometry a grandeur associated with the mysteries, with power (both sacred and secular), and with political clout. The idea of Geometry as holding within it the kernel of all advancement, all truth, and the ultimate mysteries of Wisdom itself elevated that art or science to the highest pinnacle in the respect and awe of Mankind: Geometry was a kind of First Cause, a touchstone of power and knowledge, and the means by which mighty expressions of the truth could be realised. It held within it the possibility to re-create the Divine in building, the lost Temple of Solomon itself, and even, on a grander scale, the City of God. It follows, therefore, that the creators of stone monuments such as great churches and the like, enjoyed a certain status and that the Architects and Builders of Houses of God on such a spectacular scale as those of the mighty Cathedrals of the Middle Ages were no ordinary artisans, and were clearly far more mobile than members of other Crafts with different skills.

Early documents prized by Freemasons contain legends that relate to the very beginnings of Geometry. Obviously, as already emphasised, Geometry, Masonry, and Architecture were inter-connected, but Geometry was considered to have been discovered even before the Flood by Jabal, inventor of tents[44], who was promoted in the *Cooke MS* to the position of Master Mason responsible for the building of Enoch, the first city mentioned in the Bible, for his client, Cain[45]. From the Hebrew *Apocrypha* and from Flavius Josephus's *Jewish Antiquities*[46] comes the legend that Abraham instructed the Ancient Egyptians in Arithmetic and Astronomy, the source of similar twelfth-century claims by Honorius (*or* Henricus) Augustodunensis[47]. However, neither the last nor Peter Comestor[48], both of whom are recorded in the *Cooke MS*, mentions Euclid.

Later versions of these convoluted matters grant Euclid the distinction of having founded Geometry, in the basic principles of which he had been instructed by Abraham, despite the fact that Abraham had been dead some millennium-and-a-half before Euclid had the happiness to be born. Here, then, is an example of syncretism in which Jewish legend and aspects of Antique civilisation merge: this will be a process (in which chronology plays little part) that will become familiar throughout this study, and is a common feature of texts purporting to be serious histories of Freemasonry. However, tendencies to telescope historic events and to create improbable connections by ignoring the time-gap of hundreds, even thousands, of years, are not unusual features of the Mediaeval world, and indeed syncretism, by which various real figures were merged with deities or mythical personages (and by which deities themselves became identified with other deities and personages), was a strong feature of Classical Antiquity itself[49].

An interesting legend is that which claimed Geometry was invented as a corollary of Nilotic flooding: this

---

32 Isidore of Seville (2006) esp. Bk. **iii**.
33 Hiscock (2007) 11-12.
34 *See* his (sometimes known as Chalcidius) *Timaeus*. *See* Calcidius (1962).
35 Marcobius (1952), in which he discoursed on number, symbolism, oracles, moral virtue, astronomy, music, geography, and the soul, vindicating Plato against Aristotle.
36 *See* his *Septem Artes Liberales* (*c*.420) in Capella (1971-7).
37 Aurelius Augustine, Bishop of Hippo (from 395). *See* Augustine (1888), in the translation by Marcus Dods.
38 Boethius (1983).
39 Cassiodorus (2004).
40 *See* Grosseteste (1942, 1996) *passim*, and O'Carroll (*Ed.*) (2003) 151-79.
41 Hugh of St Victor (1991) **ii** 7.
42 Renewal of Platonic philosophy by Plotinus, whose writing influenced later Mediaeval authors.
43 Hiscock (2007) 8-63 is an excellent introduction to this thorny subject, a shut book to followers of shallow Modernism in all its forms.
44 Although *Cooke MS* calls them 'dwelling howsis'.
45 *Genesis* 4: 17. Enoch was Cain's son, after whom the city was named.
46 Josephus (2006) *passim*.
47 'Honorius Augustodunensis' was probably someone called Solitarius or Inclusus. *See* Trethewey (*Ed.*) (1939): *De Imagine Mundi*.
48 *See* Sherwood-Smith (2000) and Migne (*Ed.*) (1844-65) **clxii** col. 138.
49 *See* Curl (2005) *passim*, and Witt (1971) *passim*.

attribution was recorded by Diodorus Siculus[50], whose *Bibliotheca* included much of interest dealing with the history and mythology of the Ancient Egyptians. Diodorus Siculus noted that the Egyptians divided the inundated mud-covered lands by means of measured sections[51], and that this marked the beginnings of Geometry: the essence of his writings was disseminated by Bishop Isidore of Seville. The good Bishop (whose massive *Encyclopaedia* was one of the most influential books of the Middle Ages), however, omitted any mention of Abraham in this weighty matter, for through Diodorus Siculus the Great Geometer became Hermes the Messenger, no less. Nilotic flooding, and measurement by Cubits[52] (the units by which the amount of flooding was calculated) became associated with the Masonic legend in which Hermes Trismegistus and Euclid were identified as one and the same. The Hellenistic Hermes was Egyptianised through contact with the Egyptian Thoth. On the celebrated Rosetta Stone Hermes Thoth was described as 'the Great, the Great' but the epithet *Trismegistus* occurs only rarely outside the 'Hermetic' texts: the prefix *tris* appears from the Roman period. According to Titus Flavius Clemens (Clement of Alexandria), Hermes Trismegistus was the author of forty-two fundamental texts dealing with Egyptian religion, including astrological, cosmological, geographical, medical, and pedagogic books, as well as hymns to the deities and liturgical instructions[53]. This Hermes Trismegistus was identified with the Roman god Mercury, and with the Egyptian deity Thoth, inventor of hieroglyphs, protector of Osiris, and guardian of sacred knowledge. He was also identified with the Instructor of the Great Goddess Isis (whose tears for the murdered Osiris caused the Nile to flood) in many matters, including Geometry[54]. Diodorus Siculus is the source for the idea that instruction in Mathematics and Geometry was given to the sons of priests alone, and thus the idea of Geometry, the root of Masonry, as an exclusive and secret art or science, handed down to the deities, to an élite, or to a specific class, has an obvious connotation with Freemasonry in later times.[55]

So even before the Sack of Constantinople in 1453 brought scholars and books to the West, interest in Greek texts and in Egypt had been aroused. The connection between the Egyptian Horus and the Graeco-Roman Apollo was once more revealed[56] when Greek texts known as *Horapollo* dealing with Egyptian matters were rediscovered by Cristofero Buondelmonte of Florence in 1419: what had actually been found was a Mediaeval version of a Greek original called *Hori Apollonis Hieroglyphica*, and the writings were attributed to Hermes Trismegistus, who was thought to be a contemporary of Moses. Their translation into Latin and Italian in the fifteenth century encouraged the flowering of Neo-Platonist ideas current in the third and fourth centuries in Alexandria to early-Renaissance and late-Mediaeval Europe. These texts became important to scholars throughout the civilised world, and were perceived as links between Christian doctrine and philosophical and magical practices going back to Ancient Egypt. However, these so-called 'Hermetic' texts appear to have been by various Alexandrian authors written between the first and third (or fourth) centuries of our era: Hermes was certainly not *Contemporaneus Moysi* (as he is described in the famous historiated marble pavement at the West end of the Cathedral dedicated to the Assumption of the Virgin at Siena).

The world of the Renaissance Humanists was greatly influenced by pagan philosophy, but Christianity was not rejected as a result: rather, it was reinterpreted in the light of the wisdom of ancient texts, and the basic similarities of all known religions and philosophies were explored. Marsilio Ficino was a follower of Platonic ideas, and indeed saw in the works of 'Hermes Trismegistus' much that was redolent of Christianity (which is not surprising as they date from after the foundation of the Christian religion): he translated the texts into Italian, and these were published in 1471. The works were seen as containing profound truths that *predicted* Christian belief, and that established a thread of wisdom from Ancient Egypt to the Jews, the Greeks, and the Romans: the 'Hermetic' truths, regarded as going back to the time of Moses, or even Abraham, were a source of spiritual and intellectual stimulation that cannot be overestimated (despite their dodgy provenance), and had a profound effect on the study of Egyptian artefacts and on the legends of Freemasonry[57].

Guilds, Fraternities, Chantries, and Religious Observance

All sections in Chapter I have attempted to outline three identifiable strands in an interpretation of the term 'Freemason' in relation to 'Operative Masonry', which means that connected with working stonemasons. As is evident from the above, there is a mass of competing and conflicting views and theories, exacerbated by Masonic obsessions about the origins of the Craft. So how and why did organisations and associations associated with a working Craft become transmogrified into so-called 'Speculative Freemasonry'?

It is important to recognise and understand that Fraternities, Guilds, and Incorporations in the Mediaeval period held the religious side of their activities to be as important as the economic and trade aspects, and in some respects even more so. Feast-Days of Patron Saints, great religious festivals, and Craft pageants would find groups

---

50 Diodorus Siculus (1933-67, 1990).
51 Knoop & Jones (1948) 66.
52 Unit of linear measurement based on a sixteenth of the level by which the Nile rose in flood, and subsequently based on the distance from the elbow to the tip of the middle finger.
53 Festugière (1949-54), Fowden (1993), Hermes Trimegistus (1995), Nock (*Ed.*) (1945-54). For the Rosetta Stone *see* Parkinson, Diffie, Fischer, & Simpson (1999) *passim*.
54 Knoop & Jones (1948) 66; Curl (2005) 80-1 and *passim*.
55 Knoop, Jones, & Hamer (*Eds.*) (1938).
56 Sbordone (*Ed.*) (1940).

57 *See* Curl (2005) xxvi, 80-1, 86, 89, 90, 128, 132, 136, and *passim*.

of liveried men taking part in processions, plays, and meals. Many Guilds and Fraternities maintained altars and even chapels in great churches (and paid for Chaplains to perform the Offices), for although none but the richest could afford to endow a Chantry (an establishment, endowment, or foundation for the daily or frequent saying of Masses on behalf of the souls of the founder, founders, or other persons intended), as groups this could be made possible, so prayers for the dead and Chantries were available to the Guilds, which, if sufficiently wealthy, could actually have their own chantry-chapels, often set apart from the rest of the church by means of screens, or built as an extension to the church proper. These days visitors to very large churches often marvel at the size, and assume that this was because of vast congregations in times past: this is not so, for the body of a church was often subdivided by means of screens to enclose chantry-chapels (each with its own altar): the very large Church of St Laurence, Ludlow, Shropshire, still displays evidence (such as *piscinae* for washing out the sacred vessels after Mass in the walls of the aisles) that it once had an interior subdivided for the accommodation of such chapels[58]. One of the most important of the bases of Fraternities during the Middle Ages, then, was the doctrine of Purgatory which necessitated the frequent offering of *Obits* or Masses to free souls from its toils, so this in turn caused Chantries to be richly endowed as a variety of insurance-policy for the hereafter[59].

The English Parliament expressly abolished Purgatory[60], and the Crown confiscated Chantries in the sixteenth century: there were similar disruptions in every region where Protestantism triumphed, for the Reformed religion held that no intervention by the living could affect what happened to the souls of the dead, and new burial-grounds were established unattached to churches, in order to sunder the dead from the living and assist in the suppression of Roman Catholic beliefs and customs[61]. Although many chantry-chapels for individuals survived in England (in Winchester Cathedral, for example), chapels used by Guilds soon lost their associations, so that the mass of the populace no longer know what they were, nor what they were for. It should also be remembered that churches were once themselves sepulchres, and if a person were sufficiently well-off could specify in his or her Will where he or she wished to be buried or entombed (often near a statue of a favourite Saint or near a certain altar)[62]. Protestantism attempted to prevent this practice (albeit somewhat stripped of its popular religious connotations), but it nevertheless continued for reasons of social status, and even funerary chapels or 'aisles' were added to churches for the burial of whole families, without the trappings of Roman Catholic practice[63], so such places were sometimes termed 'mortuary chapels', and would not have been furnished with altars. It was nineteenth-century concerns about hygiene that largely put paid to the custom of burial within churches, except for the Great and Good (Lord Mountbatten of Burma[64] was entombed in Romsey Abbey, Hampshire, in 1979, at his own request), and encouraged the formation of large cemeteries, laid out on orderly and hygienic principles, with appropriate landscape-design[65]. With problems of church-upkeep, dwindling congregations, and so on, it might be appropriate to reconsider the use of churches as places where the dead could rest, even as calcined remains[66], which would not only bring in income, but help to make churches once again significant buildings in communities. The beautiful columbarium (1999) in the Church of St Mary, Bourne Street, Westminster, designed by John Roderick Warlow Gradidge, shows how this could be achieved in a positive and enhancing way.

The impact of Protestantism (especially in its more extreme Calvinist forms) left a huge void, for processions, the celebrations of great festivals, and even religious activities by groups such as Guilds were suppressed. Altars associated with Patron Saints were destroyed or removed, and a rich mix of custom, symbol, devotions, and pageant was abandoned. The Reformation, therefore, dealt a severe blow to participation in ceremony, and dented the connection of collective bodies of Guilds with formal religious observance. Indeed, the Guilds and Fraternities tended for a while to remain faithful to the old religion, though in time they were obliged to conform, while often retaining in their grand titles (as in the Livery Companies of the City of London) a clear connection with a Roman Catholic past.

As Guilds and Fraternities could no longer keep their own altars and chapels within churches, the churches themselves were stripped of much of their richness, and must have looked, quite suddenly, shockingly empty and bare, over-large for their purpose (as is painfully clear in a vast number of instances today). From places ablaze with colour and lighted tapers, many altars and screens, and plentiful imagery, churches became mere shells of what they had been. The impact on the populace as a whole, let alone the Guilds and Fraternities, must have been profoundly unsettling. Those who decry 'empty church-buildings' today should be made aware that the reasons

---

58 There were probably as many as sixteen chantry-chapels. *See* David Lloyd: *The Parish Church of St Laurence: A History and a Guide* (Ludlow: Parochial Church Council 1980) 4.

59 For an outline of the architectural implications *see* Colvin (1999) 152-89.

60 The *Articles of Religion* (1562) of the Anglican Church (xxii) declare that 'The Romish Doctrine concerning Purgatory, Pardons, Worshipping and Adoration, as well of Images as of Reliques, and also invocation of Saints, is a fond thing vainly invented, and is grounded in no warranty of Scripture, but rather repugnant to the Word of God'. Purgatory was actually abolished in 1543, and the final blow came with the Dissolution of Colleges (i.e. Chantries) (1 Edw. VI *c*. 14) in 1547 (hence the term 'Collegiate Church').

61 *See* Ariès (1981) for a detailed discussion of these matters.

62 *See* Duffy (1992) for illumination.

63 Colvin (1999).

64 Louis Francis Albert Victor Nicholas, 1st Earl Mountbatten of Burma from 1947.

65 Curl (2000*c*).

66 Cremated remains are not 'ashes': they are ground-up calcined bone fragments.

are not concerned primarily with 'falling congregations' (for it is doubtful if the vast East Anglian churches, for example, were ever crammed to bursting), but with the removal of many functions for which they were designed. These monuments were not conceived as preaching-boxes for static, trapped congregations to hear 'The Word': they were built for processions, elaborate ceremonies and observances, and for participation by Fraternities, Guilds, and other bodies in ceremonies and rituals associated with the security of the future life of the dead. Once churches ceased to be not only sepulchres (which happened only much later) but places where the living, in associations, could intervene on behalf of their dead Brethren and Sisters, a very large part of their *raison d'être* evaporated.

The Scottish Dimension

It seems, therefore, that the Reformation had the effect of forcing some Crafts to develop secret ceremonies and rituals of their own, for, as Stevenson has emphasised, the Reformed Churches discouraged religious worship and ceremony by the Guilds themselves[67]. It does seem to have been this aspect that was one of the most important elements in the evolution of what has become known as 'Speculative Freemasonry', a term that is perhaps unfortunate, and about which there has been much heated debate.

Now it is true that during the sixteenth century Scotland was a small, relatively poor, relatively backward, and disordered country, but many enterprising and educated Scots travelled on the Continent, bringing back influences from Italy, France, and elsewhere, because Scotland, for many reasons, was obliged to form closer connections with Europe than with its larger, richer, and often aggressive neighbour to the South; in particular, Scotland looked to France, and Scots traders had settlements far from home, even by the River Vistula, where, to this day, there exist large and handsome granaries near Kazimierz Dolny with which Scots merchants had interests.

Those familiar with the Architecture of Scotland will know how remarkably widespread was the impact of Renaissance detailing, and indeed that the late-fifteenth and early-sixteenth façades of the Royal Palaces at Stirling and Falkirk are among the earliest coherent Renaissance designs in the British Isles. Following the accession of King James VI a period of peace and stability occurred after the appalling religious and political upheavals that were such a sorry feature of the reign of Mary Queen of Scots. Certainly the Arts (including the Art of Memory[68]) flourished at Court, encouraged by the intelligent and cultured Danish Queen Anne, and during the late-sixteenth and early-seventeenth centuries there was a remarkable upsurge of building activity, not so much by the Crown, but by the nobility, by landowners, and by burgesses, all of whom had clearly benefited from the new and unaccustomed stability. Merchants and craftsmen also built, and the material used was almost exclusively stone. Several things strike the observer: first, how overtly Christian themes in the decorations are eschewed (probably to avoid accusations of 'idolatry' or 'Popery'); second, how emblems and lush iconography informed stone-carving, all inspired by Renaissance patterns; third, how often elaborate symbolism, frequently with seemingly occult echoes, occurs; and fourth, how very individually Scottish in character is the Architecture — it does not look anything like contemporary Architecture in England (or anywhere else, for that matter, unless one includes nineteenth-century Revivals or buildings erected by 'Planters' for Scotland in early-seventeenth-century Ulster). And among the most lavish examples of decorative work are fire-surrounds, over-mantels, ceilings, doorways, carved heraldic devices, and funerary monuments[69].

This confident upsurge of building activity required the services of numerous stonemasons, and probably encouraged a very considerable increase in the number of apprentices being taken on to learn the Craft. With this came a new pride in work and achievements, keeping certain traditions alive, but absorbing new Renaissance influences while expunging anything suggesting idolatry or the old religion: nevertheless, stonemasons reacted in several ways to the changes brought by the Protestant Reformation, which not only altered religious belief but changed the way in which religion was seen and what it was for.

Masonic organisation and ritual in Scotland seem to have evolved in a response to stern Reformation principles: they were attempts to fill the void caused by the abolition of colour, ritual, and ceremony by a grimly dour and Calvinist Church[70]. The post-Reformation Craft of Masonry developed more elaborate rituals than did other groups, but then it was already quite a distinct Craft *before* the Reformation, with its own guarded recognition methods and a mythology, 'history', and series of legends of rich complexity. The evolution of the Craft when esoteric knowledge (e.g. the study of Alchemy, Astronomy, Emblems, and much else which seems to have engaged many at that time) and the search for it were producing a ferment of ideas in the Renaissance period (including a harking back to Vitruvian and earlier principles of Antiquity), attracted many who were not stonemasons to the Lodges, perhaps in order to satisfy a need for ritual that the new Church ignored[71]. Stevenson has suggested that in the relationship of Scottish Lodges with the Reformed Church may lie the beginnings of distinctive features of later Freemasonry[72]; 'the exclusion of overt religious elements' from Lodge activities 'while at the same time clearly accepting the existence of God and the truth of Christianity'[73] can explain much.

---

67 Stevenson (1988*b*) 117-124 for an excellent summary of this.
68 *See* Yates (1966).
69 *See* the admirable *Buildings of Scotland* series; the indispensable MacGibbon & Ross (1877-92 and 1896-7) *passim*; Dunbar (1966) 51-2; Breeze (*Ed*.) (1984); and Dunbar (1999) *passim*.
70 Stevenson (1988*b*) 123.
71 *Ibid*.
72 *Ibid*.
73 *Ibid*.

Stevenson went on to point out that 'the emergence of Freemasonry in seventeenth-century Scotland as a system of morality illustrated by symbols, allegories, and rituals does not indicate any precocious deistic or tolerant attitudes to religion, but simply acceptance' that the Lodge 'was not a valid place' for stonemasons in which to indulge their (orthodox) religious inclinations. In the long term, of course, 'this exclusion from' Lodges of 'open commitment to any one brand of religion opened the way for the adoption of heterodox ideas and the admission of members with divergent religious beliefs'[74]. The Church of Scotland, Stevenson argued, accepted the existence of Lodges, and of rituals to be held within them or by them, on condition they were not *religious* rituals: this certainly goes a long way to explaining the tolerance the Reformed Church showed towards the Lodges, in marked contrast to the suppression of all drama and play-acting, not only because of Papist and Pagan associations, but also because of the fundamentalist position in representing images of other people. The Reformed Church in Scotland allowed some legitimacy to the Arts but only provided they were sundered from religious observance[75]. Masonic ritual, seen as *unimportant in religious terms*, and as a harmless activity not in competition with the Church, was not denounced from the pulpit: it was ceremony and formula, without dangerous religious connotations. If this had not been the case it would not have survived in the ultra-Protestant climate of late-sixteenth- and seventeenth-century Scotland[76], and it is essential to grasp this point. Those who claim Freemasonry is a 'religion', or is in some way religiously suspect, ignore this significant fact. What is of immense importance is that the nascent tenets of Freemasonry that emerged in Scottish Lodges seem to have informed several features of later Freemasonry: religious toleration, support for Deism, and *the profound connection of the Craft with the Enlightenment of the eighteenth century*[77], something far too many commentators ignore, dispute, or arrogantly dismiss.

And there was another aspect, and this, too, cannot be overlooked in the present context. Freemasonry had within it the potential of becoming something like a new religion, for it gave a new sense of belonging to those who were disillusioned with the Christian Churches, with notions of Providence, and with belief in the Supernatural (benign or not). Freemasonry, as it evolved, could offer a philosophy perhaps similar to a Natural Religion based on observations of the powers of Nature, Reason, and Wisdom. Ceremony and ritual were present in Lodge meetings, and the Craft claimed descent from mysteries older than Christianity, linking the greatness of Ancient Egyptian civilisation with the Temple of Solomon (Wisdom again), and the very beginnings of Time itself.

Stevenson has claimed[78] that it is in Scotland that we find the beginnings of what we now understand as Freemasonry. In 1583 William Schaw was appointed Master of Works, responsible for all Royal castles and palaces for life, by James VI. Schaw was a man of substance, a 'grit maister of all and sindrie his hines palaceis, biggingis and reparationis, and grit overseer'[79]. Most important, from our point of view, was that he reorganised the Craft in Scotland, and gave it enhanced stature and meaning throughout the Kingdom. As Stevenson observed. 'in doing so he created' modern Freemasonry[80], a statement that has clearly caused discomfort South of the Border and elsewhere (and may, it is true, be a somewhat oversimplified view). Schaw's position enabled him to issue two Codes of Statutes in 1598 and 1599 in which regulations for the organisation and practice of the Craft of stonemasonry through a system of Lodges were laid down. Now these 'Lodges' were unlike the Mediaeval ones previously described (i.e. buildings erected for a specific purpose during a contract): instead, they were intended to contain all the Operative Masons in a Burgh[81] or District, and not just those who happened to be employed on a particular site. These 'Lodges' were intended to be permanent institutions governed by elected officials under the supervision of a Grand Warden (at first Schaw himself)[82]. In other words rituals, rules, and binding ordinances were to be established nationally, administered through local Lodges. Mason Marks were mentioned, and these were to be recorded in Lodge Minute-Books. Masons were not supposed to be allowed to labour with Cowans (or semi-skilled men who nevertheless undertook certain works involving stone). Cowans were clearly not permitted to work with lime-mortar, and they may not have been permitted to cut or carve stone[83]. As Cowans were 'without the Word'[84], they were not initiated into the esoteric rituals of Masonry.

The Second Schaw statutes of 1599 were altered to take account of local conditions, recognising precedence, but they also refer to the importance of Masters most perfect and worthiest of memory testing others in their Art, Craft, Science, and Ancient Memory, and to those wishing to become Fellow Crafts having to give proof of Memory. In particular, the Warden of Kilwinning Lodge was ordered to test every Entered Apprentice and Fellow Craft in the 'Art of Memorie and Science thair of'. Now although the Art of Memory, as a technique[85], had been known since Classical Antiquity, by the Middle Ages and Renaissance

---

74 Stevenson (1988b) 124.
75 *Ibid*.
76 Where all was not Sweetness and Light, for superstition was widespread, and Witchcraft was widely believed in (and horribly punished after farcical hearings). James VI himself wrote a treatise on Witchcraft called *Daemonologie* (1597), but he seems to have been mostly a sceptic concerning that subject.
77 Stevenson (1988b) 123. My italics.
78 Stevenson (1998a and b) *passim*.
79 Paton (*Ed.*) (1957-82) **i** xvii. *See* also Imrie & Dunbar (*Eds.*) (1957-82) **ii** *passim*.
80 Stevenson (1988b) 32. *See* ODNB **xlix** (2004) 206-7.
81 Scots equivalent of a Municipality or Borough.
82 Stevenson (1988a) 3.
83 Stevenson (1988b) 42.
84 Carr (1961) 133.
85 To be outlined later.

periods it had become imbued with Symbolism and had Occult resonances.

Thus in reorganising Scottish Masonry, Schaw had more than mundane and bureaucratic matters in mind, for there was another agenda to it all: there is ample evidence that Schaw was covertly seeking to revive and encourage Mediaeval Masonic mythology and rituals, reconstituted within a framework profoundly influenced by the new Renaissance ideas[86]. Schaw defined the two 'grades' or 'ranks' of Masons within the Lodges: Entered Apprentice and Fellow Craft, which became standard in Non-Operative Freemasonry until, in the late-seventeenth and early-eighteenth centuries, a separate Grade of Master was created, giving the three 'Degrees' of later Freemasonry. The Statutes suggest that there were ceremonies of initiation to these Grades, and, as Stevenson has reminded us, although no Scottish copies of the 'Old Charges' are known before the middle of the seventeenth century[87], the Statutes suggest that that the Mediaeval legends were as familiar to Scots Masons as they were to their English colleagues[88]. Lodges began to keep regular Minutes of meetings, and in them initiations were recorded. Schaw's encouragement of Lodge-members to become involved in the latest philosophical concerns and esoteric ideas, and to take a wide interest in all manner of intellectual themes (including Rosicrucianism, another fashionable movement of the time), was significant.

Schaw's concerns with injecting into the traditional legends and institutions of the Craft a rich soup of Renaissance preoccupations were not just personal whims, but reflected many of the obsessions of the time in which 'secret' societies thrived throughout Europe, many concerned with finding solutions to the wars and religious upheavals which were doing so much damage (and it should be recalled that Scotland had not been unscathed by these events). Many of the members of these Societies believed that in the Lost Wisdom of ancient civilisations lay the keys to a new understanding that would lead to universal Harmony. A widespread Renaissance belief in the superiority of those ancient civilisations over the Mediaeval period was pronounced in the 'Hermetic' movement, as was the hope that in Astrology and Alchemy lay paths to the recovery of that which had been lost.

As Ancient Egyptian was earlier than Graeco-Roman civilisation, so the argument went, it must therefore have held within it the means of finding true Wisdom once again. In the effusions of the supposed 'Ancient Egyptian' sage Hermes Trismegistus (identified with Euclid) it was believed the rediscovery could be made. Egyptian hieroglyphs[89], however, could no longer be read in the sixteenth century, and indeed had not been decipherable in the West since at least the fall of the Western Roman Empire, but it appears they may still have been readable (for a time) by Islamic scholars until they, too, lost the necessary knowledge. Those hieroglyphs were thought to contain much connected with Ancient Wisdom, and many sought to decipher them, attempting to be 'scientific' in so doing. Hermetic quests were therefore partly historical (no matter how shaky were the techniques), but they were also concerned with spiritual enlightenment, purification, and the things of the mind: in all such endeavours, not involving the profane was important, for only initiates, working on higher intellectual and spiritual planes in secrecy, were judged capable or worthy to unlock and reveal Ancient Wisdom to their Brethren. The myths of the Craft included origins in Ancient Egypt, and, given the widespread enthusiasm for Hermeticism in Europe at the time, Masons must have been very aware of the importance of having a deity-like figure enshrined in their 'histories': mere verifiable historical truths played little part in the matter, something that might arouse the impatience and ire of post-Enlightenment opinion, but that is the way it was then.

The fact that at the core of the ritual in Schaw's recently created Lodges lay aspects of the Hermetic quest for Lost Knowledge (for that was important, if not *essential* to the future of civilisation and the human race), is the key as to why so many persons who were not stonemasons, or even connected with the Craft, were attracted to the Lodges, and joined them[90]. Sir Robert Moray[91] was one such intellectual, and he was but one of many. Eventually, gentlemen-Freemasons were to dominate the membership of the Scottish Lodges, so much so that the origins of those Lodges in the sixteenth-century 'Operative' Craft would become obscured.

Some commentators (mostly English) have airily assumed that Scottish Freemasonry in the seventeenth century was purely concerned with the organisation of the Mason's trade, and from which the philosophical dimension evident in eighteenth-century English Free-masonry was absent. Such a view dismisses the undoubted concerns of men like Moray (himself a Scot), and ignores the very real evidence of esoteric traditions in Scotland, including the Contract or Agreement of the Masters, Freemen, and Fellow Crafts Masons resident in the Burgh of Perth in 1658. They and their predecessors as Masons enjoyed, since the building of the Temple of Temples (i.e. the Temple of Solomon), 'ane uniforme communitie and unione throughout the whole world'. This document contains three significant points: first, it has the first known reference in Scottish Masonic documents to the myth of Solomon's Temple as the source of the skills and achievements of the Craft; second, it recognised the claim

---

86 Stevenson (1988a) 4.
87 And those that have survived were clearly derived from the English originals.
88 Stevenson (1988a) 4.
89 Of which many could be seen on obelisks and other objects in Rome, so a dangerous journey to Egypt was not necessary. *See* Curl (2005) *passim*.
90 If this point is accepted, it explains much. Stevenson's work in this respect has been of immense importance, and the present writer acknowledges Stevenson's kindness and generosity in sharing his knowledge and permitting quotations from his works to appear here.
91 ODNB **xxxix** (2004) 8-10. Moray had become a Freemason in 1641.

of the Kilwinning Lodge to be the first such in Scotland, but that the Perth Lodge was *derived* from Kilwinning, and therefore acquired kudos; and third, the Perth Lodge had originated with the building of the great Abbey of Scone[92], which had acquired a colony of Augustinian Canons from Nostell Priory, West Riding of Yorkshire, in 1122, at the behest of King Alexander I.

Stevenson has pointed out that in Scotland there is evidence for the continuous operation of recognisable Masonic Lodges since 1599: in England the evidence is fragmentary concerning seventeenth-century Freemasonry, though it includes notes of the initiation of Elias Ashmole at Warrington and Randle Holme, the herald painter, at Chester[93]. In Ashmole's case, his passion for Alchemy and Astrology is well-attested and it is known he took a strong interest in magical signs: in 1652 he brought out his *Theatrum Chemicum Britannicum*, a collection of English alchemical poems, annotated by him, which is one of the key sources for the history of Alchemy, and he was also fascinated by John Dee, the Mathematician, Astrologer, and Antiquary, who dabbled in magic and 'angelic conversations'. Dee managed to have an audience with Emperor Rudolf II in Prague in 1548, and it should be remembered that this Emperor was greatly interested in Alchemy, Astrology, Astronomy, and Chemistry, as well as being a Patron of that curious character, Tycho Brahe, and Johann Kepler.

Now Brahe's earlier Patron had been Frederick II, King of Denmark and Norway (from 1559), and Frederick was father of Princess Anne of Denmark, the future Queen of Scotland, England, and Ireland, and Consort of James VI and I. King Frederick had granted Brahe the island of Hven, in the Sound between Denmark and Sweden, in 1576: there was established Uraniborg, Brahe's dwelling, observatory, research-institute, alchemical laboratory, and museum.

Royal and Other Connections

A Danish match for King James was under discussion from 1581, and in 1589 a marriage was arranged between him and Princess Anne (she always called herself 'Anna'). In August of that year a proxy marriage-ceremony took place in the Great Hall of Kronborg Castle, George Keith (4th Earl Marischal) standing in for the King. Things had started badly, however, for King James had selected Jane Kennedy (who had attended his mother, and had gently bound Queen Mary's eyes before her beheading at Fotheringhay in 1587) to be among the group of courtiers to be sent to Denmark to accompany his bride on her journey back to Edinburgh, but the boat in which she travelled from Burntisland to Leith (to join the ship bound for Denmark) collided with another vessel, and she and many others perished[94].

After the celebrations, Anne's flotilla set sail for Scotland on 25 September, but one of the cannons saluting the new Queen exploded, killing two gunners, and another cannon blew up on board her own ship, killing the gunner and wounding several of the crew[95]. Then, what should have been a straightforward voyage almost ended in disaster, for ferocious storms forced the fleet to seek shelter in the fjords of Southern Norway. The 'impatient and sorrowful' King set sail for Norway in search of his Queen on 22 October, and located the Danish ships near what is now Oslo. James and Anne then went through a religious wedding-ceremony at the Bishop's Palace, and, the weather still being stormy, the Royal Party repaired to Kronborg, arriving there on 21 January 1590. During their stay they also visited Copenhagen, Roskilde, Frederiksborg, and Tycho Brahe's island retreat, and did not finally sail from Denmark until 21 April 1590, landing safely at Leith on 1 May to a lavish and colourful welcome, and a magnificent display of pageantry.

Schaw had travelled to Norway with the King, but returned to Scotland to make preparations for the Queen's arrival in her new Kingdom. The King had presented his bride with a Charter of the Regality of Dunfermline as a Morrowing Gift, and Schaw supervised major works of repair and redecoration at the Palace and Abbey of Dunfermline, as well as at Holyrood Palace, Edinburgh, and Stirling Castle (where he was also responsible for the new Chapel Royal erected for the Baptism of Prince Henry Frederick in 1594).

The new Queen of Scots was not only intelligent, but educated and acutely aware of current trends in European thought: she was a fine linguist, had a wide appreciation of the Arts, and, most importantly for our purposes, had a lifelong passion for Architecture. She was, unsurprisingly, a powerful influence on Scottish Court culture, notably Architecture, and became friendly with William Schaw, whose works at her residence in Dunfermline had pleased her. The Queen was nominally a Lutheran, and the Scots had agreed that she would continue in that faith: gradually, however, her religious leanings attracted criticism, not least from the General Assembly of the Church of Scotland in 1596, for it was noticed that there were many Roman Catholics within Royal circles, especially that around the Queen. Prominent among those Roman Catholics was the King's cousin, the chief Lady of Anne's household from November 1590: she was Henrietta Stewart, Countess of Huntly, who was fired with Counter-Reformation zeal. Finding grim Calvinism uncongenial (not least the carping criticisms from the Kirk about her 'ungodly' behaviour and calls for her lifestyle needing 'to be reformit'[96]), she displayed leanings towards Roman Catholicism in 1593, and by 1596 she was worshipping as a Roman Catholic,

---

92 For these matters *see* Stevenson (1988a) 101-7. For resistance to Stevenson's impeccable research *see* Ars Quatuor Coronatorum **cvii** (1994) 53-84.

93 I am indebted to Andrew Prescott for discussing these matters with me. For Holme *see* ODNB **xxvii** (2004) 774-5, and for Ashmole *see* ODNB **ii** (2004) 661-5.

94 *See* Fraser (1969) 539, 550, and Stevenson (1997) 25 and *passim*.
95 ODNB **ii** (2004) 192.
96 *Ibid*. 195.

and so had probably been converted by then, although the Danes in her household continued to attend Lutheran services presided over by the Queen's Pastor, John Sering.

After Dunfermline became the Queen's preferred residence, where she could surround herself with like-minded (and Roman Catholic) friends in comparative privacy, her Master of Works, William Schaw, further extended the Palace there, building a 'Queen's House' and, most significantly, an Oratory for her Privy Chamber. Schaw also worked for Robert Seton (6th Lord Seton from 1586 and later [1600] 1st Earl of Winton) and his brother, Alexander Seton[97] (1st Earl of Dunfermline [from 1605]): the Setons were also Roman Catholics, and their support for Schaw undoubtedly helped to keep him in good odour at Court. Schaw's creations at Dunfermline earned him the Queen's trust and friendship, and he became her Chamberlain.

Apart from Stevenson, many commentators have failed to notice the enormous importance of Schaw as a major figure (quite apart from his place in the history of Freemasonry), which is very odd. He travelled to France in 1584 with George Seton (5th Lord Seton from 1549) as part of a mission to renew ties of friendship between Scotland and France, a sub-plot of which was the furtherance of Roman Catholic interests and the eventual restoration of the old religion and of Mary, Queen of Scots, to the Throne with Continental help. Alexander Seton, fourth son of the then Lord Seton, was also a member of the mission, and was well-versed in Mathematics: he was said to be skilled in Architecture as well as in Greek and Latin, so Schaw was the ideal travelling-companion for one who wished to extend his knowledge of Architecture. Alexander had been a student at the Jesuit-run German College, where he received a first-class Classical education, and managed to survive all attacks on him (he was what the English called a 'Church Papist', outwardly Conforming, but privately devoted to the old faith). In 1593 he became Chairman of a Committee charged with managing the Queen's property, and was so successful that the King made this the nucleus of an eight-man group to manage all the Royal finances. Called 'The Octavians', this group consisted almost entirely of 'Papists known or inclining to Popery or Malignancy'[98], and Seton himself was dubbed 'that Romanist president, a shaveling and a priest'[99], even though there is no evidence that he took Holy Orders. However, his connections and shrewdness led to his appointment as guardian (1600-4) to the infant Prince Charles. As a lawyer and a person of urbane distinction and polish, he was appointed in 1604 as chief negotiator of the proposed Anglo-Scottish union after the Union of the Crowns in 1603, and, even though political union[100] did not materialise until 1707, Seton won the friendship and respect of Sir Robert Cecil (1st Earl of Salisbury from 1605), and in 1604 he was rewarded with the Lord Chancellorship of Scotland and in 1605 the Earldom of Dunfermline.

Queen Anne continued to practise her Roman Catholicism after she moved to London as Queen of England. As noted above, the cultivated circle around her at Dunfermline was an important catalyst for the raising of the tone at the Scottish Court, and in England, with more money available, was able to develop her interests, originally formed in Denmark, and further evolved during her years in Scotland. She played a major part in putting on magnificent Court Masques, and between 1604 and 1611 she commissioned and *performed in* six Masques at Hampton Court and Whitehall Palaces. Most of these were designed by Inigo Jones, who seems to have acted for her in a similar rôle to that Schaw had performed in Scotland, for the Queen employed Jones for architectural projects, including the astonishingly innovative Queen's House, Greenwich (1616-19), completed (1630-5) for her daughter-in-law, Henrietta Maria, Consort (from 1625) of King Charles I (reigned from 1625, executed 1649). Other architectural works by Jones for Queen Anne included the Great Gate at the Park, the Silk-Worm House, and Gateway to the Vineyard at Oatlands House, Surrey (1616-17 – demolished); alterations at Somerset (later Denmark) House, the Strand, London (from 1609 – all demolished 1776-90); and (possibly) improvements to her apartments at Greenwich Palace after 1613 (demolished). Thus Queen Anne was an important figure in the first English Palladian Revival.

Now Jones had travelled to Denmark in 1603 with Roger Manners[101], 5th Earl of Rutland from 1588 (who had been charged with the bestowing of the Garter upon King Christian IV). The Danish King was Queen Anne's brother, and Jones appears to have worked for him for a brief period before returning to London in 1604 to collaborate with Ben Johnson on Masques, the first of which, *The Masque of Blackness*, was given in the old Banqueting House at Whitehall Palace on 6 January 1605. Between 1605 and 1609 Jones's drawings improved enormously, so that by the end of that period his draughtsmanship

---

97 Seton held the title of Prior of Pluscarden from the age of nine. He should not be confused with the famous Alchemist, also 'Alexander Seton' (d. 1604), who was said to have carried out successful transmutations of metal, and who was pursued by many Princes in Germany (*see* Trevor-Roper [2006] 95).

98 *ODNB* **xlix** (2004) 799.

99 *Ibid.*

100 James envisaged a full legal, administrative, and parliamentary union, but by 1607 this ambitious plan was dead.

101 Rutland graduated from the University of Padua in 1596, an odd choice for an Englishman. Rutland's brother, Francis (6th Earl of Rutland from 1612), married Cecily Tufton, a recusant, and he, his daughter (by his first wife) Katherine, and his sister all became Roman Catholics. In 1624 he and his wife were top of a list of 'suspected Popish Recusants' drawn up by the Commons, and he fell into the category of a 'Church Papist' (*ODNB* **xxxvi** [2004] 462). Katherine married in 1620 George Villiers (1st Duke of Buckingham from 1623), for whom Inigo Jones carried out works at Whitehall Palace (1619-28) and York House, The Strand (c.1625). After Buckingham's assassination, Katherine reverted to the Roman Catholicism she had been obliged to renounce on her marriage, and in 1635 married Randal MacDonnell, Viscount Dunluce, later 2nd Earl (from 1636) and 1st Marquess (from 1645) of Antrim, one of Ireland's greatest magnates, and a Roman Catholic. Katherine Manners was one of the most influential women at the Caroline Court, and was related through her Villiers connections with the Earls of Arundel, Desmond, Hamilton, Nithsdale, Northampton, Pembroke, and Suffolk.

showed he had acquired an accomplished Italianate style: he *may* have visited Italy in 1605-6, but the remarkable development in his technique and his grasp of Classicism may owe more to careful study and to the encouragement of the Queen. He was appointed Surveyor of Works to Henry, Prince of Wales, in 1610, and in 1613 travelled in the train of Thomas Howard, 14th Earl of Arundel from 1595, as part of the official entourage escorting Frederick V, Elector Palatine of the Rhine from 1610, and his new wife, Princess Elizabeth, daughter of James VI and I and Queen Anne, to the Elector's seat at Heidelberg. Having safely delivered the Elector and Electress, Arundel and his party travelled south to Italy, a journey that was of enormous importance to the architectural education of both Jones and himself[102].

Meanwhile, the Prince of Wales, a young man of great promise, had died, and Prince Charles became heir to the Throne. After his return to England in 1614/15, Jones became Surveyor of the King's Works, and began to make use of the results of his Italian tour, for he had not only met the elderly architect Vincenzo Scamozzi, but acquired various books by celebrated authors, including the *Quattro Libri* (1601 edition) of Andrea Palladio. Thus equipped, Jones introduced an Architecture to England that was strongly influenced by the works of Palladio and Scamozzi[103]. His work, in turn, influenced the Second Palladian Revival led by Richard Boyle (3rd Earl of Burlington and 4th Earl of Cork [from 1704]), Colen Campbell, and their contemporaries, so it cannot be overestimated in importance. Jones, indeed, was a main figure of the First Palladian Revival, and was a catalyst for the Second. And behind Jones was the figure of the Queen.

Pl. II.1 Monument of William Schaw in Dunfermline Abbey (MC. B080708).

It was not only in Architecture and theatrical displays that Anne was influential: she established an extensive collection of paintings which was greatly expanded under Charles I, she was passionately interested in Music, and she was a discerning Patron of writers. Indeed, she was far more culturally sophisticated than was her husband (although he was a remarkable phenomenon: a King with an enormous and unrivalled literary output covering an astonishing range of subjects, including poetry and translations), and her support for Architecture, Art, Literature, Music, and Theatre in both Scotland (as far as was possible, with a disapproving Kirk always vigilant) and England should be better recognised[104]. Indeed, she has been most unfairly and unjustly treated by commentators, having been accused of anonymity, frivolity, stupidity, and of being uninteresting, but recent publications are attempting to reassess her reputation. In the context of this study her support for Schaw and Jones is of overwhelming importance.

---

102 The travels of Arundel and Jones have parallels with those of Seton and Schaw. Arundel aroused some suspicion in his lifetime as one unduly close to the Papacy, and although he outwardly Conformed, he remained very sympathetic to Roman Catholics (*see Archivo General*, Simancas, Libro 374, 2, vii, 1621). He continued to be identified with Roman Catholic interests at Court in the years preceding the Civil War, and he died a Roman Catholic in exile in Padua, where his heart and entrails were entombed in the Basilica of St Anthony, though his body was returned to England for burial in the Fitzalan Chapel, Arundel, Sussex. Jones acted as Arundel's Architect for works at Arundel House, The Strand (demolished c.1768), and had many Roman Catholic Patrons: indeed, he was said (on the authority of Sir Christopher Wren, no less), to have died a Roman Catholic. However, Jones was a Member of Parliament and a Justice of the Peace, and so must have Conformed, in public at least (Colvin [2008] 588).

103 *See* Colvin (2008) 584-93; *ODNB* **xxx** (2004) 527-38; and Turner (*Ed.*) (1996) **xvii** 633-9.

104 *ODNB* **ii** (2004) 191-9.

So Schaw had the ear of the Queen, and was her Chamberlain and Master of Ceremonies: he was not only her personal Architect, but a national figure of great significance in architectural terms, and with Royal Patronage and as a protégé of the powerful Seton family, he was a force with which to be reckoned. After he died in 1602 the Queen instructed Seton to commemorate him, and a large funerary monument was duly erected (probably after 1605) in Dunfermline Abbey. The inscription (in Latin) is of immense interest, and begins with the formula D O M (*Deo* or *Domino Optimo Maximo* – God (or the Lord) the Best and Greatest [or God Most Holy and Most High]), normally associated with Roman Catholicism. It goes on to celebrate Schaw as a man illustrious for his rare experience, admirable rectitude, unmatched integrity, and consummate qualities, and refers to his eagerness to improve his mind by foreign travel: we are also informed that he was accomplished in 'every liberal art', that he 'excelled in architecture', and that 'Princes… esteemed him for his conspicuous gifts'[105] (see **Pl.II.1**, p.29).

This memorial, though Classical, is very coarse, and compares very unfavourably with contemporary work South of the Border. Given his various connections through the Setons, the Queen, and the Sinclairs (see below), it is highly likely that he was a closet Roman Catholic: he has been described as 'evidently… one of the small circle of [Roman] Catholics who survived at court with the connivance of James VI'[106]. He may have been the William Schaw for whom black velvet was bought in 1560 in order to make his cloak, part of his Court dress (probably for mourning) as a page to Mary of Guise (Queen Dowager, Regent of Scotland, and mother of Mary, Queen of Scots)[107]. After the death of the Regent, nothing much is known of Schaw until his appointment (21 December 1583) as Master of Works to the King. Subsequent references to him as an Architect are among the earliest uses of the word in Scotland[108]. His elevation as Master of Works was probably possible during the reaction to extreme Protestantism which brought more conservative men to power[109]. Nevertheless, Schaw was ordered to appear before the Edinburgh Presbytery in 1588 as a suspected Papist, and in 1593 an English agent identified him as a 'suspected Jesuit'[110].

There seems to have been little doubt that Schaw was indeed a Roman Catholic, and managed a cunning balancing-act in order to survive (as did his friends, the Setons). Where was he between 1560 and 1583, however? Was he educated on the Continent, perhaps by Jesuits?

The answer is that we simply do not know, but that is not surprising, because a Jesuit-educated Scotsman at a time of religious upheaval leading to the effective deposition and execution of Queen Mary would not have encouraged him to seek what is nowadays known as a 'high profile'. Nevertheless, Schaw acquired an education *somewhere*, and it is not unreasonable to hazard a guess that he did so in Europe. Certainly he was held in such high regard that not only did he travel to France with Seton on what was more than a diplomatic mission, but one connected with support for Roman Catholicism (and, probably, the exiled Mary, Queen of Scots). He was placed in charge of the entertainments for the Danish Ambassadors in 1585 (in which capacities he designed the settings and acted as Master of Ceremonies), and, as we have seen, accompanied the King to Norway in 1589, after which he returned to Edinburgh to make preparations for the new Queen's reception. Thus he was in an unusually powerful and influential position, and a Papist too.

That Schaw was 'inspired by the Renaissance exaltation' of Architecture as 'the greatest of' the Arts, and 'built on old traditions of the primacy' of Masons (as the agents of Architects) 'to claim a special status for them' cannot be doubted. Whilst much of his proposed reorganisation of the Craft concerned 'the working practices' of Masons, 'there are also hints at secrecy and rituals', mixing Mediaeval and Renaissance elements. Furthermore, the 'issue of the two sets' of Statutes 'evidently followed meetings' of Masons held on the day of their Patron Saint, St John the Evangelist (27 December). 'The development' of these Lodges 'and their rituals was to be central to' the emergence of Freemasonry[111].

The most widely accepted Patron Saint for the Craft was St John, but there is more than a little confusion (here and elsewhere in Masonic investigations) about whether this was St John the Baptist (d. *c*.30 – Feast-Day 24 June) or St John the Evangelist *or* Apostle[112] (Feast-Day 27 December). Before the Reformation, the Incorporation of Masons and Wrights had been responsible for the upkeep of the Chapel of St John the Evangelist in the great church of St Giles, Edinburgh, and most seventeenth-century Lodges convened their main assembly of the year on 27 December[113]. Many Mediaeval Guilds held their Saints in high regard as Patrons, but neither St John appears to have had any special connection with the building-trades or with Masonry. Richard Wagner, in *Die Meistersinger von Nürnberg* (1861-7, first performed on 21 June 1868 in Munich), brings the action to its climax on St John's Day (24 June – which was also the Name-Day of the character of Hans Sachs, the cobbler, who actually existed), the *Johannesfest*, at which *all* the Guilds gather, including the Shoemakers and Leather-Workers, whose Patrons were Sts Crispin and Crispinian (Feast-Day 25 October).

---

105 *Grand Lodge of Scotland Year Book* (1982) 68. *See* also *ODNB* **xlix** (2004) 206-7; Stevenson (1988*b*) *passim*; *Ars Quatuor Coronatorum* **l** (1937) 220-6; and Howard (1995) **ii**. Schaw may have been involved in some way with the design of Fyvie Castle, Aberdeenshire, Seton Palace, Lothian (destroyed), and Pinkie House, Musselburgh, Lothian, all properties connected with the Seton family.
106 *ODNB* **xlix** (2004) 206.
107 Paul (*Ed.*) (1916) 23.
108 *ODNB* **xlix** (2004) 206.
109 Stevenson (1988*b*) 28.
110 *Calendar of State Papers relating to Scotland* for *1589-93* 620 and for *1593-5* 18.

111 *ODNB* **xlix** (2004) 207. The *ODNB* entry is by David Stevenson, to whose impressive work this study is indebted.
112 Also known as the Divine. *See* Baring-Gould **xv** (1914) 307-10.
113 Stevenson (1988*b*) 43.

The two St Johns' Feast-Days mentioned above are known as 'The Two Great Parallels', but although St John the Divine (or the Evangelist) was associated with the Masons who held important gatherings on 27 December, St John the Baptist (an immensely popular Saint in the Middle Ages, to which the numbers of churches named after him testify) was associated with the Knights Hospitallers, whose principal work it was to guard the Holy Sepulchre in Jerusalem, and therefore, by further association, he was connected with the lost Temple of Solomon. It is possible, however, that both these Saints were confused with St John the Almsgiver or Almoner, Patriarch of Alexandria (Feast-Day 23 January), perhaps because of a vague notion that, as Patron of the Knights of Malta, he was connected with the Craft of Building. Other Saints who have claims to be connected with the Craft are Sts Barbara, Virgin-Martyr (Feast-Day 4 December, whose Emblem was a three-windowed tower), and Thomas the Apostle (Feast-Day 21 December, whose Emblems are a builder's Rule or Square). Barbara was recognised as Patroness of Architects and Builders, and Thomas claimed to be a Carpenter and Architect[114]. Much honoured throughout the Mediaeval period were the Four Crowned Martyrs (*Quatuor Coronati* – Feast-Day 8 November – whose Emblems were the Saw, Hammer, Mallet, Compasses, and Square)[115]. It is therefore unsurprising that the first Grand Master of the Premier Grand Lodge was elected and installed on St John the Baptist's Day, 1717, and installation-days are still referred to in some areas as 'St John's'. St John the Baptist has been identified with Hermes/Mercury, and therefore with the 'Messenger', the 'One Who Went Before'.

Acutely aware that his theory is only a hypothesis, the present writer hazards a suggestion that what Schaw may have been attempting was not only a restoration of colour and ritual (badly dented by Calvinistic prohibitions) into the Craft, but vast improvements in its status by insisting that Cowans and others should be excluded from Masonry and from knowledge of anything of its mysteries that were claimed to link it with Antiquity. By enshrining techniques such as the Art of Memory into his Statutes, Schaw may have been trying to bring the Craft into line with advanced Renaissance ideas, believing that, through Masonry (the Craft or Art or Science distinguished by its familiarity with Geometry and other ancient lore [as noted earlier]), aspects of Roman Catholicism and of ancient traditions could be preserved and restored in times of momentous and destructive change. In other words, his agenda was of far greater import than it might appear on the surface.

Perhaps frustrated by his failure to obtain *official* Royal approval for the Craft, Schaw seems to have turned to Sinclair of Roslin in an attempt to obtain such approval through a different channel. The Sinclairs, of course, had some claims to be Patrons of the Craft connected with the unfinished church begun by William Sinclair, Earl of Caithness and Orkney, and his son in the fifteenth century. However, the Sinclairs of Roslin were only a junior branch of the family that had commenced this remarkable building, known as St Matthew's Chapel, of which only the clerestoreyed choir with north, south, and eastern aisles, the east walls of the transepts, and a vaulted chamber (called the Lower Chapel, Sacristry, or Crypt) to the east at a low level, were realised[116].

The foundations of what was to have been the nave and transepts of a very grand private Collegiate Church have been investigated, but what has caused the choir and its aisles (the eastern aisle was clearly intended to house a chapel or chapels) to become famous is the elaborate stone-carving that covers almost every part of the structure. In nearly any location this would be worthy of notice, but in the context of late-Mediaeval Scotland (where even ambitious buildings tend to be plain, even severe), it is extraordinary. For comparable fantastic and sculpture-encrusted Gothic architecture 'one must go to Belém or Batalha or S. Juan de los Reyes in Toledo'[117]. Much nonsense has been written about Roslin, but it was to be a lavish Collegiate Church in which members of the family were to be commemorated (and entombed) and prayers offered for the repose and welfare of their souls. The association of the Chapel with the legend of the murdered Mason will be described later[118].

In 1600-1, Schaw supported what is known as the First St Clair Charter, whereby the Masons were to recognise William Sinclair of Roslin as their Patron and Protector[119]. There were precedents in that several Scots Lairds had become protectors of itinerant tradesmen in their localities, and there is evidence of an Aberdeenshire Laird confirmed by James VI as Warden of the Masons of North-East Scotland in 1590, so the Sinclair claims to be Patrons and Protectors were not without historical respectability. Sinclair Patronage was renewed in the Second St Clair Charter of 1627-8, addressed to Sinclair's son, William, but by the 1630s the rival claims of the Royal Masters of Works and the Sinclairs caused such difficulties that Schaw's Lodge system was left to evolve on its own.

Schaw's death in 1602 and the removal of the Court to London on the Union of the Crowns in 1603 prevented attempts to win the King's support. Why did Schaw select

---

114 For these see *Bulletin of the John Rylands Library* **x** (1926) 80-111 **xi** (1927) 20-50; Medlycott (1905) *passim*; Delehaye (1931) 658-9; Migne (*Ed.*) **cxvi** (1857-1904) 301-16; *Analecta Bollandiana* **lxxvii** (1959) 5-41. See also Jones (1986) 338-43; Baring-Gould (1914); and Farmer (1992).

115 Jones (1986) 342. *See* also Farmer (1992) 184-5.

116 *See* MacGibbon & Ross **iii** (1897) 149-79 (with drawings), and The Earl of Rosslyn (1997): *Rosslyn Chapel* (Rosslyn: Rosslyn Chapel Trust).

117 McWilliam (1978) 411-2. The Franciscan convent of San Juan de los Reyes, Toledo, Spain, was founded in 1477. Santa Maria, Belém, Portugal, was begun 1502, and the Capillas Imperfectes, Batalha, Portugal, a mortuary-chapel, was designed 1434.

118 *See* Cooper (2006) for a splendidly robust refutation of the vast accretions of nonsense that have become glued to an unfinished Collegiate Church, and for an injection of sober facts and sound common sense, freed from lurid fantasies about Holy Grails, Templars, or anything else. The fact is that the Church is really about family kudos and piety. *See* also MacGibbon & Ross **iii** (1897) 149-179, which points out that Roslin had a Provost, six Prebendaries, and two 'singing boys' or choristers: absurd legends and improbable connections are prudently eschewed.

119 Stevenson (1988*a*) 5. St Clair is also spelled Sinclair, and Roslin Rosslyn. *See* Cooper (2006) 278-81 for a transcription of the Charters.

Sinclair as Patron in any case? Certainly the realised fragment of the Chapel had amazed and awed generations of Masons who saw it, and so a connection was made between the Craft and the family. But there was another factor: William Sinclair was a Roman Catholic, and had been in constant trouble with the Church of Scotland over images, altars, and 'uther monuments of idolatrie'[120]. By 1592 however, the altars had been demolished, but many of the carved figures (surprisingly) were allowed to remain. Sinclair's connection with Schaw probably began through building-works at Rosslyn Castle, but, apart from his religion, it is difficult to understand why Schaw chose Sinclair as a possible Patron, as he (Sinclair) was an heroic fornicator, notorious for his 'lewdness'. Sinclair's son (also William, but a different kettle of fish, being a solid citizen, Justice of the Peace, a Knight, a Sheriff, and [outwardly at least] a Conformer in religious matters[121]) sought to maintain his family's connection with the Craft, and the result was the Second St Clair Charter of c.1627-8.

However, the claims of the Sinclairs were hotly disputed, despite the tradition that from 1600 to 1736 they were hereditary Patrons of the Mason Craft. In 1636 at a meeting in Falkland, Sir Anthony Alexander (who had 'acquired skill in architectorie'[122], was a member of a Lodge of Mary's Chapel, Edinburgh, and who was Master of Works) attempted a major reorganisation of the building-trades through what became known as the Falkland Statutes. On Alexander's death the Sinclairs once again attempted to reclaim their position. Such squabbles about who was Patron or Top Dog ceased to be of much importance as Civil War moved closer, but in 1736 the then William St Clair[123] resigned his and his heirs' claims over the Craft, in return for which he was elected the first Grand Master of Scotland[124].

There was more to Alexander's reorganisation. He appears to have been prompted by the curious syncretic mixture of traditional and Renaissance ideas that Schaw had attempted to bring to the Craft in order to enhance its status (and perhaps for other reasons as well). In addition, Alexander may have tried to widen the organisation of the Lodge system to embrace other building-crafts, yet keep them subordinated to Masonry. As observed earlier, the Vitruvian concept of Architecture was that it was the most important among all the Arts, yet there is nothing explicit in the Falkland Statutes concerning Craft superiority, or references to rituals, secrets, or esoteric matters. Nevertheless, the attempt to impose the Statutes on the Lodges suggests that some kind of central authority was still being sought, even as the Monarchy tottered towards disaster, and Civil War disrupted everything.

From the above, therefore, it would seem that sixteenth-century developments of the Craft in Scotland may have included attempts to give it great status by means of massive injections of esoteric lore, connections with ancient mysteries, and the Renaissance Art of Memory, as well as making it the guardian of secrets and creating an impressive series of rituals in place of the banned observances relating to Chantries and the like. But, given the religious dimension in such dangerous times, was it possible that Schaw, connected as he was with the Setons, Sinclairs, and even the Queen, was attempting to use a reorganised Craft to lay the foundations of some kind of revival of Roman Catholicism or Roman Catholic practices (or at least pre-Reformation customs), perhaps not unconnected with Counter-Reformation currents? The search for That which was Lost, and the guardianship of ancient knowledge, after all, led back before the Reformation to times capable of creating glorious works of Architecture, like Roslin Chapel or the Temple of Solomon. From an early twenty-first-century viewpoint, a world in which various branches of Christianity were literally at each other's throats, and when professing one faith could easily lead to ruin and cruel death at the hands of another version of it, is beyond the comprehension of most, but there can be no doubting the central place religious controversy, power-politics with religious affiliations, and esoteric belief played in the sixteenth, seventeenth, and early eighteenth centuries.

What is certain is that, if one wished to reform the world, leading it back to happier times, and do so in reasonable security, Architecture was as suitable a vehicle as any to use for that purpose, and the Lodges offered an elite membership and secret series of meetings to achieve deeply-held aims that might be too dangerous to air outside a select company where the climate could be hostile and murderous.

---

120 Quoted in Stevenson (1988b) 55.
121 His father probably left for Ireland in or around 1617 (accompanied by a miller's daughter), where he supposed life would be easier for him as a Roman Catholic.
122 Stevenson (1988b) 61.
123 As the family then spelled its name.
124 Stevenson (1988b) 66.

CHAPTER III

Hermeticism, Memory, Legends, and Syncretism

The Hermetic Tradition; Mnemonic Techniques; The Hiramic and Other Legends; Syncretism and Mysteries; Concluding Remarks

'Memoria est thesaurus omnium rerum e custos.'[1]
MARCUS TULLIUS CICERO (106-43 BC):
De Oratore (55 BC) **i** sec. 5.

'Memory is to us the hearing of deaf actions, and the seeing of blind... what wonders it performs in preserving and storing up things that have passed, or, rather, things that are!'
MESTRIUS PLUTARCHUS (PLUTARCH)
(before AD 50 – after AD 120):
Morals: On the Cessation of Oracles sec. 39.

'The severe Schools shall never laugh me out of the philosophy of *Hermes*, that this visible World is but a Picture of the invisible, wherein as in a Pourtraict, things are not truely, but in equivocal shapes, and as they counterfeit some more real substance in that invisible Fabrick.'
SIR THOMAS BROWNE (1605-82):
Religio Medici **i** sect. 12.

The Hermetic Tradition

Neo-Platonism (the philosophical and religious system, mainly composed of a mix of Platonic ideas and Egyptian/Asiatic Mysteries, which originated in Alexandria in the third century, and is perhaps best represented in the works of Plotinus, Porphyry, and Proclus) permeated much of Renaissance thought, and blurred distinctions between matter and spirit: it was, of course, fundamentally Pantheistic (a fact obscured by Christian apologists). The whole of the cosmos was seen as an *entity*, and special attributes were accorded to Symbols, Numbers, Colours, and Letters: everything merged with the Divine, and the stars in the firmament were seen to be joined to Man's fortunes. Indeed, a harnessing of forces for the benefit of Mankind was the aim of the Occultists, Alchemists, Astrologers, and Magicians[2] who were associated with the remarkable rediscovery of Neo-Platonic thought that had tended to be hidden away in the dark after the death of Emperor Julianus Flavius Claudius (Julian 'The Apostate'). Julian's surviving writings show him to have been both learned and capable of fluent expression, and his brief reign saw a general religious toleration as well as a vigorous programme to restore Hellenism, a fusion of Greek and non-Greek culture, together with a revival of ancient pagan Cults. Even more interesting was his proposal to rebuild the Jewish Temple in Jerusalem, possibly part of his attempts to marginalise Christianity as well as to demonstrate his essential tolerance of religions (not something shared by Christians). Julian himself was devoted to Isis, most universal of deities, which perhaps says much about his stance.

A search for esoteric knowledge through Alchemy[3] became a European obsession in the sixteenth and seventeenth centuries before Newtonian physicists put paid to such notions (although Alchemical ideas persisted in certain quarters almost until the end of the eighteenth century, as we will see). In this connection, materialistic

---

1 Memory is the treasury and guardian of all things.

2 *See* Yates (1972) *passim*, for discussions on these matters. *See also* Yates (1979) *passim*.
3 *Ibid*.

ideas born of Rationalism have been unfair to the Age of the Alchemists, for the seeking of The Philosopher's Stone was more a striving for some form of moral and spiritual Rebirth than a short-cut to coining gold in the vulgar sense[4]. Alchemists desired to find a reality behind the physical world, and strove mightily to find a means of controlling Forces of nature in order to give Mankind powers beyond his imagining[5]. Renaissance Alchemists sought a Perfection of the Spirit, a Union with the Divine in the Universe, and a God-like state of Pure and Revealed Knowledge: if they did not go about this in the right way, it was not for want of trying or of a passionate and deeply-felt desire for something transcendental.

Poetry of the period (often termed 'Metaphysical' for very good reasons) was frequently ecstatic, concerned with the attainment of some unspoiled and spiritual plane of blinding revelation and clarity unknown to everyday prosaic experience. Thomas Traherne, for example, in his *Centuries of Meditation* [6], spoke of never enjoying the world aright

> 'till the sea itself floweth in your veins, till you are clothed with the heavens, and crowned with the stars: and perceive yourself to be the sole heir of the whole world, and more than so, because men are in it who are every one sole heirs as well as you.'[7]

There is certainly an ecstatic quality in his description of corn as 'immortal wheat, which never should be reaped, nor was ever sown', and in his thought that it had 'stood from everlasting to everlasting'[8]. Such notions are foreign to an age obsessed by measurement in which the unmeasureable is ignored, as though it does not exist simply because it cannot be measured. One cannot imagine the fatuities of 'cost-benefit analysis' flourishing in the Graeco-Roman world.

Aspects of Neo-Platonic occult ideas were considered in secrecy, not only because of possible dangers from orthodoxy or from powerful individuals or groups, but because, if understanding of the hidden meanings of the universe were to be grasped, that knowledge could not be made public in order to prevent its misuse, for only the pure and initiates were worthy vessels to hold such power. Thus secret societies existed, and were associated with the search for knowledge and the guardianship of spiritual truths too precious to be bandied about. Masonic 'secrecy' was thus nothing unusual, for it grew from the need for the Craft to preserve its Mysteries, Wisdom, and Signs, and evolved at a time when exclusive and significant knowledge was treasured: sharing this with all would not only devalue it, but could be dangerous if it fell into the wrong hands, for, after all, as Alexander Pope correctly observed, a 'little learning is a dangerous thing', because 'shallow draughts intoxicate the brain'[9]. The legend of the Garden of Eden remained powerfully influential, but, as T. H. Huxley wrote, if 'a little knowledge is dangerous, where is the man who has so much as to be out of danger?'[10].

Emblems, Symbols, and Hieroglyphs were valued by thinkers of the Neo-Platonic moulds, for they were like perceived truths of the universe: they had meanings that could be interpreted, but those meanings could also be disguised in decent obscurity to keep them from the uninitiated. The sages of the time believed that the eternal truths of Divine Revelation had been known in Antiquity, notably by the Ancient Egyptians whose hieroglyphs offered intellects an endless source of contemplation and puzzlement (all the more so as many accessible hieroglyphs were Roman or Italian works in the Egyptian Taste, and were of the bogus or decorative kind)[11]. Many attempts were made to decipher hieroglyphs, of which the most interesting were those of the German Jesuit, Athanasius Kircher, whose relevant works are listed in the Select Bibliography[12]. Although barking up wrong trees, they at least demonstrate a reasoned attempt to codify Egyptian and Egyptianising monuments and artefacts using the exemplars in Rome itself (the importance of Egyptian religion in the Roman Empire, the elevation of Roman Emperors as deities in conformity with Egyptian custom, and the fashion for Egyptian artefacts led to a very large collection of Egyptian and Egyptianising objects being gathered together in Rome during Imperial times: from the Middle Ages, and especially during the Renaissance, a great many of these were disinterred, and these may still be seen today).

Interpretation of hieroglyphs was based on the belief that sacred and eternal truths had been concealed therein, and that their meaning was inadequately expressed in mere words. This notion was derived from a consideration of obscure passages (of which there are many) in Scripture and other writings, for the more opaque, the more minds strove to interpret meanings. From the awe felt for hieroglyphs grew the evolution of the Emblem and Symbol as means of expressing ideas, truths, and meanings which had to be concealed from the ignorant and the profane, but which could be read by the pure and the initiated: it is hardly surprising that the literature on Emblems of the period is enormous. Emblems consist of a picture incorporating Symbols, Hieroglyphs, and a Composition with figures, designs, and the like, and had to have texts explaining the meanings. Emblems codified certain ideas by means of conventions, just as Masonic ritual used a pictorial set of Emblems and a verbal Catechism to suggest its truths. The invention and interpretation of Emblems became a not insignificant part of late-Renaissance

---

4   Evans (1973) *passim*. Evans and Yates remain interesting reading for an understanding of European Renaissance thought, despite Yates's misreading of many connections, especially with regard to the British. See Churton (2007).
5   *Ibid*. See also the works of Yates cited in the Select Bibliography. See also Gilbert (*Ed.*) (2007).
6   Traherne (1950).
7   *Ibid*. *First Century* Section 29.
8   *Ibid*. *Third Century* Section 3.
9   *An Essay on Criticism* (1711) 215-7.
10   *On Elementary Instruction in Physiology* in *Collected Essays* **iii** (1895).
11   See Curl (2005) *passim*.
12   Kircher (1636, 1643, 1647, 1650, 1652-54, 1666, 1676, 1679). See also Godwin (1979a, 2009).

searchings for Truth and Revelation, and involved layers of meaning with different aspects of Truth, so much so that Truth itself was often made even more elusive: obfuscation became an end in itself, and the unravelling of onion-like layers developed as a desirable occupation. The obscure and the secret were perceived as virtues, for had not the Creator concealed the secrets of the very universe? Thus much literature of the period is many-layered, as though to secrete important truths in obscurantist texts. In such a world, elements of Architecture, geometrical forms, and even the tools of the Masons' Craft were valued far beyond what they were in actuality, and were given additional symbolic significances. The Mason in the Lodge, considering the implications of the Square, the Triangle, the Compass, or the Plumb-Line, for example, was saturated in Neo-Platonist ideas, and shared much of his outlook with the Astrologer, the Alchemist, and the Seekers after the Philosopher's Stone. However, as Jan Snoek has pointed out, the notion of secrecy, or of secret societies, can create negative reactions in the public mind, and that phenomenon has unquestionably contributed to what has been termed Freemasonry's 'Bad Press'[13].

The Renaissance Hermetic tradition appears to have developed through Marsilio Ficino and Pico della Mirandola, and gained a new lease of life in the seventeenth century[14]. Robert Fludd[15] was an adherent of the philosophy of the so-called 'Egyptian priest', Hermes Trismegistus (who, as noted previously was identified with Euclid, Thoth, Mercury, and even with St John the Baptist)[16], as is apparent in *Tractatus Apologeticus*[17] and other works[18], which set out matters developed by Pico della Mirandola when he added elements from the Cabbala[19] (the name given in post-Biblical Hebrew to the oral tradition handed down from Moses to the Rabbis of the *Mishnah* [Jewish oral law] and the *Talmud* [fundamental code of Jewish civil and canon law][20] and also applied from the beginning of the thirteenth century to the supposed tradition of the mystical interpretation of the Old Testament. It also means an unwritten tradition, a mystery, or an esoteric doctrine or art) to the revival of Hermeticism, encouraged by Ficino's interpretation of the recovered Hermetic texts.

Bruno and Michael Maier figure prominently in a kind of proto-Enlightenment strongly spiced with Egyptiana. Maier, the author of *Arcana Arcanissima*[21], was close to the Court of Emperor Rudolf II[22], who was devoted to Alchemy, Astrology, Astronomy, Chemistry, and Magic, and was the Patron of Brahe and Kepler. The title-page of Maier's *Arcana Arcanissima* (1614) features two obelisks, each set on four balls on pedestals, with figures of Osiris, Typhon (identified with the Egyptian Seth), Isis, Hercules, Dionysus, and representations of an ibis, a *cynocephalus* (humanoid figure with a dog's head, or a dog-faced baboon, probably connected with initiation into Ancient Egyptian Mysteries), and the Apis-Bull (a bull-deity, 'son of Isis', herald of Ptah, closely associated with Osiris [who became the Graeco-Roman Osorapis or Serapis/Sarapis]). Maier's *Symbola Aureae*[23] is a volume not entirely innocent of Egyptian or Egyptianising ideas, containing material in *Hermetis Ægyptiorum Regis et Antesigniani Symbolum*. Both Maier and Fludd's works were published in Oppenheim, and both had connections with Great Britain, The Netherlands, and the Court of the Holy Roman Empire of the German Nations. Maier, like Fludd and Dee, did much to promote 'Hermetic Truth': his *Symbola* contains praise for the Wisdom of Hermes, celebrates the sacredness of the Virgin Queen Chemia[24], and ends with a hymn to Regeneration[25]. Chemia is obviously the protean Isis in another of her many guises, the fount of Wisdom: however the notion of the Virgin Queen was powerful in Elizabethan times, for Queen Elizabeth I of England and Ireland became an icon to replace the Papist Virgin Mary (yet another instance of the prohibition of a universally loved Mediaeval Roman Catholic image leaving a void that had to be filled by beleaguered Protestantism: Isis returned in yet another form). Hermetic-Egyptian ideas can also be found in the works of Edmund Spenser.

However, despite the curious undercurrents present in the Elizabethan Age, the main esoteric movements were Continental, and, by extension, Scottish, for men like Fludd were outsiders in an English context, and even Dee's influence remained marginal. One of the most important centres for esoteric thought was the University of Tübingen[26], where Andreae and his friends, Tobias Hess and Christoph Besold, studied Hermetic ideas, Alchemy, Renaissance Neo-Platonism after Pico della Mirandola, the writings of Bruno, and much else. The Bohemian thinker, Comenius[27], acknowledged the importance of the Tübingen circle in passing the 'torch' illuminating the 'Way of Light', and, as the founder of universal education, was a powerful influence on educational and social reform in England, The Netherlands, and Sweden. Indeed, the late Hugh Trevor-Roper, created Lord Dacre of Glanton in 1979, named Comenius and two others as the real philosophers of the English Revolution, whose influence and books supported the foundation of the Royal Society in 1661. The other two named by Trevor-Roper were

---

13 Bogdan (2007) 25.
14 Yates (1964) *passim*.
15 Godwin (1979b).
16 Godwin (1981).
17 Fludd (1617).
18 *See* Fludd (1617-24) and Godwin (1979b).
19 Also *Cabala, Qabbalah*.
20 The *Talmud* includes the *Mishnah* and the later *Gemara*, or Commentary, forming an explanatory, illustrative, and discursive complement to the *Mishnah* (which itself was codified *c.*AD 200).
21 Maier (1614).
22 Yates (1964, 1972, 1975).

23 Maier (1617).
24 Yates (1972) 85.
25 *Ibid*.
26 Founded by Eberhard Im Bart (Graf [Count] and later 1st Duke [from 1495] of Württemberg) in 1477, the University adopted the Reformed faith in 1534. Philipp Melanchthon lectured there 1512-18.
27 Johann Amos Komensky.

CPl.III.I *Scenographia* or Panorama of the *Hortus Palatinus* at Heidelberg. On the left is the long walk of the Upper Terrace. In the foreground the two circular layouts are (*left*) the Labyrinth and (*right*) the Bed of the Seasons. Three different types of parterre are evident: knot-parterres with strip-patterns; *parterres de pièces coupées* with shaped flower-beds; and *parterres de broderie* where patterns are formed of coloured earth or gravel. Immediately to the left of the Labyrinth is a parterre with the hollows filled with water instead of raised areas. The Bed of the Seasons was designed with 72 individual beds in which the distribution of the plants was determined by the time of year in which they were in flower. The garden was intended to contain numerous *fabriques*, including a large grotto, a belvedere, portals, monuments, and constructions intended to trigger by allusion all sorts of memories and thoughts. Painting (before 1620) by Jacques Foucquier (or Fouquier) (KMH B1146).

Samuel Hartlib[28], agriculturalist and educational reformer, and graduate of the University of Königsberg in East Prussia, and John Dury, a Scot, who graduated from the University of Leiden, and became Minister to the English Company of Merchant Adventurers[29] in Elbing by 1628 where he met Comenius, Hartlib, and Thomas Roe, British diplomat involved in futile attempts to save the Company from Danish tolls and Polish seizure of property. Dury and his colleagues shared a vision of Protestant Reunion and Universal Reformation of the World in which Educational Reform was central. Dury was the son of Robert Durie (who had been granted the Portership of the Outer Port of Dunfermline Abbey for life in 1592), and the grandson of John Durie (who had been a Benedictine monk at Dunfermline Abbey, but embraced Protestantism shortly after the Reformation).

Throughout this study reference will be made to the significance of Protestantism, Hermeticism, Symbolism, and Syncretism (among much else) in connection with Freemasonry. There was at least one extraordinary artefact that may have some sort of link with Scotland, Emblems, Labyrinths, Symbolism, the Reformation, and an ill-fated bid to establish a Protestant Kingdom in Bohemia, in the heart of the Holy Roman Empire itself. Frederick V, Elector Palatine, with his Electress, Princess Elizabeth, daughter of King James VI and I and Queen Anne, established a garden at the *Schloß*, Heidelberg, that, to Protestant-Renaissance minds, was the Eighth Wonder of the World. After the death of Henry, Prince of Wales,

---

28 Born in Elbing, Western Poland, of a mother who was the daughter of an English merchant in Danzig. For these matters *see* Trevor-Roper (2006) 338 and *passim*. *See* also ODNB **xxv** (2004) 623-6.

29 Known as the English Eastland Company.

Salomon de Caus, a French garden-designer and hydraulic engineer, who had been in the service of both Queen Anne and Prince Henry, was employed by the Elector and Electress to lay out the gardens, and the designs were published[30] by Johann Theodore De Bry, including a panorama by Matthäus Merian[31] based on a painting by Jacques Fouquier showing English knot-gardens, *broderies* (or 'embroidered' gardens), fountains, grottos, and a Labyrinth of clipped hedges (**CPl.III.I**).

The complex iconography, a programme involving a belief in Universal Harmony, and the Euclidian, Platonic, and Pythagorean systems of numbers have been adequately described elsewhere[32]. One interpretation would have it that the soul moves through various states represented by parts of a garden, through the Maze (representing the confusion of Life's Journey), to the new Harmony of the Orange Parterre where even Nature was transformed and understood by the Intellect, and on to a new plane of Revelation through Astrology and the Mysteries of Divine love. Such a programme suggests an idealised Reformation and a proto-Enlightenment based on Hermetic ideas.

At Heidelberg the gardens evoked marvels by such means as mechanical fountains which emitted musical sounds. De Caus employed systems of design in which Architecture, Hydraulic Engineering, Perspective, Geometry, Ideals of Proportion based on the meaning of Numbers, and Mathematical Science were all conscripted to the cause. There were grottoes, water-features, statues, and many other devices that would have conjured up the Ancient World, but, most importantly, the use of numerical studies in order to create mechanical musical instruments heralds the obsessions of the Enlightenment with gadgets, as well as evoking Antique allusions and pointing the way to industrial power in the centuries ahead. De Caus seems to have employed steam power for some of his ingenious machines, which he based on Vitruvian and Pythagorean precedents, and which looked forward to the mammoth organs and water-displays of nineteenth-century Europe and America. The *Hortus Palatinus* was a Symbol of proto-Enlightenment that embraced universal systems of Harmony and Proportion: it was a series of experiences through which one could pass and reflect, and it had its parallels – though not its exact antecedents or derivatives – in ancient and later gardens.

Following the arrival of Princess Elizabeth at Heidelberg (the Arundel-Jones connection was previously noted), the Electoral capital became for a time (1612-20) the centre of a brief idyll of Culture, Enlightenment, Learning, and Toleration. When Frederick unwisely accepted the Throne of Bohemia, thereby incurring the wrath of the Emperor[33] and of Roman Catholic Europe, the Thirty Years' War was sparked, and Frederick lost both his Bohemian Throne and

---
30 Caus (1620).
31 Who married De Bry's daughter, Maria Magdalena, in 1617.
32 Yates (1972) 85 and Patterson (1981).
33 Ferdinand II had been chosen King of Bohemia in 1617, but Bohemian Protestants, fearing their civil and religious liberties were under threat, declared him deposed and elected Frederick in his stead.

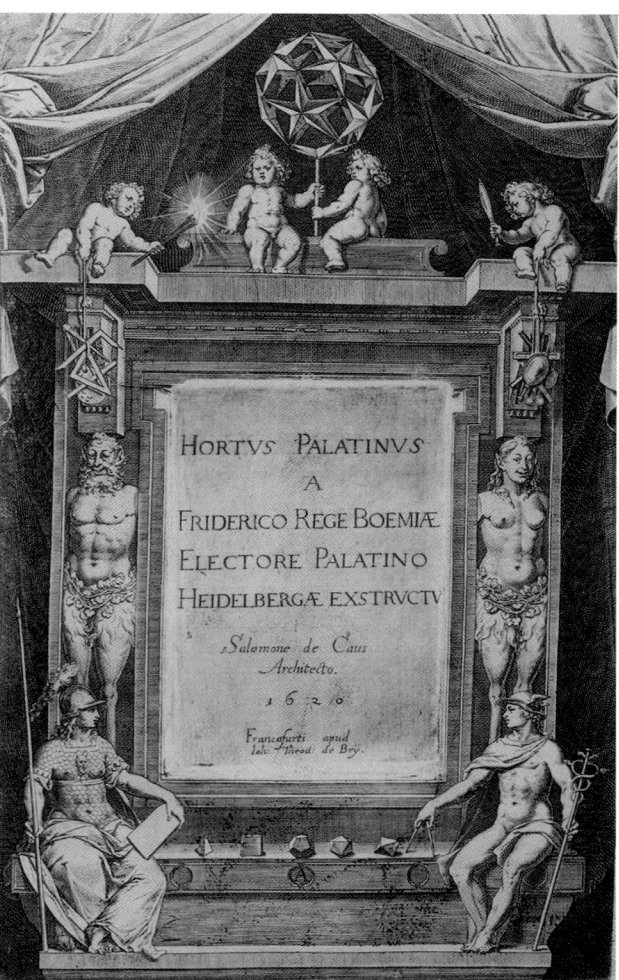

Pl.III.1 Title-page of *Hortus Palatinus* (*University of Glasgow 0746139 DSC_0028-1 LR00225011*).

his Palatinate. He and his wife were dubbed 'The Winter King and Queen', and went into exile in The Netherlands. Habsburg forces used the *Hortus Palatinus* as an artillery base from which the *Schloß* was bombarded: plundering and vandalism over many years did the rest. So the forces of reaction, allied to those that had condemned Bruno to the Stake, stemmed the tide of inquiry in Protestant Europe[34].

If the design of the Heidelberg garden is startling, the title-page of *Hortus Palatinus* is even odder (**Pl.III.1**). A massive, blocky, primitivist, almost Neo-Classical architrave with bold crossettes and plain oversailing cornice framed the lettering. On the cornice a *putto* dangled a square, set-square, compasses, and other implements used in Architecture, whilst holding in his left hand a torch for Illumination, Exposition, and Truth. Two *putti* in the centre carried a polyhedral form composed of five-pointed stars, and another *putto* on the right dangled a mirror and other attributes. At the base Minerva faced Hermes with *caduceus* and dividers, and between these

---
34 Curl (1988), McIntosh (2005) 71-74, Yates (1972) 9-12, Yates (1964) *passim*.

two seated figures were pyramid, a cube, and various polyhedral forms. Flanking the inscription panel were male (*left*) and female (*right*) faun-like creatures. The design could well have been a Masonic frontispiece.

Now although these extraordinary gardens were never completed (de Caus himself tells us that work was stopped as a result of the Bohemian War), they were not initially subjected to systematic destruction, and visitors in the latter part of the seventeenth century reported that one fountain was still operational[35]. Much destruction took place at the behest of King Louis XIV (who was keen to expunge all traces of Protestantism where ever he could), and thereafter the silence imposed by the Thirty Years' War on late German Humanism submerged the *Hortus Palatinus* in obscurity. Some commentators have dismissed the Heidelberg gardens, some even claiming that we do not know if they were ever realised: this is nonsense, for, as noted above, de Caus pointed out that War prevented work from proceeding, but work had most certainly begun, and there were still aspects of the gardens visible some eighty years later until the French wrecked them. The point is that we have a detailed description of the *designs* for the gardens, showing how they were *intended* to look when completed[36]. Because certain emphases in the work of the late Frances Yates relating to the impact of Rosicrucianism in England have been questioned, even refuted, that does not invalidate the importance of the *Hortus Palatinus*, and it must be remembered that we are talking about a *German* Protestant proto-Enlightenment and a garden designed by a *French* Huguenot. When the National Socialists denounced certain composers such as Franz Schreker and Erich Wolfgang Korngold as 'degenerate', it was enough to drive their works into obscurity: only in the last few years have they started to be rediscovered. Masterpieces such as *Der ferne Klang* (1903-10) and *Das Wunder der Heliane* (1927) have been recorded in recent times, and have proved to be richly rewarding musical experiences. It would be foolish to dismiss aspects of the *Hortus Palatinus* just because Yates got some things wrong and that Patterson and others followed her findings: the main source is the 1620 publication, and that offers rich enough pickings for anybody. The fact is that de Caus's extraordinary book is one of the finest records of a garden-design to come down to us from the seventeenth century, and it is not just about gardening either. It has many allusions and enormous cultural resonances that only the most obtuse can ignore with equanimity.

Giordano Bruno preached a Reformation of the World based on a return to 'Egyptian' wisdom and religion as revealed in Hermetic writings. Religious differences were to be overcome through love and magic, and Bruno's ideas were carried throughout Northern Europe. Bruno was to die at the stake, partly for his conviction that the wisdom of Ancient Egypt was greater than that displayed by a repressive Roman Catholicism that burned dissidents.

His denial of the unique nature of Christianity included the observation that even the Cross with Nimbus was a Symbol invented by the Egyptians (the *Ankh*), and he saw clearly the debt that Christian belief and practice owed to the ancient Cults of Isis and Osiris, including giving birth by supernatural means, and the abilities to resurrect the dead, heal the sick, and restore sight. As noted previously, the attributes and names of Mary and Isis were identical. Bruno must have smiled a wryly cynical smile when considering that the Inquisition demanding his life could ignore the fact that the Vicar of Christ had claimed descent from Osiris through the disreputable 'researches' of Annius (*or* Annio) of Viterbo, who connected the Medicis by descent from Noah after the Flood, and Rodrigo de Borja y Borja[37] (reigned as Pope Alexander VI) from none other than Osiris. The decorations of the *Appartamento Borgia* in the Vatican, featuring the Apis-Bull carried in procession with the head of Hermes, Isis, and Osiris, Hermes Trismegistus, Moses, are no accident, nor are they mere decoration: they were part of a programme[38]. There were other Egyptianising phenomena, one of the strangest of which to survive is the illuminated Missal[39] of Pompeo Colonna, created Cardinal in 1517 by Pope Leo X[40]: but then the Colonna clan also claimed improbable descent from Osiris[41].

The religion of the Egyptians was held to contain prophecies of Christianity (though this could never be admitted by the Church, what ever the Popes might claim or do in private), and seen as the 'imperfect harbinger', though modern scholarship has tended to vindicate Bruno and others. As already noted, 'Hermetic' writings were later than Christ (though this was not recognised in late-Mediaeval or Renaissance times), but the ideas in Hermeticism concerned with the spiritual journey and the searchings of the individual found favour in Protestant circles. Renaissance minds looked back to Antiquity with admiration, and the seeking after Ancient Wisdom was paralleled by the study of the Art and Architecture of the Ancients. The 'purified' religion of the Reformation sought inspiration from the examples of the Early Christians and from texts of Antiquity in which wisdom of a spiritual nature was enshrined.

Religious strife, persecution, bloody and destructive war between Protestant and Counter-Reformation forces, and fragmentation among the Protestant ranks led to a growing tendency towards private contemplation and covert observance. It seems apparent that Conformity with what ever was regarded as orthodox often disguised devotion to Hermetic ideas that were felt to be older, nobler, purer, and truer than the warring (and revoltingly barbarous) factions of Christianity (the record of which, in

---

35 Patterson (1981) 68.
36 *Ibid.* and Caus (1620).
37 Borgia in Italian.
38 Curl (2005) 86-91.
39 John Rylands University Library of Manchester, Rylands Latin MS. 32, fol. 79r). Reproduced in Curl (2005) 97.
40 Giovanni de'Medici.
41 *See Mitteilungen des Österreichischen Instituts für Geschichtsforschung* **lv** (1942).

terms of open-mindedness and tolerance, was negligible). Bruno, however, did not keep his Hermeticism secret, but argued for a sort of Egyptian Reformation mixed up with ideas about Good Works and Utilitarianism for the benefit of Mankind[42]: he also deplored the passing of many of the best features of Mediaeval organisation, including the charitable and social cohesion given by the ancient Guilds.

Frances Yates, in her *Giordano Bruno*, wondered where could be found a 'combination… of religious tolerance, emotional linkage with the past, emphasis on good works for others, and imaginative attachment to the religion and symbolism of the Egyptians'[43]. The answer she came up with was Freemasonry, for Hermetic ideas and Freemasonry have points of closeness that cannot be dismissed. As Stevenson has pointed out, the period saw 'the peak of the Hermetic striving for enlightenment and the spiritual rebirth of mankind, based on secret knowledge and secret societies or cults. When a system of lodges emerges in Scotland with secret rituals and identification signs, just as the great esoteric Hermetic movement was sweeping across Europe, there surely must be a link between them. This is all the more the case as the masons had long possessed a tradition, enshrined in the Old Charges, that Hermes had played a major part in preserving knowledge of the mason craft and transmitting it to mankind after the flood, and that a key development in craft history, the teaching of masonry by Euclid to the sons of the nobility, had taken place in Egypt. Any educated man of the day would have some knowledge of Hermetic lore, and would pick up the reference to Hermes in the Old Charges and thus be likely to see masonry as a Hermetic art bound up with one of the great intellectual movements of the day'[44].

Quite so: there must indeed be a link, and the strong Egyptian flavour in much Masonic design must stem partly from this and from the idea that obscure hieroglyphical inscriptions (which nobody could read) held sacred truths. Yet much Isiac allusion was actually preserved in the Church as part of the Marian *cultus*, and other ideas, such as the connections with Daedalus and the Labryinth, were openly illustrated by Mediaeval Masons in Cathedral floors, such as those of Chartres and Rheims. Is there, therefore, some possibility of truth in the Masonic claims that much ancient lore was actually passed on through the Lodges themselves from Antiquity? This may not be as far-fetched as has been suggested by some hitherto, although there must have been a new injection of Hermeticism during the Renaissance period which gave new life and meaning to old customs. A view might be offered that something *did* survive, and that it was re-interpreted and *revived* from the sixteenth century, but that the *survivals* were overlaid, embellished, obscured, and perhaps corrupted. Yet the Daedalus-Labyrinth connection with Antiquity is irrefutable, as is God as Architect (Imhotep-Ptah), and Isis transformed as Mary, so the Egyptian themes were there all the time. When we read that it was Hermes, the Preserver of Knowledge, who not only treasured the Wisdom and methods of the Craft, but in due course passed on the heritage to Mankind, syncretic bells ring, for many sets of legends overlap, interlock, and merge with each other.

Mnemonic Techniques

Central to any basic understanding of Freemasonry is the rôle of Memory. The Lodge itself was a mnemonic of the Temple, of a lost ideal, and much else. Esoteric knowledge, too, was not safe in the hands of the ignorant or the profane, so it was safer for initiates to remember such material, possibly using Emblems as aids to memory, rather than to commit secrets to a page. The trouble with passing on traditions orally, however, is that Memory plays tricks, and things can get jumbled or distorted.

Among the many facets of ancient knowledge to be rediscovered and reinterpreted during the Renaissance period was the method used in Classical Antiquity for improving memory. This interesting mnemonic technique was closely associated with Hermeticism, and was not only extremely useful, but had overtones of the Divine, of Cosmic relevance, and of striving towards Perfection. In Scotland Fellow Crafts were not admitted to the Lodge without 'pruife of memorie and art of craft'[45]. Persons obliged to speak or perform in public (e.g. actors, musicians, orators, politicians, etc.) needed to develop methods of memorising a vast range of material. It may startle some to learn that Graeco-Roman mnemonic methods employed works of Architecture (not mere buildings) in which the interiors were organised, ordered, and sufficiently complex (i.e. where Geometry and Mathematics were used as the basis for their arrangement, together with a literate architectural *language*, complete with adequate vocabulary)[46], as vehicles for the technique. Frances Yates devoted a whole book to what is known as *The Art of Memory*[47], so only the barest outline is possible here, and indeed a précis was given earlier. The method used involved the detailed and careful study of a large building with architectural pretensions: the student would note the plan, the disposition of rooms, features, sculptures, finishes, and details, and would commit these to memory, perhaps only after several visits. Of course the process would involve a journey through the building, so the rooms, spaces, compartments, and so on were visited and viewed in a definite and logical order, involving a progression or a route, an important point, as we will see later. When memorising a text, a play, a speech, or a sequence of facts or points to be made, the student had to remember the *route* through the building, so that the rooms, with their features, became associated with key elements in the text, with concepts, with faces, or even with specific words or phrases. The order of the

---

42 Yates (1964) 273-4 and *passim*.
43 *Ibid*.
44 Stevenson (1988b) 85.

45 Jones (1956) 129.
46 Yates (1966). What follows is derived from her work.
47 Yates (1966) for a clear and comprehensive exposition.

images retained in the memory, obviously, had to correspond with the order of the contents of the speech, and the remembered images then prompted a triggering mechanism to release associations with thoughts, ideas, words, abstractions, and so on.

Such a technique allowed considerable scope for detailed personal observation, permitting tailor-made memory-routes tuned to personal taste or convenience. Relationships between images (and, of course, types of image), places, and content might be extremely obscure (or even incomprehensible) to all except the person involved in the exercise[48]. During the 'play-back' a student proceeded in his mind through the building complex, permitting each room, corridor, space, architectural detail, material, colour, etc., to prompt an *association* whereby the desired phrase, point, fact, etc., could be 'triggered'. Highly skilled and practised perambulators through building groups as organised and as vast as Roman *Thermae* apparently could associate almost every word of a speech with the images of the sequences of the route, and prodigious examples of successes for the method were claimed[49]. Such a mnemonic technique could encourage associations, abstractions, and identification by Symbol and Attribute in a built environment lavishly decorated and embellished with architectural enrichment and statuary that themselves were derived from a sophisticated *vocabulary* and fully-developed *language* of *literate* design. This point must be emphasised, for the technique would work with Classical Architecture, or perhaps with fine Gothic specimens (provided they were rich enough), but it would stand very little chance of any success with the more feeble products of Modernism since 1945, most of which hardly rate as Architecture at all. The Art of Memory would also work in a richly contrived Garden of Allusions, with varied treatments and numerous *fabriques* (building in landscaped gardens, such as eye-catchers, so-called follies, temples, statuary, rock-work grottoes, obelisks, and other structures [bridges, etc.]), and is connected with Associationism[50], an important aspect of the aesthetic categories of the Beautiful, the Picturesque, and the Sublime[51].

The Art of Memory could also involve elaborate Symbols or Emblems, many of which were familiar throughout the Ancient World, notably in the Roman Empire. Just as the deities of Antiquity had Attributes which helped to identify them and jog the memory concerning their activities and powers, or 'specialisations', so Christian iconography absorbed much that already existed: George Norman Douglas's crack that Christianity was partly a 'quaint Alexandrian *tutti-frutti*'[52], the success of which had been assured by an intellectual dissolvent made possible by oriental introspectiveness that culminated in the 'idly-splendid yearnings of Plato'[53], tainting 'the well-springs of honest research for two thousand years'[54], is not, perhaps, too far off the mark in this respect. Christian Saints were depicted with Virtues, Instruments of Martyrdom, and so in order that they could be identified, and contemplation (based on memories of their deeds) encouraged[55]: St Catherine with her Wheel, St Laurence with his Grid-Iron, St Andrew with his Saltire Cross, and St Bartholomew with Flaying-Knife, are but four examples of a truly remarkable catalogue of horrors. It is perhaps worth noting, *en passant*, that most Saints' Days record the date of Martyrdom, of physical death: in Christian belief, however, this death is a true birth, for Saints are 're-born' by Martyrdom and enter Eternal Life among the Blessed. The Masonic idea of a 'death' and a 'new life' on Initiation is a parallel, and both ideas are very ancient, owing much to the developed notions of death and rebirth in Antiquity. A Mediaeval Cathedral, with its Labyrinths, many images, thousands of carvings, stained-glass windows, shrines, chapels, and amazingly complex iconography, served also as a vast Temple of Memory (reminding the pilgrim of the Temple of Solomon, of Biblical stories, of the Deeds of the Saints, and of formulae for prayer and devotion), a point that goes a long way to explaining the extraordinary complexity of such buildings, which were also gigantic Reliquaries and places of entombment and commemoration, as well as having Chantry-Chapels, special Chapels for the veneration of certain Saints, and much more besides.

Mnemonic methods, involving perambulation through a sequence of spaces in which architectural features would be memorised, was developed further by placing *imaginary* pictures or details on parts of rooms as aids to memory[56]: there were many variations using similar techniques that could be used to suit individual tastes and requirements. This 'Art of Memory' was revived during the Renaissance period, and, called 'Artificial Memory', 'Science or Art of Mnemonics', or 'System of Mnemonic Devices', was discussed in a number of Renaissance texts, including *Foenix. Domini Petri Ravennatis Memoriae Magistri* by Petrus of Ravenna[57]; *The Art of Memory, that Otherwyse is called The Phenix*, a translation by Robert Copland of Petrus Ravennas's work[58]; and *The Castel of Memorie* by Guglielmo Gratarolo[59] in an English translation by William Fulwood (which defines 'Artificiall Memorie' as a 'disposying or placing of sensible things in the mynde by imagination, whereunto the naturall Memorie hauing respect, is by them admonished'). Abraham Cowley spoke of his mistress's 'Parts becoming to him "a kind of Art of Memory"', which might (to some) be a more agreeable methodology to adopt by those of less architectural turns

---

48 Stevenson (1988*b*) 37-96.
49 *Ibid*.
50 *See* Alison (1811).
51 Curl (2006*a*) 75, 578, 751-2.
52 Douglas (1915) 311.

53 *Ibid*.
54 *Ibid*.
55 Stevenson (1988*b*) 87-96.
56 *Ibid*.
57 Petrus of Ravenna or Petrus Ravennas (1533). The *Foenix* first came out in 1491.
58 Copland (*Tr.*) (*c.*1545).
59 Gratarola (1562).

of mind, while Edmond Hoyle, in his *A Short Treatise on the Game of Whist*, advised mnemonic methods to assist in the game in the additional part entitled *An Artificial Memory: Or, An easy Method of Assisting the Memory of those that play at the Game*[60]. So the Art of Memory was a well-known and ancient technique that was revived during the Renaissance period as part of a general rediscovery of Antiquity, and was embraced by many groups and individuals in search of esoteric knowledge, using elaborate Emblems, Charts, Frontispieces, and the like. The Phoenix, as a Symbol of the Art of Memory, is not an unfamiliar motif, and apparently was used earlier by the Knights Templar to denote Resurrection or Continuity[61].

Considerations of Architecture were essential elements of the Neo-Platonic themes of the Renaissance period, notably aspects of Hermeticism and the rediscovery of Classical memory techniques. The Art of Memory, as a so-called 'occult' art, became an important element in European intellectual life. One Giulio Camillo is credited with the invention of a theatre of memory based on Vitruvian principles with Biblical (especially Solomonic) additions: he made objects designed to jog the memory which he set as 'memory-places'[62]. Not only could memory techniques be improved, Camillo claimed, but his system was supposed to be able to control the forces within the firmament itself by using the pattern of the stars and the signs of the Zodiac as a wider, universal theatre of memory.[63] However, the Art of Memory's usefulness could also extend to Sermons: it was used by several well-known preachers including Lancelot Andrewes, Bishop of Winchester from 1618, and John Donne, Dean of St Paul's Cathedral, London, from 1621[64].

The Hiramic and Other Legends

Various versions of this story exist, but the variant in which the Master of the Works at King Solomon's Temple was murdered by means of three blows (with a hammer, a level, and a plumb) to the head by three Masons (sometimes referred to as Apprentices and sometimes by Fellow Crafts) in attempts to obtain from him the secrets of a Master Mason (including the 'Mason Word') has become important to Freemasonry. The legend was probably known in the 1720s when Anderson brought out his *Constitutions*, but the oldest known form appears to be that recorded in Prichard's *Masonry Dissected* (1730)[65]. The Master Mason is usually referred to as Hiram Abif or Abiff: when he was missed, fifteen Fellow Crafts were ordered to search for him, and those involved in the search agreed that if they did not manage to find the 'Word' on or about him, they would take the first thing they found as being the 'Word'. The body was duly found buried with a covering of green moss and turf, and the King ordered it should be 'taken up' or 'raised' and decently interred. As Hiram's body was putrefying, when the Masons attempted to raise him by gripping his forefinger, the skin came off, so a firmer grip was taken of his hand, and the body was raised 'hand to hand', 'foot to foot', 'cheek to cheek', 'knee to knee', and 'hand to back': these are called the Five Points of Fellowship.

A slightly different variation of the legend was related in the so-called *Graham MS*[66], a version of the 'Old Charges' written in 1726. In this the three sons[67] of Noah, determined to find a clue to some valuable secret their father had possessed when alive, went to the grave, having agreed in advance that if they did not find what they were looking for (a common feature of old legends), the first thing they discovered would be to them the secret. It should be remembered that all things valuable for the new world were preserved on the Ark by Noah at the Time of the Flood, according to legend (the parallels with the 'Pillars' surviving Fire and Water are obvious), so the sons desired the key to them (though it does not seem to have occurred to the fabricators of the legend that there was no point in preserving them if they were not passed on). All that was in the grave was Noah's dead body, but when they tried to 'raise' it the finger they had gripped came away, and the same thing happened with the wrist and elbow, so the whole putrefying body was raised, supported by setting foot to foot, knee to knee, breast to breast, cheek to cheek, and hand to back[68]. One of the sons remarked that there was still 'mar[r]ow in this bone', the second said there was only a 'dry bone', and the third perceptively observed that 'it stinketh', and so they gave it (the bone) 'a name as it is known to free masonry to this day'[69].

The similarities between the Hiram Abiff tale and that of Noah's corpse are obvious: each is concerned with attempts to obtain secret knowledge from a dead body, and each comes up with a substitute secret when the real one cannot be found. Thus the legends are necromantic in character, necromancy being the magical art of obtaining knowledge (especially of future events) from the dead: in Classical Antiquity secrets were obtained by summoning the shades of the dead rather than by digging up bodies[70]. In Classical times the dead were feared, and had to be appeased: they were kept away from the living, and bodies were regarded as unclean. In the Middle Ages, however, Relics were everywhere and were venerated, so dead bodies of Saints were prized and collected rather than hidden away.

The Noah story may be a corruption of the tale of his drunkenness[71], when Ham saw his father lying naked in a stupor, but Shem and Japheth 'took a garment, and laid *it* upon both their shoulders, and went backward, and covered the nakedness of their father; and their faces *were*

---

60 Hoyle (1750).
61 Mackey (1919 edn.) 420.
62 Yates (1966) 128-72.
63 Stevenson (1988*b*) 90.
64 Guite (1993).
65 Prichard (1730).

66 Knoop, Jones, & Hamer (*Eds.*) (1963) 92-3.
67 Shem, Ham, and Japheth.
68 Knoop & Jones (1948) 89.
69 *Ibid.* 89-90.
70 Stevenson (1988*b*) 144.
71 *Genesis* 9: 19-27.

backward, and they saw not their father's nakedness'[72]. As a result, when he came to, Noah cursed Ham and blessed the other two. There are, however, Biblical accounts of the raising of dead bodies involving the restoration of life when prophets lay down full-length on the corpses and breathed into their faces. One example is that of Elisha, who went into the room where a dead boy lay upon a bed, and shut the door 'and lay upon the child, and put his mouth upon his mouth, and his eyes upon his eyes, and his hands upon his hands: and he stretched himself up on the child; and the flesh of the child waxed warm'[73]. Later, Elisha, having walked about, went into the room yet again, 'and stretched himself upon' the child, who then obligingly 'sneezed seven times' and 'opened his eyes'[74]. Elisha then restored the living child to his mother, a Shunammite woman.

Then there was Elijah, who raised the widow's son by carrying his body up to the loft where he (Elijah) 'abode', and laying it upon his bed: he then 'stretched himself upon the child three times' who revived[75]. Then, in the New Testament, we find Eutychus, who fell asleep during a long bout of preaching by Paul, and fell 'from the third loft', after which he was pronounced dead. Paul 'fell on him' and embraced him, 'And they brought the young man alive, and were not a little comforted'[76].

So there was a Biblical tradition of bringing the dead back to life, but by the sixteenth and seventeenth centuries the idea survived 'only as necromancy'[77]. Ham, Noah's son, was associated with the Black Arts, and possibly with necromancy. These murky matters were chronicled by Reginald Scot[78] and Vincent de Beauvais[79]. However, there are records of yet another case, involving a woman who cured a man who believed himself to be bewitched: she came into his bed and stretched herself above him, her head to his head, her hands over him, and so forth, all the while mumbling words he could not understand. This occurred in 1623 when belief in witchcraft was rife in Scotland (and elsewhere), and was meticulously recorded by Robert Pitcairn, Writer to the Signet[80].

By the early part of the seventeenth century the Rosicrucians, who took their name from Christian Rosenkreutz[81] (the supposed founder of the specifically Protestant variant of Hermeticism, who is probably a symbolic figure, yet may have actually been based upon Philipp Theophrastus Bombast von Hohenheim), were making their presence felt through various strands of Hermeticism: their influence began to filter through to Scots Lodges[82]. Known as Paracelsus, whose philosophy was based on visionary Neoplatonism, Hohenheim regarded the life of Man as inseparable from that of the Universe, and introduced many new ideas (many of them dangerous nonsense) to medicine. Martin Luther adopted the Emblem of a Cross emerging from a Rose, so the Christian/Protestant aspects of the movement are obvious, but the Red Cross was also associated with the Cross of St George, and, in combination with the Rose, had connotations with the Tudor dynasty, and may also have been connected in some way with the Union and with Protestant attempts to roll back the Roman Catholic Counter Reformation[83]. It should be emphasised that the Rosicrucian movement began in Germany, and although it was exported, by the time it reached the British Isles it was almost wholly stripped of its politico-religious aspects, even though it had an impact on certain intellectuals.

However, the Rose is also a symbol of silence and secrecy, and anything spoken *sub rosa*, or 'under the rose', is confidential[84]: it was the Emblem of Harpocrates (who is often depicted with his finger to his lips), the God of Silence and Secrecy, who has been identified with Horus, son of Isis, born after a necrophilous union with the dead Osiris. By a ruse, Isis obtained the secret name of the powerful sun-god Re, knowledge of which conferred limitless power, and passed it on to Horus, who thereby became one the almighty Egyptian Trinity of Isis, Osiris, and Horus. The legend of the passing on of the secret name or word has its parallels in Freemasonic lore[85].

The followers of 'Christian Rosenkreutz' agreed that their Fraternity should remain a secret for a century, and after 120 years the secret tomb of 'Rosenkreutz' was discovered containing the perfectly preserved corpse together with many documents and symbols, after which the tomb was re-sealed and hidden[86]. The Rosicrucians, it seems, like many others, aimed at a Universal and General Reformation of the Whole Wide World[87]. The discovery of Rosenkreutz's corpse was supposed to be in 1604, and when the vault was opened, the 'inner sun' revealed a new Enlightenment. Rosicrucianism, which claimed an ancient lineage, was primarily associated with Protestantism, but when Frederick V, the Prince-Elector who was married to Princess Elizabeth of Great Britain, failed in his venture to challenge the authority of the Empire and Roman Catholicism, interest in the Fraternity declined. Nevertheless, aspects of Rosicrucianism were absorbed into the general culture of the times, notably in Scotland, where Sir Robert Moray was steeped in Rosicrucian lore, and Sir David Lindsay, 1st Lord Lindsay of Balcarres (from 1601– who was also immersed in Alchemy, Hermeticism, and Rosicrucianism), appears to have been a key figure

---

72 *Genesis* 9: 23.
73 II *Kings* 4: 32-34.
74 *Ibid.*: 35. One can almost hear the sharp intakes of breath from certain quarters in these politically correct days, when paedophiles are said to lurk in every corner: spiced with a dose of necrophilia as well, the reptiles of the media would have a field-day with this story if it were reported nowadays.
75 I *Kings* 17: 19-22
76 *The Acts of the Apostles* 20: 9-12.
77 Knoop & Jones (1948) 91.
78 Scot (1886). *See* the 1930 edn. 222.
79 Vincent de Beauvais (1473) **ii** ch.ci.
80 Pitcairn (1833) 537. Recorded, indeed, without any indication of a raised eyebrow anywhere.
81 That is, 'Rosy Cross'.

82 Stevenson (1988b) 97.
83 Yates (1972) 267 and Waite (1924) 107.
84 Browne (1912) **ii** 266-7.
85 Curl (2005) 438, 440-1.
86 Andreae (1973).
87 Yates (1972) 72-5.

in transmitting Rosicrucian ideas to that country[88]. In England Ashmole was also interested in the Fraternity. A connection between the Craft and Rosicrucianism is underlined by the story of the finding of the vault containing Rosenkreutz's body, for the discoverer was an Architect engaged in carrying out alterations to the Fraternity's headquarters. Thomas Vaughan[89], Alchemist and Moray's *protégé*, published an English version of the *Fama* of Andreae in 1652[90], from which many readers would have become convinced that a secret Brotherhood already existed which possessed the knowledge that had eluded Man from Time immemorial. So a search for Enlightenment might switch from grasping at arcane straws to seeking out some sort of tacit Brotherhood that was steeped in Ancient Wisdom. As the discoverer of Rosenkreutz's body was an Architect, he was also a Mason[91]. There is also a strange link (or series of links) between the Stuart Court, Schaw, Dee, Brahe, the Electoral Court at Heidelberg, Inigo Jones, Arundel, Rosicrucianism, Roman Catholicism, Protestantism, Moray, Ashmole, and many others, which points to what Stevenson called 'the already mixed bag' of Masonic lore – 'the myth of Egypt, Solomon's Temple, the Hermetic quest, the art of memory' – to which the addition of another myth, that of 'the secret order of invisible brethren, dedicated to seeking ultimate truths and to understanding the mysterious universe'[92], emerged as a heady, if at times incoherent, brew. And a further link was a necromantic one: the seeking of secrets from corpses, which one might regard as a curious preoccupation to be pursued by those in search of spiritual and scientific Enlightenment[93].

So where does all this get us? To return to the legend of Hiram Abiff[94], when he was attacked by the three Masons, each blow was delivered at a different door of the Temple, and after each battering, Hiram tried to escape, leaving a trail of blood around the floor or ground until he died in the East: this trail of blood may be the origin of some of the designs round Masonic tracing-boards and some documents and images. Originally (as previously noted), there had been fifteen conspirators, but twelve drew back (Recanters), and these twelve men were to bring Geometry and Architecture to the world (*see* **Pl.III.2**, p.44). Now in this story the number of multiples of three should be noted: the Three buried the body; the Fellow-Crafts sought it, and agreed that if they did not find the secret (the Word) in or about Hiram, then the first word associated with the finding of the body should become the Master Word (the latter being like a Rabbinical Tradition', in way of comment upon Jachin and Boaz, with the addition of some secret sign delivered by hand to hand, by which Freemasons recognise each other, as the Rev. Robert Kirk, Minister at Aberfoyle, Stirlingshire, noted in 1691)[95].

The body of Hiram Abiff was found under some green moss on which a sprig of Acacia had been placed. Jewish priests were not allowed to walk over graves, so it was necessary to mark places of burial by some means, and Acacia bushes were supposed to be associated with this idea: the Acacia is also a symbol of innocence, rebirth, and immortality. The putrefying corpse of Hiram was discovered because the five seekers pulled on the sprig of Acacia when climbing, but it came away in the grip, indicating that the sprig had been placed there recently, and this led to the finding of the body, for Acacia was planted to dissuade the curious, and marked where cadavers lay, so travellers would pass by and not disturb the sprig. The five finders, of course, represent a third of the original fifteen: when they attempted to lift the body from the grave, as noted above, the skin of the forefinger came off (The Slip), and so it was raised by means of the Five Points of Fellowship. Hiram Abiff was reburied in the precincts of the Temple, possibly suggesting human sacrifice or even the sanctity conferred by interring the bodies of Saints in a church. Tombs and shrines are often one and the same, after all, and in ancient times human sacrifices were often made in order to consecrate some important building.

In the Noah story the discovery of marrow in one of the bones by one brother led to the 'naming of the bone'. Marrow, of course, also means 'partner' or 'fellow', but it was also seen as the seat or source of animal vitality and strength, as the inmost or central part, the essence, so associated with inner meaning and secrets. Given that mnemonics played such an important part in the past, notably in Antiquity and during the Renaissance, the bone remark could have been a means of reminding Masons of the objectives of Fellowship, and that Fellowship was an essential part of Freemasonry: 'marrow' could also have been a mnemonic for *mahabyn*, supposedly the Master's Word[96], which was divided into two words: the first two syllables (*Maha*) said by one person, and *byn* by another.

A short catechism known as *The Trinity College, Dublin, MS* (1711) informs us that 'Boaz' was the Word for Apprentices, and various other sources make it clear that initiations of Entered Apprentices and Fellow Crafts involved separate Words and secrets[97]. The Dublin MS states that 'Jachin' was the Word for the Fellow Craft, so the Fellow Craft was in possession of two Words for use in the Five Points of Fellowship embrace. Boaz, as noted above, was the column on the right-hand of the Temple's portal as one approached it (left as one departed from the Temple): it is associated with the First Degree of Entered Apprentice, with Strength, and with the Senior Warden.

---

88 McLean (1979).
89 Or Vaughn.
90 Vaughan (1923) 20 and *passim*.
91 Stevenson (1988*b*) 104.
92 *Ibid.* 105. Yates (1972) suggested that Rosicrucianism had its origins in the alchemical-spiritual questings of John Dee, and that the *Fama Fraternitatis* had its genesis in the political ambitions of Frederick V, Elector Palatine: neither suggestion holds much water.
93 For Rosicrucianism *see* especially McIntosh (1987, 1992), but Roberts (1969, 1972) is useful on Secret Societies generally, and on the possibilities of Freemasonic history. *See* also Churton (2007) for a useful corrective view.
94 *See* Snoek (2003) and Ward (1925).

95 Knoop & Jones (1948) 88. *See Transactions of the London and Middlesex Archaeological Society* New Series **vii** (1933) 139, and Kirk (1933).
96 *Sloane 3329 MS* of *c*.1700. *See* Knoop, Jones, & Hamer (*Eds*.) (1963)
97 Stevenson (1988*b*) 149.

Pl.III.2 *The Foundation of the Royal Order of the Free Masons in Palestine A.M. 4037*. Engraving by D. Lambert of 1789 showing the Murder of Hiram by the Three, and the Recanting Twelve who were to bring Geometry and Architecture into the world in four groups of three, armed with the Signs and Words. Note the two columns on either side of the arched entrance. Rods, squares, and Masonic tools are in evidence, as is the Globe. The object partially shown in the bottom left seems to be based on a polyhedral sundial, somewhat inaccurately observed, and has a vague resemblance to the Scottish sundials described elsewhere (UGLE).

Jachin was the column on the left-hand of the Temple portal as one approached it (right as one left the Temple): it is associated with Establishment, Legality, the Second Degree of Fellow Craft, and with the Junior Warden. The Dublin MS gives the third word (*Mahabyn* [c.1700]) as *Matchpin* (1711), and other variants are *Maughbin* (1723), *Magboe and boe, marrow in the/this bone* (1725, 1726), *Machbenah* (1730, 1738), *macbenac* (1744, 1745, 1751), *makbenak* (1747, 1748), *mahhabone* (1760, 1762), the Caledonia-looking *Mac Benack* (1762), and so on. Even *marrowbone* turns up from time to time. In I *Chronicles* 2: 49, in one of those tedious genealogical lists which blight the Bible, can be found the name *Machbenah*, which, according to Christopher Barker's edition of the *Geneva Bible* published in 1580, might mean several things, e.g. 'poverty of understanding', or 'the smiting of the builder', an obvious connection with the murder of the Master Builder or the Father-Figure. According to Wallace McLeod[98], *Mah* is the Hebrew interrogative meaning 'what?', and the *Journal of the Grand Lodge of the State of Israel* is called *Haboneh Hahofshi*, which is said to mean *The Free Mason* [99]. McLeod has cast doubts if the originators of the seventeenth-century so-called 'secrets' of Freemasonry would have known Urdu: unfortunately for McLeod's claim, the word *Mahael* appears in English in 1638 in Sir Thomas Herbert's *Travels*[100] and *Moholl* in Samuel Purchas's *Pilgrimes*[101], so it is by no means impossible that the seventeenth-century 'originators' would have known of it, and associated it with the famous (and controversial) Word.

The 'marrow' as Fellow, Colleague, Partner, etc. makes some sense, but *mahabyn*, etc., do not, unless we take

---

98 To whom the present writer is indebted for these remarks in a personal communication.
99 That is, The Builder, The Free – Aubrey Newman helped to check this.
100 Herbert (1638) 71.
101 Purchas (1625) I iv 428.

the *Sloane 3329 MS* as true, and accept *maha* and *byn* as two words. Even then the ground is very shaky, so what follows is merely an hypothesis. The seventeenth-century Ideal Lodge was orientated East-West, contained two columns by reference to the names Jachin and Boaz, and held the grave of Hiram the Architect: for was not the first Lodge situated in the portico of the Temple? The work of Freemasons in the Lodge was mystical, and involved the Building of the Temple, or the reconstruction of a lost Ideal Community in a setting worthy of it, where the Architect and the Craftsmen mixed freely, and social distinction was broken down from the highest echelons of society to the lowest. This high/low progression idea, according to Stevenson, may help to explain the apparently nonsensical *mahabyn/matchpin/marrowbone* of the Hiramic Legend, for an Entered Apprentice in the Catechism was 'in the "hall"', which might be interpreted as follows: if the 'hall' is the Lodge (*mahal*, an Urdu [Arabic] word meaning private apartments or lodgings in a palace), and *ben* (Middle English *binne*, related to *bin*, or *binnan*, or *bihnen*), meaning within, towards the inner part, or into the chamber from the kitchen (e.g. *but-and-ben*, meaning outer and inner apartments of a house), then the Masonic connotations become less murky. The Master had access to the far, innermost chamber (*far ben*), and the Word therefore suggests this privilege. Stevenson, however, has suggested a slightly different meaning by which words exchanged were reminders in architectural terms that the Fellowship of Freemasonry overcame social distinctions[102].

Stevenson was not convinced about the 'marrow' explanations, and found it difficult to accept that *mahabyn* could be a distortion. He has suggested that, as Architecture/Masonry combined theory and practice, it joined the province of the upper echelons of society with the realms of the artisan: John Mylne, who became a Fellow of Craft in the Edinburgh Masonic Lodge in 1733 and Master Mason to the Crown in 1636, was celebrated in an inscription for being able to

> '…unite in one
> Highest and lowest occupation.
> To sit with Statesmen, Councillors to Kings
> To work with Tradesmen, in Mechanick things,'[103]

so could not *mahabyn* refer to 'from the highest to the lowest', that is, from the grand palatial apartment to the inner chamber of a humble dwelling?

It is unclear if the Master's Word was the same as the Mason Word: it does seem, though, that the Mason Word was around for a long time, that it was used with the Five Points of Fellowship for ceremonies, and that it had some profound resonances, partly mnemonic of secret knowledge and treasured wisdom. This does not mean that the mysterious Mason Word was used to distinguish a skilled stonemason from the Mediaeval equivalent of a 'cowboy' contractor: that could have been done far more reliably by means of a practical demonstration with stone and chisel. It seems to have been more an indication that a craftsman who knew it accepted certain rules, and also had certain privileges because he was a member of a body: it was *not*, therefore, evidence of technical ability, but of some kind of position in an association or incorporation with rules, requirements, privileges, and obligations. A Mason with the Mason Word could therefore have a better chance of finding work, and could also claim relief if he fell on evil times. Certainly in Scotland it appears that the Mason Word (which appears to have been two words) was used to protect the craftsmen from persons who had not been apprenticed. The very term 'Word', with a capital W, suggests the significance of Scripture (the Biblical Word or the Word of God) as used in the Reformed Church in Scotland, and endows the Mason Word with extra properties of significance, meaning, mystery, and awe[104]. There is another point to be borne in mind, as was hinted at earlier: the Reformation ended the Cults of Saints and the Veneration of Relics. It may well be that the bone stories were connected with the importance given to Relics in earlier times, and to the need to give Freemasonry a powerful *inner* secret as potent as were Saints' bones in former days.

Although *Machbenah*[105] is a Hebrew word, it is improbable that *mahabyn* has a Hebrew origin, although it has very definitely been associated with building, the builder, and the body of Hiram. If the murdered Mason's body lay in a Lodge of the mind or imagination, its secrets unrevealed (because raising the corpse failed to discover the *real* secret, so a substitute chosen arbitrarily became the secret instead), then although the initiated Mason was admitted to some secrets, much greater scope for acquiring knowledge, important secrets, and illumination remained. If 'marrow' in the bone is accepted as a possible mnemonic, then it *could* refer to a secret within, and it may, like *maugh*, refer to a colleague or a partner. But bone itself has a meaning related to the innermost part or the core, and physically bones consist partly of salts or carbonate and phosphate of lime, which might support a relationship with lime-mortar and therefore with the trowel. *Maught* means strength, might, power, and ability, so could this, too, allude to masonry joined by means of lime-mortar?

If the importance once given to associationism and to mnemonics is accepted, an intriguing possibility concerning *mahabyn* is suggested by the techniques of mnemonics and the associations of the trowel, lime-mortar, and sound masonry. After all, as William Preston, in his *Illustrations of Masonry*[106], reminds us, the trowel teaches that nothing can be united without proper cement, and that the perfection of a building must depend on the proper disposition of that cement: thus Charity, the bond

---

102 Stevenson (1988b) 150-1.
103 Quoted in Colvin (2008) 718.
104 Stevenson (1988b) 135-69 discusses these points: Stevenson is excellent on the ramifications of early Freemasonry in Scotland.
105 Smith (*Ed.*) (1863) **ii** 182.
106 Preston (1775) *passim*.

of perfection and social union, must link separate minds and separate interests. It also teaches that, like the radii of a circle which run from the centre to every part of the circumference, the principle of universal benevolence may be diffused to every member of the community[107].

The name *mahoe* is given to several trees, and is applied with qualifications to similar plants of various genera: it can also mean a malvaceous tree, *Paritium tiliacum*, and *tileaceous* means belonging to the Natural Order *Tiliaceae*, typified by the genus *Tilea*, the lime or linden-tree (*Tilia Europaea*). If *mahabyn* suggests something like inner meaning among trees, then it could allude to lime-mortar, as the great binding agency used in Masonry, holding all Masons together from the highest to the lowest, but *not* used by Cowans or the profane. *Mahabyn*, therefore, may be a mnemonic for lime, and especially lime-mortar, but this is offered only as a hypothetical explanation for a word that *appears* to be nonsensical, at least on the surface. It is not insignificant that the trowel is used when jointing stones with lime-mortar, and that this tool, as Preston reminds us, has other meanings. Furthermore, marrow is a vascular fatty substance found in the cavities of bones, that is the inmost or central part, or something which makes a pair with something else. *To marrow* is to join, associate, match, or pair, or to resemble or be equal to something. Now the basis of all lime is calcium, which abounds in the form of carbonates: lime is made from limestone, chalk, shells, and *bones* of animals, all of which have to be calcined, then hydrated, to make an alkaline caustic substance[108]. The purest, white lime, which slakes rapidly and expands from two to three times its original bulk during the process, has a high degree of plasticity, and is therefore termed 'fat': for mortar it is mixed with sand and, possibly, crushed stone to obtain the required colour. Could the 'marrow' refer to pure, white *fat*, or rich lime?

An even simpler explanation could be that the 'marrow-in-the-bone' aspect of the Hiramic legend may be an Art-of-Memory technique for remembering the word itself. However, the lime-mortar aspect seems to the present writer to offer a reasonably plausible hypothesis. Lime-mortar is a binding-agent, and the trowel is the means by which it is applied to masonry, but not by Cowans. Lime-mortar, tempered and slaked, is a significant Symbol, and indicates that passions and fiery temperaments are under control, transformed by the process. Untempered mortar indicates that the lessons of the Craft have not been assimilated. Lime is the most important constituent of traditional mortar used when building stone walls, so, symbolically, it is a powerful binding-agency in Masonry. A Cowan was a builder of dry-stone walls (that is, without using mortar), and was without the Word, uninitiated in the secrets of the Craft, and therefore profane. His status was not as high as that of a Mason, and the key to his status was his lack of possession of the Word and his familiarity with dry-stone work rather than with masonry bound with lime-mortar. Indeed, mortar (and therefore lime) implies connections by binding (like the rope or indented tuft), and the attributes of the Craft. Lime in French is *Chaux*, hence the Ideal Town of Claude-Nicolas Ledoux, published in 1804[109]. If mnemonic techniques are accepted as part of Freemasonry, the lime-tree can be associated with mortar, as can the lemon-tree (*Citrus Limonium*) and the Acacia (especially the locust-tree or carob [*Ceratonia Siliqua*] or False Acacia [*Robinia Pseudacacia*]). Lime is also associated with Chalk, an old Masonic Symbol.

A few more remarks on *mahabyn* are necessary. Stevenson referred to *mahal* in the sense of palace, and mentioned one celebrated building, the Taj Mahal (163148), as an example where the word appears. Now the Taj Mahal at Agra was built as a mausoleum for the Emperor Shah Jehan's favourite wife, Arjumand Banu Begum, and its name is a corruption of the Queen's title Mumtaz-i Mahal (chosen of the Palace). Snoek has suggested[110] that *mahabyn* means the inner room of the mausoleum where Hiram was entombed and to which only Master Masons had access. Perhaps he was right, but the whole business is strange, and doubtless will exercise scholars for many years yet, but the theory offered here (*pace* Snoek[111] *et al.*) in all humility is, it is submitted, really quite as plausible as any other.

Syncretism and Mysteries

Considering the syncretism of deities and cults of the Ancient World, there is reason to suppose that the Hiramic legend *may* also be a kind of memory of or allusion to consecration-sacrifices common in the Middle East, and associated with the worship of Astarte-Ashtoreth-Ashtaroth-Ishtar. Solomon was rather keen on women, including Egyptians, Moabites, Ammonites, Edomites, Zidonians, and Hittites, and 'clave unto these in love'[112], with the result that the King built places for the worship of Ashtoreth, Milcom, Chemosh, Molech, and other deities[113]. Ashtoreth was identified with Aphrodite-Venus and with Hathor, and was also associated with Adonis, so it is difficult to disentangle one legend from another. Adonis, for example, was identified as Damuzi, Tammuz, Baal, and Ešmun.

The murder of the Egyptian deity Osiris and the search for him, subsequent finding of the dismembered corpse by Isis, and her necrophilous union with him to produce Horus is a remarkable myth. During the festival of Adonia, statues of Adonis were laid out as corpses, and then 'raised' to permit him to spend half of the year with Aphrodite: this myth was associated with the death and

---

107 I am indebted to my old friend, Terence O. Haunch, for drawing my attention to this, and for correcting several of my many howlers. *Mea culpa*... Any that remain are my fault, and mine alone.
108 Papworth (*Ed.*) (1852-92) **v** 89-91.
109 Ledoux (1804); Vidler (1987, 1990).
110 Snoek (2002) 10.
111 My old friend Jan Snoek is as open-minded a colleague as one could wish for, so I know he will not take umbrage.
112 I *Kings* 11: 1-2.
113 II *Kings* 23: 13. *See also* Smith (*Ed.*) (1863) **i** 122-3.

renewal of vegetation. There are certain similarities to the Hiramic legend in both. Yet in all initiation ceremonies there is at least an allusion to a symbolic death and a rebirth: an Apprentice finishing his Apprenticeship with some splendid work, and then 'dying', is a way of pointing to the death as an Apprentice and resurrection as a Master, and recurs in many Mysteries. It does, however, raise the *possibility* that the Hiram legend was a remembrance of a consecration sacrifice, with the further possibility that the Temple of Solomon could at one time have been dedicated to something other than tradition holds. After all, the Old Testament lists several deities to which Solomon erected temples and shrines.

The Masonic problem is compounded by the fact that there was more than one Hiram, and that these were confused, not only with each other, but with other legends (the Noah story is one of many). There is nothing peculiar to Freemasonry about this, for throughout Antiquity and the Middle Ages legends overlapped, got mixed up, or were otherwise inextricably tangled. Matters were also complicated by scribes who, when copying the work of some other crabbed hand, misread, misinterpreted, or embellished the original: multiplying those problems would create a bewildering variety of stories, whilst the imaginative graphics of interpreters also would create brand-new ideas, legends, and even 'histories'.

In the Hiramic Legend context mention should be made of a very curious plate in Benedictus Arias Montanus's *Exemplar: sive de sacris fabricis Liber* of 1572[114] showing Noah's Ark as a coffin containing the body of Christ with Stigmata, perhaps emphasising the Ark as a container and means of Salvation in the real and mystical sense. The image occurs again in versions of the Holy Bible published from that date. Such ideas and images show how very complex was the world of Renaissance Symbol, Allegory, Emblem, and Idea: as in Classical Antiquity very many legends intermingled, so that in the end Hiram, Noah, Christ, Osiris, Rosenkreutz, and Hermetic-Egyptian themes coalesced[115].

This section will deal briefly with Mysteries in the sense of secret religious ceremonies which were allowed to be witnessed only by the initiated, rather than in the sense of an occupation, Craft, or Art, or Livery Company. Mystery-religions are of great antiquity, but in the Masonic context the most interesting are those of Ancient Egypt invented by Isis Herself, the Great Goddess of a Myriad Names, the *Magna Mater*[116]. The Egyptian cults, Geometry, and even the Great Architect have Masonic connections that cannot be avoided. Rituals included references to secrets that were not seen or heard, but handed down, and these secrets were presided over by the jackal-headed Anubis who, significantly, taught Isis the way when she was searching for the dismembered Osiris. Isiac mysteries were participated in by certain Roman Emperors, and involved purification, personal piety, and a variety of symbolic journeys, with a trial and degrees. Hadrian is known to have gone through ceremonies at Eleusis that had Isiac-Egyptian connotations. Enlightenment (*photismos*), initiation as a *mysterion*, and *symbolon* (password) are terms that recur in Antiquity. The term *mysterion* signified the obtaining of esoteric wisdom after some kind of endurance-test involving trials, or ordeals, had been passed. Many cults in the Graeco-Roman world required initiates to await enlightenment whilst being kept isolated in darkness, and there were rules concerning silence, patience, and fortitude. The concept of being reborn in the presence of the Great Goddess Isis after a symbolic death was part of the Isiac cults[117]. An initiate, once 'reborn', would join a sacred band of chosen ones who would be informed of the divine mysteries by being entrusted with esoteric knowledge. Mozart's O *heiliges Band der Freundschaft treuer Brüder*[118](K.148) perfectly suggests Masonic ideas of fraternity and a 'sacred band', but was apparently written long before he became a Freemason: the words were by Ludwig Friedrich Lenz[119], and appear in a Regensburg Masonic songbook[120]. Some have suggested that Mozart actually wrote this song in the 1780s, but he kept company with Masons from his Salzburg days, and did not have to wait to join the Craft before he could set the words. Such ideas of sacred fraternities and so on had been around for a very long time, often just beneath the surface, such was the strength of survival of the ancient mysteries in one form or another.

The Greek historian Herodotus of Halicarnassus identified Hephaestus with Ptah, the Egyptian God of Fire and Architect of the Universe, and the demi-gods, the Cabiri, as his (Hephaestus-Ptah's) sons who were born in Egypt. Late theology of Antiquity established links between the Great Goddess Isis and Memphis, where the temples of the Cabiri and of Ptah could be found. Isis, as sister-consort of Osiris, was also Mother of the God and of the Apis-Bull associated with Ptah and Osiris. Certainly it seems that Isis was firmly ensconced, through her connections with the Cabiri, in Thessalonica as early as the third century BC[121]. Isis was linked to Imhotep, a real figure, chief Architect to King Zoser (Djoser) and designer of the celebrated step-pyramid and mortuary complex at Saqqara[122], who was known as 'son of Ptah' and identified with Asclepius: he was eventually deified as Architect of the Universe and one of the Trinity, with Horus and Isis. Imhotep is credited with the invention of building with cut and dressed masonry, was an accomplished author, and a healer, versed in medicine. Imhotep and Isis had a temple dedicated to them at Epidaurus which is unsurprising, as both were devoted to medicine and to the occult. Eventually Imhotep achieved precedence over Ptah, the creator

---

114 Arias Montanus (1572).
115 Illustrated in Rosenau (1979) 109.
116 *See* Curl (2005) 12-22 and *passim*.

117 Merkelbach (1962) 187 and *passim*.
118 O sacred band of friendship's truest brothers.
119 Ballin (1960).
120 Thomson (1977) 26, 43-4, 176.
121 Witt (1970).
122 Erman (1927).

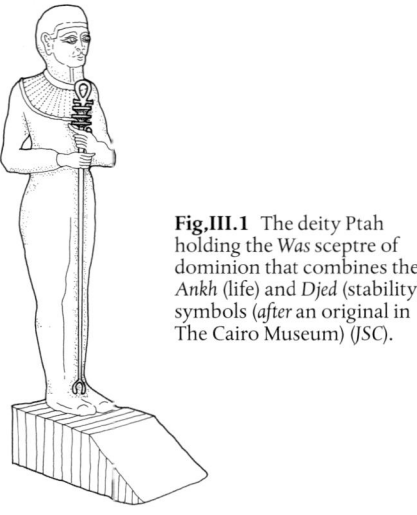

Fig.III.1 The deity Ptah holding the *Was* sceptre of dominion that combines the *Ankh* (life) and *Djed* (stability) symbols (*after* an original in The Cairo Museum) (JSC).

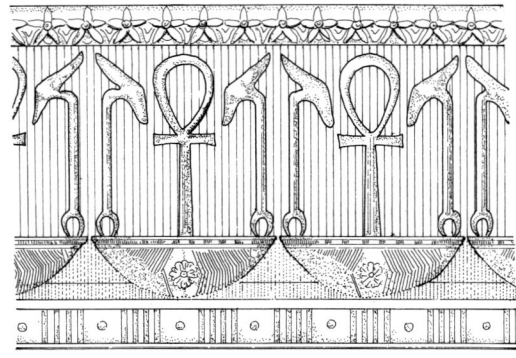

Fig.III.2 *Was* sceptres alternating with *Ankh* symbols set above a series of stylised wicker-work baskets (*after* a decorative frieze in the Temple of Hathor at Dendera of the Ptolemaïc period [probably after 116 BC]) (JSC).

of skills in architectural design, who had been closely associated with the stupendous works of Architecture of Ancient Egypt[123], and so the creator of the Saqqara complex became the Great Architect of the Universe: the Master-Mason, as Architect had himself become a God. He was not the only one, for Amenhotep, who rose to prominence as an overseer of the Royal Works and who appears to have been the Architect of many significant buildings at Thebes and in Nubia, was so important that he was given Pharaoh Amenhotep III's (reigned c.1391-c.1353 BC) eldest daughter as wife, as well as a mortuary-temple in Western Thebes, otherwise exclusively reserved for Royalty. He was deified in the Ptolemaïc period (304-30 BC), and declared to be the inseparable brother of Imhotep.

Now these points seem to have escaped many Masonic commentators, but they do go a long way to explain the importance of Masonic and Egyptian attributes as mystical objects. Yet it is clear that they must be taken into account in any consideration of the history, legends, and rituals of Freemasonry, for the Craft has claims to incorporate the Mysteries of later Antiquity within its activities. The initiates follow the ways of the Cabiri of old, and indeed of Isis herself, who searched for That which was Lost, Osiris. The syncretic aspects of myths are clear, for Osiris, resurrected as Ptah (who began and ended the day, and who was the deity of Masons and Architects engaged on building temples and tombs), was also identified with, and eventually superseded by, Imhotep, who decreed that a building should be *firmly established*. Thus Ptah/Imhotep often had a sceptre of dominion (*Was*) (**Figs.III.1 & 2**) that combined the *Ankh* (symbolising life and resurrection) and the *Djed* (symbolising stability), but he may also be associated with the *Djed* column (**Fig. III.3**), representing strength *and* stability, attributes of Boaz (though *establishment* is connected with Jachin[124]). In Hebrew Jachin is associated with firmness, is 'he shall

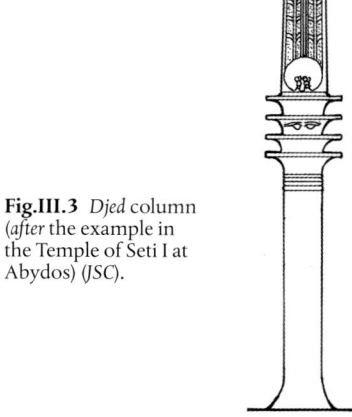

Fig.III.3 *Djed* column (*after* the example in the Temple of Seti I at Abydos) (JSC).

establish', and Boaz, associated with strength and stability, means 'in it (or him) is strength'. The present writer has been criticised for suggesting an Egyptian influence and syncretism: but the evidence is quite clear, for Osiris/Ptah/Imhotep had a column as his attribute, and there are many other connections. One critic[125] said that 'any significance the alleged meanings' of Jachin and Boaz 'need to be traced no further back' than Biblical Hebrew. Why? If such critics would trouble themselves with Ancient Egyptian Symbolism and Theology (for a start) they would find that the associations are *much* earlier than 'Biblical Hebrew', which is unfortunate for their agendas, but the *facts* are that these matters go back far further than the Bible. Crude assumptions that Christianity, or the Judaeo-Christian tradition are the be-all and end-all of things will not wash, and indeed there is a great deal of evidence that Christianity itself owes as much to the Nile as it does to the Jordan[126]. Those whose myopia, closed minds, and refusal to consider the remarkable absorption of Ancient Egyptian

---

123 *See* Curl (2005) 417, 442, 444, 456-7.
124 Witt (1971) 157.

125 In a personal communication.
126 *See* Curl (2005) for an introduction to this subject. *See also* Witt (1971) *passim*.

myths, ideas, connections, and even design motifs at least from the time Egypt became a province of the Roman Empire, usually cannot see beyond their Christian noses.

The facts that Jachin is associated with foundations and establishment and that Boaz is identified with strength and stability indicates a syncretism so widespread as to be of considerable importance, and that Ancient Egypt is indeed of exceeding significance in the mythology of Freemasonry. Images of the Great Architect, of God as Divine Architect, and of Christ as Creator may by syncretic visions based on Osiris/Ptah/Imhotep, which is not at all strange when we consider how very closely Mary the Madonna, Mother of God, resembles Isis, the Great Goddess, with whom, indeed, she shares a remarkable number of attributes[127].

During the Ptolemaïc period, and thereafter, in the Roman Empire, Isis, her Consort Osiris, and Horus/Haprocrates, had become a Trinity associated with the rising and setting of the sun. They were skilled practitioners in Mathematics, Geometry, and inventions; controllers of fire and bringers of heat, light, and life; dissolvers of darkness; and resurrectors of the dead (quite apart from their impressive skills as Healers and as Architects). It is of vital importance to recognise (despite the discomfort of those who adhere to rigid Christian beliefs) that the veneration of Isis, Osiris[128]/Serapis[129], Ptah/Imhotep, Horus/Harpocrates, and so on, was not confined to Egypt, but became widespread in the Graeco-Roman world, until Christianity concealed, prohibited, or absorbed it. Isiac legends (or Theology) point to an interesting parallel with Freemasonry: the murder of Osiris at the hands of the protean Seth (who was associated with Ashtoreth) was the great forerunner, but in the rites associated with the Cabiri one of the brothers was killed by other brothers, suggesting the death of Hiram. Apuleius tells us of Degrees of Trials, of Oaths, of Secrecy, of Passwords of Hidden Truths, of passages from Darkness to Light, and of a Victory over Death in the Isiac mysteries[130]. Abstinence, fasting, patience, and endurance of long periods in the dark were part of the Isiac mysteries (the term *incubare* refers to the custom of sleeping in a sanctuary where oracular responses were sought through dreams or necromancy). The candidate was then led to a chamber and thus participated in a ritual journey, passing through all the 'elements', until at midnight the blazing sun was seen, and the Gods themselves appeared. Yet Apuleius, who speaks of journeys to the verge of death, does not tell us of any disclosures, for the rites were secret, and betrayal of them would bring punishment. In due course Apuleius translated his Initiate to the great *Isaeum* in the Campus Martius in Rome (one of the greatest of all temples of Imperial Rome[131]), where he was admitted to a new Degree of Isis and Osiris, who were joined in their mother's womb as brother and sister, as husband and wife, in attributes, and in ritual. And, possessing the All-Seeing Eye, was the mighty Osiris the Resurrected, the Invincible, the Almighty, who was also Ptah/Serapis/Ammon and much else: he was quite something.

Indeed, for the Third Degree the candidate was guided by Osiris himself, the Highest among the Greatest, and the Greatest among the Highest, in a mystic union where two became one and the candidate was alone with the Alone in a sanctuary where Serenity, Stillness, and Silence ruled like Gods. So the journey Apuleius outlined was part of the Isiac mystery, and that which the Neo-Platonist writer Plotinus connected with an ecstatic elevation of the soul to the Divine: it could not be revealed, but involved a ritual purification by water, the ducking of the head seven times, a prayer to the Queen of Heaven, Isis, and the donning of different garments or vestments for each of the regions through which the candidate would pass. During this ritual journey the candidate would undergo the *mors voluntaria*, or voluntary death, yet hoped for rescue and resurrection by Isis[132].

The idea of a journey through various compartments, with vestments for each stage, before a goal is reached, is not confined to ancient esoteric Egyptian mystery-cults. Daedalus, the cunning artificer, was revered by the artists' Guilds of the ancient world, especially in Attica. An accomplished Architect, Daedalus was supposed to have invented the axe, awl, and bevel. His nephew, who invented the saw, the potter's wheel, the lathe, and other tools (and so appeared likely to surpass him in inventiveness and originality), attracted the jealousy of Daedalus, who slew him and buried the body, in which act he (Daedalus) was detected. The parallels will be obvious. Daedalus fled to Crete where he designed and built the Labyrinth of Gnosus (Knossos) for the Minotaur: he entrusted Ariadne with certain secrets (symbolised by the clue of yarn[133]) by which she guided Theseus through the Maze (note the Isiac notion of a guide through dark passages)[134]. And the Labyrinth, as we will see, recurs as an important element in this study.

The Labyrinth as an emblem or as a form is a number of communicating passages, arranged in great complexity, through which it is difficult to find one's way without guidance: it is also called a Maze, and is an intricate, tortuous arrangement of features designed to mystify. It is suggested by the key-pattern, Greek key, fret, maze, or meander (a geometrical ornament consisting of horizontal and vertical fillets joining at angles, a variety of fret called *grecque* or *labyrinthine*, like a series of key-shapes on bands [usually friezes and string-courses] in Classical Architecture, so related to the Swastika)[135].

---

127 For these matters expounded upon in detail *see* Curl (2005) *passim*.
128 Sometimes called Osorapis or Serapis/Sarapis in the Graeco-Roman world. See Curl (2005) 15.
129 *See* Hornbostel (1973) *passim*.
130 Apuleius Madaurensis (1924).
131 *See* Curl (2005) xxiii, 16, 30-9, 47, 50, 51, 70, 75, 80, 110, 114, 401-2, etc.

132 Witt (1971) 157f.
133 Yarn, or rope, of destiny is woven by the three Norns during the Prologue of the *Götterdämmerung* (first given 1876) by Richard Wagner. It is also associated with the Skirret.
134 Seyffert (1899) 171. For Ariadne *see* 64.
135 *See* Curl (2006a) *passim*.

Pl.III.3 Labyrinth in the centre of the nave of Chartres Cathedral, which measures some 13 metres (43 feet) in diameter, and is similar to a labyrinth illustrated in Villard de Honnecourt's thirteenth-century notebooks. This labyrinth once contained a signature-plate of the Architect or Master-Builder, and the way to the central point was 230 metres (775 feet) long, representing a journey, a ritual pilgrimage, progress through life itself, with all its false turnings, and even the Holy Grail. Significantly, Parsifal, in Wagner's *Bühnenweihfestspiel*, asks 'Who is the Grail?', and Gurnemanz points out that no earthly path leads to it, and none could tread it unless guided by the Grail itself (JSC).

A Labyrinth is also planting in a garden arranged as hedges between labyrinthine paths leading to a centre, a feature of seventeenth-century garden-design (e.g. at Hampton Court). It can be a place laid out for ritual pilgrimage in a church (e.g. the inlaid labyrinth of blue and white stones in the nave-floor of the Cathedral of Notre-Dame, Chartres, in France [**Pl.III.3**]): the centre of such a Labyrinth was the *Jerusalem* or *Paradise*, the Holy City of God to which the pilgrim aspired. Certain mazes were also formed in turf, as at Wing, Rutland, or Saffron Walden, Essex, similar to the designs in churches, which have led to a Christian interpretation being applied to them, but they may have had a non-Christian origin.

Labyrinthine patterns were among the ancestors of the 'knots', or ornamental patterns, found in gardens of the fifteenth and sixteenth centuries. By the end of the fifteenth century a knot was synonymous with a maze. Even the Greek-key pattern is derived from a labyrinthine form, and maze-like patterns recur in the art of many ancient civilisations. Apart from their complex decorative possibilities, labyrinthine designs had symbolic and even magical connotations, for they could be protective (by leading potential enemies or evil spirits literally up the garden path), and they could also suggest the journey through life itself, with its many dead-ends, wrong turnings, and misleading signs, until the correct way could be found and the prize gained. In this last sense, a labyrinth could be a symbol of a journey through one's existence, with all its mistakes, until a Paradise or a rebirth could be attained[135].

In the case of labyrinthine designs set in the floors of some Mediaeval cathedrals for ritual pilgrimage there were some curious customs associated with them, including the obscure maze-dance by clergy, connected with an allegory of a journey through Life to the City of God. Maze-patterns in paving (as at Chartres) repeat those of turf or hedge, but tend to be more refined, and of course hedge-mazes of topiary were themselves enclosed gardens[137]. In some of the greatest cathedrals of the Mediaeval period large areas of nave-floor were given over to labyrinthine patterns that sometimes even contained the names and portraits of the Architects responsible. Only images of the Labyrinths of Amiens (which has been partially reconstructed) and Rheims (**Pl.III.4**) survive to portray the Architects and Bishops who laid the foundation-stones. The Chartres Labyrinth[138] (which still exists) has lost its signature-plate from the centre, but it is clear that the Mediaeval Architects were not only providing a pattern which could be used for prayer, for ritual pilgrimage, for curious maze-dances, and as an allegory of life's journey, with its trials and tribulations, but were showing they were the heirs of Daedalus, the Builder of the Labyrinth and the Architect of so many buildings supposedly in Egypt, Sicily, Sardinia, Greece, and Italy[139]. A Labyrinth not unlike the pattern of that in Chartres was incised into the innermost pier of the west façade (twelfth century) of the Cathedral of San Martino, Lucca, Italy, and was probably associated with the pilgrim-culture of Mediaeval times, suggesting not only a pilgrimage, but the erring paths of human life. A penitent could trace a way through the Labyrinth with a finger in such a position, rather than having to walk it, as at Chartres.

So, inevitably, by the familiar process of syncretism[140], Architects identified with Daedalus (who is shown flying from the Labyrinth in a relief[141] from the *campanile* of Florence Cathedral probably by Andrea Pisano, though Giotto di Bondoni was the Architect who designed the structure), for a Mason named Anselmus signed the reliefs of the Porta Romana (now Castello Sforzesco), Milan, with the inscription ANSELMUS DEDALUS ALTER, meaning that he saw himself as a second Daedalus[142]. Some have identified this Anselmus as Anselmo da Campione, Master of the Works at Milan Cathedral (consecrated 1184)[143].

Mediaeval Architects (or Master-Builders), then, were not anonymous nobodies, but had status, and in some cases were duly celebrated by means of sculpted figures. Matthias of Arras was commemorated at St Vitus Cathedral, Prague (to which he had been called to build it); Peter Parler is also portrayed in Prague Cathedral; very

---

136 Curl (1988).

137 *Ibid.*

138 Known as *La Lieue* because the total length of its paths is said to be a *League*, it served as a penitential path for the faithful. However, a League (1.376 English miles [2.215 km] or 2.764 French miles [4.448 km]) would seem to be far too great a measure, so the nickname may suggest that the total length of the path is great. The actual diameter is *c*.12.2 metres.

139 Svanberg (1983) 144 f. For Labyrinths *see* Turner (*Ed.*) (1998) **xviii** 584-5.

140 Fusing or blending, as by identification of deities, or reconciliation of, or attempts to reconcile, different systems of belief.

141 The originals are now in the Mus. Opera Duomo, Florence.

142 Svanberg (1983) 146.

143 Turner (*Ed.*) (1998) **ii** 129, and **v** 549-51.

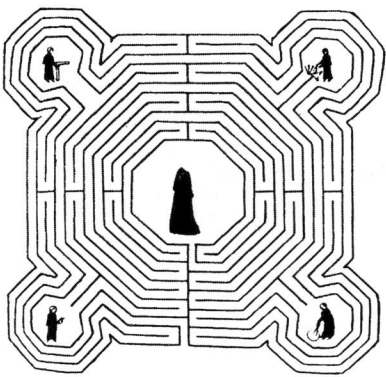

Pl.III.4 Labyrinth in Rheims Cathedral from a sixteenth-century representation (it was destroyed in the eighteenth century). Four Master Masons were named and shown with compasses and square, while the Archbishop was depicted in the centre (JSC).

realistic carved portraits of Master-Masons were carved for the funerary monuments of Nikolaus von Büren and Konrad Kuene[144]: the von Büren figures survive in the Diocesan Museum, and the heavily restored monument of Kuene may be seen in the Cathedral of Sts Peter and the Virgin Mary, Cologne; and under the organ-loft of the Cathedral of St Stephen, Vienna, is an astonishingly realistic (and coloured) portrait, supposedly of Anton Pilgram, holding a square and compasses (1513). The Architect added another self-portrait under the pulpit of the same church (1515): he appears to be leaning out of a carved window-opening, and again holds compasses in his right hand. Adam Kraft also left portraits of himself in the Schreyer-Landauer monument, St Sebald, Nuremberg (begun 1490), and as one of the figures supporting the tabernacle in the Church of St Lorenz, Nuremberg (the other two figures were those of Kraft's assistants). Henry Wy was portrayed on one of the spandrels of St Alban's Cathedral, Hertfordshire, and the late John Hooper Harvey identified several other portraits of English Mediaeval Architects[145].

Masons, Carpenters, and Architects are depicted in stained-glass windows, sculptured reliefs (the Cathedral-Church in Münster, Westphalia, is especially rich in this respect), illuminated manuscripts, ceiling-bosses where rib-vaults converge, individually sculpted figures (such as those from the van Büren tomb in Cologne), and painted portraits. Thus, from the above and many other examples, such as the magnificent incised slab that once covered the grave of Hue *or* Hugues Libergié *or* Libergier in the Abbey-Church of St-Nicaise, Rheims (destroyed), and is now in Rheims Cathedral, it is clear that Master-Masons were held in high regard. Libergier's slab shows the Architect holding a model of a church and his staff of office, and there are a square and compasses on either side of his feet:

the inscription styles him 'Maistre'[146]. Another Architect, Pierre de Montreuil, was buried in St Germain-des-Prés, Paris, where the inscription informed readers that he was *Doctor Lathomorum* (Doctor of Masons, a very grand title, which also meant 'teacher of Masons'). The Architect of the Romanesque Cathedral of Pisa, Buscheto *or* Busketus *or* Boschetto, was compared with Daedalus, and judged his superior in an inscription in Pisa (now set in the northernmost arch of the Cathedral façade)[147]. Finally, mention should be made of Villard *or* Wilars *or* Vilars de Honnecourt *or* Honecort, French draughtsman, author of a portfolio of some 250 drawings, about a sixth of which are of architectural subjects. It has been claimed that this is the most important Mediaeval architectural treatise to survive. Called the 'Lodge-Book', it has been suggested it was designed to assist Apprentices and others. It includes sections on Architecture, machinery, figures, sculpture, theory, and drawings of animals. Now in the *Bibliothèque Nationale*, Paris[148], the 'Lodge-Book' contains plans of actual buildings as well as unrealised designs, inaccurate records of buildings and architectural details seen, and much else. Paul Frankl has gone so far as to dub Villard the 'Gothic Vitruvius'[149], a grotesque exaggeration, as Villard's drawings demonstrate he knew very little about design, stereotomy, or construction. The collection is probably no more than a record of the interests of a reasonably curious and well-travelled thirteenth-century gentleman from Picardy, but as a book of instruction for Apprentices (or anyone else) it would have been useless. Sir Nikolaus Pevsner called Villard an 'Architect', and claimed his work was 'invaluable as a source'[150]: this demonstrates the pitfalls when an art-historian, who obviously knew very little of how buildings were constructed, pontificated on architectural matters. Villard's work is nothing more than an eclectic scrap-book, with notes about many impressions and objects, but it is certainly not a manual of any use whatsoever to 'pupils' or 'Apprentices'. The collection does, however, contain a drawing of a Labyrinth similar to that in Chartres Cathedral.

Given the undoubted status of the Mediaeval Architect, it is not surprising that even God became *Architectus Mundi* in thirteenth-century representations, showing him with compasses, an image revived by William Blake and others much later. This, perhaps subliminal, memory of Ptah-Imhotep as Sublime Architect is not an uncommon idea or image, recurring in numerous illuminated Biblical texts of the Middle Ages. So Osiris, Ptah, Imhotep, Daedalus, God as *Architectus Mundi*, and Mediaeval Cathedral Architects have similar attributes. In these connecting themes and motifs from Antiquity, Freemasonry has certain roots, perhaps partly spurious, but they exist nevertheless: of that there can be no doubt. The actual *processes* by which certain ideas recurred remain obscure, but the rediscovery of

---

144 Kuene is referred to as *Magister Operis* (Master of the Works) on his funerary monument.
145 Harvey (1987) 375-6.
146 Turner (*Ed.*) (1998) **xix** 308.
147 *Ibid.* **v** 291-2.
148 Bib. N. MS. Fr. 19093.
149 Turner (*Ed.*) (1998) **xxxii** 569-71.
150 Pevsner (1960) 141-2.

'Hermetic' texts, the importance of Graeco-Roman writings that had survived the centuries (not *least* the bonfires of destructive Christian zeal), the continuing presence of certain elements in design, the handing down of legend by word of mouth, and the continuing mechanisms of identification, of taking over of attributes, and of widespread syncretism unquestionably played their parts.

These complex processes, mind-boggling in their scope, can begin to be understood (at least in part) by studying the development of the Cult of the Virgin Mary, the Initiator, the Unfading Rose, the Heifer who brought forth the Spotless Calf, the Chariot of Fire, the Star-Flaming Queen, the Haven and the Anchorage, the Mistress of the Word, the Queen of Heaven, the Great Virgin, the Mother of the God, the Garden Enclosed, the Fountain (sealed or playing): Isis remained what She ever was, as the Source of Grace and Truth, the Resurrection and the Life, and the Great Goddess, who stealthily became the Virgin Mary. Isis-Sophia, the Wise, the Sister of God and His Spouse, is also Mary, the Sister and Spouse of God, the Sister of Christ, the Wearer of Diadems, the Cornucopia of All our Goods, the Fructificatio, the Lighthouse of the World, the Salvatrix, Inventrix, and Justitia, She is the Moon, the Crescent, the Swallow, the Bow, the Deer, and an infinite number of other things as well. The amazingly comprehensive Aretalogy of that incorrigible enthusiast, Hippolytus Marraccius (Ippolito Marracci), entitled *Polyanthea Mariana*, if perused with clear eye and unclouded mind, will satisfy any doubters as to the astonishing absorption of Isiac attributes by the Marian *Cultus*[151], for he covered the topic without a hint of irony, humour, or wavering of belief, all in exhaustive and exhausting detail.

The not unreasonable claims of Giordano[152] Bruno that the most acceptable Theologies had developed in the Egypt of Antiquity, and that the Cult of Isis exerted a formative influence on Christianity itself, should not offend any but the most closed of limited minds: Christianity, with its Saints, Emblems, Veneration of the BVM, and complex Iconographies, is indebted to Ancient Egypt in the evolution of its Cults and its Arts. Bruno was an important figure in the rise of Neo-Platonism, and was significant in Hermeticism and late Humanism. His Pantheism and wide-ranging learning did not endear him to the Establishment, and he was burned at the stake in Rome during the Pontificate of Clement VIII[153].

Despite burnings of 'heretics' (Clement had some thirty such burned during his Pontificate) and many other attempts to suppress that which was unpalatable to orthodox opinion, the whole of Christendom is permeated with ideas born in Antiquity, with Hermetic notions, and with themes derived from the Graeco-Roman-Egyptian Cults. It is hardly surprising, therefore, that Freemasonry, too, has taken on board some of those themes: a vast organisation with a code of conduct, rituals, a system of morality in which Allegory and Symbol play their parts, with concepts of Trials, Degrees, Initiations, and Secrecies, and with the ideas of Ritual Journeys, Death and Rebirth after Ordeals, and much else besides, has claims to connections (however tenuous they might appear today) with the Mysteries of Graeco-Roman-Egyptian Antiquity. The All-Seeing Eye of Ptah, the Isiac Mysteries, and the Resurrection of Osiris the Mighty, the Invincible, are not very far removed from the centre of Freemasonry: Ptah's column is not unrelated to Boaz and Boaz's inner meaning, and it should always be borne in mind that Ptah was superseded by Imhotep, a real Architect, who himself was deified.

Concluding Remarks

Bruno worked on aspects of memory, and argued that Man might achieve union with the Divine through a revelation of Ancient Egyptian knowledge[154]. Alexander Dickson, a Scot and follower of Bruno, published in 1584 a work based on Bruno's ideas in which Antique techniques revealing the Art of Memory were given overt Egypto-Hermetic settings[155]: this was denounced on religious grounds by a Cambridge scholar[156] and defended by Dickson[157]. One of Dickson's techniques was to get his students to memorise places and images from a building in groups of ten, the images in each set of ten were linked by visual associations to enable them to be memorised in the correct sequence[158]. Stevenson gives an example of this: if, say, a lute were to be followed by a fire, then the image of the lute should be burning[159]. Despite all the high-mindedness, Sir Hugh Plat, one of Dickson's students, used the Art of Memory when learning stories or playing cards[160].

Stevenson has suggested[161] that Dickson probably promoted Hermetic-Brunonian ideas in Scotland, and we know Schaw insisted that Masons should be thoroughly tested in the Art of Memory, which was and is (or ought to be) of particular interest to Freemasons: it was, after all, as previously noted, based on the idea of studying a large and complex building, and it was recognised as giving new powers by developing mnemonic skills for acquiring knowledge and storing facts by means of allusions and associations. Yates saw the connection between the Art of Memory (using Architecture as a vehicle in the striving for Wisdom) and Freemasonry[162]. She went so far as to suggest that the Renaissance occult Art of Memory was the source of an Hermetic and mystical movement which used the imaginary, legendary, or speculative elements of

---

151 *See* Marraccius (1648, 1710).
152 He was baptised Filippo, but became Giordano on becoming a Dominican friar. *See* papers by Frances Yates (1938, 1940) in *Journal* of the Warburg and Courtauld Institutes, **ii** and **iii**.
153 Ippolito Aldobrandini, who enlarged the Index (1596) in which Jewish books were banned, and sharpened the severity of the Inquisition.
154 Yates (1979) 128-70.
155 Durkan (1962).
156 'G. P. Cantabrigiensis' (1584).
157 Dickson (1584).
158 Stevenson (1988*b*) 87-96.
159 *Ibid.* 90.
160 Plat (1594). *See also* Yates (1966) 284-5.
161 Stevenson (1988*b*) 92.
162 Yates (1966) 286-7 and *passim*.

the *Architecture* held in memory as vehicles for teaching moral and mystical ideas directed towards and from the Great Architect of the Universe[163]. Stevenson reminds us[164] that the Warden of the Lodge of Kilwinning in 1599 was ordered to test every Entered Apprentice and Fellow Craft in the 'art of Memorie and Science thairof', and that punishments were to be instituted for those who 'lost any point thairof'. Masters most perfect in the Art of Memory were to test other Masons in aspects of the Art, Craft, Science, and Ancient Memory[165]. Thus it is clear from what are known as the Second Schaw Statutes that Hermetic Renaissance ideas were introduced to the Craft, indeed they were almost *imposed* by the Master of Works himself, and that there are definite links between Bruno, Dickson, and Schaw, as Stevenson has demonstrated. This must also clarify why ideas concerning mystical Enlightenment through an ancient technique not only developed aspects of Masonic custom, but profoundly influenced the often baffling and very peculiar iconography of the Craft.

These points comprise significant parts of the history of Freemasonry, linking Hermetic strands of 'Ancient Egyptian Wisdom' with the Mason Craft. The Enlightenment interest in Egyptian Architecture and Mysteries *before* the scientific surveys of Egyptian buildings thus makes much more sense: the Hermetic ideas permeated Scotland, and it was through Scotland that much later Masonic custom was filtered. It is in Scotland, too, that we find tangible and visible evidence of how deeply Renaissance themes had penetrated that country: that evidence is so startling and so strange that it cannot be dismissed as artistic licence or as mere chance. It will form part of the next Chapter.

If we look again at Dickson, various strands start to fall into place. He was loyal to Roman Catholicism, and, indeed to the dethroned Mary Queen of Scots until her execution in 1587. In the late 1580s and early 1590s he was involved in murky negotiations in France and the Spanish Netherlands, and his presence at the Court of James VI worried English agents sufficiently to have him watched. He was questioned by the General Assembly of the Church of Scotland for attending Mass and making no secret of his loyalty to Rome, but, like many others, he enjoyed the favour and protection of the King, even though he was a 'papistical papist'. Dickson was not the only Brunonian at Court: William Fowler, Secretary to Queen Anne, was also an expert on the 'Art of Memorye', and indeed probably taught that Art to the Queen. Fowler had attended St Leonard's College, St Andrews, as did Dickson, so they were probably acquainted at least since the 1570s. Fowler had been involved in the marriage negotiations between James and Anne, and in 1589-90 travelled to Denmark to pursue those: Dickson was also in the party. In the 1590s he travelled in Italy, notably to Padua and Venice, and we have already noted connections with Padua[166]. Both Fowler and Dickson had to survive in a dangerous world of politico-religious intrigue: Dickson's adherence to Rome led to a great deal of difficulty for him, and he seems to have been a double-dealer, intriguing with both the English and Roman Catholic powers; Fowler's Protestantism eventually soured his relations with the Queen. But Schaw's relations with Fowler were close, for Fowler, as the Queen's Secretary, and Schaw, as her Chamberlain, had to work together in their professional capacities[167]. Fowler recorded James's decision to rebuild the Chapel Royal at Stirling Castle for the Baptism of the infant Prince Henry in 1594: Fowler was in charge of arrangements for the pageants associated with the Baptism, and Schaw was not only in charge of the 'new chappell' but was Master of Ceremonies at the event[168].

Bruno was to be incinerated for heresy only two months after the issue of the Second Schaw Statutes. So how do we reconcile the Fowler-Dickson-Schaw axis, the Art of Memory, and Bruno? All were outsiders, for Bruno's unorthodox views were unacceptable to the Church (even though, as we have seen, grandees of that Church could claim descent from Osiris and surround themselves with Egyptianising images and ideas, so there was, at least, more than a whiff of hypocrisy about it all); Dickson was a Roman Catholic trying to survive in a country where Calvinist Protestantism was in the ascendant; Fowler was a Protestant serving a Roman Catholic Queen and working with the Roman Catholic Schaw; and Schaw, as a Roman Catholic, was endeavouring to inject elements of Hermeticism into the Mason Craft, including the Art of Memory, intended to lead to spiritual renewal. Thus the Lodge may eventually have become a sort of Temple of Memory, an imaginary place where images set in position within it were Art of Memory aids to remind Masons of the rituals of Initiation and the secrets of the Craft. And if something precious had been lost, such an organisation as Masonry could be a means of keeping it alive, despite repression by one type of 'Christianity' or another.

If all this business about mystic numbers, Signs of the Zodiac, and Revelations concerning Ancient Knowledge seems fishy today, we must remember that there are plenty of people around who consult Astrologers, study Horoscopes, look for Signs, and put faith in Numbers some three centuries *after* supposed Newtonian Enlightenment, and plenty of believers in the literal truth of Scripture a century-and-a-half after the publication (1859) of the epoch-making *Origin of Species* by Charles Robert Darwin. The late-sixteenth and the seventeenth centuries were dangerous times in which to live, and the foundations of orthodox faith turned out to be more shifting sands than solid rock, yet the iron certitudes of one confession could demand utter conformity with them from its adherents and the destruction of those who could not accept them. The past, and especially the past in Antiquity, must have

---

163 Yates (1966) 286-7 and *passim*.
164 Stevenson (1988b) 49 and *passim*.
165 *Ibid*.
166 *ODNB* **xx** (2004) 598-9.
167 For Fowler *see* Fowler (1914-40).
168 Fowler **ii** (1936) 169-70, and **iii** (1940) 172, 176, 181.

seemed to offer anchors and safe harbours to those adrift on the stormy seas of religious controversy, so we should attempt to understand the uncertainties and dangers that beset so many at the time, no matter if they were Protestant or Roman Catholic. Force and terror were used by both sides, and not to their credit either, for *all* monotheistic religions are essentially intolerant: it is in that context that we need to consider the emergence of Freemasonry.

The Age of the Alchemical Magus, of the Faustian Seeker, of the Wanderer, did not have the benefit or otherwise of Newtonian physics and all that came after it, but it did have something else that perhaps recognised the importance of spiritual, unmeasurable, ecstatic values. And if those values were equated with a Craft and with Moral Work, Special Knowledge, and a seeking to find something infinitely precious that required patient rebuilding in the hearts of Mankind, some sort of caution would have seemed prudent. The Reformation of the World cannot be undertaken by anybody: only those with certain skills are capable of even trying, and their work, if scrutinised by every fool on earth, could easily be misinterpreted and lead to trouble. There can be no arguing with that, for it has happened, again and again and again, with depressingly destructive results.

CHAPTER IV

Early Artefacts, Jacobites, and Hanoverians

Introduction; Visible Evidence of Early Freemasonry in Artefacts in Scotland; England, Scotland, Jacobites, and Hanoverians; The Two Pillars or Columns

'…the mere discovery of the writings on which reliance was apparently placed, does not convert… legendary matter… into authoritative history…'

DOUGLAS KNOOP (1883-1948) &
GWILYM PEREDUR JONES (1892-1975):
The Genesis of Freemasonry
(Manchester: Manchester University Press, 1948) 70.

'A good Memory is the best Monument. Others are subject to Casualty and Time, and we know that the Pyramids themselves doting with age have forgotten the names of their Founders.'

THOMAS FULLER (1608-61):
The Holy State, Book iii *Of Tombes*,
last paragraph, lines 1-4
(Cambridge: Roger Daniel 1647).

Introduction

Thus, from the above, it should be clear that Scotland played an important part in the curious matters considered in this study, not only because of the colossal changes introduced as a result of the Reformation, but because of the unification of the Crowns in 1603 and the removal of the Stuart Court to London in a period of considerable religious and political instability. The first years of the seventeenth century were dangerous times. Freemasonry was certainly something many intellectuals took seriously, and the Craft grew in importance and influence, especially towards the end of the seventeenth and the beginning of the eighteenth century. This Chapter will outline some aspects relevant to these convoluted affairs.

Visible Evidence of Early Freemasonry in Artefacts in Scotland

The Knights Templars, or Military Order of the Poor Knights of Christ and of the Temple of Solomon[1] comprised a military and religious Order, consisting of Knights, Chaplains, and men-at-arms, founded in 1119, chiefly for the protection of the Holy Sepulchre and to escort Christian pilgrims visiting the Holy Land. The Order was called thus because it occupied a building (the al-Aqsa Mosque) on the massive Temple platform in Jerusalem, which the Crusaders believed was part of the Temple of Solomon. The Order became immensely wealthy, with vast estates and properties throughout Western Europe, and was suppressed in 1312, having been accused of all manner of blasphemies, heresies, and wicked practices. The suppression by an administrative ordinance (*Vox Clamatis*) was carried out at the instigation of King Philippe IV[2] of France, who leaned on the Pope, Philippe's puppet Clement V, to dissolve the Order[3]. The destruction of the Templars had three fateful consequences: it facilitated conquests by the Turks and therefore the spread of Islam

---
1 *Pauperes Commilitones Christi Templique Salomonici.*
2 Known as 'The Fair'.
3 *See* Barber (2003).

into Europe; it set a vile precedent for the revoltingly cruel criminal procedures of France which lasted until the Revolution; and it gave the seal of approval at the highest level to belief in witchcraft, sexual fantasies involving the Devil, and sanctioned the use of appalling tortures to extract confessions concerning repulsive perversions dreamed up in the diseased minds of the accusers, who were obsessed with what can only be described as Pious Filth, thus sparking the horrible persecution of 'witches' well into the eighteenth century.

For a time the Templars were regarded as the most effective and dangerous of the enemies of Islam. However, they were unable to prevent the collapse of the Crusader Kingdom when Acre fell in 1291, and many began to blame the Templars for this disaster. Power and wealth attracted envy, and soon the Templars were in trouble, largely fomented by King Philippe, who was covetous of their wealth and jealous of their power. Arrests of Templars began in 1307, and the Pope attempted to take over responsibility for proceedings himself (finding the Papal powers were being usurped by secular forces controlled by the King of France). Clement V therefore issued a Bull, *Pastoralis Præeminentiæ* (22 November 1307), which ordered the arrests of Templars throughout Latin Christendom. One version of the Bull was sent to King Edward II of England, who at first refused to believe the fearful accusations, but eventually fell into line, and so the Templars were arrested in England and their property confiscated. The Pope made his decision about Templar property in the Bull *Ad Providam* (2 May 1312): it was to be transferred to the Order of Hospitallers (Knights of the Order of the Hospital of St John of Jerusalem). Clearly the attraction of acquiring riches from confiscated property appealed to many individuals, and the whole business of trials for heresy, etc., reeks of acquisitive greed. To judge from proceedings against Templars in Ireland, only fourteen appear to have been interrogated, and in Scotland only two (and both of these were Englishmen)[4].

The Templars suffered many losses, but numerous Knights and others seem to have got away, either melting into the populace at large, or joining other Orders. It has been suggested that some may have escaped to Scotland and to the Western Isles and Ulster, where the Papal writ was not prevalent or all-powerful, and where the political and legal frameworks at the time of Robert I 'the Bruce' were sufficiently confused to permit members of the Order to survive[5]. It has been pointed out that there are surviving funerary monuments featuring what have been described as Masonic Squares, Masonic tools, and Templar swords and crosses at Garway (Herefordshire), Kilmartin (Argyll), Kilmory Knap (also Argyll), and other sites that have affinities with Templar memorials in the Holy Land, but of those three named sites, only St Michael's, Garway, can be identified with certainty as having been a Preceptory of the Templars, founded in the 1180s, which originally had a circular nave (of which the chancel arch is the only part that survives). There does not appear to be irrefutable evidence that places such as Kilmartin or Kilmory Knap had any Templar connections at all. Yet the fact that the Bruce was very much a law unto himself, and wished to restore an independent Kingdom of Scotland, it has been claimed, meant that the secular agents of the Papacy could not enforce Papal policy, and so surviving Templars may have gone to ground in Scotland[6]. This is a possibility that few accept, yet it is by no means *entirely* fanciful. We know that the Templars owned ships, a fleet, in fact, but we do not know what happened to them or it, and there *are* stones inscribed with what resemble Templar crosses (a type of *formy*, *paty*, or *patée* cross, not unlike the Prussian Iron Cross) in Highland churchyards and churches, but that is not by any means proof, and these are not necessarily Templar stones.

However, it seems highly unlikely that any surviving members of the Order simply vanished (although they must have adopted a low profile): they were probably subsumed in some way into Scots and other societies. Quite possibly some Masonic legends and concerns, such as ritual, the iconography of the Temple, and certain signs and symbols, derive from Templar practices, for there are rather too many signs in common for this to be entirely accidental. Obviously documentary evidence is somewhat lacking, but the visual evidence on tombstones and in sculpture does suggest that certain aspects of speculative Freemasonry may owe *something* (however tenuous) to the Templars, or to the *idea* or *legends* of the Templars. The idea of loss, for example, is particularly apposite in the type of the Temple itself: the lost headquarters, the lost arts, the lost Architecture, and the lost power are all encapsulated in the Temple and its iconography. The Templar connection, and the importance of Scotland in the history of Freemasonry, mnemonics, Renaissance-Hermetic ideas, and the

---

4 Barber (2003) 236-7. *See* also Baigent & Leigh (1989) 64-5.
5 Baigent & Leigh (1989) 87-102.

6 Baigent & Leigh (1989), *passim*. Much conventional academic opinion rejects any survival of the Templars, and some commentators have more or less accepted the evidence of the transcripts of the trials as clinching the guilt of the Order. However, individual Templars were not permitted to give evidence for the defence, and confessions extracted under torture should not be accepted as true. Just before they were due to receive their sentences of life imprisonment in 1314, Jacques de Molay, Grand Master of the Order from c.1295), and Gaufrid (Geoffroi) de Charney, Preceptor of Normandy, publicly withdrew their 'confessions' and protested to the assembled thousands in front of Notre Dame in Paris the innocence of the Order. King Philippe did not wait to consult the Church any further: he had both men burnt at the stake. *See* Barber (2003) *passim* for the Trial, and *see* Cooper (2006) 227-35 and *passim* for a robust refutation of Templar stories and the supposed evidence of tombstones. Walker and Sinclair (2000) do not mention any Templar connection at all in connection with Kilmartin and Kilmory Knap. As Cooper (2006) 235 has observed, 'there are major difficulties to be resolved before it can be argued that such graveslabs etc. actually have any connection' with the Mediaeval Order of Knights Templar. I have taken the trouble to inspect many of these supposed Templar artefacts, and have come to the conclusion that the various Schools of carvers of graveslabs (e.g. Iona, Kintyre, Loch Sween, and Loch Awe Schools, each with its distinct style) produced great numbers of such carvings, and in such quantities that, if the Templar connection is accepted, this must mean that Scotland was the refuge for huge numbers of Templars after 1307. This, I believe, is not a sustainable position, and, anyway, if the Templars had gone to ground to escape persecution, it is unlikely they would advertise their presence by means of such means as carved graveslabs, crosses, and the like. Anonymity is not generated by grand funerary monuments.

Reformation cannot be overlooked. A singular significance of Scotland in arcane matters (not necessarily anything whatsoever connected with Templars or legends of the Templars) is reflected in the proliferation of architectonic and sculptural curiosities that cannot be entirely explained in terms of function or climate[7], but not all of these are by any means tombstones or funerary monuments, although the tools of the Mason often feature on headstones.

Some remarkably common sculpted types of artefacts survive in Scotland which indubitably display Masonic allusions. Examples of tombstones and memorials with Masonic emblems on them abound in the churchyards and cemeteries of Scotland, but the most elaborate surviving artefacts with Masonic connotations are sundials, which is an odd aspect of a rainy, frequently overcast land, not to be explained in so-called 'functional' terms[8]. Two very unusual sundial types deserve comment here, although sundials can be found in an incredible number of positions on buildings or as detached objects; the two are obelisk- and lectern-shaped sundials. Obelisk-sundials have overt Egyptian allusions, but Egyptian obelisks themselves were believed by some to have been gnomons, that is the 'pin' of a dial the shadow of which points the hour. These strange objects have square shafts rising from a stepped or plain base, the shaft being divided on each side into five panels, thus presenting twenty compartments to the viewer as he walks around it. These compartments are ornamented with cup-shaped, heart-shaped, triangular, and other incisions, which are usually lined to mark the hours: the sharp edges of the figures cast the shadows, while stone gnomons or metal stiles are also fixed in the hollows. At the top of the compartmented shaft is a block which bulges out on corbelled forms to create an octagon on plan, while above and below each facet over the four sides of the shaft are sloping faces, which also have dials. The triangular pieces formed by the meeting of the square and the octagon are cut out, forming dark shadows. Above the octagon, which returns to the square plan, is an obelisk or a finial, again subdivided vertically into panels (although there does not seem to be a commonly agreed number of these, unlike the square shafts which nearly always have five). Examples include those at Mount Stuart (Bute) (**Pl.IV.1**), Leven (Fife), and Tongue (Sutherland) (**Pl.IV.2**).

Lectern-shaped sundials are even odder, consisting of a pedestal or shaft on which is an elaborately carved and hollowed stone containing several sundials, the whole ensemble bearing a resemblance to a lectern or elaborate music-stand with a sloping top in the equatorial plane, usually with a star on top. These dials (also known as Masonic sundials) were said by Thomas Ross to be based on the form of Petrus Apianus[9] of Ingolstadt's *Torquetum*, an instrument invented in the sixteenth

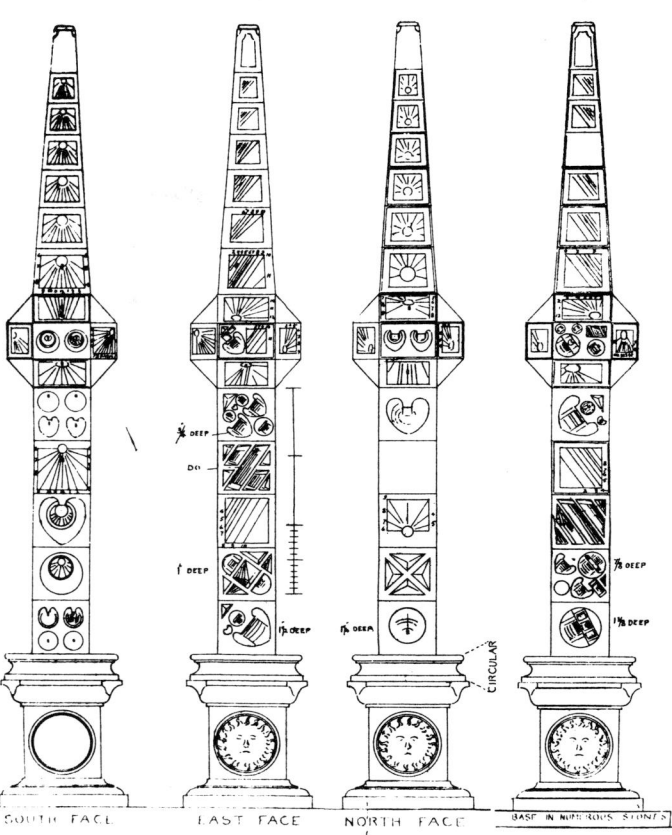

Pl.IV.1 Seventeenth-century obelisk-sundial from Mount Stuart, Bute, from MacGibbon & Ross **v** (1892) 416 (*Collection JSC*).

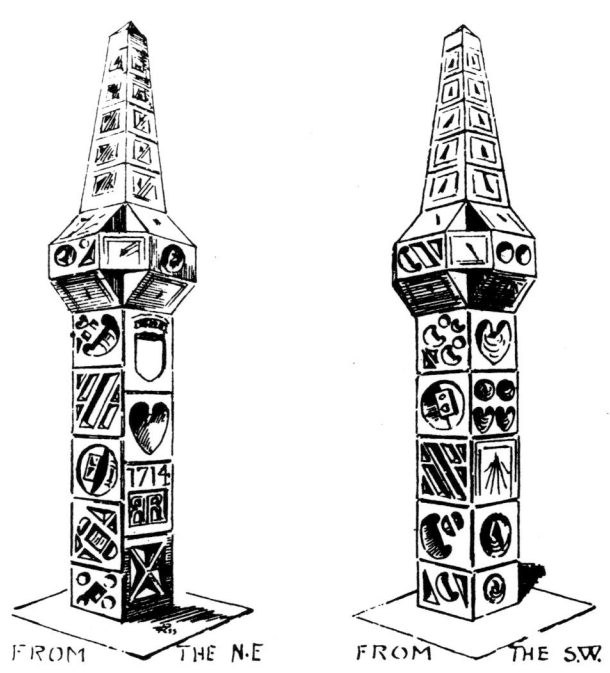

Pl.IV.2 Obelisk-sundial at Tongue, Sutherland, probably of 1714, from MacGibbon & Ross **v** (1892) 423 (*Collection JSC*).

---

7 But *see* Cooper (2006) 156, 173, 213, 223-5, 227-5, 247-9.
8 MacGibbon & Ross (1892) **v** 357-514. *See* also Gatty & Lloyd (Eds.) (1900) *passim*.
9 Born Peter Bienewitz *or* Bennewitz, and *called* Peter Apian. *See* Apian (1533). I am grateful to Professor Gerard L'E. Turner for discussing various Renaissance scientific instruments with me.

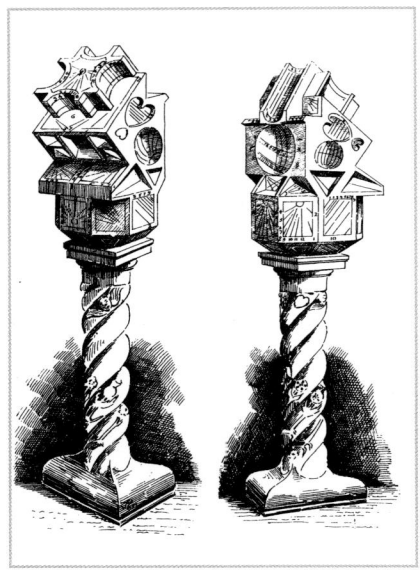

Pl.IV.3 *(far left)* Lectern-shaped sundial from Woodhouselee, near Penicuik, Midlothian. Such sundials have strong Masonic allusions, and are based on the *Torquetum*, an instrument invented in the sixteenth century by Peter Apian of Ingolstadt for calculating the position of the sun, moon, and stars. The *Torquetum* is the model for many lectern-shaped sundials found especially in Scotland. The idea of a petrified astronomical instrument is somewhat bizarre, but the sun-moon-stars imagery is strong in Freemasonry. Note also the spiral form of the pedestal: the spiral alludes to the Solomonic Temple. *See* Gatty & Lloyd (*Eds.*) (1900). From MacGibbon & Ross **v** (1892) 423 (*Collection JSC*).

Pl.IV.4 *(right)* Lectern-shaped sundial from Neidpath Castle, Peeblesshire. From MacGibbon & Ross **v** (1892) 426 (*Collection JSC*).

century for calculating the positions of the sun, moon, and stars. Apian's design was published in his *Book on Instruments* of 1533. This similarity must be regarded as superficial, however, as the *Torquetum* is mobile, unlike the massive, heavy lecterns of masonry. Good examples from Woodhouselee (Midlothian) (**Pl.IV.3**), and Neidpath Castle, near Peebles, Peeblesshire (**Pl.IV.4**), have been catalogued by a number of writers. At Lamancha House, near West Linton, Peeblesshire, an extraordinary lectern-sundial was placed on a capital in the form of a wicker-work basket filled with fruit; the basket resembles an Egyptian bell-capital, but it may also have allusions to the 'net-work' and 'pomegranates' of the 'chapters' of the Solomonic Temple (**Pl.IV.5**).

A further variant is the facet-headed dial, polyhedral or extremely irregular, set on a baluster that is usually spiral or twisted. This spiral form, as will be described below, has strong Masonic connotations, and is associated with the Solomonic Temple as well. One of the most complicated – so irregular that no two sections through it would be alike – was at Haddington, East Lothian (**Pl.IV.6**), and should be compared with the design in the Foundation of the Royal Order print (*see* **Pl.III.2**, p.57). Sundials were created in a huge variety of shapes and sizes: that from Newbattle Abbey, Midlothian (*c.*mid-seventeenth century) combines winged sphinx-like figures, grotesque faces with protruding tongues as scrolls, and a crowning obelisk set above an octagonal structure on which are dials, coroneted initials of the Lothian family, Arms, and a Crest (**Pl.IV.7**).

Why were such extraordinary and complex objects created in such numbers in a land not renowned for its clear skies? The Architect/mathematician/astronomer/diallist derives from Renaissance Vitruvian ideals, and it is probable that working Masons designed these sundials both to show off their practical skills as craftsmen, and to suggest their acquaintance with the higher learning and their Craft's guardianship of complex truths, knowledge,

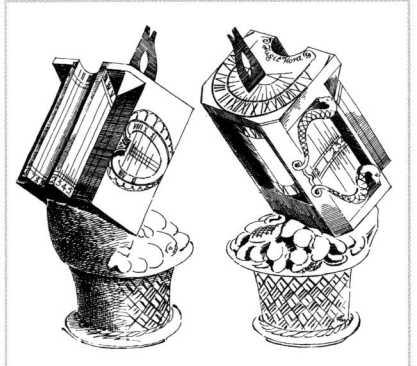

Pl.IV.5 *(left)* Lectern-shaped sundial (*c.*1700) from Lamancha House, near West Linton, Peeblesshire. From MacGibbon & Ross **v** (1892) 430 (*Collection JSC*).

Pl. IV.6 *(right)* Multi-faceted dial from Haddington, East Lothian. Note the spiral form of the pedestal. From MacGibbon & Ross **v** (1892) 466 (*Collection JSC*).

sciences, and mysteries. The connection between the Craft, the Heavens, the Earth, the Firmament, and the way in which advanced ideas, knowledge of complex instruments, and enlightenment were communicated to craftsmen, embraces a vast series of notions of cooperation, fellowship, mystical and scientific themes, and the importance of the Master-mason-cum-Architect as a Renaissance *Uomo Universale*[10]. It also underscores the intellectual/mystical/higher learning/and arcane aspects of 'Operative' Masonry which persons who were *not* Stonemasons found intriguing: the fact that designers, who also realised their designs with their own hands (sometimes with the assistance of others less skilled *as designers*), were versed in uncommon matters concerning Geometry, Mathematics, Astronomy, and so on, had a profound attraction for those seeking Knowledge and the

---

10 MacGibbon & Ross **v** (1887-92) 357-512. Stevenson (1988*b*) 113-8. *See* also Somerville (1987, 1994).

Pl.IV.7 Sundial from Newbattle Abbey, Midlothian (*c.* mid-seventeenth century) (MC. C080708).

Key to Understanding of many phenomena. The *practical* side of *Operative* Masonry, however, must be emphasised.

Yet the whole idea of a petrified astronomical instrument is itself bizarre, but can make more sense if seen in the light of Schaw's activities, those of Dickson, and other matters discussed above. When the Calvinist ethic of abhorring decoration and demanding a function for it is considered, this may also have contributed to the genesis of these strange objects. There seems to be little doubt that the sundials had a far greater significance than the merely functional one of telling the time, for in their complexity and multiplicity of facets and dials they suggest a welding together of a variety of forms and shapes symbolically implying the healing of the schisms in Christendom, and encapsulating the desire for an all-embracing and benevolent enlightenment that could repair the disasters of religious difference, superstition, intolerance, and cruelty. Needles, hearts, and stars which feature in so many sundials suggest not only the influence of the stars on the fate of Man, but Masonic and Marian imagery. The compass needle, for example, has associations with the Stella Maris, and hence is both Marian and Isiac.

David Stevenson, in his study of Scottish Freemasonry of 1988 cited in the footnotes and bibliography of this book, sheds new light on Schaw and others, identifies these sundials as demonstrating connections between Masons, mathematicians, astronomers, and ideas, and places events in Scotland firmly in the forefront of Masonic history. His book is indispensable, for he develops various themes previously discussed by Frances Yates, and takes those firmly within a Masonic milieu. Significantly, although sundials ceased to be fashionable in Scotland around 1750, it is precisely from that period that elaborate dials became popular on the European Continent: it was then that Continental Freemasonry developed and became widespread. That such sundials are Masonic cannot be doubted, for they recur in numbers in The Netherlands and in Central Europe during the phenomenal rise of Freemasonry in the Age of the Enlightenment. Some spectacular sundials have been recorded in Alsace and in Hungary. R. R. J. Rohr[11], E. Zinner[12], and others have noted many examples.

England, Scotland, Jacobites, and Hanoverians

So in England and in Scotland, in the late sixteenth century, a Craft mythology and initiation ceremonies, inherited or adapted from the Middle Ages, evolved, responding to the religious climate of the time. Records of The Masons' Company of London from 1619 contain references to the 'making' of Masons and to Masons being 'accepted', and there is also mention of meetings about 'acception' and the holding of 'acception dinners'[13]: there are also, as has been noted above, remarks about men who were members of the Company being 'accepted' or 'made' Masons by being initiated into a group *within* the Company[14]. Admission to the Acception was recorded in 1619-20, 1630-1, 1638-9, 1645-6, 1646-7, 1649-50, 1663-4, and there were probably other instances, but the records are incomplete[15]. So initiations to an organisation were carried out *within* a Livery Company in London, but in Edinburgh, the Lodge concerned with initiations into secrets existed *parallel* to the Incorporation or Guild, and was apparently separate from it. In Scotland Masons who were Masters of a Guild were able to join a Lodge, as were Apprentices and Journeymen, but in London only a minority of members of the Company could be 'accepted' or 'made'[16], which suggests some kind of Higher Learning, or a more illustrious status *within* the organisation.

According to Robert Plot, the custom of admitting men into the 'Society of Free-Masons' was widespread by 1686[17], and involved admission, secret signs, presentation of gloves, and a collation. Fellows of the 'Society' were called 'Accepted Masons'[18]. John Aubrey, in his *Natural History of Wiltshire*, written 1656-91, but not published until 1847[19], referred to the 'Fraternity of adopted-Masons' and

---

11 Rohr (1971, 1986).
12 Zinner (1964) *passim*.
13 *See* Conder (1894) for these matters.
14 *Ibid. See* also *Ars Quatuor Coronatorum* **ix** (1896) 29-37 and Knoop & Jones (1948) 146-7.
15 Knoop & Jones (1948) 147.
16 Stevenson (1988*b*) 218.
17 Plot (1686) §§ 85-86.
18 *See* Baxter (1908) for a transcript.
19 Aubrey (1847), and *see* Knoop, Jones, & Hamer (*Eds.*) (1945) 41-2.

described how Masons (the manner of whose Adoption was 'very formall') were known to each other by 'Signes and Watch-words'. Aubrey was followed by Richard Rawlinson in his memoir of Elias Ashmole printed in the Introduction to Ashmole's *Antiquities of Berkshire* (1719)[20], and in all three sources the possibility of friendly benefits being made available to relieve distressed members is mentioned: this *may* also have been a *factor* in attracting persons to seek admission to the Craft, but it clearly was not the only one. Ashmole, as previously noted, was admitted as a non-'Operative' Mason in 1646 in Warrington, but Nicholas Stone (the Sculptor and Architect, who was Warden of The Masons' Company in 1627 and 1630, and served as Master in 1633-4) was admitted to the Acception in 1638-9, and, in terms of widely-accepted definition, was clearly an 'Operative' Mason.

Those who cannot grasp how gifted and intelligent men could have become involved in esoteric matters should not regard their beliefs or searchings as 'mistaken'[21]. Christopher Wren, for example, following his father's[22] example, was devoted to the élite Fraternity of the Order of the Garter, and in 1691 is said to have become a member of a Fraternity of Accepted Masons, probably at the *Goose and Gridiron* Tavern in St Paul's Churchyard[23]: this, probably, was the beginning of the Lodge of Antiquity No. 2, where, in 1717, the first Annual Assembly of Grand Lodge was held, when four London Lodges amalgamated. However, claims that Wren had become a Freemason derive not only from an Addendum to Aubrey's *Wiltshire* on the manuscript[24]. We know that Sir Robert Moray, Wren's earliest Court Patron after 1660, was a Freemason, and he may have aroused the great man's interest in the more arcane side of the Craft: furthermore, there is a letter from Wren to David Gregory at Oxford[25] advising him on repairs to the Bodleian Library and the Divinity Schools, dated July 1700, in which reference is made to 'Brother Wallis'[26]. This has been interpreted to mean that all three men were Freemasons[27], but Wren could have been using 'Brother' in a jocular way as all three men were Fellows of the Royal Society. But, as they were interested in Geometry, they *could* all have been Freemasons. Wren was supposed to be Master of his Lodge for the second time in 1710, and to have held that position until 1716: the amalgamation was said to have occurred because the Master of one of the Lodges had become very ancient and infirm, and the new Grand Master of the composite Lodge would be drawn from each of the original Lodges in rotation. The ancient Master may have been Wren[28], but this connection between the Craft and Wren is by no means proved beyond all doubt[29]. Nevertheless, given the claims of the Craft and its attractions for those seeking illumination and knowledge of Ancient Wisdom, it is beyond dispute that many intellectuals of the seventeenth and eighteenth century *were* initiated.

Some commentators hold that 'Free and Accepted or speculative Masonry had its origins in England'[30], but others have been convinced it began in Scotland[31]. A useful summary of the two cases has been provided by Jan Snoek[32], but, as the arguments for and against would fill (and have done so) several books, there is no place for a comprehensive rehearsal of them here. Having read widely and waded through some turgid stuff, some sort of synoptic view can be offered, however. The key to the whole thing would seem to lie in the huge changes that came about as a result of the Calvinistic 'Reformation' in Scotland and the Break with Rome and subsequent destruction of traditional religious practices in England. Towards the end of the sixteenth century in Scotland some sort of rudimentary rituals were evolved in Lodges, perhaps in an attempt to replace lost religious observance with something else that nevertheless was solemn and food for thought (but could not attract the opprobrium of the Reformed Church of Scotland). In 1598-9, influenced by Schaw, who had powerful Royal and aristocratic connections, Lodges were organised on a national basis, with initiation rites into the 'Degree' of Fellow Craft or Master Mason during which secrets were communicated. This ritual had a necromantic character[33], and also included the presentation of gloves, a banquet (paid for by the candidate), and the passing on of the Mason Word (about which more later), together with a Grip, the words 'Jachin' and 'Boaz', and the Five Points of Fellowship.

In England before 1646 a ritual was evolved for the 'making' or 'accepting' of a Mason, and the meetings were referred to as Lodges, presided over by Wardens. The ritual seems to have been accompanied by an opening prayer, presentation of gloves, a meal (again paid for by the candidate), the reading of the 'Old Charges', the taking of an oath, the communication of secret signs and words, and a closing prayer. It appears that some Lodges were formed within existing organisations, and that there was a Lodge of elite members of The Worshipful Company of Masons of the City of London to which persons such as Nicholas Stone belonged.

At some period in the latter part of the seventeenth century rituals were created in Scotland for the 'Degree' of Entered Apprentice, and this 'Degree' was derived

---

20 Ashmole (1719).
21 Jardine (2002) xvi.
22 Christopher Wren (1589-1658), Dean of Windsor.
23 This has often been described as having taken place in St Paul's Church (i.e. Cathedral), but this seems unlikely.
24 Jardine (2002) 468. *See* also Archives of the Royal Society Misc. MS. 92, f.277, and *Ars Quatuor Coronatorum* **xi** (1898) facsimile opposite p.10.
25 Gregory was a Scot, a Mathematician, and an Astronomer, who became a Fellow of the Royal Society in 1692. His *A Treatise of Practical Geometry* was not published until 1745, and a ninth edition came out in 1780.
26 John Wallis, Geometrician and Mathematician, a founder-member of the Royal Society.
27 Jardine (2002) 469.

28 *Ibid*. 470.
29 *See* Castells (1917) for this thorny matter.
30 Hamill (1986) 27. Hamill (1994) 31 repeats this statement.
31 Stevenson (1988a and b).
32 Scanlan (*Ed.*) (2002) 1-19.
33 Necromancy, as noted previously, was the art of gaining knowledge from the dead, or from dead bodies.

from that for the Fellow Craft or Master's Degree. It, too, had a necromantic character. During the last quarter of the seventeenth and the first quarter of the eighteenth century the English rituals for the 'making' of a Mason and for the Scots Entered Apprentice somehow melded, and the Scots ritual for the Fellow Craft/Master Mason was taken on in England. Thus two 'Degrees' existed. For the Entered Apprentice prayers, the presentation of gloves, and an apron, the reading of the 'Old Charges', the taking of an oath, the communication of secrets, a meal, the rehearsing of the 'catechism', and a closing prayer seemed to have formed the basis of the ritual. For the higher 'Degree' there was a rehearsal, a meal, a prayer, an oath-taking, communication of secrets (including the Five Points of Fellowship), rehearsal of the 'catechism', and a closing prayer. Around 1700, a new 'Degree' was created in Scotland, which included the 'Master's Word', and soon after 'Jachin' and 'Boaz' became associated with the 'Degree' of Entered Apprentice.

In or about 1725 in London the essence of the 'Degree' of Entered Apprentice was divided: one part became the new Entered Apprentice 'Degree', and the other the 'Degree' of Fellow Craft. The former 'Degree' of Fellow Craft or Master Mason became that of Master Mason. 'Jachin' and 'Boaz' were associated with the first two 'Degrees', a system known as the Moderns. In 1751 in London, Masons initiated in Ireland according to the Scots tradition created a new Grand Lodge calling itself 'Antients', and in 1816 the United Grand Lodge of England adopted a revised ritual, largely 'Antient', but with variations. Certain Lodges remained more or less laws unto themselves, and so there are often no clear coherent lines of development[34].

However, this is not a study of the arcane details of countless rituals and ceremonies: such an investigation would be of limited interest (except to Freemasons), and indeed would be tedious to excess. The most significant aspects will be abstracted. Freemasonry and its development *cannot* be considered without taking into account the Reformation (in its various manifestations), the Roman Catholic elements at work in Scotland in the 1590s, the Union of the Crowns in 1603, the *Act of Union* in 1707[35], the Accession of Georg Ludwig, *Kurfürst* (Prince-Elector) of Hanover from 1698, as King George I of Great Britain and Ireland in 1714 on the death of Queen Anne, the 1715 Jacobite Rebellion in support of the exiled House of Stuart[36], the rather more serious Jacobite Rebellion of 1745-6 led by Charles Edward Louis John Casimir Silvester Severino Maria Stuart (styled King Charles III from 1766), and the French Revolutionary and Napoleonic Wars.

Thus the Revolution that was the Reformation not only altered features once familiar in Mediaeval life, such as observances by Guilds and Fraternities during religious festivals, but created a void in which new forms of ceremony and ritual could be developed in the secrecy of meetings such as the Lodges. The enormous impact of the English Revolution of the 1640s and 1650s clearly left ideas of Republicanism and Radicalism that had a considerable effect throughout the eighteenth century, especially through The Netherlands. The Scientific Revolution that began with Nicolaus Koppernigk (Copernicus) had reached new heights with the publication (1687) of Newton's *Philosophiae Naturalis Principia Mathematica*[37], a work that had the profoundest effects on the Enlightenment, and especially on the French *philosophes*. Radicals of the eighteenth century learned from the Newtonian Revolution a new reverence for Nature, but the move to disengage the clergy and established Churches from Government that had begun with the English Revolution soon became a part of Continental radicalism[38]. Although there was an undercurrent of English Republicanism in the eighteenth century, many shied away from this (with memories of the Commonwealth): Newton[39] and Boyle[40], for example, chose a liberal and moderate undogmatic type of Christianity in preference to the radicalism of the Puritan sectaries.

Freemasonry in England, firmly associated with Whiggery from 1717, provided a social institution that could promote cultural, political, and undogmatic notions. Members of the Craft would acknowledge the God of the new science, the Great Architect, who was no longer a figure of rage, vengeance, and wrath, but the embodiment of Order, Measurement, and Stability: the Great Architect was a Creator, benevolent, truthful, full of grave wisdom, and part of the natural order of things.

During the early part of the eighteenth century organised Freemasonry became widespread in both the British Isles and on the Continent. This spread is closely connected with the rise of the Whig oligarchy and with the growth of British economic and military power. Freemasonry was fashionable in The Netherlands and in the Holy Roman Empire (notably in Austria), which is not surprising, for both were allies of Britain in the power-struggle with France, and both were aware of British prosperity, of the remarkable constitutional structure, and of the new stability in Britain that came after the Act of Settlement of 1701[41]. That Freemasonry was intensely political can hardly be doubted. The Craft may have been brought to Vienna in the wake of Prince Eugen[42] of Savoy, the great military commander and ally of Britain, who had many Freemasons in his entourage[43]. The Duke of Lorraine, Francis Stephen, later (1745) to become

---

34 Scanlan (*Ed.*) (2002) 17-18.
35 6 Ann. *c.*11 and 40 (England) and Anne *c.*7 (Scotland).
36 In the person of James Francis Edward Stuart (styled James VIII and III by his supporters), the Roman Catholic claimant to the three Thrones.
37 Newton (1687).
38 Jacob (1981, 1991).
39 Sir Isaac Newton.
40 Robert Boyle, natural philosopher.
41 12 & 13 Will. III *c.* 2.
42 François Eugène, or Franz Eugen, Prince of Savoy, who gained singular success against the French, and who decisively defeated Turkish forces, thereby greatly weakening Ottoman power in Europe and raising Austria to the position of a great European power.
43 Jacob (1981) *passim*.

Holy Roman Emperor[44], was initiated as a Freemason at the Ambassadorial Residence in The Hague of Philip Stanhope[45], 4th Earl of Chesterfield (from 1726) by none other than Desaguliers, and in the following year (1731) was raised as a Master Mason at Houghton Hall, Norfolk, the seat of Sir Robert Walpole, Prime Minister from 1721 to 1742[46]. At the same time as Franz's Coronation in 1745, it seems that a Freemasonic ceremony was held at Frankfurt-am-Main at which various dignitaries from The Netherlands were initiated[47]. That no less a personage than the 'Roman Emperor' himself had been initiated as a Freemason says much about the pervasiveness of the Craft during the eighteenth century.

In England during the eighteenth century Freemasonry was approximately Protestant, and was not seen as posing any threat to the Established Church or to the State: on the contrary, it tended to support both. Yet on the Continent Freemasonry was often denounced as subversive, especially where the Roman Catholic Church was concerned, and it was also perceived as Republican and Radical. The reasons for this are clear: Freemasonry on the Continent tended to be supported by those of a liberal bent who admired England and English institutions, who revered Newton and his philosophies, and who abhorred Absolutism and the clerical and intellectual stranglehold of the old régimes. It was this precise connection with Protestantism and with anti-Absolutism (spelling a threat to both Church and Divinely-Ordained Monarchy) that condemned Continental Freemasonry in the eyes of the Church.

Freemasonry claimed links with the mysteries of Antiquity, but it clearly was also a link with Renaissance Hermeticism, Newtonian Science, and the Guilds of the past. With its aprons, tools, and other emblems, it evoked a world of the noble craftsman, the dignity of labour, and the creation of inspired Architecture. It also broke down social barriers, for within the Lodge the aristocrat hob-nobbed with non-aristocrats, and if aprons and tools were anything to go by, he would soon be rubbing shoulders with artisans in the confines of the Lodge. An easy socialising that had been a feature of English custom thus spread to the Continent, and threatened the rigid stratification of society. In fact, Freemasonry portended a social revolution of Continental import. Thus Freemasonry on the Continent began to be seen as subversive, quite unlike its parent organisation. Sundials in The Netherlands and in Central Europe would appear to be a memorial to the spread of British Freemasonry among her Continental allies in the military struggles with France, the epitome of Absolutist Monarchy.

Masonic imagery is varied, catholic, and curious. It is worth reflecting on how much of the above affected the design of Masonic Lodges, for many Lodges met in buildings used for other purposes. To some extent, therefore, Freemasons had to set up their emblems and images in rooms acquired for meetings and so the décor was of a temporary nature, indicating perhaps a Lodge of the imagination, with objects and signs placed in certain positions as an aid to remembering rituals, secrets, and the Mason Word. Lodges, in a sense, therefore, were places where the Hermetic Art of Memory could be practised. It is also clear from Masonic rituals and catechisms that there was an Ideal Lodge, a symbolic building, that Freemasons shared in imagination. Seventeenth-century meetings in hired rooms involved the markings of plans of this imaginary Lodge on floors, and there also seem to have been cloths marked with positions which were laid for specific ceremonies. Lodges of the mind contained the grave of the Master Hiram in a trough under the west window looking to the east, and this grave contained a secret or a potential substitute secret.

We have looked at the impact of the Reformation, at the Roman Catholic elements that appear to have been involved in Schaw's attempts at reform, and at the St Clair Charters, but the importation of aspects of what was to become Freemasonry into England with the Court of King James VI and I must have been significant, and the connection between the Roman Catholic Queen Anne (James's Consort) and figures such as Inigo Jones deserves greater scrutiny.

Despite the evidence, some writers have difficulty in accepting that 'Speculative' Freemasonry evolved from the 'Operative' Lodges at all, but consider that it developed only because groups of men sought esoteric knowledge of Antiquity and Enlightenment derived from so-called 'Hermetic' Wisdom (which we know was not all that ancient). As Freemasonry grandly claims to guard knowledge passed down from the times recorded in *Genesis* via Ancient Egypt, those who sought the eternal truths of lost mysteries gravitated towards the Craft. As noted, Ashmole (a figure of some stature) was initiated in 1646, and in 1682 he attended a meeting of a Lodge at Masons' Hall at which several people were admitted into the Fellowship of the Free Masons[48]. Numerous sources suggest that Antiquarians, Scientists, and other Gentlemen possessing curiosity about the world they inhabited, became Freemasons in the 'Accepted' sense during the course of the seventeenth and early eighteenth centuries, and that several Societies and Fraternities of Freemasons came into existence. However, as has been explained above, 'Accepted' seems to have meant an upper echelon of 'Operative' Masonry at one time, and was not something set apart from practical stonemasonry. In all this hunger for knowledge, the hiatus of the Civil War, the joyless Puritan 'Commonwealth' (when even Maypoles and Christmas festivities were frowned upon), and the disruption of so much (not least

---

44 Kaiser Franz I, Roman Emperor from 1745, and Grand Duke of Tuscany, married in 1736 Archduchess Maria Theresia, daughter of Charles VI, who became Queen of Hungary and Bohemia on her father's death in 1740. On the death (1745) of the Elector of Bavaria (who claimed the Empire as Charles VII), Francis Stephen was elected Emperor.

45 Freemason, initiatied 1721 at Stationers' Hall. See Scanlan (*Ed.*) (2002) 38; Surtees (1817-92) **lxxiii** 64.

46 Scanlan (*Ed.*) (2002) 38. See also Anderson (*Ed.*) (1738) 129; Gotch (1991) 20-1; Pick & Knight (1983) 127; Frere (*Ed.*) (1967) 268.

47 Jacob (1981) 111 quoting Grand Lodge of The Netherlands MS. Kl. 1062.

48 Knoop, Jones, & Hamer (*Eds.*) (1945) 40-41 and Knoop & Jones (1948) 15.

in terms of religion), must have been catalysts. A huge upsurge of interest in scientific and cultural matters occurred with the Restoration of the Monarchy in 1660, and this coincided with much activity associated with what was to become known as 'Speculative Freemasonry'.

The brief reign of James II and VII (and the 'Glorious Revolution' leading to the reigns of William and Mary, William III, and Anne (during which the *political* Union of England and Scotland occurred) prompted further changes that were soon to be of considerable importance. It was the accession of George I in 1714 which seems to have had an immense impact on the development of Freemasonry, for in 1715, as noted above, there was a Jacobite Rebellion. Grand Lodge was formed in 1717, and in 1723 Anderson's *Constitutions*[49] appeared. Now Anderson was a Scot, a Presbyterian Minister, and a Freemason, and Scots influences on the Craft were obvious (*pace* Hamill *et al.*) as it spread throughout England in the early eighteenth century. Anderson's work undoubtedly helped English Masons to acquire an elaborate mythological history in addition to that they already possessed in the 'Old Charges'. As Stevenson pointed out, the 'compilation of the two works which were to prove so influential in forming' eighteenth-century Freemasonry, 'the *Constitutions* of 1723 and 1738[50], was entrusted primarily to a Scot', so this must be 'surely itself significant'[51]. Also 'significant' is the fact that twelve of the Grand Masters of England in the eighteenth century were Scots[52], and that when French Freemasons 'invented many higher degrees and rituals they felt the best way to give them legitimacy was to call them the "*Rite écossais*"'[53].

All this would seem *very* odd, for Scots were not exactly flavour of the month in eighteenth-century England, for various reasons. First of all, the *Act of Union* gave Scots influence in English affairs that was resented[54], and revived memories of William III's honouring of Dutchmen and James VI and I's support for his Scots courtiers. The 1715 Rebellion had not endeared Caledonia to the English either (matters were to be exacerbated in 1745-6 when the Jacobite army [which would have looked very foreign, rough, and uncouth to English eyes] invaded England and got as far South as Derby). Furthermore, even after the 1707 *Act of Union*, Scotland was closer to France than to England, and not only because of the executions of Mary, Queen of Scots (1587) and Charles I (1649). Even the Restoration of Charles II, who had been exiled in France, and the presence of Stuarts resident first in France and then in Rome, led a considerable number of Scots to have divided loyalties, despite the Stuart connections of William III and the Hanoverians[55]. And the English could not forget the potential menace of Mary, Queen of Scots, and the support given to her by the Roman Catholic powers, especially Spain.

Anderson's imaginative compilations were mostly about creating a mythology, peopling past centuries with Freemasons, and even giving English Freemasonry more than its fair share of Royal and noble connections. If he had produced a mythology in which Scots predominated, English Freemasonry would never have accepted it, for Scots were sometimes despised and even feared. There is something else in all this that needs to be understood. Much that was to become Freemasonry had come South with the Scots Court, and through Scots connections: Roman Catholicism had been embedded within it, and it was associated with the House of Stuart and with pre-Reformation organisations. It had to be cleansed of any whiff of Jacobite sympathies (especially after 1715-16 and 1745-6), and so required some sort of publications that would give it respectability and an acceptable 'history' to place it above suspicion, firmly in the Hanoverian camp, but it was also steeped in *tradition*, and so represented continuity, legitimacy, and historical links with the past, and even with a pre-Reformation past at that.

So, following the formation of Grand Lodge in 1717 in London, Freemasonry enjoyed a remarkable growth, and not only in the British Isles. It was exported to the Low Countries, France, Spain, Russia, and even India in the 1720s, and a decade later there were Lodges in the German Lands, Italy, Portugal, and Sweden. In this spread, there were changes of emphases, for in France (at least at the beginning), Freemasonry seems to have drawn its membership from the aristocracy. In Britain, however, Freemasonry (like other societies which evolved during the eighteenth century) was largely convivial: one reads of 'Free Masons and other Learned Men, that used to get drunk'[56] in the English translation of a French tome by Albert-Henri de Sallengre in praise of drunkenness[57], and it appears that the Brotherhood of the Craft was often in its Cups during the Georgian Age. This does not mean, of course, that Freemasons were more given to Bacchic excess than were other Societies and Fraternities of the period, for most convivial gatherings of the time seem to have drunk deep, and indeed it was a national tendency to drink so heavily that visitors from Continental countries could hardly fail to notice the fact. One might observe that little has changed in that respect. It was not only obeisance to Bacchus that engaged the Freemasons of Georgian Britain, however, for lectures on Architecture and Geometry were often given at Lodge meetings (and the importance of Geometry as a source of knowledge must be stressed). However, there exist in Freemasonic collections numerous cautions against the imbibing of excess alcohol, and these can be found in literally hundreds of pamphlets, booklets, speeches, and books, far too many to be listed here.

---

49 Anderson (*Ed.*) (1723).
50 Anderson (*Ed.*) (1738).
51 Stevenson (1988b) 231.
52 Frere (*Ed.*) (1967) 265-75.
53 Stevenson (1988b) 231.
54 A less vocal resentment could be detected from 1997 when the 'New Labour' Governments of Blair and Brown had a strong Scots representation that was not to everyone's taste.
55 *See* Scanlan (*Ed.*) (2002) 25 on these matters.

56 *See* Knoop, Jones, & Hamer (*Eds.*) (1945) 108.
57 *See* Sallengre (1723), published by the irrepressible Edmund Curll (1682/3-1747), who rarely missed a trick when it came to bringing out diverting books. *See* Curl (2008).

So Freemasonry in England, as promoted by Grand Lodge from 1717, seems to have been committed to the Hanoverian (and therefore Whig) cause, and promoted 'latitudinarian ideals of tolerance'[58]: it also had a tendency to Deism[59] and Natural Religion[60]. Freemasonry attracted intellectuals interested in the new sciences: this was the period when the hero of the Enlightenment, Isaac Newton, was advocating Empiricism, and his many discourses were transforming Mathematical Optics and Mechanics. However, Newton was also interested in Alchemy, and assembled a huge library dealing with the subject: he also concerned himself with Theology, and his prodigious reading read himself out of orthodoxy, rejecting Trinitarianism and much else. These facts, and Newton's growing involvement in the interpretation of prophecies, may shock, but they were not unusual among intellectuals of the time. His Arianism[61] nearly cost him his academic career at Cambridge, and his resistance to James II and VII's attempts to install a Roman Catholic majority in the University of Cambridge caused him to be called before the notorious George Jeffreys (1st Baron Jeffreys of Wem from 1685), which could also have been extremely awkward for him. Newton was elected President of the Royal Society in 1703, and in that capacity introduced J. T. Desaguliers (mentioned earlier) as an experimentalist to the Royal Society in 1713. Desaguliers became Curator in 1717, and in 1719 was elected Grand Master of the recently formed Grand Lodge.

Thus the Royal Society, Natural Philosophy, Freemasonry, the Court (for Desaguliers had preached before the King and was Chaplain to Frederick Lewis [Prince of Wales from 1729]: indeed Desaguliers[62] presided over the ceremonies in 1737 when the Prince himself was initiated as a Freemason, thereby beginning a long-standing connection between the House of Hanover [and later Saxe-Coburg-Gotha and Windsor] with the Craft), and the social and intellectual élites of the capital became linked. As M. D. J. Scanlan has observed, 'it was probably Desaguliers's enthusiasm' for the Craft 'that induced many members' of the scientific Establishment 'to seek membership' of a Lodge[63]. Between 1723 and 1730, eighty-nine of the first 250 Fellows of the Royal Society were Freemasons[64]. Many political figures also became members of the Craft[65].

So if we can accept that some sort of Order (albeit much of it myth and invention) was created by Anderson and Desaguliers out of the 'Old Gothic' Chaos, then we also must face up to the fact that much of their attempts to grant the Craft respectability and history must be regarded as curiously fanciful for persons of supposedly scientific and rational bent. When we find Lord Justice Gerald Fitzgibbon, the prominent Irish lawyer, who became a Freemason in 1876 (Trinity College Lodge), stating 'I am convinced that long before the transition from Operative to Speculative Masonry, probably for centuries, possibly even before the days of Solomon, the Craft existed as an organized Society or Guild'[66], we are not reading the deranged utterances of some batty Irishman, but a typical view propounded by innumerable Freemasons who had swallowed the sort of mythology produced by Anderson, Desaguliers, and very many others. Fitzgibbon may have been paraphrasing the opinions of Augustus Frederick Fitzgerald, 3rd Duke of Leinster (from 1804), Grand Master of Irish Freemasons (1813-74), but such opinions seem to have been (and are) widely held.

Thus, from the end of the seventeenth century, and especially from the beginning of the eighteenth, Freemasonry became the Craft or occupation of Freemasons: it enshrined the principles, practices, and institutions of Freemasons: it was a quasi-secret or tacit Brotherhood, capable of instructive sympathy. Freemasonry grew into a Brotherhood of men joined together through initiation-rites that were supposedly secret, the members of which recognised each other by covert methods of identification (such as hand-grips or signs), and which was organised in groups called Lodges. A Lodge came to mean the group of Freemasons comprising a branch of the Brotherhood; the place of meeting for members (whether it was a permanent building, or a suite of rooms set aside for such meetings, or a temporary marked-out space in a room); and the meeting itself.

Yet a connection between organisations of stonemasons in Mediaeval times and Freemasonry since c.1700 is often infuriatingly obscure, although modern scholarship has attempted to shed light in some extremely dusty corners. It is clear that there were many organisations of bodies of Masons for one reason or another: religious, professional, regulatory, and economic. Various *Corps de Métiers* and *Compagnonnages* existed in French-speaking parts; there were the *Steinmetzen* (literally stonemasons) in the German Lands; there were Guilds of stonemasons in Flanders and in the Free Cities of Europe; there were Architect-Mason Companies in Italy; there were Lodges and Incorporations of Masons in Scotland; and there were Assemblies, Craft-Guilds, and Companies in England[67].

The key to any attempt to understand this arcane world lies in a knowledge of the upheavals of organisation and observance caused by the Reformation (and it should be remembered that the Scottish Reformation was a very different affair from the English version), and the peculiar climate in which sundry attempts to rediscover lost

---

58 Scanlan (*Ed.*) (2002) 37.
59 Belief in a Supreme Being, but not through Revealed Religion: Deism rejected the supernatural Doctrines of Christianity.
60 Derived from Reason without Revelation: 'The Things knowable concerning God, and our Duty, by the Light of Nature are called natural Religion', as Isaac Watts defined it. See Watts (1725) ii v § 3. See Roberts (1972) 20-21.
61 Arius (fourth century), a Presbyter of Alexandria, who denied that Christ was of the same substance or essence with God.
62 Desaguliers became an Anglican Deacon in 1710 and Priest in 1717. In 1716 he was appointed Chaplain to James Brydges (1st Duke of Chandos from 1719), who proved to be a generous Patron. With Anderson, Desaguliers was instrumental in drawing up the *Constitutions*.
63 Scanlan (*Ed.*) (2002) 38.
64 *Ars Quatuor Coronatorum* **lxxx** (1967) 110-20.
65 Scanlan (*Ed.*) (2002) 38.
66 Edge (1912) 12-13.
67 Knoop & Jones (1948) *passim*.

knowledge were attempted, often with very odd results. We enter the strange world of 'Hermetic Wisdom', of the Magus, and of lost 'Egyptian' (and therefore doubly obscure, because very little was known of Egypt, even of hieroglyphs) knowledge. However, we should not regard Freemasonry as bunk, dismiss it as unworthy of notice, or try to avoid taking it into account. The fact is that far too many persons (who were definitely of considerable intellectual stature, or had clout in one way or another) were interested in the Craft, were Brethren, or took it seriously: this suggests that any attempt to justify ignoring it (as far too many have done) might be foolish.

Thus the next step will have to be to examine some important legends of the Craft and some artefacts that have survived. There is nothing to be gained by wading through the *minutiae* of Freemasonic lore: the Select Bibliography at the end of this book suggests further reading which should satisfy (and weary) the stoutest hearts.

The Two Pillars or Columns

Let us define our terms, because 'Masonic' writers (and others) frequently get 'column', 'pier', and 'pillar' hopelessly confused. A *pillar* is a *pila*, a plain, unmoulded, undecorated, detached solid structure, square or rectangular on plan, with no allusions to the Orders of Architecture whatsoever. It can also be a *pier*, as in the nave-arcade of a church, although this usage can be confusing, and some writers avoid it. A pillar is *not* a free-standing column, such as the Nelson so-called 'Pillar' in Trafalgar Square, London (1839-43), which is actually a *column* of the Corinthian Order set on a pedestal and supporting a statue of Admiral Lord Horatio Nelson[68] on top: it was designed by William Railton. So a *column* is a detached upright slender structural member, sometimes monolithic, usually circular on plan, but can also be polygonal or square on plan, normally carrying an entablature or lintel, but sometimes standing on its own. In the Classical Orders (*see* Select Glossary at the end of this book), a column consists of a base, shaft, and capital (except for the Greek Doric Order, which has no base), and the shaft tapers towards the top in a gentle curve called *entasis*. Columns are therefore distinct from piers and pillars.

A *pier* is a detached mass of construction, generally acting as a support, such as the solid part of a wall between two openings, or a massive element from which arches spring, as in a bridge. It can be a support, such as a pier in a repetitive nave-arcade varying from sturdy, oversized Romanesque examples to the lighter, taller, more slender, multi-moulded late-Gothic types. Piers are very much more massive than columns, and are not monoliths.[69]

The 'Two Pillars' play a significant part in early Masonic Legend in the manuscripts known as the 'Old Charges'[70]. They are *not* the same as the two *columns* that are frequently shown as the 'pillars' erected in the porch of Solomon's Temple, although the latter, by the familiar process of syncretism and association, became confused with the legendary 'pillars'. These 'Two Pillars' of Masonic Legend were supposed to be the medium by which secret knowledge was saved from destruction by Fire and Water[71]. The story can be found in the Hebrew *Apocrypha*, but appears to have had a Babylonian origin[72]: in this version a Babylonian priest had a premonition of a flood, and proceeded to work a history of the beginning, procedure, and end of all things on clay tablets, which were then baked hard in a fiery furnace. These tablets were buried in the City of the Sun at Sippara, and were the basis of knowledge upon which the rebuilding of Babylon was made possible[73]. In Hebraic versions Eve instructed Seth[74] and his siblings to record on tablets of stone and baked clay the words of the Archangel Michael when he brought the command to vacate the Garden of Eden: thus Eve's tablets would survive whether fire or flood destroyed the world[75]. Later versions of this granted Adam the credit for prophecy: the tablets were transformed into 'pillars' on which were carved the discoveries made by the descendants of Adam and Eve[76]. The idea goes back to the beginning of things, and to a lost Paradise itself (it should be noted, furthermore, in the light of what follows in a subsequent Chapter, that the Lost Paradise was a *Garden*). Later, we are told that astronomical discoveries made by Seth were recorded on the 'pillars', and in even later versions only music was carved by Jubal on them (which by then consisted of one marble 'pillar' and one of brick[77]). Such legends display a curious (or even wilful) ignorance of the nature of marble (which would become quicklime if burned, and eroded if subjected to the action of water), and of a brick 'pillar' (which might survive a fire, but hardly a flood). Then there is another version in which Lamech's children carved information that would be of practical use to Mankind. Other sources then came up with the proposition that Zoroaster (Zarathustra) caused the entire canon of Seven Liberal Arts to be cut into fourteen pillars (which wobble into the category of column): seven were of brass and seven of brick, and these monuments were

---

68 He was created Baron Nelson of the Nile and of Burnham Thorpe in 1798, Viscount Nelson of the Nile and of Burnham Thorpe in 1801, and Duke of Bronté in Sicily from 1799. In recent years, as 'education' becomes more and more corrupted, facts are no longer regarded as 'relevant'. The monument is now thought to commemorate Nelson Rolihlahla Mandela (1918-), especially by 'schoolteachers' showing their charges the sights of London: I have actually heard a female 'teacher' make that absurd claim in Trafalgar Square, and was denounced abusively when I had the temerity to correct her.

69 For definitions of architectural terms, *see* Curl (2006a).
70 Knoop & Jones (1948) 67.
71 *Ibid*. It is strange how the 'Two Pillars' of Masonic Legend were displaced in the Craft by the two 'Pillars' of King Solomon's Temple, although the originals do still figure in at least one quite ancient Freemasonic Order (my thanks to T. O. Haunch for this).
72 *Ibid*.
73 Smith (1876) 43.
74 The third son of Adam, and father of Enos (*see* Smith [*Ed*.] [1863] **iii** 1218): he is not to be confused with the Egyptian Seth (*see* Curl [2005] 462).
75 Charles (*Ed*.) (1913) **ii** 152.
76 Knoop & Jones (1948) 68.
77 Gaster (*Ed*.) (1899) 50.

constructed to preserve knowledge from the outcome of a vengeful God[78]. The 'pillars' inscribed by Jubal and Zoroaster are recorded in *The Chronicles of Jerameel*[79], and the Lamech and Zoroastrian legends were mentioned in the twelfth-century *Historia Scholastica* of Comestor[80].

Later Mediaeval versions made fanciful claims that after the Flood two 'pillars' were found, one by Pythagoras and the other by our old friend Hermes Trismegistus who, between them, passed on the secret knowledge they had acquired[81]. However, the alleged authority for this, the *Polychronicon* of Ranulf Higden, failed to mention it, and another important early history, the *Polycraticus* of John of Salisbury, Bishop of Chartres, was silent on the matter[82]. The *Cooke MS* does indeed contain the prophecy of Fire and Flood, and records the work of the children of Lamech in preserving the Seven Liberal Arts which were carved on seven 'pillars'. The Pythagoras/Hermes invention in the *Cooke MS* is repeated again and again[83], and from *Cooke* we gather one 'pillar' was of marble, and the other of *lacerus* (a misreading of *lateres*, signifying burnt or baked clay). The compiler of the manuscript informs us that marble was used because it will not burn: every Mason who used mortar would know that marble, if burned, produces quicklime, so perhaps the scribe was a Cowan. He also tells us that 'lacerus' was used to make the other 'pillar' to prevent it from sinking, but this, like much else, is clearly nonsense.

Thus the 'pillars' in the 'Old Charges' represent a variant on the widespread notion of preserving (and searching for) knowledge from the past, and may have had Babylonian origins. The early introduction of threats by Fire and Water should be noted, for, as we will see, these play an important part in many significant eighteenth-century works, including those by the Abbé Jean Terrasson, Jean-Jacques Lequeu, and Emanuel Schikaneder.

Somewhere and at some time, these 'pillars' began to merge with the 'pillars' of the Solomonic Temple in Masonic legend. The latter were free-standing, and stood on either side of the entrance to the Temple: this was a usual feature of temples of the period (e.g. the Syrian temple at Tell Tayinat[84] [tenth century BC]), and it was also common that they should be given personal names. The Solomonic 'pillars' were described as follows:

'And king Solomon sent and fetched Hiram out of Tyre.
 He *was* a widow's son of the tribe of Naphtali,
 and his father *was* a man of Tyre, a worker in brass:
 and he was filled with wisdom, and understanding,
 and cunning to work all works in brass.

And he came to king Solomon, and wrought all his work.
 For he cast two pillars of brass,
of eighteen cubits[85] high apiece:
and a line of twelve cubits did compass
either of them about.
 And he made two chapiters[86] *of* molten brass,
to set upon the tops of the pillars:
the height of one chapiter *was* five cubits,
and the height of the other chapiter *was* five cubits:
 And nets of checker work, and wreaths of chain work,
for the chapiters which *were* upon the top of the pillars;
seven for the one chapiter, and seven for the other chapiter.
 And he made the pillars, and two rows round about
upon the one net-work, to cover the chapiters
that *were* upon the top, with pomegranates:
and so did he for the other chapiter.
 And the chapiters that *were* upon the top of the pillars *were*
of lily work in the porch, four cubits.
 And the chapiters upon the two pillars *had* pomegranates
also above, over against the belly which *was* by the net-work:
and the pomegranates *were* two hundred in rows
round about upon the other chapiter.
 And he set up the pillars in the porch of the temple:
and he set up the right pillar, and called the name thereof
 Jachin: and he set up the left pillar, and called the name
 thereof Boaz.
 And upon the top of the pillars *was* lily work:
so was the work of the pillars finished.'[87]

The capitals, then, were very tall, if they were five and the 'pillars' eighteen Cubits high, so they must have looked extremely top-heavy. Tall capitals, however, occurred at Persepolis, in the 'Hall of the Hundred Columns' (sixth to fifth century BC), and there was plenty of decoration that could be described as 'lily-work' at that great complex, a fine example of Persian Architecture[88]. Even allowing for the notorious problems associated with deciphering architectural descriptions, the Biblical accounts do pose difficulties. More convincing is the account in *Chronicles*:

'…he made before the house two pillars of thirty and
five cubits high, and the chapiter that was on the top of
each of them was five cubits.'[89]

In *Chronicles* we also read that Solomon asked 'Huram, the king of Tyre' to send a man 'cunning to work in gold, and in silver, and in brass, and in iron, and in purple, and crimson, and blue, and that can skill to grave with the cunning men' he had at his disposal[90].

---

78 Gaster (*Ed.*) (1899) 70.
79 *Ibid. passim*.
80 Comestor (1987) xxxix.
81 Knoop & Jones (1948) 69 referring to the *Cooke MS*.
82 *See* Higden (1865-86) and John of Salisbury (1479-81).
83 *See* Knoop & Jones (1948) 69. For the Seven Liberal Arts *see* the scholarly paper by Mooney (1993) which deals with a Middle English text at Trinity College, Cambridge (MS R.14.52), dating from c.1458-85, and numbered 922 in M. R. James (1900-4): *The Western Manuscripts in the Library of Trinity College, Cambridge: A Descriptive Catalogue* (Cambridge: Cambridge University Press) ii 338-9. I am grateful to Andrew Prescott for drawing my attention to Linne Mooney's work.
84 *See* Hamblin & Seely (2007) 30 and *passim*.
85 An *Egyptian Cubit* was based upon the sixteen measures by which the Nile flooded when Isis wept for Osiris. There is a celebrated statue of the Nile, Cornucopia, and sixteen Cubits (represented by *putti*) in the Vatican. The Cubit was also based on the length of the human forearm, and varied: the *Egyptian Cubit* was about 52.42 cm., whilst the Roman *Cubitus* was about 44.19 cm. In addition, there was the *Salomonic* or *Royal Cubit*, which, according to *Ezekiel* (Ezekiel 40: 5), consisted of the length of a forearm plus a hand's breadth: the *Royal Cubit* was the basis of measurement for several important buildings, such as Holkham Hall, Norfolk, and the Old Schools, Oxford. *See* Schmidt, Keller, Jaeger, & Burman (*Eds.*) (2001).
86 A capital of a column.
87 I *Kings* 7: 13-22.
88 *See* Smith (*Ed.*) (1863) ii 876-7.
89 II *Chronicles* 3: 15.
90 II *Chronicles* 2: 3, 7.

We also know from Biblical and other sources (notably Josephus) that the capitals were finished with 'lily-work', that is architectural ornament similar to the fleur-de-lys or the lotus-flower so widely used in Ancient Egyptian Architecture. Josephus[91] also mentions network interwoven with small palms made of brass[92], which suggests the palmette ornament found with many variants in Antiquity. It therefore seems not unlikely that the capitals of the two 'pillars' (which must have been columns) had architectural similarities to Ancient Egyptian capitals featuring lotus, papyrus, and palm motifs. It is also probable that the 'pillars' were set on bases, perhaps pedestals[93].

One 'pillar' on the 'right hand' was called Jachin, and the other, 'on the left', was named Boaz: Jachin probably refers to the establishment of the Throne of David, and his Kingdom and his seed, so it is a name associated with foundations or establishments, and may mean 'He Shall Establish'. Boaz perhaps suggests that in the 'Strength of God (Yahweh) the King shall Rejoice', and probably means 'in it [or Him] is Strength': Boaz, of course, was supposedly the great-grandfather of King David[94], although some Biblical scholars have suggested many more generations were involved in the genealogy[95]. The problem here, of course, is to decide which was right and which was left. The 'pillars' were at the east entrance to the Temple (the Holy of Holies was to the west): on the *right*, as one approached, was Boaz (at the north-east of the entrance), and on the *left* was Jachin (to the south-east of the entrance). When we think of Jachin and Boaz as on the 'left' or 'right', we have to do so heraldically, and consider how they would be viewed by someone *leaving* the east entrance to the Temple. It is quite wrong, therefore, to think of an elevation of the Temple with Jachin on the right and Boaz on the left: it was the other way round[96]. Most Masonic diagrams do indeed show Jachin on the left and Boaz on the right: the curious thing is that the Lodge is orientated with the Master's place and the Bible at the *east*, and the 'Two Pillars' at the west. So if Masonic Lodges are laid out with the Temple in mind, the left-right problem becomes acute because the orientation is back-to-front, and it is arguable that with this mirror-image, as it were, Jachin ought to be on the right and Boaz on the left. The difficulty lies, of course, in the overlaying of Christian ecclesiastical orientation on that of the Jewish Temple. The simile of the Craft is that the sun rises in the east to bring the day, just as the Master in the east opens the Lodge and instructs the Brethren in Freemasonry (**Pl. IV.8**). Syncretism brings problems as well as solutions, and often obscures[97].

---
91 Flavius Josephus was a Jewish soldier who became a Roman citizen, was presented by Emperor Titus (reigned 79-81) with many rare books after the Sack of Jerusalem, and who wrote several important works including his tome on Jewish Antiquities. *See* Josephus (2006).
92 Jones (1986) 357.
93 *See* Hamblin & Seely (2007) *passim*.
94 Ruth 4: 21-22, Matthew 1: 5-6
95 Smith (Ed.) (1863) **i** 222.
96 Ibid. 358.
97 *See Journal of Biblical Literature* **lviii** (1939) 143-9 for an erudite paper on Jachin and Boaz.

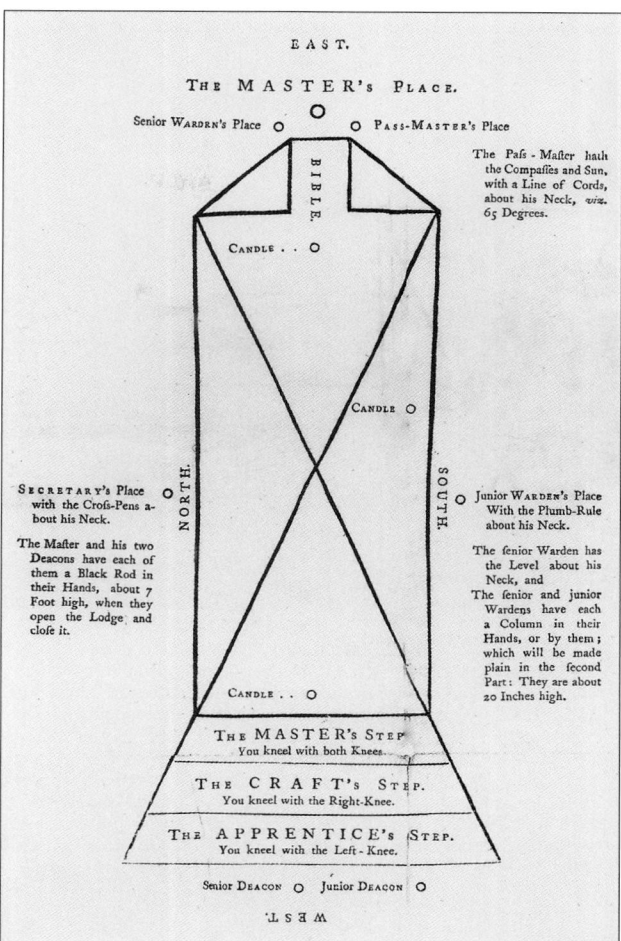

Pl.IV.8 Freemasons' Lodge layout from *The Three Distinct Knocks, Or the Door of the Most Antient Free-Masonry, Opening to All Men, neither Naked nor Cloath'd, Barefoot, nor Shod, Ec. Being an universal Description of all its Branches, from In its first Rise to this present Time, As it is deliver'd in all Lodges...* etc. in the 1763 edn. (UGLE).

The Solomonic Temple seems to have exercised the minds of many scholars in the early part of the Middle Ages as well as later, and the sense of acute loss implied by the destruction of the Temple certainly existed. Like the Garden of Eden mentioned earlier, the lost Temple was a potent idea. Indeed, perhaps unlike any other building in history, it captured the imaginations of men and women, and suggested the time when God dwelt among us.

Two very strange Mediaeval columns with multiple shafts and weird serpentine enrichment (*see* **Pl.IV.9**, p.68) were erected at the Cathedral-Church of St Kilian, Würzburg[98]: these are actually inscribed 'Jachin' and 'Boaz', and seem to have been associated with an attempt to allude to the Temple of Solomon in the Architecture of the Würzburg *Dom*. It is from the inscriptions that these curious columns, with their interlacing detail, show an early association in the minds of European Masons with some kind of draped column, or a column round which plants or spiral ornament were wrapped: the allusion, as

---
98 *See also* Böcher (1960). The twelfth-century Synagogue at Worms also had columns so inscribed.

Pl.IV.9 *Jachin* (left) and *Boaz* (right) in Würzburg Cathedral: two Mediaeval columns, made by the *Steinmetzen*, probably in the thirteenth century, though they may be twelfth-century in date, and some opinion holds that they are eleventh-century carvings. The most likely date, however, is early thirteenth or late twelfth century. Stieglitz opined that they were an overt reference to the Fraternity, but other explanations include certain theological symbolism: Boaz, being tripartite, represents the Trinity, while the shafts, with their curious coiled formations, allude to the Deity without a beginning or an end, as well as to the binding of ties; Jachin represents body and soul, united by a mysterious bond, while the capital, formed of another endless bond, represents the spirit and eternity. The persistence of serpentine, spiral, or twisted columns in representations of the Temple and of Lodges should be noted. Similar knotted shafts can be found at the east end of the *Broletto* in Como, where one of the *bifore* contains two such examples dating from around 1215, which ties in with the most likely Würzburg date (*Bischofliches Ordinariat Würzburg*).

will be demonstrated later in this study, became more pronounced with the Renaissance and Baroque periods. Serpentine ornament, therefore, especially when associated with columns, was identified very early in European iconography with the Solomonic Temple, and later with Freemasonry. It also seems to have had links with a School of Masons based on Lake Como from the time of the Roman Empire in the West (the so-called Comacine School): similar serpentine ornament to that of the columns in Würzburg occurs in the façade of the *Broletto*, completed 1215, in the City of Como itself, and on two tiers of arcades on the west front of the Church of San Michele, Lucca (thirteenth century, restored in the nineteenth). Other examples may be found in Italian Romanesque architecture.

The two columns (which is what they were and are) have also been interpreted as representing the physical powers of generation or creation (i.e. a phallic symbol), as the spiritual power of regeneration (i.e. salvation), and as allusions to the stone 'pillar' of Jacob at Bethel, with names suggesting strength and firmness. However, the left-right problem also occurs in churches, for the Gospel was read from the left (i.e. north side) and the Epistle from the right (south): the Gospel concerns Christ and the Jews, and the Epistle Paul and the Gentiles, so there was a tendency to connect the left with Judaism/Old Testament and the right with Christianity/New Testament[99]. Thus Jachin and Boaz had connotations with the Old and New Testaments, Sts Peter and Paul, and Jews and Gentiles[100].

The *Broletto*, Lucca, and Würzburg columns could be said to have knots on their shafts, and there are countless variants of spirals, twisted shafts, and decorated shafts of many kinds, some of which will be discussed below. There are also columns associated with the Solomonic idea consisting of bases, shafts, capitals, and globular objects on top: a pair can be found flanking the portal of the twelfth-century Church of Santa Maria Maggiore, Tuscania, Latium. Again, this type will be further examined later.

The variation of meaning of columns is complicated, and it will not be profitable to list them here. The significance of Jachin and Boaz, as far as this study is concerned, is their importance as markers and guardians of entrances, as mnemonics of the Temple and of the legends of how esoteric knowledge was preserved, and as sources for the design of columns, especially in the Renaissance and Baroque periods. Columns twisted like barley-sugar sticks, or with spirals wound round them (or both) can be found in reconstructions of the Temple, in the *Baldacchino* over the high altar in the Basilica of St Peter, Rome, and in the décor of Continental Freemasonic Lodges, to give but three examples. The spiral shaft, even from very early Mediaeval times, was used for columns or piers associated with an altar or an important shrine. It is also found at Roslin Chapel, the fifteenth-century unfinished church of remarkable richness virtually encrusted with elaborate carving. At Roslin (associated with the Sinclairs as previously described), the piers dividing the ambulatory from the east chapel are spectacular, but that to the south, with a spiral band of carved ornament winding around it, is called the Prentice Pillar (from an apparently recent story that it was carved by a talented apprentice who was killed by a jealous Master-Mason). The parallel with the Hiram legend (*see* below) is obvious, but it is curious that the pier has four strips of stylised carved foliage draped around the shaft in spiral around 180 degrees, starting from each of the Cardinal points of the compass at the base and finishing at the opposite Cardinal points at the top. Winged serpents with entwined necks bite their own tails at the foot. One of the carved heads sports a dent in its forehead, and is supposed to be the murdered apprentice: however, the dent is not Mediaeval, and the head once had a beard (removed after 1845)[101]. The Sinclairs of Roslin, as we have seen, were

99 Onians (1988) 102.

100 Cahn (1976) 51.
101 Cooper (2006) 146.

associated with Freemasonry from the seventeenth century, and it would seem that much phoney legend has been tacked on to their Chapel: matters have got a lot worse in recent times with stories of the Holy Grail, the Templars, and so on, subjects with which Robert Cooper has dealt, firmly, sensibly, and without over-statement[102].

However, the spiral, or Solomonic form of column enjoyed a significance as something special, even from the Middle Ages, and probably before then. But not all columns were either spiral or had spirals draped around their shafts. Many were straight, but had globes on top of the capitals (like those on either side of the portal of Santa Maria Maggiore, Tuscania, Latium, referred to above). In Masonic legend two pairs of 'pillars', those containing knowledge, and those of Solomon's Temple, became one single pair by a process of syncretism and confusion. Yet there was a third pair that would have meant far more to any reasonably educated person of the sixteenth and seventeenth centuries: in ancient times the mountains on either side of the passage from the Mediterranean to the Atlantic (known as the Straits of Gibraltar) were known as the 'Pillars of Hercules'. They were associated with the motto *Ne Plus Ultra*[103], meaning 'nothing beyond it', or 'nothing more beyond', but Charles V, Holy Roman Emperor from 1519 (crowned 1520) and King of Spain from 1518, also had an immense Empire in America, so he adopted as his Emblems the two columns with the motto *Plus Ultra*, or 'More Beyond', for there *was* a New World across the seas. Furthermore, modern Europe was confident, and was outstripping the achievements of Antiquity.

Charles V's Emblems struck chords: they were widely adopted, sometimes with references to the Temple of Solomon, and sometimes connected with the idea of Empire[104]. They may be seen carved on the exterior of the *Capilla Real* in the Cathedral-Church of Santa María de la Asunción, Seville (1550-70), a project in which Charles V took a keen personal interest, and the most stunning architectural manifestation of the Emblems occurred at the *Karlskirche*, Vienna (from 1715), which will be described in detail later. These memorable Emblems may also be found in numerous printed works, of which the engraved title-page[105] of *Instauratio Magna* (1620) by Francis Bacon[106] is one of the most arresting: his columns are inscribed *Plus Ultra*, and the image includes a ship sailing out far beyond them, suggesting, of course, the limited boundaries of the Ancient World and the outward-looking possibilities offered by exploring new seas and territories (not only physical, but of the mind as well)[107]. Bacon's goal was to enlarge the bounds of Reason 'and to endow man's estate with new value'[108]. What Bacon attempted was to reorganise Natural Philosophy, correcting what he perceived as errors in the Aristotelian scheme of things: Bacon observed that a weakness of the old Aristotelian logic was that it leapt from empirical particulars to axioms, and he emphasised the importance of experiments and tests, for he did not accept that experience gives the human mind the means by which things can be understood, for human senses are not reliable. He argued for the need for methodological assistance to provide sound, reliable information: received opinion, the senses, and casual observation all needed support from experiments. Underlying Bacon's philosophy lay his desire to reorganise the Sciences and to restore to Man that command over Nature which he believed had been lost by the Fall and the expulsion from Eden. So again we find the idea of Loss, the search for that which was Lost, at the core of his work. What indeed Bacon seems to have been seeking was, as Peter Dawkins has observed, nothing less than 'the universal and general Reformation of the Whole Wide World through the Renewal of all Arts and Sciences'[109].

Such aims could hardly fail to have a strong appeal for Masons, so much so that in addition to the merging of two sets of legends concerning 'Pillars', a third pair of 'Pillars' was added to the fecund mix. As 'Pillars' flanked the entrance to the Temple and the Lodge, then by entering a Lodge the Mason would not only enter a special place, acquiring lost secrets and knowledge, and passing from the known world into a new, mysterious one[110]. It should be emphasised that Emblems were immensely potent in the sixteenth and seventeenth centuries, and although they (and much else) mean nothing to the vast majority of people today, that does not invalidate their importance in the past.

There is yet another pair of 'Pillars' that can probably be considered as a *fourth* component of the brew: the earth and the heavens were said to be supported by 'Pillars'. Heaven was seen as a 'curtain'[111], 'tent'[112], or 'canopy' supported by 'pillars', and the earth was carried on 'pillars' as well[113]. Yet other interpretations compare 'pillars' with certain early Christian figures: Paul, for example, said that James, Cephas, and John 'seemed to be pillars'[114]. Bases of columns could be interpreted as the sacred texts on which rest the doctrines of the preachers, and the columns themselves might represent the Apostles and the teachers of the Gospel. Two columns, such as those suggested by those made by Hiram, might stand for those who by their preaching gave both Gentiles and Jews the knowledge to bring them into the Church, and they (the columns), standing on either side of the doorway, mark the entry into the Kingdom of Heaven for both Jews and Gentiles. Jesus claimed that He was *the* door through which anyone who entered would be saved[115], and nobody could go to

---

102 Cooper (2006) *passim*.
103 Sometimes given as *Non Plus Ultra*.
104 Yates (1975) 23, 57-8, 123-4, 138-146.
105 *See* Burnett (1998).
106 Bacon (1620). *See* also Spedding, Ellis, & Heath (*Eds.*) (1857-74).
107 Hooykaas (1972) 63.
108 Spedding, Ellis, & Heath (*Eds.*) (1857-74) **xiv** 119-22.
109 Dawkins (1983).
110 The 'Pillars of Hercules' allusion.
111 *Isaiah* 40: 22; *Psalms* 104: 2.
112 *Isaiah* 40: 22.
113 I *Samuel* 2: 8; *Psalms* 75:3.
114 *Galatians* 2: 9.
115 *John* 10: 9.

the Father other than through Him[116]. The two capitals or 'chapiters' were the minds of the teachers, and also the Old and the New Testaments. The dimensions of the capitals, said to be five Cubits high, were held to be correct because the Law of Moses was contained within five books, and the sequences of the New Testament could be said to be five periods. Chains and nets on capitals might suggest the spiritual values among the Saints, the varied characters of the Elect, offering an elaborate interconnection of ideas and themes.

Such notions were put about by Hrabanus Maurus (Rabanus Magnentius Maurus, Abbot of Fulda from 822 and Archbishop of Mainz from 847), whose *De Universo* can be justly regarded as one of the most influential of all encyclopaedias, specifically Christian in character, which helped to lay down the intellectual foundations of the Middle Ages[117]. So now not only were the columns or 'pillars' held to contain knowledge, but specifically Christian and Jewish knowledge; they had names (Jachin and Boaz), and were anthropomorphic; they represented Apostles and teachers of the Gospel; they guarded the way to something new, marvellous, and splendid, the *Plus Ultra* of the New World, New Life, Transformed Existence, Enlightenment, and even Paradise; and they were especially prized in Freemasonry, as mnemonics of the Lost Temple, and much else[118].

Jachin and Boaz sufficed by name as mnemonics of the 'Pillars' (either the Solomonic/Hiram 'Pillars' or the 'Two Pillars' of even greater antiquity in legend by which the Word, in the sense of essential esoteric knowledge, was preserved) for Apprentices and Higher Grades, it is clear that at some time in the seventeenth century separate signs for recognition (grips or handshakes) were evolved for Fellow Crafts and Masters,[119] so that three distinct Grades or Degrees developed, possibly as a result of English Freemasons embracing Scottish rites, but more likely because the three Grades or Degrees actually developed in Scotland by the end of the seventeenth century[120].

Early rituals point not to two, but to Three Pillars, supporting Wisdom, Strength, and Beauty, and reminding Masons of Solomon (who caused the Temple to be built), of Hiram, King of Tyre (who gave men and materials), and of the other Hiram (who built and adorned the Temple); the last is usually, and erroneously, referred to as Hiram Abiff. Wisdom/Solomon/the Master is represented by the Ionic Order; Strength/King Hiram/the Senior Warden is represented by the Doric, and Beauty/Hiram the Master/Builder/Junior Warden is represented by the Corinthian. However, before the Union of the two rival eighteenth-century Grand Lodges in 1813 (which gave us the United Grand Lodge of England), the attribution was slightly different, with the Orders arranged in seniority. As with much else in the arcane realms of Freemasonry, the reasons for the change are unclear: perhaps it was because the parvenu 'Antients' insisted on getting their way on this and many other aspects. The Premier (1717) Grand Lodge, shortly after George, Prince of Wales, was elected Grand Master in 1791, commissioned chairs with instructions to

> 'make the Columns or Pillars of the Chairs strictly conformable to the Order and Usage of the Society, viz. the Grand Master's to be of the Doric Order, the Senior Warden's the Ionic Order, and the Junior Warden's the Corinthian Order.'[121]

This is the suite of chairs which may still be seen in the Museum at Freemasons' Hall, London.

Such 'Warden's Columns' are also associated with floor candelabra, and were sometimes themselves the candleholders.[122] Pillars also support hour-glasses (passing time and the transitory nature of life), and sometimes carry globes (or interpreted as two superimposed lavers, or bowls, sometimes as Heaven and Earth, but more probably derived from sixteenth-century representations of Solomon's Temple showing globes on top of Jachin and Boaz). So, there seem to have been three sets of the 'Two Pillars': the 'Pillars' used to record knowledge and secrets; the Solomonic Temple 'Pillars' of Hiram; and the 'Pillars' of Hercules (the last common emblematic devices of the Renaissance period). In addition, however, there were Doric, Ionic, and Corinthian Columns, and some or all of these got confused at some time or another.

The notion of the 'Pillars' of Hercules (the Straits of Gibraltar) symbolised by two columns, certainly became significant during the Renaissance, and, in some instances, acquired globes on top. This motif seems to have been absorbed into Freemasonry, and became identified with Jachin and Boaz and with the confused and confusing ideas of 'Pillars' generally. It is all really a wonderful example of syncretism, and, given that modern Freemasonry seems to be not a survival from Antiquity, but something which emerged around the time of the Reformation and developed in the ensuing centuries, gives pause for thought about how certain aspects of religion also absorbed, confused, changed, and merged into myths, legends, and themes from Classical Antiquity into a kind of Mediterranean soup. This is not to invalidate Religion or Freemasonry, of course: it merely points to obvious instances where interpretation and time have played significant parts in creating something completely new out of something very ancient. It is all a fascinating, baffling, infuriating, and entertaining business.

---

116 *John* 14: 6.
117 *See* Migne (*Ed.*) (1844-65) **cxi** 9-614.
118 For a detailed account of a range of meanings Western culture has assigned to columns, in their various manifestations, *see* Onians (1988) *passim*.
119 Stevenson (1988b) 150-1.
120 *See* Carr (1962) and the same author's work on the Word and the Catechisms in *AQC* (1970, 1971, and 1972). *See also* Stevenson (1988b) 151.

121 Information kindly provided by T. O. Haunch, to whom the author is indebted.
122 Jones (1956) 355-6. In II *Chronicles* 4:16 the Hebrew name is given as *Huram*, and again in II *Chronicles* 2:13: in these instances Huram is 'his father' and 'my father's' respectively. 'Hiram Abif' or 'Abiff' is therefore 'Hiram the father'.

CHAPTER V

The Great Prototype

*Introduction: The Jewish Temple; The Decline and Destruction of Solomon's Temple; Zerubbabel's Temple; The Herodian Temple; Representations of the Temple; Fischer von Erlach; The Case of the **Karlskirche**; The Spiral Columns; Afterword: Into the Abyss*

'And the king commanded, and they brought great stones, costly stones, *and* hewed stones, to lay the foundation of the house.

And Solomon's builders and Hiram's builders did hew *them*, and the stonesquarers: so they prepared timber and stones to build the house.'

I Kings 5: 17, 18.

'Now in the second year of their coming unto the house of God at Jerusalem, in the second month, began Zerubbabel the son of Shealtiel, and Jeshua the son of Jozadak, and the remnant of their brethren the priests and the Levites, and all they that were come out of the captivity unto Jerusalem; and appointed the Levites, from twenty years old and upwards, to set forward the work of the house of the LORD.'

Ezra 3: 8.

Introduction: the Jewish Temple

The Jewish so-called 'Temple' (*templum* means an area, demarcated and consecrated by the augurs for the taking of auspices, set apart, or used for sacred purposes; it can mean an area of sky or land, heaven or earth, or both, as well as a building consecrated to a deity or deities) had a strong axis leading from the entrance to the Holy of Holies and the Ark of the Covenant, and did not contain a cult statue: it therefore differed from most pagan temples.

After a long period in captivity in Egypt, Israelite worship was formalised through revelation to Moses, with Divine instructions to make a sanctuary 'that I may dwell among' the people[1], so the Tabernacle was a dwelling-place and a sanctuary. It was conceived as a moveable tented shrine set within a rectangular court. Every important dimension was either 5 cubits or a multiple of 5 cubits. Assuming a cubit was the length of a man's forearm from the elbow-joint to the tip of the extended middle finger, a cubit measured 18 Greek inches, or just over 18 English inches[2]. Thus the Tabernacle was 30 cubits long and 10 cubits wide, so about 45 feet long and 15 feet wide, and the court in which it was situated was separated from the rest of the camp by a partition of curtains hung from poles. This sacred space was 100 cubits (150 feet) long and 50 cubits (75 feet) wide, with a 20-cubit-wide entrance on one of the shorter sides[3], that to the east, for the long axis lay east-west (see **Fig.V.1**, p.72).

So there was a special rectangular space enclosed by linen hangings supported by 'brass' (i.e. probably bronze) posts[4] fitted with silver hooks and fillets. One of the shorter sides of this court lay to the east, with linen hangings 15 cubits wide on each side of the 20-cubit-wide entrance which was hung with 'blue, purple, and scarlet, and fine twined linen, wrought with needlework'[5]. The curtains around the court were 5 cubits high.

---

1 *Exodus* 26: 8.
2 *See* Smith (*Ed.*) (1863) **iii** 1451 n.
3 So the Tabernacle was about 13.7 metres long and 4.6 metres wide, and the court was about 46 metres long and 23 metres wide. *See Exodus* 27.
4 Called 'pillars' in the King James Bible.
5 *Exodus* 27: 16.

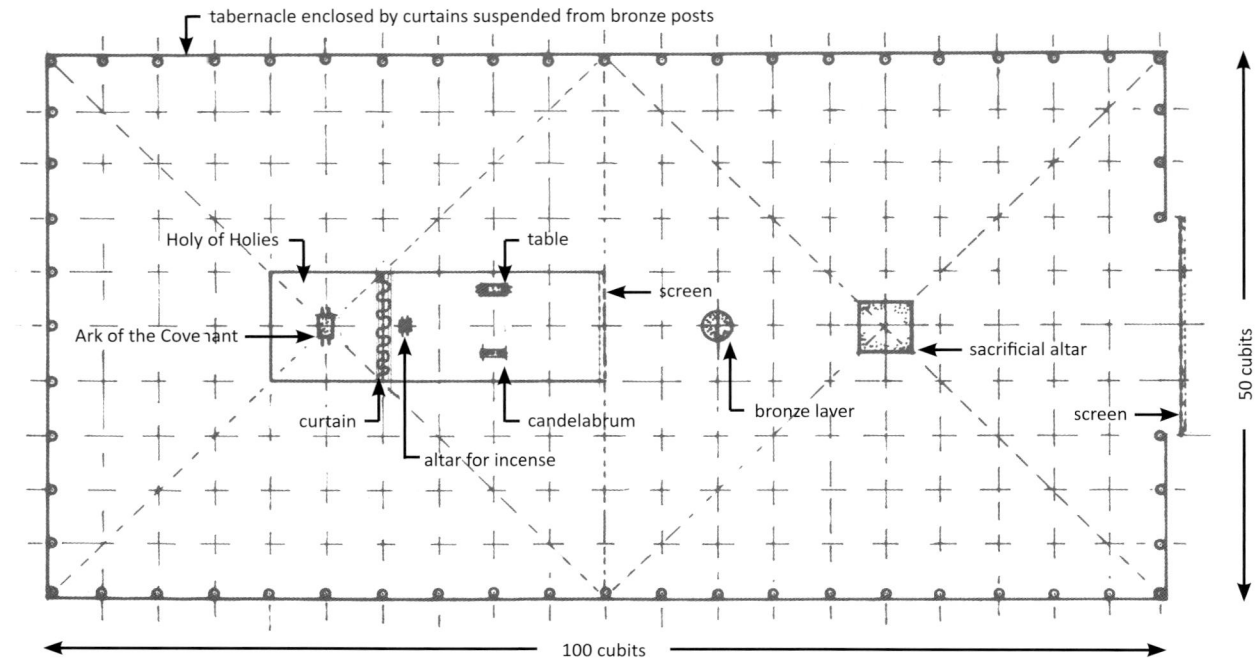

Fig.V.1 Reconstruction of the layout of the Jewish Tabernacle plan (JSC).

The court had two zones, each 50 cubits square. In the centre of the eastern part was the sacrificial horned altar, with its 'network of brass'[6], 5 cubits long and 5 broad, 3 cubits high: this altar was made of *shittim* (Acacia) wood, overlaid with 'brass', which again was probably bronze. Bronze rings were fitted to receive long handles (or 'staves') of Acacia-wood covered with bronze so that the altar could be lifted and carried.

Between the altar for burnt offerings and the Tabernacle was a large bronze laver for ritual purification[7] by the priests. The Tabernacle itself (constructed of three walls of gold-plated Acacia-wood covered with linen cloth) was situated in the western part of the court, and consisted of an eastern rectangular room 20 cubits by 10, separated by a curtain from the 10 x 10 cubit Holy of Holies. This curtain (or veil) was of 'blue, purple, and scarlet, and fine twined linen; *with* Cherubims made... of cunning work'[8], and in front of it, on the eastern side, was an altar on which to burn incense: it was one cubit square on plan, and 2 cubits high, made of Acacia-wood overlaid with pure gold. This altar too, was portable, and had rings into which poles could be placed to carry it[9]. This room, the Holy Place, also contained the Table of the Bread[10] of the Presence (again of Acacia-wood overlaid with pure gold), and the *Menorah*, or seven-branched candelabrum, made of pure gold. The Holy Place had a curtain at its eastern end, which was similar to the 'veil' between it and the Holy of Holies[11]. The whole of the Tabernacle was protected by a large tent.

Within the perfect cube of the Holy of Holies was the Ark of the Covenant, containing relics of the Exodus: the Tablets of the Law; Manna[12]; and Aaron's Rod[13]. Now this Ark was a rectangular box of Acacia-wood covered with pure gold, 2½ cubits long, 1½ cubits wide, and 1½ cubits high: like everything else associated with the Tabernacle, it was portable. On top of the rectangular box was a 'mercy-seat' (probably a misleading term, but associated with Antonement and the Throne of God), actually the lid of the Ark on which were two golden Cherubims facing each other, with outstretched wings touching[14]. The winged Cherubims suggest those Ancient Egyptian winged figures that may be found on portable shrines and elsewhere, associated with Egyptian deities and Kingship.

The Tabernacle, the Ark, and other furnishings accompanied the Israelites during their migrations and entry into the Promised Land. It was set up at Shiloh[15], but the Ark eventually moved to Jerusalem 'in the midst of the tabernacle that David had pitched for it'[16] when Israel was established as a Kingdom in one place under King David. Subsequently, Solomon brought the Ark and Tabernacle to the new, permanent site of the Temple[17], where it appears the Levites kept the charge of the Tabernacle[18], probably

---

6 *Exodus* 27: 4-8.
7 *Exodus* 30: 18-21.
8 *Exodus* 36: 35.
9 *Exodus* 30: 1-6.
10 2 cubits long, 1 wide, and 1½ high.
11 *Exodus* 26: 30-37.
12 It was white, like coriander-seed, and tasted like wafers made with honey (*Exodus* 16: 31).
13 *Exodus* 16: 33-34; 25: 16; *Numbers* 17: 1-13.
14 *Exodus* 25: 10-22. *Cherubim* is also plural.
15 *Joshua* 18: 1.
16 II *Samuel* 6: 2-17.
17 I *Kings* 8: 4.
18 I *Chronicles* 23: 32.

destroyed when the Jerusalem Temple was burned by the Babylonians in 586 BC.

Solomon's Temple was erected c.968BC, and was of stone with cedar-wood roof and internal furnishings (it was lined with timber so that 'there was no stone to be seen'[19]. Like the Tabernacle, it was orientated east-west, was rectangular, and contained a cubic Holy of Holies at the west end. However, the Solomonic Temple's dimensions were double those of the original nomadic Tabernacle: the Holy of Holies cube was 20 cubits each way; the Holy Place was 40 cubits long and 20 wide; and the porch at the east end was 10 cubits deep[20]. Instead of the sloping tent-roofs, around three sides of the rectangular building were small chambers 5-7 cubits wide disposed on three storeys, so the main body of the Holy of Holies and Holy Place rose up above these chambers, probably with some kind of clerestorey openings[21]. The Bible confirms the length of the Temple as 'threescore cubits', and the breadth thereof twenty *cubits*, and the height thereof thirty cubits[22], with a porch 'before the temple... twenty cubits' wide and 10 cubits deep. Now all this sounds reasonable until we come across an assertion in *Chronicles* that 'the porch *was* in the front *of the house*, the length *of it was* according to the breadth of the house, twenty cubits, and the height *was* an hundred and twenty: and he overlaid it with pure gold'[23]. There is also a statement that the upper chambers were 'overlaid' with gold[24], and even a reference to 'altars that were on the top of the upper chamber'[25], which suggests something very odd, possibly confirmed in the Talmud and by Josephus that there was some sort of superstructure on the Temple that was equal in height to the lower part, and that the total height was 120 cubits[26]. Could this, perhaps, have meant that, like the platform (or *talar*) that existed on the roofs of the palace temples at Persepolis as shown on the façade of the Tomb of Darius I[27] at Naksh-i-Rustam, near Persepolis (c.485 BC)[28], altars were erected on some kind of superstructure that stood on at least part of the Temple (that portion above the porch)?

According to *Kings*[29], the so-called 'pillars' of 'brass' were 18 cubits high, with circumferences of 12 cubits, and 'chapiters' 5 cubits high. In addition, above this there was a further 'chapter' of 'lily-work' 4 cubits high[30], in which case there would have been some sort of 9-cubit-high element on top of the 'pillars', which would have rendered them somewhat top-heavy. Perhaps the additional 4-cubit-high element was, in fact, an entablature, possibly not unlike the decorative entablatures at Persepolis[31], where again the complex capitals were about half the height of the shafts. In short, it is possible that the columns at Persepolis may have resembled Jachin and Boaz more than any other type of column and capital known to us from Antiquity.

Most commentators have been content to accept a roof-span of 20 cubits for the Holy of Holies and the Holy Place, but that is 30 feet or so[32], which suggests either enormous cedarwood beams, very technically advanced trusses, or, more likely, internal supports in the form of columns. Given the geometry, it is likely there were 4 columns inside the square Holy of Holies, probably 8 inside the Holy Place, 2 in the porch, and either two more between the Holy Place and the Holy of Holies or some kind of pilaster or pier arrangement with a solid wall between them, for, unlike the Tabernacle, the two compartments were separated by a wall with a doorway rather than by a 'veil'[33], although a 'veil of blue, and purple, and crimson' and 'fine linen, and wrought Cherubims thereon' screened the Ark in some way[34]. The doors were of olive-wood, carved with Cherubims, palm-trees, and 'open flowers'[35], overlaid with gold.

The Holy of Holies (otherwise known as the 'Oracle') contained the Ark of the Covenant, as before, but in addition to the Cherubims on the Ark itself, Solomon caused two gigantic Cherubims[36] to be made of olive-wood, covered in gold, with outstretched wings (the tips of which touched) guarding the Ark: 10 cubits high, with 5-cubit-long wings, the furthermost tips of which were 10 cubits apart, so the wing of one touched one wall, and the wing of the other touched the other wall[37]. The faces of the Cherubims were turned towards each other[38]. The walls were carved with figures of Cherubims, palm-trees, and open flowers, 'within and without'[39].

As for the Holy Place, it was again furnished with an altar on which to burn incense, a table for the bread, and, rather than one candelabrum, ten of these, of gold[40]. Bowls, censers, pans, hinges, snuffers, ladles, and other artefacts were made of solid gold[41]. To the east of the Holy Place was a porch or vestibule, probably some kind of transitional space with walls on three sides (that on the west with a doorway or doorways), and that on the east probably a distyle *in antis* arrangement with the two columns[42]. On the other hand, the two columns could have stood in front of the vestibule wall, perhaps as a kind of primitive portico. In *Chronicles* however, it seems quite

---

19 I *Kings* 6: 18.
20 So about 100 feet long and 30 feet wide.
21 The tall rectangular main body of the temple seems to have been about 30 cubits high (45 feet) with the parts containing the chambers on three sides of this block about 20 cubits high.
22 I *Kings* 6: 2.
23 II *Chronicles* 3: 4.
24 II *Chronicles* 3: 9.
25 II *Kings* 23: 12.
26 Josephus (2006) **viii** 3 §2.
27 Known as Hystaspes.
28 Smith (*Ed.*) (1863) **iii** 1456-7.
29 I *Kings* 7: 15-16.
30 *Ibid.*: 19.

31 *Ibid.*: 22.
32 9.1 metres.
33 I *Kings* 6: 31-2.
34 II *Chronicles* 3: 14.
35 Presumably resembling a stylised rosette.
36 From the beginning of the seventeenth century *Cherubim* was preferred as the plural, rather than *Cherubims*, but for clarity the latter form is used here.
37 I *Kings* 6: 23-28.
38 II *Chronicles* 3: 13,
39 I *Kings* 6: 29.
40 I *Kings* 7: 49.
41 *Ibid.* : 50.
42 I *Kings* 6: 3.

clear that the 'pillars' were 'before' the Temple, 35 cubits high, with 5-cubit-high 'chapiters'[43].

A vast 'brass' altar for burnt offerings, 20 cubits square, ten cubits high, was erected in the courtyard to the east of the Temple (we do not know how big was this court, but it was probably of 100 cubits north and south and 200 cubits east and west, if it followed the increase of sizes of the Tabernacle itself. According to I *Kings* 6: 36 the court was surrounded by a low wall of stone topped by a row of cedar 'beams', probably richly decorated [these 'beams' were probably thick posts placed closely together])[44]. Between the Temple-front and the altar was a 'molten sea of ten cubits from brim to brim, round in compass, and five cubits the height thereof', with a circumference of 30 cubits[45]. This vast basin of cast bronze was supported on the backs of 12 bronze oxen, three of which each faced north, south, east, and west[46]. As well as this enormous basin for priestly ablutions, there were ten 'brass' lavers mounted on wheels[47]. This metalwork was all made by 'Hiram', 'of the tribe of Naphtali'[48].

Another aspect of the Temple which tends to get glossed over is the application of what appears to have been three tiers or storeys of small chambers around the north, south, and western sides of the taller structure containing the porch, Holy Place, and Holy of Holies. The lowest storey had chambers 5 cubits wide; the next storey had chambers 6 cubits wide; and on the topmost storey the chambers were 7 metres wide. What were these chambers for? They were probably quarters for the priests and others who served the Temple. The diminution of wall-thickness with height enabled the floors of the chambers to be carried on off-sets to avoid having to cut into the stonework of the Temple to support the joists. There must have been means of communication between floors, and these were very likely spiral staircases. The plan of the so-called Palace of Darius at Persepolis has small chambers on either side of a square columned hall and a porch: two chambers flank a tetrastyle portico. This kind of arrangement (narrowed to distyle) could provide clues as to how the Temple was laid out.

Finally, there is no clue in the Bible concerning any porticos or gateways which may have embellished the wall and court surrounding Solomon's Temple, although there is mention of certain names applied to 'gates' of the Temple, but these are obscure[49].

So the Tabernacle was re-interpreted in permanent form, as Architecture, in Solomon's Temple, which stood for nearly four centuries as a potent reminder of the presence of God and the Covenant with Israel and the Royal House of David.

The Decline and Destruction of Solomon's Temple

After the death of Solomon Israel was divided into a southern Kingdom (Judah with its capital at Jerusalem) and a northern Kingdom (Israel – with its capital in Samaria). The northerners strayed from strict observance of Jewish Laws, and, according to Biblical accounts, took to worshipping Canaanite deities such as Baal. Retribution was great, for the Assyrians invaded Samaria and took it in 722 BC.

Under Hezekiah attempts were made to unite Israel once more, to drive the Assyrians out, and to give the Israelites a spiritual centre by focusing religious observance on the Temple of Solomon, for it seems that a great many Jewish Kings (including Solomon) had taken up with cults and practices abominated by orthodoxy. Images, sacred groves, and pagan altars were all destroyed[50]. However, the attempt to remove the Assyrian yoke was unsuccessful, and King Sennacherib attacked, destroying virtually everything except Jerusalem in 701. After Hezekiah was succeeded by Manasseh (who again turned away from the Lord God of Israel), syncretising types of worship which Hezekiah had abolished (and therefore, to some, had been responsible for the devastation wreaked by the Assyrians) were restored. It is quite clear from Biblical accounts that Manasseh (like other Jewish kings) encouraged pagan worship even in the Temple[51]: he was said to have 'used enchantments, and dealt with familiar spirits and wizards'[52], among much else. In other words, he adopted an eclectic attitude to various cults.

Needless to say, Jewish prophets thundered mightily against such tendencies, promising retribution, which duly came in the form of Nebuchadnezzar II, King of Babylon, who is famous for his Hanging Gardens, and is vilified for his destruction of the Temple and for his conquest of Judah[53] in 587-6 BC. However, the prophets clearly held the site of the Temple in high esteem (although they abhorred what had gone on in the Temple itself under various Kings), and Jeremiah not only prophesied the destruction of the Temple and the looting of its contents, but a time in the future when the captive Israelites would return from Babylon and restore the Temple as a habitation of justice and mountain of holiness[54].

The prophet Ezekiel appears to have been taken prisoner before the Babylonian destruction of the Temple, yet foresaw its demise[55] and that of Jerusalem, when God departed leaving the Temple undefended[56]. However, in the context of this study, Ezekiel's detailed descriptions of a Temple of the future are important, for they had a very considerable influence on *Christian* as well as *Jewish*

---

43 II *Chronicles* 3: 17.
44 II *Chronicles* 4: 1.
45 Ibid.: 2.
46 Ibid.: 4. See also I *Kings* 7: 23-26.
47 I *Kings* 7: 38; I *Chronicles* 4: 6. The fountain in the Court of the Lions, at the Alhambra, Granada (late fourteenth century) perhaps alluded to Solomon's Temple with reference to the 'sea' on the backs of oxen.
48 I *Kings* 7: 13-14.
49 I *Chronicles* 9: 18, 19, 21, 22, 23, etc. See Smith (Ed.) (1863) **iii** 1459.

50 II *Chronicles* 31: 1.
51 2 *Kings* 21.
52 Ibid.: 6.
53 Prophesied in *Jeremiah* 25: 11 and mentioned in *Daniel* 1: 1-2. See also II *Kings* 25 and *Jeremiah* 39.
54 *Jeremiah* 31: 23.
55 *Ezekiel* 8, 9, 10, 11. See also II *Kings* 25.
56 Ibid.: 11.

theology, iconography, and much else[57]. It has to be said that Ezekiel's description is both prolix and obfuscatory, although the dimensions given are exactly those of Solomon's Temple. Some dimensions are given in *reeds*, which appear to have been equivalent to 6 *Babylonian* cubits (i.e. an ordinary cubit plus a hand's breadth, or 21 inches), so a *reed* was about 10½ feet: if Ezekiel's improbable dimensions are followed exactly, we find the court (at 500 reeds per side) would have covered an area greater than the entire city of Jerusalem[58].

Zerubbabel's Temple

In captivity, the Jews recalled the days long past, and, by the 'rivers of Babylon', they 'sat down' and 'wept' when they 'remembered Zion'[59]. Deliverance was to come from an unexpected source. Cyrus became Pasargadian King in 559 BC and, after a successful rebellion against the Median Empire (553 BC), styled himself 'King of the Persians': despite attempts by Babylon, Egypt, Lydia, and Sparta to bring him to heel, he increased his power and prestige until, in 539 BC, he destroyed the mighty Babylonian Empire and in 538 granted to the captive Jews the return to Palestine and permission to rebuild Jerusalem and the Temple. Led by Sheshbazzar, Prince of Judah, the Jews carried some of the Temple treasures back from Babylon to Jerusalem[60], and Zerubbabel and Jeshua 'began to build the house of God which *is* in Jerusalem'[61]. Thus the Second Temple (which may have been a partial rebuilding of Solomon's Temple) is also known as Zerubbabel's Temple, and was completed around 516 BC after Cyrus's death when Darius I was King of the Persians, who proved to be as generous to the returning Jews as had been Cyrus.

It would seem that Zerubbabel's Temple was 60 cubits wide and 60 cubits high, and consisted of three stone-built storeys (probably the chambers surrounding the Temple proper) with one timber storey on top (probably a type of *talar*)[62]. So Zerubbabel's Temple building was actually 20 cubits wider than Solomon's, but there is no reason to suppose that the Holy of Holies or the Holy Place were larger, so it is probable that the rebuilt Temple had a wide porch with 20-cubit wide chambers all round, including the thickness of the walls, but this might be explained if corridors were created between the chambers and the Temple proper, to permit access to individual rooms rather than having to pass through one room to reach another. Thus Zerubbabel's Temple must have been 100 cubits long by 60 wide. The Temple court was enclosed by a wall, and was 100 cubits wide, so must have been about 300 cubits long: we also know that the altar was 20 cubits square and 10 high, so was enormous[63].

The generosity of Cyrus and Darius enabled many artefacts to be returned to Zerubbabel's Temple, but a great deal had been lost. The Ark of the Covenant with the Cherubims had disappeared, and so the Holy of Holies was empty. Until 332 BC Judaea remained under Persian domination, and during that time the Jews could practise their religion. Alexander 'the Great' of Macedon (356-323 BC) defeated the Persians after sustained campaigns in 332, but, although Temple worship continued, yet again aspects of non-Jewish religions invaded the sacred precincts[64]. In 320 BC Ptolemy I Soter of Egypt took possession of Jerusalem, and, despite occasional upheavals, the Ptolemies were established as rulers. This undoubtedly helped a Hellenistic Judaism to evolve, of which the leading exponent was Philon, or Philo Judaeus (*c.*30 BC-*c.* AD 40): this had a profound influence on the development of Christianity. Under Ptolemy II Philadelphus were the beginnings of the Septuagint[65] Bible, and from that period date several synagogues in Egypt.

Under Seleucid rule, Antiochus IV Epiphanes attempted further Hellenisation by despoiling the Temple and destroying the remains of Jewish separatism by merging the local religious practices into a syncretistic pagan mixture: the Jewish God, for example, was identified with Zeus, whose image was set up in the Temple. At the same time, attempts were made to suppress traditional Jewish rites. Such events prompted revolt in 167 BC. Under the able command of Judas Maccabaeus and his sons and followers, a guerrilla war was waged which retook the Temple and re-dedicated it in 165 BC. Indeed, after a campaign which lasted until 142 BC, the Maccabees (or Hasmonaeans) secured freedom of worship and a degree of autonomy that lasted until Judaea became a client Kingdom of Rome after Jerusalem was captured in 63 BC by Gnaeus Pompeius Magnus (Pompey), an event that laid the foundations for subsequent Roman reorganisation.

The Herodian Temple

In *c.*42 BC Marcus Antonius became master of Asia, and in Rome Herod the Great was recognised as ruler of Jerusalem and Judaea, and became known as a great builder and patron of the arts, especially as the renovator of the Temple (mostly for political reasons). This huge work of beautification is unusually well-documented, and it was in the Herodian complex that Jesus is supposed to have preached. Work began in 19 BC and continued until AD 63: it involved the complete reconstruction of Zerubbabel's Temple, keeping the original dimensions of the plan, but enlarging the courts by extending the already vast platform on the Temple Mount[66].

For this last and greatest of the Jewish Temples we are indebted to the words of Josephus and to the *Talmud*

---

57 *See* Ezekiel 40-48.
58 Ezekiel 40: 5 and *passim*.
59 Psalms 137: 1.
60 Ezra 2: 7-11.
61 *Ezra* 5: 2. It was influenced by Persian Architecture.
62 Ezra 6: 3-4. *See* also Josephus (2006): **xi** 4 § 6.
63 Smith (*Ed.*) (1863) **iii** 1459.

64 *Malachi* 1 and 3.
65 The Old Testament in Greek, attributed to 72 translators working in Alexandria.
66 For a discussion on the Temple and its iconography, *see* Rosenau (1979). *See* also Hamblin & Seely (2007) 42-9.

(actually the Rabbinical texts known as the *Mishnah*). It appears that the Temple itself was based upon Zerubbabel's building, but surrounded by a huge wall of great strength 180 cubits by 240, and adorned by porches and ten gates of some architectural magnificence. Beyond this there was an outer enclosure, some 400 cubits square, adorned with porticoes of great splendour: it would seem that something very akin to the Classical Orders was used for embellishment. The most impressive parts of the Temple appear to have been the vast ranges of colonnades in the outer court, and the Temple's inner court on a raised platform was approached through architecturally grand gateways, the finest of which was the eastern gate leading from the Court of the Women to the Upper Court. Just inside this gateway was the huge Altar of Burnt Offerings, 50 cubits square and 15 cubits high (but, according to *Middoth*, smaller).

However, the Temple itself differed from earlier versions in having a very wide front with wings or shoulders, and was 100 cubits wide, the same as the length. In the centre of this front, according to Josephus and *Middoth*, was a large arch, probably 40 cubits high[67]. Biblical and other architectural descriptions are notoriously difficult to unravel, so the opening may not have been an arch at all, but a horizontal-headed opening (the more likely type). Unfortunately, we do not know much about how the rest of the front was treated, whether it was plain, had pilasters, or a series of arcades (like the Palace, Ctesiphon, Mesopotamia). The most likely architectural flavour was probably Hellenistic, and almost certainly with a pronounced Roman flavour.

Thus the Temple proper was a T-shape on plan, with a massive, wide, tall front approached by a flight of steps. Numismatic and other evidence suggests that the Temple either had four massive columns supporting a triangular pediment, or that the columns were engaged (i.e. partially buried in the front wall), or that it had pilasters supporting a pediment. It would seem that gold was liberally applied, but exactly how is uncertain: it was probably a means of embellishing capitals and bases, but whether these were of columns or pilasters is not known.

It is also uncertain if the whole of the T-shaped Temple was the same height as, or if the front was taller than, the rest of the building. However, the wide front element contained a vestibule with an elaborate entrance to the Holy Place, probably flanked by columns. This entrance was hung with a multi-coloured 'veil' behind which was the Holy Place at the western end of which another 'veil' screened the Holy of Holies. As before, the Holy Place contained the table for the Bread of the Presence, the Altar for incense, and the seven-branched candelabrum: its walls were hung with plates of gold. As the Ark had been lost, the Holy of Holies was empty, except for the gold plates on the walls, although tradition has it that a bedrock on the floor was the place where the world began, and so this rock was sprinkled with sacrificial blood by priests on the Day of Atonement. This rock is probably the same as that within the so-called 'Mosque of Omar' or 'Dome of the Rock', completed in AD 691: the Rock is also associated with Jacob's Ladder, with the Ascent of Mohammed, and with much else of great significance for the Abrahamic religions.

It is clear that Herod's Temple was a huge building of great architectural magnificence. The wall that surrounded the site was of plain ashlar up to the level of the courts (part of this is the Wailing Wall), with a series of repetitive pilaster-strips, a monumental theme visible today at the wall of the Herodian shrine of Hebron which surrounds the Tombs of the Patriarchs. Somewhat unnervingly, Albert Speer followed a similar arrangement at the *Haupttribüne*, *Zeppelinfeld*, Nuremberg (from 1934 – partly destroyed)[68], although square columns rather than pilaster-strips were exploited. Herod's fidelity to Rome made the Kingdom of Judaea an important factor in the defences of the Empire. Herod's son, Archelus, failed to guarantee anything like security, so Rome assumed direct control, although Herod Agrippa I once again briefly stabilised loyalty. However, the imposition of direct Roman rule inflamed Jewish nationalism, and the First Revolt (AD 66-70) caused much damage to Jerusalem by rival Jewish factions: this, however, was insignificant to the wholesale destruction caused when Titus (reigned as Emperor AD 79-81) sacked Jerusalem, destroyed the Temple, and enslaved many Jews. The Arch of Titus in Rome (AD 71) shows processions in which loot from the Temple is carried in triumph.

Among the artefacts alleged to have been brought to Rome by Titus were twelve spiral columns supposedly from the Herodian Temple: these, however, appear in fact to have been introduced to Rome by Constantine the Great to support the canopy over the tomb of the Apostle Peter in the old Basilica of St Peter, Rome (c.324-30). Nevertheless, they have somehow been associated with the Temple, and the twisted form is called 'Solomonic', particularly connected with Jewish architecture, and especially with the Solomonic Temple[69].

During the reign of Hadrian attempts were made to restore Jerusalem as a great Graeco-Roman city, but the Jews again rose in rebellion under Bar Kochba in the Second Revolt (AD 131-5): this was crushed, Jerusalem was re-named Aelia Capitolina, and only Gentiles were allowed to reside there. The remains of the Herodian Temple were used as a quarry for new buildings, some of which were removed by Constantine when he established Jerusalem as an important place of pilgrimage. The city surrendered to Muslim forces in 638, and subsequently suffered many vicissitudes which are beyond the scope of the present work.

The short reign of the Emperor Flavius Claudius Julianus, known as Julian The Apostate, attempted to restore polytheism, perceiving (with ample justification) that monotheistic religions such as Christianity were forces of persecution and intolerance. Conscious of the position Christians took *vis-à-vis* the Jews, Julian allowed the Jews

---

67 Smith (*Ed.*) (1863) iii 1464.

68 Arndt, Koch, & Larsson (1978) 11-17.
69 *See* Ward-Perkins (1952).

to settle in Jerusalem once more, and gave government aid to rebuild the Temple. However, earthquakes and storms held up the works (to the satisfaction of Christians), and Julian's early death in battle against the Persians put paid to the scheme. Christianity was restored, Julian's death was hailed as righteous punishment for his apostasy, and the Jews were once more subjugated.

In the seventh century the Jews again saw in a Persian invasion of Byzantine territory some hopes of recovering lost ground, but the Emperor Heraclius recaptured Jerusalem (629) and oppressed the Jews, thus ending any hopes of restoring the Temple, although the Muslim conquest in 636-9 gave the Jews renewed expectations as Byzantine power waned, for the Caliph Omar (Umar) permitted the Jews to resettle in Jerusalem, and the Temple Mount (which had been deliberately defiled by Christians) was cleansed. Even the erection of a mosque on the site of the Temple seems to have been at least partially accepted, for after the viciousness of the Christians the Muslim conquerors seemed to be relatively benevolent. Indeed, it appears that, until around 720 or thereabouts, Jews cleaned the mosque, cared for its lamps, and acted as caretakers. But as Islam and Judaism inevitably grew more antagonistic towards each other, all realistic Jewish hopes for a restoration of the Temple waned, and no further attempts were made to rebuild it.

What *is* significant, however, is that the destruction of the Temple[70] represented a huge Loss, and it was so for both Jews and Christians. Notions of prophecies concerning the rebuilding of the Temple and the restoration of Jerusalem (not just physically, but as a home for the Jews) were the subjects of much study. Christians had to re-evaluate what their attitudes towards the Temple should actually be, but for both religions the loss of the actual Temple created a mystical idea of a celestial Temple to be found in the mind, in contemplation, in the imagination. Freemasonry has long revered the Temple as a symbol of what has been lost, as an ideal, as the model for the Lodge, and as an inspiration of what might be reconstructed. The Knights Templars also held Solomon's Temple in considerable reverence, and it is difficult to accept that there was absolutely no connection between Freemasonry and the Templars, although the evidence is obscure, not surprisingly. These matters will be outlined below.

Representations of the Temple

Illustrations showing the Temple in Classical Antiquity tend to depict aediculated forms or the entrance portico of what are clearly Classical compositions, and do not concern us here[71]. After the destruction of the Temple, it remained important to Jews, surviving through images, tradition, descriptions, and iconography. Daily religious readings helped to preserve ideas of the Temple, not only

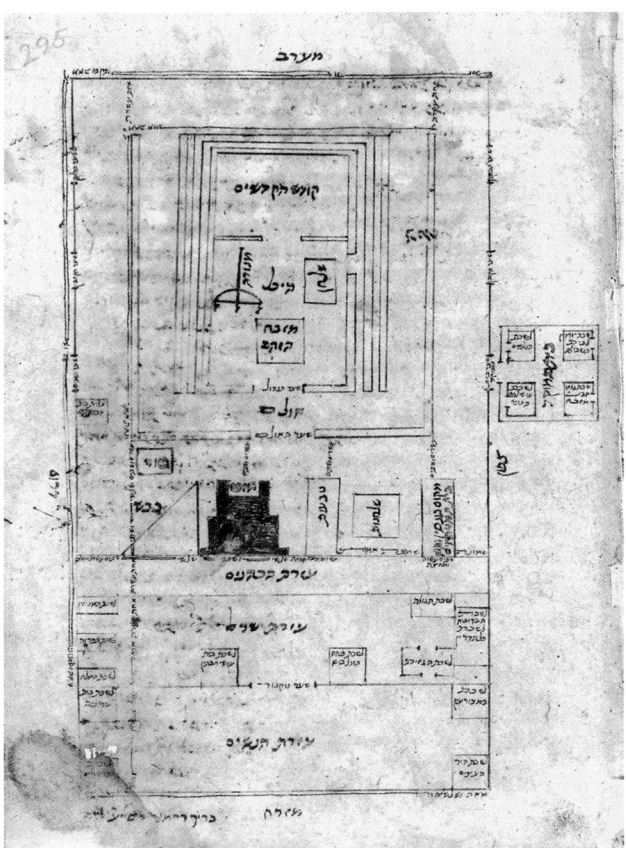

Pl.V.1 Moses Ben Maimon's plan of the Temple, a twelfth-century version based on *Mishnah* (BO. MS. Pococke. fol. 295 R).

the building itself, but the rituals carried out within it and its precincts.

Of considerable importance in the preservation of tradition was the commentary and codification of the oral law passed down through many generations. Moses Ben Maimon (better known, perhaps, as Maimonides), was a singularly important figure as an interpreter of the Jewish Code of Laws, and was the author of the *Mishnah* (or *Mishneh*) *Torah*, or Code of Maimonides[72], a kind of *summa theologiae* of Judaism. Maimonides included drawings to illustrate his description of the Temple and its artefacts, not just as an historical record, but as an attempt to prepare Jews for a time in the future when the Temple could be reconstructed. These illustrations were captioned in Hebrew (**Pl.V.1**) even though the main parts of the texts of his Commentary on the *Mishnah* and the *Book of Commandments* were in Arabic.

Maimonides's *Mishnah Torah* secured him a commanding position in the evolution of Rabbinical Law, and represents the first of a series of authoritative Codes: it was translated into Latin by Louis Compiègne de Veil as *De Cultu Divino, ex Mosis Majemonidae secunda Lege seu Manu Forti Liber*

---

70 Goldhill (2005).
71 Rosenau (1979). *See* especially Dr Rosenau on the Synagogue of Dura-Europos and others.

72 *See* Yale Judaica Series **xii** (1957): *The Code of Maimonides, Book Eight. The Book of Temple Service* (New Haven CT & London: Yale UP). *See* also Danby (Tr.) (1933).

VIII... published in Paris in 1678, and reprinted in *Fasciculus sextus Opisculorum quae ad historiam ac philologiam sacram spectant* in Rotterdam in 1696. Another Rotterdam version has a slightly different title: *De Cultu divino ex R. Majemonidae secundae legis, seu manus fortis libro VIII.*

Maimonides's illustrations and those of Richard of St Victor[75] attempted to reconstruct the Temple, including waters gushing from under the buildings. Richard of St Victor, in his *De Templo Salomonis ad litteram* and in his *De Aedificia Ezechielis*, occasionally called *In Visionem Ezechielis*, went into the problem at length: his plan has a distinct vestibule, the Temple with altar in the centre, and the Holy of Holies beyond. These versions show highly organised buildings, and have a pronounced architectonic quality. In the case of Richard of St Victor he was among the very first to attempt explanations of the sense of the Scriptures, and he was the first to provide drawings (a plan, with three views showing, as would be expected of the period, a Romanesque building). Reproductions of these were printed in Richard's *Opera Omnia*, published in Paris in 1518, in Lyons in 1534, in Venice in 1592, and later in 1650.

Of course there are notorious problems facing the draughtsman who has to work from descriptions alone. The case of the Mausoleum at Halicarnassus is typical and celebrated, for although we have bits of that great Hellenistic building, know much about Greek Architecture, and have a description from Pliny, the variations of interpretation have been many[74]. The difficulties with the Solomonic Temple are compounded by the differences between the accounts of the building in I *Kings* 6 & 7 and those in II *Chronicles* 3 & 4, not to mention the fact that we do not know nearly as much about Jewish Architecture before the Graeco-Roman ascendancy as we do about the Classical language of Architecture[75]. Certain commentators, including Moses Ben Maimon, thought that the Second Temple (that of Zerubbabel, reported in *Ezra*) was largely a rebuild of the Solomonic Temple with additions from the Ezekiel account.

The late thirteenth- and early fourteenth-century Franciscan, Nicolaus de Lyra, acquired his reputation by interpreting the Temple in his *Postilla litteralis* and *Postilla mystica seu moralis*; it is clear he knew Maimonides and other Jewish and Christian sources, but his great

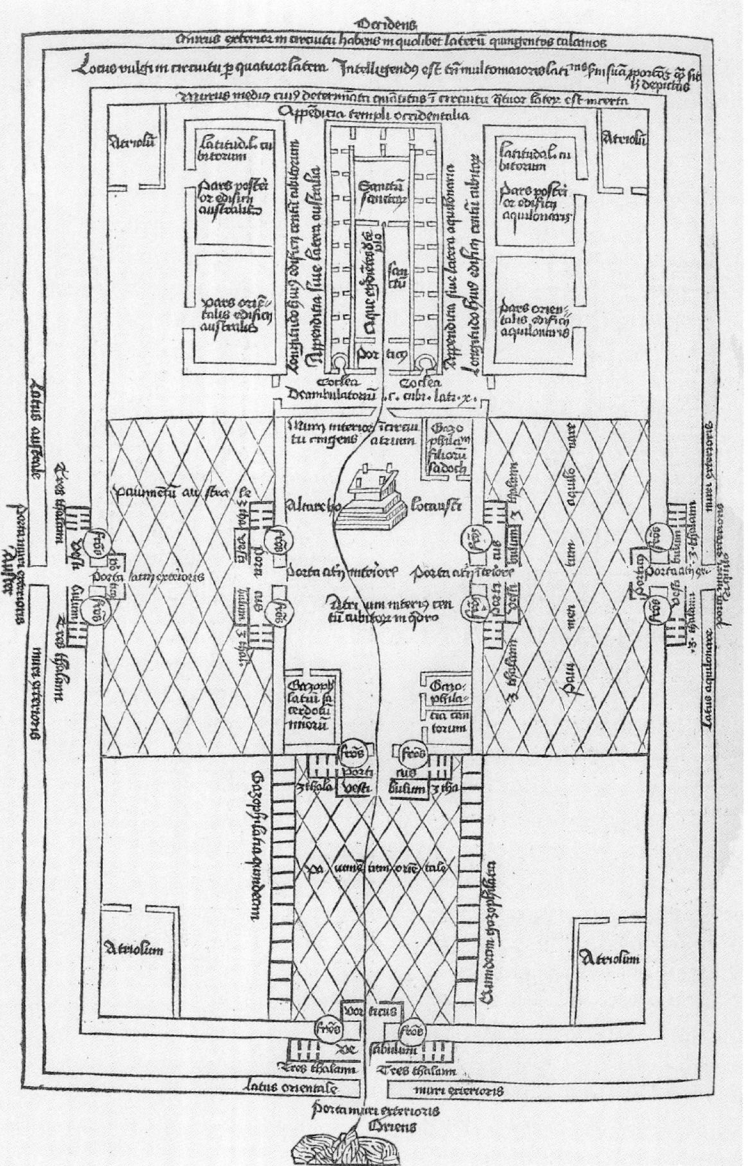

Pl.V.2 Plan of the Temple and precincts in Jerusalem. From Nicolaus de Lyra, *Prologus Primus... fratris Nicolai de Lira in testamentum vetus, et... Explicit postilla...* printed by Koburger, or Koberger, in Nürnberg in 1481 (*BL. IC. 7206*).

importance lies in his attempts to illustrate the complete Temple complex.[76] Moses Ben Maimon's diagram of the Temple seems to have been the model for Nicolaus de Lyra's clear plan, although de Lyra goes into much greater detail, showing a symmetrical ramp to the altar, columns *in antis*, and a highly organised architectonic arrangement of elements.[77] De Lyra's *Postillae* were printed with all the illustrations in the edition of the Bible published by Anton Koberger as *Postillae super Biblia cum additionibus Pauli Burgensis* in Nuremberg in 1481, 1485, and 1493; other early printed editions include those of Basel (1498 and 1502), Venice (1489 and 1588), and Lyons (1502). The *Postillae*

---

73 Richard became Prior of the Abbey of St Victor, near Paris, an Augustinian foundation. He probably came from the Diocese of Carlisle, and some hold that he was a Scot.

74 See Curl (1980) 28-30.

75 The Biblical accounts make one long for an Editor-in-Chief of these prolix, contradictory, and also repetitive descriptions that are infuriatingly difficult (and infinitely tedious) to decipher.

76 BN. MS. Latin 358 and 461. *See* Nicolaus de Lyra (1481).

77 Rosenau (1979) *passim*.

Pl.V.3 Version of Franciscus Vatablus's (François Vatable) designs for the Temple of Solomon (which originally appeared in the Estienne Bible published in Paris in 1540), from the edition published in Venice in 1648. Similar illustrations were printed in the François Perrin/ Antoine Vincent Bible of 1567, and there were many other close copies made over the years. Note the fact that the roof is removed (*left*) to permit the Ark and Cherubim to be seen. Jachin and Boaz, with globular 'chapiters', stand in front of the main façade. The view of the Temple with courts and altar (*right*) bears a strong resemblance to the illustrations of Masonic Lodges published in the 'exposures' of the eighteenth century (*UGLE*).

illustrations were not only based on Biblical sources, but were once much admired for their quality.[78] Koberger's ground-plan of the Temple is only one of several versions of de Lyra's images, and his woodcuts follow quite closely original illustrations in manuscripts (**Pl.V.2**).

It is perhaps significant to record that John Calvin used the term 'temple' to designate churches devoted to his cause not only to differentiate Calvinist churches from those of other denominations, but to emphasise the Biblical roots of Protestant faith in that he saw his own ministry as a continuation of ancient pre-Roman Catholic priesthood. By the time of Denis Diderot's *Encyclopédie* (from 1751) the French regarded the words 'temple' and 'church' as synonymous, but 'church' was not necessarily applied to Protestant places of worship: in other words a 'church' was not always Protestant, but a 'temple' was if used to describe a Christian place of worship. This fact is very significant when we consider the honours accorded to the Protestants and to Protestantism in Masonic circles in Roman Catholic countries during the Enlightenment.

Now 'temple' used as a term for a Protestant church suggests a connection with the Temple, and indeed the associations of the Temple of Solomon with circular or polygonal buildings stems from the perceptions of buildings such as the Dome of the Rock or the Church of the Holy Sepulchre, which had a profound influence *because* they were associated with Biblical Antiquity[79]. Besides, circular or centrally-planned buildings such as Dresden's *Frauenkirche* (1722-43, reconstructed 1996-2005), by Georg Bähr[80], lent themselves to congregational static worship

and to the hearing of The Word: the basilican arrangement, later translated into Romanesue and Gothic buildings, was wholly unsuited to this form of worship.

Just as the Renaissance turned to Antiquity, so did the Reformation turn to Biblical sources for 'truth' and *Ur*-texts. Franciscus Vatablus (or François Vatable), held a Chair in Hebrew at the College de France in Paris: he appears to have had Protestant leanings, for he was denounced for heresies at one stage, and indeed seems to have had contact, direct or indirect, with Ulrich (Huldreich) Zwingli, the Protestant theologian. Robert Estienne, the publisher, produced an edition of the Bible in 1540 to which he added Vatablus's commentaries that included chapters on Ezekiel together with Vatablus's woodcuts of the Temple (these wood-cuts subsequently reappeared in other editions, notably the *Biblia Sacra* of 1573 published in Paris). Variants recur in a 1567 Bible brought out by François Perrin and Antoine Vincent, and in a Venetian version of 1648 (**Pl.V.3**). Not only is the Temple shown with the roof off so that the Ark could be depicted, but Jachin and Boaz are indicated with globes on top as 'chapiters'. Now these illustrations are very significant, for the details are proto-Masonic, while the method of illustration and presentation seem to herald later illustrations of Freemasons' Lodges. The Vatablus woodcuts appeared again in the editions of the Bible published by Estienne in 1545 and 1546, and in another published in Geneva in 1557: they were also used by Jean de Tournes in a French Bible of 1551 published in Lyons, and in a Frankfurt-am-Main Bible of 1571. Another Geneva edition by Estienne of 1560 (this time a translation) also included an aerial view of the Temple with a key.

Matthias Hafenreffer produced a *Templum Ezechielis*[81] in Tübingen in 1613 (*see* **Pl.V.4**, p.80) based on an axial

---

78 Rosenau (1979) 39. I am grateful to Dr Rosenau for discussing these matters with me. *See* Nicolaus de Lyra (1481).
79 Colvin (1991) *passim*.
80 Drummond (1934) 29, 31, and *passim*. Frauenkirche = Church of Our Lady.
81 Hafenreffer (1613).

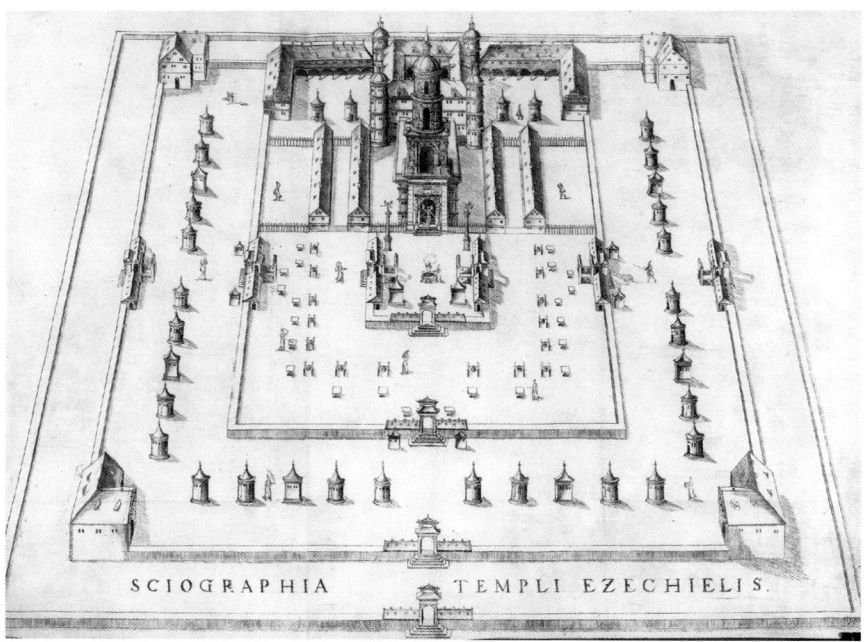

Pl.V.4 Bird's-eye view of Hafenreffer's version of the Temple from his *Templum Ezechielis* published in Tübingen in 1613 (*BL. 690 g. 4*).

scheme with Solomon's Palace situated behind the Temple. Hafenreffer was a Protestant Pastor, Mathematician, and Natural Scientist, who favoured an ordered axial arrangement for his 'reconstruction' based on Ezekiel, but he clearly knew Vatablus's work, for he used one of his designs in his own book. Hafenreffer was a teacher and friend of Johann Kepler (who attended the University of Tübingen from 1588, became assistant to Tycho Brahe at the Prague Observatory, and, in 1627, gave the *Rudolphine Tables* to the world which remained for a century or so the best aid to the study of Astronomy). Hafenreffer's commentaries on Ezekiel can be regarded as the Protestant view of the Temple (compared with Roman Catholic investigations such as those of the Jesuit Villalpando which will be described below). Hafenreffer proposed a Sublime Geometry of Harmony and Proportion, and his investigations dealing with the quadrature (or squaring) of the circle and the determination of the value of π were deduced from the geometrical relationships of the Temple as reconstructed[82]. In the *Appendix Geometrica* of his *Templum Ezechielis*, Hafenreffer's claim that the Prophet had provided enough detail to set out the geometric principles on which the design of the Temple was based was apparently arrived at after discussions not only with Kepler but with Michael Maestlin (Kepler's mentor, who taught Mathematics at Tübingen from 1583).

Further plans of the Solomonic and Ezekiel Temples were published, notably by Sébastien Chatillon in his Bible published in Basel in 1551 with subsequent editions. Hector Pinto, in his *In Ezechielem Prophetam commentaria*, published in Salamanca in 1568, merged various ideas, including those of Richard of St Victor and of Hugh of St Cher's *Postillae in sacram scripturam...* printed in the Basel Bible of 1498. Benedictus (Benito) Arias Montano, in his *Exemplar*, published in Antwerp in 1572 in the Antwerp Polyglot Bible, included three illustrations of the Temple which were subsequently reprinted in Leiden in 1593, in London in 1660, and in Amsterdam in 1698. He included much material from the *Middoth*[83] and clearly considered all three Jewish Temples (those of Solomon, Zerubbabel, and Herod) as real, rather than symbolic, ideal, or visionary buildings.

While Protestants had certainly concerned themselves with matters relating to the Temple, investigation of the subject received a considerable boost when the Jesuits Hieronymo (Jerónimo) de Prado and Juan Bautista Villalpando produced their *In Ezechielem Explanationes et Apparatus Urbis ac Templi Hierosolymitani, commentariis et imaginibus illustratus* in Rome from 1596 to 1631. The illustrations in the volume entitled *De Postrema Ezechielis Prophetae Visione* (Rome, 1631) showed the Temple with a highly organised plan and elevations of considerable grandeur; in fact, they were certainly a cut above any earlier designs, but they were based on absurd assumptions that the Temples of *Chronicles, Kings,* and *Ezekiel* were one and the same, and that the Herodian Temple was a myth (*see* **Pls.V.5 & 6**, opposite and p. 82). Villalpando insisted on the claim that the Solomonic Temple was designed by God, was therefore perfect, and was the great forerunner of the Christian church: the idea that the Architects of the Temple had been divinely inspired, and that Classical Orders derived from the Temple, and therefore from God, was firmly planted. Furthermore, Villalpando proposed that only by producing accurate architectural drawings of the Temple could the essence of the prophetic visions in the Bible be understood: this seems to be an allusion to the Art of Memory, in a somewhat roundabout way[84].

The odd thing about Villalpando's version of the Temple is that it is more a grandiose Renaissance building than a reconstruction based on historical analysis. Villalpando's Temple was a stunning image *in Renaissance terms* of the Architecture which he imagined God had created: not only the forms and proportions, but the Orders of Architecture, were designed from the divinely inspired Order of the Temple. He connected Classicism, Vitruvius, and Holy Writ in an attempt to demonstrate that Christian Revelation and Classical Antiquity were compatible, and there are indications that the whole process of disentangling an

---

82 Reich & Knobloch (2002) 157-183.

83 *See* Epstein (*Ed.*) (1948).
84 *See* Villalpandus (1596 and ff).

Architecture from the clues in the Bible was seen in similar terms to proceeding through a labyrinth. It is interesting that the descriptions in Ezekiel were called *mysteriorum Dei labyrinthum* by St Jerome himself in his *Commentariorum in Ezechielem Prophetam,* while allegorical meanings were also the concern of St Gregory in *Homiliarum in Ezechielem,* of Bede in *De Templo Salomonis,* and of other early commentators.[85] Themes recur, merge, and overlap.

Villalpando's plan resembles that of the Escorial Palace, near Madrid (see **Pl.V.7**, p.82), designed by Juan Bautista de Toledo and Juan de Herrera for King Philip II, and which again has a curious iconography, discussed at length by René Taylor elsewhere.[86] In the Escorial ideas of the Temple, the tomb, the monastery, the palace, and the pattern combine with symbols of martyrdom, with the Signs of the Zodiac, and with Hermetic-Alchemical-Astrological ideas. The religious and mystical nature of the King, his ascetic habits, his devotional routine, his interest in Relics (he had a vast collection amassed not only from piety, but for reasons of belief in their beneficent and medicinal qualities), and the various uses of the Escorial (including that of mausoleum for the Roman Catholic monarchs of Spain) all found a place on the extraordinary building. Even the angle-towers of the Escorial and the form of the plan have been suggested to represent the bases and design of the grid-iron on which St Laurence suffered his martyrdom (Pope Gregory XIII presented a pot full of the melted fat of St Laurence to the King of Spain, which may help to explain this complicated allusion)[87].

Herrera himself is known to have been a Lullist, that is influenced by Raimon Lull, who was a mystic, philosopher, and who sought to unite Roman Catholic, Jew, and Moslem by means of their common philosophical, mystical, and scientific beliefs. Lull was

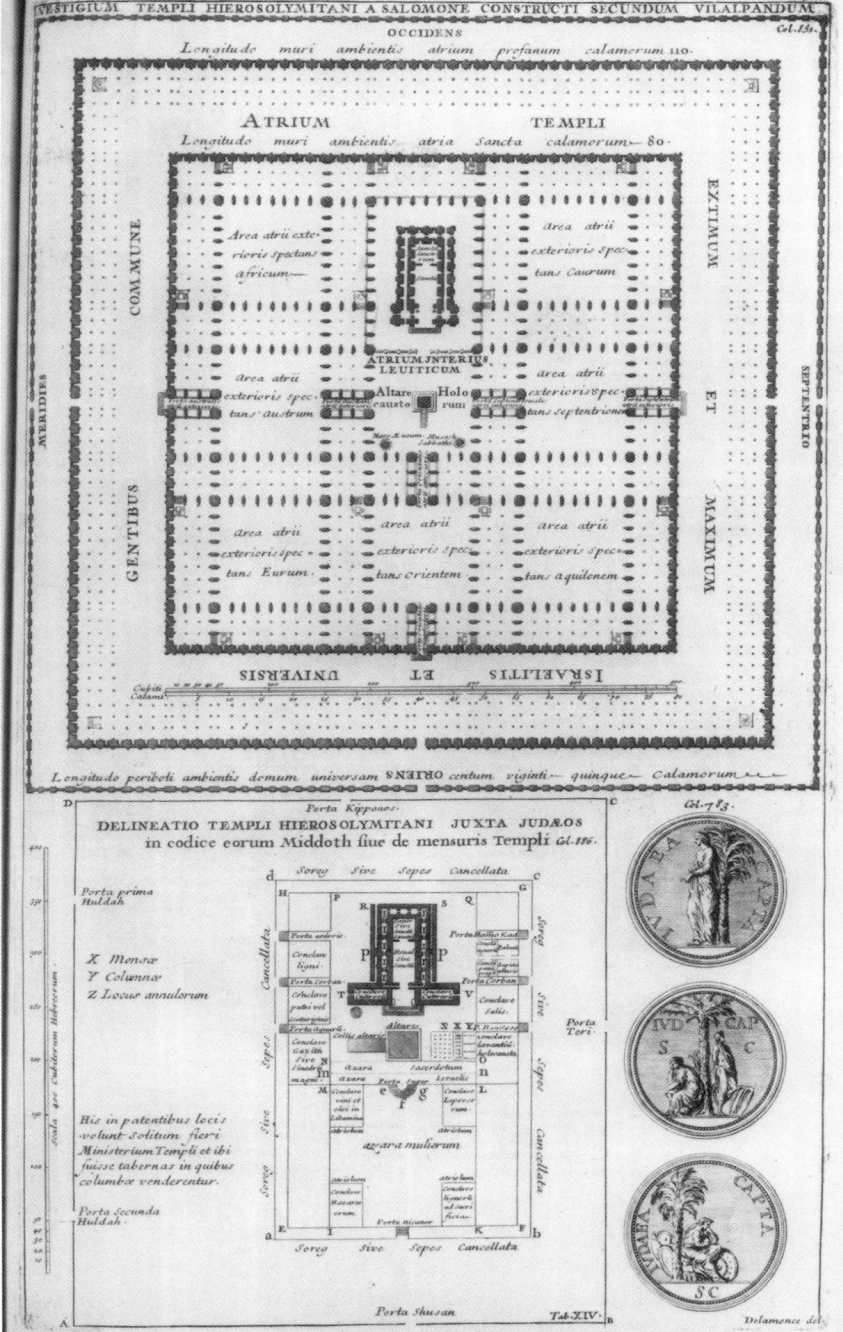

Pl.V.5 Plan of the Temple and its precincts in Jerusalem by Juan Bautista Villalpando from his *De Postrema Ezechielis Prophetae Visione,* published in Rome in 1631. The highly regular plan should be noted. This version of Villalpando's Temple is from Plate XIV of Lamy (1720). As well as Villalpando's plan this plate shows (*bottom*) a plan based on *Middoth*: note the wide front of the Temple, similar to the version proposed by Perrault (BL. 691. k. 15).

a Christian Cabbalist, and some of his ideas permeated Renaissance Neoplatonism.[88] Herrera himself owned a large collection of Hermetic writings, and had taught Villalpando. Both Juan Bautista de Toledo and Herrera were involved in astrological investigations, and in studies

---

85 See Hermann, Wolfgang (1967): 'Unknown Designs for the "Temple of Jerusalem" by Claude Perrault' in Fraser, Hibbard, & Lewine (Eds.) (1967) 143-158.

86 Taylor, René (1967): 'Architecture and Magic: Considerations on the *Idea* of the Escorial' in Fraser, Hibbard, & Lewine (Eds.) (1967) 81-109.

87 Baring-Gould (1914) **ix** 109-10.

88 Yates (1979) 9-15.

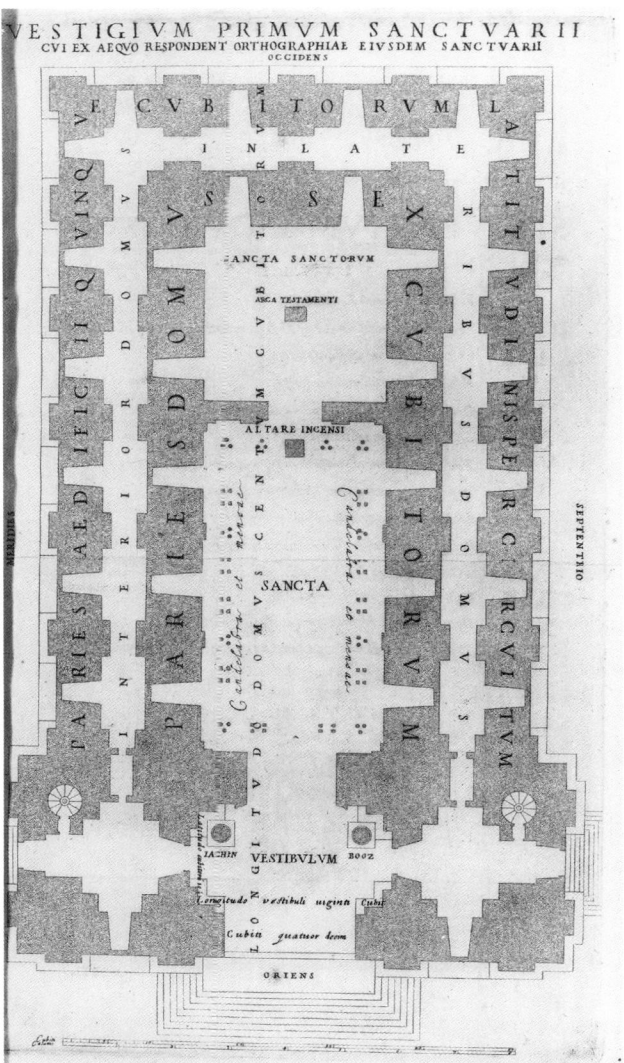

Pl.V.6 Detail of the plan of the Temple by Villalpando showing the porch and Jachin and Boaz, from his *De Postrema…* (UGLE).

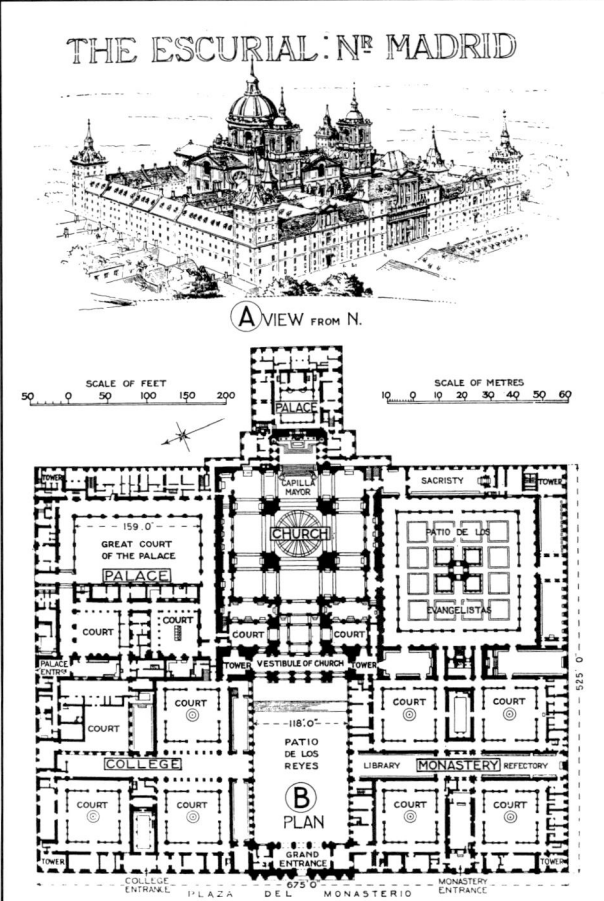

Pl.V.7 The Escurial (Escorial), near Madrid, showing the plan and a view from the north. The plan has certain close affinities with Villalpando's interpretation of the Temple in Jerusalem. From Fletcher (1954) 759 *(Collection JSC/RIBA)*.

of the occult, and it seems obvious that the Escorial designs may have influenced Villalpando for the illustrations of the Temple in his *In Ezechielem Explanationes*. Through Herrera and other influences Villalpando was steeped in Vitruvian ideas, and was concerned to interpret descriptions in *Chronicles* and in *Ezekiel* as part of a syncretic Biblical/ Christian/ Architectural study.

It also must be considered whether or not the Escorial was itself influenced by descriptions of the Temple: from the complexities of intermingled iconographies prevalent at the time it would seem highly probable. The Escorial was certainly influenced by Lullism, by Vitruvian patterns, and by ideas concerning the order and harmony of the universe. It is a design so full of astrological, magical, religious, geometrical, and other allusions that it cannot be discussed at length here. René Taylor[89] covers the Hermetic and other aspects in considerable detail and with enormous erudition.

If it is so that the Escorial *was* actually based on the Temple, then Philip of Spain was identified with Solomon himself, and indeed that was so, for Fray José de Sigüenza, in his *Tercera parte de la Historia de la Orden de San Geronimo*, published in Madrid in 1605, refers to the new Temple of Solomon and to the fact that Philip attempted to imitate Solomon in his works.[90] Villalpando's Temple, like Herrera's Escorial, was a symbol of the Almighty's creation, and held within it systems of hierarchy and of universal order. Its connection with the design of the Escorial is interesting, for that curious pile has strong astrological allusions, and mixes Hermetic, Solomonic, Christian, Jewish, and other symbols and connections with ideas of harmony, organisation, syncretism, and Vitruvian architecture. In this respect it is a very interesting problem to compare attempts to recreate the Solomonic Temple as the palace-cum-church of a Roman Catholic monarch with an eighteenth-century church of enormous verve and Baroque swagger in which ideas of Imperial grandeur mingle with allusions to Antiquity and to the Temple: this will be discussed shortly.

---

89 *See* footnote 86.

90 Quoted in Taylor *(see* footnote 86 above).

The impact of Villalpando's images was enormous, and had a profound influence on many interpreters, including Guglielmus Surenhusius, although the latter's *Mishnah* (or, properly *Mischna*) included a version of the Temple plan (**Pl.V.8**) that owes more to Maimonides than to Villalpando. The elevational treatment of the buildings, however, is derived from Villalpando, while the early eighteenth-century plates by Jan Luyken (**Pl.V.9**) are also strongly influenced by the earlier images.

Matthaeus Merian the Elder produced an extraordinary version in his collection of illustrations to the Bible (known as *Icones Biblicae*) published (*c*.1650) in *Historiae Sacrae Veteris et Novi Testamenti*. Like the Escorial and Hafenreffer's vision, Merian's is a unified composition of some grandeur, owing more to free interpretation and imagination than to precise adherence to Biblical sources (*see* **Pl.V.10**, p.84). Yet these examples were by no means rare, for no less a figure than Sir Isaac Newton devoted *A Description of the Temple of Solomon* to a study of the measurements of the Temple which was published in 1728 in *Chronology of Ancient Kingdoms Amended*; it contains a plan of the Temple symmetrically arranged. It is extraordinary to consider the attitudes of Newton, the hero of the Enlightenment, for his stance on architectural history was based more on his Unitarian and anti-Papist principles than on reason. The book attempts to determine the dates of events in Antiquity from astronomical considerations, and mixes mythological and historical happenings.

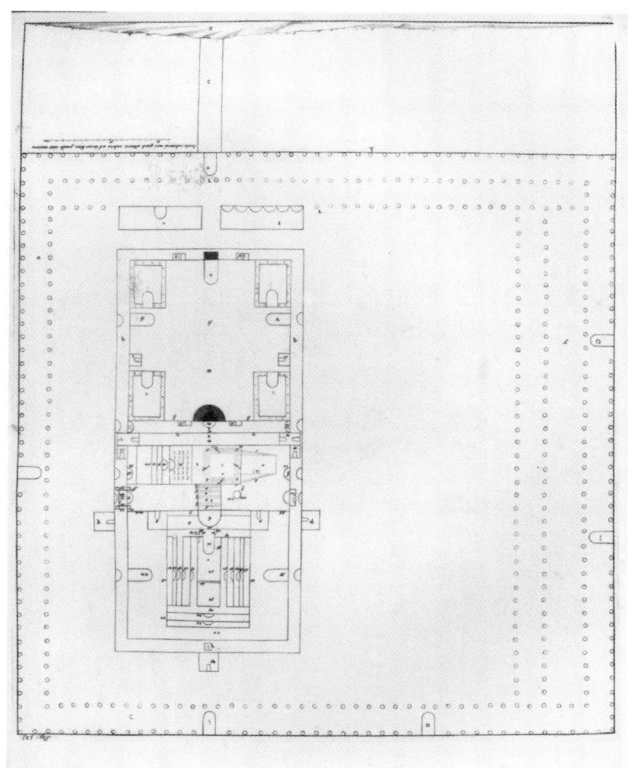

Pl.V.8 Plan of the Temple and its court by Constantinus L'Empereur from Part 5 of Guglielmus Surenhusius's *Mishnah sive Legum Mischnicarum liber qui inscribitur Ordo Sacrorum, etc...* (Amsterdam, 1702). This is based on Moses Ben Maimon, and the parallels with designs for Lodges will be clear. (*BL.15c. 7-12*).

Pl.V.9 The inner courtyard of the Temple in Jerusalem with the Temple Façade, altar, and the two columns of brass, from *Histoire les Plus Remarquables de l'Ancien et du Nouveau Testament*, published by Jean Cóvens and Corneille Mortier (Amsterdam, 1732). This plate, by Jan Luyken (*or* Luiken), is from the French version of *Afbeeldingen der merkwaardigste Geschiedenissen van het Oude en Nieuwe Testament* published in 1729. The Temple is based on Villalpando's work, except that it also has Jachin and Boaz, which signify the Solomonic rather than the later Temple. The plate also shows the Ark with Cherubims in the Holy of Holies, the altar, and the 'molten sea' carried on two rows of oxen (*UGLE*).

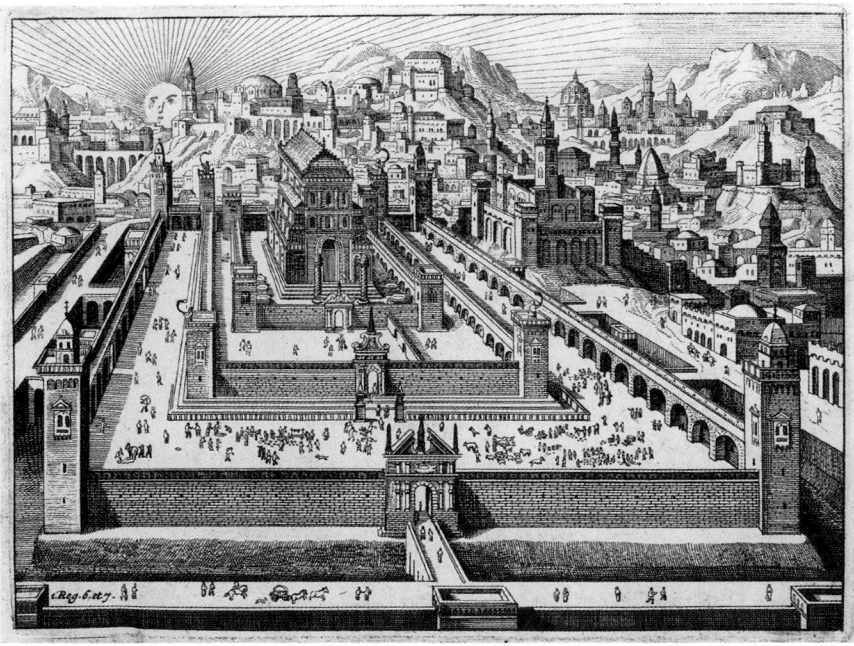 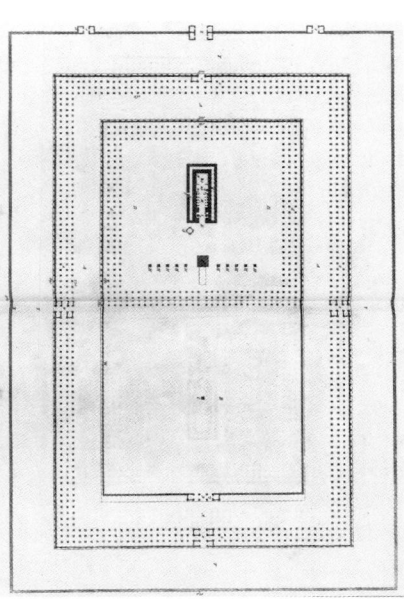

Pl.V.10 View of the Temple in Jerusalem by Matthias Merian, from his *Icones Biblicae*. This copy is from a scrapbook collection of engravings at Freemasons' Hall assembled by Antoine-Louis Moret and entitled *Recueil de vignettes religieuses et maçonniques...* (UGLE).

Pl.V.11 Plan of the Temple in Jerusalem and its precincts by John Wood, from Wood (1741) Plates 24-25 (UGLE).

Newton's volume had a profound influence on John Wood the Elder (also Unitarian and anti-Papist), the man who brought Palladianism to Bath, Bristol, and Liverpool, and author of *The Origin of Building: or, the Plagiarism of the Heathens Detected*, published in Bath in 1741. Wood was obsessed by Masonic symbolism and by mystic considerations. He saw Solomon's Temple as a hieroglyph of Jewish history, and built up the importance of Jewish planning and Architecture in preference to Vitruvian writings, of which he was profoundly suspicious because Vitruvius was a 'pagan' and, in Wood's view, had plagiarised Jewish ideas. In *The Origin of Building* Wood speaks of Lodges being dug in the mountains, and of rocks as symbols of soundness and the foundations of wisdom. Wood wallowed in Celtic prehistory, and seems to have accepted notions that the Orders were divinely ordained and first used in the Temple of Solomon. He saw Bath as a place with temples to the sun and moon, the capital of the Ancient Britons, and as Troy. The new city, with its square, terrace, crescent, forum, and circus, was, in fact, a series of mystical symbols, clothed in Classical Orders that were (to him) not Graeco-Roman but Divine. Royal Crescent was connected with the crescent-moon of Isis-Minerva-Diana-Onca, and King's Circus was a mixture of an Ancient British Temple of the Sun and the Zerubbabel Temple in Jerusalem (an idea derived from the circular visions of the Temple promoted by the Dome of the Rock, the Church of the Holy Sepulchre, Templar churches, and illustrations of the Temple as circular Pantheons by Heemskerck and others). In this book is a plan of King Solomon's Temple that seems to show a rigidly symmetrical scheme owing more to Classical Antiquity and to Newton than to the plans of Constantin L'Empereur or Maimondes (**Pl.V.11**).

Yet, if Vitruvian principles and Classical Architecture were claimed to have derived from the Temple of Solomon and from God, this was hardly surprising. Classical Architecture, anticipated in Biblical times, with the Classical Orders Divinely inspired, was also the theme of Villalpando's thesis in his commentaries on Ezekiel. What was the reason for this? It was clearly to free Classical Architecture from the stigma of pagan origins and thus enable it to be used in Christian churches and in Christian cities (whether Roman Catholic or Protestant). Wood constructed a Classical church within the ruined nave of Llandaff Cathedral in 1734-52 (demolished 1850), which was a hypothetical reconstruction of the inner court of the Solomonic Temple. The masonry of Llandaff's choir was to Wood Romano-Christian, and thus a direct descendant of the Temple built by Hiram using proportions and measurements that had esoteric and Divine symbolism. According to Wood, Bath Abbey had the dimensions of Noah's Ark, of the Tabernacle, and of Solomon's Temple. These matters are discussed further by Mowl and Earnshaw[91].

More extraordinary because of the stripped-down, primitivist, and forward-looking plates, was Bernard Lamy's[92] *De Tabernaculo Foederis, de Sancta Civitate Jerusalem, et de Templo EJUS*, published in Paris in 1720, which depicts a vast stepped platform (**Pl.V.12**) on a scale worthy of the work of Étienne-Louis Boullée, while the Temple itself is a severe, almost Neo-Classical, design (*see* **Pls.V.13-15**,

91 Mowl & Earnshaw (1988).
92 Lamy (1696, 1720).

below and p.86). The wide vestibule and Ledoux-like[93] character of the building point to the *Karlskirche* and to Chaux, both, as we will see, with strong Masonic connections. There are certain stylistic similarities to Claude Perrault's treatment of the same theme in Compiègne de Veil's *De Cultu Divino...*[94]

Fischer von Erlach

It is clear from published sources alone that during the sixteenth-, seventeenth-, and early eighteenth-century periods Jewish, Catholic, Protestant, and other traditions influenced each other, mingling with Hermetic, symbolic, and many other themes at the

---

93 Reminiscent of the severe designs of Claude-Nicolas Ledoux.
94 Compiègne de Veil (1678).

Pl.V.12 *(above)* Plate X from Lamy (1720). This Sublime reconstruction of the Temple in Jerusalem has overtones of Fischer von Erlach, and anticipates the scale of designs by Boullée (BL. 691. k.15).

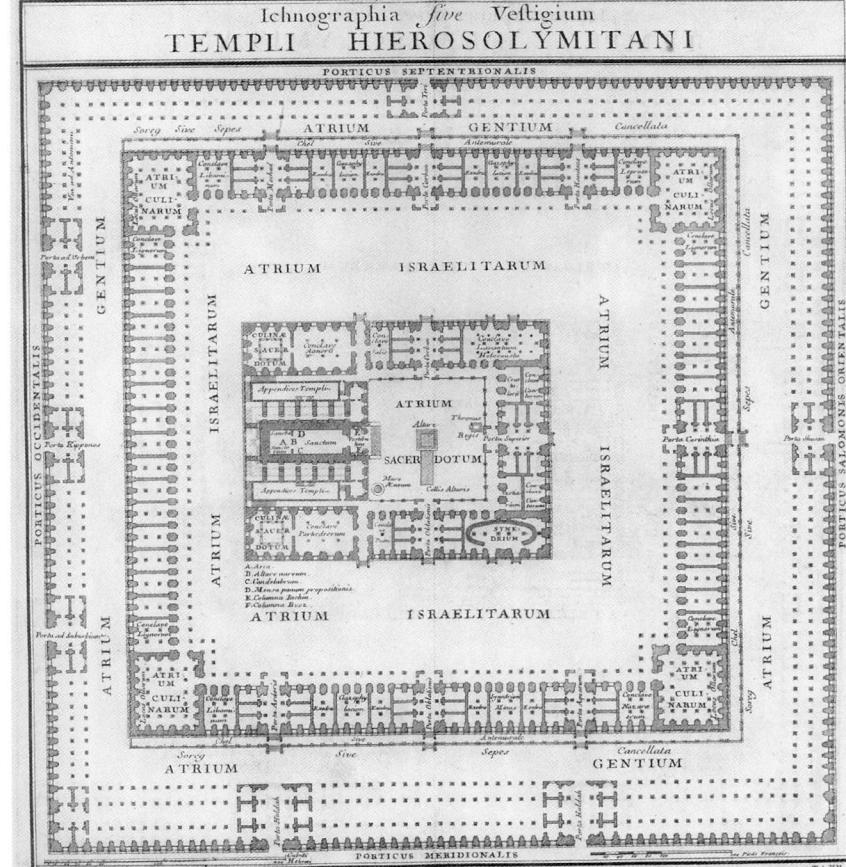

Pl.V.13 Plate XII from Lamy (1720). The plan of the Temple in Jerusalem differs from the influential work of Villalpando; indeed Lamy had little regard for Villalpando, and returned to *Chronicles* for his sources as well as to the *Mishnah*. Jachin and Boaz are shown in the Temple vestibule, and, significantly, they are not indicated as free-standing, but are *in antis* (BL. 691. k. 15).

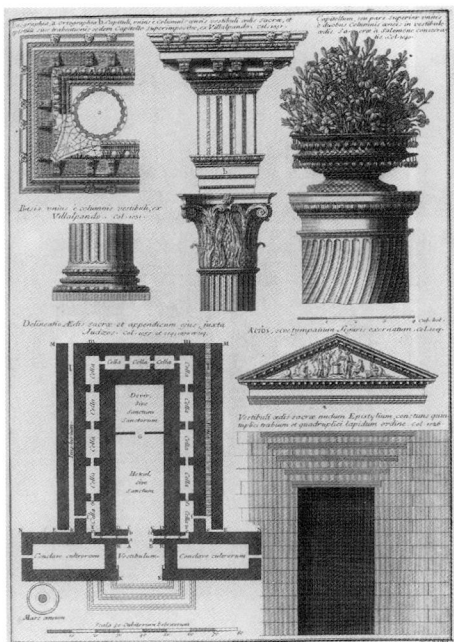

Pl.V.14 Plate XVIII from Lamy (1720). Details of Lamy's reconstruction of the Temple, showing the 'chapiters', a plan of the Temple, and certain comparisons with Villalpando's work. Note the spiral fluting of the column (BL. 691. k. 15).

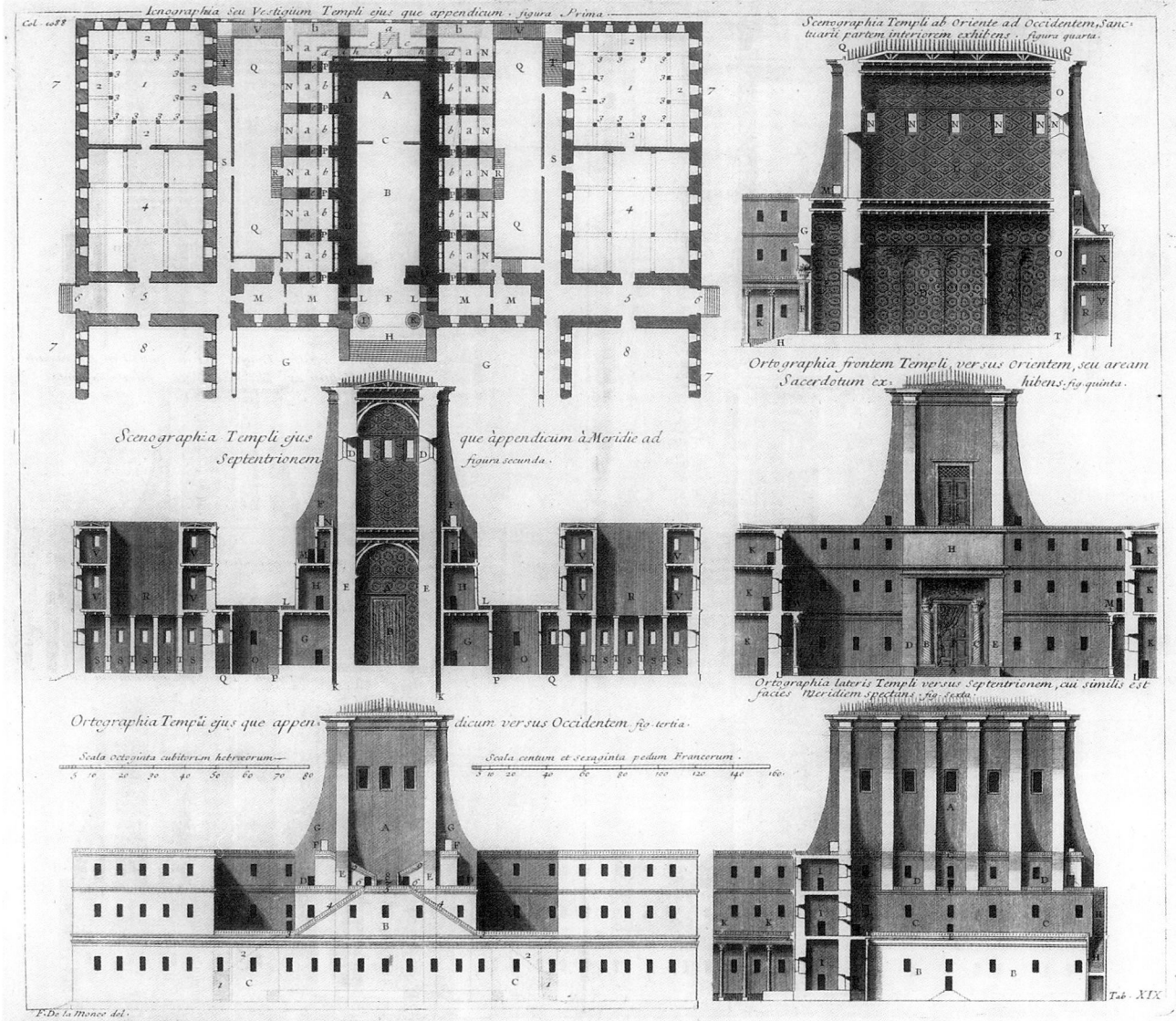

Pl.V.15 Plate XIX from Lamy (1720). The extraordinary details of the Temple, showing the severe proto-Neo-Classical style. The plan (*top*) and elevation (*middle right*) show Jachin and Boaz in the vestibule with their spiral flutings and 'chapiters' (see **Pl.V.14**, p.85) (BL. 691. k. 15).

same time.[95] We have noted the curious coming together of ideas in the Palace of a Roman Catholic King at the Escorial, but there is another great masterpiece of triumphalist Roman Catholic Architecture that hints at Temple and Masonic undertones.

Johann Bernhard Fischer von Erlach[96] met the scholarly Jesuit Athanasius Kircher in Rome[97]. Kircher was one of the first to attempt serious studies of Egyptian and Egyptianising artefacts in Rome, and himself owned a vast collection of such objects. Fischer absorbed many theories while in Rome, as well as acquiring a thorough grounding in the Architecture of Italy and France: among those he met were Giovanni Lorenzo Bernini and Carlo Fontana.

His *Entwurff Einer Historischen Architektur* of 1721[98], however, contains interpretations of Egyptian Architecture that owe more to imagination than to fact, yet had an influence on later Architects such as Boullée, whose vast pyramids with ramps up the sides are clearly derived from Fischer's plates. Fischer believed that Classical Architecture derived from the Temple of Solomon (**Pl.V.16**), and this partially Masonic idea was further expanded in his work by tracing the development of Architecture in Ancient Egypt, Persia, Greece, and in non-European countries. Fischer clearly knew his written sources well, and gives chapter and verse for them (his versions of the Temple of Solomon are based on Villalpando). Where possible, he tried to get drawings of buildings or of ruins, and this helped him to achieve some accuracy. He was acquainted with the philosophy of Gottfried Wilhelm Leibnitz and derived from it his own

95 *See* Yates in the Select Bibliography, and Rosenau on the *Temple* and on *Ideal Cities*. *See also* Stevenson (1988b) and Jones (1956).
96 For Fischer von Erlach *see* Aurenhammer (1973) and especially Sedlmayr (1976).
97 *See* Curl (2005) *passim*. *See also* Godwin (2009).

98 But *see* Fischer von Erlach (1725).

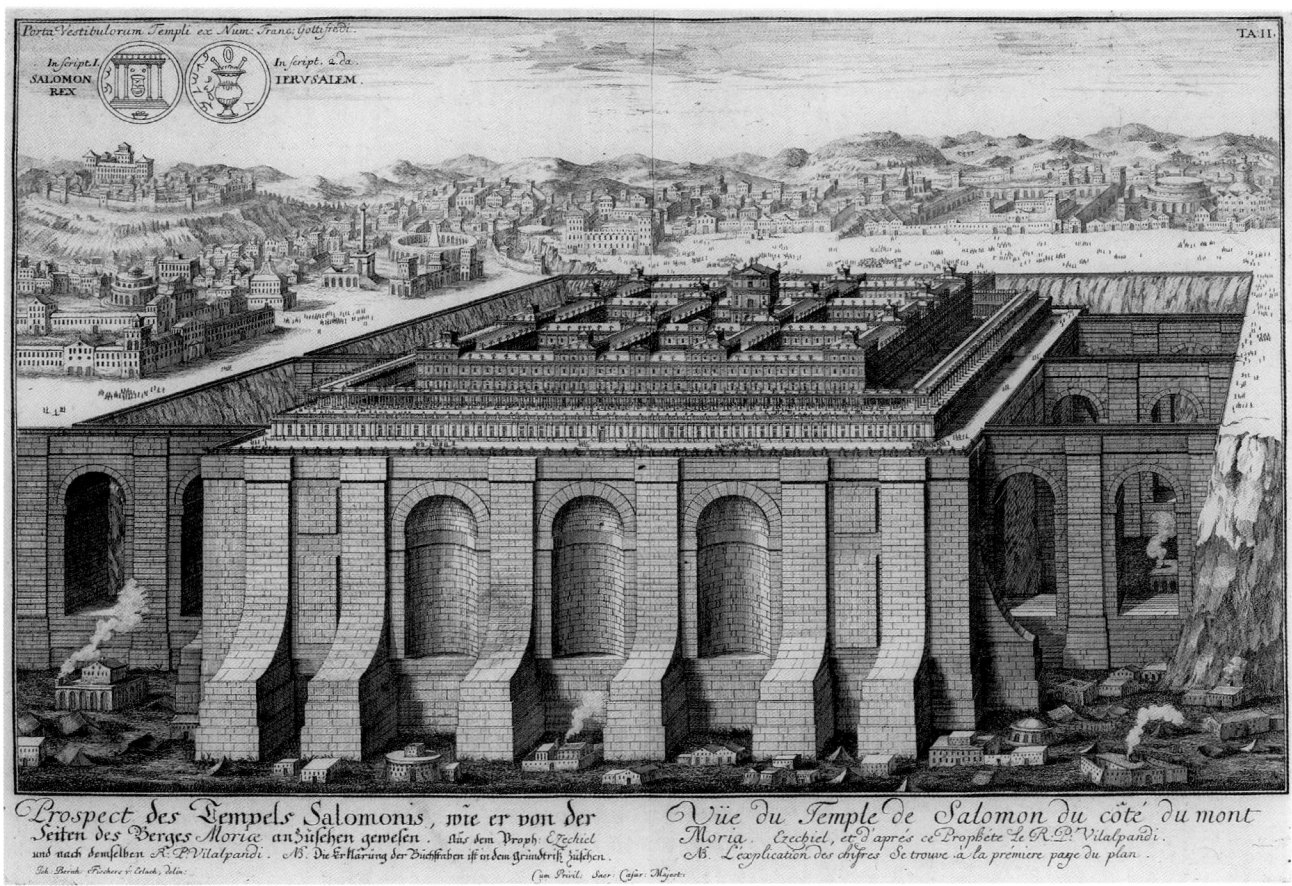

Pl.V.16 Version of Villalpando's Temple of Solomon from Fischer von Erlach (1725) (*Collection JSC*).

theocentric ideas of the world, where God was the greatest of all Architects (a significantly Masonic and Isiac notion).

His enthusiasm for Antiquity was perhaps fired by the antiquarians he had met in Rome (c.1671-84) at the Court of the exiled Queen Christina of Sweden, and his cosmopolitan circle of friends included many in Protestant Northern Europe (notably in Prussia, The Netherlands, and England). It is more than likely that he met Christopher Wren when he visited London in 1704, and it is most unlikely that he avoided all contact with Freemasonry, for indeed some of the ideas expressed in his *Entwurff*, and especially his looking back to the Temple of Solomon and to Egypt, might suggest that he was a Freemason himself. It will be recalled that there were many Freemasons in Prince Eugen of Savoy's entourage, and, as noted previously, that Freemasonry seems to have reached Vienna partly through Masonic influences in The Netherlands[99]. Fischer's use of architectural elements was eclectic in the extreme: one has only to analyse the brilliant *Karlskirche* in Vienna to find many strands that add up to something quite extraordinary which cannot be explained without taking into account several themes that coalesce in a great work of art.

The Case of the *Karlskirche*

In 1713 Plague raged in Vienna. Seeking Divine intercession, the Emperor Charles VI vowed to build a great and magnificent church to deliver his capital from the pestilence. The building was to be dedicated to the Emperor's Patron Saint, St Charles Borromeo[100], and was to be a memorial to the last Habsburg King of Spain and to the dream of uniting the Crowns of the Empire and of Spain, as Charles V had done. The *Karlskirche* draws on elements from several sources which Fischer harmonised in one composition. The Temple in Jerusalem is well to the fore, as would be expected from one who believed that it was the basis from which Architecture itself developed, but it is alluded to in an astonishing way: two massive columns on either side of the great prostyle hexastyle Corinthian portico look like Trajanic columns, but they carry on their spirals reliefs representing scenes from St Charles Borromeo's life and the miracles he performed after his death[101] (*see* **Pls.V.17-20**, pp.88-9).

Now Jachin and Boaz, as well as being associated with the Two Pillars enshrining knowledge of Masonic Legend,

---

99 *See* Jacob (1981) 37, 55-6, 61, 102, 111, 120, 147, 170, 183-5, 188, 202-3, 216, 224-5, 228, 231-2, 261, 274. Some commentators have been dismissive of Jacob's claims.

100 As Archbishop of Milan, Charles Borromeo organised relief in his Plague-stricken diocese in 1576. His was a major force of the Counter-Reformation, and he was canonised in 1610.

101 Aurenhammer (1973) 132.

with the Temple of Solomon, and with Biblical references to earth and heaven supported on pillars (the probable origin of the image of two columns with spheres on top), were also identified with the Pillars of Hercules at the Straits of Gibraltar, which stood *at the end of the world* in the Middle Ages, but signified the gateway to the New World in Renaissance times, with ideas of endless expansion, wealth, knowledge, and a triumphal development of European societies. The motto that there was nothing beyond, in fact, as noted earlier, had become *Plus Ultra*, and recurs in devices of the Holy Roman Emperor himself, of Queen Elizabeth, of the Kings of France, and of many other Renaissance figures[102]. In Masonic thought, therefore, the Two Pillars signified the entrance to the Temple/Lodge not only as a memory of the Temple in Jerusalem, as a reminder of the seeking, finding, and keeping of lost wisdom, but also as a mark of the ending of an old world or existence and the moving from a known world to a new one (in many senses)[103]. As will be seen, the Two Pillars played an enormously important part in Masonic iconography, art, and Architecture, but they were also common and popular emblems during the sixteenth century, as Frances Yates and others have demonstrated. They recurred in one of the grandest of Imperial Baroque Churches in Central Europe. These *columns* were also the Emperor's own emblem, inherited from Charles V: the 'Pillars' therefore carry the Crown of Spain flanked by the eagles of the Holy Roman Empire. The deeds of St Charles also allude to the *Constantia Et Fortitudo* of the Emperor Charles VI: Leibnitz had proposed that ancestors and namesakes of the Emperor should also be celebrated, and their deeds represented on the shafts of the columns, but this was not realised.[104] The columns also allude to Jachin and Boaz, and so to the Solomonic Temple, and their spirals are not only Trajanic, but Masonic and Solomonic, as will be made clear in this study.

The great portico, reminiscent of Antiquity, with the dome behind, recalls the Roman Pantheon; but also derives from images of the Temple as a domed form with the Two Columns standing in front of the steps, as in Maarten van Heemskerck's drawing of the Temple of Jerusalem. Van Heemskerck used Corinthian columns for the Two Pillars, but twisted 'barley-sugar' types for the portico of the Temple itself (**Pl.V.21**). The allusion is further reinforced by Leon Battista Alberti's constant references to temples in his *De re aedificatoria*: temples to the sun should be circular, while the temple of Vesta should be like a ball, he observed, and he calls all places of worship 'temples'. The circular form of the church of the Holy Sepulchre in Jerusalem and the circular Templar churches modelled on it and on the so-called Dome of the Rock (which was used as a church by the Templars and which stood on the great rock associated with the Temple) had potent symbolic, allusory, and visual properties. Other important circular or polygonal structures include the great church at Aachen built by Charlemagne[105], San Stefano Rotondo in Rome, and many Renaissance and Baroque designs (many of which never got off the drawing-board). This important connection between the Dome of the Rock, the church of the Holy Sepulchre, Templar churches in London, and round churches

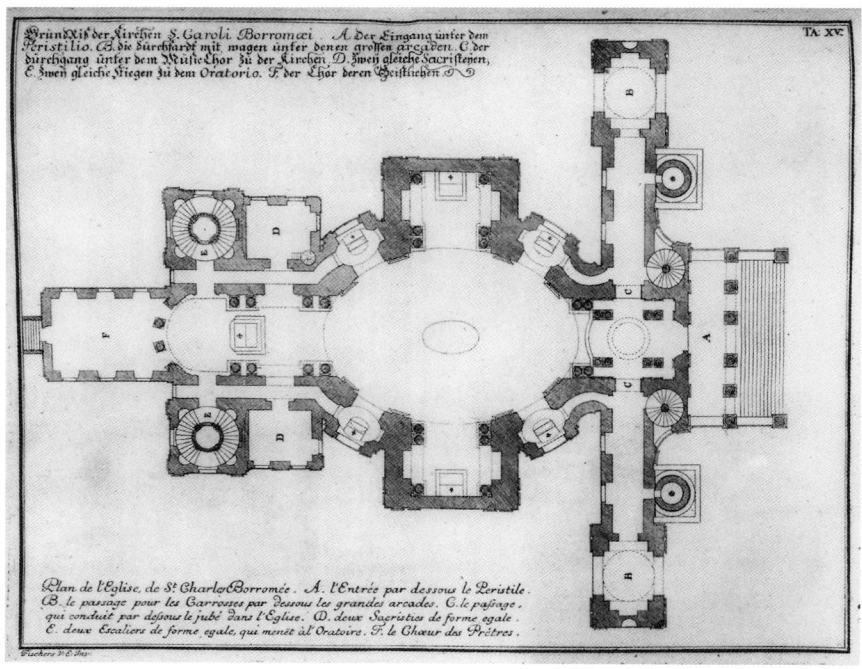

Pl.V.17 Plan of the *Karlskirche*, Vienna, showing the wide front with hexastyle portico flanked by two columns, elliptical body of the church, surrounded by chapels, and narrow chancel. From Fischer von Erlach (1725) (*Collection JSC*).

(Cambridge, Ludlow Castle, and the Holy Sepulchre in Northampton are but three examples) must be stressed, for ideas of round churches persisted as holy places for Orders and Brotherhoods: Montsalvat in *Parsifal* is one example, and there were others[106]. Round forms suggest wholeness, completeness, and the protection of the outer circumference; they are apposite to Closed Orders or to meeting-places, as is amply demonstrated by the polygonal plans of so many English Chapter Houses. The circular form of the Roman Pantheon and that of the cathedral at Aachen both suggested Imperial connotations with Antiquity and with the beginnings of the Holy Roman Empire itself.

---

102 *See* Yates (1975) *passim*. *See also* Stevenson (1988*b*) 148.
103 Stevenson (1988*b*) 148.
104 Aurenhammer (1973) 135.

105 Crowned Emperor in Rome by Pope Leo III in 800.
106 Doukhan (1997-8) 565-74.

Pl.V.18 Prospect of the liturgical west front of the *Karlskirche*, Vienna, from Fischer von Erlach (1725). This extraordinary building employs the concave front flanked by Baroque towers and dominant dome of Borromini's *Sant' Agnese in Agone* in Rome, but applies a prostyle portico in the Antique manner of the Pantheon, together with two spiral columns (which allude to Antiquity through the Trajanic model, to the deeds of Saint Carlo Borromeo, to the Pillars of Hercules, to the Imperial theme of *plus ultra*, to Jachin and Boaz, and to the Solomonic Temple). The long narrow passage linking the towers is a clear reference to the porch or vestibule of the Temple in Jerusalem, and indicates that Fischer von Erlach probably knew some of the illustrations to the Code of Maimonides. The *Karlskirche* is an extraordinary synthesis of Baroque, Borrominiesque, Biblical, Imperial, Antique, Talmudic, and iconographical themes all in one building (*Collection JSC*).

Pl.V.19 (*far left*) Side (liturgical south) elevation of the *Karlskirche*, Vienna, from Fischer von Erlach (1725) (*Collection JSC*).

Pl.V.20 (*right*) East-west section through the *Karlskirche*, Vienna, from Fischer von Erlach (1725) (*Collection JSC*).

Pl.V.21 (*left*) Maarten van Heemskerck's version of the destruction of the Temple of Solomon in Jerusalem in an engraving by Philipp Galle. Note the Two 'Pillars', the twisted 'barley-sugar' columns *in antis* of the porch, and the domed form of the building, an image which seems to have entered European consciousness from associations with the Dome of the Rock in Jerusalem, despite Biblical descriptions. The doubling of free-standing columns on pedestals *and* twisted columns *in antis* is a clear example of drawing on several sources, and, possibly, 'overkill' (*Collection JSC*).

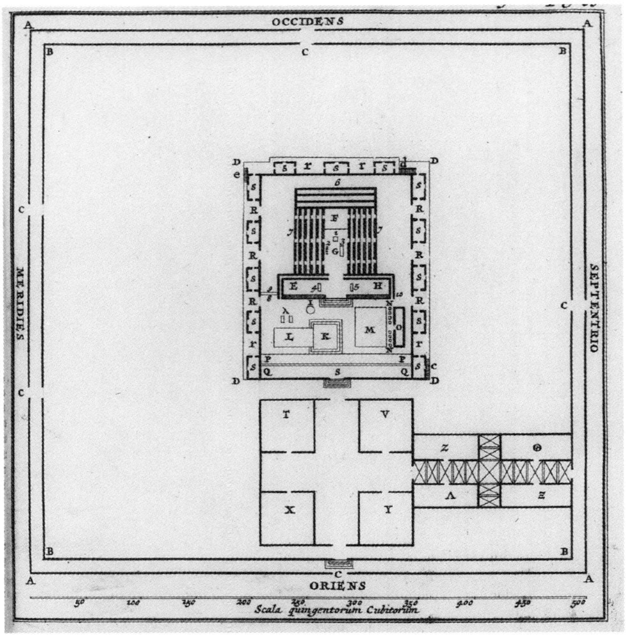

Pl.V.22 Plan of the Temple in Jerusalem by Claude Perrault, from Maimonides (1678). Note the extremely wide vestibule (*BL. 3129. aa.20*).

Pl.V.23 Elevations of the Temple in Jerusalem by Claude Perrault, from Maimonides (1678). Note the primitivist pylon-like front to the Temple, heralding Neo-Classical stripped simplicity of more than a century later (*BL. 3129. ca. 20*).

The Temple allusion of the *Karlskirche* is reinforced by the statues of Church and Synagogue placed on either side of the steps leading to the portico, and the reference to Roman Antiquity is further emphasised by the resemblance of the pedimented portico of the *Karlskirche* to that of the Temple of Concordia that stood in the *Forum Romanum*. Within the tympanum is sculpture depicting Vienna's deliverance from the Plague as a result of St Charles's intervention, while at the apex of the pediment is a statue of the Saint as Intercessor for Mankind, and therefore embodying one of the Three Theological Virtues, namely Charity. The other two Virtues, Faith and Hope, stand on top of the towers. The precedents of Hagia Sophia in Constantinople and of St Peter's in Rome also played their parts, but there is another precedent that is quite clear: Francesco Borromini's and Carlo Rainaldi's Church of *Sant' Agnese in Agone* (from 1644) in the *Piazza Navona* in Rome, with its concave front, flanking towers, and dome. Fischer himself had experimented with a concave front earlier in Salzburg, at the very much smaller, but impressive *Dreifaltigkeitskirche* (Church of the Holy Trinity), completed in 1702. The composition is similar, and the elliptical plan of the great dome derives from Roman Baroque precedents, notably the work of Borromini. Certain echoes of Wren's work at St Paul's Cathedral, London, also occur, but the influence of Borromini is stronger. Fischer's eclectic composition glorified the Emperor as a second Solomon and as the successor to the Roman Emperors (an idea we have already encountered at the Escorial, and in reference to Aachen and the Pantheon in Rome), and this complex iconographical notion was fully understood by contemporaries[107].

There is another odd aspect of the plan that seems to have escaped commentators: the very wide front, with its terminating tower-pavilions and passages to which the Two Columns are attached is strange in the extreme. Why is it like that? A probable explanation is that the porch of the Temple was wider by thirty cubits than the House proper behind it, and resembled a bema or transept[108]. This wide porch is shown (**Pls.V.22 & 23**) in Claude Perrault's illustrations of the Temple from the *Mishnah Torah*, or Code of Maimonides, translated into Latin by Louis Compiègne de Veil, and published in Paris in 1678. Perrault showed a stark, blank wall with a vast entrance-door reminiscent of the Neo-Classicists' work of a century and more later, but Perrault's drawing shows something else: the vast porch could become two Egyptian pylons with very little alteration. Thus the wide porch had Egyptianising connotations that would have been obvious to those Architects working at the end of the eighteenth and beginning of the nineteenth centuries when the great Egyptological publications came out[109]. Other influences were probably Parisian: the façade of the *Église des Minimes* as designed (1657) by François Mansart, with its wide front and flanking bell-towers, and possibly the the *Dôme des Invalides* (1676-91), by Jules Hardouin Mansart, certainly seem to have informed the design to some extent.

A further device is found inside the church (which on plan and elevation has certain phallic properties): this is the equilateral triangle with the sign of Yahweh set in a burst

---

107 Aurenhammer (1973) 136.
108 *Tractate of the Mishnah, Middoth Cap 4, Mishnah 7*. See Rosenau (1979) 187. See Hollis (1934).
109 For these *see* Curl (2005).

Pl.V.24 *(left)* Plate II of Chamoust (1783), engraved by Schmitz, showing the garlanded spiral form of the proposed French Order, based on the spirals associated with Continental Lodges, with the Temple, and with Antiquity. *(Top)* Type of the French Order showing its origin, and *(bottom)* the French Order Developed, showing the triple columns used in an arcade and the triple, garlanded columns in the circular temple (*Butler Library, Columbia University in the City of New York*).

Pl.V.25 *(right)* Plate III from Chamoust (1783), engraved by de la Gardette, showing the triple form of the French Order, that is three columns on a triangular base. This triangular base, three columns, and the spirals, make the French Order indubitably Masonic (*BL. CUP. 22. s. 14*).

of radiant light[110]. Thus the *Karlskirche* contains within its composition and iconography many features familiar in Masonic design, and it is an astonishing, fascinating, and remarkable building, completed under the direction of Fischer's son, Joseph Emanuel Fischer von Erlach, who made many subtle changes to the realised work which are clear when it is compared to the elder Fischer's published designs.

The Spiral Columns

One more point needs to be made concerning the *Karlskirche* and the two 'Trajanic' or 'Hercules' columns. The spiral form has itself Solomonic connotations, for the twisted, barley-sugar, or spiral column was illustrated by a number of artists in representations of the Temple. Heemskerck used twisted columns as did Jean Fouquet in Flavius Josephus's *Antiquités Judaïques* illustrations now in the Bibliothèque Nationale[111] in Paris. Raphael also used twisted columns in the cartoon showing the Healing of the Lame at the Beautiful Gate now in the Victoria and Albert Museum in London. Bernini employed twisted columns in his *Baldacchino* in St Peter's, Rome, but these were allusions to the Antique columns, some of which were supposedly looted from the Temple[112], that adorned the Constantinian basilica. Indeed, the basilica had twelve spiral columns

---

110 This was a common device, and does not, in this case, suggest Freemasonic connotations, though in other locations it might well do just that.

111 BN. MS. fr. 247.
112 Wittkower (1973) 115 and 347.

Pl.V.26 A design for a Masonic certificate for Lodges under the Grand Orient of Egypt and dependencies, from a nineteenth-century printer's sample-book. On the left is Jachin and on the right Boaz, both with Hathor-headed columns. Note the pyramid, obelisk, Nilotic trees, elephant, and Doric temple with winged disc with *uraei* in the tympanum. Of particular interest is the way in which the columns are entwined with flowers and foliage arranged as spirals, indicative of the Masonic significance given to spiral columns: these spirals recall Ribart de Chamoust's French Order illustrated in **Pls.V.24 & 25**, p.91 (*UGLE*).

in the sanctuary over the tomb of St Peter, so they were part of a monument with a prestige unmatched anywhere else in Western Christendom[113]. It is clear that the twisted 'Solomonic' form was seen as exotic, eastern, Biblical, sacred, and associated with holy places, which explains to some extent why it recurs in Romanesque columns and piers, and in the Baroque period, notably on altarpieces and in canopies over altars.

A variant is the column with vines twined around, or the column around which serpents twisted. Ribart de Chamoust's *L'Ordre François trouvé dans la Nature* of 1783[114] proposed a 'French Order' in which plants twine around the shafts of columns, and where Nature is the begetter of the Order, an idea derived from the Abbé Marc-Antoine Laugier and others (*see* **Pls.V.24 & 25**, p.91). Of course the spiral garland or snake wound round pillars suggests the forms found in circular labyrinths, just as the Greek-key forms derived from square labyrinths. Serpents are associated with wisdom (very Isiac), while in a circular (*ouroboros*) form, that is with their tails in their mouths, they symbolise eternity or everlasting life. The *caduceus* of Hermes, with its twining serpents, was an enchanter's wand, producing prosperity and wealth, but it also signified influences over the living and the dead. Asclepius, who could heal, and even resurrect the dead, is associated with snakes, the symbols of rejuvenation and prophecy, which are often depicted twined around his staff. Incubation-cures were sought in the temples of Asclepius, who later became identified with Serapis, the Graeco-Roman version of Osiris (incubation involved sleeping within temple precincts, or in special rooms in the temple compound set aside for the purpose)[115]. However, the garlands wound on spirals around columns are variations on the twisted-columns theme, and, apart from their spectacular effect in Ribart's designs, recur in countless Lodge Certificates (**Pl.V.26**), a subject closely studied by Terence Haunch[116].

---

113 *See* Ward-Perkins (1952). *See also* Fernie (1989).
114 Chamoust (1783).
115 Curl (2005) 15, 69.
116 Haunch (2008), *AQC* **lxxxii** 169–242, and personal communications. Haunch's many papers in *AQC* are recommended.

Afterword: Into the Abyss

It is clear that the Temple of Solomon has been the object of countless Jewish and Christian cosmic speculations for many centuries. It has also been extremely important in Freemasonry, and recurs in many forms on thousands of illustrations associated with the Craft. Just one image from Travenol (1749) purporting to show a Lodge of Master Masons (**Pl.V.27**), features an interpretation of the Temple clearly derived from Hafenreffer's imaginative 'reconstruction' (see **Pl.V.4**, p.80), an influential work which recurs in the literature, no matter what the Biblical accounts might indicate. Problems of interpreting the building from the few confusing (and contradictory) descriptions have exercised many minds, especially in relation to the long descriptions in *Ezekiel*. From the above it will be clear that the Biblical sources are the most important for any information on the Temple to which we have access. The Temple (or the idea of it) is a living tradition in two major religions and in Freemasonry, but the Biblical sources are very vague in far too many respects and they ought to be read with extreme caution, given that the Bible comprises a library that was built up, written, and edited with various aims, not least those concerned with politics and power. That the Temple was a hugely significant political construct in the united Kingdom created by David and perfected and completed by a consummate political operator in Solomon must be taken into account.

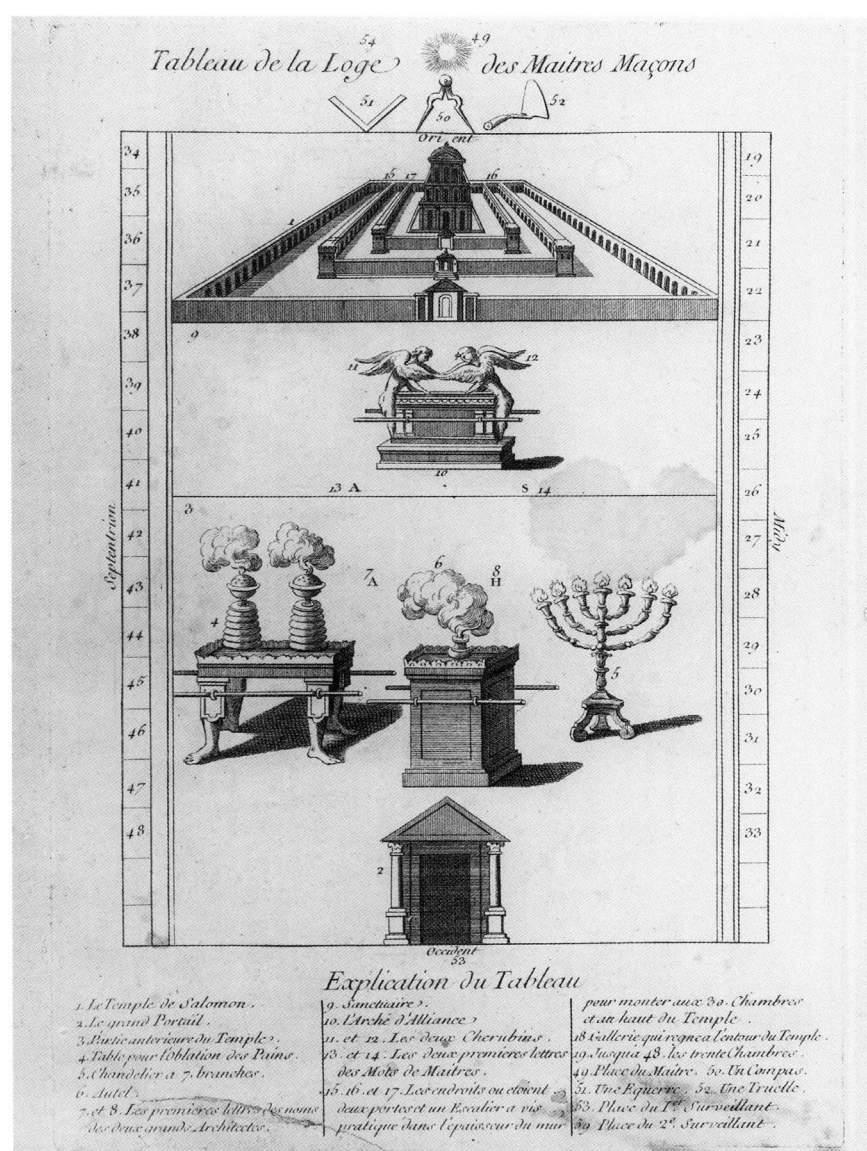

Pl.V.27 Plate from Travenol (1749) showing a Lodge of Master Masons with the Temple of Solomon (*top* – obviously based on Hafenreffer's work [*see* **Pl.V.4**, p.80]), the Ark of the Covenant with Cherubim (*centre*), altar for burning incense, table for offerings of bread, candelabrum, and portal (*UGLE*).

The major political problems of any united Kingdom concerned the interconnections and relationships between three distinct parts: these were Judah (Hebrew/Nomadic); Israel (Hebrew/Agricultural); and Jerusalem (Canaanite/Urban). Those three parts were identified with powerful symbols: Judah with the Ark of the Covenant; Israel with the Tent of Meeting; and Jerusalem with the Cherubim. Thus, within and by means of the Temple, three distinct and conflicting traditions were brought together, so the Temple was the Symbol (i.e. it was what it represented) of Unity, of political Clout, of Power, and of Reconciliation. With the destruction of the united Kingdom after the death of Solomon, the Temple ceased to be associated with Unity and Reconciliation: in other words, the Symbol began to lose part of its meaning. The Temple stood in the Capital of Judah, and the Ark of the Covenant became its primary Symbol. The Tabernacle in turn became a symbolic re-interpretation of the Tent of Meeting, and was associated with a portable Temple evolved during the reign of Hezekiah at the end of the eighth and beginning of the seventh centuries BC.

Given such major problems associated with attempts to unify disparate functions and traditions, and the difficulties of maintaining some sort of independence when faced with aggressive, expansionist powers, it is not an outrageous claim to interpret the vision of the Temple in *Ezekiel* and the description in *Chronicles*, for example, as politically motivated, with an agenda concerned to promote religion, social cohesion, and national power. When the Temple stood it thus played an important part in Jewish consciousness, and, after its destruction, its sacred memory (it was nothing less) remained, kept potent and real by means of the written word, iconography, rituals, and tradition[117]. More recently, further layers of meaning or resonances have been added, many of them profoundly disturbing and deeply shocking.

In front of the Temple proper stood the altar on which the burnt offerings were made: these sacrifices were wholly consumed by fire, and the term *holocaust* (from the Greek for *whole* and *burnt*) describes them, although it can also mean a sacrifice on a large scale, the complete destruction of a large number of people. Professor Robert Jan van Pelt[118] has carried out investigations of a very unnerving nature in which he has demonstrated the relationships of the developments of the notorious camp at Auschwitz-Birkenau, the settlement patterns, the town, and a rural 200-square-mile area of the region. In a perceptive essay entitled 'Into the Suffering City: Considerations of the *German Series*'[119], van Pelt has written about the deeply unsettling images created by the architect and artist, Melvin Charney[120], and in the context of the present study, about one image in particular (1986) entitled *Visions of the Temple (after Matthias Hafenreffer's "Reconstruction of the Temple of Jerusalem" published in Tübingen in 1631)*[121]. Van Pelt has considered 'the story of the Temple..., a story that concentrates on two moments of actual destruction – in 587 BC and AD 70 – and one moment of symbolic destruction'[122]: 'Jesus, when he had cried again with a loud voice, yielded up the ghost. And, behold, the veil of the temple was rent in twain from the top to the bottom; and the earth did quake, and the rocks rent; And the graves were opened; and many bodies of the saints which slept arose, And came out of the graves...'[123]. In the confusing yet fascinating history of the Temple, the 'seeming exaltation of completion masks Divine withdrawal', and 'the agony of oblation offers epiphany'[124].

What Charney did in his 1986 drawing was to take a vision of Ezekiel's Temple as interpreted by a distinguished seventeenth-century German Lutheran mathematician (*see* **Pl.V.4**, p.80) and overlay it with an image of part of the extermination-camp at Auschwitz-Birkenau. From the seemingly innocuous gate (cynically designed to look like rural farm-buildings) to the centrepiece of the entire shattering image, the crematorium chimney, runs a railway-track, a powerful axis. Thus the Holy of Holies becomes the Altar of the Burnt Offerings, the crematorium, on that main axis. Then the word *Holocaust* takes on an even more horrifying set of associations, with *Architectural* and *Planning* implications for National Socialist[125] obsessions concerning Jews and Freemasons (**CPl.V.I**).

Many persons today shy away from reading Adolf Hitler's book, *Mein Kampf* (My Struggle)[126], but a careful study of that work (together with awareness of the building up of the Hitler cult in the 1920s and 1930s), demonstrates that not only did Hitler set out to deify himself as Saviour of the German People, but that what he created was a nihilistic secular religion devoid of moral restraint or transcendental hopes. There can be no doubt that *Mein Kampf* had a *theological* logic (within its own terms, what ever one might think of it), demanding total power and utter ruthlessness to achieve and retain that power, yet all within restricting limitations of time.

Charney's drawing seems to propose that the huts of the camp could expand forever on either side of the main gateway-crematorium axis. Indeed, his drawing suggests that the real shrine of Naziism was a death-camp, an industrial factory of death that could be extended infinitely over swampy Silesian ground. It also posits an interesting question: why did the extermination programme continue for so long, consume so many resources, and even take precedence over the war-effort[127] in many respects? Was the Nazi obsession with mass-murder a form of Diabolism, sacrificing victims daily as a Burnt Offering in a ghastly parody of the daily sacrifices at the Temple in Jerusalem? But then, as 'Ulrich', the 'Man Without Qualities' of Robert Musil's great novel observes, 'if Mankind could dream collectively, it would dream' the brutal murderer Moosbrugger, the embodiment of all sinister qualities[128]. Might it even dream mass-murder? Or worse? Or was the programme of extermination a vast bureaucratic machine that simply continued under its own momentum, defying all reason, all logic, every humane argument, all economic sense, and even military necessity, once it had been started?

Although the Jews had suffered from vicious pogroms and persecution throughout the period when they were dispersed throughout Europe, it is perhaps not well known that the secularisation promoted by the French *philosophes* of the Enlightenment, the Revolutionaries, and nineteenth-century Liberalism, had its dark side. Voltaire considered that it would not be surprising if the Jews 'would not some day become deadly to the human race', and deserve 'to be punished', for that was their 'destiny'[129]. Later, Houston Stewart Chamberlain, in his *Die Grundlagen*

---

117 I am indebted to Robert Jan van Pelt for the above. *See* also van Pelt's contribution in Ramírez (*Ed.*) (1991a) which drew on the work of other scholars, including Th. A. Busink, Frank Moore Cross, Richard Elliott Friedman, Baruch Halpern, and Menahem Haran.
118 *See* van Pelt (1984, 1991), and van Pelt & Dwork (1996).
119 Van Pelt (1991) 35-53.
120 Charney (1991).
121 *Ibid*. 165.
122 *Ibid*. 47.
123 Matthew 27 50-53.
124 Charney (1991) 47.

125 The NSDAP (*Nationalsozialistische Deutsche Arbeiterpartei* [National Socialist German Workers' Party]), with both 'Socialist' and 'Workers' in its title, has been fatuously termed 'right-wing': it was nothing of the sort.
126 *See* Hitler (1925-7). The word 'struggle' is a favourite among Leftists.
127 Van Pelt & Dwork (1996) 197-235.
128 Musil (1979). In German, the novel is *Der Mann ohne Eigenschaften*, published in three parts (1930, 1932, and 1978).
129 Himmelfarb (2008) 157, quoting Voltaire's *Essai sur les mœurs*.

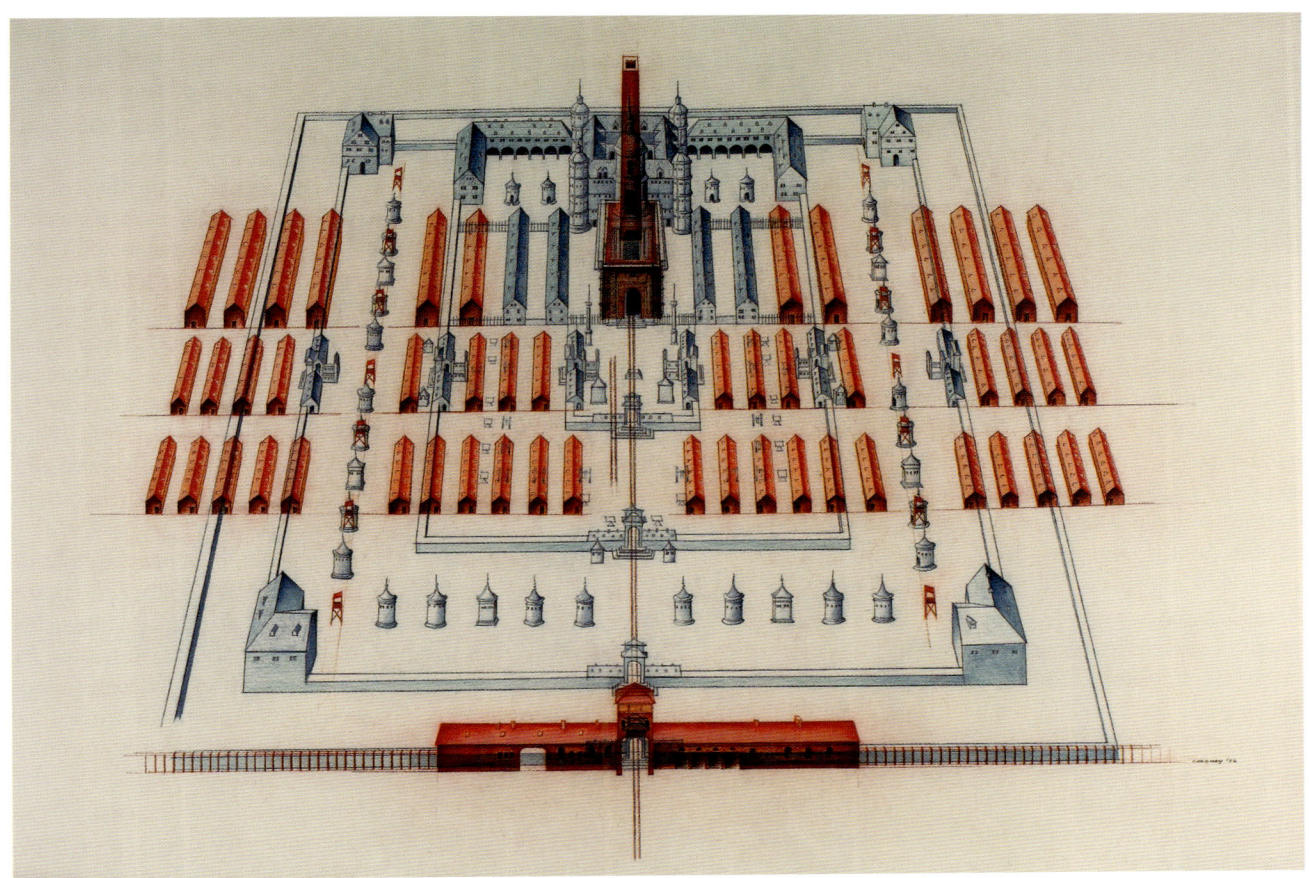

CPl.V.I 'Visions of the Temple' (after Matthias Hafenreffer's "Reconstruction of the Temple of Jerusalem", published in Tübingen in 1631 [*see* **Pl.V.4**, p.80]). Drawing in pastel on paper by Melvin Charney showing the crematorium and some of the huts at the extermination-camp of Auschwitz-Birkenau superimposed on Hafenreffer's image (NGC).

des neunzehn Jahrhunderts of 1899[130], argued that nineteenth-century Europeans had lost their senses of national and religious identity, yet the Jews, because they preserved the idea of Zion and hopes of re-creating the Temple, had preserved their 'sense of purpose and destiny'[131]. The realisation of such hopes, Chamberlain argued, lay in acquiring power over Gentiles and preserving a racially pure people[132]: thus Jews aimed at world domination, and they had as their allies in this nefarious plan the Freemasons and Liberals who, championing Liberty, Equality, and Fraternity, had actually removed everything that had successfully blocked the Jewish 'conspiracy' until the very end of the eighteenth century. Thus, for those who defended so-called 'Christian civilisation', the Enlightenment ideal of recovering the Lost Temple in a world dominated by religious tolerance, international cooperation, and benevolent Freemasonry was only a misleading smoke-screen, hiding the real purpose of establishing a Jewish World Temple from which all power would emanate. So world-wide Freemasonry was perceived by paranoid fantasists as the dangerously sinister ally of the World Jewish Conspiracy: as it was international, it was therefore the natural ally of the Jew against Christianity, and its desire to re-create the Lost Temple within the hearts of Men was really a diabolical plot for the Jews to rebuild *their* Temple at the seat of world-power in Jerusalem[133]. Freemasonry was fondly imagined to be a sort of 'screen' for the Jews in their objects: thus images, reconstructions, and scholarly attempts to establish what the original Temple looked like were also viewed with suspicion, so any Masonic book with material about the Temple in it was regarded as proof of a conspiracy, and of the dangers of studying the Temple. The range of loony fantasies is huge, and there was no country in which such poisonous notions were not disseminated. The French were certainly not guiltless, nor the Belgians, nor any other country, but the Russian, Sergei Aleksandrovich Nilus, produced one of the most unpleasant specimens, widely known as *The Protocols of the Elders of Zion*[134], a pamphlet still very much in print, notably in its English translation by Victor Emile Marsden. The *Protocols* 'revealed' that 'Gentile Masonry' was really only a screen

---

130 Issued in English translation as *The Foundations of the Nineteenth Century* in 1911-12. See Chamberlain (1911-12).
131 Van Pelt (1991) 49. The Temple point condemned Masons too.
132 Chamberlain (1911-12) **i** 330-1, a vile work.

133 For this, and other poisonous stuff, *see* Katz (1970) 150 and *passim*, and Nilus (1972) 30 and *passim*.
134 Nilus (1972).

for fiendish Jewish plots[135]. After the catastrophe of 1914-18 Marxists were also credited with the position of dupes working for Jewish World Domination.

In Germany, an obscure Saxon lawyer, Eduard Emil Eckert (who blew his brains out in 1866, and who was probably deranged), published a series of vicious diatribes against Freemasonry, which he claimed was seeking (like the Jews) the destruction of Christianity and its replacement with Paganism[136]. Eckert's poisonous books are not well known among English-speaking readers, but they were widely read in Francophone countries as well as throughout German-speaking lands. He saw the restored Temple rising from destroyed Christian civilisations after an apocalyptic upheaval that left the Jew victorious. His fantasies were certainly absorbed by Adolf Hitler, who saw himself as acting according to the will of the Creator by setting up defences against the Jew[137]. The hideous legacy of anti-Jewish and anti-Masonic scribblings has been admirably chronicled by the late Norman Cohn[138], and Eckert's publications have also been dissected by scholars brave enough to wade through such turgid stuff.

So, if the French Enlightenment, encouraged by the anti-Jewish Voltaire, Diderot, Holbach, and others[139], had managed to unseat God from the Heavenly Throne, the supposed champions of that unseated God, who feared the Temple as a goal of World Jewry and who perceived the Lost Ideal of international Freemasonry as another manifestation of a conspiracy to dominate the world, determined on a response, a solution to the problem, by building a temple at Auschwitz-Birkenau, 'and there they broke and sacrificed... the devils... of their own making. In the final analysis, the pandemonium of Auschwitz became some kind of perverse' realisation of the 'prophetical Temple. The rows of shacks became a universal shrine'[140].

The Inferno that was Auschwitz-Birkenau, a Hell on Earth, was not an accident. Its vast crematoria with 'triple-muffle' furnaces[141] were *designed*, as were the wholly inadequate latrines which constituted an excremental assault on the unfortunate inmates. The chief architect was SS-Sturmbannführer[142] Karl Bischoff[143], but he had in his team other Architects. They included Austrian-born SS-Obersturmführer[144] Walther Dejaco (one of whose drawings[145] in the Auschwitz Museum shows the main entrance-gatehouse) and SS-Untersturmführer[146] Friedrich (Fritz) Karl Ertl[147], who designed the regular layout of the camp which Charney illustrated in his evocative drawing. Ertl had studied (1928-31) at the Dessau *Bauhaus* under Hannes Meyer (who insisted that building was not an aesthetic process, and that everything depended on the marriage between function and economy). Meyer's Collectivist approach (he made Marxism and Leninism essential studies) alienated many, but gained him kudos in Leftist circles. After Meyer was dismissed as Director in 1930[148], he was succeeded by Ludwig Mies van der Rohe[149], so Ertl had the benefit of instruction under two heroes of the 'Progressive' Left. Hitler himself was a Modernist who despised tradition and the past: he also scorned Himmler's obsessions with mystic cults, and cannot be seen by any rational processes as a man of the Right in terms of politics. He was unquestionably a Leftist Revolutionary and Nihilist, a destroyer of tradition and a despiser of conservatism[150].

It is perhaps of some note that the ideologies of the *Bauhaus* have been Establishment Orthodoxy ever since 1945, and that they inform virtually all architectural education in the twenty-first century, which may go some way to explaining why almost all towns and cities have been transformed into hellish dystopian uninhabitable places, where incessant noise, violent pornographic 'entertainment', and other attendant horrors attend the habitat of an uncivilised, dangerous, self-absorbed population. An inhumane world dreamed up by Modernism begat Auschwitz-Birkenau: it threatens to engulf us all[151].

---

135 Nilus (1972): 30. However, event the *Protocols* lacks originality, for it appears to be plagiarised from Maurice Joly's *Dialogue aux Enfers entre Machiavel et Montesquieu*, a satire (Dialogue in Hell between Machiavelli and Montesquieu) published (1864) by A. Mertens in Brussels: this 'indebtedness' has long been recognised, at least since just after the 1914-18 War, and probably before. See *Times Literary Supplement* **5522** (30 January 2009) 6.
136 Eckert (1852, 1855a, 1855b), for example. See also Katz (1970) *passim*.
137 Hitler (1925-7) *passim*.
138 See, for example, his *Warrant for Genocide* (Cohn [1967]).
139 Himmelfarb (2008) 157.
140 Van Pelt (1991) 51. I am grateful to Robert Jan van Pelt for permission to quote. Pandemonium was the capital of Hell in Milton's *Paradise Lost* (first printed 1667): without a capital 'p' it is a tumultuously noisy, disorderly place or assembly.
141 With three openings, so bodies could be burnt more quickly and economically. They were designed by Kurt Prüfer of the J. A. Topf und Söhne firm based in Erfurt.

142 Paramilitary rank of the Nazi Party, literally 'Storm Unit Leader' (equivalent to a Major), *Sturmbann* was equivalent to a Battalion, *SS* stands for *Schutzstaffel* (literally 'Protection-Squad').
143 Born Neuhemsbach, near Kaiserslautern, Germany. At Auschwitz from 1941.
144 Paramilitary rank of the Nazi Party, literally 'Senior Assault (or Storm) Leader' in charge of between 50 and 100 men, regarded as equivalent in rank to an *Oberleutnant* (First Lieutenant) in the Regular Army.
145 Reproduced in van Pelt (1991) 43.
146 Junior Storm Leader, i.e. Lieutenant. He was promoted SS-Hauptsturmführer (equivalent to Captain) while at Auschwitz.
147 Born at Breitbrunn, near Linz, Austria, his SS number was 417.971.
148 He was heaped with honours and privileges in the Soviet Union where he remained until 1936.
149 Mies's gnomic remark that architecture is the 'Will of the Epoch translated into Space' was quoted almost *verbatim* by Hitler, many of whose *ex cathedra* sayings were very close to those spouted by the *Bauhäusler*. Mies attempted a *rapprochement* with the Nazis, but, as the economy became orientated towards war, he left Germany, and in 1938 settled in Chicago IL. Ertl claimed after the 1939-45 war that the most important influences on him had been various Bauhäusler heroes of the Modern Movement.
150 See Spotts (2002) *passim*.
151 Salingaros et al. (2004) *passim*.

CHAPTER VI

Lodges, Designs, Architecture, and Symbols

Introduction; The Lodge; Tracing-Boards; Women and Freemasonry, Papal Disapproval, and Mopses; Certificates and Architectural Elements; Freemasons' Hall in London; Other Masonic Buildings; Epilogue

'It cannot be too strongly asserted that Masonry is neither a religion nor a substitute for religion. Masonry seeks to inculcate in its members a standard of conduct and behaviour which it believes to be acceptable to all creeds, but studiously refrains from intervening in the field of dogma or theology. Masonry is therefore not a competitor with religion though in the sphere of human conduct it may be hoped that its teaching will be complementary to that of religion.'

JOHN M. HAMILL (1947-):
'Freemasonry and religion – the English view' in TREVOR STEWART (*Ed.*) (2006): *Freemasonry and Religion: Many Faiths, One Brotherhood. The Canonbury Papers* **iii** (London: Canonbury Masonic Research Centre) 1, quoting *Proceedings* of the United Grand Lodge of England (12 September 1962).

'A Lodge is a Place where *Masons* assemble and work: Hence that assembly, or duly organiz'd Society of Masons, is call'd a LODGE, and every Brother ought to belong to one…'

BERNARD EDWARD JONES (1879-1965):
Freemasons' Guide and Compendium (London: Harrap 1956) 345, quoting from JAMES ANDERSON (*Ed.*) (1723): *The Constitutions of the Free-Masons* (London: John Senex & John Hooke).

Introduction

Freemasonry, among many other things, is a society of men[1] who came to believe in a 'Supreme Being', but the name of that Being is the business of the person becoming a Freemason who accepts his obligations on a volume he holds sacred: in other words every Freemason follows the form and beliefs of his own religion, and sectarian arguments are not allowed at Freemasonic meetings. So, although Freemasonry is not a 'religion, nor is it a substitute for religion', it could be described, in its more serious moments, as a kind of philosophical companion to religion[2].

The Lodge

The Craft disseminates its messages, or 'teachings' by means of dramatic staged 'rituals' which are termed *Degrees* conferred in a *Lodge*, the essential unit of organisation of Freemasonry, which is associated with a particular place or geographical area. Even in prisoner-of-war camps, Lodges were specially established to maintain the work of the Craft and give succour to Brethren (this was as true of French prisoners during the Napoleonic Wars as it was of Allied prisoners in Germany in the 1939-45 War). Teaching also employs a complicated system of symbols that owe their origins to the tools and instruments of the stonemason's trade, some of which were familiar to architects and engineers before the advent of computers. Every Lodge is subservient to a Grand Lodge, the main governing organisation for Freemasonry in a country. In the United States of America, for example, there is a Grand Lodge in each State.

A Lodge is the place (a room or a building) in which Freemasons meet, but it is also the society, or body of Freemasons itself, and it is the meeting of that body. It has previously been noted that a Lodge was the building set aside for the use of Masons on a building-site, and was often

---

1 During the eighteenth century, androgynous Orders were established which admitted both sexes to 'Lodges of Adoption'. More recently, exclusively female Lodges have been formed.

2 For lectures and other matters concerned with the First Degree (Emulation Working) *see* Redman (2007) *passim*.

the workshop, refectory, meeting-room, and dormitory rolled in one. Every Lodge of Speculative Masonry has a name and number, and the number indicates precedence. Every Lodge makes an annual return to the Grand Lodge of its subscribing members, and also remits the names of the Master, Wardens, and Past Masters[3].

The chief *raison d'être* of a Freemasonic Lodge, then, is to confer the Three Craft Degrees on Brethren: these are Entered Apprentice, Fellow Craft, and Master Mason Degrees, and the rituals connect with the legends supposed to have been associated with the building of Solomon's Temple. These rituals (accompanied by lectures) clarify the essential teachings of Freemasonry. In addition, there are so-called 'Higher Degrees' to which only Master Masons may aspire: these include Mark Masonry, the Knights Templar, the Holy Royal Arch, and probably number over a thousand[4]. In essence, however, these Higher Degrees (each with special rituals and symbols) only enlarge upon aspects of the Three Craft Degrees and emphasise details. Take the Mark Mason Degrees, for example: Operative Masons were provided with marks once their Apprenticeships were over, and they cut these into stones to identify work done in order to be paid for it. However, in Freemasonic terms, the Mark Degrees emphasise that what a Freemason does can be identified as his action, so it is important to ensure probity and quality. The Mark Degrees seem to have been connected with the Fellow Craft, as a completion or addendum, and the Holy Royal Arch Degree was a sort of continuation of the Master's Degree[5]. However, the subject of Higher Degrees is vast, and deserves a volume to itself, so it is really beyond the scope of this study[6].

Every new Lodge has to be constituted, and opened in Three Degrees. The officer scatters corn (Plenty), pours wine (Joy and Cheer), pours oil (Peace and Concord), and sprinkles salt (Fidelity and Friendship) before dedicating the Lodge. The Chaplain takes a censer three times around the Lodge and offers prayers. Three candles and a box containing the Warrant and Constitutions have also played their parts in the making of the legitimacy of a Lodge. Lodges have not met in private houses for many years, presumably for purposes of secrecy,[7] although this was once very common, as was the custom of holding Lodge meetings in public-houses.

Lodges were orientated East-West, with the Master's place at the East (as opposed to the Temple, where the Holy Place was in the West), and so followed ecclesiastical practice. The East, after all, is associated with Light, the New Day, and Life, and the West with Darkness, Death, and the Sunset. Learning originated in the East, so the principal entrance to a Lodge room ought to face East because the East is a place of light, a symbol of mental and spiritual illumination. As the sun rises in the East to bring life to the day, so the Master is placed in the East to open the Lodge and give instruction and illumination to the Brethren in the Craft of Freemasonry[8], thereby bringing Enlightenment.

Some early Lodges were not always 'oblong squares' and some seem to have been triangular, while others were cruciform.[9] This is not to say that the actual rooms or buildings were triangular or cruciform, but that the imaginary, mystical, symbolic or remembered Lodge was *marked on floors* to plans of those shapes. It is known that Brethren were not regarded as being in the Lodge until they had stepped within the chalked or otherwise defined limits. Now if Lodge floor-plans had to be marked on real floors in the meeting-rooms (often inns), certain substances had to be employed for the purpose, and those substances were necessarily removed at the end of meetings. There were, of course, precedents in the designs formed on the floors by Mediaeval Masons in order to cut the stone to precise shapes for, say, tracery. One can imagine that drawings using chalk, charcoal, etc., on floors would not always be capable of removal, even with soap, mop, and water, and would leave a mess. Thus other means of delineating the plan of the Lodge had to be evolved, including the invention of the portable floor-cloth with the design already on it. The floor-cloth was a canvas, painted, which developed into a composite picture of symbols, and had a limited life. It was transmogrified into the Lodge-board or tracing-board, which became common around the end of the eighteenth century.

Tracing-Boards

A *tracing-board* is an emblem of the drawing- or tracing-board of the Mediaeval Masons on which plans and details were drawn. A tracing-board of operative Masons was a board on which parchment might be fixed, or it might be a flat stone or slate on which drawings might be made, or it might even be the floor itself on which the Master Mason would lay out details to be made by the craftsmen.[10] Tracing-boards, then, were not necessarily boards on which a semi-transparent skin or paper might be placed for tracing purposes: tracing meant more than copying, and, in fact, signified the process of designing, devising, detailing, drawing, or planning. The root of the term is the Latin *Tractus*, meaning a drawing or a track.[11] Gothic 'tracery' is derived from this, and indeed had to be set out on large surfaces for full-size detailing, so the floor became a tracing-board for such designs. It is important to realise that Mediaeval drawings had to be accurate: the setting out of a vast Second-Pointed piece of window tracery, or the complex

---

3 This stems from various enactments in the reign of King George III to keep tabs on 'secret societies' during a period which saw the American War of Independence, the Irish Rebellion of 1798, and the French Wars.
4 Coil (1961).
5 *See* McNulty (2006); Prescott (*Ed.*) (2006); Alexander & Morrison (2997); Tatton-Brown & Munby (*Eds.*) (1996).
6 *See*, however, McNulty (2006) 181-213, which discusses Higher Degrees.
7 Jones (1956) 348.

8 Jones (1956) 349.
9 *Ibid.*
10 *Ibid.* 399.
11 *Ibid.*

Pl.VI.1 *(top)* Assembly of Freemasons for the Reception of Apprentices. The apprentice enters on the left, his breast bare, blindfolded, with shoelaces undone and knee exposed. Note the Master seated and the Brethren with aprons. On the floor is a cloth with Jachin and Boaz, the seven steps leading to the Temple, the Mosaic Pavement, the west window, the flaming star, the east window, the indented tuft (or tessellated border), the sun, the perpendicular, and other emblems. From Plate I of Bernigeroth (1745) (*UGLE*).

Pl.VI.2 *(centre)* Reception of Apprentice. The Brethren are in position around the cloth; the candidate kneels on the stool, and swears with his hand on the Bible never to reveal the mysteries of Freemasonry. This appears to be a mirror-image of an earlier plate, which shows the candidate kneeling with his left knee, probably reflecting techniques of copying images on engraved plates. From Plate 2 of Bernigeroth (1745) (*UGLE*).

Pl.VI.3 *(bottom)* Lodge assembled for the Reception of Master Masons. The Master is seated, and the lights are tripled. Note the floor-cloth design. From Plate 3 of Bernigeroth (1745) (*UGLE*).

geometry of a lierne vault, needed precise drawings to make them possible at all. Records survive to show that considerable quantities of skins were used to make the full-size working-drawings for a number of major buildings such as the cathedral at Exeter.[12]

The tracing-board of Speculative Freemasonry therefore developed as an emblem. The process seems to have been as set out below. Early in the history of so-called Speculative (i.e. Non-Operative) Freemasonry, it seems to have been usual to trace out the form of the Lodge on the floor of the room in which the meeting took place. The necessity of chalking or otherwise marking up an area and then of erasing the marks (as noted above) proved troublesome and cumbersome. Use of chalk, charcoal, and clay to mark out (or trace) the Lodge had symbolic connotations: chalk represented Freedom, for it was free for the use of Man, left a trace, yet could be erased; charcoal was Fervent, able to destroy or change metal; while clay was Zealous, representing the earth and the grave. Such materials must have been difficult to apply and even worse to remove, especially where it was necessary to delete all traces in borrowed premises such as rooms in inns or private houses. Drawings of Lodge layouts were often made with chalk, stone-blue (a compound of indigo with starch or whiting, used by laundresses), and charcoal mixed, and one of the first tasks of a newly-initiated Freemason was to take a mop and clean the tracing until nothing remained.[13]

Various designs, including the Mosaic Pavement, or chequerboard-pattern (signifying something upon which

---

12 Jones (1956) 400.

13 *Ibid.* 395.

Pl.VI.4 *(top)* Assembly of Freemasons for the Reception of Master Masons. The Master sits beneath a canopy. The new member or member-elect is the figure second from the right with the guardian's (or watcher's) sword pointing at his breast. The figure beneath the covering on the left is a candidate to whom the Master has not yet bestowed the accolade. Note the floor-cloth with emblems of Death. From Plate 4 of Bernigeroth (1745) (UGLE).

Pl.VI.5 *(centre)* Assembly of Freemasons for the Reception of members to the Degree of Master Mason. On the right are three hooded seated figures (recipients who have not yet received the accolade). The candidate is being laid on the coffin as a symbol of his death before Enlightenment and new life. From Plate 5 of Bernigeroth (1745) (UGLE).

Pl.VI.6 *(bottom)* The next stage of Initiation. The candidate lies on the 'coffin' or grave on the Lodge, his face covered by a linen the colour of blood, while the Brethren point their swords at his body. The other candidates lie covered on the right. From Plate 6 of Bernigeroth (1745) (UGLE).

Pl.VI.7 *(right)* The Master 'raises' the candidate from his symbolic Death whilst granting the Mason Word. From Plate 7 of Bernigeroth (1745) (UGLE).

and instruments; the tomb of Hiram; and others were included. Clearly the trouble taken to trace such patterns (and clean them up afterwards) must have been considerable, and in due course (apparently in the early part of the eighteenth century) cloths with the various emblems and plans of Lodges painted on them were introduced as floor-cloths or even carpets. Lodges of the Three Degrees required different cloths: the latter appear to have been of painted canvas and cannot have had a long life. Consequently the floor-cloths were translated to the status of table-cloths, or even hung on walls. As a wall-diagram the tracing-board became the Lodge Board, containing a composite set of emblems (*see* **Pls. VI.19-21**, p.107), and its origins became obscured. The floor-cloth (used either on the floor, on a table, or placed on a wooden roller and suspended from a wall) seems to have been called such until around 1800, when the tracing-board (sometimes the framed or suspended floor-cloth) came into general use.

The tracing-board of speculative Freemasonry is now remote from the floor-cloths, carpets, and practical drawing-boards of yesteryear. In French Masonic literature the *Planche à Tracer* is sometimes called *trace*, or outline, or

the Freemasons drew ground draughts, or draughted a symbolic building, or representing the chequered existence of Man who had to face Good and Evil); the Laced or Indented Tuft (called *La Houpe Dentelée* or *Die Schnur von starken Faden* [the rope or cord of strong thread] with tassels, representing the Four Cardinal Virtues); Masonic tools

layout. Occasionally, as on some French representations of layouts, tracing-boards in the original operative sense are seen, with pinpricks representing the outline of the tracing.[14]

During the eighteenth century several 'exposures' of Masonic activities and 'secrets' were published, many of them of French origin, and most of them dependent upon each other, even to the extent of mirror-imaging the plates. Straight or mirror-image, however, many of these 'exposures' feature tracing-boards. Eighteenth-century plans of Lodges show typical layouts. These have three steps (one for the First Degree [or Entered Apprentice, kneeling with the left knee], one for the Second Degree [or Fellow Craft, kneeling with the right knee], and one of the Third Degree [or Master, kneeling with both knees]), three candlesticks, and the Master's place at the east end. Other illustrations from eighteenth-century 'exposures' of the Craft show Masonic activities on floor-drawings, cloths, or carpets (**Pls.VI.1-7**, pp.99-101). A curious feature of these publications is not only the tendency for wholesale copying, but the fact that many of the plates are actually mirror-images of earlier plates, and thus give a false view (left and right becoming confused). Whether this was deliberate obfuscation or (more likely) expediency caused by the processes of copying engravings is difficult to assess.

 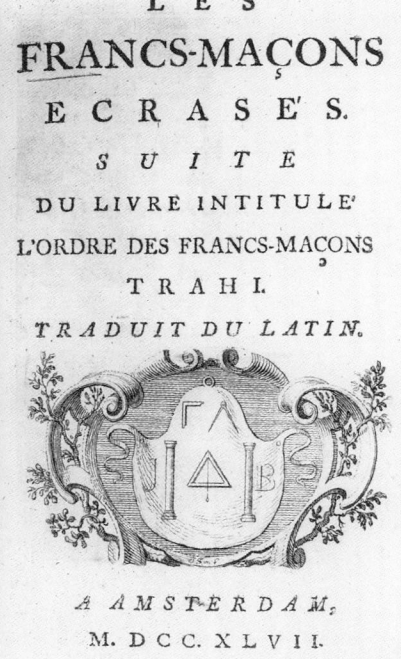

Pl.VI.8 Frontispiece and title-page of Larudan (1746), designed and engraved by Simon Fokke. The title means 'The Freemasons ruined', and the picture shows a Lodge falling down, complete with Masonic emblems. The front of the Lodge bears more than a passing resemblance to some Renaissance imaginary reconstructions of the Temple in Jerusalem. This was one of the most celebrated of the French 'exposures' (*UGLE*).

---

14 Jones (1956) 398-403.

Pl.VI.9 Plate I from Larudan (1746). It purports to show a Lodge or a layout for the Reception of an Apprentice (*UGLE*).

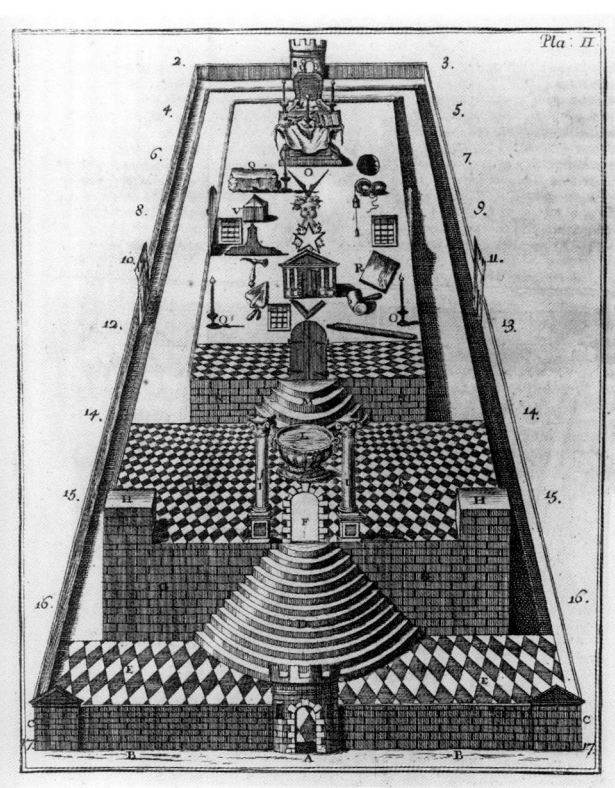

Pl.VI.10 Lodge layout or floor-cloth for the Reception of a 'Compagnon' Mason. Plate II from Larudan (1746). The remarkable resemblance to sixteenth-century depictions of the Temple of Solomon should be immediately apparent (*UGLE*).

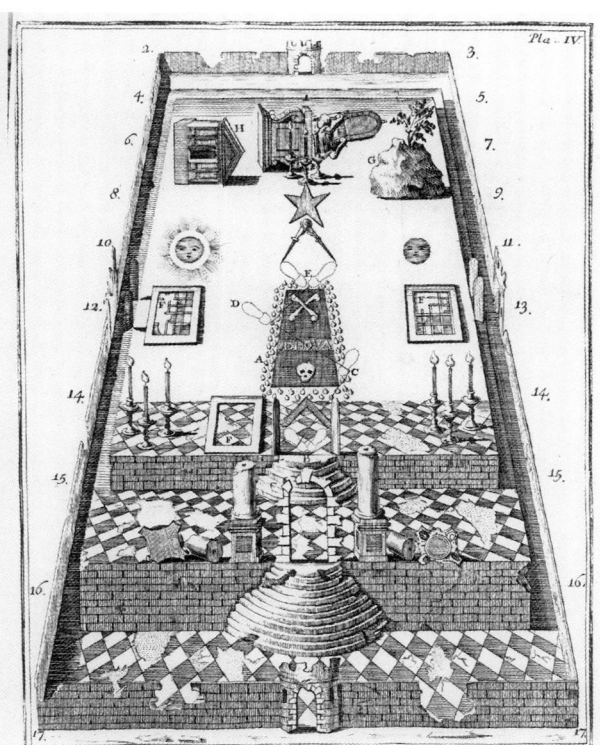

Pl.VI.11 Lodge layout or floor-cloth for the Reception of a Master Mason. Plate IV from Larudan (1746). Note the triple lights, the acacia bush, the grave, and other Masonic emblems. Again, the resemblance to the Solomonic Temple should be noted: its ruined state suggests that becoming a Master is only a stage in the search for perfection (*UGLE*).

One of the most remarkable of these exposés was *Les Francs-Maçons Écrasés*, published following a work entitled *L'Ordre des Francs-Maçons Trahi*, and supposedly translated from the Latin[15]. *Les Francs-Maçons Écrasés* was by the Abbé Larudan, and the frontispiece showed the 'ruin' of a Masonic Lodge (**Pl.VI.8**, p.101). The same volume depicted layouts of the Lodges that were obviously derived from sixteenth-century reconstructions of Solomon's Temple, complete with Jachin and Boaz, chequered floors, steps, lights, compasses, and other familiar emblems (**Pls.VI.9-11**). Another important 'exposure' was that of 'Léonard Gabanon', pseudonym of Louis-Antoine Travenol, whose *Nouveau Catéchisme des Francs-Maçons* appeared in several editions in the 1740s (**Pl.VI.12**). Travenol[16] also included some interesting plates in his *Catéchisme*, comprising a Reception of Apprentices (**Pl.VI.13**), a Reception of 'Compagnons' (**Pl.VI.14**, p.104), a Reception of Masters (**Pl.VI.15**, p.104), a dinner for Freemasons (**Pl.VI.16**, p.104), a plan of a Lodge of an 'Apprentif-Compagnon' (**Pl.VI.17**, p.105), a True Plan of a Lodge for the Reception of an 'Apprentif-Compagnon' (**Pl.VI.18**, p.105), and a Plan of a Lodge of Master Masons (see **Pl.V.27**, p.93). Travenol it was who published some of the earliest printed designs

---

15 See Larudan (1746) and *Istituzione Riti e Ceremonie dell'Ordine de' Francs-Maçons* (1785).

16 Travenol appears to have been a musician as well as a writer.

Pl.VI.12 Frontispiece and title-page of Travenol (1749). Note the Masons in their aprons. The Angel of Fame has floor-cloths or tracing-boards as banners on his trumpets. This was an important French 'exposure' of Freemasonry (UGLE).

of floor-cloths in his first 'exposure', *Le Catéchisme*[17]. He also appears to have been the first to depict the *Houpe Dentelée* as a Tasselled Cord, serving as a frame. Larudan criticised Travenol's design as inexact, but he nevertheless retained the *Houpe Dentelée* without any changes. So what does the *Houpe* suggest?

In his *Désolation*[18], Travenol described the *Houpe* as *une espèce de Cordon de Veuve* (a species of border [or strand, or girdle] of a widow) which surrounds (or encompasses) the upper part of the design. So what does the reference to a 'Widow' signify? The answer appears to lie in European rituals current in the 1740s in which Freemasons were described as 'Sons of the Widow'. By an extension of this, the Craft itself became the Widow, and the floor-cloth her Blazon of Arms. An investigation into French Heraldry reveals that Widows bear the Arms of their late husbands, which are *surrounded by an intertwined cord*[19]. This cord, knotted and twisted, is joined in a knot at the base, with two tassels flowing from it right and left. It is uncertain if Travenol invented this cord, or if he reported something he had seen: he seems to have been the only French writer of the time who used the *Cordon de Veuve* explanation[20].

Many illustrations of Lodge interiors, therefore, were copies of other images, often mirror-images, and varying in quality. Some are crude (like the repetitive texts

17 Travenol (1744).
18 Travenol (1747).
19 *See* Larousse (1928-33) under 'blason'.
20 Carr (Ed.) (1971) 320. I am most grateful to my friend, T. O. Haunch, for drawing Carr's Digression on the *Houpe Dentellée* (sic) to my attention.

Pl.VI.13 Reception of Apprentices from Travenol (1749). Note the floorcloth (UGLE).

Pl.VI.14 *(top left)* Reception of 'Compagnons' from Travenol (1749). Note the floorcloth (*UGLE*).

Pl.VI.15 *(top right)* Reception of Master Masons from Travenol (1749). Note the candidate, the floor-cloth with 'tears', the triple lights, and the skull (*UGLE*).

Pl.VI.16 *(left)* Dinner for Freemasons, from Travenol (1749) (*UGLE*).

of the 'exposures'), but others have aesthetically acceptable qualities. Some of the most attractive illustrations of Lodges appeared as engravings by the German artist, Johann Martin Bernigeroth, and these were reproduced in several publications and in pirated form (see **Pls.VI.1-7**, pp.99-101). However, Bernigeroth's book on the Costumes of the Freemasons in their assemblies, 'principally for the reception of Apprentices and Masters, all newly and honestly discovered', published in Leipzig[21] shows floor-cloths, ceremonies, dress, and much else, superbly delineated in engravings of the highest quality: no apology is offered for reproducing so many of them here, for they are lovely things, infinitely superior to many of the amateurish efforts in sundry eighteenth-century pamphlets.

Floor-cloths, which appear to have replaced the crude markings in chalk, charcoal, and clay, and could be rolled up and removed after the Lodge meeting had closed, were obviously walked upon, and, as previously noted, would have had a strictly limited life. So the tracing-board was evolved which provided illustrations appropriate for the

---

21 Bernigeroth (1745, 1746).

LODGES, DESIGNS, ARCHITECTURE, AND SYMBOLS / 105

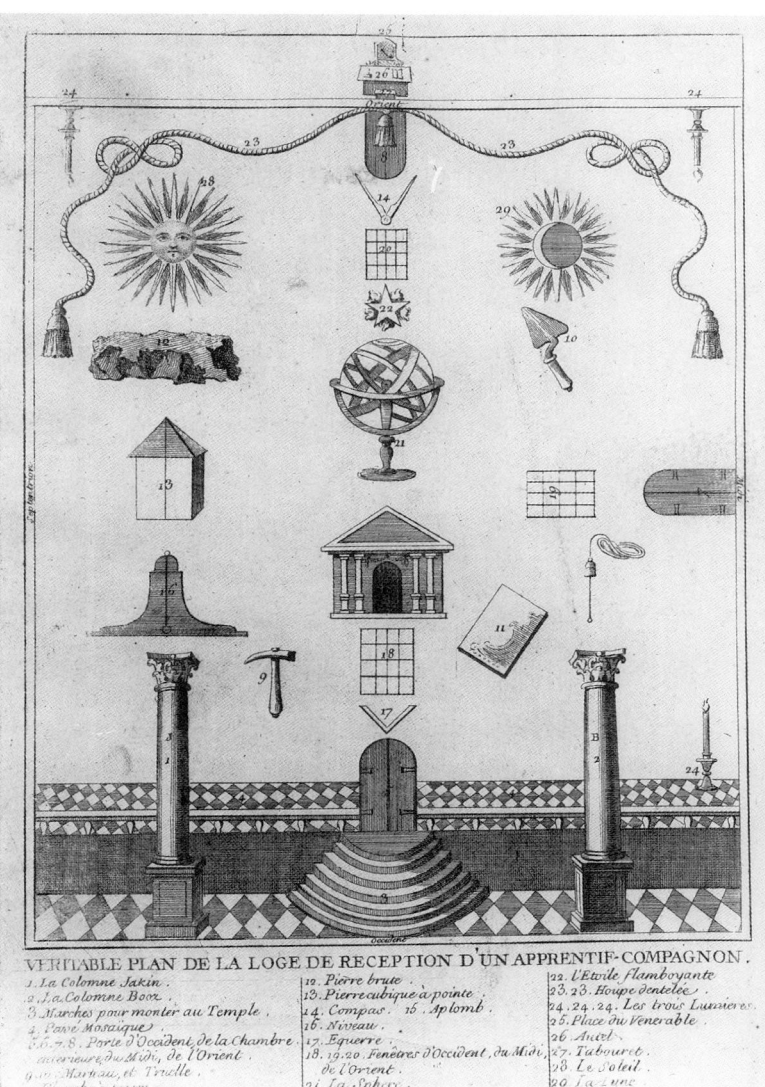

Pl.VI.17 *(left)* Plan of a Lodge of 'Apprentif-Compagnons' from Travenol (1749). Note Jachin and Boaz, the steps, the architectural centerpiece, and the Masonic emblems (*UGLE*).

Plate VI.18 *(right)* True Plan of a Lodge for the Reception of an 'Apprentif-Compagnon', from Travenol (1749), showing (1 & 2) Jachin and Boaz; (3) the steps to the Temple; (4) the Mosaic Pavement; (5) the western gate; (6) the gate to the interior chambers; (7) the southern gate; (8) the eastern gate; (9) the scappling-hammer; (10) the trowel; (11) the tracing-board or table with outlines of profiles; (12) the uncut stone; (13) the cubic ashlar with pyramid; (14) the compasses; (15) the plumb; (16) the level; (17) the square; (18, 19, 20) the western, southern, and eastern lights; (21) the globe; (22) the flaming star; (23) the *houpe dentelée*; (24) the three lights; (25) the seat of the Master; (26) altar; (27) the stool; (28) the sun; (29) the moon (*UGLE*).

three basic Craft Degrees (**Pls.VI.19-21**, p.107). That for the First Degree (**Pl.VI.19**) pictured the essential symbols, including the three basic Classical Orders of Architecture (Doric, Ionic, and Corinthian)[22] associated with Strength, Wisdom, and Beauty, and various other common Masonic motifs. The chequered or 'Mosaic' pavement

(Good and Evil in life); the Rough Ashlar (stone fresh from the quarry that has to be cut, so that it represents Man in his unperfected state, the Apprentice who has to work to perfect himself); the Perfect Ashlar, or stone worked and polished ready to be placed in the building (so represents the Apprentice who has been trained and is ready to advance to the Second Degree); Jacob's Ladder[23] by which the candidate makes his mystical ascent via the Three Steps of Faith (with Book and Cross), Hope (with Anchor), and Charity (with children), Charity being the last step[24]; the Key to the Lodge, representing the Words that could identify the Mason and open the Lodge to him; the Sun and Moon (representing Duality); the Realms of the Physical World and of the Spirit (Heavens) with other Realms between the two; the All-Seeing Eye of the Deity; Euclid's 47th Proposition (**CPl.VI.I**, p.106 – in any right-

---

22 However, there are *eight* distinct types of Classical Order: Greek Doric, Roman Doric, Greek Ionic, Roman Ionic, Greek Corinthian, Roman Corinthian, Tuscan (also known as the Gigantic Order), and Composite, although before the systematic rediscovery of Greek Architecture in the eighteenth century, the canonical *five* Orders (Tuscan, Roman Doric, Roman Ionic, Roman Corinthian, and Composite) were accepted, codified by Leon Battista Alberti and illustrated by Sebastiano Serlio in *Regole Generale* of 1537. *See* Curl (2006a) 13-15, 540, 705. Visitors to the great collections of architectural fragments from Classical Antiquity (such as the Pergamon Museum, Berlin), will observe that there were further variations on the eight Classical Orders, often displaying much graceful invention.

23 The Ladder is usually shown standing between two parallel lines, the paired opposites of the two Saints John of Midsummer and Midwinter.

24 They are called the Theological Virtues.

CPl.VI.I Board c.1801) surrounded by a Greek Key pattern featuring various Masonic tools with symbolic significance. Euclid's 47th Proposition is top left, demonstrating that in any right-angled triangle the squared hypotenuse equals the sum of the other two sides squared (UGLE).

Junior Warden asks for a Password, and indicates that before the climb can begin the candidate must be properly motivated and also must have completed all required tasks. Tools (such as the Plumb-line, Level, and Square) are often featured, signifying Licence, Restraint, and the Balance between the two. Prominent is usually an Ear of Corn (Wisdom and Enlightenment, so often included in Initiation Rituals), representing also natural maturation. Both Wardens wear Aprons, the first Gift bestowed on an initiated Apprentice, an emblem of Purity in Life and Conduct. The All-Seeing Eye is usually featured, representing Superintending Providence, knowing All and seeing All. It is an emblem of the Degree of Master Mason, for God or the Deity is All Eyes. A Bridge over water, or a waterfall, may also be depicted, the Arch of Masonry by which one can pass safely to the other side. A Triangle may also be shown, and a Hebrew letter in the Middle Chamber, although this may sometimes be given as a 'G'. This G is assumed by many Freemasons to refer to God, but as it appears in French images, this would not make a great deal of sense[25]. Some commentators say it represents Geometry, one of the Seven Liberal Arts, and others that it is a Neo-Platonic reference to the Deity[26]. The problem with this rather flimsy explanation is that the emblem of interlocked square and compasses with G in the middle first appears in an edition of Ptolemy's *Geographia*[27] dated 1522, and only resurfaces in Freemasonry early in the eighteenth century[28]. And in 1522 it stood *neither* for God *nor* for Geometry. So what *did* it represent? The answer, which will surprise many, is that it stood for *Geography*[29].

angled triangle, the hypotenuse [longest side] equals when squared the sum of the squares of the other two sides): it is this *relationship* which gives a craftsman the means of constructing a right angle of 90°. If a line, say 4 units long is drawn, and compasses set to 3 units are set at one end of the base-line, an arc will be formed. If the compasses are then set to 5 units, using the other end of the base-line as the centre, an arc intersecting the other arc will provide the point from which a straight line can be drawn down to join the base-line, and a right-angle is formed); the square (a symbol of moral probity, and a tool by which great exactness in building can be achieved); a plumb-line (an instrument for erecting perpendicular lines, symbolising upright codes of conduct); compasses (a measure of life and conduct, keeping passions within bounds); and the Book of the Law (setting out Rules for Conduct), often indicated as the Bible.

The tracing-board of the Second Degree (**Pl.VI.20**) illustrates the task to be tackled by the Fellow Craft. Dominant are the Two Columns (Jachin and Boaz, really the Lost Perfection of Solomon's Temple, capped by the earthly and celestial spheres) between which is a Winding Stair leading to a building where the Mosaic Pavement is prominent. The Senior Warden guarding the Middle Chamber is usually depicted at the top of the Winding Stair, and the Junior Warden guards the bottom. The

Finally, there is the tracing-board of the Third Degree (**Pl.VI.21**), which alludes to the processes by which a candidate becomes a Master Mason. It concerns a ritual by which the 'dead' are raised to new life: if life, as we know it, is 'like death', because we live unenlightened ever since the expulsion from the Garden of Eden and our consequent remoteness from the Divine Presence, the elevation to

---

25 A reference to God (*Dieu*) in French would logically be 'D'.
26 Prichard (1730) and Thorp (*Ed.*) (1907).
27 Ptolemy (1522).
28 Impens (2002).
29 I owe this to David Stevenson, in a generous personal communication. It demonstrates how accretions tend to obscure, rather than illuminate: the 'G-for-God' association obviously does not stand up. G for 'Geography', however, makes more sense (*Geographie* in German, *Géographie* in French), and 'Geometry' also works as *Geometrie* in German and *Géométrie* in French. 'G', representing the Great Geometer, would seem to be a more sensible explanation than 'God'.

Pl.VI.19 *(left)* English early-nineteenth-century tracing-board associated with the First Degree, showing the basic Orders of Architecture (Doric, Ionic, and Corinthian), although Ionic is incorrectly identified with Strength (which is properly associated with Doric) instead of Wisdom. Various Masonic attributes are also shown (*UGLE*).

Pl.VI.20 *(centre)* English early-nineteenth-century tracing-board associated with the Second Degree, showing Jachin and Boaz surmounted by globes, with the winding stair leading to a chequer (so-called Mosaic) pavement with canopied aedicule, flanked by four columns, probably representing the Temple (*UGLE*).

Pl.VI.21 *(right)* English early-nineteenth-century tracing-board associated with the Third Degree, showing a coffin, allusions to Death, a chequered pavement, two columns supporting an arch, a square, compasses, and other Masonic tools, and the initials M. B. (standing for the so-called 'Mason Word'), and TBC for TuBal Cain, 'the first artificer in metals' (*UGLE*).

the Master's Degree is regarded as a means by which we can regain the consciousness of something Lost, so the ritual does not involve actual death, but a ritual, mystical death and rebirth. As with Ancient Mystery Cults (such as that of Isis and Osiris), when a ritual death in the Temple was followed by a 'resurrection' leading to perfection and regeneration in the presence of the awesome deities themselves, so the 'death' and 'raising' of a Freemason to the Degree of Master Mason represents a new beginning in a state of enlightened perfection[30]. Tracing-boards (as with all three Degrees) vary in detail, but common features are the skull and crossbones, a coffin, the entrance to the Holy of Holies flanked by columns (the Order varies), the chequered or Mosaic Pavement, the Square, Compasses, Plumb-line, Level, and a Maul or Mallet (frequently called a Gavel). To be clear about this, a Maul is a heavy hammer-like implement such as a Mallet, used to tap a chisel to dress stone: it is used by Masons and Sculptors for fine work. A Chairman's Mallet or Master-Mason's Gavel is a wooden Mallet cut so that its ends are triangular in shape (*gavel* is another word for a *gable*, in architectural terminology), so suggests a type of axe used to hew stone. Thus *Maul* and *Gavel* are often confused, and the Gavel is associated with the instrument by which a Chairman or Master keeps order at a meeting. In the Third Degree rituals the correct instrument should be the heavy *Maul*[31], the tool with which Hiram was slain, according to the myth. Just to add to the confusion, both *Gavels* and *Mauls* have been termed *Hirams*, but some representations seem to depict not *Mauls* but *Beetles* (instruments with heavy heads, usually of wood, with handles or stocks, used for driving pegs, wedges, etc., or for crushing, bruising, breaking, flattening, or smoothing, or for ramming down paving-slabs). The *Maul* especially associated with the Third Degree, however, is the round-headed *Setting-Maul*, for fixing ashlars in place. The *Setting-Maul* is a tool enacting the Ritual Death after which a candidate is 'Raised' to the Level of the Spirit. Third-Degree tracing-boards have West at the top or head of the coffin, whereas First-Degree boards have East at the top: this alludes to the Master Mason, having completed a journey to the East in search of Knowledge, returning to the West in order to help other Freemasons in their seekings and journeys. Also present in such boards is the image of a Sprig of Acacia: this is a sign of Life, a living vegetable that can grow to its full potential, like the Freemason. The Acacia, of course, is also a symbol of the never-failing hope of Divine Guidance and Protection, and of Rebirth, but it is also associated with the hurried burial of Hiram and with the discovery of his decomposing body. Tracing-boards can also feature the Tablets inscribed with the Ten Commandments or give some indication

---

30 For the Craft Degrees *see* Wilmshurst (1923, 1948).

31 *Mauls* are sometimes called *Mells* or *Keevils*.

CPl.VI.II (*top left*) Plate made in Belleek, County Fermanagh, showing Masonic symbols (*UGLE*).

CPl.VI.III (*bottom left*) French prisoner-of-war plaque (*c*.1800) showing most of the symbols of the Craft Degrees (*UGLE*).

CPl.VI.IV (*top right*) English toast-rack (twentieth century) featuring the Square and Compasses with Levels as feet (*UGLE*).

of these Commandments by various means (such as a book with initials). For these arcane matters the works of Walter Leslie Wilmshurst go into the meaning of Freemasonry and Masonic Initiation in depth, and point out that Freemasonry is both a Science and an Art, the first concerned with Understanding of Self and Enlightenment, and the second with work of Self-Purification and living Life according to certain principles[32].

From the above, it will be understood that the implements and tools illustrated in or on Masonic documents or objects have associations and meanings. Even the border of a plate may be liberally decorated with obvious Masonic symbols (**CPl.VI.II**), and other artefacts associated with the table may also be overtly Masonic (**CPls.VI.III-IV**). But it is with the tools themselves that we find all sorts of allusions and triggers (**CPls.VI.V-VIII**), for they have profound meaning for the Craft, as well as offering marvellous opportunities to designers for fanciful constructions (**CPl.VI.IX**, p.110) or the decoration of sundry objects, from aprons (**CPl.VI.X**, p.111) to jewellery (**CPl.VI.XI**, p.111). This application of Masonic symbols was extremely common in the eighteenth, nineteenth, and twentieth centuries, but not so usual was the use of simple images to suggest Masonic commandments: a good example, however (**CPl.VI.XII**, p.111), is the snuff-box of 1846, commanding the Mason to 'Hear, See, and Be Silent'.

So how do tracing-boards reflect the plans of Lodges? Numerous diagrams of Lodge layouts were published in various pamphlets[33] throughout the eighteenth century, and we know from descriptions that these reflected fact. A 'Gentleman Belonging to the Jerusalem Lodge' and Charles Warren[34] both published a 'Plan of the Drawing on the Floor at the making of a Mason' which seems to offer some sort of idea of how a Lodge was arranged (**Pl.VI.22**, p.111). The Canongate Kilwinning Lodge plan was rectangular: the Master was at the east; the Senior and Junior Wardens in the West, with triangular pedestal themselves set at the points of a triangle; the Secretary was on the Master's

---

32 *See* Wilmshurst 1923, 1948). Some modern Masonic historians have been critical of Wilmshurst's work, however, so caution is advised.

33 See, for example, Gentleman Belonging to the Jerusalem Lodge (1762); Pass'd Master (1765); V-n (1760); Warren (1765); and Jackson (Ed.) (1986) for a surfeit of English Masonic 'Exposures' sufficient to satisfy all enthusiasts.

34 *See* Bibliography.

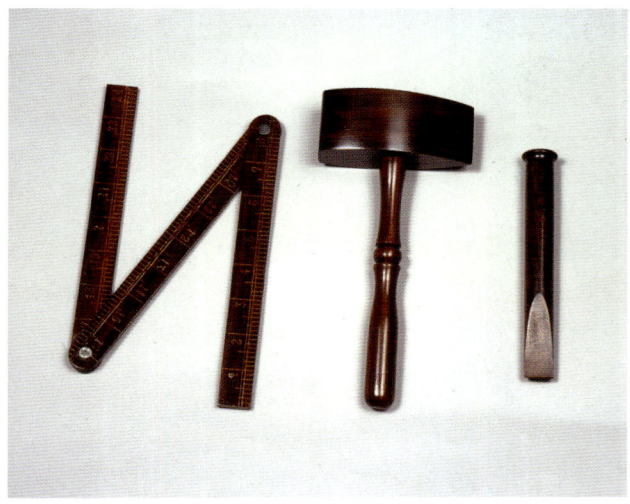

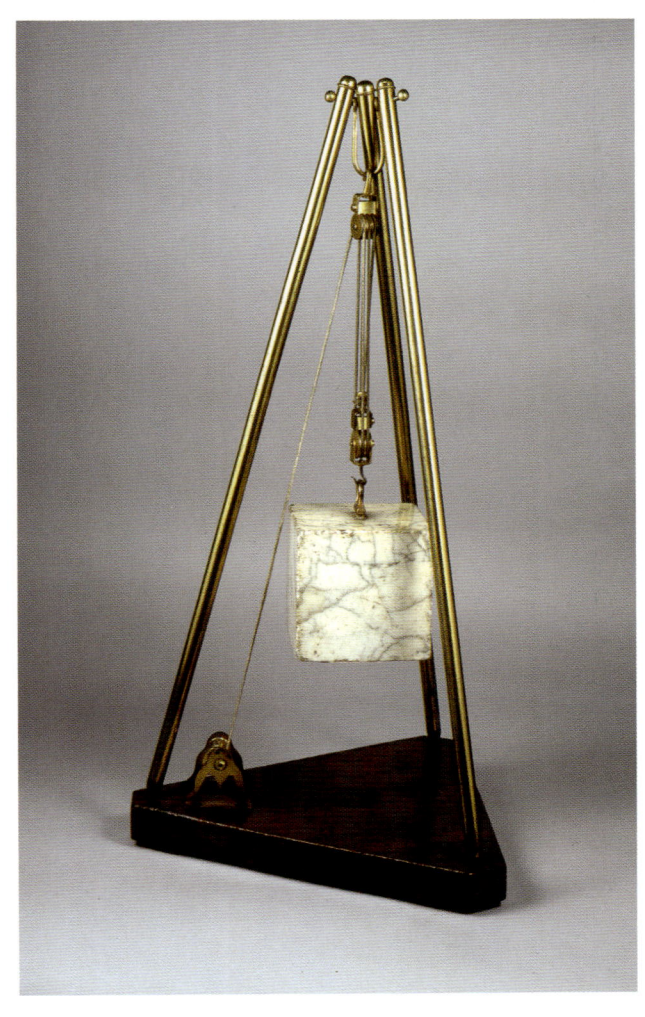

CPl.VI.V (*top left*) Ceremonial 'tools' of the First Degree: the Gauge (*left*), 24 inches long, represents the hours of the day in which Intellect and Skills may be developed, as well as suggesting exactness; the Chisel (*right*) which is used to work stone, also represents Education and the ability to classify and analyse; the last balances Passion, represented by the Gavel (*centre*), which can represent Force or Energy. All three are symbolic 'working' tools of the Degree of Apprentice, representing Action, and date from the 1930s (*UGLE*).

CPl.VI.VI (*centre left*) Ceremonial 'tools' of the Second Degree: the Plumb-line (*left*) has obvious uses in building, but in Freemasonry it is associated with Licence, in contrast to Restraint as suggested by the Level (*centre, bottom*), a tool used to ensure correctness when laying stones. The Square (*top*) is a right-angle, and suggests a Balance between the other two implements. All three are symbolic 'working' tools of the Degree of the Fellow Craft, representing the practice of Morality and Probity, and keeping a Balance, and they date from the 1930s (*UGLE*).

CPl.VI.VII (*bottom left*) Ceremonial 'tools' of the Third Degree: the Skirret (*left*), a line on a reel, enables straight lines to be formed for building purposes, but in Freemasonry it teaches restraint; the Compass (*centre*) is used to describe circles, but can also measure repeated lengths, so is a symbol of Proportion, balancing the straight line made possible by the Skirret and the Freedom given by the Pencil (*right*). All three are concerned with Design, and therefore connected with Creativity and with Architecture, so are tools of the Master Mason. They date from the 1930s (*UGLE*).

CPl.VI.VIII (*bottom right*) Model (*c.*1830) of a Lewis in action, suspended from a tripod and supporting an ashlar cube. This is a metal device which is set into a recess in ashlar to enable it to be lowered into position, something impossible if a rope were wound around the stone. Once the stone is properly placed, the Lewis can be removed without damaging the ashlar (*UGLE*).

left, and the Treasurer on his right, while positions were defined for the two standard-bearers and the Bible Bearer, and for the Master of Ceremonies (on the Master's left) and Senior Deacon (on the Master's right). The Junior Deacon was positioned near the Senior Warden, and the Inner Guard near the Junior Warden.[35] The Brethren were seated along the sides of the Lodge in lines between the positions of the Treasurer and Senior Warden and Brethren, the

---

35 Jones (1956) 353.

CPl. VI.IX 'A Free Mason Form'd out of the Materials of his Lodge': it is inscribed with the verse:

> 'Behold a *Master-Mason* rare,
> Whose *mystic Portrait* does declare
> The *Secrets* of *Free Masonry*,
> Fair for all to read and see,
> But few there are to whom they're known,
> Tho' they so plainly here are shown'.

The Apron, the Two 'Pillars', Compasses, the Square, the Lewis, the 47th Proposition of Euclid, and so on are shown within a charming Rococo frame. Drawn by A. Slade and published by W. Tringham (1754) (*GLFI*).

CPl.VI.X English Apron of *c.*1813 decorated with figures of Faith (*right*), Hope (*left*), and Charity (*top*), familiar Masonic Personifications (*UGLE*).

CPl.VI.XII Papier-mâché box (probably for snuff), showing an ear, an eye, and locked lips, signifying 'Hear', 'See', and 'Be Silent', the Motto of the United Grand Lodge of England. It dates from 1846 (*UGLE*).

CPl.VI.XI Brooch made by French prisoners-of-war *c.*1800 depicting many Masonic symbols (*UGLE*).

Secretary and the Junior Warden. Two large columns (mis-named 'pillars') stood on either side of the long axis marking the entrance to the Lodge inside the room enclosure. In the centre, half-way between the columns and the Master, was the Altar, a reminder of the Temple, of the injunction to build Altars in the Bible, and the need to have a focus, a table, a mnemonic of many things. A Lodge itself was regarded as an Ark, or repository of Wisdom and Secrets, but many Lodges had Arks, or boxes containing the Warrant, Regalia, and so forth; in the case of travelling Lodges (for example those connected with the Army) Arks were doubly necessary. The Ark, in another sense, of course, was Noah's.

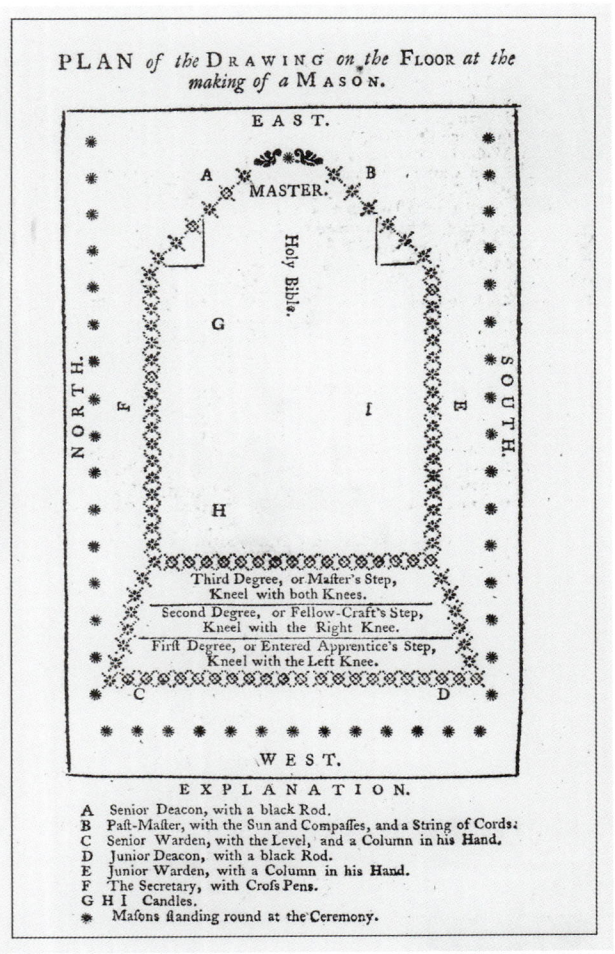

Pl.VI.22 Masonic Lodge layout from *Jachin and Boaz*, published in London in 1776. This is a version of a diagram in *The Free Mason stripped Naked; or, the whole Art and Mystery of Free-Masonry, Made Plain and Easy to all Capacities*, by Charles Warren, published in Dublin (1765) (*UGLE*).

Candles were symbols of spiritual light or illumination, and have connotations with Consecration, Gratitude, and the Keeping of Promises. Mediaeval Craft-Guilds, as has been mentioned, maintained altars in churches and kept them well supplied with candles. Three candles have a clear religious significance (the Trinity etc.), but they also can suggest Silence and Secrecy, as in *Tace*, the Latin for 'Be Silent'. This is alluded to in William Dampier's *Voyages* as 'Trust none of them for they are all Thieves, but Tace is Latin for a Candle',[36] and by Henry Fielding as '"*Tace*, Madam", answered Murphy, "is Latin for a candle; I commend your prudence."'[37] This curious phrase is a humorously veiled hint to keep silent. Candles were therefore reminders of Masonic secrecy, and the three candlesticks were often arranged to stand on the points of a triangle. (In an eighteenth-century plan two points are set to form a parallel line with the north wall of the Lodge, while the 'apex' points south. In the same plan three steps for the First, Second, and Third Degrees are shown to the West, while the Master and Bible are placed within a triangular form to the East.) The three candles also represent the Volume of the Sacred Law, the Square, and the Compasses (the Greater Lights), whilst the Lesser Lights were the candles of the Master and Wardens.

One of the most attractive and comprehensive of illustrations (as far as Masonic emblems are concerned) is the frontispiece of *Jachin and Boaz*[38], published in London in

[36] Dampier (1697) 356.
[37] Fielding (1751) **i** x. See also Sir Walter Scott, Bt., in his *Familiar Letters* (see Scott [1894] **ii** 115) 24 February 1821.
[38] Gentleman Belonging to the Jerusalem Lodge, originally published in 1762.

Pl.VI.23 (*above*) Frontispiece of *Jachin and Boaz* published in London in 1776 (UGLE).

Pl.VI.24 (*right*) Frontispiece and title-page of *Les Secrets de L'Ordre des Francs-Maçons, Dévoilés & mis au jour par Monsieur P****, showing a candidate for the Degree of Apprentice being blindfolded, from the first part of Pérau (1745c) (UGLE).

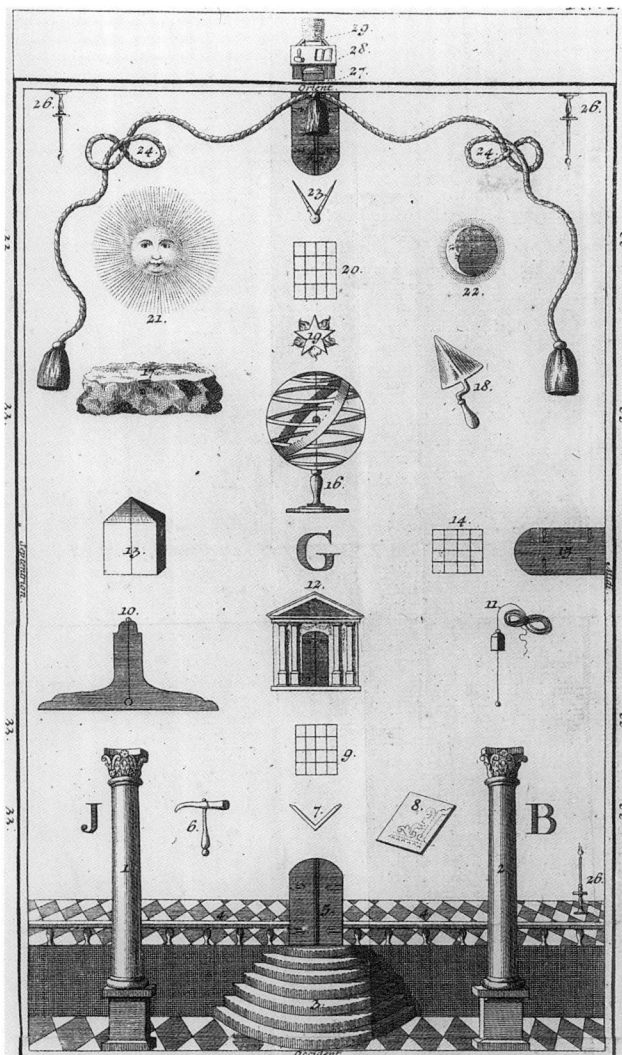

Pl.VI.25.1 A true plan of a Lodge for the Reception of 'Apprentif Compagnon'. (1) Jachin; (2) Boaz; (3) the Seven Steps to ascend to the Temple; (4) the Mosaic Pavement; (5) the western gate; (6) the Masons' hammer or mallet; (7) the square; (8) the floor to be delineated upon (tracing-board); (9) the west window; (10) the level; (11) the perpendicular line, or plumb-line; (12) the portal of the inner chamber; (13) the pointed cubical stone (i.e. pyramid on cube); (14) the south window; (15) the south door; (16) the sphere; 17) the rough stone; (18) the trowel; (19) the flaming star; (20) the east window; (21) the sun; (22) the moon; (23) the compass; (24) the indented tuft; (25) the east door; (26) the three lights; (27) the stool; (28) the table; (29) the Master's chair; (30) the Senior Warden's chair; (31) the Junior Warden's chair; (32) the three Masters' seats; (33) the three Fellow-Crafts' seats (except the last Member received); (34) the Junior Warden's plumb-line. From Pérau (1745c) (UGLE).

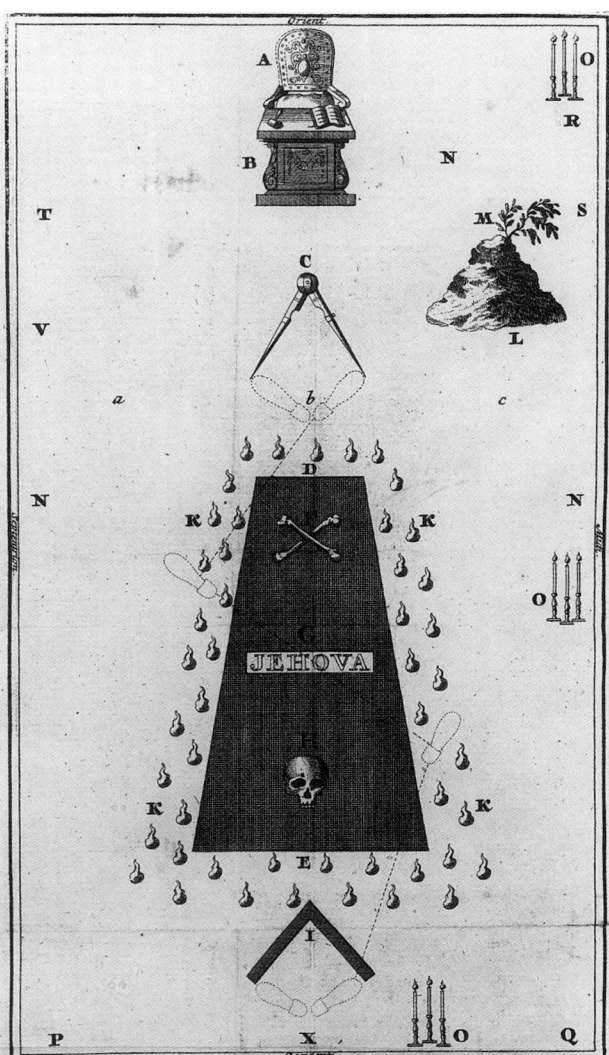

Pl.VI.25.2 A true plan of a Lodge for the Reception of a Master (A) the Master's seat; (B) the altar with Bible and mallet; (C) the compass; (D, E) the coffin; (F) bones across; (G) the ancient word of the masters; (H) a death's head; (I) the rule; (K) three tears, or *guttes*; (L) a mountain; (M) a branch of acacia; (N) three Brethren holding rolls of paper; (O) the nine lights placed three by three; (P) the Senior Warden; (Q) the Junior Warden; (R) the Speaker; (S) the Brother Visitors; (T) the Secretary; (V) the Treasurer (X) the Receiver. The positions marked a, b, and c are where the sun, flaming star, and moon are placed on some cloths, but this custom seems to have been mostly used for the reception of Apprentices and Fellow Crafts. From Pérau (1745c) (UGLE).

1776 (**Pl.VI.23**), a volume that also contains a diagram of a Lodge layout (see **Pl.VI.22**, p.111). In fact, the historian of Freemasonry can delve deeply into the literature of eighteenth-century Freemasonry, and find there much to delight, both visually and intellectually. One of the keys to the Enlightenment can be found among seemingly esoteric publications, yet the unclosed mind and the unclouded eye will have no difficulty in recognising themes from sixteenth-century representations of the Temple of Solomon to the sweetest gardens of the European revolution in sensibility.

Women and Freemasonry, Papal Disapproval, and Mopses

'Exposures' of the eighteenth century were many, and featured illustrations such as those mentioned above. Similar decorations embellished *L'Ordre des Francs-Maçons Trahi, et Le Secret des Mopses Révélé* (The Order of Free-Masons Betrayed, and the Secret of Mopses Revealed), included in the Abbé Gabriel-Louis-Calabre Pérau's *Les Secrets de L'Ordre des Francs-Maçons Dévoilés & mis au jour* (The Secrets of the Order of Free-Masonry Unveiled and Laid

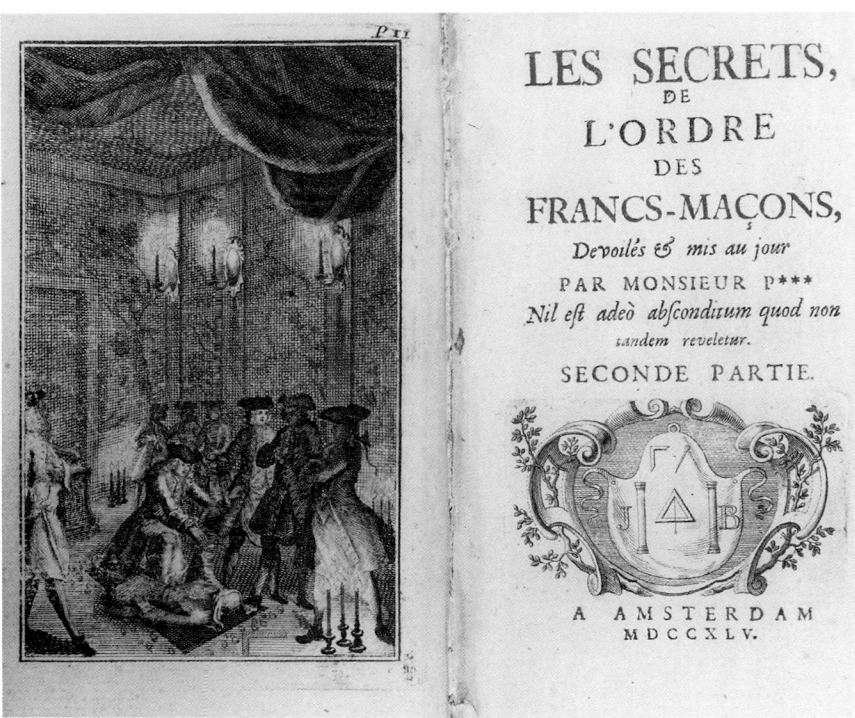

Pl.VI.26 (*left*) Frontispiece and title-page of Pérau's *Les Secrets de L'Ordre des Francs-Maçons Dévoilés & mis au jour par Monsieur P****, showing the Master 'raising' a new Master Mason, from the second part of Pérau (1745c) (UGLE).

Pl.VI.27.1 (*below left*) Plan of a Lodge for the Reception of an Apprentice. This design purports to be correct, but is not. (1) Jachin; (2) Boaz; (3) seven steps to enter the Temple; (4) Mosaic Pavement; (5) west window; (6) tracing-board for the Masters; (7) flaming star; (8) south window; (9) plumb or perpendicular; (10) east window; (11) level; (12) unhewn stone; (13) square; (14) cubic stone, with point (pyramid); (15) indented tuft; (A) Master; (B) First Inspector, Watcher, or Guardian; (C) Second Watcher; (D) altar; (E) foot-stool; (F, G, H) the three lights. In this, as in other French designs, Jachin is associated with Strength, and Boaz with Wisdom. From Plate IV of Pérau (1745c) (UGLE).

Pl.VI.27.2 (*below right*) Inexact plan of a Lodge for the Reception of a Master. Note the Acacia on the coffin, the position of the skull and crossbones, and the liberal scattering of tears, or *guttes* (incorrectly described as 'gutters' in some curiously inaccurate 'Masonic' publications). From Plate V of Pérau (1745c) (UGLE).

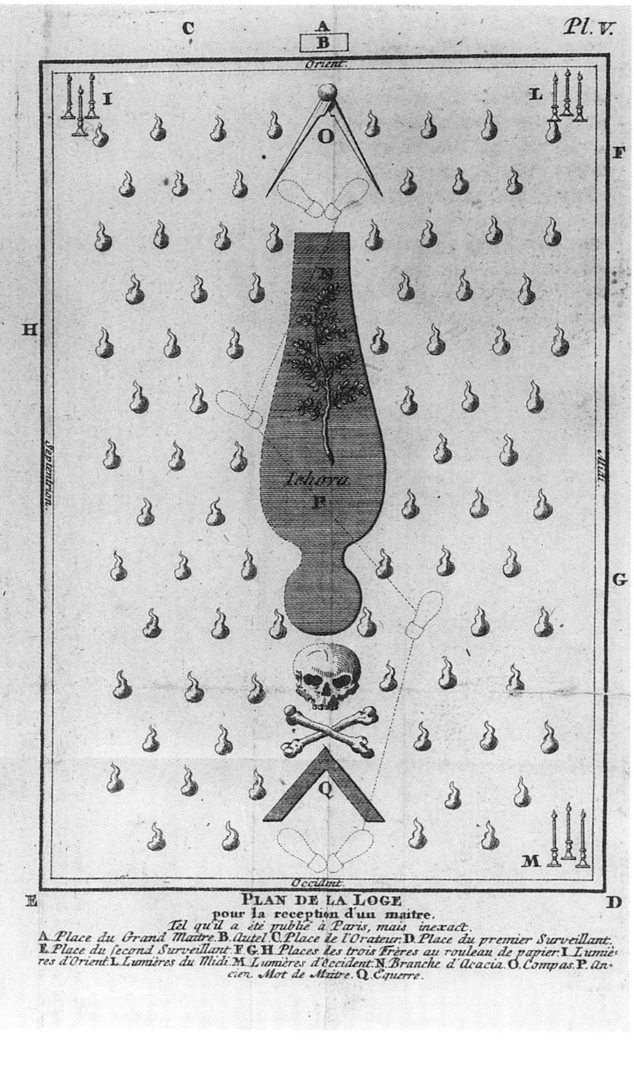

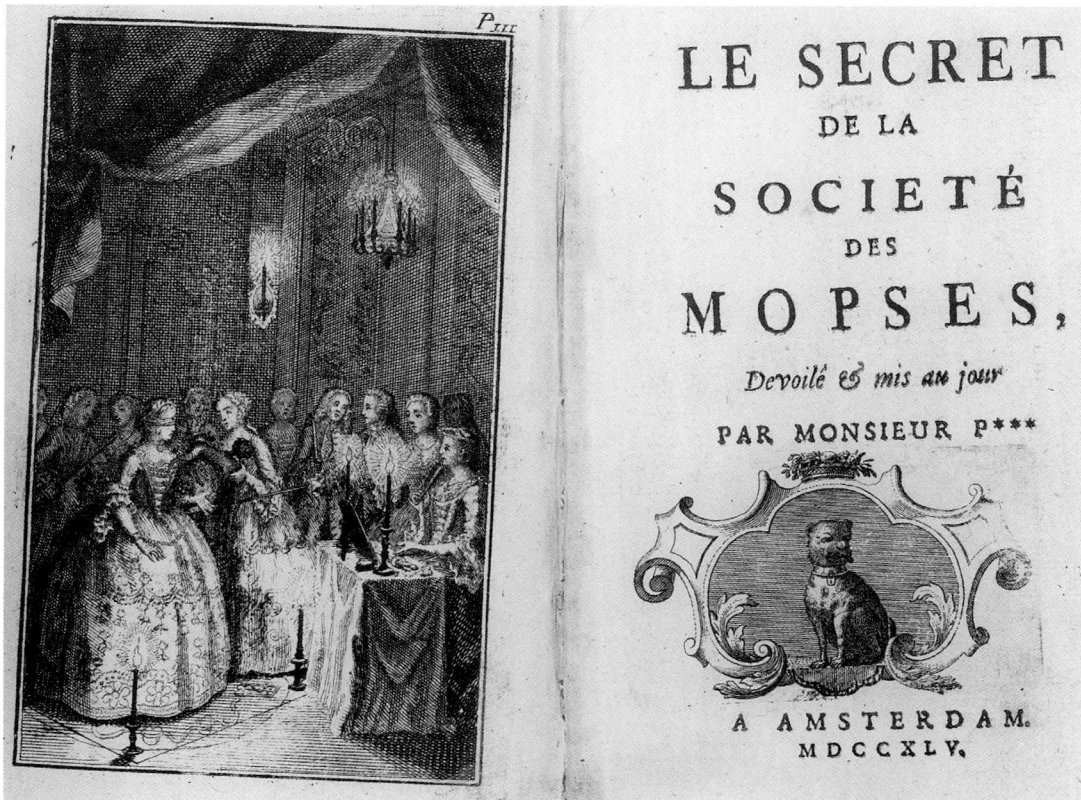

Pl.VI.28 Frontispiece and title-page of *Le Secret de la Société des Mopses Dévoilé*. The frontispiece shows the Reception of a female Apprentice into a Lodge of Mopses, The Order of Mopses (from the German *Mops*, meaning a Pug-dog) was an androgynous society founded in 1739-40, and the name is taken from that of a young Mastiff-type of dog with a Pug-like face, noted for its courage and faithfulness. As the plate comes from *L'Ordre des Francs-Maçons Trahi* (Betrayed), *et Le Secret de la Société des Mopses Dévoilé* (Amsterdam 1745), the widely believed claim that women were admitted only after 1776 is clearly incorrect, for the Grand Mistress is seated, and a woman Apprentice is being initiated (although the rite of initiation appears to be less than savoury, and is probably scurrilous) from Pérau (1745b) (UGLE).

Open), published in two parts in 'Amsterdam' in 1745 (**Pl. VI.24**, p.112). Pérau's book shows 'true plans' of Lodges for the Receptions of both an 'Apprentif-Compagnon' and a Master Mason (**Pls.VI.25.1 & 2**, p.113). Pérau's second part (**Pl.VI.26**) of *Les Secrets...* shows the Master 'raising' a new Master Mason from the 'dead' as well as plans of Lodges (**Pls.VI.27.1 & 2**). Pérau also produced *Le Secret de la Société des Mopses Dévoilés & mis au jour par Monsieur P**** published in 1745 (**Pl.VI.28**). The plan of a Lodge of Mopses (see **Pl.IX.23**, p.229) differs from other tracing-boards or floor-cloths previously described[39].

So what was a Lodge of Mopses? Freemasonry is mostly associated in the popular mind with men only, but women were also close to the Craft through various associations. The first female Freemason (**Pl. VI.29**) proper appears to have been Elizabeth Aldworth[40], whose father, the Rt. Hon. Arthur St Leger, was 1st Viscount Doneraile, of County Cork, a leading Freemason who conducted Lodge meetings

Pl.VI.29 'The Hon: Mrs Aldworth, the Female Freemason', published in *Freemason's Quarterly Review* (September 1839) (UGLE).

---

39   See Pérau (1745 *a*, *b*, & *c*).
40   She married Richard Aldworth of Newmarket, County Cork.

Pl.VI.30 'The Free-Mason's Surpriz'd or the Secret Dis-Cover'd: a true tale from a Mason's Lodge in Canterbury', printed for T. Wilkins, 1754. The inscription referred to the fact that 'Parson & Clerke, with their sanctified Faces, Had a Peep at Molls Rouser' (*UGLE*).

at his residence (not an uncommon practice at that time), probably shortly before the formation of Grand Lodge (1717). Elizabeth, who would have been very young at the time (probably a teenager), is supposed to have witnessed a Degree ritual when eavesdropping, so the members of the Lodge decided to induct her as a Freemason so as to ensure her silence. She is said to have become Master of the Lodge in due course[41].

Less respectable, perhaps, was the case of 'Moll', a girl who secreted herself in a garret above a Lodge in Canterbury, Kent, in order to ascertain the secrets of Freemasonry. Unfortunately, her knowledge of building construction was less than sound, and she broke through the lath-and-plaster ceiling and was suspended there, revealing her stockinged legs and naked backside to the startled Brethren, some of whom appeared more amused than shocked (**Pl.VI.30**).

However, female interest in the Craft was one of the features of the eighteenth century, and especially of the Age of the Enlightenment: as a result, Lodges of Adoption (or Adoptive Lodges) were formed which operated under the direction of a normal Lodge, and they conferred Degrees which differed from the usual three Craft Degrees. When Pope Clement XII, noted for his political naïvety, attacked Freemasonry's natural bias, secret oaths, religious attitudes, and much else in the Constitution *In eminenti* (28 April 1738), this was the first official Papal statement concerning Freemasonry, but it was a *Bulla* of the *Mandamenta* class, that is an Act of Condemnation (**Pl.VI.31**): what the Papacy found particularly worrying was Freemasonry's indifferentism, which, to Freemasons, was actually tolerance. The Roman Catholic Church was concerned about the expansion of English (and therefore Protestant) trade and influence throughout Europe, and Freemasonry was perceived as yet another aspect of this phenomenon. However, political differences between the Holy See and various parts of Europe meant that the Bull carried no legal authority even in countries that were predominantly Roman Catholic. In certain states (notably Poland, Portugal, and Spain) the Inquisition acted against Freemasonry when and where ever it could. In Lisbon in 1744, for example, a Swiss Protestant Freemason diamond-cutter, one John Coustos, was arrested and tortured, although he was rescued from a sentence of four years' servitude in the galleys through the intervention of the British Envoy to the Court at Lisbon, Charles Compton, who invoked the name of King George II to secure Coustos's release. Coustos issued an account of his experiences which went into several editions (including ones in French and German)[42]: the timing is significant, for the Jacobite Rebellion had broken out in 1745, and anti-Roman Catholic feelings in Britain were running high[43].

Matters were further exacerbated by the Bull *Providas Romanorum Pontificum* of 1751, issued by Pope Benedict XIV: this renewed the condemnation of Clement XII, and also denounced various writings of the Enlightenment, including those of Charles-Louis de Secondat, Baron de la Brède et de

---

41 MacNulty (2006) 226.

42 Coustos (1746).
43 *See* Gilbert (2006).

Montesquieu, whose *L'Esprit des Lois* (or *Loix*) came out in Geneva in 1748[44]. The renewed antagonism of the Papacy towards Freemasonry prompted predictable fights carried out in print, including defences of Freemasonry[45] and attacks (in which support for the Papal position was spelled out[46]). There was a veritable avalanche of published material, much of it repetitive, but a succinct outline of the friction between Freemasonry and the Roman Catholic Church can be found in the *Canonbury Papers*[47].

One of the by-products of Papal disapproval of the Craft was the blossoming not only of Freemasonry, but of Lodges of Adoption, including the Order of Mopses in the Holy Roman Empire. The Order of Mopses took its name from the German *Mops*, meaning a Pug or young Mastiff type of dog with a Pug-like face, noted for its courage and fidelity. This Order, founded shortly after the 1738 Bull, kept alive ideas of private association in the German-speaking lands, and admitted women to all offices except that of Grand Master. There was, however, a 'Grand Mistress', and the male and female heads of the Order alternately assumed for six months each the supreme position within the Order. An illustration showing the Reception of a female Apprentice into a Lodge of Mopses was published in 1745 in Pérau's exposure[48], not in 'Amsterdam' as claimed on the title-page, but in Frankfurt-am-Main: it shows the presiding Mistress seated, and the blindfolded candidate's face in close proximity to the dog's backside[49] (see **Pl.VI.28**, p.115). The plan of the Lodge in Pérau's scurrilous book (see **Pl.IX.23**, p.229) has a *Mops* (*doguin* in French, meaning a Mastiff-pup or whelp) in the very centre[50]. As will be explained later, the Order of Mopses had particular resonances in Poland[51].

Now the last-named country was closely connected with part of Germany when the second son of the Elector of Saxony, Johann Georg III, succeeded his brother (Johann Georg IV) as Elector Friedrich August I (b. 1670) in 1694. On the death of the King of Poland, John III Sobieski, Friedrich August was elected King in 1697, and took the name Augustus II. From 1704 to 1709 he was replaced by the protégé of King Charles XII of Sweden, Stanisław (Stanislaus) I Leszczyński[52], but regained the Throne and held it until his death, when it, like the Electorate, passed to his only legitimate son, Friedrich Augustus II of Saxony, who reigned as Augustus III of Poland, although Stanisław Leszczyński unsuccessfully attempted to regain the Throne for himself.

The Absolutist Court of Augustus the Strong (as Friedrich August I was known, not least for his legendary number of mistresses) created the conditions in which

Pl.VI.31 The Papal condemnation of Freemasonry, *In eminenti*, of 1738 (UGLE).

the first European hard-paste porcelain was invented, the outcome of a collaboration between Johann Friedrich Böttger, Gottfried Pabst von Ohain, Ehrenfried Walther von Tschirnhaus, and others[53]. Böttger was kept virtually a prisoner by the Elector, who charged him with manufacturing gold: as it turned out, the attempts were unsuccessful, but porcelain was invented, and it turned out to be extremely lucrative. An Edict was issued from Dresden in 1710, and a factory was established at the Albrechtsburg in Meissen: the first Director was Michael Nehmitz, and designers included Johann Jacob Irminger, Johann Benjamin Thomae, Paul Heermann, but with the appointment as modeller of the Court Sculptor, Johann Joachim Kändler, in 1731, an enormous range of enchanting and elegant figures was produced, often with humorous overtones, and these are among the prettiest creations

---

44 Montesquieu (1748).
45 Clarke (1751).
46 Hondt (1752).
47 Stewart (*Ed.*) (2006) 75-91.
48 Pérau (1745*a*).
49 A version of this illustration is reproduced in McNulty (2006) 226.
50 Pérau (1745*a*) Plate VIII.
51 Curl (1995, 2004, 2006*b*, 2006*d*).
52 Who, in 1725, became father-in-law of King Louis XV of France when the latter married his daughter, Maria.

53 Including David Köhler, Paul Wildenstein, and Samuel Stöltzel.

CPl.VI.XIII *(top left)* Meissen group, probably by Kändler, of 1743, showing a couple: the woman is sewing an apron, leaning over her is a young man perhaps indicating silence, and under the table is a *Mops* (UGLE).

CPl.VI.XIV *(top right)* Female figure holding a Pug, probably by Kändler (UGLE).

CPl.VI.XV *(left)* Pug-dog of porcelain (UGLE).

of German Rococo[54]. Loosely known as 'Dresden' china figures, they were actually made in Meissen, and the best examples date from the 1740s and 1750s. Among them, four objects relevant to this study deserve mention. The first is a delightful group called *Masonic Lovers*, showing a young woman seated at a table, sewing an apron: standing beside her, and leaning over her is a young man perhaps indicating silence; and seated partly under the table is a *Mops*. Dated 1743 (**CPl.VI.XIII**), it is attributed to Kändler, and probably suggests that the group is associated with the Society of Mopses. The second object shows a woman alone, with a Pug, and is probably of a similar date, very likely also by Kändler (**CPl.VI.XIV**). The third, which may or may not be from Meissen, is a *barbonnière* (a small receptacle modelled to resemble a bearded face, with a hinged back) in the form of a head of a Pug-dog, also probably associated with the Society of Mopses. The fourth is a Pug, beautifully modelled (**CPl.VI.XV**). These four items are held by the superlative Library and Museum at Freemasons' Hall (United Grand Lodge of England), which contains a rich array of Masonic material: from this collection it is clear that many figurines were created to support various allusions to Freemasonry (Adoptive or otherwise) by various porcelain factories, quite apart from the exquisite Rococo exemplars from Meissen. The Berlin factory also turned out several Masonic figurines[55], and it was not alone in its endeavours: the Craft was ever-present in all sorts of artefacts, illustrations, designs, and indeed its presence was widespread. And some of the most charming of all objects associated with the Craft were those connected with, or alluding in some way with, the Society of Mopses or to women and the fringes of Freemasonry[56].

---

54 *See* Turner (*Ed.*) (1998) **xxi** 62-67, and related articles mentioned therein.

55 *See,* for example, Duriegl & Winkler (*Eds.*) (1992) 225. The same source (327-339) has information on women and Freemasonry.

56 For women and the Craft *see* Anonymous (1791), Chevalier de tous les Ordres Maçonniques (1807), Jacquelin (1812), Madame xxx (1744), and A Sister Mason (1765).

Certificates and Architectural Elements

To be an Accepted Mason became socially respectable by the end of the seventeenth century in England (as is obvious from the numerous members of the Establishment who had joined the Craft), although gentlemen in Scotland had been members of Lodges much earlier. Lodges evolved into social and convivial societies, and by the second decade of the eighteenth century, four London Lodges united to form a Grand Lodge with the objects of promoting benevolence and brotherly sentiments, and of giving help to Brethren (Grand Lodge also seems to have been formed with the object of purging Freemasonry of Jacobite tendencies after the 1715 Rebellion and to consolidate English Freemasonry in the Whig and Hanoverian cause). King George I was not exactly universally loved, but he served a useful purpose: he would ensure the maintenance of the Settlement that had resulted from the 'Glorious Revolution' of 1688 and he would keep the Pope well at bay.

This London Grand Lodge was the progenitor of other Lodges at home and abroad, and from 1717 it began to regulate the constitutions of the various groups in existence. In 1721 James Anderson was appointed to oversee the production of a *Book of Constitutions* to contain the history, charges, regulations, and Master's Song which duly appeared in 1723[57]. Anderson (a Scot, as has been previously noted) had been commissioned when John Montagu, 2nd Duke of Montagu, was Grand Master. Montagu was a scholar, a Fellow of the Royal Society, and was admitted a Doctor of Physic at the University of Cambridge in 1717. A Knight of the Garter (1718) and a Fellow of the Royal College of Physicians, he was Grand Master of Grand Lodge 1721-2. His Whig and intellectual credentials were impeccable, therefore, but there was discontent among the Tories.

In 1721 Philip James Wharton, Duke of Wharton, was admitted into the Society of Freemasons at the *King's Arms Tavern*, St Paul's Churchyard, and in 1722 he was installed as Grand Master. Now in 1716 Wharton had visited James Francis Edward, Stuart Pretender to the Thrones, and was created Duke of Northumberland on 22 December by the Pretender, an event calculated to infuriate Whig and Hanoverian opinion. As Marquess of Catherlough he took his seat in the Irish House of Lords in 1717 and became a Privy Councillor in the same year. From 1719 to 1723 he was Chairman of the Hellfire Club, an organisation dedicated to the promotion of dissolute behaviour and parodies of established religion[58]. Once installed as Grand Master, Wharton seems to have distinguished himself by having the band play *Let the king enjoy his Own Again*, a popular Jacobite tune (*ODNB* claims he sparked controversy by 'singing a strongly pro-Stuart ballad', but this was probably an aspect of his reckless 'profligacy perhaps unparalleled in Augustan England'[59]). Wharton converted to

Pl.VI.32 Frontispiece by John Pine of *The Constitutions of the Free-Masons* published in London in 1723. This appears to have been the first printed constitution of any speculative Freemasonic body (i.e. Premier Grand Lodge of England, founded 1717). The figure holding the *Constitutions* is John, 2nd Duke of Montagu, and the figure facing him is Philip, Duke of Wharton, both eminent Freemasons. Note the proof of Euclid's 47th Proposition on the pavement, and the Five Roman Orders of Architecture (*UGLE*).

Roman Catholicism in 1726 in Spain, and died impoverished, a hopeless drunk, despised by Jacobites and everyone who knew him.

However, he has enjoyed immortality in Freemasonic circles, for he is shown with Montagu in the celebrated frontispiece (**Pl.VI.32**) by John Pine in *The Constitutions of Freemasonry* (1723), the first printed Constitution of any speculative Freemasonic body. It was Wharton, too, who signed off Anderson's *Constitutions*, approving the document for printing, but he probably did not realise the full impact (or was too drunk to do so). Given that a notorious pro-Jacobite rake had been Grand Master, it is hardly surprising that the Freemasons were keen to distance themselves from any whiff of disloyalty to the Government and Ruling House. The leading figures among this cleansing exercise were Desaguliers, Anderson, and Francis, Earl of Dalkeith, Grand Master 1723-4. Wharton, in Vienna in 1726, declared for James III & VIII, and denounced what he claimed were the 'usurpers' of Accepted Freemasonry[60].

Eighteenth-century Masonic certificates[61] and printed summonses (in themselves a major study, for hundreds [and probably thousands] survive) are often, or even

---

57 Anderson (*Ed.*) (1723).
58 *ODNB* **lviii** 367-371. Not to be confused with the Club later associated with Sir Francis Dashwood.
59 *ODNB* **lviii** 367. 'Reckless profligacy' seems to refer to his addiction to the Bottle.

60 For these matters *see* Churton (2006).
61 *See* Haunch (2008).

usually, embellished with emblems and motifs, including the Tuscan, Doric, Ionic, and Corinthian Orders of Architecture. A summons of the West India & American Lodge of the Most Ancient and Honourable Society of Free & Accepted Masons of 1760 shows pairs of columns of Corinthian, Tuscan (although the bases are not Tuscan, so the Order might more accurately be described as unfluted Roman Doric), and Ionic Orders on which stand the Theological and Cardinal Virtues (**Pl.VI.33**). Other summonses feature various familiar Masonic motifs (**Pls.VI.34 & 35**). The three sets of columns of three Classical Orders derive from mixing some of the associations of 'columns' and 'pillars' as outlined above with ideas of Strength, Wisdom, and Beauty: Doric for Strength; Ionic for Wisdom; and Corinthian for Beauty seem to have been the allusions. On occasion Masonic certificates and summonses will show columns (Jachin and Boaz) of two different Orders, each supporting a globe, the iconography of which has previously been discussed. With Wisdom on one side and Beauty on the other, the original associations of Jachin and Boaz became obscured and mixed up. One suspects that the problem here was that Palladian and Rococo sensibilities tended to be removed from the intensities of Renaissance-Hermetic ideas, and there was a general dilution and confusion of Symbol and Emblem, although the objects themselves were often of great beauty, and were finely crafted.

As many of these interesting summonses make clear, Freemasons generally met in taverns during the eighteenth century, for only gradually did Lodges acquire property as permanent venues for meetings. Some Lodges met in private houses, often quite humble dwellings, as is obvious from descriptions of a Lodge which met regularly in the roof-space of a lowly County Down cottage[62]: this cannot have been unusual.

Pl.VI.33 A Summons to attend the duties of the West India & American Lodge of the Most Ancient & Honourable Society of Free & Accepted Masons at the *Queen's Arms Tavern* in St Paul's Churchyard, 1760. Note the Corinthian, Tuscan, and Ionic Orders of Architecture: in Masonic iconography Doric is equated with Strength, Ionic with Wisdom, and Corinthian with Beauty. On the left are the Three Theological Virtues of (*from left*) Charity (with children), Hope (with Anchor), and Faith (with book), while on the right (*from the left*) are Fortitude and Wisdom as Minerva, Strength as Hercules, and Beauty as Venus (presumably). Other Virtues in Masonry are Prudence, Temperance, and Justice, whilst Initiates are taught the importance of Secrecy, Fidelity, and Obedience. Note the palm-trees as Nilotic motifs, an allusion to Egypt (*Noble Collection LMA*).

Freemasons' Hall in London

As was previously noted, the Grand Lodge of England (the Premier Grand Lodge of the World) was created on St John the Baptist's Day, 1717, at the *Goose and Gridiron* Ale-House[63], St Paul's Churchyard, in the City of London.

---

62 *See* W.G. Simpson (1926). I am indebted to Lorraine Frazer of Archbishop Robinson's Library, Armagh (Armagh Public Libraries) for this item. *See* also Edge (1912).

63 Demolished 1894.

Pl.VI.34 A Summons to attend the duties of the Lodge of Unity at the *Horn Tavern*, Doctor's Commons, St Paul's, of 1813. Like that of the West India and American Lodge there are three Orders and an arch. The figure of Charity has acquired an Egyptian head-dress, and the chequered floor is Masonic, consisting of a multiplicity of squares, symbolising the chequered life of man, and alluding to crafted floors of Antiquity. The Nilotic theme is emphasised by the cornucopia (a symbol of Isis and the fecundity associated with the flooding of the Nile). Beehives represent industry, and, of course, the ability to build crafted structures of great complexity. It has been claimed that the beehive fell from favour because it was adopted by the Jacobites as an emblem of their continuing potency after 1745, but this is clearly nonsense from its adoption by a City of London Lodge, which would have been anything but Jacobite. Beehives represent immortality, and, of course, are associated with the Virgin Mary and with Isis, with Christ the aethereal, and with sovereignty (*Noble Collection LMA*).

Pl.VI.35 A Summons to attend the Lodge of Harmony. There are three steps (the Three Grades), the chequered floor, Faith (*left*), Hope (*right*), and Charity (*above*). The Two Columns (one Ionic and one Corinthian) have globes on top, clearly derived from sixteenth-century views of the Temple, and owing nothing to Jewish Antiquity, but much to Rome, where a column with globe was preserved. The All-Seeing Eye is a symbol of the Deity. The Ladder is that of Jacob as a symbol of moral, intellectual, and spiritual progress: the number of rungs was usually depicted as seven, representing Temperance, Fortitude, Prudence, Justice, Faith, Hope, and Charity. There are also Seven Stars or Planets, a roughly hewn block of masonry, Masonic tools and instruments, and a recurring theme of three (*Noble Collection LMA*).

The location was actually London House Yard, which no longer exists (**Pl.VI.36**, p.122). For over half a century, Grand Lodge met in Livery Company Halls, taverns, and inns. We know that the first aristocratic Grand Master (the Duke of Montagu) was installed at a Feast at Stationers' Hall in 1721, but the Hall of The Merchant Taylors was the most favoured venue from 1723, the year in which the first Minute-Book of Grand Lodge was opened.

However, it became apparent that a more permanent Hall would be desirable, and in 1768, during the Grand Mastership of Henry, 5th Duke of Beaufort, plans were laid for the 'most effectual Means for raising a Fund to build a Hall and purchase Jewels, Furniture, &c. for the Grand Lodge'[64]. It was not until the Grand Mastership (1772-6) of Robert Edward, 9th Baron Petre[65], that the project was revived, and, stimulated by Petre's dynamic leadership and personal generosity, premises at No. 61 Great Queen Street, Lincoln's Inn Fields, were purchased[66] consisting of a 'Front House' facing the street, a 'Back' or 'Rear' House separated from the 'Front House' by a small courtyard, and a rear garden lying to the south-east. The garden was to become the site of Freemasons' Hall. It was decided to use the upper floors of the houses for offices and meeting-rooms, and the 'Front House' was let: it became the *Freemasons' Tavern* and Coffee-House, and the tenant, one Luke Reilly (presumably of Hibernian extraction), was permitted to put up a sign decorated with the Freemasons' Arms and the Motto *Vide, Audi, Tace*[67].

The Architect appointed was Thomas Sandby, himself a Freemason, and his splendid designs for Freemasons' Hall were realised 1775-6, probably his finest architectural work (**Pl.VI.37**, p.123). Sandby was an interesting character. He was employed in the military drawing-office

---

64 Stubbs & Haunch (1983) 10.
65 Petre, with his connections to the family of the Dukes of Norfolk, was a Roman Catholic.
66 The frontage lay between the main entrance to the Connaught Rooms and the eastern end of the present Freemasons' Hall. The price paid was 3,000 guineas.
67 Subsequently, after 1813, rearranged in order.

Pl.VI.36 London House Yard, City of London, showing the *Goose and Gridiron* shortly before its demolition in 1894 (*Norman Collection LMA*).

in the Tower of London in the 1740s, and from 1743 he was attached to the Commander-in-Chief, William Augustus, Duke of Cumberland: he was present at the Battles of Dettingen (1743) and Culloden (1746). In 1750 he was personally employed by the Duke, and became Deputy Ranger of Windsor Great Park, which gave him financial independence for the rest of his life. Sandby remained in good odour with the Royal Family after the Duke's death, and was the first Professor of Architecture at the Royal Academy (1770)[68].

Money (£3,000) was raised by subscription, and the foundation-stone was duly laid in 1775. Subscribers who gave £25 received in acknowledgement a silver medal (1780) (**CPl.VI.XVI**), designed and engraved by another Freemason, Edward Parker: the dies were sunk and the medals struck by Lewis Pingo, Chief Engraver from 1780 to the Royal Mint[69]. In May 1776 the Hall was dedicated. With its Order of robust Roman Doric, lavish entablature, elegant lunettes, and elaborate ceiling, the Hall[70] was the setting for many of the most important meetings that eventually led to the Abolition of Slavery, to the establishment of the first effective attempts to improve the conditions of the urban poor, and to other significant reforms of the first decades of the nineteenth century (including the formation of the first cemeteries[71]). Not until the 1860s was the Hall used solely for the purposes of Freemasonry alone[72], when it was designated the Grand Temple.

The symmetrical façade of the eighteenth-century *Freemasons' Tavern* was five windows wide, three storeys high (over a basement), with the entrance to the Tavern in the centre, and the approach to the Hall on the right (north-western side). A Giant Order of six Corinthian pilasters rose through the two upper storeys, carrying an entablature and a parapet. Entry to the offices above the Tavern was by the door on the left (**Pl.VI.38**). The Tavern was rebuilt in 1786-9 on a much grander scale, with Attic storey, to designs by William Tyler[73] (**CPl.VI.XVII**, p.124).

Now there was nothing particularly Freemasonic about any of these buildings, inside or out (apart from the Arms of the Freemasons which announced the Tavern), although in Sandby's great Hall there were Masonic Emblems in the metopes of the Doric frieze, and in the centre of the ceiling was a golden sun with Signs of the Zodiac. There is an extraordinary illustration by Giovanni Battista Cipriani[74] which shows Sandby's Hall with various allegorical figures in attendance: in Cipriani's vision, where the reality of the Architecture is intermingled with Masonic allusions, two

---

68 *See* Colvin (2008) 896-8. Sandby was appointed Grand Architect to the Freemasons in 1775.
69 *ODNB* (2004) **xliv** 367.
70 Actually really only a Hall of Assembly, for many years it was let out, often for public meetings, usually non-Masonic gatherings, concerts, readings, dinners, and so on.
71 Curl (*Ed.*) (2001b).
72 Stubbs & Haunch (1983) 13.
73 Britton & Pugin (1825) **i** 331n. *See also* Colvin (2008) 1063-4. Tyler is better known as a sculptor (*see* Gunnis [1968] 403-4, and Papworth [*Ed.*] [1892] **viii** 109).
74 Turner (*Ed.*) (1998) **vii** 339-40.

LODGES, DESIGNS, ARCHITECTURE, AND SYMBOLS / 123

Pl.VI.37
Freemasons' Hall, by Thomas Sandby, in 1900 (NMR. *Bedford Lemere.* 15810/6).

CPl.VI.XVI Silver medal (1780) designed by Edward Parker and struck by Lewis Pingo, presented to Thomas Sandby in acknowledgement of his contribution to the building of Freemasons' Hall (*UGLE*).

Pl.VI.38 'Elevation of Free Masons Tavern', drawn by Sandby in 1783 and engraved by F. Allen. Sandby's Hall lay to the rear of the Tavern and was entered via the doorway on the right. The Tavern itself was entered by the central doorway, and the doorway to the left offered access to the offices above the Tavern (*UGLE*).

CPl.VI.XVII The *Freemasons' Tavern* as rebuilt (1786-9) to designs by William Tyler: it is shown on this remarkable serving-dish, embellished with Masonic Symbols. First half of the nineteenth century, manufactured for *Freemasons' Tavern* (UGLE).

globes are set on a table with compasses, a trowel, and other paraphernalia (**Pl.VI.39**). In this respect it is interesting to note the block of stone suspended from the apex of a tripod: this represents Earth, the heaviest and most inert of the four alchemical Elements, and Earth is the Foundation of the material selected by God from which Mankind can be fashioned in His Image. But a block is something more when it becomes a cube, for a cube, as one of the basic forms of Geometry, is derived from the square, is equated with Earth, and is a hieroglyph, in Hermetic terms, of the Divine Will. The cube, for example, appears in the ceiling of the choir of the church in the Escorial, and on it God the Father and the Son rest their feet. And there is even more to the tripod, for it demonstrates the Lewis, a metal device placed in a recess in a Perfect Ashlar: the stonemason's Lewis is a grapnel, for which a shaped socket is cut into the top of the block of stone. The Lewis consists of two wedge-shaped steel keys between which is a steel spacer with parallel sides, and a shackle-pin is passed through the upper parts of all three pieces and provides the hold for the loop of metal to which the rope or lifting-chain is fixed. Once the stone is lowered into position, the pin can be removed, the central spacing-piece is withdrawn, and the two wedges can then also be extracted. So the Lewis is a Symbol of Strength, and the name has been given to the son of a Mason[75] (see **CPl.VI.VIII**, p.109).

Two other objects in Cipriani's illustration[76] deserve comment: on the left is an Orrery, showing the circulation of the planets, and on the right, on the stand, the very odd-looking object which looks a bit like some sort of boiling-device, is probably supposed to be an air-pump. There is a letter in the archives of the Library at Freemasons' Hall in London[77] from Thomas Sandby to Cipriani with suggestions as to what should be depicted in the illustration from which it appears that this strange-looking apparatus does indeed represent an air-pump. Apparently Sandby was not sure what such a pump actually looked like, so what we see now is the result of Cipriani's interpretation of Sandby's vague instructions.

So why an air-pump? There seems to have been considerable interest in air-pumps in the latter part of the eighteenth century. Such interest began with experiments carried out by Robert Boyle with his *Machina Boyleana* or 'Pneumatic Engine' of 1659[78], and continued, almost as a kind of mania thereafter, often involving considerable cruelty to living creatures. Joseph Wright of Derby, in his *A Philosopher Lecturing at the Orrery* (1766)[79] and *Experiment on a Bird in an Air Pump* (1768)[80], showed to great dramatic effect the fascination provided by a consideration of the

---

75 See Jones (1986) 414-194.
76 Stubbs & Haunch (1983) 10.
77 10/B/6. I owe this to my generous friend T. O. Haunch.
78 Derived from Otto von Guericke's experiments in pneumatics.
79 Derby Museum and Art Gallery.
80 London: Tate Gallery.

Pl.VI.39 Freemasons' Hall, Queen Street, Lincoln's Inn Fields, of 1775-6, designed by Thomas Sandby. Allegorical print drawn by Giovanni Battista Cipriani and Thomas Sandby and engraved by Francesco Bartolozzi and James Fitler (*or* Fittler), showing the interior of the Hall with Masonic figures in attendance. At the top is Truth (sometimes identified as Prudence), with her mirror reflecting its rays on diverse ornaments of the Hall, as well as on the globes, Masonic instruments, and furniture. Truth is attended by the Three Theological Virtues, Charity (*left*), Hope (*with Anchor*), and Faith (*with Book and Chalice from which shines the Cross*), while the Genius of Freemasonry, commissioned by Truth and her attendants, is descending into the Hall bearing a lighted torch in his right hand and carrying on his left arm the ribbon with a pendant medal with which the Grand Master will be invested in token of the divine approbation of a building sacred to Charity and Benevolence. This illustration was used as the Frontispiece to the 1784 *Book of Constitutions* (*LMA*).

Pl.VI.40 Design (1813) by Soane for the Ark of the Masonic Covenant as part of the furnishings for Freemasons' Hall. Note the triangular form and the use of the three Orders of Architecture (with corresponding entablatures), and typical Soanesque capping using the segmental arch associated with Isis (*SJSM*).

Universe and of natural phenomena, such as a vacuum. Demonstrations with air-pumps were not confined to learned societies, but were also common in private and public gatherings, so the appearance of the Orrery and the Air-Pump in Cipriani's illustration is a reminder that eighteenth-century Lodges often had lectures, demonstrations, and talks on scientific subjects at a time when 'Natural Philosophy' was an important part of the Enlightenment and a general hunger for knowledge[81]. Sandby's Hall, complete with allegorical figures, featured as the Frontispiece of the 1784 *Book of Constitutions*: Sandby and Cipriani were responsible for the design, and Francesco Bartolozzi and James Fittler for the engraving.

John Soane (he was not knighted until 1832) had been approached in 1812 to survey and value the property adjacent to the *Freemasons' Tavern* in Great Queen Street, and as soon as he became a Freemason in 1813 he was commissioned to design a new Ark of the Masonic Covenant for the new United Grand Lodge of England (also 1813) following the Union of Grand Lodge (founded 1717) and the Antient Grand Lodge (founded 1751). The Ark has certain similarities to the triangular pedestals of Soane's designs for the Pitt Cenotaph at the National Debt Redemption Office (1818)[82]. The Ark is shown in

---

81 I owe this important point to T. O. Haunch.

82 *See Ars Quatuor Coronatorum* **cv** (1992) 203-15 and Frere (*Ed.*) (1967). Soane's Ark owed something to his earlier design for the Simeon Monument, Reading, Berkshire (1804). *See* Bold & Chaney (*Eds.*) (1993) 271-82. *See Architectural History* **xii** (1969) 28-29 and Fig. 21d.

CPl.VI.XVIII Perspective of Soane's Council Chamber, Freemasons' Hall, London, from a painting (1828) by J. M. Gandy: daylight view. Note that the room is viewed as though through a proscenium, with theatrical curtain framing it (*SJSM SM P89*).

the painting (1828) of Soane as Grand Superintendent by John Jackson, RA (*see* **CPl.Int.I**, p.xxv): it consisted (it was destroyed in a devastating fire of 1883) of a structure on a triangular plan at the points of which were columns of all three basic Orders (Roman Doric, Ionic, and Corinthian) supporting fragmentary entablatures. On top was a capping-block with Soane's favourite device of segmental pediment (in the tympana of which were radiating elements suggesting the All-Seeing Eye), and the whole was surmounted by a strigillated short column or altar-pedestal, over which was a flame (**Pl.VI.40**, p.125).

Soane worked closely with the Duke of Sussex to arrive at suitable designs for the new Masonic Hall, but some dozen years were to pass following the ceremony of Union of the Lodges at which his Ark was consecrated before Soane's proposals began to be realised. After the Square, the Plumb, the Level, and the Mallet were delivered to the Grand Masters, they gave Three Knocks with the Mallet, saying:

> 'May the Great Architect of the Universe enable us to uphold the Grand Edifice of Union of which this Ark of the Covenant is the Symbol, which shall contain within it the Instrument of Brotherly Love, and bear upon it the Holy Bible, Square, and Compass, as the Light of our Faith and the Rule of our Works may He dispose our Hearts to make it perpetual.'

At this, the two Grand Masters placed the Act of Union within the Ark. Then the Cornucopia, Wine, and Oil were presented to the Grand Masters, who, 'according to antient rite, poured forth Corn, Wine, and Oil' on the Ark. It was at this ceremony too, in 1813, in Sandby's Hall, decorated by Soane for the occasion, that the Duke ceremonially installed Soane as Grand Superintendent of Works[83].

Soane recommended the purchase of further property in Great Queen Street in 1814-15, and he proposed a series of designs for new accommodation from 1826[84]. What emerged was a rectangular room with two chimneypieces on each of the long sides, arched centrepieces containing an organ in one and a ceremonial throne in the other, while the shorter sides were articulated with Ionic columns set between tall pedimented recesses. In the centre of each of the short sides were a throne and an entrance. The ceiling, however, as often with Soane, articulated the complex room even further, with its two broad segmented coffered arches and unsupported canopy like the inside of Soane's 'sarcophagus lid' motif in the centre of which was the circular opening allowing light to penetrate from above. Soane was deeply interested in the possibilities of using coloured glass to create effects of lighting in his interiors, so the glazed panels of the truncated cone of the lantern were decorated with Signs of the Zodiac in yellow glass. The four large windows over the fireplaces were glazed with strongly coloured glass consisting of yellow diaper-patterns in orange grounds. Glass in the four segmental-headed clerestorey openings above the central elements of each wall contained painted representations of the Five Roman Orders of Architecture (Tuscan, Doric,

---

[83] *AQC* **xcv** (1983) 194-202.
[84] *See* Watkin (1995).

CPl.VI.XIX Perspective of Soane's Council Chamber, Freemasons' Hall, London, from a painting (1832) by J. M. Gandy: evening view. Note the curtain again (*SJSM SM P268*).

Ionic, Corinthian, and Composite)[85]. These Five Orders appear to have made their way into the English system of Freemasonry through the influence of William Preston (1742-1818), and are familiar elements in Craft Certificates, Summonses, and Invitation-Cards of English Lodges in the eighteenth century[86].

Grand Superintendent of Works Soane worked on the designs for a new Hall for several years, but it was not until 1826 that his proposals more or less gelled, and building-works continued from 1828 until 1831. Soane's extraordinary room (**CPl.VI.XVIII**) (called 'The Temple' or Council Chamber) had a short life, for it was demolished in 1864. Yet, as David Watkin has observed, the 'hall was not only the climax of Soane's preoccupation with the poetry of domed top-lit spaces; as a building hemmed in an all sides by others, it was characteristic of the circumstances which produced many of his finest works'[87]. Watkin also pertinently noted that 'though long perceived as an important commission in Soane's career, his Masonic Hall... has never been fully discussed by historians of architecture'[88]. This demonstrates the curious attitudes of so-called 'academics' who shy away from any whiff of Freemasonry, and treat it as though it has a bad smell.

Soane's Council Chamber, 'with its top- and side-lighting, its coloured glass, and its organ', was a 'hermetic interior of emotional intensity in which Soane gave romantic expression to his preoccupation with coloured light, music and poetic effects'[89]. These 'effects' were enhanced by the perspective of the Chamber by Joseph Michael Gandy, especially his *Interior of the Edifice Devoted Exclusively to Freemasonry.. an Evening View* (1832), in which the splendid room is 'theatrically framed by curtains parted to unveil an ethereal sanctuary, glowing in a mysterious, other-worldly light'[90] (**CPl.VI.XIX**). The room 'also challenged all expectations of constructional propriety: in the extreme corners' four large glazed windows above the fireplaces apparently supported the thrust of the low segmental vaults, and in the centre of the ceiling, over the Ark, Soane placed a vault apparently springing from four *unsupported* pendent ornaments from each of which was suspended a chandelier. In the centre of this disconcerting vault was a circular truncated glazed cone decorated with astrological signs below a glazed lantern[91].

The curious 'floating vault' in the centre of the room has its origin in the lids found on Antique cinerary chests for the reception of calcined human remains: such forms were used by Soane for pier-caps at the gateway to Pitzhanger Manor, Ealing, Middlesex (1800-3), where the front parlour had a 'floating ceiling' like the underside of such a form. Perhaps the most celebrated use of the 'urn-lid' was at Soane's own tomb (1815) in the new-burial ground of St Giles-in-the-Fields, adjacent to Old St Pancras churchyard,

---

85 *AQC* (1969) 35-50. For the Orders *see* Select Glossary of the present work.
86 *Ibid*. 169-253. *See* also Haunch (2008).
87 Watkin (1995) 402.
88 *Ibid*.

89 Watkin (1996) 423.
90 *Ibid*.
91 Lukacher (2006) 165-7. The windows were illuminated by light from two small courts.

Pl.VI.41 Sir John Soane's mausoleum in the new burial-ground of St-Giles-in-the-Fields adjacent to Old St Pancras churchyard in London. Note the Isiac segmental pediments, serpent twined round the drum at the top, and the incised wavy line (JSC).

in London[92]. This so-called 'monopteral temple' consists of a block of stone under a canopy carried on four Ionic columns: a simple pediment surmounts each face. This little canopy is sheltered by a bigger canopy carried on square columns, and the canopy is one block of stone cut to form a massive capstone with segmental pediments on all four sides. Each segmental pediment has a wavy line incised on its flat surface, a very curious device. On top of this capstone is a drum around which a serpent with its tail in its mouth is carved (in this respect it should be remembered that the memorial of Herder in Weimar also featured a coiled serpent or *ouroboros*). On top of the drum is a pine-cone finial (**Plate VI.41**).

Soane's extraordinary house at Lincoln's Inn Fields, with its collections of casts, pictures, books, and *objets d'art*, is itself a reminder to visitors of an enormous range of cultures in European civilisation, while the mysterious tomb-like qualities of parts of the house, the routes, and the complex spatial inter-relationships, with folding walls, point to a mind steeped in theories of mnemonics and a passion for exemplars. Soane's tomb has a number of

---

92 For an introduction to Soane and his obsessions with motifs connected with death *see* Summerson (1978).

Masonic allusions mixed with his stern, quirky variety of stripped Classicism, but the essence of the design had a very long life, for it was the inspiration for the cast-iron telephone-boxes designed by Sir Giles Gilbert Scott in 1924 and 1935[93].

Now we know that Soane, who rose rapidly[94] to the upper echelons of Freemasonry after his initiation, owned certain books connected with the Craft[95]. In one volume[96] is a collection of Masonic songs, poems, and toasts, including:

'The solemn temples [*sic*] cloud capt-towers,
Th' aspiring domes are works of ours'

and

'When stately palaces arise,
When columns grace the hall,
When tow'rs and spires salute the skies,
We owe to masons all.'[97]

Soane appended Shakespeare's original lines to Gandy's perspective of the Rotunda of the Bank of England in ruins, and he designed a miniature version of the canopy and lantern at his 'New Hall' or 'Temple' at his Museum in Lincoln's Inn Fields.

There can be no doubt that Soane took Freemasonry (and his own connection with the Craft) very seriously indeed. The contents of his extensive Library demonstrate that he was steeped in various aspects of the French Enlightenment, and he had apparently given much thought to 'Baron d'Hancarville's' work[98], especially with regard to the common origins of various types of religious experience, a concern of much Enlightenment thought. Indeed, what might be termed Soane's vision of some kind of world order owed much to contemporary Freemasons, and we know that Soane searched for and experimented with appropriate simplified ornament suitable for modern buildings[99]. Soane also owned a copy of the mighty *Encyclopédie* of Denis Diderot and Jean Le Rond d'Alembert[100], and we have previously noted that he also possessed a copy of *La Franche-Maçonnerie* by Alexandre-Marie Lenoir, the scholar who established the Musée des Monuments Français in the former Convent of the Petits Augustins in Paris from 1791 (opened to the public in 1796), a sort of cultural retirement-home for Mediaeval, Gothic France, disowned by the Revolutionaries. It should be remembered that the Church was nationalised in France in 1789, the religious houses were closed and their contents confiscated, and even the funerary monuments of the Royal Family in Saint-Denis Abbey were dismembered (and the bodies flung on rubbish-heaps). Christianity itself was abolished in 1793. Lenoir managed to save, re-assemble, and dis-

---

93 Stamp (1989).
94 Taylor (1982).
95 Among them Gentleman Belonging to the Jerusalem Lodge (identified as R. S.) (1762 – in the 1812 edn.) and Lenoir (1814).
96 Gentleman Belonging to the Jerusalem Lodge (1812 edn.) 43-6.
97 *Ibid*. Derived from Prospero's speech in *The Tempest* **iv** sc. 1 l.148 ff.
98 *See*, for example, Hugues (1785).
99 For Soane's reading, *see* Watkin (1996).
100 *See* Diderot & d'Alembert (1751-80). *See also* Diderot & d'Alembert (1782-1832).

play a vast range of treasures uprooted from their original habitats, and was partially successful in saving much from the Taleban-like zeal of revolutionary vandals, although his personal safety was often endangered in the process. Unfortunately we do not know for certain if Soane visited the Museum of sculpture and architecture, but it undoubtedly 'afforded a number of visual and intellectual parallels with his own house and museum in Lincoln's Inn Fields'[101].

Soane also owned a copy of Ledoux's *L'Architecture considerée*[102], and indeed copied out passages of the text in which Ledoux proposed a new town based on social ideals derived from Freemasonic-Enlightenment sources[103]. Other works in Soane's Library included *Monde Primitif*[104] by Antoine Court de Gébelin and *Lettres sur l'architecture des anciens et celles moderns* by Charles-François Viel de Saint-Meaux[105]: both French writers seem to have derived ideas from similar sources as did d'Hancarville, especially regarding Allegory and Symbolism, in which ideas were promoted about an Architecture that would be enriched with allusions to cosmology, myth, and religion. Court de Gébelin, especially, saw the dramas of initiation-rites as providing an obvious link of continuity through from Ancient Egypt through Ancient Greek myths to modern Freemasonry. Some of these ideas were explored in other books with which James Christie (better known as an Auctioneer) was concerned: these were his works on Etruscan Vases[106] and Idolatry[107], and his comments on Count Uvarov's book on the Mysteries of Eleusis[108]. Christie, like Lenoir and Soane, was deeply interested in the possibilities of lighting in interiors, particularly associated with the Mysteries of Eleusis[109].

When Soane acquired the sarcophagus of Seti I, discovered by Giovanni Battista Belzoni in 1817, he decided to invite selected guests to a special showing by lamplight of this beautiful object[110]. Belzoni[111] himself was a Freemason, close to Augustus Frederick, Duke of Sussex[112], who was a friend of Soane, and was probably responsible for getting Soane involved in the building-work at Great Queen Street. The Duke had been educated at the University of Göttingen, where he was taught by the prominent Freemason, Professor Friedrich Ludwig Wilhelm Meyer: he became a Freemason in the Lodge of Glorious Truth, Berlin, in 1798[113].

To Soane[114], influenced as he was by Continental (and especially by French) ideas, allegorical and metaphorical aspects were invested with great significance. Architectural history was equated with the development of society, and Architecture was seen as a means of establishing a just and ordered system. Continental Freemasonry proposed that exemplars and basic theories of Architecture and society were inextricably linked. Order and Geometry were therefore associated with the *structure* of society, and especially with a lost ideal: the Temple was the greatest achievement of Architecture and ancient society, and so the preliminaries of a purification of modern society and a reconstruction of the lost or submerged values of that ancient society were achievable by reconstructing the Temple in hundreds of locations and thousands of minds. This is a remarkable idea, and very important in an understanding of an aspect of the Enlightenment not often aired in Britain: yet it was not new, for it was there in Renaissance times and earlier.

The great Soane had an ambition to create some sort of unity of the arts, something his fellow-Freemason, Nicolas Le Camus de Mézières[115], had also sought: his belief that architectural character could be created by the mysterious effects of light was something Soane shared. Indeed, Soane quoted Le Camus liberally in his Royal Academy lectures[116]. In his superlative designs for the Hall for the Freemasons Soane created a work that rose far above most contemporary interiors, and exploited the possibility of light. It is clear that he, like Mozart, was deeply affected by the Craft, for it embodied a type of ethical code for living in *this* world, something that was essentially secular in its search for ideas. Freemasonry brought the ideals of the Enlightenment into its rituals and rules of conduct, instilling notions of civility, loyalty, benevolence, and much else in an attempt to create a new way of life for its adherents. Yet there was 'an all-pervasive religiosity' about Masonic sociability. 'In it we may find that "heavenly city" offered by the new secular philosophies of the eighteenth century to their worldly and cosmopolitan followers'[117]. Freemasons sought a return to simple, primitive, elemental truths, and a reconstruction of a noble, unfalse, altruistic progress from those truths along the civilised paths of architectural history in which the Language of the Orders, the ideal of the lost Temple of Solomon, and Reason would play their parts. Freemasons desired to rebuild a moral edifice, no less, as an exemplar of what was noble and splendid and true in the first ages of the world, and within it they tried to conserve the ecumenical catholicity of the Freemasonic Tradition as a way forward to progress and benevolent development of the whole of Mankind. Freemasons saw themselves as endeavouring to reconstruct the dissipated parts of the Temple, to seek again the original proportions in all their purity, and to

---

101 Watkin (1995) 402. *See* also Fyfe & Law (*Eds.*) (1988) 39-64. For the contents of Lenoir's Museum *see* Lenoir (1795-1806).
102 Ledoux (1804).
103 *See* Vidler (1976, 1987, 1990). However, *see* also Rykwert (1983), for an early study (the first edn. was 1980) in which links between Architecture and Freemasonry during the Enlightenment were explored.
104 Court de Gébelin (1776 – Soane possessed the 1777 edn.).
105 Viel de Saint-Meaux (1787).
106 Christie (1806).
107 Christie (1814).
108 Uvarov (1817).
109 Watkin (1995) 404. *See* also *Georgian Group Journal* (1991) 26-35.
110 *See* Mayes (2003) 295. *See* also Weisse (1880). John Adam Weisse's book on *The Obelisk and Freemasonry* remains interesting reading.
111 *See AQC* **xcviii** (1985) 1-12.
112 *See* Gillen (1976).
113 *AQC* **lxxv** (1962) 37-45.

114 *See* Dean (2006), Stroud (1984), Summerson (1952, 1978), and Watkin (1995, 1996).
115 Camus de Mézières (1780).
116 Watkin (1996).
117 Jacob (1991) 22.

Pl.VI.42 (right)
F. P. Cockerell's new Freemasons' Hall in Great Queen Street, as completed in 1869. To the left is the new *Freemasons' Tavern*. From *The Illustrated London News* (12 June 1869) (GLCL).

Pl.VI.43 (below) Banqueting Hall by Cockerell. From *The Illustrated London News* (12 June 1869) (GLCL).

re-establish a hierarchy of ornament harmonious with the structure[118]. There are thus similarities to the ambitions of King Philip II in building the Escorial, and to many earlier ideas and theories. The staggering point with which to come to terms is that so many syncretic threads from Antiquity, and especially from the Graeco-Roman world, survived to play such a significant role in the last half millennium.

Soane's work for the Freemasons embraced many of these themes. He also provided various other rooms, and a large kitchen situated beneath the 'New Hall', which, unfortunately, only lasted as designed by Soane until 1838 when Philip Hardwick added an apse[119]. In 1863 Soane's wonderful, exquisite creation was destroyed, and a new building was erected to designs by another Freemason, Frederick Pepys Cockerell, who, as David Watkin has observed, 'should have known better'[120] than to demolish a masterpiece by a far greater architect, a 'more complete physical expression of Masonic metaphor than anything achieved by Soane's contemporaries'[121]. Now we know that Cockerell's father, Charles Robert Cockerell, was very interested in theories concerning the Craft[122], as his lecture-notes for the Royal Academy prove, and was a fastidious and sensitive Architect, so it is regrettable that his son's interventions at Great Queen Street were not of a higher quality and did not respect Soane's brilliant work.

Although Sandby's 'Grand Temple' survived Cockerell's drastic rebuilding, little else did. A separate Tavern would be built, and a new, rather overblown Classical design (**Pl.VI.42**) was provided (part of which survived in 2011) with sculpture by William Grinsell Nicholl[123].

---

118 Curl (1991d) 118.
119 *Civil Engineer & Architect's Journal* **i** (1837-8) 204.
120 Watkin (1995) 414.
121 Ibid.
122 I am indebted to Frank Albo, who has investigated C. R. Cockerell's papers.
123 Who had carved the tympanum sculptures (1850-1) and recumbent lions (1855-6) at St George's Hall, Liverpool, and the Neo-Classical reliefs (1838) on the front of the Oxford and Cambridge Club, Pall Mall, London (1836-8) by Sir Robert Smirke.

Cockerell also designed the new Banqueting Hall[124] of *Freemasons' Tavern*, a somewhat coarsely detailed space (**Pl.VI.43**), now the Grand Hall of the *Connaught Rooms* (named after the then [1909] Grand Master, Prince Arthur, 1st Duke of Connaught and Strathearn). The foundation-stone of Cockerell's grandly symmetrical building was laid in 1864 by Thomas Dundas, 2nd Earl of Zetland, Grand Master, and the new Hall was inaugurated in 1869. It was intended to provide a 'proper and dignified home for English Freemasonry which should be entirely unconnected with Tavern or Tavern influence'. Cockerell's building was extended Westwards in 1899-1900, the new wing matching the façade of the rebuilt Tavern to the East[125] (**Pl.VI.44**).

Before the international catastrophe of 1914-18, there had been talk of further expanding Freemasons' Hall as a memorial to King Edward VII, who had been Grand Master from 1874 until his accession to the Throne. A small levy on all Brethren of the Craft had been collected since 1908, but after the War it was decided to finance the project on a voluntary basis with an appeal for funds for a completely new building to be called the Masonic Peace Memorial. Thus part of the complex of buildings that had formed Freemasons' Hall in London, and in which so many important meetings were held that had shaped the nation in the course of the nineteenth century, was superseded by the magnificent Masonic Peace Memorial. A two-stage architectural competition was held in 1926, judged by Sir Edwin Landseer Lutyens, Walter Frederick Cave, and Alexander Burnett Brown, and this was won by Henry Victor Ashley and Francis Winton Newman who had been in partnership since 1907, and who were both Freemasons. The Memorial consists of a Hall and a Temple, with administrative, executive, meeting, and display rooms, including a large and impressive Library and Museum (to which this study is indebted). Ingeniously arranged on an awkward

Pl.VI.44 Cockerell's symmetrical Freemasons' Hall (1864-9) with *Freemasons' Tavern* to the left. The matching building to the right of the Hall was erected 1899-1900. Only part of Cockerell's façade survives in 2011, that to the left of the arched centrepiece, leaving part of the crowning open-bottomed pediment ludicrously unresolved. Photograph of 1900 (*NMR. Bedford Lemere. 15810/1*).

Pl.VI.45 Perspective of the Masonic Peace Memorial, headquarters of the United Grand Lodge of England in Great Queen Street, London. The building was designed by H. V. Ashley and F. Winton Newman in 1926. Note the *in antis* arrangement of the columns, and the mighty pile-up of masonry. The tower is an interesting composition, with its aedicules (these should be compared with the upper stages of the tower of the St Vincent Street Church in Glasgow, by 'Greek' Thomson), *in antis* columns, and arched forms (*UGLE*).

---

124 *Illustrated London News* (12 June 1869).
125 Stubbs & Haunch (1983) 16.

Pl.VI.46 Original drawing of a detail of the façade to Great Queen Street of the 'Masonic Peace Memorial' (Freemasons' Hall), designed by Ashley & Newman. The use of *in antis* columns is significant, suggesting the Solomonic Temple (*UGLE*).

site, the massive pile-up of Neo-Classical motifs at the corner of Great Queen Street and Wild Street remains a familiar London landmark (**Pl.VI.45**, p.131). It has been described as flaunting 'extremes of theatrical display' in a 'flamboyantly' Classical exterior, with a 'grandiosely Egyptian central hall'[126]. To some, it is 'bewilderingly self-possessed, in gleaming Portland stone, with a corner frontage like the Port of London Authority[127] and all the detail in an embellished Classical Revival'[128]. Such criticisms might be judged unfair, for the internal detailing is sumptuous, and the materials rich and beautifully incorporated. Unfortunately, the demolitions necessary for the rebuilding involved the destruction of two-thirds of Cockerell's work, leaving only a three-bay portion and the lower part of the central crowning triangular pediment ludicrously left hanging, as it were.

Among the fine sculptures within Freemasons' Hall are those of the Dukes of Sussex (1846) and York (1827) by Edward Hodges Baily; King George IV and the Duke of Sussex (1830) by Sir Francis Leggatt Chantrey; and King William IV (1832) and the Duke of Kent (1833) by John Francis. Portraits include a fine one of H. R. H. Arthur, Duke of Connaught and Strathearn (Grand Master 1901-39) by Sir Arthur Stockdale Cope, an impressive George IV by Sir Thomas Lawrence, and H.R.H. George, Duke of Kent (Grand Master 1939-42) by Simon Vincent Edmund Paul Elwes. In the First Vestibule is the War Memorial Shrine and Window, an exquisite work of Walter Gilbert, another Freemason, who was also responsible for much work in Liverpool Anglican Cathedral[129].

Sandby's Hall had an apse at one end in which Baily's statue of the Duke of Sussex was placed. In 1883 the Hall was damaged in a fire (which destroyed Soane's Ark), but it was restored and survived until 1933, when it was demolished at the time of the erection of the present great building by Ashley & Newman (**Pl.VI.46**).

Other Masonic Buildings

Purpose-built Halls for Freemasons became usual during the nineteenth century as Lodges found meeting in public-houses increasingly inconvenient, not least because pubs were no longer regarded in the same light as formerly: there had, in fact, been an extraordinary religious revival[130] following the end of the French Wars in 1815, and Freemasonry could hardly go against the immense flow, although by the time Matthew Arnold wrote his *Dover Beach* (1867), the 'Sea of Faith' had started to ebb, and Arnold, like others, could

> '... only hear
> Its melancholy, long, withdrawing roar,
> Retreating, to the breath
> Of the night-wind, down the vast edges drear
> And naked shingles of the world.'[131]

So Freemasons determined to erect purpose-made Halls. William Wilkins designed one of the first, in York Street, Bath, erected 1817-19[132] (**Pl.VI.47**). As the author of

---

126 Cherry & Pevsner (1998) 70. It suggest, perhaps, a lighthouse, and the four shrine-like elements of the tower are not unlike the four openings of the tower of 'Greek' Thomson's St Vincent Street Church, Glasgow, mentioned and illustrated in Chapter XI.

127 Actually the former offices of the Port of London Authority, Trinity Square, City of London, built 1912-22 to designs by Sir Thomas Edwin Cooper.

128 Cherry & Pevsner (1998) 267.

129 Kennerley (1991).

130 *See* Curl (2007a) Ch. 2.

131 *Dover Beach* (1867) l. 24-8. *See* Curl (2000c – 2004 edn.) 258-65.

132 It was only used by the Freemasons for a very short time (1818-23), and then became a venue for various functions, including the exhibition of works of art. By the early 1830s it was a Nonconformist Chapel, and from 1842 was Bethesda Chapel. In 1866 it became a Meeting-House for the Society of Friends. *See* Ison (2000) 83-4. Figures of Faith, Hope, and Charity were originally intended to stand at the apex and ends of the pediment, and the architrave of the blind doorway bore the inscription FREEMASONS' HALL A. L. 5817. It is unclear if the statues were ever erected, for they are not shown on the engraving (1818) of the building by Henry Sargant Storer. In March 1978 the Society of Friends decided to sell the building but it was obliged to take it off the market. Various attempts to find new uses were made, until at last, in 2008, detailed proposals for the conservation of the building were prepared by McLaughlin Ross llp. I am indebted to David McLaughlin, Conservation Architect, for information.

Pl.VI.47 'Free Mason's Hall' in York Street, Bath, designed by William Wilkins, erected 1817-19. Drawn and engraved by Henry Sargant Storer and published 1818 by Sherwood & Co. Note the *in antis* arrangement of the columns (*Collection JSC*).

The Antiquities of Magna Graecia (1807)[133] and the Architect of Downing College, Cambridge (1807-20 – the Grecian style of which had been backed by Thomas Hope[134]), Wilkins was suitably versed in Grecian Architecture[135], and the severe Greek Revival style was considered at the time to be of strict Masonic appearance. Now why should this be? Clearly the Greek Revival style was untainted by associations with Absolutism, or, indeed, with any European style connected with Absolutism, Revolution, or the Church, so it lent itself to the Craft, with its benevolent, liberal ethos: but there was another obvious connection, and that was the distyle *in antis* arrangement of the columns between the *antae* of the portico which suggested Solomon's Temple (the twin columns Jachin and Boaz) in its Renaissance variants, while the battered Graeco-Egyptian architraves, triangular knockers, and Egyptianising chimney-pots in the shape of Egyptian pylon-towers also suggested the Antique origins of Freemasonry. This distyle *in antis* motif is a particularly Masonic element: it was found in Sandby's Hall and recurs in many places in Freemasons' Hall, Great Queen Street – the most important Masonic building in Britain – and is common to a great number of Masonic Halls throughout the United Kingdom. That is not to suggest that a distyle *in antis* arrangement is *always* indicative of a Masonic connection, for that would not be true. However, its recurrence in buildings erected specifically for Masonic purposes indicates that the Solomonic Temple as an idea could be alluded to by this subtle means, not overtly, but perhaps slyly, missing those who were uninformed.

Buildings where ceremonies of the Craft take place are necessarily inward-looking, so that frequently Masonic Halls are top-lit (if illuminated by daylight at all): Wilkins's Masonic Hall in Bath still has its fine roof-lights. Any fenestration in outside walls therefore occurs where office, executive, or non-ceremonial uses are required. Soane used top lighting for parts of his Museum at Lincoln's Inn Fields, and, of course, at the Bank of England, where the severe interiors and windowless exterior walls (necessary to protect the Bank from the notorious gin-soaked London Mob) had certain Masonic resonances. Both the Greek and Egyptian styles of Architecture, of course, lent themselves admirably to the windowless façade, but Egyptian styles especially suggested the early history and legends of Freemasonry in which Abraham, 'Hermetic Wisdom', Egyptian Learning, Solomon, Hiram, Euclid, Enoch, Jabel, and many others feature. One of the most overtly Egyptian of all British Masonic Halls, with fine architectural qualities, was erected at Mainridge, Boston, Lincolnshire, in 1860-3. The building, of gault brick with stone dressings, again has the distyle *in antis* arrangement of columns (this time with palm capitals and tall *abaci*): it is based on Ancient Egyptian prototypes, part-pylon, and part-temple façade (though much shortened and paraphrased) from Edfu, Dendur, and Philae, as illustrated in the seminal works of Baron Dominique Vivant Denon[136], of the Commission des Sciences et Arts d'Égypte[137], of Carl Richard Lepsius[138], and of artists such as David Roberts[139]. The interior was coloured chocolate, with Egyptianising ornaments of gilt-bronze (e.g. winged globe with *uraei*, scarab, lotus, eternal serpent, etc.), and the ceiling (or 'Masonic Canopy') was dark blue, with gilt stars. Eschewing all modesty, the splendid, tough, assertive, pylon-tower-like front proclaims in hieroglyphs that its foundation dates from 1860[140]. In the coved cornice is the winged solar globe with *uraei* (**Pl.VI.48**, p.134).

This building is so fine, and the hieroglyphs and details so archaeologically correct, that someone in the know must have been involved in the design: a possible candidate could be Joseph Bonomi Jr. (a distinguished

---

133 Published by Longman, Hurst, Orme, & Rees. It was also published in Cambridge by the University Press.
134 *See* Watkin & Hewat-Jaboor (*Eds.*) (2008).
135 Though not in its startling polychrome guises – that was to be understood later, notably by Jakob Ignaz Hittorff and Karl Ludwig Wilhelm von Zanth.
136 Denon (1802).
137 Commision des Sciences et Arts d'Égypte (1809-28).
138 Lepsius (1844-59, 1853).
139 Roberts (1855-6),
140 'In the Twenty-Third Year of the Reign of Her Majesty the Royal Daughter Victoria, Lady Most Gracious, this Building was Erected'. As Victoria became Queen on 20 June 1837, the inscription must refer to the *commencement* of the building, rather than its *completion* (which would have been in the twenty-sixth year of her reign).

Pl.VI.48 Freemasons' Hall, Mainridge, Boston, Lincolnshire, of 1860-3. Of gault brick with stone dressings, this pylon-like front with a distyle *in antis* arrangement (recalling Jachin and Boaz before the Temple) of palm-leaf capitals has an inscription in hieroglyphs which states when it was built. Note the winged disc with *uraei*. Although it is based on published sources such as Denon's *Voyage...*, with the Nubian temple at Dendur clearly in evidence, the palm-capitals have extra non-Egyptian ornament which may be attempts to introduce architectural enrichment as allusions to the 'chapiters' of Solomon's Temple as described in the Bible (*JSC*).

chronicled by Eugène Warmenbol and others[143]. Paul Bonduelle was responsible for the *Grote Temple, Les Vrais Amis de l'Union et du Progrès Réunis*, at 79 *Lakenstraat*, Brussels (1909-10), which was liberally decorated with Egyptianising detail[144]. The Egyptianising interiors were rich and scholarly. More severe, perhaps, was the *Temple de La Flandre* in Brugge, of 1912, by Ernest Callebout. The fine building which housed *Les Amis du Commerce et la Persévérance Réunis* in the *Meistraat*, Antwerp, was designed by Pierre-François Laout and Jean-Laurent Hasse[145], with Egyptianising stucco-work by Henri Verbuecken[146]. It was destroyed in 1982. Several Belgian Lodges adopted Egyptianising décor and tended to reject aspects of Freemasonry inherited from the British Isles, namely specific references to Christianity, preferring, instead, to make their connections with something far older. Antiquity and Ancient Egypt in particular had more attractions than had the Bible, when Continental Freemasons *transformèrent leurs locaux de la façon la plus heureuse en reconstituant le cadre historique antique des temples véritables*[147].

It seems that Lodges built under the aegis of the Grand Orient of Belgium between 1870 and 1914 were particularly affected by Egyptianising design, reflecting the friction between the Roman Catholic Church and Freemasonry. The Temple of Perfect Union (*La Parfait Union*) in Mons, for example, designed by Hector Puchot, was intended to remind all who saw it that the Mons Lodge would work for the moral and intellectual emancipation of the community. An Egyptianising style would allude to a great culture that pre-dated Christianity (which itself owed much to Ancient Egypt[148]) and would be a badge of Anti-Clericalism. The Mons Lodge, in the *rue Chisaire*, was inaugurated in 1890, and has numerous Egyptianising motifs: indeed the whole front is a variation on the pylon-tower theme[149].

The Freemasonic Temple in the *boulevard d'Avroy*, Liège (Luik), houses the Lodge *La Parfait Intelligence et l'Étoile Réunies*,

Egyptologist who became Curator of Sir John Soane's Museum), responsible for the Egyptianising Temple Mills, Marshall Street, Leeds, Yorkshire (1842), and the lodges and gates at Abney Park Cemetery, Stoke Newington, London (1840)[141], but the documentary evidence is lacking.

An Egyptianising timber doorcase survives at 3 High Street, Warwick, and consists of columns supporting a somewhat heavy semicircular pediment, and the entire ensemble is richly embellished with lotus-and-papyrus-enrichment, although colouring is absent: it appears at one time to have been associated with a Freemasonic Lodge. A connection between Freemasonry and Egyptomania was amply demonstrated in Belgium, where several rather startling exemplars were built, including the Grand Temple of the *Amis Philanthropes* Lodge (1877-9), *rue du Persil*, Brussels, by Adolphe Samyn[142], and there were many

---

141 See Curl (2005) for these matters.
142 For Belgian examples *see* Humbert & Price (*Eds.*) (2003); Celis (1984); Warmenbol (2005); various items by Warmenbol listed in the Bibliography; Warmenbol & Wasseige (1990).
143 See Bibliography.
144 *M & L. Momumenten & Landschappen*. 3 Jahrgang **iii** (May-June 1984) 33-5.
145 Gubel *et al* (1995) 33.
146 Grieten (*Ed.*) (2002) 285-306. I am grateful to Petra Maclot and Eugène Warmenbol for this.
147 Mallinger (1978) 23; Warmenbol (2001) 60.
148 Curl (2005) discusses this theme in detail.
149 Warmenbol (2001) 62.

and has a handsome Egyptianising doorcase of *c.*1910[150]. This may have been by Arthur Snyers, who was to go on to design the scholarly Egyptianising *Palais du Royaume d'Égypte* at the *Exposition Internationale* at Liège (Luik) in 1930. At Namur, in the *rue Félix Wodon*, is the Freemasonic Temple (inaugurated 1908), designed by Jules Malevez: it has a monumental and vigorous Egyptianising portal[151].

Beyond Belgium there are many examples of Egyptianising Freemasonic Architecture, 'but in no other part of the world can one find such a high density of Masonic temples reproducing the "Sanctuaries of Memphis"'[152]. At Valenciennes, for example, a new Egyptianising Temple was erected in 1840, complete with obelisks, supposedly based on illustrations in the *Description de l'Égypte*, designed by an architect named Bernard[153], but only fragments of it remain. Outstanding among Egyptianising interiors was that of the Masonic Temple at Douai (1824), sumptuously decorated by Félix Robaut, and of course there is the celebrated *Temple du Droit Humain*, 5 *rue Jules Breton*, Paris XIIIe, of *c.*1912, a Lodge for Women: over the entrance-door *Ordo ab Chao* (Order out of Chaos), a Freemasonic Motto, is inscribed, and the gallery at first-floor level is partially carried on hefty consoles above which is a plain horizontal element inscribed with the legend:

Pl.VI.49 Temple *Le Droit Humain*, 5 *rue Jules Breton*, in Paris (1912), an Egyptianising façade, designed by Charles Nizet, on which is an inscription extolling the rights of women. Over the door is the inscription 'Order out of Chaos' much favoured in French Masonic circles from 1802. Note the Egyptianising coved cornice and the vaguely Moorish crenellations (*UGLE*).

'DANS L'HVMANITE LA FEMME A LES MEMES DEVOIRS QVE L'HOMME

ELLE DOIT AVOIR LES MEMES DROITS DANS LA FAMILLE ET DANS LA SOCIETE'[154]

eschewing accents. Rising from this horizontal beam-like element are seven somewhat elongated palmiform columns, two of which (at the ends of the colonnade) are engaged: between the columns is a balustrade composed of alternate *Ankhs* and *Djed* columns. The crowning gorge-cornice is embellished with stylised vertical leaves and two winged triangles. Somewhat incongruously, there is a crowning crenellation of vaguely Moorish type[155] (**Pl. VI.49**). This is an unusually overt and very handsome admission of Freemasonic affiliation for either France or the United Kingdom: the Architect was Charles Nizet. Belgium, however, tended to be less inhibited, even aggressive, in its Egyptianising Masonic iconography. In Scandinavia, too, Freemasonic architecture is generally reticent (apart from some symbolic devices placed discreetly on façades): an exception was the Lodge at Norrköping, Sweden (1868-9), which had an Egyptianising doorcase (with winged globe), a sphinx in a panel, and another winged globe on the attic storey[156].

There are several Egyptianising Freemasonic Halls in Australia, including Emulation Lodge, 3 Rochester Road, Canterbury, Victoria of 1928-30, designed by Dunstan Reynolds, and the Sandringham Masonic Centre, 22 Abbott Street, Sandringham, Victoria, of 1931, designed by Gordon John Sutherland (where two columns are set *in antis*). Pronounced Egyptianising detail was added to the Zetland Temple, Kyneton, Victoria, in 1905-11, to designs by Thomas Fisher Levick[157].

---

150 Warmenbol (2001) 63.
151 *Ibid.* 65
152 Humbert & Price (*Eds.*) (2003) 219.
153 *Ibid.* 214.
154 Woman has the same duties as Man in Humankind: she is owed the same rights in the family and in Society.
155 Humbert (1998) 168-9.

---

156 Eklund (*c.*1880).
157 Humbert & Price (*Eds.*) (2003) Chapter 9.

Of course, Freemasonry created numerous very grand buildings in the United States of America, and to include them would require a second or even a third volume. Readers are therefore advised to consult books specifically dealing with the United States[158]: among the most spectacular exemplars may be mentioned the Headquarters for the Scottish Rite Southern Jurisdiction, Washington DC, completed 1916 to designs by John Russell Pope, the greatest academic Classicist of his time in the USA. This magnificent building is in the Greek Ionic style, and is loosely based on the Mausoleum of Halicarnassus (fourth century BC). The serene but rich Classical interiors are among the greatest of Pope's creations. Other great Neo-Classical Freemasonic buildings erected in the twentieth century include the Scottish Rite Cathedral, San Antonio, TX (1925), the Masonic Temples of St Louis, MO, and Cincinnati, OH, and the George Washington Masonic National Memorial, Alexandria, VA (1922-32), by Harvey Wiley Corbett. The last has a fine hexastyle Greek Doric prostyle portico, a vast tower with stages of three superimposed Orders, and a stepped pyramidal roof. The interior is splendidly severe and correct. There were many more huge Masonic buildings erected between 1915 and the beginning of the Second World War, including the vast Masonic Temple, Detroit, MI (vaguely Gothic)[159]. Curiously, several American Masonic buildings have a strongly Islamic influence, including the Kismet Temple, Brooklyn (1910), by R. Thomas Short, the Lu Lu Temple, Philadelphia, PA (1904), by Frederick Webber, the Kalurah Temple Mosque, Binghamtown, New York (1917-18), by Arthur T. Lacey, the Al Malaikah Temple, Los Angeles, CA (1925-6), by John C. Austin, the Yaarab Temple, Atlanta, GA (1925-30), by Marye, Alger, & Vinour[160], and the Mecca Temple, 56th Street, New York (1922-24), by Harry Percy Knowles, completed by Clinton & Russell[161]. The enormous Temple in Philadelphia, PA, by James H. Windrin, is vaguely Romanesque outside, but has Classical interiors of great richness, Renaissance, Gothic, and Ionic Temples, and a truly superb and stunningly rich Egyptian Temple (1889).

To return to the British Isles, the Masonic Hall at the rear of 74 Queen Street, Edinburgh, of 1894, was by George Henderson, of Hay[162] & Henderson, Architects, but it did not rate highly with the critics, who felt the interior was 'treated much after the manner of the shopkeeper's saloon'[163]. No. 75 led to the Masonic Temple (1900-1), designed by Peter Lyle Barclay Henderson, a Freemason who practised independently as an Architect in Edinburgh from 1873. It was 'one of the most remarkable interiors in Edinburgh'[164] until the late 1970s, when the elaborate, strongly-coloured Egyptianising decorations were painted out with pastel colours. In 1984 the Hall and Temple were demolished.

Now this act of philistine vandalism (not an unusual occurrence in Scotland at the time, when far too many fine buildings were either demolished, 'went on fire', or were ruined by hamfisted alterations) destroyed what was described on the back of a fine pencil-and-watercolour perspective (1901) by Robert Forbes Sherar (**CPl.VI.XX**) as 'No. 1 Title New Chapter Room 78 Queen St Edinburgh for the Supreme Grand Royal Arch Chapter of Scotland'. 'The thoroughgoing use of Egyptian motifs extends even to the carpets and furniture'[165]. The architectural press remarked (1901) that the 'Chapter-Room is in the style of an ancient Egyptian Temple... It has been suggested that [the figure decoration] should represent the story of Isis and Osiris... or be simply reproductions form the Book of the Dead... The ceiling is carried on timber trusses, the details of which are Assyrian in style. The upholstery of the seats is deep crimson, and forms a sort of dado all around... The capitals of the large columns and the ceiling over the dais are in brilliant colours after the style of a peacock's tail'[166].

Of course this extraordinary lost interior was not alone, as Marcel Celis, Petra Maclot, Eugène Warmenbol, and others have pointed out[167]. Many Halls of Freemasons on both sides of the Atlantic (though some of the most scholarly examples were in Flanders) were built in an Egyptianising style, drawing on sources such as the massive publication of the Commission des Sciences et Arts d'Égypte, Denon, Lepsius, and the great *Histoire de l'Art Égyptien* (1878-9) by Achille-Constant-Théodore-Émile Prisse d'Avennes[168]. In these buildings lavish polychrome decorations often reached high levels of inventiveness, and frequently the scale of the interiors was impressive too.

Many Halls for Freemasons in the twentieth century became very grand. The 'finest Masonic Temple in London', as the Abercorn Rooms on the first floor of the Great Eastern Hotel, Liverpool Street, London (1911-12), were described in *The Freemason*[169], was completed by Hampton & Sons to designs by Messrs Brown and Barrow[170], and was indeed lavish. It has been described as 'admirably mysterious, glowing with mahogany and rich green marble, with much display of columns around the walls'[171]. Facing thrones are set in elaborate Classical aedicules, and there is a large sunburst on the ceiling. The former Temple in the Great Eastern Hotel was in the Egyptian style, and was in the basement: the new 1911-12 Temple was in the purest Greek, with features representing Wisdom, Strength, and Beauty. Its Grecian motifs included Doric and Ionic aedicules that incorporated the All-Seeing Eye and acted

---

158 *See*, for example, Moore (2006) and Tabbert (2005).
159 *See* Tabbert for these and a comprehensive series of references.
160 P. Thornton Marye, Richard W. Alger, & Olivier J. Vinour.
161 Moore (2006) is full of detail concerning these buildings.
162 William Hay (1818-88).
163 Quoted in Gifford, McWilliam, & Walker (1984) 321.
164 *Ibid*.
165 Conner (*Ed*.) (1983) 96.
166 *Building News* (26 July 1901) 105. *See* also Conner (*Ed*.) (1983) Catalogue item 206; Humbert, Pantazzi, & Ziegler (*Eds*.) (1994) 458-9; Humbert (*Ed*.) (1996) 355.
167 Celis (1984); Maclot & Warmenbol (1984).
168 All listed in the Bibliography below.
169 9 November 1912.
170 Alexander Burnett Brown and Ernest Robert Barrow. Brown was a Freemason, and he was in partnership (1897-1930) with Barrow.
171 Bradley & Pevsner (1997) 312.

CPl.VI.XX The Chapter Room at 78 Queen Street, Edinburgh, for the Supreme Grand Royal Arch Chapter of Scotland, designed by P. L. B. Henderson, built 1900-1, demolished 1984. The Royal Arch Halls are shown in an exhibition drawing (pencil and watercolour) by Robert F. Sherar, 1901. The use of Egyptian motifs extended to the carpets and furniture. (RCAHMS EDD/846/CN).

as canopies for the ceremonial chairs. This opulent and very beautiful Temple was photographed by Harry Bedford Lemere on completion (**Pls.VI.50-52**, p.138).

However, Masonic allusions are not always overt in the Architecture of Freemasonry, especially that of the exteriors of Masonic Halls: it is as though the Lodges wished to carry their 'secrets' into architectural anonymity, though that is clearly not the case with the triumphant and noble pile of the 'Masonic Peace Memorial' (now Freemasons' Hall, Great Queen Street, London). Masonic Halls in certain areas, such as Ulster, are immediately identifiable: like the Gillespie monument in Comber, County Down (*see* below), they are adorned with Masonic Symbols. Masonic bashfulness is not a concern in that part of the world, and many Halls have Masonic Emblems displayed in prominent positions to make the buildings identifiable. Unfortunately, that has proved to be a problem, for the buildings have often been subjected to attack. Many Masonic Halls in Ulster are similar in general form to Nonconformist Churches, where a decent

Pl.VI.50 *(top)* Masonic Temple in the Abercorn Rooms, Great Eastern Hotel, Liverpool Street, London, photographed (1912) by Bedford Lemere (21911) (*LMA*).

Pl.VI.51 *(left)* Detail of Ionic aedicule in the Masonic Temple in the Abercorn Rooms, Great Eastern Hotel, Liverpool Street, London, photographed (1912) by Bedford Lemere (21914). Note the motto *Audi, Vide, Tace* over the pediment (*LMA*).

Pl.VI.52 *(bottom right)* Detail of Greek Doric aedicule in the Masonic Temple in the Abercorn Rooms, Great Eastern Hotel, Liverpool Street, London, photographed (1912) by Bedford Lemere (21913) (*LMA*).

CPl.VI.XXI Interior of Royal Arch Chapter Room, Freemasons' Hall, Molesworth Street, Dublin. The curious capitals are clearly attempts to convey the idea of 'lily-work chapiters' of the Temple of Solomon (*GLFI*).

understated Classical simplicity predominated in the nineteenth century[172]. However, such examples rarely rise to architectural heights of splendour, and, as a building-type, Masonic and other Halls, of, say, the Orange and Hibernian Orders, tend to be relatively unpretentious, and there is little one can say about them.

The interiors of some of the grander Lodges in the British Isles, however, in terms of Architecture, are exceedingly ambitious. The Grand Royal Arch Chapter Room of Freemasons' Hall (Masonic Grand Lodge), Molesworth Street, Dublin, for example, is in a powerful Graeco-Egyptianising style. The building itself was designed by Edward Holmes, and decorated by Thomas Earley & Henry Powell. It dates from 1866 and has been described as a 'theatrical tour-de-force that survives in pristine condition internally'[173]. There is a splendid Grand Lodge Room of the Corinthian Order, two startling Gothic rooms (Knights Templar Chapel and the much larger Prince Mason's Room), but the Royal Arch Chapter Room is extraordinary, with its painted engaged columns with reeded and foliated capitals supporting five ceiling compartments with deep foliated cornices. Between the columns seven-branched gasoliers spring from Egyptianising heads. The exotic focus of the room, a kind of Egyptian canopy on four columns, is guarded by brightly-coloured *couchant* sphinxes, and flanked by a pair of free-standing columns (an obvious reference to Jachin and Boaz)[174] (**CPl.VI.XXI**). Facing Molesworth Street, the exterior of the building is articulated over its three storeys by superimposed Orders, and in the crowning pediment is the All-Seeing Eye, Square, and Compasses set in a roundel in the centre of the tympanum[175] (**CPl.VI.XXII**, p.140).

There can be no argument. There is a vast wealth of Architecture realised to accommodate activities by Freemasons, yet this has been for the most part ignored by architectural historians[176]. As Marcel Gossé has correctly pointed out, many eighteenth-century Architects concerned themselves with the design of imaginary Temples, really Ideal Temples of the Mind, goals to be aspired to, longed for, and given honoured places in an intellectual Utopia. As Gossé observed, a Temple should reflect the World and Order of the Universe: a return to sources

---

172 Curl (1980*b*).
173 Casey (2005) 490.
174 For a full description of this fine building, *see* Casey (2005) 490-1.
175 For details of the architecture of numerous Masonic Halls *see* Culot *et al.* (2006). For Arthur Square, Belfast, *see* Leighton (1927).
176 With the exceptions of Culot *et al.*, Warmenbol, and others listed in the Bibliography.

CPl.VI.XXII Exterior of Freemasons' Hall, Molesworth Street, Dublin, designed by Edward Holmes. Note the three superimposed Orders of Architecture and the resemblance of the façade to Renaissance images of the Temple (*see* **Pls.V.9, V.10, V.16, VI.8**) (*GLFI*).

Pl.VI.53 'Bath' furniture in the possession of Loyal Lodge No 251, Barnstaple, Devon. Note Jachin and Boaz, complete with 'lily-work chapiters' and bowls, and the relationship with sixteenth-century images of the Temple (*UGLE*).

is very necessary (something a Modernist could never contemplate, as the *tabula rasa* is the only source available to him, apart from ill-thought-out cribs from the latest fashionable 'celebrity' designer). In Gossé's own designs the Classical Language of Architecture is ever-present, and his *Temple en Utopie* (1993-2000) draws on the distyle *in antis* arrangement of columns, clearly alluding to the Solomonic Temple, both inside and outside[177]. His *Temple de Style Dorique* of the 1990s, is depicted in finely rendered drawings, and in 1995 he also produced a *Projet de Petit Temple de Style Égyptien*, with variations in the Ionic (1994-5) and Corinthian (1999) styles. He has produced admirable studies of obelisks, Jachin and Boaz, and interpretations of the Orders[178].

Among the most superlative items in any Freemasons' Hall must be listed the 'Bath' furnishings of the Lodge Room of the Loyal Lodge No. 251, Barnstaple, Devon: Jachin and Boaz, brass columns with 'lily-work chapiters' and bowls were justly celebrated for their magnificence and quality. From the bowls hang chains from which are suspended brass balls suggesting pomegranates: these remarkable columns date from the end of the eighteenth century. Even finer are the two globes of 1799: they were the work of the well-known William and John Cary, no less. These globes stand on extraordinary Rococo pedestals[179] (**Pl.VI.53**).

Epilogue

So, throughout Europe and the Americas are literally thousands of Masonic buildings, some outstandingly fine and rich, some moderately interesting, and others of only mediocre quality, yet nevertheless of considerable importance to the Brethren. It is odd that this great legacy of buildings, furnishings, and artefacts has received relatively scant attention from serious historians. However, there are many articles in *Transactions* of Lodges, in *Ars Quatuor Coronatorum*, and other Masonic publications. The Reverend Neville Barker Cryer[180] has given us a useful book on Lodges, and this may be used with profit by all desirous of pursuing the subject.

The next step in the present volume is to turn to a wider consideration of developments on the Continent, bearing in mind that the Enlightenment had many different facets, and therefore produced many very curious and diverse responses to Freemasonry and to ideas filtered through the Craft. It is a complex business, and the ramifications are many and fascinating.

---

177 Culot *et al.* (2006) 180-193.
178 Illustrated in Culot *et al.* (2006) 180-193.
179 For this Lodge *see* Pook (1933). For the furnishings *see* Oliver (1947) and Norman (1946). Oliver's paper was based on Norman's.
180 Cryer (1989*a*, *b*, & *c*, 1990*a* & *b*).

CHAPTER VII

Freemasonry, Neo-Classicism, Egyptian Rites, and Problems with the Enlightenment

Introduction; Freemasonry in Europe; Freemasonry and Neo-Classicism; Freemasonry and Egyptian Elements in Neo-Classical Architecture; Ledoux and Lequeu; Conclusion

'La pensée politique, en France, est rétrospective ou utopique.'[1]
RAYMOND ARON (1905-83):
L'opium des intellectuels (Paris: Calmann-Levy 1955) Ch. 1.

'La Révolution française... a considéré le citoyen d'une façon abstraite, en dehors de toutes les sociétés particulières de même que les religions considèrent l'homme en général, indépendamment du pays et du temps.'[2]
ALEXIS CHARLES HENRI MAURICE CLÉREL, COMTE DE TOCQUEVILLE (1805-59):
L'Ancien Régime in *Oeuvres Complètes*
J.-P. MAYER (Ed.) (Paris: Gallimard, from 1951) **ii** 89.

Introduction

The *Philosophes* of France lived in a country which, at the time, was not autocratic, yet was not free: censorship was applied erratically and inconsistently, and it is important to grasp the fact that France had not gone through the momentous changes of Church and State which had occurred in Britain, and which had made the British Enlightenment possible. The French indulged in flights of fancy, uninhibited by practicalities: they could theorise, untrammelled by any immediate likelihood of having to implement their ideas[3].

The great monument of the French Enlightenment was the *Encyclopédie*, published, between 1751 and 1772, in seventeen volumes of text and eleven volumes of fine explanatory plates: seven additional volumes came out between 1776 and 1780[4]. Diderot stated that the aim of the *Encyclopédie* was to collect all the knowledge then available, to publish it, and to disseminate it to contemporaries and to future generations in order to make them wiser and happier. D'Alembert, in his *Preliminary Discourse* in the *Encylopédie* claimed that the great work was an attempt to provide a systematic analysis of the order and inter-relations of human knowledge.

The *philosophes* were not only assiduous collectors of facts, but were fascinated by abstractions, especially principles: and one principle they held in the highest esteem above all others. That was Reason. Diderot said of the *Encylopédie* that it was the tool of a philosophical and reasoning age[5], but it should be remembered that it was an Englishman, Thomas Paine, who coined the phrase 'The Age of Reason'[6]. However, significantly, Paine subtitled his great book on the subject *Being an Investigation of True and Fabulous Theology*, and that part of the title is usually omitted when Paine's publications are mentioned. To the *philosophes* Reason was what Grace is to the Christians: wading through entries in that mighty work, the *Encylopédie*, it is clear that, to Diderot and his colleagues, Reason

---

1 Political thought, in France, is retrospective or utopian.
2 The French Revolution... considered the citizen as an abstract proposition set apart from all particular societies in the same way as religions considered Man in general, independent of country and time.

3 Himmelfarb (2008) 150.
4 Diderot, d'Alembert, *et al.* (1751-80).
5 *Ibid.* **xii** 510 and Diderot (1956) 291, 312-13.
6 *See* Paine (1794-5).

was elevated to a status equivalent to a religion. They were opposed to an authoritarian and repressive Church allied to an authoritarian and repressive State; to a faith which defied Reason; and to any form of institutionalised religion. Some of the articles in the *Encylopédie* proposed that religion was an invention by priests in order to intimidate and terrorise the ignorant and ill-educated: not a few commentators, however, have perceived such a mechanism as a prudent tool to keep the Mob docile. The problem, of course, was that once that mechanism became disabled, the ignorant and ill-educated masses were transmogrified into a dangerous and destructive force, something that became all too apparent during the Revolution and subsequent upheavals.

Loathing of *l'infâme*, it is clear, was directed towards the Roman Catholic Church, and against Christianity itself, in any form. Many *philosophes*, however, were Deists: they just had a detestation of Christianity. Voltaire himself claimed that any sensible fellow with a sense of honour must hold the Christian 'sect' in horror[7]. Not so the masses, however, for the beastly *canaille* would not be trusted in matters of Reason: it was stupid, prejudiced, ignorant, cruel, and wicked[8]. Friedrich von Schiller would have agreed: *mit der Dummheit kämpfen Götter selbst vergebens*[9], after all. The *philosophes*, with good reason, distrusted the Mob, the *canaille*, the vulgar rabble that is given so much credence in the twenty-first century. The majority, that key to 'democracy', cannot be relied upon to reason at all, for, as Eugene Victor Debs observed, it is 'always wrong'[10]. Henrik Ibsen agreed: *Flertallet har aldrig retten på sin side*[11].

Although the *philosophes* had a good stab at verbally bashing the Church and Christianity, Paine was more persuasive. His *Age of Reason* is a trenchant and unwavering attack on Christianity and all organised religion, although Paine himself believed in a Divinity, in one God[12]. He claimed that all 'national institutions of churches, whether Jewish, Christian, or Turkish'[13] were 'no other than human inventions, set up to terrify and enslave mankind, and monopolise power and profit'[14]. He also wrote that anything which 'everyone is required to believe' should be subject to proof and evidence available to all[15]. Paine, widely read and ferociously intelligent, could find nothing to warrant a belief in Christianity, but established many grounds for suspecting imposture. His eloquent denunciation should be required reading in these perilous times, when Unreason seems to be on the march, and the Mob (with its repulsive beliefs and values) is becoming or has become dominant everywhere. He wrote that when 'we read the obscene stories, the voluptuous debaucheries, the cruel and torturous executions, the unrelenting vindictiveness, with which more than half the Bible is filled, it would be more consistent that we called it the word of a demon than the Word of God'[16].

Paine had been influenced by Benjamin Martin and James Ferguson, so his Deism was formed partly from his understanding of what might be termed 'celestial mechanics', and partly from a study of the conflicting stories and claims found in the Bible: his rejection of Biblical teaching was based on the improbability of such stories and claims, and the fact that many are both contradictory and ludicrous.

Many *philosophes*, with their antipathy towards Christianity (albeit in the form to which they were accustomed, namely the Roman Catholic Church), reacted to the Bull *In eminenti* of 1738 against Freemasonry by joining the Craft[17]. And the tendency among the *philosophes* to embrace utopian ideas and a longing for some system other than Christianity propelled those who were Deists to investigate an organisation which accepted the notion of The Great Architect of the Universe. This was a very different atmosphere, therefore, to that which existed in the British Isles: thus it is unsurprising that there was much in Continental, and especially in French, Freemasonry that was more extreme, more exotic, and more alienated from the religious and political Establishments.

Freemasonry in Europe

In the centuries before 1717 there had been systems for the binding of men together for some common purpose. There seems to have been a considerable movement of Rosicrucians on the Protestant side in the seventeenth century, while the Jesuits appear to have employed some of the techniques of the Rosicrucians in the opposing camp[18]. Something of differing interests lingered in Freemasonry: in 1688 the Royalists in Britain were divided in opinion, and certain Jacobite Freemasons took the Craft abroad with them, establishing Lodges in which the Stuart cause was still supported. Freemasonry in England itself, however, abandoned the Stuarts and became Hanoverian, and it is from this period that the Craft was established on a settled basis, undergoing a considerable metamorphosis in that it became almost entirely 'speculative': in the process the connection between Architecture and craftsmen-operative Masons was weakened. The many societies that existed in the seventeenth century could, in fact, play parts in any cause, and the establishment of Grand Lodge and the 'gelling' of a ritual and constitution mark a point

---

7 Gay (1967) **i** 391-2.
8 Diderot, d'Alembert, et al. (1751-80) **x** 860.
9 With stupidity the Gods themselves struggle in vain (*Die Jungfrau von Orléans* [1801] Act 3 sc. 6).
10 Debs (1928) 66.
11 The majority never has right on its side (*An Enemy of the People* [1882] Act 4).
12 Paine (1945) **i** 464.
13 By 'Turkish' he meant 'Muslim'.
14 Paine (1945) **i** 464.
15 *Ibid*. **i** 468.

16 *Ibid*. **i** 474. For repulsive torments and tortures *see* Fr. Antonio Gallonio's excruciating volume (Gallonio [1930]) illustrated by Giovanni de Guerra and engraved by Antonio Tempesta: it should satisfy depraved appetites at least for a time.
17 For Freemasonry and the Roman Catholic Church *see* Gilbert (2006).
18 *See* Yates (1972) for details too broad in scope to be discussed here. *See also* Webster (1924), although this work should be used with caution.

when Freemasonry in England was reformed, registered, and cleansed of Jacobite intrigue. Essential to this was the removal of differences of religion, rank, and interest: concord, fraternity, and tolerance were to be encouraged. For the British, the chasms between classes were tending to be bridged by the moral and common sense that (at that time) was held to be innate in everyone, no matter to what class a person might belong. To the *philosophes*, however, those constituting the *canaille* were incapable of possessing either moral or common sense.

Freemasonry, with its Great Architect, reverence for Natural Order, and connections with Newtonian figures and with Whiggery and the post-1689 Settlement, encouraged a *form* of religiosity, but it was protean, undogmatic, and liberal. For this very reason it was to incur the displeasure of the Roman Catholic Church, whilst its connections with Protestantism were hardly likely to endear it to that Church. Some Continental Lodges appear to have grown from formations by exiled Jacobites, but the remarkable spread of Freemasonry in Europe is not unconnected with Britain's influence among her allies, notably in The Netherlands and in the Holy Roman Empire of the German Nations. Certainly among many Europeans there was a climate of opinion that admired British institutions, British Order, Liberalism, science, and undogmatic stances in matters of religion. It is no accident that Protestants and Protestantism were to be treated with respect in Continental Masonic circles, notably at Maupertuis, at Franconville-la-Garenne, and even in a chorale in *Die Zauberflöte*, on which topics more will be said below. The very fact of Freemasonry's associations with religious toleration was enough to condemn it in the eyes of the Roman Catholic Church, while its overt admiration for the achievements of Protestantism and for an increasingly protean type of religious belief was bound to lead to trouble.

It is all the more interesting to consider Austrian Freemasonry[19] in this light, for, as noted earlier, the husband of Maria Theresia had become a Freemason and seems to have remained devoted to the Craft thereafter[20]. Prince Eugen of Savoy's circle had its fair share of Freemasons who had been initiated in The Netherlands, and who were in close touch with British Freemasons during the wars with France. A Lodge had been founded in The Hague as early as 1710[21], and many Brethren were Huguenot refugees involved in the book-trade and in publishing. Huguenots were also numerous in London and Berlin, where they played a considerable part in commercial and intellectual life. Most importantly, however, their experiences at the hands of Absolutist Monarchies and Roman Catholics in their native land led many of them to start to question orthodox Christian doctrine. Masonic Lodges offered a tolerant milieu for such persons, and the undogmatic nature of Freemasonry had attractions for those holding many and disparate beliefs: all those beliefs could co-exist and survive. The point about Freemasonry was that it offered a clubbable, discreet means by which meetings could be held and enlightened ideas floated without fear of reprisals. Opponents of Absolutism and sceptics in matters of religious dogma found in Freemasonry a club to which they could belong: what is more, it was an international club, and grew steadily year by year. By its very internationalism, however, it posed a threat (or was perceived to pose a threat) to Absolutism and to the Roman Church.

Prince Eugen of Savoy's circle in The Hague seems to have been a centre for all manner of libertarians, free-thinkers, and even radicals[22]: it was also remarkable for its liberal content, and the Prince's interests (if his own intact collection of books in Vienna is anything to go by) included the late-Renaissance Neo-Pagans, with Giordano Bruno well to the fore. The Prince's Belvedere Palace in Vienna (1714-24), designed by Fischer von Erlach's great rival, Johann Lukas von Hildebrandt, is a Baroque masterpiece, but, in its strangely orientalising roofs, seems to have an affinity with the delectable 'Indo-Chinese' Schloss Pillnitz (1720-3)[23] on the Elbe, upstream from Dresden, designed by Matthäus Daniel Pöppelmann. These buildings, in which eclecticism played such an important part, were examples of the use of deliberately wide-ranging styles associated with the Enlightenment and with advanced modern ideas. Universalism, tolerance, interest in the writings of people the Church regarded as 'heretics', and borrowing from 'exotic' cultures such as those of China and India, were features of the Enlightenment and of the tastes of those eighteenth-century figures who were to find philosophical and spiritual satisfaction in Freemasonry. That the Craft was intimately connected with Architecture is clear, but it is not generally appreciated that in the eighteenth century certain stylistic aspects of Architecture and Design were also closely interwoven with Freemasonry.

Mention was made previously of the significance of Scotland in the history of 'speculative' Freemasonry[24]: the Craft, through Schaw and others, was closely connected with the Royal House of Stuart, so much so that it became known as the 'Royal Art'. The reign of King James VI and I saw the rise of Inigo Jones, whose championship of Italian Renaissance Architecture based on the work of Palladio introduced some remarkable modern buildings to a Britain used to a somewhat clumsy and over-elaborate style derived from Northern European exemplars. Jones's Palladianism did not take root after the fall of the Monarchy, for it was too deeply associated with the Stuart cause. When Lord Burlington and his circle revived an interest in Jones's work in the early eighteenth century, however, and the Palladian style became *de rigueur* for the

---

19 *See*, for example, Düriegl & Winkler (*Eds.*) (1992).
20 Jacob (1981) 111, 127, 242, and *passim*.
21 Although the *official* establishment of Freemasonry in The Netherlands when a Lodge was affiliated constitutionally with Grand Lodge did not occur until 1734.

22 Jacob (1981) 147.
23 One of the largest eighteenth-century European buildings in an orientalising style.
24 *See* Cooper (2006) and Stevenson (1984, 1988a, 1988b, 1997), for example.

country-houses of the Whig oligarchy as well as for many public buildings, not only was that style associated with a Royalist cause, but it was almost a deliberate attempt to show that the Hanoverian Succession followed naturally from the House of Stuart, and so Architecture was brought into play as evidence of continuity and even of legitimacy. This time, however, unlike the First Palladian Revival of the period *c*.1610 to *c*.1637, the associations were with the Whigs, and, inevitably, with Freemasonry[25]. Walpole's Houghton Hall in Norfolk is a case in point. Later, Wörlitz in Anhalt was to acquire a *Schloß* (1769-73) of impeccable Palladian proportions set in a magical Garden of Allusions: that the *Schloß* bore a strong resemblance to Claremont, Surrey (1771-4), by Lancelot 'Capability' Brown and Henry Holland (a Freemason) cannot be disputed. Here was England-by-the-Elbe, not a mere stylistic conceit, but a political, social, intellectual, and moral statement. This is not to underestimate, however, the legacy of English Republicanism, passed to the Continental Lodges through The Netherlands, which eventually found its way to France: after the Restoration of the Stuart Monarchy in 1660 Republicanism went underground, but it did not die, and found fertile soil in The Netherlands, which, in any case, had a Protestant Republican tradition[26].

There occurred, in Northern Europe, and notably in the British Isles, something remarkable in the seventeenth and eighteenth centuries: it involved the separation of theological and political theory which probably began with Thomas Hobbes, was refined by Benedictus (*or* Baruch) Spinoza in The Netherlands and by John Locke (who lived for a time in The Netherlands), and further developed by David Hume and Adam Smith, the last two both giants of what became known as the Scottish Enlightenment. These great men helped to evolve a view of religion as a *projection* of human fears and desires: thus the possibility was created by which Mankind could be freed from the tyranny of transcendent religion, superstitious belief, and clerical repression, with parallel developments of *private* religion and a political life divorced from religion. With such undercurrents and shifts of perception, it is understandable how Freemasonry came to offer so many so much in the course of the eighteenth century.

There would appear to be three distinct strands in Freemasonry: the Royalist Stuart legitimist strand, with a strong content of nostalgia for Roman Catholicism; the moderate, liberal-minded, Whig strand with its loyalty to the Royal House of Hanover and the anti-Absolutist post-1689 Settlement; and the Republican strand that was more radical and that certainly had a powerful effect on the Lodges of France and the Low Countries[27]. Even in the Roman Catholic countries the Lodges were the meeting-places for those of advanced opinions, interested in science and in natural phenomena, and more involved in attempting to improve the lot of Mankind by rational means than by relying on religion in any organised sense. To some, Protestantism was seen as a first phase in the breaking of the power of the Clergy and the Church, so Protestant hero-martyrs (like Admiral Gaspard de Châtillon, Comte Coligny [who was vilely murdered during the infamous massacre of St Bartholomew's Day]) were remembered with respect as the great forerunners of the Enlightenment. European Freemasons, however, tended to become sceptics, holding secular opinions, aware of aspects of the Great Architect's creation in themselves as part of the natural order of things, but eschewing the supernatural and the intervention of Providence, the Saints, or indeed much of the complex apparatus that had been developed over the centuries by the Church.

There were other aspects of endeavour in Europe that had distinct Freemasonic associations. One was the design of gardens, based on English exemplars, which became fashionable in France, Germany, and elsewhere. The Garden of Allusions with poetic elements, associations, and 'natural' aspects, was to give birth to the Movement to found Cemeteries, and this will be discussed later[28]. Another important British export to the Continent was the encyclopaedia: the first encyclopaedia of the eighteenth century was the *Cyclopaedia* of Ephraim Chambers, published by subscription in London 1728. Chambers had been apprenticed (1714-21) to John Senex, and was probably a Freemason[29]: his great work was indebted to some extent to the pioneering dictionaries of Louis Moréri and Pierre Bayle, and reflected the Masonic desire for knowledge, to encourage learning, and to establish facts. We know that the publication of the *Cyclopaedia* was encouraged by a number of Freemasons, and indeed Senex himself was one of the publishers: through it Newtonian

---

25 Jacob (1981) 100 and *passim*. There are, however, several puzzling aspects which might suggest the Second Palladian Revival occasionally hedged its bets. At Chiswick House, Middlesex, for example (*c*.1725-9), designed by Burlington, the influence of Andrea Palladio is obvious, but there are curious features that suggest Burlington's family connections with the exiled Stuarts were maintained. At Chiswick he used oak-leaves instead of laurel on friezes; there are Jacobite Roses and Thistles on the friezes of the chimney-pieces in the Green and Red Rooms; a probable portrait of Maria Clementina Sobieska, wife of the Jacobite Pretender (James Francis Edward Stuart, known by Jacobites as King James III and VIII), can be found on the ceiling of the Summer Parlour; and the Red, Blue, and Green Rooms suggest Craft levels. In particular, the Red Room features Masonic implements, an allegory of the Resurrection of the Fallen Arts (represented by Hermes accompanied by *putti* carrying a cornucopia and Masonic emblems, and by a fallen bust of Inigo Jones), and a Rainbow over Hermes and an Arch below him (*see* Hewlings [2009] 50). We know that Burlington had many Jacobite contacts and friends, that his name occurs in Jacobite cypher-lists, and that he resigned from all his Court posts in 1733, an event perhaps prompted by a conflict of loyalties. If, in fact, he *was* a closet Jacobite (and the door of that closet, to judge from the iconography at Chiswick House, was not by any means firmly shut), his cult of Palladianism, far from reflecting any Whig ideology, could be seen as a deliberate reversion to the architectural style favoured by the Stuart Court at the time of Inigo Jones, so was a statement of continuity and revival. The widespread adoption of the Second Palladian Revival by others, however, would seem to be connected with a desire to give legitimacy to the Settlement and Hanoverian Succession by connecting it with legitimacy through the Stuart maternal line, so was predominantly a Whig phenomenon.

26 *See* Jacob (1981) for these matters.

27 *See* Jacob (1981, 1991).

28 *See* Curl (1984b, 1988, 1994a, 1995, 1997, 2004, 2006c, 2006d).

29 *See Quatuor Coronatorum Antigrapha* **x** (1913) 122. *See* also Taylor (1966) 143.

ideas were disseminated, and, very significantly, it carried an account of British Freemasonry which was copied by many Continental sources.

Chambers's work, therefore, can be regarded as a major Masonic project: furthermore, a 'French translation of large parts of its content was used in the compilation of Diderot's and d'Alembert's *Encyclopédie*'[30], which started out as a revision of Chambers's work, but soon took on a flavour of its own and became very much more comprehensive. The many contributors to the *Encyclopédie* included almost everyone of any note in intellectual circles in France at the time. Diderot commissioned a frontispiece from the Freemason Charles-Nicolas Cochin II, drawn in 1764, and engraved in 1772 by Benoît-Louis Prévost, which some claim is Masonic and others do not[31]. Even the first volumes of the *Encyclopédie* were adorned with Emblems of Wisdom and Light, but the main connection between Diderot's work and Freemasonry would appear to be through contributors who had contacts with Huguenot exiles in The Netherlands, and through the Amsterdam publisher, Swiss-born Marc-Michel Rey, who seems to have had financial and distributing interests in the *Encyclopédie*. Rey, who, like Rousseau, hailed from Geneva, became one of the most distinguished publishers of the Enlightenment, handling works by many luminaries, including Rousseau and Paul Heinrich Dietrich, Baron von Holbach[32], author of anti-Christian works such as *Christianisme dévoilé*[33] and *Système de la Nature*[34]. The facts that, although Holbach and his circle were based in Paris, but that their books had to be published under false imprints outside France, say much about the paradoxes of the *ancient régime*. Rey's acquaintances included many Freemasons. It is partly through Rey, the Abbé Claude Yvon, and the Abbé Jean-Martin de Prades[35], that there were connections between the *Encyclopédie* and Freemasonry. Yvon himself was a Freemason, and de Prades corresponded with a number of active Freemasons. There can be no doubt that Encyclopaedism had close links with the Craft, and that the attitude to intellectual endeavour implicit in the collation of information was fostered in many Freemasonic circles. We have already established the important Freemasonic links that were associated with Ephraim Chambers's *Cyclopaedia*, a work which had its many Continental admirers. Andrew Michael Ramsay, Scots philosopher and Jacobite sympathiser (who became a Baronet in the Jacobite creation of 1735), was converted to Roman Catholicism in 1710 under the influence of François de Salignac de la Mothe Fénelon (Archbishop of Cambrai from 1695), Christian Neo-Platonist, who was seen by some commentators as a *philosophe*, but in whose writings there is no trace of any belief in liberty of conscience attributed to him by eighteenth-century admirers. In this respect Fénelon's somewhat chilly character pre-echoed attitudes of later *philosophes*. Ramsay arrived in The Netherlands in 1710, where he met numerous exiled Scots, before proceeding to Cambrai for instruction by Fénelon (whose biography he was to publish in French and English in the 1720s), and moved to Paris in 1716, where he made the acquaintance of the Jacobite Court-in-exile, and became tutor to the young Prince Charles Edward Stuart in 1723[36]. In common with many exiled Jacobites, Ramsay became a leading figure in French Freemasonry as a member of the Lodge of St Thomas. In 1737 he delivered *A Discourse Pronounced at the Reception of Freemasons*[37], which stressed the Craft's aims to unify all humanity through the love of virtue, and argued that Freemasonry had originated during the Crusades[38]. Ramsay was also admitted to the Horn Lodge in London in 1730, so it would appear that his devotion to toleration and free sharing of intellectual matters made his stance acceptable to the Whigs (whose religious affiliations could be described as undogmatically Christian, in contrast to a growing anti-Clericalism in certain Continental circles). He advocated a new encyclopaedia[39], but it was not to be anything resembling the production of Diderot and d'Alembert: on the contrary, it was to be a vehicle for the dissemination of a specifically Christian Enlightenment imbued with Freemasonic ideals. On the other hand, people like Yvon contributed to the *Encyclopédie*, inserting a strong flavour of materialism and rationalism into articles dealing with the Soul, Polytheism, and other weighty matters[40], presumably reactions to the obscurantist religious atmosphere prevalent in the *Ancien Régime*.

The formation of the London Grand Lodge in 1717 had significant effects outside England, for from about 1717 to 1740 many Freemasonic Lodges were established throughout Northern Europe. With the approval of London's Grand Lodge, the Grand Lodge of France was established in Paris in 1725[41], and for a number of years French Lodges 'performed cultural functions to promote Enlightenment concepts'[42]. The ex-Jesuit Jean-Baptiste-Louis Gresset certainly saw Freemasonry as a 'cultural vehicle' of the Enlightenment, for initiates could use Reason to erect Spiritual Temples and thereby to improve the tone of Society[43], a specifically Freemasonic notion.

Thus, when we consider figures such as Desaguliers and Ramsay, we can describe them as Freemasonic Enlighteners, convinced that the Craft owed much to the

---

30 *ODNB* **x** (2004) 980.
31 *See* Jacob (1981) 257; *Diderot Studies* (1973) 171-3; and Barber *et al.* (1967) 223-37.
32 Otherwise Paul-Henri Thiry, Baron d'Holbach, although he was a German, born in the Palatinate.
33 Holbach (1767).
34 Holbach (1770).
35 Both of whom were published by Rey, and both of whom had to flee to The Netherlands in 1752 an account of their robust materialistic and rational views.

36 *ODNB* **xlv** (2004) 915-7.
37 Voltaire (1738) 58-61. *See also* Oliver (1847-50).
38 *ODNB* **xlv** (2004) 917.
39 Ramsay (c.1729). *See also* Luquet (1963) 157-8.
40 Jacob (1981) 256. For contributors to the *Encyclopédie see* Lough (1973).
41 Weisberger, McLeod, & Morris (*Eds.*) (2002) 299. *See also* Chevallier (1974) 3-7, Coil (1967-8) **i** 230-4, and *AQC* **xlvii** (1934) 87-114.
42 Weisberger, McLeod, & Morris (*Eds.*) (2002) 301.
43 Chevallier (1964) 60.

Ancients. Ramsay, in his *Voyages de Cyrus*[44], claimed that Ancient Egyptians, King Solomon, Cyrus, and others from Antiquity were steeped in the Mysteries, and thereby laid the foundations for modern 'Speculative Freemasonry'. Ramsay, of course, as noted above, was a Roman Catholic convert and Jacobite[45], yet he believed that the principles of Freemasonry not only reflected essential doctrines of Roman Catholicism, but that it was compatible with other major world religions[46]: his was an unusually open-minded position, which goes far to explain why he was acceptable to English Whigs. Desaguliers had come from a persecuted Huguenot background to Anglicanism, yet his views did not differ all that widely from those of Ramsay. In a nutshell, there were many eighteenth-century thinkers who saw nothing incompatible between the principles of Freemasonry and established religions[47]. Ramsay, in particular, claimed that the Knights Templar promoted notions of benevolence, justice, and virtue, and lived according to the precepts of Freemasonry[48], a view at odds with the official Papal position, for an association of the Templars with the Craft proved unpalatable to the Roman Catholic Church, so it was probably difficult for Ramsay and others when *In eminenti* was issued in 1738, the first Papal condemnation of Freemasonry, attacking the Craft's naturalistic bias, its demands for secret oaths, its religious 'indifference', and its perceived threat to Church and State. Thenceforth, Roman Catholics who joined the Craft ran the risk of being excommunicated.

In spite of this, Freemasonry prospered on the Continent, and acquired new and ever more exotic 'Degrees'. From the 1730s onwards, Continental and British Freemasonry tended to become distinct in their differences, notably in relation to the ecclesiastical and secular authorities, for in Britain, as previously noted, the Craft was associated with Whiggery and the Hanoverians, but on the Continent, especially in the Roman Catholic countries, Freemasonry tended to become a vehicle for the dissemination of ideas unacceptable to reactionary forces. Certainly in France the Craft was increasingly seen as deriving from crusading chivalry, from Ancient Egyptian Mysteries, and possibly from the Templars. Various attempts were made to bring the Grand Lodge of France closer to British Craft Masonry, but violent rivalry between various factions led to seemingly interminable disputes. Under the aegis of Louis-Philippe-Joseph d'Orléans, the Anglophile Duc de Chartres (later Duc d'Orléans, called *Égalité* during the Revolution, which did not save him from the Guillotine), Grand Master[49] of the English Grand Lodge of France, it was agreed that the Grand Orient would be established as the governing body of Parisian Freemasonry, and a Constitution was prepared in 1773 by Anne-Charles-Sigismond de Montmorency-Luxembourg, Duc de Piney-Luxembourg, which transformed the Grand Orient (with which the Grand Lodge was amalgamated) into an important national body, and a learned society was set up in 1776 called the Lodge of the Nine Sisters (*Neuf Soeurs*) which played a huge part in exchanging knowledge and ideas[50]. Thereafter, French Freemasonry became a vehicle for political activism, and, ultimately, for the transmission and exchange of some of the most important features of the Enlightenment.

Needless to say, it was the very fact of Papal disapproval that drove French Freemasons to become more radical and anti-clerical: one would go as far as to say that *In eminenti* weakened the Ramsayan view of the Craft as compatible with Roman Catholicism, and made it anti-authoritarian, anti-clerical, and even anti-Christian. Once the Grand Orient had been established, French Freemasonry tended to acquire a pronounced flavour of its own, developing new rituals and Degrees, but, most importantly, fostering advanced ideas. By 1780, in spite of Papal denunciations and harassment by elements of the State, there were over 80 Lodges in Paris[51], in addition to which there were specifically military Lodges, women's Lodges (or rather Lodges with which women were associated), and schismatics of various kinds[52]. It was because of the work and influence of Montmorency-Luxembourg and Philippe d'Orléans that the Grand Orient gained, if not support from the Crown, at least tolerance, was able to attract considerable numbers of aristocratic and bourgeois members, and managed to survive attacks from anti-Freemasonic (mostly Roman Catholic) quarters. Many of the most distinguished artists, scientists, and thinkers of the time in Paris became members of the ultra-intellectual Lodge of the Nine Sisters (*Neuf Soeurs*), established (as noted above) to promote the Liberal Arts and Sciences, as an offshoot of the Grand Orient. The inspiration behind the formation of the Nine Sisters was the Astronomer, Joseph-Jérome Lefrançais de Lalande, the Orator of the Grand Orient, who believed that a fundamental task of Freemasonry was to Enlighten by such promotion: thus he saw the Lodge of the Nine Sisters as a cultural locus and as a major catalyst in the progress of the Enlightenment, and indeed, as a Learned Society. The induction of Voltaire into this Lodge in 1778 was intended to give status to the Nine Sisters and attract members. Among prominent Freemasons present at Voltaire's induction (which was a high-speed affair strictly *not* in accordance with Freemasonic practice and custom) were the American Enlightener Benjamin Franklin, the Linguist Antoine Court de Gébelin, Dr. Joseph-Ignace Guillotin (who, contrary to popular belief, did not perish by his own invention during the Terror, although he came close to it), and Count Aleksandr Sergeyevich Stroganov.

---

44 *See* the 1730 edition published by Jaques (*sic*) Bettenham in London.
45 Monod (1989) 302-4 usefully outlines connections between French Freemasonry and the Jacobites.
46 Findel (1869) 203.
47 Chevallier (1974) 19-24.
48 Weisberger, McLeod, & Morris (*Eds*.) (2002) 306 and *passim* for these and other related matters.
49 Installed 22 October 1773.

50 Weisberger, McLeod, & Morris (2002) 314-336.
51 Chevallier (1964) is still illuminating on this.
52 *Ibid*.

In 1770 Franklin[53] succeeded Lalande as Master of the Lodge, a position he occupied until 1780. Names associated with the Nine Sisters included the eminent painters Jean-Baptiste Greuze, Hubert Robert, and Claude-Joseph Vernet; the sculptor Jean-Antoine Houdon[54]; the inventors of the hot-air balloon, Joseph-Michel and Jacques-Étienne Montgolfier; a few musicians, including Niccolò Piccinni; five Architects, including Charles-Axel Guillaumot and Bernard Poyet; and members of the legal profession including Claude-Emmanuel-Joseph-Pierre, Marquis de Pastoret[55].

As far as Architects were concerned, between 1774 and 1789, over one hundred and twenty belonged to Lodges in Paris affiliated with the Grand Orient[56]. Among them may be mentioned Jean-Baptiste de Puisieux (who was involved in the building of *Ste-Geneviève* under Jacques-Germain Soufflot and who wrote an important treatise[57] on Geometry in which his interest in Freemasonry is overt). *Les Coeurs Simples de l'Étoile Polaire* Lodge seems to have had ten Architects in a total membership of ninety: they included Jean-François-Thérèse Chalgrin (who designed the severe basilica of *St-Philippe-du-Roule* [1768-74], and the enormous *Arc de Triomphe de l'Étoile* [1806-36], both in Paris); Nicolas Le Camus de Mézières (architect of the *Halle au Blé*, Paris [1763-7], and author of *Le Génie de l'architecture* [1780] in which he proposed that Architecture should be pleasing to the senses and induce elevating impressions on the heart and mind, thus leading to the concept of *architecture parlante* that had such a profound effect on numerous important Architects, not least Soane); and Charles de Wailly (Architect of the austere *Théâtre de l'Odéon*, Paris [1769-82], and the *Château de Montmusard*, near Dijon [1764-9 – the first French country-house in which the Antique flavour was dominant]).

One of the most significant aspects of the period in which Freemasonry evolved in France during the 1770s and thereafter is that many who were associated with the Humanities and the Fine Arts sought greater knowledge of, and drew on paradigms from, Classical Antiquity: the search for Enlightenment was *intimately connected* with the rediscovery of Antiquity. So, closely linked with Freemasonry were the Revivals of Roman, Greek, and Egyptian Architecture, the Classicisation of Painting, the re-creation of Arcadian landscapes, and themes concerned with Nature. Thus, what we now call Neo-Classicism was an expression of the Enlightenment and of Freemasonic ideals in the widespread and remarkably energetic attempts to recover That Which Was Lost.

To take only one example, Court de Gébelin concerned himself with Mystery Cults, Ancient Myths, and Linguistics, among much else. In particular, he drew parallels between the Eleusinian Mystery Cults and Freemasonry in his own time: both had cultural functions, and both imparted the moral doctrines and values of Antique civilisations[58]. Ideas of Virtue, Justice, and Liberty were common to both. Court de Gébelin described ancient initiation ceremonies during which candidates acquired the secrets of the Mysteries, prayers were offered to the Supreme Being, and the ceremonies ended with feasting[59]. Just as the Eleusinian Mysteries embodied cultural ideals cherished in Antiquity, so late-eighteenth-century Freemasonry encouraged the seeking after those lost cultural ideals in Architecture, Sculpture, Landscapes, Landscape Painting, respect for Nature, and much else. At Freemasonic banquets, the Brethren, all equal in the Lodge, sought origins, primitive beginnings of human happiness, and the 'first times' when Mankind was kindlier and less selfish. Repose, Virtue, and Pleasure were in alliance: all was identified with Morality, and through the Craft a new Art of Living could emerge, far-removed from both Asceticism and Debauchery[60].

Court de Gébelin drew on Classical sources to paint a vivid picture of the dramas of the Mysteries and the eventual Enlightenment of initiates. The 'horror' of the ceremonies was made more fearful by human ingenuity: thunderclaps resounded on all sides, thunderbolts fell with terrible sounds; frightening figures would be seen; the Sanctuary itself shook; and Earth herself resounded with hellish noise. Then calm descended, the 'scene' (i.e. stage) opened and extended into the distance; the end of the Sanctuary parted; and the initiates perceived agreeable meadows bathed in light. Thus the elements of Initiation alluded to descent into the Underworld, Trials and Proofs of Worth, and a new birth in sun-drenched Enlightened bliss[61].

However, Court de Gébelin's descriptions of initiation-rites, while owing much to Plutarch (Mestrius Plutarchus) and to Themistius's *De Anima*, lean more towards the Cult of Orpheus than to Eleusis[62]. We will return to Orpheus later. Carl Kerényi investigated and interpreted the spatial aspects of Eleusis and the Sanctuary of Demeter and Kore/Persephone[63]: the Temple there was a Hall of Initiation (*Anaktoron* or *Telesterion*), apparently almost square on plan[64], which was an unusual form for a Greek temple[65].

As in England, French Freemasons did not at first have purpose-built Lodges, and met in private houses, restaurants, or inns. Police raids seem to have broken up many a convivial gathering, but generally the costumes, tools, emblems, décor, and other paraphernalia had to be carted around for use by Lodges when and where required. Chequered carpets, candlesticks, and other objects were used to provide the 'sets' for ceremonies, while floor-

---

53 His induction was at the St John's Lodge, Philadelphia, PA, in 1731.
54 Who made portrait-busts of Diderot (1771), Franklin (1778), and Voltaire, among others.
55 *See* Ligou (1964), Ligou (*Ed.*) (1991), and Ligou *et al.* (2000).
56 Vidler (1987) 92-3.
57 Puisieux (1765).
58 Court de Gébelin (1773-82) **i** 306-8.
59 *Ibid.* 319-30.
60 Mauzi (1965) 611-2.
61 Court de Gébelin (1773-82) **iv** 320.
62 Mylonas (1961) *passim*.
63 Persephone/Kore was Demeter's daughter by Zeus, and was often worshipped with her mother. As Queen of the Underworld, she had connections with Orphism and to Orphic literature ascribed to Orpheus.
64 Dinsmoor (1950) *passim*, but *see* Fig. 73.
65 Kerényi (1991) *passim*.

drawings defined the areas for rituals[66]. These plans, of course, were mnemonics of Solomon's Temple, and were designed to guide initiations as well as to indicate the positions of main elements. They were distantly related in idea to the ancient Labyrinths in Cathedral floors (e.g. Chartres), or those formed in turf (e.g. Wing, Rutland, or Saffron Walden, Essex) that were routes for pilgrims to progress while in prayer, taking wrong turnings, until eventually Paradise was reached: Labyrinths, as previously described, were also allegories of the journey through life. Freemasons sought the origins of their Craft in the still centres of their Lodges, which were drawn apart from the rest of the world and shielded from prying eyes: in the Lodge and its Emblems Freemasons sought the memory of beginnings and of the Temple itself. The Lodge, therefore, was, with its iconography, a mnemonic of the Temple, and was itself a Temple to the Art of Memory.

By the second half of the eighteenth century the typology of French Lodges had become clear. The utilitarian parts of the building were at the lowest level, and the rooms of the Lodge were disposed in series: the first room was dark, with two small chambers for candidates (the parallel with Graeco-Roman Isiac rites is obvious); the second part was for purification, washing, etc. (again there is a parallel with Isiac initiations in the Graeco-Roman World); then the main hall of the Lodge for ceremonies was disposed with space for initiation. Then came the banqueting- or dining-room[67], where convivial activities would follow the more serious rites of initiation. Needless to say, the exteriors of the buildings used as Lodges were very discreet, and gave no sign of the purposes or activities within. The need to keep and store archives, records, and books in Lodges led to the provision of rooms for such purposes, and by the 1780s separate rooms appear to have been regarded as ideal for the three Grades of Initiation[68]. Proportions of the Lodges were attempts to approximate to measurements of the Solomonic Temple, while the 'Two Pillars' marked the entrance to the space of the Lodge, and the East, or Orient, was given lavish décor to mark its importance (even though, as was made clear earlier, the *orientation* of the original Temple was the other way round).

Freemasonic activities in Paris sometimes became overt and public, and the Order prospered throughout France, gaining membership in droves under the leadership of the Grand Orient. Freemasonry from the 1770s could almost be said to be popular (among the bourgeoisie and the aristocracy at any rate), appealing to a wide cross-section of French Society. The Grand Orient acquired in 1774 the former Jesuit Novitiate in the Faubourg Saint-Germain as its headquarters, and work began on the conversion of the buildings to designs by Pierre Poncet. Rooms were arranged in series, the first being hung with flowered patterns on cloth, the second decorated in watered blue and white, and the third (the main hall) had a blue ceiling, a double row of benches, triangular tables, and two columns of pure metal with capitals carrying clusters of stars[69]. The Orient itself (approached by steps) had a platform with a throne, and beyond was the banqueting-hall, decorated in blue and red, with a blue ceiling, and with a platform and chair for the Grand Master. There it was, according to Lalande, that the Freemasons sought to build a Temple to the Great Architect of the Universe and to Virtue, and in that Sacred Asylum the Orient was to give itself up to its Sublime Works[70]. The front of the Lodge was decorated for one grand festival with an 'illumination' of Gothic (*sic*) Architecture, eight twisted (presumably barley-sugar or twisted) columns, with obelisks in between[71]. So by 1776 the spiral column and exotic features (many Egyptian) were becoming common features of Masonic décor, often mingling ideas of the Solomonic Temple with motifs from Ancient Egypt.

Only a few months after his initiation into the Lodge *Neuf Soeurs*, Voltaire died, and the Temple was transformed into a Lodge of Sorrows, lavishly hung with black cloth. A pyramidal cenotaph on high steps in front of which were three broken columns, banners inscribed with sayings of Voltaire, and other trappings provided the décor for a ceremony of speeches, readings, and musical performances. Broken columns became commonly used as funerary monuments in the nineteenth century, but Bernard Jones stated[72] that although the design of the charity-box produced at each Lodge meeting 'is symbolic of death' and is in the form of a broken column, this 'has no particular' Masonic significance, 'having been copied from memorial monuments of a design common to the period of its adoption', the early 1800s. With respect to him, Jones would appear to have been wrong, for broken columns were in use in French Lodges at least as early as 1778, and were displayed in the *pompes funèbres* associated with the deaths of Brethren. However, *The Royal Masonic Cyclopaedia* states[73] that in Freemasonry 'the Broken Column is the emblem of the fall or death of one of the chief supporters of the Craft'. Some regard the use of a broken column as a charity collecting-box as 'inappropriate', something the Craft was 'landed with' by the 'commercial forces of suppliers of Lodge furniture and paraphernalia'. The broken column, however, does figure 'appropriately' in American Masonic monitors, where it is associated with the 'death... of one of the chief supporters of the Craft', that is, 'Hiram Abiff and the legend of the Third Degree'[74].

The 'catch' of Voltaire's initiation led to many more recruits to the Order, and by 1780 it is clear, what with publicity, denunciations from the Church, and many works of Masonic scholarship, anecdote, exposure, and

---

66 Chevallier (1968) *passim*, for reports and inventories.
67 Larudan (1785) describes this in detail.
68 Béyerlé (1784).
69 See État du G∴ O∴ de France (1777) **i**/4, 7, 35-6. See also Vidler (1987) 94, 209, n. 53.
70 Ibid.
71 Ibid.
72 Jones (1986) 448.
73 Mackenzie (*Ed.*) (1887b). but *see* the 1987 edn., 82-3.
74 T. O. Haunch, in a personal communication.

counter-exposure, that Freemasonry and its activities in France were hardly 'secret' any more: in fact the sheer amount of publications remains daunting to any student of the period. Many contain extraordinary illustrations of Lodges that emphasise Death and Dying (**Pl.VII.1**): these have been represented by some anti-Masonic writers as 'evidence' that the Craft is a Cult 'dedicated to the worship of Death' and that its 'philosophy' represents a 'death-wish' for civilisation. However, Death occupies a place almost beyond the register of what the living can know, a signifier that is difficult to grasp. Jacques Derrida went so far as to claim that Death is *always* the name of a *Secret*, always a *Shibboleth*, for the manifest name of a Secret is from the start a very private name, the language about Death 'is nothing but the long history of a Secret Society'. Death lies somewhere outside clear categories, for it is probably a Void that has acquired a name. All this suggests that the central place of Death in the consciousness of any sensitive and thinking person as the one Certainty in Life, can be interpreted by some as the name of a name that has no name, something sinister. But, as Mozart and others knew, the Craft actually alleviated the fear of Death[75] by helping to counteract Superstition and the more horrific, threatening claims of the Church concerning post-mortem Punishments: such a view saw Death as natural, as a friend, as normal, and to be accepted, sometimes with gratitude.

Freemasonry and Neo-Classicism

As was indicated above, Freemasonry, drawing on aspects of Antiquity for its ceremonies, initiations, teachings, and much else (not least the Classical Orders of Architecture), was not alone in its activities. The Classical Language of Architecture, in the eighteenth century, was a universal language, yet it began to be perceived as corrupted, filtered, as it were, through the Italian Renaissance. It was therefore important, it was argued, to go back to Antiquity, to real Antique models, to purify Architecture, simplify it, and cleanse it of accretions. Exemplars from the Roman World were studied, and the remains of Hellenic and Hellenistic Architecture were surveyed and the results made available in publications[76]. That simplicity led to a severe, bare Architecture, an Architecture that, like Court de Gébelin's *monde primitif*, was also elemental, stark, and even reduced to stereometrically pure forms. As the search for the Primitive continued, sources from even further back in time were sought: first from Ancient Rome, then from Ancient Greece and the Hellenistic World, then from Ancient Egypt, and finally from prehistory, where stark exemplars such as Stonehenge or Neolithic burial-chambers were exalted.

So it was with Painting, where subjects turned to the Antique, and even portraits became Classicised. In Sculpture, too, Antique paradigms informed the creation of

Pl.VII.1 French Lodge design for the Reception of a Master Mason. This lushly eerie setting has reminders of Mortality, the Grave, the Acacia, Jachin and Boaz, and other familiar elements, but the drapes with pear-shaped *guttes* or tears, give it an overpowering quality. From *Le Régulateur du Maçon*, published by the Grand Orient of France in Paris, 1801. It appears that Continental examples of the Lodge of Sorrows for deceased Brethern had similar décor, such images have been interpreted as very sinister by anti-Masonic writers (*Collection JSC*).

portrait-busts, heroic figures, and so on. And in Landscape Design, Elysium and Arcady were evoked, with temples strategically placed, mausolea erected against backdrops of trees, and monuments doubling as eyecatchers. This was the Age of Neo-Classicism, and an essential stimulant to that Age and its many achievements was Freemasonry, which also turned back to Antiquity in search of a Lost Perfection. Many Architects adopted the idea of their work being directed towards, if not Utopian, certainly ideal ends to improve the lot of Mankind. In doing so, they, whether Freemasons or not, worked at a time when Freemasonic Symbolism, ideas, and aspirations permeated much of intellectual life. It was an extraordinary, fecund, and exciting period, when creativity, informed by a secure base of profound study of Antique precedents, produced some wonderful stuff.

The search for Simplicity (albeit Classical Simplicity), of course, is associated with the Abbé Marc-Antoine Laugier, who became one of the earliest and most

---

75 *See* Derrida (1993) *passim*; Klaver (2004) 187; Lina (2004) 134-8; Morra, Robson, & Smith (*Eds*.) (2000) xx, 249.

76 For this *see* Curl (2001a).

important theorists of Neo-Classicism. His *Essai sur l'Architecture* (1753) was profoundly influential, setting out a rational interpretation of Classicism as a logical, straightforward expression of the need for shelter, derived from the 'Primitive Hut' of tree-trunks supporting a structure. He extolled the need for columns as opposed to those of the engaged variety, or pilasters, and argued for a return to Antique principles as an antidote to all the accretions from the Renaissance period onwards that had obscured the essence of the origins of columnar and trabeated construction[77]. The immediate influence of his views was on Jacques-Germain Soufflot, who had studied the Greek temples at Paestum, and whose Church of Ste-Geneviève, Paris, was greatly admired for its logic, *gravitas*, and geometrical perfection (the severe crypt was strongly influenced by Laugier's theories, and by the powerful Doric Order of Paestum). Translations of Laugier's *Essai* into English and German carried his ideas throughout Europe.

Laugier, although an *Abbé*, was independent-minded enough to respond[78] to Papal denunciations of Freemasonry, and defended the Craft against the attacks of 1738[79] and 1751 (a renewal[80] of Clement XII's condemnation by Pope Benedict XIV) in a poem published in 1779[81] and again in the Abbé Philippe-André Grandidier's *Essais Historiques et Topographiques sur l'Église Cathédrale de Strasbourg* (1782)[82]. Nevertheless, the evidence that Laugier himself may have been a Freemason is unclear and scant, although his writings would indicate that he was at least sympathetic towards the Craft and its ideals. He was certainly interested in the whole question of historical paradigms apparent in seventeenth-and-eighteenth-century architectural theory[83].

An important Architect who responded to a call for a return to the Primitive, the Original, and the Simple was Claude-Nicolas Ledoux, whose designs are astonishing in terms of their stereometrical purity and their extraordinary visionary qualities (though still firmly derived from Classicism, but a Classicism stripped to its bare essentials). In his remarkable book, *L'Architecture Considérée sous le Rapport de l'Art, des Moeurs et de la Législation*[84], he proposed several designs that are interesting from the point of view of this study, for Ledoux appears to have had connections with Masonic and crypto-Masonic societies.

William Thomas Beckford met Ledoux in 1784, and was shown a mysterious place in the suburbs of Paris, set in a garden in which was a processional route which passed between tall pyramidal wood-piles to a large pyramid: thereafter the route led through a hall, an antechamber and cottage, an elaborate cubic room, a curtain (perhaps an allusion to the Veil of the Temple), a large hall in which was a massive laver and a fire giving off aromatic scents (perhaps a reminder of the laver and altar of Solomon's Temple), then a stair, and finally a tribune and chapel[85]. There are several important points to be noted here. First, the route to some sort of Lodge with its possible mnemonics of the Temple, was in a *garden*. Second, the Primitive pyramidal huts suggest at least a nod to Laugier's ideas of the origins of Architecture. Then there was the pyramid, with its Egyptian connotations; the hall with its Mediaeval associations; the cottage with its rustic simplicity influenced by Rousseau, perhaps; the cubic room suggested Classical civilisations, then the Temple was symbolised; and finally a stair led to a kind of climactic Holy of Holies, a realm of Enlightenment and spiritual awakening after darkness (**Fig.VII.1**).

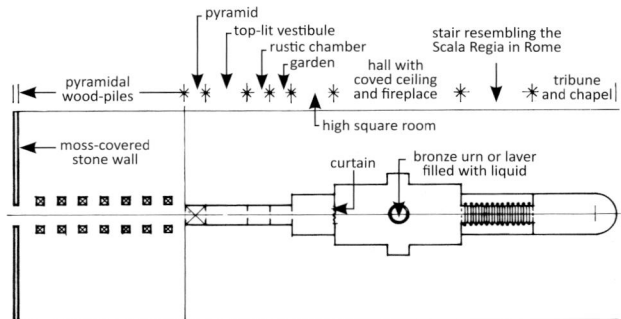

Fig.VII.1 Stylised diagram of the place visited by Ledoux and Beckford. It resembles a sequence in an Ancient Egyptian Temple (*see* **Pls.VII.10 & 11**, p.156). The various rooms could equally well have been treated as individual *fabriques* in a garden (JSC).

It is difficult to understand why Mowl was so dismissive of this in his study of Beckford: Ledoux's creations included many strange buildings for '*cultes*', and nothing in the description is any stranger than the proposals by Ledoux for his ideal town illustrated in his amazing book. Ledoux's life had a 'hidden side'[86], and he, like many of his contemporaries[87], was involved in secret or quasi-secret societies with interests in the occult, all of which might appear to be curious in what we know as the Age of Enlightenment. Was Ledoux involved in the kind of heretical Freemasonry which 'Cagliostro' (in reality Giuseppe Balsamo [alchemist, confidence-trickster, imposter, and fraud]) claimed to have founded in Naples in 1777. It is unlikely if we will ever know, but, unless Beckford indulged in flights of fancy (of which he was more than capable), Ledoux probably did take part in one

---

77 *See* Laugier (1753, 1765, 1782).
78 It is assumed that the author in question *was* Laugier. *See* Vidler (1987) 88 and 208 n.29.
79 *In eminenti* of Clement XII (28 April 1738).
80 18 May 1751. Benedict, described wryly by Horace Walpole as 'a Pope without nephews', also denounced various writings of the Enlightenment, including (13 March 1752) Montesquieu's *Esprit des Loix* (1748): such denunciations have continued ever since.
81 *Journal de Monsieur* (January 1779) 75-85 and also in *Journal de Nancy* (1779) 118-124 and 139-148. *See* also Frankl & Panofsky (1945).
82 Grandidier (1782) **ii** 417.
83 *See*, for example, Couret de Villeneuve (1748) 1-25 and *passim*. *See* also Herrmann (1962) *passim*.
84 Ledoux (1804, 1847). *See* also Vidler (1990).

85 Oliver (1932) 172-81. *See* also Vidler (1990) 338-340. Mowl (1998) admitted Beckford's account 'may contain a grain of truth', but dismissed most of it as 'nonsensical'.
86 Braham (1980) 160. Braham's study, despite its age, has stood up well to advancing Time.
87 *Ibid.* 11, 79, 155, 157, 160, 171, 186, 207-8, 216, 232, 236.

of the many societies that flourished in the last years of the *ancient régime*, and which are now being investigated by scholars.

A drawing of an eye, with the theatre at Besançon reflected in the pupil (**Pl.VII.2**), published in the collection of designs by Ledoux, recalls Leon Battista Alberti's device, the winged eye, and may have been inspired by the All-Seeing Eye which, although not exclusively associated with Freemasonry, was certainly present as an Emblem in numerous Masonic publications and designs. Ledoux employed blank walls, simplified architectural forms, and sparing ornament in his severe designs. Furthermore, the possibilities of stereometrically pure forms (such as the pyramid) were exploited by him, as in the celebrated proposal for a gun-foundry for an Industrial City near Chaux, in which Ledoux reduced the factory to a pure, logical, geometrical series of elements (**Pl.VII.3**). A comparison with the Escorial, with its corner-towers, and its astrological and symbolic allusions, not least its connection with the grid-iron of St Laurence's Martyrdom, is hard to avoid, for the pyramids at the corners of Ledoux's composition could easily be the supports for such a grid if the plans were turned upside-down.

Three enormous schemes by Ledoux will suffice to demonstrate his striving for Primitive Simplicity in Classical Architecture, a totality and wholeness of vision (as in the *Saline du Roi* at Arc-et-Senans [otherwise known as the *Saline de Chaux* of 1774-9] which he proposed to expand into an ideal town laid out on an elliptical plan), and a harmonious relationship of buildings to function, expression, and to each other. His *Barrières* of Paris, or customs-posts (of which only four of the planned fifty-plus survive), were masterworks of Neo-Classical simplicity and understatement (**Pl. VII.4**, p.152): Beckford said that from their massive, sepulchral character, they looked more like the entrances to a necropolis than to a 'city so damnably alive as this confounded capital'[88]. At

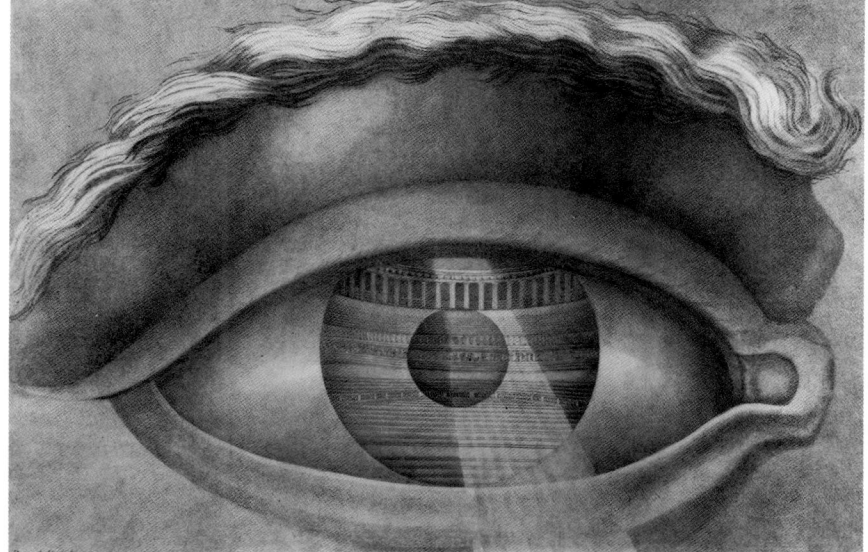

Pl.VII.2 *Coup d'oeil du théâtre de Besançon*, suggesting the All-Seeing Eye and the Theatre at Besançon by C.-N. Ledoux, a possible Masonic allusion, with certain overtones after Alberti: it illustrates Ledoux's point that the eye is the 'first frame' through which we see the world. From Ledoux (1804) Plate 113 (*SJSM*).

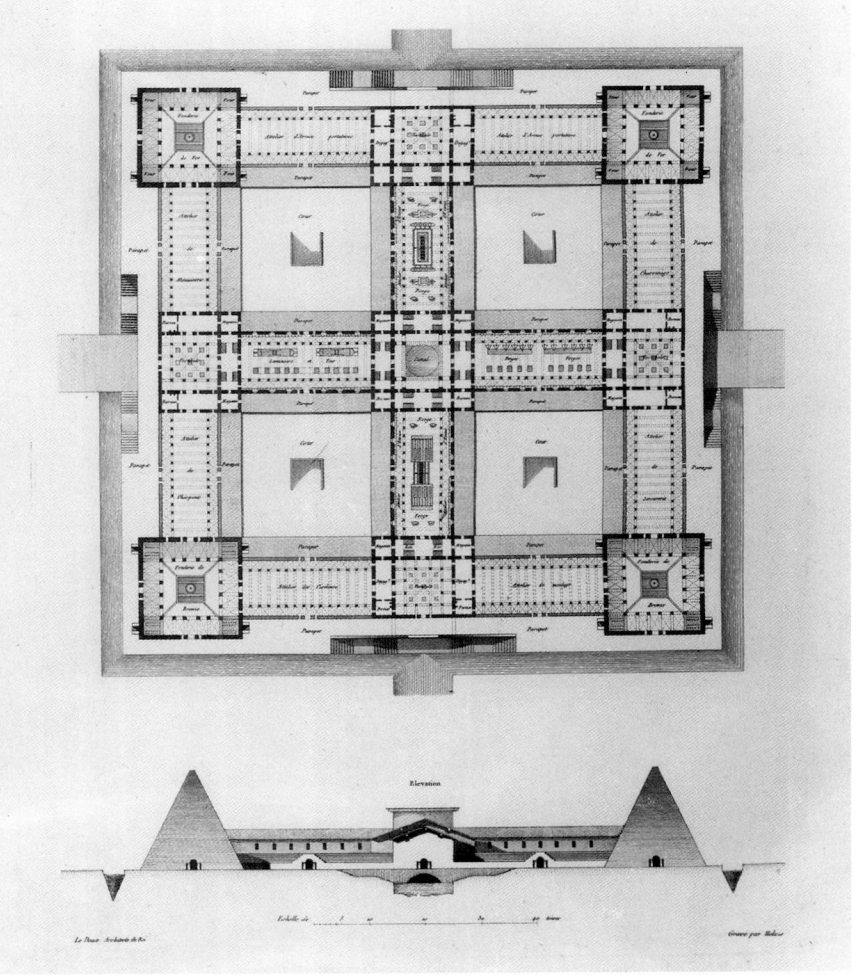

Pl.VII.3 Plan and elevation of C.-N. Ledoux's *Forge à Canons* from Ledoux (1804) Plate 124. Note the rigid grid-iron plan and use of pyramids. The form recalls Juan de Herrera's Escorial and various versions of the Temple complex in Jerusalem, notably that of Villalpando (*SJSM*).

---

88 Braham (1980) 193-4.

Pl.VII.4 *Barrière de la Villette*, Paris, by Ledoux, showing an excellent example of his simplified Classicism, reduced to elemental Geometry (JSC).

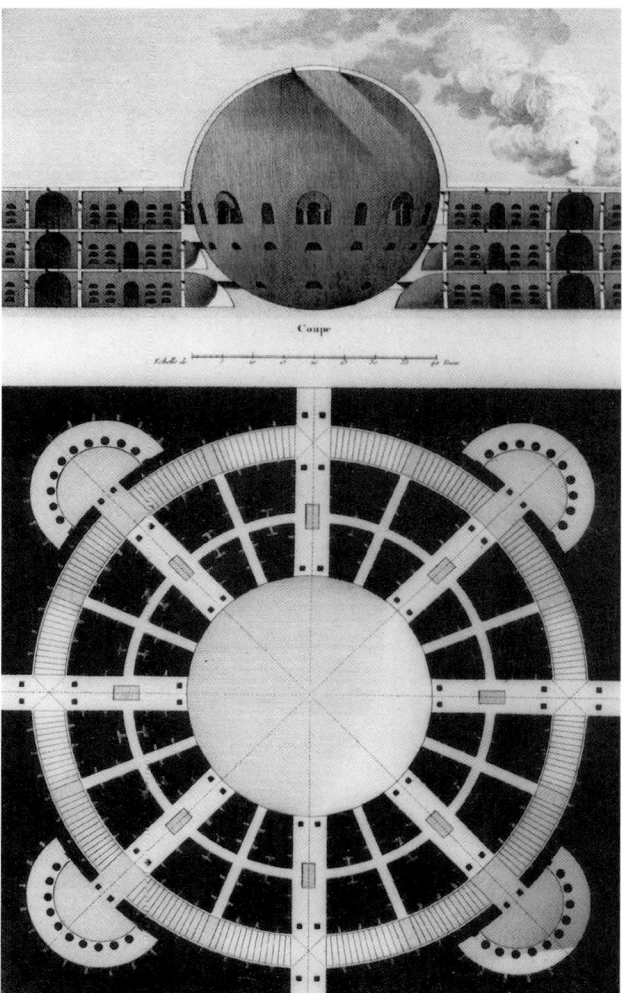

Pl.VII.5 Ledoux's design for the Cemetery at Chaux. Note the severe stereometrically pure forms and the central sphere (a favourite theme of French Neo-Classical designers imbued with Masonic ideas). From Ledoux (1804), engraved by Ransonnette (SJSM).

the *Barrière du Trône* Ledoux designed not only two severe pavilions, but two free-standing columns set on tough pedimented bases: these columns suggest the Pillars of Hercules, the World Beyond and Within, and the 'Two Pillars' of Masonic Legend based on allusions to the Solomonic Temple.

As has been pointed out. The Two Columns, wide vestibule-like front, and domed space behind with Holy of Holies to the east were employed by Fischer von Erlach in the *Karlskriche*, Vienna, and the Pantheon-type mixed with Graeco-Roman and Jewish Temple found its way into French Masonic designs (see **Pl.X.10**, p.271). The Primitive Hut, as an ideal, became associated with nobility through Rousseauesque ideas, and with Adam, who gained his knowledge from the Great Architect Himself, transforming the Primitive Hut into a sophisticated work of Architecture based on proportional systems derived from Geometry. Hence Adam became the first Freemason, the first Natural 'Primitive' Man, and the author of the exemplar of the Primitive Hut. Ideals of Classical Primitivism that came to fruition in the toughest works of the Neo-Classical period were associated, however tentatively, with Freemasonry. However, Architects *and* Freemasons began to be perceived as the representatives and interpreters of The Great Architect of The Universe: this clearly had ramifications in that the contributions of Architects in producing purified, noble, stripped Classical buildings, cleansed of all corruptions, were not without significance as Architecture influenced by Freemasonry in which it was touched by the Divine.

Many Architects and architectural theorists working in Paris alone (as noted above) in the 1770s and 1780s were known Freemasons. Many, too, including Ledoux and Jean-Jacques Lequeu, were profoundly influenced by the notion that architectural design and theory could be harnessed to the promotion of political and social change, and perceived elements of design as having potent *meanings* (or even potential *new* meanings), so that Architecture would 'speak': this was the notion of *architecture parlante* (or architecture expressive of its purpose by means of its form), a term apparently invented by Léon Vaudoyer, the son of Antoine-Laurent-Thomas Vaudoyer[89].

Late-eighteenth-century French designers had a vast vocabulary of Masonic and quasi-Masonic Emblems, Images, and Allusions on which to draw, many of which were familiar to an educated public[90]. Étienne-Louis Boullée may or may not have been a Freemason, yet his work was clearly permeated by ideas that were rife in

---

89 Bergdoll (1994b) *passim*.
90 Vidler (1987) 93.

Pl.VII.6 Ledoux's extraordinary and improbable elevation of the Cemetery at Chaux, showing his use of spheres. From Ledoux (1804), engraved by Bovinet (SJSM).

Craft circles, and Lequeu (a curious character, who was probably unbalanced) was steeped in Masonic imagery, producing numerous eclectic designs for buildings that were obviously at least partly informed by Freemasonry. A little-known source of many of the experimental architectural schemes that surfaced in France in the latter part of the eighteenth century was *La Coterie des Anti-Façonniers*, by the Abbé Laurent Bordelon, first published in 1675 and then again in 1716[91]: it described, astonishingly, groups of people in their sphere-shaped 'Lodges', and Bordelon may have influenced Ledoux when designing his spherical Lodge for Maupertuis in the 1780s (the House of the Agricultural Guards)[92], the spherical centre of the Cemetery at Chaux (*c.*1785) (**Pl.VII.5**), or the truly astonishing 'Elevation of the Cemetery of the Town of Chaux' engraved by Edmé Bovinet and published in Ledoux's *Architecture*[93], edited by Daniel Ramée (**Pl.VII.6**). This spherical theme was also taken up to spectacular effect by Boullée for his design (1784) for a Cenotaph to the Deity of the French Enlightenment, Isaac Newton: the sphere was placed in a 'cup' of concentric drums planted with rings of evergreen trees, an obvious mixing of the type of the Imperial Roman Mausoleum (e.g. that of Hadrian) with the ideal of stereometrical purity sought by so many experimenters of the Neo-Classical period (**Pls. VII.7-9**, p.154).

Freemasonry and Egyptian Elements in Neo-Classical Architecture

Giovanni Battista Piranesi had insisted that the hardness and 'simplicity' of Ancient Egyptian Architecture were not due to ignorance, but were deliberate expressions: the taste of his day saw non-naturalistic styles as 'primitive' or 'inferior', but Piranesi knew that Egyptian Art was highly sophisticated, and had tremendous possibilities for future designers in an age dominated by tyranny of Good Taste. Johann Gottfried Herder was among the first in the eighteenth century to point out what Egyptian Art might contribute to European design. Herder noted that the first great monuments in the world were those of Ancient Egypt, and that lasting buildings, using squares, triangles, and points, became the pyramids and obelisks. Impressions of grandeur and permanence, without recourse to ornament, were achieved by the Ancient Egyptians, and Herder realised the possibilities of a stark, simple Architecture, a severe expression of basic forms, in the emulation of Ancient Egyptian exemplars. The 'primitiveness' of so much late-eighteenth-century architectural experiment stemmed from philosophical ideas of Herder and Edmund Burke, and the stripped-down, Sublime images derive from Piranesi, whose gigantic, overpowering prisons, over-scaled views, improbably magnificent megalomaniac tombs, and Egyptianising eclecticism were to mingle with a growing demand for simplicity by the German Herder and the Frenchman Laugier. Architects of the last quarter of the eighteenth century were not slow to connect Laugier's call for simplicity with the potent ideas of Herder, the images of Piranesi, and the Sublime of Burke and Immanuel Kant[94]. R. F. Gould classified Herder, who was a profound

---

91 Bordelon (1716). *See* also Dinaux (1867) **i** 37.
92 *See* Vidler (1990) 314-5.
93 Ramée (*Ed.*) (1847) plate 142.

94 Key texts are Burke (1757), Herder (1774-6), and Kant (2004 and 2007). *See* also Curl (2005) 167, 187, 220, and *passim*, Piranesi (1756, 1761, 1769, 1972), and Wilton-Ely (*Ed.*) 1972, 1978*a*, 1978*b*).

154 / Freemasonry and the Enlightenment

Pl.VII.7 Elevation of Boullée's cenotaph to Newton. The pure form of the sphere sits in the 'cup' of concentric drums with rings of evergreen trees. Note the monumental stairs and simple, stereometrically pure forms. The debt to Roman Imperial mausolea is clear, but the scale is vast, far more inflated than anything in Classical Antiquity (*BN. CE. HA57, No. 7*).

Pl.VII.8 Section through Boullée's cenotaph to Newton. A blazing globe set in the centre suggests day and the sun as well as illumination in the sense of Enlightenment and the explanation of the mysteries of Nature, even though outside the sphere it is dark (*BN. CE. HA 57, No. 9*).

Pl.VII.9 Section through Boullée's cenotaph to Newton of 1784. The rings of cypress trees, the sarcophagus-shaped cenotaph, and the stereometrically pure forms should be noted. The sphere is pierced to allow light in to suggest the position of the stars, even though outside it is day. Here Neo-Classical concerns with clarity and simplicity merge with megalomaniac scale (after Piranesi), and the Architecture of Imperial Roman mausolea (*BN. CE. HA57, No. 8*).

influence on Johann Wolfgang von Goethe, as a 'writer of the Craft'[95], and indeed Herder's work contains much overt Freemasonic material. His memorial in Weimar has the Motto *Licht Liebe Leben*[96] arranged in a circle around AΩ and held within an *ouroboros*[97] behind the head of which is a Blazing Sun[98].

A later major influence on generations of French Architects was Antoine-Chrysostôme Quatremère de Quincy, whose Prize Essay submitted to the Académie des Inscriptions et Belles-Lettres in 1785 is likely to have been known to Boullée and others, although it was not published in Paris until 1803 as *De L'Architecture Égyptienne, Considerée Dans son origine ses principes et son goût, et comparée Sous les mêmes rapports à l'Architecture Grecque*. In it, he dwelt on the massiveness and brooding grandeur of Ancient Egyptian Architecture, and granted that it comprised much that was admirable: the Pyramids were rightly objects worthy of respect, whilst the architectural arrangement of temples gave an impression of greatness. The illustrations in Quatremère de Quincy's work were by Antoine-Joseph Gaitte, and show architectural detail in reasonably correct form, given that professional surveys of *echt*-Egyptian buildings were only just beginning to appear in print. Quatremère, of course, was not only powerfully influenced by his Craft convictions. His scholarly studies of Ancient Egyptian Architecture were carried out before the works of Denon[99] and the Commission[100] appeared. As Anthony Vidler has cogently remarked, Quatremère 'exhibited all the characteristics of one who was influenced by his Masonic affiliations'[101], and some of the Gaitte illustrations (**Pls.VII.10 & 11**, p.156) have parallels in the descriptions of the mysterious Lodge visited by Ledoux and Beckford (*see* **Fig.VII.1**, p.150).

The importance of Freemasonry in the history of Neo-Classical Architecture and the Enlightenment is considerable, especially where the Egyptian Revival is concerned. The idea of Egypt as a source of knowledge of building and of all wisdom enshrouded in the supposed 'Hermetic' Mysteries was well known to Freemasonry. The Craft of Freemasonry itself was traced allegedly to Egypt, the Israelites were said to have learned the skills of building in stone from the Egyptians (in another version, Abraham passed on secrets to the Egyptians), and there was a close perceived connection between the story of captivity in Egypt, the use of the Cubit as a unit of measurement, and the legends of the Craft and of the Solomonic Temple. In most of the legends, Freemasonry, as the Craft involved with Geometry, building with stone, measurement, and the creation of Architecture, was also the guardian of sacred esoteric knowledge passed to Mankind from the Creator. It should be observed that myths have often played an enormous rôle in history, for what is generally believed is a potent force, even if untrue. The evolution of a myth must necessitate invention, and its encapsulation in a story has its parallels in some sort of ritual adjustment, a kind of transformation of barbarous legend to civility, a domestication, a formalisation. If the early history of the legends of Freemasonry is obscure, it has most certainly been further enveloped in thick mists by invention and obfuscation. But myth is often a deliberate cultural construct, and so it would appear was the case with the Craft. Myth certainly flavoured the phenomenon known as the Scottish Enlightenment, which had a profoundly different taste when compared with the French Enlightenment, the German *Aufklärung*, the American, or the English Enlightenments[102].

Freemasonry in the latter half of the eighteenth century reflected many of the philosophical, moral, political, artistic, and intellectual currents of the Enlightenment in its various guises. Liberalism and progressive notions were implicit in Freemasonic ideals of the Brotherhood and Perfectability of Man[103], and many Continental Freemasons seem to have held little brief for the Roman Catholic hierarchy and its reactionary and condemnatory pronouncements: indeed, many of the threats, denunciations, Bulls, and the like seem to have had little effect during the apogee of the Enlightenment.

A ceremonial setting using motifs from Ancient Egypt would seem to be the logical result of the widespread acceptance of Freemasonry during the Age of the Enlightenment, given Freemasonic beliefs in Egypt as the source of so much skill and wisdom, yet an Egyptianising theme in Freemasonry does not appear to have surfaced much before c.1750. Although overt Egyptianising décor was used to great effect in the Grand Royal Arch Chapter Room, Freemasons' Hall, 17 Molesworth Street, Dublin, and in the design for the Chapter Room of the Supreme Grand Royal Arch Chapter of Scotland, 78 Queen Street, Edinburgh, Lodges in the British Isles do not appear to have embraced the Egyptian Revival style with much enthusiasm. Continental Lodges, however, notably those in France and what was to become Belgium, acquired a fair share of Egyptianising features, especially on the designs of Craft Certificates and the like, where pyramids, Egyptian columns, palm-trees, sphinxes, and Egyptian Hathor-or-Isis-headed capitals were much in evidence[104] (**Pls.VII.12 & 13**, pp.157-8).

Now why should this have been the case? There were four main influences in the transformation. In 1731 the Abbé Jean Terrasson published his *Séthos, histoire ou vie tirée des monumens anecdotes de l'ancienne Égypte. Traduite d'un*

---

95 Gould (1884-87) **iii** 285.
96 Light Love Life.
97 A snake in circular form, with its tail in its mouth, suggesting an eternal recurring process, or immortality.
98 Beyer & Piana (1969) plate 73.
99 Denon (1802).
100 Commission des Sciences et Arts d'Égypte (1809-28).
101 Vidler (1987) 93.

102 *See* Himmelfarb (2008) for different Enlightenments, and *see* Trevor-Roper (2008) for the myths of Scotland's identity (including pithy remarks on tartans, Clan affiliations, 'Ossian', and the curious case of the 'Sobieski Stuarts').
103 Curl (2006b) 51, Curl (2006d) 5-6.
104 I owe these to T. O. Haunch, who kindly showed me a selection of them in Freemasons' Hall in the 1980s.

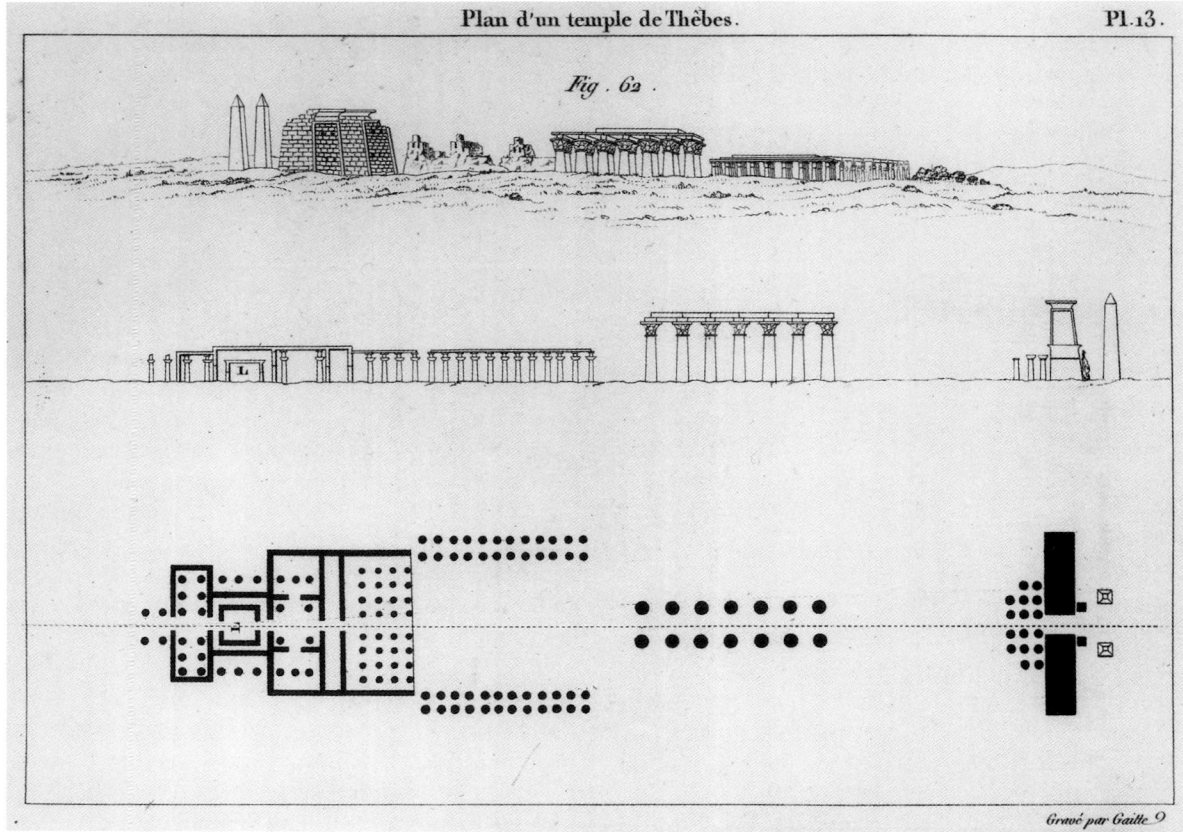

Pl.VII.10 Egyptian temple at Thebes. Engraving by Gaitte (Plate 13), from Quatremère de Quincy (1803), showing the pronounced axial routes, with pylons, obelisks, colonnades, courts, and inner parts. Such a route had its parallels in Terrasson's work and in the Lodge of Ledoux which William Beckford claimed he had visited (*see* **Fig.VII.1**, p.150). The approach to the whole complex between two obelisks suggested the Two Pillars of Freemasonry (*Collection JSC*).

Pl.VII.11 Plan of Egyptian temple at Thebes, from Quatremère de Quincy (1803), Plate 14, showing the clearly defined axial route (*after* Pococke [1743-9]) and a view of ruins at Thebes (*after* Norden [1757 and 1780]). Engraving by Gaitte. The strong axial route, progressing from the outside between two obelisks, then two pylon-towers, then into a great columned hall, then along a way defined by columns, then into a court open to the sky, and then through a series of rooms to the Holy of Holies obviously had resonances for Freemasons (*Collection JSC*).

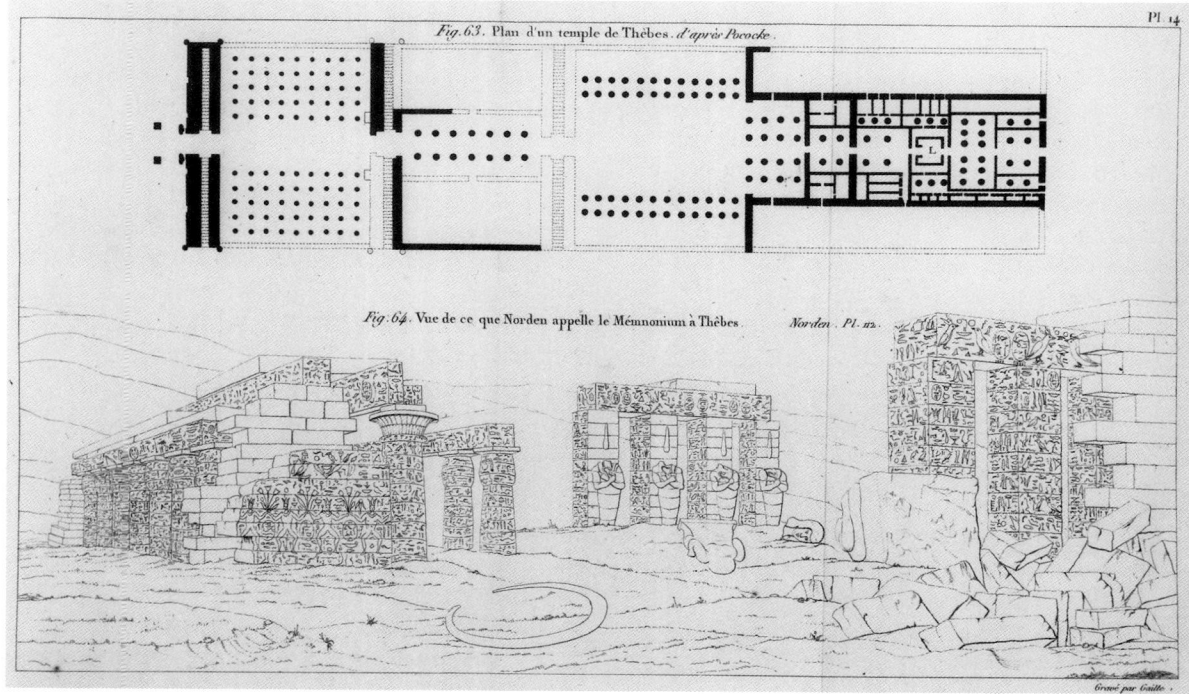

Pl.VII.12 A design for a Masonic certificate for Lodges under the Grand Orient of France, from a nineteenth-century printer's sample-book. Jachin and Boaz have acquired pomegranates in the form of Isiac lotus-crowns. Other features include the sphinx with *Ankh*, Masonic tools, pyramid, Nilotic plants, Isiac fountain, *putto* with inverted torch symbolising the extinguishing of life, winged boy with lotus-crown holding a club with serpent coiled around it (Resurrection, Harpocrates/Horus, and Silence), Serapis/Osiris, and three-headed serpent holding the Key, Crown, and Sword. Note the sarcophagus in the rock-work cave (*UGLE*).

manuscript grec[105]. This very prolix book, by a translator of Diodorus Siculus, concerns *Séthos*, an Egyptian Prince, who is initiated into ancient Mysteries, and who, after many travels and adventures, retires to a temple of initiates. The book was much read, and was often cited as if it were a standard work on Ancient Egyptian matters. English[106] and German translations appeared in 1732, an Italian version in 1734, and yet another German edition in 1777. Thomas Moore's romance, *The Epicurean* (1827) contains ideas borrowed from *Séthos*, and it was in a review of Moore's work by Thomas Love Peacock that the connection between *Séthos* and *Die Zauberflöte* (1790) appears to have been first noticed[107]. Like many other works of the period, Terrasson's book is Rococo, in the sense of its central idea being dressed up in 'exotic' garments. Yet the description of the Isiac Mysteries in *Séthos* is very long and detailed: throughout the book the idea of Ancient Egypt as the fount of all wisdom and of the 'Hermetic' tradition is stressed. *Séthos* is set in the Egypt of Antiquity, and the Prince-hero undergoes various trials for his initiation into the Mysteries of Isis. In mythology, Isis and Osiris, husband and wife, sister and brother, are mostly venerated together, but after the murder of Osiris and his dismemberment, Isis reassembled his body, although she was unable to locate his generative organs, so conceived and gave birth to Horus/Harpocrates by supernatural means. The Mysteries were those of Isis alone, although even in Graeco-Roman Egyptian cults, Serapis/Osiris and Isis were often venerated in different parts of the same temple complexes[108].

In *Séthos* various Enlightenment notions are well to the fore, including disapproval of the wielding of arbitrary (and therefore illegitimate) power by princes. Terrasson's initiates into the Isiac Mysteries even have the right to sit in judgement on dead princes to establish if their acts in life were benevolent or not: if they were not, their bodies were denied the rites of burial, and this denial, according to Terrasson, was sufficient to keep the ancient Kings within the rule of dispassionate law[109]. *Séthos*, once he has passed his various trials, has his hereditary claims

---

105 *See* Terrasson (1731).
106 Lediard (Tr.) (1732).
107 Brett-Smith & Jones (1924-34) **ix** 46-9.
108 *See* Curl (2005) *passim*.
109 Lediard (Tr.) (1732) **i** 34.

Plate VII.13 A design for a Masonic certificate for Lodges under the Grand Orient of France, from a nineteenth-century printer's sample-book. Note the pyramids, palm-trees, Masonic tools, Egyptian Architecture, and figure of Charity, with Ancient of Days. Note also the rock-work cavern with cave on the left (UGLE).

to authority confirmed by his merits[110], so the initiation into the Isiac Mysteries makes him part of a body of men all of whom have passed various tests, and all of whom are distinguished by moral and intellectual excellence. Terrasson's initiates never tell lies, but they never reveal secrets either, just as Apuleius, in *The Golden Ass*, ends his book with an initiation into the Mysteries of Isis, yet leaves his readers in some confusion about what the initiation rites or Mysteries actually were[111]. The tradition of letting on there were secrets, yet concealing them, is of considerable antiquity: it certainly existed in the Graeco-Roman World, and probably was also present in earlier civilisations. *Séthos* has copious references to authorities in Antiquity, and the book is so steeped in Classical learning that it acquired a status rather more august than perhaps it deserved.

That *Séthos* appeared at the right time was undeniable, for in Europe had begun the cult of 'Primitive' society and the attribution to it of supposedly purer morals, simpler virtues, and more 'natural' poetry than could be found in the 'artificial' 'cultivated' civilisation of the West. This was the Age of Rousseau, of Herder, and of the German *Sturm und Drang* movement: it was a new climate in which the cults of the Sublime and of Melancholy (partly to be satisfied by the outpourings of the 'Graveyard' Poets, of which more below) sought new stimuli in the search for 'Primitive Man' and his creations before the March of Progress obliterated them. This explains the mania for the supposed creations of 'Ossian' which will be discussed later[112].

As part of this curious hunger for the 'Primitive' (especially if it could be perceived as mysterious and largely unknown), things Egyptian undoubtedly had their attractions. *Séthos* was one powerful stimulus, but Cagliostro was another. An unscrupulous charlatan, 'Count' Cagliostro (or Giuseppe Balsamo) had passed a dissolute and criminal youth, and is supposed to have studied alchemy in the East. In Europe, he peddled drugs and potions, and is said to have become a Freemason in London in the 1770s, although another version is that he was initiated at the Pyramids in Egypt. He later was claimed to have become Grand Master of a Lodge in Paris to which a Temple of Isis was attached, and to be Deputy

---

110 Lediard (Tr.) (1732) **i** 187.
111 Apuleius Madaurensis (1924) 333-59.

112 Trevor-Roper (2008) Ch. 4.

of the 'Grand Kophta', who had not been seen by anyone. However, Cagliostro's Egyptian Rite acquired a Supreme Council in 1785 in Paris, the year in which he announced that both men and women should be entitled to take part in, and have knowledge of, the Mysteries of the Pyramids he claimed to have discovered in Egypt[113]. In 1785 Cagliostro was implicated in the Affair of the Diamond Necklace: briefly, Jeanne de Saint-Rémy de Valois became (1784) the mistress of Louis-René-Édouard, Cardinal de Rohan, and persuaded her lover that his attempts to ingratiate himself with the Queen[114] were welcome. The Parisian jewellers Charles-Auguste Boehmer & Paul Bassenge had spent many years collecting precious stones for a necklace they hoped to sell to Marie-Jeanne Bécu, Comtesse Du Barry, mistress of King Louis XV, but failed to do so, and turned their attention to the new Queen after 1774. Rohan's mistress, her husband (Antoine-Nicolas de la Motte), another of her lovers (Rétaux de Villette), a prostitute named 'Marie-Nicole le Guay d'Oliva', and Cagliostro were all implicated when the Cardinal was relieved of a very large sum of money and de la Motte began selling the precious stones in Paris and London. The ensuing scandal led to the arrest of the various parties: Rohan was acquitted[115], as was d'Oliva, but Jeanne de la Motte was whipped, branded, and imprisoned, while Cagliostro and de Villette were exiled. De la Motte (who had been sentenced to the galleys *in absentia*) prudently remained in London, only returning to France much later, but his wife did irreparable damage to the Queen by publishing falsehoods[116] about her sexual proclivities (these scandalous stories were eagerly lapped up by the Mob): Jeanne de la Motte died after falling from a window in London[117], so did not survive the Queen, who was guillotined in 1793.

This whole unsavoury affair was typical of Cagliostro, who eventually was imprisoned in connection with other frauds, and died in gaol. Nevertheless, his so-called 'Egyptian' rites and rituals were adopted in some French and German Lodges, although British Freemasons regarded him and his brand of supposed Freemasonry as fraudulent. In Lodges under Cagliostro's aegis the 'Egyptian' rite owed much to the legend of the descent of Orpheus into the Underworld: candidates were blindfolded, then submitted to ritual trials by Fire, Water, and Air[118]. Yet Cagliostro was not by any means alone: there were other fashionably exotic offshoots of Freemasonry with extravagant rituals that catered for a society in search of esoteric thrills[119].

The third influence in the transformation alluded to above was that of Carl (or Karl) Friedrich Köppen who published (1778) a curious work on the rites of initiation of Egyptian priests which became influential in Continental circles of the Craft[120]. It was translated into French by the Chevalier de Bérage, and into English by at least two authors. It appears in Manly Palmer Hall's work on *Freemasonry of the Ancient Egyptians*[121]. However, it seems that Köppen was not solely responsible for these texts: Bernhard Hymmen also contributed, and the result was an alternative history of Freemasonry in which the Grand Master was the Biblical Ham, who settled in Egypt and took the name Menes. Köppen and Hymmen's Order was called the *Afrikanische Bauherren*, and claimed to possess secret knowledge passed down from Ancient Egypt[122]. These hoary matters could fill a book on their own, but the subject of different degrees and the strange world of occult practices curiously rife in France during the Enlightenment can be followed in several publications[123].

From the various descriptions of 'Egyptian' rites it seems they were supposed to have been derived from Isiac ceremonies in Ancient Egypt and the Graeco-Roman World. An Antique pavement of mosaics from Antioch, for example, shows the *Mors Voluntaria*, when the initiate goes fearlessly towards the unsheathed sword, the important moment of initiation in the House of Mysteries of Isis[124]. The idea of a trial, even a voluntary death, where faith triumphs, has its parallels in the literature of Freemasonry, Isiac and Freemasonic ritual, and Christian Martyrology. We have noted the Beckford/Ledoux garden, route, and buildings, and there appear to have been other curiosities, linking the past to the present and the future, and harking back to the 'Primitive' and to mysterious themes from ancient civilisations. Justine Wynne, Countess Rosenberg-Orsini, for example, described in *Alticchiero*[125] the villa of that name which had a Canopus as well as other exotic features: she had been the mistress of the prominent Freemasons Giovanni Giacomo Casanova de Seingalt and Andrea Memmo. There had been a Canopus too at Hadrian's Villa at Tivoli, and it is clear that aspects of Freemasonry with an Egyptianising flavour could be found not only in rituals and buildings, but in gardens as well.

William Beckford moved in the circle of Justine Wynne for a time in the 1780s, and in 1781-2 he employed Philippe-Jacques de Loutherbourg to transform rooms at Fonthill Abbey, Wiltshire, into exotic 'Arabian' sets, and also to design an 'Egyptian Rout', one of Beckford's extravagant parties. Loutherbourg was involved with Alchemy, Mysticism, and the Occult, and later in his career (until 1789) offered faith-healing services through 'Heavenly and Divine Influx'[126]. Loutherbourg left England for a time with

---

113 McIntosh (1975) 30-31. See also *Collectanea* **v**/2 (1954) 165-215, and Caillet (1994) 17-19. For Cagliostro see also McCalman (2003).
114 Marie Antoinette (1755-93), formerly Archduchess Maria Antonia of Austria, Queen of France from 1774.
115 Though exiled.
116 Motte (1790) *passim*.
117 She was buried in the churchyard of St Mary, Lambeth.
118 Lalande (1964) *passim*.
119 For these curious matters *see* Forestier (1970) and Forestier (*Ed.*) (n.d.).
120 Köppen (*Ed.*) (1766) and Köppen (1821). *See also* Bérage (1776).
121 Hall (1937).
122 *The Kneph: Official Journal of the Antient and Primitive Rite of Masonry* (1882) **ii** 15-22.
123 Especially McIntosh (1975) and Bogdan (2006, 2007a, 2007b). Perceptions, therefore, that the 'Enlightenment' on the Continent was devoid of fog, are often off the mark.
124 Witt (1971) Plate 34.
125 Rosenberg-Orsini (1787). Sometimes Wynne is known as Orsini-Rosenberg.
126 *ODNB* **xxxiv** (2004) 489-90.

Cagliostro, so there was a definite connection between 'Egyptian Masonry' and Beckford through Cagliostro and Loutherbourg. There is a further Freemasonic link in that the great Soane designed Loutherbourg's handsome monument in the churchyard of St Nicholas, Chiswick, Middlesex.

Beckford admired the work of Piranesi too, seeing in it Sublime and 'Gothic' qualities. As the theories of Laugier and Herder, the influence of Piranesi, and the rediscovery of the Antique, first of Roman (given further impetus by the rediscovery of Herculaneum, Pompeii, and Stabia), then of Greek, and finally Egyptian examples, drew Architects away from the frivolities of the Rococo to a more severe expression, clear geometrical shapes were exploited. The frontiers of taste were pushed further towards greater ruggedness, massiveness, primitiveness, and the search for 'Simplicity' led naturally to Egyptian and even Prehistoric exemplars.

French Architects began to experiment with huge forms, simple massing, and monumental symmetry in the Academies of Paris and Rome, using public buildings, cemeteries, and vast civic structures as the vehicles for their designs. Boullée was one of the visionaries who experimented with unadorned walls, simplified forms, and massive megalomanic scale derived from Piranesi's deliberately inflated views of Rome and other engravings showing real buildings. Boullée's designs for cenotaphs and cemeteries often depicted projects in which Egyptian motifs played some part. Huge blank walls emphasised the terror and finality of Death, expressive of his ideas of an Architecture suggestive of its purpose: he designed Temples of Death, intended to chill the hearts of those who beheld them. Such buildings were intended to withstand the ravages of Time, to be perfectly symmetrical, and included enormous Neo-Classical sarcophagi (which themselves became gigantic buildings), pyramids, and funerary triumphal arches. By cutting all ornament to the very minimum, Boullée gave his buildings a chilly, immutable character. Cone-shaped cenotaphs incorporating themes based on both domes and pyramids, with obelisks and cypresses much in evidence; monuments with flat surfaces, bare and unadorned, the only 'decoration' consisting of a play of frightening shadows; and gloomy, terrifying images incorporating abstractions and paraphrases recur in his works. Terror and desolation, finality, stillness, and a monumentality of overwhelming vastness can be found in plenty in Boullée's designs which influenced a generation of young Architects. They were also a powerful influence on Albert Speer, who designed vast structures for Adolf Hitler's Third Reich.

Thus the fourth influence connected with what has been described as 'Egyptomania' was concerned with the search for the Primitive, and for an Architecture that was stripped to its essentials from which all fripperies had been eliminated. The Neo-Classical movement turned first to the study of Roman Antiquity to provide models for modern Architecture: in other words Renaissance exemplars, even those of Palladio, were perceived as corrupt, so genuine works of the distant past began to be measured, drawn, and investigated. Then the attempts to find something even more severe led to surveys of the buildings of Ancient Greece, and so, stimulated by the writings of Winckelmann and others, Hellenic models became the subject for scholarly study, and, when Architectural design went even further towards stereometrical purity and the expression of the Sublime, the possibilities offered by Ancient Egyptian and even Prehistoric structures seemed to find many admirers among Architects. Thus Egypt, a mysterious land made even more exotic by its unreadable hieroglyphs, offered attractions that could not be resisted. Its associations with *Séthos*, the Mysteries, Freemasonry, Hermeticism, and much else made it a magnet, and the first stirrings of what eventually was to lead to the French invasion of Egypt (with its important discoveries that gave birth to Egyptology) could be detected.

Ledoux and Lequeu

The work of two Architects will now be considered. Much has been written about Claude-Nicolas Ledoux[127], and there can be no doubt that he was profoundly influenced by esoteric influences current at the time. The alleys in the garden which Ledoux visited with Beckford (assuming such a visit actually occurred) were lined with piles of worked and unworked wood, and some of the piles were in the form of 'Primitive Huts' with thatched roofs: Laugier, Freemasonry, Rousseau, and others were influences one way or another. It is clear that the essence of such places was connected with association, memory, allusion, and ultimately, mnemonic ideas, and that regeneration, improvement through contact with Nature, and notions of a better society, a better world, were well to the fore.

At the Ideal Town Ledoux proposed at Chaux, Ledoux allowed for structures where various esoteric groups might meet[128]. At Chaux (which means 'lime', a fact curiously ignored by most commentators), ideas of wholeness, peace, and advancement of crafts were to be promoted in ritual 'temples' (including one phallic-shaped [on plan] whore-house, the *Oïkéma*, in which young men would be initiated in the rites of sexual congress) dedicated to them. Freemasonic emphases on the importance of keeping vows would also play rôles in promoting marital fidelity in union and harmony. There was much else besides, all conceived within a remarkably inventive series of stripped Neo-Classical buildings (**Pls.VII.14-17**, pp.161-3).

Ledoux and Chaux, therefore, can be seen as the forerunners of theorists such as François-Marie-Charles Fourier and his notion of *Phalanstères* in which the fundamental harmony to be found in society, animal

---

127 See Vidler (1990), which contains a large Bibliography.
128 Ledoux (1804) 188, but *see* also Vidler (1987) 211, n. 73 and *passim*. *See* also Vidler (1990) *passim*, a superb study of Ledoux that is hardly ever likely to be superseded.

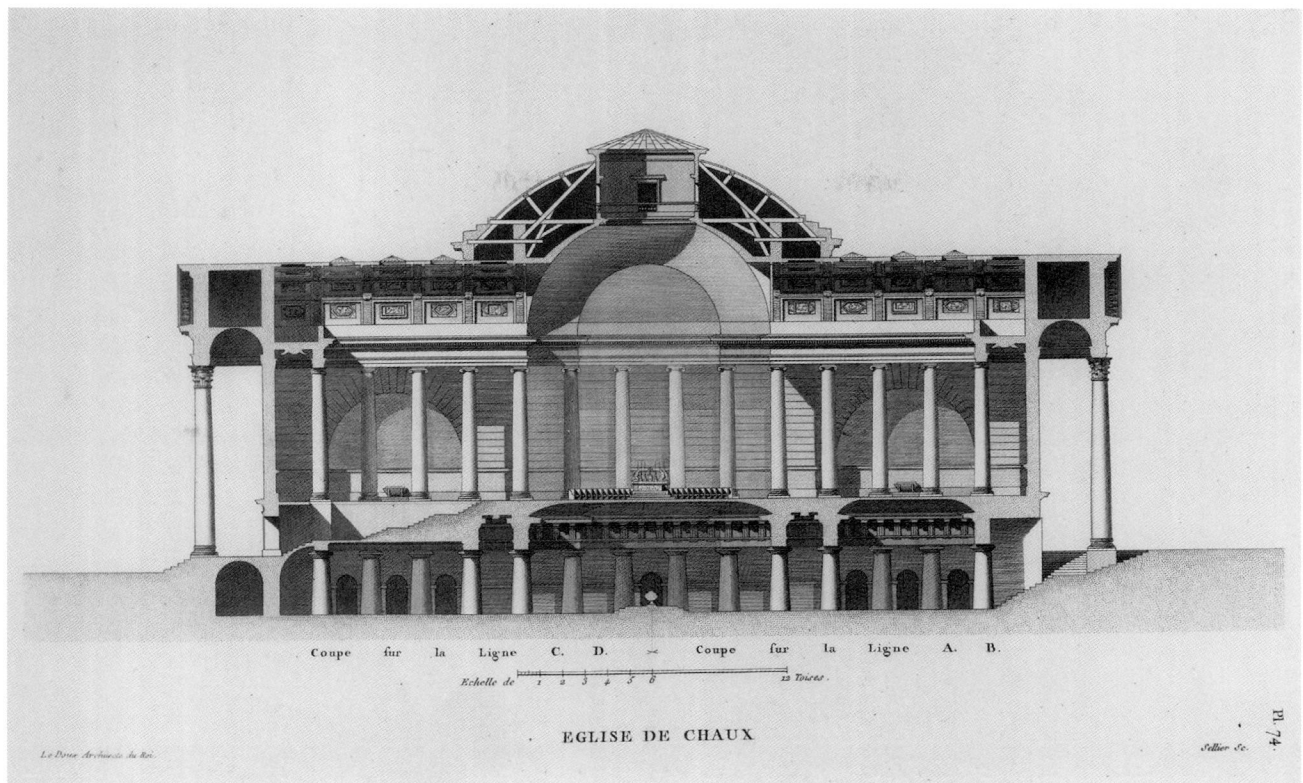

Pl.VII.14 Section through the proposed church at Chaux (Lime), engraved by François-Noël Sellier (b. 1737) from Ledoux (1804), Plate 74. The crypt, with its primitivist unfluted Doric columns, and the church interior lit only by the oculus, are more suited, perhaps, for use as Masonic Lodges than as Christian places of worship. Here the Supreme Deity might be venerated, and the crypt might well have been designed for use by a cult of some sort. The building seems to have been intended as a didactic means by which the essentials of a rational Deism might be conveyed in order to bolster individual and social morality of the proposed town (*SJSM*).

life, organic life, and the material universe would be encouraged to develop. Fourier believed that misery and vice sprang from unnatural restraints imposed on the gratification of desires, and that the only route to happiness and virtue lay through the full, free development of human nature and the unrestrained indulgence of human passions. His beliefs might be economically described as 'Natural Optimism': ultimately, though, such concerns with experimentation led to coercive notions that tried to improve untidy Humanity by means of institutionalised Totalitarianism of one sort or another. Out of supposedly 'Liberal Idealism' comes regimentation, just as out of Reason comes Irrationality, as the Terror demonstrated with awesome and irrefutable effect. Fourier himself noted that Freemasonry had been like a precious stone, disdained, warped, corrupted, and underestimated by society because its true value was not even recognised[129]. It is not widely known that Fourier perceived Freemasonry as offering a possible framework for a renewed and transformed society, and, like Ledoux, saw scope for 'associations' of people which could be expanded infinitely to lead to major social reforms (an idea central to Illuminism in Central Europe). These notions led to that chimaerical goal of the Perfectability of Man. Places where people could meet for social occasions could play a civilising rôle: by example, by association, and by regeneration, society itself would be reformed, it was proposed, on rational, harmonious, optimistic, benevolent non-superstitious lines. Some of these ideas were to be found in Fourier's exposition of his *Phalanstère*, published in *Le Nouveau Monde*[130], and Pierre-Simon Ballanche also promoted variants of them. Jean-Baptiste-André Godin, in his *Familistère*[131] at Guise, and in his *Solutions Sociales*[132] took Fourier's proposals further in terms of practical association.

If some of Ledoux's designs were startling in their imagery, the esquisses of Jean-Jacques Lequeu are even stranger. He produced an extraordinary drawing of a Lodge, which he unaccountably called a 'Gothic House' (but then Beckford associated Piranesi with Gothic too), illustrating a route along an axis based on Ancient Egyptian temples, and which is obviously derived from Terrasson's description in *Séthos* in that it shows a three-stage place of initiation (**CPl.VII.I**, p.165). Lequeu drew an elaborate section, much ornamented with quotations from Terrasson, with a huge shaft in which sits an iron cage (**Pl.VII.18**, p.164). The three-headed Cerberus guards these chambers with corbelled roofs (very Piranesian-

---

129 Fourier (1808) 195 and *passim*. See also Vidler (1987) 102 and 211 n.82.
130 Fourier (1829).
131 Curl (1983) 59, 159, 179.
132 Godin (1871).

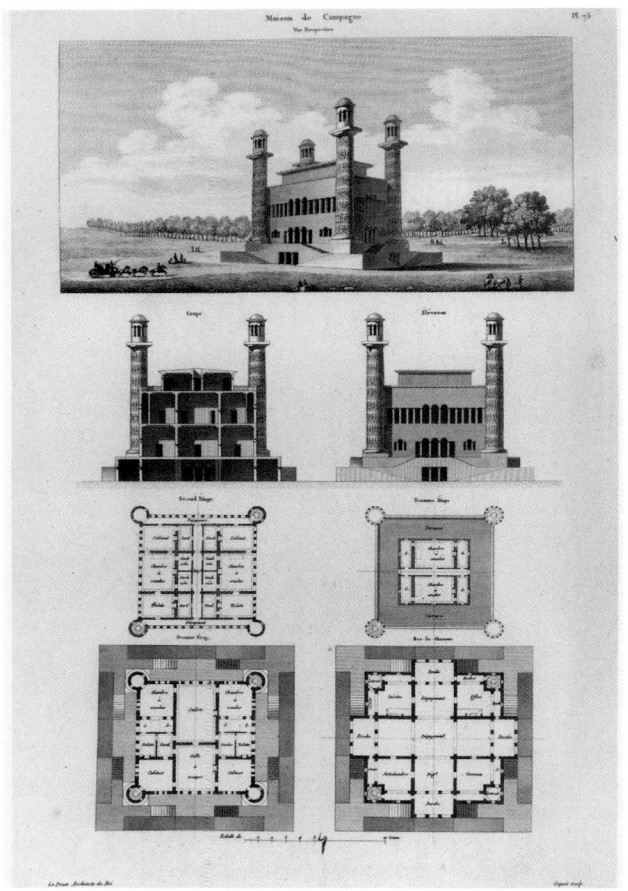

Egyptian), then the route leads to a huge chamber above which are metallic tools for torture: this huge chamber is a furnace for the Trial by Fire, and looks like a kiln (**Pl. VII.19**, p.164). Three more bays of Piranesian corbel-vaulted chambers lead to steps down to another chamber filled with water (the Trial by Water) (**Pl.VII.20**, p.164). Steps lead up to a space where the aspirant could be hoisted through the air to reach the sanctuary dominated by Isis (who looks more like Britannia, and indeed represents Wisdom/Minerva)[133]: the chamber contains Cups of Memory and Forgetfulness[134] (**Pl.VII.21**, p.164). These Cups refer to mnemonic techniques developed from the sixteenth century (and were probably a lot earlier), and we must remember that the Art of Memory was significant in Freemasonry. The Trials by Fire, Water, and Air are also illustrated in *La Franche-Maçonnerie Rendue à sa véritable Origine, ou l'Antiquité de la Franche-Maçonnerie prouvée par l'explication des mystères anciens et modernes* by Alexandre-Marie Lenoir, published in Paris in 1814[135]. The source is again obviously *Séthos* (**Pl.VII.22**, p.166).

Lequeu's was clearly a very odd case, as his curious Architecture and obscene drawings (*Figures Lascives*) would suggest. He refers to the Great Architect of the Universe in

Pl.VII.15 (*left*) The House in the Country, or Temple of Memory, engraved by Coquet, from Ledoux (1804) Plate 75. This extraordinary design recalls a fortress, Trajanic columns, Palladian architecture, Greek, Roman, and Moresque Islamic themes, and much else. It can therefore be interpreted as a mnemonic of form, Architecture, and civilisation, for Ledoux himself referred to the desirability of making the different characters of works of Architecture from various civilisations known to all. The Temple of Memory was intended to be free from the prejudices of Classically-trained Architects, and suggested a wider culture, taking elements from many centuries, languages of design, and civilisations. Around the columns (which owe a debt to Fischer von Erlach's *Karlskirche* in Vienna) were to be reliefs celebrating women as Heroines, Sustainers of Mores, and Promoters of Natural Virtues: Ledoux seems to have intended the building to be a Lodge of Adoption, conceived as a *fabrique* in the park to enshrine the Virtues of Women, Memories of Childhood, and Anticipation of Death (indeed, he envisaged it as his own tomb, where he would lie in a structure where the 'virtuous passions' were ever-present) as a memorial to his mother (*SJSM*).

Pl.VII.16 (*right*) The *Panarèthéon*, or Temple of Accomplished Virtue and School of Morals, engraved by van Maëlle and Simon, from Ledoux (1804), Plate 92. It was an academy where the duties of Man were taught. The ramps leading to the upper chamber were associated with Degrees of Perfection, and around the cubic form were sculpted personifications of the Days, Hours, Graces, Reason, Wisdom, Continence, Generosity, Justice, Love, Magnanimity, Moderation, Piety, Prudence, and Temperance (the Social Virtues). Between the figures (which were to be of 'noble simplicity' informed by Greek sculpture) were inscriptions that included quotations from Oriental and Indian sources as well as from Classical Antiquity and Western philosophers. Thus Ledoux's design was to be for a Neo-Classical Temple as a mnemonic of all that was worthy and of value to society (*SJSM*).

133 The representation of the Goddess is flanked by columns of the Ionic Order, the one associated with Wisdom.
134 Vertical Section of Cellars of Gothic House in Lequeu's *Architecture Civile*, plate 156, Cabinet des Estampes, BN.
135 Lenoir (1814).

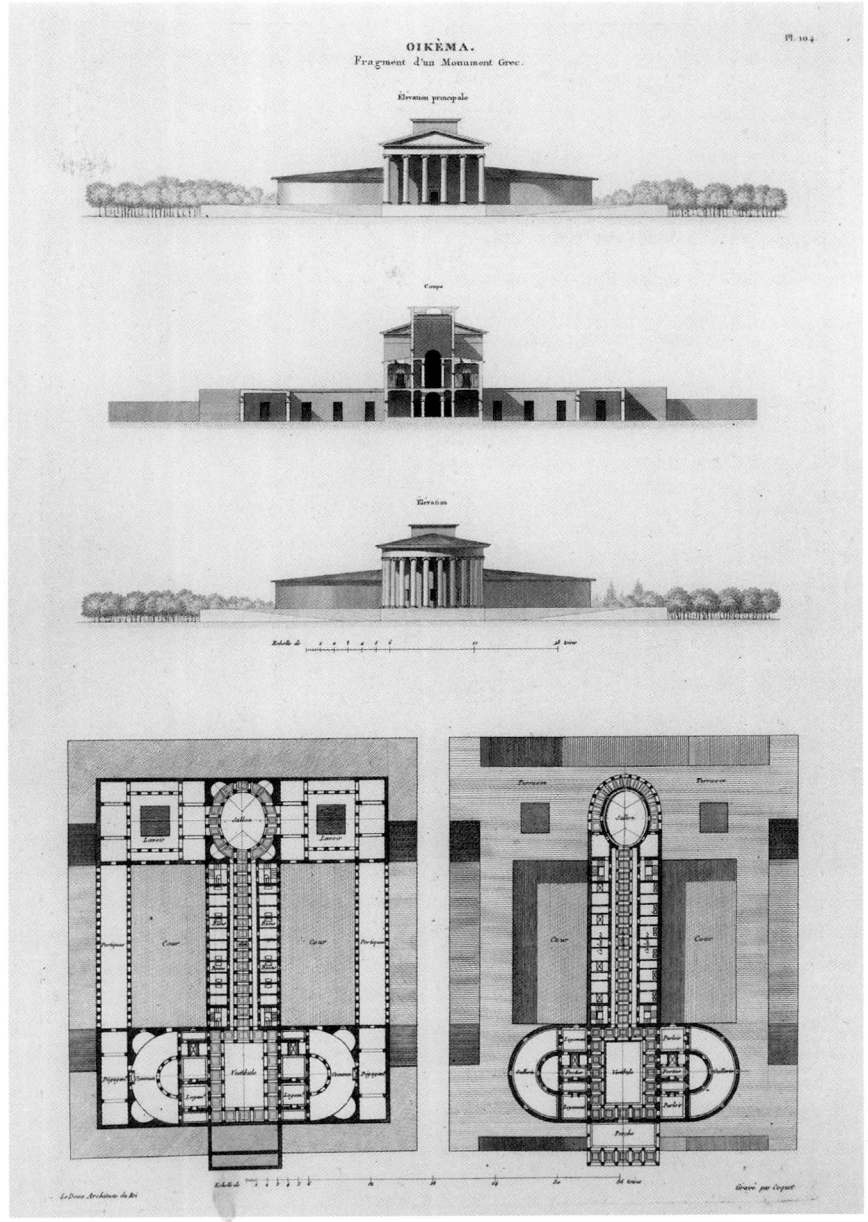

Pl.VII.17 Plans, elevations, and section of the *Oïkéma* or Temple of Sexual Instruction, at Chaux by Ledoux, engraved by Coquet. The severe Neo-Classical appearance (described by Ledoux as '*Fragment d'un Monument Grec*') belies the phallic plan-form at the upper level. In the cente of the entrance-vestibule was to be a tripod (based on that found in the ruins of the Temple of Venus) from which a pyramidal flame burned. Reliefs celebrated the 'lascivious' Roman Goddesses associated with voluptuousness, and the long corridor off which were bedrooms was a *passage d'amour* leading to an elliptical saloon from which access could be had to the baths and courts of the lower level, or to the agreeable gardens, so once again the *Oïkéma* was a *fabrique* in a designed landscape. The building only revealed its purpose in its plan, and this was a *Secret* known only to the Architect: Ledoux himself noted that the tranquil walls, with no windows, concealed the 'agitation' inside. Indeed, the *Oïkéma* was a Temple of Depravity, a Workshop of Corruption, intended to institutionalise and control prostitution as well as to instil a reaction, pointing wayward Youth towards Virtue and the Altar of Marriage. It is important to connect the concept of this *fabrique* with the myths of Virgilian Eleusinian Mysteries and Ovid's *Metamorphoses*, late-eighteenth-century eroticism, and Arcadia, suggested by the landscape in the *Val d'amour*. The Route of Initiation was thus adapted for another purpose, and although concerned with the erotic, was also intended as a teaching instrument for the encouragement of Morality and the promotion of the state of Matrimony. From Ledoux (1804) Plate 104 (SJSM).

the manuscript of 'Architecture Civile', and draws on an unexpected source, the Descriptive Geometry of Gaspard Monge, Comte de Péluse, one of the *savants* who went to Egypt with Bonaparte. Monge was Professor at the École Polytechnique in Paris, and was a member of the *Ordre des Sophisiens*, a highly élite Freemasonic Brotherhood, which seems to have had as members many of those who had been to Egypt and studied the monuments and artefacts. Monge was entombed at the *Rond-Point des Peupliers*, Père-Lachaise Cemetery, in a grand tomb in the Egyptianising style, designed by Pierre Clochard, and the mausoleum was built in 1820 (see **Pl.VIII.28**, p.198, and **XI.18**, p.300). Normand relates that those who caused the structure to be erected granted the execution to Clochard, Architect, who, in the chosen style, demonstrated the association

of Monge with the *Institut d'Égypte* and with the scientific travels and researches that resulted from its work[136]. By any standards the concept of the Egyptian Campaign (1798-1801) was extraordinary, grandiose, and breathtaking in its audacity and scope: when the French fleet sailed from Toulon in 1798, a learned Commission on the Sciences and Arts consisting of 167 eminent intellectuals under the leadership of Baron Dominique Vivant Denon accompanied the army on board. Under Denon's command were sixteen cartographers and surveyors who were to record the land and the fabric, and who were to herald the birth of modern Egyptology. These *savants* set up printing-presses, an administrative system, and drawing-offices: the work of surveying and recording had begun.

---
136 Normand (1832) 4-9.

Pl.VII.18 Detail of the first part of Lequeu's Trials by Fire, Water, and Air, shown in **CPl.VII.I**. On the left is the shaft leading down to the gate guarded by Cerberus (*BN. CE. AC, Plate 61, Fig. 156*).

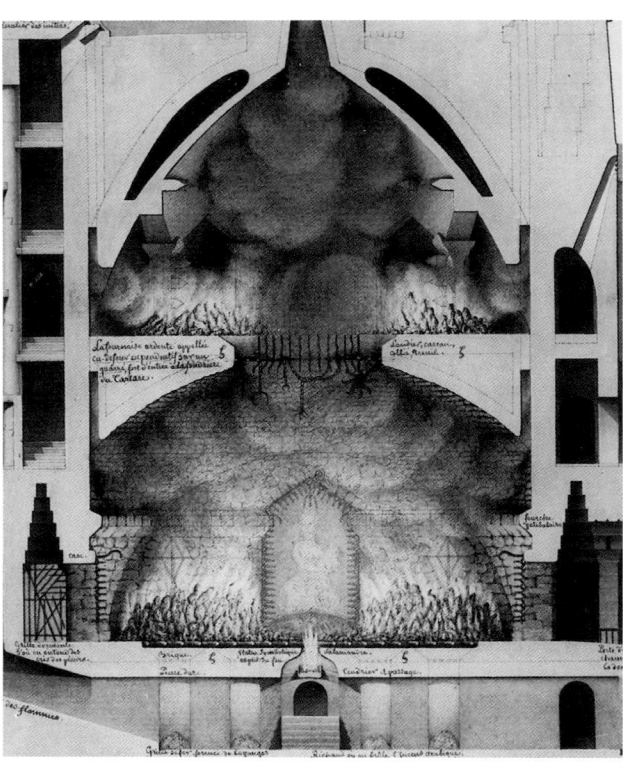

Pl.VII.19 The Trial by Fire by Lequeu, a detail from his 'Gothic House'. The form of the furnace recalls brick kilns and glass-making structures. Note the hanging chains, pincers, instruments of torture, and bays of corbelled vault in the Piranesian manner. The Trial by Fire is the '*Première Épreuve de l'aspirant*' (*BN. CE. AC, Plate 61, Fig. 156*).

Pl.VII.20 The Trial by Water by Lequeu, a detail from his 'Gothic House'. This is the '*Deuxième Épreuve*' in the tenebrous regions of the structure (*BN. CE. AC, Plate 61, Fig. 156*).

Pl.VII.21 Lequeu's *Dernière Épreuve*, or Trial by Air, in which the aspirant is hoisted up to enter the sanctuary of Wisdom in which are the brimming Cups of Memory and Forgetfulness. If the aspirant fails this last Trial he drops down into the tunnel and has to go back whence he came. This sequence of Trials (**Pls.VII.18-21**) could easily be a set for *Die Zauberflöte* (*BN. CE. AC, Plate 61, Fig. 156*).

CPl.VII.1 *Section perpendiculaire d'un souterrain de la Maison Gothique, au droit de la ligne milieu, en la largeur des mamelons et suivant la pente de la montagne.* J.-J. Lequeu's version of the Trials by Fire, Water, and Air, based on Terrasson's *Séthos*. Above the Gate of the Intrepid (*Porte des Intrépides*) is painted the inscription 'He who follows this path alone and without looking behind him' (Orpheus legend), 'will be purified by Fire and Air; and if he strives to conquer the dread of Death he will emerge from the underworld, and will behold the light once more, and will be worthy to be admitted into the company of wise men and men of valour'. On the left is a shaft leading from the Great Pyramid, then a warning inscription, the three-headed dog Cerberus, then passages with corbelled vaults (based on Piranesi's designs in *Diverse Maniere...*), then a huge kiln-like furnace for the Trial by Fire (complete with instruments of torture), then three bays of corbelled vaults recalling Piranesian forms, then the chamber for the Trial by Water. Finally, the third stage of initiation, the Trial by Air, is reached, and the initiate is hoisted to the presence of Wisdom where the brimming Cup of Oblivion and the Cup of Memory stand on an altar. This could easily be a set for *Die Zauberflöte* (BN. CE. AC, Plate 61, Fig. 156).

Laboratories, a museum, and a library were formed, and the *Institut d'Égypte* was founded. Denon's energy and enthusiasm were unbounded, and in a remarkably short time a vast amount of material had been gathered, accurate surveys had been made, and the foundations laid for the two great monuments of the campaign: Denon's *Voyage*[137] and the gigantic *Description*[138]. Apart from these wonderful publications, the campaign led to the researches that unravelled the mystery of the meaning of hieroglyphs. A piece of carved basalt was discovered in 1799 by a French engineer[139] at Fort Julien on the Rosetta north of the River Nile: it was inscribed in hieroglyphs, in a cursive script that looked something like Arabic, and in Greek. This *stele* was dated 196 BC from the reign of Ptolemy V Epiphanes. Dr Thomas Young seems to have been the first to realise that hieroglyphs included both phonetic and pictorial signs[140], sent his conclusions to the French scholar Jean-François Champollion in 1814, and published his findings in a supplement to the *Encyclopaedia Britannica* in 1819. When Giovanni Belzoni discovered (1815) an obelisk with base-block (both of which had inscriptions in hieroglyphs

137 Denon (1802).
138 Commission des Sciences et Arts d'Égypte (1809-28). *See* Select Bibliography.
139 Captain Pierre-François-Xavier Bouchard.
140 Young (1823).

Pl.VII.22 The Trials by Fire, Water, and Air for the Reception of Initiates in Memphis. A plate from Lenoir (1814), showing the ceremonies of initiation described in *Séthos*, and purporting to apply to contemporary initiation practice of Freemasons. The setting is subterranean, mysterious, and unrelentingly Egyptian. On the right an initiate passes through fire, then water, and on the left is being hoisted through the air by an apparatus similar to that shown in **Pl.VII.21**, p.164. Design by Jean-Michel Moreau (the Younger) engraved by L. Petit (*Collection JSC*).

and Greek), and brought it[141] to England for the collection of the Antiquary William John Bankes, Champollion realised Young was right, and began to enlarge Young's list of correctly identified hieroglyphs. Also working on copies of the texts on the 'Rosetta Stone' at the same time were Baron Antoine-Isaac Silvestre de Sacy and Johan David Åkerblad. By September 1822 Champollion had concluded that hieroglyphs were partly ideographic and partly phonetic, and in 1828, accompanied by Nestor L'Hôte[142] and an Italian team led by Ippolito Rosellini[143], Champollion visited Egypt to copy and collect texts. He also found he was able to read these having devised an Alphabet of Hieroglyphs which he published[144]. A centuries-old mystery had been solved[145].

The invasion of Egypt in 1798 had been planned in the greatest secrecy, and the supposed aim was to liberate Egypt from Ottoman rule and thereby menace British India and threaten British notions of the balance of power. Furthermore, it was proposed that French engineers would cut a huge canal through the isthmus of Suez, and thus spread French influence to Asia and Africa. Almost immediately Napoléon was compared with Alexander and Octavian[146]. Those in the know about where the French expedition was heading had read texts such as *Lettres sur l'Égypte*[147] by Claude-Étienne Savary (1750-88), and Napoléon himself had a copy of *Voyage en Syrie et en Égypte*[148]

by Constantin-François de Chasseboeuf, Comte de Volney, in which the monuments of Upper Egypt, largely buried in the sands, were mentioned as being ready for discovery.

However, it has to be said that the immense efforts made by the French to record Egyptian Antiquities, facts about Egypt, Ancient Egyptian Architecture and artefacts, etc., had very little to do with military strategy. The sub-plots (generally passed over in silence most commentators) were to find the secrets of the Ancients (especially the secrets concerning power) and to elevate Napoléon as a modern Alexander, a modern Augustus, over the French dream of an *Empire Mussulman*. Nevertheless, there was also an element of genuine altruism in the Egyptian enterprise which the British, then and now, have found difficult to understand or appreciate[149]. And behind that altruism was a deeply-felt passion for the acquisition of knowledge, to understand the world, and not just the modern world either: the spirit of the *philosophes* permeated the aims of the Egyptian expedition, and the very large number of the *savants* connected with the Craft of Freemasonry was no accident[150]. Although Monge's body no longer lies in his Egyptianising tomb (it was translated to the *Panthéon* in 1989), other men associated with the Egyptian campaign were also entombed at Père-Lachaise: they included Champollion himself and Joseph Fourier, first Secretary of the *Institut de l'Égypte*, and Edme François Jomard, member of the *Commission* and of the *Institut*, and one of the most important personalities (with Fourier) behind the realisation of the great *Description de l'Égypte*. Interestingly, Monge, Champollion, and Fourier were all entombed in Division No 18: eighteen is the Degree of

---

141 It was the first Ancient Egyptian obelisk of any size to reach the British Isles.
142 L'Hôte (1836, 1840).
143 Rosellini (1832-44, 1925).
144 Champollion (1822, 1833, 1841).
145 For details see Curl (2005) *passim*.
146 Herold (1962) Chapter 1.
147 Savary (1785-6).
148 Volney (1787).

149 See Clayton (1982), Conner (*Ed.*) (1983), and Marlowe (1971).
150 Eugène Warmenbol first drew my attention to this and to the *Ordre des Sophisiens*, an act of generosity for which I am most grateful.

the Rose-Croix, the number of those who watched over Hiram's grave, and three (Harmony, Friendship, Concord, Peace, and Temperance, a Perfect Number) multiplied by six (Health and Justice, and perfect because it could be divided by both two and three, and because 1+2+3=6). In other words, 18 has an esoteric significance far beyond a convenient label for a Division in a Cemetery.

Many find these curious aspects of the Napoleonic-*Savants* investigations of things Egyptian to be beyond them, preferring the more mundane strategic-military arguments. The problem is that, by ignoring what here has been termed the 'sub-plot', many artefacts produced by the French cannot be explained, for not only are there the great works of Denon and of the Commission to be accounted for, but the Egyptianising ephemera and not-so-ephemeral objects do not make sense if it were all only a matter of war, threats to interests, or geo-political planning. A case in point is the French Master-Mason's apron with busts of Cambacérès and Joseph Bonaparte set on Jachin and Boaz with an Egyptianising Temple in the centre, an obelisk, pylon-towers, and a pyramid (**Pl.VII.23**): that Freemasonry, the Bonapartes, and Egypt were closely connected is made overt by such objects which are not uncommon. Things Egyptian also informed numerous architectural designs.

Pl.VII.23 Early nineteenth-century French Master Mason's apron printed from an engraved plate. The busts on Jachin (*left*) and Boaz (*right*) are, respectively, those of Jean-Jacques-Régis Cambacérès, Duc de Parme from 1808, who replaced Louis Bonaparte as Joint Grand Master of the Grand Orient of France in 1805, and Joseph Bonaparte, nominated Joint Grand Master in 1804. Note Jachin and Boaz entwined with spirals of flowers, the Egyptian temple, obelisk, pyramid, pylon-towers, and chequerboard 'Mosaic' floor. Cambacérès became Second Consul under Bonaparte in 1799: it is likely the apron dates from *c*.1806. Note the pyramidal top to a cubic ashlar immediately to the left of Jachin, which could easily be mistaken for the top of a buried obelisk (UGLE).

Lequeu's work drew on Egyptian motifs far more than did Ledoux. It has come under scrutiny by a number of scholars[151], and is perhaps even more baffling because we know so little about the man. Duboy claimed that Lequeu 'intended to impose on his public a masonic initiation, which we can only describe as *frivolous*'[152]. All the plates in Lequeu's 'Architecture Civile'[153] are liberally annotated in his neat bureaucratic hand, but these (and the mass of newspaper cuttings and other documents in the collection) obscure rather than clarify. It does seem that in the meticulous drawings of imaginary buildings, details, instruments, weird self-portraits (reminiscent of the sculptures of Franz Xaver Messerschmidt, who probably *did* suffer from a psychotic illness), and lascivious figures, Lequeu, if not actually mad, was making some kind of protest at the way in which craftsmen were being robbed of their trade-secrets, having their skills paraded in the *Encylopédie*, and reduced to the status of slaves by newfangled machinery. Lequeu himself was from an artisan background, and never tired of saying so. His drawings certainly contain many allusions to Freemasonry, and it may be that his apparently frivolous images were some sort of veiled protest against the popularisation, vulgarisation, and even corruption of Freemasonic ideals, as he perceived them.

'Architecture Civile' seems disordered for it consists of many ideas, themes, and images that do not seem to belong: it is disturbing in its incongruity and weirdness. The productions of Boullée, Ledoux, and others were more reassuring because they were ordered, designed with flair, had a solid background in Classicism, and pointed to a Utopian future. Lequeu, on the other hand, actually follows the definitions of Architecture and its classifications as set out in the *Encyclopédie*, but, by carrying his listings to absurd lengths, actually creates mayhem[154]. It is as though Lequeu were attacking the artisan's alienation: that monument to rationality itself, the *Encyclopédie* of Diderot and his colleagues, perhaps was his target. Lequeu

---

151 *See*, for example, Duboy (1986).
152 *Ibid.* 15.
153 In the Cabinet des Estampes, Bibliothèque Nationale, Paris.
154 Duboy (1986) discusses this at some length.

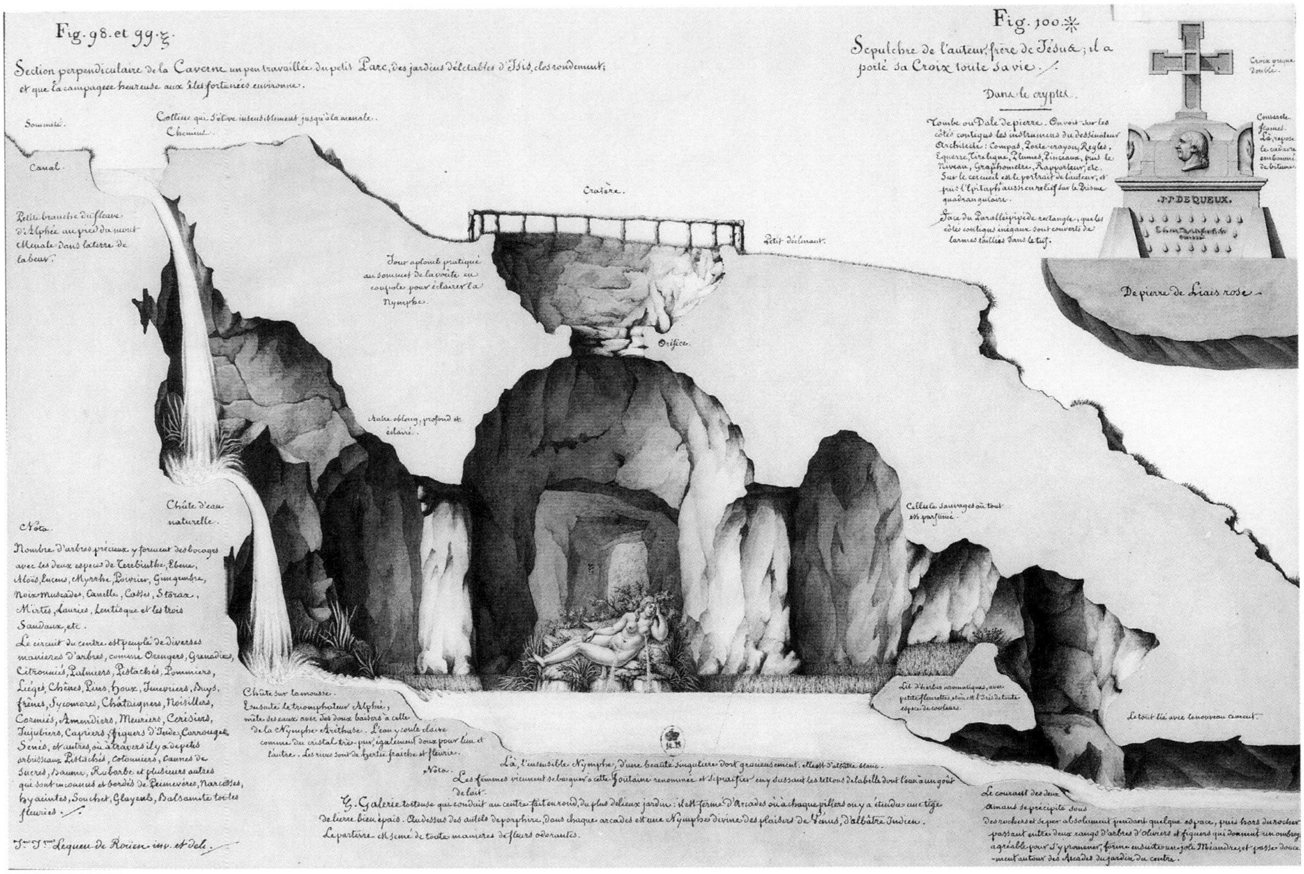

Pl.VII.24 *(top)* Lequeu's perpendicular section of the (somewhat artificially adapted) Cavern in the little Park of the delectable Gardens of Isis, completely enclosed, and surrounded by the joyful landscape of the Fortunate Isles. The vignette on the right shows the sepulchre of the author, brother of Jesus, who has carried his Cross all his life. The Isiac idea of a healing spring is depicted, and the whole resembles to some extent the ideas behind the 'Gothic House'. The female figure spouting water from her breasts was clearly suggested by the fountain-statues of Artemis of Ephesus in Italian Renaissance gardens. The fact that this is a *fabrique* for a garden should be noted (BN. CE. AC, Plate 33, Figs. 98, 99 and 100).

Pl.VII.25 *(left)* Main and lateral elevations of Lequeu's country house known as the Temple of Silence, with Harpocrates, Commerce, and Abundance in the pediment, the dogs as symbols of household guardians, the Goddesses of the Twelve Hours, turtles in the metopes, and owls by Harpocrates's feet and over the door. The lateral elevation had views over 'Meudon, Bellevue, and St Cloud and the smiling plains watered by the Seine'. There was also a Chinese Garden. From Krafft (1812) Plate 39 (SJSM).

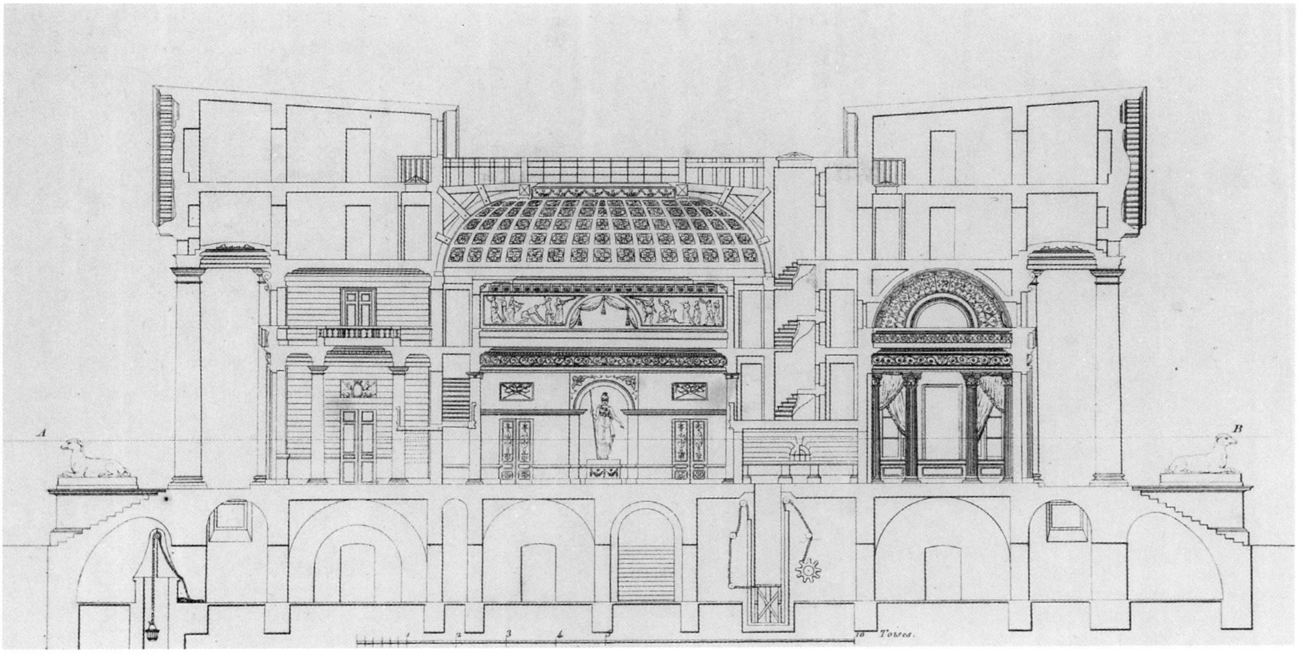

Pl.VII.26 Section of Lequeu's Temple of Silence, showing the central dining-room that could also double as a hall. Note the lifting devices, recalling the Trial by Air shown in **Pls.VII.20 & 21**, p.164. From Krafft (1812) (SJSM).

identified with Christ as Artisan and also with James the brother of Christ, who bore his cross all his life (**Pl.VII.24**). However, Duboy has argued that the present catalogue of Lequeu's works bears little relation to the inventory of the donation to what was the Royal Library in 1825: he states that, in his opinion, some person or persons has or have deliberately modified Lequeu's work 'to give it that air of a complex game it now has'[155]. In relation to this matter, Duboy suggests that Marcel[156] Duchamp and Raymond Roussel may have tampered with Lequeu's drawings to make them even more surreal: his interpretations take us into the realms of Fourier and Jean-Anthelme Brillat-Savarin (whose gastronomic writings Fourier elevated to the plane of 'Gastrosophy'), and from there to the Dadaists, Surrealists, and Futurists, particularly the circles of 'Le Corbusier'[157] and Duchamp (who despised Le Corbusier and all he stood for). However, with respect to Duboy, Lequeu's drawings are quite odd enough without further Surreal overlays.

Lequeu designed a country-house near 'Portenort' in 1786 for the 'Comte de Bouville'[158], supposedly a wealthy Freemason. It was an amphi-prostyle octastyle temple with Tuscan columns and a Roman Doric entablature (**Pl.VII.25**): in the tympanum of one of the pediments was a relief of Harpocrates/Horus, the God of Silence, with serpents, and in the other (over the entrance-front) was Harpocrates again, flanked by 'Commerce' and 'Abundance'. Over the door was an owl, emblem of Night and Death, and in the metopes were turtles, associated with dark powers. Owls were also symbols of moral transformation of the sinful Flesh by means of the Spirit; of Wisdom, Skill, and Power; of Concentration and Meditation; and of Mediaries between Heaven and Earth[159]; inside there was a sequence of rooms giving access to the Gallery, and this sequence could also be approached from subterranean passages (**Pl.VII.26**).

This 'Temple of Silence' was situated to the West of Paris and had views over Meudon, Bellevue, and St-Cloud: Johann Carl (*called* Jean-Charles) Krafft illustrated it in his *Recueil d'architecture civile...*[160]: it appears to have been intended as a dwelling-house and as a Masonic Temple. Two dogs, symbolic of tutelary household gods, guarded the porticoes: dogs could also be guardians of the realms of Silence and the Dead, the Guiders of Souls or Mediators between the Worlds of the Dead and of the Living. Each portico sheltered six pedestals bearing the Goddesses of the Twelve Hours, the Gatekeepers of Heaven, and the long sides of the Temple had engaged columns, making the Temple theme more obvious, yet the plan (**Pl.VII.27**, p.170) owes something to the work of Andrea Palladio. Krafft apparently had some difficulty in understanding

---

155 Duboy (1986) 35.
156 Actually Henry-Robert-Marcel Duchamp.
157 Pseudonym from 1920 of Charles-Édouard Jeanneret, Modernist Architect, self-publicist, coiner of messianic slogans, and promoter of an architectural vocabulary widely copied after 1945 with disastrous consequences for countless towns and cities. *See* Curl (2006a) 198-201. *See* also Birksted (2009) for the Corbusier who has been obscured (mostly by the man himself, in his attempt to set himself up as a messianic figure for the cult of Corbusianity).
158 There was a 'Count of Bouville' in *The Castle of Wolfenbach* (London: William Lane 1793) by Eliza Parsons, one of the 'horrid novels' mentioned in *Northanger Abbey* (London: John Murray 1818) Chapter 6 by Jane Austen.

159 For Symbolism *see* Becker (1992).
160 Krafft (1812) Pls. XXXVII-XXXIX.

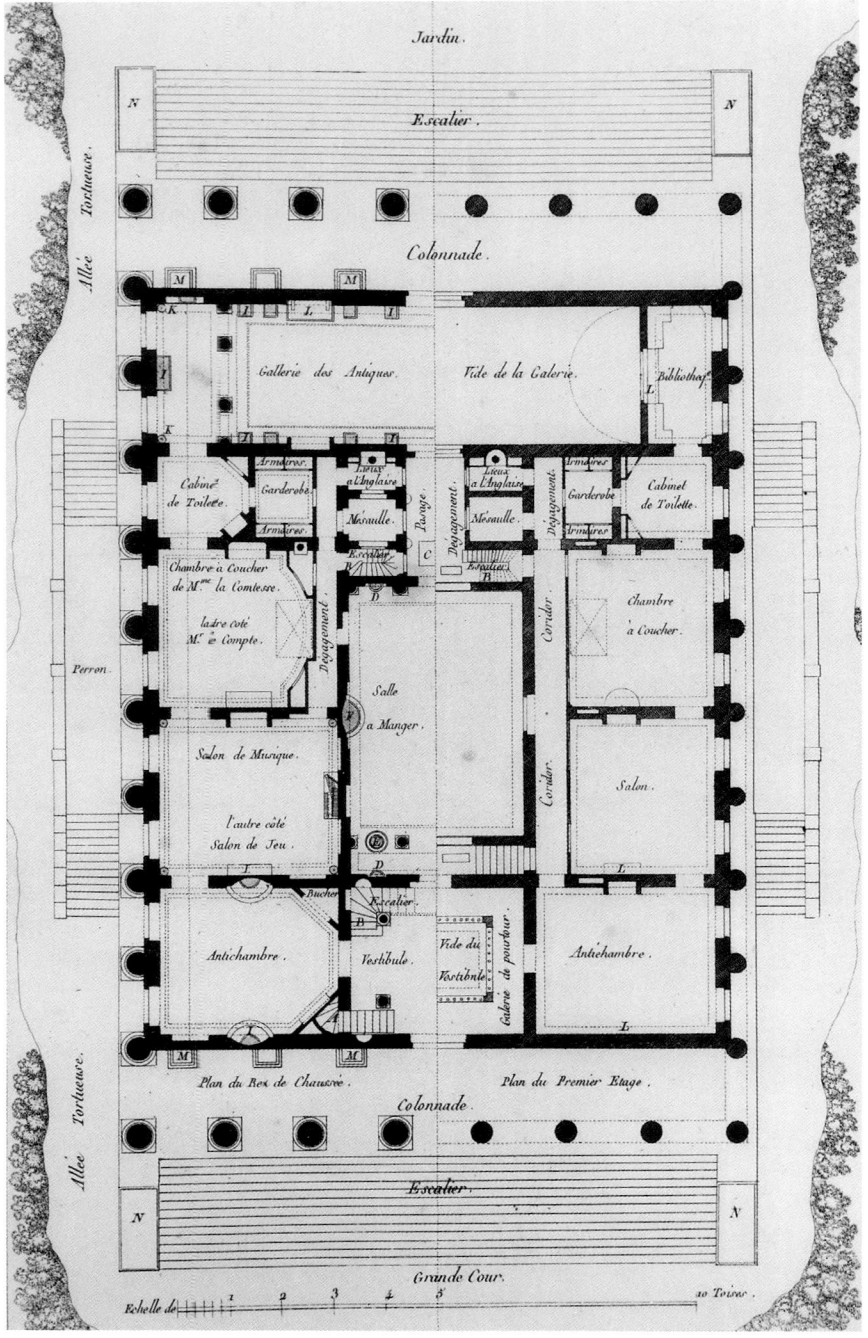

Pl.VII.27 Plan of the House of Pleasure in the Antique style, called the Temple of Silence, by J. J. Lequeu, Architect. From Krafft (1812) Plate 37 (SJSM).

Lequeu (who lived for a time in a brothel) seems to have wallowed in the possibilities that designs for temples, monuments, and Lodges offered (**Pls.VII.28-34**, pp.171-4), for his use of motifs and Masonic allusions is highly inventive: he obviously knew Terrasson, if not Mozart's *Die Zauberflöte*, for his design for a 'Gothic House' could easily be used as as a stage-set for that Sublime *Singspiel*. With Lequeu we enter a deeply disturbing world. Even Ledoux's designs have a chilly strangeness about them, but the case of Lequeu is very peculiar indeed.

Conclusion

Michel Foucault regarded Heterotopias as spaces that function in non-hegemonic conditions: they are spaces of otherness, which are neither here nor there, such as a representation of Utopia, and have many more layers of meaning than are immediately apparent. The problem with them, however, is that they can undermine Syntax, Order, and Reason, threaten Grammar, tear Mythology apart, and end in Futility and Chaos. At some time in the 1770s French Freemasonry was bedevilled by a series of defections, by the establishment of quasi-Freemasonic societies (often very odd), and by the attractions of mystical, occultist, and other rites. The trouble with Reason was that eventually it reasoned Reason out of existence, and the replacement of the Church and its teachings by 'rational' ethical systems left the need for Mystery, Belief, and Miracles unsatisfied. Franz Anton Mesmer, with his theories of 'animal magnetism' and astrology, Cagliostro, with his 'Egyptian Rites', and the infiltration of many societies by the Bavarian Illuminati and other organisations were manifestations of disturbing undercurrents: the Grotesque, the Irrational, the Sensational, and the Terrible offered attractions to those weary of Progress, Reason, and Science.

why Lequeu had given the name, design, and character of a temple to what was a building intended as a residence. Lequeu responded by showing the *Temple du Silence* re-erected as a Temple at the gates of Paris. Krafft also illustrated Lequeu's designs for a house at s'Grawensel, the 'Cazin de Terlinden', for the Dowager of Meulenaer in Belgium, an extraordinary house with a very ingenious plan[161].

And what Gertrude Himmelfarb has called 'The Ideology of Reason'[162] produced its own horrors. The French Revolution was not in any case a 'social' revolution, and the Terror had nothing to do with compassion: rather it

---

161 Krafft (1812) Pls. LV-LX.

162 Himmelfarb (2008) 147-187.

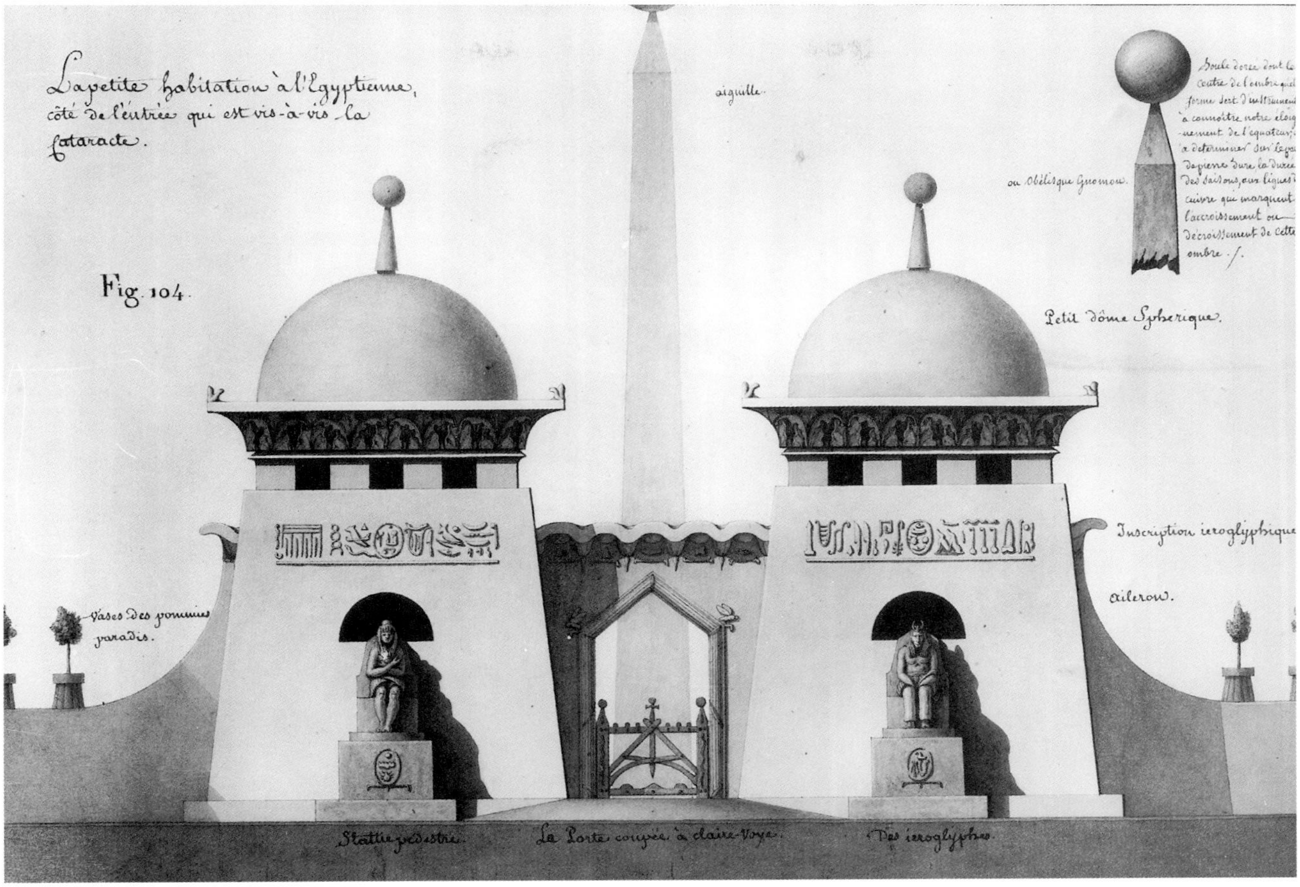

Pl.VII.28 *(top)* The small dwelling in Egyptian Style, showing the entrance that faces the waterfall, by Lequeu. This could almost be the set for the scene with Two Men in Black Armour in *Die Zauberflöte*, and clearly marks the beginning of some sort of route, the axis of which is marked by an obelisk (BN. CE. AC, Plate 35, Fig. 104).

Pl.VII.29 *(right)* Temple of Verdure of Ceres by Lequeu. Note the identification with Artemis of Ephesus, and therefore with Isis, the spiral form of the columns (identified with Freemasonry), and the fountains (again Isiac). This *fabrique* has an inscription stating that 'True Happiness is in the Country' (BN. CE. AC, Plate 57, Fig. 149).

was an hysterical, paranoid phenomenon concerned, not with so-called 'public safety', but with the preservation of the régime in power. *Le Peuple* was not The People, but an Abstraction, represented, not by 'The People', but by the will of demagogues concerned with so-called 'Equality' and 'Justice', blithely ignoring Liberty. It is, sadly, a familiar phenomenon, and shows every sign of becoming widespread.

Continental thinkers of the Enlightenment betrayed the separation of theological and political thinking that had evolved from Hobbes, through Locke, and then through Hume: this is why there is such a remarkable difference between the pragmatic, common-sense, benevolent British Enlightenment, and the oddly dictatorial and frequently unpleasant Continental version, especially the French Enlightenment. Rousseau's sentimentality, Kant's God of Reason, and Hegel's almost Sanctified State

Pl.VII.30 (*top*) Temple of Divination (i.e. Prediction), by Lequeu. The building suggests Trials by Fire, and was intended to form the northern extremity of an Elysium (*BN. CE. AC, Plate 63, Fig. 158*).

Pl.VII.31 (*middle*) Porch or vestibule which leads to the underground chambers and Pluto's dwelling, facing the right-hand side wall of the Temple of Wisdom, and (*bottom*) main entrance of the Temple of Wisdom. Both these Lequeu drawings show pronounced Egyptianesque leanings. Note the canted section of the vestibule, which is a favourite 'Egyptian' motif adopted by designers of the time. The Temple tympanum celebrates the statement that Happiness, Welfare, or Prosperity lie in the angle, quoin, or corner where the Wise are assembled: it is therefore unquestionably Masonic (*BN. CE. AC, Plate 67, Figs 164 and 165*).

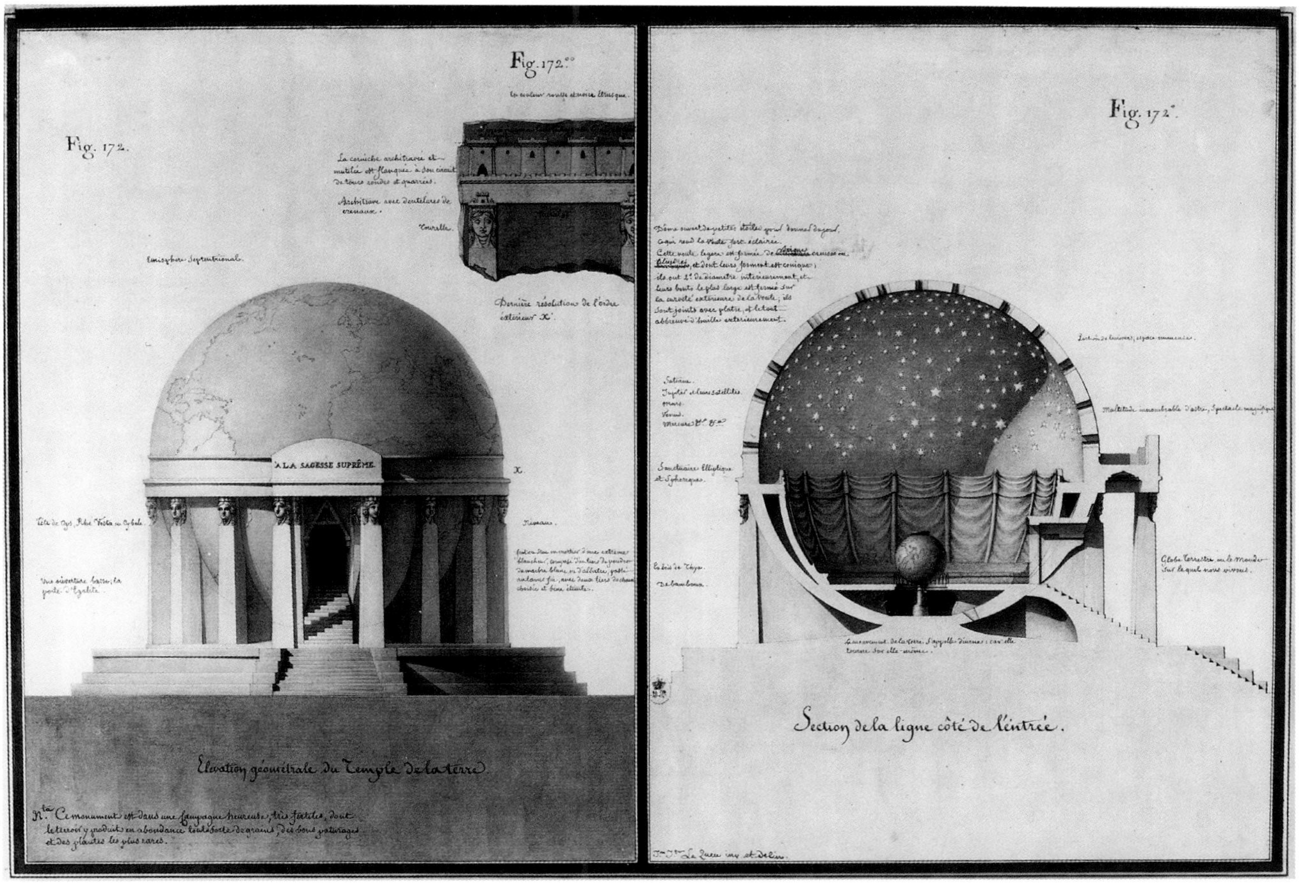

Pl.VII.32 *(top)* Elevation and section of a Temple of the Earth by Lequeu. Note the use of the sphere as an emblem of Wisdom and Nature, a theme also pursued by Boullée, Ledoux, and other Architects of the late-eighteenth century. The segmental-headed block over the entrance is inscribed to the 'Supreme Wisdom'. The sphere, pierced to suggest the stars from within, and with a map of the world on the outside, should be compared with Boullée's Cenotaph for Newton (BN. CE. AC, Plate 72, Figs 172, 172°, 172°°).

Pl.VII.33 *(right)* Monument to a number of illustrious men of the city... for Victory Square, exhibited in Liberty Hall. The Time when human victims were being sacrificed to liberty, 1794. Design by Lequeu, showing his use of the garlanded column form, partly phallic, partly suggested by those entwined columns derived from the spiral or 'Solomonic' types (BN. CE. AC, Plate 72, Fig. 176).

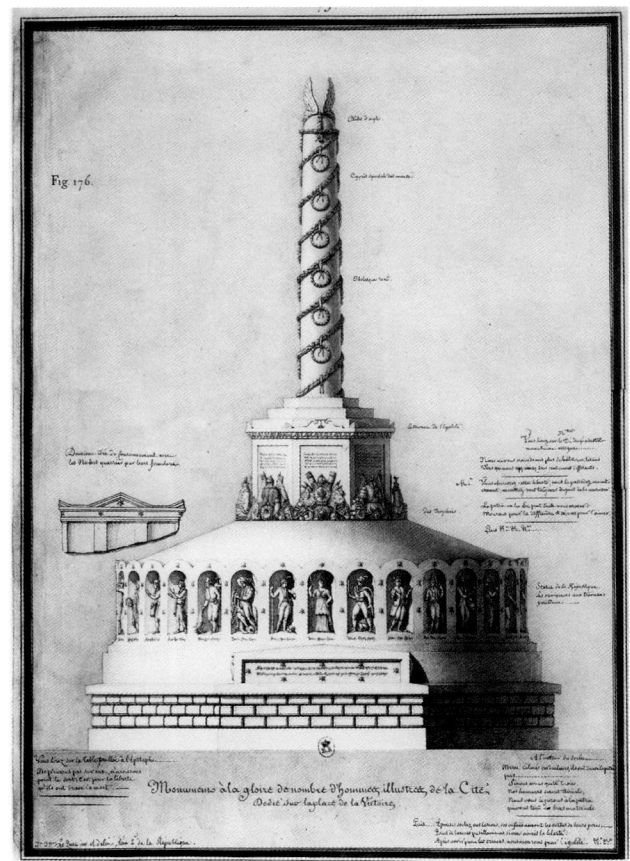

all infected political developments with concepts of what might be described as Secular Religion, corrupted with a transformed notion of what was Sacred. The Gods could not be tamed or even domesticated by Reason set up on a pedestal: separated from the organisation of a Church and its authority, the Gods quickly reverted to pagan mischiefs during the European Enlightenment, hurling thunderbolts willy-nilly at the mortals who had unleashed them, or perhaps, as in Wagnerian story-telling, they changed into dragons. This appalling mayhem caused by Continental rejection of the Hobbesian liberal tradition led to Barbarism: the Terror of the 1790s, the secular religions of National Socialism and Communism, and the horrors associated with those régimes are just some manifesta-

Pl.VII.34 Interior of the Cool Room of a house in the Egyptian Taste by Lequeu. Various Masonic hints are suggested by the source of the living waters leaving the *Rocher*. Note the darkened room, the hieroglyphs, the canted fanlight (itself suggestive of the Square and Compasses), the two herms (with Egyptianising head-dresses and hieroglyphs on the pedestals), and the flowing waters on either side of the passage to the mysterious door (*BN. CE. AC., Plate 58, Fig. 150*).

tions. One suspects that there was much in the 1780s, as with later revolutions, that derived from envy: the foolish attempts to propitiate the spiteful rages of dragons by sacrifices (usually of Truth, Logic, and even of victims from Man's own species) bring forth but new horrors. Those fortunate enough to have basked in the British Enlightenment developed more earthily than did their Continental cousins: they did not become oracular, and realised that certain disagreeable beasts cannot be mollified by kindness or by sacrifice: instead, they treated them with honest contempt, and the dragons obligingly went to ground. It is a source of disquiet that they seem to be re-emerging, more deadly than they ever were, from their gloomy and unsavoury lairs in the twenty-first century.

CHAPTER VIII

Elysian Fields and Garden Transformations

Introduction; The Eighteenth-Century Landscape, Politics, and Meaning; The 'Graveyard Poets'; The International Significance of Night Thoughts; *Narcissa's Burial; The Arcadian Landscape and the Tomb; Burial and Commemoration in Gardens: The Emergence of the Cemetery; The Landscape Garden and Freemasonry; Fabriques; Hadrian's Villa at Tivoli; Some Other Significant Gardens*

'One likes to think of scholars as courageous, adventurous individuals, resolute in their search for truth. But there are two subjects in particular which scholars tend to avoid: mysticism... and secret societies... Now... Curl has offered us an explanation of the artistic and architectural influence of the Freemasons.. [his work]... on the landscape garden and on cemeteries... will no doubt prove the most controversial,... but... [if] the *jardin anglais* or *anglo-chinois* was an imitation of English models, why did the Continent not follow the English line of development, leading to the simplified Edenic landscapes of Capability Brown? Why the heavy emphasis on tombs and symbolic garden buildings, to the extent of seeming a discordant clutter to the English eye?... Curl's interpretation in terms of Masonic tradition makes better sense of the Continental landscape than the previous accounts I have found. It also reveals a curious blind spot in the work of previous historians of the subject... Curl deserves our thanks for having opened the subject up, and any future studies on the Continental landscape garden and on the emergence of garden cemeteries will have to take his work into account.'

BRENT ELLIOTT (1952-):
Review of *The Art and Architecture of Freemasonry: An Introductory Study* (London: Batsford 1991) in *Garden History: The Journal of The Garden History Society* **xx**/2 (Autumn 1992) 207-8.

'Amid the green glades and gloomy cypresses which surround and overshadow the vast variety of sepulchral ornaments of *Père La Chaise*, the contemplative mind is not only impressed with sentiments of solemn sublimity..., but with those of the most tender and heart-affecting melancholy... There, the instability of all human affairs is most emphatically and eloquently taught by the dread silence of the tomb, and unquivocably beheld in the mere change which a few years have produced on the garden itself...'

JOHN STRANG (1795-1863):
Necropolis Glasguensis; with Observations [sic] *on Ancient and Modern Tombs and Sepulture* (Glasgow: Atkinson & Co. 1831) 29-30.

Introduction

The English landscape garden[1] was one of the greatest creations of these islands to be exported, and its influence was widely disseminated during the eighteenth and nineteenth centuries. It was informal, asymmetrical, and 'natural' in the sense that it was *designed* to look unforced: among its most celebrated creators were Lancelot 'Capability' Brown[2], who, with Charles Bridgeman[3] and William Kent[4], created the 'naturalisation' of the park at Stowe, Buckinghamshire. Bridgeman was credited with introducing the 'ha-ha'[5] to England in 1719 at Stowe: this was a boundary to a garden designed not to interrupt a view from, for example, a country-house. It consists of a ditch with perpendicular or slightly battered side or revetment nearest the viewpoint, faced with brick or stone, and the other side sloped and turfed: it kept animals away from the area contiguous to the house, yet was concealed, so did not spoil the ideal of bringing the country into the picture. The 'English garden' was designed to be 'Picturesque', an aesthetic category, or standard of taste, largely concerned with landscape and with emotional responses to associations evocative of passions or events[6]. From *Pittoresco* ('in the manner of the painters'), it was also associated with carefully contrived landscape-paintings, particularly those of Claude Lorraine, Salvator Rosa, and the two Poussins. Essentially an anti-urban aesthetic concerned with sensibility, it was linked to notions of pleasing the eye with compositions reminiscent of those in paintings. To Sir Uvedale Price the Picturesque comprised all the qualities of nature and art that could be discerned in paintings since the time of Titian, and argued in his *Essay on the Picturesque* (1794) in favour of 'natural' beauty[7].

---

1 The subject is vast, and a Bibliography large enough to do it justice is not possible here.
2 Stroud (1984*a*).
3 Willis (2002).
4 Hunt & Willis (*Eds.*) (1988), Hunt (1987), Mowl (2006).
5 It was described by Antoine-Joseph Dézallier d'Argenville in his *Théorie* of 1709 (*see* Dézallier d'Argenville [1709]) and may have been first used in England by Guillaume Beaumont at Levens Hall, Westmorland, around 1698.
6 *See*, for example, Knight (1805) and Burke (1757).
7 Price (1794-8).

Now many paintings of Classical landscapes included buildings, such as temples, altars, and so on, thus English gardens acquired them too. John Vanbrugh designed important garden-buildings at Stowe, but was also responsible for the Obelisk (1714), Pyramid Gate (1719), and Belvedere Temple (1725-8) at Castle Howard, Yorkshire, for Charles Howard, 3rd Earl of Carlisle[8]. Nicholas Hawksmoor designed the Pyramid (1728), the severe and nobly monumental Mausoleum (1729-36), and the Temple of Venus (1731-5 – demolished), also at Castle Howard[9]. Henry Flitcroft was the Architect of the Temple of Ceres (now Flora – 1744-5), the Temple of Hercules (1754-6 – based on the Pantheon in Rome), and the Temple of Apollo (*c*.1765 – based on the Round Temple at Baalbek) at Stourhead, Wiltshire, in the magical garden created by Henry Hoare[10]. Horace Walpole, the English virtuoso and wit, described Stourhead (essentially a landscape with temples around an artificial lake) as 'one of the most Picturesque scenes in the world', and he was not far off the mark[11].

Pl.VIII.1 *(top)* Mausoleum at Castle Howard, Yorkshire (1729-35), designed by Nicholas Hawksmoor, with base (1737-42) by Daniel Garrett (*CL, CIA, photograph AFK, K.4.8911*).

Pl.VIII.2 *(below)* Gothick Temple, or Temple of Liberty, at Stowe, Buckinghamshire, by James Gibbs, with lantern pinnacle-towers by Sanderson Miller (*CL, CIA, photograph AFK, K.G.27852*).

Stowe, however, with Vanbrugh's garden-buildings erected for Richard Temple, 1st Viscount Cobham, differed from Stourhead in numerous ways. Vanbrugh's garden-buildings (*c*.1719-25) were the Lake Pavilions (re-sited 1764), the Rotunda (altered), the Temple of Bacchus (demolished), the Temple of Sleep (demolished), Nelson's Seat (demolished), the Cold Bath (demolished), Queen Caroline's Monument (a tetrapylon), and the Pyramid (demolished). Later, Kent added the Temple of British Worthies (*c*.1735), the Temple of Ancient Virtue (*c*.1735-7), Congreve's Monument (1736), and other structures[12].

So there was a massive mausoleum doubling as an eye-catcher at Castle Howard (**Pl.VIII.1**), and there were monuments to real people at Stowe. When Bridgeman and Kent flooded the valley at Stowe and created a glade around it, they called the result 'Elysian Fields' in which statues of Saxon Gods and famous Britons were erected. The Temple of British Worthies, too, celebrated a *political* point in that it was a memorial to Whiggery. In 1741-4 James Gibbs designed and built the Gothick Temple (or Temple of Liberty) at Stowe (**Pl.VIII.2**): triangular on plan, it was intended to celebrate the 'Gothic Liberties' that Cobham and his Whig allies perceived (rightly or wrongly) as threatened by the Prime Minister (1721-42), Sir Robert Walpole (created 1st Earl of Orford in 1742). The 'Temple' was dedicated to the 'Liberty of Our Ancestors', alluding

---

8 Colvin (2008 – which includes further reading) 1067-74.
9 *Ibid*. 496-502.
10 *Ibid*. 379-84.
11 Woodbridge (1970). Stourhead and Stowe were influential.
12 Etlin (1984) 183-97.

to the freedoms which Tacitus had claimed for the English and the Germans, and it contained an inscription:

'I THANK GOD I AM NOT A ROMAN'

suggesting that Roman Catholicism had been abjured, that the building was not subject to either ecclesiastical or Imperial Rome, but a statement of Gothic Freedom, and that the style of the building was also very definitely not Roman, but Gothic[13]. The individual who thanked God he was not a Roman was Temple himself, the creator of the 'Temple' of Liberty, who indeed saw himself as that Temple of Liberty, and had the vault of the 'Temple' decorated with bogus heraldic devices to show his family could be traced back to times when the 'Gods, of a Nation, Valiant, Wise, and Free', guided the Anglo-Saxons[14].

Architecture in landscapes, therefore, could suggest ideas, and could make powerful political and other points. Sanderson Miller, the Squire of Radway, designed a battlemented and machicolated Gothic Tower at Edgehill, Warwickshire (1745-7): it resembles the Mediaeval Guy's Tower at Warwick Castle, so is probably the first Gothic eyecatcher/belvedere to derive from a real Mediaeval precedent (**Pl.VIII.3**). Now the Tower affords a spectacular view from the ridge of Edge Hill over the site of the first battle of the English Civil War (1642), and the allusion to Warwick Castle was probably intended to trigger memories of a series of earlier English Civil Wars, those of the Roses (1455-87), and the power behind the Throne, Richard Neville, 16th Earl of Warwick and 6th Earl of Salisbury, known as the 'Kingmaker': Miller's Tower is really an invitation to consider the making and unmaking of Kings and Constitutions, from the Wars of the Roses, to the Civil War, and to the defeat of the Jacobite Army of Charles Edward Stuart at Culloden (1746). The type of historical engagement it offers, however, is elegiac and reflective, not triumphalist, for it takes no sides[15].

Now such convoluted allusions are beyond the comprehension of most people today, and a visit to an eighteenth-century garden with its many *fabriques*[16] (as the French call garden-buildings) will not mean much unless explanatory notes are provided, and even then interpretations will be so foreign to contemporary blunted sensibilities that they are probably a waste of time[17]. Nevertheless, that many gardens were not without *meanings* is accepted by many save the most pusillanimous, and such creations deserve the closest study.

The most important aspect to be noted about gardens such as Stowe and Castle Howard is that they had commemorative and elegiac qualities. At Stowe, especially, were aspects of meaning that were profound, redolent of politics, power, and steeped in mythology. Not least of these were those concerned with national identity.

Pl.VIII.3 The Gothick Tower, Edgehill, Warwickshire, by Sanderson Miller (*JSC*).

The Eighteenth-Century Landscape, Politics, and Meaning

If Italian Renaissance authors had identified Gothic with the 'barbarians' and the destruction of Classical Antiquity, it should also be recognised that to Northern Europeans the invaders of *their* territories were the Romans, and so Mediaeval Architecture began to be associated with emerging nationhood. Classicism, on the other hand, represented foreign invasion, colonisation, and repression, thus North European sixteenth-century historians began to *reinvent* an *interpretation* of Gothic. Cornelius Tacitus, the Roman historian, had compared contemporary Roman society with that of the Germans, not always to the advantage of the former: his Germans were devoted to Liberty, elected their rulers, arrived at decisions by consensus, were hospitable and generous, were brave and steadfast, their society was free from the sexual licentiousness that was common in Rome, and they were straightforward and free from guile[18]. Constructors of Northern national identity were also influenced by the sixth-century work of Jordanes, historian of the Goths, who preserved precious information concerning the Teutonic peoples that came to pre-eminence, and, with their origins in 'Scandza' or 'Scanzia' (Sweden), colonised

---

13 Curl (2007a) 34.
14 The quote (1732) is from the work of Gilbert West (1753).
15 Brooks (1999) Chs. 3 & 4, Curl (2007a) 36.
16 Mosser (1991). *See* also Calder (*Ed.*) (2006) for a general study of how to look at eighteenth-century gardens.
17 *See*, for example, Macpherson (1998).

18 Tacitus (1999) on the Germans.

much of Europe and brought about the downfall of Rome. This construct was attractive to sixteenth-century religious Reformers, who could see analogies between free, liberty-loving, moral Teutons who had brought down a corrupt Roman tyranny, and the German Protestants who had struggled successfully against the oppression of the Papacy. Such allusions were adopted by other countries, and concerning England the Antiquary, Richard Verstegan (*alias* Rowlands), published in Antwerp[19] a work in which he argued that the Angles, Jutes, and Saxons who colonised England after the withdrawal of the Romans were sound, Liberty-loving Teutons. In France, too, the jurist and convert to Protestantism, François Hotman (*or* Hotomanus), published his *Franco-Gallia* (1573)[20] in which he claimed that the Gauls and Franks were also Teutons.

In England, Parliamentarians realised that many of the ideas floated during the German Reformation, and by authors such as Hotman and Verstegan, were important in creating precedents for their own aspirations, including the right of Parliament to curtail the power of the Monarchy. Verstegan had demonstrated that English reverence for Liberty reflected Teutonic origins and virtues that Tacitus himself had described. Saxon Kings, it was claimed, were elected by a Sovereign Assembly (which had the final say in matters of law), and the powers of those Kings were subject to control. This *Witenagemot*, or National Assembly or Council of the Anglo-Saxons, was comprised of *Witan* or wise men, and was clearly, to Antiquarians, the successor to the tribal councils described by Tacitus. Parliamentarians of the seventeenth century perceived themselves as the heirs of that ancient Anglo-Saxon (and therefore Gothic) system: such a position had to be tenable, so Antiquarians were employed to create well-researched arguments based on precedents. The Puritan, Nathaniel Bacon, set down powerful arguments against the claims of the Royal Prerogatives and hierarchical pretensions, and claimed that no nation earth preserved 'so much of the ancient Gothique law' as did England[21].

Once the Protestant Succession through the Hanoverian line had been secured following the deposition of James II and VII by various enactments[22], a Constitutional Monarchy limited in its powers was established. The principle of Parliamentary authority was firmly put in place by law, and numerous publications argued that those fundamental changes in the governance of Britain were based on the historical precedents of Anglo-Saxon tribal elections to Kingship. Among them may be cited the political dialogues by James Tyrrell[23], the *Discourses* by Algernon Sidney (who had been executed for treason [he had had the temerity to confirm the lawfulness of deposing Kings at a time when to openly express such opinions was unwise])[24], and the *Preface* to the translation of Hotman (1711) by Robert Molesworth (an admirer of Sidney)[25], which was later reprinted (1775) under the title *The Principles of a Real Whig*[26]. In essence, these writers were among the begetters of an argument that English Liberty, with its origins in the Anglo-Saxon *Witenagemot* (which, in turn, had derived from the Councils of the Goths), had matured and reached its apogee in the post-1689 Settlement. Compared with the political situation elsewhere in Europe, there was a lot to be said for this point of view. John Oldmixon, for example[27], denounced those factions that had brought Europe to the brink of slavery by advancing the power of France, and in his *Memoirs of Ireland* (1716)[28] he exposed attempts by the Stuarts and 'Papists' to undermine the British Constitution and the Protestant religion. He claimed[29] (like Bacon) that 'Gothick Governments' were all free, and that no nation had preserved its 'Gothick Constitution' better than had England. Verstegan and others had argued that the Anglo-Saxons had been landowners, but that their rights had been usurped by the Norman conquerors, who had altered things so that feudal tenure, by which land was held by tenants of the Crown, replaced the more free 'Gothic' system. James Harington (or Harrington) had argued[30] that power depends on the balance of property, normally of landed property, and that the principle of landed property should be vigorously defended. Gothic Liberty was fine, but it had to take account of the landed interest, for the stability of that interest was essential to the workings of the free Gothic political system. Thus Whiggery absorbed Gothic theory, for it was realised that stability had to be restored after the seventeeth-century upheavals, and the landed interest seemed to hold the key.

Evidence had to be provided to legitimise the Settlement, for, after all, an anointed King had been deposed, and there were still questions in the air. The ecclesiastical historian John Inett, for example, demonstrated[31] that there had been 'Papal Aggression' against the 'Liberties' of the English Church, but argued that the Reformation had restored ancient religious and political rights that had been curtailed or usurped under 'Popery'. Thus the Mediaeval Church in England had been reformed, yet remained part of the Holy Catholic and Apostolic Church, and was closely associated with political institutions and with the Monarchy. And the glue for Anglicans, Parliamentarians, and others sore wearied by instability, upheavals, and strife, was Gothic in its many forms, and in its sundry guises.

The new post-1689 Settlement could claim continuity with the Mediaeval Church and State, and could also insist

---

19 Verstegan (1605). Verstegan was a Roman Catholic who worked as a publishing and intelligence agent for the superiors of the English mission. See ODNB **lvi** (2004) 381-2.
20 *See* Molesworth (1711).
21 Bacon (1647-51).
22 1 Will. & Mar. sess. 2 *c*.2., 12 & 13 Will. III *c*.2, 13 &14 Will. III *c*.6, 1 Ann. *c*.16, 6 Ann. *c*.41, 10 Ann. *c*.8.
23 Tyrrell (1979).

24 Sidney (1698).
25 Molesworth (1711).
26 Molesworth (1775).
27 Oldmixon (1712).
28 Oldmixon (1716).
29 Oldmixon (1724-6).
30 Harrington (1656).
31 Inett (1704-10).

on a connection with the freedoms of Gothic history. Central to stability, however, was the landed interest, for land was power, and landowning had to be protected to maintain equilibrium. In order to support and give respectability to the landed interests, Historians and Antiquarians were again called upon for their services. There was an enormous upsurge in genealogical and heraldic investigations of the time, which, by recording births, marriages, and deaths, could support the bases of property inheritance. Thus researchers assumed a position of immense importance in the landed interest, disinterring Mediaeval monastic records and ancient wills, and recording inscriptions and Achievements of Arms on tombs and monuments.

The new climate established with the Accession of King George I in 1714 was one in which Architecture as political propaganda was very much on the agenda. Anthony Ashley Cooper (3rd Earl of Shaftesbury from 1699), ardent Whig and friend of Molesworth (who, as an Irishman, had every reason to detest James II and VII and the Jacobites, as he had lost much during the Wars in Ireland [1689-91]), wrote in c.1712 *A Letter concerning the Art, or Science of Design*[32] in which he argued for the necessity to establish a 'National Taste' avoiding corrupting influences, notably emanating from France. The Second Palladian Revival promoted largely by Richard Boyle (3rd Earl of Burlington and 4th Earl of Cork) and Colen Campbell (whose *Vitruvius Britannicus* containing designs in the Palladian style started to appear from 1715) not only linked Architecture of the Hanoverian period to that of the reigns of James I and VI and Charles I (the First Palladian Revival of which Inigo Jones was the master), thus emphasising continuity and legitimacy, but distanced British Architecture from the 'affected and licentious' Baroque of Absolutism and Popery in favour of a dignified 'Antique Simplicity'.

It should be remembered also that in 1715 the first Jacobite Rebellion against the Hanoverian Succession occurred, so there was a desire to stabilise that Succession after the Rebellion, and the Whigs were behind such stabilisation. These trends, movements, ideas, and personalities ensured that the landed gentry and aristocracy identified with the Settlement and with their position by erecting vast Palladian houses on their estates, landscaped to provide suitable settings for their new, gravely dignified piles. The grandees who built such houses saw themselves as representatives of a New Augustan Age, connecting themselves with Antiquity not only through the new Architecture, but through the obligatory Grand Tour and a Classical education.

However, Georgian building endeavours were not all Classical and Palladian, for Gothic structures were also built, notably in the new, carefully contrived gardens. The first eighteenth-century Gothic garden-building was erected at Shotover Park, Oxfordshire, in 1716-17, for James Tyrrell, no less, author of *Discourses*[33],

---
32 *See* Cooper (1714).
33 *See* Tyrrell (1979).

Pl.VIII.4 Gothic Temple at Shotover Park, Oxfordshire (1716-17) (*CL, CIA, photograph AFK, K.G.28907*).

previously noted (**Pl.VIII.4**). The dates are significant: the Hanoverians had succeeded in 1714 and the 'Old Pretender's' Rebellion of 1715 had failed (thereby swinging popular support behind the Hanoverians), so the Gothic 'Temple', essentially an eye-catcher, was a celebration of Whig victory and of the success of the post-1689 Settlement. The crenellated building, with its arcade, rose-window, pinnacle, and turrets, could not be mistaken for a Mediaeval structure, and owes little to scholarship, so belongs to that rather whimsical eighteenth-century style known as 'sham' or even as 'Carpenters' Gothick'. But there was nothing sham about the sentiments or reasons behind its creation: Tyrrell's garden-building celebrated 'Gothic Liberty', yet *suggested* an origin far back in time (and therefore represented continuity and historical respectability), and begat generations of Gothic *fabriques* in gardens. Contrary to much belief, such so-called 'follies' were of great ideological importance. They were wholly unlike seventeenth-century Gothic Revival buildings (which had been mostly ecclesiastical or collegiate), for there were very few precedents for anything like Gothic garden-buildings (unless ruined Mediaeval monastic buildings in gardens could be included), and so Gothic began to be used in completely new contexts, could acquire new meanings, and could be employed for sundry reasons, whilst always retaining something of its allusions to Mediaeval and earlier pasts.

So at Shotover we have a Gothic garden-building erected at the very start of the Georgian period, just after the 1715 Jacobite Rebellion, and completed just as Freemasonry was also being consolidated and regularised in the Hanoverian cause. At Stowe, the later Gothick

CPl.VIII.I Nicolas Poussin's second version of the *Et in Arcadia Ego* theme, known as Arcadian Shepherds (oil on canvas) (*Louvre, Paris/Giraudon/BAL*).

Temple or Temple of Liberty by Gibbs was associated with a statement of Whig principles and with claims that Cobham himself was a Temple, standing for Liberty. Then there was Sanderson Miller's Tower at Edge Hill, offering allusions and reflections after the defeat of the 1745-6 Jacobite Rebellion: it was anything but whimsical.

A detailed examination of all the Gothic *fabriques* of Georgian England cannot be attempted here, but it is important to grasp that such *fabriques* once had political, cultural, and other meanings, and that Gothic was extremely flexible as a means by which associations could be passed on. Gothic was also important in that it increasingly came to be associated with a national style, with ideas about the English landscape, and with English history. There were also subtle changes in the widely-held older perceptions of what had been Anglo-Saxon England. No longer were free Germanic spirits held to have been ordinary fellows, proto-democrats, but proud members of a landowning nobility. This view of the libertarian landowning classes was confirmed by several studies such as those of Thomas Madox[34]. Parliament, as a result of these new perceptions, came to act for the interests of a landowning class that, axiomatically, was seen as identical to the interests of the nation.

Once more, therefore, it was important to emphasise the legitimacy of the claims of those landowning classes to the ownership of the land. To this end, Architecture again came into play, for a built ruin, a new, Georgian idea, could give additional *gravitas* to a landscape, and therefore to an estate, and could even help a squire to *create* a past (and thus give a necessary sense of historical continuity to ownership). Like heraldry and documentation, ruins could be useful to establish legitimacy, a history, and respectability: Georgian Gothic was no laughing matter, despite the sneers of later commentators. It was a deadly serious business, with powerful agendas.

A good (and justly celebrated) example of a sham ruin was Sanderson Miller's Hagley Castle, Worcestershire, consisting of a castellated circular tower (1747-8), the base of an apparently (but built that way) second tower, and a wall, pierced by a doorway, joining the two, erected for Sir George Lyttelton, Bt. (created 1st Baron Lyttelton in 1756). This 'ruined' castle was a huge success, admired by many, and created a vogue for Miller's services as an embellisher of houses and parks. Horace Walpole pronounced that Hagley had the 'true rust of the Barons' Wars', a remark that is not as innocently connected with aesthetics as it might seem, for the Lytteltons were major players in the bloody battles for power during the Middle Ages, especially in the

---

34 *See* Madox (1736), reissued 1741.

Barons' Wars of 1263-7. Furthermore, Miller's client had close political connections with Cobham of Stowe, so, by a process of association[35], familiar then but not now, Miller's Gothic 'ruin' linked notions of Whig Liberty with Mediaeval History, with the thirteenth-century Barons' Wars, and with the wider post-Culloden political climate: in addition, the cunningly contrived 'Castle' transformed its site into 'historical ground' in the words of William Shenstone[36]. After these pioneering works, Gothic 'ruins' arose in some variety throughout the land, no doubt creating a sense of historical connections with estates acquired, perhaps, not that long before. Furthermore, where substantial real Mediaeval ruins survived (e.g. at Fountains Abbey, West Riding, and Rievaulx, North Riding, both in Yorkshire), they could become important elements in newly designed landscaped parks (e.g. Studley Royal, West Riding of Yorkshire).

In essence, the English landscape garden had many meanings: it was contrived to look like a Classical scene in a painting, complete with *fabriques*; it was intended to set off a fine house and look as though it had always been there, connecting the family who owned it and the house with the land, with the history of the country, and with Classical Antiquity; its garden-buildings had *meanings*, sometimes political, sometimes elegiac, and sometimes to trigger thoughts, memories, and allusions; and the whole was about legitimacy, power, and the Establishment. Many of the ideas about Liberty, Constitutional Monarchy, and Checks and Balances to prevent Absolutism were deeply embedded in Freemasonry, and the Craft, as a force for Enlightenment in the eighteenth century, should not be underestimated. If important ideas about Liberty, Politics, and Power could be expressed in garden-buildings, so could Freemasonry play a part in the iconography of the garden.

The 'Graveyard Poets'

Certain literary themes had begun to surface in the sixteenth and seventeenth centuries in, for example, the works of Edmund Spenser[37] and John Milton[38], where some Gothic tendencies and aspects of the cult of Melancholy may be detected. Spenser's 'ghastly Owle' shrieking a 'balefull Note', his references to the 'dark, doleful, dreary' and 'greedy grave'[39] and Milton's evocations of the 'dim religious light'[40] of Mediaeval buildings can be said to have Gothic pre-echoes, perhaps precursors of what we would now call Romanticism.

It was in the eighteenth century, however, that Gothic 'Gloomths' (as Horace Walpole called them) came into their own. Alexander Pope delved into Gothic on occasion: the 'grots and caverns shagged with horrid thorn', the 'moss-grown' buildings with 'spiry turrets crowned', the 'awful arches', and the 'dim windows' shedding a 'solemn light' in *Eloïsa to Abelard*[41], conjure a Gothic past, but, the 'twilight groves and dusky caves', 'Black Melancholy', 'death-like silence', 'dread response', 'gloomy presence', and 'browner horror'[42] of the woods point to a genre that was to link the Supernatural, Gothic, Melancholy, and Horror in the Romantic Gothic novels of Walpole[43], Matthew Gregory Lewis[44], William Beckford[45], and others. Although these rather dreary fictional effusions are pure hokum, they struck chords, and were immensely successful and influential.

At the beginning of the twenty-first century, when landscapes appear to be valued no longer, it is worth remembering that the rediscovery of their aesthetic, poetic, and emotional aspects (influenced by the writings of Publius Vergilius Maro [Virgil] and the paintings of Claude Gellée [*called* Le Lorrain(e)], Nicolas Poussin, and Salvator Rosa) was essentially an eighteenth-century phenomenon. James Thomson, whose verse demonstrates his fondness for landscape (e.g. *The Seasons* [1726-30]), was to refer specifically to all three painters in his *The Castle of Indolence* (1748):

> 'Whate'er Lorraine light-touched with softening hue,
> Or savage Rosa dashed, or learned Poussin drew.'

Thomson, indeed, was one of the first poets to inaugurate a new feeling of Nature and Landscape.

However, the great trio of 'Graveyard Poets' (Robert Blair, Thomas Gray, and Edward Young) had the most impact[46]. The Romantic Movement had its source in Archaeology, to some extent, but it is clear that there developed something like a delight in decay during the second half of the eighteenth century. There was something about the crumbling parish-churches and ruined monasteries of the English landscape that struck an answering chord. Freed from the imminent threat of 'Popery' and a restoration of the 'Papist' Pretender (especially after Culloden in 1746), the remains of a Romanist past could be viewed with kindlier eyes.

Gray's *Elegy in a Country Churchyard*, begun in 1742 and published in 1750, emphasised Death as the Leveller, respecting neither social position nor age, and reflected an the lost talents of those whose humble status precluded greatness. Much more 'Gothic' was *The Grave*, a didactic poem by Robert Blair, published in 1743, in which he celebrated Death, the solitude and horrors of the Tomb and the Dank Vault, and the anguish of Bereavement.

> '... The grave, dread thing!
> Men shiver when thou'rt nam'd: Nature appall'd,
> Shakes off her wonted firmness...'

Blair set his scene with great power, conjuring the 'wreck

---

35 Alison (1790).
36 For Shenstone's importance *see* Curl (2004).
37 *The Faerie Queen* (1589-96).
38 *Il Penseroso* (1645).
39 *The Faerie Queen* **i** xi 33.
40 *Il Penseroso* 160.

41 *Eloïsa to Abelard* (1717) 20 142-4. *See* Pope (1717).
42 *Ibid.* 163-70.
43 *The Castle of Otranto* (1764).
44 *The Monk* (1796).
45 *Vathek, An Arabian Tale* (1786). *See* Mowl (1998).
46 Blair (1826); Curl (2000c); Gray (1912); Young (1989). For Thomson *see* Thomson (1763).

of things which were', the 'dreary' sound of howling wind, the 'gloomy aisles', and the 'low vaults', where 'nought but silence reigns'. To Blair, nobody was safe: even the beautiful young woman is imagined with her 'head low laid', while 'surfeited upon' her 'damask cheek' the 'high-fed worm, in lazy volumes roll'd', freely rioted.

However, even more important for the purposes of this study was Edward Young, whose fame was to be based on the publication of his *The Complaint: or, Night Thoughts on Life, Death, & Immortality* from 1742[47], the whole nine parts of which came out in 1750, with many subsequent editions[48]. From the time of its publication Young's *Night Thoughts* was acclaimed as a masterpiece: it was translated into every European language (including Magyar and Turkish), and was of very great significance in the Europe of the Enlightenment, notably in France and the German-speaking lands. As the distinguished editor, Stephen Cornford, has noted, for more than a hundred years *Night Thoughts* was 'one of the most influential, praised, and well-known poems in the English language'[49]. Even more important, from our point of view, is the fact that it was a 'seminal work' in the 'secular cult of sepulchral melancholy'[50].

Night Thoughts is a long poem suffused with the Sublime, reflections on a passing time, and the transience of life, love, and fame, and the decline of worldly power: it contains considerations of infinity, limitlessness, the universe, and the eternal presence of the Deity. It also involves notions of the continuing perfectibility of the human mind, an optimistic eighteenth-century illusion we might find dubious today. Central to *Night Thoughts* are ideas concerning morality and judgement, and the poem is full of feeling, sensibility, and an all-pervasive, gentle melancholy: its kernel is all about death and dying, and Young attempted to assuage the fear, terror, and desolation associated with Blairite death by encouraging aspirations towards the 'good death' and the observance of prudent Christian virtues. Thus contemplation of death is demonstrated to be a suitable corrective to careless living and as a perfectly sensible, proper preparation for the inevitable.

The International Significance of *Night Thoughts*

In its triumphant progress throughout Europe 'Youngism' acquired certain changes of emphasis which deserve our closest attention. *Night Thoughts* was essentially, in its original, English version, a work of Georgian Christian Protestant orthodoxy, yet it went through subtle metamorphoses to become a key work in the fashionable cult of sepulchres, melancholy, and ruins. In its Continental transformations, it became part of a European taste centring on remembrance, memorials, and contemplative reveries as earthly substitutes for notions of immortality. Death was perceived as a prerequisite for the cultivation of emotions connected with ideas of change, inevitability, and silent melancholy freed from all thoughts of Heaven or Hell. Associated images of graveyards, solitary mourners visiting the silent tomb for contemplation, night scenes, owls, and ruined abbeys, had a powerful appeal.

A remarkable alteration of mood was primarily due to Pierre Prime Félicien Le Tourneur, whose free adaptation and translation, *Les Nuits de Young*, came out in 1769[51]. Not only did this version re-arrange the order of Young's nine books into twenty-four sections, but most of the Christian allusions were expunged, tiresome theological expositions were relegated to notes, and the poem was transformed into an evocation of the solitary poet's personal grief as he wandered alone among the tombs[52]. However, as Forster[53] has described, the tide of 'Youngism' that washed over Europe flowed in two separate waves: the German and the French. *Night Thoughts* had been rendered into German by Johann Arnold Ebert, published in 1751/2, with further editions in 1753 and 1756[54], and 1752 saw another German translation by Christian Bernhard Kayser[55]. Ebert produced a very handsome edition with the original English text facing the translation, copiously embellished with learned notes, and Kayser also brought out a revised edition of his translation at the same time. Young's poem had a profound influence on the *Sturm und Drang*[56] movement, and it was greatly admired by many intellectuals, including Friedrich Gottlieb Klopstock (who wrote an *Ode* to Young), Gotthold Ephraim Lessing (who regarded *Night Thoughts* as a masterpiece of the Sublime), Johann Gottfried Herder (the decisive influence on Goethe), and the great man himself, Johann Wolfgang von Goethe (who used *Night Thoughts* as his English reader and whose tender and wistful novella, *Die Wahlverwandtschaften*[57], contains themes clearly derived from Young's work): in short, *Night Thoughts*, in the German translation (*Nachtgedanken*), was a powerful element of the *Aufklärung*[58], and indeed in the whole German Romantic Movement. One might suggest that certain paintings by Caspar David Friedrich (e.g. *Entrance to the Cemetery* [1825][59]) or by the Swiss artist Marquard Wocher (e.g. the *Epitaph for Chrischona Staehelin* [1799][60]), were profoundly influenced by the *Nachtgedanken*. Goethe himself acknowledged the influence of Young's work on his own phenomenally

---

47 *See* Young (1989).
48 *See* Curl (1994a).
49 Young (1989) ix.
50 *Ibid*. 17.
51 Tourneur (1769).
52 Young (1989) 18.
53 Forster (1986) 387.
54 Ebert (1753).
55 Published in Hanover by Johann Wilhelm Schmidt.
56 Storm and Stress.
57 *The Elective Affinities*, published by Cotta in Tübingen. *See* Goethe (1809) *passim*.
58 Although it is used to signify the Enlightenment, its meaning in German is slightly different, as it signifies more 'Illumination', 'Clarification', 'Instruction concerning Facts', and 'Elucidation'. It also means 'Reconnaissance' in a military sense. *Zeitalter der Aufklärung* is the term meaning the Age of Enlightenment but the nuances of *Aufklärung* also suggest 'clearing up', 'shedding light on', 'explaining', and 'making clear', so it has a very different meaning in Germany.
59 Now in the *Staatliche Kunstsammlungen, Gemäldegalerie*, Dresden.
60 Now in the *Kunstmuseum*, Basel.

successful *Die Leiden des jungen Werthers*[61]. So numerous were the German-speaking imitators of *Night Thoughts* that they were called 'Younglings' (a jest on *Jüngling*, meaning a youth, young man, or stripling).

Forster[62] has referred to the 'conscientious Germans' trying 'to render the *Nights* as faithfully as possible in their translations' and being duly followed by the Scandinavians and the Dutch, but the later French less faithful versions were more widely disseminated, not least because the French language was understood through a greater part of Europe than was German. Thus the Frenchified *Night Thoughts* was in turn further corrupted in translations into Italian, Spanish, Portuguese, Russian, Polish, Czech, modern Greek, Magyar, Turkish, and Maltese. It created major changes in the 'literary atmosphere of the various countries'[63] in which it became common currency.

The first French translations were not those of Le Tourneur, but prose versions of *Night I* (1762) and *Night II* (1764) by Claude de Thyard, Comte de Bissy. The Count was much affected by the Sublime touches in Young's poem, and indeed went so far as to compare the Englishman with Pindar and Homer 'in point of grandeur'[64], but his Gallic sensibilities were offended by what he felt were lapses into Bad Taste, Exaggeration, and Obfuscation. Le Tourneur, in the *Preface* to his 1769 edition of the 'complete' *Night Thoughts* (actually much boiled down to neat sections), commented on what he regarded as the numerous faults in the original, but allowed that Young's text was a 'Sublime Elegy' on the miseries of the human condition[65]. However, he made no bones about his intention to paraphrase Young in order to please the French, and the plan worked: Le Tourneur's fellow-countrymen approved of the results, and even Voltaire gave his *imprimatur* to the re-ordering of the work: the French version was an immediate success and 'Younglings' had arrived in France. By 1789 *Night Thoughts*, in its various guises, had become a success on a European-wide scale, despite its critical stance regarding Roman Catholicism, not least in the famous episode of 'Narcissa's burial' in *Night III* which captured the European imagination and created a vogue for burial in gardens that was the single most powerful factor in the nascent movement to create garden-cemeteries.

Narcissa's Burial

The events described in *Night III* were based on real happenings. 'Narcissa' has been identified as Young's stepdaughter, Elizabeth Lee, who married (1735) Young's friend Henry Temple (elder son of Henry Temple, 1st Viscount Palmerston from 1722-3). The Temples, with Young and his wife, had travelled to France in 1736, seeking a more agreeable climate for young Elizabeth's 'Consumption', but the journey was in vain, for the eighteen-year-old girl died, and was buried in the graveyard of the *Hôtel-Dieu* in Lyons at eleven at night[66]. Young dramatised this, suggesting the gloom and horror of a burial in the darkness in a grave stealthily dug and probably already occupied (so he called it 'a stolen grave'). Le Tourneur interpreted Young's line that he 'bore her nearer to the Sun'[67] as located 'à Montpellier', and went so far as to provide an illustration showing the poet secretly laying 'Narcissa' at midnight in her 'stolen grave'.

Young's rage and grief were expressed in denunciations of the 'Strangers to Kindness' whose eyes 'let fall Inhuman Tears' 'While *Nature* melted', and 'Superstition rav'd'. Spirits 'nurst In blind Infallibility's embrace' denied 'the Charity of Dust... a Charity their Dogs' enjoyed. What could the desperate Young do? 'With pious Sacrilege' he stole a grave, and 'More like her Murderer, than Friend', he crept 'In midnight Darkness', whispered his last sigh, and silently mouthed what should have been loudly declaimed. His grief was matched by rival indignation, and 'half-execration mingled' with his prayers: he 'sore-grudg'd the Savage land her Sacred Dust', stamped upon 'the curst Soil', and with a humanity, denied to poor Narcissa, wished all the bigots and cold-hearted French a grave[68].

Now this was savage, powerful stuff, denouncing the heartless 'Papist' French who denied the young 'heretic' Englishwoman what they gladly gave even to their dogs. This celebrated episode, made even more memorable by gloomy images, had a tremendous impact throughout Europe. The burial of Protestants (or 'non-Catholics', as some prefer) in Roman Catholic countries often created difficulties and unpleasantnesses. In the rapidly changing climate of the eighteenth-century Enlightenment, however, the 'Narcissa episode' aroused all sorts of responses, many of far-reaching implication.

Legends abounded. The Keeper of the *Jardin Royale* at Montpellier, taking his cue from Le Tourneur, invented a story (probably with a beady eye on the Main Chance) in which his predecessor was bribed by Young to dig a grave, and 'Narcissa' was carried, wrapped only in a sheet, to the secret resting-place[69]. Further credence was given to this implausible tale by Francis Garden (Lord Gardenstone from 1764) in his *Travelling Memorandums*[70], who reported that 'some generous and liberal-minded French persons of distinction' had contributed funds to erect a monument over the spot in a 'little gloomy grove', but that there had been objections from those who took exception to *any* memorial being erected over unconsecrated ground to the memory of a 'heretic'. In due course, Thomas Pitt (1st Baron Camelford from 1784) is said to have authenticated the Montpellier site by exhuming some bones there, and a 'tomb' inscribed PLACANDIS NARCISSAE MANIBUS was erected which became a tourist attraction, doubtless

---

61 *The Sorrows of Young Werther*, published in Leipzig by Weygand. *See* Goethe (1774).
62 Forster (1986) 387.
63 *Ibid.*
64 *Ibid.* 389.
65 Tourneur (1769) **i, vi, lii, lvi**.
66 Forster (1986) 150.
67 Young (1989) **iii** 119.
68 *Ibid.* 150-188.
69 Forster (1986) 151.
70 Garden (1791-5) **i** 187.

to the great satisfaction of the Keeper, despite the existence of a real tombstone at the *Hôtel-Dieu* in Lyons. Matters may have been further confused by the surreptitious burial of 'Lady Wildair' at Montpellier in the play *Harry Wildair* (1701) by George Farquhar: Her Ladyship's servant, 'Dick', tells us that those 'cursed barbarous devils, the French, would not let us bury her... She was a heretic woman and they would not let her corpse be put in their holy ground... [We] carried her out upon our own shoulders through a back door at midnight and laid her in a grave that I dug for her myself with my own hands'[71]. The points should be emphasised that the supposed grave-site was in a *garden* at Montpellier, and that well-connected Frenchmen desired to erect a monument there to demonstrate their responses to the story and to the charges of bigotry.

However, Young's French biographer, Walter Thomas[72], attempted to counter the charges of inhumanity, bigotry, and lack of feeling which the English poet had laid against the French. He pointed out (perfectly correctly) that burial at night was usual[73] for Protestants, and that Young's only cause for serious complaint was the exorbitant fee of 729 *livres* 12 *sous* demanded by the Provost of the Merchants who controlled the burial-ground. Although interment at night was not at all unusual at the time, in most cases these appear to have been within churches, and became fashionable partly to avoid the expense and formality of heraldic funerals, and partly to afford greater degrees of intimacy between mourners more appropriate to private grief than to public display. What ever the truth of the 'Narcissa episode'[74], there can be no denying its importance in the histories of gardens and of cemeteries[75].

The Arcadian Landscape and the Tomb

Classical Arcadia is a mountainous region of Greece in the centre of the Peloponnese. The idealised notion of Arcadia, where the God Pan dwelt, with its pastoral landscape peopled by contented shepherds, derives from the Roman poet Virgil, who set his *Eclogues* in Arcady[76], influenced by the *Idylls* of the Greek pastoral poet Theocritus (first half of the third century BC).

The meaning of the well-known phrase *et in Arcadia ego* is disputed, but seems to suggest 'even in Arcady am I', the 'I' being Death. Giovanni Francesco Barbieri, known as *Il Guercino* (The Squinting One), was one of the first to paint the subject, and depicted a skull set on a pedestal inscribed *et in Arcadia ego* which two shepherds have discovered: the meaning is clear, for the skull is Death, speaking through the inscription to the effect that, even in Arcadia, Death holds sway. Thus *Il Guercino*'s painting is really a thinly disguised Classicising Mediaeval *memento mori*. On occasion the phrase became *et ego in Arcadia*, meaning 'I too lived in Arcady', and expressing great happiness lost for ever. Nicolas Poussin, in his second version of the *et in Arcadia ego* theme (c.1635-6) featured shepherds in Arcady carefully studying the inscription on a very simple, severe tomb set in the landscape (**CPl.VIII.I**, p.180). Overt references to Death (e.g. the skull) were expunged: the shadow of the kneeling shepherd cast on the tomb alludes to the spirit, or the Classical *Manes*, but the image became a powerful one for eighteenth-century protagonists of the elegiac landscape. The memorial in a garden could not only evoke the shade of the departed, but ideas of Arcady too, the Land of Lost Happiness: most importantly, all references to the horrors of decay, bones, putrefaction, and the dank, unwholesome graveyard or vault were banished. Here was a peaceful, beautiful ideal, a place fit for reflection and memories where Death was civilised[77].

As Richard Etlin has noted, with the beginnings of the Picturesque landscape, 'the tomb entered the garden'[78]. However, as early as the seventeenth century, English poets had alluded to modest tombs set in gardens, harking back to Classical Antiquity and the Elysian Fields celebrated by Hesiod, Homer, Virgil, and others. Abraham Cowley, for example, expressed his desire in verse to be buried in his own garden, 'free from noise and pain', with the beauties of the landscape invoking Paradise itself[79].

One of the first major landscaped gardens to suggest the Elysian Fields was that at Castle Howard, Yorkshire: there, the pleasant groves and lush countryside were mnemonic of a Virgilian landscape, and the great Mausoleum containing the dead of the family was a magnificent ornament to the composed setting of the house. Alexander Pope created a garden of 'memory and meditation' at Twickenham (1719-44) that included a grotto embellished with geological specimens (presented by friends and admirers) serving as mnemonics of those who had given them to him, and an obelisk set in a cypress grove (a monument to his mother). The elegiac character of Pope's garden, with its visual and emotional climax in the memorial obelisk, was greatly admired, notably by Christian Cajus Lorenz Hirschfeld in his huge *Theorie der Gartenkunst*[80]: it was Hirschfeld who famously gave credit to the English for introducing to gardens memorials in the form of urns, columns, and buildings, and Pope's obelisk was one of the first such memorials through which the

---

71 Farquhar (1930) **i** 172-3.
72 Thomas (1901) *passim*.
73 During the seventeenth and eighteenth centuries it was also common in England.
74 O'Connor (1919).
75 Curl (1994*a*) for the first detailed discussion of this. William Hutchinson (1775) associated *Night Thoughts* with Masonic sentiments, and indeed Young, for a short time, was closely connected with Philip, Duke of Wharton. Hutchinson's daughters were known to some as Faith, Hope, and Charity, but to their detractors they were called, unhappily, Plague, Pestilence, and Famine. See ODNB **xxix** (2004) 36-7, and **lx** (2004) 882-7.
76 *See* Hornblower & Spawforth (*Eds*.) (1996) 138-9, 1602-7, and Howatson (*Ed*.) (1989) 48-9.

77 Curl (1994*a*). I am grateful to Taylor & Francis Ltd. For permission to quote from this paper.
78 Etlin (1994) 163. Etlin's admirable book (which I had the pleasure of reviewing in *Progressive Architecture* [August 1984] 125-6) when it first came out, is the most comprehensive study of the topic.
79 *Ibid*. 171.
80 Hirschfeld (1779-85): also published as *Théorie de l'art des Jardins* by the same Leipzig publishers. It was brought out again in 1973 by Minkoff Reprints of Geneva.

poet sought to retain the presence of his mother near him by means of allusions, mnemonics, and the artful composition of a landscaped garden.

One of the most significant figures in the transformation of the garden was the English poet, William Shenstone, whose elegiac writings, lamenting lost youth, friendship, life, or love, disseminated notions of memorials set in evocative landscapes. Etlin has observed that in Shenstone's works the 'connection between elegiac sentiment and the landscape could not be made more explicit'[81], and indeed Shenstone intended that his published elegies would be illustrated with scenes from his own garden. This was The Leasowes, Halesowen, Worcestershire (of which very little survives), intended to evoke an idealised Virgilian Arcady. In Virgil's fifth *Eclogue* the raising of a lasting memorial to the dead Daphnis is mentioned, and this is alluded to by an image of a funerary urn set in a grove used as a vignette by Robert Dodsley (publisher, too, of Young's *Night Thoughts*), in his posthumous edition of Shenstone's writings in 1764[82]. Shenstone celebrated his friends in what was essentially a Garden of Remembrance. Creations such as Shenstone's provided exemplars, and the urn, the marker, and the memorial became essential ornaments of the garden, part of the eighteenth-century attempts to evoke elegiac sentiments, trigger associations, and Classical Antiquity in Northern Europe. However, Shenstone, obsessed by the idea of *et in Arcadia ego* as 'and I was once an inhabitant of Arcadia', contributed to a transformation of the *memento mori* concept behind the paintings of *Il Guercino* and Poussin, so that the phrase signified the dead who had once known the joys of life in a peaceful landscape. The spirits of the dead remained, therefore, in the gardens, and through Death the living passed into an evocation of Arcadia, the land of perpetual Spring. Just as Pope retained the presence of his mother in his garden, so Shenstone and his contemporaries kept their dead friends, loves, and pasts enshrined by allusion and mnemonic means in elegiac gardens.

In the gardens at Stowe the emphasis was slightly different: there, not only individuals, but public virtues and ideals were commemorated. The Elysian Fields at Stowe attempted a re-creation of a landscape of Virgilian groves, sweetly-watered meadows, and still lakes. Kent set the elegiac tone with his Temple of British Worthies, and the numerous monuments erected in the gently-contoured landscape commemorated national figures. Virtues of the British were celebrated in the Temples, and a host of triggers for contemplation was created. Stowe was of enormous importance because it demonstrated how commemoration and ideas could be contained within a pastoral setting that evoked Arcady and Elysium. Stowe was inspiring, reminding visitors of Nationhood, Liberty, and cherished Ideals, all by means of buildings, monuments, man-made landscapes, vistas, and sequential episodes in a vast garden. Hirschfeld saw Stowe as a superb model for future developments, inspiring noble ideas through mnemonics, and linking Classical Antiquity to the recent past and the future. Continental visitors admired such English landscapes, and a potent series of themes began to emerge.

Night Thoughts proved to be an important influence on Salomon Gessner, whose *Idyllen* came out in 1756, with a subsequent French edition of 1762[83]. Gessner's pastoral poetry enjoyed one of the most sensational successes in the literary history of Europe, and was admired by Hirschfeld and many others for whom it greatly surpassed in excellence the poetry of Antiquity, even that of Virgil. Many Continental aristocrats who had laid out celebrated gardens were profoundly influenced by Gessner's work. This Swiss author celebrated the virtues, not of heroes, but of ordinary life, such as family affection, mutual respect, gratitude, consideration, and fidelity. His *Idylls* did not preach, but inspired virtuous behaviour through sensibility: throughout, tombs set in charming, gentle landscapes were significant catalysts in promoting appropriately tender feelings.

In the twentieth century there were disapproving voices raised against this sort of thing. Norman Douglas unfairly dismissed Gessner as a 'derivative bore..., moralising in some decorous Paradise amid flocks of Dresden-China sheep and sugary-watery youths and maidens. Who can read his much-translated masterpiece without unpleasant twinges?'[84]. Douglas also recalled, with distaste, 'an infinity of kissing' in Gessner's tome that 'could not but end in slobber and *Gefühlsduselei*'[85], but then by that time Douglas had no sympathy with gynerasts. True, tears are not bitter in the *Idylls*, and there is little in Gessner's work to suggest that any shepherd, sporting with Amaryllis in the shade, behaved indecorously. However, it seems that Gessner *was* widely read, and his writings helped in no small measure to promote the idea of the visit to the tomb of a loved one, and the 'weeping pastoral' was widely quoted. Tombs in landscapes began to be regarded as essential elements in visions of Arcadia. In Gessner's idealised world the tomb in the garden was a place where the living could weep moderate tears, recall the dead to mind, reflect, remember, and keep the departed 'alive' in some way in thought and spirit. Gessner's *Idylls* have many references to graves in beautiful landscapes, surrounded with honeysuckle, willows, and creeping ivies, where the living could pour libations and remember their dead in a way that almost suggested their continuing presence. The Gessnerian tomb in the Arcadian landscape therefore stood as an evocative and potent marker, a sort of talisman, between two worlds (either of which, in the Youngian sense, could be more 'real' than the other), where the living could derive inspiration, happiness, moral uplift, and tender feelings from visits. Sentimental Gessner may have been, but his work should be considered in the context of how the dead

---

81 Etlin (1984) 176.
82 Shenstone (1764).
83 *See* Gessner (1756, 1762).
84 Douglas (1915) 315.
85 Sentimental mush.

Pl.VIII.5 Plan of the *Jardin de Monceau*, Paris, belonging to the Duc de Chartres. Note the three Mazes, or Labyrinths, and the Yellow, Rose, and Blue Gardens to the North (*left*) of which is the *Bois des Tombeaux*. Drawn by Carmontelle and engraved by Bertand. Plate I from Carmontelle (1779) (*Collection JSC*).

were disposed of at the time: insanitary, malodorous, overcrowded, ugly, repulsive, and horrible burial-grounds have been amply described in numerous publications[86], and there is little point in repeating those sagas of revolting and disgusting vileness here.

From 1773 to 1778 Louis Carrogis[87], known as Carmontelle, laid out the landscape of allusions at Monceau, near Paris, for Louis-Philippe-Joseph d'Orléans, the Anglophile Duc de Chartres and Grand Master of the Grand Orient of France. What is now the *Parc Monceau* was one of the first 'naturalistic' French gardens, but it contained (and still contains) a *Bois des Tombeaux* where pyramids, pedestals, and urns were set among the trees (**Pls.VIII.5 & 6**). Much later, in 1801, Nicolas-Thérèse-Benoît, Comte Frochot, made a proposal that the *Parc* should be converted into a public cemetery because real tombs could augment the cenotaphs in Carmontelle's *Bois des Tombeaux*: this was never realised, but it is worth tracing how the idea evolved.

Burial and Commemoration in Gardens

Various themes outlined above began to coalesce in the 1770s. At Ermenonville, René-Louis, Marquis de Girardin, Freemason, created an *Élysée* which he modelled on The Leasowes (he had visited Shenstone's garden in the 1760s) and on the description of 'Julie's' garden in *La Nouvelle Héloïse*[88], the popular novel by Jean-Jacques Rousseau. Now Rousseau had been born a Protestant, and his unorthodox ideas marked him out as being unacceptable to certain elements of the *Ancien Régime*. He spent the last weeks of his life at Ermenonville, and when he died Girardin had his body buried in the centre of a small island in the *Élysée* lake: there, surrounded by poplars (hence *Île des Peupliers*), a temporary tomb-marker, consisting of a Classical pedestal topped by an urn, was erected (**Pl.VIII.7**).

The burial was reported in the press, and a view of the *Île des Peupliers* was published and became widely distributed. Not long afterwards Hubert Robert, the landscape-painter, designed a permanent stone tomb in the form of an Antique sarcophagus which again was recorded in images and became familiar throughout Europe[89]. Hirschfeld approved, finding nothing disagreeable or sombre about Rousseau's burial, for the poet appeared to be 'sleeping' on the island: indeed, Hirschfeld hailed Rousseau's grave as a model for a new system of burying in gardens rather than within overcrowded churchyards and churches (**Pls. VIII.8 & 9**, p.188).

This very influential tomb, however, was much more than a gesture of friendship. First of all, it was a monument to Nature and Truth; secondly, it evoked English exemplars; and thirdly, perhaps even more importantly, the Marquis was making a public statement about his open-mindedness and lack of bigotry by burying a 'heretic' in his own garden. Girardin thus responded in a dramatic, public, and practical way to the 'Narcissa episode' in

---

86 *See*, for example, Curl (2000c), Etlin (1984), and other titles listed in the Select Bibliography.
87 Carmontelle (1779) *passim*.

88 Rousseau (1761).
89 Girardin (1777). *See* also Ermenonville (1788).

ELYSIAN FIELDS AND GARDEN TRANSFORMATIONS / 187

Pl.VIII.6 View of the *Bois des Tombeaux, Parc Monceau*, Paris, designed by Carmontelle and engraved by L. Lesueur. Plate XII from Carmontelle (1779) (*Collection JSC*).

Pl.VIII.7 The temporary tomb of Jean-Jacques Rousseau on the *Île des Peupliers*, or *Élysée*, in the gardens of the Vicomte de Girardin at Ermenonville. View dated 1778 by Jean-Michel Moreau (*Collection JSC*).

Pl.VIII.8 The *Île des Peupliers* at Ermenonville, showing the later permanent tomb of J.-J. Rousseau, designed by Hubert Robert and sculpted by Le Sueur. From Ermenonville (1788): illustrated by Mérigot Fils (*Collection JSC*).

Pl.VIII.9 Detail of Rousseau's tomb on the *Île des Peupliers* at Ermenonville by Hubert Robert (*Collection JSC*).

Young's *Night Thoughts*. Soon the *Élysée*, partly influenced also by Stowe, became so frequently visited that Girardin had to limit access to it in order to protect it. Tourists were advised to view the island from the shore of the lake, but even then the greenswards became bald, and the *Élysée* somewhat tired-looking around the edges of the lake.

The author of the official guidebook to Ermenonville, Stanislas-Cécile-Xavier-Louis, Comte de Girardin, Vicomte d'Ermenonville, was not backward in pointing out that the park could easily have provided Gessner with settings for his *Idylls*. Furthermore, the abstractions of Stowe were developed by celebrating Humanity, Justice, Light, Nature, Physics, and Satire by means of monuments to, respectively, William Penn, Charles-Louis de Secondat, Baron de la Brède et de Montesquieu, Sir Isaac Newton, J.-J. Rousseau, René Descartes, and François-Marie Arouet, better-known as Voltaire. On another island was the grave of the painter Georg Friedrich Meyer, and there were numerous cenotaphs and memorials, including a truncated pyramid commemorating Theocritus, Virgil, James Thomson, and Gessner, the four poets who had celebrated the sweet images of Nature. Near by was a monument inscribed in English to Shenstone's memory.

Ermenonville, therefore, was an exemplar of great significance, recognised as such by Hirschfeld in his influential work on garden-design, which also drew attention to other tombs in gardens such as those of Johann Georg Sulzer (who had promoted the landscaped 'English' garden in Germany[90]) near Berlin, and of the *Landgräfin* Henrietta Caroline of Hesse-Darmstadt in the *Herrengarten*, Darmstadt. Sulzer's tomb was an obelisk on a pedestal set by a quiet pool surrounded by trees, and that of the *Landgräfin* was a simple funerary mound covered with ivy and shaded by willows, yews, and dark conifers in a spot where she was wont to visit and meditate when alive (her tomb acquired a funerary urn embellished with an inscription by the Freemason King Friedrich II of Prussia). These, and other peaceful, charming, and affecting examples were described by Hirschfeld, who noted with approval that there was nothing grisly or terrible about them.

Other writers also changed perceptions. The Abbé Jacques Delille brought out his important poem *Les Jardins* in 1782[91] in which he praised Poussin's version of Arcady as a model, and emphasised the importance of trees, water, and plants to provide proper settings

---
90 Sulzer (1771-4).
91 Delille (1782).

Pl.VIII.10 The Pantheon-temple at Franconville-la-Garenne, engraved by Lepagelet after a drawing by F. Marie de Lussy, from Lussi (1784) (BL.282.d.17).

Pl.VIII.11 *Bosquet de l'Amitié* at Franconville-la-Garenne, drawn and engraved by Lepagelet, from Lussi (1784) (BL. 282. d.17).

for tombs. He proposed an Elysium which would be a commemorative park embellished with statues. However, it was Bernardin de Saint-Pierre who carried ideas for transforming the commemorative garden even further[92]: he proposed landscaped *Élysées* as the burial-places of the Great and Good, and public cemeteries (essentially landscaped gardens where the dead would be buried and, if prosperity allowed, monuments erected). Specifically, Bernardin denounced contemporary churchyards and burials in churches as harmful to the living, hygienically indefensible, and aesthetically disgusting. He proposed that Paris should follow the examples of Classical Antiquity, the Chinese, and the Ottoman Turks by burying its dead in the countryside. Public cemeteries should be created in the vicinity of the city, planted with cypresses, pines, and fruit-trees, and monuments erected in such a setting could only induce profound moral feelings and tender melancholy in those who visited them. The living would thus derive benefit from perambulations of such Arcadian places, whereas any unfortunate who stumbled upon foetid and revolting churchyards could only experience horror, disgust, and an assault on any tender feelings.

Bernardin proposed that a garden-cemetery should have its own sepulchral chapel for funeral services, and that the design of tombs would be the choice of individuals. In his suggestions for landscaped *Élysées* he envisaged large landscaped parks beautified by columns, obelisks, pyramids, urns, statues, pedestals, domed buildings, temples, and sculptures of all sorts, with a great variety of stones to vary the colours as much as possible. Overcrowding of monuments would be avoided, and the principles of the informal 'English' Picturesque landscape would be applied. Throughout, trees and shrubs selected would be plentiful, and chosen with care for the best possible visual effects[93].

These themes were gathered together in the entry on cemeteries in the *Encylopédie* contributed by Antoine-Chrysostôme Quatremère de Quincy, Freemason, architectural theorist, and key figure in the formation of the first landscaped cemeteries. However, literary efforts largely concerned with records, theories, and the dissemination of ideas were one thing, but exemplars were another, for the gardens actually laid out were among the most important precedents for the Elysian cemetery of the future. And central to the creation of such plans were reactions to *Night Thoughts*, men of the Enlightenment, and the ideals of Freemasonry.

---

92 Bernardin de Saint-Pierre (1784).

93 Etlin (1984) *passim*, but *see* especially 214-5.

Pl.VIII.12 *Rocher*, or artificial rock, at Franconville-la-Garenne, engraved by Lepagelet after a drawing by F. Marie de Lussy, from Lussi (1784) (*BL.282.d.17*).

Pl.VIII.13 'La Piramide' (a memorial to the Comte d'Albon's ancestors) at Franconville-la-Garenne, engraved by Lepagelet after a drawing by Angélique Charlotte, Comtesse d'Albon, from Lussi (1784) (*BL.282.d.17*).

Claude-Camille-François, Comte d'Albon, created an extraordinary and evocative garden at Franconville-la-Garenne in the 1780s. Several views of this beautiful elegiac garden were drawn by Angélique Charlotte de Castellane, Comtesse d'Albon, and these, with other illustrations by F. Marie de Lussy engraved by Lepagelet (Le Pagelet), were published[94]. This stunning Picturesque garden contained numerous *fabriques*, including a Pantheon-like Temple (a common motif in Freemasonic iconography) (**Pl.VIII.10**, p.189), an Obelisk, a Temple of the Muses, a *Bosquet d'Amitié* (Grove of Tender Affection) (**Pl. VIII.11**, p.189), a Cascade, a Temple of the Dawn, a Primitive Hut (alluding to theories concerning the origin of Architecture by Laugier *et al.*), a Priapus, an Isle, a Chinese Kiosk, a *Rocher* (artificial rock, in this case with waterfalls [**Pl.VIII.12**]), a Fountain, a Statue of Pan, a Devil's Bridge (to be oecumenical), an Asylum for Shepherds (being Arcadia, an essential shelter in inclement weather), a Column, and a Pyramid (commemorating the d'Albon ancestors [**Pl.VIII.13**]). Such wide-ranging allusions to many styles, ideas, and civilisations were not only intended to be mnemonic, but the eclecticism was indicative of open-mindedness, a Freemasonic virtue. Even more startling was the monument to 'William Tell' and other allusions to Switzerland (and therefore indicating approval of freedom from oppression, of national aspirations, and of democracy).

Three other elements in d'Albon's garden deserve the closest attention. The first of these was the cenotaph of the Swiss botanist and physiologist, Albrecht von Haller, consisting of a mound like a truncated pyramid with an urn on its flat top and four poplars planted around the mound (**Pl. VIII.14**). The second was the tomb of Court de Gébelin, Linguist, Protestant, Freemason, and author of *Monde Primitif* [95], who had inspired many aspects of the garden with his ideas. Taking themes from Rousseau, Court de Gébelin had contrasted earlier, simpler, more primitive times with his own day, and saw many virtues lacking in the France of his times. His tomb had an Antique 'primitive' air about it, with four 'ruined' columns set as sentinels around the blocky sarcophagus, an arrangement that was not unlike that of Haller's cenotaph (**Pl.VIII.15**). Thus d'Albon deliberately arranged for his friend, a 'heretic' and a Freemason, to be buried in his own garden, partly

---

94 Lussi (1784) and Lepagelet & Lussi (1790). Lussi is given as 'Lussy' on the illustrations in 'Pinx', but as Lussi in print.

95 Court de Gébelin (1773-82).

in emulation of Girardin's burial of Rousseau[96] (the poplars of Haller's cenotaph and the 'ruined' primitive columns with poplars near by allude to the *Île des Peupliers* at Ermenonville), and partly to show that he was a civilised creature of the Enlightenment, unlike the unfeeling bigots described by Young in the 'Narcissa episode' of *Night Thoughts*. The third element was the *Caverne d'Young*, an artificial cave or grotto erected in memory of the English poet, High Priest of the Cult of Sepulchral Melancholy, and critic of bigots who refused 'Narcissa' the rights they gave their dogs (**Pl.VIII.16**, p.192). So Franconville-la-Garenne was a demonstration that an aristocratic, enlightened, sensitive, French Freemason, by tenderly burying a 'heretic' and fellow-member of the Craft on his estate, could show the world that he was capable of responding to Young's strictures by kindness, benevolence, freedom of thought, and the rejection of religious bigotry (all Freemasonic virtues).

The Rousseau and Court de Gébelin examples made it clear that the commemoration of men and ideas by means of monuments could be far more telling if real bodies lay beneath them. Sometimes it was not possible to acquire the cadavers, so cenotaphs[97] had to suffice. Anne-Pierre, Marquis de Montesquiou-Fézensac, influential Freemason, had employed Ledoux to rebuild the house and remodel the park at his estate of Maupertuis (Manche) in the 1760s, and later, in the 1770s, commissioned Alexandre-Théodore

Pl.VIII.14 'Le tombeau d'haller' (it was actually a cenotaph) at Franconville-la-Garenne, engraved by Lepagelet after a drawing by F. Marie de Lussy, from Lussi (1784) (*BL.282.d.17*).

96 Rousseau died 2 July 1778. His body was '*déposé*' on the *Île des Peupliers* 4 January 1779, but later '*transporté*' to the *Panthéon* in Paris 13 October 1791.

97 Empty tombs.

Pl.VIII.15 '*Tombeau*' [actual] *de Court de Gébelin transporté à Franconville et inhumé dans les jardins de M^de La Comtesse d'Albon le Dix Juillet 1784*', engraved by Lepagelet after a drawing by F. Marie de Lussy, from Lussi (1784). Court de Gébelin, Protestant and Freemason, was the distinguished author of *Le Monde Primitif*. The form of the tomb with the four markers appears to have Masonic significance for it recurs in several eighteenth-century designs, and is associated with marking out of territory (*BL.282.d.17*).

Pl.VIII.16 *Caverne d'Young* at Franconville-la-Garenne, drawn and engraved by Lepagelet, from Lussi (1784). Edward Young was the author of *Night Thoughts*, the poetic work highly influential in France and Germany (*BL.282.d.17*).

Brongniart to design the 'ruined' pyramid to stand by the lake in the *Élysée* set within the gardens. A well-known view of this pyramid was published by Alexandre-Louis-Joseph, Comte de Laborde[98], but few have commented on some aspects of the illustration that are worth mention. The pyramid was used for various meetings and ceremonies of a Freemasonic or quasi-Freemasonic nature, and Brongniart (himself a Freemason) alluded to Hermetic-Egyptian mysteries by means of the segmental pediment in primitive Doric columns. The segmental pediment was unknown in Classical Architecture before the first century AD, and was particularly associated with Nilotic cults, especially the worship of Isis, the goddess of the moon (so the crescent-moon is suggested by the shape of the pediment)[99]. To the left of the Pyramid in the illustration (drawn by Constant Bourgeois[100]) is a Neo-Classical mausoleum-like building, actually a monumental cenotaph commemorating the Protestant Admiral Gaspard de Châtillon, Comte de Coligny, who was murdered on St Bartholomew's Day, and whose dead body was displayed on a gibbet where it suffered further indignities (**Pl.VIII.17**). Now this is very significant, for

---

98 Laborde (1808-15).
99 Curl (2005) *passim*, but *see* especially 17, 31-4, 36, 52, 95, 114, 175, 194, 286.
100 And engraved by Madame Massard.

the Marquis was making overt his disapproval of bigotry and intolerance by responding to Young's description of the 'Narcissa episode' in *Night III*: he demonstrated that he could (and would) commemorate 'heretics' and would bury them with decency (if he could) in his own garden, but if he had no corpse to inter, he would still solemnly commemorate 'heretic' dead by erecting cenotaphs. The Coligny cenotaph was commented upon by the Scots landscape-gardener, Thomas Blaikie, who observed that the presence of the cenotaph demonstrated that the Marquis was no friend 'of those catholick persicutions which is looked upon by most reasonable people as a disgrace to France. Here about this part of the country are a great Many protestant familly although not tolerated in France yet they are much respected'[101].

Jean-Joseph, Marquis de Laborde, also a Freemason, created another *Élysée* in his garden at Méréville (Essonne): there, by the lake, he erected a rostral column to commemorate two of his sons who had died on the fatal expedition of Jean-François de Galaup, Comte de la Pérouse, which came to grief in the Samoan Islands and on reefs north of the New Hebrides (**Pl.VIII.18**). In order to show his even-handedness and open mind, he also erected four grave Antique Greek Doric columns, supporting a rudimentary entablature as a shelter for the funerary urn and pedestal in memory of Captain James Cook, who lost his life in Hawaii during his third great voyage of exploration (**Pl.VIII.19**). The Méréville ensemble was also designed by Hubert Robert (who succeeded the Architect François-Joseph Bélanger, responsible for the general plan), and the positions of the two monuments by the lake-shore were intended to allude to the distant sea-shores on which both the British and French expeditions had met nemesis. A further allusive mnemonic touch was provided by the sea pine and other carefully chosen plants, whilst the weeping-willows and poplars contributed to the sad, elegiac qualities of the landscape. All too soon the Marquis himself was to perish by the Guillotine.

A.-L.-J. Laborde, son of the Marquis, in his celebrated and very beautiful book[102], listed and illustrated many important French gardens, including Ermenonville, Méréville, Maupertuis, and Morfontaine (with Weymouth Pine[103] and black marble tomb on a high pedestal set on an artificial mound [**Pl.VIII.20**, p.194]; *bosquet* and altar-like tomb at the entrance of the Little Park [**Pl. VIII.21**, p.194]; and rock-work [*Grand Rocher*] inscribed with verses by Delille [**Pl.VIII.22**, p.195]). Morfontaine or Mortefontaine (Oise) was the property of Louis Le Peletier de Morfontaine, Marquis de Montmélian, until purchased by Joseph Bonaparte in 1798, yet another Freemason. Laborde also described the garden at Plessis-Chamand, where the wife of the owner was buried in a fine tomb set in the park, surrounded by shrubs and trees[104] (**Pl.VIII.23**. p.195).

---

101 Blaikie (1931) 206.
102 Laborde (1808-15).
103 The New English larch, introduced to England in 1705, named after Sir Thomas Thynne, 1st Viscount Weymouth.
104 *Vues pittoresques*... (1787).

Pl. VIII.17 The 'ruined' pyramid in the *Élysée* at Maupertuis designed by Brongniart. Note the Doric columns carrying the segmental pediment (a form associated with Isiac cults). On the left is the cenotaph in memory of Admiral Gaspard de Coligny, the Protestant murdered on St Bartholomew's Day 1572. From Laborde (1808-15), drawn by Constant Bourgeois and engraved by Madame Massard (*DO, HU*).

Pl.VIII.18 Rostral column at Méréville, from Laborde (1808-15), Plate 54, drawn by Constant Bourgeois and engraved by F. Gamble (*DO, HU*).

Pl.VIII.19 'Tomb' (actually cenotaph) in memory of Captain James Cook at Méréville, from Laborde (1808-15), Plate 55, drawn by Constant Bourgeois and engraved by F. Gamble (*DO, HU*).

Pl.VIII.20 Weymouth Pine and black-marble tomb set on an artificial mound in the Little Park at Morfontaine, from Laborde (1808-15), Plate 16, drawn by Constant Bourgeois and engraved by Mlle Olimpe Neveu (*SJSM*).

Pl.VIII.21 *Bosquet* at the entrance to the Little Park at Morfontaine, from Laborde (1808-15), Plate 15, drawn by Constant Bourgeois and engraved by Mlle Olimpe Neveu (*SJSM*).

Pl.VIII.22 *Grand Rocher* at Morfontaine, inscribed with a quotation from Delille (1782), from Laborde (1808-15), Plate 20, drawn by Constant Bourgeois and engraved by F. Gamble (*SJSM*).

Pl.VIII.23 Tomb in the garden at Plessis-Chamand (Oise), from Laborde (1808-15), Plate 68, drawn by Constant Bourgeois and engraved by de Villiers the Younger (*SJSM*).

The Emergence of the Cemetery

Thus it was that the Arcadian landscape-garden, embellished with *fabriques*, became a desirable exemplar for burial of the dead when compared with unsavoury, even vile, urban churchyards. Yet politicians moved slowly, and it was some time before the idea was officially adopted. Under the *Ancien Régime* the Churchyard of the Innocents in Paris which had been in use for centuries, was closed. For many years its condition had been scandalous, and in the 1780s the Church of the Innocents and the *charniers* (charnel-houses) surrounding the putrid ground were demolished. In 1785 the transfer of bones began from the Innocents to underground ossuaries in worked-out quarries under the Plaine De Montrouge in Montparnasse, but contemporary descriptions suggest they were places of nightmares, worlds of darkness and silence broken only when new cartloads of bones from other closed crypts and churchyards were tipped in. There Chaos reigned, with Destruction and Death.

However, from 1810, Prefect Frochot (who also proposed the conversion of the *Parc Monceau* into a cemetery) and the Inspector-General of Quarries, Louis-Étienne-François Héricart-Ferrand, later Vicomte de Thury, created Order (a skill of Freemasons and [once] of Architects) in this Kingdom of Death and Chaos by arranging bones and skulls in carefully constructed walls lining corridors and spaces with all the precision and severity of Neo-Classical taste. There, the visitor was exhorted to be quiet, and to contemplate vain grandeur, nothingness, and the Silences of Death[105] (**Pls.VIII.24 & 25**, p.196).

The Freemason and Theorist, Quatremère de Quincy, favoured the establishment of catacombs, and he was the leading light in the transformation of Soufflot's great church of Sainte-Geneviève (secularised 1791) into the national *Panthéon*. Charles-Michel de la Villette, Marquis du Plessis (who burned his patents of Nobility in an act of political correctness and was the protégé of Voltaire, who dubbed him 'the French Tibullus'[106]), became Deputy for the Département of Seine-et-Oise, and supported the concept of converting the building into a national tomb for the Great and Good. Villette opined that Parisian burial-grounds were hideous, and that something drastic should be done about them. He favoured the idea of establishing cemeteries or 'sleeping-places', doubtless with the garden at Plessis-Chamand in mind. For a time it was hoped to create a vast public cemetery around the *Panthéon*, but this was never realised, so the building stood for several years in a somewhat bald open space. Quatremère de Quincy, who was very much aware of the concept of *types* of buildings, was instrumental in the blocking-up of the windows of the former Church in order *to give it the character of a mausoleum*. This has been completely misinterpreted by some, including John Summerson, who wrote that 'the windows had to be blocked' because 'the factor of safety proved too low'[107].

The Architect Antoine-Laurent-Thomas Vaudoyer proposed transforming the promenade of the *Champs-Elysées* into a linear cemetery resembling the *Via Appia Antica* outside Rome, but much grander, lined with noble mausolea and statues of illustrious Frenchmen. Vaudoyer also hinted at an educational programme in this proposal, whereby History would be taught and the place of the dead in that history demonstrated in many ways. It is perhaps regrettable that this idea of a *Voie Sacrée* was never realised, for given the period and the grandeur of its Architecture, it would have been stunningly beautiful, effective, and moving (as well as instructive).

However, the notion of a cemetery as a *Champ de Repos* seems to have evolved as part of the anti-clericalism and egalitarianism of the Revolution. The dead were to be severed from churches, Christian symbols were to be removed, and the new cemeteries were to become a means of social engineering, promoting the ideals of the Revolution: at the secular tomb contracts could be signed, promises sworn, and discord smoothed. Cemeteries were to be the catalysts in the promotion of tender feelings in

---

105 Héricart-Ferrand (1815). *See also* Saint-A... (1816) 188-243.

106 Anonymous pamphleteers promoted him as 'Grand Commander' of a quasi-Freemasonic Order. One publication, *Les Enfants de Sodome à l'Assemblée Nationale, ou Députation de l'Ordre de la Manchette aux représants tous les Ordres* made much of his homosexuality.

107 Summerson (1980) 93. Howard Colvin (1919-2007) complained of Summerson's 'factual carelessness', as well he might: I have read more student essays than I care to remember, in which the windows blocked up were ascribed to a need to strengthen the structure, all stemming from Summerson's text. For a detailed study of the *Panthéon* see Middleton & Baudouin-Matuszek (2007).

Pl.VIII.24 View in the *Crypte de Saint-Laurent* in the Paris Catacombs by Cloquet from Héricart-Ferrand (1815), Plate 6. The inscription is taken from the First Epistle of Paul the Apostle to the Corinthians, Ch. 15, v.52-3, referring to the sounding of the Last Trump (*Canet Tuba*), the Dead being raised incorruptible, the corruptible putting on incorruption, and mortals putting on immortality (*Collection JSC*).

Pl.VIII.25 *Vue Intérieur des Catacombes* showing the bones as arranged in a chamber by Héricart de Thury from 1810. From St.-A (1816), opposite page 188, engraved by Dubois (*Collection JSC*).

the Elysian Fields which would be dramatically contrasted with Church-controlled burial-grounds where skulls, bones, foetor, horror, and loathsomeness were to be found in plenty. Agreeable philanthropic ideals and sweet reason were to replace despair, terror, hellfire, superstition, and disgusting sights and smells. Death was to became Eternal Rest, or Sleep, and all ghoulish images in Baroque and Christian Art were to be banished. Those gleefully animated skeletons on Baroque funerary monuments, brandishing spears, scythes, and hour-glasses, were to be eliminated: Death would be tamed, and the garden-cemetery, with its Freemasonic, Youngian, and anti-clerical connotations, would weaken the forces of reaction, superstition, and the past. That, in a nutshell, was the theory.

The official Decree of 23 Prairial, Year XII (12 June 1804) drew up the rules for French cemeteries that have remained essentially the same until our own times. It prohibited burial in churches and towns and ordered the establishment of cemeteries outside urban limits, planted with trees and shrubs. Regulations were drawn up concerning modes of burial, the erection of tombs, and monuments, and so on. The Decree was the culmination of much debate, indecision, and fierce differences of opinion: as Ariès noted[108], it was far more than a legal text, but a kind of secular 'Ten Commandments' of a new cult, the Cult of the Dead, although the moral and religious aspects of the Decree have been gradually whittled away, so that eventually it became more or less a set of regulations for public health. A further metamorphosis was that the banished, distant cemetery only impinged but little on the physical realities and spiritual awareness of the living: within a few decades, though, not only did the cemetery, as it was beautified and the idea of the landscape-garden dotted with *fabriques*, in its transformed state as a *Champ de Repos*, become a place of resort for the living, but towns could not be seen as viable social organisations without it[109].

The Administration of Public Works in Paris proposed four new cemeteries for the city, in rural settings, as the concept of large, airy, and well-planned places of burial gained credence. Nevertheless, it was not until 1804 that Frochot was able to instruct Brongniart, by then Chief Inspector-General of the Second Section of Public Works for the *Département* of the Seine and the City of Paris, to develop land at Mont-Louis as a great cemetery to the east of the city. This became the famous cemetery of Père-Lachaise. Brongniart proposed a large pyramid (never realised) on the main axis, combined formal and naturalistic elements in the designs (**Pl.VIII.26**), and created circuitous carriageways with a *rond-point* at carefully selected positions[110].

Père-Lachaise, designed by a prominent Freemason, was the prototypical nineteenth-century funerary garden, and soon became world-famous. It was visited by many who were interested in the problems of burying and commemorating the dead in a civilised fashion, and its influence was enormous throughout Europe and

---

108 Ariès (1981) 516.
109 *Ibid., passim.*
110 For details on the evolution of Père-Lachaise *see* Etlin (1984) 303-58, an invaluable contribution.

America. Its many designs for superb monuments and mausolea were published in illustrated books[111], and were copied on both sides of the Atlantic. However, there was a curious aspect of the early history of Père-Lachaise Cemetery: just as once it had been desirable to be buried in churches near the Relics of Saints, post-Revolutionary, supposedly rational France sought to bury its dead in Arcadian gardens given a secular seal of approval by having the cadavers of famous people translated to them. Thus to Père-Lachaise the corpses of Jean de la Fontaine, Jean-Baptiste Poquelin, called Molière (**Pl.VIII.27**), and even the supposed remains of the Mediaeval lovers, Pierre Abélard and Héloïse, were transferred in 1817: the ill-fated last-named pair are commemorated by the canopied Gothic tomb moved from the Abbey of Paraclet under the direction of Alexandre-Marie Lenoir, and restored for the cemetery under the direction of Étienne-Hippolyte Godde (who was also responsible for the chapel and entrance-gate of the Cemetery)[112].

Pl.VIII.26 Brongniart's proposals (*c*.1810) for the Cemetery of Père-Lachaise in Paris, showing the main entrance and the vast pyramid set in the landscaped grounds (*MVP Carnavalet Inv. No. D96697, Photo No. 86 CAR 0250*).

The *Grand Rond* at Père-Lachaise was designed to be surrounded by poplars[113], so it was a deliberate allusion to Rousseau's tomb at Ermenonville: in Section 18 (a significant number in Freemasonry, as previously noted) stands the Egyptianising mausoleum of Gaspard Monge[114] and the obelisk of Champollion (**Pl. VIII.28**, p.198). Not far away are the Classical monuments of Brongniart and Delille, designed respectively by Louis-Hippolyte Lebas and Philippon (perhaps after a proposal by Hubert Robert), set, appropriately in a quiet glade[115] (**Pl.VIII.29**, p.198). Brongniart and Delille thus lie in a charming *bosquet* in the cemetery which they helped to create: it was a terrestrial Paradise, an Elysium, and an Arcady, where the enchantments of the Landscape Garden, Nature, Art, and Architecture alleviated the gloom of the grave. Delille himself had written in *Les Jardins* of an 'invitation' to visit him in his 'dark retreat,... where bending branches gently wave', his 'poetic tomb... set in a place of peace, love, and mourning'. There, perhaps, a visitor might 'shed a tear or two' upon his grave, and from 'each falling drop

Pl.VIII.27 The tombs of Molière and La Fontaine in Père-Lachaise Cemetery, Paris. These literary figures were translated to the new Cemetery in order to give it status and create a demand for burial there. Image drawn by Antoine-Félix Boisselier and engraved by Louis-Marie Normand fils. From Normand (1832) Plate 43 (*Collection JSC*).

would roses spring'. Here, therefore, was a new kind of Romantic sensibility, for nobody would have considered any urban burial-ground or churchyard (such as the sordid Innocents, with its *charniers*) as a 'place of peace, love, and mourning' by any stretch of the imagination. Thus, with the establishment of Père-Lachaise nothing less than a revolution had occurred, and the cemetery became *the* exemplar of an entirely new culture of nineteenth-century Death that transformed the disposal of corpses in many countries thereafter. As has been outlined above, however, the cemetery movement owed much to Young's *Night Thoughts*, to the English landscape garden, and to Freemasonry, all of which contributed to it, and to the taming and civilising of Death.

111 For example, in Normand (1832).
112 *Ibid.* 3, Plates 2, 20.
113 *Ibid.*, Plate 19.
114 *Ibid.*, Plate 52.
115 *Ibid.*, Plate 61.

Pl.VIII.28 *(top)* The Rond-Point des Peupliers in Père-Lachaise Cemetery, Paris, with Gaspard Monge's Egyptianesque mausoleum on the left, designed by Pierre Clochard. Image drawn by Boisselier and engraved by Normand fils. From Normand (1832) Plate 19 (*Collection JSC*).

Pl.VIII.29 *(left)* The tombs of Brongniart *(left)*, by Louis-Hippolyte Lebas, and of Jacques Delille *(right)*, by Philippon, perhaps after a proposal by Hubert Robert, in Père-Lachaise Cemetery, Paris. Brongniart's *Bourse* in Paris is shown in relief on his tomb: he was the Architect of the Cemetery, and the Abbé Jacques Delille was the author of *Les jardins, ou l'art d'embellir les paysages* (1782) an influential work that helped to create the climate of opinion in which garden-cemeteries were first laid out. Image drawn by Boisselier and engraved by Normand fils. From Normand (1832) Plate 61 (*Collection JSC*).

The Landscape Garden and Freemasonry

Suggestions that Freemasonry might have impinged on the design of the landscape garden have met with some opposition, and the topic has been denounced as an 'error' and as a 'dead end' leading 'down the garden path'[116]. Yet many scholars (none of whom may be regarded as being of unsound mind)[117] have looked at the matter in a sober and serious light, and have concluded that there are indeed, in certain instances, some sorts of connection or connections between Freemasonry and garden-design. Man, on many occasions and in many eras, has attempted to create around him surroundings that reflect or project his own concerns, feelings, or thoughts. Thus, as has been observed often, Art influences Nature, and it should be remembered that *all* Art is contrived. A garden, therefore, may provide mnemonics of those ideas, feelings, thoughts, or concerns, and give clues about the culture in which it was created. Garden History may be just as instructive about a civilisation as are the Architecture, Literature, Painting, Poetry, Sculpture, or other creative Arts. Jean-

---

116 Macpherson (1998). For insights into how the eighteenth-century garden was viewed, *see* Calder (*Ed.*) (2006).

117 *See*, for example, Buttlar (1982, 1989), Curl (1991*d*, 1995, 2004, 2006*b*), Olausson (1985), Pochat & Wagner (*Eds*) (1987) 96-116, Schwartz (1975), Vidler (1987, 1990), and many others. *See* Select Bibliography.

Jacques Rousseau, after all, proposed a natural landscape as the place for Mankind to begin his regeneration[118], so the use of a garden for purposes other than growing vegetables, fruit, or flowers, is not implausible.

Joseph Rykwert, too, considered aspects of the links between Architecture, Neo-Platonic ideas, Freemasonry, and concepts leading to a possible transformation of society in which political and religious differences would be, if not resolved, at least reconciled[119]. The distinguished French art and architectural historian, Monique Mosser, has written that 'it cannot be denied that many' of the most celebrated Picturesque French gardens of the 1770s and 1780s were created by or for aristocratic Freemasons[120], and it has been suggested that gardens such as the *Désert de Retz*, Yvelines, and the *Parc Monceau*, Paris (both designed for prominent Freemasons[121]), contained layouts and *fabriques* informed by Freemasonic ritualism and symbolism[122], although in the case of the former garden, its owner seems to have been more interested in Alchemy than the Craft, but we should not forget that Alchemy was a concern of many contemporary Continental Freemasons.

The eighteenth century was the great age of garden-design, especially in relation to the evolution and proliferation of the English landscape garden, the *jardin anglais* or *jardin anglo-chinois*, found in many places in Europe: it was also, as Olausson has reminded us, 'the great era of Freemasonry'[123]. At the beginning of that century, Freemasonry was hardly a secret at all, but later, from around 1750, especially in the Roman Catholic countries, the Craft came under attack, not only from the Papacy, but from the authors of several 'exposures', from those opposed to any suggestion that free-thinking, tolerant, enlightened minds might promote notions of equality, rationalism, and 'natural religion', and from those who could not accept ethics based on Reason rather than on Superstition policed by Fear. And there is no doubt that those in the vanguard of the European Enlightenment were either Freemasons themselves or were closely involved with Freemasons and Freemasonic ideals. Given such hostility, it is little wonder that the Craft became a lot more secretive, and evolved complicated rituals, partly for protection, and partly to give *gravitas* to ceremony.

Fabriques

In any discussion of these weighty matters it should be emphasised yet again that Continental Freemasonry is not the same as British Freemasonry, any more that the French Enlightenment, say, is similar to the British or American Enlightenments[124]. Parts of the initiation-ceremonies of Continental Freemasonry are considered as a symbolic journey (e.g. the circumambulation of the room in which the ceremony takes place), and there are unquestionably other parts of the ceremony 'for which a garden setting would be most appropriate. For example, at a certain point during the initiation ceremony the candidate', still blindfolded ('hooded'), 'is led out of the lodge room and made to follow a convoluted route, after which he is led back to the lodge and enters it bending down as if going into a cave or grotto'[125]. Even more interesting is the possible 'use of garden settings for some of the "higher degrees". The staging of these degrees as exemplified in American usage is often based on gardens, pergolas, Greek temples, and other structures that could be found... in a large garden'[126]. Thus, the interiors of Lodge-rooms would be decorated to look like a garden or gardens, complete with *fabriques*, specifically for ceremonies. It is obvious that, 'instead of building a stage decoration of a garden, a real garden could... be.. used for these... ceremonies, using permanent or temporary structures to represent temples, grottoes, peristyles, etc.'[127]. It has also been noted by another authority that 'theatrical techniques were... employed to create the *mise-en-scène* for the initiation ceremony of the Freemasons which was sometimes performed in a garden'[128]. The point is that eighteenth-century designs for interiors of *fabriques* actually were made, and the evidence of these and various routes in gardens exists, so the connections made here are not based on wishful thinking, speculation, the loony fringe of occultism, or anything other than hard fact.

As noted above, Anthony Vidler[129] has discussed initiation areas and routes in eighteenth-century contexts, and has reminded us of the description of the route and *fabriques* visited by Beckford and Ledoux, which, by any standards, was extraordinary. Most British commentators have shied away from this, or regarded it as fiction, probably because there is a whole world of the occult and the mysterious in the France of the so-called Enlightenment which frightens them to death, and of which they are woefully ignorant. In recent years have come to light drawings by the French Architect and *Ornemaniste*, Jean-Demosthène Dugourc[130], among which is a design for a

---

118 Rousseau (1761) *passim*.
119 Rykwert (1983).
120 Mosser & Teyssot (*Eds*.) (1991) 274 and *passim*. Mosser has also specifically referred to the connection between Freemasonry and landscape-gardening in 'Le Rocher et la Colonne – une thème d'iconographie architectural au XVIIIe siècle' *Revue de l'Art* **lviii-lix** (1982-3) 55-74.
121 *Le Désert de Retz* near St-Germain-en-Laye was owned by François-Nicolas-Henri Racine de Monville and the *Parc Monceau*, as previously noted, was laid out by Louis Carrogis, known as Carmontelle, for Racine de Monville's friend, the Anglophile Louis-Philippe-Joseph, Duc de Chartres, Grand Master of the Grand Orient of France. *See* Carmontelle (1779).
122 Adams (1979) 118, Vidler (1976).
123 Olausson (1985) 413.

124 *See* Himmelfarb (2008).
125 Leon Zeldis in Macpherson (1998) 72.
126 *Ibid*.
127 *Ibid*. *See* also the *Catalogue* of the Exhibition *Theatre of the Fraternity: Staging the Ritual Space of the Scottish Rite of Freemasonry 1896-1929* (Minneapolis MN: Frederick R. Weisman Art Museum 1996) 85, 88, 96, and *passim*.
128 Adams (1979) 114.
129 Vidler (1990) 337-40. Also described by Gallet (1980) 24, 269-71.
130 Guilmard (1880-1), Hartmann (1978), Montaiglon (1877), Trévise (1925).

fabrique which has what Monique Mosser calls 'disturbing parallels'[131] with Beckford's account. Dugourc was the brother-in-law of François-Joseph Bélanger, Architect of many *fabriques* in several gardens, including those of Beloeil, Belgium (for Charles-Joseph, Prince de Ligne), Bagatelle, Bois de Boulogne, Paris (for Charles-Philippe, Comte d'Artois [later King Charles X]), and Méréville, near Étampes (for Jean-Joseph, Marquis de Laborde). It looks as though Beckford's description might have been based on an experience that actually happened, especially as it is known that there are several designs for *fabriques* in more than one European country which do not appear to have been mere whims on the parts of their creators. Monique Mosser has also mentioned the resemblance of Dugourc's strange *fabrique* to the 'Regeneration' Lodge, built by Cagliostro (founder, as mentioned above, of the so-called 'Egyptian' ritual) near Basel for the Banker Jacob Sarasin. There, the candidate was to live in the company of his hierophant[132] for forty days before his initiation[133], precedents for which may be found in Isiac practices in the Roman Empire, in the 'incubation' custom followed by Emperors devoted to Queen Isis[134], suggestions in Apuleius[135], and parts of Terrasson's *Séthos*[136].

The Prince de Ligne in his *Coup d'oeil sur Beloeil et sur une grande partie des jardins de l'Europe* (1781)[137], observed that visitors to his garden who did not wish to think (he described them as not 'provoked to thought') could only have to accept the entire garden as groves and paths amid mere shrubs and flowers with the occasional building (*fabrique* – the more exotic the better), which, designed to prompt the imaginations of those who had any, could, nevertheless, be observed blankly by the untutored, or by those deficient in brain or sensibility, as a mere structure, without associations. On the other hand, *fabriques* could provide part of the *scenery* for what, in effect, was a series of stage-sets to be viewed by the *intelligent* visitor (in the dual rôles of actor and decoder) as he or she perambulated the garden. Beloeil was, in fact, a huge allegorical garden triggering thoughts that traced life from the 'cradle of childhood' to the 'chamber of death', with *fabriques* in which many eclectic themes could be found within the formal syncretism of the whole. Urbane and civilised, at ease with a vast range of subjects, from battlefields to informed contemplation of the erotic, de Ligne saw *fabriques* as means by which the iconography of the garden might be *interpreted*, with the arousal of many complex emotions, appeals to sentiment, and the expression of a kaleidoscope of ideas, intentions, and allusions. *Fabriques* (de Ligne did not care for the term) might be regarded as mere *buildings*, devoid of Architectural significance, by the dim-witted, but to those with cultivated minds and with eyes connected to their brains, they had *meanings*, and could have powerful resonances and play profound cultural rôles: recollections of friendship, of love, and of much, much more besides were given mnemonic stimuli by the temples, tombs, cenotaphs, altars, funerary urns, grottoes, caves, rock-work constructions, memorials, and so on in gardens. A primitive hut made of tree-trunks and branches, covered in moss, might serve as a reminder of debates about the origins of Architecture itself[138]; grottoes of rock-work would serve to recall to mind Antique pagan cults and river-deities, the rough foundations of sophisticated structures, early attempts to build by primitive Man, or even Man in his imperfected state; whilst a temple dedicated to a pagan Deity, a Gothic House, a Chinese bridge, an urn on a pedestal, and a cenotaph were all elements that could remind a visitor of Antiquity, of the Middle Ages, of the Exotic East, and of the inevitability of Death (and thus emphasise the importance of living full, interesting, moral lives in which probity was essential). *Fabriques* in gardens provided an architectural vocabulary linked to History, Literature, Antiquity, Feeling, Sentiment, Melancholy, and much else: they were episodes and essential elements in a microcosmic landscape designed to stimulate learned associations, enriching the spirit and encouraging the imagination to make wide-ranging connections, so the more stylistically and typologically varied they were, the richer that vocabulary would be. An eighteenth-century Garden of Allusions[139], cleverly laid out and embellished with many and varied *fabriques*, could become an encyclopaedia of the cultures, ideas, and histories of the world, and a walk through it could provide lessons in Architecture, Civilisation, and History, or could become an Allegory of the Journey through Life itself, an encapsulation of a vast range of cultural triggers to be experienced in a few hours. Thus a Gothic House, a Roman Aqueduct, a Synagogue, or a Grotto of the Sybil all had sound reasons for being there, and were not plonked down without thought. It is *essential* to understand that such a garden was not simply a series of Picturesque views composed to give frivolous amusement, but a complex mnemonic device, prompting literary, emotional, and historical associations, all imbued with *feeling*. And even the Picturesque views themselves might evoke paintings, places in Italy or Greece, or the mythology of Classical Antiquity. In short, such a garden could be regarded as a concise version of the *Encyclopédie*: it was certainly not a mere frivolous conceit. A garden-building, perceived today as a 'mere' 'ruined temple' in the Antique style, may not have been intended as such when it was built, but rather as a monument to that chimaerical Enlightenment ideal of the Perfectibility of Man, which only future generations (which had achieved a Higher State of sophistication and development) might complete and make a Classical, perfect whole: it could also, of course, be an elegiac tribute to a lost civilisation or conquered nation; to a Deity superseded by later Gods; or to dead individuals. The possibilities were enormous. And from a 'ruined' *fabrique* a

---

131 Mosser & Teyssot (*Ed*.) (1991) 274, illustrated 272.
132 Teacher, expounder, or one who reveals sacred things.
133 Mosser & Teyssot (*Eds*.) (1991) 276.
134 Curl (2005) 30.
135 Apuleius Madaurensis (1924) 333-59 (Book **xi** xlvii).
136 Terrasson (1731).
137 *See* Ligne (1922) from which all the quotations are taken.

138 Laugier (1753), for example.
139 Curl (1988, 1994a, 1995, 1997, 2000c) and Curl (*Ed*.) (2001b).

visitor might look out towards some enchanting vision of Perfection.

The widely-travelled and cultured de Ligne's advice was sought throughout Europe by those keen to create gardens. Bored by repetition, he perceived *fabriques* as offering antidotes to tedious architectural correctness, and the more original, eclectic, and exotic they were, then so much the better. Peruvian huts, Laplanders' shelters, and little palaces from the Caucasus offered more scope for mnemonics than the reconstruction, from pattern-books, of a limited range of Antique Roman temples. *Fabriques*, therefore, have an honourable place among Asylums of Libertinage, and a Garden of Allusion can be regarded as an Ideal, removed from the tedium of the prosaic world, spurring the imagination, and providing a setting for forays of the mind and spirit. *Fabriques* were definitely *not* mere ornamental buildings without meaning: they were created for *many* reasons, and were intended to speak to visitors to gardens. To claim, as some have done, that certain garden-buildings were only undertaken to give employment to unskilled out-of-work ex-soldiers, is indicative of ludicrously bleak and materialistic outlooks on life, and of woefully inadequate opinions concerning eighteenth-century gardens. The problem has been exacerbated by Modernist stripping of all *meaning* from Architecture, which, in the twenty-first century can no longer be said to have a vocabulary, let alone a language: to many today, therefore, the concept that a garden could have any serious meanings at all is difficult, if not impossible, to grasp. We should not judge eighteenth-century garden-buildings from the limited viewpoints of our own times.

De Ligne was a member of several Freemasonic Lodges in the Austrian Netherlands, was affiliated in France to the Lodge *St-Jean de Montmorency-Luxembourg*[140], and invented a cryptic vocabulary for his gardens that led to the creation of an enormously complex puzzle composed of *fabriques* in their settings. The sport, for the visitor, was to decode the messages and unravel the meanings. De Ligne was disgusted by those who could not begin to comprehend his gardens, but matters have got a lot worse since his day, as there are many who refuse to acknowledge that such complex gardens have any meanings at all. Yet Gardens of Allusions have been around for a long time, so mention of just a few of them will be necessary here, simply as a reminder that they are not figments of the fevered imaginings of an elderly historian.

Hadrian's Villa at Tivoli

In many periods of history, gardens have been designed with the *intention* of *conveying* ideas beyond the obvious pleasures of plants, paths, shady arbours, and water. Nearly all great civilisations have produced gardens that were *not only* concerned with the need to grow plants for food, fuel, cooking, perfumes, or medicinal purposes, but were also intended to appeal to the spirit, to the emotions, and to the intellect. Gardens of Allusion *with layered meanings* have been known since Antiquity. The *Villa Adriana* at Tibur (Tivoli), for example, had elaborate gardens that were specifically *designed to suggest*, among other things, the diversity of the Roman Empire during the reign of Hadrian: one of the most evocative sections of the garden was the Euripus or canal embellished with sculptures of Nilotic subjects and a *Serapaeum*[141], intended as a mnemonic of the Egyptian Canopus[142]. As the *Scriptores Historiae Augustae* relate[143], Hadrian created a marvel of Architecture and Landscape-Gardening: to the different parts he assigned the names of... buildings and localities, such as the *Lycaeum*, the *Academy*..., the *Canopus*, and *Tempe*, while in order that nothing should be wanting, he even constructed a representation of *Tartarus* (or *Hades*)[144]. However, the Canopus at Tivoli was not completed in its final form until 134-8, when it seems to have been lavishly beautified as a memorial to the Emperor's 'favourite' (as he has been coyly known), Antinoüs, who was drowned in the Nile during Hadrian's second visit to Egypt. The Bithynian youth's death has been variously claimed as a ritual sacrifice, as an accident, and even as an act of self-worship (the Narcissus myth hovers near), but what ever the reasons for his premature demise, he was extravagantly mourned by the Emperor, deified, and commemorated by means of statues, cults, shrines, temples, and festivals. He even had a new town in Egypt (Antinöopolis) created in his memory by the banks of the Nile, opposite Hermopolis Magna[145]. Several representations of Antinoüs existed at Tivoli, as we know from excavated material, so very many things were suggested by the gardens and *fabriques* there, not least the Egyptian Deities, the deified Antinoüs, the Nile, Canopus, a Province of the Roman Empire, and homosexual love[146]. In particular, part of the *Villa Adriana* grounds had an *Antinöeion* consisting of two prostyle tetrastyle temples facing each other (one appears to have had a segmental pediment), with an obelisk between them and a semicircular colonnade set on the axis marked by the obelisk. This complex (only recently discovered at Tivoli) was erected to one side of the grand official entrance to the Villa, and the gardens around the two temples were planted with palm-trees to evoke the landscape along the Nile in which Antinoüs perished[147]. Thus this *Antinöeion* to Antinoüs resurrected as Osiris (and therefore shown

---

140 Mosser & Teyssot (*Eds.*) (1991) 274. *See also* Curl (1995).

141 Shrine of Serapis, the Graeco-Roman version of Osiris, also *Serapaeion* or *Serapeion*.

142 *See* Curl (1997) and Curl (2005) 47-54.

143 United at an uncertain date into a single collection, the *Scriptores* consist of biographies of Roman Emperors by (perhaps) six authors, one of whom (Spartian) appears to have been active during the reign of Diocletian (Gaius Valerius Diocletianus [c.240-c.321]). Some scholars do not give much weight to the collection, regarding it as a series of forgeries or otherwise suspect, and it has even been suggested that the 'six' authors were, in fact, pseudonyms for one person, who may have written the lot in the reign of Theodosius I. Nevertheless, 'Spartian' on Hadrian does accord with much of what we know of this remarkable, widely-travelled, and urbane Emperor.

144 *See* Curl (2005) 48. *See also* Magie (*Tr.*) (2005) 41 (section xxvi).

145 These matters are discussed in Birley (1997) 235-58.

146 For the *Villa Adriana* and other matters *see* Curl (2000a, b). *See* also Opper (2008) 168-91.

147 Opper (2008) 178.

with *Nemes* head-dress and *Shendyt* kilt-like garment) was a powerful mnemonic of many aspects of Hadrian's life, loves, and Empire.

So a garden in Antiquity (and an enormously important one) was not just a place of recreation, but had significant buildings, sculptures, water-features, and so on which alluded to a huge number of references, so was an example of a sophisticated creation in which mnemonic techniques were used to trigger many thoughts, memories, allusions, ideas, and so on. Water carried sacral connotations in Hellenistic times, but at Tivoli the water-works were extensive and varied, and included virtually the 'whole typology of Roman water architecture'[148]. Indeed, water was the unifying element of the entire Hadrianic complex (as it was with numerous other, later gardens), and was included not only to add pleasure by providing visual delights, but to cool visitors, and to soothe them with the sounds of running water, as well as suggest power, control over the environment, and the triggering of thoughts about the vast Empire and its many and varied riches.

Some Other Significant Gardens

One of the most extraordinary books to have emerged during the Renaissance, as noted in a previous Chapter, was *Hypnerotomachia Poliphili*, subtitled *The Strife of Love in a Dream*, supposedly by Francesco Colonna, a Friar of dubious reputation. Published in Venice in 1499 by Aldus Manutius, it was an important volume which included descriptions of hieroglyphs and of many buildings of Antiquity: although a work of imagination, it drew on Antique literature, and the woodcuts remained influential for long afterwards, especially as prime sources for Renaissance ideas concerning both buildings and gardens. In the book, Poliphilo is clearly obsessed by Antiquity: its remains speak to him of a period infinitely superior to his own in every way. In Book I, the climax resembles Book XI of Apuleius's *Metamorphoses* in which he witnesses the Mysteries of Isis and Osiris. What is most significant, however, is that the Dream of Poliphilo involves numerous objects in a wondrous garden, where fountains, groves, and *fabriques* of all sorts could be found. For an elegant modern translation Godwin's admirable work is recommended[149].

Other studies have pointed out the influence of *Hypnerotomachia Poliphili* on garden-design throughout Europe[150]. The author, it has been claimed, was not the friar, but another Francesco Colonna, of noble birth, and that the book is an encapsulation of the views of an enlightened Humanist faction. It certainly would seem to describe some sort of initiatory journey, with possibly an allusion to the hill on which stands the remains of the Roman Temple of Fortuna Primigenia at Palestrina (the Roman Praeneste), which would have been familiar to Prince Colonna[151]. However, as Colonna was referred to as 'Frater', the friar attribution seems to be that mostly accepted. One aspect of Colonna's book is striking in the present context, and that is its connections with traditions of memory systems that had survived from Antiquity. As the Art of Memory, or 'The Phoenix' was closely connected with *metonymy*, a figure of speech which consists in substituting the name of an attribute of a thing (or something closely related to it) for the name of the thing or object itself: metonymy in essentially a *trope* in which the name of one thing is substituted for another related to it, the effect for the cause, and so on. It was also associated with metaphor, a figure of speech in which a name or a descriptive word is transferred to some other object that differs from, but is analogous to, that to which it is properly applicable. In gardens, for example, a route might suggest Life, or even the Journey through Life to Death, and so could convey the idea of a Pilgrimage.

A mnemonic device, of course, is one intended to aid the memory, and 'mnemonic' means 'of or pertaining to memory'. Many creators of gardens appear to have shared a concern for gardens in which *meaning* was carefully encoded, often by means of allusions (indirect references). The point is reiterated, simply because so many commentators simply fail to see how a garden can have connections with memory, allusions, arcane subjects, or connections with literature, poetry, Antiquity, or, for that matter, anything else. It is unfortunately true that allusions are ignored, and the richness of certain gardens is not recognised by visitors unable to decode the meanings so carefully suggested. No Garden of Allusions can begin to be understood unless it is realised that the visitor to it was both actor *and* spectator, and that the various scenes or episodes within it were intended to arouse responses[152]. Many gardens were created with carefully planned routes, scenes, episodes, buildings, and monuments all concerned with mnemonics. Noble ideas, distinguished personages, evocations of grand events or distant lands (not just distant geographically, but distant in terms of time as well), and lost perfection (notably Arcadia) could be conjured up by associations, jogging cultural themes in the mind by means of visual allusions. Emotions, passions, and melancholy thoughts could be aroused by means of garden-design, and the *fabriques* were intended expressly to inspire thoughts and jog memories. Indeed, an entire cultural programme could be encapsulated in a garden. Man's progress through life, from birth to the inevitable grave, was a theme found in many gardens, but astonishingly complex ideas evolved in the Continental gardens of the Renaissance and especially of the Enlightenment, yet the seeds were there already in distant Antiquity.

Bomarzo, near Viterbo, for example, created for Pier Francesco 'Vicino' Orsini from *c.*1552, was partly conceived as a memorial to Giulia Farnese, Orsini's wife, and has weird *fabriques*, including the *Mouth of Hell*, siren-like creatures, and

---

148 Ehrlich (1989) 161.
149 Godwin (1999).
150 Kretzulesco-Quaranta (1986) among them.

151 McIntosh (2005*a*) 53, quoting Kretzulesco-Quaranta (1986).
152 Hunt (1991) 233.

a giant grotesque head supporting a sphere with a castle on top. The themes of History, Time, and Deception are evident, and Etruscan civilisation is alluded to throughout. But one obvious influence was *Hypnerotomachia Poliphili*, as well as the universal themes of Love and Death[153]. Certainly there was an intended itinerary, a route, with inscriptions addressed directly to the visitor: one asks the person entering the garden to observe it piece by piece, and tell the Sphinx under whom the inscription is cut whether so many marvels were created for deception or only for art[154]. The predominant atmosphere of Bomarzo is that of Melancholy: it is palpable, like a distorted and frightening dream.

Far less weird or creepy is the garden created under Cardinal Ippolito d'Este between 1550 and 1572 to designs by Pirro Ligorio and others. Now Ligorio was an antiquarian, and carried out major archaeological investigations at the site of the *Villa Adriana*: he recorded the artefacts recovered from Hadrian's gardens, and his drawings became known through copies. Steeped in history, myth, and legend, he interwove allusions to Antique Tiburtine cults into the iconography of the gardens of the Villa d'Este, where Memory is a major theme, for historical understanding of any part could be jogged by a series of triggers. The fountains were intended not only to beautify the gardens and delight the beholder, but to contain meanings suggestive of the nature and deities of the region, and indeed harked back to Hadrian's great Villa not far distant. Those meanings are not at all obvious, and derive from the placing of the principal fountains on a system of alignments with various Antique sites in the surrounding landscape[155].

In short, the gardens of the Villa d'Este are not only strange and wonderful in themselves, but have formal relationships with the surrounding landscape, and especially with the principal sites of Classical Antiquity in the vicinity. The subject is of immense complexity and can only be touched upon here, but certain scholars[156] began investigations that point to rewarding interpretations. Even pagan deities were given Christian associations by Renaissance intellectuals in a process of syncretism worthy of the Graeco-Roman world in the early years of the Empire. Connections with Diana/Artemis, the *Villa Adriana*, St Paul, the Virgin Mother, the generative Earth, and Egypt, among other allusions, are made at the Villa d'Este by the fountain-statue of Artemis of Ephesus transformed and identified with the Sybil of legend, who was in turn to become *Mater Matuta*, the Goddess of the Dawn.

There were many other Renaissance gardens designed, as Christopher McIntosh has rightly observed, 'to provide richly symbolic journeys'[157]: they must include the *Hortus Palatinus*, Heidelberg, laid out, as previously noted, by Salomon de Caus for Frederick V, Elector Palatine of the Rhine (reigned 1610-20). Although never completed, de Caus recorded the entire project[158], which was to include English knots, *broderies*, fountains, grottoes, and an elliptical labyrinth of clipped hedges. The complex iconography, the programme involving ideas about universal harmony, and the Euclidian, Platonic, and Pythagorean systems of numbers have been discussed at exhaustive length elsewhere[159].

During the eighteenth century, however, many gardens were created that embraced not only ideas that had been around since Classical Antiquity, but the mysterious, darker side of the Renaissance and the delightful concept of the 'natural', Picturesque garden invented in England, but transformed on the Continent. Several French gardens, including that at Maupertuis (with which both Brongniart and Ledoux were involved), have been mentioned above. Another series of garden-pavilions and Egyptianising ornaments was proposed for the park at Étupes designed by Jean-Baptiste Kléber for the Duke of Württemberg-Mömpelgard[160] in 1787: the ensemble included an Egyptian Island approached by a bridge, and on the island was a swing, benches, ornaments, and a bath-house, all in the Egyptian manner[161]. As Major-General Kléber, Military Governor of Alexandria, this gifted Architect was assassinated is Egypt during the aftermath of the Napoleonic Campaign, and has many *avenues*, *boulevards*, and *places* named after him today: a bronze statue of him as an heroic General standing in front of a reclining sphinx was put up in the *Place Kléber*, Strasbourg, sculpted (1838) by Philippe Grass. Kléber was a Freemason, and, like many of his generation, was fascinated by the stereometrical simplicity of Egyptian Architecture: he designed a pyramid to enshrine the calcined remains of General François-Severin-Desgraviers Marceau (1769-96) at Koblenz.

Thus the second half of the eighteenth century saw the creation of numerous important gardens which contained many references of many kinds to many ideas, persons, and much else. It is impossible here to describe them all, but a selected few will suffice to demonstrate that there was far more to Gardens of Allusion than a superficial glance at them would suggest. These will feature in the next Chapter.

---

153 *Journal of Garden History* **iv** (1984) whole issue.
154 Ibid. 36. See also McIntosh (2005a) 68.
155 Dernie (1956) 20-25.
156 *See*, for example, Coffin (1960, 1964). *See* also Curl (1997, 2000a, 2000b).

157 McIntosh (2005a) 55. *See* also McIntosh (2005b).
158 Caus (1620).
159 McIntosh (2005a) 71-4, Mosser & Teyssot (*Eds*.) (1991) 157-9, Patterson (1981).
160 Mömpelgard was part of the Württemberg lands until 1793 when it passed to France, and is now known as Montbéliard.
161 Carrott (1978) Plates 3, 5, Humbert (1989a) 40, Krafft & Dubois (1809-10) 17, 31-5.

CHAPTER IX

Landscapes, Allusions, and Meanings

Introduction; Wörlitz; Arkadia; The Garden of Allusions at Arkadia Considered; Schwetzingen; Conclusion

'The completion of the building is the responsibility of many Crafts... but the foundation is the Mason's business, and... is the chief business of the entire undertaking. It is an earnest labour... Here, within this narrow excavated space you honour us by appearing as witnesses of our secret labour. Soon we shall lay this well-hewn stone... the perpendicular and horizontal of which denote the trueness of the walls without and within... Here, too, there must be lime and cement: for as men who are inclined to one another hold together better when they are cemented by the Law, so too... [stones]... are better united by this binding force... Then Charlotte and others... with a threefold blow blessed the union of the stone and the earth.'

JOHANN WOLFGANG VON GOETHE (1749-1832):
Die Wahlverwandtschaften (1808): freely translated.

'A sort of cell, built of rough stone fragments, shaded by trees, emerges... the Cell of the... Mystagogue. Two ways lead out of it: one, leading right, can be likened to the unreflective, toilsome way of the person without knowledge or intellectual culture... The other, leading left, is the arcane path of the mystic, the apprentice in exalted wisdom... In these journeyings one can believe one speaks the language of the Mysteries, and that one stands on the threshold of Proserpine, the boundary between Life and Death.'

AUGUST VON RODE (1751-1837):
Beschreibung des Fürstlichen Anhalt-Dessauischen Landhauses und Englischen Gartens zu Wörlitz
(Dessau: H. Tänzer 1814): freely translated.

Introduction

The two translated quotations from Goethe and von Rode at the beginning of this Chapter concern the building-works in a small German State and a description of part of the Garden of Allusions at Wörlitz in Anhalt. Goethe's *Die Wahlverwandtschaften* (from which the first quotation is taken) also contains descriptions of the laying out of a landscape garden around a lake, clearly influenced by the extraordinarily beautiful *Gartenreich*, which will be mentioned below. Goethe observed that 'although the Mason's work continues above ground, it is still concealed, or, where it is not hidden, is carried out for the sake of what cannot be seen... As he who has done evil must fear that, in spite of all precautions, his deeds will be found out, so he who has done good in secret must expect that, contrary to his intentions, that, too will be revealed'[1]. This, and the quotation at the Chapter-head, suggest a Freemasonic influence, and as we know Goethe himself was deeply impressed by the *Gartenreich* laid out at the behest of a cultivated Prince and partly designed by one of the most sensitive Architects working in Germany during the second half of the eighteenth century, it is not unreasonable to propose that Masonic ideals may have played a part in the genesis and development of the beautiful and fascinating gardens at Wörlitz. It is also important to remember that the intellectual and cultural climates of the eighteenth century in a small German Principality differed hugely from those of Anglophone countries at the beginning of the twenty-first century, and so such places require a modicum of understanding based on research and study before they can begin to be appreciated. We need to have an inkling of how to look at things, using our eyes, hearts, and brains rather than our ears. This requires a degree of sensitivity and quite a lot of homework in order to grasp what various allusions suggest[2].

Three important Continental gardens will feature in this Chapter: two are in Germany and one is in Poland. All three, although *influenced* by English exemplars, are

---

1 Goethe (1809) Ch. 9, freely translated by the Author.
2 For an introduction, *see* Calder (*Ed.*) (2006) and Curl (1995, 1997, 2004, 2006b). *See also* Lee (2007) *passim*.

markedly different in many respects from gardens in the British Isles, and embrace many themes and ideas that were concerns of their civilised creators, and which will not be familiar to many Anglophone readers. Indeed, they must all be viewed with open minds and eyes, for all three invite visitors to look at them by rediscovering old ways of so doing, for they carry transformative signals and have many mystical, philosophical, and other meanings. However, any attempt to 'read' the meaning of a garden such as those described here can be rather like trying to study an old text, some pages of which may be missing or illegible, and others couched in language no longer clear to us. In a Prosaic Age it is important to grasp that many gardens on the European Continent had meanings that transcended the ordinary, but there is not a great deal of literature available that explains this complex problem. There is one publication, though, which whilst being a beautiful thing in itself, reveals much, and indeed is a truly comprehensive survey of garden history: it was written by Marie Luise Schroeter Gothein, Prussian scholar, gardener, and author, who lost her sons in the murderous catastrophe of 1914-18, and was a graduate of the University of Breslau (now Wrocław). She wrote on a number of topics, including Indian Gardens, John Keats, William Wordsworth, and the work of her husband, Eberhard Gothein, but her masterpiece is undoubtedly *Geschichte der Gartenkunst*[3], which first appeared in 1914. A sumptuous, beautiful pair of volumes, handsomely produced by Eugen Diederichs in Jena, the updated version of 1926 was translated into English, and appeared in 1928. It was comprehensively illustrated, and its intelligent, humane, scholarly, and humorous tone is thoroughly admirable.

The gardens with which we are concerned unquestionably have aspects to them which cannot be explained by mere fashion or whimsy. It should also be remembered that, at the time of their creation, there was a widespread interest in Antiquity and in things esoteric as well as rational. Freemasonry, with its interest in ideas of Ancient Wisdom and in metaphors taken from Architecture, was also in the ascendant at the time: it would therefore have been very odd if certain metaphors, symbols, and notions connected with the Craft had *not* impinged upon the design of gardens. And in certain gardens there is clear evidence of Freemasonic influences[4]. Christopher McIntosh has pointed out that it 'might seem strange that, among the gardens with masonic elements, few of them show evidence of an attempt to represent an actual masonic lodge. However, it only takes a moment's reflection' to realise why this is so. 'The lodge is a private space where only the specially invited are allowed to enter, whereas a garden is a place that is difficult to make totally secret. So what we would expect to find in a masonic garden would be rather a symbolic reflection of the ideas and world view of the Mason'[5]. Given that some of the motifs of that world-view include Architecture and Building (particularly the Temple of Solomon, treated as a metaphor for the 'inner work' of moral development undertaken by individual Freemasons) and the search for Lost Wisdom which informed the Architecture of Antiquity, if a heady brew of Hermeticism, Alchemy, and Astrology is added and a symbolic, initiatory journey planned for, we detect some of the themes found in certain gardens of the Enlightenment.

Sources for what McIntosh has aptly described as the 'symbol-strewn landscape'[6] must include the many illustrations on Craft Certificates, Summonses, and even title-pages of books dealing with Freemasonry, for in gardens we find them: the domed circular Temple with Classical portico, Sphinxes, Pyramids and Obelisks, Serpents twined around globes, ruined arches, broken columns, and so on. To take the domed Temple with portico alone, it recurs many times in Freemasonic decorations, so what does it mean? Curiously, although we have Biblical descriptions of the Solomonic Temple as an essentially rectangular building, ever since the Crusades an alternative Temple of circular or polygonal form had entered the European imagination. This is because, as noted previously, the Islamic 'Dome of the Rock' (known erroneously as the 'Mosque of Omar') became the *dominant image* of the Jewish Temple for Westerners, as can be seen in *The Marriage of the Virgin* by Raphael Sanzio), in which the Italian Renaissance interpretation of the Temple was clearly based on the Dome of the Rock[7]. That is how ideas and icons become accepted as reality: it is a complex business.

Wörlitz

Gardens outside France will now be discussed, both of which are richly endowed with *fabriques* and saturated in meaning. Take the *Gartenreich*[8] in the tiny Principality ruled by Prince Leopold III Friedrich Franz von Anhalt-Dessau (reigned from 1758) (**Pl.IX.1**, p.206). There, at Wörlitz and elsewhere, a magical garden was created, an 'England by the Elbe'[9], designed by the Prince, his Architect (Friedrich Wilhelm, Freiherr von Erdmannsdorff)[10], and his gardeners (Johann Leopold Ludwig Schoch the Elder, Johann Georg Schoch the Younger, and Johann Friedrich Eyserbeck). This Garden Kingdom extended over 300 square kilometres, and work began in 1764: it was influenced by the journeys the Prince made to England in 1763-4, 1768-9, 1775, and 1785 (**Pl.IX.2**, p.206). From the start, he insisted on the *educational* programme of his wonderful creation: all designs followed the 'advice of Horace' to combine 'the useful with the beautiful', and

---

3 *See* Gothein (1928). Its English version (1928) was entitled *A History of Garden Art*. I thank Peter and Eleanor Inch for this.
4 McIntosh (2005a) 92.

5 *Ibid*.
6 *Ibid*. 93.
7 Goldhill (2005) 120.
8 *See* Alex & Kühn (1988).
9 Trauzettel (1996).
10 *See* Schweinitz (1999) 126, 175, 253, 268, for further information about Erdmannsdorff's influence.

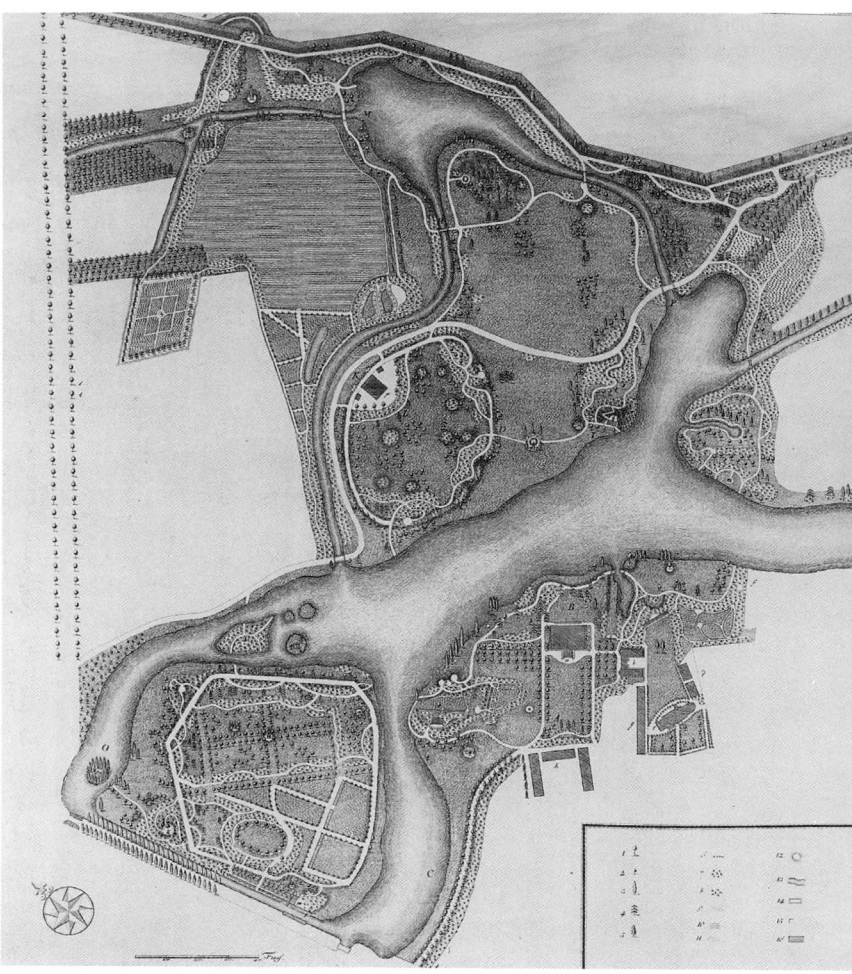

Pl.IX.1 *(above)* Prince Leopold III Friedrich Franz von Anhalt-Dessau surveys his *Gartenreich*. In the distance behind him is the Gothic House (*JSC*).

Pl.IX.2 *(right)* Erklärung des Grundrißes des Gartens zu Wörlitz (Explanation of the ground-plan of the gardens of Wörlitz) of 1784 drawn by Johann Christian Neumark and engraved by Israel Solomon Probst of Dessau. The *Rousseau-insel* is the island in the lake on the left (Wörlitz, Inv. No IV, 354).

'nothing was included which did not have a purpose'[11]. The Iron Bridge, for example, erected in 1791 (**Pl.IX.3**), is a quarter-scale reproduction of the celebrated Iron Bridge at Coalbrookdale in Shropshire, erected in 1777-9 to designs by Thomas Farnolls Pritchard (**Pl.IX.4**), but it is only one of 'an instructive series of buildings whereby the development of bridge-building of all styles is shown and the solution of thirty-one technical problems demonstrated'[12]. Now if the intelligent and enlightened Anglophile Prince only intended the 'numerous building projects' to give work to his people (including 'a lot of unskilled lads disbanded from war')[13], why would he go to the trouble of demonstrating all those different technical solutions? Such an interpretation is untenable.

Wörlitz 'is as much a waterscape as a landscape – a series of lakes', canals, and inlets 'formed by a salient of the River Elbe'[14]. It was the first major German garden to be laid out in the English style, and it was enormously influential. By selecting this style the Prince was keen to appear modern and Enlightened, and looked to England for his inspiration. Debts to Stowe and Stourhead are 'obvious in the flowing curves of the park and in many of the features, such as the Pantheon, the Gothic House, and the Temple of Flora'[15]. The Prince did not wish to be a Prince at all, for he wanted to move to Richmond-on-Thames and live the life of an English gentleman: however, he settled for the next best thing, and brought England to Wörlitz. Unfortunately, he destroyed most of his papers, so we do not know if he had ever been initiated as a Freemason, but we do know he was in contact with several Freemasons, and he was certainly influenced by ideals of the Craft, many of which permeated cultivated European aristocracy during the Enlightenment. Certainly the notions of a route and an initiation theme are present: these emerge from the guide-book to the Park, written by August von Rode[16], first published in 1788, with subsequent revisions of 1798 and 1814. Rode had translated Apuleius's *Golden Ass* into German, and his guide-book is instructive. The so-called Neumark Garden at Wörlitz contains a Labyrinth of rockwork, representing the individual's journey through life (**Pl.IX.5**, p.208): a narrow path leads to a clearing shaded by Acacias (connected with the Freemasonic legend of Hiram Abiff), and the way leads through a rock-work

---

11 Trauzettel (1996) 222.
12 *Ibid*. 225.
13 Macpherson (1998) 56.
14 McIntosh (2005a) 96.

15 *Ibid*. 97.
16 Rode (1996).

construction bearing the legend (**Pl. IX.6**, p.208)

'WAEHLE WANDRER
DEINEN WEG
MIT VERNUNFT[17]'

which sounds very like the exhortations in the words of some of Mozart's Masonic music, notably the so-called *Lied zur Gesellenreise* (K.468)[18], in which the candidate for the new Degree is urged to be firm as he wanders on his way, because he knows it is the path of Wisdom, bathed in Light, and the songs *Zur Eröffnung der Freimaurerloge* (K.483) and *Zum Schluß der Freimaurerloge* (K.484)[19], in which thanks are given to those who guided the Brethren 'on every step of their Masonic way', and the leaders of the Lodge are asked to point the Brethren towards the paths of Wisdom, rejoicing in the chains of Brotherhood that bind them together. The same poet wrote the words for the last-mentioned two songs[20]. In *Die Zauberflöte* (K.620 of 1791), Act II, Scene 1, there is a moving prayer to Isis and Osiris, asking the deities to bestow Wisdom on the young couple as they begin their journey towards initiation[21], and it is now generally accepted that Mozart's celebrated *Singspiel*[22] was at least *partly* influenced by aspects of Freemasonry[23], even though this may not be entirely palatable in certain quarters. If Freemasonry could play some sort of rôle in the genesis of a late-eighteenth-century German *Singspiel*, why could it not also be a significant element in a late-eighteenth-century German garden? If, as some have dogmatically claimed, Wörlitz was merely a project designed to provide work for former troops[24], why, at the very beginning of the journey around the gardens at Wörlitz, would the visitor be encouraged to choose between the path of the 'ignorant and uncultured man' and the 'mysterious way of the mystagogue, *apprentice in divine knowledge*' [25]. Does that not sound very like something with at least some Freemasonic overtones?

Pl.IX.3 *Eiserne Brücke* at Wörlitz, with rock-work abutments, of 1791. This is based on the original Iron Bridge of 1778 at Coalbrookdale on the Severn in Shropshire. The Wörlitz version is scaled down (it is 7.75 [25 feet] metres in span), and is part of a vast scheme of eclectic references intended as mnemonics of the best of culture and knowledge, and as celebrations of achievements (JSC).

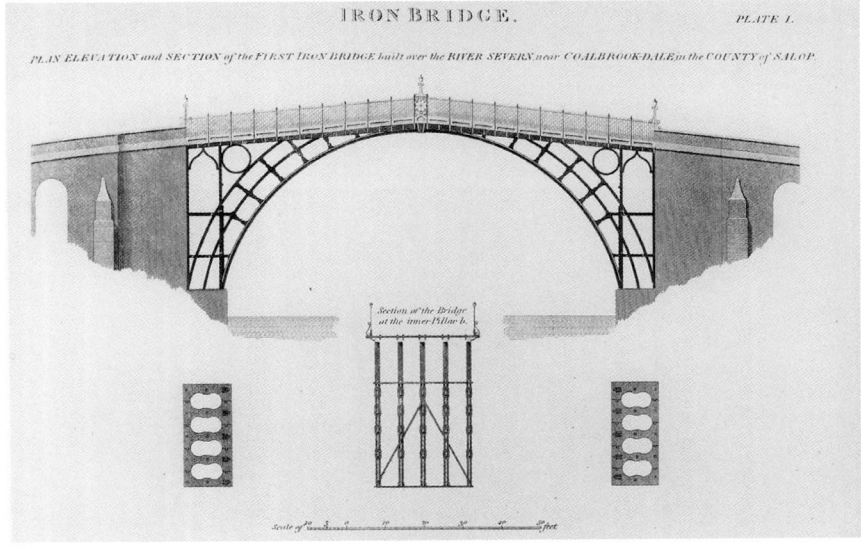

Pl. IX.4 The 'First Iron Bridge' built over the River Severn, near Coalbrook-Dale, in the County of Salop', designed by Pritchard and erected 1777-9. Drawn by Peter Nicholson and engraved by J. Bacon (1819) (*Collection JSC*).

Between 1788 and 1794 an island (*Der Stein* [The Stone]) was created in the lake at Wörlitz intended to allude to memories of Italy, and therefore to the Grand Tour undertaken by the Prince, his younger brother, Johann Georg, Georg Heinrich von Berenhorst, and

---

17 Choose, Traveller, your Path with Reason.
18 *See* next Chapter. Text by Josef Franz von Ratschky (*see* Ratschky [1791]).
19 *See* next Chapter.
20 August Veith von Schittlersberg.
21 The celebrated *O Isis und Osiris schenket / Der Weisheit Geist dem neuen Paar!*
22 A play with musical numbers. *See* the following Chapter for more detail.
23 *See* Thomson (1977), 155-68 and *passim*; and Landon (1982).
24 Macpherson (1998) 56. Others have sneeringly asserted that those trying to establish a connection between gardens and Freemasonry are suffering from 'delirious illusions' (Macpherson [1998] 68).

25 My italics. *See* Rode (1996).

Pl.IX.5 *(left)* Rock-work entrance to the 'Labyrinth' at Wörlitz (*RA*).

Pl.IX.6 *(above)* Exhortation inscribed on a stone, set into the rock-work entrance to the 'Labyrinth' at Wörlitz. It reads *Choose, Traveller, your Path with Reason* (*Waehle Wandrer deinen Weg mit Vernunft*). It could easily form part of the entrance to Trials of Initiation to be read by a potential candidate (*RA*).

Pl.IX.7 The Stone Island (*Insel Stein*) at Wörlitz, with rock-work 'Vesuvius' erupting with fireworks. Aquatint by Wilhelm Friedrich Schlotterbeck *after* Karl Kuntz, 1797 (*SGD, Inv.-Nr. G. 416*).

Erdmannsdorff from 1765, during which the party met, among many others, Johann Joachim Winckelmann (the leading historian of Antiquity at the time, and a major influence on Neo-Classicism), Charles-Louis Clérisseau (draughtsman, scholar, and Architect who also had a profound effect on the evolution of Neo-Classicism, and was one of the most important influences on Robert Adam), and Sir William Hamilton (British emissary to the Court of Naples and enthusiastic collector of antiquities, including Greek vases). The *Stein* and its immediate vicinity incorporate a representation of the geography of the Gulf of Naples, and towering over the grounds (largely covered with rock-work grottoes), is a rock-work 'Vesuvius', which could be filled with fireworks and illuminated to suggest an eruption (**Pl.IX.7**). In addition to the reproduction of the grotto-filled volcanic landscape in the vicinity of Naples, there is a Temple of Day and Night, an amphitheatre, a columbarium, Roman Baths, and the 'Villa Hamilton', a replica of the summer-house of Sir William (**Pl.IX.8**). The ensemble also suggests the archaeological discoveries at Pompeii and elsewhere in the region that were such powerful stimuli to Neo-Classicism, the dominant language of the architectural citations in the *Gartenreich*, especially in the works of Erdmannsdorff[26].

Pl.IX.8 Villa Hamilton (1791-94) by F. W. von Erdmannsdorff, and rock-work cone of 'Vesuvius' on the Stone Island (*Insel Stein* of 1788-96) at Wörlitz. Rock-work had significance as a symbol of Soundness and as the foundation of Wisdom. The Villa celebrated the collection of Sir William Hamilton, diplomat and archaeologist, who witnessed and described the eruptions of Vesuvius, and who was an expert on volcanoes and volcanic rocks. He was a kinsman of William Beckford, and made several major collections of Greek and Roman antiquities, notably vases (*Wörlitz*).

Elsewhere in the garden at Wörlitz are allusions to the famous garden at Ermenonville, laid out, as previously noted, for the aristocratic Freemason, René-Louis, Marquis de Girardin, in which was the *Île des Peupliers* in the *Élysée* where Rousseau had been entombed: at Wörlitz is an island, predictably called the *Rousseauinsel*[27], complete with poplar-trees and a funerary urn set on a pedestal (**Pl.IX.9**, p.210). Now the uninformed would regard this as a 'mere pastiche' (a term misused by Modernists, the ignorant, and the idle, as in its original meaning it is *not* pejorative at all), a copy, a conceit, but there is far more to it than that. It is also an allusion to those enlightened, aristocratic, French Freemasons, who erected cenotaphs to Protestants in their gardens to demonstrate their rejection of bigotry. As mentioned above, cenotaphs[28] were one thing, but it occurred to some that the emotional impact and mnemonic resonances would be even greater if real bodies of real 'heretics' could be buried in gardens and commemorated by means of actual sepulchral monuments. The most famous of such burials was Rousseau's entombment on the island at Ermenonville, so the Prince (who had met Rousseau) was not only associating himself with the open-minded attitudes of Girardin and other enlightened French Freemasons, but alluding to the description of 'Julie's' garden in Rousseau's novel, *La Nouvelle Héloïse*[29], which first came out in 1761. In turn, Girardin had got some of *his* ideas for his garden from The Leasowes, Worcestershire, laid out for William Shenstone, whose elegiac works promoted the idea of memorials set in gardens[30]. And the catalyst, as has been emphasised above, for such burials of 'heretics' was Young's *Night Thoughts*[31].

Furthermore, the Prince of Anhalt-Dessau was distantly related to the Protestant Admiral Gaspard de Châtillon, Comte Coligny, victim of the massacres of St Bartholomew's Day, who was commemorated, as previously noted, by a cenotaph erected by an aristocratic Freemason in the *Élysée* of his celebrated garden at Maupertuis, overshadowed by the enormous 'ruined' Graeco-Egyptian-Primitivist pyramid designed by Brongniart, another Freemason. An inventory[32] of the *fabriques* at Maupertuis, made in 1795, mentions a 'subterranean grotto in rusticated stone... surmounted by a façade in the form of a pyramid'[33], and Vidler has stated that the *fabriques* there 'may well have marked stages along

---

26 Bode *et al.* (1997) 133, nos. 67 and 68.
27 Rousseau Island.
28 From the Greek *kenos* and *taphos*, meaning an empty tomb, or a funerary monument in memory of a person or persons whose bodies lie elsewhere.
29 Rousseau (1761).
30 Etlin (1984).
31 *See* O'Connor (1919) and Curl (1994*a*).
32 *Inventaire des fabriques* (21 Prairial an III).
33 Vidler (1987) 210 n.72.

Pl.IX.9 The *Rousseauinsel* at Wörlitz of 1782 (JSC).

Pl.IX.10 *Nymphaeum* at Wörlitz of 1767-8 by Erdmannsdorff (JSC).

a kind of ritualistic route through the *jardin-anglais*, called by Mountesquiou "Élysée"[34]. At Wörlitz, Rousseauesque social, political, and philosophical notions, together with the cult of Nature, were embraced, and the *Rousseauinsel* there was a deliberate expression of identification with open-minded, unbigoted ideals, compassion, and hatred of oppression.

A similar theme connected with open-mindedness, fairness, and compassion was behind the erection of the circular Synagogue at Wörlitz. Emancipation of the Jews was 'represented most notably in the state school and synagogue completed in 1799'[35], a charming building that doubles as a garden *fabrique*. It also spells out tolerance, and expresses the idea of a Temple in that during the seventeenth and eighteenth centuries non-Roman Catholic churches were referred to as 'Temples', and were often circular in form. This was true of Protestant churches, which were even called *'temples'* in France. But the Synagogue, whilst suggesting these connections, would also have been a mnemonic of the Temple of Solomon, as many representations of the Jewish Temple in the previous two centuries before 1799 had been of circular buildings, and that form also appears on countless specifically Freemasonic engravings, images, and other illustrations. This association of certain 'temples' with circular plans seems to have gained momentum through the influence of Leon Battista Alberti and his constant references to them in his *De Re Ædificatoria*, first published compete in 1486[36]. And, as has been mentioned above, the circular form of the church of the Holy Sepulchre in Jerusalem and the circular Templar churches modelled on it and the centrally-planned, octagonal, so-called Dome of the Rock[37] (which was used as a church after the capture of the city by Crusaders and which stood on the great platform associated with the Temple of Solomon) had potent symbolic, allusory, and visual properties with many resonances. During the Christian occupation of Jerusalem the Dome of the Rock became known as *Templum Domini*[38], and that seems to have been the original source of the very curious association of a wonderful Islamic building with the Lost Ideal of the Temple of Solomon, and therefore the reason why circular buildings purporting to be the Temple appear on so many Freemasonic illustrations. Thus there is far more to the circular form than is immediately obvious to the eye, and it also alludes to the Vestal Temple on the banks of the Tiber near Rome, so connects the Wörlitz ensemble with Classical Antiquity as well. A further acknowledgement of Classical Antiquity was apparent in the *Nymphaeum* (**Pl. IX.10**), a beautiful design by Erdmannsdorff of 1767-8, dedicated to the water-nymphs (*Naiads*), and served as a sheltered portico where the wanderers in the garden could

---

34 Vidler (1987) 130.
35 Bode *et al.* (1997) 13.
36 Alberti (1486). *See* Rykwert *et al.* (1988).
37 *See* Goldhill (2004) 109-124. Although octagonal outside, with an aisle octagonal on plan all round the central space, the drum and innermost arcade supporting it are circular on plan.
38 Temple of Our Lord. *See* Goldhill (2004) 120.

rest and enjoy the view across the lake to the *Englischer Sitz* in the *Schlossgarten*. This *Nymphaeum* was a favourite spot for the poet Friedrich von Matthisson, remembered today as the author of *Adelaide*, one of Beethoven's most celebrated songs[39]. Matthisson died at Wörlitz. The Synagogue-*fabrique* at Wörlitz, incidentally, only escaped destruction at the hands of a Nazi mob in 1938 through the courage of a civil-servant who shared some of the Prince's ideals and saw the intolerance and philistinism of the period as an affront to the Prince's memory[40], and indeed as an attack on the entire fabric of the European Enlightenment.

There is another aspect to the Synagogue (which is visible at the end of the *Elbewall* [Elbe Dike or Ditch] with Memorial Urn to the foreground): the circular Synagogue, related as noted above to notions of the Solomonic Temple and Classical circular types, was contrasted with the Gothic Revival Church of St Peter (1804-10 – designed by Georg Christoph Hesekiel), the steeple of which alludes to English types, such as the Church of St James, Louth, Lincolnshire (*c*.1440-5 and 1501-15). The last has flying buttresses between the four pinnacles and the spire. So the Church, the steeple of which is the tallest structure in Wörlitz, is again English in inspiration, and the Protestant Church was seen as a *modern development* from the Synagogue, transformed in style, and alluding, not to Antiquity or to Classicism, but to English Gothic, for England was the Prince's ideal. It is a poetic idea, perfectly realised in the magical *Gartenreich*, where the influence of England, ideas of Freedom, and much else inform the whole ensemble (**Pl.IX.11**). On the opposite side of the *Elbewall* is the Warning Altar, erected as a memorial to Erdmannsdorff: it is inscribed with an instruction to the visitor cut into a raised band around the middle of the cylindrical structure featuring reliefs of Artemis/Diana and Phoebus/Apollo above the band and of the Nine Muses below. The inscription (in German) may be translated as 'Wanderer, heed Nature and Art, and protect their works'. It is a moving monument to a great man.

Goethe, universally recognised as one of the most important intellectuals of the *Aufklärung*, as noted earlier, visited Wörlitz (in fact he 'was often a guest there'), and imbibed much from the heartrendingly lovely *Gartenreich*: 'he praised the father and ruler of what he referred to

Pl. IX.11 View of the *Elbewall* at Wörlitz from the Mound with Memorial Urn, showing the Synagogue in the distance (immediately beyond the bridge) and the Gothic Church to its right, framed by trees. On the right of the picture is the Warning Altar, Erdmannsdorff's memorial (Wörlitz, photograph PK).

as a "well-governed and at the same time outwardly beautified country"'[41], and found the park (where the 'gods had allowed the Prince to create a dream around himself') 'infinitely beautiful'. The gardens at Wörlitz were essentially realisations of Arcady, celebrations of Enlightened Reason, and, in the opinion of Christoph Martin Wieland, the 'ornament and epitome of the age'[42], but they were also far, far more than that. Goethe recognised that the individual parts of such a garden had meanings, and that the compositions were revealed to the visitor as he progressed along paths and water-ways, evoking associations and emotions in the beholder. 'The landscape scenes and architecture described' in Goethe's exquisitely tender novella *Die Wahlverwandtschaften* (*The Elective Affinities*) 'were inspired by much of what the poet had seen in the expansive garden'[43], as any reasonably diligent reader of the book who has visited Wörlitz will immediately recognise. Goethe was a Freemason, and, decisively influenced by Herder (another prominent and

---

39 1795, published 1797.
40 Bode *et al.* (1997) 13.

41 *Ibid.* 11.
42 *Ibid.* 10.
43 *Ibid.* 10.

distinguished German Freemason who greatly admired the works of Young), he absorbed many ideas from his studies of the English poet's works, for elegiac and tenderly expressed themes from Young are very evident in *Die Wahlverwandtschaften*[44]. It is also significant that yet another German Freemason, Lessing, held *Night Thoughts*[45] in high esteem, and there can be no doubt that the work of Edward Young was a formative and decisive factor in the German Enlightenment and the early Romantic period, especially in respect of the design of gardens and their transformation into places of commemoration and burial of the dead. Now Goethe not only appreciated the meanings and nuances in the *Gartenreich*[46], but took seriously the libretto of *Die Zauberflöte*. His 'enthusiasm for *Die Zauberflöte* undoubtedly depended more upon the initiate value' that he recognised 'in the libretto than upon love for the music'[47], for the evidence suggests that Goethe was not, in fact, very musical at all. Goethe observed that the 'high significance [of *Die Zauberflöte*] will not escape the initiates'[48], and insisted that more 'knowledge is required to understand the value of this libretto [that of *Die Zauberflöte*], than to mock it'[49]. Quite so, and more culture, knowledge, and imagination are required by those who fail to even begin to understand the layers of meaning in eighteenth-century Gardens of Allusion.

The Prince de Ligne advised gardeners, painters, poets, and philosophers to go to Wörlitz, for there he saw his ideas perfected in the design of routes with *fabriques* that jogged many associations, memories, and thoughts. It would be no exaggeration to claim that the Garden Kingdom by the Elbe is a 'true encyclopædia of the cultural history of the eighteenth century that has no equal'[50]. In other words, a powerful and highly intelligent Freemason, who lamented the insensitive dimness of those visiting his own gardens of Beloeil because they were incapable of or uninterested in deciphering his elegantly eclectic stimuli to the imagination (let alone appreciating the visual delights), praised Wörlitz, the garden which gave shape to the vision of Arcadia and entranced an entire generation with its beauties and resonances. The Garden Kingdom (or Realm) attracted de Ligne's approval because it was, among many things, an ever-changing series of stage-sets for a sophisticated theatre of the mind. Although we do not possess documentary evidence to prove that either the Prince of Anhalt-Dessau or his Architect and friend, Freiherr von Erdmannsdorff, were actually Freemasons, it is highly improbable that they would have avoided all contact with the Craft, especially as they travelled widely, and the Prince visited England on several occasions where Freemasonry

Pl.IX.12 View along one of the waterways at Wörlitz to the Temple of Venus in the distance (JSC).

was certainly embraced by numerous intelligent members of the aristocratic and professional classes. We do know, however, that Prince Franz of Anhalt-Bernburg was a Freemason, as were Dukes Friedrich Ferdinand and Heinrich of Anhalt-Köthen[51], and it would appear that the Craft was well-established among the upper echelons of Anhalt society. For what ever reasons (probably prudence), the Prince of Anhalt-Dessau, as noted above, destroyed many of his papers, and only parts of Erdmannsdorff's records of the trips abroad have survived[52]. Nevertheless, given Goethe's connection with the Prince and with the Craft, it is simply beyond belief that Freemasonry did not impinge upon the idealistic and intelligent creator of the *Gartenreich* or upon the sensibilities of the equally bright and sensitive Erdmannsdorff: there are so many themes and motifs at Wörlitz which connect with the Craft that a dogmatic rejection of such a link is absurd.

Let us look at the remarkably pure circular Temple of Venus intended by Erdmannsdorff as an allusion to the

---

44 Analyses of these matters would provide the basis for a very substantial scholarly paper, and so cannot be elaborated upon here.
45 See Cornford (Ed) (1989), Curl (1994a), Ebert (1753), Forster (1986), Kind (1906), Shelley (1914) and Wicker (1952).
46 Now a World Heritage Site, and properly justified in being so designated.
47 Chailley (1972) 47.
48 Ibid. 7.
49 Massin (1959) 562 quoted in Chailley (1972) 297.
50 Bode *et al.* (1997) 10.

51 Lennhoff & Posner (1932), column 547. *See* also Schletter, Zille, *et al.* (1900), Vol. **i**, 39-40. Reference kindly provided by Herr Werner Schwartz, Grossarchiv of *Grosse National-Mutterloge* (Mother-Lodge) '*Zu den drei Weltkugeln*' (Three Globes), Berlin (Charlottenburg).
52 For example, Anhalt Provincial State Library, Dessau, HS 10012, and the Travel Notes from 1764, reproduced in Bode *et al.* (1997) 37-71. Destruction of papers coincided with a period of reaction.

CPl.IX.I Gothic House at Wörlitz (1773-1813) designed by Hesekiel and Erdmannsdorff (*JSC*).

Pl.IX.13 Portal of the new cemetery (*Der Neue Begräbnisplatz*) in Dessau, the public non-denominational communal cemetery unattached to a church laid out to designs by Erdmannsdorff in 1787-9. Etching by Christian Friedrich Wiegand. The inscription reads *Tod is nicht Tod, ist nur Veredlung sterblicher Natur*. The figures in the niches represent the twin brothers Sleep and Death, while Hope with her Anchor crowns the composition (*SGD, Schloss Georgium, Inv. No. G.660*).

Temple of the Sibyl at Tivoli: built in 1794 it completes the mystical garden in which the entire place is pervaded with Symbolism. The Wörlitz Temple of Venus stands on foundations integrated as part of a dyke, and it should be remembered that Venus, born of the Sea, personifies the Element of Water. It can be seen as the tantalising terminus of a view along a narrow stretch of water (**Pl.IX.12**), and, with the Grottoes of Vulcan and Aeolus as mnemonics of the Elements of Fire and Air, has many overtones. From the Temple of Venus can be seen the Gothic House, so within the garden, the Gothic House and the Temple of Venus formed a connection[53]. If Gothic in England had been associated with English Freedom and Liberty (and this was clearly the case), then the Gothic House at Wörlitz (1773-1813 – designed by Georg Christoph Hesekiel[54] with Erdmannsdorff's collaboration [**CPl.IX.I**]) was also intended to evoke England and Freedom (its interior alludes to Lincoln Cathedral and other English sites): it was there, in that Gothic House, that the Prince's gardener's daughter, Leopoldine Luise Schoch, gave birth to his children, so the House represented Freedom in many things, not least

that of Love (although there were also political aspects that alluded to the Prince's position as an advocate of the Mediaeval Constitution of Estates in opposition to the overweening ambitions of a militaristic Prussia and the pretensions of the Habsburgs). Thus the ever-present deity in the Gothic House, visible too, was Venus. It is also worth noting that the Prince and Erdmannsdorff visited Stowe on at least two occasions, and also knew Rousham. But the presiding genius at Wörlitz was Lessing, Freemason and advocate of religious and general tolerance, who held Young's work in the highest regard, and the influence of England, through its gardens, its *fabriques*, its architecture, and Young's poetry, is beyond all dispute[55].

Before we leave the *Gartenreich* it is worth considering for a moment the new Cemetery (*Der Neue Begräbnisplatz*) at Dessau which Erdmannsdorff designed. It was laid out in 1787-9, and, like other cemeteries of the period, was part of a general attempt to improve hygiene and treat the dead as equals, without regard to rank or station. Erdmannsdorff himself was buried there. The entrance-gateway, a simplified Neo-Classical design, is crowned by a figure of Hope with her Anchor and two swagged urns. In the niches were the twin brothers, Sleep and Death,

---

53 I am grateful to Reinhard Alex for elucidating on these matters.
54 As noted above, Hesekiel's Gothic parish-church at Wörlitz (1804-10), a key building of the German Gothic Revival, was obviously intended to allude to England.

55 See McIntosh (2005a) 96-102. I am most grateful to Christopher McIntosh for sharing his views on these and other matters with me.

CPl.IX.II Princess Helena Radzwiłłowa, from a painting by E. Gebauer (MNA. Nr. Inw. NB 286.WP).

the Church was advocated[56]. Research within the last two decades in Poland[57] has demonstrated that there were, among Polish Freemasons, many theorists and creators of garden-layouts in the advanced modern style, with many *fabriques* intended to trigger associations and suggest *meanings*. Among them were August Fryderyk Moszyński, Ignacy Potocki, Stanisław Kostka Potocki, and Simon Gottlieb (or Szymon Bogumił) Zug. The Garden of Allusions at Arkadia was created over some forty years by Princess Helena Radziwiłłowa[58] (**CPl. IX.II**), who was a member of the Grand Adoption Lodge of Warsaw (subordinated to the Polish National Lodge or Grand Orient), which later became the Grand Charity Lodge of the Grand Orient of Warsaw. Princess Helena was initiated into Adoptive Freemasonry (a branch of the Craft established for women sometimes confused with the Society of Mopses)[59] in 1782, in which year her friend, Princess Izabela Czartoryska[60], was initiated to membership of the same Lodge (which would also boast Izabela Lubomirska as an initiate). All three women were 'devoted advocates of the new-style gardens'[61], and created fine examples of the genre, of which only and the inscription to the effect that Death is not Death, only a part of the natural and noble order of things, has profoundly Enlightenment-Freemasonic overtones with its references to an ennobling or refinement of dying Nature. One could hardly have a clearer signal of the influence of ideals held by the Craft: considering that the *Begräbnisplatz* or *Stadtgottesacker* is one of the earliest planned, humane, civilised cemeteries of Enlightened Europe, the allusions are obvious (**Pl.IX.13**, p.213).

Arkadia

During the reign of Stanisław August Poniatowski (King of Poland 1764-95) Freemasonry became very important in that country, for not only was the King a Freemason, but the Craft greatly influenced the proceedings of the Four-Year *Sejm* (Parliament) and the progressive Third-of-May Constitution of 1791. Rationalism was disseminated, together with other ideals of the Enlightenment, Obscurantism and clerical Privileges were opposed, and reform of

---

56 See Zamoyski (1992); Piwkowski (1998) 546.
57 Swirida (1993) in *Ars Regia* **ii**/3 (reference kindly provided by Lucas Elkin). I am grateful to Ewa Święcka for discussing these matters with me.
58 *Née* Przeździecka, who, in 1771, married into the Radziwiłł family, thereby acquiring one of the highest social positions in the Kingdom (*see* Wegner [1954]). Related by marriage to the Prussian Royal House and to another Polish magnate family, the Czartoryskis, she was also a friend of King Stanisław Poniatowski, Catherine II (of the princely family of Anhalt-Zerbst), and Alexander I of Russia. She was an outstanding collector and bibliophile. Her husband was Prince Michał Hieronim Radziwiłł. For S.K. Potocki *see* Polanowska (2009).
59 See Chapter VI. The Society of the Order of Mopses (formed, as previously noted above, as a result of the hostile *In eminenti* [1738]), specifically attempted to avoid and refute any reasons for denunciations (including accusations of Sodomy): however, it was then reproached for being libertine. The Society reached Poland from Vienna, and, as previously noted, was named after the German *Mops*, a Pug-dog noted for its courage and fidelity. Adoptive (or Adoption) Freemasonry is a term normally applied to the form of Freemasonry found in France from *c*.1745, which found favour throughout Europe, and in which women were initiated as *Maçonnes*: it was recognised by the Grand Orient of France in 1774 as true Freemasonry. So there has to be a distinction made between Adoptive or Adoption Freemasonry and the Mopses, although the attribute of the Pug-dog seems to have found its way into Adoptive Freemasonry as well. I am grateful to Jan Snoek for his illuminating notes on these matters.
60 *Née* Fleming. She was the daughter of Count Jerzy Detloff Fleming and Princess Antonina Czartoryska. She married Prince Adam Kazimierz Czartoryski in 1761.
61 Piwkowski (1998) 547.

Arkadia survives in any way intact. Freemason-poets such as Józef Sierakowski, Tomasz Kajetan Węgierski, Stanisław Trembecki, and Kazimierz Brodziński formulated opinions on garden-design and celebrated the benefits and charms of the landscape-garden, redolent with meaning, mnemonics, and hidden agendas. The most important of these poets in promoting the New Sensibility were Franciszek Karpiński and Franciszek Dionizy Kniaźnin, who played a significant part in the lives of Isabela Czartoryska, her second daughter (Maria Anna Wirtemberska), and Helena Radziwiłłowa, and in the creation of the concept of 'sentiment' (meaning a 'moral reflection' or a 'thought, often an elevated one, influenced by emotion, a combining of heart with head or an emotional impulse leading to an opinion or principle' rather than simply a 'feeling' or emotion)[62] in Poland. The Czartoryska garden at Puławy was clearly a major catalyst in the creation of Maria Anna Wirtemberska's novel *Malvina, or the Heart's Intuition*[63], first published in Warsaw in 1816, just as Wörlitz very obviously inspired part of Goethe's *The Elective Affinities*[64]. Izabela Czartoryzka's passion for the art of landscape-gardening embraced a wide imaginative, spiritual, and cultural programme, not simply copying fashions or dealing with the practicalities. She published her own *Various Thoughts on the Method of Planning Gardens*[65] in 1805, and it is clear that one of the most significant influences on her ideas (and those of her daughter) was the French poet Jacques Delille, author of the hugely important *Les Jardins, ou l'Art d'embellir les Paysages* (1782)[66]. Indeed, the Princess corresponded with Delille for several years[67], and a further connection lay in the fact that Karpiński, High Priest of the 'New Sensibility' taught Maria Anna at the time (1782-3) he was translating Delille's *Jardins* into Polish as *Ogrody*: Karpiński used this task as a classroom exercise, and part of the Polish version of *Les Jardins* was Maria Anna's work. To be sure, the Czartoryska-Delille traffic was not just one way: Izabela Czartoryska provided descriptions of the gardens at Puławy for Delille, and Maria Anna knew Delille's poem *L'Imagination* (1806), from which she quoted a couplet at the beginning of her *Malvina*, dedicated to her brother, Adam Jerzy Czartoryski:

Pl.IX.14 Temple of Memory (later called the Temple of the Sybil) at Puławy. Chrystian Piotr Aigner, Architect (JSC).

'*Enfin quand la raison hésite et flotte encore,
Souvent l'instinct rapide a déjà pris l'essor,*'[68]

a sentiment that might be applied to gardens too[69].

The gardens at Puławy were created by Princess Czartoryska, it is true, but others assisted her to realise he vision: among them were the Painter Jan Piotr Norblin (Jean-Pierre Norblin de la Gourdaine) and the Architect Chrystian Piotr Aigner. It had *fabriques* (some of which survive), including a Temple of Memory (later called Temple of the Sybil [1798-1801] – based on the famous circular Temple at Tivoli [**Pl.IX.14**]), a Gothic House, and a rotunda-church with portico (1800-3) based on the Roman Pantheon (the significance of which in the context of centralised plans referred to above has been largely overlooked by most commentators). Unfortunately the badly damaged and considerably eroded garden is difficult to 'read' today, but central to its genesis was the concept of drawing on the past to point to the future, and to draw strength and comfort from the traditions and history of Poland after the nation and country had been torn apart[70]. Thus Puławy was not just a garden, but had a programme, even a political agenda. Puławy was therefore a major centre of 'sentiment'.[71]

---

62 Todd (1986) 7.
63 Wirtemberska (2001). Wirtemberska's father was Prince Adam Kazimierz Czartoryski.
64 Wörlitz also influenced the making of the splendid gardens at Weimar: Goethe had visited Wörlitz with Karl August, reigning (from 1775) Grand Duke (*Großherzog*) of Saxe-Weimar-Eisenach, who had summoned Goethe to Weimar almost immediately he assumed power. Karl August's tutor from 1771 was Christoph Martin Wieland. As Grand Duke, he summoned Herder to Weimar to improve education, and under his aegis the University of Jena achieved great stature as a seat of Enlightened Learning. To say that Freemasonry had considerable influence in the Grand Duchy would be an understatement, and the Grand Duke himself became a Freemason in 1782. Karl August was also responsible for breeding the Weimaraner, a gun-dog still well-known today.
65 Aleksandrowicz (1998). Czartoryska's work appeared as *Myśli różne o sposobie zakładania ogrodów*. See Czartoryska (1805).
66 Delille (1782). See also Klemperer (1954), an important and perceptive paper curiously undervalued in Anglophone circles. It is worthy of study. See also Maunde (Tr.) (1801).
67 Aleksandrowicz (1998) 29-79.

68 Delille (1806) i Chant I lines 1 and 2 on page 25. At last (or Finally) when Reason falters and wavers again, Often fleet Instinct has already taken flight.
69 Wirtemberska (2001) ix-xxxxvi.
70 Wojcikowski (1978).
71 Todd (1986) 7. See also Aleksandrowicz (1998) for a discussion of Puławy.

That Arkadia and its sister-gardens had indeed hidden meanings is recognised in Poland, for the laying out of gardens and Freemasonic activities were at the time considered a Royal Art, at the source of which stood the Great Architect of the Universe and the Creator of the Garden of Eden, the Garden of Paradise, and it is an indisputable fact that most of the theorists of Polish garden-design and of the New Sensibility, as well as the owners of the estates for whom gardens were laid out, were Freemasons. 'Gardens occupied a prominent place' in the symbolism and rituals of Freemasonry: the idea of transforming the world was enshrined in exemplary *fabriques* as well as in the 'immemorial cycles of the dying and reviving of Nature'[72]. At Arkadia various associations from Freemasonic symbolism can be found, including the contrasting opposition of Darkness and Light, Night and Day, Death and Life, as well as Chaos in the form of a ruin juxtaposed with the order of Classical architecture.

In many passages in *Malvina* there are so-called '"Ossianic" references and imagery, intended mainly to inspire longing and melancholy'. Malvina's form, like her name, evoked the girls who once shimmered through Fingal's Halls and were celebrated by 'Ossian' in his verses. One of the most popular works of literature that captured the imagination of the time (it was mentioned, for example, in Goethe's *Werther*[73]) was the supposed translation of the poems of 'Ossian', the third-century Gaelic bard, by James Macpherson, who seems to have invented most of 'Ossian's' *oeuvre*. The Czartoryskis and Radziwiłłs were familiar with 'Ossian' through translations by Karpiński (1782), Konstanty Tyminiecki (1791), Ignacy Krasicki (c.1794, 1803), and Kniaźnin (before 1795)[74]. Macpherson's work (in spite of its fraudulent aspects) had a profound effect on European sensibility, and its influence on the evolution of early Romanticism should not be underestimated, for, as Ursula Phillips has pointed out[75], the cult of Ossian did not only imply a love of wild mountains, mists, moonlight, and lonely graves, as well as a predisposition to melancholy and a sense of transience: another important element in the poetry of Ossian was the 'cult of chivalry, and the strong sense of national identity evident among Ossian's ancient warriors. The revival of chivalric values, and the interconnection made – especially by the incumbents of Puławy' – between those values and the contemporary situation in Poland also finds various manifestations in *Malvina*[76]. Isabela Czartoryska actually made a journey to England and Scotland between 1789 and 1791 to enable her to see the landscapes associated with her literary heroes, not least of whom was 'Ossian'[77].

Ossianic themes recur in Arkadia too, in the primitivist 'Amphitheatre' designed by Henryk Ittar which includes constructions of interlocking eight-sided blocks of stone, suggesting cyclopean masonry. Now such shaped stones (an octagonal pillar [probably part of the shaft of a Hellenistic column] representing Niobe stands not far from the north-eastern end of the Circus) not only suggest primitive masonry, but intricate net-like lockings, symbolically showing how a building fabric is constructed as a whole form from apparently difficult and disparate elements. Thus the fabric of society, made up of many-faceted individuals, but bound by the tempered mortar of Freemasonry, is represented. *Fabriques* might be constructed to suggest 'Ossian' and ancient Gaelic literature, not only by primitivist constructions such as the 'Grotto of the Sybil', but by means of allusions to the strange polygonal rock-formations of the Giant's Causeway in County Antrim and of 'Fingal's Cave' on the island of Staffa in the Hebrides (even though the pillar may have been brought from Delos, its shape was not one usually associated with Classicism). Ittar's polygonal masonry and the lone pillar also allude to the lost world of 'Ossian' and to Gaelic mythology as well as to Niobe and the social cohesion created by Freemasonry.

Arkadia, for which Princess Helena wrote her own guide[78], had a sophisticated programme. It is one of the best examples of a garden, full of encoded messages, of the Classical-Romantic era. The main themes are Love, Beauty, Happiness, and Death: it is full of Virgilian sorrows and regrets, as well as Youngian[79] sepulchral melancholy; it has dissonances between idyllic surroundings and human suffering; it is a sanctuary of personal memories; and it encapsulates the Primitive, Antiquity, the Middle Ages, and the elegiac concerns of late eighteenth-century sensibility[80]. The garden has been described in detail elsewhere[81] with its Aqueduct, Temple of Diana, High Priest's Sanctuary, Grotto of the Sybil, Gothic House (of course an allusion to Poland's lost independence [English Gothic Freedom again]), Isle of Offerings, Greek Arch, Isle of Poplars (a nod to Rousseau), Cenotaphs, Tombs, Margrave's House, Amphitheatre, Circus with obelisk, and Ossianic themes. Arkadia is literally full of meaning, and its Freemasonic credentials are clear and documented. Obviously it owes something to Wörlitz too, which is not surprising, as Zug, a member of the Temple of Isis Lodge in Warsaw, hailed from Saxony, and Ittar was heavily influenced by both Piranesi[82] and the advanced

---

72 Piwkowski (1998) 548. The inscription on Erdmannsdorff's fine entrance to the *Neue Begräbnisplatz* at Dessau expresses similar sentiments.
73 Goethe (1774).
74 Wirtemberska (2001) xxv-xxvii.
75 Ibid. xxvii.
76 Ibid. But for an *exposé* of 'Ossian' see Trevor-Roper (2008), meticulous in its dissection and biting in its wit.
77 She had also met Rousseau, Voltaire, and Franklin, and in 1801 she opened one of the first museums in Poland, which she called 'The Temple of Memory', a significant choice of terminology: it was also called 'The Gothic House', a term also used by Lequeu.
78 Radziwiłłowa (1800).
79 That is, Edward Young, whose significance has been described above: his influence in Europe cannot be over-stated.
80 *Album Literackie* 1 (1848) 143-54, and *see* also Piwkowski (1998) 558-61.
81 Curl (1995, 2004).
82 And Charles-Louis Clérisseau, a close friend of Piranesi, Winckelmann, and other significant members of the international circle interested in the Antique, in turn influenced (as noted above) not only Sir William Hamilton but Erdmannsdorff himself. Hamilton is commemorated at Wörlitz by the *Insel Stein* and the 'Villa Hamilton' (see **Pls.IX.7 & 8**, pp.208-9).

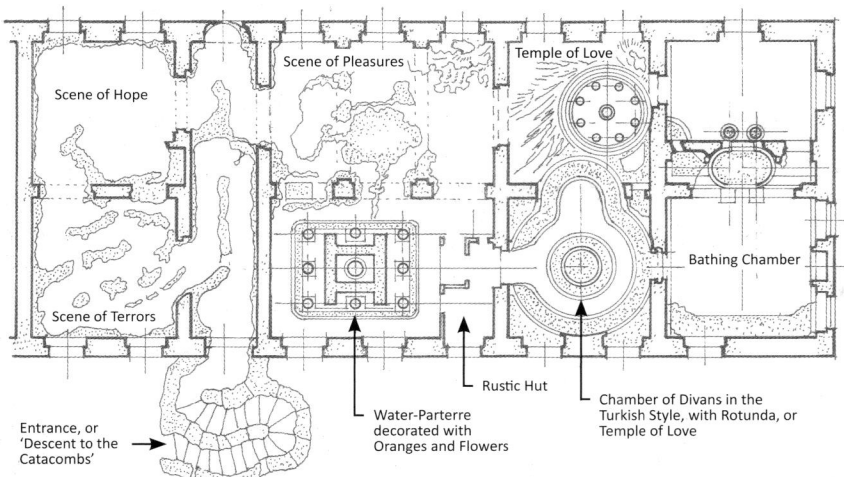

Fig.IX.1 Plan of a labyrinthine route at the Mniejszy Palace, Warsaw, by Zug. The entrance, or 'descent to the catacombs' led into the building from a garden. The first spaces were a 'Scene of Terrors' which led the perambulator into a 'Scene of Hope', the décor of which was influenced by Piranesi. Then came a rock-work grotto which led to a garden with streams pouring from a cascade into a pool. Beside a water-parterre decorated with oranges and flowers was a rustic primitive hut, which, despite its innocent appearance, concealed the entrance to the 'Chamber of Divans in the Turkish Style', a rotunda with fountain, from which access could be add to the 'Bath Chamber' and vast divan. Note the T-H motif in the water-parterre (JSC after a drawing by Zug in the Print Room, University Library, Warsaw).

Neo-Classicism of the French Academy in Rome, where Freemasonic connections ran everywhere.

It seems clear that the literary imagination drew on real locations and artefacts, and that, going the other way, some architects of the later eighteenth century were inspired by literature. Zug, who had settled in Poland in 1762, was ennobled in 1768, and designed in 1775-7 an extraordinary garden, part-real, part-*trompe-l'oeil* for the basement of the Mniejszy Palace in Warsaw, in which he violated the strict geometry of the plan by weaving a labyrinthine route through it and creating cavernous spaces in which the décor drew upon images in *Diverse Maniere* (1769)[83] by Giovanni Battista Piranesi as well as on images of rustic huts, grottoes, cascades, and plants[84] (**Fig.IX.1**). The facts that the design featured a *water-garden* with cascade and rivulets *inside* a building, and that elements such as the rustic hut, luxurious bathing-chamber approached through a Temple of Love (a rotunda), and a *route* through places evoking Terror, Hope, and so on, are significant, and point to a great difference between Continental and British Freemasonry. But the most remarkable aspect of the design is that it involves a *garden* and completely subverts the geometries of the building. That Zug was influenced in these designs for a garden of Horror, Pleasure, and Hope by descriptions in Denon's *Point de lendemain* (1777)[85] and in *Séthos* (1731)[86] seems clear: the latter book appears to have provided the bases for some of the more arcane rites practised in the higher degrees of Continental Freemasonry. Denon's *Voyage*[87] had a huge impact, triggering the Egyptian Revival[88], but his novel seems to describe a progression, an initiation-route, and is reminiscent of passages in Apuleius[89] in which an initiation in the Temple of Isis is described. It contains a description of a country estate with a sanctuary for initiates that suggested a perfumed garden, grotto, and velvet lawns, but was actually *within* a building (or a series of buildings). As previously noted, Denon was a member of the *Ordre des Sophisiens*, an élite Freemasonic Brotherhood closely associated with the *savants* and their work on Egyptian Architecture and artefacts[90].

Now Zug was a convinced Freemason, and the Craft was a thriving force in the Poland of Stanisław Poniatowski[91] (who was a pillar of Warsaw's Freemasonry, and went under the name of Salsinatus). Before Partition in 1795 Freemasonry impinged on many aspects of upper-class life in Poland: with names like *Prejudice Overcome* and *True Patriotism*, the Lodges attempted not only to reform society but to bring a rational education system to a country freed from the more repressive and obscurantist fetters of the Church. After Partition, the beleaguered Craft became a focus for Nationalism and the dream of re-establishing Poland as an independent State. Apart from his great importance as an exponent of Neo-Classicism in Polish Architecture[92], Zug was a significant practitioner and theorist of garden-design, was the co-author (with August Fryderyk Moszyński) of the very interesting but little-known (in Anglophone circles) *Essay* [sic] *sur le Jardinage Anglois* of 1774[93], and contributed the article on the splendid gardens of Warsaw published (1784) in the immensely influential, useful, and very informative *Theorie der Gartenkunst* by Christian Cajus Lorenz Hirschfeld[94]. Zug's work at Arkadia, near Nieborów[95], is of considerable importance.

In 1807 the Princesses Helena Radziwiłłowa and Izabela Czartoryzka entered the Eden Adoption Lodge that functioned under the then Duchy of Warsaw's Grand Orient. In 1806 and 1807, when Napoléon defeated

---

83 Piranesi (1769).
84 The drawings are in the Print Room, University Library, Warsaw. See Mosser & Teyssot (1991) 270-1.
85 Denon (1995).
86 Terrasson (1731). *See also* Lediard (Tr.) (1732).

87 Denon (1802).
88 Curl (2005).
89 Apuleius Madaurensis (1924).
90 I am indebted to Eugène Warmenbol for this.
91 Zamoyski (1992).
92 Lorentz & Rottermund (1984).
93 Moszyński (1977).
94 Hirschfeld (1779-85). *See* v 340-64. Zug is referred to as 'Mr. Zugk, Architecte de la Cour Electorale de Saxe à Varsovie, artiste qui réunit aux connoissances de l'architecture d'autres connoissances & un goût rare en fait de l'art des jardins'.
95 Wegner (1954).

Prussia and engaged in a war with Russia, the Duchy was created, but despite the addition of Austrian territory (Kraków and part of Galicia) in 1809, it was too small to be self-supporting. Nevertheless, its Constitution was framed on the French model and on very advanced lines, with absolute religious toleration and a well-developed local autonomy, and owed much to Freemasonic ideals, notably in the educational and economic spheres. Napoléon made (1807) the King of Saxony, Friedrich August I (reigned 1806-27), Duke of Warsaw, and the Duchy raised an Army Corps of nearly 98,000 men (an impressive figure given the total population) for Napoléon's War against Russia, but the catastrophe of 1812 sealed the fortunes of any independent Poland. Despite this, Polish and Saxon troops followed Napoléon during the campaign of 1813-14, and their commander, Marshal Prince Józef Anton Poniatowski[96], was killed in covering the Emperor's retreat after the Battle of the Nations at Leipzig, after which the Duchy was occupied by Russian forces. Polish hopes for the future were frustrated after the Congress of Vienna, for independence was illusory until the end of 1918.

So we have to consider the gardens at Arkadia and Puławy in the light of Poland's tragic history, but we also must always bear in mind the importance of Freemasonry in that country at the end of eighteenth and the beginning of the nineteenth centuries[97]: the impact of the Craft cannot be underestimated.

Norblin was also involved in the creation of Arkadia. He made conceptual drawings for the *fabriques*, and carried out some of the painted decorations in the Temple of Diana (designed by Zug) there. His pupil, the draughtsman, painter, and graphic artist, Aleksander Orłowski, also helped to decorate the interior of the Temple of Diana, and made sketches of the *fabriques* known as the 'Margrave's House' and 'Gothic House' (realised by Zug). Orłowski is reckoned to have had an immense influence on Polish and Russian art[98]. Another artist attached to Norblin's studio was Michał Płoński, who assisted his master with the paintings in the Temple of Diana, and made hundreds of sketches of the gardens.

However, one of the key figures in the creation of Arkadia was Józef Sierakowski, author, historian, diplomat, amateur artist, water-colourist, engraver, and Freemason. He was a member of the Warsaw Lodge of the Temple of Isis, and was involved in other societies concerned with science, arts, and progressive ideas. He appears to have been a generator of ideas for the garden, and actually made a design for the Tomb of Illusions at Arkadia which was superseded by the later designs by Henryk Ittar, who was of Italian-Polish stock, trained in Rome, and influenced by Piranesi and by the work of advanced Neo-Classicists at the French Academy in Rome. Ittar came to Poland in the 1790s and worked for Helena Radziwiłłowa at Arkadia from 1799 to 1804, designing the extraordinary *fabriques* known as the Circus, the Amphitheatre, and the Tomb of Illusions, none of which survives intact, although the drawings do, and give an idea of how advanced and innovative his ideas were[99]. The garden-overseer, for much of the time, was Wojciech Jaszczołd.

The Garden of Allusions at Arkadia Considered

Some thirty hectares of flat fields began to be transformed into a park in the 'English' style in 1778. The first task was to stabilise the banks of the River Łupia, then hundreds of trees and shrubs were planted and circuitous paths were created, winding in and out of *bosquets* and clearings. From points on these paths, *fabriques* could be seen. Routes were cunningly contrived so that the park seemed to be larger than it actually was. Huge granite stones were collected from the surrounding countryside, and an artificial lake was made, complete with islands, by damming the river. By 1781 the waters of the Łupia were diverted into the lake, and the landscape began to take shape. From 1782 work began on the *fabriques*, and continued until Princess Helena's death in 1821 (**CPl.IX.III**).

The choice of Arkadia as a name deserves a word of explanation. It evokes an ideal Classical landscape, unspoiled days of innocence, and Virgilian joy in the countryside. The Arcadian myth also provided allusions to death, happiness, and love that are interwoven through the park. Nicolas Poussin, as noted previously, created an image of Arcadia in his celebrated painting *Et in Arcadia Ego*, in which shepherds are shown examining a Classical tomb in an idyllic landscape (*see* **CPl.VIII.I**, p.180): the painting suggests that the person buried there was once happy, and in Arcadia too, but that those contemplating the tomb and its inscription would also die one day. The famous inscription can also be interpreted in a more sombre way: it suggests that 'And I too' (meaning Death) 'am in Arcady', so that even in a landscape of almost unbearably beautiful loveliness, the inevitable is always there, lurking among the groves, like some noontide Demon of Antiquity. The inscription was cut into a sarcophagus in Arkadia itself, situated on an island created by the diversion of the waters, clearly an allusion to Rousseau's tomb on the *Île des Peupliers* at Ermenonville, and to its charming copy, the *Rousseauinsel* at Wörlitz. Certainly, a sense of melancholy, of loss, and of vanished joys pervades this hauntingly lovely garden, exacerbated by years of neglect. Many *fabriques* invoke sentiments, communion with Nature, and a connection with Antiquity. Arkadia was intended to provide an exemplar of the programmatic garden in which Love, Death, Tranquillity, Antiquity, Nature, Art, and Memory would be evoked. There were allusions to Resignation (drawing on Schiller), and to the notion that in Arcady the first day began (meaning the first day of Enlightenment,

---

96 A nephew of the last King of Poland.
97 The following is based on Radziwiłłowa (1800), on notes made during a visit to Arkadia, on discussions with Ewa Święcka (who carried out conservation work in the Temple of Diana in the early 1990s), and on sources such as Ciołek (1978) and Piwkowski (1998).
98 Piwkowski (1993) 556.

99 Cowell & Święcka (*Eds.*) (1995).

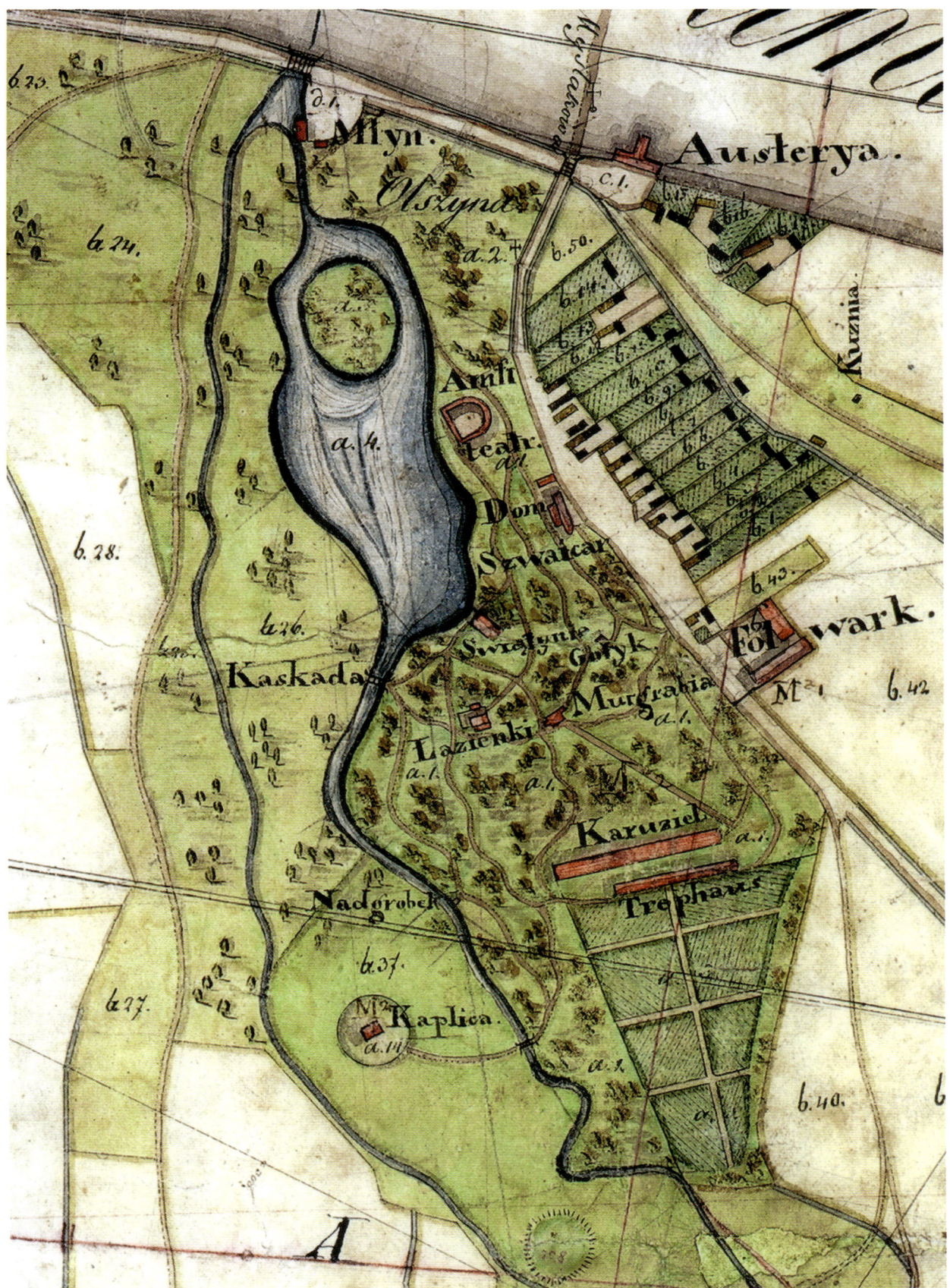

CPl.IX.III Fragment of a plan of Arkadia by J. Ostrowski, 1839, showing the lake with island, cascade under the aqueduct, and location of *fabriques* marked in carmine. At the bottom is the *Karuziel* or Circus (MNA.Zb., Inw. NB 2787.WP).

Pl.IX.15 *(top left)* Two Tuscan columns carrying the ruined arch at the High Priest's Sanctuary, Arkadia, with Hope feeding the Chimaera (by Staggi) (JSC).

Pl.IX.16 *(top right)* Arched niches by the Chimaera fountain in Arkadia, suggesting funerary niches in an Antique columbarium (JSC).

Pl.IX.17 *(left)* Detail of the construction of the High Priest's Sanctuary, showing the deliberate suggestion of an Antique building converted to peasant use, with fragments of its former glory still visible (JSC).

both Freemasonic and in terms of the *Aufklärung*). Whilst Arcady itself was suggested, so was Mythology, for the park was laid out as a place of reverie and reflection in which a rich menu of themes could be found.

At the very entrance was a fountain and fruit-trees, a mnemonic of the story of Philemon and Baucis, the aged couple who lived in a poor cottage in Phrygia and entertained Zeus and Hermes when the gods travelled *incognito* over Asia: for this deed their cottage was miraculously transformed into a great temple in which the couple became priest and priestess. After their deaths (in the same hour) they were changed into trees the boughs of which intertwined. The fountain and fruit-trees also suggest Lavinia and Palemon in *The Seasons* by James Thomson, a work known to Princess Helena. At Arkadia the two little houses or lodges at the entrance-gates (designed by Norblin) were actually called Philemon and Baucis to emphasise the point, and suggested hospitality and generosity of heart. The side of the garden associated with Baucis might prove admonitory to those lacking in sentiment and feelings, whilst the Philemon side was a passage leading to a temple of Nature. The French inscription could be translated as:

'happiness is the lot only of those who share it.'

The first buildings were constructed in 1781, starting with the sluice and the building beside it, decorated by Norblin: this was a mill. Across the lake a cascade was created. The first of the important *fabriques* went up in about 1783, and was called the High Priest's Sanctuary or the Roman Bath: it is an eclectic building in the form of an artificial 'ruined' work of Roman Antiquity. It is embellished with Mediaeval and early Renaissance sculpture brought from the palace of the Primate of Łowicz (demolished at the time). Herms, rosettes, and other Classical-Renaissance details taken from the destroyed chapel at Łowicz Collegiate Church were also incorporated within the *fabriques*: these fine sculptures were carved by Jan Michałowicz. On the north side of the 'sanctuary' is a 'ruined' semicircular arch carried over two Tuscan columns between which is a Neo-Classical bas-relief by Gioacchino Staggi depicting Hope feeding a Chimæra (**Pl.IX.15**): beneath it is a panel with two lion-mask water-spouts set over a basin above which is the inscription

'L'espérance nourrit une Chimère et la Vie s'écoule'
(Hope nourishes a Delusion and Life slips by).

The 'ruined' wall to the left of the fountain has arched niches resembling those in an ancient columbarium, or scaled-down *arcosolia* in a *hypogeum* or catacomb, so Death is suggested (**Pl.IX.16**). Elsewhere, in this strange and evocative building, are architectural fragments set into the walls that awaken thoughts of Roman Antiquity, vanished glories, and lost meanings. On the eastern side of the Sanctuary was a sheep-pen (constructed of arches to shelter the flocks that grazed peacefully in the gentle landscape) above which was a colonnaded loggia at first-floor level (**CPl.IX.IV**). On the western side of the Sanctuary the masonry evoked Roman work, with thin tile-voussoirs over blocked arches (emphasising change and decay), and other deliberately mnemonic details. This extraordinary Sanctuary was intended to read as though it were a Classical building of Antiquity that had been added to at various times, partially ruined, and then adapted by the shepherds of Arcady for their own pastoral use (**Pl. IX.17**). But the meaning becomes clear when we consider the ideas implicit in sacrificial altars, funerary columns, basin for the blood of sacrificial victims, and columbaria niches: as Princess Helena herself tells us, the horrors suggested in this shrine of Death are overlaid by the change of use and part ruination carried out by Arcadian shepherds who soon afterwards *set up the rule of the Golden*

CPl.IX.IV Colonnaded loggia at the Sanctuary (WP).

Age in its majestic vaults[100]. The notion of Transformation is obvious.

Also in 1783 work began on the Temple of Diana to designs by Zug: it was composed to be seen from several positions, each view of which would suggest a different building. To the south-east for example, the Temple, framed by trees, looked like a circular structure, for a *pteron* of six Ionic columns (signifying Wisdom) led to one of the entrances (see **Pl.IX.19**, p.224). On the frieze of this semicircular portico was inscribed words from Horace in an Italian translation:

'M'INVOLO D'ALTRVI PER RITROVAR ME STESSA'
(I part from others in order to find myself again).

However, the view across the lake from the west revealed a tetrastyle Ionic portico (sacred to the Name of God and

---

[100] Radziwiłłowa (1848) **i** 143-54. This was a translation of the French text published as a limited edition of only 100 copies in Berlin in 1800 by Georg Decker. *See also* the translation by Edward Kmiecik in Piwkowski (1998) 558-61.

to Wisdom) crowned with a triangular pediment below which, on the frieze, was an inscription from Petrarch (Francesco Petrarca):

> 'DOVE PACE TROVAI D'OGNI MIA GVERRA'
> (Where I found Peace from all my Tribulations).[101]

Pedestals on either side of the steps leading up from the waters of the lake to this portico were surmounted by an Egyptianising lion on the right side and a sphinx on the left (**CPl.IX.V**). This composition, flanked by trees, and mirrored in the waters, was reminiscent of paintings by Claude, Poussin, and others. A screen of Poplars and Acacias (redolent of Freemasonic allusions to Death, Burial, Innocence, and Immortality), partly concealed the north wall.

Inside the Temple was a miniature Pantheon-like rotunda with an altar for the offerings of visitors, whilst a circular bedroom (expressed in the projection on the long south wall) was embellished with mural paintings of Powązki, the garden created by Zug for Princess Helena's

CPl.IX.V Portico of Temple of Diana with steps leading down to the lake flanked by a sphinx and lion. Note the inscription (WP).

friend, Izabela Czartoryska. This southern projection was also host to a shrine of Pan, the woodland deity whose shade and presence haunted Arcady. Yet even in this apparently sunlit Neo-Classical Temple, allusions to Death were never very far away. The goddess of the Fields and Forests was the Patroness of the Park, but she was also the goddess of Night and of Hunting. Young's elegiac poetry, Melancholy Night, and the sombre darkness where Death stalked were all connected with this Temple. Artemis-Diana killed not only animals, but people, as the motif of Niobe mentioned above reminds us: Niobe was the tragic mother who boasted of her superiority in fecundity over the goddess Leto, the mother of Apollo and Artemis, whereupon the siblings killed all Niobe's children. Niobe wept for her offspring until she was turned into a column of stone. So Death hovered, even in the most delightful building in Arkadia, as the inscription beyond Niobe's head reminded the visitor:

> 'QVAM RAPVIT IN VITA MORS RESTITVTA'
> (Whom, when Life had been restored [to her], Death snatched away).[102]

This must refer to one of the Princess's daughters, probably Krystyna, whose promise was cut off by her premature death, and may be an oblique reference to Eurydice, the most familiar version of whose story is in Virgil's *Georgics* IV: it does not appear to be a readily identifiable quotation. Norblin and his pupils created the Apolline decorations, and the beautiful interiors drew on Pompeian, Roman, and other precedents. However, a detailed consideration of this Temple is not possible here, except to note that the connection with the goddess Isis was also made overt, for Artemis-Diana was identified with Isis, and therefore with the Egyptian Mysteries in Terrasson's *Séthos*. Asymmetrical Neo-Classicism can be very subtle, and it is clear that the Temple of Diana was designed to present different climaxes to different views within the park.

If we turn to Princess Helena's own description of the gardens at Arkadia, she emphasised meanings and intentions. The garden of Baucis was a place where 'copious sacrifices' could be made 'to that isle inaccessible to the insensitive who would dare trespass this holy shrine of passion'. The garden of Philo 'is the passage through to the shrine devoted to nature, in homage deserved for the beauty conferred upon these places. Art has surrounded it with ever blooming wreaths'. Yet when we read on, we find the astonishing statement that the 'fount' is 'open only to the

---

101 Durling (*Ed.*) (1976), Poem 300, line 4, 478-9.

102 I am grateful to Professor E. J. Kenney for discussing this with me, although we both think the comparison with the Eurydice legend is apt, there appears to be no echo of the Virgilian text in the inscription, which is a very curious construction.

chosen' and that the visitor, 'willing to be one with' the 'chosen' should 'tread the path ever more deeply shrouded in coniferous shadows as the grotto of the Sybil draws near'.[103]

Now this sounds like a call to potential initiates. When we come to the Grotto of the Sybil itself, we find a primitive structure of 'immense boulders, suspended as though by Titans'[104] resembling some megalithic dolmen built at the base of the mound on which stood the *fabrique* known as the 'Knight's Dwelling' or 'Gothic House' (**Pl.IX.18**). This Sublime primitive portal looks like the entrance to some place of foreboding, where initiates have to pass trials, and indeed it leads to a steep path connecting the Grotto with a place of unhappiness, the Gothic Sanctuary of Adversity and Sadness, the design of which seems to have been by Aleksander Orłowski. So what was the meaning of this? The primitivist Grotto certainly alludes to prophecy and the Sybil, but it also gives a nod to 'Ossian'. The Gothic House began to be associated with Princess Helena's son, Michał Gedeon Radziwiłł, who had taken part in the Napoleonic campaign of 1812 as Brigadier-General of the Warsaw Duchy Army, so it became a symbolic residence of a 'gallant knight'[105] who had defended the crossing of the Dźwina river near Połock, and also the fortress of Gdańsk when it was besieged by the Prussians.

As noted previously, after the final partition of Poland by Austria, Prussia, and Russia, there was a brief period when it looked as if some degree of independence would be gained by backing Napoléon against his enemies, and the short-lived Duchy of Warsaw was established. The repression of independence, and the bravery of the Poles who had fought for independence against their oppressors, are therefore remembered in the Gothic House or refuge, 'the seat of *disaster* and *melancholy*'[106]. Inside the Gothic House were portraits of Polish commanders of the Napoleonic period, military objects, Achievements of Arms, and much else: there was also an inscription in Polish which can be translated as:

> 'if this memento conveys your virtues to posterity, my beloved son,
> it will also testify that your mother keeps your image deep in her heart.'

Pl.IX.18 Massive primitive Grotto of the Sybil (*right*) at Arkadia, with the Gothic House (described as a 'chapel' behind, drawn by Zygmunt Vogel, engraved by Jan Zachariasz Frey (1806). Note the kneeling hermit (*MNA. Zb.WP*).

The visitor left the Gothic House through an 'open gallery of sharply pointed arches' that struggled 'with the surrounding trees for primacy, as to which is more ancient or rises more lofty'[107]. The path led 'to an arch, a bold Greek-style structure which so far neither the Goths nor vermin managed to better. This arch, victorious in its struggle against passing time, though in part by earth buried, caps a wide panorama which serves it as a magnificent backdrop. The picture all around shows ever flourishing groves, in the fold of which one sees the rotund shape of the temple'[108]. In fact, the Classical Temple is a serene contrast to the Gothic House, with the 'Greek' Arch (1783) spanning the path between them (**Pl.IX.19**, p.224), although there is nothing 'Greek' about the Arch at all (so the Arch must have an esoteric significance). The main axis of the view from the Arch to the semicircular portico of the Temple lies east-west, so, at the turn of Spring and Summer, when Nature starts bearing fruit, the sun rises exactly within the arch's frame, and illuminates the interior of the Temple with its first rays. The view of the Temple of Diana (also known as the *Temple of Love*, the *Temple of Friendship*, the *Temple of Nature*, and the *Temple of Wisdom*) framed by the Arch was shown to perfection in the drawing by Zygmunt Vogel (a Freemason) engraved by Jan Zachariasz Frey (also a Freemason). This familiar engraving was published in 1806 and dedicated to Helena Radziwiłłowa. Within the Arch are five figures: the Princess is shown, Frey holds the Dedication, and Vogel points to it. Thus at least three personages closely

---

103 Radziwiłłowa (1800).
104 Ibid.
105 The term 'gallant knight' was used by Maria Wirtemberska in *Malvina* to describe Polish patriots rallying to the colours, and contemporary soldiers were associated with knights of Gothic chivalry.
106 Radziwiłłowa (1800).
107 Ibid.
108 Ibid., *passim*.

Pl.IX.19 View of the semicircular *pteron* of the Temple of Diana at Arkadia, framed by the 'ruined' so-called 'Greek' arch. Drawing by Zygmunt Vogel, engraved by Jan Zachariasz Frey, showing the vision of Perfection from the ruins, an Enlightenment idea that recurs (*Collection JSC*).

connected with Freemasonry are depicted under the Arch, beneath the vault, with a Temple associated with Wisdom and much else in the distance on the main axis. The six Ionic columns of the semicircular portico also represent health and justice, and the number was perfect because it could be divided by both two and three, and because one, two, and three added together equals six (*aliquot* parts).

Passing through the tetrastyle west portico (four [the *tetragrammaton*] suggested the Deity) the visitor would have a view over the lake to the Elysium, lavishly planted with trees, and to the Isle of Offerings, his next stop after a visit to the Knight's Tent, an octagonal structure erected on an artificial mound and consisting entirely of large glass planes held in mahogany frames, with draperies of Moroccan muslin. Access to the Isle of Offerings was by boat guided by ropes attached at one end to an anchor, the attribute of Hope, sited close to a tree carrying a shield with Achievements of Arms set over the Knight's Tent: the other end was run through a ring held in the teeth of a sphinx (suggesting the secrets of the Island). Once across the water, on the Island, the visitor could find various altars and mnemonic devices, including altars to the ideas of Friendship, Hope, Gratitude, and Remembrance, on which votive offerings of flowers picked at the entrance to the park could be laid, and could also enjoy enticing prospects of the Temple of Diana.

In 1784 the 'Roman Aqueduct' was constructed by the cascade at the point where the river flowed into the lake, not far from the temple of Diana (**CPl.IX.VI**): it gave access across the water to the Elysium and yet evoked the grandeurs of Roman engineering, including the huge aqueducts bringing life-giving waters across the Campagna to the capital of the ancient world. This was reconstructed by Gerard Ciołek in 1951. The dam itself created a miniature cascade, the water of which made a soft, continuous, murmuring sound to lull to sleep present cares, replacing them with dreams of the past and hopes for the future. Ittar made drawings of the Aqueduct in 1800.

An artificial Island of Poplars was created in the river on an axis formed between the lakeside portico of the Temple of Diana and the south-western façade of the High Priest's Sanctuary and projected further to mid-river. On this Island was erected a cenotaph in the most severe Neo-Classical style consisting of a battered plinth, a monolithic die with a curved recess cut into it, a monolithic sarcophagus-lid with Greek horns (**Pl.IX.20**), and a draped urn surmounting the entire composition. Within the recess was a copy (probably by Gioacchino Staggi's brother, Pietro) of the recumbent statue (1599) of St Cecilia in the church of St Cecilia in Trastévere, Rome, by Stefano Maderno, formerly thought by some to be by Giovanni Lorenzo Bernini. On one side was the inscription:

'ET IN ARCADIO EGO'

and on the other:

'J'AI FAIT L'ARCADIE ET J'Y REPOSE',[109]

a reference to Princess Helena herself (**Pl.IX.21**, p.226).

In the 1790s the architectural furnishing of the garden was greatly expanded. At the beginning of the decade the 'Margrave's House' (a deliberate evocation of an Italian farmhouse constructed with fragments taken from grander buildings) was erected adjacent to the great Arch

---

109 I have made Arcadia and there I rest. For further light on the rural ideal *see* Grimm & Hermand (1989). I am indebted to Colin T. Clarkson for this reference.

(**Pl.IX.22**, p.226), and other *fabriques* of that era included the Gothic House (1795-7), the Knight's Tent, and other structures demonstrating a wider palette of styles and materials. The Margrave's House was raised and given crenellations in the middle of the nineteenth century, probably by Franciszek Maria Lancie. It was when Henryk Ittar succeeded Zug as chief architect, however, that a severe stripped Neo-Classicism emerged just before 1800 (**CPl.IX.VII**, p.226). Although Zug had explored the possibilities of erecting a sepulchral chapel or mausoleum in the park, it was Ittar who would realise this in his extraordinary design for the so-called Tomb of Illusions erected in the Elysian Fields. The catalyst was the death of Helena Radziwiłłowa's daughter, Krystyna Magdalena, who was endowed with many talents, and was a pupil of Norblin and Płoński. Later, two other daughters, Aniela and Róża were also commemorated in this Tomb. Ittar's design (for which there

CPl.IX.VI *(right)* 'Roman Aqueduct' at Arkadia (*WP*).

Pl.IX.20 *(below)* Isle of Poplars with Neo-Classical tomb, evoking Rousseau, drawn by Zygmunt Vogel, 1795 (MNA ZB. Inw. 153.WP).

Pl.IX.21 Tomb on the Isle of Poplars, drawn by Zygmunt Vogel, 1795 (MNA. Pałac. Inw. NB 123. Por. il. XXXIX.30.WP).

Pl.IX.22 (*above right*) 'Margrave's House' adjacent to the 'Greek' Arch, shown in a drawing by Zygmunt Vogel, 1795. The Temple of Diana may be seen through the Arch (MNA. ZB. Inw. NB 157.WP).

CPl.IX.VII (*left*) Severe Neo-Classical preliminary design by Ittar for the Tomb of Illusions at Arkadia, of 1799-1800, showing primitive Doric and Egyptianising elements (MNA.Zb., Inw. NB 3519.WP).

were several proposals before one was realised) employed bare cubic masses, a sparing use of architectural detail, and a noble severity rarely found, even at that time. Furthermore, the Tomb was sited beyond the formerly enclosed boundaries of the garden in the meadow situated at the far side of the river (referred to as Lethe, the river of oblivion) in the Elysian Fields shadowed by weeping willows. In Princess Helena's words the tomb was a 'symbol of suffering and misfortune which so painfully deprive life of hope and illusion'[110], and on it was inscribed:

'CELUI QUI SÈME[111] DANS LES PLEURS, RECUEILLE DANS LA JOIE' (One who sows in tears shall reap in joy[112]).

The Tomb of Illusions contained nothing terrifying concerning death: instead, quotations from various

---
110 Radziwiłłowa (1800).
111 Given as se'me in several Polish texts, including Piwkowski (1998) 561.
112 *Psalm* **cxxvi**, verse 5 (or 6 in the Authorised Version).

CPl.IX.VIII Remains of the *spina* of the Circus at Arkadia, showing the obelisk and the primitivist elemental monoliths marking the centres of the turning-circles (*WP*).

writers, including Edward Young, were inscribed. As the Princess noted, it is 'difficult to read all these grand truths and be able to revert to earlier illusions about life. Hence, from here one should move in the direction of the waterfall, to complete the pondering of Young's thoughts to the calm murmur of falling water'[113]. This sounds very much like a rejection of conventional religion and the acceptance of resignation, rationalism, and kindly benevolence, but once again the influence of England should be emphasised.

Ittar was also responsible for the design of two subsequent and very original structures, the Amphitheatre and the Circus, vast buildings that have few parallels in any landscape garden. Clearly informed by Piranesi's interpretations of the architecture of Ancient Rome (as published in *Antichità Romane* [collected in four volumes in 1756]), Ittar took as his precedents the ruins of the theatre at Pompeii and the *spina* of the Circus on the *Via Appia Antica* outside Rome, and, influenced by his training at the

---

113 Radziwiłłowa (1800).

French Academy in Rome, used elementary geometrical solids, absolutely rigorous logic in the juxtaposition of forms, and ruthless elimination of all decoration.

The 'Amphitheatre' was not an amphitheatre at all, but a semicircular theatre, a quarter of the size of a real Antique theatre, and, as already indicated, Ittar suggested severity and Primitivism by constructing parts of the building with eight-sided blocks of stone, a reference to cyclopean masonry. Several architects (e.g. Alexander 'Greek' Thomson at the plinth of Caledonia Road church in Glasgow [1856] and Leo von Klenze) employed irregularly shaped very large blocks of stone, sometimes approximating to polygons, dressed sufficiently for them to fit tightly together, called *Megalithic* or *Pelasgic*, to suggest very early origins, or rock-like foundations. As indicated above, this kind of primitive masonry visibly demonstrates intricate interlockings, and therefore a society composed of many-faceted individuals, bound together by the tempered mortar of Freemasonry. It seems also, as noted above, to have alluded to 'Ossian' by acting as a mnemonic of the rock-formations of the Giant's Causeway and 'Fingal's Cave'.

Unfortunately, the Amphitheatre was a casualty of the vast and irreversible damage caused by Zygmunt Radziwiłł, son of Michał Gedeon Radziwiłł and his wife, Aleksandra Stecka, so Princess Helena's grandson, Zygmunt Radziwiłł, after 1864, demolished Ittar's Tomb of Illusions, Amphitheatre, and Circus, and sold off the stone. He also disposed of the entire Arkadia park in 1869, though Michał Piotr Radziwiłł, Zygmunt's nephew, repurchased the garden in 1893.

The Circus, constructed in 1801, was a quarter full-size, with a semicircular south-western end. Its *spina* was adorned with an obelisk and a series of severe Neo-Classical constructions, including a sarcophagus, columns, phallic-shaped elements (**CPl.IX.VIII**, p.227), altars, a sculpted head of a racehorse named 'Arcadius', statues, etc. At one end was a primitivist construction of two unadorned uprights and a lintel with a pitched top (**CPl.IX.IX**). An inscription on the base of the obelisk records:

'MVNIFICENTIAE AVGVSTI HELENA POSVIT',

a reference to the generosity of Tsar Alexander I who permitted the building of the Circus and provided some of the ornaments that graced the *spina* from the Imperial collections at St Petersburg.

So what was the meaning of the Circus? Death stalked that *fabrique* too, where Ancient Rome, Ancient Egypt, and Primitivism were evoked, and with them thoughts about vanished civilisations and fallen Empires. Life was seen as a competition, a race, and the runner the individual going through life, passing a series of mnemonics that triggered many thoughts and associations. Perhaps the Circus has a parallel in Antiquity in the *Euripus*, or formal stretch of water flanked by architectural constructions, statuary, etc., as at the *Canopus* of the *Villa Adriana*, Tivoli (134-8), intended as a mnemonic of the town in Ancient Egypt, celebrated for its canals and beauty [114].

Princess Helena intended the Circus to be the last *fabrique* to be seen by the visitor on the way out, so it was a concentrated series of mnemonic triggers pulling many ideas, impressions, and memories together by means of a series of markers along Lethe's stream. Unfortunately, she does not tell us much about the Circus, which appears to have been connected with the idea of vanished civilisations, and therefore with the loss of Poland's independence. It is therefore not surprising that she did not spell this out, given the subservient position of her nation at the time. Today, we can only imagine the Circus (though Ittar's drawings for it and the constructions and ornaments survive), because Zygmunt Radziwiłł's vandalism destroyed it, and the position of the *spina* is only suggested by two monolithic *cippi* and by the obelisk in the middle. Some fragments of the other ornaments on the *spina* survive in the park, but much has been lost (see **CPl. IX.VIII**, p.227).

CPl.IX.IX Ittar's design of 1800 for the main gate to the Circus (MNA. Zb. Inw. NB 3541. T.Żołtowska.WP)

---

114 See Curl (2000*a*) 53-64; and Curl (2000*b*) 123-35.

Over the last twenty years of Princess Helena's life further *fabriques* were erected, including the Swiss Chalet with conservatory (an allusion to William Tell and to the fight for national freedom in the face of the oppressor), and the long orangery parallel to the Circus. There is one last element to Arkadia that should be mentioned, and it is important. The Swiss Chalet was intended to link the garden to a new village constructed on the opposite side of the Nieborów-Łowicz road. This village, regularly laid out, represented the final phase of the design of Arkadia in which nationhood was expressed in the folk and peasant traditions of Poland. The Polish language, the essence of folk traditions, and the connection between the People and the Soil were emphasised. Furthermore, the happy shepherds in Arcady of old could be identified with Polish peasants in Arkadia in the unhappy present, a means of asserting nationality.

Thus the elegiac character of the park became ever more poignant, for Arkadia began to represent the sorrows of a life, provided mnemonics of past events and persons close to the Princess, encapsulated an eclectic reference to the ideals of a lost Enlightenment, and attempted to show that a wide range of cultural influences (from the dim Gaelic mists of the time of 'Ossian' and beyond, through the glories of Classical Antiquity, a Mediaeval past, and change [suggested by the transformation of the place of pagan sacrifice into the abode of gentle Arcadian shepherds]) could be found in Poland, and in one small park. Arkadia was all about memories, reveries, regrets, and keeping civilisation and culture alive in difficult times.

Arkadia, long neglected, is one of the most remarkable elegiac Gardens of Allusion in Europe, and was recognised as such by Delille[115]: there, feelings and sensibility are given expression with sad eloquence. It is of considerable cultural importance for all Europeans, and it is hoped that the works of conservation that are slowly taking place will start to make it intelligible again. Much needs to be done, however, before it will truly be appreciated.

The Abbé Gabriel-Louis-Calabre Pérau published[116] a 'Plan of a Lodge of the Order of Mopses' which has a 'Temple' or 'Palace of Love' (one of the names by which the Temple of Diana at Arkadia was known) (**Pl.IX.23**).

[115] Delille (1782).
[116] Pérau (1745).

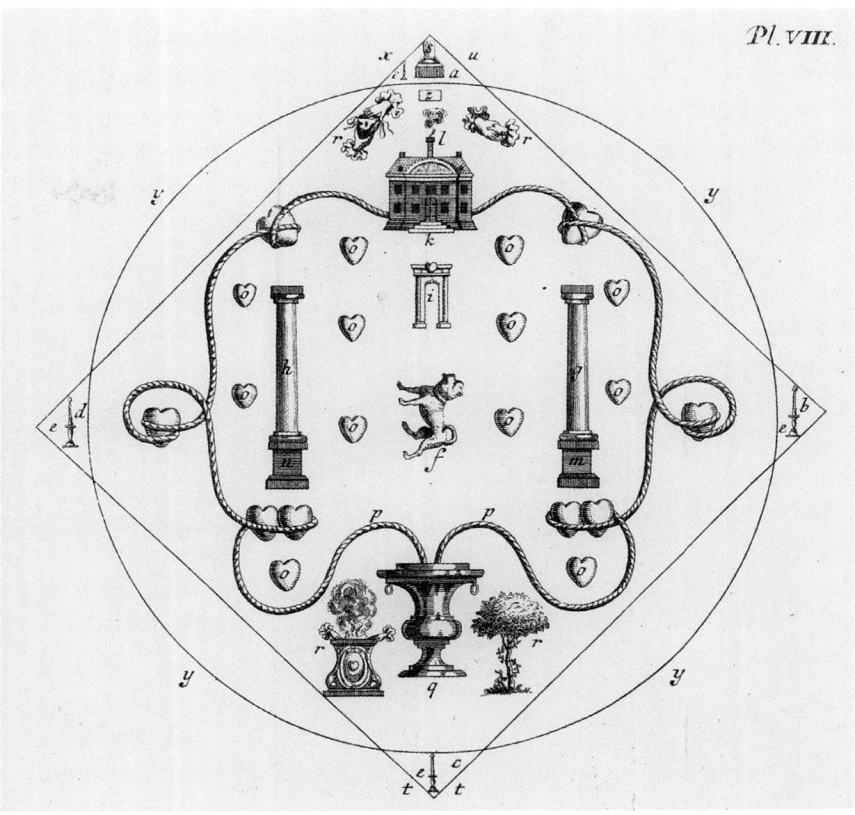

Pl.IX.23 Plan of a Lodge of the Order of Mopses. Key: (a) east; (b) south, meridian; (c) west; (d) north and the seven stars; (e) four lights; (f) *Mops* (Pug) or *Doguin* (whelp of a Mastiff), representing Courage and Faithfulness; (g) Fidelity; (h) Friendship; (i) door or portal to the Palace of Love; (k) Palace of Love; (l) chimney of Eternity; (m) Sincerity; (n) Constancy; (o) four scattered (or strewn) hearts; (p) strand of rope indicating Kindness, Courtesy, and Free-Will, linking the hearts; (q) Vase of Reason from which flows the strand; (r) four symbols of Friendship; (s) Master of the Lodge, or Grand Mopse, seated before the Table; (t) Watchers or Guardians; (u) Outsiders (male and female); (x) Officers and Officials; (y) Brothers and Sisters, placed informally around the circle and square; (z) position in many Lodges where the candidate, blindfolded, was elevated in the air. From Plate VIII of Pérau (1745*b*) (*UGLE*).

In front of this Temple, on axis, is the door to the Palace of Love, and this arch is in the same relationship to the Temple as is the 'Greek' Arch to the Temple of Diana at Arkadia. Out of a 'Vase of Reason' flows a strand of rope indicating kindness, courtesy, and free-will, linking all human hearts. There are pedestals under columns (signifying Sincerity and Constancy), and the columns themselves represent Fidelity and Friendship. There are other attributes of Friendship, including Clasped Hands, and Hands on an Altar, and in the centre of the plan is a Pug-dog or young Mastiff (*Mops* in German) representing (as noted previously) Courage and Faithfulness. Is it altogether fanciful to see the strand of rope as the agency binding many ideas together and suggesting the meandering paths of a garden? At Arkadia is not the whole idea behind the garden connected with Fidelity and Courage, especially in keeping alive the soul of the subjugated Poland? On Pérau's plan the attribute of Faithfulness and Courage stands in the exact centre of the illustration, and at Arkadia those admirable qualities were poignantly celebrated.

CPl.IX.X Portrait of Anna Karolina Orzelska, with Pug, probably by Louis de Silvestre or by an anonymous painter in the studio of Antoine Pesne (c.1726) (MNA Nr. Inw. NB 485).

Interestingly, at Nieborów[117], the Radziwiłł seat not far from Arkadia, has been found the head of a *Mops* carved in wood, and also in that palace is a portrait of c.1735 (from the studio of Antoine Pesne) of Countess Anna Karolina Orzelska (illegitimate daughter of Friedrich August – Elector of Saxony [from 1694] and King [August II] of Poland [from 1697], known as 'August the Strong' – and Henryka [Henriette] Rénard) in which the young lady (who is startlingly like her father in looks) holds a *Mops* in her right arm (**CPl.IX.X**). One could hardly have the specific connection more clearly spelled out.

Schwetzingen

On 19 July 1763 (Johann Georg) Leopold Mozart wrote a letter from *Zum roten Haus* in Schwetzingen to his friend Hagenauer in Salzburg that his children (Wolfgang and Nannerl) had 'set all' the town 'talking'[118]. He also found that his Bavarian money did not convert easily (a frequent and annoying problem in the German lands in the eighteenth century), and seems to have been uncomfortable with the lack of overt Roman Catholicism where the family stayed[119]. Indeed, he disapprovingly remarked that four religions (Roman Catholic, Lutheran, Calvinist, and Jewish) co-existed in the places through which the Mozarts were passing. These were the somewhat fragmented territories of the Palatinate, over which the extraordinary Karl (or Carl) Theodor had ruled as Elector since 1742. From 1720 the capital of the Electorate was Mannheim, and the Court spent the Summers at Schwetzingen. Any discussion of the Elector's creations at his Summer residence must take into account certain features of his character and of his territories. It will be remembered that the Palatinate had been the realm of the 'Winter King' of Bohemia, the Elector Frederick V, and that Heidelberg had been the seat of the Court, the same Heidelberg where had been created the great Renaissance Garden with its allusions to the Reformation of the World[120]. After 1705 the political settlement of the region led to a reasonably stable balance between religious denominations that lasted throughout the eighteenth century, although the Roman Catholic Electors established a privileged aristocratic minority of the same religious persuasion within their realms. Heidelberg, however, was dominantly Calvinist, and it seems to have been that fact which determined the then Elector, Karl Philipp, to move his Court to Mannheim.

Like many of his contemporaries, Karl Theodor was educated, intelligent, and interested in new ideas, but he was also a Roman Catholic, so tended to be both conservative and progressive at the same time, trying to balance Absolutism with Enlightenment ideals. As an example of this, he not only corresponded with Voltaire[121], and offered him hospitality at Schwetzingen during the writing of *Candide*[122] (in which orthodox beliefs and attitudes were ridiculed, and the optimism of Jean-Jacques Rousseau and Gottfried Wilhelm Leibniz was satirised), but gave conservative Jesuits asylum after they were expelled from France in the reign of Louis XV in 1764. These apparent ambiguities were, in fact, typical of Karl Theodor: a sceptic, his scepticism also embraced modernity, and if he could dismiss some of the more unlikely events recorded in the Lives of the Saints[123] as lies, he was also unwilling to unquestioningly and uncritically accept the doctrine of Progress, seeing (correctly, as it turned out) that the worship of Reason might cause new

---

117 Piwkowski (1989, 1998, 2005). Piwkowski & Moniatowicz (2001). I acknowledge the help of Włodzimierz Piwkowski.

118 Anderson (Ed.) (1989) 25, letter 13.

119 Salzburg was the fiefdom of a Prince-Archbishop of the Empire. Protestants had been driven out from the city in 1731, thereby benefiting Prussia, which offered asylum to Protestant refugees. Such expulsions were stock examples of the folly of persecution, and were quoted as such during the Enlightenment. Salzburg's suffocating atmosphere may have appealed to the conformist Leopold Mozart, but it certainly did not to his vastly more talented son, who detested the place.

120 *See* Patterson (1981), though many do not accept his interpretation. McIntosh (2005a) xviii, 6, 16, 71-74, however, has perceived a great deal in this garden, and I tend to agree with many of his views.

121 Francois-Marie Arouet.

122 Published 1759.

123 See Baring-Gould (1914) for a sober and relentless account of grotesque improbabilities.

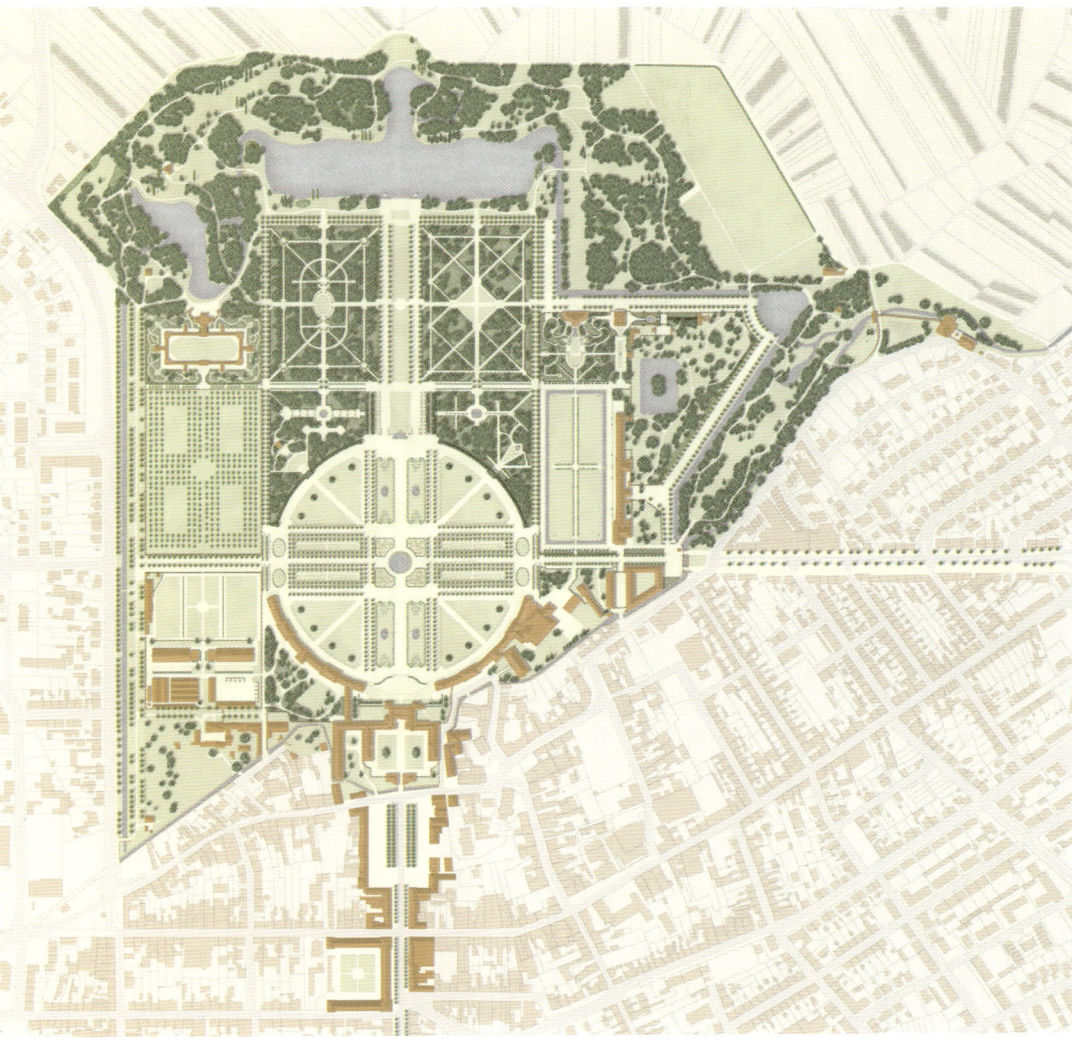

CPl.IX.XI Plan of the Gardens at Schwetzingen showing the cruciform and radiating pattern. In the centre is an inverted Latin Cross, the head of which coincides with the *Schloß*, on the right the layout of the canal suggests Compasses, and on the left, before the construction of the 'Mosque', a canal in the form of a right-angled 'Square' suggested some kind of syncretism. At the top is the later informal 'English' garden (*Struve & Partner, Atelier für Grafik-Design Heidelberg*).

problems, and that something unpleasant might evolve from too much optimistic belief in the widely trumpeted but chimaerical Perfectability of Man. In many ways, he was a most attractive personality, bright, tolerant, and wisely sceptical: like many of his contemporaries of similar rank, he was no democrat, and was essentially a Prince of the Enlightenment, capable of a truly catholic (in the sense of universal) embracing of many influences, ideas, and meanings. Most importantly, though, he recognised the significance of history and the best of the past, because the *tabula rasa* (the ideal of destructive revolutionaries) was anathema to him. That love of history, of mythology, of precedent, and of many-layered meanings is amply demonstrated at Schwetzingen, the gardens of which were greatly admired by Leopold Mozart (and which were to be revisited by his son, Wolfgang, in 1790)[124]. As part of his civilised, cultivated Court, Karl Theodor[125] also established what was to be recognised as 'undeniably the best' orchestra 'in Germany'[126], and, what is more, one composed of players not given to excessive drinking or dissipation[127]. There are very many examples of Karl Theodor's open-mindedness: to give refuge to persecuted Jesuits, yet have as his guest a noted anti-clerical intellectual such as Voltaire says much about his stance. It is therefore not surprising that he would have done what many others were doing in the eighteenth century: express a multitude of important ideas in his gardens, for, just as in England those who supported liberty, the post-1689 Settlement, and the Hanoverian Succession as an antidote to Stuart Absolutism (with the threat of a restoration of Roman Catholicism) created gardens with Gothic *fabriques* to spell out their affiliations with what was thought of as Ancient Liberties[128], so, in Germany, an enlightened Prince subtly pointed the way to many allusions, references, and ideas in his spectacular gardens at Schwetzingen.

So Karl Theodor had feet in many camps: his Court was splendid, yet he encouraged scholarly and scientific

---

124 Anderson (*Ed.*) (1989) 947, letter 590.
125 For Karl Theodor and Mozart see Gutman (2000) *passim*.
126 Leopold Mozart in 1763.

127 W.A. Mozart expressed almost the same opinions in a letter to his father from Paris, dated 9 July 1778. *See* Anderson (*Ed.*) (1989) 562, letter 313.
128 This matter is discussed in Curl (2007), Chapters I & II.

CPl.IX.XII View over the fountain in the centre of the cruciform arrangement of the Gardens at Schwetzingen, looking over the Lake towards the distant hills (*AF*).

pursuits, built up a fine library and collections, established a progressive theatre (open to the public), had the best orchestra in Germany, and his realms were noted for their toleration of religious persuasions. When, in 1777, Karl Theodor became Elector of Bavaria and his Court moved to Munich, the inhabitants of Mannheim despaired for their future well-being: however, the Electress Elisabeth Augusta stayed on in Mannheim (which also remained an important seat of government), and the National Theatre became a significant institution. Furthermore, Mannheim developed an intellectual climate conducive to the propagation of new ideas, and Freemasonry (with other esoteric societies) flourished.

At Schwetzingen, however, the gardens of the *Schloß* were developed, first on formal models derived from French exemplars, and the most important designer (from 1748) was Nicolas de Pigage, who had worked with his father, Anselm, at Lunéville, before studying in Paris and travelling to complete his education (notably in England). A major input to the design of the gardens was that of Johann Ludwig Petri from 1753. However, the presence of the Sun King can be detected, not only in the formality of the gardens, but in the repeated references to Apollo, the Sun God, throughout.

So what can we perceive at Schwetzingen, other than the obvious French influences in the formal geometries and Apolline allusions, and the looser, more informal 'English' layouts created by Friedrich Ludwig von Sckell from 1777, though still under the overall control of Pigage? The most obvious is the geometry of the circle with cruciform arrangement of paths stretching into the distances (an important aspect of design, also found in earlier times and in English work), with the diagonal vistas created by the superimposition of the saltire (or St Andrew) cross. This great circle with its radiating paths suggests both the Sun (and therefore Apollo) and Christianity (the top of the Latin cross at the east coinciding with the *Schloß*)[129] (**CPl.IX.XI**, p.231). But we find also a remarkable collection of statuary in which there are many references to the Sun, and also to Wisdom, in the personification of Minerva, identified also with Isis, with whom water is closely connected. Fountains, gardens enclosed, roses, and other attributes were associated with the Great Goddess of the Egyptians, who also became the most widely revered of all Goddesses in the Graeco-Roman World[130]. And water, obviously, is one of the most important and ever present aspects of the gardens at Schwetzingen (although the channels have been much altered since the eighteenth century as a result of changes to the drainage-system).

A perambulation of the gardens reveals a great range of statuary, ornamental vases and urns, and several *fabriques* (all of which are not quite straightforward garden-buildings, but have curious aspects to them which deserve comment). The elaborate geometric patterns of planting and paths and the presence of water everywhere have, of course, parallels elsewhere, but Heidelberg immediately springs to mind as an early seventeenth-century precedent, and what more appropriate than an eighteenth-century Elector re-creating complexes of paths, geometries, fountains, and water features at Schwetzingen to emphasise some sort of continuity? A Roman Catholic Elector not only acknowledging the extraordinary achievement of

129 I am grateful to Jan Snoek for elaborating on this point.
130 *See* Curl (2005) *passim*.

his Protestant predecessor, but overlaying it with a mighty Cross (the triumph of Roman Catholic orthodoxy, perhaps?), and superimposing allusions to Classical Antiquity suggests continuity, legitimacy, and, of course, power. Again and again we find allusions to Minerva and to the Sun: Apollo, as the deity of the Sun, suggests Enlightenment, and his symbol, the sunburst, is repeated over and over again, as is that other powerful symbol, the star with flames, emblem of Divinity, of resurrection, and therefore of Minerva-Isis, the Moon-Goddess[131]. The Sun and the Moon represent Wisdom, Power, and Goodness, emphasising omnipresent rule by night and by day, and of course the Sun had associations with the Sun King, Louis XIV, Absolutist ruler *par excellence* of the early-eighteenth century. And an Absolutist ruler should show Wisdom, be something better than Louis XIV, indeed a latter-day Solomon.

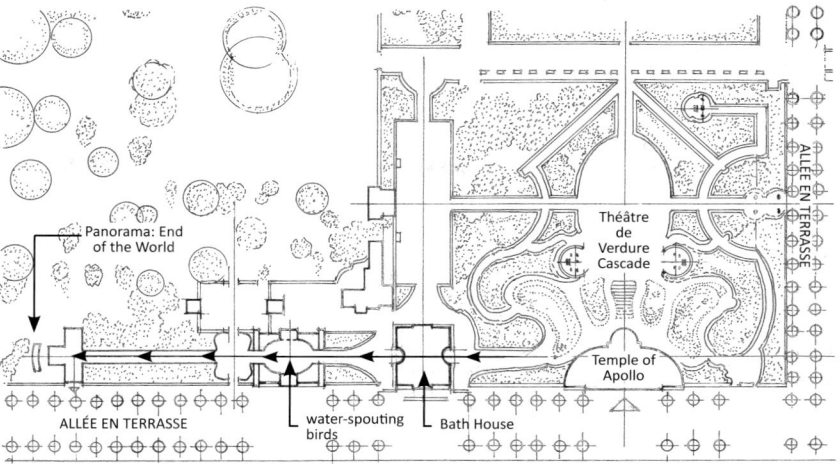

Fig. IX.2 Possible route linking the Temple of Apollo to the vision of the Paradise Garden (JSC *with acknowledgements to AF*).

That Schwetzingen alludes to earlier exemplars cannot be in doubt, for not only is Heidelberg suggested, but Tivoli too: Antinoüs himself presided over part of the garden. So Graeco-Roman Antiquity informs the garden, and the design is anchored in the landscape by means of vistas leading out to distant hills (**CPl.IX.XII**), thus local topography plays its part (although much damaged by some twentieth-century developments which are insensitively sited, block vistas, and injure the overall concept, a not uncommon feature of Modernist design, which rarely takes context into account). Important too is the Hunt, emphasised by sculptures of stags being brought down by hounds, and by the allusions to Diana/Artemis (identified with Isis and therefore with Minerva as well).

However, apart from the vast range of allusions to Classical Antiquity and mythology, to the Elements, to Nature, to Wisdom, to healing, to the powers of water, and to much else at Schwetzingen, the presence of rocks cannot be ignored. Rocks symbolise soundness, and are the foundations of Wisdom: they are associated with grottoes, labyrinths (themselves symbols of pilgrimages and of life's journey), and, in their rough, uncut state, with unperfected, untutored, uneducated Man, capable of improvement. Thus they support the perfected superstructures of, for example, the temples of Minerva, Apollo, and Mercury, all *fabriques* at Schwetzingen.

It would be tedious to catalogue all the statuary in the gardens, except to point out that themes concerned with Antiquity, Tivoli, mythology, and much else are alluded to over and over again. It is when we examine the *fabriques* however, that we start to find many things that are extraordinary, unusual, and evocative. Take the exquisite *Louis Seize* Bath-House, for example. It is entered through a porch with *in antis* columns, and this arrangement we know from English examples is often associated with Masonic Lodges, suggestive of Jachin and Boaz, the two elements particularly evocative of the Temple of Solomon. Pigage's enchanting little building has allusions to Wisdom, and the interior décor is a charming example of the *Louis Seize* style. The elliptical salon of the building has a ceiling featuring Dawn or Aurora overcoming Night, perhaps an allegory of the Enlightenment. So far there is nothing extraordinary about this *fabrique* apart from its obvious architectural quality and its beauty: what is absolutely strange is the Bath itself, sunk as an elliptical form within a room in which actual curtains frozen in stillness by being dipped in plaster of Paris can be seen[132]. The oddest features are the metal serpents linked with the supply of water: now serpents are linked with healing, with Wisdom, with Resurrection (because a serpent could discard its skin), and so in this instance are connected with benevolent deities and notions. One is therefore tempted to suggest that the Bath is more than a bath as such, but may be associated with ritual cleansing or with the idea of purification before a journey[133]. What could be more desirable than the cleansing waters of the Bath-House, and the suggestion of cleansing, not just that of the body, but of the mind as well?

All gardens require perambulation in order that their complexities and delights can be fully enjoyed, so are suggestive of longer journeys, even a lifetime of searching, and it was often the purpose of gardens to trigger memories in educated minds, to suggest new thoughts by

---

131 In this respect, the *Sternflammende Königin* in Mozart's *Die Zauberflöte* should be recalled (*see the following Chapter*).

132 Similar tricks can be found at Castle Ward, County Down, Ireland (1760-73), where hats, musical instruments, baskets, etc., were dipped in plaster of Paris and then applied to the walls as part of the décor.

133 The Trials by Water, described in the Abbé Terrasson's *Séthos* (1731), recur in Mozart's *Die Zauberflöte* (1791), so perhaps it is just possible that the bath may be connected with esoteric ritual, or perhaps it is only a *reference* to such rather than actually *intended* for esoteric use: an *allusion*, therefore.

CPl.IX.XIII *(above)* View from the Bath-House at Schwetzingen through the trellis-work towards the distant painted landscape (BH. RPS/LAD).

CPl.IX.XIV *(above right)* Trellis-work, two pavilions, and four aviaries outside the Bath-House surrounding a pool at Schwetzingen: in the centre is an eagle-owl with its prey, and around the top of the circular trellis are several water-spouting birds protesting with water-jets about the cruelty. The songs of real birds in the aviaries added to the poignancy of the scene which could be viewed from the pavilion (BH. RPS/LAD).

CPl.IX.XV *(right)* Diorama showing the 'End of the World', a vision of an enchanting landscape, at the end of the trellis-lined walk from the Bath-House at Schwetzingen. It is illuminated by natural light (BH. RPS/LAD).

means of allusion, and to stimulate, enlighten, evolve, and propose. However, there is an interesting possibility here: the main entrance to the Bath-House may not have been any of the obvious openings, but perhaps the large portal on the west façade of the Temple of Apollo which would have been accessible by coach from the major *allées*. If this, as Andreas Förcerer has suggested, is so, then the visitor would enter the Temple of Apollo, ascend the stairs, select a direction, walk through rough, dark vaults, and then arrive at the sunlit terrace on which stands the Temple. From that position the Bath-House can be seen, and the visitor could understand in which direction to travel. Inspection of the plans drawn by Nicolas de Pigage himself demonstrates that the elliptical space in the centre of the Bath-House (which suggests an open space with a heavenly vision on the ceiling) was conceived as part of a route leading from the Temple of Apollo through the Bath-House and outside again to the most delightful and amazing spaces (**Fig.IX.2**, p.233). From darkness, therefore, the visitor ascends to light, and then proceeds to the Bath-House, an elliptical Hall which has a ceiling painted as though it is a sky, with Aurora dispelling Night. From this space, the visitor could enter several charming rooms, including the Elector's study, the Chinese Tea-Room, the Elector's bedroom, or, indeed, the luxurious Bath. The parallels with Zug's plan mentioned earlier are interesting.

So, cleansed and enlightened, the visitor could proceed out of the Bath-House (**CPl.IX.XIII**) through two more *in antis* columns, along a magical route defined by paths and trellis-work, the vista emphasised by theatrical perspective. He or she would then come to a sunlit elliptical space in the centre of which is a pool and an eagle-owl attacking

CPl.IX.XVI 'Roman Water Fort', Obelisk, and Ruined Aqueduct at Schwetzingen by Pigage (1779) (BH.RPS/LAD).

a frightened bird, but all around are birds as fountains, in attitudes of protest, showing compassion for the victim of the eagle-owl (**CPl.IX.XIV**). Two little secluded seating-areas permit contemplation of this moving scene. The long avenue (*berceau en treillage*) then leads down to a distant view of a paradisical garden, a vision of Eden, painted on a wall and illuminated from above, a truly dramatic and theatrical element known as The End of the World (**CPl.IX.XV**). The two rooms to either side have ceilings with paintings of trellis-work and birds, and these rooms lead out of the route. It is one of the most strange and delightful features in any garden in all Europe: a marvellous, extremely ingenious, and wondrous place. Cleansed, the perambulator passes through transformed Nature to a vision of unspoiled natural loveliness, where all appears 'inexpressibly rare and delightful', and all things are 'spotless, pure, and glorious'[134].

The aqueduct, with 'Roman ruins' and obelisk (**CPl.IX.XVI**) suggests not only ancient Rome and the great engineering works associated with that city, but is again closely associated with water, and water is an element strongly represented at Schwetzingen, notably at the Temple of Apollo, where water flows down a cascade, viewed by sphinxes (**CPl.IX.XVII**, p.236). Now Apollo's statue is protected by a rotunda of Ionic columns (associated again with Wisdom) arranged in four groups of three, and three suggests Harmony, Friendship, Concord, Peace, and Temperance, and is regarded in Masonic lore as perfect. It is also the Trinity, Isis, Horus, and Osiris, the Three Lights, the Three Jewels, the Three Degrees, the Three Principal Orders of Architecture, the Three Knocks, the Three Fellow Crafts, and much else. Four was sacred to the name of God, so four times three has especial significance. And the whole Temple is based on rocks, and raised up, with dark vaults underneath, yet has a sunlit terrace above, the realm of Apollo and Enlightenment. The emblem of the Sun is again repeated, in Sunbursts, and the circle recurs in the openings.

Then there is the Botanic Temple, with its strange bark-like exterior (**CPl.IX.XVIII**, p.236), and entrance guarded by sphinxes. Inside is a statue (by Francesco Carabelli) of Demeter, the corn-goddess (or Ceres, often also identified with Isis), who founded the Eleusinian

---

[134] Thomas Traherne, English mystic, in Traherne (1981) Sect. 2. There are parallels between the Schwetzingen *fabriques* of Bath-House, routes, etc., and the *Grand Rocher* in the gardens of Baudard de Saint-James at Neuilly-sur-Seine, designed by Bélanger: Baudard was a Freemason. For this garden see Krafft (1801 etc.) No. 19, Plate 109. I am grateful to Andreas Förderer for sharing his views on this with me. See also Grötz & Quecke (Eds.) (2006): in a paper entitled *Badehäuser – Ein Thema der Architektur um 1800* in that work (99-121), Susanne Grötz and Klaus Jan Philipp discuss bath-*fabriques* at Łazienki Palace, Warsaw, as illustrated by Jan Chrystian Kamsetzer, and at other places where there were parallels with Schwetzingen.

CPl.IX.XVII (*above*) Temple of Apollo at Schwetzingen by Pigage (1762) (*BH.RPS/LAD*).

CPl.IX.XVIII (*left*) Botanic Temple at Schwetzingen, by Pigage (1778), with sphinxes (by Johann Konrad Linck), showing the bark-like exterior of the cylindrical building (*BH.RPS/LAD*).

Mysteries. The coffered dome with central light and vaulted underground chamber may also allude to those ancient Mysteries, and therefore to eighteenth-century initiation-rites. Again, it should be noted that there is a very expensive underground vault, which must have been built for a purpose: if it had only been intended to give the Temple prominence by raising it up higher than ground-level, this could have been done without resorting to such a costly solution, so the vault must be there for a reason. The Minerva Temple, a perfect Classical building with tetrastyle portico of the Corinthian Order (representing Beauty), also has an underground vault, and again features the circular openings for illumination: the perfection of the Temple suggests some kind of victory over the darkness below, but it should also be remembered that Minerva was the goddess of crafts and trade-guilds, so has obvious connections with Freemasonry. That is not to claim that there is a *definite* link with the Craft: only that the *fabriques* were clearly intended to be more than mere garden embellishments.

In respect of these vaults, it should be pointed out that the area around Schwetzingen was once very marshy, indeed malarial, and that even the course of the River Rhine was altered to try to improve matters, much work being carried out under the direction of Johann Gottfried Tulla. The little Leimbach was also much changed, so there were major drainage schemes to rid the area of malaria, improve navigation, and encourage a general increase of salubrious conditions. It has been suggested by some that the vaults and other structures at Schwetzingen might have been created in order to provide places of rest and protection from the heat and rain for gardeners during the Summer months, but a riposte to that might perhaps be that this was a rather profligate solution to such problems, and that, although the vaults might be so used, that does not mean their *primary purpose* was to enable gardeners to take their ease. *Even if* the vaults *were* designed to raise the buildings above floods, and to make them more aesthetically dominant in the gardens, other means, less costly, could be found to achieve these ends, so the vaults might seem to have had other meanings and reasons for being there: after all, explaining a garden such as that at Schwetzingen in purely 'functional' or 'rational' terms is clearly difficult, and, arguably, unreasonably blinkered.

A *vault* is essentially any arched structure of stone, brick, concrete, etc., primarily a ceiling over a volume, but may also be a roof, and it may carry a floor or a roof: it is constructed so that the stones or other materials of which it is composed support and keep each other in their places. Any volume covered by means of a *vault* or *voussure* is said to be *vaulted*[135]. Now secret things, or things secret except to the few initiates, are said to be *cryptic*, and in Freemasonry, the word is associated with a *crypt* or a *vault*[136]. There were vaults under the Temple in Jerusalem[137], and such a vault has associations in legend with the entombment of Hiram, the supposed master-builder of the Temple. This may also allude to the widespread custom in Antiquity of human sacrifice to ensure the stability of a building. It is not an unreasonable hypothesis to suggest that the vaults under *fabriques* in Schwetzingen may indeed allude to those under the Temple, and to the idea that after the discovery of the murdered Hiram's body, it was entombed somewhere in the Temple precincts, so that these buildings with their vaults have some sort of connection with the lost Temple, and therefore with legends of Freemasonry.

There are plenty of descriptions of the Jewish Temple[138], including the earliest Tabernacle[139], the Temple of Solomon[140], the Temple of Zerubbabel[141], Ezekiel's vision of the Temple[142] and the Herodian temple[143]. Josephus largely repeats Biblical accounts[144] of the Tabernacle and other matters, but he is illuminating in others, especially when the Bible dwells at tedious length on dimensions in Cubits, and descriptions of buildings are notoriously difficult to interpret anyway. However, the key to the mysterious persistence of vaults would appear to lie with the writings of the ecclesiastical historian, Philostorgius, the originals of which appear to be lost, but which were recorded by Photius, Patriarch of Constantinople 858-67 and 878-86. In this literature we are told that, under the Temple, in a cave cut out of the rock in the form of a perfect square, stood a column or a pillar on which was a book wrapped in oiled linen: this turned out to be the *Gospel* according to St John[145]. Now if we are to understand that the *Gospel* had been placed there at some very early date, *it would pre-date itself*, and therefore pass into the realms of the miraculous, but even if we are to glean that the text was corrupt, and the *Gospel* was somehow hidden and preserved within the Temple precinct, in some dark rock-hewn cave, then that, too, is remarkable, and explains much about the importance of St John as the Messenger, the one Who Went Before, Hermes-Mercury, and much else. Therein, I am convinced, lies the key.

It is when we come to the 'ruined' Temple of Mercury (**CPl.IX.XIX**, p.238) that we find more overt Freemasonic references, for the plan is constructed on the geometries of the equilateral triangle, the three dots of Masonic abbreviation (∴) and symbol of the Godhead, Perfection, and of Trinities, and there is a circular or winding stair[146] leading upwards (**Fig.IX.3**, p.238). Again, this *fabrique* is constructed as a 'ruin' on a rough rock-work base with

---

135 *See* Curl (2006a) 811-4.
136 Jones (1956) 291.
137 *Ibid.* 514.
138 *See*, for example, Smith (*Ed.*) iii (1863) 1450-64.
139 *Ibid.* 1451-4. See *Exodus* xxvi, xxvii, xxxvi 8-38, and Flavius Josephus in Josephus (1981) 3, 6.
140 II *Chronicles* ii-vi, I *Kings* vi-vii, and Josephus (1981) 3, 6.
141 *Ezra* vi; Josephus (1981) 12, 3
142 *Ezekiel* xl, xli, xlii, xliii, etc.
143 Josephus (1981) 15.
144 *See* Kühnel (*Ed.*) (1997/1998).
145 *See* Jones (1975), 128; and *see* also Snoek (1997) 23-33.
146 Suggestive of the way up to the middle chamber of the Temple.

CPl.IX.XIX 'Ruined' Temple of Mercury at Schwetzingen by Pigage (1787-92) (*BH.RPS/LAD*).

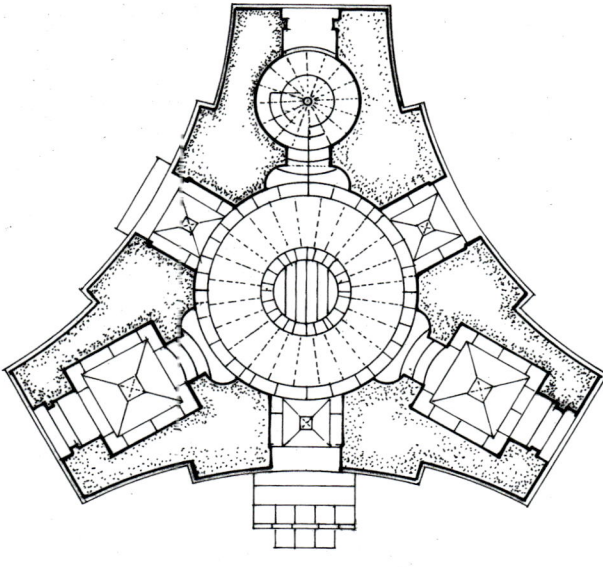

Fig.IX.3 Plan of the Temple of Mercury at Schwetzingen, showing its relationship to a Masonic abbreviation (∴) (*JSC*).

more hewn stone above, and thirty-three steps[147] lead up to a place from which a view may be had over the lake to the so-called 'Mosque' from part of the Temple which is constructed to look as though it has collapsed. Now this is all very interesting, for Mercury is identified with St John, the Messenger, and also with Thoth, who instructed the great Isis herself, notably in Geometry, and Geometry is the basis of all Architecture, all conscious design, the complexities of which were known to the Craft of Freemasonry. The temple also suggests a ruined Antique mausoleum, perhaps that of Hermes Trismegistus, the 'thrice-great', supposed inventor of hieroglyphs, identified with Euclid and Pythagoras, after whom so-called

[147] That the upper winding stair in the Temple of Mercury would have 33 steps was predicted by Jan Snoek and found to be so on 25 September 2005. I am grateful to Professor Snoek for pointing this out to me during our visit there on 18 February 2006. Winding staircases, supposedly derived from Solomon's Temple (*see* I Kings vi, 8), point to or lead to hidden knowledge which can only be attained by those who ascend to celestial things. Yet the winding stair leads to we know not what: it hides what comes next, but when climbed can reveal truth. So the revelation at the platform at the top of the stair is important, as is the number 33, which has especial Freemasonic and Rosicrucian significance, and Our Lord lived for 33 years on Earth.

'Hermetic' or 'Egyptian' Wisdom is named. Now Mercury is also the One Who Came Before, and St John the Baptist, as the One Who Came Before Christ, is therefore important in Freemasonic legend. Indeed St John the Baptist, St John the Evangelist, and St John the Almoner (or of Jerusalem) have all been claimed to be Patron Saints of Freemasonry, as previously noted, and Mercury is identified with Hermes Trismegistus. Now if the Temple of Mercury, as the forerunner, was an imperfect ruin, symbolising an attempt to be a harbinger of perfection, it nevertheless stands on a triangle, on three dots arranged as a triangle, and therefore is built upon a Freemasonic abbreviation. The broken part of the upper structure affords a view over the lake to the 'Mosque', so from the ruin is seen a vision of a perfect building. Thus the 'ruined' trial building, the experiment, the precedent, gives way to the completed vision, where Biblical, legendary, exotic, stylistically catholic all-embracing, and many other aspects coalesce. From the ruins of one culture the future can be seen, in all its completed glory.

So what is this so-called 'Mosque'? Sir William Chambers had experimented with exoticism with some success, notably with his *fabriques* at Kew, where the 'Alhambra' and 'Mosque' purported to be in the 'Moorish' style. The 'Alhambra', a five-bay building of 1758, was based on a design by Johann Heinrich Müntz, the balustrade of which obviously was the precedent for the entrance-building to the cloister of the Schwetzingen 'Mosque': Chambers had published his *Plans, Elevations, Sections, and Perspective Views of the Garden Buildings at Kew in Surrey* in 1763, which included illustrations of both the 'Alhambra' and the 'Mosque', and his 'Mosque' had two free-standing minaret-like features and ogee arched openings (the latter owing much to Batty[148] and Thomas

CPl.IX.XX (right) 'Mosque' at Schwetzingen by Pigage (c.1786-95), viewed across the Lake (AF).

CPl.IX.XXI (below) Flaming five-pointed Star over the entrance to the 'Mosque' at Schwetzingen (AF).

Langley, whose *Ancient Architecture, Restored, and Improved* came out in 1741-2[149]. The Langleys' work owed little to Mediaeval precedent, and they invented a new style, something we call today 'Georgian Gothick', also known, somewhat pejoratively, as 'Carpenters' Gothick'. The columns in the Schwetzingen cloister are vaguely similar to Batty Langley's Order IV or Second Gothick Entablature).

Although others experimented with Gothick, notably William Kent and Thomas Wright, it was a preEcclesiological Gothick, owing more to fancy than to Archaeology, and Gothick was seen at the time to be

---

148 Batty Langley was a convinced and active Freemason, and called four of his sons Euclid, Vitruvius, Archimedes, and Hiram (the last the builder of the Temple in Jerusalem, in Freemasonic lore).

149 Langley (1747). *See* the new edition (Gregg Press Ltd.) Farnborough, Hampshire (1967).

CPl.IX.XXII Interior showing the dome with its humane aphorisms and other features (*BH.RPS/LAD*).

exotic, like *Chinoiserie* or the so-called 'Moresque' style. Thus Gothick, in what purported to be a 'Mosque', was not peculiar, for it was perceived as part of the vocabulary of the rare, the odd, the strange, the unusual. Therefore the *mixture* of stylistic devices at the Schwetzingen 'Mosque' was what should be expected of the time, and it should also be remembered that an embracing of a great variety of styles (known as Eclecticism) was regarded as indicative of open-mindedness and freedom from bigotry.

The first remarkable thing about the 'Mosque' is the distribution of elements, for the two minaret-like towers recall, in their relationship to the front portico, the triumphal columns of the *Karlskirche* in Vienna, Fischer von Erlach's masterpiece, begun 1715 (**CPl.IX.XX**, p.239). As has been described elsewhere[150], the *Karlskirche* alludes to Roman Antiquity, the Temple in Jerusalem, the life of St Charles Borromeo, King Solomon, the Habsburg motif of *Plus Ultra*, and combinations of Baroque, Borrominiesque, Biblical, Imperial, Antique, Talmudic, and complex iconographical themes, all in the one building (*see* **Pl.V.18**, p.89). The 'Mosque' at Schwetzingen, too, suggests the reconstructed Temple of Solomon (especially the circular domed forms alluding yet again to those notions derived from the Dome of the Rock in Jerusalem[151]), and the five-pointed flaming stars (**CPl.IX.XXI**, p.239) that recur in the building have many resonances. The two 'minarets', the stars, the tetrastyle portico with its curious three triangular pediments (Harmony, Friendship, Concord, Peace, Temperance, Perfection, and the Sacred Name of God), and its Geometry suggest Jachin and Boaz, Strength, Establishment, and Legality, and therefore the Temple of Solomon itself, the Lost Ideal, the longing for perfection epitomised in the inscriptions within (**CPl.IX.XXII**). Instead of pulpits and a prayer-recess (which one would expect in a real Mosque), one finds stars[152], humane aphorisms[153], and a passage to a cloister, where the floor-patterns repeat geometries found elsewhere in the garden. There, in the cloister, around the 'Turkish Garden' (**CPl. IX.XXIII**), the moon in its phases presides over the four corner-pavilions (**CPl.IX.XXIV**, p.242), and the moon sheds light at night, the domain of Isis, with universal meaning emphasised by the elaborate pavements (the Solomonic Temple again). Further elements are of some importance, especially the gilded crowns on the roofs of the pavilions, suggesting the Four Christians martyred under Diocletian, the *Quatuor Coronati*, after whom the journal of a Research Lodge of Freemasonry as well as the Lodge itself takes its name[154]. And the key to so much of Schwetzingen's gardens, as with many other Renaissance, Baroque, and Enlightenment obsessions

150 Curl (2002d) 96-103. But *see* also above.
151 Goldhill (2004) *passim*.
152 The *Sternflammende Königin* idea again, the Queen of the Night, an Isis-Diana-Minerva amalgam. The stars at Schwetzingen were identified by Andréa Kroon on 22 January 2006.
153 *See* Udo Simon: 'Die arabischen Inschriften der Moschee im Schwetzinger Schlossgarten' Snoek, Scholl, & Kroon (*Eds*) (2006) 189-202.
154 *Ars Quatuor Coronatorum*.

CPl.IX.XXIII Cloister around the 'Turkish Garden' with Langleyesque 'Gothick' columns, trellis-work, and exquisite ceilings (*BH.RPS/LAD*).

with the Solomonic Temple is *Ezekiel*: the literature is considerable, and the interpretations many, but the Old Testament descriptions have informed the layout of the so-called 'Mosque', and the detail connects with so much Freemasonic iconography. One source which may have been extremely important for the 'Mosque', though not slavishly followed, was Matthias Hafenreffer's interpretation[155] of the Temple as imagined by Ezekiel, a sort of ideal. There are other volumes, too, many of which were major source-books[156] at one time, which appear to have had some sort of influence on the extraordinary and rather wonderful 'Mosque' at Schwetzingen, which may be a rarefied, exotic, and marvellous attempt to suggest the Temple, or at least allude to it in an oblique way, yet filtered through accretions that had evolved since the Middle Ages. Certainly, as a *fabrique*, it is huge and ambitious: it consists of a circular space over which is a domed ceiling and a tall domed element over that capped by an onion-shaped top. On either side of the circular space are two square rooms and these are linked by quadrants to the two minaret-like towers. The circular hall is entered through a prostyle tetrastyle portico, and leads to a rectangular room which gives access to the impressive rectangular cloister that surrounds the 'Turkish Garden'. The layout is shown in **Figs.IX.4 & 5**, p.243: by any standards this is one of the largest and most impressive of all eighteenth-century

155 Hafenreffer (1613).
156 They are given in the Select Bibliography of the present work.

CPl.IX.XXIV Corner-pavilion and ogee-arched cloister (by Pigage [1777984]), around the 'Turkish Garden' behind the 'Mosque' at Schwetzingen (*AF*).

fabriques, a *tour-de-force* of wit and elegance, remarkably beautiful and serene. It is no mere folly, and indeed none of the *fabriques* at Schwetzingen can be seen as anything less than a very considerable work of Architecture, which should be food for thought.

Karl Theodor was a Prince of the Enlightenment who believed that through Benevolence he could benefit his people and his realm. His garden at Schwetzingen, continued even after he had left for Munich, is exemplary. It has a complex and deliberate plan of statuary which is not merely decorative: it has meaning, linking the elements of Fire, Water, Earth, and Air, with progress from the darkness to the light, from deep vaults and labyrinthine ways to light-filled rationality, from the Ancient Egyptian Mysteries (hinted at by obelisks, sphinxes, lions, etc.) to the Wisdom of Minerva, the Sun of Enlightenment, and the Lost Perfection of the Temple of Solomon itself, joining the Old and the New, linking Ancient Wisdom to Modern Aspirations, and, most of all, making connections closely interwoven with Christianity. These were themes that ran through the all-embracing tolerant systems of eighteenth-century Freemasonry, and which are expressed in the garden at Schwetzingen. That is not to say that Karl Theodor *was* a Freemason: we simply do not know, but an eminent Freemason *was* closely connected with his Mannheim Court, as will be mentioned in the following Chapter, and another with his establishment in Munich.

And round this splendid garden, tying it all together as with a binding thread, is the waterway, joining the allusions and the symbols in a coherent whole. The Garden Enclosed, an attribute of the Blessed Virgin Mary, the Mother of God, is, of course, connected with the Great Forerunner, Queen Isis, and therefore with Minerva as well, for all the attributes are shared.

With such extraordinary allusions, what do we know about Karl Theodor's connections with the Illuminatists and Freemasonry? A Prince of the *Ancien Régime* had to be seen to be a Prince, and could not, in the ordinary way of things, hob-nob with lesser mortals. However, as a Freemason, within the Lodge, all were equal, and discourse among equals could take place. It was therefore through Freemasonry and other esoteric 'secret' societies that many aristocrats and princely families could meet intellectuals of lower social rank who could converse freely with them without fear of trouble. One astonishing image may point the way to Karl Theodor's involvement with Freemasonry: in the Vienna *Karlskirche* an equilateral triangle containing the name of God set in a sunburst occurs over the High Altar, and over many eighteenth-century altars can be found the All-Seeing Eye with sunburst held within an equilateral triangle[157]. Now this motif is also known in Freemasonry, denoting Superintending Providence, knowing and seeing all: it is an emblem of the Degree of Master-Mason, for God is All Eyes, and represents T∴G∴A∴O∴T∴U∴ (The Great

---

[157] A good example of its use in the normal Roman Catholic context may be seen in the Rococo Church of St Peter, Mainz. I am grateful to Hans-Detlef Mebes for showing me this building (though no interpretations anywhere in this present work are due to him).

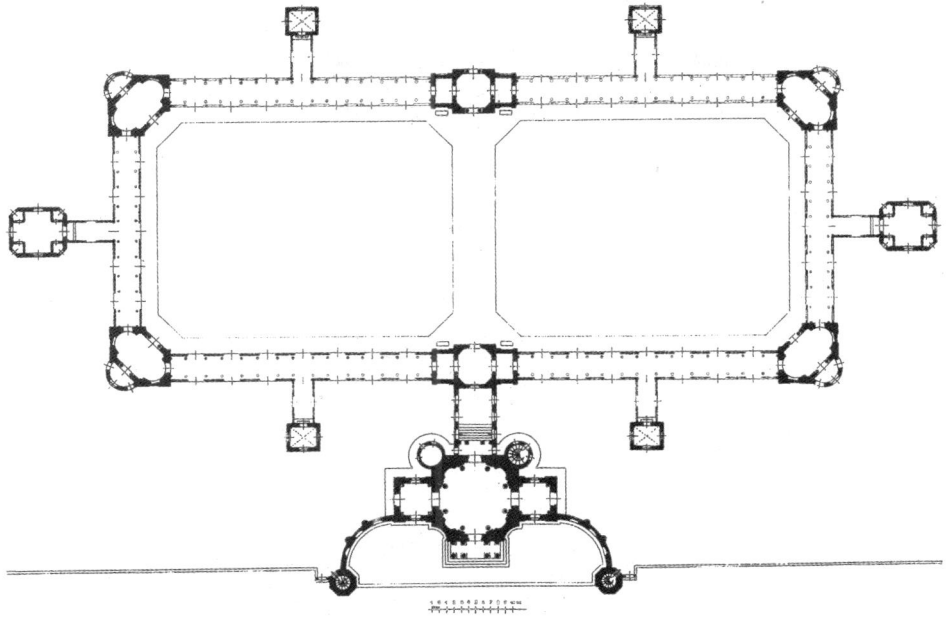

Fig.IX.4 Plan of the 'Mosque' and cloister surrounding the 'Turkish Garden' at Schwetzingen. Note the corner-pavilions and other small rooms, and the concave front of the 'Mosque' with 'minarets' (*From Martin [1933]* – see *Select Bibliography*).

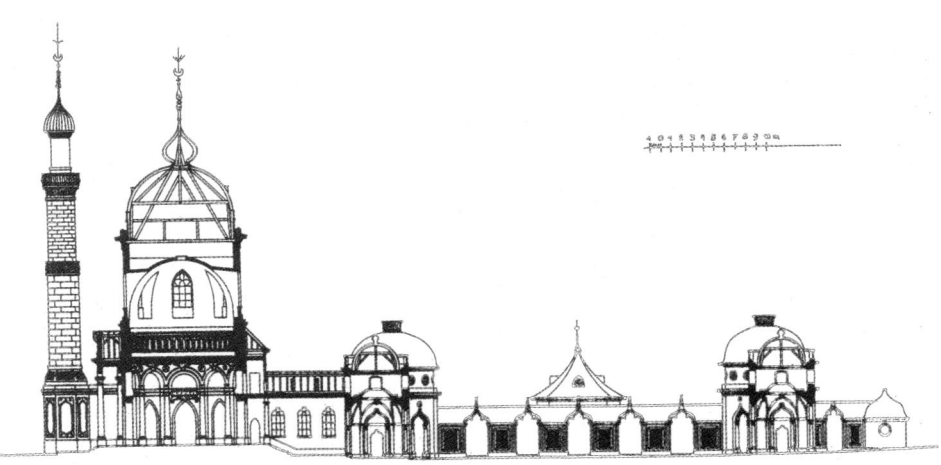

Fig.IX.5 Section through the 'Mosque' and cloister at Schwetzingen, showing the domed circular space, 'minarets', and pavilions of the cloister-walk (*From Martin [1933]* – see *Select Bibliography*).

Architect of the Universe). It is therefore very peculiar to find the All-Seeing Eye within the triangle set on an urn above a pedestal on which is a portrait of Elisabeth Augusta: this is in a painting by an unknown artist of 1761 showing an allegory on the death of the new-born Franz Ludwig Joseph, the Elector's only son.[158] Indeed, it is most unusual, so much so that it deserves comment:

it must refer to Superintending Providence as it does not occur where it should in Roman Catholic iconography, and therefore probably has a Freemasonic aspect. And this, together with the curiosities of the garden, suggests some kind of esoteric interest, most likely Freemasonic, on behalf of the Elector.

There are further ramifications. One of the key figures in the later life of Karl Theodor was Sir Benjamin Thompson, born in Massachusetts, but an American

---

158 Number 1.4.5 in Probst *et al.* (1999) (Band II) 33. I am grateful to Jan Snoek and to Monika Scholl-Frey for drawing my attention to this item.

Loyalist (that is, loyal to King George III), who entered the Elector's service in 1784. Thompson became a Colonel in the Bavarian Army, and applied scientific principles to the problems of feeding and clothing soldiers. He also introduced workhouses so that beggars could be employed to make suitable cloth, and he invented improvements in the design of heating, concerning himself with efficiency and the saving of fuel. He introduced potatoes into the Bavarian diet, applied scientific approaches to nutrition, and promoted the laying out (from 1789) of the celebrated English Garden in Munich for the recreation of the inhabitants: it was designed by Sckell. Thompson became Minister for War, Minister of Police, Major-General in the Bavarian Army, Chamberlain, and Councillor of State: his services were recognised when he was created Graf von Rumford[159] in the Nobility of the Holy Roman Empire in 1792. In 1796, when Munich was threatened by French and Austrian armies, Rumford (as he then was) managed to persuade both not to attack the city, and indeed the threat passed. He was a prime mover in setting up the Royal Institution in London, attempted to establish a similar Institute in Bavaria, and married (1805) Marie-Anne Paulze, the widow of the brilliant French scientist, Antoine-Laurent Lavoisier, who had perished by the Guillotine during the Terror. Now we know Thompson was a Freemason[150], and became one at the St John's Lodge No 1, Portsmouth, New Hampshire, on 12 November 1772[161], so it is *entirely unlikely* that he did not carry his Freemasonic ideals with him to Karl Theodor's Court. The notion of a garden, open to the public, and created to raise tone, civilise, and educate the population is very much in tune with Freemasonic principles of the time. In relation to Karl Theodor, the influence of Count Rumford should not be overlooked, neglected, or under-estimated. If *Ezekiel* had been the main influence on Pigage's designs for the cloister (with strong doses of Batty Langley and Chambers), Rumford's influence on the rest of the 'Mosque' from 1786 to 1796 should not be discounted, nor should his connection with Sckell.

The gardens at Schwetzingen, remarkably complete, have many *fabriques*, but their complexities cannot be explained in terms of utility, 'functionalism', or even the water-table, let alone for reasons of pleasure, frivolity, or mere aesthetics: with their substructures they were much more expensive than strictly speaking necessary if they were only to shelter gardeners, to keep the buildings above water, or for eye-catching purposes, and so it is logical to propose that they must have been constructed for esoteric or mnemonic reasons. The figure of Minerva is ever-present, associated with Isis, Diana, and the Moon, and so with fountains and healing waters (both obvious ingredients at Schwetzingen). If a journey in a complex garden can suggest a journey through life, or travels in search of Truth, Beauty, and Meaning, then Schwetzingen is a superb example of the type. It links Antiquity and ancient gardens, and, through its amazing diversity, suggests the longing for Enlightenment that was such a feature of the epoch. In all this, the binding element (apart from water) is the ideal, and in that lies the spirit of Freemasonry, one of the most significant strands that informed the European Age of Reason. If Freemasonry sought to re-fashion the world, to reform it, the garden is as good a place as anywhere to start. And there is no doubt that the Prince de Ligne, the Prince of Anhalt-Dessau, and Princess Helena Radziwiłł, among many others, had agendas rather than outdoor work-relief schemes on their minds, and even left evidence of the improving, moral, educational, and other notions with which they were concerned. The Prince de Ligne, in particular, was scathing about those whose sensibilities were so atrophied that they could not be bothered to decipher the encoded messages at Beloeil.

One last thing needs to be mentioned, and that is the importance of views *from* the garden at Schwetzingen. Distant hills, routes, and openness have been partially obscured by modern developments that do nothing but erode Karl Theodor's vision (which owes much to the Villa de'Este and to Kent's 'leaping' of the 'fence' to call 'all Nature a garden')[162]. As the circles recurring in plans and in *fabriques* (e.g. the openings) suggest wholeness, so should that wholeness of the entire ensemble be respected and enhanced as part of any future management-plan.

There can be no question that the magnificent Garden of Allusions at Schwetzingen is one of the great achievements of enlightened, benevolent rule in the German lands, and it clearly should be recognised as a place of world importance.

Conclusion

Despite the amount of research I have undertaken into aspects of garden history, I am conscious of only having glanced at a forgotten subject that seems to be of vast extent: there do appear to be many submerged allusions to which I have drawn attention, and I do not think they can be dismissed as airily as some have tried. If one takes Arkadia alone, the Freemasonic connections are quite clear. Of course a journey in search of knowledge, a progressive path, a choice of options, or mnemonics are all very ancient ideas, and may not necessarily have any Freemasonic connections at all, but sometimes they do seem to have such links, and of that there can be no argument. During the period in which the gardens I have mentioned were created, the first-century AD text known as the *Tablet of Cebes* was widely known. This concerned a votive tablet in a temple carved with many characters and several scenes. In the explanation of its meaning, the text describes how each person enters Life, and after many

---

159 Rumford was the township from which his first wife's (Sarah Walker) family came: it is now Concord, NH.
160 *See* Foss (1972).
161 Curl (2004) 122.

162 As Horace Walpole wrote (1782) of William Kent. See Walpole (1995) 43-4. *See also* Mowl (2006).

Trials, Temptations, and false turnings, if that person makes sound decisions and choices, he may eventually ascend the steep, rocky path leading to Happiness and Enlightenment through Education. Very well, and there are plenty of ideas that have come down to us from Antiquity that were eagerly taken up during the eighteenth century, not least by Freemasons.

One further point needs some emphasis here, and that is the Baroque attitude to past and future cultures which attempted *Synthesis* in a truly heroic attempt to link the diversity of historical cultural forms into a newly integrated whole. This aspect of Baroque art and architecture can be compared only with the Hellenistic and Roman Syntheses of ancient and disparate cultures (as, for example, at the *Villa Adriana*, Tivoli), and it is arguable that the Baroque Syntheses were altogether deeper, more comprehensive, and impressive even that those of Antiquity[163]. In a garden such as that at Schwetzingen we find an extraordinary aspect of garden-design as a *Compendium*, in which compressed within its boundaries is an *Encyclopaedia of References*, a vast canvas of diverse historical, symbolic, allegorical, mythological, and artistic meanings, all combined in one delightful, enchanting whole. Here we find one epoch inserted within another. Christianity and Classical pagan religion, the exotic, visions of Paradise, and much else, a huge combination with an almost infinite variety of cultural and mythological allusions, mnemonic triggers, and much, much more. It is a *Gesamtkunstwerk*[164] in which there can be found a creative tension in the synthesis of Antique architectural forms, ruins, the exotic, allusions to Classical mythology and history, esoteric legends, and elaborate geometries into a new entity reflecting perhaps, the whole of the world, and not just the world one can or could see, but the world of the spirit and mind as well. This is an example of the *Historia Universalis* so important in an attempt to understand much of what went on in the seventeenth and eighteenth centuries: a limited and impoverished Modernist viewpoint is wholly unequipped to be able to begin to understand this phenomenon[165].

A great garden such as that at Schwetzingen is all about complexity, diversity, all-inclusiveness, and much else besides: it is really a statement of open-mindedness, and that, really, is of singular importance in any consideration of this remarkable, beautiful, and enchanting place.

It is clear that the creators of these glorious and extremely interesting gardens were deeply serious people, and that they were trying to raise tone, improve society, and educate by means of their creations. There is enough material in the *Gartenreich* of the Prince of Anhalt-Dessau, the views of the Prince de Ligne on gardens and *fabriques*, the works of Princesses Helena Radziwiłłowa and Izabela Czartoryska, and the gardens of Karl Theodor to fill a very large book. Those who have claimed that 'there never was enough in this subject to make it worth pursuing'[166] might well be mistaken[167], and it might be helpful to those who have dismissed the possibility that there could be any connection between Freemasonry and gardens if they should start by perusing certain not exactly unknown Masonic texts: William Preston, for example, stated near the beginning of his seminal work that, were

> 'a man placed in a beautiful garden, would not his mind be affected with exquisite delight on a calm survey of its rich collections? Would not the groves, the grottoes, the artful wilds, the flowery parterres, the opening vistos [sic], the lofty cascades, the winding streams, the whole variegated scene, awaken his sensibility, and inspire his soul with the most exalted ideas? When he observed the delicate order, the nice symmetry, and beautiful disposition of every part, seemingly complete in itself, yet reflecting new beauties on the other, and all contributing to make one perfect whole, would not his mind be agitated with the most bewitching sensations; and would not the view of the delightful scene naturally lead him to admire and venerate the happy genius who contrived it?'[168]

Perhaps that sums it all up.

---

163 Doukhan (2001). Professor Doukhan's work is most impressive, and all students of the period can profit from reading his published papers.

164 Total Work of Art.

165 For these weighty matters *see*, for example, Schmidt-Biggemann (1983), and the same author's many works on Enlightenment culture.

166 Macpherson (1998) 59.

167 I am grateful to many people for help with this Chapter. First of all I thank the Master, Fellows, and Governing Body of Peterhouse, University of Cambridge, where the gist of it was written. I am grateful to Colin T. Clarkson and Lucas Elkin of The University Library, University of Cambridge, for generous assistance in matters of dates, quotations, and facts. Reinhard Alex, Eva Eissmann, Włodzimierz Piwkowski (of the National Museum in Warsaw and the Museum at Nieborów and Arkadia), Alan Short and Michael Foster (of the Faculty of Architecture and History of Art, University of Cambridge), Ewa Święcka (former Curator and Conservator of Arkadia), and Katarzyna Zachwatowicz-Jasieńska all helped with images, published material, and many kindnesses. My wife, Dorota Iwaniec, helped by translating from the Polish, often at short notice. John Ashby, Andreas Förderer, Robert A. Gilbert, Peter Holland, Katrina Jowett, Gavin Kelly, Georg Friedrich Kempter, and Jan Snoek all gave assistance and valuable advice. I am also indebted to Peter Hamilton Currie, who edited my paper 'The Landscape Garden and Freemasonry' (*see* Curl [2004]: it forms part of the substance of this Chapter, and the re-use of some of this material is by kind permission of QCCC Ltd). I thank J. A. M. Snoek, Monika Scholl, and Andréa A. Kroon for permission to incorporate material published in 2006 (*see* Curl [2006b]), and acknowledge the generosity of OVN (Foundation for the Advancement of Academic Research into the History of Freemasonry in The Netherlands).

168 Preston (1792) 1-2.

CHAPTER X

Mozart and Freemasonry

Introduction; Mozart's First Associations with the Craft; Later Developments; Die Zauberflöte, Freemasonic Opera?; The Music and the Libretto; Stage-Sets and Egyptian Architecture; Epilogue

'O Isis und Osiris, schenket
Der Weisheit Geist dem neuen Paar!
Die ihr Wand'rer Schritte lenket,
Stärkt mit Geduld sie in Gefahr.
Laßt sie der Prüfung Früchte sehen;
Doch sollten sie zu Grabe gehen,
So lohnt der Tugend kühnen Lauf,
Nehmt sie in euren Wohnsitz auf.'

EMANUEL JOHANN JOSEPH BAPTIST
SCHIKANEDER (1751-1812) ET AL.:
Die Zauberflöte (The Magic Flute): Act II Scene 1.

'Zerfließet heut', geliebte Brüder,
in Wonn' und Jubellieder,
Josephs Wohltätigkeit
hat uns, in deren Brust
ein dreifach Feuer brennt,
hat unsre Hoffnung neu gekrönt.'[1]

AUGUSTIN VEITH EDLER VON
SCHITTLERSBERG (1751-1811):
Song for Tenor, Mens' Chorus, and Organ,
set to music (K.483) by Mozart.

Introduction

Early in his life Mozart had written a *Singspiel* supposedly first performed in the garden of Dr Franz Anton Mesmer in 1768: it was called *Bastien und Bastienne* (K.50 [46b]), and its Libretto was by Friedrich Wilhelm Weiskern and Johann H. F. Müller, with additions by Johann Andreas Schachtner, after the parody of Rousseau's *Le Devin du Village* (premiered 1752) called *Les Amours de Bastien et Bastienne* by Marie-Justine Benoîte Favart, Charles-Simon Favart, and Harny de Guerville. The connection is therefore of some interest: Mozart, aged 12, set a work that originated with one of the significant figures of the Enlightenment that appears to have been given its first performance in the Viennese garden of a man who was to be involved with Freemasonry, Cagliostro, and other personalities of the period. More was to follow.

The playwright, Tobias Philipp, Freiherr von Gebler, Freemason, who knew Lessing, Wieland, and other Masonic writers, wrote the text of the heroic drama *Thamos: König in Ägypten* ('Thamos, King in Egypt') between 1773 and 1779. Indeed the source of the subject-matter has been claimed to have been Christoph Martin Wieland's[2] *Dschinnistan oder Auserlesene Feen- und Geister-Mährchen*[3], a curious collection that also provided the genesis of the libretto of Mozart's *Die Zauberflöte*[4], but *Thamos* is far more likely to have been influenced by *Séthos* (one of the characters in Thamos is called 'Sethos'), a German translation of which, by Christoph Gottlieb Wend, had appeared in 1732[5].

---

1 The Schikaneder text reads in English as: 'O Isis and Osiris, bestow the Spirit of Wisdom on this young couple! You, who guide the traveller's footsteps, grant Strength with Patience in time of Danger. Give them the Rewards of their Trial; but should they enter the Tomb, then honour their courageous journey, Accept them in your dwelling-place'; and the Schittlersberg as 'Today, beloved Brethren, melt into songs of delight and rejoicing, Joseph's Beneficence to us, whose hearts burn with threefold Fire, has crowned our Hope anew'.

2 Goethe gave the *Totenfeier* (funeral exequies) for Wieland at the Amalia Freemasonic Lodge, Weimar.
3 Wieland (1786-9): 'Dschinnistan or Selected Fairy- and Ghost-Stories'.
4 *See* Dent (1960) 26, 33, 225. *Die Zauberflöte* = The Magic Flute.
5 For *Séthos see* Terrasson (1731) and Lediard (Tr.) (1732).

Mozart[6] composed at least two choruses and an entr'acte for *Thamos* in 1773, but completely re-cast and expanded the score (K.345 [KE.336a])[7] for a performance of the play by the troupe of Johann Böhm in Salzburg during the 1779-80 season. Gebler mentioned Mozart's music in a letter of 13 December 1773, and his work was performed in Vienna in 1774[8] with Mozart's music described as 'beautifully written' in *Historisch Kritische Theaterchronik von Wien*[9]. It would appear that the play was given in Salzburg in 1776, complete with Mozart's music, according to Alfred Orel[10].

Thus in the 1770s Mozart came into contact with mystical ideas of initiation, Hermetic religion, and Freemasonry, which seem to have made profound impressions on him, for his *Thamos* contains solemn and noble music (comparable with severe Neo-Classical designs of the period): Otto Jahn observed of the choral writing in *Thamos* that it is grander, more free, and more imposing than that of any of Mozart's Masses of the time, and pointed out that a 'solemn act of worship was represented' on the stage. He also noted that the 'expression of reverence to the Supreme Being was heightened in effect by the Egyptian surroundings'[11]. Indeed 'Egyptian' theatrical sets, designed with varying attention to historical accuracy (this was before the scholarly French publications had appeared[12], not unconnected with the influence of Freemasonry for reasons outlined in previous Chapters), were associated with numerous productions of the time. For *Thamos*, for example, Egyptianising stage-sets were designed for a production North of the Alps, probably influenced by the stage-designs of Mauro Antonio Tesi of the previous decade. But Mozart's great music was also influenced by the works of Christoph Willibald, Ritter von Gluck, and by the innovations of the Mannheim School of musicians to which he had been exposed during his visits to the Court of the Elector Carl (or Karl) Theodor.

Mozart's First Associations with the Craft

The first Lodge in the Holy Roman Empire of the German Nations is said to have been founded in Prague in 1726. Despite Papal condemnation and the antipathy of the Kaiserin Maria Theresia to the Craft[13], Freemasonry flourished in the Empire: it will be remembered that Francis Stephen, Duke of Lorraine (Franz Stephan von Lothringen, Kaiser Franz I from 1745), had been initiated in The Hague, and had married Maria Theresia in 1736. The first Viennese Lodge was *Aux Trois Canons* or *Zu den drei Kanonen* of 1742.

Mozart himself was initiated in December 1784 as a member of the Lodge *Zur Wohltätigkeit*[14]. Now 1784 was the year in which Kaiser Joseph II (who had become joint-ruler with his mother, Maria Theresia, in 1765 on the death of Francis, and who was to be sole ruler from 1780 when the Kaiserin died) determined to ensure that Lodges within the Empire should transfer their allegiance from the foreign Grand Lodges (which had constituted them) to a new National Grand Lodge (*Große Landesloge von Österreich*) which was duly formed in 1784 with Johann Baptist, Graf Dietrichstein, as Grand Master[15]. Most Austrian Lodges had adhered to the English Ritual, but in 1781 an Imperial Decree prescribed that no spiritual *or* secular Orders were to submit to any foreign authorities, and payment of fees to any official body outside the Monarchy was forbidden. The *Große Landesloge von Österreich* from 1784 embraced seven Provinces with seventeen Lodges in Austria, seven in Bohemia, four in Galicia, two in Austrian Lombardy, three in Transylvania, twelve in Hungary, and seventeen in the Austrian Netherlands[16]. During the 1780s the Craft flourished in Austria, especially in Vienna, where leading personalities were drawn to it. Of the eight Viennese Lodges, the leading one was *Zur wahren Eintracht*[17] over which the remarkable figure of Ignaz Edler von Born (scientist, mineralogist, and writer), was Master. Mozart's Lodge was not very large, and met at the inn *Zum roten Krebsen*[18] near the

---

6 The Register of the Cathedral Parish, Salzburg, dated 28 January 1756, records the Baptism of Joannes Chrysost[omus] Wolfgangus Theophilus Mozart, born 27 January (Feast-Day of St John Chrysostom), the son of Johann Georg Leopold Mozart (Composer, Conductor, and Teacher, author of the textbook *Versuch einer gründlichen Violinschule* [see Mozart (1756)] and his wife, Anna Maria Walburga Pertl. For some years Mozart used the German 'Gottlieb' instead of 'Theophilus' before he settled for 'Amadè' or 'Amadeus' around 1777, although in Italy from 1770 he called himself 'Amadeo'. On his Confirmation, Mozart acquired the extra name of Sigismundus (*see* his letter of 14 November 1777 from Mannheim to his father), after Sigismund III Christoph, Graf von Schrattenbach, Prince-Archbishop of Salzburg (1753-71).

7 Throughout, the K. (e.g. K.626 for *Requiem*) refers to Köchel's *Chronologisch-thematisches Verzeichniss sämtlicher Tonwerke Wolfgang Amadé Mozarts* and, if further K. numbers appear after the original K. numbers, these refer to later revisions (*see* Köchel [1862]). This was the first chronological thematic presentation of all the then known works by Mozart, and was compiled by Ludwig Alois Ferdinand, Ritter von Köchel, published in 1862.

8 Deutsch (1965) 146, 148.
9 24 March, 13 April, 9 May, all 1774.
10 Deutsch (1965) 149, quoting *Acta Mozartiana* **iv**/4 (1957) 76.
11 Dent (1960) 254.
12 Denon (1802); Commission des Sciences et des Arts d'Égypte (1809-28).

13 Although she suppressed *In eminenti* in Austria, regarding such Papal action as an infringement of her privileges. Her husband also seems to have persuaded her father, Karl VI, to avoid persecuting the Craft during the period 1738 to the accession of Maria Theresia. It was Karl VI, it will be remembered, who ordered the building of the *Karlskirche* to designs by Fischer von Erlach, which, as we have seen, contains many allusions to the Temple. The protection given to the Craft, therefore, may have been due less to Franz Stephan's intervention than to a covert appreciation by the Kaiser of certain themes found in Freemasonry, its iconography, and its importance in the preservation and development of mnemonic techniques to preserve history, legend, and the lost buildings of Antiquity. It should be remembered that there had been a strong thread of mysticism in Habsburg history, not least in the concerns of Rudolph II, Karl (or Charles) V, and, of course, the Spanish connections and the Escorial. Karl VI also showed an enlightened, though not always successful, interest in the prosperity of his subjects, and from as early as 1713 he had begun to prepare for the so-called 'Pragmatic Sanction' to regulate the Succession and ensure the recognition of his daughter, Maria Theresia, as his heiress. That alone showed a remarkable capacity for breaking with established tradition.

14 Charity, or Beneficence.
15 For these matters *see* the excellent Düriegl & Winkler (Eds.) (1992).
16 Landon (1982) 8.
17 True Concord or Harmony.
18 The Red Crayfish.

Hohe Markt: it often found it convenient to work with the larger (and more influential) *Zur wahren Eintracht*, which had a couple of hundred members. Apart from Mozart's own *Zur Wohltätigkeit* and *Zur wahren Eintracht*, there were six other Viennese Lodges in 1785: these were *Zu den drei Adlern*[19], *Zur Beständigkeit*[20], *Zu den drei Feuern*[21], *Zum heiligen Joseph*[22], *Zum Palmbaum*[23], and *Zur gekrönten Hoffnung*[24], the last, like *Zur wahren Eintracht*, a large Lodge. It was in the *Zur wahren Eintracht* Lodge that Mozart was raised to the Fellow Craft, in January 1785, in a ceremony presided over by von Born. Shortly afterwards he was raised to the Third Degree, probably in the same Lodge. So 1784 was an important year for Mozart: not only did he become an Entered Apprentice of the Craft, but he began to keep a thematic catalogue[25] of his works without which we would not have the precise dates of his compositions from that time, nor would we have invaluable information concerning the music he composed for Masonic occasions[26].

Mozart, through Gebler and other influences, would certainly have been aware of the Craft in the 1770s[27], but the Master who initiated him was an old friend of the Mozart family, Otto Heinrich, Freiherr von Gemmingen-Hornberg, civil servant, diplomat, playwright[28], and admirer of Diderot, who had been Palatine Chamberlain and Privy Councillor to the Prince-Elector Karl Theodor at Mozart's beloved Mannheim[29]. However, when Karl Theodor became Elector of Bavaria and moved the Court to Munich from 1778, intelligence of which 'fell upon Mannheim like a thunderbolt, and completely extinguished, as it were, the joy' of the inhabitants[30], this must have been one of the reasons why the Baron moved to Vienna. Interestingly, von Gemmingen-Hornberg lived for a time in the *Schloß* at Schwetzingen, and was clearly involved in Freemasonry (despite *official* Electoral disapproval) in the Mannheim area. His translation to Vienna seems partly to have been because of his diplomatic skills, but he was undoubtedly attracted to what appeared to be a growing centre for Enlightenment ideas.

Several scholars[31] have established those facts about Mozart's Masonic career that have survived in documentary evidence. Mozart's father, Leopold, in 1785, was initiated as a Freemason in the Lodge *Zur Wohltätigkeit*, and at *Zur wahren Eintracht* passed to the Fellow Craft Degree, swiftly becoming a Master Mason at the same Lodge presided over by Born. It is believed that at the ceremony, Wolfgang's *Gesellenreise* (The Journey of the Fellow Craft – K.468) was performed: the words were by Josef Franz Ratschky (Orator[32] of *Zur wahren Eintracht*), and were published in a collection of his poems in 1785[33]. Two days later, the Mozarts, father and son, attended the Lodge *Zur gekrönten Hoffnung*, where Born was honoured, and Wolfgang's Cantata, *Die Maurerfreude* (The Mason's Joy, K.471), was performed. The occasion was Born's invention of a new means of separating metals which was more economical of both labour and timber, and he was created a Knight of the Realm as a result. The words of *Die Maurerfreude* were by the Bohemian priest, Franz Xaver Petran, Freemason (he was a member of *Zur gekrönten Hoffnung*) and Chaplain to Franz Josef, Graf Thun (also a Freemason, member of *Zur wahren Eintracht*, occultist, alchemist, and enthusiastic follower of Franz Anton Mesmer), who is portrayed on the frontispiece of Johann Caspar Lavater's *Protokoll über den Spiritus Familiaris Gablidone*[34]. The text of *Die Maurerfreude* starts by celebrating how Nature 'unveils' her countenance 'by degrees' to the 'unflinching eye', how she 'imbues' a Freemason with 'Lofty Wisdom to fill' his mind and 'Virtue to fill his heart'. It goes on to point to the Freemason as the 'disciple' of Wisdom and Virtue, receiving his crown from 'Joseph's hands', the joyous celebration and triumph of Masons ('Joseph' being the Kaiser): the inmost halls of the Temple would 'echo' with 'jubilant songs' telling of the gathering of laurels by 'Joseph the Wise', who, 'twisted

---

19 Three Eagles.
20 Steadfastness or Constancy. Joseph Lange, Mozart's brother-in-law, belonged to this Lodge: Lange painted (1789-90) a celebrated portrait of the composer.
21 Three Fires.
22 Saint Joseph.
23 Palm-tree.
24 Crowned Hope.
25 *Verzeichnüss* [sic] *aller meiner Werke* (Catalogue of all my works) 1784-91. See Rosenthal & Tyson (1990).
26 See Köchel (1862).
27 The song, *O heiliges Band der Freundschaft treuer Brüder* (K.148 of 1772 or 1775-6) has been doubted by some as 'Masonic'. The text was by Ludwig Friedrich Lenz, apparently in honour of the Salzburg Lodge of St John (*Lobgesang auf die feierliche Johannisloge*), and some have suggested it cannot date from before Mozart became a Freemason in December 1784. However, Freemasonry was widespread in the German Lands at the time, and, as is clear from the vast literature on the subject, was hardly a 'secret'. In the circles in which Mozart moved, it is more than likely he could have composed music for Freemasons before he became one himself. Anyway, Lenz's words, referring to the 'sacred bond of Friendship between true Brothers', 'Up, Masons, and sing: tell the World today', 'Virtue', 'nothing more glorious than our Lodges', 'the quiet Happiness to which Masons are dedicated', a 'law' which calls for Friendship and teaches Men Love', and much else, could not be more specifically Freemasonic.
28 He was the author of *Mannheimische Dramaturgie* (1779) and *Der deutsche Hausvater* (1780). He moved to Vienna in 1782. His name crops up in letters of the Mozart family. See Anderson (*Ed.*) (1989) **ii** 516, 589, 605, 631, 638, although his name is mis-spelt as 'Homberg' therein. Mozart composed music for a drama by Gemmingen-Hornberg, *Semiramis* (see Mozart's letter from Mannheim to his father, dated 3 December 1778 – see Anderson [*Ed.*] [1989] **ii** 637-9). This composition, if it was ever completed, does not appear to have survived.
29 As he referred to it in a letter of 12 November 1778.
30 Mozart, 31 July 1778, quoted in Anderson (1989) **ii** 588.

31 Among them Bauer & Deutsch (*Eds.*) (1962-75), Deutsch (1932, 1937), Deutsch (*Ed.*) (1961), Landon (1982), Smyth (1975), Thomson (1972), Till (1992), and others.
32 A Freemasonic Officer found in Continental Freemasonry, who explained the ceremonies through which candidates passed.
33 *Die in einem neuen Grade/Der Erkenntnis nun euch naht,/Wandert fest auf eurem Pfade,/Wißt, es ist der Weisheit Pfad./Nur der unverdroß'ne Mann/Mag dem Quell des Lichts sich nah'n.* (You, who are approaching a new Degree of Discernment, now walk steadfastly on your way, knowing it is the path of Wisdom. Only he who perseveres may draw near the Source of Light). The text goes on to refer to candidates as 'pilgrims' taking their Brothers' blessings with them: with caution at their side, the thirst for Knowledge should guide them as they were advised to test everything and never fall into the trap of indolent blindness. Life's journey, they were told, is hard, but sweet is the prize awaiting the wise wanderer who can learn from his travels and one day can say his path was bathed in Light.
34 Frankfurt-am-Main & Leipzig 1787 s.n. Thun's wife, Gräfin Maria Wilhelmine Thun, was celebrated for her intellectual *salon*. She was the beloved patroness of Mozart.

laurels round the brow of the wisest of Masons'. The first performance of the tenor part of *Die Maurerfreude* was sung by Johann Valentin Adamberger, opera-singer and Brother of *Zur gekrönten Hoffnung*. The Cantata was published by Pasquale Artaria with a Preface by Wenzel Tobias Epstein[35] and a handsome frontispiece (**Pl.X.1**) drawn by Ignaz Unterberger, engraved by Sebastian Mansfeld, all of whom were Brethren of *Zur gekrönten Hoffnung*, adorned the printed work.

Mozart also composed (probably 1782-3) a Canonic Adagio for two basset-horns and bassoon (K.410 [440d, 484d]) and an Adagio for two clarinets and three basset-horns (K.411 [440a, 484a]), both possibly, it is said, used for Freemasonic ceremonies[36]. They were very likely written with Anton Paul Stadler and his brother, Johann Nepomuk Franz Stadler, in mind: both were excellent performers on the clarinet and basset-horn, and from 1781 both were employed in the Court Orchestra in Vienna. The clarinet and basset-horn solos in *La Clemenza di Tito* (K.621 of 1791) were written for Anton Stadler, and it was for the modified clarinet favoured by Anton that Mozart wrote his Clarinet Quintet (K.581 – 1789) and Clarinet Concerto (K.622 of 1791). Anton Stadler was a Freemason, and member of *Zur gekrönten Hoffnung*, but that does not make basset-horns or clarinets 'Masonic': in fact Mozart employed basset-horns for an aria to be inserted in a revival of *Le Nozze di Figaro* in 1789. This was *Al desio di chi t'adora* (K.577) and sung by Adriana Ferrarese del Bene, née Francesca Gabrielli. He also used one such instrument in the aria *Non più di fiori vaghe catena* in *La Clemenza di Tito* (K.621 of 1791). In neither case was there any connection whatsoever with Freemasonry.

Of very great importance among Mozart's compositions that were definitely for the Freemasons is his *Maurerische Trauermusik* (Masonic Funeral Music of 1785 [K.477 (479a)]), written, it is claimed by some, for a Lodge of Sorrows or Memorial Service for two eminent Freemasons, Georg August, Herzog von Mecklenburg-Strelitz[37], and Court Chancellor Graf Franz (Ferenc)

Pl.X.1 Title-page of Mozart's Masonic Cantata *Die Maurerfreude* (K.471), in the Viennese first Artaria edition of 1785, engraved by Sebastian Mansfeld after Ignaz Unterberger. The text was by Franz Petran, and the piece was written in honour of Ignaz von Born, Grand Master of the *Zur wahren Eintracht* Lodge. Emblems of Truth, Harmony, and Crowned Hope can be seen, all referring to Viennese Lodges (BL. Music Library, Hirsch IV, 84).

Esterházy von Galántha[38]. With its two oboes, clarinet, three basset-horns, two horns, contrabassoon, and string quartet, it is a short but powerfully evocative work, and features the plainchant *tonus peregrinus* drawing on the Lamentations used in Passion Week and in the *Miserere* of the *Requiem* Mass. This *tonus peregrinus* (or 'wandering tone') was associated with the Psalm *In exitu Israel* (114 in the *Book of Common Prayer*), but the *cantus firmus* used in this intense Adagio has connections with the penitential Psalm 51 (*Miserere mei, Deus*[39]) and is found in that mine of information, Abraham Zvi Idelsohn's *Songs of the Babylonian Jews* in the Series *Thesaurus of Oriental Hebrew Melodies*[40]: it is obvious that Mozart placed enormous importance on this, for he quoted the *cantus firmus* in full at the end of his autograph score, as though to spell out the allusions. Not for the first time, the Roman Catholic composer, a creature steeped in the Enlightenment and in the tenets of Freemasonry, was to draw on music that had resonances *beyond* Roman Catholicism. Graf Esterházy was a member of *Zur gekrönten Hoffnung*, and Herzog Georg August was an Honorary Member of *Zu den drei Adlern*: the taut music,

---

35 Who was of Jewish origins.

36 Though some dispute this: the facts that Mozart knew performers capable of playing the instruments well, and liked the sounds they made, doubtless inspired him to write the music.

37 Whose sister was Princess Charlotte Sophia of Mecklenburg-Strelitz (Queen of King George III). He was Major-General in the Imperial Army.

38 He had been Hungarian-Transylvanian Court Chancellor (*Hofrat*), and was known as *Quinquin*, a nickname that may have prompted Hugo von Hofmannsthal to use it as a nickname for Graf Oktavian in the libretto of *Der Rosenkavalier* (Op. 59), set to music by Richard Strauss in 1909-10 and first given in Dresden in 1911. Some authorities (e.g. Thomson [1977] 82) have held that the *Maurerische Trauermusik* was probably written for the ritual ceremony of Death and Resurrection rather than *for* the Lodge of Sorrows, although we know it was *performed* at such.

39 Have mercy upon me, O God, after thy great goodness: according to the multitude of thy mercies blot out my transgressions, etc., known as *Miserere mei Deus*.

40 Idelsohn (1923).

remarkable for its depth of feeling, its masculine calmness, and its acknowledgement of solemnity in the presence of Man's inevitable end, perhaps refers to that Hope in the *Tierce de Picardie* with which it finishes[41]. The first part of the *cantus firmus* is, in fact, the Gregorian Lamentation Chant *Incipit Lamentatio Jeremiae*, and obviously meant a great deal to Mozart, for he used variants of it again in the *Te decet* of his D Minor *Requiem* of 1791 (K.626) and in *Die Zauberflöte* (K.620) during the strange Scene 31 of Act II when the Two Men in Black Armour sing

'Der, welcher wandert diese Straße voll Beschwerden
Wird rein durch Feuer, Wasser, Luft, und Erden'[42],

and in both the *Maurerische Trauermusik* and *Zauberflöte* examples the *cantus firmus* is a deliberate slow march: in the case of the scene with *Zwei schwarzgeharnischte Männer* ('Two Men in Black Armour' – not, as most BBC announcers and opera-house programmes would have it, 'Two armed Men'), the slow march is the *Protestant* chorale, *Ach Gott, vom Himmel sieh' darein, Und lass dich's doch erbarmen!* ('Ah, God from Heaven look on them and yet grant them thy mercy!) a paraphrase by none other than Martin Luther of Psalm XI in the Vulgate version, first published 1524, and used by numerous composers, including the great Johann Sebastian Bach in his Cantata BWV2. Mozart's score and other evidence in the National Library, Vienna, point to the fact that the extraordinary passage with the Two Men in Black Armour in *Die Zauberflöte* was meticulously worked on by the composer who probably saw the tune in *Kunst des reinen Satzes* published in Berlin in 1771-6 by Johann Philipp Kirnberger[43]. It is clear that the music of this scene, of the *Maurerische Trauermusik*, and of the *Requiem* is all interconnected, and obviously meant much to its creator. Mozart's elegiac *Maurerische Trauermusik* has a dark, mysterious atmosphere, the musical equivalent of some Neo-Classical designs, like those of Louis-Jean Desprez[44]: this short orchestral work is permeated with the figure three, not only in its tripartite form, but in its sixty-nine measures with the *Te decet hymnus* plainsong used by Michael Haydn in his *Requiem pro defuncto Archiepiscopo Sigismundo* (1771) with which Mozart was familiar. Mozart's orchestration in the *Maurerische Trauermusik* anticipates that of the opening pages of his own unfinished *Requiem* (K.626) of 1791.

In the year in which Mozart became a Freemason, Joseph von Sonnenfels of the *Zur wahren Eintracht* Lodge, wrote a piece on the 'Influence of Masonry on Civil Society' in which he claimed that the Craft had been the means by which the ideals of the Enlightenment had been disseminated[45], and others have asserted that nearly all those who figured in the 'Josephinian Enlightenment' were Freemasons, and indeed that about eighty percent of members of the Austrian senior bureaucracy in the 1780s were involved in the Craft[46]. The so-called Josephinian Enlightenment, however, was short-lived. Joseph II's reign as Kaiser saw the blossoming of Freemasonry as an agent for a radical programme of reform in which society was perceived as autonomous, even responsible for its own regulation, guided by an idealised type of secular virtue. To many minds of the Enlightenment, a consideration began to evolve that Christianity, after all, might not be an agent for and promoter of moral authority and truth, and could be seen as profoundly superstitious, stifling inquiry, and fostering unthinking obedience to dogmas. Some perceived the Christians as agents of fanaticism and oppression, and sought instead to establish some sort of system of ethics stripped of the supernatural: the Churches claimed that without God Mankind would never be virtuous, but the eighteenth-century *philosophes* pointed out, not without good reason, that Christianity had had sufficient time to promote virtue, yet Mankind still behaved vilely, cruelly, dishonestly, and immorally. As Jacob Laib Talmon noted, the *philosophes* had no doubt they sought a paradoxical secular religion[47].

The 'Enlightened' Joseph II, however, believed in a paternal despotism that functioned for the good of all. From 1780 he completed the emancipation of the serfs, begun by his mother, introduced religious toleration, restricted Papal authority to spiritual matters only, secularised Church lands, suppressed certain religious Orders and transferred monasteries from the jurisdiction of the Pope to that of Diocesan Bishops, subjugated the Clergy to the lay State, and promoted the compulsory use of the German language throughout the Empire. He established asylums, hospitals, orphanages, schools, and institutions to train and educate. He reformed the fiscal system and the administration of the law, but his anti-clerical innovations so alarmed the Papacy that Pope Pius VI (who was deeply concerned about the rising tide of Atheism and Secularism, and especially about Febronianism [the German equivalent of Gallicanism which Johann Nikolaus von Hontheim of Trier promoted under the pseudonym of 'Justinus Febronius']) visited Joseph in 1782 to attempt to dissuade the Kaiser from the path he had chosen, but without success.

However, Joseph was still a Roman Catholic, but attempted to curtail Papal influence, thus his obedience to the Holy See was not absolute. He never went as far as King Friedrich II of Prussia (who robustly declared that Christianity was the invention of priests, and that it was an old

---

41 For an interesting discussion of this *see* Landon & Mitchell (*Eds.*) (1956) 153-5. A *tierce de picardie*, or 'Picardy Third' is a *major* third in a tonic chord at the end of a composition which is otherwise in the *minor* key.

42 He who travels this path with burdens, is purified by Fire, Water, Air, and Earth.

43 *See* Jahn (1856) **iv** 617.

44 Curl (2005) 153, 174-6, 184, 253, 365. Desprez settled in Sweden in 1784, a country in which the Craft was 'intimately controlled and directed by the Royal Family', having been called there from Rome by King Gustavus III, whose brother was Grand Master of the Grand Lodge of Sweden. The King promoted many men of humble birth, but who had talent, to positions of prominence and power (Gould **iii** [1884-87] 198).

45 *Journal für Freymaurer* **i** (1784) 135-92. *See* also Sonnenfels (1783-87).

46 *See* Bodi (1977) 77. *See* also Winter (1971) 191 and *see* Winter (1962) for a sound analysis of Josephinism.

47 Talmon (1986) 21, and *passim*. Talmon's brilliant 'Totalitarian Democracy' encapsulates what has happened since the eighteenth century.

metaphysical fiction, stuffed with miracles, contradictions, and absurdities, spawned in the fevered imaginations of the Orientals and then spread to Europe, where some fanatics espoused it, some intriguers pretended to be convinced by it, and some imbeciles actually believed it[48]), and indeed he back-tracked, bowing to pressure from the Clergy in relation to Freemasonry, as will be described below.

In the course of its advancement through Europe the Craft had acquired many accretions, and very quickly it departed from British Freemasonry, embracing Higher Degrees and much else involving arcane practices, pretensions to be heirs of the Templars, and more. By the 1780s Freemasonry in the German lands was infiltrated by Rosicrucianism and thereby acquired tendencies to mysticism and the occult. In Vienna, particularly, many Lodges were pronouncedly Rosicrucian in character[49], which Born resisted, as it appears he hoped to use *Zur wahren Eintracht* as a catalyst for the formation of an equivalent to the Royal Society in London (which had, of course, been connected with both the Craft and with a particular type of Deism associated with Sir Isaac Newton). Not only was Born's Lodge involved in scholarly publications, but had a large library, and could boast some of the finest minds of the time among its members. One of Born's colleagues in this extraordinary movement was Freiherr Gottfried van Swieten, Diplomat, Imperial Librarian, and Government Official, who was closely involved in musical life, and an intimate of Mozart, Haydn, and others. Born's circle was in contact with many important figures of the Enlightenment, including Wieland, Schiller, and others[50].

Till has pointed out that Mozart's Lodge, *Zur Wohltätigkeit*, was 'specifically the meeting place for those who believed in a *Catholic* Enlightenment in Vienna. It was, undoubtedly, for this reason that Mozart chose to join Gemmingen's Lodge rather than the more radical and secular[51] *Zur wahren Eintracht*'. Well, perhaps, but Mozart often attended meetings in *Zur wahren Eintracht*, and indeed was raised to the Second Degree there (and probably to the Third Degree as well, although documentary evidence is missing). It is far more likely that Mozart joined *Zur Wohltätigkeit* because of his previous connections with Gemmingen at Mannheim, a *Residenzstadt* where he had been happy and creative.

Pl.X.2 Design for an Egyptian tomb (c.1779-84) by Louis-Jean Desprez in pen and ink, with watercolour over black chalk. This is the Neo-Classical Kingdom of Death, where a seated crowned skeletal figure with Egyptianising head-dress presides. Note the *loculus* with cadaver feet on the right, the segmental form of the vault, and the segmental sarcophagus with bogus hieroglyphs. Desprez, clearly, was influenced by Piranesian images. The relationship of the crescent-moon of Isis and bow of Diana is obvious. Here is Sublime Terror. Desprez was called from Rome to Stockholm in 1784 to serve King Gustavus III of Sweden, whose brother, Karl, was Grand Master of the Grand Lodge of Sweden from 1773 (C-HM No. 1938-88-3951).

To some, of course, the whole notion of a 'Catholic Enlightenment' was absurd, and many regarded the prospects for the Enlightenment in Roman Catholic Austria as unpromising. And unpromising they turned out to be, for Joseph II seems to have alienated rather too many interests for comfort, and towards the end of his life his 'reforms' started to go into reverse gear. Friedrich II of Prussia's remark that Joseph was a 'sacristan'[52] had more than a ring of truth about it.

Also closely involved with von Born and van Swieten was Aloys Blumauer (journalist, poet, and satirist)[53]. Mozart set one of Blumauer's verses to music: this was the *Lied der Freiheit* ('Song of Freedom' – K.506) of 1785. Blumauer was a Freemason, a member of *Zur wahren Eintracht*, later amalgamated with the *Zur Wahrheit* Lodge.

Later Developments

Joseph II started to move back from his reforms as early as December 1785, when, pressurised by various interests, not least the Clergy, he decreed that there should be no more than three Lodges in each of the main cities, and that these should periodically submit detailed lists of Brethren to the authorities for official inspection[54]. However, there may have been a reason, unrelated to

---

48 For Friedrich's views see Preuss (*Ed.*) (1846-56).
49 Till (1992) 121.
50 *Ibid*. 122-5 expands on these connections.
51 *Ibid*. 124-5.

52 Cragg (1960) 219. For Freemasonry in Josephinian Vienna *see* the brilliant Rosenstrauch-Königsberg (1975, 1984).
53 For Blumauer *see*, for example, Rosenstrauch-Königsberg (1984).
54 Smyth (1975) 43.

any anti-Craft aspects, for this: by then Freemasonry was infected by Cagliosto's so-called 'Egyptian Rites', and by the Order of Illuminati of Johann Adam Weishaupt[55], who was convinced the Egyptian pyramids were Temples of Initiation, and evolved a philosophy that was anti-monarchical and opposed to conventional Christianity. Although he had become a Freemason in 1777, his increasingly radical programmes incurred the displeasure of the authorities in the Bavaria of Karl Theodor, and the Society of Illuminati was banned in 1784. Weishaupt settled in Gotha under the protection of Herzog Ernst II of Saxe-Gotha-Altenburg, and produced several books on Illuminism[56]. The infection of Freemasonry, of course, had long alienated the Craft in the British Isles, and British Freemasons looked on Continental developments with the gravest suspicion, as well they might.

So, given these problems, the Viennese Lodges were contracted and amalgamated: *Zur wahren Eintracht*, *Zum Palmenbaum*, and *Zu den drei Adlern* formed a new Lodge named *Zur Wahrheit* (Truth); *Zur gekrönten Hoffnung*, *Zur Wohtätigkeit*, and *Zu den drei Feuern* became *Zur neugekrönten Hoffnung* (New-Crowned Hope). *Zum heiligen Joseph* and *Zur Beständigkeit* closed and some of the Brethren joined the new Lodges, although *Zum heiligen Joseph* seems to have been resurrected for a brief period in 1790.

The unified Lodges prompted Mozart to new musical works for Masonic occasions: these were *Zerfließet heut' geliebte Brüder*[57] (K.483) and *Ihr unsre neuen Leiter* (K.484): the first (subtitled *Zur Eröffnung der Freimaurerloge* [For the Opening of the Freemasons' Lodge]), welcoming the newly-formed Lodge, tells of Joseph's Beneficence (*Wohltätigkeit*) towards the Brethren, whose breasts are aflame with threefold Fire (*dreifach Feuer* – a play on *drei Feuern*), and to the fact that the Kaiser had 'crowned our Hope anew (*hat unsre Hoffnung neu gekrönt* - an obvious reference to *Zur neugekrönten Hoffnung*). The words go on to praise 'Joseph... who has bound us more closely together... and is crowning us with a loving hand'.

The second work, welcoming the newly-elected Grand Master of the united Lodges, was composed *Zum Schluß der Freimaurerloge* (For the Closing of the Freemasons' Lodge) and refers to the 'new leaders', to an oath to build a Great Edifice, to 'wings of truth', to the 'Throne of Wisdom', to Charity (*Wohltätig*), and to 'Envy of the Profane'. The words of both were by Augustin Veith Edler von Schittlersberg (Orator of *Zur Wahrheit*), and both date from the end of 1785. The first Master of *Zur neugekrönten Hoffnung* was none other than von Gebler, who may have been the first to interest Mozart in the Craft.

In 1786, too, Mozart worked on the Cantata *Dir, Seele des Weltalls, O Sonne* ('O Sun, Soul of the Cosmos', K.429 [468a]), to words by Lorenz Leopold Haschka (a former Jesuit, who became a poet[58]), a work which he never finished. From 1786 there seems to be a paucity of known works composed by Mozart for Masonic occasions, which may suggest that several have been lost[59]. Some commentators have detected Masonic allusions in the Andante of the String Quartet in A (K.464), in the String Quartet in C (K.465), in the Piano Concerto in C (K.467), and in other works by a composer who was fascinated by numbers. However, this vast subject cannot be covered here[60], and the present writer remains sceptical. There are, nevertheless, some late compositions that are specifically Freemasonic, including the so-called 'Little German Cantata' (1791), *Die ihr des unermeßlichen Weltalls* (K.619): the text refers to the Creator of the Universe (whether called Jehova, God, Brahma, or Fu), asks for the ennobling effects of clarity of mind, and exhorts Brethren to break the bonds of Illusion, to tear down the veil of Prejudice, and to take off the robe which hides Humanity in sectarian disguise. Apart from other commendable instructions, it suggests the Brethren should create the Garden of Eden from the Desert, when everything in Nature will shine on those who love Order, Harmony, and Concord, and Life's True Happiness will be achieved. The words of this Cantata were by Franz Heinrich Ziegenhagen, and, although many hold the work was not intended for the use of the Lodges, its sentiments, full of oecumenical open-mindedness, are worthy of Freemasonry. Furthermore, the reference to the re-creation of a Garden, the lost Paradise, suggests Masonic ideals as well as pointing to the *garden* as a significant metaphor for improvement of Mankind.

In November 1791 Mozart completed the so-called *Eine kleine Freimaurerkantate* (K.623) for the inauguration of the new premises of *Zur gekrönte Hoffnung* (the Lodge had reverted to this name after the amalgamation): the words are supposed to be by Johann Georg Karl (Charles) Ludwig (Lewis) Giesecke (who had formerly been known as Johann Georg Metzler), an interesting character, who was a Mineralogist with strong interests in the theatre (he

---

55 Interestingly, in the light of earlier history, a graduate of the University of Ingolstadt.

56 *See* Robison (1797) for attacks on Illuminati, 'Free Masons', and 'Reading Societies'. Weishaupt has been the subject of many absurd imaginings that are beyond the scope of this present study.

57 Today, beloved Brethren, melt.

58 His best-known work was the Austrian Imperial National Anthem, *Gott erhalte Franz den Kaiser* (God preserve Francis the Emperor – known as *Das Kaiserlied* [The Emperor's Song]), which was set to music (1797) by Franz Josef Haydn to provide the Nation with an adequate expression of the fidelity of the people to the Throne during the French Wars. The idea came from Mozart's friend Baron van Swieten, and Haydn himself became a Freemason in the Lodge *Zur wahren Eintracht* in February 1785. The great theme was later used by those with aspirations to unify Germany, and became *Deutschland, Deutschland über Alles* (Germany, Germany before everything – which – contrary to Received Opinion, does not refer to militant notions of conquest or to superiority over all, but to the need for loyalty to the ideal of a united Germany replacing fragmented loyalties to tiny and impotent princely States). The words of *Das Lied der Deutschen* were by August Heinrich Hoffmann von Fallersleben, written in 1841, and the third stanza of the poem set to Haydn's music is now the German National Anthem.

59 *AQC* **lxix** (1957) 23. This, however, is unlikely, given Mozart's own Thematic Catalogue.

60 *See*, for example, Grattan-Guinness (1992). But *see* also Chailley (1972) and Thomson (1977) for detailed examples. All should be treated with caution, tested, and carefully examined.

wrote the libretto[61] for *Oberon der Elfkönig* [Oberon the Elf King, sometimes called *Oberon, König der Elfen*] with music by Paul Wranitsky, first staged in 1789 at the *Theater auf der Wieden* in Vienna). His later career brought him to Scotland, where his portrait was painted by Henry Raeburn, and in 1814 was elected to the Chair of Mineralogy at the Dublin Society[62]. He carried out mineralogical surveys of Counties Antrim, Donegal, Down, Londonderry, Mayo, and Tyrone, all of which were published. For his work in Greenland he was knighted by the King of Denmark in 1816, in which year he was elected a member of the Royal Irish Academy. He died in Dublin and was buried there[63].

If Giesecke were, in fact, the author of *Laut verkünde unsre Freude* (Proclaim aloud our Joy), he inspired Mozart to write one of his most felicitous compositions: the walls of the Lodge resounded as the Brethren consecrated the place by the Golden Chains of Brotherhood and the True Union of Hearts as the Temple. The Brethren gathered for the first time in the 'New Seat of Wisdom and Virtue', dedicated as a Sanctuary of Masonic Work, where Beneficence (*Wohltätigkeit*), the Queen of All Virtues, was 'enthroned in silent splendour'. The text goes on to speak of the Almighty Power which, in Silence, bestows its Blessings upon Mankind. This '*Stille Gottheit*' (Silent Godhead) warmed the Mason's heart with 'gentle sunshine'. The celebrations in the Lodge were to be a 'monument' (*Denkmal*) to 'renewed and firmly-sealed Union', and all Envy, Covetousness, and Slander were to be banished for ever in a place where Harmony (*Eintracht*) tied the precious bonds created by Brotherly Love. In the final duet between the Tenor and Bass, reference is made to '*diese Mauern*' (these walls) bearing witness to Freemasons' Work, and the *Mauern* were consecrated in Harmony. In that place, where hearts were tuned to Virtue, Envy would be silenced, and the Wish fulfilled which 'Crowns Our Hope' (*und der Wunsch so ganz erfüllet, welcher unsre Hoffnung krönt*).

Perhaps the last *specifically* Masonic work to be composed by Mozart was the so-called *Kettenlied* (Chain Song – K.623a) with a text supposedly by Emanuel Schikaneder (or, more likely, by Giesecke) beginning *Laßt uns mit geschlung'nen Händen Brüder* ('Brethren let us join hands'): it refers to the chain encircling the Lodge and the entire world, and to the Light in the East, West, South, and North. However, K.623a, which was published in 1792 as an Appendix to K.623, is regarded as of 'doubtful authenticity', which is unsurprising, as it is uninspired, and has nothing of the musical qualities of K.623. It is the music of the present-day Austrian National Anthem, with new words, *Land der Berge* (Land of Mountains) written by Paula von Preradovic in response to a competition of 1947. Perhaps the music was by Johann Holzer, who was also a member of the same Lodge, or perhaps it actually *was* by Mozart, who was ill at the time, and very soon to die.

K.623 rings all sorts of bells. In *Die Zauberflöte* (K.620)[64] the words of Sarastro's great aria *In diesen heil'gen Hallen* (Within these holy [or sacred] Halls) contain the phrase *In diesen heil'gen Mauern*: this is usually translated as 'Within these walls so holy' or 'Within these sacred (or holy) Walls'[65], and there are references in the works by Mozart that we know *were* Masonic to *dieser Mauern* (these walls), *Maurer* (Mason or Masons), *Maurers Brust* and *Maurerbrust* (Mason's Breast), *Maurergang* (Masonic or Mason's Way), *Maurerfreude* (Mason's Joy), *Maureraugenweide* (a feast for Masons' eyes), *dem Weisen der Maurer* (of the wisest of Masons), and so on. The text of *In diesen heil'gen Hallen* and much else in *Die Zauberflöte* suggests a strong Freemasonic influence, and the implication of *In diesen heil'gen Mauern* is that the walls referred to are of stone and themselves have Masonic significance: there are also aspects of the libretto that display similarities to the words of music composed specifically for Masonic occasions.

Freemasonry, in its various flavours, it would appear[66], was a focus for Austria's intelligentsia, and that the Viennese Lodges especially numbered Brethren among their members who were eminent in all branches of life. The Lodges were also significant in that many Brethren held 'advanced' opinions, and were well aware of the problems likely to develop if the colossal gaps between rich and poor were perpetuated. The prevailing opinion among Freemasons was that through Enlightenment, Education, Knowledge, Reason, and an understanding of Nature, Society as a whole could be improved, raised in tone, and could benefit everyone, not least the lower orders. However, the so-called Josephinian Enlightenment, by 1786, was starting to show distinct signs of authoritarianism, very likely as part of a general paranoia about the growth of 'secret' societies in late-eighteenth-century Europe. Nevertheless, one of the benefits of the Kaiser's regulation of the Craft is that some of the lists of members of Lodges that were required to be drawn up have survived, including two for *Zur gekrönten Hoffnung* of 1790 (the *neu*, as noted above, had been dropped in or around 1789): it includes Mozart's name as well as those of Prince Nikolaus Josef (Miklós József) Esterházy (Franz Josef Haydn's Patron), Johann Baptist, Graf Esterházy, Franz Seraphim, Graf Esterházy (the son of 'Quinquin'), Johann Nepomuk, Graf Esterházy, Ignaz Alberti (the Viennese artist), Karl Ludwig Giesecke, Anton Alois, Fürst von Hohenzollern-Sigmaringen, and other persons of note in the Vienna of the time, including high-ranking personages in the Civil Service, the legal world, publishing, the Church, landowners, soldiers, musicians, artists, craftsmen, and members of the highest aristocracy. A painting attributed to Ignaz Unterberger (**CPl.X.I**, p.261) in the former *Historisches Museum der Stadt Wien* (now *Wien*

---

61 It was based on Friederike Sophie Seyler's libretto, *Hüon und Amande*, which was in turn derived from Wieland's poem, *Oberon* (1780), and was set to music (1789) by Karl Hanke.

62 Later Royal Dublin Society.

63 ODNB **xxii** (2004) 114-5. It has been suggested that his Dublin appointment owed much to his Freemasonic connections. I am grateful to Maurice Craig for discussing Giesecke with me in Dublin in 1978.

64 Act II Scene 13 Number 15.

65 *See* Giesecke (n.d.) 28, Mozart (1973).

66 From texts such as Landon (1982, 1988, 1989), Landon (*Ed.*) (1990), Landon & Mitchell (*Eds.*) (1956), Smyth (1975), Thomson (1977), Till (1992).

Museum) shows a Viennese Lodge in c.late 1780s-1790: like other representations of Freemasonic rooms, it is viewed as though an opening revealed by drawn-back curtains. According to H. C. Robbins Landon[67], the Rainbow in the picture, as the sign of Hope, with the Sun, probably suggest Crowned Hope, so the Lodge very likely represents *Zur gekrönten Hoffnung*, with Prince Nikolaus Esterházy as Master of Ceremonies. Two clerics are depicted, one an Abbot in white (probably Johann Lambert von Hanotte), and the other a monk in a brown habit (very likely Pater Ignaz Faber, a Franciscan). Landon has suggested that Ignaz Alberti, Giesecke, Wenzel Tobias Epstein, and Mozart can also be identified in the painting.

Another picture (**CPl.X.II**, p.262), supposedly of a Lodge interior, also featuring a man of genius, shows Robert Burns, as Poet Laureate of the Lodge Canongate Kilwinning, on 1 March 1787. It is interesting to compare these images showing two almost exact contemporaries, both of whom became world-famous as creative artists, as dedicated Freemasons in their Lodges, revered by their Brethren. We do know who painted the Burns picture: it is by William Stewart Watson and dates from 1846.

On the death of Kaiser Joseph II[68] in 1790 Austrian Freemasons awaited with considerable trepidation the next blow from the new Kaiser, Joseph's brother, Leopold II (reigned 1790-2). It should be remembered that repercussions from France were already starting to worry European monarchs, and the links between progressive ideas, the *philosophes*, and French Freemasons could not be ignored. In 1790, Queen Marie Antoinette warned her brother, the new Kaiser, to take care over any associations of Freemasons, for it was by means of Freemasonry that the 'monsters' in France counted on succeeding elsewhere. Landon has suggested that in the uncertainty following the death of Joseph II, Mozart and Schikaneder took the risk of producing *Die Zauberflöte*, an allegorical Opera in German that was part-*Singspiel*, intended to save the Craft by showing it in the best possible light[69]. This is probably a far-fetched notion, for, on the face of it, it is difficult to see how a *Singspiel*, given in a suburban theatre, could save the Craft by means of encoded messages in obscure numerology and fanciful allegories that only those who had been initiated could begin to understand. Indeed, Landon could be said to have over-egged the pudding, perhaps, despite his eminence as a musicologist. However, we do know that when Mozart was in Prague in August-September 1791 for the première of *La Clemenza di Tito* (K.621) as part of the Festivities relating to the Coronation of Leopold II as King of Bohemia, he visited the Lodge *Zur Wahrheit und Einigkeit* (Truth & Unity), and *Der Maurerfreude* was performed there in his honour. Mozart was deeply moved, and said he was about to render an even greater homage to the Craft, by which he very likely meant *Die Zauberflöte*[70], although he *may* have had *Laut verkünde* (K.623) in mind, but on balance the most likely candidate is *Die Zauberflöte*.

In 1791 the Craft was facing a real threat of being banned in Austria (its Light Extinguished), and in 1794 the Lodges closed voluntarily *before* the new Kaiser, Franz II (reigned 1792-1806 as Holy Roman Emperor, and from 1804-35 as Franz I, Hereditary Emperor of Austria), prohibited all 'secret' societies in his realms. By that time, of course, the former Archduchess Maria Antonia, sister of Joseph II and Leopold II, as Queen Marie Antoinette of France, had been guillotined, and the horrors of Jacobinism and the Terror had been unleashed. That there had been Freemasonic sympathisers with the ideals of the French Revolution cannot be doubted, and Freemasonic revolutionary leaders elsewhere included George Washington, Benjamin Franklin, and numerous figures involved in 1789-90 in France, although the Terror and Regicide were not on the agenda then. The problem was that they occurred, and were not inhibited by the all the claims to Benevolence, Brotherhood, and Fraternity. Reason, also, it might be thought, would make magic, superstition, and sorcery less attractive: the opposite seems to have occurred, as will be demonstrated below.

Die Zauberflöte: Freemasonic Opera?

Mozart's *Die Zauberflöte* has been identified by many writers as a 'Freemasonic' or 'Masonic' Opera[71], so it is important to re-examine these claims, which have been widely accepted by several persons, although there have been those who have already questioned them[72].

Die Zauberflöte, it should be emphasised, was only *one* of many such examples of the 'fairy-tale' or 'magical' *Singspiel* which appeared during the latter part of the eighteenth century. This form of entertainment, known as *Märchenoper* (literally 'Fairy-Tale Opera') in German-speaking countries, has not had the attention of scholars it deserves, probably because the stories were all improbable, and are partly buffoonery, partly hokum, partly dependent upon elaborate scenic effects and transformations, and shot through with supposedly magical and supernatural aspects, mixed in with portentous pseudo-solemnity in the form of wise men or 'priests' (not associated with the Church, but with some form of pagan or esoteric beliefs). All this is *very* odd, given the climate of the supposed

---

67 Landon (1982) *passim*.
68 For 'Josephinism' see Winter (1962, 1971) and O'Brien (1969). See also Sadie (*Ed.*) (1996) 3-20 and Beales (1987).
69 (Landon) (1983) 60, 131-5. See Thomson (1977) 133. There are nearly 40 works by Mozart with possible or obvious Freemasonic connections, and there were at least two more, now lost: these were songs of 1786, *Zur Eröffnung der Meisterloge* (On the Inauguration of the Master Lodge), and *Zum Schluß der Meisterarbeit* (At the Closing of the Master Work). *See also* BM. Add. MS 32596. I am grateful to John Milne for these items.
70 Strebel (1991) 166.
71 Notably by Berk (2004), Chailley (1972), Landon (1982, 1988), Nettl (1932, 1970), Thomson (1977), and others.
72 Notably Buch (2004): I am indebted to John A. Rice of Rochester MN for drawing my attention to this and other items. Among more sceptical opinions of the 'Masonic' thread are Branscombe (1965-6, 1972), Hocquard (1979, 1993), Macpherson (1987), Morehen (1981), and Wangermée (1980-1).

Enlightenment: one would expect an Enlightened society to eschew such cheap thrills, but that is not what happened. On the contrary, many productions, by several composers, were put on, and apparently enjoyed by a public not in the least concerned with high-mindedness, Freemasonic ideals, or secret agendas.

So why has Mozart's *Die Zauberflöte* been accorded special status above the many other examples of *Märchenoper* that we know existed, most of which are never, or only rarely, performed today? There are usually reasons why an artist becomes valued after his death, not always connected with the quality of his work: one thinks, for example, of the cases of the Dutch painter Vincent van Gogh (who had no success during his lifetime, but after his suicide his fame grew rapidly) and of the Scots Architect Charles Rennie Mackintosh (who was fond of the Demon Drink, and whose work was tainted with 'decadent' *Art Nouveau* [a style associated with the *fin-de-siècle* world of people like Aubrey Beardsley (whose work was suffused with pornographic images and morbid Depravity) and Oscar Wilde (whose fall from grace was spectacular)]). After his death, Mackintosh was proclaimed as a kind of proto-Modernist, a view which does not stand up to serious examination, as he had far more in common with the protagonists of the German *Jugendstil* and the Viennese *Sezession*. In Mozart's case his early death, nonsensical tales about the causes of his demise, his 'pauper's grave', and the careful 'marketing' of his work by his widow ensured his virtual deification, helped along by burgeoning German Nationalism and Mozart's own remarkable apotheosis as a 'German Master'. A nineteenth-century view of him as a transcendent artist with a God-given genius, helped along by various hagiographies, has unquestionably led to a perception of *Die Zauberflöte* as far more profound and sophisticated than its *Märchenoper* status could possibly suggest. However, that status does not depend on its libretto, but on Mozart's music, which reached a much higher level than did any other contemporary *Singspiel* of the type: indeed, it is one of his finest scores, without which later masterpieces, such as Beethoven's *Fidelio*, would be inconceivable. There is therefore a very real danger of reading into the libretto a quality of profundity as great as the music: many, it would seem, have fallen headlong into that trap, displaying in the process an ignorance (perhaps partly due to wishful thinking) of other contemporary works of the kind.

As far as can be judged, the earliest suggestion of a Freemasonic content in the *libretto* was printed in 1795[73]. This argued that, as the Craft was viewed with suspicion by women (who attempted to discover its 'secrets'), the Queen of the Night (who ruled over a realm where free-thinking was forbidden) saw Freemasonry as a menace, and because she could not have access to the Wisdom taught in the Lodges, she attempted to destroy them. This article's reference to *neugierigen Frauenzimmern* (curious women) possibly looks back to the play, *Le Donne Curiose*[74] of 1753 by Carlo Goldoni which also attacked the Craft. It seems to have been the *Hamburgisches Briefträger* article's references to the *Meister des Stuhls* (Master of the Lodge) and the Queen as *Fürstinn* (Princess) that may have suggested that Born was the model for Sarastro and Maria Theresia that for the Queen of the Night. Also in 1794, Ludwig von Batzko interpreted *Die Zauberflöte* in terms of Light *versus* Darkness, and Enlightenment *versus* Superstition: Batzko referred to some of the parts of the *Singspiel* as alluding to the 'ceremonies' of 'certain Orders', and mentioned that 'even the uninitiated' would recognise this if they had an acquaintance with the Ancient Mysteries of Antique cultures[75]. Some, however, found the 'mysteries' and 'heavy veil of allegory' insuperable obstacles for any audience which would, therefore, be incapable of finding the 'slightest interest' in the *Singspiel*: this was certainly the view of Professor Johann Jakob Engel, *Oberdirektor* (1787-94) of the Berlin *Hoftheater*, when he wrote[76] to King Friedrich Wilhelm II of Prussia giving reasons why *Die Zauberflöte* should *not* be performed in Berlin. He felt it was the author's intention to 'crowd together every conceivable difficulty for the stage designer and machinists' (true!), and that a work was created 'whose sole merit' was 'visual splendour'. Engel regretted that 'the great composer Mozart' had squandered his talent on such unrewarding, mystical, and untheatrical material'[77]. *Die Zauberflöte* was not given in the Berlin theatre until 12 May 1794.

So, almost from the first appearance of the *Singspiel* it was recognised that *something* was going on relating to the ceremonies of 'Orders' connected in some way with *Mysterien der Alten*. Nettl proposed[78] a detailed analysis of a 'Masonic' series of allegories in *Die Zauberflöte*, and his considerable contributions to the literature were further expanded by Jacques Chailley, who suggested that Freemasonry was evident in virtually every Scene of the *Singspiel* as well as in each part of the music[79]. As Buch as stated[80], however, neither 'Nettl nor Chailley demonstrated a narrative allegory; rather they proposed a symbolic complex of language, image, and music without a discernable linear plot'. Quite so, yet many writers have accepted the allegorical essence of the libretto and the music as a subtly encoded representation of the Craft[81]: however, the statement that Mozart transformed the *Singspiel* into an 'allegory of his own quasi-religious commitment to Freemasonry'[82] may not be that far off the mark.

---

73 *Hamburgischer Briefträger* (15 November 1794) 25 issued in 1795.

74 Set as an opera by Ermanno Wolf-Ferrari, and first performed as *Die neugierigen Frauen* in 1903 in Munich.
75 Batzko (1794) 366-71.
76 8 March 1792.
77 Deutsch (Ed.) (1961) in the English translation (1965) 444.
78 Buch (2004) 194, Irmen (1996), Nettl (1932, 1956, 1957), Nettl (1955) 145-54, *Opera News* **xx**/17 (1956) 8-10, Schenk (Ed.) (1932) 142-9.
79 Chailley (1972) *passim*. See also Chailley (1967, 1976).
80 Buch (2004) 194.
81 Sadie (Ed.) (1992) **iii** 489-503, and **iv** 1215-18, both by Julian Rushton.
82 *Ibid*. **iii** 491. His attitude resembles that of Soane.

Buch has pointed out[83] with truth that both Nettl and Chailley based their arguments on the 'wording of a few dialogues' in the libretto 'and the presence of Egyptian and Masonic images on the frontispiece' [sic] of the opera's original libretto. It is true that the dialogues do have some similarities to 'Masonic writings, specifically the pseudo-Egyptian French novel'[84] *Séthos*[85] by Terrasson and Born's essay on the Egyptian Mysteries. The closest resemblances between *Die Zauberflöte* and *Séthos* are in Act II, Scene 1, and Act II, Scene 31 (with the Two Men in Black Armour)[86], where Mozart's librettist(s) drew on the German translation of Terrasson's work, with some differences: for example, the 'hymns' in *Séthos* mention Horus and Isis, but not Osiris, who certainly can be found in *Die Zauberflöte*. As Buch has written[87], Schikaneder (or Schikaneder et al.) drew upon *Séthos*, but 'there is no justification to interpret' this 'in a broader allegorical context'[88]. In addition, 'at least two other' texts, with *no* claimed 'allegorical content' use 'similar language': these include the 'operas' *Der Höllenberg* (1795) by Schikaneder, with music by the Salzburg-born composer Joseph Wölfl (a pupil of Leopold Mozart and Michael Haydn); *Babylons Piramiden* (1797), again by Schikaneder, with music by Johann Georg Anton Mederitsch-Gallus (Act I), and Peter Winter (Act II) – which is rich in 'Egyptian' 'temple' scenes, with plenty of 'sacred rites', 'priests', processions, and the usual mix of 'magic' and coarse, folksy humour. Interestingly (or perhaps inevitably) the Finale of Act II of *Babylons Piramiden* has a journey through Fire and Water, so a journey and the powers of the Elements are involved. The *Singspiel, Das Labyrinth, oder der Kampf mit den Elementen* (The Labyrinth, or the Struggle with the Elements) was designed by Schikaneder as a sequel to *Die Zauberflöte*, with which it has many textual similarities: it was first given in 1798 at Schikaneder's *Freihaus-Theater auf der Wieden* with music by Peter Winter, and features the Queen of the Night who plans to send an army to destroy Sarastro's Temple (where Tamino and Pamina [by now married] are sent into opposite ends of a labyrinth to complete their final Trials of Initiation). The connections with *Die Zauberflöte* are many, yet no 'Masonic' sub-plots have attracted commentators to anything like the degree accorded to Mozart's *Singspiel*.

So *Die Zauberflöte* is based in part on *Séthos*, and it is clear that the author(s) of the libretto was/were familiar not only with Terrasson's work, but perhaps with the writings of Apuleius, Diodorus Siculus, and Lucian. Like Séthos, Tamino in *Die Zauberflöte* is a Prince, and a travelling Prince at that, who seeks education by journeying in foreign parts and by initiation into certain mysteries. But the *Flute* is not just derived from *Séthos*: like many concoctions of the period it owes debts to other works, including Gebler's *Thamos, König in Ägypten*, Wranitzky's *Oberon*, Liebeskind's *Lulu* in Wieland's *Dschinnistan* of 1786, and sundry works of Rococo *Exotica* popular at the time. In 1790 Schikaneder had presented in the *Theater auf der Wieden* in the suburbs of Vienna a *Singspiel* entitled *Der Stein der Weisen oder Die Zauberinsel* (The Philosopher's Stone or The Magic Island) which contained three brief numbers by Mozart[89]: this work as a whole consisted of arias, choruses, orchestral passages, and various ensembles by five different composers, so it was really the work of several hands, and it has some undoubted similarities to *Die Zauberflöte*. The very first scene in an Arcadian Landscape has a pyramid in the centre, and later there are Trials once again involving Water and Fire: besides, again, the story was lifted from *Dschinnistan*. *Der Stein der Weisen* had its fair share of comic figures, based on the popular *Hannswurst* character, but by the end of the eighteenth century such theatrical diversions had become formulae with elaborate mechanical tricks and comic turns, sometimes leavened with a bit of serious or pseudo-serious stuff. Eighteenth-century fiction (and popular theatre) often featured ideas connected with the 'noble savage', and the 'natural state' was considered the 'true' condition of human nature before it acquired the fripperies of civilisation. 'Men of Nature' were called *Papagenos*, and Papageno is the comic figure in *Die Zauberflöte*, a figure covered with feathers, a bird-catcher: the connection with other 'primitive' figures such as Incas, Native Americans, and so on will be obvious. Tamino, the Séthos-figure, a serious character in *Die Zauberflöte*, is given an extra-exotic aura by being credited with a *Japanese* background, although his name, and that of his female counterpart, Pamina, seem to be of vaguely Egyptian origin. It should be remembered that interest in things Egyptian was a late-eighteenth-century preoccupation, *before* the Napoleonic expedition and subsequent publications made accurate images of Ancient Egyptian Architecture and Artefacts familiar. *Die Zauberflöte*, therefore, draws on ideas of Egypt as exotic, mysterious, and associated with secrecy and, indirectly, with Freemasonry. If *Séthos* can be identified as one source for the *Singspiel*, *Dschinnistan* is another, but, perhaps, even more interesting, so is Ignaz von Born's essay[90] on the 'Egyptian Mysteries', a source virtually ignored by Anglophone commentators: it is of some significance in the genesis of *Die Zauberflöte*, not only for its content, but because it was by Born, whose influence on Viennese Freemasonry was considerable. A trawl through some of his other works will reward the diligent[91], for there is no doubt whatsoever that he was not only a leading light in the Craft, but a major force in the 'Josephinian Enlightenment'[92]. However, claims that Schikaneder plundered Born's essay when creating the scenes with the Speaker (Act I, Scene 19)[93] and Sarastro's

---

83 Buch (2004) 195.
84 Ibid.
85 Translated into German by Matthias Claudius, a Freemason, as *Geschichte des egyptische Königs Sethos*, published in Breslau (1777-8).
86 Some call this Scene 28.
87 Buch (2004) 197.
88 Ibid.
89 The duets *Nun, liebes Weibchen, Miau, Miau*, and *Fort, armer Jüngling*.
90 Born (1784), which influenced the writers of *Die Zauberflöte* in *general* terms rather than in *detail*.
91 Born (1783-88).
92 *See* Beales (1987), O'Brien (1969), Winter (1962).
93 Give in some texts as Scene 12.

second aria (Act II, Scene 13)[94], in which Friendship and Brotherhood are praised simply do not stand up to close examination. The libretto owes more to other libretti, to vague liberal sentiments, and to Freemasonic ideals, loosely expressed, than to Born's essay. In the final scene of the *Singspiel*, the praises to Wisdom, Beauty, and Strength *do* have Freemasonic resonances, but they do not connect the libretto with Born. In Born's writing, it is true, is a reference to a Serpent attacking Horus, but that comes from Plutarch: it does not make it the basis of any Freemasonic undercurrents, at least based on Born's work.

It is a fact that there are those who refuse to see *any* connections between the Craft and *Die Zauberflöte*, and there are those who see the Craft's influence or allusions to it in *every* bar. I would venture to suggest that both are mistaken. This Chapter will not overstate the case, but will propose that there *are* several interesting aspects of the *Singspiel* which cannot be ignored as being *influenced* by Freemasonry, but many also recur in other examples of *Märchenoper* of the period. If Giesecke is accepted as one of the authors of the text (as he claimed, in later years)[95], as well as Schikaneder, there we have two Freemasons involved. Add Mozart and we have three. Giesecke edited the *Regensburger Theater-Journal* (1784-6), and Schikaneder became a Freemason in Regensburg, so there was a connection there too: Giesecke was to be part of Schikaneder's troupe until he pursued his other studies. That is not to claim that Giesecke or Schikaneder placed Freemasonry in the centre of *Die Zauberflöte*, however. It might suggest, on the other hand, that they used certain *sentiments* of the Craft in the text, but that does not make the *Flute* a 'Masonic Opera'.

Alberti's decoration of the printed libretto of 1791 are of particular interest in terms of this study: one illustration (**Pl.X.3**) is often (even usually) referred to as the 'Frontispiece' but it is in fact an illustration (at least in the copies I have inspected). It is saturated with alchemical/Rosicrucian/ Freemasonic allusions. It shows a rocky grotto, a fragment of broken architectural enrichment, a steeply-pitched pyramid (or is it a fat obelisk?) with bogus 'Egyptian' symbols (although the *Ankh looks* genuine enough). On the right is what seems to be a grave, with hourglass, shovel, pick, etc. The sloping side of the 'pyramid' shows a Bull's head, the horns of which form a lyre. This is Taurus, the conjunction of Sun and Moon, when Venus is in Taurus, but it may also connect with the Apis-bull, a symbol of Ptah (associated with Osiris and with Fire and Metalwork, underlining alchemical allusions). And what about the *Ankh*-like figure? It is a cross over which is a circle, but this circle is different, because it has a centre marked as

Pl.X.3 Engraving by Ignaz Alberti, Vienna from the first edition of the libretto of *Die Zauberflöte* of 1791 (it is often referred to as the Frontispiece, but it is not). It is saturated with alchemical/Rosicrucian allusions. The Alchemical Vessel (the large vase) like much else in the illustration (apart from the pyramidal form) is copied from illustrations by Jean-Laurent Legeay (or Le Geay) which can be found in Érouart (1982). The close affinities in style with the work of Piranesi should be noted (*BL. Music Library, Hirsch N, 1385*).

a dot, thus symbolises the Sun, so the Sun is dominated by Venus over Taurus, and the bull reigns over Music[96]. At the base of the pyramid on the left are two snakes forming an approximate *Swastika*, a turning wheel, representing the transformation of the Elements[97]: they may refer to lead/Saturn, so are a direct reference to Alchemy. To the right of the snakes is an Ibis, representing the Egyptian Deity Thoth (identified with Hermes-Mercury, and with the Messenger, St John): it devours a snake, so represents the first stage of the transformation in alchemical processes. Immediately below the Bull's head are Mercury (Hermes) and Jupiter (Zeus): so here are quicksilver and tin. Some interpretations have suggested that to the right of Taurus is perhaps Mars (like a numeral 2), which may refer to Salt, to Distillation, to Red, and to Iron[98].

---

94 Given in some texts as Scene 12.
95 See *ODNB* **xxii** (2004) 144: 'he evidently co-operated with Schikaneder and others in the writing of … the libretto'. This is now discredited among several scholars, but there remains some doubt, as the matter is by no means proved beyond argument. I would suggest that the exchanges between the Speaker and Tamino (Act I, Scene 19) were probably beyond Schikaneder's capabilities: some other hand or hands may have been involved.

96 Berk (2004) 336.
97 *Ibid.*
98 See **Klossowski de Rola** (1973) 127 and Rosenberg (1972).

The vase with crouching figures possibly alludes to the Alchemical Vessel or Hermetic-Vase. It is virtually copied from an illustration by Jean-Laurent Le Geay[99] published in his *Collection de Divers Sujets de Vases, Tombeaux, Ruines, et Fontaines Utiles aux Artistes Inventée et Gravée par J.-L. Le Geay, Architecte* (1770)[100], from which it is clear Le Geay's fantastic designs and those of Piranesi had much in common: Le Geay, in fact, resided in Rome (1737-42), and influenced Piranesi who had arrived there from Venice in 1740. Le Geay worked with Piranesi and other engravers on various projects before returning to Paris where he gained a reputation as one of the protagonists of Neo-Classicism. He then went to Berlin in 1745 where he prepared plans for the Roman Catholic Cathedral of St Hedwig, and, after a spell at the Court of Mecklenburg-Schwerin, was appointed *Premier Architecte* to King Friedrich II of Prussia for whom he designed the elegant *Communs* in Potsdam. Le Geay taught Boullée and others, and through them spread the Gospel of Neo-Classicism. Although there is no direct evidence that Le Geay was a Freemason, there is no doubt that the Craft was active in Berlin and Paris when he was living in both cities, and he certainly moved in circles which had Freemasons among them.

So what does this *Vas Hermeticum* mean? Berk suggests it is where the 'mortification' process takes place leading to a renewal of life, so it is 'the vase of rebirth'[101]. However, he states that the 'death's-head' is represented on the vase twice: a close examination of the original illustration under a magnifying-glass shows no 'death's heads' at all: the upper head in a circle is a cheerful-looking face, certainly no 'death's head', and the lower one wears a crown, and does not look very skull-like (though indeed it is *more* skull-like than the cheery character above). The vase itself is flanked by two squatting figures, part-ape, part-man, with torsos that seem to be cornucopia-like forms. These are probably the 'Apes of Nature'[102], chained to the vase by ties of what appear to be varieties of bellflowers attached to their ears (thus the harmonious sounds inside the vase, according to Berk, are transmitted). Around the vase are intertwined serpents suggesting re-creation, but on top of the vase the design differs from Le Geay's illustration[103]: Alberti's version shows what appear to be two copulating dogs. These may allude to the 'sacred marriage' of Sulphur with Salt, the Sun and Moon[104], for dogs represent transforming substances. In an early (perhaps the first) performance of *Die Zauberflöte*, the scene in which Papageno was not permitted to embrace Papagena (Act II Scene 28) contained a steeply-pointed pyramid, a suspended star, two arches, *and* a large Hermetic vase[105].

Another of Le Geay's engravings features two arches, but the pyramid, suspended star, and copulating dogs are Alberti's additions: Alberti's version (which is therefore a combination of *two* images by Le Geay) differs from those of Le Geay in that it omits Le Geay's Cross and the Lantern, and substitutes a five-pointed Star with a flame in the centre, a common feature of Freemasonic illustrations (the *étoile flamboyante* not to be confused with true Blazing Star, the *Hexalpha*): it also shows part of a human figure leaning against the excavated earth, and that figure has a bare left shoulder, a possible reference to Initiation Rites. Thus this figure, Risen, as it were, though exhausted, from the Grave, may represent an Initiate (or a dead body).

Whilst the tools may refer to those necessary to open a grave, they may also allude to the three raw substances (or even principles) taken from the Earth, for after all, Alchemists were invited to visit the interior of the Earth, and while rectifying matter find the hidden Stone. Alberti's illustration shows what look like two tablets behind the hourglass: could these be the Tablets of Hermes Trismegistus, the secrets buried in the Grave? Some commentators[106] have suggested that underneath the vase is a head (supposedly Saturn, guardian of the Nether World, and Devourer of the Impure) from the mouth of which flies a bird (a pigeon or a rooster): however, the delineation of the head and bird are too feeble for the present writer to accept this, although admittedly the hourglass at the open grave may refer to Saturn-Chronos, the God of Time, but, more likely, it is a simple *Memento Mori*, a reminder of the inevitability of Death. The jug behind the pickaxe and shovel may suggest the liquid that reinvigorates those who search within the Earth. It has also been suggested that the three broken fragments at the bottom of the picture are gravestones: that nearest the pickaxe *could* be a broken ledger-stone, but the middle one is part of a Classical entablature, and the one on the left looks like an attempt to represent *guilloche* ornament as well as a series of rudimentary flutes (incised channels in stone). It is far more likely they represent aspects of Masonry, broken and imperfect, rather than tombstones.

The pier between the two arches in Le Geay's illustration is blocked (i.e. has blocks which interrupt and project from the faces of the pier) with two large blocks (cubes): in Alberti's version there are *three* such blocks, but what the decorations in the panels of these actually signify is anyone's guess, apart from that on the lowest block which depicts the Sun and Gold (large central circle), the two sexes (smaller circles), and the three 'elements' of Sulphur, Salt, and Masonry.

Nearly all those who have commented on the Alberti illustration seem to think it is subterranean, some sort of Initiation-place such as is described by Terrasson in *Séthos*. But the five-pointed star is also an alchemical symbol, the unity of 3 and 2, of masculine and feminine, and close study of Alberti's star reveals part of the letter G. Now we have seen that the G stands for several things, but in addition it

---

99 Often given as Legeay. See Eriksen (1974), Érouart (1982), Fraser, Hibbard, & Lewine (Ed.) (1967) 189-196, Turner (Ed.) (1998) **xix** 76.
100 See Geay (c.1770) in a Collection of Engravings held at the Bodleian Library, University of Oxford.
101 Berk (2004) 333 note 14.
102 See Godwin (1979b) 22, 76.
103 Berk (2004) Fig. 68.
104 Ibid. 333. See Jung **ii** (1966) 248 note 4; Jung **xiv** (1963) 147 note 280.
105 Berk (2004) Fig. 75.5.

106 Berk (2004) 341.

is the first letter of *Gamos* (meaning Marriage), as well as of *Gnosis*, meaning Knowledge: in Pythagorean systems *Gamos* represented the number 5. So what is probably referred to here is the Sacred Marriage, or Alchemical Wedding, Human Perfection, Harmony, and Completeness. The Star, however, hangs from a carved horizontal plaque: in Le Geay's version it bears a resemblance to a Roman Isiac procession, but in Alberti's has a central Pantheon-like Temple flanked by two columns (possibly an allusion to the Temple of Solomon, Jachin, and Boaz). On the extreme right of this plaque is a mound (the Grave of Hiram?), and the other figures may allude to the murder, search for the body, and other aspects of the legend. As previously noted, the *association*, ever since the Crusades, of the Islamic Dome of the Rock with the Temple of Solomon in Western iconography, led to many representations of that Temple as a *circular* building.

Berk suggests that beyond the main arch is another arch with a door in which is a smaller door (a wicket), and that the Cross over the main door represents the Four Elements marking an alchemical oven or furnace. He has also, by enlarging the curving path leading to the arch, claimed to have discovered allusions to *Mercurius* (Mercury), *Ignis* (Fire), *Aqua* (Water), so these may refer to the Trials of the Initiation as well as having alchemical associations[107], and is satisfied that the illustration is an alchemical allegory. However, the opening-within-the-opening also occurs (not in identical form) in Le Geay's illustration, as does the arched opening higher up behind which light glimmers: in Alberti's version this suggests an illuminated space behind the façade rather than a furnace. Berk has also claimed to have identified a serpent on the path just in front of the wicket, but close examination of the illustration convinces at least one observer that this is too indistinct to be of any significance: it is a case, perhaps, of reading too much into the picture. Now we know Born and others were profoundly interested in scientific knowledge, and there were those in the eighteenth century who still perceived value in subjects such as Alchemy. An esoteric-alchemical aspect to Freemasonry clearly existed in Vienna at this time, but Alberti's derivative illustration does not prove a Masonic connection nor does it clinch Mozart's intention of creating an allegory of Freemasonry. Wishful thinking is one thing: facts are another.

The Music and the Libretto

Vast amounts of print have been expended on *Die Zauberflöte*, and only a few salient points will be made here (a synopsis of the Libretto will not be given, as the *Singspiel* is very well-known). At the start of the Overture (in the so-called 'Masonic' Key of E flat Major [i.e. with three flats]), is one chord followed by two more (three with anacrusis), making five in all (in the rhythm Long-Short-Long-Short-Long), interpreted as combining the Duad and the Triad, representing the Five-Pointed Star, or Light itself. The following Adagio is seen by some as a conventional and decorous representation of the Kingdom of the Night, or Darkness and Chaos. The opening of the first fugue, however, may be *Ordo ab Chao*, Order out of Chaos, a Freemasonic skill, with a rhythm suggesting the fast tapping of scappling hammers (used to reduce faces of blocks of stone to plane surfaces without working them smooth, so important Work of Masons). The fugue breaks off for the three-thrice chords used in Austrian Freemasonry before a darker section of self-examination in the minor key with many chromaticisms (suggesting a journey, in sound) leads to the closing bars in the major key, representing the Victory of the Sun.

Now from where do the assertions come that the chords in E flat and that the repeated chords at the start of the Overture were 'Masonic'? From Nettl and Chailley[108] certainly, but the problem with this is that *evidence* of a 'Masonic' connection with E Flat[109] from the eighteenth century either does not exist, or has not yet been discovered. On the other hand, three flats as a representation of the Trinity *are* mentioned, so they have a *Christian* allusion, according to Christian Friedrich Daniel Schubart[110], and Jean-François Le Sueur also emphasised the Christian associations[111].

Buch has pointed out[112] that there are many late-eighteenth-century overtures that start with a 'call to attention' or *annonce*, which are associated with 'marvellous' or 'supernatural' operas: these *annonces* may take the form of repeated loud chords which may indicate some kind of 'magic' content thereafter, but not a Freemasonic connotation at all. Buch quotes examples by Tommaso Michele Francesco Saverio Traetta's *Armida* (1761) and Giuseppe Gazzaniga's *Circe* (1786), and proposes that the 'melodic and textural aspects' of the fugal *allegro* of the *Zauberflöte* overture 'hardly suggest Masonry': indeed, he calls it a 'cliché' to indicate the idea of a 'flight' (i.e. a chase). He also states that the 'key of E flat had been associated with the infernal realm by composers from Lully[113] to Gluck[114]. There are, however, the Three-times-Three mysterious chords (in the rhythm short-short-long, short-short-long, short-short-long) that interrupt the *allegro* of the overture: these are unusual, capture our attention, and Mozart must have had a very good reason for putting them there at all.

Throughout *Die Zauberflöte* the figure three is encountered: the 'Three Knocks' of the Overture, the key of E flat Major with its three flats, the Three Ladies, the Three Boys (or Genii), the Three Temples, and plentiful use of rhythms of three in the scoring. Tamino is the Initiate, taking vows of silence and symbolically making a journey,

---

107 Berk (2004) 348-9. However the metal mercury was called *argentum vivum*. I have examined the curving path too, but the images are too indistinct to be taken seriously as meaningful allusions.

108 *See*, for example, Chailley (1972) and Nettl (1970).
109 *See* Steblin (2002).
110 Schubart (1924) 261-2.
111 Sueur (1787).
112 Buch (2004) 215-6.
113 Jean-Baptiste Lully (1632-87).
114 *Ibid.* 217, referring to Christoph Willibald, Ritter von Gluck.

fasting, going through Trials by Fire, Water, Air, and Earth, then finally passing from Darkness into Light. Sarastro, the High Priest of the Temple, is derived from Zoroaster (or Zarathustra), and some have suggested his character was based on that of Born (who died in July 1791): it has been proposed that Sarastro was a kind of memorial to him as Master of an élite Lodge, an Academy of intellectual and scientific inquiry, which under his aegis became an important (if short-lived) element in the Josephinian Enlightenment[115]. We know that Born had no high regard for obscurantist clergy: he declared that monks were ignorant, that Jesuitry and fanaticism could be equated with roguery, ignorance, superstition, and stupidity, and that much else was deeply wrong with the times. However, as noted above, Three is a number associated with many things, not least Christianity, the Three Graces, the Three Virtues, the Three-Headed Dog Cerberus, and much else: it is not necessarily 'Masonic', but it *could* allude to the Craft. In other words, nothing is clear-cut.

There are, however, many parallels with Isiac religion in *Die Zauberflöte*: Isis transformed herself into an old hag and then into a beautiful girl, just as happens to Papagena. Papageno the bird-catcher might well have stepped from the banks of the Nile, with his reed-pipes. The magic bells may be a reference to the sacred *sistrum* and timbrels used in Isiac ceremonies[116], and indeed *sistra* replaced the bell in Ethiopian Christian liturgies, while the *crotalus* was used instead of the bell in Western European churches on Maundy Thursday[117]. So the bells, roses, transformations, and even the bird-catcher with his pipes can be seen, perhaps, to have Isiac-Egyptian connotations. Furthermore, Monostatos, whose black face and singular name pick him out as anti-social (his heart is as black as his face), represents the obscure, the dark, the hateful, and the villainous[118]. He could be loosely identified with Seth of the South Wind, the murderer and dismemberer of Osiris, especially since he hates the Temple and the High Priest Sarastro, and therefore hates Isis and Osiris as well[119]. His chains and irons represent repression that can only be lifted when his intended victims are initiated to Enlightenment. It has been suggested that he may be an emblem of the black-robed clerics who served the Church, and indeed that interpretation explains his devotion to the Queen of the Night and his servile and treacherous attitude to Sarastro and his band. Monostatos is given to lechery, to earthiness, and he is isolated: should the Night triumph, so will his carnality, and Pamina will be subjected. However, given the context of other examples of the contemporary *Singspiel* genre, all this could be incidental, and although it is agreeable to speculate, we must not lose sight of the fact

that Schikaneder was keen (like most theatrical managers) to make money: the 'magical' *Singspiel*, leavened with a bit of low *Hannswurst* comedy and some portentous seriousness in the form of 'Enlightened' moralising, worked as a money-spinner and was *popular entertainment,* not a vehicle for high-flown mysteries or crafty propaganda in favour of Freemasonry.

Now *Die Zauberflöte* is not just a re-hash of *Séthos* though *some* of it is just that. That memorable and very curious thirty-first Scene in Act II, with the Two Men in Black Armour, suggests conquering the fear of Death, rising from Earth to the Sphere of Heaven, Illumination, Consecration, and the Mysteries of Isis Herself. As with the Masonic Funeral Music, a march-like theme is used over which the Two Men sing their texts to a Lutheran chorale, perhaps to emphasise the solemn, even Biblical, nature of this extraordinary Trial scene. The Antique element is reinforced by the Two Men, who might be two *telamones* from the *Villa Adriana* at Tivoli, or even Jachin and Boaz themselves. The *telamones*, of course, were Roman work in the Egyptianising Taste, and were similar to the figure of Antinoüs, also from Tivoli. The Old Testament promises that one who passes through waters will not be overflown, and that one who walks through fire will not be burned, nor will flame kindle upon the walker[120].

Use of a Protestant[121] chorale in *Die Zauberflöte* has a curious parallel at Maupertuis, where, as previously noted, Brongniart designed the 'ruined' pyramid which dominated an *Élysée*: the segmental pediment, associated with Isis, was a feature of that *fabrique*. The *Élysée* was also identified with a monumental mausoleum (actually a cenotaph) commemorating Admiral de Coligny who had been murdered in 1572: one could hardly have a more explicit commentary on bigotry in this clear association with persecuted minorities, *in a garden,* too.

Landon[122] has pointed out that this solemn Lutheran music was very different when compared with the

---

115 Till (1992) 121-4, 132-3, 135, 19-16, 283-4, 294, 303. *See also* Berk (2004) *passim,* Thomson (1977) *passim.*

116 Witt (1970, 1971, 1975) *passim.*

117 *See* Witt (1971) 269-81. *See also* Fortescue (1948) 308 and Steiner (1980).

118 All this causes problems for the politically correct, but one cannot judge a *Singspiel* in Vienna of 1791 from the standpoint of the early 2000s.

119 Curl (2005) 250.

120 *Isaiah* 43:2.

121 Protestantism is alluded to in Mozart's *Requiem* (K.626) as well. Not only did the 'learned' fugal manner derive from Mozart's study of the works of those great Saxon Protestant composers Johann Sebastian Bach and Georg Friedrich (but also given as 'Frideric' or 'Friederich') Händel: the fugal *Kyrie* of the *Requiem* has a first subject that is perhaps a direct quotation from Händel's *Messiah* ('And with his stripes'). Now Mozart had not only prepared a new edition of *Messiah* (K.572) for none other than Baron van Swieten in 1789 (so was very familiar with Händel's work), but used an almost identical fugal subject (also in D minor) in 1780 (the *Laudate Pueri* in the *Vespers* [K.339]). Mozart had also employed the theme he exploited in the opening *Requiem* in his *Misericordias Domini* (K.222/205a) of 1775 or 1776, and, as previously noted, the Mozart *Requiem* owes not a little to Michael Haydn's *Requiem* in C minor (especially the *te decet hymnus* plainsong melody). Another work which probably influenced the design of Mozart's *Requiem* was that of Florian Gassmann in C Minor: the opening choruses of both Masses have many similarities. Thus Mozart's last (and unfinished) work embraces older styles of music, Antique and Protestant themes, and looks back to an ancient Jewish culture through the Old Testament. With its dark colouring, its quotation of Plainsong, and its use of Händelian themes and fugues, the *Requiem,* too, has associations far beyond a setting of the Mass for the Dead by an eighteenth-century composer of genius. The Protestant-Jewish-Roman Catholic connections perhaps express (or suggest) the oecumenical unity so fundamental to Freemasonry.

122 Landon (1988) 130.

CPl.X.I Interior of a Viennese Masonic Lodge in c.late 1780s-1790 attributed to Ignaz Unterberger. The central figure in the foreground with sword (the Master of Ceremonies), standing to the left of the candidate, is, according to Professor Robbins Landon (Landon [1982]), Prince Nikolaus (Miklós) Esterházy. The figure with sword to the right of the blindfolded candidate may be Wenzel Tobias Epstein. The smiling figure, seated and turning to speak to his neighbour, second from the left, is perhaps Ignaz Alberti, while the seated figure fourth from the left, shown full-face, could be Giesecke. The standing figure on the extreme left is probably Johann Nepomuk, Graf Esterházy, wearing a travelling-cloak, as he was absent. At least three events seem to be happening at once, so it is probably a composite picture, depicting not a realistic view of one occasion, but a syncretic record of several. The columns entwined with serpents *recall* the Solomonic twisted columns and the winding stair, suggesting, however, a Masonic setting (Jachin and Boaz, perhaps). The rainbow, as the sign of Hope, and the sun, suggest Crowned Hope, so the Lodge is probably *Zur (neu) gekrönten Hoffnung*. The Master (Johann Baptist, Graf Esterházy, Imperial and Royal Chamberlain) is shown with the gavel. The seated figure on the extreme right is the unmistakable figure of Wolfgang Amadeus Mozart, who seems to be in ebullient spirits, making a jest with the figure beside him. To the right of this figure one of the Brethren is taking snuff. Two clerics can be detected among the seated figures on the right: in the centre (the fifth to the left of Mozart) is a white-robed figure, possibly Abbot Johann Lambert von Hanotte, and second from the left of this seated group is a monk, possibly Pater Ignaz Faber. Note the three lights on the triangle-chandelier, Hermes-Mercurius, the Messenger (with caduceus), the rough and perfect ashlars on the tracing-board, and the various Masonic implements and symbols (*Wien Museum I.N.47.527*).

liturgical experiences of the average Roman Catholic Austrian. He also tells us[123] that the orchestral introduction to this Scene contains 'precisely eighteen groups of notes', that there are eighteen groups of priests at the very beginning of Act II (as the Libretto[124] makes clear), that the first part of the solemn chords *O Isis und Osiris* (Act II, Scene 21) is eighteen bars long, and that Papagena is eighteen years old (Act II, Scene 16), although when she claims to be this age she appears as an old hag. Eighteen is the Degree of the Rose-Croix, the number of priests who watched over Hiram's grave, and is also six times three, and six is two times three. A perusal of eighteenth-century Freemasonic booklets will make the importance of the number three clear: Three Jewels, Three Lights, Three Persons, Three Steps, Three Points, and so on[125]. However, the Numerology path is strewn with traps, and too much of it can prove unhealthy. Even though we know Mozart liked puzzles, and may have played numerical games in his music, too much introspection of this kind is unprofitable.

One point that completely eludes modern designers of this *Singspiel* is the fact that roses played an important part in early productions: the flying-machine of the Three Boys (or Genii) is covered with roses, and presumably there was scope for roses in the gardens, bowers, and other sets. Roses were used in Isiac rites: Lucius, in *Metamorphoses*[126], eats roses during his Initiation, and the Flower of Isis

---

123 Landon (1988) 130.
124 Printed in full in Berk (2004) 541-627. *See* Giesecke (n.d.).
125 *See* Gould (1884-87). *See* also Landon (1988) 130-2.
126 Apuleius Madaurensis (1924) 343 (Book **xi**).

CPl.X.II Painting by William Stewart Watson showing the Inauguration of Robert Burns as Poet Laureate of the Lodge Canongate Kilwinning, Edinburgh, in 1787 (*By kind permission of The Grand Lodge of Scotland*).

was the unfading Rose. The Mystic Rose, of course, is an Attribute of the Virgin Mary as it was of Isis Herself, the Great Forerunner[127].

The last scenes of *Die Zauberflöte* include an attack by the Queen of the Night and her accomplices on the Temple and the dissipation of the Darkness by Light. Sarastro proclaims:

'Die Strahlen der Sonne vertreiben die Nacht
Zernichten der Heuchler erschlichene Macht'
(The rays of the sun scatter the night,
Breaking asunder the might of the false dissembler).

Pamina and Tamino (who together have passed through the Trials) are welcomed by a chorus of priests with the words:

'Es siegte die Stärke und krönet zum Lohn
Die Schönheit *und* Weisheit *mit ewiger Kron*'
(*Strength* is victorious and crowns as reward
Beauty and *Wisdom* with the eternal Crown).

As noted above, *Strength*, *Beauty*, and *Wisdom* are words with powerful Freemasonic connotations, associated with the St John and also the Scottish Rite: Strength is represented in Masonic symbolism by the Doric Order; Wisdom by the Ionic; and Beauty by the Corinthian. Strength, Beauty, and Wisdom, it will be recalled, are the Three Principal Supports of Freemasonry, and are expressed in many ways, but usually by the Classical Orders of Architecture. This aspect of the libretto *does* support some sort of connection with the Craft, however tenuous.

There has been a great deal of argument as to why the Queen of the Night and her retinue were presented first as forces of good, and then as of evil. The *sternflammende Königin* (star-flaming Queen) must derive from images of the Queen of Heaven, and is therefore a figure from Antiquity, related to Isis/Astarte and the Moon. When Monostatos attempts to pounce on the sleeping Pamina, he requests the Moon to be hidden, yet his request brings the Queen at once to protect Pamina, which was the opposite of his intentions[128]. Now the 'star-flaming Queen', or Queen of the Night, is an image that would have been very familiar to Austrians: she is suggestive of the Virgin Mary, and her image on her crescent-moon surrounded by stars is one often encountered in eighteenth-century ecclesiastical Art and Architecture (*see* **Pl.X.9**, p.271). But there is a subtlety that seems to have escaped most commentators on *Die Zauberflöte*: the star-flaming Queen of the Night is a pseudo-Isis, Lady of Fire and Flames, the Fire of Hades. Could it be, given the Enlightenment's curious and retrogressive fascination for arcane and esoteric matters, that the Queen, referred to in the libretto

---

127 *See* Jameson (1907) 38-47 and *passim*. The Virgin Mary was the Rose of Sharon, and plantations of roses often occur in representations of her. She was also depicted as the Madonna of the Rose Bush.

128 Act II, Scene 8.

in terms of deceit, superstition, and trickery, represents a usurper of Isis the Benevolent, the Good, the Mistress of the Word, the Beginning, Source of Grace and Truth, the Resurrection and the Life, the Mother of God, Supreme Deity as Maker of Monarchs, Shelter of the Living and of the Dead? Sarastro and the priests invoke Isis and Osiris, and pray to them, but it is obvious from the libretto that the star-flaming Queen of the Night is *not* Isis, although she has stolen the Great Goddess's attributes of the Moon and the Stars. The Queen and her black-clad Ladies are not all bad, for they give Tamino the flute, making him into an Orpheus by that act whereby he can charm ever the fiercest animals: nevertheless the Three Ladies obscure the Truth with their Darkness, Misrepresentation, and Deceits. At the very beginning of Act I the Three Veiled Ladies (veiled because Enlightenment cannot reach them) kill the Serpent of which Tamino was terrified. Now the Serpent is associated with Wisdom and Healing, so Tamino's terror could well be interpreted as due to ignorance: if, in fact, the Ladies have attacked and chopped up an attribute of Wisdom, they are showing their true colours at the very beginning of the *Singspiel* by being inimical to Wisdom (and therefore to the Craft) and by trying to annex the young Tamino for their nefarious cause, which is to destroy the Temple and Sarastro's Order.

In respect of *Die Zauberflöte* the Orpheus connection is not fanciful. The legend is one of the earliest and most obscure in Greek Mythology. Orpheus was the Type of Poet and Musician who ventured into the Underworld, suffered great loss, originated Mysteries to which men only were initiated, was murdered, and was dismembered by Thracian women. The parallels with Osiris, the missionary going on a journey, who preaches goodness, culture, and music are clear, even in his dismemberment, and the serpent in *Die Zauberflöte* is dismembered. Tamino, in not speaking to Pamina, is undergoing a Trial that resembles the Orpheus-Eurydice legend.

We learn also that it is Pamina who leads Tamino through the Trials by Fire and Water, the way strewn with roses, while he plays the flute her father carved in a 'magic hour' from a thousand-year-old oak tree during lightning, thunder, storm, and uproar. So her father, too, was a supernatural being, like her mother (who disowns Pamina because she will not kill Sarastro). And here we should examine the case with care, for could it not be the case that the 'mother' who disowns Pamina is actually Mother Church, and therefore not her biological mother at all? As noted previously, the Church was not above ordering assassinations for its own ends (as in the cases of William the Silent, the Massacre of St Bartholomew's Day, and attempts on the life of Queen Elizabeth I of England). Pamina does not appear to be very deeply disturbed by being disowned (as she would be were the Queen truly her mother), and implores Sarastro not to punish the star-flaming Queen because the Queen's grief over losing Pamina was punishment enough. Could Pamina, therefore, be regarded as a woman who was connected with Freemasonry, perhaps through the Order of Mopses? However, Pamina, by leading Tamino through the Trials, guided herself by Love, may be showing him the Mysteries of Life in a symbolic way[129].

Now Hermes invented the lyre (the instrument of Orpheus), and was the guide to the Dead in Hades: if the flute is substituted for the lyre (Hermes also invented the shepherd's pipe), that gives Pamina a Hermetic-Egyptian connection too. However, the priestly race of the Kerykes (of the Eleusinian Mysteries) claimed Hermes as the head of their family, that is, Father, and, of course, those Mysteries were also festivals of Demeter (identified with Isis) and her daughter Persephone. The Egyptianisation of *Die Zauberflöte* was, it is suggested, more remarkable than in the cases of many other examples of the *Singspiel* in the 1780s and 1790s, and certainly the music is of a superior kind.

A not unreasonable interpretation of *Die Zauberflöte*, therefore, is that certain agents put it about that a Brotherhood is wicked and that its members are up to no good (as, of course, happened not only in Bulls but in many hysterical and paranoid publications concerning the Craft). The Truth, however, is different, for Wisdom, Strength, and Beauty are the rewards in the Enlightened precincts of the Temple, and lead to a heaven on *earth* created by an Enlightened Mankind. The Three Boys refer to a secret that is not theirs to tell, to the Sun parting the clouds of Superstition, to heaven on earth coming again, and to Man and the Gods being reconciled. In that extraordinary Transformation scene, the Three Boys lead Tamino into a grove in which stand the Three Temples of Wisdom (*Weisheit*), Reason (*Vernunft*), and Nature (*Natur*) and counsel him to be steadfast, patient and silent (*Sei standhaft, duldsam, und verschwiegen!*). The Temple of Wisdom is in the middle, and is the biggest of the three; on the right is the Temple of Reason: and on the left the Temple of Nature (see **CPl.X.V**, p.270). That is what the Libretto says, and the Three Temples are connected by means of a colonnade. This is not what is obvious in the earliest sets that were illustrated[130], probably from a Viennese production by Schikaneder of c.1794, in which Reason is shown left and Nature right. Could this be an allusion to the Jachin/Boaz problem, which is often confused between right and left? Tamino, however, declaims that the *Pforten* (portals or doors[131]) and *Säulen* (columns[132]) show that Prudence (*Klugheit* – which can also mean discretion, wisdom, intelligence, sagacity, astuteness, etc.), Work (*Arbeit*), and Arts (*Künste*) may all be found

---

129 Brophy (1988) 189. Brophy's claim that the 'nonsensical' façade of *Die Zauberflöte* was a means by which the 'utterance in code' could be cloaked is perhaps overdone. This superior (even snooty) attitude towards the eighteenth-century *Singspiel* has been typical of many who have placed Mozart and his work on a very tall pedestal. The *Singspiel* of the period under discussion should be judged for what it is, not from the values of a different age.

130 Berk (2004) Figs. 75.2, 75.3.

131 *Pforte* can also mean a gate or an entrance.

132 *Säule* also means a pillar, a support, a pile, a prop, a post, an upright, or a jamb. *See* the erudite paper by Kempter (2007).

within. Tamino is repulsed from the Temples of Reason and Nature because he, representing perhaps unperfected Spirituality, or Imperfect Man, cannot achieve Wisdom through Reason or Nature alone: in other words, those twin deities of the Enlightenment, deified Reason and Rousseauesque Nature, are not themselves up to the task of educating Mankind. It is only when he approaches the central Temple of Wisdom that the Speaker engages him in dialogue and starts to correct the false views Tamino has formed concerning Sarastro and the Temple: it is at that part of the *Singspiel* that I suggest Giesecke, rather than Schikaneder, may have played an important rôle.

From then on Tamino proceeds to Enlightenment through various Trials, until he and Pamina (the child of Superstition and Patriarchal Reason) enter the Temple presided over by Isis and Osiris, the Symbols of Nature and Reason reunited at last[133]. Johann Christoph Friedrich von Schiller warned that the very shallow Reason worshipped during the Enlightenment could not bring about a transformation of Society on its own, and Reason alone could not unveil the truth of Nature either. Wisdom, Reason, and Nature combined, though, could perhaps lead somewhere. As Leopold Engel wrote in his history of the Illuminati, Enlightenment is really about self-knowledge, about what others are, and about perceptions concerning what other members of the human race can become, but it involved helping others, sharing joys, and rejoicing in the human condition and its potential[134]. Another possible influence on some of the ideas floated in *Die Zauberflöte* was Adolf, Freiherr von Knigge, who was involved in the Illuminati and Freemasonry, and was a disciple of Rousseau. Some of his writings have parallels with the text of Mozart's *Singspiel*[135], but a detailed analysis is not possible here. However, a careful trawl through the Baron's works will reveal much of interest to the intrepid seeker of information[136].

The point about the beginning and end of *Die Zauberflöte* is that it teaches us two important truths: first, that things are not always what they seem; and, second, that the man (Tamino) who is 'more than a Prince' by being a man, learns to cast aside the darkness by venturing through portals into the Unknown, metaphorically dies, and is resurrected after Initiation and undergoing Trials, overcoming the very fear of Death itself. He also, when playing the flute, standing with the instrument in its transverse position, becomes an enigmatical representation of a word or a name by suggesting the Masonic Square. To some, this might appear far-fetched, but the intellectual climate of 1791 was not what it is in the twenty-first century, and, in view of the content of *Die Zauberflöte*, should at least be considered.

Mozart, it is known, took great comfort from views on Death held in circles associated with the Craft, as is clear from his letters to his dying father in 1787: he regarded Death as the real purpose of Life, as a Best Friend, and as a Comforter, with no terrifying connotations[137]. Mozart was grateful that he had been granted the opportunity (he noted to his father at this point that he would know what he meant) of learning that Death is the *key* which unlocks the door to true happiness. This key, of course, refers to the teachings of Freemasonry. The Craft, it would seem, gave Mozart a solace that the Church, with its terrible doctrines of Purgatory and Hellfire, could never give: sweet reasonableness, acceptance, and a reconciliation with the realities of Life seemed far more attractive than Eternal Damnation and all the other Terrors taught by the Church. The serenity of mind Mozart displayed was that of a true son of the *Aufklärung* and of a dedicated Freemason who had symbolically passed (like his father) from Death to Life in the ceremonies leading to the Degree of Master Mason, and who was wholly conversant with Freemasonic philosophies concerning Death.

It is clear from the custom of Lodges of Sorrows (for which Mozart's *Maurerische Trauermusik* probably was given) that Freemasons gave their departed Brethren a dignified memorial: Mozart himself was commemorated by a Lodge of Sorrows after his death which must have been a solemn and moving contrast to the perfunctory offices of St Stephen's Cathedral performed by priests of the Church. Now the *Maurerrede auf Mozarts Tod* given under the aegis of *Zur gekrönten Hoffnung* was actually published by Ignaz Alberti in 1792, and was by Karl Friedrich Hensler. However, this edifying ceremony, at which Mozart was praised as a benefactor, did not take place until April 1792[138]. There are many accounts of the aftermath of Mozart's death, some conflicting, some confused, and posterity has not helped by piling layer upon layer of romantic, judgemental nonsense on top of it all[139]. However, the Masonic Oration on Mozart's death referred to the 'Eternal Architect of the World' having taken one of the 'most beloved' members: Mozart was referred to as 'our transfigured Brother' whose memory should be celebrated by renewing Masonic vows of 'inviolable loyalty to Virtue at the grave of A...', by which some have claimed is meant 'Adam' (a pseudonym adopted by Mozart), but it is more likely to refer to Adoniram, supposedly an adviser to King Solomon who was slain whilst on duty: his name signifies the Highest Grade of the Scottish Rite.

This Mozart, the genius who made the eighteenth century sing for ever in our ears, died early in the morning on 5 December 1791 of 'acute miliary fever'

---

133 *See* Till (1992) 283 and Thomson (1977) 157.
134 Engel (1906) 154-6.
135 Knigge (1978-92), the volumes (**xii** and **xiii**) entitled *Freimaurer- und Illuminatenschriften*.
136 Thomson (1977) 15-16, 81, 134, 141, 157, 159, 163, 172 touched on this matter, and also found material in Engel (1906), although she called the latter 'Ludwig' instead of 'Leopold'.

137 Mozart to his father, 4 April 1787. *See* Anderson (*Ed.*) (1988) 907.
138 Gruber (1991) 5, 13-22, 56-7. *See* Deutsch (1965) 447-451. The *Maurerrede*, edited by Deutsch, was published in facsimile in *Schweizerische Musikzeitung* (Zürich, February 1956).
139 For useful material *see* Braunbehrens (1986), Deutsch (*Ed.*) (1965), Gruber (1991), Gutman (2000), Landon (1982, 1988, 1989), Landon (*Ed.*) (1990), Landon & Mitchell (*Eds.*) (1956), Sadie (*Ed.*) (1996), Solomon (1995).

probably brought on by a fatal combination of infection, a constitution weakened by overwork and worry, and the attentions of medical men. Unseasonably mild weather led to almost instant beginnings of putrefaction, and Baron van Swieten took charge of the funeral arrangements. As Mozart's *Requiem* was to be held on 10 December, the actual funeral service took place in the Crucifix Chapel, a porch-like structure over the stairs leading down to the Catacomb attached to the North wall of the Cathedral on 6 December. Under the law no corpse could be buried until 48 hours after death, so it would appear that the state of Mozart's body speeded things up. Regulations prohibited the passage of the hearse during daylight, and the disposal of the body was virtually a secular, matter-of-fact affair. In fact Mozart, dressed in a black suit, was transported in his own coffin to the recently-established suburban Cemetery of St Marx, and there was interred on 7 December in an *allgemeines einfaches Grab*'[140], not a communal (*gemeinschaftlich*) grave. This was *not* a 'pauper's grave', nor was it a communal pit with others, nor was Mozart tipped out of the parish coffin: he was buried in his own coffin (paid for by van Swieten), dressed in a suit, in his own grave. It was a leasehold grave (like most at the time). The *Wiener Zeitung*[141] reported that there were moves to set up a stone tablet over the composer's burial-place with an inscription stating that Mozart had superseded Orpheus, but there is little evidence it was ever realised. Four days after the burial of Mozart's mortal remains, solemn obsequies were celebrated in the Church of St Michael[142], and the music used seems to have included part of the unfinished K.626 *Requiem*[143].

Much has been made of the fact that nobody accompanied the coffin to the cemetery: however, this was normal. Nobody would travel outside the city in the dark, and back again, and besides, cemeteries were not pleasant places in the 1790s. The agreeable garden-cemetery, where Death was tamed, came later, as was made clear above. This point, and the programme of reform that led to the establishment of landscaped garden-cemeteries, owed much to Freemasonry, as has been commented upon earlier.

There are many other intriguing aspects to *Die Zauberflöte*. The *Palmenwalde* scenes in the *Singspiel* remind us, not only of the Nilotic setting, but of many Continental Lodges named after palm-trees (palms, like acacias, bays, chestnuts, limes, and myrtles, had powerful Freemasonic connotations in Central Europe). Mozart's use of secret codes and liking for riddles are well-known, whilst his skills with mathematical puzzles and number-games were clear from an early age, so it is not surprising that the *Flute* appears to have many symbolic number-systems and what may be coded musical messages, many of which escape the ear but become more obvious on paper[144]. It appears that Mozart himself had plans to found some sort of esoteric society with Illuminatist-Freemasonic aims, and that it was to be called *Grotto* or *Grotta*[145]. Mozart appears to have written an essay (now lost) on the subject which was referred to by his widow in 1799 and 1800[146]. We know that the Mozart family was familiar with several rock-work grottoes, and Mozart knew the so-called 'Cave of the Illuminati' at Aigen, near Salzburg, which had a waterfall[147]: it is possible that this place suggested the setting for Act II Scene 31 of *Die Zauberflöte*.

However, matters mentioned in the previous paragraphs need to be treated with caution, for there are problems. First of all, there is an unequivocal statement in the Appendix to Mozart's biography, written by Georg Nikolaus, Freiherr von Nissen, with Mozart's widow, Constanze, to the effect that the librettist of *Die Zauberflöte* intended only a parody, an apotheosis of the Freemasons' Order (*Apotheose des Freymaurer-Ordens*), a symbolic struggle (*Kampf*) of Wisdom (*Weisheit*) with Folly (*Thorheit*), Virtue (*Tugend*) with Vice (*Laster*), and Light (*Licht*) with Darkness (*Finsterniss*). Furthermore, Nissen and Mozart's widow wrote that if you want to understand *Die Zauberflöte* then you should recall Childhood (*Kindheit*), for only things which cannot be explained can enthral the soul of a child (*Kinderseele*). They went on to say there was little profit in trying to find out *how* and *why* a story (*Fabel*) came into being, for only a fairy-tale (*Märchen*) and belief in it will justify the tale at all: one should be a believer for two short hours or give up on the pleasures (*Genüße*) of a charming illusion (*holden Wahnes*), for Mozart certainly intended nothing more or less...[148] They also stated that Mozart did not 'probe into the depths of foolish Wisdom', but that his 'sweet melodies' prompted awakenings of the 'first inklings of the Divine'[149].

Secondly, the 'Trials' in Act II have been claimed to refer to Freemasonic Initiations. The problem here is that processing through Fire and Water was never part of the Craft's Initiation rituals, and a man *led* by a woman through such 'Trials' was most certainly not 'Masonic'. However, there are numerous examples of Trials in 'magic' and 'fairy-tale' stories in which Virtue, Friendship, Fidelity, and Love are put to the test[150]. Some occurred in operas, including works by Louis Fuzellier, Jean-Joseph Mouret, Pierre-Alexandre Monsigny[151], and Jean-Philippe Rameau. The last's *Zaïs* (1748 – with libretto by Jean-Louis de Cahusac) has a celebrated Trial, and his *Zoroastre* (1749 – also with libretto by Cahusac, a Freemason, incidentally) contains

---

140 Normal single Grave.
141 31 December 1791.
142 *Auszug aller europäischen Zeitungen* (13 December 1791).
143 *Der heimliche Botschafter* (16 December 1791). *See* Gutman (2000) 743-54.
144 *See*, for example, Berk (2004), Chailley (1972), Grattan-Guinness (1992), Thomson (1977), and other sources listed in the Select Bibliography below.
145 Bauer & Deutsch (*Eds.*) (1962-75) **iv** 299, 330, 360, and *passim*. *See* also Berk (2004) 426.
146 Bauer & Deutsch (*Eds.*) (1962-75) **iv** 360.
147 Illustrated in Chailley (1972) Plate 41.
148 Nissen (1828) in the 1984 edn. 112-14.
149 *Ibid*.
150 Buch (2004) 210-11 lists several examples.
151 *La Belle Arsène*, for example, of 1773.

elements of Trials and Initiation. Both the Rameau operas have been perceived as 'Masonic', something enhanced by 'Egyptian' or exotic settings, but such perceptions are too tenuous to be taken entirely seriously. Buch has examined many theatrical productions with music that are concerned with the supernatural, Trials, Initiations, and the like, and found that any 'putative Masonic scheme' for any of them is 'problematic'[152]. I agree.

The libretto of *Die Zauberflöte*, then, draws on many sources, and although there are several aspects of it which seem to have been *influenced* by Freemasonry, the work as a whole cannot really be regarded as a 'Masonic Opera'. The Trials by Fire, Water, Air, and Earth referred to in *Die Zauberflöte* seem to derive more from fanciful French images, drawing on texts of the time (such as those of Terrasson), but have little or no 'Masonic' connection.

So, if there are a *few* aspects of the libretto that seem to be inspired by the Craft and its ideals, what of the music? That it transcends the limitations of the libretto would appear to be a generally held view: it also ascends to a high level of inspiration, delights, and gives pause for reflection. It is a suitably jolly accompaniment to the comical goings-on, it is solemn and impressive during the scenes when serious matters are under consideration or being enacted, it is passionately scary when the icy Queen rages and threatens, it is deeply sad when human sorrow is conveyed, it is joyous and full of rapture when lovers are united and obstacles overcome, and it is radiantly noble and grand when the Chorus sings the praises of Sarastro in the Temple. It was Mozart who created that music, and into it he put the best of himself: given his adherence to the Craft, and the impressive music he created for Masonic occasions, it is not rash to suggest that he put some of his beliefs and feelings about the ideals of Freemasonry into the fairy-tale *Singspiel*. That does not make *Die Zauberflöte* a 'Masonic Opera': Mozart called it a *teutsche Oper*, and Schikaneder grandly named it *große Oper* (German it may be, but it is more *Singspiel* than 'Opera'). And, despite all attempts to inflate its status, *Die Zauberflöte* was written for a *popular* suburban theatre, as *entertainment*, not as some high-falutin' allegory of Freemasonry. As far as we know, neither Mozart nor Schikaneder ever mentioned the Craft in relation to *Die Zauberflöte* (unless Mozart's remark in Prague in 1791 about performing a great homage to the Craft can be relied upon as fact[153]).

It was Leopold von Sonnleithner (he knew several people who had known Mozart) who claimed (in 1857) that *Die Zauberflöte* was a glorification of Freemasonry, but his opinions do not seem to have appeared in print until 1919-20[154]. In any case they were only part of a theory of his that Schikaneder introduced a Freemasonic element into Act I because it needed changes to distinguish it from the *Singspiel Kaspar der Fagottist oder Die Zauberzither* (Caspar the Bassoonist, or the Magic Zither), with libretto by Joachim Perinet after August Jakob Liebeskind's *Lulu, oder Die Zauberflöte*, published in *Dschinnistan* **iii**, and music by Wenzel Müller, which was first given in Vienna in 1791. However, Mozart saw that *Singspiel* and did not think much of it[155]: claims that it influenced *Die Zauberflöte* are not borne out by an examination of its content[156].

It is submitted that *Die Zauberflöte*, like the extraordinarily original *Karlskirche* in Vienna, is unquestionably a work with more to it than a superficial acquaintance with it would suggest, and, like Fischer von Erlach's church, has many layers of meaning[157]. *Die Zauberflöte*, in turn, brought out the best in a whole generation of stage-designers, and their creations are rewarding to study for the sheer variety of invention they display. The Architectural and Egyptianising effects were remarkable, for *accurate* source-material relating to Ancient Egyptian design only really became available after the Expedition of Bonaparte to Egypt at the very end of the eighteenth century[158].

One last point needs to be made concerning *Die Zauberflöte*: many of the scenes take place in *gardens*. Act I Scene 1 is set in a rocky place with trees, and there is a *fabrique* in the form of a Temple. Act I Scene 17 is a grove with the Three Temples of Wisdom, Reason, and Nature connected by a colonnade, an important aspect of the garden *fabriques* in that Wisdom, Reason, and Nature have to be understood *as a whole*, even though the Temple of Wisdom is given pride of place, and it is there, in that grove, that Tamino's journey to Enlightenment begins, starting with the solemn dialogue he has with the Speaker. At the beginning of Act II, Scene 1, is a *Palmenwalde* (a wood of palm trees), and it is there that Sarastro and the priests of the Temple (18 in number altogether) enter in solemn procession. Act II, Scene 2, is set in a courtyard in front of the Temple, with broken columns, pyramidal *fabriques*, thorn-bushes, and lofty Egyptian portals, so it is part-garden, at night. Act II, Scene 8, is a garden, with a bower of flowers and rose-bushes in which Pamina sleeps, the Moon illuminating her face. Act II, Scene 14, is a large hall, but in the foreground are *zwei Rasenbänke* (two grassy banks), and the flying-machine of the Three Boys is festooned with rose-bushes and flowers (Scene 17). Act II, Scene 29, is set in a garden, transformed in Scene 31 to a mountainous region, with waterfall, a rock-work *fabrique*, and pyramids: this is the Scene with the Two Men in Black Armour, and marks the beginning of the Trials by Fire and Water at the end of which the successful Initiate, duly Enlightened, would be equipped to serve the Mysteries of Isis Herself. The Egyptianising content of the *Singspiel* prompted designers to experiment with sundry Egypt-inspired stage-sets, and it is worth mentioning a few of these below.

---

152 Buch (2004) 214.
153 Strebel (1991) 166.
154 Sonnleithner (1919-20).
155 In a letter to Constanze Mozart dated 12 June 1791.
156 It was revived at the Vienna *Kammeroper* in 1970, which proved it was a typically agreeable *Singspiel* of no great profundity. *See* Wieland (1786-7). I am grateful to the late Malcolm Davies for sharing his views with me.
157 *See* Godwin (1979c).
158 For details *see* Curl (2005) *passim*.

Stage-Sets and Egyptian Architecture

Only two years after the death of Mozart, Giulio Quaglio III designed stage-sets for a production of *Die Zauberflöte* at the *Nationaltheater*, Mannheim, in 1794, that was a considerable improvement on the original Viennese and other very early performances[159]. The set (**Pl.X.4**), probably by Giuseppe Quaglio, for the *seltsames Gewölbe* (strange vault) in Act II, Scene 20, shows sphinxes, obelisks set on balls, semicircular *loculi* with corpses à la Desprez (*see* **Pl.X.2**, p.251), and cinerary urns: it is impressive, and the earlier connections of Mannheim with Freemasonry, Mozart, and Freiherr von Gemmingen-Hornberg should be remembered. The Quaglios were involved in designing stage-sets in Dresden, Mannheim, Munich, Schwetzingen, Zweibrücken, and other centres. Giulio Quaglio III, son of Domenico Quaglio I, became official painter to the Court Theatre at Mannheim in 1785, and was a master of realistic architectural and landscape scenery. Like his brother he borrowed heavily from engravings by Piranesi (e.g. the section on Sepulchral Monuments in *Le Antichità Romane*[160], the *Vedute di Roma*[161], and *Diverse Maniere*[162]).

As has been previously mentioned, the Esterházy family were deeply involved in Freemasonry. In 1804 *Die Zauberflöte* was given at the Esterházy seat of Kismarton[163], with sets by the appropriately-named Carl Maurer, who was engaged as *Hofkammermaler* in 1802 by Prince Miklós II. Maurer's somewhat unscholarly designs (**Pls.X.5-7**, p.268) are preserved in a sketch-book, *Handzeichnungen zum Theater Gebrauch von Carl Maurer, Fürstich Esterhazycher Hof Theater Decorateur*, dated Eisenstadt 1812, and now in the Čaplovič Library: these sets attempted to suggest Egypt, but had inauthentic and ill-observed details[164], including sphinxes, bogus hieroglyphs, obelisks, a Bernini-Poliphilus elephant with an obelisk on its back, a Piranesian prison-interior, a term with six breasts over a fountain (presumably supposed to be Artemis of Ephesus), segmental-pedimented Temples based on Roman Isiac exemplars, and corbelled openings and stepped and canted arches[165], the last clearly derived from Piranesi's *Diverse maniere* (**Pl.X.8**, p.269). What makes Maurer's sets so interesting is that they not

Pl.X.4 Design, probably by Giuseppe Quaglio (1747-1828), for the *Nationaltheater*, Mannheim, production of *Die Zauberflöte*, in 1794. The subject is a 'vault inside a pyramid', for Act II, Scene 20, and shows Papageno and the crone Papagena (aged 18). The obelisks, sphinxes, torso hanging out of the *loculus* on the right, and funerary character should be noted, as should the curious use of ogee arches and the primitivist form of the opening on the left (*DT. No.S.Qi.44/II, neg. no. 2246*).

only prolonged a non-historical phase of Egyptianising design two to ten years after the publication of Denon's great work[166], but looked forward to aspects of *Art-Déco*. Nonetheless, the strong Freemasonic links with the Esterházy family must be borne in mind: the Egyptianising sets were associated with the Craft, and the allusions would not escape educated Freemasons.

Far more professional, and of a quality that is outstanding, are the sets designed by Karl Friedrich Schinkel in 1815 when Schinkel was appointed to design stage-décor for the *Königliche Schauspiele-Opernhaus* in Berlin under the general management of Karl Friedrich Moritz Paul, Graf von Brühl. *Die Zauberflöte* was given with Schinkel's magnificent sets on 16 January 1816 to celebrate the centenary of the Coronation of the first Prussian King at Königsberg and the victory (1815) after the Wars of Liberation against the French: this splendid production set new standards of excellence. Schinkel selected the Egyptian style for historical correctness as well as for the grandeur and solemnity of the occasion, and he produced a masterpiece of Neo-Classical theatre-decoration in which architectural and historical authenticity were achieved without being slavish to pedantic correctness in every detail: Ernst Theodor Wilhelm (later Amadeus) Hoffmann, in the *Dramaturgischen Wochenblatt* of 2 March 1816, waxed lyrical about them, praising the starry skies, dark vaults full of Sublime Terror, supernatural atmosphere, noble sphinxes, colossal scale of the Great Temple, and the contrast between light and dark[167]. These were published in Berlin in 1819-24 as *Decorationen auf den beiden Königlichen Theatern in Berlin* by Carl Friedrich Thiele with coloured

---

159 See, for example, *Allgemeines Europäisches Journal*, published in Brünn (now Brno) in 1795, which pictured six rather crudely-drawn scenes.
160 Piranesi (1756).
161 Piranesi (1748-78).
162 Piranesi (1769).
163 Known in German as Eisenstadt, the capital of the Burgenland, where the Esterházy Princes had a fine *Schloß*, designed by Carl(o) Martin(o) Carlone, and built 1663-72. Kismarton passed from Hungary to Austria in 1921: it should not be confused with the huge Esterházy Palace in Hungary proper (it is now called Fertöd), built 1764-84 by Prince Miklós to designs perhaps by himself and Melchior Hefele.
164 Prince Miklós incurred very heavy expenditure during the Napoleonic Wars when he raised a regiment, and his grandson, Prince Miklós III, was forced to sell part of the huge Esterházy collections. Maurer, therefore, could have been an economy.
165 Horányi (1962). I am indebted to Madam Edith Róth of the *Académiai Kiadó*, Budapest, to Professor Mátyás Horányi, and to Dr Štefan Krivuš, Director of Matica Slovenská, for help with Maurer's sketch-book in the Čaplovič Library, Dolny Kubín. I am also indebted to Milena Michalkóva for assistance with correspondence.

---

166 Denon (1802). *See* Curl (2005) *passim*.
167 Börsch-Supan & Grisebach (*Eds.*) (1981) items 210 a-h.

illustrations by Friedrich Jügel and Friedrich Christoph Dietrich after Schinkel. These memorable images include a fantastic Egyptianising Temple in a rocky grotto (Act I, Scene 1), given additional menace by the inclusion of crouching, sinister, winged figures (**CPl.X.III**), and the Hall of Stars of the Queen of the Night (Act I, Scene 6), an image of remarkable simplicity and directness (**CPl.X.IV**, p.270) alluding to the Roman Pantheon and to the Marian illustrations featuring the crescent-moon (**Pl.X.9**, p.271). Schinkel's vault as a metaphor of the Heavens had its parallels in representations of the Temple of Solomon as a Pantheon-like structure: Maarten van Heemskerck showed such a form in his vision of the Temple, and the title-page of a Prussian Masonic Song-Book of 1798-9 (**Pl.X.10**, p.271)[168] indicates how these ideas merged. The Pantheon-type of Temple also appears as an illustration to Le Régulateur du Maçon of 1801 (**Pl.X.11**, p.271).

For Act I, Scene 15, Schinkel set three Egyptianising portals in a unified composition within a lushly tropical landscape to signify the sanctuary of Wisdom, Reason, and Nature (**CPl.X.V**, p.270). Osiris presides over the central portal of the Temple of Wisdom, and the sources for the design appear to be Piranesi's *Diverse maniere...*, Denon's *Voyage...*, and Friedrich Heinrich Alexander, Freiherr von Humboldt's account of his explorations (1799-1804) of South America, and especially his studies of volcanoes. A distant view of the Temple complex at Philae (or at least a group of buildings on an island that recall the Isiac Temples at Philae) appears as a vignette in a *Palmenwalde* for Act II, Scene 1, of *Die Zauberflöte*: the Nilotic aspects of the landscape are somewhat transformed by the mountainous background, probably suggested by Humboldt's travels (**CPl.X.VI**, p.271).

Schinkel's marvellous set for Act II, Scene 8, shows a landscape (Sarastro's garden), an Egyptianising *Élysée*, bathed in moonlight, with a lake and

168 Böheim (1798-9).

MOZART AND FREEMASONRY / 269

FACING PAGE

Pl.X.5 *(top)* Carl Maurer's design (page 10 of his sketch-book [Maurer (1812)]) for *Die Zauberflöte*, showing decorations for the theatre at Kismarton (Eisenstadt). This, and other designs illustrated here, appear to have been used for a production of the *Singspiel* first given at Kismarton 10 August 1804 under the direction of Mozart's former pupil Johann Nepomuk Hummel. There are winged, breasted sphinxes, fake hieroglyphs, a steeply-pitched banded pyramid, paired columns in front of the Temple (suggesting Jachin and Boaz), and a temple-front with segmental top to the portico, a form associated with Temples of Isis in Graeco-Roman Antiquity (*Matica Slovenská*).

Pl.X.6 *(middle)* Carl Maurer's design (page 15 of his sketch-book [Maurer (1812)]) for *Die Zauberflöte*, showing a moonlit garden (Act II, Scene 8) with Nilotic flora, an obelisk divided into five panels on each flank, a six-breasted bust representing Diana of Ephesus and Isis, and the fountain, an Isiac feature (*Matica Slovenská*).

Pl.X.7 *(bottom)* Carl Maurer's design (page 16 of his sketch-book [Maurer (1812)]) for the entrance to the Trials by Fire and Water (Act II, Scene 31) of *Die Zauberflöte*. Maurer exploited the corbelled pseudo-arches which derive from Piranesi's work, and also showed primitive unfluted Doric columns (to suggest Egypt) and the canted arch (which also derives from the corbelled pseudo-arch, and was used by Piranesi). The canted and corbelled 'arches', seen here together, were to become common features in the Egyptian Revival of the nineteenth and twentieth centuries, and were popular in *Art-Déco* work. The angled 'arch', for example, recurs in bridges associated with the M1 Motorway designed in the 1930s (*Matica Slovenská*).

Pl.X.8 *(above)* Fireplace design by Piranesi from his *Diverse maniere*, featuring corbelled pseudo-arches derived from the inverted stepped-pyramid motif, with an Artemis of Ephesus over the fireplace, and supporting figures derived from the Antinoüs-*telamones* figures from the *Villa Adriana*, mixed with other Egyptianising themes derived from Antique fragments, freely interpreted. The corbelled pseudo-arch became a common theme in later designs which purported to be Egyptian or Egyptianising work, and recurs in *Art-Déco* design. The next step was to shave off the steps to provide a canted opening, another common theme of the Egyptian Revival in the early nineteenth century (*SAL*).

CPl.X.III *(below)* Schinkel's design for Act I, Scene 1, of *Die Zauberflöte* in the 1816 production of the opera at the *Königliche Schauspiele-Opernhaus*, Berlin, showing a fantastic Egyptian temple in a rocky grotto, treated quite freely, but with enormous verve. This, the domain of the Queen of the Night, has a suitably sinister flavour, appropriate for the palace of the *Sternflammende Königin*, who is also known as Astrifiammante in certain nineteenth-century versions of the *Singspiel*. The crouching figures are suggestive of futuristic science-fiction fantasies, and the cavetto cornice with small figures (with stars) at cornice level have a Piranesian flavour. Note the triangular pseudo-arch at the bottom (*Thiele* [1823] BL.1899.c.5).

CPl.X.IV Schinkel's gouache design for Act I, Scene 6, of *Die Zauberflöte* in the 1816 production of the opera at the *Königliche Schauspiele-Opernhaus*, Berlin, showing a dark vault in the form of a hemi-dome, indicated by stars that follow the lines of 'vault-ribs' terminating in an 'oculus' like that of the Pantheon in Rome. In the centre is the Queen of the Night standing on her crescent-moon, an extraordinary image that recalls the *Immaculata* from Baroque and Rococo ceilings: the Isiac and Marian allusions are clear, and the identification in such a startling manner by Schinkel of the Queen with the *Immaculata* points to an important aspect of *Die Zauberflöte*. The Queen and her allies represent the forces of Superstition, Obscurantism, and Reaction, so must have a religious connotation: *Das Weib dünkt sich groß zu sein; hofft durch Blendwerk und Aberglauben das Volk zu berücken, und unsern festen Tempelbau zu zerstören* (That woman thinks much of herself, and hopes by trickery and superstition to ensnare the people and to destroy our safe and strongly-built Temple), as Sarastro puts it. Carl Friedrich Thiele's published version was based on Schinkel's original project (Schinkel Museum SMB, KuSdZ, *c*.121.x) *(Thiele [1823] BL.1899.c.5)*.

CPl.X.V Schinkel's design for Act I, Scene 15 of *Die Zauberflöte* in the 1816 Berlin production at the *Königliche Schauspiele-Opernhaus* showing the forecourt to Sarastro's palace with a tropical landscape in the background. The three portals lead to Temples of Wisdom, Reason, and Nature, but are contained within a unified building in which Osiris presides over the central portal (Wisdom); a male priest with hieroglyphical tablet (derived from Piranesi's designs) is over the portal of Reason; and a goat (or perhaps a bull) is set above the portal of Nature. The sources for the design appear to be Piranesi's *Diverse maniere...*, Denon's *Voyage*, and Alexander von Humboldt's account of his journey to South America. Carl Friedrich Thiele's version was based on Schinkel's original project (Schinkel Museum, SMB, XII c. 118) *(Thiele [1823] BL. 1899. c. 5)*.

Pl.X.9 Ceiling of the *Stiftskirche*, Lindau-am-Bodensee, Germany, showing the Assumption of the Blessed Virgin Mary, with the figure (surrounded by stars and sunbursts, angels, cherubs) standing on the crescent-moon. From a painting (*c*.1748-51) by Giuseppe Appiani. Photograph of 1980 (*JSC*).

Pl.X.10 Title-page of *Auswahl von Maurer Gesängen mit Melodien der vorzüglichsten Componisten in zwej Abtheilungen getheilt; gesammlet and herausgegeben, von J. M. Böheim* (Selection of Masonic Songs with Melodies by pre-eminent Composers divided into Two Parts: Collected and Edited by J(oseph) M(ichael) Böheim), engraved by Carl Jäck of Berlin, and published in 1798. This Masonic song-book has a vignette of a Pantheon-like structure with an Antique Doric portico flanked by sphinxes and obelisks. The music includes works by Mozart, Pleyel, Naumann, etc. (*UGLE*).

Pl.X.11 Engraving from *Le Régulateur du Maçon* of 1801 showing a Pantheon-like structure on a base of seven steps, with G in blazing star, Masonic tools, a beehive, the seven stars, sun and moon, rough or unworked stone, and pyramid on cube. Note the cord, or 'tessellated border', known as *La houpe dentelée*, or *die Schnur von starken Faden*: this cord is intertwined with knots, and has a tassel at each end. A cord of strong threads with lovers' knots alludes to the care of Providence, which surrounds and keeps Freemasons within its protection. According to French ritual, the cord is intended to remind Freemasons that the Brotherhood surrounds the earth, and that distance does not relax the bonds: it is an emblem of the fraternal bond by which Freemasons are united. The cord should consist of sixty threads or yarns, because no Lodge (according to ancient statutes) was supposed to have more than sixty members. Four tassels were necessary to complete the symbolism of the Four Cardinal Virtues, but two are often found in French and German designs. 'Tessellated', of course, suggests the small stones used in a mosaic pavement, but the 'tessellated border' of Freemasonry seems to mean a cord of black and white threads, decorated with tassels, surrounding the tracing-board of the First Degree (which is a representation of the Lodge): it signifies the mystic tie binding the Craft (wherever dispersed), into one band of Brotherhood. The cord may also allude to the halter of ancient mysteries by which a candidate was led to initiation (*Collection JSC*).

an island on which is a mausoleum consisting of a massive Sphinx on a battered base, with palm-trees (**CPl.X.VII**, p.272). Hoffmann, in the *Dramaturgischen Wochenblatt* felt the design was serious and solemn, with a mysterious colossus looking down on the Silence of Nature. The two figures in the foreground owe something to Piranesi, and they, the palm-trees, and the reflections in the water add to the effects of serenity, of magic, and of mystery.

Also dramatic, dark, mysterious, and suggestive of vast prisons, creepy catacombs, funeral designs of Desprez, and Piranesi's *esquisses* for Egyptianising fireplaces[169] is the 'strange vault' with massive piers and a primitive structure of enormous unadorned beams. Statues representing mummified bodies are set in niches on stepped bases (**CPl.X.VIII**, p.273). Sources would appear to have included Denon's study of the Temple at Apollonopolis and certain creations of Piranesi.

Schinkel's design for Act II, Scene 31 (called 28 in Thiele), depicts the awesome entrance to the Trials by Fire and Water, above which is the mighty Temple of the

---

169 Piranesi (1769).

CPl.X.VI Schinkel's design for Act II, Scene 1 of *Die Zauberflöte* in the 1816 Berlin production at the *Königliche Schauspiele-Opernhaus*, showing the luxuriantly tropical flavour of the Nilotic landscape or 'Palmenwalde'. In the centre is a distant view of a Philae-like complex of Egyptian temples dedicated to Isis. The sources may be Humboldt's travels and Denon's *Voyage*... Carl Friedrich Thiele's version of Schinkel's original project (Schinkel Museum, SMB, Th XX) *(Thiele [1823] BL.1899. c. 5)*.

CPl.X.VII Schinkel's design for Act II, Scene 8 of *Die Zauberflöte* in the 1816 Berlin production at the *Königliche Schauspiele-Opernhaus*, showing Sarastro's garden, with lake and island on which is a mausoleum consisting of a massive sphinx placed on a battered base, with palm-trees. This '*Mondscheinlandschaft*' is one of the most evocative of the entire set of outstanding designs: it is a noble evocation of a Nilotic style, but the figures in the foreground somewhat incongruously seem to owe something to Piranesi. Carl Friedrich Thiele's version of Schinkel's original project (Schinkel Museum, SMB, KuSdZ, XXIIc, Pass BL.1899.c.5) *(Thiele [1823] BL.1899.c.5.)*.

CPl.X.VIII Schinkel's design for Act II, Scene 20 of *Die Zauberflöte* in the 1816 Berlin production at the *Königliche Schauspiele-Opernhaus*, showing the interior of a 'strange vault' with massive piers and a primitivist structure of enormous unadorned beams. Statues of mummified figures are set in niches on stepped bases. Sources would appear to have been descriptions of the 1791 Viennese production, Denon's study of the interior of the temple of Apollonopolis, and certain creations of Piranesi. Friedrich Jügel's version of Schinkel's original project (Schinkel Museum, SMB, Th. XXIII) (*Thiele [1823]* (BL.1899.c.5).

CPl.X.IX Schinkel's design for Act II, Scene 31 (called 28 in Thiele [1823]) for the 1816 Berlin production of *Die Zauberflöte* at the *Königliche Schauspiele-Opernhaus*, showing the awesome entrances to the Trials by Fire and Water, with steps leading up to the portal of the mighty Temple of the Sun, treated with great Egyptianising verve. The Architecture is derived from Denon's *Voyage...* (portico from Dendera), and from the title-page of F. Norden's *Travels in Egypt and Nubia* of 1757. Other elements are from Schinkel's own Diorama project *Das Labyrinth von Creta* of 1807, and from Mauro Tesi's *Raccoltà di Disegni Originali* published in Bologna in 1787 (Schinkel Museum SMB KuSDZ, XXII/119 and SM XVb/50- 52) (*Thiele [1823]* BL. 1899.c.5).

CPl.X.X Schinkel's design for the Closing Scene of Act II and of the whole *Singspiel* in the 1816 Berlin production of *Die Zauberflöte* at the *Königliche Schauspiele-Opernhaus* showing the interior of the colossal Temple of the Sun. In the background Osiris the Resurrected, the All-Wise, sits enthroned, flanked by Apis-Bulls. On either side are colossal Piranesian statues of priests in attitudes of adoration, and in the distance is a huge pyramid rising from the light of the sun behind the head of Osiris, with pylon-towers and obelisks on each side. The colonnades *in antis* on either side are based on Denon's *Voyage...* of 1802, while other elements derive from Piranesiesque designs, and from Schinkel's own Diorama project *Das Labyrinth van Creta* of 1807, especially the *Tempelanlage von Edfu* (SM XXII e/62). The Osiris figure mixes the Hadrianic figure of Antinoüs, elements in Denon, and Piranesian flavours as the centrepiece of a spectacular final scene in which

'Die Strahlen der Sonne vertreiben die Nacht,
Zernichten der Heuchler erschlichene Macht'
(The rays of the sun scatter the night
Breaking asunder the might of the false dissembler).

Here Strength, Beauty, and Wisdom are lauded in the final chorus: words with powerful Freemasonic connotations. So Sarastro and his priests, presiding over the Egyptian Mysteries, represent the triumph of Benevolence, Wisdom, and Freemasonry over the forces of Superstition, Lies, and Darkness (Schinkel Museum, SMB Th/3) (Thiele [1823] BL.1899.c.5).

Sun, treated with great Egyptianising verve (**CPl.X.IX**, p.273). The Architecture is derived from Denon's *Voyage…* (especially the portico from Dendera) and from the title-page of Frederick Ludvig Norden's *Travels in Egypt and Nubia*[170]. Other elements were taken from Schinkel's own Diorama project *Das Labyrinth von Creta* (1807) and Mauro Antonio Tesi's *Raccoltà di Disegni Originali* published in Bologna in 1787[171].

The final image (**CPl.X.X**) of Schinkel's sets (Act II, Scene 38) shows the colossal Temple of the Sun: presiding is a huge statue of Osiris the Resurrected, the Invincible, the All-Wise, based on the Hadrianic figure of Antinoüs with elements from Piranesi's *Diverse Maniere*. On either side are Piranesian figures in attitudes of adoration, and in the distance is a huge pyramid. The colonnaded Temple-fronts on either side are based on Denon's *Voyage*, and other elements are derived from Schinkel's Diorama *Das Labyrinth von Creta* (1807) spiced with Piranesian motifs.

These Schinkel *Zauberflöte* sets are fairly well-known, but less familiar works by Schinkel for opera-designs were also of superb quality. Among the finest were his designs for the opera *Olimpia*, with a text adapted by E. T. A. Hoffmann from the *tragédie lyrique* by Joseph-Marie Armand Michel Dieulafoy and Charles Brifaut after Voltaire's *Olimpie* and music by Gaspare Spontini: it was given in 1821 at the *Königliches Opernhaus*, Berlin, with Schinkel's splendid Neo-Classical sets. As in his earlier work for *Die Zauberflöte*, Schinkel explored many Graeco-Egyptian themes which recur in designs specifically associated with the Craft. In the *Olimpia* designs, for example, the Asiatic Artemis statue is correctly shown (**CPl.X.XI**) with the curious rings of 'breasts' that may represent eggs or

---

170 Norden (1757).
171 Tesi (1787).

CPl.X.XI *(above)* Schinkel's design for Act I, Scene 2 (Decoration II), of Spontini's opera, *Olimpia*, in the 1821 Berlin production. Friedrich Jügel after the original project in the Schinkel Museum SMB Th/15 (*Thiele* [1823] BL.1899.c.5).

Pl.X.12 *(right)* Artemis/Diana of Ephesus, mixing Graeco-Roman and other traditions. This deity was identified with Isis as a mother-goddess, and as goddess of the Moon and Night. The horned animals around the body suggest the cows' horns of Isis, whilst the wrappings suggest the bindings of an Egyptian mummified body. The disc behind her head is reminiscent of a halo. This replica of the celebrated cult-statue in Ephesus, with its symbols of fecundity, dates from the second century AD, and came from the *Villa Adriana* at Tivoli. The egg-like forms give the statue the name *multimammian*, or many-breasted, but they are not breasts, and are clearly shown hooked on to a necklace: they are probably representative of the testicles of sacrificed animals, although another interpretation is that they are eggs. Now in the *Galleria dei Candelabri* in the Vatican, Inv. 2505. Photograph of 1980 (JSC).

the testicles of sacrificed animals, while the casing of the body, wrapped like an Egyptian mummy, is embellished with the heads of horned beasts such as deer (**Pl.X.12**). The crescent-moon over the forehead of the more Grecian Artemis outside also identifies the Goddess with Isis in Act III, penultimate scene (**CPl.X.XII**, p.276).

Other interesting designs for *Die Zauberflöte* include those of Simon Quaglio. Dr Manfred Boetzkes has said[172] that 'Quaglio's stage-sets are fully equal in authority to those of Schinkel'. Quaglio, like Schinkel, sought 'inspiration from Egyptian architecture and his success in doing so may be seen from impressive studies like the Temple Forecourt and imaginative works like the Egyptian

---

172 Arts Council of Great Britain (1972) 943.

CPl.X.XII Schinkel's design for Act III, penultimate Scene (Decoration IV), of Spontini's opera, *Olimpia*, in the 1821 Berlin production. Friedrich Jügel after the original project in the Schinkel Museum SMB Th/1. The composition was influenced by that of the Brandenburg Gate, Berlin, of 1789-94, by Carl Gotthard Langhans, and also by Stuart & Revett's *Antiquities of Athens* (Thiele [1823] BL.1899.c.5).

Interior'[173]. This Quaglio was the son of Giuseppe Quaglio, and from 1814 painted Architectural scenes for the Court Theatre in Munich: in 1824 he succeeded his father as chief scene-director there, a post he occupied for the next half-century, retiring in 1877. His style was influenced by his brother, Angelo, and his father, Giuseppe, but by 1818, when he produced sets for *Die Zauberflöte* to grace the opening of the *Nationaltheater* in Munich, he was treating his themes with a mixture of Romanticism and Classicism. His Egyptian interior (Act I, Scene 13) combines Greek and Egyptian features, palm-capitals, Egyptianesque frieze, and much else (**Pl.X.13**), but his Temple forecourt (Act II, Scene 2) has massive pylon-towers, obelisks, colonnades, and colossal seated Egyptian figures, and looks convincingly Egyptian (**Pl.X.14**). The obelisks flanking the entrance are positioned as real obelisks were, rather than acting as focal points or centrepieces, but they may also subtly allude to Jachin and Boaz. Over the entrance between the pylon-towers is a stepped corbelled 'arch', a feature owing much to Piranesi. Quaglio's 'strange vault' (Act II, Scene 20) combines built forms and natural rocks, and incorporates familiar motifs such as funerary *loculi*, Egyptianising doorways, two pillars, caryatides with Egyptianising head-dresses, and stepped Piranesian forms (**Pl.X.15**).

Pl.X.13 Simon Quaglio's pen-and-watercolour design for Act I, Scene 13 of *Die Zauberflöte* for the 27 November 1818 production at the *Nationaltheater*, Munich. This 'Egyptian interior' combines Greek and Egyptian features (note the palm-capitals and frieze, the Egyptian figures, the coffering, and the extraordinary Neo-Classical glazing-bars to the window) (DT. No.S.Qu.525, neg. no. 2252).

173 Arts Council of Great Britain (1972) item 755. See S. Qu. 503, S. Qu. 532, and S. Qu. 525 of the *Clara Ziegler-Stiftung, Theatermuseum*, Munich. See also *Maske und Kothurn* (1956) **ii**.

Norbert Bittner, the Viennese Architectural painter and etcher, produced illustrations of stage-designs for *Die Zauberflöte* after Josef Ignác Platzer and Antonio di Pian for an 1818 production of *Die Zauberflöte* at the *Kärntnertortheater*, Vienna, that were nothing like as scholarly, and retrogressed to the fairground style of Egyptianisms. The *Prächtiges Zimmer in Sarastros Palast* (Act I, Scene 13) exploits corbelled forms, but does not draw on any of the publications that made dignified and convincing Egyptianising sets possible (**Pl.X.16**). Bittner's illustration for Act II, Scene 20 ('a vault between pyramids'), shows three canted 'arches', one stepped 'arch', two pylon-forms into which colonnades have been (improbably) set, and two obelisks that teeter on the verge

Pl.X.14 Simon Quaglio's pen-and-watercolour design for Act II, Scene 2 of *Die Zauberflöte* for the 1818 production at the *Nationaltheater*, Munich. The forecourt to the Temple is shown, with massive pylons, obelisks, colonnades, and colossal seated Egyptian figures. Quaglio's slightly off-axis approach should be compared with Schinkel's deliberately balanced symmetry. The two massive obelisks, while looking suitably Egyptian in their context, may subtly allude to Jachin and Boaz (DT. No.S.Qu.532,neg.no.A.1539).

Pl.X.15 Simon Quaglio's pen-and-watercolour design for Act II, Scene 20, of *Die Zauberflöte* for the 1818 production at the *Nationaltheater*, Munich. This 'strange vault' combines built forms with natural rocks, and incorporates funerary *loculi*, Egyptian doorcases, two pillars that are like circular obelisks with coffers set around their sides, stepped Piranesian forms, caryatides with Egyptian head-dresses, hieroglyphs, and a seated colossal figure (DT. No.S.Qu.530, neg. no. 2253).

Pl.X.16 Etching after Josef Platzer and Antonio di Pian by Norbert Bittner of the Egyptian Room in Act I, Scene 13, for the 1818 production of *Die Zauberflöte* at the *Kärntnertortheater*, Vienna. Note the stepped corbelled forms derived from Piranesi's work (TMK. No. G. 16939a).

Pl.X.17 Norbert Bittner's etching of a 'vault between pyramids' based on de Pian's design for Act II, Scene 20 of *Die Zauberflöte* in the 1818 production at the *Kärntnertortheater*, Vienna. No Egyptian pylons ever had columns set *in antis* within them (although in-antis distyle arrangements appear to have been seen as specifically Masonic in later times), while the canted vault (echoed in the openings in the podium supporting the fat obelisks) derives from Piranesi's designs in *Diverse maniere d' adornare i cammini*, as does the stepped form of the podium and of the doorway on the right (TMK. No.G. 16939b).

Pl.X.18 *(left)* Tempera-and-watercolour design by Beuther for the Egyptian Room in Act I, Scene 13, for the 1817 production of *Die Zauberflöte* at the *Grossherzogliches Hoftheater*, Weimar, and for the 1821 production at the *Kurfürstliches Hoftheater*, Kassel (TMK. No. G. 16927).

Pl.X.19 *(below)* Beuther's tempera-and-watercolour design for a garden with sphinx at night in Act II, Scene 8 of *Die Zauberflöte* in a production at the *Kurfürstliches Hoftheater*, Kassel, in 1821. Although the image is not as powerful as that devised by Schinkel, a strong Nilotic flavour is imparted (TMK. No.G. 16928a).

of becoming thin pyramids (**Pl.X.17**, p.277). Bittner's work was published.[174]

Friedrich Christian Beuther, originally from Alsace, worked in Bamberg, Darmstadt, Wiesbaden, and Würzburg before moving to the *Hoftheater*, Weimar, in 1815, where Goethe was involved in the management. When Goethe withdrew in 1818, Beuther moved to Braunschweig (Brunswick), then to Kassel in 1823, where he remained until his death. His designs (**Pls.X.18 & 19**) for *Die Zauberflöte* suggest that he studied history and geography and the physical characteristics of land forms. Like Goethe, Beuther recognised the importance of aesthetic Beauty and poetic Truth, and he may have appreciated the significance of stage-design as a medium by which all the visual arts combined in a totality. His *Bemerkungen und Ansichten über Theatermalerei* (Observations and Views on Scene Painting) remains an interesting work for the insights it can give us of notions current in the period 1815 to c.1840 through the influence of Goethe[175].

Die Zauberflöte provided the inspiration for numerous designs from the time of the first performance. Throughout the nineteenth and twentieth centuries it prompted many solutions to the problems of staging it, some successful, some mediocre, and some less than satisfactory. As late as 1978 David Hockney designed Egyptianising sets for a production by the Glyndebourne Festival Opera which returned to pyramidal compositions, obelisks, and canted arches (**Pls.X.20 & 21**).

There have been many studies written about *Die Zauberflöte* alone, but there is scope for further research on Mozart as a Freemasonic artist, taking into account the layers of meaning[176] in words as well as music. So it is with Masonic ideas expressed in Architecture and in designed Landscapes: in the eighteenth century much of European cultural life was permeated by Freemasonry, and earlier, Freemasonry played various roles we are only beginning to understand.

---

174 Bittner (1818).
175 *See* Beuther (1833a, 1833b) and Jung (1963).

176 *See* Godwin (1979a). Godwin and I have both used 'layers of meaning' in this context, quite independently, long before either of us was aware of the other's work.

Epilogue

Mozart, composer of Elysian harmonies, left another masterpiece in his last three symphonies of 1788, which can be seen as a whole design, and perhaps herald *Die Zauberflöte*. These symphonies (the first of which begins in the key of E flat major), like *Die Zauberflöte*, suggest a journey towards some sort of goal (an Initiation, perhaps). The E flat major symphony (K.543) has an electrifying opening with the use of a knocking rhythm, then a massive dissonance before the Allegro (in which the basic rhythm is three beats to a bar). This dissonance in the preliminary Adagio may be a representation of Chaos, like the Overture to *Die Zauberflöte*, the introduction to Franz Josef Haydn's *Die Schöpfung* (The Creation)[177], and the Adagio beginning of Mozart's 'Dissonance' String Quartet in C major (K.465) of 1785, which some have identified specifically as being connected with Freemasonry[178], although there are doubters. The second movement of the symphony, an *Andante con moto*, has the deceptively simple lyrical quality of much of *Die Zauberflöte*. Symphony No. 40 (K.550) in the dark key of G minor, with its restless, musical opening and extraordinary *Andante* in a six-eight knock-like rhythm, suggests the fear and despair of the night. Finally, No. 41 (K.551) in C major, with its miraculously complex counterpoint resolved in the glorious sun-like key of C major, suggests the light after the darkness, and reception into the Temple set in Elysian Fields. The last movement of the symphony features a four-note theme (C, D, F, and E) which derives from the Gregorian Chant: this theme seems to have haunted Mozart for much of his life, and he used it to great effect in the *Missa Brevis* in F of 1774 (K.192 [186f]) known as *The Little Credo Mass* wherein the sequence is used again and again in the *Credo* (I believe). The theme was also a feature of the *Sanctus* of the so-called *Credo* Mass (K.257) and of the development section of the first movement of Symphony No. 33 in B Flat major (K.319). The finale of the symphony No. 41 may therefore be some sort of statement of belief: the late Edward Joseph Dent quoted the opinion of 'Herbert J. Ellingford'[179] that this music was

Pl.X.20 David Hockney's design (1978 Glyndebourne production) for an Egyptian Room, showing the form of the chamfered or canted 'arch', a favourite *Art-Déco* motif derived from the Piranesian interpretation of the Egyptian style (GG.0968-15).

Pl.X.21 David Hockney's design (1978 Glyndebourne production) for the entrance to a pyramid (GG.0969-16).

---

177 Composed 1797-8 (Hob. XX1:2). It should be remembered that Haydn was a Freemason and that the text of *The Creation* was by none other than Baron van Swieten.

178 *See* Hjelmborg & Sørensen (*Eds.*) (1962) 283-7, a contribution by Chailley. *See also* Thomson (1977) 86-7.

179 This appears to be a misprint for Herbert Frederick Ellingford.

'incontestably Masonic'[180]. If we regard Mozart's last three symphonies as a journey in sound, leading from Chaos through Darkness to final Enlightenment (emphasised by the repeated four-note theme he had used elsewhere, notably for the words *Credo, Credo*), comparing it with the story of a journey from Confusion, through Darkness, to final acceptance among the Initiates in the Temple, the journeyings in certain gardens with a programme of allusions through *fabriques* certainly have parallels. The case of Mozart is reasonably well documented, and there is no doubt whatsoever that Freemasonry was very important to him. Not only did he write music *for* the Craft, but he absorbed lessons *from* it and seems to have put many allusions *to* it in a great many of his works, not just those with words, but in his symphonic, chamber, and other compositions[181]. However, this enormous[182] subject offers considerable scope for investigation that cannot be pursued to a conclusion here: it may suggest paths to be explored by others.

One other possible masterpiece that deals with a journey, and ends on a suitably desolate note appropriate for the *Hochmitternacht*[183] of Austrian Freemasonry, is *Winterreise* (Winter Journey) by Wilhelm Müller set to music 1827-8 (D.911) by Franz Peter Schubert. Müller's verses include a lime-tree, fountains, waterfalls, rocky chasms, a *Letzte Hoffnung* (last hope), a graveyard, funerary wreaths, and three suns, all of which can be perceived as having Masonic connotations. Chailley suggested that 'all appearances' pointed to Schubert probably having been a Freemason, but as the Craft was then in bad odour with the authorities[184], nobody would be overt about being a Brother. I am inclined to agree, but even more interesting is the case of Müller who, like Lord Byron, was associated with Greek Independence, was of a liberal turn of mind, and yet in 1824 became Privy Councillor (*Hofrat*) at the court of Duke Leopold IV of Anhalt-Dessau (reigned 1817-63). It will be recalled that under the Prince of Anhalt-Dessau the fascinating *Gartenreich* had been created, including the original Garden of Allusions at Wörlitz. The Principality of Anhalt-Dessau became a Duchy in 1807, and, as has been noted above, the Craft certainly existed in that part of the world, where even some members of the House of Anhalt-Bernburg were Freemasons[185]. What is certain, however, is that Schubert was coming to terms with his own mortality as he composed *Winterreise*, and was increasingly disillusioned with conventional Christianity. Just as Mozart viewed Death as the 'true goal' of existence[186], so Schubert (who became ferociously anti-clerical) admired Nature and deplored attachment to 'puny' human life[187]. It is highly unlikely that Schubert, like Beethoven, was wholly unaffected by Freemasonry, even if the Craft had been suppressed and officially did not exist. Ideas can survive, even in times of oppression. And Mozart's music has survived the attention of ignorant egotistical directors who inflict their misinterpretations on the productions. Yet once there were designers who tried to give us visual accessories that respected the words and the music: some of their creations grace this Chapter. It is a pity their example cannot inform productions in the twenty-first century[188].

---

180 Dent (1960) 232.
181 *See* Chailley (1972), Hjelmborg & Sørensen (*Eds.*) (1962), and Thomson (1977), for example. Thomson's bibliography is also useful.
182 *See*, for example, the very thorough study of songs, music, and musicians associated with Freemasonry in The Netherlands during the period 1730-1806 (Davies [2005b]). The late Malcolm Davies's contributions to the subject have been immense (*see* Davies [2005. 2005a]), and I am very grateful to him for discussing the work of several composers in relation to the Craft during a conference he organised in Den Haag in 2008.
183 High or deep midnight.
184 By 1795 Austrian Freemasonry had, at least on the surface, ceased to exist. The Lodges had closed voluntarily in 1794 and the Craft was officially suppressed in 1795. It is interesting that the Nazis, who could hardly fail to acknowledge Mozart as a great 'German Master', found themselves in some difficulty concerning his Masonic music, and altered the words accordingly. Similarly, they also removed references to Abraham, etc., in Mozart's *Requiem* (K.626), to conform to their obscene ideology.
185 For Schubert, etc., *see* Chailley (1965).
186 4 April 1787.
187 Deutsch (*Ed.*) (1947) 436.
188 I am indebted to T. O. Haunch who was kind enough to encourage my work on Mozart: his comments helped me to arrive at some of the content of this Chapter, although he is in no way responsible for my theories or interpretations. I also acknowledge the scholarly work of David J. Buch, especially Buch (2004), and of John A. Rice, one of whose studies (Rice [2006]) I had the pleasure of reviewing in *Garden History* **xxxv**/2 (Winter 2007) 243-4. For remarks concerning music and the Enlightenment *see* Agnew (2008). Finally, this Chapter is dedicated to the memory of my father.

CHAPTER XI

Conclusion

Monuments and Mausolea; Cemeteries; Opposition and Attacks; The Case of 'Greek' Thomson; Is there a Masonic Style?; Epilogue

'To subsist in lasting Monuments, to live in their productions, to exist in their names, and prædicament of *Chymera's*, was large satisfaction unto old expectations and made one part of their *Elyziums*.'

SIR THOMAS BROWNE (1605-82): *Hydriotaphia* in *The Works of Sir Thomas Browne* **iii** (Edinburgh: John Grant 1912) 144.

'All that is good, and kind, and charitable, it [Freemasonry] encourages; all that is vicious, and cruel, and oppressive, it reprobates.'

ALBERT GALLATIN MACKEY (1807-81): *A Lexicon of Freemasonry* (London: Charles Griffin & Co., 1883) 109, quoting an address by DeWitt Clinton (1769-1828) at the installation of Grand Master Stephen van Rensselaer (1765-1839) in 1825 (which Mackey gives incorrectly as 1852).

'[Freemasons] are now boldly rising up against God Himself. They are planning the destruction of holy Church publicly and openly, and with the set purpose of utterly despoiling the nations of Christendom... [Some] have plainly determined... that, artfully and of set purpose, the multitude should be satiated with a boundless license of vice... the whole principle and object of the sect lies in what is vicious and criminal...'

POPE LEO XIII (1878-1903): *Humanum Genus* (Encyclical Letter on Freemasonry dated 20 April 1884) GERALD C. TREACY, SJ (*Ed.*): Rockford IL: TAN Books, 1978) 2, 12, 18.

Monuments and Mausolea

It is in the Monument that we often find Masonic allusions set out: many are in cemeteries such as Père-Lachaise in Paris[1], but others stand proudly in positions where they are not hidden, obscured, or lost among a wealth of memorials. One of the most amazing is the tall object in the Square at Comber, County Down, in Ireland, commemorating Major-General Sir (Hugh) Robert Rollo Gillespie, who came from an old Scots family which had acquired lands in Down early in the eighteenth century. He had an adventure-filled life, and eventually was appointed to command at Meerut. In 1814, during the war against Nepal, with the Meerut Division of the Bengal troops, before the fortress at Kalunga in the foothills of the Himalayas, he was killed in the attempt to take it. He is supposed to have shouted, as he led the attack, 'Now, Kennedy, for the Honour of Down'[2].

In 1816 a statue of Gillespie by Francis Leggatt Chantrey was erected in the south transept of St Paul's Cathedral, London (**Pl.XI.1**, p.282), and a column on a pedestal was put up over his grave in Meerut. Now Gillespie had become a Freemason in 1783, probably in the 3rd Irish Horse Regimental Lodge No. 577, and it seems to have been this connection that prompted the formation of a committee in 1843 to raise funds for a monument in Comber. A design was prepared by 'Mr Johnston of Belfast', but unfortunately in Francis C. Crossle's Masonic Notes he is spelled 'Johnson', and *The Newry Telegraph* of 26 June 1845 (when the monument had been completed) once again called him 'Johnson', a spelling repeated by Crossle[3]. Gunnis states that in 1845 'Johnston, —, of Belfast' carved the statue that crowns the memorial[4]. Contemporary newspaper reports inform us that the foundation-stone was laid on St John's

---

1 Normand (1832 and 1847).
2 This was Charles Pratt Kennedy, who served in the British Army 1808-65, and was related to the well-known Ulster family of McCausland. Kennedy wrote 'A True Account of the Action at Kalunga' (1834), a copy of which is in Freemasons' Hall, Molesworth Street, Dublin.
3 MS dated 1888 in Freemasons' Hall, Dublin, 83, 87. I am grateful to Rebecca Hayes for showing me these documents.
4 Gunnis (1968) 220. Roscoe *et al.* (2009) 669, 671.

Pl.XI.1 Statue (1816) of Major-General Sir Robert Rollo Gillespie by Chantrey. It stands in the south transept of St Paul's Cathedral, London (*GLFI*).

Pl.XI.2 Monument (1845) of Major-General Sir Robert Rollo Gillespie in Comber, County Down. Note the five panels on the shaft, which, taking into account the cap, can be read as seven rungs (*JSC*).

Day 1844, and that the monument was dedicated in 1845. At these ceremonies the Rector of Comber cautioned the 'multitude' against 'indulging in ardent spirits', for this was the period that saw the beginnings of the Temperance Movement[5]. The design of what is actually a square (rather than circular) vaguely Tuscan column (**Pl.XI.2**), with its shaft divided into five panels (inscribed with the names of the places in which Gillespie saw action)[6] on each face, thus alluding to ladders (which, with the capital below the statue, could be read as having seven rungs), it has been suggested might have been the responsibility of the Engineer and Surveyor, James Johnson (or Johnston) of Cromac Place, Belfast[7], but it is highly unlikely that an Engineer or Surveyor could have carved the statue, so if Gunnis is right, Johnston or Johnson, a sculptor, designed

either all or part of the monument. As will be seen below, this appears to have been the case.

The die of the pedestal contains a panel on each of its four faces: two have inscriptions, one has Arms (referring to the Order of the Bath) and Trophies (with the Motto *Auspice Deo*), and one has Masonic emblems. One of the inscriptions reads:

THIS TABLET
HAVING REMAINED BLANK SINCE THE ERECTION OF THE MONUMENT IN 1845,
IT SEEMS FITTING TO THE MASONIC BODY AND TOWNSMEN OF COMBER TO RECORD
ON IT THAT THE BRILLANT [sic] REPUTATION OF SIR ROLLO, WAS MOST WORTHILY
MAINTAINED BY HIS GRANDSON
MAJOR-GENERAL ROBERT ROLLO GILLESPIE, C.B.
WHO FOR OVER 40 YEARS SERVED HIS COUNTRY
WITH THE SAME BRAVERY AND FIDELITY AS HIS ILLUSTRIOUS ANCESTOR,
AND WON DISTINCTION IN THE FOLLOWING PLACES
RESHIRE, BUSHIRE, KUOSAB, KULAPORE, ELMAGFAR,
TEL-EL MAHUTA, KASSASSIN, TEL-EL KEBIR, BIKANIR.
HE DIED ON THE 17TH NOV. 1890, IN COMMAND OF THE

---

5 Aiken McClelland, 'Sir Rollo Gillespie and His Monument', an article in Freemasons' Hall, Dublin. See also R. E. Parkinson (1977).
6 ODNB **xxii** (2004) 260-2.
7 Bendall **ii** (1997) 280.

MHOW DIVISION OF THE BOMBAY ARMY[8]

JULY 5TH 1893 JOHN FRAZER[9] COUNTY SURVEYOR] INSPECTORS
WILLIAM WALKER, ARCHITECT

The other inscription reads:

ROBERT ROLLO GILLESPIE
MAJOR-GENERAL AND KNIGHT COMMANDER OF THE MOST
HONORABLE MILITARY ORDER OF THE BATH,
BORN AT COMBER, A.D. 1766;
AFTER A BRIEF BUT GLORIOUS CAREER,
FELL IN BATTLE BEFORE THE FORTRESS OF KALUNGA. 24th OCTOBER, 1814.
HIS LAST WORDS WERE –
"ONE SHOT MORE FOR THE HONOR OF DOWN!"
A MONUMENT AT MEERUT IN THE EAST MARKS THE GRAVE WHERE HIS ASHES REST
A STATUE IN THE CATHEDRAL OF SAINT PAUL IN THE CITY OF LONDON,
VOTED BY BOTH HOUSES OF PARLIAMENT, ATTESTS THE GRATITUDE OF THE NATION –
HIS OWN COUNTRYMEN,
PROUD OF THE ACHIEVEMENTS WHICH HAVE SHED LUSTRE UPON HIS NATIVE LAND,
WITH A FEW OF HIS OLD COMPANIONS IN ARMS, HAVE RAISED THIS COLUMN
WITHIN THAT COUNTY WHICH CLAIMED HIS LATEST REMEMBRANCE,
TO PERPETUATE HIS MEMORY AT THE PLACE OF HIS BIRTH.

In very small letters at the bottom right-hand of this inscription can be found

JOHNSTON
STEAM MARBLE WORKS
BELFAST

This was John Johnston, whose residence and place business was the Steam Marble Works, 49 Great Patrick Street, Belfast (according to the 1861 Belfast/Ulster Street Directory), but who, in 1843, was described as a 'Stone Cutter', and was at 55 Great Patrick Street. This clinches it: the Gillespie monument, and probably the statue as well, were made by John Johnston, Stone Cutter, of the Steam Marble Works, Great Patrick Street, Belfast. The probable *Architect*, responsible for the design of the structure, was William Walker, about whom very little appears to be known.

A third panel (**Pl.XI.3**) contains two columns each on three steps, with globes on top; Masonic tools and instruments, the All-Seeing Eye, the *Hexalpha* with the Triple *Tau* (T over H, suggesting *Templum Hierosolymae*), the Sun and Moon, the Seven Stars, the Proof of Euclid's Forty-Seventh Proposition (the sum of the squares of two sides of a right-angled triangle equals the square of the hypotenuse), the Pentalpha surrounding G, the Square and Compasses (both Legs Under), surrounding the letter

Pl.XI.3 Panel on the die of the pedestal of the Gillespie monument in Comber, County Down, showing Masonic emblems. The Two 'Pillars' (Jachin and Boaz) with globes on top (an incorrect and unhistorical device which derives from sixteenth-century representations of Solomon's Temple), Masonic tools and instruments, Euclid's Forty-Seventh Proposition, the *Hexalpha* with the Triple *Tau*, the Pentalpha with G (supposed to suggest God or Geometry, but this cannot be sustained), and Mottoes. On the open book on which rest the Compasses and Square with G is inscribed (not visible in the photograph) 'St John's Gospel' (JSC).

G, superimposed on an open book inscribed 'St John's Gospel', the Plumb-Line, Levels and Rules, the Apron, and the Mottoes *Audi, Vidi, Tace* (Hear, See, be Silent) and *Sit Lux et Lux Fuit* (Let there be Light: and there was Light[10]). It would be hard to find a more overt Freemasonic expression anywhere.

In respect of the five panels on each face of the shaft of the square column, five, of course, is one of the sacred numbers of Freemasonry, and is formed of a combination of the Duad with the Triad, of the first even number with (excluding Unity) the first odd number, two plus three. In the School of Pythagorean Number Systems, five represents Light, so the Gillespie monument can be read as a beacon or a lighthouse. A five-pointed star is a symbol of health (Triple Triangle), and, of course, there are Five basic Roman Orders of Architecture.

The Comber monument, therefore, is certainly one of the most interesting and least obscure of all Masonic commemorative edifices, and its iconography (in spite of mistreatment by paint-sprayers and slogan-writers) can be studied today with benefit. That it is related to obelisks, lighthouses, Caledonian sundials mentioned earlier, and Pythagorean theories adds to its interest. Whilst Scottish tombstones and sundials often have clear Masonic attributes, it is not very often that a public memorial actually advertises its Masonic connections, yet there is such a monument at Comber, and it is an amazing example.

With sundry Egyptian associations and early-nineteenth-century Egyptomania, the pyramid and the obelisk were recruited for commemorative purposes. Examples are many, and include the Wellington

---

8 This Gillespie was supposedly Sir Robert Rollo Gillespie's grandson, but the evidence for the precise family connection is elusive. The places listed were battles of the Anglo-Persian war of the 1850s, the Ahmed Arabi (*or* Orabi) Revolt in Egypt in the 1880s, and campaigns in India.

9 A John Frazer is noted by Bendall **ii** (1997) 188 as having been 'of Downpatrick', and that he was a Civil Engineer and County Surveyor, but his dates are given as *fl.*1838-42. He does not seem to have been active in 1893, so why are his name and that of Walker inscribed? One explanation is that the tablet 'having remained blank' since 1845, acquired the inscription after the second Gillespie's death, and that the names of the original County Surveyor and Architect were added then as 'Inspectors', but the presence of the date, 1893, confuses matters regarding authorship.

10 *Genesis* 1 verse 3.

Pl.XI.4 The Wellington Testimonial, Phoenix Park, Dublin (1817-22) (JSC).

Pl.XI.5 Massive granite obelisk with Egyptian pedestal incorporating a steeply battered die at Rostrevor, County Down. The bold cavetto cornice contains winged orbs with uraei on each side, and the relief on the die shows a sarcophagus draped with flags and military trophies and flanked by inverted torches. The monument was erected in memory of Major-General Robert Ross in 1826, and was designed by William Vitruvius Morrison (JSC).

Testimonial in Phoenix Park, Dublin (1817-22) (**Pl. XI.4**), designed by Robert Smirke[11], Freemason, as a tribute to Arthur Wellesley, 1st Duke of Wellington from 1814, who had been initiated in Lodge No. 494, Trim, County Meath, and whose brother, Richard Wellesley, 2nd Earl of Mornington from 1781, became Master of the Grand Lodge of Ireland[12]. Another spectacular obelisk was erected at Rostrevor, County Down, in 1826 to commemorate Major-General Robert Ross, designed by William Vitruvius Morrison (**Pl.XI.5**). Now Ross had seen service in Egypt in 1801, and members of his family had held high office in the Grand Lodge of Free and Accepted Masons of Ireland in the 1780s[13]. The massive obelisk with its battered Egyptianising pedestal was paid for by Ross's former Army colleagues and by the gentry of County Down: among both groups were several members of the Craft.

Yet a further column (this time a circular one with a palm-capital) stands at the Fontaine de la Victoire, *Place du Châtelet*, Paris, which is inscribed with the names of battles won by Napoléon Bonaparte (**Pl.XI.6**). It was designed by François-Jean Bralle with sculptures by Simon-Louis Boizot. Erected between 1806 and 1808, the Egyptianising palm-capital was intended to evoke the Nile campaign by Napoléon. The handsome sphinxes with the double basins were added in 1858 to designs by Gabriel-Jean-Antoine Davioud and sculpted by Henri Alfred Marie Jacquemart, giving an extra Egyptian flavour to the more subtly Nilotic column. But the column itself has clearly seven subdivisions (the topmost being the palm-capital), so may allude to Jacob's Ladder, by which Freemasons hope to reach the Canopy of their Lodge. The monument, like many others in Paris, is a reminder of the Napoleonic campaigns, and that the French Army was permeated with

---

11 He was knighted in 1832.
12 Lepper & Crossle (1925) 216.
13 A Colonel Robert Ross is recorded as a member of Grand Masters Lodge, Dublin, from 1785. Information kindly provided by Rebecca Hayes.

Pl.XI.6 *Fontaine de la Victoire, Place du Châtelet, Paris*, with its *Colonne du Palmier* inscribed with the names of fifteen battles won by Napoléon, erected 1806-8, with sphinxes and fountains added 1858 *(JSC)*.

Pl.XI.7 Monument to J. C. J. van Speijk, of 1839, by J. D. Zocher *(RIBA)*.

Freemasonry, as a visit to the Cemetery of Père-Lachaise is sufficient to demonstrate. A comparison of lists of Freemasonry with the names of illustrious dead in the parts of the Cemetery where Napoleonic officers lie will prove the point. *L'égyptomanie* meant far more than an enthusiasm for a fashionable architectural style: it was an emblem of a way of life, of a philosophy, of a system that almost swept through and vanquished the world through the force of French Arms, and it was a reminder of the power and potency of progressive, revolutionary ideas. Masonic zeal to improve the world, to bring Light where before there was Darkness, and to establish Harmony throughout Europe and beyond was a powerful incentive among the officer-corps of the Napoleonic armies. One further possible interpretation of the Châtelet column is that it is not merely a reminder of the campaigns, and a monument to victories, but that it is specifically a mnemonic device to suggest the Nilotic adventures by reference to the Pharos of Alexandria and to the desire of Freemasons to arrive at Enlightenment.

As far as lighthouses are concerned, one of the most spectacular is that designed by Jan David Zocher[14] as a memorial to the Dutch naval hero, Jan Carel Josephus van Speijk[15], whose gunboat was about to be seized by Belgian Nationalists during the Revolution to separate what is now Belgium from The Netherlands: rather than have his ship fall into the hands of insurgents he blew it up, killing himself and several Belgian Seceders as well. The original design consisted of a Tuscan column on a massive, battered Grecian base, with the lighthouse lantern on top, above the capital (**Pl.XI.7**). A variant of the design was erected 1838-40 at Egmond aan Zee.

Freemasons are the 'Sons of Light', and the Light of the Craft emanates from the Source of all Purity and Perfection: Masons, coming from Darkness into the Light

---

14 Who had been a pupil of Louis-Hippolyte Lebas. Zocher was a member of *La Charité* Lodge, Amsterdam. I am grateful to the late Malcolm Davies for this information.

15 J. C. J. van Speijk applied to join the Lodge *Vriendschap* in Soerabaja in 1827, but left Soerabaja before his initiation. Again, thanks are due to the late M. G. Davies for this help.

of Initiation, are admonished to let the Light within them shine out before all men, so that their Good Works can be seen, and the Great Fountainhead of that Light glorified[16]. In respect of lighthouses, the use of highly simplified unfluted Doric for the shaft, with Graeco-Egyptian doorcases and other Egyptianising features was a characteristic of the splendid series of buildings erected around the waters of the British Isles during the first half of the nineteenth century. Good examples are those designs by Alan Stevenson including buildings at Cromarty (1846), Fortrose (1846), Noss Head, Caithness (1849), and Eilean Glas, Scalpay (c.1845)[17].

Pyramids, too, have powerful associations with Death, with 'Egyptian' rites, and, mostly through Continental sources, with Freemasonry. A pyramid-monument in the churchyard of St Anne, Limehouse, London, has certain resonances suggesting aspects of some of the Scottish sundials discussed earlier: it is very sharply pitched, and comes closer to being either a very thin pyramid or a fat obelisk, but is divided vertically into five panels, and is inscribed 'The Wisdom of Solomon' in English and Hebrew, with much-weathered Achievements of Arms below: it formerly stood on a square plinth[18], and is eighteenth-century in date (**Pl.XI.8**). If it does have a Freemasonic connection (apart from the Solomonic inscription) it is a very early and remarkable example.

From the Mediaeval period pyramids and obelisks had been confused, as is clear from the 1499 printed edition of *Hypnerotomachia Poliphili*[19] where an obelisk of sorts is placed on top of a steeply-pitched stepped pyramid (**Pl.XI.9**). In Architecture the Image is more influential than the Word (although pretentious jargon seems to have impressed far too many designers in recent times), so it is unsurprising that the obelisk-on-top-of-the-steeply-pitched-pyramid recurs: two examples will be cited here, the first being 'The Pyramid to contain Five Millions of Individuals. Designed for the Centre of the General Cemetry [*sic*] of the Metropolis by Thomas Willson, Architect, of *c.*1824 or

Pl.XI.8 Pyramid in St Anne's churchyard, Limehouse, London. Note the panelled effect, and compare with the Scottish sundials described above (*JSC*).

*c.*1825, published in *c.*1831[20] (**Pl.XI.10**), and the second the pyramidal mausoleum for the assassinated James Abram Garfield, 20th President of the United States of America and Freemason, designed (1882) by Thomas Willson of London, another variation of the *Hypnerotomachia Poliphili* theme, with rows of Egyptianising lions, a domed interior inside the pyramid, and a battered Egyptianesque entrance

---

16 Mackey (1919) 195.

17 Gifford (1992), 62, 124, 347, 399, 418, 626, 629, and Plate 122. See also Curl (2005) 275.

18 It should be compared with the Raine monument in the churchyard of St George-in-the-East, Cannon Street Road, London.

19 Colonna (1499), but *see* Godwin (*Ed. & Tr.*) (1999) 26.

20 Its base was to cover 18 acres, and the whole structure would have been equivalent to 1000 acres of cemetery land. Willson was involved in a scheme to lead a party of emigrants to South Africa (1819-20), but quarrelled with his companions and returned to London in 1822-3. He petitioned Parliament with his Pyramid proposal (*see Journal of the House of Commons* **lxxxv** [1830] 216-23), but got nowhere. He revised his plans for an Australian version in *c.*1850 (*see* Staffordshire Records Office, Gower papers, D 593 Q/1/6). We know that there was a four-year-old Thomas Willson (the Architect's son) in the emigrant party, which would put his birth-year as *c.* 1815 or possibly *c.* 1814.

Pl.XI.9 *(right)* Illustration from *Hypnerotomachie*, the French version (Paris: Keruer, 1561) of *Hypnerotomachia Poliphili*, which attempts to show an obelisk on top of a stepped pyramid, a combination that owes little to Antiquity, but which had a profound effect on Renaissance and later imagery (*SJSM*).

Pl.XI.10 *(far right)* 'The Pyramid to contain Five Millions of Individuals. Designed for the Centre of the General Cemetry [*sic*] of the Metropolis' by Thomas Willson, Architect, engraved by Charles Whiting. The steeply-pitched pyramid crowned with an obelisk is inflated to megalomaniac scale, and is derived from the image in *Hypnerotomachia Poliphili* (1499) (*GLCL*).

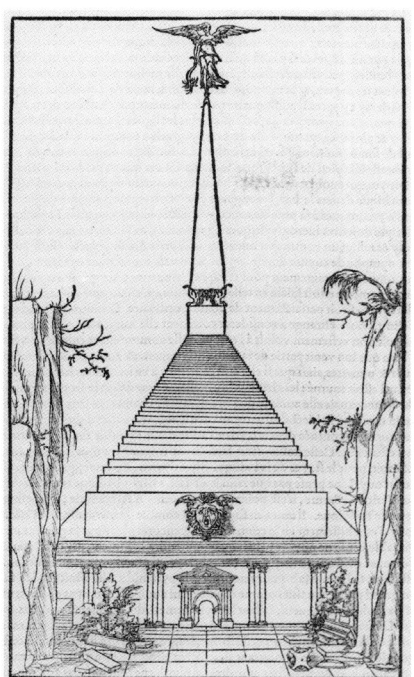
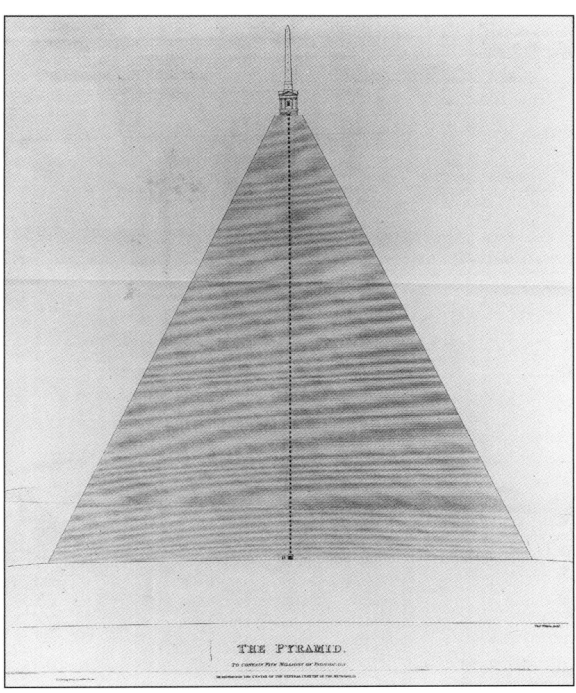

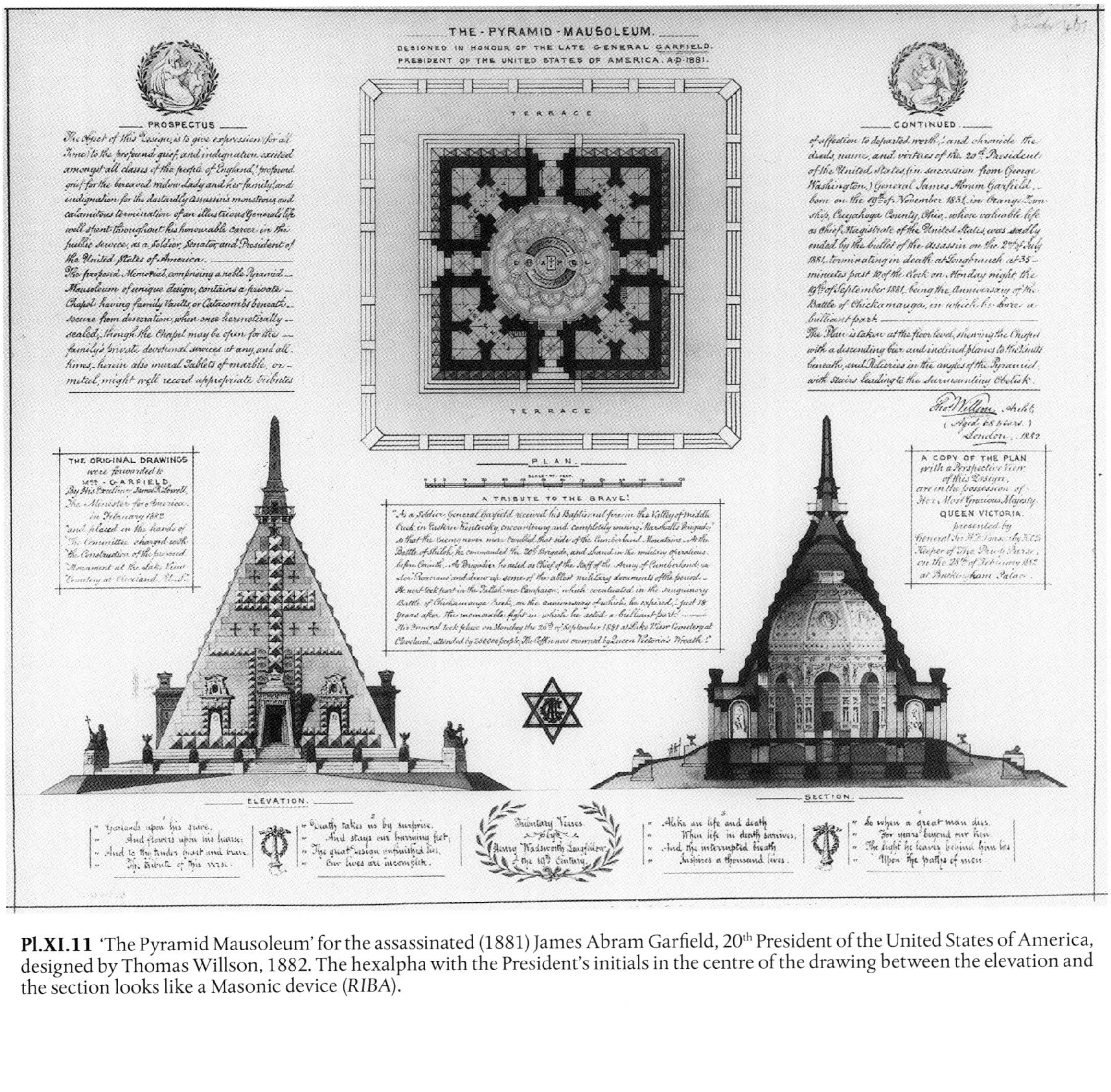

Pl.XI.11 'The Pyramid Mausoleum' for the assassinated (1881) James Abram Garfield, 20th President of the United States of America, designed by Thomas Willson, 1882. The hexalpha with the President's initials in the centre of the drawing between the elevation and the section looks like a Masonic device (*RIBA*).

Pl.XI.12 Design for a *Grabstætte* or Mausoleum for the Counts of Henckel-Donnersmarck, by Julius and Otto Raschdorff, 1897 (*RIBA*).

to each face[21] (**Pl.XI.11**, p.287). The initials IAG are held within a hexalpha on the drawing, and the prominence given to the G suggests a Masonic device.

There were numerous other experiments featuring pyramids with porticoes on all four sides produced by Architects of the Neo-Classical period. Friedrich Gilly, for example, the decisive influence on the great Karl Friedrich Schinkel, designed such a monument in 1791, and the essentials recurred in numerous designs, although, as the nineteenth century neared its end, the purity of form was submerged in a welter of ornament, as in the designs for a *Grabstætte* (burial-place or tomb) for the Counts Henckel-Donnersmarck (1897) by Julius Karl Raschdorff in collaboration with his son, Otto. The Henckel-Donnersmarck mausoleum was to have had banded Tuscan columns on all four sides, and the design was rather typical of the heavy style favoured during the Second Reich of Kaiser Wilhelm II[22]. Wilhelm Ludwig Viktor, Graf Henckel von Donnersmarck, General-Leutnant in the Prussian Army, had been Grand Master of the National Grand Lodge of All German Freemasons from 1838 until his death[23], but the Raschdorff design (**Pl. IX.12**) was apparently prepared at the behest of Guido Georg Friedrich Erdmann Heinrich Adalbert, Graf[24] (*Fürst*[25] from 1901) Henckel von Donnersmarck: the Raschdorffs also designed the Gothic mortuary chapel and tomb at the Henckel-Donnersmarck estates of Schloß Neudeck in Silesia (now Świerklaniec, Poland).

Cemeteries

The Cemetery of Père-Lachaise in Paris quickly found its admirers[26], and in the 1820s the Barrister George Frederick Carden[27] began his campaign to form hygienic modern cemeteries outside built-up areas to replace the unsavoury and overcrowded churchyards, crypts, and burial-grounds of London. The immediate proposal by Carden and his associates was for a new London cemetery on Primrose Hill (a site not unlike that of Père-Lachaise), and this stimulated several Architects (including Willson) to suggest designs. However, Willson's ideas did not appeal to the promoters of the new cemeteries: it savoured too much of the vast Neo-Classical designs for built cemeteries by the Architects of the French Academies of Rome and Paris, and these were tainted by the excesses of the Terror and of the French Revolution (which, arguably, set back the various progressive causes in Britain alone by at least a generation).

A scheme influenced by Père-Lachaise was favoured (after all, that great cemetery had been profoundly influenced by English landscape gardens), and this led to a public gathering in June 1830 in (appropriately) the *Freemasons' Tavern*[28], chaired by 'Lord Viscount Milton'[29]. A new Joint Stock Company was announced, to be called The General Cemetery Company, and those present at the meeting included Andrew Spottiswoode, Sir John Dean Paul, Bt., and Lord Lansdowne[30]. Supporters of new cemeteries came from a pronouncedly 'progressive' side of the national spectrum of opinion, and Freemasons were well to the fore. At the 1830 meeting a splendid bird's-eye perspective of a proposed 'Grand National Cemetery' designed by Francis Goodwin was shown, which consisted of a vast rectangular space enclosed by colonnades, with chapels in the form of Greek temples, and Towers of the Winds at each corner of the colonnades[31].

Cemeteries and burial-grounds, unattached to churches, owed their first origins to Protestantism and then to

---

21 Curl (2005) 306-7. As Willson was 68 when he submitted the designs in 1882, he cannot have been Thomas John Willson (1824-1903), as he would have been born c.1814. It is unusual for an Architect to state his age on a drawing, but Willson did so on the Garfield proposal: unfortunately no known Willson fits a birth-date of 1814, so the only candidate must be the son of the Thomas Willson who led the party to South Africa in 1819-20 (*see* Nash [1987] *passim*, and Note 20, p.286).

22 Friedrich Wilhelm Viktor Albert, abdicated as German Emperor and King of Prussia 1918.

23 Gould **iii** (1884-87) 258.

24 Count.

25 Prince.

26 *See* Etlin (1977, 1982, 1984) and Curl (1993, 1994*a*, 2000*c*, 2002*b*, and Curl (*Ed.*) (2001*b*).

27 *ODNB* **x** (2004) 18-19. *See also* Curl (*Ed.*) (2001*b*).

28 The 'Tavern' and the 'Hall' were terms used synonymously, so the meeting actually occurred in Sandby's Hall.

29 Charles William Wentworth Fitzwilliam became 3rd Earl Fitzwilliam in 1833.

30 Henry Petty-Fitzmaurice, 3rd Marques of Lansdowne and 4th Earl of Kerry, Benthamite and pupil of Dugald Stewart.

31 For a detailed history of the General Cemetery Company *see* Curl (*Ed.*) (2001*b*) 26, where Goodwin's proposals are illustrated.

the concerns of persons of liberal and progressive ideas, many of whom, of course, were Freemasons. Norwich acquired its non-denominational Rosary Cemetery in 1821 (but mostly patronised by Dissenters); then Liverpool gained the Low Hill Necropolis of 1825, and, from 1825-9, the much larger Cemetery of St James, laid out in a disused stone-quarry to designs by John Foster at a cost of £21,000 by a Joint Stock Company. St James's Cemetery was determinedly Neo-Classical, with ramps leading down to the floor of the quarry, a perfect Greek Revival temple as the mortuary-chapel, routes carved through the solid rock (providing Sublimely Aweful effects), catacombs in the battered sides of the ramps, and a circular Greek Revival mausoleum of William Huskisson, M.P. (killed at the opening of the Liverpool and Manchester Railway). The planting was in clumps, and was by John Shepherd, possibly assisted by his nephew, Henry Shepherd, employing the *bosquet* ideas prevalent in French elegiac gardens of the eighteenth century and later used at Père-Lachaise. Liverpool, of course, had a strong Evangelical and Dissenting element among its leading citizens, and Freemasonry was also influential there. The inter-denominational Glasgow Necropolis was formed by the Merchants' House of the city by prominent citizens, many of whom had Masonic affiliations. This severe and dramatically-sited Neo-Classical cemetery is the most Sublime of all such places in the British Isles[32], and its formation was largely due to the efforts of John Strang, whose *Necropolis Glasguensis* was published in 1831.

With the examples of Glasgow and Liverpool to emulate, The General Cemetery Company in London determined to press ahead with its proposals, and in 1832 a Bill for establishing a cemetery in the neighbourhood of the metropolis received the Royal Assent. Passage of the Bill was no doubt smoothed by the fact that in October 1831 the first of a series of ferocious cholera epidemics struck, and, apart from the chaos caused in the already obscenely overcrowded churchyards, an added incentive to form cemeteries was provided by the belief that the epidemics were caused by evil 'miasmas' that arose from the burial-grounds (not an entirely illogical opinion given the appalling effluvium described so vividly by contemporary commentators)[33]. Furthermore, the gratifyingly high dividend paid to shareholders by the Joint Stock Company in Liverpool doubtless encouraged the wheels to turn.

Full details of the history of The General Cemetery of All Souls at Kensal Green, London, have been published elsewhere[34], so repetition would be superfluous here. It will be sufficient to say that the spacious landscaped layout[35] and Greek Revival buildings by John Griffith of Finsbury began to attract attention and custom, so by 1839 The General Cemetery Company was flourishing, and the original shares had doubled in value. The Cemetery acquired many handsome monuments in the Neo-Classical mode, and was adorned with a wide variety of flowers and evergreens to augment the original landscape design. Like Père-Lachaise (to which the remains of persons of distinction had been translated in order to give a secular seal of approval to the place, replacing an earlier desire to be buried near the bones of Saints or votive statues), Kensal Green pulled off a coup when it acquired the bodies and memorials of three Royals: these were H.R.H. Augustus Frederick, Duke of Sussex, illustrious Freemason, his sister, H.R.H. Princess Sophia, who opted for burial near her favourite brother, and H.R.H. George William Frederick Charles, 2nd Duke of Cambridge. Both Royal Dukes elected for burial at Kensal Green in order to be at rest with their morganatic wives (neither marriage was recognised under the Royal Marriages Act[36]), but Princess Sophia had had a child by an equerry, Major General Thomas Garth, and had most of her own fortune embezzled by that curious *eminence grise* of the young Princess Victoria's youth, Sir John Ponsonby Conroy, Bt., who was Comptroller of the Duchess of Kent's household, and called 'King John' by William IV[37]. The Duke of Sussex had another reason for wishing to be buried at Kensal Green: he was so appalled by the condition of the vaults at St George's Chapel, Windsor, that he refused to countenance being entombed there. His niece, Queen Victoria, wanted him to be placed in the Royal vaults, but the possibility of 25,000 Freemasons invading Windsor Castle for the funeral concentrated minds, so Queen Victoria gave her consent to interment at Kensal Green[38], and the Duke's widow, Lady Cecilia Letitia, joined him in the tomb[39] on her death.

The Duke of Sussex had lived on the Continent, and had studied at the University of Göttingen. He gave his support to all the progressive causes of his time, including Abolition of the Slave Trade, Catholic Emancipation, removal of all civil disabilities of Jews and Dissenters, Abolition of the Corn Laws, and Parliamentary Reform. His interest in the advancement of the Arts and Sciences was genuine and enlightened, and lent his influence to promote schemes of benevolence[40]. In short, this true Prince of the *Aufklärung* behaved as a convinced member of the Craft should. He was probably the most intelligent of all the children of King George III and Queen Charlotte. His real intellectual tastes and his deeply-held Masonic beliefs (he only relinquished his leadership of Grand Lodge on his death) involved him with most of the great issues of the day. His

---

32 Curl (2000c).
33 See Curl (2000c) and Curl (Ed.) (2001b) for details.
34 Curl (Ed.) (2001b).
35 Various individuals were involved: see Curl (Ed.) (2001b) 287-96. Among them were Hugh Ronalds, Richard Forrest, the Hon. Thomas Liddell, John Griffith, and others mentioned in Curl (Ed.) (2001b).
36 12 Geo. III, *c*. 11.
37 One of Victoria's first acts on becoming Queen in 1837 was to dismiss Conroy, whose knighthood was Guelphic, and whose Baronetcy dated from 1837. He was rumoured to have been the lover of Queen Victoria's mother as well as of her Lady-in-Waiting, Lady Flora Elizabeth Hastings. In fact, Lady Flora died of a malignant tumour on her liver which had been misdiagnosed as a pregnancy. Queen Victoria's treatment of her was both cruel and vindictive, and does her no credit.
38 Plot 5268/**114**/PS. For details of the funeral at Kensal Green see Curl (Ed.) (2001b) 112-116.
39 Designed by Matthew Wharton Johnson, it cost £312, and was completed in 1845.
40 *ODNB* **ii** (2004) 950-51.

Pl.XI.13 Entrance to the Egyptian Avenue at St James's Cemetery, Highgate, by J. B. Bunning, 1839 (JSC).

'whole heart was bent on accomplishing that great *desideratum* of Masons, the Union of the Two Fraternities who had been mistermed *Ancient* and *Modern*'[41]. The Duke's interests were fully in accord with what one would expect of a well-educated Freemason in the period 1780-1840, and his burial at Kensal Green, like the interments of his fellow-Masons at Père-Lachaise, was wholly consistent with the man and his views. One might hazard the observation that he might have proved an admirable King.

In terms of allusion, British cemeteries are less obviously Masonic than those of France or Italy, although Highgate Cemetery (laid out by The London Cemetery Company to designs by Stephen Geary and James Bunstone Bunning from 1836 to 1842) has its spectacularly Sublime Egyptian Avenue (**Pl.XI.13**) and Cedar of Lebanon Catacombs, all in a powerful Kingdom-of-Death Egyptianising style that would provide a marvellous setting for Act II of Mozart's *Die Zauberflöte*. The West of London and Westminster Cemetery at Brompton, designed by Benjamin Baud, a pupil of Francis Goodwin, contains a highly formalised avenue and circus, with a polygonal domed chapel on the main axis and circular galleries over the catacombs: it appears to be a watered-down reference to the colonnades in front of St Peter's Basilica in Rome incorporating the Pantheon type discussed above.

Entrance-gates and lodges in the Egyptian Revival style at Abney Park Cemetery, Stoke Newington, London, designed by Professor William Hosking and Joseph Bonomi, were more overtly Masonic, and the Architecture of the entrance was archaeologically correct and scholarly. Abney Park was the only Cemetery of the period not to have any part of it consecrated for use by the Established Church of England. It had a complicated scheme of planting by George Loddiges, a complete arboretum in which all trees and shrubs were clearly labelled for the education of visitors, a fact much admired by John Claudius Loudon[42]. 'Churchyards and cemeteries', wrote Loudon, 'are scenes not only calculated to improve the morals and the taste, and by their botanical riches to cultivate the intellect, but they serve as *historical records*'[43]. 'The country churchyard was formerly the country labourer's only library, and to it was limited his knowledge of history, chronology, and biography'[44]. Strang had earlier opined that a 'garden cemetery and monumental decoration... are not only beneficial to public morals, to the improvement of manners, but are likewise calculated to extend virtuous and generous feelings... A garden cemetery is the sworn foe to preternatural fear and superstition...'[45].

Cemeteries, then, were perceived as educational and morally uplifting, and this exemplary concept owes an immense amount to Freemasonry. Walking in the garden-cemetery the uninstructed could learn about varieties of trees and shrubs[46], study the latest creations of the sculptor's art, acquire knowledge of Architecture and styles, and improve sensibilities by becoming acquainted with the iconography of Death and its Symbolism, as well as by reading affecting inscriptions and admonitory homilies. Thus would Benevolence and Wisdom be disseminated (a powerful Masonic notion), and the idea of the Cemetery as part of a scheme of social engineering found roots in Britain as well as on the Continent. The Masonic connections are clear. Ideas of suggestion were promoted by Loudon in his book on cemeteries[47] in which he insisted that the planting of such places should have a distinctive character quite unlike that of the public park or a pleasure-garden: he recommended evergreens, dark-leaved yews, and fastigiate trees found in Italian or Classical cemeteries because of their more Sublime forms, and because they had long been *associated* with places of sepulture.[48]

Opposition and Attacks

The vast literature on Death is an almost inexhaustible mine of material, especially those works in French that put the Anglo-Saxon world to shame. Philippe Ariès[49] has described how, through Masonic ideas, the notion

---

41 Gould **ii** (1884-87) 491.
42 *See* Loudon (1843).
43 *Ibid*. 13.
44 *Ibid*.
45 Strang (1831) 58-9.
46 Curl (2000c) *passim*.
47 Loudon (1843).
48 *Ibid*. 20-21.
49 Ariès (1981) *passim*.

of granting the dead to be dealt with by a benevolent Nature gained strength. He also demonstrated that Roman Catholic writers in the 1870s were fulminating against cemeteries:

> 'the sophists of that shameful age [the Enlightenment of the eighteenth century] demanded... that the cemeteries be banished from the habitations of the living. Concern for public health was the mask behind which they hid... The banishment of the cemeteries, demanded by the ungodly... was... nothing but an empty excuse... Concealed under the guise of public hygiene was an attack on the Catholic Church... The banishment of cemeteries was a good way promptly to extinguish the sense of filial piety toward the dead... To separate the cemetery from the church was to disturb one of the finest and most salutary harmonies that religion ever created... With two strokes of the pen[50], the pagan mind abolished the custom of centuries...'

Furthermore, it was specifically Freemasonry which demanded

> 'the banishment of the cemetery to ten leagues from the capital and the establishment of a railroad for the dead... And people persist in denying the disastrous influence of classical studies...
>
> The nineteenth-century cemetery is the last arena of the desperate struggle between Satanism and Christianity... A nation that forgets its dead is a nation of ingrates.'[51]

Thus Monsignor Jean-Joseph Gaume, in his tediously bigoted *Le Cimetière au dix-neuvième Siècle: ou le dernier mot des solidaires* (The Cemetery in the nineteenth century: or the last word on the fellowships)[52], quoted by Ariès in his magisterial volume. Gaume clearly recognised the powerful Masonic victory in establishing cemeteries and weakening the ties between the Living and the Dead, thereby threatening the authority of the Church.

Certainly the viler attacks on Freemasonry originated from Roman Catholic sources, although others joined in the sport of bashing the Craft. *A Catholic Dictionary*, for example, by William Edward Addis and Thomas Arnold, revised by Thomas Bartholomew Scannell and Philip Edward Hallett, with *Nihil Obstat* and *Imprimatur* of 1950[53], suggests much that would be obnoxious if it were not such patent nonsense. Freemasonry, we are told, is anti-Christian, leads to religious indifference, is politically subversive, has extensive power everywhere, spreads like *merulius lachrymans*, destroys legitimate authority, and brings all governments into contempt. Jews, of course, were admitted to Freemasonry, which prided itself on being tolerant, and Tolerance is not something for which the Church has been especially noted in its history, as Giordano Bruno and others knew full well, so it is but a short step for anti-Masonic 'Literature' to suggest that Freemasonry is a 'secret society' manipulated by Jews, that Communism was an invention of Jews and Freemasons, and that Jewish-Masonic conspiracies could be found everywhere.

Nesta Helen Webster, however, whose background was partly Anglican and partly Plymouth Brethren, became influenced by the writings of Françoise Éléonore Dejean de Manville, Comtesse de Sabran, and convinced herself she was a reincarnation of someone who had experienced the French Revolution and that the cataclysmic events of 1789 to 1800 had been brought about by 'Illuminated Freemasonry' led, of course, by Jews. She was supported by Alan Ian Percy, the anti-Semitic 8th Duke of Northumberland, and by the notoriously pro-Nazi and anti-Semitic Sir Barry Edward Domvile, to name but two. Thus Webster, another Christian, but not herself from the Roman Catholic camp, shared (with many members of the British Establishment) prejudices and fantasies with those who were firmly Romanist, which suggests that deeply embedded within Christianity lies an anti-Jewish seam, no matter what the variety of Christian opinion. Webster, in her *Secret Societies and Subversive Movements*, talked of 'Jewish Perils' and other such poisonous stuff[54], and claimed that the authenticity of *Protocols of the Elders of Zion* was an 'open question': furthermore, she asserted that even if the *Protocols* proved to be a forgery, nevertheless it showed what the Jews were *capable* of plotting, so they could be blamed anyway. A Fascist sympathiser and conspiracy-theorist, she claimed Hitler had successfully halted the Jewish attempt to control the world, and she contributed to Northumberland's violently anti-Semitic journal *The Patriot*, claiming that a perennial 'Judaeo-Masonic' Plot based on international finance was always behind any disturbance or unpleasantness. Since her death assorted conspiracy-theorists, anti-Semites, and anti-Masons have built a vast edifice of nonsense on her incontinent ramblings[55] which detected a Jewish cabal everywhere, using the Freemasons *and* the Jesuits (frequent bedfellows in such scribbling) as a smokescreen for its nefarious activities. Her belief that the Illuminati, Freemasons, and Weishaupt had been behind the worst excesses of the French Revolution convinced many, who should have known better. One of her books was *The Cause of World Unrest* (1920), which claimed that for centuries there had been a hidden 'conspiracy', chiefly Jewish, the objects of which included Revolution, Communism, and Anarchy[56].

The Reverend Edward Cahill, SJ, published several works in which his loathing of Freemasonry was clear. His *Freemasonry and the Anti-Christian Movement*, published

---

50 This refers to the Decree of Prairial, Year XII.
51 Ariès (1981) 546-47.
52 Gaume (1873). There was, however, more than a grain of truth in the essence of Gaume's attacks: by establishing burial-grounds physically unattached to churches, Roman Catholic practices of Prayers for the Dead, etc., were weakened, and there is no doubt the separation was part of a deliberate policy by sixteenth-century and later Reformers to stamp out such practices and beliefs in Purgatory and the like.
53 Addis & Arnold (1957) 362.
54 Webster (1924).
55 *ODNB* **lvii** (2004) 894-5, for a condensed version of the less than fragrant career of an 'entirely unremarkable woman'.
56 Published by Grant Richards. It contained an Introduction by the Editor of *The Morning Post*, Howell Arthur Gwynne, whose obscene paranoia and anti-Semitism earned him credit among the unbalanced.

in 1929[57], described the Craft as a 'child of the Protestant pseudo-Reformation', and went on to attack it from several angles, mostly, of course, because of its *tolerance* in matters of religion: he therefore advocated a counter-movement inspired by supernatural and religious (i.e. Roman Catholic) beliefs. How Voltaire would have recognised the tone! Cahill, as an Irish Nationalist, also claimed that the British Army in Ireland was permeated by Freemasonry[58], and that the Ulster Rebellion led by Edward Henry Carson and James Craig was 'engineered largely through Masonic intrigue'. Whilst Freemasonry was certainly supported by the Anglo-Irish 'Ascendancy', it should be remembered that in the earlier part of the nineteenth century the majority of Irish Freemasons were Roman Catholics[59], including Daniel O'Connell, who was initiated in 1799, the year in which he began his career as a Barrister on the Munster Circuit[60]. However, the Irish Roman Catholic Hierarchy denounced the Craft, and O'Connell (mindful of his political standing) ceased to be a Freemason in the 1820s. Why did this come about? The answer lies in the Rebellion of 1798, the leaders of which had been undoubtedly inspired by the French Revolution: after the Rebellion had failed, the Roman Catholic Archbishop of Dublin (from 1786), John Thomas Troy[61], was placed in the difficult position of defending the Church from an anti-Roman Catholic reaction, so he excommunicated the rebels and then turned his attention to Freemasonry, which he saw as involved with both the French and Irish upheavals. The Archbishop persuaded O'Connell to relinquish his membership, and the 'Liberator' did so, but only revealed the facts in 1837, citing the oaths as his main objection to the Craft. Nevertheless, O'Connell was on record as claiming 'Freemasonry in Ireland' had 'no evil tendency'[62]. A further factor in the decline of membership among Roman Catholics was nervousness following the passing of the *Unlawful Oaths (Ireland) Act* of 1823[63] which prompted the Church to pressurise the Faithful to abandon the Craft.

There had been numerous publications which purported to reveal the intrinsic wickedness of Freemasonry, notably the hysterical effusions of the Abbé Augustin Barruel which appeared in 1797 and in an English translation (1798)[64], but there were also denunciations by persons of religious persuasions other than Roman Catholicism: a good example was the *Proofs of a Conspiracy* by John Robison also of 1797[65]. Barruel and Robison proved to be influential, and their books inflamed anti-Masonic prejudice.

Ever since Pope Clement XII's *In eminenti* of 1738, the first Papal condemnation of the Craft, the Roman Church has been hostile: Benedict XIV renewed Clement XII's denunciation in 1751[66]; Pius VII again condemned Freemasonry (1821)[67]; Leo XII again denounced it (1825)[68]; Pius VIII railed against the influence of the Craft (1829, 1830)[69]; Gregory XVI attacked religious indifferentism, and denounced the toleration of religions by Freemasonry[70]; Pius IX (*Pio Nono*) perceived the hand of Freemasonry behind any radical movement in Europe, notably the revolutions of 1848 and the shift towards Italian Unification, and this led to his denunciation[71] of Freemasonry for conspiring against God, the Church, and Civil Society, and a further attack[72] which accused Masonic bodies of being among the evils from which the 'Synagogue [sic] of Satan' was formed to join 'battle against the Church of Christ'[73]; and then Leo XIII unleashed his vicious pronouncement on the Craft in 1884[74] which specified the types of Humanity that were of the Kingdom of God and those that were of the Kingdom of Satan. Freemasons were *specifically* 'of the Devil', proposing that the 'multitude should be satiated with a boundless license of vice', and their principles lay in what was vicious and criminal. The Craft was denounced in the most intemperate manner, not least because it favoured the secularisation of education, the promotion of civil marriage and divorce, and much else that many would regard as sensible and humane. Religious segregated education controlled by the Church has not been noticeably successful in promoting Harmony in places like Ireland, but then Harmony was not high on the agenda: Control and Power were.

As Gilbert has observed in his measured account of Papal paranoia[75], 'from the tenor of' Leo XIII's encyclical, the Pope was 'fearful of losing spiritual as well as temporal power, and it is noteworthy' that he (the Pope) offered 'no evidence at all – except to refer in general terms to "exceptional and onerous laws imposed upon the clergy" – in support of the damnation of Freemasonry'. The Faithful 'continued to be at once fearful and ignorant of Freemasonry', while Freemasons 'either ignored or derided

---

57 Cahill (1929). He also published *The Truth about Freemasonry* (Melbourne: Australian Catholic Trust Society 1936). The *Truth* part of the title cannot be excused or defended. R.A. Gilbert (*see* Gilbert [2006] 87) has described Cahill, with accuracy, as 'mendacious', whose work is 'replete with misunderstanding and misinformation'. Having waded through Cahill's appalling prose, I can assent to Gilbert's views.
58 It was no more permeated by the Craft in Ireland than it was in other parts of the Empire.
59 Chetwode Crawley (1911) 58.
60 Edge (1912) 38 and *passim*.
61 ODNB **lv** (2004) 450-52.
62 Parkinson **ii** (1957) 107.
63 4 Geo. IV *c*.87 This was actually aimed against violent agitators.
64 Barruel (1797).
65 Robison (1797).

66 *Providas Romanorum Pontificum* (1751).
67 *Ecclesiam a Jesu Christo*.
68 *Quo Graviora Mala*, which held the Craft was a threat to lawful Governments and to the Church.
69 *Traditi Humilitati* (1829) and *Litteris Altero* (1830). It contains 'putrid impiety' among its unpleasant phraseology.
70 *Mirari Vos* (1832), in which book-burning is recommended, an activity concerning which Heinrich Heine warned could lead to the burning of human beings (*see* quotation at the beginning of the Bibliography).
71 *Multiplices Inter* (1865).
72 *Etsi Multa* (1873).
73 So much for claims concerning *Pio Nono*'s 'liberal', 'moderate progressive', and other supposed virtues.
74 *Humanum Genus* (1884). *See* the version edited by Gerald C. Treacy, SJ (Rockford IL: TAN Books, 1978), listed under Leo XIII in the Select Bibliography.
75 Gilbert (2006).

the encyclical[76]. This was largely true of the British Isles, but the encyclical provoked rage in the United States of America, where it was seen as an attack on Protestantism, free education, and constitutional restraints on arbitrary power: in fact a 'Declaration of War against the Human Race'. The Papacy was denounced as having an 'intolerant, persecuting, cruel, inhuman spirit' which flamed out 'as ferociously as ever from its bloody eyes'[77]. The author, Albert Pike, was a prolific Masonic writer with trenchant views, and his reactions were echoed in the outraged responses in many European countries, notably France (where the Grand Orient had eliminated [1877] from its constitutions any requirement for its members to believe in God in any case, but the Holy See condemned the whole of Freemasonry, even though most Grand Lodges severed relations with the Grand Orient de France as a result of its actions in 1877) and Belgium. The hostility of the Vatican provoked anticlericalism in France, so that by 1912 the majority of French Deputies and Senators were anti-Roman Catholic Freemasons. It is therefore unsurprising that in France the secularisation of education, constant attacks on clergy, and curtailment of Parish and Diocesan activities resulted in a country reacting to the reactionary absurdities of *Humanum Genus*[78].

Matters then became truly vicious in France, largely through the unpleasant publications of Marie-Joseph Gabriel Antoine Jogand-Pagès, who wrote under the *nom-de-plume* of 'Léo Taxil': his effusions appealed to those devoid of critical faculties. His considerable output, though lacking in intellectual rigour, was poisonous, and 'Toxin' might have been a more appropriate pseudonym for him: he also used further disguises, including 'Miss Diana Vaughan' and 'Dr Bataille'[79]. Jogand-Pagès's offerings included *Le Diable au XIXe Siècle* and lurid inventions concerning so-called 'Palladiste' Masonry, a Satanist outfit from the evil clutches of which 'Diana Vaughan' (allegedly a 'High Priestess of a Female Masonic Order') had escaped in order to return to the arms of a compassionate and ever-loving Mother Church.

This sort of nonsense was eagerly embraced by the Church in France, and Taxil's pornographic tales of blasphemy and debauchery were incorporated in numerous anti-Masonic publications (which were also, it should be noted, violently anti-Semitic), including those by Monsignor Johann Gabriel Léon Louis Meurin, SJ[80], and Abel Clarin de la Rive[81]. Even though 'Taxil' admitted in 1897 (much to Clarin de la Rive's disgust) that 'Diana Vaughan''s confessions had been a complete fabrication, and that his true aim was to make the Church look silly, a very large number of gullible fools swallowed his drivel whole, and believed in it. To make matters worse, Clarin de la Rive, in his 1894 book[82], published a fictitious so-called 'Instruction' by the American Albert Pike, allegedly of 1889, in which it was claimed Lucifer was God. For those who wish to pursue the unsavoury Taxil affair, the most reliable texts are those by Arthur Edward Waite[83] and Eugen Joseph Weber[84].

The anti-Semitic aspects of these ghastly publications were to bear fruit, not only in the terrible atmosphere created in France and elsewhere in the 1890s (the affair of Alfred Dreyfus is a case in point), but in the lasting effects that were to lead to the enthusiastic rounding-up of Jews in *unoccupied* France after the defeat of that country in the 1939-45 war. Among the most hysterical of anti-Masonic writers was Monsignor Ernest Jouin, whose *Le Péril judéo-maçonnique* of 1920-25 in five volumes persuaded himself and far too many of his readers that Judaism and Freemasonry constituted the Ultimate Evil[85]. Jouin believed that unless Roman Catholicism could 'lift' Christian civilisation to some imagined new level, 'Judeo-Masonry' would drag everything down to the horrors of barbarism and decadent Paganism. He claimed that the 'City of Evil' was named 'Judeo-Masonry', and his views were wholeheartedly supported by the Holy See. Pope Benedict XV, for example, commended Jouin for his work against the 'enemies' of religion, and Pius XI re-affirmed the view that Freemasonry was the 'mortal enemy' of the Church[86]. Under Benedict XV those 'who give their names to the Masonic sect' (sic) by that act incurred Excommunication, and in 1983 (under John Paul II) the irreconcilability of Freemasonic 'associations' with the doctrine of the Church was re-stated, and the Faithful who enrolled in 'Masonic associations' were declared to be in a state of 'grave sin'[87].

Since then animosity towards the Craft is still palpable. In 1996 Freemasonry was once again declared to be 'incompatible' with Christian Faith and Practice, 'whether or not' a Masonic organisation appeared to be engaged in activities against the Church. In other words, it did not matter if a Mason displayed animosity towards the Roman Catholic Church or did not: his adherence to the Craft was enough to ensure the threat of Excommunication existed. That this clarifying letter to Bishops in the United States of America was issued by Cardinal (from 1985) Bernard Francis Law, Archbishop of Boston from 1984, is not without interest, for his actions (and inactions) over the sexual misconduct of priests in his Archdiocese led to his resignation in 2002, after which the Pope appointed him to several positions in Rome[88].

---

76 Gilbert (2006) 83.
77 Pike (1884) 7. Pike's views were as intolerant as were those he attacked.
78 See Flavien Brenier: 'Freemasonry and its Modern Activities' *Oxford and Cambridge Review* (1912). See also Cahill (1929) 24.
79 See Bataille (1896), Vaughan (1895-7 and 1896), and Taxil (1895).
80 Bishop of Port-Louis, Mauritius, and titular Archbishop, no less, of Nisibis. See Meurin (1893).
81 Clarin de la Rive (1894).
82 Ibid.
83 Waite (2003).
84 Weber (1964).
85 Jouin (1920-25).
86 See Gilbert (2006) 86-87.
87 *Quaesitum est* of 26 November 1983 issued by the Congregation for the Doctrine of the Faith, the Prefect of which was Cardinal Joseph Ratzinger, who became Pope Benedict XVI in 2005.
88 See Gilbert (2006) for an admirable summary of relations between Freemasonry and the Roman Catholic church.

A sojourn in any great Library, such as the Bibliothèque Nationale, the British Library, or the Library and Museum of Freemasonry in London, will be sufficient to demonstrate to the most incredulous the existence of a vast 'literature' that is both anti-Masonic *and* (almost axiomatically) anti-Semitic: that a great deal of this disreputable stuff was prompted by attitudes prevalent in the Roman Catholic Church is really beyond dispute, but the *effects* have been worse than unfortunate. That such terrible material played no small part in the industrialised murder of European Jewry can hardly be denied, though there are deniers in plenty, as will be obvious to any clear-eyed observer. In addition, there have been disturbing pieces of evidence concerning appropriation: many hoped the Church would behave differently, but when Pope John Paul II stood between the ruins of Crematoria II and III at Auschwitz-Birkenau and referred to 'six million Poles' losing their lives 'during the Second World War: a fifth of the nation'[89], he seemed to suggest that the Jews were being 'mourned on a par with others'[90], but his remarks have been perceived by some as a distortion of history, for they appear to 'eliminate questions about the Poles' own' attitudes 'towards the Jews'[91]. The spectre of Kielce hovers near[92]. Dwork and van Pelt have much to say about disquieting ambivalences that appear to survive in the Roman Church to this day[93].

Without wishing to labour the point further, four illustrations should be sufficient to suggest to the dullest and least perspicacious of minds that poisonous 'literature' can lead to horrible things. These are the front cover of an eight-page pamphlet published by Librairie Hayard in Paris, dated 20 November 1934, entitled *Le Grand Secret dévoilé des Francs-Maçons suivi de la Liste des Députés & Sénateurs Francs-Maçons* (The Great Secret of the Freemasons Unveiled followed by the List of Freemason Deputies and Senators) (**CPl.XI.I**). This capitalised on the *Affaire Stavisky*, a massive financial scandal which had political implications. Briefly, Serge Alexandre Stavisky, a Russian Jew, fraudster, confidence-trickster, and manager of municipal pawnshops in Bayonne, who was involved with numerous Government ministries, was exposed, and died as the result of what was either suicide or murder, but the ensuing scandal, whipped up by anti-Semitic, anti-Masonic, conservative, Roman Catholics, led to an attempted *coup d'état* and the fall of the Prime Minister. In three riots there were several deaths, and Édouard Daladier became Prime Minister for a few weeks before he, too, had to resign, though he once more came to power in 1938 and was under no illusions about German

CPl.XI.I *Le Grand Secret dévoilé des Francs-Maçons suivi de la liste des Députés & Sénateurs Francs-Maçons* published by Librairie Hayard, Paris, 20 November 1934 (UGLE).

ambitions to dominate Europe. He was arrested by the Vichy Government after the German invasion in 1940, and imprisoned until 1943 when he was sent to Buchenwald Concentration Camp where he remained until 1945, and managed to survive.

The attitude of the political forces opposed to Daladier and which were anti-Masonic, anti-Semitic, and defeatist severely weakened France's will to fight, and led to the inglorious collapse in war and the establishment of Vichy[94]. In 1941 French Government propaganda was overtly anti-Masonic, anti-Jewish, and anti-de Gaulle[95], as is obvious from a poster of 1941 showing the wolves of Freemasonry, the Jew, and de Gaulle threatening a French couple attempting to place a new plant[96] in the soil under the caption 'Leave us in peace!'. Also shown on the attack is a three-headed serpent 'Le Mensonge' (the Falsehood or Lie). It is interesting that the male figure's face looks slightly like Hitler's (**CPl.XI.II**).

Then there is a propaganda leaflet dropped by the Germans over France in 1943. Its message is clear: 'Tsar' Joseph Vissarionovich Stalin[97], with Freemasons' Apron, his arm around de Gaulle (deliberately made small), marches into Europe beneath a canopy of swords held by Franklin Delano Roosevelt, Churchill, and others. The

---

89 See Sergio I. Minerbi in Bauer *et al.* (*Eds.*) (1989) **iii** 2976.
90 Bauer *et al.* (*Eds*) (1989) **i** 147.
91 *Ibid. See* Dwork & van Pelt (1996) 369.
92 The murder of 37 Polish Jews by Poles in 1946: the fact that these were among 200 Holocaust survivors, and that the pogrom in Kielce took place as a result of allegations of 'blood-libel' as spread in 'literature' not unlike that discussed above, shocked international opinion.
93 Dwork & van Pelt (1996) 354-78, which is a sobering and accurate assessment of events that ought to be regarded with at least the greatest of distaste, as well as with considerable alarm.

94 Vichy France, which called itself *État Français*, existed from 1940 until 1944. Its leader was Marshal Henri Philippe Benomi Omer Joseph Pétain, who headed a reactionary programme of the so-called *Révolution Nationale*, supposedly an attempt to 'regenerate' France, but in reality a vehicle for persecuting Jews, Freemasons, Protestants, Gypsies, foreigners, homosexuals, Communists, etc., a familiar roll-call. From 1942, when Pierre Laval directed Vichy as Pétain's mental powers failed, the régime became more overtly collaborationist with the Germans. It is no accident that the French Resistance was predominantly Communist.
95 Charles André Joseph Marie de Gaulle, leader of the Free French forces 1940-44 and Prime Minister of the Provisional Government of the French Republic 1944. He was President of the Fifth Republic from 1959 to 1969.
96 It looks like an allusion to the *fleur-de-lys*, so represented the Old France (that the Republic had displaced) being re-created.
97 His real name was Dzhugashvili: he adopted 'Stalin' (Man of Steel) in 1913.

CPl.XI.II *(left)* *Laissez-nous tranquilles!* French Government poster of 1941 with strong anti-Jewish, anti-Masonic, and anti-de Gaulle messages. The man (whose face bears a passing resemblance to that of A. Hitler) and woman are placing a young plant in the soil that symbolises 'traditional' France in the *fleur-de-lys* (UGLE).

CPl.XI.III *(below)* *Judéo-Ploutocratie et Bolchévisme*. A crude German propaganda leaflet (1943) associated Roosevelt, Stalin, de Gaulle, and Churchill with Freemasonry and Jews (UGLE).

interlaced triangles on the ceiling (*Hexalpha*) were known in Freemasonry, but, conveniently for the propagandist, they are also known as the Star or Shield of David, or even as the Seal of Solomon. The triangle and eye complete the allusions, linking Judaism, Freemasonry, Plutocracy, and Bolshevism in the same camp (**CPl.XI.III**).

Finally, the front cover of a 30-page booklet published *c.*1935 by the NSDAP[98] in Berlin, and selling for 10 *Pfennigs*, entitled *Enthüllte Welt-Freimaurerei* (World-Freemasonry Unveiled) may be shown: illustrated with photographs of Masonic ceremonies, it was intended to connect a 'World Conspiracy' of Freemasons and Jews, the link emphasised by the title-page of *Le Talmud de Babylone*[99] shown behind the blindfolded figure in top-hat and apron with hands held up in submission (**Pl.XI.14**, p.296). The title of the Nazi booklet may have been suggested by the best-selling *Weltfreimaurerei, Weltrevolution, Weltrepublik* (World-Freemasonry, World-Revolution, World-Republic) by Friedrich Wichtl first published in Munich in 1919, with later editions. Wichtl also published works that connected Freemasonry, Zionism, Communism, the Spartacist Movement, and Bolshevism[100]. Now Wichtl was one of the most important of those writers who sought scapegoats to blame for the catastrophe of 1914-18: he found them among anyone different from the majority, and so predictably turned on Jews and Freemasons. He was not the only one[101], however, but the attempted connections between Jews, Freemasons, and World Hegemony owe their origins to France's Third Republic (where Jews were supposed to be giving the orders and Freemasons were alleged to carry them out). For further insights into the realities of this frightful *genre* the writings of Johannes Rogalla von Biberstein are recommended[102], together with

---

98 **Na**tionalso**zi**alistische Deutsche Arbeiter**partei** (National Socialist German Workers' Party), known as Nazi.

99 This appears to be *Le Talmud de Babylone traduit en Langue Française et complété par celui de Jérusalem et par autres monumens de l'antiquité Judaïque, par l'Abbé L. Chiarini* (Leipzig: J. A. G. Weigel 1831). Luigi Chiarini was censor of Jewish books in Poland, and his approach to the Talmud was hostile. His work was intended to reform Jewish practice, but he published the 'blood-libel' of accusations relating to ritual murder among Jews, which shows him as an anti-Semite. See *Studia Judaica* **vii** (2004) 2 (14) s.237-248, an excellent paper by Roman Marcinkowski of Warsaw University.

100 Wichtl (1919, 1921).
101 *See,* for example, Heise (1919), for a dreadful insight.
102 *See* Rogalla von Biberstein (1992, 2002).

Pl.XI.14 Front cover of *Enthüllte Welt-Freimaurerei* combining anti-Semitic and anti-Masonic insinuations (*UGLE*).

those of Cohn[103] and Lüthi[104]. There have been other useful *exposés* of the thousands of vile tracts, booklets, and books which undoubtedly helped to stoke the fires of hatred and attitudes that led to the destruction of much of European Jewry, but the cited volumes contain useful references and bibliographies that help to make an excellent case against those bigots and fools who disgraced European culture. What happened, one might ask, to the European Enlightenment of the eighteenth century? The forces of reaction did it immense damage, and the events of the nineteenth and twentieth centuries almost extinguished its promise of Illumination. The prognosis for the twenty-first century does not look promising either, and for this state of affairs one does not have to look far to perceive the sources from which disaster sprang[105].

Let us turn to more agreeable topics.

The Case of 'Greek' Thomson

Alexander 'Greek' Thomson, the Scots Neo-Classical Architect, probably among the greatest of his time, and a formidable and original designer, has been well-served by historians[106], though not by the City of Glasgow, which has treated his great legacy with a cavalier disregard for its quality that is a national disgrace.

Thomson was unusual among Architects in that he was an articulate speaker and writer as well as a designer of the first rank. He was also very interested in German ideas, something that comes out in his Architecture, for there are clear links between his work and that of the brilliant Prussian Architect, Karl Friedrich Schinkel. Thomson declared that if some inhabitants of a distant planet had the 'means of scanning in detail the features of our planet', they would 'not fail to *assign to the mason the very first place amongst those who live and labour*[107] on the face of this fair world[108]. Thomson strove to understand the 'laws upon which' Architecture rested and often mentioned 'eternal laws' and 'divine harmonies' of ideal proportions[109]. There was a mystical side to Thomson that is undeniable: he was to write of the 'mysterious power of the horizontal element in carrying the mind away into space, and into speculations about infinity'[110].

Gavin Stamp has suggested there 'may be more to Thomson's buildings than meets the eye'[111], and indeed Thomson claimed that the 'form of a temple was not controlled by any utilitarian considerations..., so the highest powers of the greatest minds were taxed in symbols and in abstract forms and combinations of lines which resulted in the sacred architecture of the ancient Egyptians and Greeks'[112]. Thomson designed three great 'temples' for the United Presbyterians of Glasgow, of which only one, St Vincent Street Church (1857-9), survives more-or-less intact. The Caledonia Road Church (1856-7) 'went on fire' (as Historic Buildings often do in Glasgow), so only part of it still exists, and the Queen's Park Church (1868-9) was destroyed in the 1939-45 war (**Pl.XI.15**). All three were constructed on platforms, as in published images of the Temple of Solomon, and there appear to be proportional systems in all three designs that connect with sacred geometry. The extraordinary capitals in St Vincent Street Church may represent an attempt to create a new Semitic Order to suggest continuity with the Temple tradition (**CPls.XI.IV-VI**, p.298). At Queen's Park, especially, Egyptianising elements were well to the fore, and at both Queen's Park and St Vincent Street the towers seem almost Indian, and certainly suggested something more Oriental than Greek.

Thomson employed Cyclopean masonry in the plinth of the Caledonia Road Church in Glasgow, and also for the plinths of his monuments to the first[113] and second[114]

---

103 Cohn (1967).
104 Lüthi (1992).
105 A considerable number is listed in the Select Bibliography.
106 *See* McFadzean (1979), Stamp (1999), Stamp (*Ed.*) (1999), Stamp & McKinstry (*Eds.*) (1994), for example.

107 My italics. It should be emphasized that the German ideas which attracted Thomson (and figures of what has become known as the Scottish Enlightenment) were thoroughly humane, steeped in the *Aufklärung*, and had no connection whatsoever with the sort of stuff embraced by the anti-Semites, Hitlerites, etc.
108 Stamp (*Ed.*) (1999) 6.
109 *Ibid.* 7.
110 *Ibid.* 8.
111 *Ibid.*
112 *Ibid.*
113 The Reverend Alexander Ogilvie Beattie.
114 The Reverend George Marshall Middleton.

Pl.XI.15 Queen's Park Church, Glasgow (destroyed), showing the Graeco-Egyptian-Orientalising style of the building. Bryan & Shear photograph M3395 (*Collection JSC*).

Ministers of St Vincent Street Church, both erected (*c*.1867-70) in the Glasgow Necropolis. Now *Cyclopean* masonry consists of irregularly shaped very large blocks of stone, sometimes approximating on the finished face to polygons, dressed sufficiently for them to fit tightly together, and it is also termed *Pelasgic* or *Megalithic* masonry. Its presence would never be noticed by most people, yet it is difficult to cut and fit together, so why go to all that trouble? It was used by some nineteenth-century Architects to suggest rock-like foundations and very early historical origins, perhaps to allude to the Rock on which the Church was built, and so has a powerful symbolic *meaning* that deserves to be taken seriously.

At St Vincent Street Church the mixture of Greek, Egyptian, and Oriental motifs suggests that Thomson could just as easily have been dubbed 'Semitic' as 'Greek'. The extraordinary tower, for example, has two Classical heads facing each other within a T-shaped opening (a *Tau* cross) (**Pl.XI.16**, p.298), alluding, perhaps, to the Cherubims within the Temple. Furthermore, there are aspects of the tower and its openings that suggest the T can be read over an H, which *could* refer to *Templum Hierosolymae*, THomson, or even Hiram of Tyre. After all, the Old Testament tells us that the faces of the Cherubims '*shall look* one to another' (*Exodus* 25, 18-21) and they are 'within the inner house' (I *Kings*, 6, 27), that is within the Temple: at St Vincent Street there they are, looking at each other within the T on each face of the tower, and the *Tau* is an important mnemonic of the Lost Temple. There is a further factor about this amazing tower: the facing of the structure up to just under the cross-bar of the T is deliberately archaic, of the pseudoisodomic kind, that is

with alternate bands of ashlar, one about half the height of the other, and the lower bands project slightly beyond the face of the taller bands[115]. Again, the topmost stage of the tower proper, under the circular element that crowns the entire composition, has an Egyptianising opening on each face (**Pl.XI.17**, p.299), similar in composition to the shrine-like elements on the tower of the Masonic Peace Monument at Great Queen Street, London. There are many other very odd things about the building that might suggest it was some sort of mnemonic of the Solomonic Temple, but that is a convoluted story[116].

Thomson also employed various devices in his domestic architecture that deserve note: among them were stars on one ceiling and a sunburst on another. Now stars suggest the Canopy of Heaven, and therefore the Covering of the Lodge: in this sense the room becomes a mnemonic of the Temple of Solomon and of the origins of Architecture itself. Stars suggest Fellowship, Divinity, Resurrection, and Light shed in the Night. The stars, therefore, preside over illuminating conversation in good Fellowship, an appropriate symbolism, one feels, for a drawing-room. The sun at its highest point suggests High Twelve or Noontide, when work stops and Refreshment is taken (an obvious theme for a dining-room). The sun also represents Enlightenment, Wisdom, Power, and Goodness or Benevolence, and its warmth is likened to Hospitality, Good Cheer, and the ever-present Deity. It also suggests the Master Mason,

---

115 This, perhaps, was intended as a subtle kind of emphasis, to suggest the H below the T.

116 See for example, *The Alexander Thomson Society Newsletter* **xi** (October 1994) 5; **xii** (January 1995) 6-8, 12; **xiv** (December 1995) 5, 9; **xvi** (May 1996) 15-16; **xviii** (February 1997) 5; **xxv** (August 1999) 5-16; **xxvi** (February 2000) 4-14; **xxvii** (September 2000) 19-27; **xxviii** (February 2001) 16.

CPl.XI.IV Capital of cast-iron columns supporting the gallery in Thomson's St Vincent Street Church, Glasgow (*RCAHMS. SC956560*).

CPl.XI.V Capital of cast-iron columns supporting the clerestorey in Thomson's St Vincent Street Church, Glasgow (*RCAHMS. SC956561*).

CPl.XI.VI Capital of cast-iron columns in the narthex of Thomson's St Vincent Street Church, Glasgow, possibly an attempt to transform Antique precedents, responding to Biblical decscriptions (*RCAHMS. SC956563*).

watching with Wisdom over the proceedings, and presiding over the Fellowship and the Lodge. In such contexts the colours (and therefore materials) of fire-surrounds may also be important. White, representing Purity, Truth, Innocence, and Hope, is therefore the colour of a Freemason's Apron. Black can symbolise Grief, Sorrow, and Death, but in Masonic terms it can refer to Prudence, Wisdom, Silence, and Secrecy. Wisdom in conviviality and guarding against idle chatter for mischievous purposes might be suitable for a dining-room, after all. Thomson designed such rooms, with white and black fire-surrounds,

Pl.XI.16 Two Cherubims facing each other within a *Tau* Cross opening in the tower of St Vincent Street Church, Glasgow, designed by 'Greek' Thomson and probably carved by John Mossman. Note the pseudoisodomic masonry on either side of the upright of the T (*JSC*).

and he was a thoughtful, brilliant Architect, one of the greatest of the nineteenth century: his creations did not spring to realisation without meaning. Nor, it is submitted, did *fabriques* in gardens, nor any work of Architecture mentioned here or above. Unfortunately the evidence of membership of Lodges in Scotland is very incomplete, and we do not know for certain if Thomson was a Freemason or not: many of his acquaintances and contemporaries were, however, including his professional partner, John Baird[117].

Finally, after consideration of the rich architectural palette employed by Thomson and others there is the problem of Modernism: if the vocabulary, grammar, and language of the great tradition of Classical Architecture were jettisoned by Modernism, how relevant can Freemasonry (drawing meanings and lessons in so many ways from tools and implements used by Craftsmen working in Stone and by Architects who could draw and who understood an Architecture that was realised in Stone) actually be today? I would suggest that there has been a fatal sundering, and that an Architect knowing nothing about masonry (usual today), who cannot draw (as he or she depends on computers), and has no grasp of the great and rich language of Classicism, will not be able to comprehend the elaborate moral symbolism of the Craft. As was also shown in an earlier chapter, those Architects trained in the *Bauhaus* in the tenets of Modernism who went on to design parts of the murder-factory of Auschwitz-Birkenau, clearly could

---

117 Other nineteenth-century Architects working in Scotland who were Freemasons included David Bryce, William Burn, David Hamilton, Thomas Hamilton, George Meikle Kemp, William Henry Playfair, and John Thomas Rochead.

have no grasp of the ethical and moral teachings of the Craft that were rooted in a traditional skills of masonry and the Classical language of Architecture. Some have suggested that figures such as the self-publicist Charles-Édouard Jeanneret, who, in conformity with the totalitarianism fashionable in the 1920s, reinvented himself as 'Le Corbusier', was profoundly influenced by the Loge L'Amitié in La Chaux-de-Fonds[118], Switzerland, where he grew up. 'Le Corbusier' was later to describe the ideas promulgated by this Francophone Lodge as providing his guide, his choice of the path he would travel, from time-honoured ideas ingrained and deeply-rooted in the intellect, like entries from a catechism[119]. Admittedly, that does sound familiar, but the linking thread was actually severed: it is very doubtful if it can be joined together again, for the Enlightenment seems to have lost its lustre, and indeed Darkness is obscuring any surviving Light.

Is there a Masonic Style?

There is not much more to be said, for this book is essentially an *introduction* to numerous subjects connected with the Craft. Any of the aspects that have been touched upon could be expanded into a major book, and the parameters have been restricted by the difficulties involved in publishing such a all-embracing theme. The Masonic tombs in the Cemeteries of Père-Lachaise (**Pl.XI.18**, p.300), Montmartre, and Montparnasse alone[120], for which lack of space has prevented coverage here, could fill a major volume, and the mnemonic side of things, the elegiac gardens of allusion, and the iconography would each account for a very large tome. One is conscious of skimming the surface, of merely offering tantalising glimpses, but it is hoped that this study, such as it is, proposes a few vignettes of a vast world that is unaccountably left unmentioned in most investigations. Several standard and (up to a point) scholarly reference-books dealing with Architecture and Architects very oddly do not mention Freemasonry at all, except obliquely if an Architect is known to have designed a Lodge or a Masonic Hall of any quality. One looks in vain for mention of Masonic affiliations in such works,

Pl.XI.17 St Vincent Street Church, Glasgow, by Thomson, from a photograph of the 1870s or 1880s by Thomas Annan, showing the massive plinth and extraordinary tower with the Egyptianising openings on each face immediately under the circular topmost stage (*Collection JSC*).

although in some cases (as in Soane's, as previously mentioned) these are well-known, and there is no reason for concealment. The *Oxford Dictionary of National Biography*, published only in 2004, contains a great many entries on figures known to have been Freemasons, yet in far too many instances there is not a single reference to membership of the Craft, even though such a connection might be important in one way or another. One suspects that, to a certain type of English academic mind, Freemasonry, like Rosicrucianism and Alchemy, is so suspect that it is seen as easier just to ignore it. Yet to do so distorts the picture, and there is no reasonable need to avoid the topic, for there is an enormous amount of material available (though care must be exercised to concentrate on real publications, actual images, and scholarship rather than to make use of any of the peculiar ravings [notably those polluting the

---

118 Chaux again!
119 Birksted (2009).
120 *See*, for example, Normand (1832, 1847).

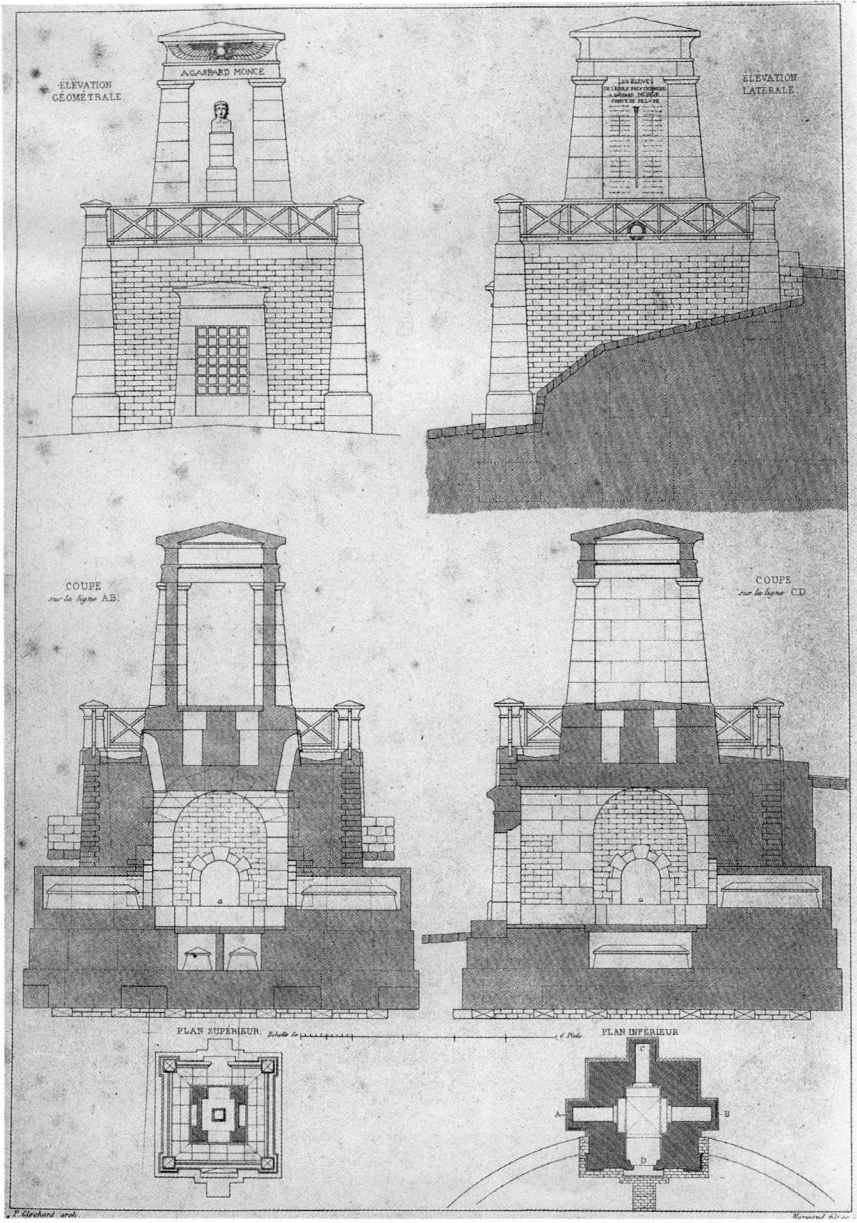

Pl.XI.18 Gaspard Monge's Egyptianising mausoleum of 1820, in Père-Lachaise Cemetery, designed by Clochard. Monge was Professor at the *École Polytechnique*, and member of an élite Lodge associated with the Napoleonic investigations into Ancient Egypt. From Normand's *Monumens Funéraires*... (JSC).

and other attributes do not constitute a style, whilst two columns or two pillars (with or without globes on top) may or may not be Masonic. However, there is a wealth of Masonic jewellery, ornaments, details, and so on that deserves the attention of scholars, and adequate records of these, with illustrations of them, if discussed in any thorough, professional way, would fill several substantial volumes. Clocks and watches decorated with Masonic symbols, for example, may be found in plenty, and the Library and Museum of Freemasons' Hall in London alone has a fine collection (**Pl.XI.19**), as have other major Masonic Institutions, such as those in Germany, Austria, the United States of America, and Ireland.

In landscape-design an elegiac note is struck, and varied allusions are made, as at Monceau, Wörlitz, Maupertuis, Arkadia, and other gardens mentioned above. Those gardens have a grave beauty and serenity, a balance that is also perhaps paralleled in Mozart's music: their eclectic, œcumenical, and stylistic vagaries testify to open minds, a rejection of bigotry and cant, and a celebration of various aspects of past and present. Walking by the lake at Wörlitz, a sense of ineffable loss is experienced: memory is jogged, places and people are recalled to mind, and ideas are floated in gracious solitude. Somehow in those enchanted gardens, sunlit mischiefs and the regrets of farewell are amalgamated, just as in much of Mozart's music even the most mellifluous passages have dark tones and disturbing nuances. The Garden of Allusions, with its Temples of Memory, whispers of some radiant truths: there is a benevolent thread that draws us together, that suggests affection and calm, which flows through those luminous demesnes. An eighteenth-century Garden of Allusions, with all its gentle melancholy and many pointers to Antiquity, Myth, and Perfection, seems to heal tendencies to introspection, and gently reminds the visitor that what is here, what is felt, what is seen, what is beautiful, can be the basis for resignation and acceptance not only of life as it is, but of what it might be: it is wholesome, true, and entirely rational, humane, and natural. It does not depend on the clergy, on obfuscation, on superstition, or on cant. The same spirit that pervades Mozart's music may also be

Internet] that make investigations more difficult than enlightening over the years). Again, the figure of Soane should be mentioned, for avoidance of a consideration of his Masonic beliefs and connections makes understanding his highly idiosyncratic and peculiar Architecture almost impossible, yet rather too many commentators on Soane have been guilty of such avoidance.

In the cause of researching and writing this book, an awareness of certain stylistic aspects has developed, but these are extremely hard to define, for they depend on hints, on feeling, and on mood as much as anything. Overt displays of Compasses, Squares, All-Seeing Eyes,

Pl.XI.19 Collection of watches and clocks with Masonic allusions. Note the triangular forms, Jachin and Boaz, and Masonic implements and signs. Time, through which we pass, is important, and the Mason, setting his alarm clock at night, would be reminded of the Craft and its lessons before going to sleep and when rising in the morning (*UGLE*).

Pl.XI.20 The Eben Mausoleum in *Kirchhof I der Jerusalem- und Neuen Kirchengemeinde*, Berlin, probably designed by Franz Ephraim Eben and Johann Ephraim Eben, possibly with advice from Friedrich Gilly. Karl Friedrich Schinkel admired it and drew it: it is a remarkable example of the stark and primitive Neo-Classical severity of the 1790s (*JSC*).

detected in such places, and helps us to feel kinship with the past, present and future: futilities and dissonances are far away, and can be abandoned as unnecessary baggage.

And what of the offspring of such places, the early cemeteries? There, too, the style (humane, sound, of the earth, with allusions to a great past and to the recent present) mingles formal structures derived from Classical Antiquity with Elysian Landscapes of the Imagination and of Allusion. In Père-Lachaise, for example, may be found a land of austere simplicity on the surface, mixed with hints of the Garden of Memory, the Memorial against the dark bank of foliage, the *Peupliers* of Rousseau's island at Ermenonville, the Acacias of Ancient Times.

In Architecture, laboured Egyptianisms and other exotica, as we have seen, *can* be Masonic, but a truer Masonic style is suggested by the simplified unshowy Neo-Classicism of the *Fürstengruft* in Weimar[121] where Goethe and Schiller lie side-by-side, in the Portal to the Cemetery at Dessau by Erdmannsdorff, in the Eben Mausoleum in Berlin-Kreuzberg[122] (**Pl.XI.20**), and in the ultra-stripped Classicism of Ledoux. Heroic yet humane (like the musical key of E flat Major) might be the best way of describing it, and there is no question that the simple Geometry and the

---

121 Designed by Clemens Wenzeslaus Coudray and built 1823-7, it has a centrally planned interior with a domed lantern carried on primitivist almost Egyptianesque columns.

122 See *Garden History* **xxxv**/1 (Summer 2007) 92-109 Figure 5.

absence of unnecessary frippery or show suggest a style appropriate to a gravity of mind, a seriousness of purpose, and to the virtues of Thought, unassuming Gentility, and Sensibility without Sentimentality.

Egyptian Architecture, with its stereometrically pure forms, blank walls, and massive simplicity, entered into the canon of Neo-Classical design, and coincided with a high point of Masonic influence in France and Germany: it is not surprising, therefore, that a simplified stripped Classicism, much influenced by the Architecture of Ancient Egypt, found favour with the *avant-garde*, many members of which were Freemasons. A severe Neo-Classical language of Architecture was felt appropriate for many institutional buildings after the Napoleonic Wars, for it was not associated with Absolutism, Royalty, Aristocracy, or the Clergy, but with a group or groups that generally lacked clout in previous centuries, but which rose to prominence in the second half of the eighteenth century. These groups might be described as intellectual aristocrats, and would include such giants as Franklin, Haydn, Thomas Jefferson, Mozart, George Washington, and many others. A Masonic Style might include the Constitution of the United States of America; many of Goethe's works (notably *Die Wahlverwandtschaften*); Classical Architecture reduced to its bare essentials in which Geometry and Proportion are elevated above Decoration, and even the Orders are either

Pl.XI.21 The crypt under the rotunda of the Capitol, Washington DC, by Latrobe, showing the primitivist Paestumesque Greek Doric columns, with massive simplified entablatures carrying the severe vaulting system, the Geometry of which derives in part from that of the Roman mausoleum now known as Santa Costanza. The mausoleum-like character of this remarkable space is intentional, for it might have been George Washington's tomb, and has resonances with the Temple and with Freemasonic legend (*Courtesy, Office of Architect of the Capitol*).

eschewed or simplified (the type of Architecture misnamed 'Revolutionary'); or the dark colouring of musical works such as the *Maurerische Trauermusik* of Mozart which are the musical equivalents of green funereal garlands of Neo-Classical cemeterial design and the dark vaults of Desprez or Héricart de Thury.

Few persons realise that the great Rotunda of the United States Capitol in Washington DC was intended not simply as an entrance-hall, but as a symbolic centrepiece under which George and Martha Washington were to lie in death. The Architect, Benjamin Henry Boneval Latrobe, English-born, German-educated, and Moravian, who absorbed advanced Neo-Classical ideas, partly through Freemasonry, introduced an austere, advanced architectural style to the United States. He emphasised the funereal character by creating a crypt based on the general arrangement of the mausoleum of the daughter of Constantine, Santa Costanza, in Rome (mid-fourth-century AD): the Capitol crypt-vaults spring from an unfluted variety of the primitive Greek Doric Order from Paestum, a powerful and evocative arrangement suggesting a Masonic Canopy as well as the spartan character of the Founding Father. The design also relates to those circular images associated with the Temple, with Freemasonic legend, and with the matters referred to above (**Pl.XI.21**).

Now Latrobe had studied at the Moravian School at Niesky, north-west of Görlitz in Oberlausitz, and later transferred to the Seminary at Barby, north of Halle, between Magdeburg and Dessau. While in Germany he was befriended by the artistic and cultivated Freiherr Karl Adolf Gottlob von Schachmann, a true spirit of the *Aufklärung*. We know that Latrobe was indeed a Freemason and that he has been identified as a Brother present at the laying of the corner-stone of the Virginia State Penitentiary[123]. It should also be remembered that on 18 September 1793 Washington, wearing his Masonic Apron and Sash, laid the corner-stone of the Capitol, escorted by his own Alexandria, VA, Lodge No. 22[124].

Of course, Washington was never entombed within the Capitol, but the intention was there: it would have been a powerful symbol for a new Nation to have the Founding Father permanently present in the very centre of the building where the elected representatives met to govern. If these ideas were startling, perhaps even more so is the design of the headquarters of the Royal Institute of British Architects at 66 Portland Place, London: it was built 1932-4 to designs by George Grey Wornum, and it is described as 'a rectangle of Portland stone with a formal front displaying large bronze doors… and an even larger window above. *Two odd free-standing pillars to the l. and r. with aspiring but otherwise obscure statues on top*'[125]. These were carved by James Woodford, and they might suggest an allusion to Jachin and Boaz at the entrance to the new Temple of Architecture (**Pl.XI.22**). This is not as far-fetched as it might appear, for Wornum was a Freemason, initiated 1923 and 'raised' 1924. He was one of the founders of Manor of Bosham Lodge No. 6297, Chichester, in 1946. From 1920 he worked with Louis-Emmanuel-Jean-Guy de Savoie-Carignan de Soissons[126], and together they submitted an unsuccessful design for the Masonic Peace Memorial Competition of 1925, won by H. V. Ashley and F. W. Newman.

So a Masonic Style is an amalgam of many things, but it has a distinctive flavour that can be recognised once the subject has been studied in depth and understood. It is a Style that pervades the last quarter of the eighteenth century and the first two decades of the nineteenth: it is, in fact, the essence of Neo-Classicism, the kernel of a movement that changed the essence of Architecture and much else, and indeed might have gone on changing things had not Reaction, Retrogression, and Bigotry replaced what seemed to be a genuine dawning of true Enlightenment.

Two further designs might be mentioned here in conclusion of this section, although they are only *representative* of a huge number that could just as well be selected to make the points. The first is an Architecture of supreme Neo-Classical simplicity at the corner of the *Rue de la Bourse* and the *Rue des Colonnes*, Paris, developed between 1793 and 1795 to designs by Nicolas-Jacques-Antoine Vestier, based on an earlier proposal by Habert Thibierge. The buildings rest on arcades for which the supports are primitive unfluted Greek Doric columns

---

123 *See* Hamlin (1955) 13, 15, and Charles P. Rady (1888): *History of Richmond Randolph Lodge No. 19* (Richmond VA: The Lodge). Latrobe seems to have known Washington through the Craft.
124 *Columbian Mirror and Alexandria Gazette* (25 September 1793). For details of this and other matters *see* Kennon (*Ed.*) (1999).
125 My italics, but quote from Cherry & Pevsner (1991) 648.
126 Comte d'Ostel, Baron Longroy.

(based on the Doric Order from Paestum), with square columns at the corners (the square echinus of the capitals was a form not used by the Greeks) (**Pl.XI.23**). The combination of arcuated forms with these columns, of course, is very un-Greek, but Neo-Classicism tended to explore such mixes. Some authorities have credited Bernard Poyet (a Freemason) with the design of the *Rue des Colonnes*, dating it to 1798, but the Architect does indeed seem to have been Vestier[127], whose sons, the appropriately named Archimède and Phidias, also became Neo-Classical Architects of some distinction. It would be difficult to find a more uncompromising design, with all the virtues of Antique severity, purity, and masculine toughness, stripped of all fripperies to the bare minimum[128]. The choice of names for Vestier's sons, too, has echoes of the Freemason Batty Langley's sons' names (Archimedes, Euclid, Hiram, and Vitruvius).

Pl.XI.22 Headquarters of the Royal Institute of British Architects (1932-4), designed by G. G. Wornum. Note the two 'pillars' (*CL.CIA, AFK, A83/970*).

The second design is a set of playing-cards published by Rudolf Ackermann in 1819 (**Pl.XI.24**, p.304). Called *Pictorial Cards in Thirteen Plates, Each containing four subjects, Partly Designed from the Subjoined Tale of Beatrice; or The Fracas*, these curious designs, 'by an artist of Vienna' have a strong individual flavour, and have affinities with the world of *Die Zauberflöte*. 'The figures', observed Ackermann, 'are beautifully drawn, the architecture well-imagined, and the *accessories* of every description are introduced with a peculiarly tasteful feeling. The Nine of Diamonds is made to form an Egyptian sepulchre; two obelisks form the entrance, leading to a massive pyramid, which composes the background of the picture, and the diamonds are converted into characteristic embellishments'[129]. Bogus hieroglyphs and winged globes complete the picture. The Six of Hearts has two seated Egyptianising figures holding inverted obelisks (so they look rather like terms) on either side of a portal leading to a darkly menacing Route: the sources must have been Piranesi's *Diverse maniere*, much modified, or similar images derived from the inventions of Le Geay and/or others. The Four of Spades features a canopy carried on four columns sheltering a pyramid and a globe, and the Two of Diamonds features pyramids and a fountain (very Isiac). This odd series of designs contains many allusions to funerary Architecture, to tombs and temples, to Egypt and to Neo-Classical subterranean vaults. Freemasonic stars, a crescent-moon, tripod,

Pl.XI.23 Buildings at the junction of the *Rue de la Bourse* and the *Rue des Colonnes*, Paris. Note the primitivist unfluted Doric columns, the square columns at the corners, the arches with anthemion motifs above each abacus, and the miniature Doric columns under the first-floor windows (*JSC*).

---

127 *Architects' Journal* **cxc** (12 July 1989) 32-41, a useful paper by Werner Szambien and Martin Meade, and *Archives de l'Art Français* **xxiv** (1969) 309-21. For Poyet as Freemason, I am indebted to Cécile Révauger.

128 Curl (2001a) 23.

129 I am grateful to Ralph Hyde for having drawn this and other material to my attention. *See* Ackermann (1819).

Pl.XI.24 Four pictorial cards from R. Ackermann's *Pictorial Cards, in Thirteen Plates...* of 1819. These curious designs 'by an artist of Vienna' have a strong Masonic flavour similar to Alberti's decorations for the libretto of *Die Zauberflöte* of 1791. Top left is the Four of Spades, top right is the Six of Hearts, bottom left is the Two of Diamonds, and bottom right is the Nine of Diamond (*The Worshipful Company of Makers of Playing Cards/LMA*).

square, two pillars, and other familiar emblems can be found in these strange cards. Ackermann paid for supplies for Simón Bolívar's campaigns of liberation from Spanish rule, and published numerous books in Spanish which played an important part in the education of the newly-established South American Republics. Bolívar, like many of the significant figures of the revolts against Spanish rule in Latin America, was a Freemason, and it should be remembered that Freemasonry played an important part in the foundation of the United States of America, in the breaking up of the Spanish Empire in Central and South America, in Nationalist aspirations in the German Lands, in the lead-up to the French Revolution, in the Napoleonic campaigns in Egypt, in the reorganisation of Europe by Napoléon in the early years of the nineteenth century, and in Italian Unification, to name but a few immensely significant facts, none of which would have endeared the Craft to the forces of Reaction. In terms of Architecture, so closely connected with Freemasonry in historical terms, the impact of the Craft during the Enlightenment on design, both of buildings and gardens, was enormous, whilst as has been discussed, many new ideas, such as those connected with the genesis of the garden-cemetery, were largely Masonic in concept. That France and Scotland should have played such major parts is not very surprising, because both countries were tied by systems of historical alliances, and relations between the two were close. It was, however, in England, at the beginning of the eighteenth century, that Freemasonry really began to evolve as a true catalyst for the Enlightenment, and from England its influence spread worldwide (with help from Ireland and Scotland, of course), but it was England, with its growing power, wealth, and energy, that was the most important begetter of Universal Freemasonry, even though the flavour and ethos of the Craft changed in the process of dissemination, notably in France.

The examples cited above eloquently sum up the essence of a visual Masonic style, but, as this book has attempted to demonstrate, there are many facets, many places, and many instances in which the influence of Freemasonry impinges, sometimes very subtly, but on other occasions overtly: that such an influence *existed* can hardly be doubted, and on the whole it has been creative and benevolent. For that, Freemasons in the British Isles, and especially in England, should hold their heads high.

Epilogue

Beneath the conventional histories that purport to deal with the Renaissance, the Baroque, and the Neo-Classical world of the eighteenth-century Enlightenment, lurk strange themes that are only recently being explored in any systematic way, though there is an immense amount still to be done. From the fifteenth century to our era the Hermetic, or Egyptian, tradition began to play an important rôle in cultural affairs. Future Enlightenment was hoped for, and sought, through the 'Hermetic' texts, the Cabbala, and Alchemy during the Renaissance period in the pre-Newtonian centuries: somehow, through a study of hieroglyphs, Hermeticism, and much else, the ancient Wisdom the Egyptians were thought to have possessed would be uncovered. The delvers into Hermetic-Egyptian labyrinths seem to have believed there were unseen irrational forces that had to be recognised as part of the cosmos: by ignoring them it was felt that those of a more rational, 'scientific' bent could miss essentials. Hermetical-Alchemical-Cabbalistical investigations developed a sense of exclusiveness and secrecy, for the sharing of esoteric knowledge with the profane, unworthy, corrupt, immoral, or stupid was seen as far too dangerous. Those who had been introduced to Isiac Mysteries in Antiquity kept things to themselves, for the mystical experiences they had could not be shared with the profane: a similar sense of secrecy was apparent among those pursuing Hermeticism, Alchemy, and Cabbalistic studies, and later among those who moved in Rosicrucian or Freemasonic circles. At the centre of it all was a sense of being guardians of esoteric and ancient Wisdom (how else does one explain the extraordinarily complex sundials found in Scotland, a land not noted for its bright weather?). During the sixteenth century, indeed, something like a radical reformation that envisaged a basic change in society, education, and sensibility, embracing every aspect of human activity, seems to have taken root and blossomed. In the later phases of the Enlightenment the symbolic and allegorical aspects of Antiquity began to be seen as presiding over much that was admired, and the ceremonies and systems of Freemasonry were explored as keys to the understanding of Antiquity itself.

What is starting to emerge is that during the Enlightenment many philosophers and others were thinking of Freemasonry and its organisation as possible means of what has become known as 'social engineering'. Fourier's *Phalanstère* was envisaged in Masonic terms: there would be Harmony between the interests of rich and poor based on Association that would be reached after *seven* historical periods or phases had been gone through. Benevolence, Equality, and individual Interests in the *Phalanstère* as a whole would be encouraged, although enforced Egalitarianism would be eschewed since variety would be possible through differing qualities and abilities of the people themselves, if brought about by encouragement and charitable actions.

Freemasonry, then, was seen as an agency for improvement, for creating an ideal society with buildings and landscapes that themselves would reflect the aspirations of the Brotherhood. Sociability, Groups, Associations, and the Good Fellowship of the Lodge were to play their parts in the foundations of a New Society. The Asylums of Happiness and Prosperity found in the Elysiums of landscape gardens and in Lodges were to become the corner-stones of a new state of mind, and through Architecture and its results (the strongly-built and firm structures of Masonry) not only would the grandeur and lost Antiquity be rediscovered, but an Ideal World based on that Antiquity grow again to renewed Perfection. It should also be remembered, however, that Freemasonry was only one of numerous societies at the time that encouraged exchanges of ideas in convivial surroundings.

Yet the Enlightenment had more of the darker, imagined side of things within it than the *philosophes* of France and the Augustans of England could ever admit: to them, basking, as it seemed, in the clear meridian splendour of Reason, Superstition and Obfuscatory Reactionary Religion were absurd, and had been discarded like some futile incantations uttered by those displaying a lack of rigour in mental matters. In spite of its rationalist pretensions and its confident belief in Progress and in the Perfectability of Man, the Enlightenment harboured, in the words of Paul-Charles-Joseph Bourget, *Le Démon du Midi*[130] (though Bourget suggested by this title of his novel more the vicious cruelties of the Middle Ages). Psalm 90, in the *Vulgate*, speaks terrifyingly of the Demon of Mid-Day in *Non timebis a timore nocturno... ab incursu et demonio meridiano...*, when the noontide demon, bringing fright and a

---
130 Bourget (1914).

CPl.XI.VII HRH Albert Edward, Prince of Wales (King Edward VII [reigned 1901-10]), as Grand Master (1874-1901). Portrait of 1885 painted by Louis William Desanges (*UGLE*).

sudden chill, passed by, something half-seen in the corner of the eye, something primaeval and incredibly old, rustling behind the Acacias and the Bay-leaves, and seeming to darken the sun itself. It can be sensed in the work of Lequeu, in Viennese pictorial cards, in the Kingdom of Death as envisaged by several Neo-Classical artists, and indeed in some Gardens of Allusion, such as Arkadia. Is it altogether fanciful to detect aspects of something more than mere darkness in the chilly schemes of Boullée, in some of the designs of Piranesi, in the stark geometries of Ledoux, in the *bosquets* behind the *fabriques* of a garden by an artificial lake, an *Élysée*, in the bare essentials of the *Rue des Colonnes*, in the dark woodwinds of some *Trauermusik*, in the moonlit garden of *Le Nozzo di Figaro*[131] when deceptively beautiful music holds within it an ineffable sadness, in the desperate, cynical gaiety of *Così fan tutte*[132], and even

---
131 K. 492.
132 K. 588. The libretti of both *Figaro* and *Così* were by Lorenzo da Ponte (*né* Emanuele Conigliano).

in that magical *fabrique* at Schwetzingen, where birds protest at murder? I think not. For all that the marvellous advances of the *philosophes* in late-eighteenth-century France seemed to herald a new world, Rationalism and Enlightenment were obviously not enough. So it was in the 1790s, when the euphoria of Liberty passed to the anguish of Terror: gone was that ancient and longed-for equipoise. From the tenebrous realms of Occultism and Hermetic Mysteries, from the longing for a Paradise on Earth, from the removal of the Supernatural in matters of Religion, something emerged, but it was not Rationalism.

For a brief period in the eighteenth century, Freemasonry was at the heart of much of the Enlightenment, much that was forward-looking, and which promised a regeneration, a reformation of the World. The energetic, scholarly, and earnest searches for Wisdom, to rediscover Antiquity, to replace Superstition by Reason, to better Mankind, and to find expressions for a New Age in Architecture, Music, and all the Arts, reached their zenith in the last years of the long eighteenth century, which might be said to have ended not in 1800, but in 1815. However, the Promised Land did not materialise, in spite of Napoleonic successes which raised hopes that some, at least, of Masonic ideals would be realised.

Eternal verities and ageless serenities are suggested by the splendours, starknesses, riches, and apparent simplicities of many of the artefacts discussed here. The iconographical, decorative, architectural, and allusive manifestations of Freemasonry are only a few aspects of an influence which has permeated European and American civilisation, yet has not attracted the attention it deserves.

In conclusion, it is of considerable importance to record that the immense changes that occurred in the United Kingdom at the end of the eighteenth and the beginning of the nineteenth centuries owed much to Freemasonry, and indeed many of the meetings that ensured those great changes would happen were held in Sandby's Freemasons' Hall. That should be a source of enormous pride for Englishmen, and for those other nations that form the United Kingdom. That Freemasonry was not only a force for Enlightenment, but stabilisation after the upheavals of the seventeenth century and the receding threat of a Jacobite return after the failed Rising of 1715, cannot be doubted. The Establishment and the Craft became enmeshed, and Royal associations were established, not least during the time when HRH Prince Augustus Frederick, Duke of Sussex, was Grand Master. An eloquent testimony to the close connection between the Craft and the Establishment can be seen in the fine portrait of HRH Albert Edward, Prince of Wales in full regalia as Grand Master (**CPl.XI.VII**, p.305).

One last artefact draws various threads together. This is connected with The Medical Society of London, a discussion-group of which one of the original founders was Dr John Coakley Lettsom, and is a Coade Stone medallion the design of which depicts a pyramid of the Cestius type forming the background of the principal

Pl.XI.25 Coade Stone panel with medallion now in the meeting-room of The Medical Society of London. It is marked *COADE LITHODIPYRA 1787*. The (unfortunately damaged) figure of Isis-Hygeia stands on a severe block embellished with an inscription in Greek framed by an *ouroboros* and flanked by sphinxes. Behind the goddess is a steeply-pitched pyramid. The palm-tree emphasises the Nilotic connection. Behind the sphinx on the left is a toppled broken Ionic column, suggesting the Received Wisdom (holding that the History of Medicine began, not with the Greeks, but with the Egyptians. The bridge links Egypt with the Classical culture of Greece and Rome (MC. A3/051202).

figure (the Great Goddess Isis of Saïs, or Isis-Hygeia) standing on a severe block on either side of which is a Sphinx (signifying Mystery) (**Pl.XI.25**). On the block is an *ouroboros* (an attribute of Eternity) surrounding a Greek inscription which translates as:

'I am all that has been and shall be created,
And no mortal has ever removed my robe.'

The bridge visible to the right of the pyramid allegorically links Egypt (note the palm) with the Classical civilisations of Greece and Rome, and the toppled Ionic column (itself an attribute of Wisdom) emphasises that claims for Medicine originating in Greece were superseded by knowledge that Egypt was the true begetter of that Science. These references to Egypt were deliberate, and had great significance in the context of eighteenth-century ideas[133].

It is an eloquent image with which to conclude this preliminary study, which, it is hoped, may prompt further investigations into what is an enormous subject. There is certainly no shortage of material.

---

[133] To most people today, the carefully composed design of the Coade Stone panel would not mean very much, for the Classical allusions no longer have resonances with generations for whom Classical Antiquity is a closed book. It is suggested, too, that the encoded messages in Gardens of Allusion will be equally impenetrable to those *made* (by watered-down education) unaware of European culture, mythology, history, and languages. Lettsom kept up an extensive correspondence with, among others, George Washington, Benjamin Franklin, and Albrecht von Haller, all of whom had impeccable Masonic credentials. He also published works on bee-hives, on the promotions of Beneficence, and on mangelwurzels. *See* Lettsom (1796, 1801) and Lettsom (Tr.) (1787).

Select Glossary of Terms

'...beyond the obvious facts that you are a bachelor, a solicitor, a Freemason, and an asthmatic, I know nothing whatever about you.'

SIR ARTHUR CONAN DOYLE (1859-1930):
The Return of Sherlock Holmes: The Adventure of the Norwood Builder (London: George Newnes 1905) 33.

This brief list is by no means exhaustive, but may help readers to identify some of the more common motifs found in the iconography of Freemasonry, Those who wish to delve into every Masonic or quasi-Masonic term are referred to Kenneth Mackenzie (*Ed.*) (1987): *The Royal Masonic Cyclopaedia* (Wellingborough: Aquarian Press), to Bernard E. Jones (1956): *Freemasons' Guide and Compendium* (London: Harrap), to the same author's (1969): *Freemasons' Book of the Royal Arch* (London: Harrap), to Albert Gallatin Mackey (1919): *A Lexicon of Freemasonry* (London: C. Griffin & Co.), to (1933): *The Oxford English Dictionary* (Oxford: OUP), to Joseph Gwilt (1903): *An Encyclopaedia of Architecture Historical, Theoretical, and Practical* (London: Longmans, Green, & Co.), to C. Lenning (1900-1): *Allgemeines Handbuch der Freimaurerei* (Leipzig: Max Hesse's Verlag), to the same author's (1822-8): *Encyclopädie der Freimaurerei* (Leipzig: Brockhaus), and to my own (2006): *Dictionary of Architecture and Landscape Architecture* (Oxford: Oxford UP) and (2005): *The Egyptian Revival: Ancient Egypt as the Inspiration for Design Motifs in the West* (London & New York: Routledge): a combination of these sources is recommended. Further information may be found in the items listed in the Select Bibliography.

Aaron. The Initiated, Aaron's Rod is associated with the Royal Arch and is one of the Three Holy Things kept in the Ark.

Abaciscus. A square compartment enclosing a part or the entire pattern or design of a Mosaic Pavement.

Abacus. The slab at the top of a capital, crowning the column. In the Tuscan, Doric, and Antique Ionic Orders it is flat and square, but in the richer Orders (Later-Roman, Ionic, Corinthian, and Composite) its four sides are concave (*see* **Corinthian**, **Doric**, **Ionic**, and **Tuscan Orders**).

Abbreviations. A Masonic abbreviation is distinguished by three points in a triangular form (∴) following a letter, and may refer to the Three Lesser Lights. The Three Points were often used by the Grand Orient of France, A few examples are given here:

A∴C∴ Year of Destruction, associated with the Knights Templar; A∴Dep∴ Year of Deposit; A∴E∴ In the Egyptian Year, used in the Hermetic Fraternity. It is obtained by adding 5044 to the ordinary or *vulgar* date; A∴H∴ In the Hebrew Year, obtained by adding 3760 to the ordinary date; A∴Inv∴ Year of the Discovery; A∴L∴ Year of Light (+4000); A∴L∴G∴D∴G∴A∴D∴L∴U∴ *À La Gloire du Grand Architecte de L'Univers*; A∴L'O∴ To the East; A∴M∴ Year of the World; A∴O∴ Year of the Order, associated with the Templars; B∴A∴ Burning Bush (*Buisson Ardente*); B∴B∴ Burning Bush; C∴C∴ Celestial Canopy; E∴A∴ Entered Apprentice; F∴ Brother (French); F∴C∴ Fellow Craft; FF∴ Brethren (French); G∴ Grand; G∴L∴ Grand Lodge; G∴M∴ Grand Master; I∴T∴N∴O∴T∴G∴A∴O∴T∴U∴ In the Name of the Great Architect of the Universe; J∴W∴ Junior Warden; M∴M∴ Masonic Month (March in France); M∴∴ Master Mason, but sometimes also found as M∴M∴; M∴W∴ Most Worshipful; R∴A∴ Royal Arch; R∴+∴ Rose Croix; R∴ ▢ *Respectable* (Worshipful) *Loge* (Lodge); R∴W∴∴ Right Worshipful Master; S∴S∴S∴ Three Greetings, or *Salut* x 3; S∴W∴ Senior Warden.

A rectangle ▢ is a Lodge; two overlapping rectangles ▭ are Lodges. A triangle (Δ = delta) is the emblem of the Chapter in Royal Arch Masonry, and represents a Trinity, The Latin Cross is the Cross of the Passion (and is distinguished from the Greek Cross by having one leg longer than the other three). The Templar Cross is like a Maltese Cross, but with straight ends to the arms rather than V-shaped, The Swastika is associated with the Hermetic Mysteries, A Templar Cross over a Delta is a sign of the Rose-Croix and signifies the Lodge of St John (*see* **Cross**).

Abditorium. A secret place for hiding records, associated with the columns of Solomon's Temple, which were supposed to be hollow.

Abracadabra. An amulet in the form of a triangle.

```
A B R A C A D A B R A
 A B R A C A D A B R
  A B R A C A D A B
   A B R A C A D A
    A B R A C A D
     A B R A C A
      A B R A C
       A B R A
        A B R
         A B
          A
```

Abraxas. The Supreme Deity using the Pythagorean system of numbers: α = 1, β = 2, ρ = 100, α = 1, ξ = 60, α = 1, ζ = 200, totalling 365, i.e. the Ancient Length of Days in a Year.

Acacia. *Mimosa Nilotica* or *Acacia Vera*, associated with grave-markings, with immortality, and with innocence. Jewish priests were not permitted to pass over graves, so it was necessary to mark the places of burials with Acacias. Routes where it *was* possible to walk might therefore be lined by Acacias, which is the reason for avenues of Acacias at Père-Lachaise Cemetery.

Acanthus. A plant (*Acanthus Spinosus*) with leaves that are the model for those in the Corinthian Order (see **Corinthian Order**).

Accepted. Initiated, meaning the acceptance by the Operative Masons of others adopted into the Order, or who have received the Freedom, as of a Guild or a Livery Company. It also appears to have signified working (or 'Operative') stonemasons who had reached the higher echelons of their Craft, so 'Accepted' does not necessarily mean something only associated with 'Speculative' Freemasonry.

Acclamation. Words used in connection with the 'battery' or 'firing', or breaking of glasses after a toast, or banging of glasses or beakers after such a toast.

Acknowledged. Candidates invested with the Masters' Degree.

Adoptive Masonry. Organisation established for the initiation of females.

Adytum. A secret, impenetrable chamber; the Holy of Holies (so associated with the Temple of Solomon); the place where oracles were delivered.

Affiliated. A Mason who joins a Lodge other than that he first joined. One of the Profane (Cowan, i.e. non-Mason) is *initiated*, while a Mason is *affiliated*.

African Architects. Eighteenth-century Masonic research society in Prussia, founded under the aegis of Frederick the Great, a celebrated Freemason.

Age. Apprentice three years, Fellow Craft five years, Master Mason seven years.

All-Seeing Eye. Superintending Providence, knowing and seeing all. It is an emblem in the Degree of Master Mason, for God is All Eyes, and represents T∴G∴A∴O∴T∴U∴.

Almond. The tree which budded was Aaron's Rod and an almond.

Alpha and Omega. The beginning and the end, the first and last (A, Ω).

Alphabet. Hebrew and Greek alphabets have numerical equivalents. As this matter would fill a book in itself, readers are referred to Mackey and Mackenzie for further Enlightenment.

Altar. A cube or double cube with four horns with Bible, Square, and Compasses (the Three Great Lights), surrounded by Three Lesser Lights, from which the grateful incense of Brotherly Love, Relief, and Truth rise. It is sometimes synonymous with 'pedestal', but this is corrupt.

Ancient Craft Masonry. Degrees of Entered Apprentice, Fellow Craft, and Master Mason.

Androgynous Masonry. Degrees of initiation of both sexes, imitative of the Degrees of Freemasonry: they appear to have originated in France, associated with Lodges of Adoption (see **Adoptive Masonry**).

Ankh. A *Tau* Cross surmounted by a circle (☥), used in Ancient Egyptian hieroglyphs, and sometimes identified with the Nimbus and Cross of the Crucifixion. It is also known as the *Crux Ansata* and is associated with Eternal Life (see **Cross**).

Anniversaries. Festivals of SS John the Baptist (24 June) and Evangelist (27 December).

Anno Lucis. In the Year of Light, used in Masonic dates, abbreviated as A∴L∴.

Antis, In. An *Anta* is a species of pilaster used in Classical Architecture to terminate the side walls of temples. When the pronaos or porch in front of the cell is formed by the projection of the side walls terminating in *antae*, with columns between, those columns are described as being *in antis*. The base and capital of *antae* differ from those on adjacent columns. *In antis* two-column arrangements are common in the Architecture of Freemasonry because of the suggestion of the porch of the Solomonic Temple and association with Jachin and Boaz (see **portico**).

Aphanism. Part of the Legends of the Craft in which a concealed dead body was subsequently found or 'resurrected'.

Apis. The sacred Egyptian Bull, associated with Osiris/Serapis.

Apprentice. Entered Apprentice is the First Degree.

Apron. The first gift bestowed on a newly initiated Apprentice. Of white leather, or lamb's skin, it is an emblem of purity in life and conduct. F∴C∴ aprons have two blue rosettes, but those of M∴M∴ have three, and have blue edging and tassels. There are other variants.

Arch of Heaven. An arch carried on two columns, signifying the Higher Degree or Royal Arch. The columns signify Wisdom of the Supreme Architect and the Strength of the Universe's stability.

Architecture. The art or science of building or designing edifices of any kind that gives them intellectual and poetic qualities over those of mere buildings. An Architect is (or used to be) a skilled professor of the art of building who designs and frames any complex structure. An Architect is also the Creator.

Arithmetic. The science concerned in measurement, and therefore in building. Freemasons are required to add to their knowledge, never to subtract, always to multiply Benevolence, and to divide assets with poor Brethren. Many numbers have emblematic significance.

Ark. The chest containing the Commandments, associated with the Jewish Temple. The term is used in Freemasonry to mean the Lodge, or even a chest containing Masonic warrants, jewels, and emblems. It is also associated with Noah and Safety.

Ark and Anchor. Hope and a Good Life.

Arts, Liberal. Grammar, Rhetoric, Logic, Arithmetic, Geometry, Music, and Astronomy, associated with the F∴C∴.

Ashlar. Stone in its rough state is ignorant, unpolished Man. The fully dressed Ashlar, smoothed and squared, represents expanded intellect, controlled passions, and purified life: it is symbolic of the initiated Mason taking his place in the Lodge. *See* **Jewels.**

Ass. Stupidity and ignorance.

Astrology. A system of divination by studying the planets in their relations to each other and to the earth, much used by Alchemists, Occultists, and Hermetic Philosophers.

Astronomy. Images of the Sun and Moon suggest the regularity and precision of Wisdom and Prudence; the Blazing Star in the East is the Divine Being or Providence, the *Hexalpha*, but also suggests the inundation of the lands by the Nile (and therefore Resurrection), and the Seven Stars are the Seven Planets which completed the astronomical system.

Atelier. A French Lodge.

Audi, Vide, Tace. Hear, See, Be Silent.

Aufklärung. Enlightenment: the spirit and aims of eighteenth-century intellectuals in imparting or receiving mental or spiritual Light through Reason, the acquisition of Wisdom, and the study of and respect for Nature. Light in this sense is identified with Freemasonry. *Aufklärung* has a slightly different meaning when compared with the English 'Enlightenment': it refers more to Elucidation, Illumination, Clarification, and Instruction.

Austria. A great many intellectuals and artists were Freemasons in eighteenth-century Austria, notably in Vienna, where Mozart and Haydn attended Lodges. Freemasonry was a major vehicle for the *Aufklärung* in Austria.

Babel. Confusion, where Language was confounded and the Science of Masonry lost. It was the name given to the celebrated Tower which was destroyed by the Almighty.

Baldachin. Canopy over the Oriental Chair in the Lodge: it signifies the Covering of the Lodge.

Beauty. One of the three principal Supports of Freemasonry, represented by the Corinthian Order. It is also represented by the Junior Warden, the Meridian Sun, and the third in rank of the Masters of the Temple. In another meaning, it is an eighteenth-century aesthetic category (*see* Curl [2006a]).

Beehive. Industry and Regeneration: an emblem of the Ark.

Bible. A Greater Light of Freemasonry from which, in the centre of the Lodge, Divine Truth is poured forth upon the East, the West, and the South. It symbolises the Will of God.

Black. Grief and Mourning, associated with the death of the Master at the Temple.

Blazing Star. Divine Providence bringing blessings and giving Life and Light; Prudence; associated with Hermeticism. The Sun, Enlightenment, and Blessings upon Mankind. The *Hexalpha*.

Blue. The colour of the first Three Degrees of Craft Masonry, signifying Friendship, Benevolence, and the Heavens.

Blue Lodges or Blue Masonry. Degrees of Entered Apprentice, Fellow Craft, and Master Mason are called Blue Masonry; Lodges in which the Degrees are conferred are called Blue Lodges, associated with the decorations associated with those Degrees.

Boaz. The column on the right-hand of the Temple as one approached the portal (left as one left the Temple). It signifies Strength. It is also associated with the First Degree of Apprentice, and with the Senior Warden in its meaning of Strength.

Bone. This is supposed to refer to the Builder, Hiram. The word also signifies a core or inmost part. A bone consists of animal matter and the salts of carbonate and phosphate of lime, so obviously is related to mortar and to chalk.

Book of Constitutions. *The Book of Constitutions of the Freemasons* edited by James Anderson, published in 1723 (*see* Select Bibliography). Also known as the *Old Charges*, it contains the Rules, Regulations, and Legends of the Craft.

Book of the Law. The Bible.

Brazen Serpent. Redemption, Mediation, but mostly associated with the Royal Arch.

Broken Column. The fall of a supporter of the Craft. Life ended or cut off, especially associated with the killing of Hiram and the Legend of the Third Degree. Death. Its meaning is disputed: its use as a collecting-box for Charity, for example, would appear to be inappropriate, unsupported by historical evidence.

Brother. The term given by Freemasons to each other. It is also used by members of other bodies, such as The Art Workers' Guild, where females are called 'Brother' as well as males.

Brotherly Love, Relief, and Truth. The three great Principles of the Craft, associated with Virtue and involving Benevolence, helping those in need, and Uprightness. Brotherly Love is the 'Foundation' and 'Copestone', the 'Cement', and the 'Glory' of the Craft.

Burning Bush. The Source (B∴B∴) of Masonic Light, or Truth out of which the Communicable Name of God (*Tetragrammaton*) was delivered to Moses.

Cabbala (sometimes given as Cabala). Mystical interpretation of the Scriptures, and metaphysical speculations. The oral tradition handed down from Moses to the Rabbis of the *Mishnah* and the *Talmud*. An unwritten tradition, a secret and esoteric Doctrine. In the Cabbala words and letters have numerical values in the *Gematria* system. A vast subject, worthy of several volumes on its own.

Cabiri. Inventors of Shipbuilding and Navigation, who founded Mysteries. One of them was murdered by the other three (shades of Hiram), and this murder was commemorated in the ancient secret rites, involving the wearing of an Apron and an Olive Branch. The Mysteries of the Cabiri were still being enacted in the Graeco-Roman world in the first century of our era, and seem to have become identified with Isiac and other Mysteries: they would appear to have impinged on Freemasonry in some way as yet not entirely clear.

Cable Tow. A cord with four tassels enclosing a tracing-board referring to the Four Cardinal Virtues and the bonds of affection uniting the Brethren. It is associated with the Entered Apprentice Degree.

Caduceus. The wand of Hermes in the form of an olive staff entwined with serpents: it signifies the Messenger, Immortality, and Peace.

Cagliostro. Founder of an 'esoteric' Egyptian rite in eighteenth-century Paris in which Alchemy and Mesmerism mixed, and men and woment were admitted to Lodges. It was fashionable for a period during the latter part of the eighteenth-century, notably in France and in the German-speaking lands, although it was also known in England. Cagliostro's Seal was an S-shaped serpent pierced by an arrow. (*see* McCalman [2003]).

Calendar. The Masonic Calendar varies according to the different rites. Usually 4000 is added to the actual date, so 2009 would be A∴L∴6009; Ancient Craft + 4000; Scottish Rite + 3760; Royal Arch + 530; Knights Templar - 1118.

Capestone. A Copestone.

Capitular Degrees. 1. 4° = Scottish Rite, Secret Master; 5° = Perfect Master; 6° Intimate Secretary; 7° Provost and Judge; 8° Intendant of the Building; 2. 9° Scottish Rite, Master Elect of Nine; 10° Grand Elect of Fifteen; 11° Sublime Knight Elect; 3. 12° Scottish Rite, Grand Master Architect; 13° Knight of the Royal Circle; 14° Scotch Elect; 4. 15° Scottish Rite, Knight of the East; 16° Prince of Jerusalem; 17° Knight of the East and West; 18° Knight of the Rose Croix. This system is French.

Carbonari. An Order of Charcoal Burners organised on similar lines to Freemasonry that was closely involved in the ideals of a United Italy, and had close connections with Scotland and with France.

Cardinal Virtues. Prudence, Fortitude, Temperance, Justice.

Carpet. Emblems of a Degree. A floor- or tracing-board.

Cassia. Acacia (corruption of).

Catafalque. A wooden bier decorated with funereal emblems, used in a Lodge of Sorrows. It is also associated with the Third Degree in French Rites.

Centre, Opening on. A Lodge in the Third Degree is Opened at the Centre, for all stand upon the same Level, and every point on the circumference of a circle is the same distance from the Centre.

Cephas. A cube of stone.

Chain. A circle of Brethren holding hands with arms crossed (i.e. right-hand to left-hand of neighbour), known as *chaine d'union*.

Chalk, Charcoal, Clay. The three qualifications for the servitude of an Entered Apprentice used to Mark the Lodge, emblematic of Freedom, Fervency, and Zeal. Chalk is also associated with lime, as used in mortar. Chalk, Charcoal, and Clay (*Kreide, Holzkohle, und Erde*) are old Masonic symbols.

Chamber of Reflection. A room furnished in sombre fashion (often with symbols or emblems of Death) where the Candidate is placed for meditation.

Chapiter. A capital of a column.

Charges. The Laws of the Craft as set out in the *Book of Constitutions*.

Charity. One of the Ecclesiastical Virtues, usually shown as a Personification, with children. A Cornerstone of the Masonic Temple, a cementing Bond of Freemasonry.

Cherubim. The Second Order of the Angelic Hierarchy. Two Cherubims were set over the Ark of the Covenant, covering it with their wings, with their faces looking one upon the other.

Chisel. A Masonic tool, an emblem of the effects of Education on the Mind, for the Mason transforms the rude Block of stone to the finely squared Ashlar.

Circumambulation. Procession around the Altar.

Circumspection. A duty in Freemasons to be cautious in words and carriage.

Closing. The Closing of the Lodge is an important ritual, for the Master alone can dismiss the Brethren.

Cock. Courage and Resurrection, an emblem of the Sun and of Life.

Coffin. The Pastos or Bed, signifying symbolic Death: deliverance is termed Rising from the Dead. An emblem of the Master's or Third Degree.

Colours. Each Grade has a colour. Green = Immortality, Hope; Blue = First Three Degrees, signifying universality of the Heavens and Truth; Red = Royal Arch Masonry, Fire, Ardour, Zeal, Regeneration, Purity, and the Reconstruction of the Temple; Purple = Mark, Past, and Most Excellent Masters, compounded of Blue (=Craft Masonry) and Red (=Royal Arch Masonry); White = Purity; Black = Suffering, Grief, Mourning, and Death; Crimson = Fervency and Zeal, associated with Royal Arch Masonry.

Column. That part of the Order of Architecture that is upright, and supports the entablature. It has a base, shaft, and capital, except for Greek Doric, which has no base (*see* **Composite**, **Corinthian**, **Doric**, **Ionic**, and **Tuscan Orders**).

Compasses. A symbol of the Sun, (like the Pyramid), and an Architectural and Masonic implement. Virtue, the measure of Life and Conduct, the additional Light to instruct in Duty and keep Passions within bounds.

Composite Order. One of the Five Orders, mixing Ionic and Corinthian, combining Wisdom and Beauty (**Fig.Gl.1**).

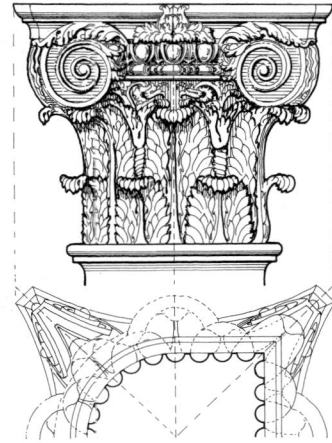

Fig.Gl.1 The Composite capital, a mixture of Ionic volutes and Corinthian acanthus-leaves (JSC).

Consecration Elements. Corn, Wine, and Oil (Health, Plenty, Peace), associated with Nourishment, Refreshment, and Healing (or Joy).

Copestone. The last stone laid. To Celebrate the Copestone is to mark the completion of the Edifice.

Corinthian Order. One of the Five Orders of Architecture, with a distinctive capital of acanthus leaves, stalks, and small scrolls at the corners. It signifies Beauty, and is associated with the South. There are two distinct types, the Greek and the Roman versions (**Fig.Gl.2 [a] & [b]**).

Cornerstone. First stone in the Foundation, laid in the North-East.

Cornucopia. The Horn of Plenty, a symbol of Abundance and Fecundity; it is associated with the Nile, and with the tears of Isis. Associated also with Refreshment and Conviviality.

Covering of the Lodge. The Canopy of Heaven with innumerable stars.

Cowan. One of the Profane, i.e. uninitiated. It seems to mean a Roughmason, Dry-stone Waller, or one not permitted to work with lime.

Craft. The whole body of Freemasonry.

Select Glossary of Terms / 311

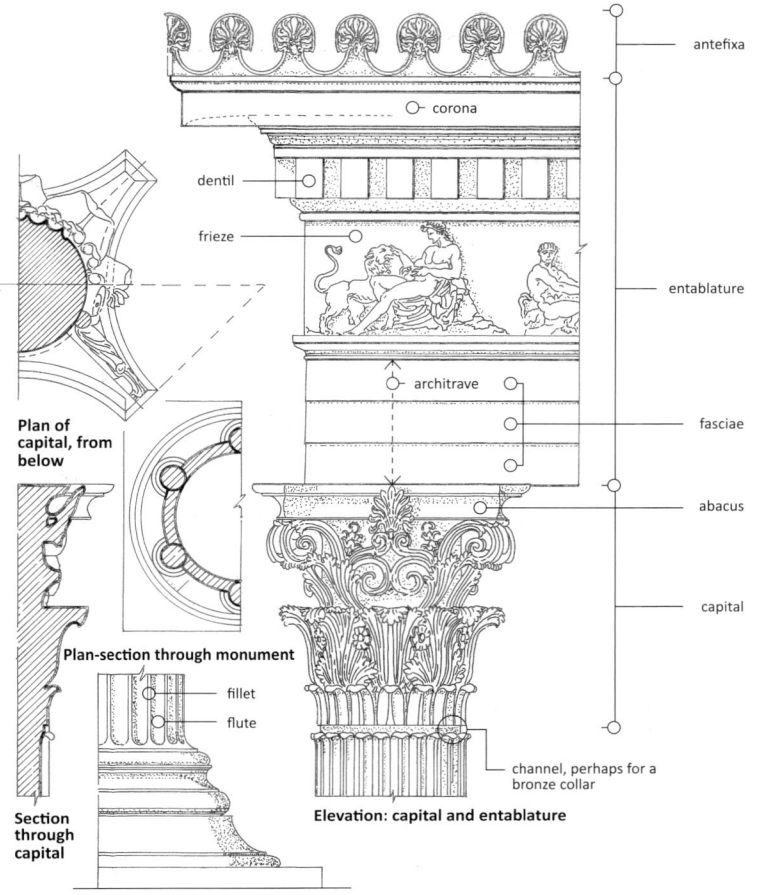

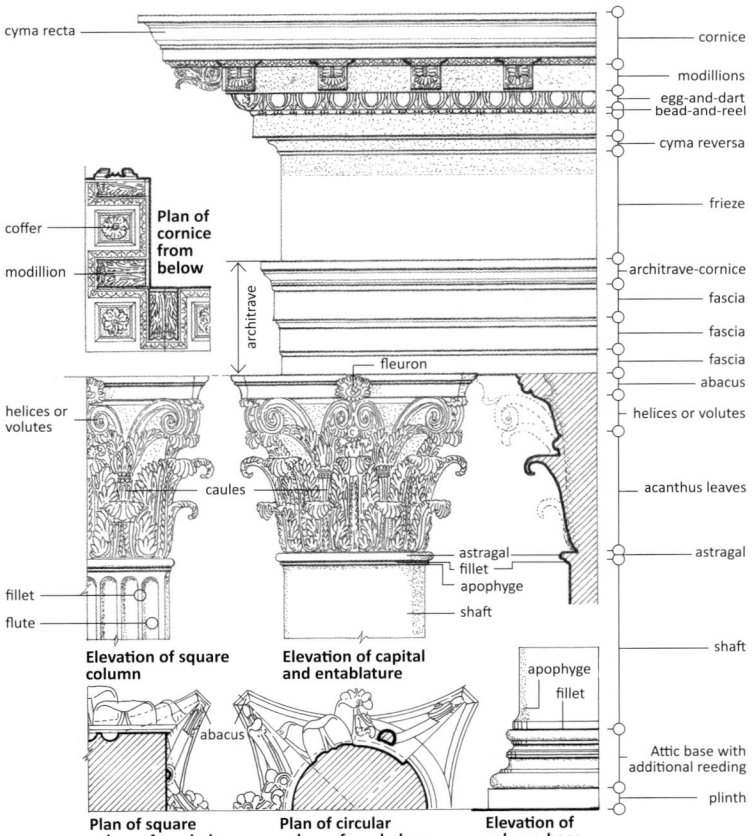

Fig.Gl.2.1 *(top left)* Greek Corinthian Order from the Choragic Monument of Lysicrates (344 BC) (JSC after Normand [1852]).

Fig.Gl.2.2 *(bottom left)* Roman Corinthian Order from the Pantheon, Rome, probably recycled from an early C1 temple and re-erected in the early C2 (JSC after Normand [1852])

Crata Repoa. An Egyptian Rite of Seven Degrees.

Cross. Different types of cross are shown here (**Fig. Gl.3**).

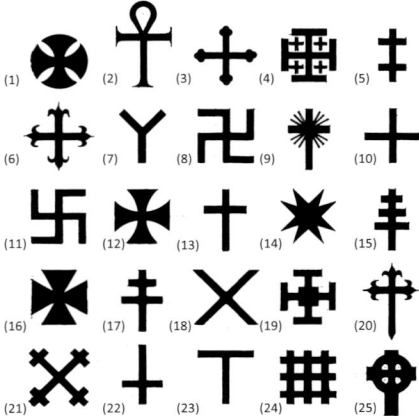

Fig.Gl.3 Cross
(1) alisée patée or Pattée. (2) Ancient-Egyptian Ankh. (3) bottonée or clover-leaf. (4) Crusader's or Jerusalem. Without the four small crosses it is a Potent cross. (5) double. (6) fleurée or fleury. If the centre leaf of each arm is omitted, it becomes a Moline. (7) forked. (8) fylfot or swastika. (9) glory. (10) Greek. (11) Hakenkreuz or potent rotated. (12) Iron or *Eisernes Kreuz* of Prussia. (13) Latin. (14) Maltese. (15) papal. (16) patée formée. (17) patriarchal. (18) St Andrew's or saltire. (19) St Chad's. (20) St James's. (21) St Julian's. (22) St Peter's. (23) *Tau* or St Anthony's. (24) triparted. (25) wheel-head or Celtic. (JSC)

Cross charged with a Rose. Rose-Croix Masonry emblem, usually with an Eagle and a Pelican at its foot.

Crow. A bar to raise weighty stones.

Crux Ansata. A cross surmounted by a circle, known as the *Ankh* (see **Cross**).

Cube. An important Masonic emblem, the Perfect Ashlar. The Perfect Lodge should be a Double Cube.

Cubit. A measure of length based on the distance from the elbow to the middle fingertip. A **Royal Cubit** was the length of the forearm plus the width of a hand, but the Cubit seems to have varied in several cultures. *See* main text and footnotes.

Cynocephalus. Man with a dog's head.

D. Door.

Dagger. Vengeance.

Darkness. Ignorance, a state of preparation, an emblem of Chaos, the state of Man before birth, the state of the uninitiated. The Kingdom of Night, or Chaos.

Degrees. Ancient Craft Masonry, or St John's Masonry, has Three Degrees of Entered Apprentice, Fellow Craft, and Master Mason. There are other Degrees in other rites, but they need not overly concern us here, as they require a volume of their own to do them justice (see **Capitular Degrees**).

Delta. A Triangle (the Greek Δ): it is also the luminous equilateral Triangle enclosing the Ineffable Name.

Design. The search for Truth.

Doric Order. The oldest of the Orders, prized for its sturdiness and simplicity. It is associated with Strength. There are two distinct types, the Greek and Roman versions (**Figs.Gl.4 [a] & [b]**).

Drop Cloth. Raising-sheet used in the Third Degree.

Duad. Two, or a line between two points.

Eagle, Double-Headed, Crowned. With a wavy sword in the claws. An emblem of Scottish Rite Masonry. A single-headed Eagle is the emblem of St John.

Ear of Corn. Plenty.

East. Where the Sun rises, dispensing Light (Wisdom).

Egg. An emblem of the creation of the world and of wholeness. It is associated with the *Ankh* (see **Cross**), with the *Vesica Piscis*, with the Kneph, and with Immortality.

Egyptian Mysteries. Ancient rites described in Graeco-Roman texts, involving the Mysteries of Isis and the final Mysteries of Osiris. They were probably the models for some esoteric Masonic ceremonies, and are described by Terrasson in the eighteenth century, an influential source for Continental Freemasonry as well as for theatrical productions (e.g. *Die Zauberflöte*).

Egyptian Triangle. See **Forty-Seventh Proposition**.

Eleusinian Mysteries. The most sacred and august of the Mysteries of the Graeco-Roman world, like Isiac Mysteries much concerned with Wanderings, Trials, Death, and Light.

Emblem. An occult representation of something by a sign.

Enlightenment. See *Aufklärung*. The spirit of certain progressive ideas in the eighteenth century, with a belief in Reason and Human Progress, and a questioning of Dogma, Received Opinion, Orthodox Religious Beliefs, and Superstitious notions.

Enoch. The builder of Two Pillars to record the principles of Knowledge, identified with Hermes Trismegistus, builder of cities.

Entered. One who has received the First Degree.

Epopt. One who has passed through the great Mysteries and has seen the Light.

Euresis. The discovery of the Body, perpetuated in the Third Degree.

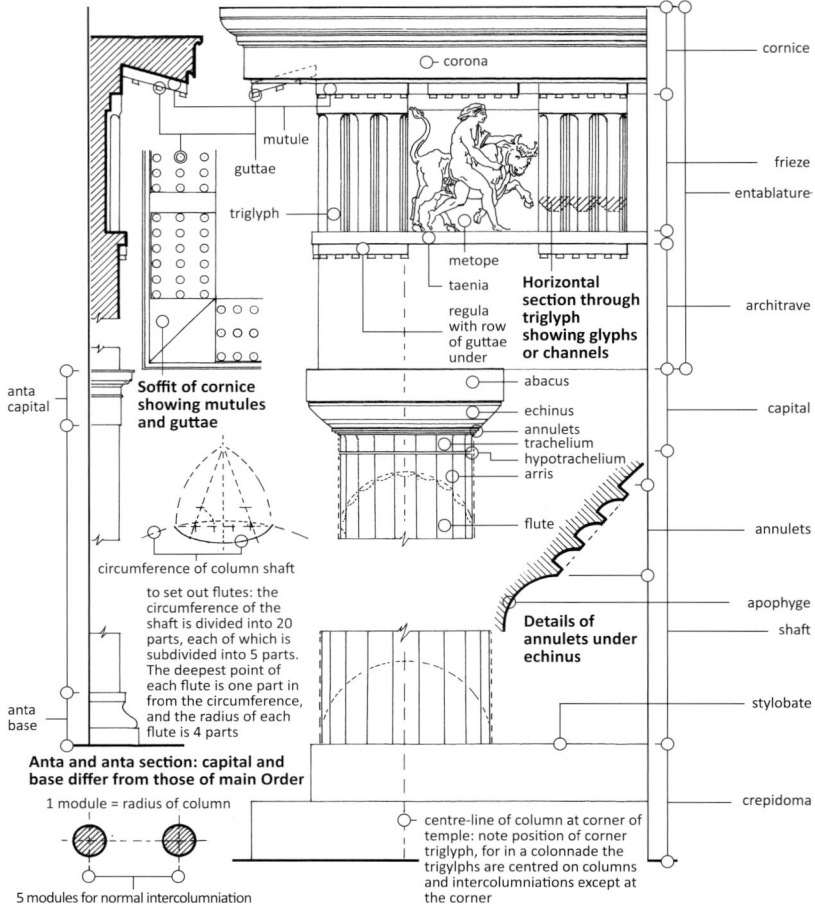

Fig,Gl.4.1 C5 BC Greek Doric Order from the Temple of 'Theseus', Athens (*JSC after Normand* [1852])

Faith. The lowest round in the Theological Ladder, frequently Personified by a female figure holding a Cross.

Fellow Craft. Second Degree of Craft Masonry, also called *Compagnon*.

Five. A sacred number, combining the Duad and Triad (the first even with the first odd, excluding Unity). It represents Light, and is symbolised by the five-pointed Star of the Triple Triangle (*Pentalpha*). There are Five Orders of Architecture, Five Points of Fellowship, and Five Senses (Hearing, Seeing, Feeling, Smelling, and Tasting). Five was also the number of knocks of the Lodges of Adoption, was associated with female Orders, with the Virgin Mary, and with Spirit, Air, Earth, Fire, and Water. It should not be confused with the Blazing Star (*Hexalpha*). Five chords commence the overture to *Die Zauberflöte*.

Fixed Lights. Three windows in the East, South, and West.

Flaming Sword. A sword with a spiral, wavy, or twisted form, used by the Tyler or Tiler when guarding the Lodge.

Flooring. A board or canvas on which the emblems of a Degree are depicted, also called Carpet or Tracing-Board. The floor of a Lodge should properly be covered with alternate squares of White and Black, symbolising the Mosaic Pavement of King Solomon's Temple. The chequer-board pattern refers to the vicissitudes of Life, or the chequered existence, and also to the Trials of a candidate.

Form. An oblong square (rectangle), with the greatest length lying East-West. A Double Cube. It represents the Lodge, the Temple, and the World.

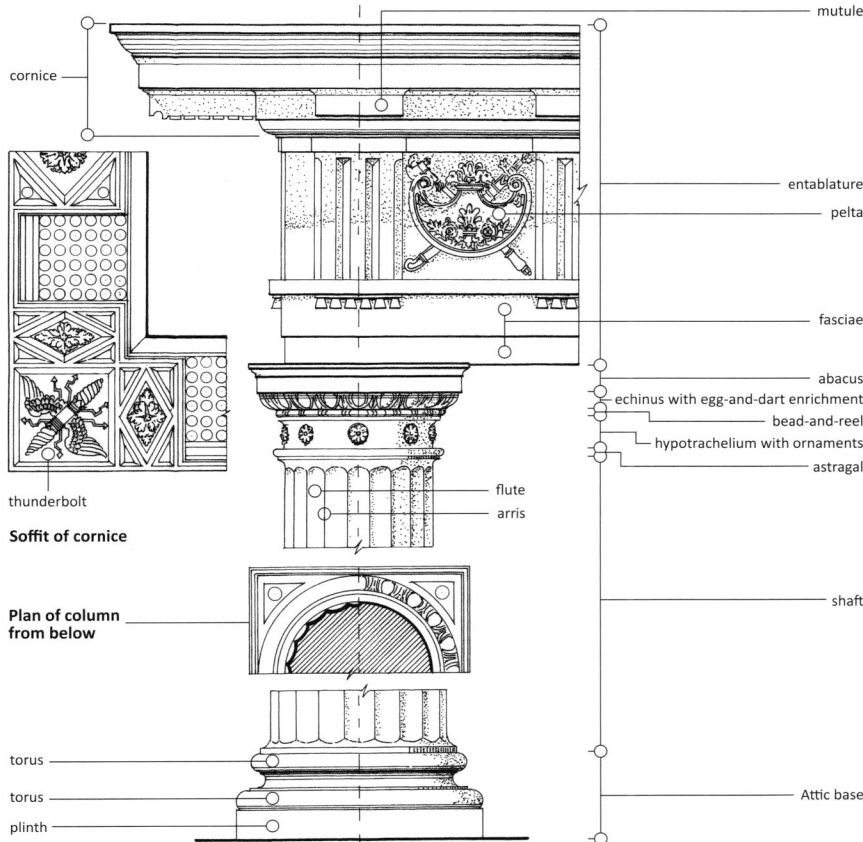

Fig.Gl.4.2 Roman Doric 'mutule' Order of Vignola (JSC after Normand [1852]).

Fortitude. One of the Four Cardinal Virtues.

Forty-Seventh Proposition. In any right-angled triangle the square described on the side opposite the right angle is equal to the sum of the squares described on the sides containing the right angle. This discovery is credited to Euclid (who is identified with Hermes Trismegistus) and to Pythagoras. The 3-4-5 Triangle was called the *Egyptian Triangle* by Plutarch. The base represented Osiris, the perpendicular Isis, and the hypotenuse Horus. The principle is fundamental to Surveying and to Architecture because by setting out a triangle with sides proportional to 3, 4, and 5, a right angle can be accurately arrived at. It is called *Euclid's Forty-Seventh Proposition*, and recurs in Masonic iconography.

Forty-Two. The number of judges before whom a dead Egyptian had to appear. The Chorus *O Isis und Osiris* sung by the priests of the Temple in Act II of *Die Zauberflöte* is forty-two bars long.

Fountain. An Isiac and Marian emblem associated with Purity and with Healing.

Four Crowned Martyrs. Four Christian Masons who were martyred in the reign of Diocletian. Pope Melchiades (or Miltiades) ordered them to be commemorated as the *Quatuor Coronati* (see main text and footnotes).

Fourteen. An important number, including the Fourteen Saints, the Fourteen Days of Burial in the Master's Degree, the Fourteen Pieces into which Osiris was cut by Seth or Typhon, and the Fourteen Days between the Full Moon and the New. The Moon (Isis) at the end of Fourteen Days after the Full Moon, enters Taurus and becomes united with the Sun from which she collects Fire on her Disc during the Fourteen Days which follow.

France. Of immense importance in the history of Freemasonry and its influence on the developments of Architectural theories and a variety of primitive Neo-Classicism, a short entry on France cannot do it justice. The huge contributions of France and of French Masonic Architects in the development of stereometrically pure forms, Graeco-Roman-Egyptian syntheses, the *Elysée,* and the cemetery are discussed in the text. The size of that contribution will be evident in the Select Bibliography. France also produced three of the most influential works associated with the Egyptian Revival and with the spread of an Architecture associated with Freemasonry: Quatremère de Quincy's *De l'Architecture Égyptienne...* of 1803, Denon's *Voyage dans la Basse et la Haute Égypte...* of 1802, and the Commission des Sciences et Arts d'Égypte's *Description de l'Égypte...* of 1809-28 (see **Select Bibliography**).

Freemason. A member of a class of skilled workers in stone; a member of the Fraternity of Free and Accepted Masons; one Free of a Company, Guild, Incorporation, or Fraternity (see the first Chapters of this book).

Freemasonry. A system of Morality, veiled in Allegory, and illustrated by Symbols; a secret or tacit Brotherhood. An organisation based on a Lodge, with unique and elaborate rituals and secrets, with members drawn to it by the rituals and by the significance of the Craft.

G. Equals 400 or, with a line over it 40,000. G is associated with one of the sacred names of God, but this explanation does not hold much historical water, as explained in the main text, because it appears in French iconography, and if the 'God' explanation were true, in France it should be a 'D'. Historically, it appears to stand for Geography, but *Geometry/Géométrie/Geometrie* would suggest the G would be appropriate in English, French, and German, and Geometry is a significant aspect of the Craft.

Gavel. A metal axe-like tool for breaking off corners of rough stone, or for roughly trimming it, with a cutting edge: a stonemason's hammer, called *Hiram* by Freemasons. Mason's Setting Maul. A Mallet. A Gable.

Geometry. The science which teaches the properties of what can be measured, and which enables figures to be set up in precise relation to each other. Geometry is of fundamental importance in Surveying and in Architecture, which may explain the letter G, in part, at least.

Germany. A most important country in Masonic terms, which produced some of the most distinguished Masonic writers, including Begemann, Bode, Findel, Herder, Kloss, Krause, Lenning, Lessing, Moritz, Schneider, and many others. Germany, in the wider eighteenth-century sense, also produced Mozart and his Masonic masterpieces. It also produced Johann Wolfgang von Goethe who became a Freemason in 1780. His writings have Masonic allusions, and are imbued with the spirit of the Fraternity. His influence on the creation of the Elysian *Weimarer Friedhof* (Cemetery) in 1818 was considerable, and he lies with Schiller in the stern Neo-Classical Graeco-Egyptian mausoleum in the form of an Antique temple designed by Clemens Wenzeslaus Coudray (whose tombstone sports the Square and Compasses as he, too, was a Freemason). Also in Weimar are buried the eminent Freemasons Johann Joachim Christoph Bode (his gravestone features a cornucopia and an obelisk), and Johann Gottfried von Herder, who was one of the first writers of the eighteenth century to see the relevance of Egyptian Architecture to the striving for Primitivism. His tombstone features an *ouroboros* (see **Serpent**), a blazing sun, Alpha and Omega, and the words 'Light, Love, Life'. Weimar, in fact, was one of the chief centres of Freemasonry in Germany, as a visit to the churchyards and the cemetery will make clear, for Masonic symbols on the memorials abound. The intellectual, artistic, and progressive liberal views of the princely family ruling Saxe-Weimar created a climate in which the *Aufklärung* flourished. The Prussian Royal House was also closely involved in Freemasonry.

Girdle. A symbol of Chastity and Purity, analogous to the Masonic Apron, and associated with Strength and Power. Graeco-Roman cult statues of Isis show the Goddess with a girdle tied with the Isiac or mystic Knot at the front, just under the breasts.

Globe. The Supreme Being. In Freemasonry the celestial and terrestrial Globes are indicators of the universal claims of the Craft, and of the widespread need for Charity. A Globe is an emblem of Power and Enlightenment, is associated with the Winged Disc with *uraei* of Egypt, and represents the Earth and the Heavens.

Golden Ass of Apuleius. The *Metamorphoses* contain an important story in which many allusions to ancient Mysteries are made, with Trials, Initiation, and so on. The connections with Isiac rituals, with Graeco-Roman Initiation Rites, with *Séthos*, with *Die Zauberflöte,* and with aspects of Freemasonry are interesting.

Grammar. One of the Seven Liberal Arts and Sciences which, with Logic and Rhetoric, form a Triad, the support of Language.

Grand, or Great Architect of the Universe. The Deity, the Grand Geometrician, Kneph the Maker, Demiurgos of the Platonic system, and a double form of Divinity and Humanity.

Grand Lodge. Every Lodge was once independent. Grand Lodges were established to regularise practice. The matter is complex, and the histories of Grand Lodges and the Grand Orient may be studied in several standard works. A Grand Lodge is really a supervising central authority, and is the Court of Appeal in case of dispute.

Grand Master. The presiding officer of the Craft with extensive powers.

Ground Floor of Lodge. The plan of the Lodge based on the Temple of Solomon. It has an Altar (a remembrance of Abraham's Sacrifice, of David's Altar, and of Solomon's Altar – known as the Three Grand Offerings).

Hand. A symbol of a Builder. The left hand is the symbol of Equity.

Harpocrates. God of Silence and Secrecy, identified with Horus the Enlightener, son of Isis. Isis, as the fount, and as Navigatrix, is also an Enlightener.

Hermes. The Messenger, identified with Hermes and Thoth, and by Diodorus Siculus as the Secretary of Osiris. The second Hermes was Hermes Trismegistus, the Thrice Great (note the Masonic and Isiac Three), who invented hieroglyphs, who is identified with Euclid (and hence with Pythagoras), and after whom Hermetic (or Egyptian) Wisdom is named. Also identified with St John as the One who went Before, and therefore is of significance to the Craft.

Hermetic Rite. A system for teaching Alchemy and the Rites of Hermes Trismegistus.

Hexalpha. A six-pointed Star formed of two interleaved equilateral Triangles. It is the Blazing Star, and is associated with Solomon's Seal and the Shield of David. It is called *Hexalpha* because it has six equilateral triangles as the points of the star. It represents the Universe, the Sun, and the Planets. It is a representation of the Trinity, among much else (**Fig.Gl.5**).

Fig.Gl.5 Hexalpha, or six-pointed star, formed of two overlapping or interlaced equilateral triangles. Its six equilateral triangular points give it its name. It is known as the Blazing Star (*JSC*).

Hieroglyph. Design representing a meaning, a word, or a sound, forming elements in a type of writing found in Ancient Egyptian monuments. When they were unreadable they were given a status of awesome importance, and were the subject of innumerable studies of a speculative nature. A *hierogrammatist* was someone entrusted with the keeping of records, and with the superintendence of monumental inscriptions. Hieroglyphs were supposed to have been invented by Hermes Trismegistus.

High Twelve. Noontide, when the Craft was called from Labour to Refreshment. It is referred to in Richard Wagner's *Parsifal*.

Hiram. The Gavel of the Worshipful Master. 'Hiramites' are Freemasons. Hiram, King of Tyre, sent Solomon men and materials to build the Temple. Hiram the Builder was supposed to be the Architect and Builder of the Temple, and was murdered by the Three with Three Blows during attempts to extract secrets from him.

Hochmitternacht. High Midnight, when the Craft was proscribed in Austria, and Freemasonry fell on hard times.

Hope. The second round (*or* rung) in the ladder. She, as a Personification, is depicted with an Anchor.

Hour-glass. The transitory nature of Life.

Illuminati. A Bavarian society founded by Weishaupt in the 1770s that was supposed to be anti-Clerical, and was denounced as anti-Christian. It infiltrated Freemasonry on the Continent, and saw Ingolstadt (where Weishaupt had the Chair in Canon Law) as Eleusis, Austria as Egypt, Munich as Athens, and Vienna as Rome. It played an important role in promulgating Enlightenment ideas throughout the Holy Roman Empire and beyond.

Illustrious Elected of Fifteen. A Degree that commemorates the Fifteen Conspirators, the Twelve who recanted, and the Three killers of Hiram.

Implements. Those tools used in Operative Masonry that are used in Speculative Masonry for instruction. They include the Gauge, the Gavel, the Chisel (Apprentice), Square, Level, Plumb (Fellow Craft), and the Trowel (Master Mason), symbolising the skills and Degrees. The Trowel, of course, was used to lay mortar for jointing, and implies a skill not possessed by a Cowan: mortar binds all Freemasons in one common Fraternity.

Indented Tassel. The rope around the pavement, frequently knotted and tasselled.

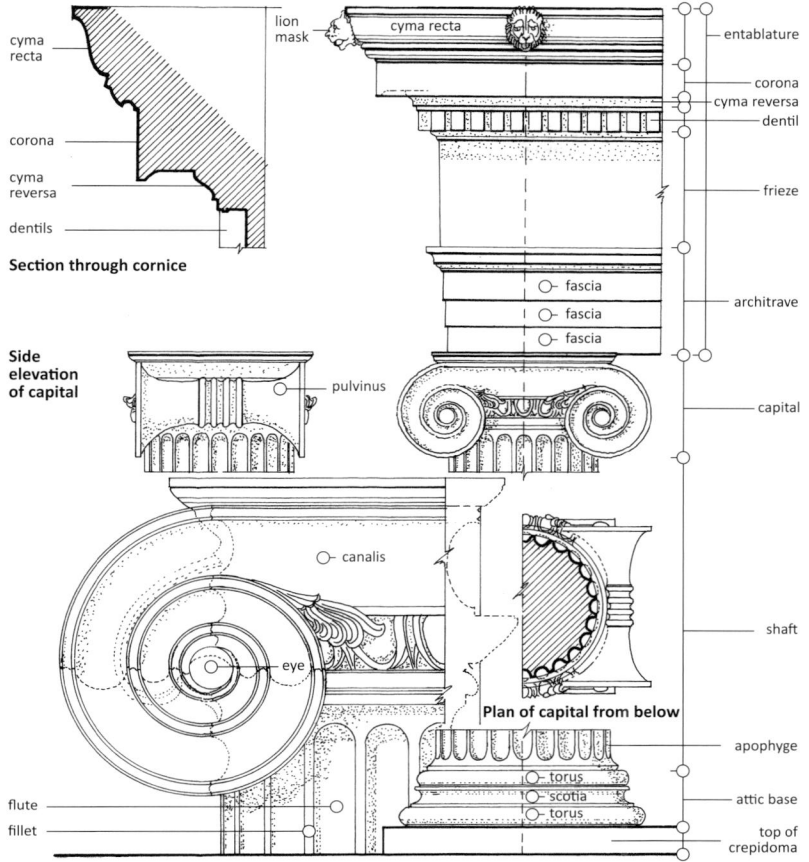

Fig.Gl.6 Greek Ionic Order from Eleusis (JSC after Normand [1852]).

Ionic Order. One of the Five Orders of Architecture, distinguished by its volutes. It represents Wisdom, and is placed in the East. The Greek Ionic Order differs slightly from the Roman version (**Fig.Gl.6**).

Isis. Egyptian Goddess who was sister and bride of Osiris. She resurrected Osiris when he was killed and dismembered by Seth, and she conceived Horus by supernatural means. Her tears caused the Nile to flood, she could blind with a stroke of her *sistrum*, and her fountains could restore sight. Her attributes are the Moon, the Cow's Horns, the Rose, the Fountain, the Lotus, and much else, and she is clearly a forerunner of the Marian *cultus* of the Christian Church. Her Mysteries have interesting parallels with Masonic rituals, and she is discussed by a number of writers in Antiquity, including Diodorus Siculus and Plutarch (*see* Curl [2005]; Witt [1971]).

Italy. Freemasonry was closely associated with liberal-progressive ideas from the eighteenth century, when a Lodge was established in Florence. Garibaldi set up a Grand Orient based on the Scottish Rite, and the Craft was closely associated with Italian Unification, and with French Freemasonry.

Jachin. The name of the left-hand column when viewed from front (right-hand when leaving) of the Solomonic Temple. It is associated with Establishment and Legality, with the Junior Warden, and with the Fellow Craft.

Jacob's Ladder. A Masonic symbol, usually of seven rounds, but sometimes a ladder of five is depicted, although this does not appear to be the Jacob's variety.

Jehovah. The *Nomen Tetragrammaton*, or ineffable name of God.

Jerusalem. The Ideal City, the City of God, Paradise, seat of the Temple, something that is longed-for, was lost and destroyed, but exists as a symbol of the Ideal. The centre of a Labyrinth was termed 'Jerusalem'.

Jewels. All Lodges have six Jewels, three fixed, and three movable: in American usage the movable Jewels are the Rough Ashlar, the Perfect Ashlar, and the Trestle-Board, while in England they are the Square, Level, and Plumb-Line; the fixed Jewels in America are the Square, Level, and Plumb, while in England they are the Rough and Perfect Ashlars, and the Tracing-Board. Why they are reversed is unclear. Jewels are also the names of the emblems worn by officers of the Fraternity as badges of office.

Jumper. A long chisel or lever.

Justice. One of the Four Cardinal Virtues, shown Personified with scales and bandaged eyes, but in Freemasonry it can be suggested by other means associated with Uprightness and by the left hand.

Key. Silence. Also a symbol of the disclosing of the Conscience before the Judges. It means the Tongue, and is often made of ivory. A keystone is the wedge-shaped stone at the top of an arch which completes the arcuated system.

Knee. Knee to knee is one of the Five Points of Fellowship, and is associated with Support.

Kneph. A winged Egg or Globe enclosing Masonic emblems, and surrounded by a serpent; it was the emblem of the Antient and Primitive Rite, and signifies the creative Principle, or the Great Architect of the Universe, the Maker, Divinity, Humanity, and the Divine in Man.

Labyrinth. A symbol of a journey or a pilgrimage or even of Life itself with all its wrong turnings and false starts. Found in gardens and in the floors of cathedrals such as Chartres. Its centre is called a 'Jerusalem' or 'Paradise'.

Landmarks. It was the custom to mark the boundaries of lands by means of stone markers. Columns carrying a canopy, as over a shrine or a tomb, do the same. Landmarks are upright stones but they are also principles. Masonic Landmarks are modes of recognition, the Degrees of Freemasonry, the Government of the Fraternity, prerogatives of the Grand Master, and much else described by Mackey, Mackenzie, *et al.* They are also associated with funerary and commemorative designs.

Level. An emblem of Equality and Probity, and a Masonic implement that ensures accurate Working of masonry.

Lewis. A metal wedge-shaped cramp inserted in a cavity in stone whereby a heavy piece of masonry can be lifted into place. It also means the son of a Freemason. A *Louveteau* means a young wolf: in the Isiac mysteries Initiates wore a wolf's mask, so a wolf was a Candidate, therefore a *louveteau* also means, like Lewis, a Mason's son. The *cynocephalus* figures of Ancient Egypt may be connected with allusions to Initiation.

Light. The object of all ancient Mysteries, in the sense of Illumination. A Lighthouse is a symbol that Freemasons have passed from Darkness into Light, for the Light shines before all men that in Good Works may be seen. Light issuing from a triangle within a dark circle is an emblem of the Knights of the Sun. Lesser Lights are the Lights placed East, West, and South, and are often in the form of columns of the three Orders. Fixed Lights are dormer-windows to the East, West, and South. The Three Great Lights are the volume of the Sacred Law, the Square, and the Compasses.

Lily. An emblem of Purity, and part of the ornaments of the Temple. It was similar to the lotus in Egyptian art, and had profound symbolic meaning, associated with the Isiac religion and with the Virgin Mary.

Lime. A tree (*see* **Trees**), but also the mortar or cement used in building. When limestone (carbonate of lime) is submitted to a red heat the carbonic acid is driven off, leaving quicklime, a powerful alkaline substance which, if mixed with water, gives off heat and forms hydrated or slaked lime, the most important part of mortar used in masonry. A Cowan was a builder of dry-stone walls (that is, without using mortar), and was without the Word, uninitiated in the secrets of Freemasonry, outside the Craft, or profane. His status was not as high as that of a Mason, and the key to his status was his lack of possession of the Word and his familiarity with dry-stone work rather than with masonry strongly bound with lime-mortar. Needless to say, mortar (and lime) implies connections by binding (like the rope or indented tuft), and the attributes of the Craft. Lime in French is *Chaux*, hence Ledoux's ideal town. If mnemonic techniques are accepted as part of Freemasonry, the Lime-tree can be associated with mortar, as can the Lemon-tree, and the Acacia (especially the Locust-tree or False Acacia with its lemon flowers). Significantly, a trowel teaches that nothing can be united without proper mortar, and that the soundness and perfection of a building depends on the proper disposition of that mortar, and so Charity, the Bond of Perfection and Social Union, must link separate minds and separate interests. Well-tempered and slaked lime for mortar was significant in Continental Masonry during the Enlightenment. Lime is also associated with Chalk, an old Masonic symbol.

Line. Any means of describing a straight line by stretching a cord between two points, or establishing a vertical by fixing a weight to a cord. It represents Moral Rectitude.

Lodge. A room in which Freemasons assemble. The Masons assembled. It represents the world and the Temple. It is also the Ark in which the warrants and other precious objects are kept. A Lodge room ought to be orientated East-West, should be isolated from other buildings, and should preferably be on an upper floor. Decorations should be Masonic emblems, Triangles, Triple Tau, Square, Compasses, Death's Head, and so on, and the floor should be carpeted, or designed with reproductions of the Mosaic pattern. Ceilings should represent the 'clouded canopy'.

Logic. One of the Seven Liberal Arts and Sciences.

Mahabyn. A secret word, the origins of which are obscure. It is also described as *Maughbin, Magboe and Boe, Mahhabone, Marrow in this Bone, Mac Benac*, and *Mackbenah*. Marrow may refer to a secret within the bone, and it may, like *Maugh*, refer to a colleague or a partner. One interpretation is that the word refers to the rotten flesh coming from the bone during the Raising of Hiram, or to decay extending even to and within the bone, but *Mahabyn* or its variants do not seem to have a Hebrew origin, although it has been associated with building, the builder, and the body of Hiram. A bone itself has a meaning related to the inmost part or the core, and bones consist partly of salts or carbonate and phosphate of lime, which might suggest a relationship with lime-mortar and the trowel which have obvious Masonic resonances. *Maught* means Strength, and *Maugrabin* apparently refers to a man of the West, or even to an African Moor. It also may signify Universality, in the sense of from the Highest to the Lowest. If there is any derivation from *mahal*, meaning private lodgings (*halla* means to lodge in Arabic), or a palace, and *bin* or *byn* derives from *ben*, meaning an inner or best room, the strange word *mahabyn* may indicate the accessibility of innermost rooms or innermost secrets to those who were initiated to the Degree of Master Mason. Boaz seems to be the word relating to the Apprentice Grade, and Jachin that of the Fellow Craft. According to the Sloane Catechism the third word is *Mahabyn*, and is associated with the Third, or Master's Degree. However, a further intriguing possibility is suggested by the techniques of mnemonics, and the associations of the trowel with mortar. The word *Mahoe* is the name of several trees, and is applied with qualifications to similar plants of various genera: it can also mean a malvaceous tree, *paritium tiliaceum*, and tileaceous means belonging to the Natural Order *Tiliaceae*, typified by the genus *Tilia*, the lime or linden-tree. If *Mahabyn* means something like the inner meaning among trees, then it could refer to lime-mortar, as the great binding agency holding all Masons together, and not used by Cowans or the profane. In other words, *mahabyn* may be a mnemonic for lime, and especially lime-mortar, but this is only a hypothesis which I offer as a possible explanation for a word that appears to be nonsensical, on the surface. My explanation is as reasonable as any other, and it is not insignificant that a trowel is used when jointing stones with lime-mortar. The explanation may be even simpler, however, in that the 'marrow-in-the-bone' aspect of the Hiramic legend may be an Art-of-Memory technique for remembering the Word itself (*see* the main text for further information/theories).

Mallet. A tool emblematic of correcting irregularities, depressing malignity, and moderation. It is often confused with the Gavel, but is quite different, as it has a large round head, while the Gavel has a small one with a triangular pointed edge, resembling a gable (*see* **Gavel**).

Mark. A device given to a particular Mason. It enabled work by any Mason to be identified, and helped in the administration of building contracts.

Masons, Worshipful Company of. A London Livery Company, thirtieth in Order of Precedence, founded in the Middle Ages.

Memory, Art of. A system of mnemonics evolved in Classical times, using large and complex buildings and routes through them as triggering mechanisms for Memory.

Monde Primitif. Antoine Court de Gébelin, himself a Freemason, produced in his remarkable book of this title, an evocation of a Primitive World, with accounts of the ancient Mysteries.

Moon. An Isiac symbol, indicative in Freemasonry of the Light shed in the Night, for the Lodge has a universal meaning.

Mopses. A variety of German Adoptive Freemasonry (androgynous from 1776), found in Roman Catholic States. From *Mops*, meaning a Pug-dog or Mastiff, indicative of Fidelity.

Mortar. Lime-mortar is an important symbol in Continental Freemasonry as a binding agent. The trowel is associated with it, and the Cowan cannot work with lime. Mortar, tempered and slaked, is a significant symbol, and indicates that passions and fiery temperaments are under control, transformed by the process. Untempered mortar indicates that the lessons of the Craft have not been fully assimilated. The symbolism is complex and varied.

Mosaic Pavement. A floor of small differently coloured stones. The term seems to have been applied to the chequerboard pattern of black and white squares on floors, but this usage must have started with a misunderstanding, for chequerboards have large slabs rather than small *tesserae*.

Nine. A significant Masonic number, involving the important 3, consecrated to the spheres (360° = 3 and 6 and 0 = 9).

Noah. Involved in rescuing with the Ark, and keeper of a secret, who was 'raised' by his sons.

North. Darkness and Night. Ignorance.

Numbers. Pythagorean number systems are far too complex to be discussed here, and excessive time spent on them can soften the brain. Only a few numbers will be mentioned. Equal numbers are female and odd ones are male because even ones can be divided, so suggest generation. One equals God, the point within the circle, Love, Concord, Piety, Fidelity, etc., because it is indivisible. It is associated with Harmony, preserving Light, and Friendship. Two, on the other hand, was evil and dark. Three was again Harmony, Friendship, Concord, Peace, and Temperance, and is regarded as perfect. Four was sacred to the Name of God (the *tetragrammaton*). Five was Light, Nature, Marriage (female = two plus male = three), and is associated with the Triple Triangle or *Pentalpha* (it is a significant beginning of the overture to *Die Zauberflöte*). Six was Health and Justice, and was perfect because it could be divided by both two and three and because one, two and three added equal six (*aliquot* parts). Seven was associated with Creation. Eight was a cube (two x two x two), and meant Friendship, Prudence, Justice, Counsel; it was associated with Nature and Equality. Nine was Perfection, and was three + three + three or three x three as well as the gestation period in months for humans. Ten, as the union of one, two, three, and four was Perfect and represented Heaven.

The first three numbers (one, two, three) are called Monad, Duad, Triad. The Monad is male and creative. The Duad is female, ever-changing, and is matter capable of form. Monad plus Duad equals Triad, which is the world formed by the creative principle out of matter, and is the basis for the Pythagorean right-angled triangle and the squaring of the sides. The Isiac connections are clear.

Obelisk. A monolith, square on plan, tapering slightly towards the top, which terminates in a small pyramid or *pyramidion*. Hieroglyphs were carved on all four faces. Obelisks were associated with the sun, were both phallic and gnomons, and were symbols of Continuity, Power, Regeneration, and Stability. As markers of axial routes they appear in Masonic iconography, usually in association with Continental Masters' Degrees (*see* Curl [2005]; Curran, Grafton, Long, & Weiss [2009]).

Oblong Square. A parallelogram or four-sided figure, all of which angles are equal, with two sides longer than the others. A symbol of the Lodge, the Ark, the Temple.

Octagon. Some representations of the Temple showed circular or polygonal buildings, clearly derived from the Dome of the Rock, the Holy Sepulchre in Jerusalem, and the Pantheon. Octagons were used in this respect, and also suggest the Crosses of the Knights of St John and of the Templars, as well as the Eight Beatitudes.

Ogee. An arched form composed of two convex and two concave curves, rising to a sharp point, like two *cyma reversa* sections meeting at a point. It occurs in various eighteenth- and nineteenth-century designs with Masonic connections (often in association with Egyptian or Classical elements, which is odd, for the ogee arch is Gothic), but its precise meaning remains obscure. It *may* refer to the Outside Guardian (O∴G∴). It is found in the cloister of the 'Mosque' at Schwetzingen, one of the largest and finest garden *fabriques* of the eighteenth century.

Operative Mason. A stonemason who practises his craft by working with stone, as opposed to a 'Speculative' Mason. However, this Operative-Speculative usage is questioned by several scholars.

Orders of Architecture. There are *eight* distinct types of Classical Order: Tuscan, Greek Doric, Roman Doric, Greek Ionic, Roman Ionic, Greek Corinthian, Roman Corinthian, and Composite, though before the systematic rediscovery of Greek Architecture in the eighteenth and early nineteenth centuries, the canonical Five Orders (Tuscan, Doric, Ionic, Corinthian, and Composite) were accepted. An Order consists of bases (except for Greek Doric which has no base), shafts, capitals, and entablature. Columns include the bases, shafts, and capitals, and entablatures consist of architraves, friezes, and cornices (*see* **Composite**, **Corinthian**, **Doric**, **Ionic**, and **Tuscan**).

Ordo ab Chao. Order from Chaos, an important Masonic motto, once suggesting the Art of Architecture itself.

Orient. The East. The supreme Masonic bodies on the Continent are called Grand Orients.

Oriflamme. The Royal Standard of France based on the banner of the Basilica of St Denis, of red silk, it was a banderole of two or three points, sometimes powdered with golden flakes of fire. Various Masonic bodies possess banners on poles or lances which are called Oriflammes, and have tassels of silk as well.

Ornaments. Mosaic Pavement, Indented Tassel, and Blazing Star.

Orphic Mysteries. Further Mysteries of the Graeco-Roman world, again involving remembrance of a murder (this time of Bacchus). Interesting from our point of view was the crowning of Initiates with poplar and the carrying of Serpents in the rituals.

Osiris. Husband/brother of Isis, he was infinitely wise, went on journeys, was murdered and dismembered by Seth (Typhon), put together again, and resurrected by Isis. Osiris is the lost Sun, Monarch of the Infernal Regions, Supreme Judge, and the Embodiment of Wisdom. His emblem was the sun, and goodness was his manifestation. Like Isis, he is of great importance in Freemasonry, notably in Continental rites, while the Egyptian Rites of the eighteenth century accord him great significance. One of his symbols is the Apis Bull. In the Graeco-Roman world he became Serapis, and his temples often had a Lady Chapel attached which was dedicated to Isis.

Ouroboros. *See* **Serpent**.

Paestum Doric. Doric Order found at the Greek temples at Paestum, south of Naples: its proportions contributed to its robust, primitivist appearance, which appealed to advanced Neo-Classicists of the late eighteenth and early nineteenth centuries (**Fig.Gl.7**).

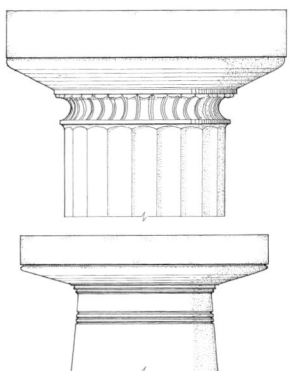

Fig.Gl.7 Paestum Doric capitals (*JSC after Normand* [1852]).

Parallel Lines. SS John the Baptist and Evangelist, the Patrons of Masonry.

Pastos. A chamber or a couch, the Ark, a coffin, emblems of Mortality. Aspirants in Antiquity were sometimes placed in a cell called a *Pastos* which commemorated the death of a god.

Pedal. Feet (*pes* = foot) planted firmly on the principles of Right cause a man to be upright and just. It symbolises Justice.

Pedestals. When the columns of Wisdom (East), Strength (West), and Beauty (South) are not erected in the Lodge, the pedestals represent them, and at these the three superior Officers sit.

Pediment. The triangular gable set over columns or pilasters. The form makes it Masonically significant. *Segmental* pediments were associated particularly during the Roman Empire with Isiac cults (the crescent-moon bow of Diana, horned form, etc.), and recur in Masonic Architecture and Art (e.g. the works of Soane).

Pelican. The Redeemer, or Charity.

Pentalpha. A geometrical figure with five points formed of three triangles. It must not be confused with the *Hexalpha* or Blazing Star, although on the Continent it often is found as such. It is an emblem of Air, Earth, Fire, Spirit, and Water, of the Five Senses, of the Five Wounds of Christ, and has long been regarded as a Talisman for protection against Evil and Ill-Health (**Fig.Gl.8**).

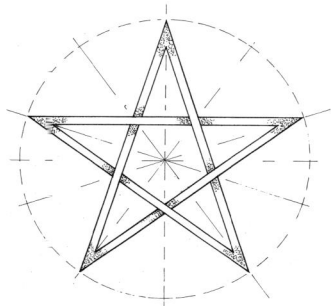

Fig.Gl.8 Pentalpha or Five-Pointed Star, really three identical triangles, but usually shown interlaced (JSC).

Perpendicular. Upright and erect, Justice, Fortitude, Prudence, Temperance, associated with the Plumb, Level, Triangle, and Square.

Phallus. The erect male member, associated with the Gnomon, the Obelisk, the Pillar, the Column, and Point within a Circle.

Pickaxe. Working tool to lift stones and break them. An emblem in Royal Arch Freemasonry.

Piece of Architecture. Any literary work dealing with Freemasonry.

Pillar. Obelisks. Free-standing vertical elements, not to be confused with columns (which would conform to an Order).

Pillars of the Porch. The two of brass erected at the Solomonic Temple by Hiram, with capitals of lily-work (lotus), one called Jachin (God-established) and the other Boaz (in Strength). These did *not*, it seems, have globes on top. Between these Pillars the Fellow Craft is encouraged to seek and acquire knowledge.

Plumb. An instrument for erecting perpendicular lines consisting of a cord and a weight. It symbolises upright codes of conduct.

Points of Fellowship. The Pentalpha or Triple Triangle.

Point within a Circle. The individual Brother within the boundaries of his duty. The phallus, or fecundity. The Universe.

Pomegranate. Used on the capitals of the Solomonic Temple 'pillars' (Jachin and Boaz), it appears to have been associated with Fruitfulness.

Pommel. A sphere on a column.

Portico. Covered ambulatory consisting of a series of columns placed at regular intervals supporting a roof, normally attached as a kind of colonnaded porch to a building. The volume so created can be open or partly enclosed at the sides, stand before a building such as a Temple, and often have a pediment over the front, in which case it is described as a *temple-front*. A Classical portico is found as:

engaged: with the ensemble of columns, entablature, and pediment embedded in the front wall;

in antis: with the columns set in a line between the projecting walls enclosing the sides of the portico (i.e. between the *antae*);

prostyle: with the columns set in a line standing before and detached from the front wall (**Fig.Gl.9**).

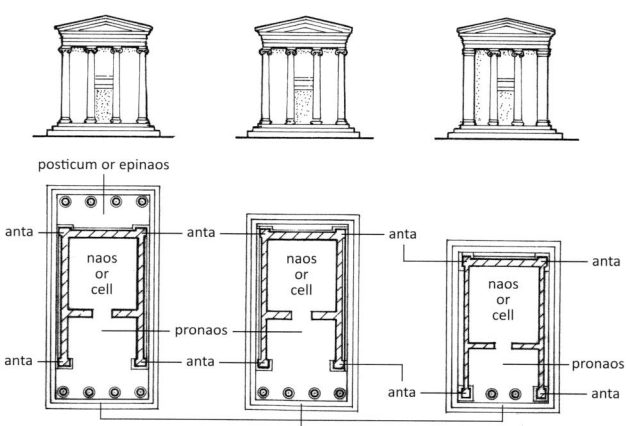

(*left*) amphi-prostyle tetrastyle, or amphi tetra-prostyle, i.e. with four columns standing in front of and at each end of the cell

(*middle*) prostyle tetrastyle, or tetra-prostyle, i.e. with four columns standing in front of the cell

(*right*) distyle *in antis*, i.e. with two columns standing in front of the cell set between the *antae* terminating the projecting cell walls. It is an arrangement found only in small temples, tombs, or shrines in Antiquity, but was subsequently widely used

Fig.Gl.9 Column arrangements in temples (JSC).

Prudence. One of the Four Cardinal Virtues.

Prussia. An important country in the history of Freemasonry, not least because of the membership of the Fraternity of several members of the Royal House. King Friedrich William III, for example, promoted much building (the masterpieces of Schinkel), and was patron to many painters and sculptors. Thanks to Royal Patronage, the famous expedition of Dr Karl Richard Lepsius to Egypt took place in 1842-5, and produced the beautiful and magisterial *Denkmäler aus Aegypten und Aethiopien*, published in Berlin in 1849-59, one of the greatest works ever devoted to a detailed study of Antique remains.

Pythagoras. Students of Pythagoras and his system of numbers (as Sage of Croton) had to go through various tests and trials that sound something like the Isiac and other Mysteries. Indeed the various Institutions established by Pythagoras resembled

Masonic themes in many ways. There were secret signs, much symbolism, and admonitory injunctions to keep silent. Right angles were moral and just; equilateral triangles were God, Light, and Truth; the Square was Divine; the Cube was the mind of Man, purified by Piety; the Point within the Circle was the Universe; the Triple Triangle was Health; and much else. Pythagoras evolved an eclectic system in which there was much that was Egyptian, and much that seemed to stem from more Eastern notions. His chief importance is his development of Geometry.

Rainbow. A sign of Hope, often used in Central European Freemasonry during the *Aufklärung*. It also seems to have been associated with the stair and with arcuated construction.

Raised. The reception into the Third Degree, or Resurrection. Hence Raising Sheet.

Red. The colour of Mark Masonry and Royal Arch Masonry.

Rhetoric. One of the Liberal Arts, associated with the development of Language.

Right Angle. Two lines meeting at ninety degrees embrace a right angle, or quarter of a circle. It represents Virtue and Uprightness.

Right Hand. Fidelity and Inviolability.

Rising Sun. Worshipful Master.

Rock, Rocks. Symbols of Soundness. Foundations for Wisdom. Rock-work is frequently associated with Grottoes, Labyrinths, and Gardens of Allusion.

Rose. Associated with Isis and Horus/Harpocrates, the rose is the flower of Silence and Secrecy, hence *sub rosa*. It is the emblem of the Virgin Mary and of Isis.

Rosicrucians. Some claim that the Rosicrucians, or Fraternity of the Order of the Rosy Cross, influenced Freemasonry. The subject is discussed at length by Frances A. Yates in her *The Rosicrucian Enlightenment* (*see* **Select Bibliography**). Rosicrucians seem to have been involved in Hermetic Wisdom, Alchemy, and other activities, and their organisation was not unlike that of the Jesuits. Rosicrucianism probably heralded a kind of proto-Enlightenment, and, despite indignant claims by Masonic writers that Rosicrucians had no connection with the Masonic Fraternity, careful reading of the evidence of sixteenth-century intellectual movements before the Newtonian revolution seems to point to several cross-influences that indicate Renaissance-Hermetic-Cabbalist-Alchemical ideas permeated a number of groups. It does seem unlikely that Freemasonry escaped unscathed.

Royal Arch. Royal Arch Masonry has been described as the 'root, heart, and marrow of Masonry'. It appears to satisfy Master Masons because it repairs a Loss. It is the quintessence of Masonic philosophy, and it contains symbolism of the most elaborate variety. It is concerned with discourses of Light and Truth, and is associated with the keystone of an arch without which the whole edifice collapses (*see* Jones [1969]: *Freemasons' Book of the Royal Arch* [London: Harrap]).

Rule. The instrument that enables straight lines to be drawn, proportion to be ascertained, and measurements made. The Master observes his duty, and veers neither to left nor to right.

St John's Masonry. A term like 'Ancient Craft', which means the three basic Degrees.

St John the Almoner. Otherwise known as St John of Jerusalem, he has been claimed as a Patron Saint of Freemasonry, but there are other candidates (*see* below).

St John the Baptist and St John the Evangelist. Usually regarded as the Patron Saints of Masonry, but the claims of St John of Jerusalem are also interesting in this respect.

Scallop. With staff and sandals, is part of the emblems of a Masonic Knight Templar.

Schaw Manuscripts. A code drawn up at the end of the sixteenth century by William Schaw for the conduct of Operative Masons in Scotland.

Scotland. A country of immense importance in the history of Freemasonry, for it was in Scotland that much of what became modern Freemasonry seems to have originated, though much refined and codified in England. The Scottish Rite is called the Ancient and Accepted Rite (*see* the works of David Stevenson cited in the **Select Bibliography**).

Scythe. Death.

Seal of Solomon. The *Hexalpha* or a double triangle. Some authorities have said it was the *Pentalpha*, but that view is disputed.

Seeing. The Mason sees with special sight, for the uninitiated are in darkness, and are blind.

Serpent. Wisdom. With tail in mouth (*ouroborus*) it is Eternity (**Fig.Gl.10**). Winged globe and *uraei* symbolise the trinity of the deities. A serpent is also a symbol of healing.

Fig.Gl.10 *Ouroboros (JSC)*

Setting Maul. Instrument of the Third Degree: it is a wooden hammer to set the stones, and was associated with the murder of Hiram. It should not be confused with the Gavel, although the latter would make a much more satisfactory murder-weapon.

Seven. A sacred number, much so in Freemasonry. The Creation, the Deluge, the companions of Noah, the Ages of Man, the Sabbath, the Seventh (Sabbatical) Year, Temperance-Fortitude-Prudence-Justice-Faith-Hope-Charity, and the seven years for the building of the Temple are but a few examples. The Seven Stars represent the Pleiades, the mystical Seven Churches, Jacob's Ladder, and the Apocalypse, among other things.

Shibboleth. A test-word to distinguish the Ephraimites (who could not pronounce *sh*) from the Gileadites; therefore a word used to detect the profane or the uninitiated, associated with the Fellow Craft and with Jachin, Plenty, Ears of Corn, and a Waterfall.

Shovel. Tools of Royal Arch Masonry. A shovel removes spoil, so in Speculative Freemasonry it symbolises the casting off of dross.

Skeleton. Reminder of Mortality: the skeleton at the feast, often found in eighteenth-century French décor.

Skirret. An instrument which acts on a centre pin, from which a line is drawn to mark out the extremities of the new building.

That line is determined by a chalked cord which leaves a white impression.

Skull. The seat of the Soul, symbol of Mortality, an emblem of Death and the Grave.

Solomonic Column. A twisted, spiral, or barley-sugar column, associated with the Temple. The form is found in columns or piers near particularly sacred sites, such as altars or shrines in cathedrals, e.g. the *Baldacchino* in St Peter's in Rome. This sacred imagery makes the form important in Masonic iconography.

Sorrow Lodge. A commemorative Lodge held for departed Brethren.

South. The Sun is at its Meridian so Refreshment can be taken. Beauty, Junior Warden, and the Corinthian Order.

Speculative Masonry. Using the tools and implements of Operative Masonry, Speculative Masonry instils a moral system by referring to the symbolic meaning of those tools and implements. The Speculative Mason is taught to build a spiritual work of Architecture, pure, strong, beautiful, and a fit Temple. It is a progressive process, and not to be attained in any Degree of perfection except by time, patience, and considerable application and industry. No candidate can be admitted to the profoundest secrets or the highest honours of Freemasonry until he has imbibed the lessons of Secrecy and Morality. The term has received criticism from some scholars.

Sphinx. An enigma in the form of an Egyptian statue of a woman's head on a lion's body. It is a symbol of Mystery, and as such is adopted by Freemasons, especially on the Continent.

Spiral or Twisted Column. Columns of the barley-sugar type, or that are garlanded or covered with spirals, are associated with the Temple and with the Winding Stair. Also called *Solomonic*.

Square. An angle of ninety degrees which enables great exactness in building to be achieved. It is also a symbol of moral probity, and is one of the Three Great Lights. Masons meet 'on the Square', with a moral meaning (to act honourably) enhanced by the chequer-board patterns of floors.

Square and Compasses. Emblems of Ancient Craft Masonry.

Star. Five points of Fellowship, suggested by the *Pentalpha*. The Blazing Star (*Hexalpha*) is an emblem of Divinity, and of the Universe. The Seven Stars are the Pleiades.

Steps. Three Degrees; Youth, Manhood, Old Age; Life, Death, Immortality.

Strength. A principal support. The Doric Order. The Senior Warden. Hiram King of Tyre. Boaz.

Sun and Moon. With the Master, are associated with the Three Lesser Lights. The Sun and Moon represent Wisdom, Power, and Goodness, and emphasise the omnipresent rule by Night and by Day.

Supports. Wisdom, Strength, and Beauty support the Lodge in the forms of Ionic, Doric, and Corinthian columns.

Tassels. The Four Cardinal Virtues attached to the cord forming the border of a Tracing-Board. Also the four Principal Points: the Guttural, Pectoral, Manual, and Pedal.

Tau. A Greek T, symbolising Eternal Life. It is associated, with the halo over it, with the *Ankh*. A Triple *Tau* is three crosses meeting at a point, and therefore looks like a T over an H, the emblem of the Deity, and Jewel of the Royal Arch. It also stands for *Templum Hierosolymae*, as a monogram of Hiram of Tyre, and as a corruption of *Shin*, the sacred abbreviation of God's name (**Fig.Gl.11**).

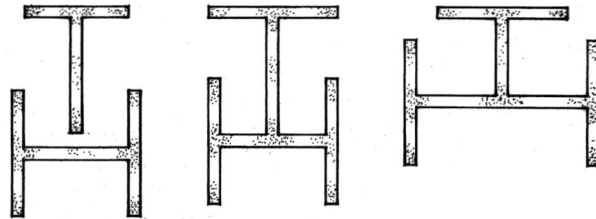

Fig.Gl.11 *Tau* cross over an H (*left*), supposedly an abbreviation for *Templum Hierosolymæ* (Temple of Jerusalem). The T then joined the H (which can be read as two Ts on their sides, sharing the same upright turned through 90°) (*middle*). When the 'Moderns' and 'Antients' amalgamated in 1817 it became three *Taus* (*right*), sometimes found in the centre of an equilateral triangle set within a circle (*JSC*).

Tears (*Guttes*). In Continental Lodges, and in most of the Higher Degrees, tears are strewn on the hangings of the Lodge.

Telamones. Male figures used to support an entablature: the male equivalent of *caryatides*. Two celebrated *telamones* from the Villa Adriana now in the Vatican have Egyptian head-dresses and appearance (*see* Curl [2005]).

Temperance. One of the Four Cardinal Virtues.

Temple of Solomon. The model for Lodges, the perfect building which was lost, and that was built supposedly under Divine Guidance through Hiram. It was destroyed by the Babylonians. It was built by the Wisdom of Solomon, the Strength of King Hiram's wealth and power, and adorned by the Beauty of Hiram the Builder's workmanship.

Temple of Zerubbabel. When the Jews were liberated they built a second Temple under Zerubbabel. Descriptions of this have played a part in the iconography of the Temple and the Lodge. According to some authorities, this Temple was a restoration of the Solomonic Temple, which was not completely destroyed.

Tessellated Border. Laid with various small stones, properly, but it also has come to mean the *houpe dentelée* or cord of strong thread intertwined with knots, at each end of which is a tassel, signifying the fraternal bonds and the Cardinal Virtues.

Tetragrammaton. A word of four letters, the ineffable name of God.

T∴G∴A∴O∴T∴U∴. The Great or Grand Architect of the Universe.

Theological Virtues. Faith (with book and Cross), Hope (with Anchor), and Charity (with children), the principal rounds of the Masonic Ladder.

Third Degree. That of Master.

Three. A sacred number: the fork, Cerberus, Fates, and Furies, the Trinity, and Isis, Horus, Osiris. In Freemasonry the Three Lights, Three Tenets, Three Jewels, Three Rounds, Three Working Tools, Three Degrees, Three Principal Orders of Architecture, Three Knocks, Three Fellow Crafts, and many others testify to the importance of Three.

Three Globes. The Lodge that became the Prussian Grand Lodge in 1765.

Three Steps. Three stages of life and the Three Degrees.

Tiler. Officer with drawn sword guarding the door of the Lodge.

Tracing-Board. Each Degree has its tracing-board, which shows the emblems for that Degree.

Trees. Certain trees have Masonic connotations, including the palm (with its Nilotic and Biblical overtones) and the Acacia, or Egyptian Thorn (*Acacia Vera*), associated with funeral-wreaths, graves, immortality, and the Tree of Paradise (with Serpent). The Acacia has also been identified with *Mimosa Nilotica* (i.e. with clear Egyptian Associations), and is an emblem of innocence. This False Acacia has lemon-coloured flowers. Acacias were planted in gardens and cemeteries (e.g. Père-Lachaise) to remind us of the ancient custom of marking graves with Acacias so that nobody would walk over them, of Initiation, of the Journey, and of Immortality. The Palm is coincident with the Acacia, and is associated with the Egyptian Mysteries of certain Continental rites. The Myrtle seems to have had similar associations for the Greeks, and so also has Masonic connotations. The German *Myrte* seems also to be a mnemonic for *Mörtel*, meaning mortar made from lime.

The Lime-tree is also Masonic (at least in eighteenth-century Continental terms), and, like the Palm, was used as the name of Lodges, notably in German-speaking countries. The German *Linde, Linden* is associated with the Lime-tree (as in the Berlin *Unter den Linden*), but the French *Limonier* is also found in Masonic contexts, such as Père-Lachaise Cemetery. The German *Zitronen*, as in Goethe's *Mignon*, is usually translated as 'lemon-trees', but, if we consider the lines

> 'Kennst du das Land, wo die Zitronen blühn,
> Im dunkeln Laub die Gold-Orangen glühn,
> Ein sanfter Wind vom blauen Himmel weht,
> Die Myrte still und hoch der Lorbeer steht?'
> (Do you know the country where the lemon-trees flower, where golden oranges glow among the dark leaves, where a gentle wind blows from the blue heavens, where the still myrtle and the high bay stand?)

we find allusions to Limes, Myrtles, and Bay-trees (the latter associated with Triumph and with the Higher Degrees of the Scottish Rite). Goethe's poem has other Masonic allusions, including a blue sky, the glowing golden elements (the stars, perhaps?), the roof or canopy resting on pillars, the marble statues, and a reference to dragons and streams (fire and water). Beloved, Protector, and Father are not without significance either (*see* **Lime** and **Mahabyn**).

Trestle-board. The board on which the Master lays designs. Symbolic of the erection of Temples in the Heart and Mind.

Triangle. Double triangles forming the *Hexalpha* (which has six points) are symbols of the Deity, the Universe, and Perfection, while triple triangles (*Pentalpha*) are symbols of Health.

Triple Tau within Triangle. Emblem of Royal Arch Masonry (*see* **Tau**).

Trowel. Tool symbolic of the binding together of the parts of a building, and therefore of Freemasonic Fellowship. Significantly, a trowel is used to apply lime-mortar. A trowel in a triangle is an emblem of cryptic Masonry.

Tubal Cain. Supposedly the inventor of brass and/or bronze, and a password.

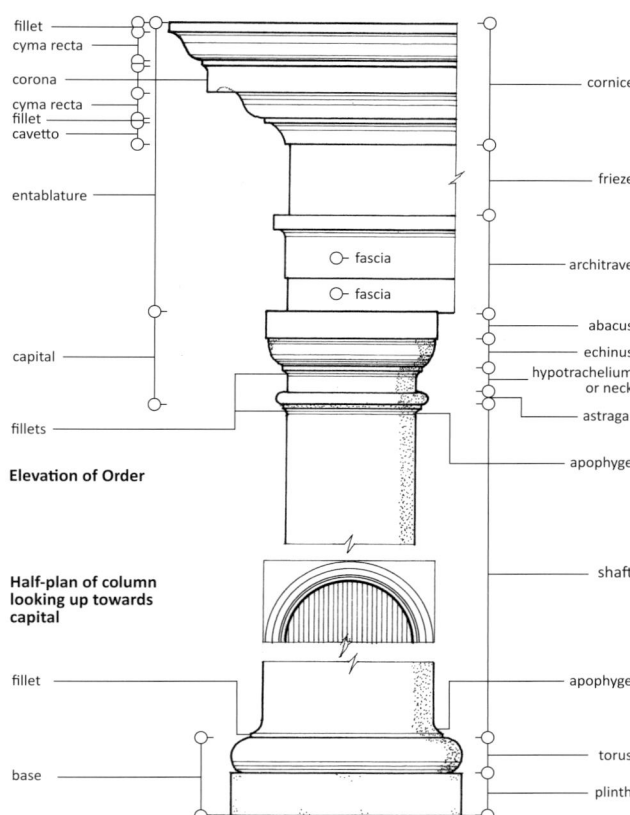

Fig.Gl.12 Tuscan Order (*JSC after Palladio*).

Turtle. Conjugal Affection and Constancy, perhaps confused with the turtle-dove and only significant in esoteric French use.

Tuscan Order. The simplest and most primitive of the Orders, it is like Roman Doric, but is unfluted, and there are no triglyphs and metopes (**Fig.Gl.12**).

Two Knights on One Horse. Poverty, associated with the Knights Templar.

Waterfall. Plenty, the Fellow Craft, and Jachin. A fountain, an Isiac Attribute.

Widow's Son. Hiram the builder.

Winding Stair. A way up to the Middle Chamber of the Temple, suggested by spiral columns or by garlanded columns, which therefore have Masonic significance.

Year of Light. The era of Creation.

Zerubbabel. Building of the sacred Temple. Called after the founder of the Second Temple.

Select Bibliography

'Dort, wo man Bücher verbrennt,
verbrennt man auch am Ende Menschen.'

(It is there, where they burn books, that eventually they burn people too).

HEINRICH HEINE (1797-1856):
Almansord: A Tragedy (1823), 1. 2245.

This list has no pretensions to comprehensiveness, but is an attempt to suggest further reading to expand on information in the text. The literature on Freemasonry is vast, as any perusal of the Library of Congress Catalogue makes clear. Every item to which this study is indebted is listed, however, and it is hoped that the following will aid those who wish to pursue further those themes that are alluded to in the text. Inclusion of any item does not signify the unqualified approval of the present writer: it is only there for information.

Abbreviations:
AJHS: American Jewish Historical Society
AQC: *Ars Quatuor Coronatorum*, being the *Transactions* of Quatuor Coronati Lodge No. 2076
CMRC: Canonbury Masonic Research Centre
HMSO: His or Her Majesty's Stationery Office
N.S. New Series
ODNB: *Oxford Dictionary of National Biography*
QCL: Quatuor Coronati Lodge No 2076
UAHS: Ulster Architectural Heritage Society
UP: University Press
USA: United States of America

The following abbreviations have been adopted for States in the USA. They follow standard American usage:

AL	Alabama	KY	Kentucky	OH	Ohio
AK	Alaska	LA	Louisiana	OK	Oklahoma
AR	Arkansas	ME	Maine	OR	Oregon
AZ	Arizona	MD	Maryland	PA	Pennsylvania
CA	California	MA	Massachusetts	RI	Rhode Island
CO	Colorado	MI	Michigan	SC	South Carolina
CT	Connecticut	MN	Minnesota	SD	South Dakota
DE	Delaware	MS	Mississippi	TN	Tennessee
DC	District Of Columbia	MO	Missouri	TX	Texas
		MT	Montana	UT	Utah
FL	Florida	NE	Nebraska	VT	Vermont
GA	Georgia	NV	Nevada	VA	Virginia
HI	Hawaii	NH	New Hampshire	WA	Washington
ID	Idaho	NJ	New Jersey	WV	West Virginia
IL	Illinois	NM	New Mexico	WI	Wisconsin
IN	Indiana	NY	New York	WY	Wyoming
IA	Iowa	NC	North Carolina		
KS	Kansas	ND	North Dakota		

ABBATE, FRANCESCO (*Ed.*) (1968): *Il Neoclassicismo* (Milan: Fabbri).
ABDOUN, SALEH (1971): *Genesi dell'Aïda* (Parma: Quaderni dell'Istituto di Studi Verdiani).
ACADÉMIE DE FRANCE À ROME (1976): *Catalogue* of the Exhibition *Piranèse et les Français: 1740-1790* (Paris, Rome, & Dijon : Académie de France à Rome [Villa Medici]).
ACADÉMIE DES BEAUX-ARTS (1787-96): *Collection des prix que la ci-devant Académie d'architecture proposoit et couronnoit tous les ans* (Paris: Basan, Joubert, & van Cléemputte). Issued in 20 *cahiers* of 6 plates each, except no. 18 which has 7 plates. Edited first by A.-P. PRIEUR, and then by P.-L. VAN CLÉEMPUTTE.
————— (1806): *Projets d'architecture et autres productions de cet art, qui ont mérités les Grands Prix accordés par l'Académie*. The engraved title-page reads *Grands Prix d'architecture. Projets couronnés par l'Académie d'architecture et par l'Institut de France. Gravés et publiés par Allais, Détournelle, et Vaudoyer* (Paris: Allais, Détournelle, & Vaudoyer).
————— (1818-34): *Grands Prix d'Architecture. Projets couronnés par l'Académie Royale des Beaux-Arts de France* (Paris: A.-L.-T. Vaudoyer & L.-P. Baltard).
ACERRELLOS, R.S. (*pseudonym*): *see* REGHELLINI – of SCIO.
ACHEN, SVEN TITO (1975): *Symboler omkring os* (Copenhagen: Gad).
ACKERMANN, RUDOLF (*Ed.*) (1809-28): *Repository of Arts, Literature, Commerce, Manufactures, Fashions, and Politics* (London: R. Ackermann).
————— (1819): *Pictorial Cards, in Thirteen Plates each containing four subjects… etc.* The set is entitled *Beatrice, or, The Fracas* (London: R. Ackermann).
ACQUIER, HIPPOLYTE, & COMBES D'AURIAC, FRÉDÉRIC (1852): *Les Cimetières de Paris, ouvrage historique, biographique, et pittoresque* (Paris: Albert).
ACTA LATOMORUM OU CHRONOLOGIE DE L'HISTOIRE DE LA FRANCHE-MAÇONNERIE FRANÇAISE (1815): (Paris: Dufart).
ACTES DU 113e CONGRÈS NATIONAL DES SOCIÉTÉS SAVANTS (1991): (Paris: Éditions du Comité des travaux historiques et scientifiques).
ACTES DU 114e CONGRÈS NATIONAL DES SOCIÉTÉS SAVANTS (1990-2): (Paris: Éditions du Comité des travaux historiques et scientifiques).
ADAMS, WALTER MARSHAM (1898): *The Book of the Master, or the Egyptian Doctrine of the Light born of the Virgin Mother* (New York: Putnam).
ADAMS, WILLIAM HOWARD (1979): *The French Garden 1500-1800* (London: Scolar Press).
ADDIS, WILLIAM EDWARD, & ARNOLD, THOMAS (1957): *A Catholic Dictionary* (London: Routledge & Kegan Paul).
ADLER, GERHARD (*Ed.*) (1953-79): *see* JUNG, CARL GUSTAV.
ADLINGTON, WILLIAM (1924): *see* APULEIUS MADAURENSIS, LUCIUS.
AGE OF NEO-CLASSICISM: *see* ARTS COUNCIL OF GREAT BRITAIN.
AGNEW, VANESSA (2008): *Enlightenment Orpheus: The Power of Music in Other Worlds* (New York: Oxford UP).

AGULHON, MAURICE (1968): *Pénitents de Francs-Maçons de l'ancienne Provence* (Paris: Fayard).

AIKIN, ARTHUR (Tr.) (1802): see DENON, BARON DOMINIQUE VIVANT.

AIKMAN, LONNELLE (1991): *We, The People: The story of The United States Capitol – its Past and its Promise* (Washington DC: U.S. Capitol Historical Society).

ALBERTI, LEON BATTISTA (1486): *De Re Ædificatoria* (Florence: Lorenzo Alamani. *See* also the version entitled *On the Art of Building in Ten Books* JOSEPH RYKWERT, NEIL LEACH, & ROBERT TAVERNOR (*Trs.*) (Cambridge MA & London: MIT Press 1988).

ALBON, CLAUDE-CAMILLE-FRANÇOIS, COMTE D' (1785): *Éloge de Court de Gébelin* (Amsterdam & Paris: Moutard).

ALBON, COMTESSE D': see LUSSI & LEPAGELET.

ALBRECHT, THEODOR (1914): *Freimaurers Weltreise* (Leipzig: s.n.).

ALEKSANDROWICZ, ALINA (1998): *Izabela Czartoryska. Polskość i europejskość* (Lublin: Marie Curie UP).

ALEMBERT, JEAN LE ROND D': see DIDEROT, DENIS.

ALEX, REINHARD, & KÜHN, PETER (1988): *Schlösser und Gärten um Wörlitz* (Leipzig: Seeman).

ALEXANDER, JENNIFER S., & MORRISON, KATHRYN A. (2007): 'Apethorpe Hall and the Workshop of Thomas Thorpe, Mason of King's Cliffe: A Study in Masons' Marks' *Architectural History: Journal of the Society of Architectural Historians of Great Britain* **l** 59-94.

ALEXANDER, ROBERT L. (1958): 'The Public Monument and Godefroy's Battle Monument' *Journal of the Society of Architectural Historians* **xviii** 19-24.

——— (1974): *The Architecture of Maximilian Godefroy* (Baltimore MD: Johns Hopkins UP).

ALFÖLDI, ANDRÁS (1934): 'Die Ausgestaltung des monarchisten Hofzeremoniells am römischen Kaiserhof' *Mitteilungen des Deutschen Archäologischen Instituts, Römische Abteilung* **xlix** 1-118.

——— (1937): 'A Festival of Isis in Rome under the Christian Emperors of the IVth Century' *Dissertationes Pannonicæ* Ser. II fasc.7 (Budapest: Institute of Numismatics and Archæology of the Pázmány University).

——— (1954): 'Isiskult und Umsturzbewegung im letzten Jahrhundert der römischen Republik' *Schweizerische Münzblätter* **v** 25-31.

——— (1965-6): 'Die alexandrinischen Götter und die Vota Publica am Jahresbeginn' *Jahrbuch für Antike und Christentum* **viii-ix** 53-87.

ALFÖLDY, G. (1989): 'Die Krise des Imperium Romanum und die Religion Roms' *Religion und Gesellschaft in der römischen Kaiserzeit, Kölner Historische Abhandlung* **xxxv** 53-102.

——— (1990): 'Der Obelisk auf dem Petersplatz in Rom' *Sitzungsberichte der Heidelberger Akademie der Wissenschaften* phil.-hist. Klasse 1990. 2.

ALGAROTTI, CONTE FRANCESCO (1791-95): *Opere* (Venice: C. Palese).

ALISON, ARCHIBALD (1790): *Essays on the Nature and Principles of Taste* (Edinburgh: Bell & Bradfute, & London: J. J. G. & G. Robinson).

ALLAIS, L.-J.: see ACADÉMIE DES BEAUX-ARTS.

ALLGEMEINE MUSIKALISCHE ZEITUNG (from 1798) (Leipzig: Breitkopf & Härtel).

ALLGEMEINES HANDBUCH DER FREIMAUREREI (1900): See SCHLETTER, HERMANN THEODORE, & ZILLE, MORITZ ALEXANDER (Leipzig: Max Hesse's Verlag).

ALLINSON, ALFRED RICHARD (Tr.) (1930): see GALLONIO, ANTONIO.

ALLYN, AVERY (1831): *A Ritual of Freemasonry* (Philadelphia PA: John Clarke). Also published (1837) as *A Ritual and Illustration of Freemasonry, and the Orange & Odd Fellows' Societies, etc.* (London: Renshaw & Kirkman).

ALMÉRAS, HENRI D' (1904): *Cagliostro (Joseph Balsamo). La franc-maçonnerie et l'occultisme au XVIIIe siècle* (Paris: Société Française d'Imprimerie et de Librairie).

——— (1910): *La Vie Parisienne sous la Révolution et le Directoire* (Paris: A. Michel).

ALTENMÜLLER, BRIGITTE H. (1975a): 'Anubis' in *Lexikon der Ägyptologie* **i** (Wiesbaden: O. Harrassowitz) c. 327-33.

——— (1975b): 'Bes' in *Lexikon der Ägyptologie* **i** (Wiesbaden: O. Harrassowitz) *c.* 720-24.

——— (1975c): 'Buto' in *Lexikon der Ägyptologie* **i** (Wiesbaden: O. Harrassowitz) *c.* 887-9.

——— (1975d): 'Djed-Pfeiler' in *Lexikon der Ägyptologie* **i** (Wiesbaden: O. Harrassowitz) *c.* 1100-1105.

——— (1975e): 'Falke' in *Lexikon der Ägyptologie* **ii** (Wiesbaden: O. Harrassowitz) *c.* 93-97.

ALTHEIM, FRANZ (1938): *A History of Roman Religion* H. MATTINGLY (Tr.) (London: Methuen).

ALTICK, RICHARD DANIEL (1978): *The Shows of London* (Cambridge MA: Belknap Press).

AMBELAIN, ROBERT (1978): *Cérémonies et Rituels de la Maçonnerie Symbolique* (Paris: Éditions Robert Laffont).

AMERICAN JEWISH HISTORICAL SOCIETY (from 1893): *American Jewish Historical Quarterly* also called *Publications of the AJHS* (New York: AJHS).

AMERICAN JOURNAL OF ARCHÆOLOGY, THE (from 1897): The Journal of the Archæological Institute of America (Baltimore MD etc.).

AMERICAN JOURNAL OF SEMITIC LANGUAGES AND LITERATURE (1884-1941) (Chicago IL: University of Chicago Press).

AMERICAN MONTHLY MAGAZINE, THE (1833-38) (New York: Bancroft, Hill, & Carvill).

AMERICAN QUARTERLY REVIEW, THE (1827-37): (Philadelphia PA: Carey, Lea, & Carey).

AMIABLE, LOUIS (1897): *La Respectable Loge: Les Neufs Sœurs* (Paris: Félix Alcan).

———, & GUIEYSSE, PAUL (1988): *L'Égypte ancienne et la franc-maçonnerie* (Paris: Trédonie).

ANDERSON, EMILY (*Ed.*) (1988): *The Letters of Mozart and His Family* (London: Macmillan).

ANDERSON, JAMES (1739): *News from Elysium or Dialogues of the Dead* (London: J. Cecil etc.).

——— (*Ed.*) (1723): *The Constitutions of the Free-Masons: containing the History, Charges, Regulations, &c. of the Most Ancient and Right Worshipful Fraternity. For the Use of the Lodges* (London: John Senex & John Hooke).

——— (*Ed.*) (1738): *The New Book of Constitutions of the Antient and Honourable Fraternity of Free and Accepted Masons* (London: C. Ward & R. Chandler). This important source-book is known as *Anderson's Constitutions*. See also W. J. HUGHAN'S Introduction to the 1890 facsimile edition of Anderson's work in *Quatuor Coronatorum Antigrapha,* **vii.**

ANDERSON, M. S. (1961): *Europe in the Eighteenth Century, 1713-1783* (New York: Holt, Rinehart, & Winston, Inc.).

ANDRÉ, ANNE (1987): 'Paris: pharaons-sur-Seine' in *L'Evénement du Jeudi* **cxxii** (5-11 March) 92-93.

ANDRÉ, CHRISTIAN KARL (*Ed.*) (1790-96): *Der Freymeurer, oder Compendiöse Bibliothek alles Wissen würdigen über geheime Gesellschaften* (Göttingen, Gotha, Halle, and Eisenach: Johann Christian Dieterich & Johann Jacob Gebauer).

ANDREAE, JOHANN VALENTIN (1973): *Fama Fraternitatis* [1614]: *Confessio Fraternitatis* [1615] *Chymische Hochzeit: Christiani Rosenkreutz Anno 1459* [1616] RICHARD VAN DÜLMEN (*Ed.*) (Stuttgart: Calwer).

ANDREWS, C. (1988): see QUIRKE, STEPHEN.

ANNALI DELL'INSTITUTO DI CORRESPONDENZA ARCHEOLOGIA (from 1829): (Rome).

ANONYMOUS (1724): *The Temple of Solomon with all its Porches, Walls, Gates, Halls, Chambers, etc.* (London: s.n.).

——— (1791): *Free Masonry for the Ladies; or, the Grand Secret Discovered* (London: W. Thiselton).

——— (1812): *O ∴ ou Histoire de la fondation du Grand Orient de France* (Paris: s.n.).

——— (1878): 'Cercle Artistique: Les Antiquités Égyptiennes de M. Allemant' *Le Précurseur* Year 43/329.

——— (1891a): 'Consécration du Nouveau Temple de la R[espectable] [Loge] La Parfaite Union, Rue Chasaire, à l'Or[ient] de Mons' *Bulletin du Gr[and] Or[ient] de Belgique* **xviii** 84-116.

——— (1891b): 'R[espectable] [Loge] Les Amis de la Parfaite Intelligence, à l'Or[ient] de Huy' *Bulletin du Gr[and] Or[ient] de Belgique* **xviii** 126-149.

——— (1909): 'R[espectable] [Loge] La Bonne Amitié à l'Or[ient] de Namur'. Compte rendu de la Fête d'Inauguration de Nouveau Temple' *Bulletin du Gr[and] Or[ient] de Belgique* **xxxvii** 157-76.

——— (1911): 'Tenue du 10 mars 1911' *Bulletin des Travaux du Suprême Conseil de Belgique* **liv** 8-14.

——— (1920): 'In memoriam Hector Puchot' *Bulletin des Travaux du Suprême Conseil de Belgique* **lviii** 165.

——— (1994): 'Influencia egipcia en la pintura europea de los siglos XVII y XVIII', *Saber ver, lo contemporaneo del Arte* **xviii** (September-October) 6-48.

ANQUETIL, GILLES (1989): 'Egyptomania' *Le Nouvel Observateur* **mcclxiv** (26 January) 26-35.

ANSIEAU, JOËLLE: (1983): 'Deux Sculptures de Georges Lacombe: Isis et le Christ' *La Revue du Louvre et des Musées de France* **iv** 287-295.

ANTICHITÀ DI ROMA (1647-71): contains works by DUPÉRAC, ROSSI ET. AL. (Rome: s.n.).

L'ANTIQUITÉ CLASSIQUE (from 1932): (Brussels etc.).

APIAN, PETER (1533): *Folium populi: Instrumentum...* (Ingolstadt: P. Apian).

APULEIUS MADAURENSIS, LUCIUS (1924): *Metamorphoseon libri XI*. Various editions, but see the edition WILLIAM ADLINGTON (Tr.) F. J. HARVEY DARTON (Ed.) (London: Navarre Society).

ARAGO, M. (1838): 'Éloge Historique de M. Joseph Fourier, par M. Arago, Secrétaire Perpétuel, lu a la Séance publique du 18 Novembre, 1833' *Memoires de l'Académie Royale des Sciences de l'Institut de France* **xiv** xcii xciii.

ARCHÆOLOGY (from 1948): (Cambridge MA: Archæological Institute of America).

L'ARCHÉOLOGIE ET SON IMAGE (1988): Colloquium, VIIIe rencontres internationales d'archéologie et d'histoire d'Antibes (29-31 October 1987 [Juan-les-Pins]). Contains contributions from ADAM, ALEXANDRE-BIDON, CHANTE, ELOY, & HUMBERT.

ARCHITECTURAL MAGAZINE, THE (1834-38): (London: Longman, Rees, Orme, Brown, Green, & Longman).

ARCHITECTURAL PUBLICATION SOCIETY (1853-92): see PAPWORTH, WYATT ANGELICUS VAN SANDAU.

ARCHITECTURAL REVIEW, THE (from 1896): (London). Also the American *THE ARCHITECTURAL REVIEW* (Boston MA: Bates, Kimball, & Guild, etc. [from 1891]).

ARCHITEKTONISCHE STUDIEN DES KAISERLICH DEUTSCHEN ARCHÆOLOGISCHEN INSTITUTS **iii** (1889).

ARGAN, G. C. (1988): 'Il pensiero dell'antico nell'arte occidentale' *Storia dell' Arte* **lxii** 13-23.

ARIAS MONTANUS, BENEDICTUS (1572): *Exemplar: sive, de sacris fabricis liber* (Antwerp: Christopherus Plantinus).

ARIÈS, PHILIPPE (1981): *The Hour of our Death* (London: Allen Lane).

ARIZZOLI-CLEMENTEL, PIERRE (1972): 'Le Mausolée de Turenne aux Invalides' *Revue de la Société des Amis du Musée de l'Armée* **lxxvi** 5-12.

——— (1976): 'Les Sourtouts Impériaux en Porcelaine de Sèvres, 1804-1814' *Keramik-Freunde der Schweiz, Mitteilungsblatt* **lxxxviii** (May) 17 f.

——— (1978): 'Charles Percier et la Salle Égyptienne de la Villa Borghèse' *Actes du Colloque 'Piranèse et les Français'* (12-14 May 1976) (Rome) 1-32.

ARNAUD, C.-P. (1817): *Recueil de tombeaux des quatres cimetières de Paris.* (Paris: Arnaud).

ARNDT, KARL, KOCH, GEORG FRIEDRICH, & LARSSON, LARS OLOF (1978): *Albert Speer: Architektur. Arbeiten 1933-1942* (Frankfurt/M: Propyläen Verlag).

ARNOLD, C. L. (1858): *The Rationale and Ethics of Freemasonry, or the Masonic Institution considered as a means of social and individual progress* (New York: Robert Macoy).

ARNOLD, DIETER (1985): 'Moses und Aïda. Das alte Ägypten in der Oper' *Ägypten-Dauer und Wandel* 173-180.

ARNOLD, THOMAS (1957): see ADDIS, WILLIAM EDWARD.

ARS QUATUOR CORONATORUM (AQC) (various dates): Transactions of the Quatuor Coronati Lodge No. 2076 (London: QCL).

ART BULLETIN, THE (from 1913): (New York etc: College Art Association of America).

ARTS COUNCIL OF GREAT BRITAIN (1972): *The Age of Neo-classicism.* The *Catalogue* of the fourteenth Exhibition of the Council of Europe (9 September - 19 November 1972) (London: The Arts Council of Great Britain).

——— (1978): *Piranesi. Catalogue* of the Exhibition by

JOHN WILTON-ELY (London: The Arts Council of Great Britain).
THE ARTS UNDER NAPOLEON (1978): *Catalogue of the Exhibition* (New York: Metropolitan Museum of Art).
ASHMOLE, ELIAS (1719): *The Antiquities of Berkshire* etc. (London: Edmund Curll).
ASSMANN, JAN (1984): *Ägypten: Theologie und Frömmigkeit einer frühen Hochkultur* (Stuttgart: Kohlkammer).
AUBREY, JOHN (1847): *The Natural History of Wiltshire* (London: J. B. Nichols for the Wiltshire Topographical Society).
AUGÉ, PAUL (Ed.) (1928-33): *see* LAROUSSE, PIERRE.
AUGUSTINE, AURELIUS, SAINT, BISHOP OF HIPPO (1888): *The Works of Aurelius Augustine, Bishop of Hippo* MARCUS DODS (Ed. & Tr.) (Edinburgh: T. & T. Clark).
AULARD, F.-V.-A. (1892): *Le Culte de la Raison et le Culte de l'Être Suprême 1793-94* (Paris: F. Alcan).
AUNE, L.J. (1929): *Frimureriet: Dets Historie i Skandinavien* (Copenhagen: H.C. Bakkes Boghandel).
AURENHAMMER, HANS (1973): *J.B. Fischer von Erlach* (London: Allen Lane).
AUTEXIER, PHILIPPE (1997): *La Lyre Maçonne: Haydn, Mozart, Spohr, Liszt* (Paris: Detrad/A.V.S.).
AVERLINO, ANTONIO DI PIERO (1965): *see* FILARETE, ANTONIO AVERLINO.
AVRIL, JEAN-BAPTISTE (1794): *Rapport de l'Administration des Travaux Publics sur les cimitières…* etc. (Paris: s.n.).
AXTELL, HAROLD LUCIUS (1907): *The Deification of Abstract Ideas in Roman Literature and Inscriptions* (Chicago IL: University of Chicago Press).
AZIZA, CLAUDE (1996): 'Les romans de momies: fantasme(s) d'archéologie ou d'histoire?' HUMBERT (Ed.) (1996) 553-83.
BABINGTON, C (Ed.) (1865-86): *see* HIGDEN, RANULF.
BACLER D'ALBE, LOUIS-ALBERT-CHRISTIAN (1822): *Promenades pittoresques et lithographiques dans Paris et ses environs* (Paris: G. Engelmann).
BACON, FRANCIS (1620): *Francisci de Verulamio… Instauratio Magna* (London: Apud Joannem Billium).
BACON, NATHANIEL (1647-51): *An Historicall Discourse of the Uniformity of the Government of England* (London: Walbancke).
BADAWY, ALEXANDER M. (1966): *A History of Egyptian Architecture* (Berkeley CA: University of California Press).
——— (1975): 'The Approach to the Egyptian Temple in the Late and Græco-Roman Periods' *Zeitschrift für ägyptische Sprache und Alterumskunde* **cii** 79ff.
BADENHAUSEN, ROLF (1938): *Die Bildbestände der Theatersammlung Louis Schneider* (Berlin: Selbstverlag der Gesellschaft für Theatergeschichte).
BAECHLER, J. (1959): *Recherches sur la diffuson des cultes isaïques en Italie du IIe s. av. J.-C. au IIe s. ap. J. C.* Dissertation (University of Strasbourg).
BAGGERMAN, ARIANNE, & DEKKER, RUDOLF (2009): *Child of the Enlightenment: Revolutionary Europe Reflected in a Boyhood Diary* DIANE WEBB (Tr.) (Leiden & Boston: Brill).
BAIGENT, MICHAEL, & LEIGH, RICHARD (1989): *The Temple and the Lodge* (London: Guild Publishing by arrangement with Jonathan Cape).
BALDUS, H. R. (1991): 'Zur Aufnahme des Sol Elagabalus-Kultes in Rom, 219 n. Chr.' *Chiron* **xxi** 175-8.
BALLIN, ERNST AUGUST (1960): *Der Dichter von Mozarts Freimaurerlied 'O Heiliges Band'* (Tutzing: H. Schneider).
BALLOU'S PICTORIAL DRAWING-ROOM COMPANION (1851-59) (Boston MA: Gleason).
BALTARD, LOUIS-PIERRE (1807): *Athenaeum, ou Galerie française des productions de tous les arts…* (Paris: Frères Piranesi).
——— (1818-34): *see* ACADÉMIE DES BEAUX-ARTS.
BALTRUŠAITIS, JURGIS (1952): 'Eighteenth-Century Gardens and Fanciful Landscapes' *Magazine of Art* **xlv** (April) 172-81.
——— (1955): *Le Moyen-âge fantastique; antiquités et exotismes dans l'art gothique* (Paris: A. Colin).
——— (1957): *Aberrations. Quatre essais sur la légende des formes* (Paris: O. Perrin).
——— (1967): *La Quête d'Isis. Introduction à l'Égyptomanie. Essai sur la légende d'un mythe* (Paris: O. Perrin).
BALZER, GEORG (1966): *Goethe als Gartenfreund* (Munich: Bruckmann).
BANDIERA, JOHN D. (1983): 'The City of the Dead: French eighteenth-century designs for funerary complexes' *Gazette des Beaux Arts* **mccclxviii** (January) 25-32.
BANVARD, JOHN (1880): *The Origins of the Building of Solomon's Temple* (Boston MA: Howard Gannett).
BAQUÉS ESTAPÉ, L. (1975-80): 'Improntas de diez escarabeos egypcios de supuesta procedencia ibicenca' *Ampurias* **xli-xlii** 377-90.
BÄR, CARL (1966): *Mozart: Krankheit, Tod, Bergräbnis.* (Basel, Paris, London: Bärenreiter).
BARBEGUIÈRE, J. (1784): *La maçonnerie mesmérienne* (Amsterdam: s.n.).
BARBER, MALCOLM (2003): *The Trial of the Templars* (London: Folio Society).
BARBER, WILLIAM HENRY, ET AL. (1967): *The Age of the Enlightenment. Studies Presented to Theodore Besterman* (London & Edinburgh: Oliver & Boyd for the University Court of St Andrews).
BARING, SIR THOMAS, BART. (1838): *A Bibliographical Account and Collation of La Description de l'Égypte, presented to the Library of the London Institution, by Sir Thomas Baring, Baronet, President: etc.* (London: privately printed).
BARING-GOULD, SABINE (1914): *The Lives of the Saints* (Edinburgh: John Grant).
BARNEY, STEPHEN A. (Tr.) (2006): *see* ISIDORE OF SEVILLE.
BARRIER, JANINE (1997): 'Bélanger et Angleterre' CONSTANS, MARTINE, ET AL. (1997a) 135-166.
BARROUX, ROBERT (1959): 'Statue et légende d'Isis à Saint-Germain-des-Prés' *Le Moyen Age* No. 3 (**lxv** fourth series t. xiv).
———, & MARIUS (1956): 'Les origines légendaires de Paris' *Paris et île-de-France* (Paris: Robert Barroux).
BARRUEL, ABBÉ AUGUSTIN (1797): *Abrégé des Mémoires pour servir à l'histoire du Jacobinisme* (London: P. Le Boussonier & Co.). It came out (1798) as *Memoirs, illustrating the Antichristian Conspiracy* ROBERT CLIFFORD (Tr.) (Dublin: William Watson & Son, and London: E. Booker).
BARTA, WINFRIED (1980): 'Funktion und Lokalisierung der Zirkumpolarsterne in den Pyramidtexten' *Zeitschrift für Ägyptische Sprache und Altertumskunde* **cvii** 1-14.
——— (1984): 'Re' *Lexikon der Ägyptologie* **v** (Wiesbaden: O. Harrossowitz) c. 156-80.
BARTHÉLEMY, J. J. (1757-60): *see* BARTOLI, PIETRO SANTI.
BARTHES, ROLAND (1971): *Sade, Fourier, Loyola* (Paris: Éditions du Seuil).
BARTHOLDY, PAUL (1886): *Bericht über das Kaiserfest i. O. Strassburg i. E. am 12. September 1886* (Neuwied/Rhein: Louis Heuser).
BARTIER, JOHN (1981): *Laïcité et franc-maçonnerie* (Brussels: Éditions de l'Université de Bruxelles).
——— (1987): *see* LIGOU, D. (Ed.).
BARTOLI, JEAN-PIERRE (1996): 'À la recherche d'une représentation sonore de l'Égypte antique: l'égyptomanie musicale en France de Rossini à Debussy' HUMBERT (Ed.) (1996) 481-506.
BARTOLI, PIETRO SANTI (1757-60) but see the edition of (1783-7): *Recueil de peintures antiques trouvées à Rome* (Paris: Molini et de Lamy). Contains J. J. BARTHÉLEMY'S 'Explication de la mosaïque de Palestrina' printed in the 1757-60 edition for the first time.
BARZUN, JACQUES (Tr.) (1956): *see* DIDEROT, DENIS.
BASAN (1787-96): *see* ACADÉMIE DES BEAUX-ARTS.
BASSI, ELENA (1936): *Giannantonio Selva, architetto veneziano* (Padua: Milani).
BATAILLE, DR (1896): *Le Diable au XIXe Siècle, ou les Mystères du Spiritisme. La franc-maçonnerie lucifériene. Révélations complètes sur le palladisme*, etc. (Paris: s.n.). 'Bataille' was a pseudonym of Jogand-Pagès and Charles Hacks.
BATHAM, C.N. (1970): *see* TUNBRIDGE, PAUL.
——— (1973): 'A Famous French Lodge' *AQC* **lxxxvi** 312-17.
BATLEY, EDWARD M. (1969): *A Preface to the Magic Flute* (London: Dennis Dobson).
——— (2005): ' "The Master of Masters"—the Genius of Goethe and the Manifestations of Freemasonry in his Work' STEWART, TREVOR (Ed.) (2005) 15-28.
BATTEAUX, CHARLES (1746): *Les Beaux-arts réduits à un même principe* (Paris: Durand).
BATZKO, LUDWIG VON (1794): 'Allegorie aus der Zauberflöte' *Journal des Luxus und der Moden* **ix** (19 April) 366-71.
BADOUIN-MATUSZEX, MARIE-NOËLLE (2007): *see* MIDDLETON, ROBIN.
BAUER, WILHELM A., & DEUTSCH, OTTO ERICH (Eds.) (1962-75): *Leopold Mozart: Briefe und Aufzeichnungen* (Kassel & New York: Bärenreiter).
BAUER, YEHUDA, ET AL. (Eds.) (1989): *Remembering for the future* (Oxford: Pergamon Press).
BAUMGARTEN, SÁNDOR (1958): *Le Crépuscule Néo-Classique. Thomas Hope* (Paris: Didier).
BAX, MARTY (Ed.) (2005): *see* KROON, ANDRÉA A.
BAXTER, RODERICK HILDEGAR (1908): *General and Historic Notes on Freemasonry* (Rochdale: James Clegg).
BAYLOT, JEAN (1965): *Dossier français de la Franc-Maçonnerie régulière* (Paris: Vitiano).
BEALES, D. (1987): *Joseph II* (Cambridge: Cambridge UP).
BEAN, JACOB (1960): *Les Dessins italiens de la collection Bonnet à Bayonne* (Paris: Éditions des Musées nationaux).
BEAUCOUR, FERNAND ÉMILE (1983): *La Campagne d'Égypte (1798-1801) d'après les dessins inédits de Noël Dejuine* (Levallois: Société de sauvegarde du château impérial de Pont-de Briques).
———, LAISSUS, YVES, & ORGOGOZO, CHANTAL (1989): *La Découverte de l'Égypte* (Paris: Flammarion).
BEAUJEU, J. (1955): *La religion romain à l'apogée de l'Empire* (Paris: Société d'édition des Belles Lettres).
BEAUTHEAC, NADINE, & BOUCHART, FRANÇOIS-XAVIER (1985): *L'Europe Exotique* (Paris: éd. du Chêne).
BEAUVALLET, PIERRE-NICOLAS (1804-7): *Fragmens d'architecture, sculpture, et peinture, dans le style antique* (Paris: Joubert).
BECHER, ILSE (1965): 'Oktavians Kampf gegen Antonius und seine Stellung zu den ägyptischen Göttern' *Das Altertum* **xi** 40-7.
——— (1966): *Das Bild der Kleopatra in der griechischen und lateinischen Literatur* (Berlin: Akademie Verlag).
——— (1970a): 'Der Isiskult in Rom – ein Kult der Halbwelt?' *Zeitschrift für ägyptische Sprache und Altertumskunde* **xcvi** 81-90.
——— (1970b) 'Antike Heilgötter und die römische Staatsreligion' *Philologus* **cxiv** 211-55.
BECHTOLDT, FRANK-ANDREAS, & WEISS, THOMAS (1996): *Weltbild Wörlitz: Entwurf einer Kulturlandschaft* (Ostfildern-Ruit: Gerd Hatje).
BECKER, FELIX (1950-53): *see* THIEME, ULRICH.
BECKER, UDO (1992): *The Continuum Encyclopedia of Symbols* LANCE W. GARNER (Tr.) (New York & London: Continuum).
BEENKEN, HERMANN THEODOR (1952): *Schöpferische Bauideen der Deutschen Romantik* (Mainz-am-Rhein: Matthias-Grünewald Verlag).
BEGEMANN, GEORG E. WILHELM (1906): *Die Tempelherrn und die Freimaurer* (Berlin: E.S. Mittler u. Sohn).
——— (1909-10): *Vorgeschichte und Anfänge der Freimaurerei in England* (Berlin: E. S. Mittler u. Sohn).
——— (1911): *Vorgeschichte und Anfänge der Freimaurerei in Irland* (Berlin: E. S. Mittler u. Sohn).
——— (1914): *Vorgeschichte und Anfänge der Freimaurerei in Schottland. Die alten schottischen Werklogen* (Berlin: E. S. Mittler u. Sohn).
BÈGUE, F.-T. (1844-8): *see* CLAVEL.
BEINLICH, HORST (1984a): 'Räucherarm' *Lexikon der Ägyptologie* **v** (Wiesbaden: O. Harrassowitz) c.83.
——— 'Seelen' *Lexikon der Ägyptologie* **v** (Wiesbaden: O. Harrassowitz) c.8046.
——— 'Sterne' *Lexikon der Ägyptologie* **vi** (Wiesbaden: O. Harrassowitz) c.1114.
BELGRADO, JACOPO (1786): *Dell' Architettura Egiziana, dissertazione di un Corrispondente dell' Accademia delle Scienze di Parigi* (Parma: Dalla Stamperia Reale).
BELIDOR, BERNARD FOREST DE (1737): *Architecture hydraulique* (Paris: C. A. Jombert).
BELL, SIR HAROLD IDRIS (1954): *Cults and Creeds in Græco-Roman Egypt* (Liverpool: Liverpool UP).
BELLAIGUE, GEOFFREY DE (1968): 'Martin-Eloy Lignereux and England' *Gazette des Beaux-Arts* **lxxi** (May-June) 283-294.

BELLERMAN, JOHANN JOACHIM (1821): *Geschichtliche Nachrichten aus dem Alterthume über Essäer und Therapeuten* (Berlin: F. Maurer).
BENDALL, SARAH (1997): *Dictionary of Land Surveyors and Local Map-makers of Great Britain and Ireland 1530-1850* (London: The British Library).
BÉNÉDICT, JEAN J. (1976): *Le Temple de Solomon* (Typescript in Freemason's Hall, London, containing reconstructions by many authors).
BENINCASA, COUNT (1787): see ROSENBERG-ORSINI, JUSTINE (WYNNE), GRÄFIN VON.
BENOIT, FRANÇOIS (1897): *L'Art François sous la Révolution et l'Empire* (Paris: L. H. May).
BENSKIN, MICHAEL (Ed.) (1986): see MCINTOSH, ANGUS.
BENYOVSZKY, KÁROLY (1926): *Das alte Theater* (Bratislava [Pressburg]: K. Angermayer).
——— (1929): *Theatergeschichtliche Kleinigkeiten* (Bratislava [Pressburg]: S. Steiner).
——— (1934): *Johann Nepomuk Hummel, der Mensch und Künstler* (Bratislava [Pressburg]: Eos-Verlag).
BENZAKEN, JEAN-CHARLES (1991): 'Iconographie du monnaies et médailles de la Fête du 10 août 1793' *Actes du 113ᵉ et du 114ᵉ congrès national des sociétés savants* (Paris: Éditions du Comité des travaux historiques et scientifiques) 291-312.
——— (1993): 'David et la numismatique' *Actes du Colloque David contre David*, edited by RÉGIS MICHEL (Paris: La Documentation française) 965-985.
BÉRAGE, CHEVALIER DE (1776): Supposed author (actually Tr.) of *Les Plus Secrets Mystères des Hauts Grades de la Maçonnerie Dévoilés* KARL FRIEDRICH KÖPPEN (Ed.) (Berlin: Haude & Spener). See the reprint of the 1774 edn., with Introduction and Notes, by RENÉ LE FORESTIER (Paris: Dorbon-Ainé 1915).
BÉRANGER, J. (1953): 'Recherches sur l'aspect idéologique du principat' *Schweizerische Beiträge zur Altertumswissenschaft* **vi** (Basel: Reinhardt).
BÉRANGER, PAUL (1819): see SAINT-ALBIN, J. S. C. DE
BERGDOLL, BARRY (1994a): *Karl Friedrich Schinkel: An Architecture for Prussia*, with photographs by ERICH LESSING (New York: Rizzoli).
——— (1994b): *Léon Vaudoyer: Historicism in the Age of Industry* (New York: Architectural History Foundation, and London: MIT Press).
BERGER, PETER L. (1967): *The Sacred Canopy. Elements of a Sociological Theory of Religion* (Garden City NY: Doubleday).
BERGH, W. VAN DEN (1957): see ZOO.
BERGMAN, JAN (1968): *Ich bin Isis. Studien zum memphitischen Hintergrund der griechischen Isisaretalogien*. Historia Religionum 3 (Uppsala: Universitetet; Stockholm: Almqvist & Wiksell).
——— (1970): *Isis-seele und Osiris-Ei. Zwei ägyptologische Studien zu Diodorus Siculus* **i** 27, 4-5 (Uppsala: Universitetet; Stockholm: Almqvist & Wiksell).
——— (1980): 'Isis' *Lexikon der Ägyptologie* **iii** (Wiesbaden: O. Harrassowitz) c. 186-203.
BERK, MATHEUS FRANCISCUS MARIA VAN DEN (2004): *The Magic Flute: Die Zauberflöte. An Alchemical Allegory* J. BERKHOUT (Tr.) (Leiden & Boston MA: Koninklijke Brill NV).
BERKHOUT, J. (Tr.) (2004): see BERK.
BERLIOZ, HECTOR (1903): 'La Flûte Enchantée et les Mystères d'Isis' *Les Musiciens et la Musique* ANDRÉ HALLAYS (Ed.) (Paris: Callmann-Lévy).
BERNAL, MARTIN (1987): *Black Athena: The Afroasiatic Roots of Classical Civilization*, **i**: *The Fabrication of Ancient Greece 1785-1985* (New Brunswick NJ: Rutgers UP).
——— (1991): *Black Athena: The Afroasiatic Roots of Classical Civilization* **ii**: *The Archæological and Documentary Evidence* (New Brunswick NJ: Rutgers UP).
BERNARD, J.-P.: 'Métro Pyramides' *Silex* **xiii** (Le rêve égyptien) 131-6.
BERNARDIN DE SAINT-PIERRE, JACQUES-HENRI (1784): *Études de la Nature* (Paris: Didot).
BERNIER, CLAUDE-LOUIS (1798): see PERCIER, CHARLES.
BERNIGEROTH, JOHANN MARTIN (1745): *Les Coutumes des Francs-Maçons dans leurs assemblées, principalement pour la réception des apprentifs et des maîtres, tout nouvellement et sincerement découvertes* (Leipzig: B. C. Breitkopf).
——— (1746): see LARUDAN.
BERNOYER, FRANÇOIS (Ed.) (1976): *Avec Bonaparte en Égypte et en Syrie, 1798-1800* (Abbeville: Les presses françaises).
BERTIER DE SAUVIGNY, GUILLAUME DE (1977): *La Restauration, 1815-1830* (Paris: Hachette).
BERTRAND, ELIE (1754): *Essai sur les Usages des Montagnes, avec une Lettre sur le Nil* (Zürich: Heidegger & Co.).
BETBUCH FÜR FREYMAURER IN HOCHWÜRDIGSTE PROVINZIALLOGE VON BÖHMEN UND ALLEN FREIMÄUREN DIESES SPRENGELS (1784) (Prague: s.n.).
BETZ, JACQUES (1954): *Bartholdi* 123-4, 268. (Paris: Éditions de Minuit).
BEUREN, OTTO (*pseudonym*) (1884): see RAICH, JOHANN MICHAEL.
BEUTHER, FRIEDRICH CHRISTIAN (1833a): *Über Licht und Farbe, die prismatischen Farben und die Newton'sche Farbenlehre* (Kassel: Beuther).
——— (1833b): *Kurze Anweisung zur Linear-Perspektive,etc.* (Kassel: Beuther).
——— (1963): see JUNG, OTTO.
BEYER, GÜNTHER & KLAUS, & PIANA, THEO (1969): *Weimar: Stätte Lebendiger Tradition* (Berlin & Weimar: Aufbau-Verlag).
BÉYERLÉ, JEAN-PIERRE-LOUIS DE (1784): *Essai sur la Franc-Maçonnerie* (Latomopolis [? Paris]: Chez Xiste Andron).
BIANCHI, ROBERT STEVEN (1980): 'Not the Isis Knot' *Bulletin of the Egyptological Seminar* **ii** 2-31.
——— (1981): 'Two Ex-Votos from the Sebennytic Group' *Journal of the Society for the Study of Egyptian Antiquities* **xi** 31-36.
——— (1988): *Cleopatra's Egypt: age of the Ptolemies* (Brooklyn NY: Brooklyn Museum).
BIET, LÉON-MARIE-DIEUDONNÉ (1925-50): see GOULIER, CHARLES-PIERRE.
BIGELOW, JACOB (1860): *A History of the Cemetery of Mount Auburn* (Boston & Cambridge MA: J. Munroe & Co.).
BIHAN, ALAIN LE (1966): *Francs-Maçons Parisiens du Grand Orient de France* (Paris: Bibliothèque Nationale).
BIRKSTED, J. K. (2009): *Le Corbusier and the Occult* (Cambridge MA & London: MIT Press).
——— (1967): *Loges et Chapitres de la Grande Loge et du Grand Orient de France (2ᵉ moitié du XVIIIᵉ siècle)* (Paris: Bibliothèque Nationale).
BIRLEY, ANTHONY RICHARD (1997): *Hadrian: The Restless Emperor* (London & New York: Routledge).
——— (Tr.) (1999): see TACITUS, CORNELIUS.
BIRRELL, FRANCIS (Ed.) (1931): see BLAIKIE, THOMAS.
BISCHOFF, ERICH (1913-14): *Die Elemente der Kabbalah* (Berlin: Barsdorf).
BITTNER, NORBERT (1818): *Theaterdekorationen nach den Original Skizzen des K.K. Hoftheater Mahlers Anton de Pian. Radirt und verlegt von Norbert Bittner* (Vienna: Bittner).
BIVER, COMTESSE MARIE-LOUISE (1963): *Le Paris de Napoléon* (Paris: Plon).
BJÖRKMAN, G. (1977): 'Harsiese' in *Lexikon der Ägyptologie* **ii** (Wiesbaden: O. Harrassowitz) c. 1018-20.
BLACK, ANTONY (1984): *Guilds and Civil Society in European Political Thought from the Twelfth Century to the Present* (Ithaca NY: Cornell UP).
BLACKMAN, A. M. (Tr.) (1927): see ERMAN, ADOLF.
BLAIKIE, THOMAS (1931): *Diary of a Scotch Gardener at the French Court at the End of the Eighteenth Century* FRANCIS BIRRELL (Ed.) (London: George Routledge & Sons).
BLAIR, ROBERT (1826): *The Grave* (Edinburgh: Stirling & Kenney; London: Longman etc.).
BLAVATSKY, HELENA PETROVNA (1877): *Isis Unveiled: a master-key to the mysteries of ancient and modern science and theology* (New York: J.W. Bouton).
BLEEKER, CLAAS JOUCO (1963): 'Isis as Savior Goddess' *Festschrift E. O. James* (Manchester: Manchester UP).
——— (1967): *Egyptian Festivals. Enactments of Religious Renewal* (Leiden: E. J. Brill).
——— (1973): *Hathor and Thoth: Two Key Figures of the Ancient Egyptian Religion* (Leiden: E. J. Brill).
BLOCH, H. (1945): 'A New Document of the Last Pagan Festival in the West, 393-394 A.D.' *Harvard Theological Review* **xxxviii** 199-244.
BLOCH, OLIVIER & PORSET, CHARLES (1992): *Le Matérialisme des Lumières. Dix-Huitième Siècle* **xxiv** [Special Issue] (Paris: Presses Universitaires de France).
BLOK, J. H. (1995): *The Early Amazons. Modern and Ancient Perspectives on a Persistent Myth* (Leiden: E. J. Brill).
BLOM, ERIC (Tr.) (1947, 1961): see DEUTSCH, OTTO ERICH (Ed.).
BLOMME, A. (1909): 'L'Égyptologie en Belgique' *Annales de l'Académie Royale d'Archéologie de Belgique* **lxi** 6 series 1 (Antwerp: J. van Hille-de Backer) 569-658.
BLONDEL, JACQUES-FRANÇOIS (1754): *Discours sur la nécessité de l'étude de l'architecture* (Paris: Jombert).
——— (1771-7): *Cours d'Architecture* (with PIERRE PATTE) (Paris: Desaint).
——— (1774): *L'Homme du monde éclairé par les arts* (Amsterdam: Monory).
BLONDEL, SPIRE (1887): *L'Art pendant la Révolution* (Paris: H. Laurens).
BOAS, GEORGE E. (1935): see LOVEJOY, ARTHUR ONCKEN.
——— (1950): *The Hieroglyphics of Horapollo* (New York: Pantheon Books).
BÖCHER, OTTO (1960): 'Die Alte Synagoge zu Worms' *Der Wormsgau* **xviii** (Worms: Verlag Stadtbibliothek).
BODE, URSULA, CLARE, DANIELA, QUILITZSCH, UWE, STÜRMER, MICHAEL, & WEISS, THOMAS (1997): *For the Friends of Nature and Art: the Garden Kingdom of Prince Franz of Anhalt-Dessau in [the] Age of Enlightenment* (Ostfildern-Ruit: Verlag Gerd Hatje).
BODI, LESLIE (1977): *Tauwetter in Wien: zur Prosa der Österreichischen Aufklärung 1781-1795* (Frankfurt-am-Main: Fischer). A new edn. (1995) was published in Vienna by Böhlau.
BOEHME, ADAM FRIEDRICH (1778): *Alphabetisches Verzeichnis aller bekannten Freimäurer-Logen aus öffentlichen Gesellschaft zusammen getragen* (Leipzig: Adam Friedrich Boehme).
BOETHIUS, ANICIUS MANLIUS SEVERINUS (1983): *Boetian Number Theory* MICHAEL MASI (Tr.) (Amsterdam: Rodopi).
BOGDAN, HENRIK (2006): 'An Introduction to the High Degrees of Freemasonry' *Heredom* **xiv**.
——— (2007a): 'Secret Societies and Western Esotericism' ROBERT A. GILBERT (Ed.) (2007) 21-29.
——— (2007b): *Western Esotericism and Rituals of Initiation* (Albany NY: State University of New York Press).
BOHDAN, CAROL L. (1980): 'Egyptian-inspired Furniture, 1800-1922' *Art and Antiques* **iii**/6 (November-December) 64-71.
BÖHEIM, JOSEPH MICHAEL (Ed.) (1798-99): *Auswahl von Maurer Gesängen mit Melodien mit den vorzüglichsten Componisten in Zweij Abtheilungen getheilt* (Berlin: s.n., but later by 'F. Maurer', 1817-19).
BOISSIER, GASTON: (1909): *La fin du paganisme* (Paris: Hachette). A later edition of 1987 was published in Hildesheim).
BOITARD, PIERRE (1834): *Manuel complet de l'architecte des jardins…* (Paris: Encyclopédie Roret).
BOLD, JOHN, & CHANEY, EDWARD (Eds.) (1993): *English Architecture, Public and Private: Essys for Kerry Downes* (London & Rio Grande OH: Hambledon Press).
BONAPARTE EN ÉGYPTE (1938): Exhibition *Catalogue* (Paris: Musée de l'Orangerie). See also 'Au Musée de l'Orangerie: Bonaparte en Égypte' *L'Illustration*, No. 4982 (27 August 1938), 541-543. The *Catalogue* was prepared by MAXIME KAHN & MAURICE SERRULAZ.
BONGIOANNI, ALESSANDRO & GRASSI, RICCARDO (1994): *Torino, L'Egitto e l'Oriente: fra Storia e Leggenda* (Turin: Angelo Manzoni).
BONNEFOY, YVES (Ed.) (1981): *Dictionnaire des Mythologies et des Religions des Sociétés traditionelles et du Monde antique* (Paris: Flammarion).
BONNET, HANS (1952): *Reallexikon der ägyptischen Religionsgeschichte* (Berlin & New York: De Gruyter). See also the later 1971 edition.
BONNEVILLE, NICOLAS DE (1791): *De l'esprit des religions* (Paris: Impr. Du Cercle social).
BOOR, J. (1952): *Masonería* (Madrid: s.n.).

BORD, GUSTAVE (1908): *La Franc-Maçonnerie en France des Origines à 1815* (Paris: Nouv. Librairie Nationale).

BORDELON, LAURENT (1716): *La Coterie des Anti-Façonniers* (Amsterdam: Aux dépens de la Compagnie). This imprint is false: it was actually published in Paris, but there was an earlier edition (supposedly published in Leiden: Jean Sambix le Jeune 1675).

BORGHOUTS, J. F. (1966): 'Op zoek naar het graf van Imhotep' *Phoenix* **xii** 360-7.

BORN, IGNAZ EDLER VON (1783-88): *Physikalische Arbeiten der einträchtigen Freunde in Wien* (Vienna: Loge zur wahren Eintracht).

——— (1784): 'Über die Mysterien der Ägypter' *Journal für Freymaurer* (Vienna: '5784') 15-132.

BÖRSCH-SUPAN, HELMUT, & GRISEBACH, LUCIUS (Eds.) (1981): *Karl Friedrich Schinkel. Architektur, Malerei, Kunstgewerbe* (Berlin: Staatlichen Schlösser und Gärten).

BOS, AGNÈS (Ed.) (1998): see HEALEY, CATHERINE.

BOUCHART, FRANÇOIS-XAVIER (1985): see BEAUTHEAC, NADINE.

BOURGET, PAUL-CHARLES-JOSEPH (1914): *Le Démon du Midi* (Paris: Plon).

BOULLÉE, ÉTIENNE-LOUIS (1968): *Architecture, Essai sur L'Art* (Paris: Hermann).

BOURGEOIS, EMIL (1930): *Le Style Empire* (Paris: Laurens).

BOURKE, JOHN WILLIAM PATRICK (1961): *Baroque Churches of Central Europe* (London: Faber & Faber) 124-5.

BOURRIAU, J. (1984): 'Salbefässe' *Lexikon der Ägyptologie* **v** (Wiesbaden: O. Harrassowitz) c. 362-366.

BOUSSEL, PATRICE (1969): *Guide de l'Île-de-France mystérieuse* (Paris: Tchou).

BOUSSET, WILHELM (1906): *Die Offenbarung Johannis* (Göttingen: Vandenhoeck).

BOWEN, RALPH H. (Tr.) (1956): see DIDEROT, DENIS.

BOWIE, KAREN (Ed.) (1998): see HEALEY, CATHERINE.

BOWMAN, ALAN K. (1990): *Egypt after the Pharaohs: 330 B.C. – 642 A.D.* (Oxford: Oxford UP).

BOYLAN, PATRICK (1922): *Thoth: the Hermes of Egypt* (London: H. Milford for Oxford UP).

BRADLEY, SIMON, & PEVSNER, NIKOLAUS (1997): *London 1: The City of London* (London: Penguin Group).

BRADSHAW, HENRY (1887): *The Life of Saint Werburge of Chester* CARL HORSTMANN (Ed.) (London: Trübner).

BRADY, THOMAS ALLEN (1935): *The Reception of the Egyptian Cults by the Greeks* (Columbia MO: University of Missouri Press).

BRANSCOMBE, PETER (1965-6): 'Die Zauberflöte: Some Textual and Interpretative Problems' *Proceedings of the Royal Musical Association* **xcii** 45-63.

——— (1972): *Music & Letters* **liii** 434-6.

——— (1991): *W. A. Mozart: Die Zauberflöte* (Cambridge: Cambridge UP).

——— (Tr.) (1961) see DEUTSCH, OTTO ERICH (Ed.)

BRAUNBEHRENS, VOLKMAR (1986): *Mozart in Vienna 1781-1791* (London: André Deutsch).

BREASTED, JAMES HENRY (1959): *Development of Religion and Thought in Ancient Egypt* (New York: Harper).

——— (Ed.) (1962): *Ancient Records of Egypt* (New York: Russell & Russell).

BRECCIA, EVARISTO (1970): *Le Musée gréco-romain d'Alexandrie 1925-1931* (Rome: 'L'Erma' di Bretschneider).

BREEZE, DAVID JOHN (Ed.) (1984): *Studies in Scottish Antiquity* (Edinburgh: Donald).

BREMER, JOHANN GOTTFRIED (1793): *Die symbolische Weisheit der Aegypter aus dem verborgensten Denkmälern des Alterthums; ein Theil der ægyptischen Maurerey, der bis noch nicht verbrannt worden* KARL PHILIPP MORITZ (Ed.) (Berlin: K. Matzdorff).

BRENGUES, JACQUES (1973): *La Franc-Maçonnerie du bois* (? Rennes: s.n.).

BRETT-SMITH, H.F.B., & JONES, C.E. (Eds.) (1924-34): *The Works of Thomas Love Peacock* (London: Constable).

BRINKS, JÜRGEN (1973): 'Die Ägyptisierenden Nachzeichnungen und Entwürfe des Klassizistischen Architekten Georg Ludwig Friedrich Laves' *Niederdeutsche Beiträge zur Kunstgeschichte Wissenschaft* **xii** 81-116.

BRITTON, JOHN, & PUGIN, AUGUSTUS CHARLES (1825): *Illustrations of the Public Buildings of London* (London: J. Taylor).

BRODER, N. (Tr.) (1956): see EINSTEIN, ALFRED.

BRONGNIART, ALEXANDRE-THÉODORE (1814): *Plans… du Cimetière Mont-Louis…* etc. (Paris: A.-T. Brongniart).

BROOKS, CHRISTOPHER (1999): *The Gothic Revival* (London: Phaidon).

BROPHY, BRIGID (1988): *Mozart the Dramatist. The Value of His Operas to him, to his age, and to us* (London: Libris).

BROSE, J. (1978): see QUATREBARBES, E. DE.

BROWN, PETER ROBERT LAMONT (1978): *The Making of Late Antiquity* (Cambridge, MA: Harvard UP).

BROWN, WILLIAM MOSELEY (1958): *From Operative to Speculative* (Masonic Service Association [29 January]).

BROWNE, SIR THOMAS (1912): *The Works of Sir Thomas Browne* CHARLES SAYLE (Ed.) (Edinburgh: John Grant).

BROWNLEE, DAVID (Ed.) *Friedrich Weinbrenner: Architect of Karlsruhe* (Philadelphia PA: University of Pennsylvania Press).

BRUNET, M. (1953): see VERLET, PIERRE.

BRUNNER-TRAUT, EMMA & HELLMUT, & ZICK-NISSEN, JOANNA (1984): *Osiris, Kreuz, und Halbmond: die drei Religionen Ägyptens* (Mainz-am-Rhein: P. von Zabern).

BUCH, DAVID JOSEPH (1997): 'Mozart and the Theater auf der Wieden: New attributions and perspectives' *Cambridge Opera Journal* **ix**/3 195-232.

———(2004): 'Die Zauberflöte: Masonic Opera, and Other Fairy Tales' *Acta Musicologica* **lxxvi** 193-219.

BUCK, JIRAH DEWEY (1911): *Mystic Masonry; or, the symbols of Freemasonry and the Greater Mysteries of Antiquity* (Chicago IL: Ezra A. Cook). See also the later (1946) edn. entitled *Symbolism of Freemasonry or Mystic Masonry and the Greater Mysteries of Antiquity*.

BUDDE, HENDRIK (Ed.) (1989): see SIEVERNICH, GEREON.

BUDISCHOVSKY, M.-C. (1977): *La diffusion des cultes isaïques autour de la mer Adriatique* (Leiden: E. J. Brill).

BUHL, M. L. (1947): 'The Goddesses of the Egyptian Tree Cult' *Journal of Near Eastern Studies* **vi** 80-97.

BUILDER, THE (from 1842): *An illustrated weekly magazine for the architect, engineer, archæologist, constructor, sanitary reformer, and art-lover* (London: The Builder).

BULLETINO DELLA COMMISSIONE ARCHEOLOGICA COMUNALE DI ROMA (from 1872): (Rome: later editions published by L'Erma di Bretschneider).

BULLOCK, STEPHEN C. (1996): *Revolutionary Brotherhood: Freemasonry and the Transformation of the American Social Order, 1730-1840* (Chapel Hill NC: University of North Carolina Press).

BUNYAN, JOHN (1756): *Solomon's Temple Spirituali'd* (London: James Schofield).

BURKE, E. L. (Tr.) (1971-7): see CAPELLA, MARTIANUS MINEUS FELIX.

BURKE, EDMUND (1757): *A Philosophical Enquiry into the Origin of Our Ideas of the Sublime and Beautiful* (London: R. & J. Dodsley).

BURKERT, WALTER (1987): *Ancient Mystery Cults* (Cambridge MA & London: Harvard UP).

BURMAN, P. (Ed.) (2001): see SCHMIDT, LEO.

BURNETT, DAVID (1998): *The Engraved Title-Page of Bacon's Instauratio Magna: An Icon and Paradigm of Science and its wider Implications* (Durham: Thomas Harriot Seminar Occasional Paper **xxvii**).

BUSINSK, T. A. (1970): *Der Tempel von Jerusalem von Salomo bis Herodes* (Leiden: E. J. Brill).

BUTTLAR, ADRIAN VON (1982): *Der Englische Landsitz, 1715-1760. Symbol eines liberalen Weltenwurfs* (Mittenwald: Mäander).

——— (1989): *Der Landschaftsgarten, Gartenkunst des Klassizismus und der Romantik* (Cologne: DuMont

CABRIÈRE, JUSTIN (1899): *Court de Gébelin, défenseur des églises réformées de France* (Cahors: A. Coueslant).

CAHILL, REV. EDWARD (1929): *Freemasonry and the Anti-Christian Movement* (Dublin: M. H. Gill & Son).

CAHN, WILHELM (1976): 'Solomonic Elements in Romanesque Art' GUTMANN, JOSEPH (Ed.) (1976).

CALCIDIUS (1962): *Timaeus* J. H. WASZINK (Ed.) (London: Warburg Institute).

CALCOTT, WELLINS (1769): *A Candid Disquisition of the Principles and Practices of the Most Antient and Honourable Society of Free and Accepted Masons…* (London: James Dixwell, for the Author).

CALDECOTT, W. SHAW (1908): *Solomon's Temple: its History and its Structure* (London: Religious Tract Society).

CALDER, MARTIN (Ed.) (2006): *Experiencing the Garden in the Eighteenth Century* (Oxford & Bern: Peter Lang).

CAMUS DE MÉZIÈRES, NICOLAS LE (1780): *Le genie de l'architecture: ou l'analogie de cet art avec nos sensations* (Paris : The Author).

CAPELLA, MARTIANUS MINEUS FELIX (1971-7): *Martianus Capella and the Seven Liberal Arts* WILLIAM HARRIS STAHL, RICHARD JOHNSON, & E. L. BURGE (Trs.) (New York & Guildford: Columbia UP).

CAPPE, AUGUST WILHELM HEINRICH (1801): *Authentische Geschichte der Freymaurerey im Orient von Hildesheim* (Hildesheim: s.n.).

CARMIGNIANI, JUAN CARLOS (1988): see TRANIÉ, JEAN.

CARMONTELLE, LOUIS CARROGIS, called (1779): *Jardin de Monceau, près de Paris, appartenant à … M. le duc de Chartres* (Paris: Delafosse).

CARR, HARRY (1954): *The Mason and the Burgh. An Examination of the Edinburgh Register of Apprentices and the Burgess Rolls* (London: W. J. Parrett for QCL).

——— (1961): *The Lodge Mother Kilwinning, No. 0. A Study of the Earliest Minute Books, 1642 to 1842* (London: QCL).

——— (1962): *The Minutes of the Lodge of Edinburgh, Mary's Chapel, No. I, 1598-1738* (London: QCL).

——— (1976): *The Freemason at Work* (London: The Author).

——— (Ed.) (1971): *The Early French Exposures* (London: QCL).

CARROGIS, LOUIS (1779): see CARMONTELLE.

CARROTT, RICHARD G. (1961): 'The architect of the Pennsylvania Fire Insurance Building' *Journal of the Society of Architectural Historians* **xx**/3 (October) 138-139.

——— (1966): 'The neo-Egyptian style in American architecture' *Antiques* (October) 482-488.

——— (1978): *The Egyptian Revival. Its Sources, Monuments, and Meaning. 1808-1858* (Berkeley CA, Los Angeles CA, & London: University of California Press).

CASEY, CHRISTINE (2005): *Dublin* in The Buildings of Ireland Series (New Haven CT & London: Yale UP).

CASSARD, ANDRÉS (1932): *Manual de la Masonería; ó sea El tejador de los ritos antiguo escocés, francés y de adopción* (Barcelona: Editorial B. Bauzá).

CASSIODORUS, MAGNUS AURELIUS (2004): *Institutions of Divine and Secular Learning* JAMES W. HALPORN (Tr.) (Liverpool: Liverpool UP).

CASSIRER, ERNST (1955): *The Philosophy of Enlightenment* (Boston MA: Beacon Press).

CASTELLS, FRANCIS. DE PAULA (1971): *Was Sir Christopher Wren a Mason?* (London: G. Kenning).

——— (1931): *English Freemasonry in its Period of Transition, A. D. 1600-1700* (London: Rider & Co.).

CAUS, SALOMON DE (1620): *Hortus Palatinus a Friderico Rege Boemiae Electore Palatino Heidelbergae exstructus* (Frankfurt: J. T. De Bry).

CAYLUS, ANNE-CLAUDE-PHILIPPE DE THUBIÈRES, COMTE DE (1752-67): *Recueil d'Antiquités Égyptiennes, Étrusques, Grecques, et Romaines* (Paris: Desaint & Saillant).

CELIS, MARCEL (1984): 'De egyptiserende maçonnieke tempels van de Brusselse Loges "Les Amis Philanthropes" en "Les Vrais Amis de l'Union et du Progrès Réunis"' *M & L. Monumenten en Landschappen* **iii**/3 (May-June) 25-41.

ČERNÝ, JAROSLAV (1952): *Ancient Egyptian Religion* (London: Hutchinson's University Library).

CHABAS, FRANÇOIS-JOSEPH (1877): see COOPER, WILLIAM RICKETTS.

CHAILLEY, JACQUES (1965): 'Le Winterreise de Schubert, est-il une oeuvre ésotérique?' *Revue d'Esthétique* 113-24.

——— (1967): 'Die Symbolik in der Zauberflöte' *Mozart-Jahrbuch* 100-110.

——— (1972): *The Magic Flute: Masonic Opera. An Interpretation of the Libretto and the Music* H. WEINSTOCK (Tr.) (London: Gollancz).

——— (1976): 'La Flûte Enchantée, Opera Maçonnique' *L'Avant-Scène Opéra* **i** 82-89.

CHAMBERLAIN, HOUSTON STEWART (1911-12): *The Foundations of the Nineteenth Century* JOHN LEES (Tr.) (London: John Lane at the Bodley Head).
CHAMBERS, EPHRAIM (Tr.) (1723-4): see CLERC, SÉBASTIEN LE.
CHAMOUST, CHARLES-FRANÇOIS RIBART DE (1783): *L'Ordre François Trouvé dans la Nature* (Paris: The Author).
CHAMPIGNEULLE, BERNARD (1961): *Promenade dans les jardins de Paris, ses bois, et ses squares* (Paris: Club des libraires de France).
CHAMPOLLION, JEAN-FRANÇOIS (1822): *Lettre à M. Dacier* (Paris: Didot).
———— (1833): *Lettres écrites d'Égypte et de Nubie en 1828 et 1829* (Paris: Didot).
———— (1841): *Dictionnaire Égyptien en écriture hiéroglyphique* (Paris: Didot).
CHANEY, EDWARD (Ed.) (1993): see BOLD, JOHN.
CHARLES, ROBERT HENRY (Ed.) (1913): *The Apocrypha and Pseudepigrapha of the Old Testament in English* (Oxford: Oxford UP).
CHARNEY, MELVIN (1991): *Parables and Other Allegories: The Work of Melvin Charney 1975-1990*, with contributions from PHYLLIS LAMBERT, ALESSANDRA LATOUR, PATRICIA C. PHILLIPS, & ROBERT-JAN VAN PELT (Montréal: Centre Canadien d'Architecture, & Cambridge MA & London: The MIT Press).
CHARPENTIER, JOSANE (1980): *La France des lieux et des demeures alchimiques* (Paris: Retz).
CHASTEL, ANDRÉ (1966): 'The Grand Eccentrics: The Moralizing Architecture of Jean-Jacques Lequeu' *Art News Annual* **xxxii** 70-83.
CHASTEL, ÉTIENNE-LOUIS (1857): *Histoire de la Destruction du Paganisme dans l'Empire d'Orient* (Paris: Académie des Inscriptions et Belles-Lettres).
CHAUSSARD, PIERRE-JEAN-BAPTISTE (1800): *Monuments de L'heroïsme français; nécessité de ramener à un plan unique ... etc.* (Paris: C.-L.-F. Panckoucke).
CHERRY, BRIDGET, & PEVSNER, NIKOLAUS (1991): *London 3 North West* in *The Buildings of England* Series (London: Penguin Group).
———— (1998): *London 4 North* in *The Buildings of England* Series (London: Penguin Group).
CHETWODE CRAWLEY, WILLIAM JOHN (1895-1900): *Cœmenteria Hibernica* (Dublin: W. McGee).
———— (1898): see SADLER, HENRY.
———— (1911): 'The Old Charges and the Papal Bull' *AQC* **xxiv** 58ff.
CHEVALIER DE TOUS LES ORDRES MAÇONNIQUES (1807): *La Vraie Maçonnerie d'Adoption* (Paris: Grand Orient de France).
CHEVALLIER, PIERRE (1964): *Les Ducs sous l'Acacia; ou, Les Premiers Pas de la Franc-Maçonnerie française, 1725-1743* (Paris: J. Vrin).
———— (1966): *Nouvelles recherches sur les francs-maçons parisiens et lorrains* (Nancy: Berger-Levrault).
———— (1968): *La Première Profanation du Temple Maçonnique, ou Louis XV et la Fraternité, 1737-1755.* (Paris: J. Vrin).
———— (1971): *Études Maçonniques* (n.p.: Imp. Paton).
———— (1974): *Histoire de la Franc-Maçonnerie française. La Maçonnerie: école de l'égalité, 1725-1799* (Paris: Fayard).
CHRISTIANSEN, ERIK, & DAHL HERMANSEN, BO (Eds.) (2001): *Arven fra Ægypten II: Genopdagelse. Mystik og vidensa* (Aarhus: Tidsskiftet Sfinx).
CHRISTIE, JAMES (1806): *A Disquisition upon Etruscan Vases* (London: W. Bulmer & T. Becket).
———— (1814): *An Essay on that Earliest Species of Idolatry, the Worship of the Elements* (Norwich: Stevenson, Matchett, & Stevenson).
———— (1817): see UVAROV, COUNT S.S.
CHURTON, TOBIAS (2006): 'Anderson's Constitutions, 1723 and 1738: Heretical or Revolutionary?' STEWART, TREVOR (Ed.) (2006) 26-49.
———— (2007): 'The First Rosicrucians' GILBERT, ROBERT A. (Ed.) (2007) 72-9.
CIAPPONI, L. A. (1980): see COLONNA, FRANCESCO.
CIOŁEK, GERARD (1954): *Ogrody Polskie* (Warsaw: Budownictwo i Architektura). Another edn. (1978) was published in Warsaw by Arcady).
CLARE, DANIELA (1997): see BODE, URSULA.
CLARET, G. (1840): *Ceremonies of Initiation* (London: G. Claret).
———— (1847): *The Whole of Craft Free-Masonry* (London: G. Claret).
CLARIN DE LA RIVE, ABEL (1894): *La Femme et l'enfant dans Franc-maçonnerie universelle* (Paris & Lyon: Delhomme & Briguet).
CLARK, H. F. (1943): 'Eighteenth-Century Elysiums: the Rôle of "Association" in the Landscape Movement' *Journal of the Warburg Institute* **vi** 165-89.
CLARK, PETER (2001): *British Clubs and Societies, 1580-1800: The Origins of an Associational World* (Oxford: Oxford UP).
CLARKE, BERNARD (1751): *An Answer to the Pope's Bull: with a Vindication of the Real Principles of Free-Masonry* (Dublin: John Butler for The Author).
CLAUSEN, ERNST ALEXANDER (1914): *Die Freimaurer; Einführung in das Wesen ihres Bundes* (Berlin: Alfred Unger).
CLAVEL (actually BÈGUE, F.-T.) (1844-8): *Almanach pittoresque de la franc-maçonnerie pour l'année 5844-5848* (Paris: Pagnerre).
———— (1845): *Historie Pittoresque de la Franc-Maçonnerie et des Societés Secrètes* (Paris: Pagnerre).
CLAWSON, MARY ANN (1989): *Constructing Brotherhood: Class, Gender, and Fraternalism* (Guildford NJ: Princeton UP).
CLAY, JEAN (1980): *Romanticism* (New York: The Vendome Press & Oxford: Phaidon).
CLAYTON, PETER A. (1982): *The Rediscovery of Ancient Egypt. Artists and Travellers in the Nineteenth Century* (London: Thames & Hudson).
———— (1994): *Chronicle of the Pharaohs* (London: Thames & Hudson).
CLÉBERT, JEAN-PAUL (1958): see ROCHEGUDE, FÉLIX, MARQUIS DE.
CLÉEMPUTTE, P.-L. VAN (1787-96): see ACADÉMIE DES BEAUX-ARTS.
CLEMEN, CARL CHRISTIAN (1912): *Primitive Christianity and its non-Jewish Sources* (Edinburgh: T. & T. Clark).
———— (1913): *Der Einfluss der Mysterienreligionen auf das älteste Christentum* (Giessen: A. Töppelmann).
———— (1914): 'Der Isiskult und das Neue Testament' *Heinrici Festschrift: Neutestamentlichen Studien* (Leipzig: J.C. Hinrichs).
———— (1931): *Religions of the World, their Nature and their History* (London: G.G. Harrap).
CLERC, SÉBASTIEN LE (1723-4): *A Treatise of Architecture* EPHRAIM CHAMBERS (Tr.) (London: R. Ware).
CLÈRE, MARCEL LE (1978): *Cimetières et Sépultures de Paris; Guide Historique et Practique* (Paris: Hachette).
COFFIN, DAVID (1960): *The Villa d'Este at Tivoli* (Princeton NJ: Princeton UP).
———— (1964): 'Ligorio on the nobility of the arts' *Journal of the Warburg and Courtauld Institutes* **xxvii** 191-210.
COGLAN, THOMAS (1813): *An Improved System of Mnemonics: or, Art of assisting the Memory simplified ... with a Dictionary ... etc.* (London: C. Cradock & W. Joy; John Hatchard). The illustrations in this (only the first volume was published) are interesting.
COHEN, A. (Tr.) (1927): see LESSING, GOTTHOLD EPHRAIM.
COHEN-HADAD, BERNARD (2001): *Respectable Loge Demain* (Paris: EDIMAF).
COHN, NORMAN RUFUS COLIN (1967): *Warrant for Genocide: the Myth of the Jewish World-Conspiracy and the Protocols of the Elders of Zion* (London: Eyre & Spottiswoode, & New York: Harper & Row). See also the German translation with commentary by MICHAEL HAGEMEISTER (1998): (Baden-Baden: Elster Verlag).
COIL, HENRY WILSON (1961): *Coil's Masonic Encyclopedia* (New York: Macoy).
———— (1962-8): *Freemasonry through Six Centuries* (S.I.: Macoy Pub.).
COLE, JUAN (2007): *Napoleon's Egypt: Invading the Middle East* (New York & Basingstoke: Palgrave Macmillan).
COLONNA, FRANCESCO (1499): *Hypnerotomachia Poliphili* (Venice: Aldus Manutius). see also *Hypnerotomachie, ou discours du songe de Poliphile* (1963: a facsimile of the 1546 French edition (Paris: Club des libraires de France). See also GODWIN, JOSCELYN (1999), and the critical edition of 1980, with commentary by G. POZZI & L. A. CIAPPONI (Padua: Antenore).
COLVIN, HOWARD MONTAGU (1991): *Architecture and the After-Life* (New Haven CT & London: Yale UP).
———— (1999): *Essays in English Architectural History* (New Haven CT & London: Yale UP).
———— (2008): *A Biographical Dictionary of British Architects 1600-1840* (New Haven CT & London: Yale UP). See also the 1995 edn. published by Yale and the 1978 edn. published by John Murray).
COMAY, JOAN (1975): *The Temple of Jerusalem* (London: Weidenfeld & Nicolson).
COMBES, ANDRÉ (2003): *Adolphe Crémieux 1796-1880: Le grand maître du rite écossais, l'avocat et homme politique, le président de l'alliance israélite universelle* in *Encyclopédie maçonnique* **xli** (Paris: Éditions maçonniques de France).
COMBES D'AURIAC, FRÉDÉRIC (1852): see ACQUIER, HIPPOLYTE.
COMESTOR, PETRUS (1987): *Genesi* (Milan: Jaca Book).
COMMISSION DES SCIENCES ET ARTS D'ÉGYPTE (1809-28): *Description de l'Égypte, ou, Recueil des observations et des recherches qui ont été faites en Égypte pendant l'expédition de l'armée française.* The volumes dated 1809-13 had the imprint 'Imprimerie impériale', and the title continued *publié par les ordres de sa Majesté l'empereur Napoléon le Grand*; those dated 1817-28 had the imprint 'Imprimerie Royale', and the title continued *publié par ordre du gouvernement*. The editor was EDMÉ-FRANÇOIS JOMARD. The text is in this order: *Antiquités-Descriptions* 1809-18 (2 vols.); *Antiquités-Mémoires* 1809-18 (2 vols.); Plates 1809-22 (5 vols.); *État moderne* 1809-22 (2 vols. in 3); plates 1809-17 (2 vols.); *Histoire naturelle* 1809-28 (2 vols.); plates 1809-17 (2 vols. in 3); *préface et explication des planches* (c. 1828) (1 vol.); *Carte topographique de l'Égypte* 1818 (1 vol.); oversize plates from *Antiquities* and *État Moderne* (2 vols.). Thus there were 9 volumes of text and 11 volumes of plates, or 21 volumes in 23, depending on the arrangement of the binding. Some bibliographies have recorded 25 volumes, and matters are further complicated by the three sizes of folio. The usual agreed number of volumes is 21, but the different sizes of folios required special book-cases to be constructed, as at the Benedictine Abbey at Salzburg (*see* HUMBERT, PANTAZZI, & ZIEGLER [Eds.] 1994), 264-6, 326-7). See also the edition published in Paris by C.-L.-F. Panckoucke, 1820-30, with atlases.
COMPIÈGNE DE VEIL, LOUIS (Tr.) (1678): *Mishnah Torah.* Illustrated by CLAUDE PERRAULT (Paris: G. Gaillou). The full title is *De Culto divino, ex Mosis Majemonidæ secunda Lege seu Manu Forti liber VIII etc ... Hunc librum ex Hebraeo Latinum fecit ...Ludovicus de Compiègne de Veil ...* See MAIMONIDES.
CONAN, MICHEL (2005): *Baroque Garden Cultures: Emulation, Sublimation, Subversion* (Washington DC: Dumbarton Oaks Research Library and Collection).
CONDER, EDWARD, JR. (1894): *Records of the Hole Crafte and Fellowship of Masons* (London: Swan Sonnenschein & Co.). See also the reprint of 1988 (Bloomington IL: The Masonic Book Club).
CONNAISSANCE DES ARTS (from 1952): (Paris: Société d'études et publications artistiques).
CONNER, PATRICK (1979): *Oriental Architecture in the West* (London: Thames & Hudson).
———— (Ed.) (1983): *The Inspiration of Egypt. Its Influences on British Artists, Travellers, and Designers, 1700-1900.* Catalogue of the Exhibition of that title held at Brighton Museum (7 May - 17 July 1983) and at Manchester City Art Gallery (4 August - 17 September). (Brighton: Brighton Borough Council).
———— (1985): 'Wedding Archæology to Art: Poynter's Israel in Egypt' *Influences in Victorian Art and Architecture* (see MACREADY, SARAH).
CONNOISSEUR, THE (from 1901): (London: National Magazine Co.).
CONSTANS, MARTINE, ET AL. (1997a): *Bagatelle dans ses jardins* (Paris: Action artistique de la ville de Paris).
———— (1997b): 'Le château du comte d'Artois' *Bagatelle dans ses jardins* (Paris: Action artistique de la ville de Paris).
COOKE, MATTHEW (Ed.) (1861): *The History and Articles of Freemasonry: now first published from a MS. in the British Museum* (London: Richard Spencer).
COOPER, ANTHONY ASHLEY (1714): *Characteristicks..., the second edn., corrected,*

containing *A Letter Concerning the Art, or Science of Design* THOMAS MICKLETHWAITE (*Ed.*) (London: John Darby).

COOPER, L. H. (2003): 'The "Boke of Dure Charges": Constructing Community in the Masons' Constitutions' *Journal of the Early Book Society* **vi** 1-39.

COOPER, ROBERT L. D. (2006): *The Rosslyn Hoax? Viewing Rosslyn Chapel from a New Perspective* (Hersham: Lewis Masonic).

COOPER, WILLIAM RICKETTS (1873): *The Horus Myth in its relation to Christianity* (London: Hardwicke & Bogue).

——— (1877): *A Short History of the Egyptian Obelisks, with translations of many of the hieroglyphic inscriptions, chiefly by M. FRANÇOIS CHABAS* (London: S. Bagster).

COPENHAVER, B. P. (*Ed.*) (1995): see HERMES TRISMEGISTUS.

COPLAND, ROBERT (Tr.) (c.1545): *The Art of Memory, that Otherwyse is called the Phenix* (London: William Myddylton).

CORNET, J. (1849): *Die Oper in Deutschland* (Hamburg: Meissner & Schirges).

CORNFORD, STEVEN (*Ed.*) (1989): Preface to his splendid edn. of YOUNG, EDWARD.

CORSU, FRANCE LE (1977): *Isis mythe et mystères* (Paris: Les Belles Lettres).

COULET, HENRI (1984): 'Quelques aspects du mythe de l'Égypte pharaonique en France au XVIIIᵉ siècle' *Le Miroir égyptien* (Marseilles: Actes des Rencontres Méditerranéennes de Provence) 21-28.

COULTON, GEORGE GORDON (1918): *Social Life in Britain from the Conquest to the Reformation* (Cambridge: Cambridge UP).

COUNTRY LIFE (from 1897): (London: Country Life).

COUPÉ, JACQUES-MICHEL (1795): *Des Sépultures en politique et en morale* (Paris: Imprimerie Nationale).

COURET DE VILLENEUVE, MARTIN (supposed author) (1748): *L'École des Francs-Maçons…* ('Jerusalem' [? Amsterdam]: s.n.).

COURT DE GÉBELIN, ANTOINE (1773-82): *Monde Primitif, analysé et comparé avec le monde moderne* (Paris: Court de Gébelin).

COUSSILLAN, AUGUSTE ANDRÉ (1966): see HILLAIRET, JACQUES.

COUSTOS, JOHN (1746): *The Sufferings of John Coustos, for Free-Masonry, and for his refusing to turn Roman Catholic, etc.* (London: The Author).

COWELL, FIONA, & ŚWIĘCKA, EWA (*Eds.*) (1995): *Arkadia: The Illusion and the Reality. Exhibition at the Polish Cultural Institute, London (8 December 1995 – 24 January 1996)* (London: Polish Cultural Institute).

CRAGG, GERALD ROBERTSON (1960): *The Church and the Age of Reason 1648-1789* (Harmondsworth: Penguin). *See also* subsequent revised edns., especially 1990.

CRAIG, MAURICE (1982): *The Architecture of Ireland from the Earliest times to 1880* (London: B. T. Batsford).

CRAIGIE, JAMES (*Ed.*) (1914-40): see FOWLER, WILLIAM.

CROSNIER-LECONTE, MARIE-LAURE (1998): see VOLAIT, MERCEDES.

CROSS, JEREMY (1819): *Masonic Chart* (New Haven CT: Cross).

CROSSLE, PHILIP: see LEPPER, JOHN HERON.

CRYER, NEVILLE BARKER (1989a): *Masonic Halls of England: The North* (Shepperton: Lewis Masonic).

——— (1989b): *Masonic Halls of England: The South* (Shepperton: Lewis Masonic).

——— (1989c): *Masonic Halls of England: The Midlands* (Shepperton: Lewis Masonic).

——— (1990a): *Masonic Halls of North Wales* (Shepperton: Lewis Masonic).

——— (1990b): *Masonic Halls of South Wales* (Shepperton: Lewis Masonic).

CULLUS, PHILIPPE (*Ed.*) (2000): see DESPY-MEYER, ANDRÉE.

CULOT, MAURICE, CURL, JAMES STEVENS, GOSSÉ, MARCEL, HENNAUT, ERIC, HEUDE, BERNARD, PESSON, WILLIAM, & TOULIER, BERNARD (2006): *Architectures Maçonniques* (Brussels: Archives d'Architecture Moderne).

CUMONT, FRANZ VALÉRY MARTIN (1911): *The Oriental Religions in Roman Paganism* (Chicago IL: Open Court Publishing).

CUNNINGHAME GRAHAM, R. B. (1933): see KIRK, ROBERT.

CURL, JAMES STEVENS (1974): 'Mozart Considered as a Jacobin' *The Music Review* **xxxv** 131-41.

——— (1977): 'Europe's Grandest Cemetery?' *Country Life* (15 September) 700-701.

——— (1980a): *A Celebration of Death. An introduction to some of the buildings, monuments, and settings of funerary architecture in the Western European tradition* (London: Constable & New York: Scribners).

——— (1980b): *Classical Churches in Ulster* (Belfast: UAHS).

——— (1981): see LOUDON, JOHN CLAUDIUS (1843).

——— (1982): *The Egyptian Revival: An Introductory Study of a Recurring Theme in the History of Taste* (London: George Allen & Unwin).

——— (1983): *The Life and Work of Henry Roberts 1803-76, Architect. The Evangelical Conscience and the Campaign for Model Housing and Healthy Nations* (Chichester: Phillimore).

——— (1984a): 'Egypt in Paris' *Country Life* (12 July) 132-3.

——— (1984b): 'The Design of the Early British Cemeteries' *Journal of Garden History* **iv**/3 (July-September) 223-54.

——— (1986a): 'Du Nil à la Seine' *Connaissance des Arts* **411** (May) 80-85.

——— (1986b): 'Legends of the Craft. The Architecture of Masonic Halls' *Country Life* (21 August) 581-3.

——— (1986c): *The Londonderry Plantation 1609-1914: The History, Architecture, and Planning of the Estates of the City of London and its Livery Companies in Ulster* (Chichester: Phillimore).

——— (1987): 'Entstehung und Architektur der frühen britischen Friedhöfe' *O Ewich is so Lanck. Die Historischen Friedhöfe in Berlin-Kreuzberg. Eine Ausstellung im Landesarchiv. Berlin, 22 April 1987 bis 26 Juni 1987* (Berlin: Nikolaische Verlagsbuchhandlung Beuermann GmbH) 267-82.

——— (1988): 'The Design of Historical Gardens: Cultural, Magical, Medical, and Scientific Gardens in Europe' *Interdisciplinary Science Reviews* **xiii**/3 264-81.

——— (1991a): 'Aspects of the Egyptian Revival in Architectural Design in the Nineteenth Century: Themes and Motifs' GOVI, CURTO, & PERNIGOTTI (*Eds.*): 89-96.

——— (1991b): 'Altes Museum, Berlin' *The Architects' Journal* **cxciii**/25 (19 June) 30-49.

——— (1991c): 'Charlottenhof, Potsdam' in *The Architects' Journal* **cxciv**/4 & 5 (24 & 31 July), 22-39.

——— (1991d): *The Art and Architecture of Freemasonry. An Introductory Study* (London: Batsford & Woodstock & New York: Overlook Press). *See also* the revised edn. of 2002.

——— (1993): *A Celebration of Death* (London: Batsford).

——— (1994a): 'Young's Night Thoughts and the origins of the garden cemetery movement' *Journal of Garden History* **xiv**/2 (April-June) 92-118.

——— (1994b): *Egyptomania: A Recurring Theme in the History of Taste* (Manchester: Manchester UP).

——— (1995): 'Arkadia, Poland: Garden of Allusions' *Garden History. The Journal of the Garden History Society* **xxiii**/1 (Summer) 91-112. Deals with a remarkable garden with Freemasonic overtones.

——— (1996a): 'Les thèmes décoratifs égyptisants et la franc-maçonnerie' JEAN-MARCEL HUMBERT (*Ed.*). (1996) 347-65.

——— (1996b): Review of POPELKA (1994) under the title of 'Ephemeral Architecture' *Print Quarterly* (March) **xiii**/1 69-71.

——— (1997): 'Gardens of Allusion' *Interdisciplinary Science Reviews* **xxii**/4 325-42.

——— (2000a): 'Egypt in Rome – an Introductory Essay. I: Isis, obelisks, and the Isæum Campense' *Interdisciplinary Science Reviews* **xxv**/1 (Spring) 53-64.

——— (2000b): 'Egypt in Rome – an Introductory Essay. II: The Villa Adriana and the beginnings of Egyptology' *Interdisciplinary Science Reviews* **xxv**/2 (Summer) 123-35.

——— (2000c): *The Victorian Celebration of Death* (Thrupp, Stroud: Sutton Publishing). *See also* paperback edn. of 2004.

——— (2000d): *The Honourable The Irish Society and the Plantation of Ulster, 1608-2000. The City of London and the Colonisation of County Londonderry in the Province of Ulster in Ireland. A History and Critique* (Chichester: Phillimore).

——— (2001a): *Classical Architecture. An Introduction to its Vocabulary and Essentials, with a Select Glossary of Terms* (London: Batsford & New York: W.W. Norton, 2003).

——— (*Ed.*) (2001b): *Kensal Green Cemetery. The Origins & Development of the General Cemetery of All Souls, Kensal Green, London, 1824-2001* (Chichester: Phillimore).

——— (2002a): *Georgian Architecture* (Newton Abbot: David & Charles).

——— (2002b): *Death and Architecture. An Introduction to Funerary and Commemorative Buildings in the Western European Tradition, with Some Consideration of their Settings* (Thrupp, Stroud: Sutton).

——— (2002c): *Piety Proclaimed. An Introduction to Places of Worship in Victorian England* (London: Historical Publications).

——— (2002d): *The Art and Architecture of Freemasonry. An Introductory Study* (Woodstock, NY; Overlook Press).

——— (2003a): 'A Pinch of Freemasonic Snuff' *Country Life* **cxcvii**/4 (23 January) 48-9.

——— (2003b): 'Egyptomania' *Freemasonry Today* **xxiii** (Winter) 32-5.

——— (2004): 'The Landscape Garden and Freemasonry' *Ars Quatuor Coronatorum* being the Transactions of QCL PETER HAMILTON CURRIE (*Ed.*) **cxvi** for the year 2003 83-126.

——— (2005): *The Egyptian Revival: Ancient Egypt as the Inspiration for Design Motifs in the West* (Abingdon & New York: Routledge).

——— (2006a): *Dictionary of Architecture and Landscape Architecture* (Oxford: Oxford UP).

——— (2006b): 'Symbolism in Eighteenth-Century Gardens: Some Observations' *Symbolism in 18th-Century Gardens: The Influence of Intellectual and Esoteric Currents* JAN A. M. SNOEK, MONIKA SCHOLL, & ANDRÉA A. KROON (*Eds.*). (Den Haag: OVN) 25-67.

——— (2006c): 'L'architecture de la franc-maçonnerie dans les Îles Britanniques' *Architectures Maçonniques*. See CULOT, MAURICE, ET AL (2006). (Brussels: Archives d'Architecture Moderne).

——— (2006d): 'The Gardens at Schwetzingen: Some Investigations and Hypotheses' FÖRDERER, ANDREAS (*Ed.*) 171-86.

——— (2007a): *Victorian Architecture: Diversity & Invention* (Reading: Spire Books).

——— (2007b): review of BERK (2004) *Print Quarterly* **xxiv**/2 157-8.

——— (2008): 'Church Monuments in Hampshire: a Petrean Connection' in *Peterhouse Annual Record 2004/2005* 64-74. (Cambridge: The Master and Fellows of Peterhouse).

CURRAN, BRIAN A. (2007): *The Egyptian Renaissance: The Afterlife of Ancient Egypt in Early Modern Italy* (Chicago IL, & London: University of Chicago Press).

———, GRAFTON, ANTHONY, LONG, PAMELA O., & WEISS, BENJAMIN (2009): *Obelisk: A History* (Cambridge MA: MIT Press).

CURTO, SILVIO (*Ed.*) (1991): see GOVI, CRISTIANA MORIGI.

CZARTORYSKA, IZABELA ELŻBIETA (1805): *Myśli różne o sposobie zakładanie ogrodów* (Wrocław: s.n.). Another edn. appeared in 1808.

DACIER, ÉMILE (1911): *Le Jardin de Monceau avant la Révolution*, Société d'Iconographie parisienne Year 3 1910 **lvi**/1.

DAHL HERMANSEN, BO (*Ed.*) (2001): see CHRISTANSEN, ERIK.

DAMPIER, WILLIAM (1697): *Voyage* (London: James Knapton).

DANBY, HERBERT (Tr.) (1933): *The Mishnah* (Oxford: Clarendon Press).

DARNTON, ROBERT (1970): *Mesmerism and the End of the Enlightenment in France* (New York: Shocken Books).

DARRAH, DELMAR DUANE (1951): *History and Evolution of Freemasonry* (Chicago IL: Charles T. Powner).

DARTON, F. J. HARVEY (*Ed.*) (1924): see APULEIUS MADAURENSIS, LUCIUS.

DAUBERMESNIL, FRANÇOIS-ANTOINE (1796):

Rapport fait au nom d'une Commission spéciale, sur le inhumations (Paris: Imprimerie Nationale).
DAVID, JACQUES-LOUIS (1794): *Rapport sur la fête héroïque pour les honneurs du Panthéon* (Paris: s.n.).
DAVIES, MALCOLM (2005): 'The Muse of Freemasonry—Masonic Songs, Marches, Odes, Cantatas, Oratorios, and Operas, 1730-1812' STEWART, TREVOR (Ed.) (2005) 85-103.
——— (2005a): 'Masonic Musical. Poetical and Theatrical Heritage. Unexplored Territories in Public and Private Archives' KROON, BAX, & SNOEK (Eds.) (2005) 148-162.
——— (2005b): *The Masonic Muse: Songs, Music, and Musicians Associated with Dutch Freemasonry: 1730-1806* (Utrecht: Koninklijke Vereniging voor Nederlandse Muziekgeschiedenis [VNM]).
DAWKINS, PETER (1983): *A Commentary on the Great Instauration: the Universal and General Reformation of the Whole Wide World through the Renewal of all Arts and Sciences* (Northampton: Francis Bacon Research Trust).
DEAN, PTOLEMY (2006): *Sir John Soane and London* (Aldershot & Burlington VT: Lund Humphries).
DEBRUGE, J. (1926): 'Histoire de la R[espectable] [Loge] La "Parfaite Intelligence et l'Étoile Réunies" à l'Orient de Liège, rédigée à l'occasion de son 150ᵉ anniversaire' *Bulletin du Grand Orient de Belgique* 182-199.
DEBS, EUGENE VICTOR (1928): *Speeches of Eugene V. Debs* (New York: International Publishers).
DEBUS, ALLEN G. (Ed.) (1988): see MERKEL, INGRID.
DEBUSSCHÈRE, PIERRE (1998): 'Jules Pollet, Peintre du Temple' *Trigonum Coronatum. Jaarboek* **vi** 108-139.
DECASTRO, M. P. DE (Tr.) (1778): see LYON, JACOB JUDA.
DECHARNEUX, BAUDOUIN, & NEFONTAINE, LUC (2001): *La Franc-maçonnerie: En pleine lumière, à contre jour* (Brussels: Labor).
DEE, JOHN (1570): *The Elements of Geometrie* (London: I. Daye).
DEININGER, J. (1965): *Die Provinziallandtage der römischen Kaiserzeit. Von Augustus bis zum Ende des 3. Jahrhunderts n. Chr., Vestigia* **vi** (Munich and Berlin: Beck).
DEKKER, RUDOLF (2009): see BAGGERMAN, ARIANNE.
DELAHAYE, HIPPOLYTE (1931): *Commentarius Perpetuus in Martyrologium Hieronymianum* (Brussels: Bollandistes).
DELESPINE, PIERRE-JULES (1827): *Marché des Blancs-Manteaux…suivi du Tombeau de Newton* (Paris: A. Boucher).
DELILLE, ABBÉ JACQUES (actually MONTANIER, JACQUES, called) (1782): *Les Jardins, ou l'art d'embellir les Paysages* (Paris: Didot. See also MAUNDE, J. (Tr.) (1801).
——— (1806): *L'Imagination, Poëme en VIII Chants accompagné de Notes Historiques et Littéraires, par J. ESMÉNARD* (Paris: Giguet & Michaud) **i** Chant I lines 1&2, 25.
DELVAUX, LUC, DE PUTTER, TH., DOYEN, F., KARLSHAUSEN, CHR., PREYS, R., & WARMENBOL, E. (1993): contributions in DIERKENS & DUVOSQUEL (Eds.).
———, & WARMENBOL, EUGÈNE (1991): *Les divins chats d'Égypte: un air subtil, un dangereux parfum* (Leuven: Peeters).
DÉMEUNIER, JEAN-NICOLAS (1784-8): *Encyclopédie méthodique. Économie, politique, et diplomatique* (Paris: C.-L.-F. Panckoucke).
DENON, BARON DOMINIQUE VIVANT (1802): *Voyage dans la Basse et la Haute Égypte, pendant les campagnes du général Bonaparte* (Paris: P. Didot l'aîné). See also the English edition (1802 by E.A. KENDAL), with an account of the invasion of Egypt by the French. (London: B. Crosby). See also the version (1803) ARTHUR AIKIN (Tr.) (London: T. Longman & O. Rees).
——— (1995): *Point de lendemain* (Paris: Gallimard).
DENT, EDWARD J. (1960): *Mozart's Operas: A Critical Study* (London: Oxford UP).
DERNIE, D. (1996): *The Villa d'Este at Tivoli* (London: Academy Editions).
DERRIDA, JACQUES (1993): *Aporias: Dying – Awaiting (one another at) the 'Limits of Truth'* (Stanford CA: Stanford UP).
DESBOIS DE ROCHEFORT, ELÉONORE-MARIE (1784-8): Article on Cemeteries in DÉMEUNIER, JEAN-NICOLAS.
DESCHAMPS, REV. NICOLAS (1881): *Les Sociétés Secrètes et la Société* (Paris: Oudin, & Avignon: Seguin).
DESCRIPTION DE L'ÉGYPTE (1809-28): see COMMISSION DES SCIENCES ET ARTS D'ÉGYPTE.
DESMONCEAUX, ABBÉ (1789): *De la bienfaisance nationale* (Paris: s.n.).
DESPREZ, LOUIS-JEAN (1781): *Ouvrage d'architecture…* (Paris: Desprez).
DESPY-MEYER, ANDRÉE, CULLUS, PHILIPPE, & JACOBS, JOHAN (Eds.) (2000): *Bruxelles. Les francs-maçons dans la cité* (Gent: Tijdsbeeld & Brussels: Parcours maçonnique).
DÉTOURNELLE, A. (1806): see ACADÉMIE DES BEAUX-ARTS.
DEUTSCH, OTTO ERICH (1932): *Mozart und die Wiener Logen* (Vienna: Wiener Freimaurer-Zeitung).
——— (1937): *Das Freihaustheater auf der Wieden* (Vienna & Leipzig: Deutscher Verlag für Jugend und Volk Gesellschaft).
——— (Ed.) (1947): *A Schubert Reader* ERIC BLOM (Tr.) (New York: W. W. Norton).
——— (Ed.) (1961): *Mozart: die Dokumente seines Lebens* (Kassel: Bärenreiter). See the version published (1965) as *Mozart: A Documentary Biography* ERIC BLOM, PETER BRANSCOMBE, & JEREMY NOBLE (Trs.) (London: A. & C. Black).
——— (1962-75): see BAUER, WILHELM A. (Ed.)
DEWACHTER, MICHEL (Ed.) (1987): see GILLESPIE, CHARLES COULSTON.
——— (1996): 'Le choc en retour: L'Égyptomanie des égyptologues' HUMBERT (Ed.) (1996) 425-34.
——— (Ed.) (1990): *L'Égypte Bonaparte, et Champollion* (Figeac: Association pour le Bicentenaire Champollion).
———, & FOUCHARD, ALAIN (Eds.) (1994): *L'égyptologie et les Champollion* (Grenoble: Presses universitaires de Grenoble).
DEWANDEL, A. (1941/2): *Geschiedenes van den Isiscultus in het westersche romeinsche Rijk* (Leiden: E. J. Brill).
DEWULF, M. (1978): 'De Egyptische Zaal van het Kasteel Moeland te St.-Niklaas, opgericht als tempel der Rosenkruisers' in *Annalen de de Koninklijke Oudheidkundige Kring van het Land van Waas* **lxxxi** 34-43.
DÉZALLIER D'ARGENVILLE, ANTOINE-JOSEPH (1709): *La Théorie et la Pratique du Jardinage* (Paris: J. Mariette).
DICKSON, ALEXANDER (1584): *Heii Scepsii Defensio pro Alexandro Dicsono Arelio: adversus quendam G. P. Cantabrigiensis* (London: Francisco Coldoco).
DIDEROT, DENIS (1821-34): *Œuvres de Denis Diderot* (Paris: J.-L.-J. Brière).
——— (1956): *Rameau's Nephew and Other Works* JACQUES BARZUN & RALPH H. BOWEN (Trs.) (Garden City NY: Doubleday).
———, ALEMBERT, JEAN LE ROND D', ET AL. (1751-80): *Encyclopédie ou dictionnaire raisonné des sciences, des arts, et des metiers, par une société de gens de lettres* (Paris: C.L.F. Panckoucke).
——— (1782-1832): *Encylopédie methodique …* (Paris: C.L.F. Panckoucke).
DIDEROT STUDIES (1973): OTIS E. FELLOWS & DIANE GUIRAGOSSIAN (Eds.) **xvi** (Geneva: Droz).
DIERKENS, ALAIN (1995a): 'Le monument funéraire de la famille Goblet d'Alviella à Court-Saint-Étienne' DIERKENS (Ed.) 193-211.
——— (Ed.) (1995b): *Eugène Goblet d'Alviella, historien et franc-maçon. Problèmes d'histoire des religions* **vi** (Brussels: Éditions de l'Université de Bruxelles).
———, & DUVOSQUEL, JEAN-MARIE (Eds.) (1993): *Henri-Joseph Redouté et l'expédition de Bonaparte en Égypte* (Brussels: Crédit communal).
DIETRICH, D. (1966): *Der hellenistische Isiskult als kosmopolitische Religion und die sogennante Isismission* (Leipzig: University of Leipzig Dissertation).
——— (1968): 'Die Ausbreitung der alexandrinischen Mysteriengötter Isis, Osiris, Serapis und Horus in griechisch-römischer Zeit' *Das Altertum* **xiv** 201-11.
DIFFIE, W. (1999): see PARKINSON, RICHARD.
DINAUX, ARTHUR MARTIN (1867): *Les Sociétés badines, bachiques, littéraires et chantantes* (Paris: Bachelin-Deflorenne).
DINSMOOR, WILLIAM BELL (1950): *The Architecture of Ancient Greece* (London: Batsford).
DIODORUS SICULUS (1933-67): *Bibliotheca* C. H. OLDFATHER ET AL. (Trs.) (Cambridge MA: Harvard UP).
——— (1990): *The Antiquities of Egypt* EDWIN MURPHY (Tr.) (New Brunswick NJ: Transaction Publishers).
DOANE, THOMAS WILLIAM (1883): *Bible Myths and their Parallels in Other Religions: Being a comparison of the Old and New Testament myths and miracles with those of heathen nations of Antiquity, considering also their Origin and Meaning* (New York: W. Bouton).
DOUGLAS, NORMAN (1915): *Old Calabria* (London: Martin Secker).
DOUKHAN, IGOR (1997-8): 'Beyond the Holy City: Symbolic Intentions in the Avant-Garde Urban Utopia' KÜHNEL (Ed.).
——— (2001): 'Baroque City: The Conception of Time and History' *Acta Academiae Artium Vilnensis* **xxi** 263.
DOWNING, ANDREW JACKSON (1841): *A Treatise on the Theory and Practice of Landscape Gardening …* (New York: Wiley & Putnam).
DOYEN, F. (1993): see DELVAUX, L.
DREYFOUS, MAURICE (1906): *Les Arts et les artistes pendant la période révolutionnaire (1785-1795)* (Paris: Paul Paclot).
DRIAULT, ÉDOUARD (1927): *L'Hôtel Beauharnais à Paris* (Paris: A. Morancé).
——— (1939): *Napoléon architecte* (Paris: Presses Universitaires de France).
——— (1940): 'L'Égypte et Napoléon' in *Revue des Études Napoléoniennes* **clxxxiv** (March-April) 122 and 128.
DRING, E.H. (1916): 'The Evolution and Development of the Tracing or Lodge Board' *Ars Quatuor Coronatorum* **xxix** 243-64 275-325.
DRUMMOND, ANDREW LANDALE (1934): *The Church Architecture of Protestantism: An Historical and Constructive Study* (Edinburgh: T. & T. Clark).
DUBOIS, P.-F.-L. (1809-10): see KRAFFT, JOHANN KARL.
DUBOY, PHILIPPE (1986): *Lequeu. An Architectural Enigma* FRANCIS SCARPE (Tr.) with Foreword by ROBIN MIDDLETON (London: Thames & Hudson).
DUCHAINE, P. (1911): *La franc-maconnerie belge au XVIIIᵉ siècle* (Brussels: P. van Fleteren).
DUFFY, EAMON (1992): *The Stripping of the Altars: Traditional Religion in England c.1400-c.1580* (New Haven CT & London: Yale UP).
DÜLMEN, RICHARD VAN (1975): *Der Geheimbund der Illuminaten* (Stuttgart-Bad Cannstadt: F. Frommann).
DUNAND, FRANÇOISE (1979): *Religion Populaire en Égypte Romaine* (Leiden: E. J. Brill).
——— (1980): 'Cultes égyptiens hors d'Égypte. Essai d'analyse des conditions de leur diffusion' *Religions, pouvoir Rapports Sociaux, Centre de Recherches d'Histoire Ancienne* **xxxii** 69-148.
DUNBAR, JOHN GREENWELL (1966): *The Historic Architecture of Scotland* (London: B.T. Batsford).
——— (1999): *Scottish Royal Palaces: the Architecture of the Royal Residences during the late Medieval and early Renaissance Periods* (East Linton: Tuckwell).
——— (Ed.) (1957-82): see IMRIE, JOHN (Ed.).
DUPUIS, CHARLES-FRANÇOIS (1790): 'Initiation, initié' *Encyclopédie Méthodique: Antiquités, Mythologie* (Paris: C.L.F. Panckoucke).
——— (1822): *Origine de tous les cultes, ou Religion universelle* (Paris: E. Babeuf).
DUPUY, MARIE-ANNE (1999): see ROSENBERG, PIERRE.
DURAND, JEAN-NICOLAS-LOUIS (1797): see LEGRAND, JACQUES-GUILLAUME.
——— (1799-1801): *Recueil et parallèle des édifices de tout genre anciens et modernes, remarquables par leur beauté, par leur grandeur, ou par leur singularité, et dessinées sur une même echelle* (Paris: Gillé).
——— (1802-05): *Précis des Leçons d'Architecture données à l'École Polytechnique* (Paris: Durand). See also the *Nouveau Précis* of 1813.
DÜRIEGL, GÜNTER, & WINKLER, SUSANNE (Eds.) (1992): *Freimaurer, Solange die Welt besteht* (Vienna: Eigenverlag der Museen der Stadt Wien).
DURKAN, JOHN (1962): 'Alexander Dickson and STC 6823' *The Bibliotheck. A Scottish Journal of Bibliography and Allied Topics* **iii** 183-5.
DURLIAT, MARCEL (1974): 'Alexandre du Mège et les mythes archéologiques à Toulouse dans le premier

tiers du XIXe siècle' *Revue de l'Art* **ccxliii** 30-41.
DURLING, ROBERT M. (Ed.) (1976): *Petrarch's Lyric Poems. The Rime Sparse and other Lyrics* (Cambridge MA: Harvard UP) Poem 300 line 4 478-9.
DUTHOY, R. (1974): 'La fonction sociale de l'Augustalité' *Epigraphica* **xxxvi** 135-54.
DUVAL, AMAURY (1801): *Des Sépultures* (Paris: C.L.F. Panckoucke).
——— (1813): *Les fontaines de Paris …* (Paris: Firmin Didot).
DUVAL, PAUL-MARIE (1961): *Paris antique des origins au IIIe siècle* (Paris: Hermann).
DUVOSQUEL, JEAN-MARIE (Ed.) (1993): see DIERKENS, ALAIN.
DWORK, DEBÓRAH, & PELT, ROBERT JAN (1996): *Auschwitz: 1270 to the Present* (New York: W.W. Norton). A paperback version was issued in 2002.
DYSON, HENRY (1633): see STOW, JOHN.
EARNSHAW, BRIAN (1988): see MOWL, TIMOTHY.
'DE ECHO VAN EGYPTE' (1984): *Kunstschrift Openbaar Kunstbezit*, 28è Jg, No. 5, (September-October).
EBERS, KARL FRIEDRICH (Ed.) (1817): *Sarsena, oder der volkommene Baumeister, enthaltend die Geschichte und Entstehung des Freimaurerordens und die verschiedene Meinungen darüber…* etc. (Bamberg: Kunz).
EBERT, JOHANN ARNOLD (1753): *Dr Edward Youngs Klagen, oder Nachtgedanken über Leben, Tod, und Unsterblichkeit* (Braunschweig & Hildesheim: Ludwig Schröders Erben).
EDGE, J. H. (1912): *The Story of Irish Freemasonry* (Dublin: Ponsonby & Gibbs at the UP).
ECKERT, EDUARD-EMIL (1852): *Der Freimaurer-Orden in seiner wahren Bedeutung* (Dresden: E. E. Eckert).
——— (1855a): *La Franc-Maçonnerie dans sa veritable signification …* etc. (Liège: J. -G. Lardinois).
——— (1855b): *Der Tempel Salomonis, das heisst General-Charte des Arbeitsplanes des Revolutionsbundes mit Erklärungswort* etc. (Prague & Dresden: s.n.).
EGGER, HERMANN (1913-16): see HÜLSEN, CHRISTIAN CARL FRIEDRICH.
L'EGITTO FUORI DELL'EGITTO. DALLA RISCOPERTA ALL'EGITTOLOGIA (1991): see GOVI, CRISTIANA MORIGI.
EGYPT AND THE HELLENISTIC WORLD (1983): *Proceedings* of the International Colloquium, Leuven, May 1983. *Studia Hellenistica* **xxvii**.
L'ÉGYPTE ET L'EXPÉDITION FRANÇAISE DE 1798 À 1801 (1978): *Catalogue* of the Exhibition held at Mont-de-Marsan (October 1978 to January 1979).
ÉGYPTE-FRANCE (1929): *Catalogue* of the French Exposition (Cairo).
——— (1949): *Catalogue* of Exposition at the Musée des Arts Décoratifs, Pavillon de Marsan (October-November) (Paris: Éd. des Presses Artistiques).
L'ÉGYPTE DANS L'ICONOGRAPHIE ET LA BANDE DESSINÉE (1987): Colloquium held in Cairo at the Centre d'Études et de Documentation économique, juridique et sociale, Institut Français d'Archéologie Orientale (15-17 May 1987). Contributions by BERTHET, BRUNON, CORTEGGIANI, ENAN, JOUTARD, & VOLAIT.
'THE EGYPTIAN REVIVAL' (1984): Review in *Gazette les Beaux-Arts* **civ**/1389 (October) 22-23.
EGYPTOMANIA (1979): (New York: Metropolitan Museum of Art).
EHRLICH, TRACY L. (1989): 'The Waterworks of Hadrian's Villa' *Journal of Garden History* **ix**/4 161.
EINGARTNER, JOHANNES (1991): *Isis und ihre Dienerinnen in der Kunst der römischen Kaiserzeit* (Leiden: E. J. Brill).
EINSTEIN, ALFRED (1956): *Mozart. His Character. His Work* A. MENDEL & N. BRODER (Trs.) (Oxford: Oxford UP).
EKLUND, P. B. (c.1880): *IX Frimurare Provinsens. Byggnader* (Stockholm: Central-Tryckeriet-P.B. Eklunds Forlag).
ELBERT, CLAUDIA (1988): *Die Theater Friedrich Weinsbrenners. Bauten und Entwürfe* (Karlsruhe: Verlag C. F. Müller GmbH).
ELLIOTT, BRENT (1992): Review in *Garden History: The Journal of the Garden History Society* **xx**/2 (Autumn) 207-8.
ELLIS, ROBERT LESLIE (Ed.) (1857-74): see SPEDDING, JAMES.
EMPEREUR, CONSTANTIN L' (1630): *Talmudis Babylonici Codex Middoth sive de Mensuris Templi* (Leyden: B. & A. Elzevir).

——— (1702): see MISHNAH.
ENCICLOPEDIA DELL'ARTE ANTICA, CLASSICA, E ORIENTALE (1958-73): I-VIII e *Supplemento* (Rome: Istituto Poligrafico dello Stato).
ENCYCLOPÆDIA OF RELIGION AND ETHICS (1908-27): see HASTINGS, JAMES, ET AL. (Eds.)
ENGEL, LEOPOLD (1906): *Geschichte des Illuminaten-Ordens* (Berlin: H. Bermühler Verlag).
ENGELMANN, HELMUT (1975): *The Delian Aretalogy of Sarapis* (Leiden: E. J. Brill).
EPSTEIN, RABBI I. (Ed.) (1848): *The Babylonian Talmud* (London: Soncino Press).
ERIKSEN, SVEND (1974): *Early Neo-Classicism in France* PETER THORNTON (Ed. & Tr.) (London: Faber).
ERMAN, ADOLF (1893): 'Obelisken römischer Zeit. I. Obelisken in Beneventum' *Mitteilungen des deutschen archäologischen Instituts, Römische Abteilung* **viii** 210-18.
——— (1896): 'Obelisken römischer Zeit. II. Der Obelisk des Antinous' *Mitteilungen des deutschen archäologischen Instituts, Römische Abteilung* **xi** 113-21.
——— (1917): *Römische Obelisken* (Berlin: G. Reimer).
——— (1927): *The Literature of the Ancient Egyptians…* A. M. BLACKMAN (Tr.) (London: Methuen).
———, & GRAPOW, HERMANN (1961): *Ägyptisches Handwörterbuch* (Hildesheim: G. Olms).
ERMENONVILLE, STANISLAS-CÉCILE-XAVIER-LOUIS, COMTE DE GIRARDIN, VICOMTE D' (1788): *Promenade ou Itinéraire des Jardins d'Ermenonville* illustrated by MÉRIGOT FILS (Paris & Ermenonville: Mérigot, Gattey, Guyot, & Murray).
ÉROUART, GILBERT (1982): *Architettura come pittura: Jean-Laurent Legeay, un Piranesiano francese nell' Europa dei Lumi* (Milan: Electa). Also published in a French edition.
ESMÉNARD, J. (Ed.) (1806): see DELILLE, ABBÉ JACQUES (1806).
ÉTAT DU G∴O∴ DE FRANCE (1777): (Paris: s.n.) **i** 4.
ETLIN, RICHARD A. (1977): 'Landscapes of Eternity: Funerary Architecture and the Cemetery, 1793-1881' *Oppositions* **viii** 14-31.
——— (1982): 'The Geometry of Death' *Progressive Architecture* (May) 134-7.
——— (1984): *The Architecture of Death. The Transformation of the Cemetery in Eighteenth-Century Paris* (Cambridge MA, & London: MIT Press).
EUROPA UND DER ORIENT 800-1900 (1989): see SIEVERNICH, GEREON.
EVANS, ROBERT JOHN WESTON (1973): *Rudolf II and His World. A Study in Intellectual History, 1576-1612* (Oxford: Clarendon Press).
EXOTISCHE WELTEN, EUROPÄISCHE PHANTASIEN (1987): *Catalogue* of Exhibition (2 September - 29 November) (Stuttgart).
EYDOUX, HENRI-PAUL (1974): 'L'Égypte à Paris' *Monuments curieux et sites étranges* (Paris: Perrin).
FAIRMAN, HERBERT WALTER (1974): *The Triumph of Horus* (London: Batsford).
FARQUHAR, GEORGE (1930): *Complete Works* CHARLES STONEHILL(Ed.) (London: Nonesuch Press).
FARMER, DAVID HUGH (1992): *The Oxford Dictionary of Saints* (Oxford: Oxford UP).
FAŸ, BERNARD (1935): *Revolution and Freemasonry* (Boston MA: Little Brown).
——— (1961): *La Franc-Maçonnerie et la révolution intellectuelle du XVIIIe Siècle* (Paris: Librairie Français).
FAZZINI, RICHARD A. (1988): 'Rêve et réalité. La persistance d'une certaine image de l'Égypte' in *Le Courier de l'UNESCO* (September) 33-35.
——— (1994): 'L'égyptomanie dans l'architecture américaine' HUMBERT (Ed.) (1996) 229-278.
FELLOWS, OTIS E. (Ed.) (1973): see DIDEROT STUDIES.
FENN, THOMAS (1910): *Prince of Wales's Lodge No.259* (London: Warrington & Co.).
FERGUSON, JOHN (1970): *The Religions of the Roman Empire* (Ithaca NY: Cornell UP).
FERGUSSON, JAMES (1878): *The Temples of the Jews* (London: John Murray).
FERNIE, ERIC (1989): 'Archaeology and iconography. Recent developments in the study of English Mediaeval architecture' *Architectural History* **xxxii** 18-29.
FESCH, PAUL (1976): *Bibliographie de la franc-maçonnerie et des Sociétés secrètes* (Brussels: G.A. Deny).
FESTUGIÈRE, ANDRÉ-MARIE-JEAN (1949-54): *La*

Révélation d'Hermès Trismégiste (Paris: Lecoffre).
FICHET, FRANÇOISE (1979): *La théorie de l'architecture à l'âge classique. Essai d'anthologie critique* (Brussels: P. Mardaga).
FIELDING, HENRY (1751): *Amelia* (London: A. Millar).
FIENSCH, GÜNTHER, & IMDAHL, MAX (Eds.) (1966): *Festschrift Werner Hager* (Recklinghausen: Bongers). Contains contributions from NOEHLES ET AL.
FILARETE, ANTONIO DI PIERO AVERLINO, known as (1965): *Filarete's Treatise on Architecture* with introduction and notes by JOHN R. SPENCER (New Haven CT & London: Yale UP).
FILLIES, DOROTHEA (Ed.) (2005): *Der Vulkan im Wörlitzer Park* (Berlin: Nicolaische Verlagsbuchhandlung).
FINDEL, GOTTFRIED JOSEPH GABRIEL (1893): *Geschichte der Freimaurerei von der Zeit ihres Entstehens bis auf die Gegenwart* (Leipzig: Findel). See also the English translation by MURRAY LYON published in 1869 (London: Asher).
FISCHER, JULIUS (1984): see LESSING, ERICH, ET AL.
FISCHER, M. (1999): see PARKINSON, RICHARD.
FISCHER VON ERLACH, JOHANN BERNHARD (1725): *Entwurff einer Historischen Architektur, in Abbildung unterschiedener verühmter Gebäude, des Alterthums und fremder Völker* (Leipzig: The Author).
FLAISCHLEN, CÄSAR (1890): *Otto Heinrich von Gemmingen: mit einer Vorstudie über Diderot als Dramatiker* (Stuttgart: G. J. Göschen).
FLEDELIUS, K. (2001): 'Ægypteri hos frimurerne' CHRISTIANSEN & DAHL HERMANSEN (Eds.) 91-106.
FLETCHER, SIR BANISTER (1954): *A History of Architecture on the Comparative Method* (London: Batsford). See also subsequent editions of 1987 (London: Butterworth) and 1996 (London: Architectural Press).
FLUDD, ROBERT (1617): *Tractatus Apologeticus Integritatem Societatis de Rosea Cruce defendens ….* (Leiden: G. Basson).
——— (1617-24): *Utriusque cosmi maioris scilicet et minoris metaphysica, physica atque technica historia…* (Oppenheim: J.-T. de Bry).
FONER, PHILIP SHELDON (Ed.) (1945): see PAINE, THOMAS.
FONTAINE, PIERRE-FRANÇOIS-LÉONARD (1801): see PERCIER, CHARLES.
FÖRDERER, ANDREAS (Ed.) (2006): *Schwetzingen: A Prince Elector's Summer Residence – Garden Design and Freemasonic Allusions* (Stuttgart: Wirtschaftsministerium & Finanzministerium Baden Württemberg, with Stadt Schwetzingen).
FORDHAM, MICHAEL (Ed.) (1953-79): see JUNG, CARL GUSTAV.
FORESTIER, RENÉ LE (1914): *Les Illuminés de Bavière* (Paris: Hachette & Cie).
——— (1970): *La Franc-Maçonnerie Templière et Occultiste aux XVIIIe et XIXe Siècles* (Paris: Aubier-Montaigne).
——— (1915). *Les Plus Secrets Mystères des Hauts Grades de la Maçonnerie Dévoilés*, originally published in 1774 (Paris: Dorbon-Âiné).
FORSTER, HAROLD (1986): *Edward Young. The poet of the Night Thoughts 1683-1765* (Alburgh, Harleston: The Erskine Press).
FORTESCUE, ADRIAN (1948): *The Ceremonies of the Roman Rite described* (London: Burns, Oates, & Washbourne).
FOSS, GERALD D. (1972): *Three Centuries of Freemasonry in New Hampshire* (Concord NH: Grand Lodge of NH).
FOUCART, PAUL FRANÇOIS (1975): *Les mystères d'Eleusis* (New York: Arno Press).
FOUCHARD, ALAIN (Ed.) (1994): see DEWACHTER, MICHEL (Ed.).
FOULSTON, JOHN (1838): *The Public Buildings erected in the West of England, as designed by John Foulston* (London: J. Williams).
FOUQUIER, MARCEL (1912): *Paris au XVIIIe siècle; ses divertissements, ses moeurs, Directoire et Consulat* (Paris: Émile-Paul).
FOURIER, FRANÇOIS-CHARLES-MARIE (1808): *Théorie des Quatre Mouvements et des destinées générales* (Lyon: s.n.).
——— (1829): *Le Nouveau Monde Industriel et Sociétaire* (Paris: Bossange).
FOWDEN, G. (1993): *The Egyptian Hermes. A historical approach to the Late Pagan mind* (Princeton NJ:

Princeton UP).
FOWLER, WILLIAM (1914-40): *The Works of William Fowler* HENRY W. MEIKLE, JAMES CRAIGIE, & JOHN PURVES (*Eds.*) (Edinburgh: Scottish Text Society). In 3 volumes (**i** [1914], **ii** [1936] and **iii** [1940]).
FRANC-MAÇONNERIE (1983): *Un siècle de franc-maçonnerie dans nos régions, 1740-1840*. Catalogue of an exhibition in the Galerie CGER (17 May – 31 July 1983) (Brussels: R. Coolen).
FRANCO, BARBARA (1976): *Masonic Symbols in American Decorative Arts* (Lexington MA: Museum of Our National Heritage).
——— (1980): *Bespangled Painted & Embroidered Decorated Masonic Aprons in America 1790-1850* (Lexington MA: Museum of Our National Heritage).
——— (1986): *Fraternally Yours. A Decade of Collecting* (Lexington, MA: Museum of Our National Heritage).
FRANKFORT, HENRI (1961): *Ancient Egyptian Religion* (New York: Harper).
——— (1971): *Kingship and the Gods* (Chicago IL: University of Chicago Press).
FRANKL, P., & PANOFSKY, E. (1945) 'The Secrets of the Medieval Masons' *Art Bulletin* **xxvii** (March) 46-60.
FRASER, ANTONIA (1969): *Mary Queen of Scots* (London: Weidenfeld & Nicolson).
FRASER, DOUGLAS, HIBBARD, HOWARD, & LEWINE, MILTON J. (*Eds.*) (1967): *Essays in the History of Art presented to Rudolf Wittkower on his sixty-fifth birthday* (London and New York: Phaidon).
FREEDLEY, GEORGE (1940): *Theatrical Designs from the Baroque through Neoclassicism...* (New York: H. Bittner & Co.).
——— (1955): *A History of the Theatre...* (New York: Crown Publishers).
FREE-MASON, A. (1723): *The Free Masons: A Hudibrastick Poem* (London: A. Moore).
FREE-MASONS' MELODY, THE (1818): *Brief and General Collection of Masonic Songs* (Bury: Prince Edwin's Lodge, No. 209).
FREEMASONS' QUARTERLY REVIEW (various years): but *see* (September 1839) (London: Sherwood, Gilbert, & Piper, etc.).
FREE-MASONS SURPRIZ'D, THE, OR THE SECRET DIS-COVER'D. A TRUE TALE FROM A MASONS LODGE IN CANTERBURY (1754): (London: T. Wilkins).
FRERE, ALEXANDER STEWART (*Ed.*) (1967): *Grand Lodge, 1717-1967* (Oxford: Oxford UP for the United Grand Lodge of England).
FREY, KATIA (1995): 'L'enterprise napoléonienne' MASSOUNIE, PRÉVOST-MARCILHACY, & RABREAU (1995) 104-23.
FRICK, KARL R. H. (1973): *Die Erleuchteten: Gnostisch-Theosophische und Alchemistisch-Rosenkreuzerische Geheimgesellschaften bis zum Ende des 18. Jahrhunderts, ein Beitrag zur Geistesgeschichte der Neuzeit* (Graz: Akademische Druck - u. Verlagsanstalt).
FRISBEE, JEROME BERNARD (n.d.): *King Solomon's Temple* (Lindsay CA: Temple Publishing).
FULWOOD, WILLIAM (*Tr.*) (1562): *see* GRATAROLA, GUGLIELMO.
FYFE, GORDON, & LAW, JOHN (*Eds.*) (1988): *Picturing Power: Visual Depiction and Social Relations* (London: Routledge).
G., G. (1826): *Promenade sérieuse au Cimetière du Père La Chaise* (Paris: Imprimerie de Lachevardière fils).
G......, J...... (1776): *Mahhabone: or, The Grand Lodge Door Open'd. Wherein is Discovered The Whole Secrets of Free-Masonry, Both Ancient and Modern... etc.* (London: Johnson & Davenport).
GABANON, LÉONARD (*pseudonym of* LOUIS TRAVENOL) (1749): *Nouveau Catéchisme des Francs-Maçons* ('Jerusalem' [i.e. Amsterdam]: Pierre Mortier). The imprint is false: it was published in Paris by the Author.
——— (various dates): *see* TRAVENOL, LOUIS.
GABRIELLI, DOMENICO (2002): *Dictionnaire Historique du Père-Lachaise XVIIe-XIX siècles* (Paris: Éditions de l'Amateur).
GALLET, MICHEL (1980): *Claude-Nicolas Ledoux, 1736-1806* (Paris: Picard).
GALLONIO, ANTONIO (1930): *Tortures and Torments of the Christian Saints from the "De SS. Martyrum Cruciatibus"* ALFRED RICHARD ALLINSON (*Tr.*)

with Plates from the designs of GIOVANNI DE GUERRA OF MODENA engraved by ANTONIO TEMPESTA of Florence (Paris: The Fortune Press).
GALTIER, G. (1989): *Maçonnerie égyptienne. Rose-croix et Néo-chevalerie: les fils de Cagliostro* (Paris: Éditions de Rocher).
GALVIN, TERRANCE G. (2003): The Architecture of Joseph Michael Gandy (1771-1843) and Sir John Soane (1753-1837): An Exploration into the Masonic and Occult Imagination of the Late Enlightenment (PhD Thesis, University of Pennsylvania).
GANAY, ERNEST, COMTE DE (1949): *Les Jardins de France et Leur Décor* (Paris: Larousse).
——— (*Ed.*) (1992): *see* LIGNE, CHARLES-JOSEPH, PRINCE DE.
GANNAL, FÉLIX (1884): *Les Cimetières depuis la fondation de la monarchie française... etc.* (Paris: Muzard et fils).
GARDEN, FRANCIS, LORD GARDENSTONE (1791-5): *Travelling Memorandums made in a Tour upon the Continent of Europe in the Years 1786, 1878, and 1788* (Edinburgh: Bell & Bradfute).
GARIN, E. (1988): *Ermetismo del Rinascimento* (Rome: Editori Riuniti).
GARNER, LANCE W. (*Tr.*) (1992): *see* BECKER, UDO.
GASTER, MOSES (1899): *The Chronicles of Jerahmeel: or, The Hebrew Bible Historiale* (London: Royal Asiatic Society).
GATTY, HORATIA K. F., & LLOYD, ELEANOR (*Eds.*) (1900): *A Book of Sundials* (London: G. Bell & Sons).
GAUME, JEAN-JOSEPH (1873): *Le Cimetière au dix-neuvième Siècle: ou le dernier mot des solidaires* (Paris: Gaume). Another edn. (Paris: Corbeil) was printed in 1874.
GAY, PETER (1967): *The Enlightenment: An Interpretation. The Rise of Modern Paganism* (London: Weidenfeld & Nicolson).
GAZETTE DES BEAUX-ARTS (from 1859): (Paris: J. Claye, etc.).
GEAY, JEAN-LAURENT LE (*c.*1770): *Vasi inventione in Engravings* (Paris: s.n.).
GELDNER, FERDINAND (*Ed.*) (1965): *see* RORICZER, MATHIAS.
GENLIS, STÉPHANIE-FÉLICITÉ DUCREST DE SAINT-AUBIN, COMTESSE DE (1810): *La Botanique historique et littéraire* (Paris: Maradan).
GENS, ÉMILE (1861): *Promenade au Jardin Zoologique d'Anvers* (Antwerp: Buschmann).
GENTLEMAN BELONGING TO THE JERUSALEM LODGE (*identified as R.S.*) (1762): *Jachin and Boaz: or, an Authentic Key to the Door of Free-Masonry, both Antient and Modern* (London: W. Nicoll). Many subsequent editions, including those published in Dublin.
GEPPERT, ERNST GÜNTER (n.d.): *Das Stammbuch der Freimaurer-Logen Deutschlands 1737-1972* (Bayreuth: Forchungsgesellschaft).
GERNDT, SIEGMAR (1981): *Idealisiert Natur: Die literarische Kontroverse um den Landschaftsgarten des 18. und frühen 19. Jahrhunderts in Deutschland* (Stuttgart: Metzler).
GESSNER, SALOMON (1756): *Idyllen von dem Verfasser des Daphnis* (Zürich: S. Gessner).
——— (1762): *Idylles et Poëmes champêtres de M. Gessner* (Lyons: J. M. Bruyset).
GEST, KEVIN L. (2007): *The Secrets of Solomon's Temple* (Hersham: Lewis).
GHALI, IBRAHIM AMIN (1986): *Vivant Denon ou la conquête du bonheur* (Cairo: Institut français d'archéologie orientale du Caire).
GIEHLOW, KARL (1915): 'Die Hieroglyphenkunde des Humanismus in der Allegorie der Renaissance' *Jahrbuch der Kunsthistorischen Sammlungen des Allerhöchsten Kaiserhauses* Bd. **xxxii** Hft. 1 (Vienna: F. Tempsky) 1-232.
GIESECKE, KARL LUDWIG (n.d.): *Die Zauberflöte: Oper in zwei Aufzügen von W. A. Mozart. Dichtung nach Ludwig Gisecke [sic] von Emanuel Schikaneder* with an Introduction by MAX CONRAD (Zürich: Apollo-Verlag).
GIFFORD, JOHN, MCWILLIAM, COLIN, & WALKER, DAVID (1984): *Edinburgh* in The Buildings of Scotland Series (Harmondsworth: Penguin Books).
GIFFORD, JOHN (1992): *Highlands and Islands* in The Buildings of Scotland series (London: Penguin Books in assn. with the Buildings of Scotland Trust).
GILBERT, ROBERT A. (1986): *see* HAMILL, JOHN (*Ed.*).

——— (1987): *see* MACKENZIE, K. R. H. (1877b).
——— (1992): *see* HAMILL, JOHN.
——— (2006): 'Paranoia and Patience: Freemasonry and the Roman Catholic Church' STEWART, TREVOR (*Ed.*) (2006) 75-90.
——— (*Ed.*) (1988): *see* HAMILL, JOHN
——— (1998): *Ars Quatuor Coronatorum, Transactions* of QCL **cx**.
——— (2007): *Seeking the Light: Freemasonry and Initiatic Traditons. Transactions of the Seventh International Conference 5 & 6 November 2005. The Canonbury Papers* **iv** (London: CMRC).
GILCHRIST, AGNES ADDISON (1950): *William Strickland, Architect and Engineer, 1788-1854* (Philadelphia PA: University of Pennsylvania Press).
GILLEN, MOLLIE (1976): *Royal Duke: Augustus Frederick, Duke of Sussex 1773-1843* (London: Sidgwick & Jackson).
GILLESPIE, CHARLES COULSTON, & DEWACHTER, MICHEL (*Eds.*) (1987): *The Monuments of Egypt: the Napoleonic edition: the complete archæological plates from La Description de l'Égypte* (Princeton NJ: Princeton Architectural Press and the Architectural League of New York).
GIRARD, JOSEPH-FRANÇOIS-HENRI DE (1801): *Des Tombeaux; ou, de l'influence des institutions funèbres sur les moeurs* (Paris: F. Buisson).
GIRARDIN (GÉRARDIN), RENÉ-LOUIS, MARQUIS DE, VICOMTE D'ERMENONVILLE (1777): *De la Composition des Paysages, ou des moyens d'embellir la Nature autour des Habitations, en joignant l'agréable à l'utile* (Geneva & Paris: P. M. Delaguette).
——— (1783): *An Essay on Landscape* (London: J. Dodsley).
GIRARDIN, STANISLAS-CÉCILE-XAVIER-LOUIS (1788): *see* ERMENONVILLE.
GIRAUD, PIERRE MARIN (1801): *Les Tombeaux, ou, essai sur les sépultres... etc.* (Paris: Desenne).
GIROLLET, ANNE (2000): *Victor Schœlcher, républicain et franc-maçon* in Encyclopédie maçonnique: collection figures **xviii** (Paris: Éditions maçonniques de France).
GLEASON, F. (1851-9): *see* BALLOU'S PICTORIAL DRAWING-ROOM COMPANION.
GODIN, JEAN-BAPTISTE-ANDRÉ (1871): *Solutions Sociales* (Paris: A. Le Chevalier).
GODWIN, JOSCELYN (1979a): *Athanasius Kircher. A Renaissance Man and the Quest for Lost Knowledge* (London: Thames & Hudson).
——— (1979b): *Robert Fludd: Hermetic Philosopher and Surveyor of Two Worlds* (London: Thames & Hudson).
——— (1979c): 'Layers of Meaning in The Magic Flute' *Music Quarterly* **lxv**/4 471-92.
——— (1981): *Mystery Religions in the Ancient World* (London: Thames & Hudson).
——— (1999): *Hypnerotomachia Poliphili – The Strife of Love in a Dream*, by FRANCESCO COLONNA: the entire text translated for the first time into English, with an Introduction by JOSCELYN GODWIN, with the original woodcut illustrations (London: Thames & Hudson).
——— (2009): *Athanasius Kircher's Theatre of the World* (London: Thames & Hudson).
GOETHE, JOHANN WOLFGANG VON (1774): *Die Leiden des jungen Werthers* (Leipzig: Weygand). *See also* MICHAEL HULSE (*Tr.*) (1989): *The Sorrows of Young Werther* (London: Penguin).
——— (1809): *Die Wahlverwandtschaften* (Tübingen: J. G. Cotta).
——— (1949): *Die Zauberflöte zweiter Teil* (Vienna: Jahresgabe der Wiener Bibliophilen Gesellschaft).
GOLDHILL, SIMON (2005): *The Temple of Jerusalem* (Cambridge MA: Harvard UP).
GOMBRICH, ERNST (1951): 'Hypnerotomachiana' *Journal of the Warburg and Courtauld Institutes* **xiv** 119-122.
——— (1989): 'Le Fantôme de la Liberté - Le rêve de la Raison: le symbolisme de la Révolution française' *FMR (Franco Maria Ricci)* **xxi** (August) 1-24.
GONZENBACH, VICTORINE VON (1957): *Untersuchungen zu den Knabenweihen im Isis-Kult der römischen Kaiserzeit* (Bonn: R. Habelt).
GOODENOUGH, ERWIN RAMSDELL (1953-68): *Jewish Symbols in the Græco-Roman Period* (New York: Pantheon Books).
GOSSÉ, MARCEL (2006): *see* CULOT, MAURICE.
GOTCH, CHRISTOPHER (1991): *The Grip of Freemasonry* (Brentford: Lantern).

GOTHEIN, MARIE LUISE (1928): *A History of Garden Art* (New York: E.P. Dutton). It originally appeared as *Geschichte der Gartenkunst* in two volumes in 1914 (Jena: Eugen Diederichs), and in a revised edition from the same publisher in 1926.
GOULD, ROBERT FREKE (1884-87): *History of Freemasonry: its Antiquities, Symbols, Constitution, Customs, etc.* (Edinburgh: T. C. & E. C. Jack).
——— (1903): *A Concise History of Freemasonry* (London: Gale & Polden).
——— (1911): *A Library of Freemasonry* (Philadelphia, PA: John C. Yorston).
——— (1931): *History of Freemasonry Embracing an Investigation of the Records of the Organisations of the Fraternity in England, Scotland, Ireland, British Colonies, France, Germany, The United States of America, and Other Countries.* Revised, edited, and brought up to date by DUDLEY WRIGHT (London: Caxton). Another edition (1951) of the above, from which mention of France, Germany, and Other Countries has been dropped from the title, was revised, edited, and brought up to date by REV. HERBERT POOLE (London: Caxton). Gould, in all his editions must be used with extreme caution.
GOULET, NICOLAS (1808): *Observations sur les embellisements de Paris et sur les monumens qui s'y construisent* (Paris: Leblanc).
GOULIER, CHARLES-PIERRE, BIET, LÉON-MARIE-DIEUDONNÉ, GRILLON, EDMÉ-JEAN-LOUIS, & TARDIEU, FEU (1825-1850): *Choix d'édifices publics, projetés et construits en France depuis le commencement du XIXe siècle* (Paris: L. Colas).
GOVI, CRISTIANA MORIGI, CURTO, SILVIO, & PERNIGOTTI, SERGIO (Eds.) (1991): *L'Egitto fuori dell' Egitto. Dalla riscoperta all' Egittologia.* Atti del Convegno Internazionale, Bologna (26-29 March 1990), with contributions from CURL, HUMBERT, JAEGER, JAMES, SCHNEIDER, ET AL. (Bologna: Cooperativa Libraria Universitaria Editrice Bologna).
GRAFTON, ANTHONY (2008): *see* CURRAN, BRIAN A.
GRANDIDIER, ABBÉ PHILIPPE-ANDRÉ (1782): *Essais Historiques et Topographiques sur l'Église Cathédrale de Strasbourg* (Strasbourg: Lavrault).
GRANDJEAN, SERGE (1950): 'Le Cabaret égyptien de Napoléon au Musée du Louvre' *Bulletin des Musées de France* **iii** (April) 62-65.
——— (1953): *see* VERLET, PIERRE.
——— (1955): 'L'Influence Égyptienne à Sèvres' *Publicaties van het Genootschap voor Napoleontische Studiën*, Aflevering 8 (September) (Den Haag: A. Sijthoff).
——— (1959): 'The Wellington-Napoleonic Relics' *The Connoisseur* **cxliii** 223-230.
——— (1964): *Inventaire après décès de l'Impératrice Joséphine à Malmaison* (Paris: Ministère d'État—Affaires culturelles).
——— (1966): *Empire Furniture, 1800 to 1825* (London: Faber).
——— (1985): 'Musée de Malmaison, le "Cabaret Égyptien" de l'Impératrice Joséphine' *La Revue du Louvre et des Musées de France* **ii** 123-128.
GRAND ORIENT DE FRANCE (1801): *Le Régulateur du Maçon* (Paris: Grand Orient de France). *See* also MOLLIER, PIERRE (Ed.) (2004): *Le Régulateur du Maçon (1785-1801): La Fixation des Grades Symboliques du Rite français, histoire et documents* (Paris: À l'Orient).
GRAPOW, HERMANN (1961): *see* ERMAN, ADOLF.
GRASSI, RICCARDO (1994): *see* BONGIOANNI, ALESSANDRO.
GRATAROLA, GUGLIELMO (1562): *The Castel of Memorie* WILLIAM FULWOOD (Tr.) (London: Rouland Hall).
GRATTAN-GUINNESS, IVOR (1992): 'Counting the Notes: Numerology in the Works of Mozart, Especially *Die Zauberflöte*' *Annals of Science* **xlix** 1-32.
GRAY, THOMAS (1912): *Poems, Letters, and Essays* (London: J. M. Dent; New York: E. P. Dutton).
GRIETEN, STEFAAN (Ed.) (2002): *Vreemd Gebouwd: Westerse en Niet-Westerse Elementen in Ouze Architectuur* (with contributions from MACLOT, WARMENBOL, ET AL.) (Turnhout: Brepols).
GRILLON, EDMÉ-JEAN-LOUIS (1825-50): *see* GOULIER, CHARLES-PIERRE.
GRIMM, REINHOLD, & HERMAND, JOST (1989): *From the Greeks to the Greens: images of the simple life* (Madison WI: University of Wisconsin Press).
GRISEBACH, LUCIUS (Ed.) (1981): *see* BÖRSCH-SUPAN.
GROSSEGGER, ELISABETH (1981): *Freimaurerei und Theater 1770-1800* (Vienna: Böhlau).
GROSSETESTE, ROBERT (1942): *Robert Grosseteste On Light* CLARE C. RIEDL (Tr.) (Milwaukee WI: Marquette UP).
——— (1996): *Robert Grosseteste on The Six Days of Creation* C. F. J. MARTIN (Tr.) (Oxford: Oxford UP).
GRÖTZ, SUSANNE, & QUECKE, URSULA (Eds.) (2006): *Balnea: Architekturgeschichte des Bades* (Marburg: Jonas Verlag).
GRUBER, GERNOT (1991): *Mozart & Posterity* (London: Quartet Books).
GUBEL, ERIC, ET AL. (1995): *Egypte Onomwonden: Egyptische oudheden van het museum Vleeshuis* (Antwerp: Stad Antwerpen & Pandora). An excellent publication dealing with the collections held in the city of Antwerp, with contributions from DELVAUX, WARMENBOL, ET AL.
GUEQUIER, J. (1903): 'R[espectable] L[oge] La Liberté ` a l'Or[ient] de Gand. La construction d'un Temp[le] maçonn[ique]' *Bulletin du Gr[and] Or[ient] de Belgique* **xxi** 91-104.
GUERRA OF MODENA, GIOVANNI (1930): *see* GALLONIO, ANTONIO.
GUIEYSSE, PAUL (1988): *see* AMIABLE, LOUIS.
GUILMARD, DÉSIRÉ (1880-1): *Les Maîtres Ornemanistes* (Paris: Plon).
GUIRAGOSSIAN, DIANE (Ed.) (1973): *see* DIDEROT STUDIES.
GUITE, AYODEJI MALCOLM (1993): *The Art of Memory and the Art of Salvation: A Study with Reference to the Works of Lancelot Andrewes, John Donne, and T. S. Eliot* (Durham: University of Durham).
GUNNIS, RUPERT (1968): *Dictionary of British Sculptors 1660-1851* (London: The Abbey Library).
GUTHRIE, WILLIAM KEITH CHAMBERS (1952): *Orpheus and Greek Religion* (London: Methuen).
GUTMAN, ROBERT W. (2000): *Mozart. A Cultural Biography* (London: Secker & Warburg).
GUTMANN, JOSEPH (Ed.) (1976): *The Temple of Solomon: Archaeological Fact and Medieval Tradition in Christian, Islamic and Jewish Art* (Missoula MT: American Academy of Religion).
GWILT, JOSEPH (1903): *An Encyclopædia of Architecture, Historical, Theoretical & Practical*, revised with additions by WYATT PAPWORTH (London: Longmans).
HAFENREFFER, MATTHIAS (1613): *Templum Ezechielis* (Tübingen: Theodoric Werlin).
HALL, MANLY PALMER (1928-75): *The Secret Teaching of All Ages: An Encyclopedic Outline of Masonic, Hermetic, Qabbalistic, and Rosicrucian Philosophy* (Los Angeles, CA: Philosophical Research Society).
——— (1937): *Freemasonry of the Ancient Egyptians. To which is added an interpretation of the Crata Repoa initiation rite, etc.* (Los Angeles CA: Philosophers Press).
HALL, MURIEL (2006): *see* ISIDORE OF SEVILLE.
HALLAYS, ANDRÉ (1903): *see* BERLIOZ, HECTOR.
HALLIWELL, JAMES ORCHARD (1844): *The Early History of Freemasonry in England* (London: J. R. Smith). The first edn. came out in 1840.
HALPORN, JAMES W. (Tr.) (2004): *see* CASSIODORUS, MAGNUS AURELIUS.
HAMBLIN, WILLIAM J., & SEELY, DAVID ROLF (2007): *Solomon's Temple: Myth and History* (London: Thames & Hudson).
HAMER, DOUGLAS (various dates): *see* KNOOP.
HAMER, MARY (1994): 'The Concord Obelisk and the French Political Imaginary' DEWACHTER & FOUCHARD (Eds.) (1994) 347-54.
HAMILL, JOHN (1985): *see* SADLER, HENRY
——— (1986): *The Craft. A History of English Freemasonry* (Leighton Buzzard: Crucible).
——— (1994): *The History of English Freemasonry* (Addlestone: Lewis Masonic).
——— (2006): 'Freemasonry and religion—the English View' STEWART, TREVOR (Ed.) (2006) 1-12.
——— (Ed.) (1986): *The Rosicrucian Seer: Magical Writings of Frederick Hockley*, with a note on Hockley's manuscripts by R.A. GILBERT (Wellingborough: Aquarian Press).
———, & GILBERT, R.A (1992): *World Freemasonry: An Illustrated History* (London: Aquarian Press).
——— (Eds.) (1998): *Freemasonry: A Celebration of the Craft* (London: Greenwich Editions).
HAMLIN, TALBOT FAULKNER (1944): *Greek Revival Architecture in America* (London: Oxford UP).
——— (1955): *Benjamin Henry Latrobe* (New York: Oxford UP).
HAMMER, KARL (1983): *Hôtel Beauharnais* (Munich: Artemis Verlag).
HAMMOND, WILLIAM (1917): *Masonic Emblems and Jewels. Treasures at Freemasons' Hall – London* (London: George Philip).
HANCARVILLE, BARON D' (1785): *see* HUGUES, PIERRE-FRANÇOIS.
HANOU, ANDRÉ (1997): *Onder de Acacia* (Leiden: Astræa).
HÄNSEL-HOHENHAUSEN, MARKUS (1989): *Die deutschsprachligen Freimaurer-Zeitschriften des 18. und 19. Jahrhunderts: Bibliographie* (Frankfurt-am-Main: R. G. Fischer).
HARCOURT, FRANÇOIS-HENRI, DUC D' (1919): *Traité de la Décoration des dehors, des jardins, et des parcs* (Paris: Émile-Paul Frères).
HARDIE, JAMES (1818): *The New Free-Mason's Monitor or Masonic Guide* (New York: George Long).
HÁRICH, JÁNOS (1937): *A Kismartoni várkert története* (Budapest: s.n.).
HARLAND-JACOBS, JESSICA L. (2007): *Builders of Empire: Freemasons and British Imperialism, 1717-1927* (Chapel Hill NC: University of North Carolina Press).
HARLEZ DE DEULIN, NATHALIE DE (2008): *Parcs et jardins Historiques de Wallonie* (Namur: Institut du Patrimoine Wallon).
HARRINGTON, JAMES (1656): *The Common-Wealth of Oceana* (London: Livewell Chapman).
HARRIS, EILEEN (1986): '"Vitruvius Britannicus" before Campbell' *The Burlington Magazine* **cxxviii** 341.
HARRISON, BRIAN (Ed.) (2004): *see* MATTHEW, H.C.G.
HARTMANN, SIMONE (1978): 'L'Ornamentiste Jean Dugourc' *L'Éstampille* **xcviii** (June) 30-35.
HARVEY, JOHN (1946): *Henry Yevele c.1320 to 1400: The Life of an English Architect* (London: B. T. Batsford).
——— (1947): *Gothic England: A Survey of National Culture* (London: B. T. Batsford).
——— (1978): *The Perpendicular Style 1330-1485* (London: B. T. Batsford).
——— (1987): *English Mediaeval Architects: A Biographical Dictionary down to 1550* (Gloucester: Alan Sutton).
HASQUIN, HERVÉ (Ed.) (1981): *Hommages à La Wallonie: Mélanges de Histoire, de Littérature, et de Philologie* (Brussels: Éditions de l'Université de Bruxelles).
HASTINGS, JAMES, ET AL. (Eds.) (1908-27): *Encylopædia of Religion and Ethics* (Edinburgh: T. & T. Clark).
HATCH, EDWIN (1957): *The Influence of Greek Ideas on Christianity* (New York: Harper).
HAUNCH, TERENCE OSBORNE (1983): *see* STUBBS, SIR JAMES.
——— (2008): *English Craft Certificates: A Presentation* (CD Presentation). But *see* (1969) his 'English Craft Certificates' AQC **lxxxii** 169-242, 232n, and his 'Tracing Boards' AQC **lxxv** 182-203 and AQC **lxxvii** 264-9.
HAUSSIG, H. W. (Ed.) (1965): *Wörterbuch der Mythologie* (Stuttgart: E. Klett).
HAUTECOEUR, LOUIS-EUGÈNE-GEORGES (1912): *Rome et la Renaissance de l'antiquité à la fin du XVIIIe siècle – Essai sur les origins du style Empire* (Paris: Fontemoing & cie).
——— (1925): 'L'Éxpédition d'Égypte et l'art français' *Napoléon, Revue des Études Napoléoniennes* (Paris: January-February) 81-87.
——— (1943-57): *Histoire de l'architecture classique en France* (Paris: A. Picard).
——— (1958): *L'Art sous la Révolution et l'Empire en France, 1789-1815* (Paris: Flammarion).
HAVEN, MARC (1964): *see* LALANDE, EMMANUEL.
HAYCOCK, DAVID BOYD (2002): *William Stukeley: Science, Religion, and Archaeology in Eighteenth-Century England* (Woodbridge: Boydell).
HEALEY, CATHERINE, BOWIE, KAREN, & BOS, AGNÈS (Eds.) (1998): *Le Père-Lachaise* (Paris: Éditions

Action Artistique de la Ville de Paris).
HEATH, DOUGLAS DENON (*Ed.*) (1857-74): *see* SPEDDING, JAMES.
HEIDELOFF, CARL ALEXANDER VON (1844): *Die Bauhütte des Mittelalters in Deutschland* (Nuremberg: Johann Adam Stein).
HEISE, KARL (1919): *Entente-Freimaurerei und Weltkrieg. Ein Beitrag zur Geschichte des Weltkrieges und zum Verständnis der wahren Freimaurerei* (Basel: Ernst Finckh).
HELCK, HANS WOLFGANG (1965): 'Die Mythologie der alten Ägypter' H. W. HAUSSIG (*Ed.*) **i** 313-406.
——— (1975-85): *Lexikon der Ägyptologie* (Wiesbaden: O. Harrassowitz).
HELLMUTH, ECKHART (*Ed.*) (1990): *The Transformation of Political Culture: England and Germany in the Late Eighteenth Century* (Oxford UP for The German Historical Institute, London).
HEMBERG, BENGT (1950): *Die Kabiren* (Uppsala: Almqvist & Wiksell).
HEMPEL, DORIS (*Ed.*) (1987): *Friedrich Wilhelm von Erdmannsdorff 1736-1800* (Wörlitz/Dessau: Staatliche Schlösser und Gärten).
HENKEL, ARTHUR, & SCHÖNE, ALBRECHT (1967): *Emblemata: Handbuch zur Sinnbild-Kunst des XVI und XVII Jahrhunderts.* (Stuttgart: J. B. Metzler).
HENNAUT, ERIC (2006): *see* CULOT, MAURICE.
HENNE AM RHYN, OTTO (1869): *Das Buch der Mysterien. Leben und Treiben der geheimen Gesellschaften aller Zeiten und Völker* (St-Gallen: Altwegg-Weber zur Treuburg).
——— (1894): *Die Freimaurer; deren Ursprung, Geschichte, Verfassung, Religion, und Politik* (Leipzig: M. Spohr).
HENSLER, KARL FRIEDRICH (1792): *Maurerrede auf Mozarts Tod. Vorgelesen bey einer Meisteraufnahne in der Sehr Ehrw. St. Joh. Zur Gekrönten Hoffnung im Orient von Wien vom B^{dr} H.....r.* (Vienna: Ignaz Alberti).
HERBERT, THOMAS (1638): *Some Yeares Travels into Divers Parts of Asia and Afrique* (London: I. Blome & R. Bishop).
HERDER, JOHANN GOTTFRIED VON (1877-1913): *Sämmtliche Werke* (Berlin: Weidmann), but *see* especially *Älteste Urkunde des Menschengeschlechts* (Riga: J. F. Hartknoch, 1774-6).
HÉRICART-FERRAND, LOUIS-ÉTIENNE-FRANÇOIS, VICOMTE DE THURY (1815): *Description des Catacombes de Paris* (Paris: Bossange & Masson).
HERMAND, JOST (1989): *see* GRIMM, REINHOLD.
HERMES TRISMEGISTUS (1995): *Hermetica* B. P. COPENHAVER (*Ed.*) (Cambridge: Cambridge UP).
HÉROLD, FERDINAND (1874): *Rapport présenté par M. Hérold, ... sur le projet de création d'un cimetière parisien a Méry-sur-Oise* (Paris: s.n.).
HEROLD, J. CHRISTOPHER (1962): *Bonaparte in Egypt* (New York: Harper & Row).
HERRMANN, WOLFGANG (1962): *Laugier and Eighteenth-Century French Theory* (London: Zwemmer).
HERSEY, GEORGE L. (1976): *Pythagorean Palaces: Magic and Architecture in the Italian Renaissance* (Ithaca NY: Cornell UP).
HEUDE, BERNARD (2006): *see* CULOT, MAURICE.
HEUTEN, G. (1931): 'La diffusion des cultes égyptiens en Occident' *Revue de l'histoire des religions* **civ** 409-16.
HEWLINGS, RICHARD (2009): 'Palladio in England: Chiswick House, London' *Country Life* (28 January) 46-50.
HIBBARD, HOWARD (*Ed.*) (1967): *see* FRASER, DOUGLAS.
HIGDEN, RANULF (1865-86): *Polychronicon* JOSEPH RAWSON LUMBY & C. BABINGTON (*Eds.*) (London: Longman & Co.).
HILLAIRET, JACQUES (AUGUSTE ANDRÉ COUSSILLAN) (1966): *Dictionnaire historiques des rues de Paris* (Paris: Éditions de Minuit).
HIMMELFARB, GERTRUDE (2008): *The Roads to Modernity: The British, French, and American Enlightenments* (London: Vintage).
HIRSCH, ERHARD (*Ed.*) (2003-6): *Frühklassik von Deutscher: Dessau 2003-2006* (Dessau: Stadt Dessau).
HIRSCHFELD, CHRISTIAN CAJUS LORENZ (1779-85): *Théorie de l'art des jardins, traduit de l'allemand (Theorie der Gartenkunst)* (Leipzig: M. G. Weidmanns Erben und Reich).
HISCOCK, NIGEL (2000): *The Wise Master Builder: Platonic Geometry in Plans of Medieval Abbeys and Cathedrals* (Aldershot: Ashgate).

——— (2003): *The White Mantle of Churches: Architecture, Liturgy, and Art around the Millennium* (Turnhout: Brepols).
——— (2007): *The Symbol at your door: Number and Geometry in the Religious Architecture of the Greek and Latin Middle Ages* (Aldershot: Ashgate).
HISTOIRE ET BANDES DESSINÉES. IMAGES DE L'ÉGYPTE ANCIENNE (1987): (Besançon: Imprimerie de la Faculté des Sciences et Imprimerie du Recordat). Contains articles by BOURGEOIS, CORTEGGIANI, ELOY, and THIEBAUT, etc.
HITLER, ADOLF (1925-7): *Mein Kampf* (Munich: F. Eher). *See also* the English versions JAMES MURPHY (*Tr.*) (London: Hurst & Blackett 1939) and RALPH MANHEIM (*Tr.*) (London: Pimlico 1992).
HJELMBORG, BJØRN, & SØRENSEN, SØREN (*Eds.*) (1962): *Natalicia Musicologica Knud Jeppesen* (Hafniae [i.e. Copenhagen]: Wilhelm Hansen].
HOBBS-HALMAY, H. M. (1992): 'The Development of Egyptian Revival in San Diego County' *The Journal of San Diego History* **xxxviii**/2 (Spring).
HOCQUARD, JEAN-VICTOR (1979): *La Flûte Enchantée* (Paris: Aubier Montaigne).
——— (1993): *Mozart, de l'Ombre à la lumière* (Paris: J.-C. Lattès).
HOEBANX, JEAN-JACQUES (1980): 'L'implantation et l'expansion de la Franc-Maçonnerie à Bruxelles et en Wallonie des origins à 1980' HASQUIN, HERVÉ (*Ed.*) 293-320.
——— (2000): 'Des loges dans la cité' DESPY-MEYER, A. (*Ed.*) 10-27.
HOFFMANN, ALFRED (1963): *Der Landschaftsgarten* (Hamburg: Broschek).
HOLBACH, PAUL HEINRICH DIETRICH, BARON VON (1767): *Le Christianisme dévoilé* ('Londres' [i.e. Frankfurt]: s.n.).
——— (1770): *Système de la Nature* ('Londres' [i.e. Amsterdam]: s.n.).
HOLLERICH, M. J. (1989): 'Myth and History in Eusebius's *De Vita Constantini*: *Vit. Const.* 1.12 in its contemporary setting' *Harvard Theological Review* **lxxxii** 421-45.
HOLLIS, FREDERICK JAMES (1934): *The Archaeology of Herod's Temple. With a Commentary on the Tractate Middoth* (London: J. M. Dent).
HOLMBERG, MAJ SANDMAN (1946): *The God Ptah* (Lund: C.W.K. Gleerup).
HOLUB, ROBERT C. (*Ed.*) (1993): *see* WILSON, W. DANIEL.
HONDT, P. DE (1752): *Les Vrais Jugemens sur la Société des Francs-Maçons* (Brussels: P. de Hondt).
HONOLKA, KURT (1990): *Papageno: Emanuel Schikaneder: Man of the Theater in Mozart's Time* (Portland OR: Amadeus Press).
HOOYKAAS, REIJER (1972): *Religion and the Rise of Modern Science* (Edinburgh: Scottish Academic Press).
HOPFNER, THEODOR (1922-25): *Fontes Historiæ Religionis Ægyptiacæ* (Bonn: A. Marx & E. Weber).
HORÁNYI, MÁTYÁS (1962): *The Magnificence of Eszterháza* (London and Budapest: Akadémiai Kiadó).
HORNBLOWER, SIMON, & SPAWFORTH, ANTHONY (*Eds.*) (1996): *The Oxford Classical Dictionary* (Oxford: Oxford UP).
HORNBOSTEL, WILHELM (1973): *Sarapis: Studien zur Überlieferungsgeschichte* etc. (Leiden: E. J. Brill).
HORNE, ALEXANDER (1967): 'The Masonic Tradition of King Solomon's Temple' *AQC* **lxxx** 8-35.
——— (1972): *King Solomon's Temple in the Masonic Tradition* (London: Aquarian Press).
——— (1978): *The York Legend in the Old Charges* (London: Lewis).
HORSLEY, SAMUEL (1728): *see* NEWTON, SIR ISAAC.
HORSTMANN, CARL (*Ed.*) (1887): *see* BRADSHAW, HENRY.
HÔTE, NESTOR L' (1836, 1840): *see* L'HÔTE, NESTOR.
HOWARD, DEBORAH (1995): *Scottish Architecture: Reformation to the Restoration 1560-1660* (Edinburgh: Edinburgh UP).
HOWATSON, M. C. (*Ed.*) (1989): *The Oxford Companion to Classical Literature* (Oxford: Oxford UP).
HOYLE, EDMOND (1750): *A Short Treatise on the Game of Whist... To which is added... A Artificial Memory* (London: T. Osborne). A smaller first edition was published in 1742.
HOYOS, ARTURO DE, & MORRIS, S. BRENT (*Eds.*)

(2004): *Freemasonry in Context: History, Ritual, Controversy* (Lanham MD: Lexington Books).
HUBALA, ERICH (1972): 'Das alte Ägypten und die bildende Kunst im 19. Jahrhundert' *Welt Kulturen und Moderne Kunst*, SIEGFRIED WICHMANN (*Ed.*) (Munich: Haus der Kunst/Bruckmann).
HUBERT, EMANUELLE (1972): 'Les "mystères" de l'Égypte avant Champollion' *Archéologia* **lii** (November) 52.
HUGH OF ST VICTOR (1991): *The Didascalion of Hugh of St Victor: a medieval guide to the arts*, JEROME TAYLOR (*Tr.*) (New York: Columbia UP).
HUGHAN, WILLIAM JAMES (1871-9): *Masonic Sketches and Reprints: History of Freemasonry in York* (**i**); *Unpublished Records of the Craft* (**ii**); *The Old Charges of British Freemasons* (with Preface by A. F. A. WOODFORD (**iii**); *Memorials of the Masonic Union of A.D. 1813* (with a reprint of Dr. Dassigny's *Serious and Impartial Inquiry*) (**iv**); and *A Numerical and Statistical Register of Lodges which formed the United Grand Lodge of England* (London: G. Kenning).
——— (1895): *The Old Charges of British Freemasonry* (Second Edition) (London: G. Kenning).
——— (1909): *Origin of the English Rite of Freemasonry* JOHN T. THORP (*Ed.*) (Leicester: Johnson, Wykes, & Co.).
HUGUES, PIERRE-FRANÇOIS (called BARON D'HANCARVILLE) (1785): *Recherches sur l'origine, l'esprit et les progrès des arts de la Grèce* (London: s.n.).
HULSE, MICHAEL (*Tr.*) (1989): *see* GOETHE (1774).
HÜLSEN, CHRISTIAN CARL FRIEDRICH, & EGGER, HERMANN (1913-16): *Die römischen Skizzenbücher von Maarten van Heemskerck...* eds. (Berlin: J. Bard).
HUMBERT, CHANTAL (1983): 'L'Égyptomanie au zénith Napoléonien' *La Gazette de L'Hôtel Drouot* **xxxi** (23 September) 24-25.
HUMBERT, JEAN-MARCEL (1971a): Recherches sur les monuments égyptiens et égyptisants de Paris. Memoire of an historical study. Paris IV. Egyptology.
——— (1971b): 'Les Monuments égyptiens et égyptisants de Paris' *Bulletin de la Société française d'Égyptologie* **lxii** (October) 9-29.
——— (1974): 'Les Obélisques de Paris: projets et réalisations' *Revue de l'Art* **xxiii** 9-29.
——— (1975): L'Égyptomanie à Paris et dans la région parisienne (architecture, décoration, et mobilier) de 1775 à 1825. Doctoral Thesis (Third Cycle) presented at the Sorbonne.
——— (1985a): 'Présence de l'égyptomanie dans l'architecture urbaine, thèmes et symboles' *Résumé des communications du 110ᵉ Congrès National des Sociétés Savantes*, Montpellier, 1-5 April 1985 (Paris: Ministère de l'Education Nationale, Comité des Travaux Historiques et Scientifiques) 74. The same theme is given in *Actes du 110ᵉ Congrès National des Sociétés* published in *Études Languedociennes* (Paris: Ministère de l'Education Nationale, Comité des Travaux Historiques et Scientifiques 1985) 423-442.
——— (1985b): 'Paris liegt am Nil' (with WILFRIED WIEGAND) *Frankfurter Allgemeine Magazin* **cclxxiv** (31 May) 52-60.
——— (1987a): L'Égyptomanie, sources, thèmes et symboles. Étude de la réutilisation des thèmes décoratifs empruntés à l'Égypte ancienne dans l'art occidental du XVIᵉ siècle à nos jours. Doctoral Thesis, Letters and Humanities, Sorbonne, Paris IV.
——— (1987b): 'Panorama de quatre siècles d'égyptomanie' *Bulletin de la Société française d'Égyptologie* **cx** (October) 48-77.
——— (1987c): 'La réinterprétation de l'Égypte ancienne dans l'architecture du XIXᵉ siècle: un courant original en marge de l'orientalisme' *Actes du Colloque Pascal-Xavier Coste* (Marseilles: 27-29 November).
——— (1989a): *L'Égyptomanie dans l'Art Occidental* (Paris [Courbevoie]: ACR Édition Internationale).
——— (1989b): 'Le Symbolisme de l'égyptomanie révolutionnaire et son influence sur l'avenir du phénomène' *Actes du 114ᵉ Congrès National des Sociétés Savantes* (3 - 9 April). *See also Résumé des Communications* (Paris: 1989).
——— (1990a): 'Napoléon et l'Égypte, ou l'osmose de deux mythes' DEWACHTER, M. (*Ed.*) 1990) 31-7.
——— (1990b): L'égyptomanie: sources, themes et symboles: etude de la réutilisation des themes décoratifs empruntés à l'Égypte ancienne dans l'art occidental du XVIᵉ siècle à nos

jours: thèse de doctorat d'État (Lille 3: ANRT)
——— (1991): 'Egyptomanie et decoration intérieure aux XIXe siècle' GOVI, CURTO, & PERNIGOTTI (*Eds.*) (1991) 221-231.
——— (1993): 'Rêves d'Égypte: l'égyptomanie, mythes, et symboles' *Égyptes* **iii** 219.
——— (1994a): 'Egyptomania' *Muséart* **xxxvii** (February) 66-9.
——— (1994b): 'Les décors égyptisants des jardins: étapes d'un parcours initiatique?' in 'Le jardin du retour' *Les Carnets de l'exotisme* **xiii** (1st semester) 51-4.
——— (1994c): 'Denon et la découverte d'Égypte' HUMBERT, PANTAZZI, & ZIEGLER (*Eds.*) (1994) 200-205. *See also* Humbert's other contributions 216-9 and 450-7.
——— (*Ed.*) (1996): *L'Égyptomanie à l'épreuve de l'archéologie. Actes du colloque international organisé au musée du Louvre par le Service culturel les 8 et 9 avril 1994* (Brussels: Éditions du Gram, and Paris, Musée du Louvre). *See also* HUMBERT's own contributions 21-35 and 97-138.
——— (1997a): 'Sources multiples and incertaines: comment la redécouverte de l'Égypte s'est traduite dans l'art' *Actes du Colloque* [18-21 May 1995]: *La Redécouverte de la Grèce et de l'Égypte au XVIIIe et au début du XIXe siècle* (Nantes: Presses de l'Universitaire de Nantes) 177-189.
——— (1997b): 'Égyptomanie' *Dictionnaire européen des Lumières* (Paris: Presses universitaires de France).
——— (1998): *L'Égypte à Paris* (Paris: Éditions Action Artistique de la Ville de Paris).
———, PANTAZZI, MICHAEL, & ZIEGLER, CHRISTIANE (*Eds.*) (1994): *Egyptomania: Egypt in Western Art 1730-1930. Catalogue* (also published in French as *Égyptomanie: L'Égypte dans l'Art Occidental, 1730-1930*) of an Exhibition held at the Musée du Louvre, Paris (20 January-18 April 1994), National Gallery of Canada, Ottawa (17 June-18 September 1994), and Kunsthistorisches Museum, Vienna (16 October 1994-29 January 1995) (Paris and Ottawa: Éditions de la Réunion des Musées Nationaux, National Gallery of Canada, and Spadem, Adagp, 1994).
———, & PRICE, CLIFFORD (*Eds.*) (2003): *Imhotep Today: Egyptianizing Architecture* (London: UCL).
HUMPHRIES, D. (*Tr.*) (1721-25): *see* MONTFAUCON, BERNARD DE.
HUNT, CHARLES CLYDE (1939): *Masonic Symbolism* (Cedar Rapids, IA: Laurence Press).
HUNT, JOHN DIXON (1987): *William Kent* (London: Zwemmer).
——— (1991): '"Ut Pictura Poesis": The Garden and the Picturesque in England' MOSSER & TEYSSOT (*Eds.*) (1991) 231-41.
———, & SCHUYLER, DAVID (*Eds.*) (1984): *Journal of Garden History* **iv**/3 (July-September). Special issue devoted to cemeteries, with contributions from CURL, ETLIN, ET AL.
———, & WILLIS, PETER (*Eds.*) (1988): *The Genius of Place: the English Landscape Garden 1620-1820* (Cambridge MA: MIT Press).
HUYBERTS, C. (1702): *see* MISHNAH.
IDELSOHN, ABRAHAM ZVI (1923): *Songs of the Babylonian Jews* (Berlin: Harz).
IMDAHL, MAX (*Ed.*) (1966): *see* FIENSCH, GÜNTHER.
IMPENS, C. (2002): 'A Mason's Emblem in 1522' *AQC* **cxv** 256-62.
IMRIE, JOHN, & DUNBAR, JOHN (*Eds.*) (1957-82): *Accounts of the Masters of Works for Building and Repairing Royal Palaces and Castles* **ii** (Edinburgh: HMSO).
INETT, JOHN (1704-10): *Origines Anglicanae: or, a History of the English Church* (London: M. Wotton).
IRMEN, HANS-JOSEF (1991): *Mozart, Mitglied geheimer Gesellschaften* (Zülpich: Prisca).
——— (1996): *Mozart's Masonry and The Magic Flute* RUTH OHM & CHANTAL SPENKE (*Trs.*) (Zülpich: Prisca).
ISIDORE OF SEVILLE, SAINT (2006): *The Etymologies of Isidore of Seville* STEPHEN A. BARNEY ET AL. (*Trs.*) with MURIEL HALL (Cambridge & New York: Cambridge UP).
ISON, WALTER WILLIAM (2004): *The Georgian Buildings of Bath* (Reading: Spire Books).
ISRAEL, JONATHAN IRVINE (1999): *Locke, Spinoza, and the Philosophical Debate concerning Toleration in the Early Enlightenment: c.1670-c.1750* in *Mededelingen van de Afdeling Letterkunde* **62**/6 N.S. (Amsterdam: Koninklijke Nederlandse Akademie van Wetenschappen).
——— (1999a): *Counter-Reformation, Economic Decline, and the Delayed Impact of the Medical Revolution in Catholic Europe, 1550-1750* (London: Routledge).
——— (2001): *Radical Enlightenment: Philosophy and the Making of Modernity* (Oxford: Oxford UP).
——— (2010): *A Revolution of the Mind: Radical Enlightenment and the Intellectual Origins of Modern Democracy* (Princeton NJ: Princeton UP).
——— (*Ed.*) (1999): *The Anglo-Dutch Moment: Essays on the Glorious Revolution and its World Impact* (Cambridge: Cambridge UP).
ISTEL, EDGAR (1928): *Die Freimaurerei in Mozarts Zauberflöte* (Berlin: A. Unger).
ISTITUZIONE RITI E CEREMONIE DELL' ORDINE DE' FRANCS MAÇONS (1785): (Venice: Bassaglis). Contains LARUDAN'S illustrations of Lodges.
IVERSEN, ERIK (1961): *The Myth of Egypt and its Hieroglyphs in European Tradition* (Copenhagen: Gad). See also the 1993 edition (Princeton NJ: Princeton UP).
——— (1968): *Obelisks in Exile* (Copenhagen: Gad).
IXNARD, P. MICHEL D' (1791): *Recueil d'Architecture...* (Strasbourg: Treuttel).
JACKSON, A. C. F. (*Ed.*) (1986): *The English Masonic Exposures of 1760-1769: with full transcripts of Three Distinct Knocks, 1760, Jachin and Boaz, 1762, Shibboleth, 1765* (London: Lewis Masonic).
JACOB, MARGARET C. (1981): *The Radical Enlightenment: Pantheists, Freemasons, and Republicans* (London: George Allen & Unwin).
——— (1991): *Living tthe Enlightenment: Freemasonry and Politics in Eighteenth-Century Europe* (Oxford & New York: Oxford UP).
——— (2006): *The Origins of Freemasonry: Facts & Fictions* (Philadelphia PA: University of Pennsylvania Press).
JACOBS, JOHAN (*Ed.*) (2000): *see* DESPY-MEYER, ANDRÉE (*Ed.*).
JACOBUS DE VORAGINE (1892): *The Golden Legend* (Hammersmith: Kelmscott Press).
JACQUELIN, JACQUES-ANDRÉ (1812): *La Lyre Maçonnique, étrennes aux Francs-Maçons et à Leurs Soeurs* (Paris: Joseph Chaumerot).
JAEGER, BERTRAND (1991): 'L'Egitto antico alla Corte dei Gonzaga' GOVI ET AL. (*Eds.*) (1991) 233-53.
——— (1992): 'La création du Musée égyptien de Turin et le goût égyptisant au Piémont' *Sesto Congresso Internazionale di Egittologia, Atti.* (Turin: International Assocation of Egyptologists).
——— (1994): 'La loggia delle muse nel Palazzo Te e la Reviviscenza dell'Egitto Antico nel Rinascimento' Mantova e l'antico Egitto da Giulio Romano a Giuseppe Acerbi. *Atti del Convegno di Studi*, Mantua, 23-24 May 1992 (Florence: Leo S. Olschki Editore).
——— (1996): 'Le café Pedrocchi de Padoue et la "modification du regard" porté sur l'Égypte ancienne en Italie au XIXe siècle' HUMBERT (*Ed.*) (1996) 189-225.
JAEGER, R. (*Ed.*) (2001): *see* SCHMIDT, LEO.
JAEGHER, F. DE (1970): 'La Loge "Les Philadelphes" à Verviers' *Bulletin des Archives Verviétoises* **vi** 15-37.
JAFFÉ, IRMA B. (1972): *see* WITTKOWER, RUDOLF.
JAHN, OTTO (1856): *W. A. Mozart* (Leipzig: Breitkopf & Härtel).
——— (1882): *Life of Mozart* (London: Novello, Ewer, & Co.).
JAHRBUCH DES KAISERLICH DEUTSCHEN ARCHÄOLOGISCHEN INSTITUTS (from 1886): (Berlin: W. de Gruyter).
JAHRBUCH D. RÖMISCH-GERMANISCHEN ZENTRALMUSEUMS MAINZ (1963) **x** 214.
JAMES, JOHN (*Tr.*) (1707): *see* POZZO, ANDREA.
——— (*Tr.*) (1708): *see* PERRAULT, CLAUDE.
JAMESON, ANNA BROWNELL (1907): *Legends of the Madonna as represented in the Fine Arts* (London: Hutchinson & Co.).
JANNEAU, GUILLAUME (1964): *L'Époque Louis XVI* (Paris: Presses universitaires de France).
JANNER, FERDINAND (1876): *Die Bauhütten des deutschen Mittelalters* (Leipzig: E. A. Seemann).
JANSSEN, JOZEF MARIE ANTOON (1943): 'Athanase Kircher "Égyptologue"' *Chronique d'Égypte* **xviii** (Brussels: Musées Royaux du Cinquantenaire).
JARDINE, LISA (2002): *On a Grander Scale: The Outstanding Career of Sir Christopher Wren* (London: HarperCollins).
JOHN OF SALISBURY (1479-81): *Polycraticus* (Brussels: Fratres Vitae Communis).
JOHNSON, J. DAVID (1949): *Facts about the Building of the Temple of Solomon* (Camas WA: J. David Johnson).
JOHNSON, RICHARD (*Tr.*) (1971-7): *see* CAPELLA, MARTIANUS MINEUS FELIX.
JOLLOIS, JEAN-BAPTISTE-PROSPER (1904): *Journal d'un ingénieur attaché à l'expédition d'Égypte, 1798-1802*, G. MASPERO (*Ed.*) (Paris: E. Leroux).
JOLY, MAURICE (1864): *Dialogue aux Enfers entre Machiavel et Montesquieu: ou, La Politique de Machiavel au XIXe siècle* (Brussels: A. Mertens).
JOMARD, EDMÉ-FRANÇOIS (1809-28): *see* COMMISSION DES SCIENCES ET ARTS D'ÉGYPTE.
——— (1812): *Recueil d'observations et de mémoires sur l'Égypte* (Paris: Imprimerie Impériale).
——— (1819): *Notice sur les nouvelles découvertes faites en Égypte...* (Paris: Baudouin).
——— (1822): *Description d'un étalon métrique orné d'hiéroglyphes découvert dans les ruines de Memphis par les soins de M. le chev. Drovetti* (Paris: J. M. Eberhart).
——— (1825): 'Antiquités égyptiennes' *Bull. univ.* **iii** 225-7.
——— (1828): 'L'école égyptienne de Paris' *J. Asiatique* **ii** 96-116.
——— (1829): *Description Générale de Memphis et des Pyramides* (Paris: Imp. Royale).
JONES, BERNARD E. (1957): *Freemasons' Book of the Royal Arch* (London:Harrap). Another edn. was published in 1969.
——— (1986): *Freemasons' Guide and Compendium* (London: George G. Harrap & Co.).
JONES, C. E. (*Ed.*) (1924-34): *see* BRETT-SMITH, H.F.B.
JONES, GWILYM PEREDUR (1942): *see* KNOOP, DOUGLAS.
——— (1952): 'Building in Stone in Medieval Western Europe' *Cambridge Economic History of Europe* (Cambridge: Cambridge UP).
JONES-DAVIES, M. T. (*Ed.*) (1981): *Emblèmes et devises au temps de la Renaissance* (Paris: Y. Touzot).
JOSEPHUS, FLAVIUS (2006): *Jewish Antiquities* WILLIAM WHISTON (*Tr.*) (London: Wordsworth Editions).
JOUIN, ERNEST (1920-25): *Le Péril judéo-maçonnique* (Paris: Émile-Paul Frères).
JOURNAL OF GARDEN HISTORY **iv**/3 (1984) (July-September). A special issue entitled *Cemetery and Garden*, JOHN DIXON HUNT & DAVID SCHUYLER (*Eds.*).
JOURNAL OF EIGHTEENTH-CENTURY STUDIES **xxxii**/1 (2009) 120-1. Review of Calder (*Ed.*) (2006).
JOURNAL OF THE WARBURG AND COURTAULD INSTITUTES (from July 1937): (London: Warburg Institute, University of London).
JUNG, CARL GUSTAV (1953-79): *Collected Works* HERBERT READ, MICHAEL FORDHAM, & GERHARD ADLER (*Eds.*) (New York: Pantheon Books).
JUNG, OTTO (1963): *Der Theatermaler Friedrich Christian Beuther (1777-1856) und seine Welt* (Emsdetten/Westf.: Lechte).
JUNK, VICTOR (1899): *Goethes Forsetzung der Mozartschen Zauberflöte* (Berlin: A. Duncker).
KADATZ, HANS JOACHIM (1986): *Friedrich Wilhelm von Erdmannsdorff* (Berlin: Verlag für Bauwesen).
KAHN, MAXIME (1938): *see* BONAPARTE EN ÉGYPTE.
KAIN, ROGER (1978): 'Napoleon I and urban planning in Paris' *The Connoisseur* **cxcvii**/791 (January) 44-51.
KAISER, ERNST (*Tr.*) (1979): *see* MUSIL, ROBERT.
KANT, IMMANUEL (2004): *Observations on the Feeling of the Beautiful and the Sublime* (Berkeley CA & London: University of California Press).
——— (2007): *Critique of Judgement* JAMES CREED MEREDITH (*Tr.*) and NICHOLAS WALKER (*Ed.*) (Oxford: Oxford UP), first published as *Kritik der Urteilskraft* (1790).
KARLSHAUSEN, CHR. (1993): *see* DELVAUX, L.
KAT, W. (1974): *Een Grootmeestersverkiezing in 1756* (The Hague: Eigenuitgave van de Loge).
KATZ, JACOB (1970): *Jews and Freemasons in Europe 1723-1939* LEONARD OSCHRY (*Tr.*) (Cambridge MA: Harvard UP).
KAUFMANN, EMIL (1933): *Von Ledoux bis Le Corbusier: Ursprung und Entwicklung der Autonomen Architektur*

(Vienna & Leipzig: Verlag Passer).
——— (1952): *Three Revolutionary Architects: Boullée, Ledoux, and Lequeu.* Transactions of the American Philosophical Society, N.S. **xlii**, Part 3 (Philadelphia: American Philosophical Society).
——— (1968): *Architecture in the Age of Reason: Baroque and Post-Baroque in England Italy, and France* (New York: Dover Publications).
KELCHNER, JOHN WESLEY (1925): *A Description of King Solomon's Temple and Citadel* (Philadelphia PA: A. J. Holman).
KELLER, C. (*Ed.*) (2001): see SCHMIDT, LEO.
KELLER, LUDWIG (1914): *Die Freimaurerei. Eine Einführung in ihre Anschauungswelt und ihre Geschichte* (Leipzig & Berlin: B. G. Teubner).
KELLY, J. N. D. (1986): *The Oxford Dictionary of Popes* (Oxford: Oxford UP).
KEMPEN, WILHELM VAN (1928): *Die Baukunst des Klassizismus in Anhalt nach 1800* (Marburg: Verlag des Kunstgeschichtlichen Seminars der Universität Marburg).
KEMPTER, GEORG FRIEDRICH (2007): *Die Säule* (Winterbach: Gesellschaft für Natur und Kunst).
KENDAL, E. A. (1802): see DENON, BARON DOMINIQUE VIVANT.
KENNERLEY, PETER (1991): *The Building of Liverpool Cathedral* (Lancaster: Carnegie Publishing).
KENNON, DONALD R. (*Ed.*) (1999): *A Republic for the Ages. The United States Capitol and the Political Culture of the Early Republic* (Charlottesville VA & London: published for The United States Capitol Historical Society by the UP of Virginia). Contains much material on Freemasonic connections.
KERÉNYI, KARL (1991): *Eleusis: Archetypal Images of Mother and Daughter* RALPH MANHEIM (*Tr.*) (Princeton NJ: Princeton UP).
KHAN, SOPHIE (1996): 'De la métaphore égyptienne à l'archéologie imaginaire: les fabulations de l'art contemporain' HUMBERT (*Ed.*) (1996) 627-50.
KILPATRICK, ROSS S. (2001): see MACLENNAN, NEIL K.
KIND, JOHN LOUIS (1906): *Young in Germany* (New York: Macmillan).
KING, ALEC HYATT (1984): *A Mozart Legacy. Aspects of the British Library collections* (London: The British Library).
KINGSBURY, NOËL, & RICHARDSON, TIM (*Eds.*) (2005): *Vista: the culture and politics of gardens* (London: Frances Lincoln).
KINNANDER, MAGNUS (1943): *Svenska frimureriets historia* (Stockholm: Natur och Kultur).
KIRCHER, ATHANASIUS (1636): *Prodomus Coptus sive Ægyptiacus* (Rome: S. Cong: de Propag: Fide).
——— (1643): *Lingua Ægyptiaca Restituta* (Rome: H. Scheus).
——— (1647): *Rituale Ecclesiæ Ægyptiacæ sive Cophtitarum… ex lingua Copta et Arabica in Latinam transtulit* (Rome?: s.n.).
——— (1650): *Obeliscus Pamphilius hoc est, interpretatio nova* (Rome: L. Grignani).
——— (1652-54): *Œdipus Ægyptiacus hoc est universalis hieroglyphicæ veterum doctrinæ temporum injuria abolitæ instauratio…in three volumes* (Rome: V. Mascardi).
——— (1666): *Obelisci Ægyptiaci, nuper inter Isæi romani rudera effossi, interpretatio hieroglyphica Athanasii Kircheri* (Rome: Varessii).
——— (1676): *Sphinx Mystagoga sive Diatribe Hieroglyphica…* (Amsterdam: Jansson-Waesberg).
——— (1679): *Turris Babel; sive, Archontologia qua primo priscorum post diluvium hominum vita,…* (Amsterdam: Jansson-Waesberg).
KIRK, ROBERT (1933): *The Secret Commonwealth of Elves, Fauns, and Fairies* with Commentaries by ANDREW LANE and Introduction by R. B. CUNNINGHAME GRAHAM (Stirling: Mackay).
KISCHKE, HORST (1996): *Die Freimaurer: Fiktion, Realität, und Perspektiven* (Wien: Ueberreuter).
KLAPP, LUDWIG (1905): *Maurerische Reden* (Hamburg: Laue).
KLAVER, ELIZABETH (*Ed.*) (2004): *Images of the Corpse: From the Renaissance to Cyberspace* (Madison WI: University of Wisconsin Press).
KLEMPERER, VIKTOR (1954): *Delilles "Gärten": ein Mosaikbild des 18. Jahrhunders* (Berlin: Akademie-Verlag).
KLOSS, GEORG FRANZ BURKHARD (1844): *Bibliographie der Freimaurerei und der mit ihr in Verbindung Gesetzen Geheimen Gesellschaften* (Frankfurt-am-Main: J.D. Sauerländer).
——— (1845): *Die Freimaurerei in ihrer Wahren Bedeutung aus den alten und ächten Urkunden der Steinmetzen, Masonen, und Freimaurer* (Leipzig: O. Klemm).
——— (1848): *Geschichte der Freimaurerei in England, Irland, und Schottland aus ächten Urkunden dargestellt (1685 bis 1784) nebst einer Abhandlung über die Ancient Masons* (Leipzig: O. Klemm).
——— (1852-53): *Geschichte der Freimaurerei in Frankreich aus ächten Urkunden dargestellt (1725-1830)* (Darmstadt: G. Jonghaus).
KLOSSOWSKI DE ROLA, STANISLAS (1973): *Alchemy: The Secret Art* (London: Thames & Hudson).
——— (1988): *The Golden Game. Alchemical Engravings of the Seventeenth Century* (London: Thames & Hudson).
KMIECIK, EDWARD (*Tr.*) (1998): Translation of RADZIWIŁŁOWA (1808) in PIWKOWSKI (1998) 558-61.
KNEISNER, FRIEDRICH (1912): *Geschichte der Deutschen Freimaurerei in ihren Grundzügen dargestellt…* (Berlin: A. Unger).
KNIGGE, ADOLF FREIHERR VON (1978-1992): *Freimaurer- und Illuminatenschriften* from *Sämtliche Werke* **xii-xiii** (Nedeln: KTO).
KNIGHT, G. NORMAN (1983): see PICK, FRED LOMAX.
KNIGHT, RICHARD PAYNE (1805): *An Analytical Inquiry into the Principles of Taste* (London: Payne & White).
KNOBLOCH, EBERHARD (2002): see REICH, KARIN.
KNOOP, DOUGLAS, & JONES, GWILYM PEREDUR (1932): 'Castle Building at Beaumaris and Caernarvon in the early fourteenth century' *AQC* **xlv** 4-49.
——— (1933): 'The Building of Eton College, 1442-1460' *AQC* **xlvi** 70-114.
——— (1934): 'London Bridge and its Builders' *AQC* **xlvii** 5-44.
——— (1935): *The London Mason in the Seventeenth Century* (Manchester: Manchester UP).
——— (1936a): 'The Bolsover Castle Building Account 1613' *AQC* **xlix** 24-79.
——— (1936b): 'The Rise of the Mason Contractor' *RIBA Journal*, **xliii**, Series 3 (17 October), 1061-1071.
——— (1937a): *An Introduction to Freemasonry* (Manchester: Manchester UP).
——— (1937b): 'The decline of the mason-architect in England' *Journal of the Royal Institute of British Architecture* 3rd Series **xliv**/19.
——— (1939): *The Scottish Mason and the Mason Word* (Manchester: Manchester UP).
——— (1940): *A Short History of Freemasonry to 1730* (Manchester: Manchester UP).
——— (1941): *Begemann's History of Freemasonry* (Frome & London: Butler & Tanner).
——— (1942a): *A Handlist of Masonic Documents* (Manchester: Manchester UP).
——— (1942b): *Freemasonry and the Growth of Natural Religion* (Frome and London: Butler & Tanner).
——— (1944): *The Scope and Method of Masonic History* (Oldham: Manchester Association for Masonic Research).
——— (1948): *The Genesis of Freemasonry. An Account of the Rise and Development of Freemasonry in its Operative, Accepted, and Early Speculative Phases* (Manchester: Publications of the University of Manchester).
——— (1967): *The Mediaeval Mason. An Economic History of English Stone Building in the Later Middle Ages and Early Modern Times* (Manchester: Manchester UP).
———, & HAMER, DOUGLAS (*Eds.*) (1938): *The Two Earliest Masonic MSS* (Manchester: Publications of the University of Manchester).
——— (1945): *Early Masonic Pamphlets* (Manchester: Publications of the University of Manchester).
——— (1963): *Early Masonic Catechisms*. Revised by H. CARR (Manchester: Manchester UP).
KOBBERT, M. (1914): 'Kult' in *Realenzyklopädie der klassischen Alterumswissenschaft*, Second Series **i**/2 (Stuttgart: J. B. Metzlersche Verlagsbuchhandlung) 565-75.
KÖBERLEIN, ERNST (1962): 'Caligula und die ägyptischen Kulte' *Beiträge zur klassischen Philologie* **iii** (Meisenheim-am-Glan: A. Hain) 23.
KOCH, GEORG FRIEDRICH (1978): see ARNDT, KARL.

KOCH, RICHARD (1911): *Br∴ Mozart, Freimaurer und Illuminaten, nebst einigen freimaurerischen kulturhistorischen Skizzen* (Bad Reichenhall: The Author).
KÖCHEL, LUDWIG, RITTER VON (1862): *Chronologisch-thematisches Verzeichniss sämtlicher Tonwerke Wolfgang Amadé Mozarts* (Leipzig: Breitkopf & Härtel). An updated edn. by GRAF PAUL VON WALDERSEE was published by the same firm in 1905, and a further revised edn. by ALFRED EINSTEIN in 1937. A later edn., published (1983) in Wiesbaden by Breitkopf & Härtel, is recommended.
KOMORZYŃSKI, EGON VON (1951): *Emanuel Schikaneder. Ein Beitrag zur Geschichte des deutschen Theaters* (Vienna: L. Doblinger).
——— (1955): *Mozart, Sendung und Schicksal* (Vienna: Kremayr & Scheriau).
KOOPER, ERIK (*Ed.*) (2006): *Sentimental and Humorous Romances* (Kalamazoo, MI: Medieval Institute Publications).
KOPPELKAMM, STEFAN (1987): *Der imaginäre Orient; Exotische Bauten des achtzehnten und neunzehnten Jahrhunderts in Europe* (Berlin: Wilhelm Ernst & Sohn Verlag).
KÖPPEN, KARL FRIEDRICH (*Ed.*) (1766): *Les Plus Secrets Mystères des Hauts Grades de la Maçonnerie Dévoilés CHEVALIER DE BÉRAGE* (*Tr.*) (Berlin: Haude & Spener). See BÉRAGE.
——— (1821): *Crata Repoa: ou Initiations aux anciens mystères des prêtres d'Égypte*, translated by F. J. M. RAGON from the German *Crata Repoa: oder Einweihungen in der alten geheimen Gesellschaft der ägyptischen Priester* published in Berlin in 1778 (Paris: Bailleul). See also BÉRAGE, ——— (1776). *Crata Repoa* was also translated by R. F. WALLACE-JAMES into English as *Crata Repoa, or, Initiations of the Ancient Mysteries of the Priests of Egypt* (S. I.: s.n. 19-?). A further translation was made by John Yarker which appears in MANLY P. HALL (1937).
KORNEMANN, E. (1901): 'Zur Geschichten der antiken Herrscherkulte' *Klio* **i** 51-146.
KRAFFT, JOHANN KARL (otherwise JEAN-CHARLES) (1801-03): *Plans, coupes, élévations des plus belles maisons et des hôtels construits à Paris et dans les environs* (Paris: Krafft & Ransonnette).
——— (1809-10): *Productions de plusieurs architectes français et étrangers, relatives aux jardins pittoresques et aux fabriques de divers genres…* (with P.-F.-L. DUBOIS) (Paris: de Levrault).
——— (1812): *Recueil d'architecture civile: contenant les plans, coupes, et élévations des châteaux, maisons de campagne*, etc. (Paris: De Crapelet).
——— (1831): *Constructions, plans, et décorations des jardins de France, d'Angleterre, et d'Allemagne* (Paris: Bance aîné).
——— (1849): *Maisons de campagne, habitations rurales, châteaux, fermes, jardins anglais, temples, chaumières, kiosques, ponts*, etc. (Paris: Bance aîné).
KREINATH, JENS, SNOEK, JAN, & STAUSBERG, MICHAEL (*Eds.*) (2006): *Theorizing Rituals: Issues, Topics, Approaches, Concepts* (Leiden, etc.: Brill).
KRETZULESCO-QUARANTA, EMANUELA (1986): *Les Jardins du Songe: 'Poliphile' et la mystique de la Renaissance* (Paris: Belles Lettres).
KRISTENSSON, GILLIS (*Ed.*) (1974): *Instructions for Parish Priests: edited from MS Cotton Claudius A II and six other manuscripts* (Lund: Gleerup).
KROON, ANDRÉA A. (*Ed.*) (2003): *Vrijmetselarij in Nederland. Een kennismaking met de wetenschappelijke studie van een 'geheim' genootschap* (Den Haag: OVN).
———, BAX, MARTY, & SNOEK, JAN (*Eds.*) (2005): *Masonic and Esoteric Heritage: New Perspectives for Art and Heritage Policies* (Den Haag: OVN).
——— (2006): see SNOEK, JAN A. M.
KRYGER, KARIN (1983): 'Der Philosoph, ein raffaelisches Motiv in Wiedewelts Werk' *HAFNIA Copenhagen Papers in the History of Art* **ix** 7-24.
——— (1985): *Allegori og Borgerdyd: Studier i det nyklassicistiske gravmæle i Danmark 1760-1820* (Copenhagen: Christian Ejlers' Forlag).
——— (1986): *Frihedsstøtten* (Odense: Landbohistorisk Selskab).
KUENZL, HANNELORE (1973): *Der Einfluss des alten Orients auf die europäische Kunst besonders im 19. und 20. Jh.* (Köln: Inaugural Dissertation).
KUÉSS, GUSTAV R., & SCHECHELBAUER, BERNHARD (1959): *200 Jahre Freimaurerei in*

Österreich (Vienna: O. Kerry).
KÜHN, PETER (1988): see ALEX, REINHARD.
KÜHNEL, BIANCA (Ed.) (1997/8): *The Real and Ideal Jerusalem in Jewish, Christian, and Islamic Art: Studies in Honor of Bezalel Narkiss on the Occasion of his Seventieth Birthday. Journal of the Center for Jewish Art* **xxiii-xxiv** (Jerusalem: The Hebrew University).
KULTURSTIFTUNG DESSAU WÖRLITZ (Ed.) (2005): *Infinitely Beautiful: The Garden Realm of Dessau-Wörlitz* (Berlin: Nicolai).
KUNOTH, GEORGE (1956): *Die historische Architektur Fischers von Erlach* (Düsseldorf: L. Schwann).
KUNST UND ANTIQITÄTEN (1989): No. 3, devoted to Egyptomania, with articles by OTTILLINGER, SCHMIDT, SCHOSKE, STROMBERG, SYNDRAM, THOMAS, & WITT-DÖRRING on various aspects of the Egyptian Revival.
KUNZE, MAX (Ed.) (2005): *Kunst und Aufklärung im 18. Jahrhundert* (Ruhpolding: Rutzen).
LABORDE, ALEXANDRE LOUIS-JOSEPH, COMTE DE (1808-15): *Description des Nouveaux Jardins de France et ses Anciens Châteaux* (Paris: Delance).
LACHAT, LOUIS (1935): see LETI, GIUSEPPE.
LACOUTURE, JEAN (1988): *Champollion: une vie de lumières* (Paris: B. Grasset).
LADURIE, EMMANUEL LE ROY (Ed.) (1990): *Mémoires d'Égypte: hommage de l'Europe à Champollion* (Strasbourg: Nuée bleue).
LAFAYE, GEORGES LOUIS (1883): *Histoire du culte des divinités d'Alexandrie: Sérapis, Isis, Harpocrate et Anubis hors de l'Égypte depuis les origins jusqu'à la naissance de l'école néo-platonique* (Paris: Thorin).
——— (1904): *Les Divinités alexandrines chez les Parisii* (Paris: Société des Antiquaires de France).
LAISSUS, YVES (1989): see BEAUCOUR, FERNAND ÉMILE.
LALANDE, EMMANUEL (1964): *Le Maître Inconnu. Cagliostro, étude historique et critique sur la haute magie, par Marc Haven* (Lyon: P. Derain).
LALANDE, JOSEPH-JÉRÔME LA FRANÇAIS DE (1777a): *État du G∴ O∴ de France* (Paris: s.n.).
——— (1777b): 'Francs-Maçons' in *Encyclopédie Supplement* (Paris: C.L.F. Panckoucke).
LAMBERT, PHYLLIS (1991): see CHARNEY, MELVIN.
LAMBRECHTS, PIERRE (1956): *Augustus en de egyptische godsdienst. Mededelingen van de koninklijke vlaamse Academie voor Wetenschappen, Letteren en schone Kunsten van België, Klasse der Letteren*, **xviii** 2 (Brussels: AWLSK).
——— (1958-62): 'La politique religieuse, des empereurs romains. Leur attitude envers les cultes égyptiens et phrygiens' *Nouvelle Clio. Revue de la découverte historique*, **x**/2, 243-4.
LAMMON, DWIGHT P. (1969): *The Baltimore Glass Trade, 1780-1820* (Charlottesville VA: Winterthur Portfolio 5, UP of Virginia).
LAMY, BERNARD (1696): *Apparatus Biblicus* (Lyons: Joann Certe).
——— (1720): *De Tabernaculo Foederis, de Sancta Civitate Jerusalem, et de Templo EJUS* (Paris: J.-B. Delespine).
LANCASTER, CLAY (1947): 'Oriental Forms in American Architecture 1880-1870' *Art Bulletin* **xxix**/3 (September) 183-193.
——— (1950): 'The Egyptian Style and Mrs Trollope's Bazaar' *Magazine of Art* **xliii** 94ff.
LANDON, H. C. ROBBINS (1982): *Mozart and the Masons. New Light on the Lodge 'Crowned Hope'* (London & New York: Thames & Hudson).
——— (1988): *Mozart's Last Year* (London & New York: Thames & Hudson).
——— (1989): *Mozart: The Golden Years 1781-1791* (London: Thames & Hudson).
——— (Ed.) (1990): *The Mozart Compendium: A Guide to Mozart's Life and Music* (London: Thames & Hudson).
———, & MITCHELL, DONALD (Eds.) (1956): *The Mozart Companion* (Oxford: Oxford UP).
LANE, ANDREW (1933): see KIRK, ROBERT.
LANG, SUSAN (1956): see PEVSNER, NIKOLAUS.
LANGLEY, BATTY (1747): *Gothic Architecture, improved by Rules and Proportions. In many Grand Designs of Columns, Doors, Windows, Chimney-Pieces, Arcades, Colonades, Porticos, Umbrellos, Temples, and Pavillions &c. with Plans, Elevations and Profiles; Geometrically Explained* (London: John Millan). See also the 1967 edn. (Farnborough: Gregg).
LANKHEIT, KLAUS (1968): *Der Tempel der Vernunft: Unveröffentlichte Zeichnungen von Boullée* (Basel & Stuttgart: Birkhäuser).
LANT, ANTONIA (1996): 'L'antiquité égyptienne revue par le cinéma, ou, Pourquoi filmer les pharaons?' HUMBERT (Ed.) (1996) 587-605.
LAROUSSE, PIERRE (1928-33): *Larousse du XXe Siècle* PAUL AUGÉ (Ed.) (Paris: Librairie Larousse) with later supplements.
LARSSON, LARS OLOF (1978): see ARNDT, KARL.
LARUDAN, ABBÉ (1746): *Les Francs-Maçons écrasés. Suite du livre intitulé, L'Ordre des Francs-Maçons Trahi* (Amsterdam: s.n.). See also *Die Zerschmetterten Freymäurer* (Frankfurt and Leipzig: s.n., 1746), which also contains a plate by BERNIGEROTH.
——— (1785): see ISTITUZIONE RITI E CEREMONIE.
LASSALLE, ÉMILE (1844): *Promenades pittoresques aux cimetières du Père-Lachaise, de Montmartre, du Montparnasse et autres, ou Choix des principaux monuments élévés dans ces Champs de Repos; dessinés et Lithographiés par Lassalle et Rousseau. Texte par J^h Marty* (Paris: A. Fourmage).
——— (1846): *Les Principaux Monuments Funéraires Du Père-Lachaise, de Montmartre, du Mont-Parnasse et autres Cimetières de Paris Dessinés et Mesurés Par Rousseau, architecte, et Lithographiés Par Lassalle, Accompagnés d'une Description succincte du monument et d'une Notice historique sur le personnage qu'il renferme, Par Marty* (Paris: Amédée Bédelet).
LATOUR, ALESSANDRA (1991): see CHARNEY, MELVIN.
LATTE, KURT (1960): *Römanische Religionsgeschichte* in *Handbuch der Altertumswissenschaft* series (Munich: C. H. Beck).
LAUGIER, MARC-ANTOINE (1753): *Essai sur l'Architecture* (Paris: Duchesne).
——— (1765): *Observations sur l'architecture* (The Hague & Paris: Desaint).
——— (1782): 'Prédicateur du Roy' GRANDIDIER, PHILIPPE-ANDRÉ.
LAURENS, HENRY (1987): *Les Origins intellectuelles de l'expédition d'Égypte. L'Orientalisme islamisant en France (1698-1798)* (Istanbul and Paris: Éditions Isis).
——— (1997): *L'Expédition d'Égypte: 1798-1801* (Paris: Éditions du Seuil).
LAW, JOHN (1988): see FYFE, GORDON.
LAWRENCE, JOHN THOMAS (1912): *The Perfect Ashlar and other Masonic Symbols* (London: A. Lewis).
——— (1924): *Highways and By-Ways of Freemasonry* (London: A. Lewis).
LEACH, NEIL (Tr.) (1988): see ALBERTI, LEON BATTISTA.
LECHEVALLIER-CHEVIGNARD, GEORGES, & SAVREUX, MAURICE (1923): *Le Biscuit de Sèvres* (Paris: A. Morancé).
LECLANT, JEAN (1956): 'Notes sur la propagation des cultes et monuments égyptiens en Occident à l'époque impériale' *Bulletin de l'Institut Français d'Archéologie Orientale* **lv** 173-9.
——— (1959): 'Reflets de l'Égypte dans la littérature latine après quelques publications recents' *Bulletin de la Faculté des Lettres Strasbourg* **xxxvii** 303-8.
——— (1963): Notices in *Orientalia* **xxxii**
——— (1968): 'Histoire de la diffusion des cultes égyptiens' *Problèmes et méthodes d'histoire religions* 92-6.
——— (1969): 'En quête de l'égyptomanie' *Revue de l'Art* **v** 82-88.
——— (1972-91): *Inventaire bibliographique des Isiaca* (Leiden: E J. Brill).
——— (1985): *De l'égyptophilie à l'égyptologie: érudits, voyageurs, collectionneurs et mécènes' Comptes rendus de l'Académie des Inscriptions et Belles-Lettres.*. Séance Publique Annuele lecture (22 November) (Paris: CRAI Institut) 4e fasc. 630-47.
——— (1986): 'Isis déesse universelle' *Bulletin de Correspondence Hellénique*, Supplement **xiv** 341-54.
———, ET AL. (1992-3): *Il VI Congresso Internazionale di Egittologia*. Torino, 1-8 Settembre, 1991 (Turin: International Association of Egyptologists).
LEDIARD, THOMAS (Tr.) (1732): *The Life of Séthos, Taken from Private Memoirs of the Ancient Egyptians. Translated from a Greek Manuscript into French. And now faithfully done into English from the Paris Edition. By Mr Lediard* (London: J. Walthoe). See TERRASSON, JEAN.
LEDOUX, CLAUDE-NICOLAS (1804): *L'architecture considerée sous le rapport de l'art, des moeurs et de la législation* (Paris: The Author, printed by Perronneau).
——— (1847): *L'Architecture de Claude-Nicolas Ledoux* (Paris: Lenoir). See RAMÉE, DANIEL (Ed.).
LEE, DUNCAN CAMPBELL (1932): *Desaguliers of No 4 and His Services to Freemasonry* (London: No. 4 Lodge).
LEE, MICHAEL G. (2007): *The German 'Mittelweg': Garden Theory and Philosophy at the Time of Kant* (New York & London: Routledge Taylor & Francis Group).
LEES, JOHN (Tr.) (1911-12): see CHAMBERLAIN, HOUSTON STEWART.
LEFEBRE, DENIS (2001): *Marcel Sembat: le socialisme maçonnique d'avant 1914* in *Encyclopédie maçonnique*, **xxxv** (Paris: Éditions maçonniques de France).
LE FORESTIER, R. (1914): see FORESTIER, R. LE.
LEFUEL, OLIVIER (1970): 'L'influence de la Campagne d'Égypte sur l'art français' *Souvenir Napoléon* **cclv** (July) 26-29.
LEGNER, ANTON (Ed.) (1978-80): *Die Parler und der schöne Stil* (Cologne: Museen der Stadt Köln). See especially the contribution by BARBARA SCHOCK-WERNER entitled 'Bauhütten und Baubetrieb der Spätgotik' from page 61.
LEGRAND, JACQUES-GUILLAUME (1797): *Recueil et parallèle des édifices de tout genre anciens et modernes remarquables par leur beauté... par J.-N.-L. Durand... avec un texte extrait de l'histoire générale de l'architecture, par J.-G. Legrand* (Paris: Gillé fils).
——— (1806-9): *Description de Paris et de ses édifices* (Paris: C.-P. Landon).
LEICESTER REPRINTS *Masonic Reprints* (various dates): Lodge of Research, No. 2429 (Leicester: Lodge of Research).
LEIGH, RICHARD (1989): see BAIGENT, MICHAEL.
LEIGHTON, S. (1927): *History of the Masonic Hall, Arthur Square, Belfast* (Belfast: W. & G. Baird).
LELIÈVRE, PIERRE (1942): *Vivant Denon, directeur des Beaux-Arts de Napoléon* (Angers: Éditions de l'Ouest).
LEMAIRE, JACQUES (1998): *L'antimaçonnisme: aspects généraux (1738-1998)* in *Encyclopédie maçonnique* **vi** (Paris: Éditions maçonniques de France).
——— (2007): See LOIR, CHRISTOPHE (Ed.).
LE MOËL, MICHEL (1997): see MOËL, MICHEL LE.
L'EMPEREUR, CONSTANTIN (1630): see EMPEREUR.
LENNHOFF, EUGEN, & POSNER, OSKAR (1932): *Internationales Freimaurerlexicon* (Zürich, Leipzig, & Vienna: Amalthea Verlag).
LENNING, C. (pseudonym: actually FRIEDRICH MOSSDORF) (1822-8): *Encyclopädie der Freimaurerei, etc* (Leipzig: F. A. Brockhaus).
——— (1863-67, 1900, etc.): *Allgemeines Handbuch der Freimaurerei* (Leipzig: F. A. Brockhaus). See also the 1900-1901 edn. (Leipzig: Max Hesse's Verlag).
LENOIR, ALEXANDRE (1989): 'Les Colosses Funèbres - les pyramides éphémères de la Révolution française' *FMR (Franco Maria Ricci)* **xxi** (August) 25-50.
LENOIR, ALEXANDRE-MARIE (1795-1806): *Description historique et chronologique des monumens de sculpture réunis au Musée des Monumens Français* (Paris: Lenoir, Au Musée, rue des Petits-Augustins, Guyot, et al.).
——— (1814): *La Franche-Maçonnerie rendue à sa véritable Origine, ou l'Antiquité de la Franche-Maçonnerie prouvée par l'explication des mystères anciens et modernes* (Paris: Fournier, etc.).
LEO XIII, POPE (1978): *Humanum Genus* (Encyclical Letter on Freemasonry dated 20 April 1884) GERALD C. TREACY SJ (Ed.) (Rockford IL: TAN books).
LEPAGELET, M., & LUSSI (LUSSY) DE (1790): *Tableau Pittoresque de la Vallée de Montmorency, un des séjours le plus agreeable des Environs de Paris* (Paris: Lepagelet & Lussi).
LEPPER, JOHN HERON, & CROSSLE, PHILIP (1925): *History of the Grand Lodge of Free and Accepted Masons of Ireland* **i** (Dublin: Lodge of Research).
LEPSIUS, CARL RICHARD (1849-59): *Denkmäler aus Ægypten und Æthiopien*. 12 vols (Berlin: Nikolaische Buchhandlung).
——— (1853): *Discoveries in Egypt, Ethiopia, and the Peninsula of Sinai in the years 1842-1845* (London: R. Bentley).
LERAT, CHRISTIAN (Director), with the collaboration of MARIE-CÉCILE RÉVAUGER (2005): *Échanges intellectuels, littéraires et artistiques dans le monde transatlantique. Actes d'un Colloquium held at Bordeaux* (15-16 February 2002) (Pessac: Maison

LE ROY, LADURIE, E. (*Ed.*) (1990): *see* LADURIE, E. LE ROY.
LESSING, ERICH (1994a): *see* BERGDOLL, BARRY.
——, FISCHER, JÜRI, ET AL. (1984): *Die Übungslogen der Gerechten und Volkommenen Loge zur Wahren Eintracht im Orient zu Wien 1782-1785* (Vienna: Grossloge von Österreich).
LESSING, GOTTHOLD EPHRAIM (1925): *Werke* (Berlin: Deutsches Verlagshaus Bong & Co.).
—— (1927): *Lessing's Masonic Dialogues (Ernst und Falk)*, with Introduction by A. COHEN (*Tr.*) (London: Baskerville Press).
LESUEUR, ÉMILE (1914): *La Franc-Maçonnerie Artésienne au XVIIIᵉ Siècle* (Paris: E. Leroux).
LETI, GIUSEPPE, & LACHAT, LOUIS (1935): *L'Ésotérisme à la scène: La Flûte Enchantée, Parsifal, Faust* (Annecy: L. Dépollier et Cie).
LETTSOM, JOHN COAKLEY (1796): *Hints for Promoting a Bee Society* (London: Darton & Harvey).
—— (1801): *Hints designed to promote Beneficence, Temperance, & Medical Science* (London: J. Manman).
—— (*Tr.*) (1787): *An Account of the Culture and Use of the Mangel-Wurzel: or Root of Scarcity, translated from the French of the Abbé de Commerell* (London: Dilly & Phillips).
LEWINE, MILTON J. (1967): *see* FRASER, DOUGLAS.
LEWIS, G. WILTON (1927): *From Bible Data The House which King Solomon Built for Jehovah* (Cincinnati OH: Standard Publishing Co.).
LEXICON ICONOGRAPHICUM MYTHOLOGIAE CLASSICAE (LIMC) (from 1981): (Zürich/Munich: Artemis).
L'HÔTE, NESTOR (1836): *Notice Historique sur les Obélisques égyptiens, et en particulier sur l'Obélisque de Lougsor* (Paris: Leleux).
—— (1840): *Lettres écrites d'Égypte en 1838 et 1839* (Paris: Didot).
LIGNE, CHARLES-JOSEPH, PRINCE DE (1922): *Coup d'oeil sur Beloeil et sur une grande partie des jardins d'Europe* COMTE ERNEST GANAY (*Ed.*) (Paris: Bossard). Originally published in 1781.
LIGOU, DANIEL (1964): 'La Franc-Maçonnerie française au XVIIIᵉ Siècle' in *L'Information Historique* **3**.
—— (*Ed.*) (1991): *Dictionnaire de la franc-maçonnerie* (Paris: Presses Universitaires de France).
——, ET AL. (2000): *Histoire des Francs-Maçons en France* (Toulouse: Drivat).
LILLA, MARK (2007): *The Stillborn God: Religion, Politics, and the Modern West* (New York: Knopf).
LINA, JÜRI (2004): *Architects of Deception: The Concealed History of Freemasonry* (Stockholm: The Author).
LINDERT, WILGERT TE (1998): *Aufklärung und Heilserwartung: philosophische und religiöse Ideen Wiener Freimaurer (1780-95)* (Frankfurt-am-Main: P. Lang).
LINDNER, DOLF (1986): *Ignaz von Born, Meister der Wahren Eintracht: Wiener Freimaurerei im 18. Jh.* (Vienna: Österreichischer Bundesverlag).
LINDNER, ERICH J. (1926): *Die königliche Kunst im Bild. Beiträge zur Ikonographie der Freimaurerei* (Graz: Akademische Druck u. Verlagsanstalt).
LINGS, MARTIN (1964): *Ancient Beliefs and Modern Superstitions* (London: Perennial Books).
LITTLE, NINA FLETCHER (1952): *American Decorative Wall Painting 1700-1850* (New York: Old Sturbridge Village & Studio Publication).
LLOYD, ELEANOR (*Ed.*) (1900): *see* GATTY, H. K. F.
LOIR, CHRISTOPHE, & LEMAIRE, JACQUES CH. (*Eds.*) (2007): *Franc-Maçonnerie et Beaux-Arts* in the Series *La Pensée et les Hommes* **lxii-lxiii** (Brussels: Espace de Libertés).
LONDON MAGAZINE, THE (from 1820): (London: Baldwin, Cradock, & Joy) but see especially 1824.
LONG, PAMELA O. (2008): *see* CURRAN, BRIAN A.
LORD, EVELYN (2008): *The Hell-Fire Clubs: Sex, Satanism, and Secret Societies* (New Haven CT & London: Yale UP).
LORENTZ, STANISŁAW, & ROTTERMUND, ANDRZEJ (1984): *Klasycyzm w Polsce* (Warsaw: Wydawnictwo Arkady).
LOUDON, MRS JANE (1846): *see* LOUDON, JOHN CLAUDIUS (1833).
LOUDON, JOHN CLAUDIUS (1833): *An Encyclopædia of Cottage, Farm, and Villa Architecture and Furniture...* (London: Longman, Rees, Orme, Brown, Green & Longman). *see also* the newer edition of 1846, edited by MRS JANE LOUDON.
—— (1834-38): *The Architectural Magazine, and Journal of Improvement in Architecture; Building, and Furnishing,...* (London: Longman, Rees, Orme, Brown, Green & Longman).
—— (1843): *On the Laying Out, Planting, and Managing of Cemeteries* (London: Longman, Brown, Green, & Longmans). *See* the edition of 1981 with an Introduction by JAMES STEVENS CURL (Redhill: Ivelet Books).
LOUGH, JOHN (1973): *The Contributors to the Encyclopédie* (London: Grant & Cutler).
LOVEJOY, ARTHUR ONCKEN, BOAS, GEORGE E., ET AL (*Eds.*) (1935): *A Documentary History of Primitivism and Related Ideas* (Baltimore MD: Johns Hopkins UP).
LUCAS, O. H. (n.d.): *King Solomon's Temple and the Ark of the Covenant* (Typed text of lecture in the Library of Freemason's Hall, London).
LUIKEN, JAN (1732): *see* LUYKEN.
LUKACHER, BRIAN (2006): *Joseph Gandy: An Architectural Visionary in Georgian England* (London: Thames & Hudson).
LUKIS, WILLIAM COLLINGS (*Ed.*) (1882-7): *The Family Memoirs of the Rev William Stukeley, and the Antiquarian and Other Correspondence of William Stukeley, Roger and Samuel Gale* etc. (Durham: Publications of the Surtees Society).
LUMBY, JOSEPH RAWSON (*Ed.*) (1865-86): *see* HIGDEN, RANULF.
LUQUET, GEORGES-HENRI (1963): *La Franc-maçonnerie et l'état en France au XVIIIᵐᵉ siècle* (Paris: Vitiano).
LUSSI, M. DE (1784): *Vues des monumens construits dans les jardins de Franconville-la-Garenne, appartenans à Madame la Comtesse d'Albon, gravés d'après ses dessins et ceux de M. de Lussi* (Paris: de Lussi).
—— (1790): *see* LEPAGELET, M.
LÜTHI, URS (1992): *Der Mythos von der Weltverschwörung: die Hetze der Schweizer Frontisten gegen Juden und Freimaurer, am Beispiel des Berner Prozesses um die "Protokolle der Weisen von Zion"* (Basel: Helbing & Lichtenhahn).
LUYKEN, JAN (1732): *Histoire les plus remarquables de l'Ancien et du Nouveau Testament* (Amsterdam: Cóvens & Mortier).
LYON, DAVID MURRAY (1900): *History of the Lodge of Edinburgh (Mary's Chapel), No. I, Embracing an Account of the Rise and Progress of Freemasonry in Scotland* (London: Gresham Pub. Co.).
—— (*Tr.*) (1893): *see* FINDEL, GOTTFRIED JOSEPH GABRIEL.
LYON, JACOB JUDA (1778): *An Accurate Description of the Grand and Glorious Temple of Solomon* M. P. DECASTRO (*Tr.*) (London: W. Bailey).
LYRA (1481): *see* NICOLAUS DE LYRA.
MCCALMAN, IAIN (2003): *The Seven Ordeals of Count Cagliostro: Count Cagliostro, Master of Magic in the Age of Reason* (London: Century). Subsequently (2004) published by Arrow.
MCCAULEY, ROBERT H. (1942): *Liverpool Transfer Designs on Anglo-American Pottery* (Portland: Southworth Anthoensen Press).
MCCLINTON, KATHERINE MORRISON (1968): *Collecting American 19th–Century Silver* (New York: Scribner's).
MCFADZEAN, RONALD (1979): *The Life and Work of Alexander Thomson* (London: Routledge & Kegan Paul).
MACGIBBON, DAVID, & ROSS, THOMAS (1887-92): *The Castellated and Domestic Architecture of Scotland from the Twelfth to the Eighteenth Century* (Edinburgh: David Douglas).
—— (1896-7): *The Ecclesiastical Architecture of Scotland from the Earliest Christian Times to the Seventeenth Century* (Edinburgh: David Douglas).
MCINTOSH, ANGUS, SAMUELS, M. L., & BENSKIN, MICHAEL (*Eds.*) (1986): *A Linguistic Atlas of Late Mediaeval English* (Aberdeen: Aberdeen UP).
MCINTOSH, CHRISTOPHER (1975): *Eliphas Lévi and the French Occult Revival* (London: Rider).
—— (1987): *The Rosicrucians: The History, Mythology, and Rituals of an Occult Order* (Wellingborough: Crucible).
—— (1992): *The Rose Cross and the Age of Reason: Eighteenth-Century Rosicrucianism in Central Europe and its Relationship to the Enlightenment*. No. **29** in the series Brill's Studies in Intellectual History (Leiden, New York, & Köln: E.J.Brill).
—— (2005a): *Gardens of the Gods: Myth, Magic, and Meaning in Horticulture* (London & New York: I. B. Tauris, distributed in the USA and Canada by Palgrave Macmillan).
—— (2005b): 'The Symbol-Strewn Landscape: Esoteric and Initiatic Symbolism in European gardens in the 18ᵗʰ and 19ᵗʰ Century' KROON, BAX, & SNOEK (*Eds.*) (2005) 45-56.
MCKAY, H. A. (1994): *Sabbath and Synagogue. The Question of Sabbath Worship in Ancient Judaism* (Leiden: E. J. Brill).
MCKEARIN, GEORGE S., & HELEN (1948): *American Glass* (New York: Crown Publishers).
MACKENZIE, KENNETH ROBERT HENDERSON (1877a): *Fundamental Constitutions of the Primitive and Original Rite of Freemasonry* (London: The Author).
—— (1877b): *The Royal Masonic Cyclopaedia* (New York: J. W. Bouton). But *see* 1987 edn., with Introduction by R. A. GILBERT & JOHN HAMILL (Wellingborough: Aquarian Press).
MACKENZIE, NORMAN (*Ed.*) (1976): *Secret Societies* (London: Aldus Books).
MACKEY, ALBERT GALLATIN (1898-1906): *The History of Freemasonry* (New York: Masonic History Co.).
—— (1919): *A Lexicon of Freemasonry; containing a Definition of all its Communicable Terms, Notices of its History, Traditions, and Antiquities* (London: Charles Griffin). Other editions were published, notably that of 1883.
MCKINSTRY, SAM (*Ed.*) (1994): *see* STAMP, GAVIN.
MCLEAN, ADAM (1979): 'A Rosicrucian Alchemical Mystery Centre in Scotland' *The Hermetic Journal* **iv** (Summer) 10-13.
MACLENNAN. NEIL, K., & KILPATRICK, ROSS S. (2001): 'King Solomon & The Temple Builders: A Biblical Reading of Giorgione's Painting "The Three Philosophers"' *Heredom* **ix** 111-134.
MCLEOD, WALLACE (*Ed.*) (1986): 'The Old Charges' *AQC* **xciv**.
—— (2002): *see* WEISBERGER, RICHARD WILLIAM.
MACLOT, PETRA, & WARMENBOL, EUGÈNE (1984): 'Twee temples onder de slopershamer: aantekeningen bij de afbraak van het logegebouw van "Les Amis du Commerce et La Persévérance Réunis" te Antwerpen' (in collaboration with M. DE SCHAMPHELEIRE) *M&L. Monumenten en Landschappen* **iii**/3 (May-June) 17-24.
—— (1985): 'Bevangen door Egypte: de Egyptische Tempel in de Antwerpse Zoo in Kunsthistorisch en Historisch Perspectief' *Zoom up Zoo* (Antwerp: Royal Zoological Society, June) 359-391.
—— (1988a): 'Antwerpen aan de Nijl: Aantekeningen bij de bouw van een Egyptische tempel te Antwerpen (1855-1862)' *Antwerpen, Tijdschrift van de Stad Antwerpen* **i** 34-43.
—— (1988b): 'Tempel en stal in één: de Egyptische tempel in de Antwerpse zoo in kunsthistorisch en historisch perspectief' *M&L. Monumenten en Landschappen* **vii**/2 24-35.
MACNULTY, W. KIRK (1991): *Freemasonry: A Journey through Ritual and Symbol* (London: Thames & Hudson).
—— (2002): *The Way of the Craftsman: A Search for the Spiritual Essence of Craft Freemasonry* (London: Central Regalia).
—— (2006): *Freemasonry: Symbols, Secrets, Significance* (London: Thames & Hudson).
MACPHERSON, JAY (1987): 'The Magic Flute and Viennese Opinion' *Man and Nature / L'Homme et la Nature* **vi** 161-72.
—— (1998): '"Masonic Landscape Design": or Down the Garden Path' ROBERT GILBERT (*Ed.*) (1998): **cx** 50-74.
MACREADY, SARAH, & THOMPSON, F. H. (*Eds.*) (1985): *Influences in Victorian Art and Architecture*. Occasional Paper N.S. **vii** (London: Society of Antiquaries of London).
MACROBIUS, AMBROSIUS THEODOSIUS (1952): *Commentary on the Dream of Scipio* WILLIAM HARRIS STAHL (*Tr.*) (New York: Columbia UP).
MCWILLIAM, COLIN (1971): *see* WALKER, DAVID.
—— (1978): *Lothian* in The Buildings of Scotland Series (Harmondsworth: Penguin).
—— (1984): *see* GIFFORD, JOHN.

MADAME XXX (1744): *La Franc-Maçonne ou Révélation de Mystères des Francs-Maçons* (Brussels: s.n.).
MADOX, THOMAS (1736): *Baronia Anglia* (London: R. Gosling).
MAGENNIS, HUGH (Ed.) (2006): see WILCOX, JONATHAN.
MAGIE, DAVID (Tr.) (2005): *Lives of the Later Caesars* (London: Folio Society).
MAIER, MICHAEL (1614): *Arcana Arcanissima, hoc est Hieroglyphica ægyptio-græca...* (London: T. Creede).
——— (1617): *Symbola Aureæ Mensæ Duodecim Nationum...* (Frankfurt: L. Iennis).
MAIMONIDES (MOSES BEN MAIMON) (1678): *De Cultu divino, ex R. Mosis Majemonidae secundae Legis seu Manus Fortis libro VIII*, translated into Latin by LOUIS COMPIÈGNE DE VEIL (Paris: G. Gaillou). Later reprinted (1696) in *Fasciculus sextus Opisculorum quae ad historiam ac Philologiam sacram spectant* (Rotterdam: s.n.).
——— (1957): *The Code of Maimonides, Book Eight. The Book of Temple Service. Yale Judaica Series, Vol. XII* (New Haven CT & London: Yale UP).
MALAISE, M. (1972): *Les conditions de pénétration et de diffusion des cultes égyptiens en Italie* (Leiden: E. J. Brill).
——— (1984): 'La diffusion des cultes égyptiens dans les provinces européenes de l'Empire Romain' *Aufstieg und Niedergang der römischen Welt. Geschichte und Kultur Roms im Spiegel der neueren Forschung* **ii** 17.3 (Berlin and New York: de Gruyter), 1615-91.
MALLINGER, JEAN (1978): *Les Origines égyptiennes des usages et des symboles maçonniques* (Lille: F. Planquart).
MANHEIM, RALPH (Tr.) (1991): see KERÉNYI, KARL.
——— (1992): see HITLER, ADOLF.
MANTOVA E L'ANTICO EGITTO DA GIULIO ROMANO A GIUSEPPE ACERBI (1994): *Atti del Convegno di Studi, Mantova, 23-24 May 1992* (Florence: Leo S. Olschki Editore). Contains excellent papers by JAEGER ET AL.
MARCHANT DE BEAUMONT, FRANÇOIS-MARIE (1821): *Vues pittoresques, historiques, et morales du Cimetière du P. La Chaise...* (Paris: The Author).
——— (1825): *Itinéraire des curieux dans le Cimetière du P. La Chaise...* (Paris: Delaforest).
MARET, HUGUES (1776): Article on Cemeteries *Supplément à l'Encyclopédie, ou Dictionnaire Raisonné des sciences, des arts et des métiers, par une société des gens de lettres* **ii** (Amsterdam: M. M. Rey) 428-30.
MARGOLIN, J.-C. (1986): *Histoire du rébus* (Paris: Maisonneuve et Larose).
MARLOWE, JOHN (1971): *Perfidious Albion: the Origins of Anglo-French Rivalry in the Levant* (London: Elek).
MARRACCIUS, HIPPOLYTUS (1648): *Bibliotheca Mariana alphabetico ordine digesta...* (Rome: F. Caballi).
——— (1710): *Polyanthea Mariana, in qua libris octodecim* (Köln: F. Metternich). An earlier edition, *Polyanthea Mariana, in libros XVIII, distributa, in qua Deipara Virginis Mariæ...*, was published in Köln by P. Ketteler in 1683, and a further edition in 20 parts was published in Rome by P. Corbolletti in 1694.
MARSDEN, VICTOR EMILE (Tr.) (1972): see NILUS, S. A.
MARTIN, C. F. J. (Tr.) (1996): see GROSSETESTE, ROBERT.
MARTIN, KURT (1933): *Die Kunstdenkmäler des Amtsbezirks Mannheim: Stadt Schwetzingen* (Karlsruhe: C. F. Müller).
MARTIN SAINT-LÉON (1901): see SAINT-LÉON.
MARTY (1844, 1846): see LASSALLE, ÉMILE.
MASKE UND KOTHURN (from 1955): Quarterly journal on theatrical matters (Vienna: Institut für Theaterwissenschaft an der Universität Wien). It contains useful Bibliographies. See especially the article by W. SCALICKI: 'Das Bühnenbild der Zauberflöte' **ii** (1956).
MASPERO, GASTON CAMILLE CHARLES (Ed.) (1904): see JOLLOIS, JEAN-BAPTISTE-PROSPER.
MASSIN, JEAN & BRIGITTE (1959): *W. A. Mozart* (Paris: Au Club français du Livre).
MASSOUNIE, DOMINIQUE, PRÉVOST-MARCILHACY, PAULINE, & RABREAU, DANIEL (1995): *Paris et ses fontaines de la Renaissance à nos jours* (Paris: Éditions Action Artistique de la Ville de Paris).
MASTAI, BOLESŁAW (1973): *The Stars and Stripes* (New York: Alfred A. Knopf).
MATTHEW, H. C. G., & HARRISON, BRIAN (Eds.) (2004): *Oxford Dictionary of National Biography (ODNB)* (Oxford: Oxford UP).
MATTINGLY, H. (Tr.) (1938): see ALTHEIM, FRANZ.
MAUNDE, JOHN (Tr.) (1801): *The Rural Philosopher, or, French Georgics: A Didactic Poem translated from the original of the Abbé Delille* (London: G. Kearsley).
MAURER, CARL (1812): *Handzeichnungen zum Theater Gebrauch von Carl Maurer, Fürstlich Esterhazyscher Hof Theater Decorateur* - unpublished manuscript dated 1812, Eisenstadt.
MAUZI, ROBERT (1965): *L'idée du Bonheur dans la littérature et la pensée françaises au XVIIIe siècle* (Paris: A. Colin).
MAYES, STANLEY (2003): *The Great Belzoni: The Circus Strongman who discovered Egypt's Treasures* (London: Tauris Parke).
MEDLYCOTT, ADOLPHUS E. (1905): *India and the Apostle Thomas* (London: David Nutt).
MEIKLE, HENRY W. (Ed.) (1914-40): see FOWLER, WILLIAM.
MELLINGHOFF, TILMAN (1987): see WATKIN, DAVID.
MENDEL, A. (Tr.) (1956): see EINSTEIN, ALFRED.
MERCER, HENRY CHAPMAN (1961): *The Bible in Iron* (Doylestown PA: Bucks County Historical Society).
MEREDITH, JAMES CREED (Tr.) (2007): see KANT, IMMANUEL.
MERÉNYI, LAJOS (1895): *Herczeg Esterházy Pál nádor* (Budapest: Magyar Történelmi Társulat).
MERIAN, MATTHAEUS (c.1650): *Iconum Biblicarum or Icones Biblicae in Historiae Sacrae Veteris et Novi Testamenti* (Amsterdam?: N. Visscher). See also MERIAN (2002): *Great Scenes from the Bible* (Mineola NY: Dover).
MERKEL, INGRID, & DEBUS, ALLEN G. (Eds.) (1988): *Hermeticism and the Renaissance: Intellectual History and the Occult in Early Modern Europe* (Washington DC: Folger Shakespeare Library, & London: Associated UPs).
MERKELBACH, REINHOLD (1962): *Roman und Mysterium in der Antike* (Munich: Beck).
——— (1963): *Isisfeste in Griechisch - Römischer Zeit* (Meisenheim-am-Glan: A. Hain).
METKEN, G. (1965): 'Jean-Jacques Lequeu ou l'architecture rêvée' *Gazette des Beaux-Arts* (April) 214.
METZGER, B. M. (1984): 'A Classified Bibliography of the Graeco-Roman Mystery Religion 1924-1973, with a Supplement 1974-1977' *Aufstieg und Niedergang der römischen Welt. Geschichte und Kultur Roms im Spiegel der neueren Forschung* **ii** 17.3 (Berlin & New York: de Gruyter).
MEURIN, JOHN GABRIEL LÉON (1893): *La franc-maçonnerie, Synagogue de Satan* (Paris: Retaux).
MICHEL, A.G. (1924): *La Dictature de la Franc-Maçonnerie sur la France* (Paris: Éditions Spes).
MICKLETHWAITE, THOMAS (Ed.) (1704): see COOPER, ANTHONY ASHLEY.
MIDDLETON, ROBIN (1986): see DUBOY, PHILIPPE.
———, & BAUDOUIN-MATUSZEK, MARIE-NOËLLE (2007): *Jean Rondelet: The Architect as Technician* (New Haven CT & London: Yale UP).
MIGNE, JACQUES-PAUL (Ed.) (1844-65): *Patrologiae Cursus Completus... Series Latina* (see also Indexes published 1862-5) (Paris: Garnier).
——— (1857-1904): *Patrologiae Cursus Completus... Series Graeca* (Paris: J.P. Migne).
MILLER, THOMAS (1852): *Picturesque Sketches of London Past and Present* (London: Office of the National Illustrated Library).
MIRALA, PETRI (2007): *Freemasonry in Ulster, 1733-1813: A Social and Political History of the Masonic Brotherhood in the North of Ireland* (Dublin: Four Courts Press).
MISHNAH (1698 ff): See the celebrated edition of G. SURENHUSIUS published in Amsterdam. Part 5 of 1702 contains illustrations of the Temple by CONSTANTIN L'EMPEREUR & C. HUYBERTS.
MITTEILUNGEN DES KAISERLICH DEUTSCHEN ARCHÄOLOGISCHEN INSTITUTS. RÖMISCHE ABTEILUNG (from 1886): (Rome: Loescher).
MOËL, MICHEL LE (1997): *L'urbanisme parisien au siècle des Lumières* (Paris: Éditions Action Artistique de la Ville de Paris).
MOGES, H. (1987): 'Isis-Osiris' in LIGOU, D. (Ed.) 622-5.
MOISY, ALEXANDRE (1813): see DUVAL, AMAURY.
MOLESWORTH, ROBERT (1711): *Franco-Gallia: Or, an Account of the Ancient Free State of France, and Most Other Parts of Europe, before the loss of their Liberties*, written originally in Latin by the famous Civilian Francis Hotoman (London: T. Goodman).
——— (1775): *The Principles of a Real Whig* (London: London Association).
MOLLIER, PIERRE (Ed.): (2004): see ORIENT DE FRANCE
——— ET AL. (2002): *Images du Patrimoine Maçonnique* (Paris: Éditions maçonniques de France).
MONEY, JOHN (1990): 'Freemasonry and the Fabric of Loyalism in Hanoverian England' HELLMUTH, ECKHART (Ed.) 235-74.
MONOD, PAUL KLÉBER (1989): *Jacobitisim and the English People, 1688-1788* (Cambridge: Cambridge UP).
MONTAGLON, ANATOLE DE (1877): 'L'Autobiographie de Dugourc' *Nouvelles Archives de l'Art Français* 367-71.
MONTANIER, JACQUES (1782): see DELILLE, ABBÉ JACQUES.
MONTESQUIEU, CHARLES-LOUIS DE SECONDAT, BARON DE (1748): *De l'Esprit des Loix* (Geneva: J. J. Vernet).
MONTFAUCON, BERNARD DE (1719-24): *L'Antiquité expliquée et représentée en figures*, 10 vols (Paris: F. Delaulne). An English edition D. HUMPHRIES (Tr.) was published 1721-25.
MONUMENS DES VICTOIRES ET CONQUÊTES DES FRANÇAIS (1829): (Paris: C.-L.-F. Panckoucke). Another edition (no publisher given) was published 1822.
M & L (*MONUMENTEN EN LANDSCHAPPEN*) (1984): This journal devoted its issue No. 3, (May - June), to the subject of *Égypte et franc-maçonnerie en Belgique*. It contains articles by MARCEL CELIS, PETRA MACLOT, and EUGÈNE WARMENBOL. The same journal devoted its issue No. 2 (March - April 1988), 13-71, to the restoration of the Egyptian temple at Antwerp Zoo, and contains articles by G.J. BRAL, L. DE CLERCQ, B. DELMOTTE, L. DELVAUX, M. DUPAS, P. MACLOT, A. MALLIET, W. SCHUDEL, J. VERBEKE, E. WARMENBOL, and E. DE WITTE.
MOONEY, LINNE R. (1993): 'A Middle English Text on the Seven Liberal Arts' *Speculum* **lxviii**/4 (October) 1027-52.
MOORE, C. H. (1907): 'The Distribution of Oriental Cults in the Gauls and the Germanies' *Transactions and Proceedings of the American Philological Association* **xxxviii** 109-49.
MOORE, WILLIAM D. (2006): *Masonic Temples: Freemasonry, Ritual Architecture, and Masculine Archetypes* (Knoxville TN: University of Tennessee Press).
MORAWIŃSKA, AGNIESZKA (Tr.) (1977): See MOSZYŃSKI, AUGUST FRYDERYK.
MOREHEN, JOHN (1981): 'Masonic Instrumental Music of the Eighteenth Century: A Survey' *The Masonic Review* **xlii** 215-24.
MORENZ, SIEGFRIED (1952): 'Die Zauberflöte; eine Studie zum Lebenszusammenhang Ägypten-Antike-Abendland' *Münstersche Forschungen* **v** Heft 2 (Münster: Böhlau-Verlag).
——— (1954): *Der Gott auf die Blume. Eine ägyptische Kosmogonie und ihre Weltweite Bildwirkung* (Ascona: Artibus Asiæ, Supplement 12). Written with JOHANNES SCHUBERT.
——— (1961): 'Ägyptische Nationalreligion und die sogenannte Isismission' *Zeitschrift der deutschen morgenländischen Gesellschaft* **xxxvi** 432-6.
MORÈRE, PIERRE (1990): see RÉVAUGER, MARIE-CÉCILE.
MORGAN, LUKE (2007): *Nature as Model: Salomon de Caux and Early Seventeenth-Century Landscape Design* (Philadelphia PA: University of Pennsylvania Press).
MORITZ, KARL PHILIPP (1793): see BREMER, JOHANN GOTTFRIED.
MORRA, JOANNE, ROBSON, MARK, & SMITH, MARQUARD (Eds.) (2000): *The Limits of Death: between philosophy and psychoanalysis* (Manchester: Manchester UP).
MORRIS, S. BRENT (2006): *The Complete Idiot's Guide to Freemasonry* (New York & London: Alpha Books).
——— (Ed.) (2002): see WEISBERGER (Ed.).
——— (2004): see HOYOS (Ed.).
——— (2006): *International Masonic Periodicals 1738-2005: A Bibliography of the Library of the Supreme*

Council (New Castle DE: Oak Knoll Press, & Washington DC: Library of the Supreme Council).
MORRISON, KATHRYN A. (2007): see ALEXANDER, JENNIFER S.
MOSSDORF, FRIEDRICH (1822-8): see LENNING, C.
MOSSER, MONIQUE (1982-3): 'Le Rocher et la Colonne – un thème d'iconographie architecturale en XVIIIe siècle' *Revue de l'Art* **lviii-lix** 55-74.
——— (1991): 'Paradox in the Garden: a brief account of *Fabriques*' MOSSER & TEYSSOT (*Eds.*) (1991) 263-80.
——— (1997): 'La perfection du jardin anglo-chinois' CONSTANS, MARTINE, ET AL. (Paris: Action artistique de la ville de Paris) 135-166.
——— ET AL. (1986): *Alexandre-Théodore Brongniart, 1739-1813* (Paris: Musée Carnavalet).
———, & RABREAU, DANIEL (1979): *Charles De Wailly: peintre architecte dans l'Europe des Lumières* (Paris: Caisse Nationale des Monuments Historiques et des Sites).
———, & TEYSSOT, GEORGES (*Eds.*) (1991): *The History of Garden Design: the Western Tradition from the Renaissance to the Present Day* (London: Thames & Hudson).
MOSZYŃSKI, AUGUST FRYDERYK (1977): *Rozprawa o Ogrodnictwie Angielskim 1774* AGNIESZKA MORAWIŃSKA (*Tr.*) (Wrocław: Zakład Narodowy im. Ossolińskich Wydawnictwo Polskiej Akademii Nauk). This includes the original French text.
MOTTE, JEANNE DE SAINT-RÉMY DE VALOIS, 'COMTESSE' DE LA (1790): *Mémoire justificatif de la Comtessa de Valois de la Motte* (London: s.n. – the imprint is false: it was probably printed in Paris). See also *The Life of Jane de St. Remy de Valois...* etc. (London: J. Bew 1791).
MOWL, TIMOTHY (1998): *William Beckford. Composing for Mozart* (London: John Murray).
——— (2006): *William Kent: Architect, Designer, Opportunist* (London: Jonathan Cape).
———, & EARNSHAW, BRIAN (1988): *John Wood: Architect of Obsession* (Bath: Millstream).
MOZART, LEOPOLD (1756): *Versuch einer gründlichen Violinschule* (Augsburg: Verlag des Verfassers). See also the versions GRETA MOENS-HAENEN (*Ed.*) (2002): (Kassel & London: Bärenreiter) and EDITHA KNOCKER (*Tr.*) (1951): *A Treatise on the Fundamental Principles of Violin Playing* (Oxford: Oxford UP).
MOZART, W. A. (1973): *Die Zauberflöte. Dichtung von Emanuel Schikaneder* WILHELM ZENTNER (*Ed.*) (Stuttgart: Philipp Reclam). This contains the fragmentary sequel by GOETHE. See GIESECKE.
MOZART UND DAS THEATER (1970): Austellung zur Mozartwoche der Deutschen Oper am Rhein, Düsseldorf (21 January – 18 February) (Köln: Universität zu Köln, Institut für Theaterwissenschaft).
MUDGE, JEAN MCCLURE (1962): *Chinese Export Porcelain* (Delaware: University of Delaware Press).
MÜLLER, DIETER (1961): *Ägypten und die griechischen Isis-Aretalogien* (Berlin: Akademie-Verlag).
MÜLLER, ERNST MAX (1899): *Der Streit der Zimmermannswerkzeuge: ein mittelenglisches Gedicht* (Erlangen: Thesis for the Fakultät der Friedrich-Alexanders-Universität).
MULVEY ROBERTS, MARIE, & ORMSBY-LENNON, HUGH (*Eds.*) (1995): *Secret Texts: The Literature of Secret Societies* (New York: AMS Press).
——— (1996): 'Pleasures Engendered by Gender: Homosociality and the Club' in PORTER, ROY, & MULVEY ROBERTS, MARIE (*Eds.*) 48-77.
MUNBY, JULIAN (*Ed.*) (1996): see TATTON-BROWN, TIM.
MUNDAY, A. M. (1633): see STOW, JOHN.
MURPHY, EDWIN (*Tr.*) (1990): see DIODORUS SICULUS.
MURPHY, JAMES (*Tr.*) (1939): see HITLER, ADOLF.
MUSIC REVIEW, THE (various years).
MUSIL, ROBERT (1979): *The Man Without Qualities* EITHNE WILKINS & ERNST KAISER (*Trs.*) (London: Secker & Warburg).
MYERS, ALEC REGINALD (1959): *The Household of Edward IV: the Black Book and the Ordinances of 1478* (Manchester: Manchester UP).
MYLNE, ROBERT SCOTT (1893): *The Master Masons to the Crown of Scotland and their Works* (Edinburgh: Scott & Ferguson).
MYLONAS, GEORGE EMMANUEL (1961): *Eleusis and the Eleusinian Mysteries* (Princeton NJ: Princeton UP).

MYNORS, ROGER AUBREY BASKERVILLE, THOMSON, RODNEY MALCOLM, & WINTERBOTTOM, MICHAEL (*Eds. & Trs.*) (1998-9): *Gesta Regum Anglorum/The History of the English Kings* (Oxford: Clarendon Press).
N....(perhaps DE NOGARET) (1742, but the date is probably false): *Apologie pour l'ordre des Francs-maçons par Mr. N*** Membre de L'Ordre. Avec deux Chansons composées par Le Frère Américain* (The Hague: Pierre Gosse, & Dresden: Georg Conrad Walther).
NASH, M. D. (1987): *The Settler Handbook: A New List of the 1820 Settlers* (Diep River: Chameleon Press).
NAUDON, PAUL (1967): *La Franc-Maçonnerie* (Paris: Presses universitaires de France).
NAUDOT, JEAN-JACQUES (1746): *Chansons notées de la très vénérable confrérie des maçons libres* (Berlin: s.n.).
NAUMANN, JOHANN GOTTLIEB (1784): *Vierzig Freymäurer-Lieder* (Berlin: C. F. Himburg).
NEFONTAINE, LUC (2001): see DECHARNEUX, BAUDOUIN.
NÉGRIER, PATRICK (1994): *Histoire et Symbolisme de Légendes compagnonniques* (Le Mans: Borrego).
——— (1995): *Textes fondateurs de la tradition maçonnique 1390-1760* (Paris: B. Grasset).
——— (1996): *Le Temple de Salomon et ses origines Égyptiennes* (Paris: Éditions Télètes).
——— (1997): *Le Temple et sa symbolique: symbolisme cosmique et philosophie de l'architecture sacrée* (Paris: Albion Michel).
——— (1998): *La pensée maçonnique du XIVe au XXe siècle* (Monaco: Rocher).
——— (2001): *La Tradition Initiatique: idées et figures autour de la franc-maçonnerie* (Bagnolet: Ivoire-Clair).
——— (2002): *La Bible et l'Égypte: Introduction à l'Ésotérisme biblique* (Montmorency: Ivoire-Clair).
——— (2003): *L'Éclectisme maçonnique: suivi de, Herméneutique maçonnique et philosophie biblique* (Groslay: Ivoire-Clair).
——— (2004): *Temple de Salomon et Diagrammes Symboliques: Iconographie des Tableaux de loge et de cabinet de réflexion* (Groslay: Ivoire-Clair).
NETTL, PAUL (1932): *Mozart und die königliche Kunst: die Freimaurerische Grundlage der "Zauberflöte"* (Berlin: F. Wunder).
——— (1955): *W. A. Mozart* (Frankfurt-am-Main: Fischer)
——— (1956): *Musik und Freimaurerei: Mozart und die königliche Kunst* (Esslingen: Bechtle).
——— (1970): *Mozart and Masonry* (New York: Da Capo Press).
NETTLESHIP, HENRY (1899): see SEYFFERT, OSKAR.
NEUGEKRÖNTEN HOFFNUNG, ZUR (1986): *Verzeichnis der Brüder und Mitglieder des St Joh. zur Neugekrönten Hoffnung im Orient zu Wien* (Vienna: Loge zur Neuguekrönten Hoffnung).
NEWBERRY, THOMAS (1887): *The Temple of Solomon* (London: James Nisbet & Co.).
NEWMAN, AUBREY (1992): 'Politics and Freemasonry in the Eighteenth Century' *AQC* **civ** 32-50.
NEWTON, SIR ISAAC (1687): *Philosophiae Naturalis Principa Mathematica* (London: Royal Society printed by Joseph Streater).
——— (1728): *A Chronology of Antient Kingdoms Amended* (London: J. Tonson). See *Isaaci Newtoni Opera quae exstant omnia*, with commentary by SAMUEL HORSLEY (London: John Nichols, 1785). Vol. **v** contains *A Chronology...*
NEWTON, ROGER HALE (1942): *Town & Davis, architects, pioneers in American Revivalist Architecture, 1812-1870...* (New York: Columbia UP).
NEW YORK STATE HISTORICAL ASSOCIATION (1975): *Outward Signs of Inner Beliefs: Symbols of American Patriotism* (Cooperstown NY: New York State Historical Association).
NICHOLLS, JONATHAN (1985): *The Matter of Courtesy: Medieval Courtesy Books and the Gawain-Poet* (Woodbridge: D. S. Brewer).
NICHOLSON, BRINSLEY (*Ed.*) (1584): see SCOT, REGINALD.
NICOLAUS DE LYRA (1481): *Prologus Prima... fratris Nicolai de Lira in testamentum vetus, et ... Explicit postilla...* (Nürnberg: Anton Koberger).
NIEDERMEIER, M. (1995): *Das Gartenreich Dessau-Wörlitz als kulturelles und literarisches Zentrum um 1780* (Dessau: Kulturamt und Amt für Denkmalpflege).
NILUS, SERGEI ALEKSANDROVICH (1972): *World Conquest through World Government: The Protocols of the Learned Elders of Zion* VICTOR EMILE MARSDEN (*Tr.*) (Chulmleigh: Britons Publishing).
NISSEN, GEORG NIKOLAUS, FREIHERR VON (1828): *Anhang zu Wolfgang Amadeus Mozarts Biographie: Originalbriefen, Sammlungen alles über ihn geschrieben, mit vielen neuen Beylagen, Steindrücken, Musikblättern, und einem Facsimile* (Leipzig: Breitkopf Härtel). See the version published in 1984 (Hildersheim: Olms).
NOBLE, JEREMY (*Tr.*) (1961): see DEUTSCH, OTTO ERICH (*Ed.*)
NOCK, ARTHUR DARBY (*Ed.*) (1945-54): *Corpus Hermeticum* A. J. FESTUGIÈRE (*Tr.*) (Paris: Société d'Édition 'Les Belles Lettres').
NOEHLES, K. (1966): see FIENSCH, GÜNTHER, & IMDAHL, MAX (*Eds.*)
NOGARARET, DE (1742): see N...
NORDEN, FREDERIK LUDVIG (1757): *Travels in Egypt and Nubia* (London: L. Davis and C. Reymers). See also the French edition, published in Copenhagen in 1755.
——— (1780): *The Antiquities, Natural History, Ruins, and other Curiosities of Egypt, Nubia, and Thebes* (London: L. Davis).
NORDMANN, ELMAR, & SCHULLE, GERD (1993): *Die freimaurerische Idee in der Zauberflöte: ein Spiegelbild antiker Mysterien* (Münster: Lit).
NORMAN, GEORGE (1946): 'The Bath Furniture' *Transactions of the Somerset Masters Lodge, No. 3746* 341-372.
NORMAND, LOUIS-MARIE (1832): *Monumens Funéraires choisis dans les Cimetières de Paris et des principales villes de France* (Paris: Normand). A second volume was published in 1847.
NORTH AMERICAN REVIEW, THE (from 1815): it was first published in Boston MA, and more recently at Cedar Falls IA: University of Northern Iowa.
NOVION, RAYMOND (1955): 'Présence de l'Égypte dans la vie Française' *Le Musée Vivant* **iv** (January) 85-88.
NOWINSKI, JUDITH (1970): *Baron Dominique Vivant Denon (1747-1825): Hedonist and Scholar in a Period of Transition* (Rutherford NJ: Fairleigh Dickinson UP).
OAKLEY, EDWARD (1729): 'Speech deliver'd to the Worshipful Society of Free and Accepted Masons' at a Lodge... the 31st of December 1728' *The Ancient Constitutions of the Free and Accepted Masons* **ii** (London: Benjamin Cole) 27-36.
O'BRIEN C. H. (1969): 'Ideas of Toleration at the Time of Joseph II' *Transactions of the American Philosophical Society* N. S. **lix** pt. 7.
O'CARROLL, MAURA (*Ed.*) (2003): *Robert Grosseteste and the Beginnings of a British Theological Tradition* (Rome: Istituto Storico dei Cappuccini).
O'CONNOR, H.W. (1919): 'The Narcissa Episode in Young's *Night Thoughts*' *Publications of the Modern Language Association* **xxiv** 130-149.
ODDONE, P. (1988): *La longue nuit des francs-maçons du Nord, 1940-1944* (Dunkerque: Éditions des Beffrois).
OECHSLIN, WERNER (1971): 'Pyramide et Sphère. Notes sur l'Architecture Révolutionnaire du XVIIIᵉ Siècle et ses Sources Italiennes' *Gazette des Beaux-Arts* (April) 201-38.
OEHME, URSULA (*Ed.*) (1991): see RICHTER, BRIGITTE.
OHM, RUTH (*Tr.*) (1996): see IRMEN, HANS-JOSEF.
OLAUSSON, MAGNUS (1985): 'Freemasonry, Occultism, and the Picturesque Garden towards the end of the eighteenth century' *Art History* **viii**/4 (December) 413-33.
OLDFATHER, C.H. (*Tr.*) (1933-67): see DIODORUS SICULUS.
OLDHAM, FRANK (1954): see WOOD, ALEXANDER.
OLDMIXON, JOHN (1712): *The Secret History of Europe* (London: A. Baldwin).
——— (1716): *Memoirs of Ireland from the Restoration, to the Present Time* (London: J. Roberts).
——— (1724-6): *The Criticial History of England, Ecclesiastical and Civil: wherein the Errors of the Monkish Writers and Others are Expos'd and Corrected* (London: J. Pemberton).
OLIVER, BRUCE W. (1947): '"The Bath Furniture" and how it came to Barnstaple' *AQC* **lvii** 109-136. But see NORMAN (1946) on which Oliver's paper is based.
OLIVER, GEORGE (1846): *Historical Landmarks and other evidences of Freemasonry* (London: s.n.).
——— (1847-50): *The Golden Remains of the Early*

Masonic Writers (London: R. Spencer).
——— (1853): *A Dictionary of Symbolical Masonry... compiled from the best Masonic Authorities* (New York: Jno. W. Leonard).
OLIVER, J. W. (1932): *The Life of William Beckford* (London: Oxford UP).
OLLIVIER-BEAUREGARD, G. M. (1866): *Les divinités égyptiennes, leur origine, leur culte, et son expansion dans le monde. À propos de la collection archéologique de feu le docteur Ernest Godard* (Paris: Librairie Internationale, and Brussels: A. Lacroix, Verboeckhoven, et cie.).
ONIANS, JOHN (1988): *Bearers of Meaning: The Classical Orders in Antiquity, the Middle Ages, and the Renaissance* (Cambridge & New York: Cambridge UP).
ÖNNERFORS, ANDREAS (2005): ' "You will prise our noble companionship": Masonic Songbooks of the 18th Century—an overlooked literary sub-genre' STEWART, TREVOR (Ed.) (2005) 135-149.
OPPER, THORSTEN (2008): *Hadrian: Empire and Conflict* (London: British Museum).
L'ORDRE DES FRANCS-MAÇONS TRAHI ET LE SECRET DES MOPSES REVELÉ (1745): see PÉRAU.
ORGOGOZO, CHANTAL (1989): see BEAUCOUR, FERNAND ÉMILE.
ORMSBY-LENNON, HUGH (Ed.) (1995): see MULVEY ROBERTS.
OSCHRY, LEONARD (Tr.) (1970): see KATZ, JACOB.
OVASON, DAVID (1999): *The Secret Architecture of our Nation's Capital. The Masons and the Building of Washington, DC* (New York: HarperCollins). Another version of this was published (1999) as *The Secret Zodiacs of Washington DC: Was the City of Stars Planned by Masons?* (London: Random House UK Ltd.).
OXFORD AND CAMBRIDGE REVIEW (1912): OSWALD R. DAWSON (Ed.) (London: Archibald Constable.
OXFORD DICTIONARY OF NATIONAL BIOGRAPHY (ODNB) (2004): see H. C. G. MATTHEW & BRIAN HARRISON (Eds.)
P., G. CANTABRIGIENSIS (1584): *Libellus de Memoria, Verissimaque bene recordandi scientia, authore G. P.... Etc.* (London: R. Waldegrave).
PAINE. THOMAS (1794-5): *The Age of Reason: Being an Investigation of True and Fabulous Theology* (London: David Isaac Eaton).
——— (1945): *The Complete Writings of Thomas Paine* PHILIP SHELDON FONER (Ed.) (New York: Citadel Press).
PALOU, JEAN (1966): *La Franc-Maçonnerie* (Paris: Payot).
PANOFSKY, ERWIN (1945): see FRANKL, P.
PANTAZZI, MICHAEL (1994): 'Absolutisme et Lumières' in the *Catalogue* of the *Egyptomania* exhibition (see HUMBERT, PANTAZZI, & ZIEGLER [Eds.] [1994] 116-123.
——— (Ed.) (1994): see HUMBERT, JEAN-MARCEL.
PAPWORTH, WYATT ANGELICUS VAN SANDAU (Ed.) (1852, 1887, 1892): *The Dictionary of Architecture* (London: The Architectural Publication Society, published by Thomas Richards [**i-vi**] and Whiting & Co [**vii** and **viii**]).
——— (1879): *J.B. Papworth: Architect to the King of Wurtemburg* (London: The Author)
——— (Ed.) (1903): see GWILT, JOSEPH.
PARKER, JOHN HENRY (1853): *Some Account of Domestic Architecture in England, from Edward I to Richard II* (Oxford: John Henry Parker).
PARKINSON, ROBERT E. (1957): *History of the Grand Lodge of Free and Accepted Masons of Ireland* **ii** (Dublin: Lodge of Research C.C.).
——— (Ed.) (1977): *Transactions for the Years 1969-1975* **xvi** The Lodge of Research No. CC Ireland (Newtownabbey: Styletype).
PARKINSON, RICHARD, with contributions by DIFFIE, W., FISCHER, M., & SIMPSON, R.S. (1999): *Cracking Codes. The Rosetta Stone and Decipherment* (London: British Museum Press).
PARREAUX, ANDRÉ (1960): *William Beckford* (Paris: A. G. Nizet).
PASS'D MASTER, A (1765): *Shibboleth: or, Every Man a Free-Mason... etc.* (London: J. Cooke). Also published in the same year (Dublin: s.n.).
PATON, HENRY MACLEOD (Ed.) (1957-82): *Accounts of the Masters of Works for Building and Repairing Royal Palaces and Castles* **i** (Edinburgh: HMSO).
PATRIMOINE MONUMENTAL DE LA BELGIQUE, LE (1975a): *Patrimoine de Hainaut. Arrondissement de Mons* **iv** (Liège: P. Mardaga).

——— (1975b): *Patrimoine de Namur. Arrondissement de Namur* **v** (Liège: P. Mardaga).
——— (1990): *Wallonie. Province de Liège.. Arrondissement de Huy* **xv** (Liège: P. Mardaga).
PATTE, PIERRE (1771-7): see BLONDEL, JACQUES-FRANÇOIS.
PATTERSON, RICHARD (1981) '"The Hortus Palatinus" at Heidelberg and the Reformation of the World' *Journal of Garden History* **i**/1 (January-March) 67-102 and **i**/2 (April-June) 179-202.
PAUL, SIR JAMES BALFOUR (Ed.) (1916): *Accounts of the Lord High Treasurer of Scotland 1559-66* **xi** (Edinburgh: HMSO).
PAUL-ALBERT, NINO (1937): *Histoire du Cimetière du Père La Chaise* (Paris: Gallimard).
PEHNT, WOLFGANG (1987): 'Altes Ägypten und neue Architektur' *Bruckmanns Pantheon. Internationale Jahreszeitschrift für Kunst* **xlv** 151-160. An interesting paper in which Egyptian influences on architects, including BEHRENS, BONATZ, BREUER, LE CORBUSIER, GROPIUS, KREIS, STIRLING, *ET AL.*, are considered.
PELT, ROBERT JAN VAN (1984): *Tempel van de wereld: de kosmische symboliek van de tempel van Salomo* (Utrecht: HES).
——— (1991): 'Into the Suffering City: Considerations of the German Series' CHARNEY, MELVIN 35-53.
——— (1996): see DWORK, DEBÓRAH
PÉRAU, ABBÉ GABRIEL-LOUIS CALABRE- (1745a): 'Le Secret des Francs-Maçons'. Originally written in 1742 or thereabouts, it appeared as *L'Ordre des Francs-Maçons Trahi et le secret des Mopses révelé* (1745) ('Amsterdam' [i.e. Frankfurt]: Jean Neaulme). A German edition was published in Leipzig in the same year, and many other editions in French followed.
——— (1745b): *Le Secret de la Société des Mopses, dévoilé & mis au jour par Monsieur P****** ('Amsterdam' [i.e. Frankfurt]: s.n.).
——— (1745c): *Les Secrets, de l'Ordre des Francs-Maçons* ('Amsterdam' [i.e. Frankfurt]: s.n.).
PERCIER, CHARLES, & FONTAINE, PIERRE-FRANÇOIS-LÉONARD (1801): *Recueil de Décorations Intérieures* (Paris: The Authors).
———, & BERNIER, CLAUDE-LOUIS (1798): *Palais, Maisons et autres édifices modernes dessinés à Rome* (Paris: Ducamp).
PEREZ, ANNIE (1989): 'Dans la postérité des lumières' *Connaissance des Arts* **ccccviii** (June) 124-129.
PERNIGOTTI, SERGIO (Ed.) (1991): see GOVI, CRISTIANI MORIGI.
PÉROUSE DE MONTCLOS, JEAN-MARIE (1969): *Étienne-Louis Boullée, 1728-1799, de l'architecture classique à l'architecture révolutionnaire* (Paris: Arts & Métiers Graphiques).
PERRAULT, CLAUDE (1678): see COMPIÈGNE DE VEIL, LOUIS.
——— (1708): *A Treatise of the Five Orders of Columns in Architecture* JOHN STURT (Engraver) JOHN JAMES (Tr.) (London: Benjamin Motte for John Sturt).
PESSON, WILLIAM (2006): see CULOT, MAURICE.
PETRUS OF RAVENNA otherwise PETRUS RAVENNAS (1533): *Foenix. Domini Petri Ravennatis Memoriae Magistri* (Venice: Pietro de Hicolini da Sabbio).
PEVSNER, NIKOLAUS (from 1951): *The Buildings of England* series (Harmondsworth: Penguin).
——— (1960): *An Outline of European Architecture* (Harmondsworth: Penguin).
——— (1968): Essays including those on 'The Doric Revival' and 'The Egyptian Revival' in *Studies in Art, Architecture, and Design* (New York: Walker).
——— (1976): *A History of Building Types* (London: Thames & Hudson).
——— (1985): *County Durham* in *The Buildings of England* series revised ELIZABETH WILLIAMSON (Harmondsworth: Penguin Books).
——— (1997): see BRADLEY, SIMON.
——— (1998): see CHERRY, BRIDGET.
———, & LANG, SUSAN (1956): 'The Egyptian Revival' *The Architectural Review* **cxix**/712 (May) 242-254, later revised and republished in *Studies in Art, Architecture, and Design* (New York: Walker 1968) **i** 212-235 and 245-248.
——— (Ed.) (1974): *The Picturesque Garden and its Influence outside the British Isles* (Washington DC: Dumbarton Oaks).
PHILALETHES, EUGENIUS (1923): see VAUGHAN,

THOMAS.
PHILLIPS, PATRICIA C. (1991): see CHARNEY, MELVIN.
PFISTER, FRIEDRICH (1922): 'Religion' *Realenkylopädie der klassischen Altertumswissenschaft* **xi** (Stuttgart: J. B. Metzlersche Verlagsbuchhandlung).
PIANA, THEO (1969): see BEYER & PIAN.
PICK, FRED LOMAX, & KNIGHT, G. NORMAN (1983): *The Freemason's Pocket Reference Book*, revised by FREDERICK SMYTH (London: Frederick Muller).
PICTORIAL CARDS IN THIRTEEN PLATES EACH CONTAINING FOUR SUBJECTS... ETC. (1819): see ACKERMANN, RUDOLF (Ed.).
PIKE, ALBERT (1884): *Reply for the Ancient and Accepted Scottish Rite of Free-Masonry to the Letter "Humanum Genus" of Pope Leo XIII* (Charleston SC: Gr. Orient of Charleston).
PINK, ANDREW (2007): The Musical Culture of Freemasonry in Early Eighteenth-Century London (PhD thesis, Goldsmiths' College, London).
PIRANESI, GIOVANNI BATTISTA (1756): *Le Antichità Romane* (Rome: Stamperia di Angelo Rotili).
——— (1748-78): *Vedute di Roma* (Rome: Faustamici dei Librara al'Corso, etc.).
——— (1761): *Della Magnificenza ed Architettura de' Romani* (Rome: The Author).
——— (1769): *Diverse Maniere d'adornare i Cammini* (Rome: Salomoni).
——— (1972): *The Polemical Works, Rome 1757, 1761, 1765, 1769* JOHN WILTON-ELY (Ed.) (Farnborough: Gregg).
PITCAIRN, ROBERT (1833): *Criminal Trials in Scotland from AD. MCCCCLXXXVIII to AD. MDCXXIV, embracing the entire reigns of James IV, and V, Mary Queen of Scots, and James VI* (Edinburgh: Tait).
PIWKOWSKI, WŁODZIMIERZ (1989): *Nieborów. Arkadia* (Łódź: Krajowa Agencja Wydawnicza).
——— (1998): *Arkadia Heleny Radziwiłłowej. Studium historyczne* (Warsaw: Ośrodek Ochrony Zabytkowego Krajobrazu).
——— (2005): *Nieborów: Mazowiecka Rezydencja Radziwiłłów* (Warsaw: Muzeum Narodowe w Warszawie).
———, & MONIATOWICZ, JANUSZ (2001): *The Radziwiłł Palace in Nieborów. The Arcadia Gardens* (Jelenia Góra: Moniatowicz Foto Studio).
PLAT, SIR HUGH (1594): *The Jewell House of Art and Nature* etc. (London: Peter Short).
PLOT, ROBERT (1686): *The Natural History of Staffordshire* (Oxford: Printed at the Theater).
POCHAT, GÖTZ, & WAGNER, BRIGITTE (Eds.) (1987): *Natur und Kunst* (Graz: Akademische Druck- und Verlagsamsalt).
POCOCKE, RICHARD (1734-5): *A Description of the East and Some Other Countries* (London: J. & R. Knapton).
POLANOWSKA, JOLANTA (2009): *Stanisław Kostka Potocki (1755-1821): Twórczość architekta amatora przedstawiciela neoklasycyzmu i nurtu picturesque* (Warsaw: Instytut Sztuki Pan. Liber Pro Arte).
POOK, T. (1933): *History of the Loyal Lodge of Freemasons, No. 251, Barnstaple, 1783-1933* (Barnstaple: The Loyal Lodge of Freemasons).
POOLE, HERBERT (1951): see GOULD, ROBERT FREKE (1931).
POPE, ALEXANDER (1717): *Eloïsa to Abelard* (London: Bernard Lintot).
POPELKA, LISELOTTE (1994): *Castrum Doloris, oder 'Trauriger Schauplatz': Untersuchungen zu Entstehung und Wesen ephemer Architektur* (Vienna: Verlag der österreichischen Akademie der Wissenschaften).
PORSET, CHARLES (1987): see TOUMSON, ROGER.
——— (1992): see BLOCH, OLIVIER.
——— (1995): *Voltaire, franc-maçon* (La Rochelle: Rumeur des Âges).
——— (1998): *Hiram sans-culotte: Franc-maçonnerie, Lumières, et Révolution: Trente ans d'études et de Recherches* (Paris: H. Champion).
——— (Ed.) (1996): *Mirabeau franc-maçon* (La Rochelle: Rumeur des Âges).
——— (1998): *La Devise maçonnique: Liberté, Egalité, Fraternité* (Paris: Éditions maçonniques de France).
——— (1999): see SOZZI, MARINA.
———, & RÉVAUGER, MARIE-CÉCILE (1998): *Franc-maçonnerie et religions dans l'Europe des Lumières* (Paris: H. Champion).
PORTER, ROY, & MULVEY ROBERTS, MARIE (Eds.) (1996): *Pleasure in the Eighteenth Century* (Basingstoke:

Macmillan).
POSNER, OSKAR (1927): *Bilder zur Geschichte der Freimaurerei* (Reichenberg: Verlag der Zeitschrift *Die Drei Ringe*).
POUND, RICKY (2009): 'The Master Mason Slain: The Hiramic Legend in the Red Velvet Room at Chiswick' *English Heritage Historical Review* **iv** 133-141.
POUND, ROSCOE (1915): *Lectures on the Philosophy of Freemasonry* (Anamosa IA: The National Masonic Research Society).
POZZI, G. (1980): *see* COLONNA, FRANCESCO.
POZZO, ANDREA (1707): *Rules and Examples of Perspective* JOHN JAMES (Tr.) with engravings by JOHN STURT (London: B. Motte for John Sturt).
PRADO, JERÓNIMO (1596 and ff): *see* VILLALPANDUS.
PRESCOTT, ANDREW (2004): 'The Earliest Use of the Word Freemason' *Year Book of the Grand Lodge of the Antient Free and Accepted Masons of Scotland* (Edinburgh: Grand Lodge of Scotland) 64-67.
——— (2005): 'Some Literary Contexts of the Regius and Cooke MSS' STEWART, TREVOR (Ed.) (2005) 43-77.
——— (2005a): 'Freemasonry as a Part of National Heritage. The Conservation of Esoteric and Fraternal Heritage in Great Britain' KROON, BAX, & SNOEK (Eds.) (2005) 211-230.
——— (2006): 'Kinge Athelston That Was a Worthy Kinge of England: Anglo-Saxon Myths of the Freemasons' WILCOX & MAGENNIS (Eds.) (2006) 397-434.
——— (Ed.) (2006): *Marking Well: Essays on the Occasion of the 150th Anniversary of the Grand Lodge of Mark Master Masons of England and Wales and its Districts and Lodges Overseas* (Hinckley: Lewis Masonic).
PRESTON, WILLIAM (1792): *Illustrations of Freemasonry* (London: C. & T. Wilkie). The first edn. was published by the author in 1772.
PREUSS, JOHANN DAVID ERDMANN (Ed.) (1846-57): *Oeuvres de Frédéric le Grand* (Berlin: Decker).
PRÉVOST-MARCILHACY, PAULINE (1995): *see* MASSOUNIE, DOMINIQUE.
PREYS, R. (1993): *see* DELVAUX, L.
PREZIOSI, DONALD (2003): *Brain of the Earth's Body: Art, Museums, and the Phantasms of Modernity* (Minneapolis MN: University of Minnesota Press).
PRICE, CLIFFORD (Ed.) (2003): *see* HUMBERT, JEAN-MARCEL.
PRICE. J. D. (Tr.) (1817): *see* UVAROV, COUNT S.S.
PRICE, UVEDALE (1794-8): *Essays on the Picturesque, as compared with the Sublime and the Beautiful* (London: Mawman).
PRICHARD, SAMUEL (1730): *Masonry Dissected: Being a Universal and Genuine Description of All its Branches* (London: J. Wilford).
PRIEUR, A.-P. (1787-96): *see* ACADÉMIE DES BEAUX-ARTS.
PRISSE D'AVENNES, ACHILLE-CONSTANT-THÉODORE-ÉMILE (1878-9): *L'Histoire de l'Art Égyptien, d'après les Monumens* (Paris: A. Bertrand).
PROBST, HANSJÖRG ET AL. (1999): *Lebenslust und Frömmigkeit Kurfürst Carl Theodor (1724-1799) zwischen Barock und Aufklärung* (Regensburg: Verlag Friedrich Pustet).
PROJET DE CATACOMBES, POUR LA VILLE DE PARIS, EN ADAPTANT À CET USAGE LES CARRIÈRES QUI SE TROUVENT TANT DANS SON ENCEINTE QUE DANS SES ENVIRONS (1782): (Paris and London: Villedieu).
PRYCE, F.N. (1923): *see* VAUGHAN, THOMAS.
PTOLEMY (PTOLEMAEUS, CLAUDIUS) (1522): *Claudii Ptolemaei Alexandrini...opus geographi[a]e...* (Argentoraci (Strassburg): Ionnes Grieningerus).
PUGIN, AUGUSTUS CHARLES (1825): *see* BRITTON, JOHN.
PUGIN, AUGUSTUS WELBY NORTHMORE (1843): *An Apology for the Revival of Christian Architecture in England* (London: J. Weale).
PUISIEUX, JEAN-BAPTISTE DE (1765): *Élémens et traité de géométrie* (Paris: Jombert).
PURCHAS, SAMUEL (1625): *Hakluytes Posthumus or Purchas his Pilgrimes* (London: Henry Featherston).
PURVES, JOHN (Ed.) (1914-40): *see* FOWLER, WILLIAM.
PUTTER, TH. DE (1993): *see* DELVAUX, L.
QUAGLIA, FERDINANDO (c.1850): *Les Cimetières de Paris. Recueil des plus remarquables monuments funèbres avec leurs inscriptions, dessinées par Quaglia, gravés par Collette* (Paris: A. Lévy).
——— (c. 1854): *Le Père Lachaise ou recueil de dessins aux traits et dans leurs justes proportions des principaux monuments de ce cimetière* (Paris: Lagny Frères).
QUATREBARBES, E. DE, & BROSE, J. (1978): 'La mystérieuse pyramide de Robermont' *La Vie Wallonne* **lii** 221-5.
QUATREMÈRE DE QUINCY, ANTOINE-CHRYSOSTÔME (1788-1825): *Encyclopédie Méthodique. Architecture* (Paris: C.L.F. Panckoucke).
——— (1791): *Rapport sur l'édifice dit de Sainte-Geneviève* (Paris: De l'Imprimerie Royale).
——— (1793): *Rapport fait au Directoire du Département de Paris, sur les travaux entrepris, continues ou achevés au Panthéon français...* (Paris: Imprimerie Ballard).
——— (1803): *De l'architecture égyptienne, considérée dans son origine, ses principes et con goût, et comparée sous les mêmes rapports à l'architecture grecque* (Paris: Barrois).
——— (1830): *Histoire de la vie et des ouvrages des plus célèbres architectes du XIᵉ siècle jusqu'à la fin du XVIIIᵉ...* (Paris: J. Renouard).
——— (1832): *Dictionnaire historique d'architecture, comprenant dans son plan les notions historiques, descriptives, archéologiques... etc.* (Paris: Librairie d'Arien le Clerc).
——— (n.d.): *Rapport fait au Conseil-Général... sur l'instruction publique... l'érection de cimetières ...etc.* (Paris: s.n.).
QUILITZSCH, UWE (1997): *see* BODE, URSULA.
QUINCY (1803): *see* QUATREMÈRE DE QUINCY.
QUIRKE, STEPHEN, & ANDREWS, C. (1988): *The Rosetta Stone: Facsimile Drawing with an Introduction and Translations* (London: British Museum Publications).
RAABE, PAUL, & SCHMIDT-BIGGEMANN (Eds.) (1979): *Aufklärung in Deutschland* (Bonn: Hohwacht).
RABREAU, DANIEL (1976): 'Le Théâtre Feydeau et la rue des Colonnes (1791-1829)' in *Actes du 100ᵉ Congrès national des Sociétés Savantes* (Paris: Bibliothèque nationale), 255-273.
——— (1979): *see* MOSSER, MONIQUE.
——— (1995): *see* MASSOUNIE, DOMINIQUE.
RACINE, MICHEL (Ed.) (2001-2): *Créateurs de Jardins et de Paysages en France de la Renaissance au début du XIXᵉ siècle* (Arles: Actes Sud; Versailles: École nationale supérieure du paysage).
RADZIWIŁŁOWA, HELENA (1800): *Le Guide d'Arcadie* (Berlin: Georg Decker).
——— (1848): 'Opis Arcadji skreślony przez założycielkę księżnę Radziwiłłowa' S. ŻOCHOWSKA (Tr.) *Album Literackie* **i** 143-54. This was a translation of the French text published as a limited edn. of 100 copies (*see* RADZIWIŁŁOWA [1800]).
RAICH, JOHANN MICHAEL (real name of BEUREN, OTTO) (1884): *Die innere Anwahrheit der Freimaurerei* (Mainz-am-Rhein: Franz Kirchheim).
RAMÉE, DANIEL (Ed.) (1847): *Architecture de C. N. Ledoux* (Paris: Lenoir).
RAMIREZ, JUAN ANTONIO (Ed.) (1991a): *Dios Arquitecto: J.B. Villalpando y el Templo de Salomón* (Madrid: Ediciones Siruela). A second edition was published in 1994.
——— (1991b): *El Templo de Salomón* (Madrid: Ediciones Siruela).
RAMSAY, ANDREW MICHAEL (c.1729): *A New Cyropaedia: or The Travels of Cyrus* (Edinburgh: Company of Booksellers).
RANFT, GERTRUD (1985): *Historische Grabstätten aus Weimars klassischer Zeit* (Weimar: Nationale Forschungs-und Gedenkstätten der Klassischen Deutschen Literatur in Weimar).
RATSCHKY, J. F. (1791): *Gedichte* (Vienna: Alberti for Graffer).
RAZI, ZVI, & SMITH, RICHARD (Eds.) (1996): *Medieval Society and the Manor Court* (Oxford: Clarendon Press).
READ, HERBERT (Ed.) (1953-79): *see* JUNG, CARL GUSTAV.
REBOLD, EMMANUEL (1851): *Histoire générale de la Franc-Maçonnerie* (Paris: A. Franck).
REDMAN, GRAHAM (2007): *Emulation Working Today* (Hersham: Lewis Masonic).
REGHELLINI, — OF SCIO (S∴ M∴R∴ DE, i.e. MONSIEUR REGHELLINI OF SCIO) (1829): *La Maçonnerie, considerée comme le Résultat des Religions égyptienne, juive, et chrétienne, par le F∴M∴ Reghellini De Schio* (Brussels: H. Tarlier). *See also* the Paris edition, published in 1833 by Dondey-Dupré. A German edition, *Die Freimaurerei in ihrem Zusammenhang mit den Religionen der alter Ægypter, der Juden, und der Christen. Nach dem französischens des F. M. R. de S∴*, etc., was published in Leipzig in 1835 by J.J. Weber. ACERRELLOS, R. S., was the pseudonym of REGHELLINI OF SCIO & RÖSSLER, CARL A.
——— (1835): *Die Freimaurerei in ihrem Zusammenhang mit den Religionen der alter Aegypter, der Juden, und der Christen. Nach dem französischens des F. M. R. de S∴*, etc. (Leipzig: J. J. Weber).
——— (1840): *Précis historique de l'Ordre du Temple, origine de la F∴ Maç∴ par le F∴ M. Reghellini de Schio* (Paris: Or∴ de Jérusalem, chez le Silence, l'an de la G∴ L∴ 5840).
REICH, KARIN, & KNOBLOCH, EBERHARD (2002): 'Die Kreisquadratur Matthias Hafenreffers' in *Acta Historica Astronomiae* **xvii** (Frankfurt-am-Main: Verlag Harri Deutsch) 157-183.
REIMANN, CHRISTIAN (2004): *Vom Sinngehalt der Bibliothek im fürstlichen Landhaus zu Wörlitz* (Worms: Wernersche Verlags Gesellschaft).
REINALTER, HELMUT (Ed.) (1983): *Freimaurer und Geheimbünde im 18. Jahrhundert in Mitteleuropa* (Frankfurt-am-Main: Suhrkamp).
——— (1987): *Joseph II und die Freimaurerei im Lichte zeitgenössischer Broschüren* (Vienna: H. Böhlau).
REITZENSTEIN, RICHARD (1956): *Die Hellenistischen Mysterienreligonen Nach ihren Grundgedanken und Wirkungen* (Stuttgart: B.G. Teubner).
RESPECTABLE LOGE (1884): *R[espectable] L[oge], Chap[itre] et Aréop[age] Les Amis de Commerce et La Persévérance Réunis à l'Orient d'Anvers. Tracé de la Fête du Consécr[ation] du Nouveau Temple. Tenue du 21 é J[our] du 8e M[ois] 5883* (Brussels: s.n.).
RÉVAUGER, MARIE-CÉCILE (1990): *Le fait maçonnique au XVIIe siècle en Grande-Bretagne et aux États-Unis* (Paris: EDIMAF).
——— (1998): *see* PORSET, CHARLES.
——— (2005): *see* LERAT, CHRISTIAN.
——— (2006): 'Freemasonry and Religion in Eighteenth-Century Britain' STEWART, TREVOR (Ed.) (2006) 93-104.
———, & MORÈRE, PIERRE (1990): *L'obscur et la raison au XVIIIe siècle dans la monde anglophone* (Grenoble: Université Stendhal).
RÊVE ÉGYPTIEN, LE (1979): *see* SILEX.
REYBAUD, LOUIS, ET AL. (1830-36): *Histoire scientifique et militaire de l'expédition française en Égypte* (Paris: A.J. Dénain).
REYMOND, EVE A.E. (1969): *The Mythical Origin of the Egyptian Temple* (Manchester: Manchester UP).
REYNOLDS, DONALD MARTIN (Ed.) (1989): *Selected Lectures of Rudolf Wittkower: The Impact of Non-European Civilizations on the Art of the West* (Cambridge: Cambridge UP).
REYNOLDS, SUSAN (1977): *An Introduction to the History of English Medieval Towns* (Oxford: Clarendon Press).
RICE, JOHN A. (2006): *The Temple of Night at Schönau: Architecture, Music, and Theater in a late Eighteenth-Century Viennese Garden* (Philadelphia PA: American Philosophical Society).
RICHARDSON, MARGARET, & STEVENS, M. A. (Eds.) (1999): *John Soane Architect: Master of Space and Light* (London: R. A. Publications).
RICHARDSON, TIM (2007): *The Arcadian Friends: Inventing the English Landscape Garden* (London: Bantam Press).
——— (Ed.) (2005): *see* KINGSBURY, NOËL.
RICHER, J. (1981): 'Isis romantique. Le mythe de la mère-épouse. Hélène, Sophie, Marie' BONNEFOY, Y. (Ed.) 597-8.
RICHTER, BRIGITTE, & OEHME, URSULA (Eds.) (1991): *Mozart in Kursachsen* (Leipzig: Stadtgeschichtlichen Museums).
RIDLEY, JASPER (1999): *The Freemasons* (London: Constable).
RIEDL, CLARE C. (Tr.) (1942): *see* GROSSETESTE, ROBERT.
RIFAUD, JEAN-JACQUES (1830): *Tableau de l'Égypte, de la Nubie, et des lieux circonvoisins, depuis 1805 jusqu'au 1828...* (Paris: Treuttel & Würtz). This work also appears as *Voyage en Égypte*, etc. *see also* the German version (1830) G. A. WIMMER (Tr.) (Vienna: C.

Gerold).
RIGAUD, JEAN (1746): *Stowe Gardens in Buckinghamshire* (London: Bowles).
RINGGREN, H. (1969): 'Light and Darkness in Ancient Egyptian Religion' *Liber amicorum. Studies in honor of C. J. Bleeker* (Leiden: E. J. Brill) 140-50.
RINSVELD, BERNARD VAN (1996): 'L'Égyptomanie au service de la politique: la visite de Bonaparte à Bruxelles en 1803' HUMBERT (*Ed.*) (1996) 369-423.
RITZ, SÁNDOR (1970-71): 'Le Città Celesti dei primi Cristiani: quella dell'Apocalisse Secondo Eusebio, e quelle sul Monte Celio in Roma' *L'Urbe, rivista romana*, etc. (Rome: L'Urbe) 33-34.
——— (1967): *La Nuova Gerusalemme dell'Apocalisse e Santo Stefano Rotondo* (Rome: s.n.).
RIVIÈRE, CLÉRY (1939): *Un Village de Brie au XVIIIe Siècle: Mauperthuis* (Paris: Éditions Picard).
ROBERTS, DAVID (1855-6): *The Holy Land, Syria, Idumea, Arabia, Egypt, and Nubia* (London: Day & Son).
ROBERTS, JOHN MORRIS (1969): 'Freemasonry: Possibilities of a Neglected Topic' *English Historical Review* **lxxxiv** 323-5.
——— (1972): *The Mythology of the Secret Societies* (London: Secher & Warburg). There is also a French edn. (Paris: Payot, 1979) and a revised English edn. (London: Paladin, 1974).
ROBINET, JEAN-FRANÇOIS-EUGÈNE (1896-8): *Le mouvement religieux à Paris pendant la Révolution* (Paris: L. Cerf).
ROBINSON, D. N. (1913): 'A Study of the Social Position of the Devotees of the Oriental Cult in the Western World' *Transactions and Proceedings of the American Philological Association* **xliv** 151-61.
ROBSON, MARK (*Ed.*) (2000): *see* MORRA, JOANNE.
ROBISON, JOHN (1797): *Proofs of a Conspiracy against all the Religions and Governments of Europe, carried on in the secret meeting of Free Masons, Illuminati, and Reading Societies* (London: T. Cadell, Davies, Creech). Another edn. came out in the following year.
ROCHEBLAVE, SAMUEL (1927): *Charles-Nicolas Cochin; Graveur et Dessinateur* (Paris: Vanoest).
ROCHEFORT, ELÉONORE-MARIE DESBOIS DE (1784-8): *see* DESBOIS DE ROCHEFORT.
ROCHEGUDE, FÉLIX, MARQUIS DE, & CLÉBERT, JEAN-PAUL (1958): *Promenades dans les rues de Paris* (Paris: Club des Libraires de France).
RODE, AUGUST VON (1996): *Beschreibung des Fürstlichen Anhalt-Dessauischen Landhauses und Englischen Gartens zu Wörlitz* (Wörlitz: Staatliche Schlösser und Gärten Wörlitz). *See also*
RODE, AUGUST VON, ROSS, HARTMUT, & TRAUZETTEL, LUDWIG (1987): *Der Englische Garten zu Wörlitz* (Berlin: Verlag für Bauwesen), which includes a reprint of Rode's *Beschreibung...* in the 1798 edn. (Dessau: H. Tänzer).
ROGALLA VON BIBERSTEIN, JOHANNES (1992): *Die These von der Verschwörung 1776-1945: Philosophen, Freimaurer, Juden, Liberale und Sozialisten als Verschwörer gegen die Sozialordnung* (Flensburg: Flensburger Hefte Vorlag).
——— (2002): *Jüdischer Bolschewismus: Mythos und Realität* (Dresden: Edition Antaios).
ROGER FILS (1816): *Le Champ du repos, ou le Cimetière Mont-Louis...* (Paris: Roger Père).
ROHR, RENÉ R. J. (1971): *Les Cadrans Solaires Anciens d'Alsace* (Colmar: Éditions Alsatia).
——— (1986): *Sundials: history, theory, and practice* (Toronto: University of Toronto Press).
RORICZER, MATHIAS (1965): *Das Büchlein von der Fialen Gerechtigkeit* FERDINAND GELDNER (*Ed.*) (Wiesbaden: Pressler).
ROSCHER, WILHELM HEINRICH (*Ed.*) (1884-1937): *Ausführliches Lexikon der griechischen und römischen Mythologie* (Leipzig: B.G. Teubner).
ROSELLINI, IPPOLITO (1832-44): *I Monumenti dell'Egitto e della Nubia* (Pisa: N. Capurro).
——— (1925): *Ippolito Rosellini e il suo Giornale della spedizione letteraria Toscana in Egitto negli anni 1828-1829* GIUSEPPE GABRIELI (*Ed.*) (Rome: Tipografia Befani).
ROSENAU, HELEN (1953): *Treatise on Architecture: a complete presentation of the Architecture Essai sur l'Art, which forms part of the Boullée papers (MS. 9153) in the Bibliothèque Nationale* (London: A. Tiranti).
——— (1960): 'The Engravings of the Grands Prix of the French Academy of Architecture' *Architectural History, Journal of the Society of Architectural Historians of Great Britain* **iii** 17-180.
——— (1974): *The Ideal City, its Architectural Evolution* (London: Studio Vista).
——— (1976): *Boullée and Visionary Architecture* (London: Academy Editions).
——— (1979): *Vision of the Temple. The Image of the Temple of Jerusalem in Judaism and Christianity* (London: Oresko Books).
ROSENBERG, ALFONS (1972): *Die Zauberflöte; Geschichte und Deutung von Mozarts Oper* (Munich: Prestel).
ROSENBERG, PIERRE (*Commissaire de l'Exposition*), & DUPUY, MARIE-ANNE (*Commissaire délégué*) (1999): *Dominque-Vivant Denon. L'œil de Napoléon*. Catalogue of an Exhibition held at the Musée du Louvre, Paris (20 October 1999-17 January 2000) (Paris: Éditions de la Réunion des Musées Nationaux).
ROSENBERG-ORSINI, JUSTINE (WYNNE), GRÄFIN VON (1787): *Alticchiero*, edited by COUNT BENINCASA (Padua: s.n.).
ROSENBLUM, ROBERT (1970): *Transformations in Late Eighteenth - Century Art* (Princeton NJ: Princeton UP).
ROSENSTRAUCH-KÖNIGSBERG, EDITH (1975): *Freimaurer im Josephinischen Wien; Aloys Blumauers Weg vom Jesuiten zum Jakobiner* (Vienna & Stuttgart: W. Braumüller).
——— (1984): *Freimaurer, Illuminati, Weltbürger: Friedrich Münters Reisen und Briefe in ihren europäischen Bezügen* (Berlin: U. Camen).
ROSENTHAL, ALBI, & TYSON, ALAN (1990): *Mozart's Thematic Catalogue: British Library Stefan Zweig MS (Introduction and Transcription)* (London: British Library).
ROSS, THOMAS (1887-92): *see* MACGIBBON, DAVID.
——— (1890): 'The Ancient Sundials of Scotland' *Proceedings of the Society of Antiquaries of Scotland* **xxiv** 161-273.
RÖSSLER, CARL A. See REGHELLINI,—OF SCIO.
ROTTERMUND, ANDRZEJ (1984): *see* LORENTZ, STANISŁAW.
ROUSSEAU (1844, 1846): *see* LASSALLE, ÉMILE.
ROUSSEAU, JEAN-JACQUES (1761): *La Nouvelle Héloïse, ou Lettres de deux amans, habitans d'une petite ville au pied des Alpes* (Paris: Duchesne).
RÜFFER, MICHAEL (2005): *Das Schloss in Wörlitz* (Munich: Deutscher Kunstverlag).
RUSSELL, D. (1986): 'Emblems and Hieroglyphics: Some Observations on the Beginnings and the Nature of Emblematic Forms' *Emblematica* **i** 227-43.
RYKWERT, JOSEPH (1983): *The First Moderns: The Architects of the Eighteenth Century* (Cambridge MA & London: MIT Press).
——— (Tr.) (1988): *see* ALBERTI, LEON BATTISTA.
S ∴ M ∴ R ∴ DE (1833): *see* REGHELLINI — OF SCIO.
SADIE, STANLEY (*Ed.*) (1992): *The New Grove Dictionary of Opera* (London & New York: Macmillan Reference).
——— (1996): *Wolfgang Amadè Mozart: Essays on his Life and his Music* (Oxford: Clarendon Press).
SADLER, HENRY (1898): *Masonic Reprints and Historical Revelations*, with an Introduction by W. J. CHETWODE CRAWLEY (London: G. Kenning).
——— (1985) *Masonic Facts and Fictions Comprising A New Theory of the Origin of the 'Antient' Grand Lodge*. With an Introduction by JOHN HAMILL (Wellingborough: Aquarian Press).
SAGUAR QUER, CARLOS (1996a): 'La Egiptomania en la España de Goya' *GOYA Revisita de Arte* **252** (May-June) 367-81.
——— (1997): 'Egiptomania y Arquitectura en España (1840-1940)' *GOYA Revisita de Arte* **259-60** (July-October) 386-406.
ST.-A....., P. DE (1816): *Promenade aux Cimetières de Paris, aux Sépultures Royales de Saint-Denis, et aux Catacombes* (Paris: C.-L.-F. Panckoucke). See also the same author's *Promenade... avec quarante-huit dessins...*, published in 1825.
SAINT-ALBIN, JACQUES SIMON COLLIN DE (1819): *Voyages de Paul Béranger, dans Paris, après 45 ans d'absence* (Paris: s.n.).
SAINT-FOIX, G. DE (1912-46): *see* WYZEWA, TEODORE D.
SAINT-LÉON, ÉTIENNE MARTIN (1901): *Le Compagnonnage, son histoire, ses coutumes, ses règlements et ses rites* (Paris: A. Colin).
SALINGAROS, NIKOS, ET AL. (2004): *Anti-Architecture and Deconstruction* (Solingen: Umbau-Verlag).
SALLENGRE, ALBERT-HENRI DE (1723): *Ebrietatis Encomium: or The Praise of Drunkenness. Wherein is authentically, and most evidently proved, the necessity of frequently getting drunk; and, That the Practice of getting Drunk is most Ancient, Primitive, and Catholic. Confirmed by the Examples of... Free Masons, Gormogons, and other tope-ing Societies, and Men of Learning of All Ages by* 'Boniface Oinophilus, de Monte Fiascona, A.B.C.' (London: Edmund Curll).
SALTER, HERBERT EDWARD (*Ed.*) (1920-1): *Mediaeval Archives of the University of Oxford* (Oxford: Clarendon Press for the Oxford Historical Society).
SALTMARSH, JOHN (1937): Review of KNOOP & JONES'S *An Introduction to Freemasonry* in *The Economic History Review* **viii**/1 (November) 102-4.
SAMUELS, M. L. (*Ed.*) (1986): *see* MCINTOSH, ANGUS.
SANDE, ANTON VAN DE (1995): *Vrijmetselarij in de Lage Landen. Een mysterieuze broederschap zonder geheimen* (Zutphen: Walburg Pers).
SANDYS, J. E. (1899): *see* SEYFFERT, OSKAR.
SARASTRO CLUB BULLETIN (1962): Official Publication of the Sarastro Masonic Club (Vienna: Sarastro Club).
SAVARY, CLAUDE-ÉTIENNE (1785-6): *Lettres sur l'Égypte* (Paris: Onfroi).
SAVREUX, MAURICE (1923): *see* LECHEVALLIER-CHEVIGNARD, GEORGES.
SBORDONE, FRANCESCO (*Ed.*) (1940): *Hori Apollonis Hieroglyphica* (Naples: L. Loffredo).
SCALICKI, W. (1956): *see* MASKE UND KOTHURN.
SCANLAN, MATTHEW D.J. (*Ed.*) (2002): *The Social Impact of Freemasonry in the Modern Western World. The Transactions of the Second International Conference 4 & 5 November 2000. Canonbury Papers* **i** (London: CMRC).
SCHAMPHELEIRE, M. DE (1984): *see* MACLOT, PETRA.
SCHECHELBAUER, BERNHARD (1959): *see* KUÉSS, GUSTAV A.
SCHEIBE, JOHANN ADOLPH (1776): *Vollständiges Liederbuch für Freymaurer* (Copenhagen & Leipzig: s.n.).
SCHENK, ERICH (*Ed.*) (1932): *Bericht über die musikwissenschaftliche Tagung der Internationalen Stiftung Mozarteum in Salzburg* (Leipzig: Breitkopf & Härtel).
SCHIFFMANN, GUSTAV ADOLF (1881): *Die Freimaurerei in Frankreich in der ersten Hälfte de XVIII. Jahrhunderts* (Leipzig: Zechel).
SCHINKEL, KARL FRIEDRICH (1823): *see* THIELE, CARL FRIEDRICH.
SCHLETTER, HERMANN THEODOR, ZILLE, MORITZ ALEXANDER, ET AL. (1900): *Allgemeines Handbuch der Freimaurerei* (Leipzig: Max Hesse's Verlag).
SCHMIDT, LEO, KELLER, C., JAEGER, R., & BURMAN, P. (*Eds.*) (20v01): *Looking Forwards: The Country House in Contemporary Research and Conservation* (Cottbus: Papers of the 1999 York Conference, BTU Cottbus).
SCHMIDT, PAUL EDMOND (1908): *Court de Gébelin à Paris, 1763-1748* (Roubaix: Foyer solidarité).
SCHMIDT-BIGGEMANN, WILHELM (1983): *Topica Universalis: Eine Modellgeschichte humanistischer und barocker Wissenschaft* (Hamburg: Meiner).
——— (*Ed.*) (1979): *see* RAABE, PAUL (*Ed.*).
SCHNEIDER, L. (1990): 'Leon Battista Alberti: Some Biographical Implications of the Winged Eye' *Art Bulletin* **lxxii** 261-70.
SCHNEIDER, RENÉ (1910): *Quatremère de Quincy et son intervention dans les arts, 1788-1830* (Paris: Hachette & Cie).
SCHOCK-WERNER, BARBARA (1978): *see* LEGNER.
SCHOLL, MONIKA (*Ed.*) (2006): *see* SNOEK, J. A. M.
SCHOLZ, JÁNOS (*Ed.*) (1950): *Baroque and Romantic Stage Design* (New York: H. Bittner).
SCHÖNE, ALBRECHT (1967): *see* HENKEL, ARTHUR.
SCHÖNE, GÜNTER (1959): *see* THEATERMUSEUM DER CLARA ZIEGLER STIFTUNG, MUNICH.
SCHUBART, CHRISTIAN FRIEDRICH DANIEL (1924): *Ideen zu einer Ästhetik der Tonkunst* PAUL ALFRED MERBACH (*Ed.*) (Leipzig: Wolkenwanderer). *See the original edn.* (Vienna: Ludwig Albrecht Schubart 1806).
SCHUBERT, JOHANNES (1954): *see* MORENZ, SIEGFRIED.
SCHULER, HEINZ (1992): *Mozart und die Freimaurerei:*

Daten, Fakten, Biographien (Wilhelmshaven: F. Noetzel).
SCHULLE, GERD (1993): see NORDMANN, ELMAR.
SCHÜTZ, F. W. VON (1790): *Versuch einer vollstaendigen Sammlung Freimaurer…* (Hamburg: C. Müller).
SCHUYLER, DAVID (Ed.) (1984): see HUNT, JOHN DIXON.
SCHWABE, JOHANN JOACHIM (1738): *Der Freimäurer* (Leipzig: Bernhard Christoph Breitkopf).
SCHWALLER DE LUBICZ, R.A. (1958): *Le Temple de l'Homme: Apet du Sud à Louqsor* (Paris: Caractères).
SCHWARTZ, OTTO, (1975): *Die freimaurischen Anlage im Park des Schlosses Luisenlund* (Kiel: The Author).
SCHWEINITZ, ANNA FRANZISKA VON (1999): *Die Landesherrlichen Gärten in Schaumburg-Lippe von 1647 bis 1918* (Worms: Wernersche Verlagsgesellschaft).
SCHWERTHEIM, OTTO E. (1986): 'Orientalische Religionen in Deutschland' *Aufstieg und Niedergang der römischen Welt. Geschichte und Kultur Roms im Spiegel der neueren Forschung* **ii** 18.1 (Berlin & New York: de Gruyter) 795-813.
SCOT, REGINALD (1886): *The Discoverie of Witchcraft*: a reprint of the first edition of 1584 BRINSLEY NICHOLSON (Ed.) (London: Elliot Stock). But see the version by MONTAGUE SUMMERS (Ed.) (1930): (London: J. Rodber) re-issued (1989) (New York: Dover).
SCOTT, SIR WALTER (1894): *Familiar Letters* (Edinburgh: David Douglas).
SEDLMAYR, HANS (1953): *Verlust der Mitte: die bildende Kunst des 19. und 20. Jahrhunderts als Symptom und Symbol der Zeit* (Salzburg: O. Müller).
——— (1976): *Johann Bernhard Fischer von Erlach* (Vienna: Herold).
SEELEY, BENTON (1797): *Stowe. A Description of the… House and Gardens…* (London: J. Edwards & L. B. Seeley).
SEELY, DAVID ROLF (2007): see HAMBLIN, WILLIAM J.
SERBANESCO, DEMETER GÉRARD ROGER (1963-66): *Histoire de la Franc-Maçonnerie Universelle* (Paris: Hachette).
SÉROUX D'AGINCOURT, JEAN-BAPTISTE-LOUIS-GEORGES (1811-23): *Histoire de l'art par les monuments depuis sa decadence au IVe siècle jusqu'à son renouvellement au XVIe* (Paris: Treuttel & Würtz).
SERRULAZ, MAURICE (1938) (Ed.): see BONAPARTE EN ÉGYPTE.
SÈVRES, MANUFACTURE NATIONALE DE PORCELAINE, MUSÉE CÉRAMIQUE (1951): *Les Grands Services de Sèvres*. Catalogue of the Exhibition (25 May - 29 July 1951) (Paris: Éditions des Musées Nationaux).
SEYFFERT, OSKAR (1899): *A Dictionary of Classical Antiquities Mythology, Religion, Literature & Art*, revised by HENRY NETTLESHIP & J.E. SANDYS (London: S. Sonnenschein & Co. & New York: Macmillan).
SEZNEC, JEAN (1953): *The Survival of the Pagan Gods: the Mythological Tradition and its place in Renaissance Humanism and Art* (New York: Pantheon Books).
SHARPE, REGINALD ROBINSON (Ed.) (1913): *Calendar of Coroners Rolls of the City of London, A.D. 1300-1378* (London: Richard Clay & Sons).
SHELLEY, HENRY CHARLES (1914): *The Life and Letters of Edward Young* (London & New York: I. Pitman & Sons).
SHENSTONE, WILLIAM (1763): *The Works in Verse and Prose, of William Shenstone, Esq.* (London: R. & J. Dodsley). See also (1808): *The Poetical Works. With a Life of the Author. And a Description of The Leasowes* (London: C. Cooke).
SHERWOOD-SMITH, MARIA C. (2000): *Studies in the Reception of the Historia Scholastica of Peter Comestor* (Oxford: Society for the Study of Mediaeval Languages and Literature).
SIDNEY, ALGERNON (1698): *Discourses Concerning Government* (London: Isaac Littlebury).
SIEVERNICH, GEREON, & BUDDE, HENDRIK (Eds.) (1989): *Europa und der Orient 800-1900*. Catalogue of the Exhibition held in the Martin-Gropius-Bau, Berlin (28 May-27 August) (Gütersloh/Munich: Bertelsmann Lexikon Verlag GmbH). It contains an enormous amount of information, and articles by GILET, LEOSPO, SYNDRAM, ET AL.
SILEX (1979): On the occasion of the second world congress on Egyptology, held in Grenoble in 1979, the journal *Silex* devoted the whole of No. 13 (September), entitled *La Rêve Égyptien*, to matters Egyptian. The authors include BERNARD, BOUGNOUX, HARI, HUMBERT, LECLANT, and THEVOZ.
SIMMONS, THOMAS FREDERICK (Ed.) (1879): *The Lay Folks Mass Book, or Manner of hearing Mass: with Rubrics and Devotions for the People.* **lxxi** Early English Text Society (London: Trübner for E. E. T. S.).
SIMPSON, R. S. (1999): see PARKINSON, RICHARD.
SIMPSON, W. G. (1926): *Masonry of the Olden Time in the Comber District, County Down, Ireland* (Lisburn: Victor McMurray).
SINCLAIR, FIONA (2000): see WALKER, FRANK ARNEIL.
SIRÉN, OSVALD (1950): *China and Gardens of Europe of the Eighteenth Century* (New York: Ronald Press).
SISTER MASON, A (1765): *Womens Masonry, or Masonry by Adoption. Explaining the Making of a Masoness*, etc. (London: D. Hookham).
SKALICKI, W. (1956): 'Das Bühnenbild der Zauberflöte' *Maske und Kothurn* **ii** (Vienna: Institut für Theaterwissenschaft an der Universität Wien).
SLEZER, JOHN (1693): *Theatrum Scotiae* (London: J. Leake for A. Swalle), but see the 1718 edn. published by D. Browne, J. Senex, W. Taylor, W. Mears, J. Browne, F. Clay, & A. Johnston.
SMITH, DOUGLAS CAMPBELL (1999): *Working the Rough Stone: Freemasonry and Society in Eighteenth-Century Russia* (DeKalb IL: Northern Illinois UP).
SMITH, GEORGE (1876): *The Chaldean Account of Genesis* (London: Low, Marston, Searle, & Rivington).
SMITH, MARQUARD (Ed.) (2000): see MORRA, JOANNE.
SMITH, RAYMOND (1989): *The Worshipful Company of Masons* (London: Worshipful Company of Masons).
SMITH, RICHARD (Ed.) (1996): see RAZI, ZVI.
SMITH, WILLIAM (Ed.) (1863): *A Dictionary of the Bible* (London: John Murray & Walton & Maberly).
SMITS, J. (1988): *De Verenigde Nederlanden op zoek naar het Oude Egypte (1570-1780). De traditie gevolgd en gewogen* (Culemborg: Boekhandel Boldingh).
SMYTH, FREDERICK (1975): 'Brother Mozart of Vienna' *AQC* **lxxxvii** 37-73.
——— (1983): see PICK, FRED LOMAX.
——— (1998): *A Reference Book for Freemasons* (London: Q.C. Correspondence Circle).
SNODIN, MICHAEL (Ed.) (1991): *Karl Friedrich Schinkel: A Universal Man* (New Haven CT & London: Yale UP in assocation with the Victoria & Albert Museum. Issued to coincide with the Exhibition of 31 July-27 October 1991 at the V&A Museum).
SNOEK, JOANNES [JAN] AUGUSTINUS MARIA (1989): *Initiations: A Methodological Approach to the Application of Classification and Definition Theory in the Study of Rituals* (Pijnacker: Dutch Efficiency Bureau).
——— (1997): 'À propos de l'origine de 3 éléments fondamentaux du degré de l'Arche Royale' *Grand Chapitre de la Saint Arche Royale de Belgique. Réunion Annuelle* (19 April) 23-33.
——— (2002): 'The earliest Development of Masonic Degrees and Rituals: Hamill versus Stevenson' SCANLAN, MATTHEW D.J. (Ed.) 2002) 1-19.
——— (2003): 'The Evolution of the Hiramic Legend in England and France' *Heredom* **xi** 11-53.
——— (Ed.) (2005): see KROON, ANDRÉA A.
———, SCHOLL, MONIKA, & KROON, ANDRÉA A. (Eds.) (2006): *Symbolism in 18th-Century Gardens: The Influence of Classical and Esoteric Currents* (Den Haag: OVN).
——— (2006): see KREINATH, JENS (Ed.)
SOLOMON, MAYNARD (1995): *Mozart: A Life* (London: Hutchinson).
SOMERVILLE, ANDREW R. (1987): 'The Ancient Sundials of Scotland' *Proceedings of the Society of Antiquaries of Scotland* **cxvii** 233-64.
——— (1994): *The Ancient Sundials of Scotland* (London: Turner).
SONGHURST, W. J. (Ed.) (1913): *Quatuor Coronatorum Antigrapha*. Masonic Reprints of the QCL **x** (London: QCL).
SONNENFELS, JOSEPH VON (1783-87): *Gesammelte Schriften* (Vienna: Mit von Baumeisterischen Schriften).
SONNLEITHNER, LEOPOLD VON (1919-20): 'Über die Zauberflöte' *Mozarteums Mitteilungen* **i**/1-2 (Salzburg: Mozartgemeinde).
SØRENSEN, SØREN (Ed.) (1962): see HJELMBORG, BJØRN (Ed.).
SOZZI, MARINA, & PORSET, CHARLES (Eds.) (1999): *Il sonno e la memoria: idee della morte e politiche funerarie nella Rivoluzione francese* (Turin: Paravia Scriptorium).
SPEDDING, JAMES, ELLIS, ROBERT LESLIE, & HEATH, DOUGLAS DENON (Eds.) (1857-74): *The Works of Francis Bacon* in 14 volumes (London: Longman & Co.).
SPENCER, JOHN R. (1965): see FILARETE, ANTONIO DI PIERO AVERLINO.
SPENKE, CHANTAL (Tr.) (1996): see IRMEN, HANS-JOSEF.
SPETH, GEORGE WILLIAM (1892): *What is Freemasonry?* (London: G. Kenning).
——— (Ed.) (1888): *The Religion of Freemasonry* (London: G. Kenning).
SPOTTS, FREDERIC (2002): *Hitler and the Power of Aesthetics* (London: Hutchinson).
STAHL, WILLIAM HARRIS (Tr.) (1952): see MACROBIUS, AMBROSIUS THEODOSIUS.
——— (1971-7): see CAPELLA, MARTIANUS MINEUS FELIX.
STAMP, GAVIN (1989): *Telephone Boxes* (London: Chatto & Windus).
——— (1999): *Alexander 'Greek' Thomson* (London: Laurence King).
——— (Ed.) (1999): *The Light of Truth and Beauty. The Lectures of Alexander 'Greek' Thomson Architect 1817-1875* (Glasgow: The Alexander Thomson Society).
———, & MCKINSTRY, SAM (Eds.) (1994): *'Greek' Thomson* (Edinburgh: Edinburgh UP Ltd.).
STARCK, JOHANN AUGUST, FREIHERR VON (1782): *Ueber die alten und neuen Mysterien* (Berlin: F. Maurer).
STAROBINSKI, JEAN (1973): *1789, les emblems de la raison* (Paris: Flammarion).
STAUSBERG, MICHAEL (Ed.) (2006): see KREINATH, JENS.
STEBLIN, RITA (2002): *A History of Key Characteristics in the Eighteenth and Nineteenth Centuries* (Rochester NY: University of Rochester Press).
STERN, JEAN (1930): *À l'ombre de Sophie Arnould. François-Joseph Bélanger, architecte des Menus-Plaisirs, Premier architecte du comte d'Artois* (Paris: Plon).
STEVENS, M. A. (Ed.) (1999): see RICHARDSON, MARGARET.
STEVENSON, DAVID (1984): 'Masonry, Symbolism, and Ethics in the life of Sir Robert Moray, FRS' *Proceedings of the Society of Antiquaries of Scotland* **cxiv** 405-31.
——— (1988a): *The First Freemasons: Scotland's early Lodges and their Members* (Aberdeen: Aberdeen UP). See also the revised edition of 2001 (Edinburgh: Grand Lodge of Scotland).
——— (1988b): *The Origins of Freemasonry. Scotland's Century 1590-1710* (Cambridge: Cambridge UP).
——— (1997): *Scotland's Last Royal Wedding: The Marriage of James VI and Anne of Denmark* (Edinburgh: John Donald).
STEVENSON, W. B. (1940): 'Sundials of Six Scottish Counties, near Glasgow' *Transactions of the Glasgow Archaeological Society* **ix** 227-86.
STEWART, TREVOR (Ed.) (2005): *Freemasonry in Music and Literature. Transactions of the Fifth International Conference 1&2 November 2003. The Canonbury Papers* **ii** (London: CMRC).
——— (2006): *Freemasonry and Religion: Many Faiths, One Brotherhood. Transactions of the Sixth International Conference 6 & 7 November 2004. The Canonbury Papers* **iii** (London: CMRC).
STONEHILL, CHARLES (Ed.) (1930): see FARQUHAR, GEORGE.
STOW, JOHN (1633): *The Survey of London* revised by A. M. MUNDAY, HENRY DYSON, ET AL. (London: Nicholas Bourne).
STRANG, JOHN (1831): *Necropolis Glasguensis; with Observations* [sic] *on Ancient and Modern Tombs and Sepulture* (Glasgow: Atkinson & Co.).
STREBEL, HARALD (1991): *Freimaurer Wolfgang Amadeus Mozart* (Stäfa: Rothenhäusler Verlag).
STROUD, DOROTHY (1966): *Henry Holland: His Life and Architecture* (London: Country Life).
——— (1984a): *Capability Brown* (London & Boston MA: Faber).
——— (1984b): *Sir John Soane Architect* (London & Boston: Faber & Faber).
STUBBS, SIR JAMES, & HAUNCH, T. O. (1983): *Freemasons' Hall: The Home and Heritage of the Craft*

(London: Library, Art, & Publications Cttee. United Grand Lodge of England).
STUKELEY, WILLIAM (1717-34): *The Order of the Pillars of Solomon's Temple Demonstrated* (MS in the Library of Freemasons' Hall, London, containing fanciful reconstructions and other matter).
——— (1817-92): *The Family Memoirs of the Rev. William Stukeley* WILLIAM COLLINGS LUKIS (Ed.) (Durham: Surtees Society **lxxiii**).
STÜRMER, MICHAEL (1997): see BODE, URSULA.
STURT, JOHN (1707): see POZZO, ANDREA.
——— (1708): see PERRAULT, CLAUDE.
SUEUR, JEAN-FRANÇOIS LE (1787): *Exposé d'une musique une, imitative, et particulière à chaque solemnité* (Paris: Veuve Hérissant). See also the reprint of 1973 (Novato: Gregg).
SUMMERS, MONTAGUE (Ed.) (1930): see SCOT, REGINALD.
SUMMERSON, SIR JOHN NEWENHAM (1952): *Sir John Soane, 1753-1837* (London: Art & Technics).
——— (1978): 'Sir John Soane and the Furniture of Death' *The Architectural Review* **clxiii**/973 (March) 147-55.
——— (1980): *The Classical Language of Architecture* (London: Thames & Hudson).
SURENHUSIUS, GUGLIELMUS (1702): *Mishnah, sive Legum Mischnicarum liber qui inscribitur Ordo Sacrorum*, etc. (Amsterdam: Borstius).
SULZER, JOHANN GEORG (1771-4): *Allgemeine Theorie der schönen Künste* etc. (Leipzig: M. G. Weidmanns Erben und Reich).
SVANBERG, JAN (1983): *Master Masons* (Stockholm: Carmina).
ŚWIĘCKA, EWA (1993): 'The Romantic Park of Arkadia' *Biuletyn Informacyjny Konserwatorów Dziet Sztuki* **iv**/2 (13) 39-40.
——— (Ed.) (1995): see COWELL, FIONA (Ed.).
SWIRIDA, INESSA (1993): 'W poszukiwaniu ukrytych znaczén. Park naturalny XVIII stulecia a wolnomularstwo' *Ars Regia* **ii**/3.
SYNDRAM, DIRK (1989): *Ägypten - Faszinationen. Untersuchungen zum Ägyptenbild im europäischen Klassizismus bis 1800* (Frankfurt-am-Main: Lang).
——— (1996): 'Les sources de l'inspiration: l'influence des modèles iconographiques sur l'égyptomanie du XVIIIe siècle' HUMBERT (Ed.) (1996): 39-58 & fig. 4 (54).
TABBERT, MARK A. (2005): *American Freemasons. Three Centuries of Building Communities* (Lexington MA: National Heritage Museum, & London: New York UP).
TACITUS, CORNELIUS (1999): *Agricola and Germany* ANTONY R. BIRLEY (Tr.) (Oxford: Oxford UP).
TALMON, JACOB LAIB (1986): *The Origins of Totalitarian Democracy* (Harmondsworth: Penguin).
TARDIEU, FEU (1825-50): see GOULIER, CHARLES-PIERRE.
TATSCH, J. HUGO (1929): *Freemasonry in the Thirteen Colonies* (New York: Macoy Publishing).
TATTON-BROWN, TIM, & MUNBY, JULIAN (Eds.) (1996): *The Archaeology of Cathedrals* (Oxford: Oxford University Committee for Archaeology **xlii**).
TAUTE, REINHOLD (1886): *Maurerische Bücherkunde. Ein Wegweiser durch die Literatur der Freimaurerei mit literarisch - kritischen Notizen und Zugleich ein Supplement zu Kloss' Bibliographie* (Leipzig: J.G. Findel).
TAXIL, LÉO (1895): *Le Diable et la Révolution* (Paris: Delhomme & Briguet).
TAVERNOR, ROBERT (Tr.) (1988): see ALBERTI, LEON BATTISTA.
TAYLOR, A. B. (Ed.) (1927): *Floris and Blancheflour, edited from the Trentham and Auchinleck MSS.* (Oxford: Clarendon Press).
TAYLOR, EVA GERMAINE RIMINGTON (1966): *The Mathematical Practitioners of Hanoverian England, 1714-1840* (Cambridge: For the Institute of Navigation at the University Press).
TAYLOR, J. E. (1982): 'Sir John Soane: Architect and Freemason' *Ars Quatuor Coronatorum* **xcv** 194-202.
TAYLOR, JEROME (Tr.) (1991): see HUGH OF ST VICTOR.
TEMPESTA OF FLORENCE, ANTONIO (1930): see GALLONIO, ANTONIO.
TENENTI, ALBERTO (1952): *La Vie et La Mort à travers l'Art du XVe Siècle* (Paris: Cahiers des Annales 8).
——— (1957): *Il senso della morte e l'amore della vita nel Rinascimento* (Turin: Studi e richerche 5).
TERNER, URSULA (2001): *Freimurerische Bildwelten: Die Ikonographie der freimaurerischen Symbolik anhand von englischen, schottischen und französischen Freimaurerdiplomen* (Petersberg: Michael Imhof Verlag).
TERRASSON, JEAN (1731): *Séthos, Histoire ou Vie Tirée des Monumens Anecdotes de l'ancienne Égypte. Traduit d'un manuscrit grec* (Paris: Hippolyte-Louis Guérin). See also the 1732 edn. THOMAS LEDIARD (Tr.).
TESI, MAURO ANTONIO (1787): *Raccoltà di disegni originale* (Bologna: Nell'Instituto delle Scienze).
TEYSSOT, GEORGES (1991): see MOSSER, MONIQUE.
THEATERMUSEUM DER CLARA ZIEGLER STIFTUNG, MUNICH (1959): *Das Bühnenbild im 19. Jahrhundert*. Catalogue of Exhibition prepared by GÜNTER SCHÖNE & HELLMUTH VRIESEN (Munich: Theatermuseum).
THIÉBAUT DE BERNEAUD, ARSÈNE (1797): *Réflexions sur les pompes funèbres* (Paris: Galletti).
——— (1798): *Voyage à l'isle des peupliers* (Paris: Lepetit).
THIELE, CARL FRIEDRICH (1823): *Decoration auf den beiden Königlichen Theatern in Berlin unter der General-Intendantur des Herrn Grafen von Brühl* (Berlin: C. F. Thiele).
THIEME, ULRICH, & BECKER, FELIX (1950-53): *Allgemeines Lexikon der bildenden Künstler von der Antike bis zur Gegenwart* (Leipzig: Seeman).
THOMAS, T. (1815): *A History of the Demolition and Rebuilding of Solomon's Temple* (London: Bickerstaffe & Wilkie; Wimborne: Noon; Taunton: Norris).
THOMAS, WALTER (1901): *Le Poète Edward Young, 1683-1765: étude sur sa vie et ses oeuvres* (Paris: Hachette).
THOMPSON, F. H. (Ed.) (1985): see MACREADY, SARAH.
THOMSON, JAMES (1763): *The Poetical Works* (Edinburgh: Donaldson & Reid).
THOMSON, KATHARINE (1977): *The Masonic Thread in Mozart* (London: Lawrence & Wishart).
THOMSON, RODNEY MALCOLM (Ed. & Tr.) (1998-9): see MYNORS, R. A. B.
THORNE, ATWOOD (1926): *Pink Lustre Pottery* (London: Batsford).
THORNTON, PETER (Ed. & Tr.) (1974): see ERIKSEN, SVEND.
THORP, JOHN THOMAS (Ed.) (1907): *A Defence of Masonry* (Leicester: J. Johnson).
——— (1909): see HUGHAN, WILLIAM JAMES.
THORY, C. A. (1815): *Acta Latomorum, ou Chronologie de l'histoire de la Franche-Maçonnerie française et étrangère* (Paris: P. E. Dufart).
THREE DISTINCT KNOCKS, THE (1763): see W.-O.-V.-n.
THURY, LOUIS-ÉTIENNE-FRANÇOIS HÉRICART-FERRAND, VICOMTE DE (1815): see HÉRICART-FERRAND.
TILL, NICHOLAS (1992): *Mozart and the Enlightenment: Truth, Virtue, and Beauty in Mozart's Operas* (London: Faber & Faber).
TODD, JANET (1986): *Sensibility: An Introduction* (London: Methuen).
TOULIER, BERNARD (2006): see CULOT, MAURICE.
TOUMSON, ROGER, & PORSET, CHARLES (1998): *La période révolutionnaire aux Antilles: Images et Résonances, Littérature, Philosophie, Histoire Sociale, Histoire des Idées* (Schœlcher, Martinique: GRELCA).
TOURNEUR, PIERRE LE (1769): *Les Nuits de Young* (Paris: Chez Lejay).
TRAHARD, PIERRE (1936): *La Sensibilité Révolutionnaire (1789-1794)* (Paris: Boivin & Cie).
TRAHERNE, THOMAS (1981): *Centuries of Meditation* (Llandogo: Old Stile Press).
TRAN TAM TINH, VINCENT (1972): *Le Culte des Divinités Orientales en Campanie en dehors de Pompéi, de Stabies et d'Herculanum* (Leiden: E. J. Brill).
——— (1983): *Sérapis Debout. Corpus des monuments de Sérapis debout et étude iconographique* (Leiden: E. J. Brill).
TRANIÉ, JEAN, & CARMIGNIANI, JUAN CARLOS (1988): *Bonaparte: La Campagne d'Égypte* (Paris: Pygmalion/G. Watelet).
TRANSACTIONS OF THE MANCHESTER ASSOCIATION FOR MASONIC RESEARCH (various years).
TRAUZETTEL, LUDWIG (1996): 'Wörlitz: England in Germany' *Garden History: The Journal of The Garden History Society* **xxiv**/2 (Winter) 221-36.
TRAVENOL, LOUIS (pseudonym LÉONARD GABANON) (1744): *Catéchisme des Francs-Maçons* ('Jérusalem': The Author, & Limoges: Pierre Mortier).
——— (1747): *La Désolation des Entrepreneurs Modernes du Temple de Jérusalem, ou, Nouveau Catéchisme des Francs-Maçons* (Paris: P. Mortier).
——— (1749): *Nouveau Catéchisme des Francs-Maçons* ('Jérusalem': P. Mortier).
TREACY, GERALD, C., SJ (Ed.) (1978): see LEO XIII, POPE.
TREDE, THEODOR (1889-91): *Das Heidentum in der römischen Kirche. Bilder aus dem Religiösen und sittlichen Leben Süditaliens* (Gotha: F.A. Perthes).
TRETHEWEY, WILLIAM HILLIARD (Ed.) (1939): *La Petite Philosophie* (Oxford: Basil Blackwell).
TREVELYAN, GEORGE MACAULAY (2000): *English Social History: A Survey of Six Centuries* (London: Pelican).
TREVISE, DUC DE (1925): 'Le reapparition de Dugourc' *Renaissance de l'art français* (February) 75-84.
TREVOR-ROPER, HUGH (2006): *Europe's Physician: The Various Life of Theodore de Mayerne* (New Haven CT & London: Yale UP).
——— (2008): *The Invention of Scotland: Myth and History* (New Haven CT & London: Yale UP).
TRITHEMIUS, JOHANNES (1690): *Annales Hirsaugienses* (St Galli [St Gall]: Typis ejusdem S. Galli).
TRUMAN, CHARLES (1982): *The Sèvres Egyptian Service, 1810-1812* (London: HMSO).
TSCHUDY, THÉODORE-HENRI DE (1766): *L'Étoile Flamboyante, ou La Société des Francs-Maçons Considérée sous tous les aspects.* (Frankfurt & Paris: s.n.).
——— (1780): *Écossois de Saint-André d'Écosse, contenant le développement total de l'art royal de la franc-maçonnerie…* etc. (Paris: Le \Verité).
TUNBRIDGE, PAUL (1968): 'The Climate of European Freemasonry 1730 to 1750' *AQC* **lxxxi** 88-128.
———, & BATHAM, C. N. (1970): 'The Climate of European Freemasonry' *AQC* **lxxxiii** 248-273.
TURNER, JANE SHOAF (Ed.) (1998): *The Dictionary of Art* (London: Macmillan).
TYRELL, JAMES (1979): *Bibliotheca Politica* (New York: Garland). The first complete edn. containing the 14th Dialogue of 1702.
TYSON, ALAN (1990): see ROSENTHAL, ALBI.
TYSSENS, JEFFREY (2007): '"En vain la terre te cache": un cadre analytique pour les monuments funéraires maçonniques' *Franc-Maçonnerie et Beaux-Arts* CHRISTOPHE LOIR & JACQUES CH. LEMAIRE (Eds.) (Brussels: Espace de Libertés).
UNITED GRAND LODGE OF ENGLAND (1926): *Constitutions of the Antient Fraternity of Free and Accepted Masons, Under the United Grand Lodge of England, Containing the General Charges, Laws and Regulations*, etc., etc. (London: Harrison).
——— (1967): *Grand Lodge, 1717-1967* (London: Oxford UP).
URBAN, HUGH (2001): 'The Adornment of Silence: Secrecy and Symbolic Power in American Freemasonry' *The Journal of Religion and Society* **iii** 1-27.
UVAROV, COUNT SERGEI SEMENOVICH (1817): *Essay on the Mysteries of Eleusis* J. D. PRICE (Tr.) with Observations by JAMES CHRISTIE (London: Rodwell & Martin).
V.-n, W.- O.- (1760): *The Three Distinct Knocks: or the Door of the Most Antient Free-Masonry, Opening to All Men, neither Naked nor Cloath'd* (London: H. Serjeant). This went into several editions, including some in Dublin published by Thomas Wilkinson. See JACKSON, A. C. F. (Ed.) (1986).
VACQUIER, JULES FÉLIX (1913): *Les Anciens Châteaux de France* (Paris: F. Contet).
——— (1914-30): *Le Style Empire; décorations extérieures et intérieures...* (Paris: F. Contet).
VALTEICH, PAUL, & KELLER, HANS (1997-2003): *Die Dessauer Grünanlagen* (Dessau: Museum für Stadtgeschichte).
VAQUIER, ANDRÉ (1957): 'Les Jardins du Comte d'Albon à Franconville-la-Garenne' *Paris et Île-de-France* **viii** (Paris: Fédération des Sociétés Historiques et Archéologiques de Paris et de l'Île-

de-France) 237-97.
——— (1965): *Inventaire des Archives municipales de Franconville-la-Garenne* (Franconville-la-Garenne: s.n.).
VARTANIAN, ARAM (1953): *Diderot and Descartes. A Study of Scientific Naturalism in the Enlightenment* (Princeton NJ: Princeton UP).
VAUDOYER, A.-L.-T. (1791): *Idées d'un citoyen François sur le lieu destiné à la sépulture des hommes illustres de la France* (Paris: Didot, fils aîné).
——— (1806 and 1818-34): see ACADÉMIE DES BEAUX-ARTS.
VAUGHAN, DIANA (1895-7): *Mémoires d'une Ex-Palladiste* (Paris: s.n.).
——— (1896): *La Restauration du Paganisme* (Paris: s.n.).
VAUGHAN, THOMAS (1923): *The Fame and Confession of the Fraternity of R.C.: commonly of the Rose Cross: with a Preface etc. by EUGENIUS PHILALETHES* (pseud. VAUGHAN) with Notes etc. by F. N. PRYCE (Margate: Societas Rosicruciana).
VEALE, ELSPETH (1991): 'The "Great Twelve": Mistery and Fraternity in Thirteenth-Century London' *Historical Research* **lxiv** 237-63.
VENTURA, GASTONE (1975): *I Riti massonici dei Misraïm e Memphis* (Rome: Anator). A French edition was published in Paris in 1986.
VERARDI, LOUIS (1834): see BOITARD, PIERRE.
VERLET, PIERRE, GRANDJEAN, SERGE, & BRUNET, M. (1953): *Sèvres* (Paris: G. Le Prat).
VERSTEGAN, RICHARD (1605): *A Restitution of Decayed Intelligence; in Antiquities; Concerning the Most Renowned English Nation* (Antwerp: R. Bruney).
VERVAL, GUY (1989): *À la recherche de Jakin et Boaz: promenade dans le jardin anglais d'un franc-maçonnerie méconnue* (Brussels: Diffusion Thustier).
VIDLER, ANTHONY (1976): 'The Architecture of the Lodges: Ritual Form and Associational Life in the Late Enlightenment' *Oppositions* **v** (Summer) 76-97.
——— (1987): *The Writing of the Walls. Architectural Theory in the Late Enlightenment* (Princeton NJ: Princeton Architectural Press).
——— (1990): *Claude-Nicolas Ledoux: Architecture and Social Reform at the End of the Ancien Régime* (Cambridge MA & London: MIT Press).
VIEL, DE SAINT-MEAUX, CHARLES-FRANÇOIS (1787): *Lettres sur l'architecture des anciens: et celles des modern*s (Paris: s.n.).
VIERNE, SIMONE (2001): *George Sand et la franc-maçonnerie* in *Encyclopédie maçonnique* **xxxvii** (Paris: Éditions maçonniques de France).
VILLALPANDUS, JUAN BAPTISTA (WITH JÉRONIMO PRADO) (1596 and ff): *In Ezechielem Explanationes et Apparatus urbis ac Templi Hierosolymitani, commentariis et imaginibus illustratus* (Rome: A. Zannetti & J. Ciaconii). See especially *De Postrema Ezechielis Prophetae Visione* (1631).
VILLEDIEU, ——— (1782): *Projet de catacombs pour la ville de Paris, en adaptant à cet usage les carrières qui se trouvent tant dans son enceinte que dans ses environs* (London & Paris: chez les marchands de nouveautés).
VILLENEUVE, MARTIN COURET DE (1748): see COURET DE VILLENEUVE.
VINCENT DE BEAUVAIS (1473): *Speculum Historiale* (Strassburg: I. Mentellin).
VOGEL, HANS MARTIN ERASMUS (1928-9): 'Ägyptisierende Baukunst des Klassizismus' *Zeitschrift für Bildende Kunst* **xliii** 160-5.
VOÏART, L. (1822): *Monumens des victories et conquêtes des Français. Recueil de tous les objets d'arts…etc., consacrés à célébrer les victories des Français de 1792 à 1815* (Paris: s.n., but later published by C.-L.-F. Panckoucke).
VOLAIT, MERCEDES (1996): 'Les architectures d'inspiration pharaonique en Égypte: formes et fondements' HUMBERT (*Ed.*) (1996) 437-58.
———, & CROSNIER-LECONTE, MARIE-LAURE (1998): *Catalogue of the exhibition L'Égypte d'un architecte: Ambroise Baudry, 1838-1906* (Paris: Somogy Éditions d'art).
VOLKMANN, LUDWIG (1923): *Bilderschriften der Renaissance: Hieroglyphik und Emblematik in ihren Beziehungen und Fortwirkungen* (Leipzig: K.W. Hiersemann). A new edition was published in Nieuwkoop by De Graaf in 1969.
VOLNEY, CONSTANTIN-FRANÇOIS CHASSEBOEUF DE (1787): *Voyage en Syrie en et Égypte, pendant les années 1783, 1784, et 1785* (Paris: Desenne).
VOLTAIRE, FRANÇOIS-MARIE AROUET DE (1738): *Lettres de M. de V, avec plusieurs pièces de differens auteurs* (Den Haag [but actually Rouen]): P. Poppy).
——— (1878): *Essai sur les Moeurs*. In *Oeuvres Complètes* (Paris: Garnier).
VRIESEN, HELLMUTH (1959): see THEATERMUSEUM DER CLARA ZIEGLER STIFTUNG, MUNICH.
VUES PITTORESQUES, PLANS, ETC., DES PRINCIPAUX JARDINS ANGLAIS QUI SONT EN FRANCE: ERMENONVILLE (1787) (Paris: Simon & Guillot).
W.-O.-V.-n (1763): see V.-n, W.-O.- (1760).
W., T.: see WILSON, THOMAS.
WADE, IRA OWEN (1938): *The Clandestine Organization and Diffusion of Philosophic Ideas in France from 1700 to 1750* (London: H. Milford for Oxford UP).
WADE, JOHN (2005): 'Wolfgang Amadeus Mozart and his contribution to the Craft' STEWART, TREVOR (*Ed.*) (2005) 150-160.
WAGNER, BRIGETTE (*Ed.*) (1987): see POCHAT, GÖTZ.
WAGNER, GUY (1966): *Bruder Mozart: Freimaurer in Wien des 18. Jahrhunderts* (Vienna: Amalthea). See also the later editions of 1996, 2003, etc.
WAGNER, HANS (1980): *Freimaurerei um Joseph II: Die Loge Zur Wahren Eintracht*. Catalogue of Exhibition at Schloss Rosenau (Zwettl: Österreichisches Freimaurermuseum).
WAILLY, CHARLES DE (1819): *Projets de Reconstruction* (Paris: F. Didot).
——— (1819): *Vues sur le Panthéon* (Paris: F. Didot).
WAITE, ARTHUR EDWARD (1924): *The Brotherhood of the Rosy Cross* (London: W. Rider).
——— (1970): *A New Encyclopædia of Freemasonry* (New Hyde Park NY: University Books).
——— (2003): *Devil Worship in France: with Diana Vaughan and the Question of Modern Palladism* (Boston MA: Weiser, & Enfield: Airlift).
WALKER, DAVID (1984): see GIFFORD, JOHN.
WALKER, FRANK ARNEIL, & SINCLAIR, FIONA (2000): *Argyll and Bute* in *The Buildings of Scotland* Series (London: Penguin Group).
WALKER, NICHOLAS (*Ed.*) (2007): see KANT, IMMANUEL.
WALLACE-JAMES, R. E. (*Tr.*) (1937): see KÖPPEN, KARL FRIEDRICH.
WALPOLE, HORACE (1995): *The History of the Modern Taste in Gardening* (New York: Ursus Press).
WANGERMANN, ERNST (1969): *From Joseph II to the Jacobin Trials* (London: Oxford UP).
WANGERMÉE, ROBERT (1980-1): 'Quelques mystères de "La Flûte Enchantée"' *Revue Belge de Musicologie* **xxxiv-xxxv** 147-63.
WARD, JOHN SEBASTIAN MARLOW (1925): *Who was Hiram Abiff?* (London: Baskerville Press). Another edition was published in 1986 (London: Lewis Masonic).
WARD-PERKINS, JOHN BRYAN (1952): 'The Shrine of St Peter and its twelve spiral columns' *Journal of Roman Studies* **xlii** 21-33.
WARMENBOL, EUGÈNE (1991): see DELVAUX, LUC.
——— (1992): 'Graven van maçons en maçonnieke graven op het Antwerpse Schoonselhof' *Epitaaf* **v**/17 2-4.
——— (1993): see DELVAUX, LUC, ET AL.
——— (1995a): 'La Religion et la civilisation égyptiennes dans l'œuvre de Goblet d'Alviella. Sources, interprétations et dérivations' DIERKENS, ALAIN (*Ed.*) (1995b) 95-106.
——— (1995b): 'Alexandrië aan de Schelde' GUBEL ET AL. (1995) 27-48.
——— (1996): 'Le sphinx réfléchi ou les sources de l'égyptomanie au XIXᵉ siècle' HUMBERT (*Ed.*) (1996) 61-96.
——— (1997): 'Architectures égyptiennes et franc-maçonnerie' *Les Nouvelles du Patrimoine* **lxxii** 22-3.
——— (1998): 'De loge L'Aménité te Sint Niklaas (1817-1844) in historisch en kunsthistorisch perspectief' *Trigonum Coronatum Jaarboek* **vi** 71-107.
——— (2001): 'L'Égypte, trois points, c'est tout' *Les Cahiers d'Urbanisme* **xxxvii** (December) 60-68.
——— (2005): '19th-Century Masonic Temples in Egyptian Style in Brussels and Antwerp. Shared Responsibilities for Heritage Organizations and Masonic Orders' KROON, BAX, & SNOEK (*Eds.*) (2005) 132-147.
———, & DELVAUX, LUC (1988): 'Oud-Egyptische teksten uit de tijd van Farao Leopold I van Opper- en Neder-Belgie' *M&L. Monumenten en Landschappen* **vii**/2 63-8.
———, & MACLOT, PETRA (1988): 'Tempel en stal in één: de Egyptische temple in de Antwerpse zoo in kunsthistorisch en historisch perspectief' *M&L. Monumenten en Landschappen* **vii**/2 24-35.
———, & MACLOT, PETRA (1991): 'Tafelen met Isis en Osiris. De egyptiserende aetzaal van kasteel Moeland te Sint-Niklaas' in *M&L. Monumenten en Landschappen* **x**/6 45-59.
———, & WASSEIGE, MANOËLLE (1989): 'Egyptomanie in de 19de-eeuwse architectuur: België in de ban van Egypte' *Bulletin van de Antwerpse Verening voor Bodem- en Grotendezoek* (1990) **ii** (NEO. Recherches sur l'art et l'architecture du XIX siècle. Journée d'études du 12 Mai 1989).
———, & WASSEIGE, MANOËLLE (1990): 'À la recherche de l'Égypte perdue: l'égyptomanie en Belgique au XIXᵉ siècle' *Art & Fact. Revue des Historiens de l'art, des archéologues, des musicologues et des orientalistes de l'Université de Liège* **ix** 105-112.
——— (1998): 'L'Égypte éphémère, 1930 de notre ère. Le temple pharaonique de l'Exposition internationale de Liège' *Maisons d'Hier et d'Aujourd'hui* **xii** (December) 16-29.
WARREN, CHARLES (1765): *The Free Mason stripped Naked: or, the whole Art and Mystery of Free-Masonry, Made Plain and Easy to All Capacities…* (London: Isaac Fell). Another edn. was published in Dublin.
WASSEIGE, MANOËLLE (1990): see WARMENBOL, EUGÈNE.
WASZINK, J. H. (*Ed.*) (1962): see CALCIDIUS.
WATELET, CLAUDE-HENRI (1774): *Essai sur les jardins* (Paris: Prault).
WATKIN, DAVID (1995): 'Freemasonry and Sir John Soane' *Journal of the Society of Architectural Historians (USA)* **liv**/4 (December) 402-417.
——— (1996): *Sir John Soane: Enlightenment Thought and the Royal Academy Lectures* (Cambridge: Cambridge UP).
———, & MELLINGHOFF, TILMAN (1987): *German Architecture and the Classical Ideal 1740-1840* (London: Thames & Hudson).
———, & HEWAT-JABOOR, PHILIP (*Eds.*) (2008): *Thomas Hope: Regency Designer* (New Haven CT & London: Yale UP).
WATTS, ISAAC (1725): *Logick: or, The right Use of Reason in the Enquiry after Truth* (London: John Clark & Richard Hett, Emanuel Mathews, & Richard Ford).
WEBB, DIANE (*Tr.*) (2009): see BAGGERMAN, ARIANNE.
WEBB, THOMAS SMITH (1797-1816): *Freemason's Monitor* (Albany NY: Webb).
WEBER, EUGEN JOSEPH (1964): *Satan franc-maçon présenté par Eugen Weber: La mystification de Léo Taxil* (Paris: Collection Archives 6 [Éditions Michèle Trinckvel]).
WEBSTER, NESTA HELEN (1924): *Secret Societies and Subversive Movements* (London: Boswell).
WEGNER, JAN (1954): *Nieborów* (Warsaw: Sztuka).
WEINBERGER, KARL, WURM, SYLVIA, & ZORRER, FERDINAND (1984): *Zirkel und Winkelmass: 200 Jahre Grosse Landesloge der Freimaurer* (Vienna: Eigenverlag der Museen der Stadt Wien).
WEINSTOCK, H. (*Tr.*) (1972): see CHAILLEY, JACQUES.
WEISBERGER, RICHARD WILLIAM (1993): *Speculative Freemasonry and the Enlightenment: A Study of the Craft in London, Paris, Prague, and Vienna* (Boulder CO: East European Monographs, & New York: Distributed by Columbia UP).
———, MCLEOD, WALLACE, & MORRIS, S. BRENT (*Eds.*) (2002): *Freemasonry on Both Sides of the Atlantic; Essays concerning the Craft in the British Isles, Europe, the United States, and Mexico* (Boulder CO: East European Monographs, & New York: Distributed by Columbia UP).
WEISS, BENJAMIN (2008): see CURRAN, BRIAN A.
WEISS, THOMAS (1996): see BECHTOLDT, FRANK-ANDREAS.
——— (1997): see BODE, URSULA.
——— (*Ed.*) (1996): *Sir William Chambers und der Englisch-Chinesische Garten in Europa* (Stuttgart: Hatje).
WEISSE, JOHN ADAM (1880): *The Obelisk and Freemasonry according to the Discoveries of Belzoni and Commander Gorringe* (New York: J. W. Bouton).

WEST, GILBERT (1753): *The Beauties of Stow* [sic]; *or, a Description of the Most Noble House, Gardens, and Magnificent Buildings therein*...(London: G. Bickham).

WESTENGAARD, ERIK (2005): 'Masonic Symbolism in the Memorial Grove at Jægerspris Castle. The Importance of Understanding Masonic Symbolism in the Conservation of Private and Public Historical Gardens' KROON, BAX, & SNOEK (Eds.) (2005) 119-131.

—— (2006): 'Gedankenvolle Gärten. Eine Wanderung durch die Freimaurerische Symbolwelt dreier Gärten' SNOEK, SCHOLL, & KROON (Eds.) 263-82.

WHATELY, THOMAS (1771): *Observations on Modern Gardening* (London: T. Payne).

—— (1771): *L'Art de former les jardins modernes, ou l'art des jardins anglais*...(Paris: C. A. Jombert père).

WHISTON, WILLIAM (Tr.) (2006): see JOSEPHUS, FLAVIUS.

WHITTAKER, ALFRED (1998): 'Mineralogy and Magic Flute' *Mitteilungen der Österreichischen Mineralogischen Gesellschaft* **cxliii** 107-33.

WICHMANN, SIEGFRIED (Ed.) (1972): see HUBALA, ERICH.

WICHTL, FRIEDRICH (1919): *Weltfreimaurerei, Weltrevolution, Weltrepublik: eine Untersuchung über Ursprung und Endziele des Weltkrieges* (Munich: J. F. Lehmann). Further edns. came out in 1928, 1936, etc.

—— (1921): *Freimaurerei, Zionismus, Kommunismus, Spartakismus, Bolschewismus* (Hamburg: Deutschvolkische Verlagsanstalt).

WICKER, CECIL VIVIAN (1952): *Edward Young and the Fear of Death; a Study in Romantic Melancholy* (Albuquerque NM: University of New Mexico).

WIEBENSON, DORA (1976): 'Le Parc Monceau et ses "Fabriques"' *Les Monuments Historiques de la France* 16-19.

—— (1978): *The Picturesque Garden in France* (Princeton NJ: Princeton UP).

WIEGAND, WILFRIED (1985): see HUMBERT, JEAN-MARCEL (1985b).

WIELAND, CHRISTOPH MARTIN (1786-9): *Dschinnistan, oder auserlesene Feen- und Geister-Mährchen* (Winterthur: Heinrich Steiner). See also the new edn. HANNELORE SCHLAFFER (Ed.) (Berlin: Aufbau 2007).

WILCOX, JONATHAN, & MAGENNIS, HUGH (Eds.) (2006): *The Power of Words: Anglo-Saxon Studies Presented to Donald G. Scragg on his Seventieth Birthday. Medieval European Studies* **viii** (Morgantown WV: West Virginia UP).

WILDEROTTER, HANS (Ed.) (2006): *Schauplatz vernünftiger Menschen—Kultur und Geschichte im Anhalt-Dessau* (Dessau: Stadtmuseum).

WILKINS, EITHNE (Tr.) (1979): see MUSIL, ROBERT.

WILLIS, PETER (2002): *Charles Bridgeman and the English Landscape Garden* (Newcastle upon Tyne: Elysium Press).

—— (Ed.) (1988): see HUNT, JOHN DIXON.

WILLS, JESSE E. (1952): 'An Echo from Egypt. A History of the Building Occupied by the First Presbyterian Church, Nashville, Tennessee' *Tennessee Historical Quarterly* **xi** (March) 63-77.

WILLSON, THOMAS (c.1831): *The Pyramid. A General Metropolitan Cemetery to be Erected in the Vicinity of Primrose Hill* (London: Willson, 11 New Cavendish Street).

WILMSHURST, WALTER LESLIE (1923): *The Meaning of Masonry* (London: William Rider & Son). This book came out in many editions, including one of 1995 (New York: Grammercy Books).

—— (1948): *The Masonic Initiation* (London: John M. Watkins). A new edn. came out in 2004 (Whitefish MT: Kessinger Publishing).

WILSON, EDWARD (1987): 'The Debate of the Carpenter's Tale' *Review of English Studies* N.S. **xxxviii**/152 (November) 445-70.

WILSON, JOAN (1975): 'Little gifts keep friendship alive - An historic Sèvres dessert service' *Apollo* **cii**/161 (July) 50-60.

WILSON, THOMAS (1751): *Le Maçon Démasqué, ou Le Vrai Secret des Francs-Maçons* (London: Owen).

—— (1766): *Solomon in All His Glory: or, the Master-Mason*, etc. (London: for G. Robinson & J. Roberts). Another edn. was published in Belfast in 1772 by James Magee.

WILSON, W. DANIEL (1984): *Humanität und Kreuzzugsideologie um 1780: die 'Türkenoper im 18. Jahrhundert und das Rettungsmotif in Wielands 'Oberon', Lessings 'Nathan', und Goethes 'Iphigenie'* (New York: P. Lang).

—— (1991): *Geheimräte gegen Geheimbünde: ein unbekanntes Kapitel der klassisch-romantischen Geschichte Weimars* (Stuttgart: J.B.Metzlersche Verlagsbuchhandlung).

—— (1999): *Das Goethe Tabu: Protest und Menschenrechte im klassischen Weimar* (Munich: Deutscher Taschenbuch Verlag).

—— (1999a): *Unterirdische Gänge: Goethe, Freimaurerei, und Politik* (Göttingen: Wallstein).

—— (Ed.) (2004): *Goethes Weimar und die französische Revolution: Dokumente der Krisenjahre* (Cologne: Böhlau).

—— & HOLUB, ROBERT C. (Eds.) (1993): *Impure Reason: Dialectic of Enlightenment in Germany* (Detroit MI: Wayne State UP).

WILTON-ELY, JOHN (Ed.) (1972): see PIRANESI, GIOVANNI BATTISTA.

—— (1978a): *Piranesi* (London: Arts Council of Great Britain).

—— (1978b): *The Mind and Art of Giovanni Battista Piranesi* (London: Thames & Hudson).

WIMMER, G. A. (tr.) (1830): see RIFAUD, JEAN-JACQUES.

WINKLER, SUSANNE (Ed.) (1992): see DÜRIEGL, GÜNTER.

WINTER, EDUARD (1971): *Barock, Absolutismus und Aufklärung in der Donaumonarchie* (Vienna: Europa Verlag).

—— (1962): *Der Josefinismus: die Geschichte des österreichischen Reformkatholizmus 1740-1848* (Berlin: Rütten & Loening).

WINTERBOTTOM, MICHAEL (Ed. & Tr.) (1998-9): see MYNORS, R.A.B.

WIRTEMBERSKA, MARIA (2001): *Malvina or the Heart's Intuition* URSULA PHILLIPS (Tr.) (London: Polish Cultural Foundation).

WISCHNITZER, RACHEL BERNSTEIN (1951): *The Egyptian Revival in Synagogue Architecture*, reprinted from *Publications of the American Jewish Historical Society* **xli**/1 (September) 61-75.

—— (1955): *Synagogue Architecture in the United States; History and Interpretation* (Philadelphia PA: Jewish Publication Society of America).

—— (1964): *The Architecture of the European Synagogue* (Philadelphia PA: Jewish Publication Society of America).

WITT, REGINALD ELDRED (1970): 'The Egyptian Cults in Macedonia between Alexander and Galerius' *Balkan Studies* **xi** (Thessalonika: Institute for Balkan Studies).

—— (1971): *Isis in the Græco-Roman World* (London: Thames & Hudson).

—— (1975): 'Historical Masonry's Religious Background' *Masonic Record* **iii** (January).

WITTE, E. (1985): 'Overzicht van het onderzoek naar de Belgische vrijmetselarij in de XIXe eeuw' *Revue belge d'histoire contemporaine* **xvi**/3-4 523-42.

WITTKOWER, RUDOLF (1973): *Art and Architecture in Italy, 1600 to 1750* (Harmondsworth: Penguin).

—— (1989): 'Egypt and Europe', 'The Obelisk', 'Hieroglyphics', and 'Piranesi's Contribution to European Egyptomania' REYNOLDS, DONALD MARTIN (Ed.) 36-59, 60-93, 94-126, and 127-144.

——, & JAFFÉ, IRMA B. (1972): *Baroque Art: the Jesuit Contribution* (New York: Fordham UP).

WOJCIKOWSKI, WŁODZIMIERZ (1978): *Puławy, Kazimierz, Natęczów, and their Countryside* (Warsaw: Krajowa Agencja Wydawnicza).

WOLLIN, NILS GUSTAF AXELSSON (1939): *Desprez en Suède; sa vie et ses travaux...* (Stockholm: Bokförlags-a.-b. Thule).

WOOD, ALEXANDER, & OLDHAM, FRANK (1954): *Thomas Young, natural philosopher* (Cambridge: Cambridge UP).

WOOD, JOHN (1741): *The Origin of Building: or, the Plagiarism of the Heathens Detected* (Bath: S. & F. Farley).

WOODBRIDGE, KENNETH (1970): *Landscape and Antiquity: Aspects of English Culture at Stourhead, 1718-1838* (London: Clarendon Press).

—— (1986): *Princely Gardens: The Origins of Development of the French Formal Style* (London: Thames & Hudson).

WOODFORD, ADOLPHUS FREDERICK ALEXANDER (1871-9): see HUGHAN, WILLIAM JAMES.

—— (1874): *A Defence of Freemasonry* (London: G. Kenning).

—— (Ed.) (1872): *Freemasons' Secrets, a Portion of the Sloane MS., 3320, British Museum* (London: G. Kenning and Leeds: J. Buckton).

—— (1878a): *The Constitution Book of 1723. The Wilson MS. Constitution* (London: G. Kenning).

—— (1878b): *Kenning's Masonic Cyclopædia and Handbook of Masonic Archæology, History, and Biography* (London: G. Kenning).

WOTTON, SIR HENRY (1624): *The Elements of Architecture* (London: John Bill).

WRIGHT, DUDLEY (1931): see GOULD, ROBERT FREKE.

WURM, SYLVIA (1984): see WEINBERGER, KARL.

WYZEWA, TEODORE D., & SAINT-FOIX, G. DE (1912-46): *W. A. Mozart, sa vie musicale et son oeuvre de l'enfance à la pleine maturité* (Paris: Perrin et Cie).

YALE CLASSICAL STUDIES (from 1928): (New Haven CT: Department of Classical Studies, Yale University).

YATES, FRANCES AMELIA (1947): *The French Academies of the Sixteenth Century* (London: The Warburg Institute, University of London).

—— (1964): *Giordano Bruno and the Hermetic Tradition* (London: Routledge & Kegan Paul).

—— (1966): *The Art of Memory* (London: Routledge & Kegan Paul).

—— (1972): *The Rosicrucian Enlightenment* (London: Routledge & Kegan Paul).

—— (1975): *Astraea. The Imperial Theme in the Sixteenth Century* (London: Routledge & Kegan Paul).

—— (1979): *The Occult Philosophy in the Elizabethan Age* (London: Routledge & Kegan Paul).

YOUNG, EDWARD (1989): *Night Thoughts* STEVEN CORNFORD (Ed.) (Cambridge: Cambridge UP).

YOUNG, THOMAS (1823): *An Account of some recent discoveries in hieroglyphical literature and Egyptian antiquities* (London: J. Murray).

ZAMOYSKI, ADAM (1992): *The Last King of Poland* (London: Jonathan Cape).

ZEITSCHRIFT FÜR ÄGYPTISCHE SPRACHE UND ALTERTUMSKUNDE (from 1863): (Leipzig: J.C. Hinrichs).

ZEITSCHRIFT FÜR BILDENDE KUNST (1866-1932): (Leipzig: E.A. Seemann), but see especially 1928-1929.

ZEITSCHRIFT FÜR KUNSTGESCHICHTE (from 1932): (Berlin: De Gruyter).

ZENKERT, ARNOLD (1984): *Katalog der ortsfesten Sonnenuhren in der DDR* (Berlin-Treptow: Das Kulturbund).

ZENNER, MARIE-THÉRÈSE (Ed.) (2004): *Villard's Legacy: Studies in Medieval Technology, Science, and Art in Memory of Jean Gimpel* (Aldershot: Ashgate).

ZENTNER, WILHELM (1971): see MOZART, W. A.

ZICK-NISSEN, JOANNA (1984): see BRUNNER-TRAUT, EMMA & HELLMUT.

ZIEGLER, CHRISTIANE (1984): 'Sistrum' in *Lexikon der Ägyptologie* **v** c. 959-963.

—— (Ed.) (1994): see HUMBERT, JEAN-MARCEL ET AL. (Eds.) (1994).

—— (1996): 'L'Égypte et le décor des musées européens au XIXᵉ siècle' HUMBERT (Ed.) (1996) 139-158.

ZINNER, E. (1964): *Alte Sonnenuhren an Europäischen Gebäuden* (Wiesbaden: F. Steiner).

ŻOCHOWSKA, S. (Tr.) (1848): see RADZIWIŁŁOWA, HELENA.

ZOO ANVERS (1988): **iv** (April) 1-53 was devoted to the Egyptian temple at Antwerp Zoo, with contributions from G.J. BRAL, L. DELVAUX, G. DEMOOR, L. FORNOVILLE, B. DE GRYSE, P. MACLOT, B. VAN PUIJENBROECK, & E. WARMENBOL.

ZOO (1957): *Uitgave van de Koninklijke Maatschappij voor Dierkunde van Antwerpen*, **iii** (January) contains an article by W. VAN DEN BERGH on 'De Egyptische Tempel een Eeuw Oud' 80-83.

ZORRER, FERDINAND (1984): see WEINBERGER, KARL.

ZUCKER, PAUL (1925): *Die Theaterdekoration des Klassizismus; eine Kunstgeschichte des Bühnenbildes* (Berlin: R. Kæmmerer).

Index

Compiled by Auriol Griffith-Jones

'…the best book in the world would owe most to a good index, and the worst…., if it had but a single good thought…, might be kept alive by it….'

HORACE BINNEY (1780-1875):
Letter to Samuel Austin Allibone (8 April 1868).

Note: Page numbers in *italic* refer to illustrations; those in **bold** refer to chapter headings and those in ***bold italic*** refer to the Glossary. In dates 'reigned' or ' reigning' is abbreviated to r.

Aaron 72, ***307***
Abélard, Pierre (1079-1142), tomb 197
Abney Park Cemetery, Stoke Newington 290
Acacia 43, 46, *102*, 107, *113*, *114*, *149*, 206, 222, 302, 305, ***308***
use of wood 72
'Accepted' Masons 4, 5, 19(n), 59, 62, 119–20, ***308***
'Acception' 4, 11, 59–60
Ackermann, Rudolf (1764-1834) 303–4, *304*
Acre, fall of (1291) 56
Act of Union (1707) 61, 63
Adam, Robert (1728-92) 209
Adamberger, Johann Valentin (1740-1804) 249
Addis, William Edward (1844-1917), *A Catholic Dictionary* 291
Adoption, Lodges of 97(n), 116, 117, *162*, 214(n), ***308***
Æthelstan (893/4-939), from 924 King of the Anglo-Saxons and from 937 of England 8, 9–10
Aigen, Salzburg, Cave of the Illuminati 265
Aigner, Chrystian Piotr (1756-1841) 215
air-pump 124–5
Åkerblad, Johan David (1763-1819) 166
Alberti, Ignaz (1760-94) 253, 254, *257*, *261*, 264
Alberti, Leon Battista (1404-72) 88, 151, 210
Albon, Angélique Charlotte de Castellane, Comtesse d' (1751-*after* 1792) 190
Albon, Claude-Camille-François, Comte d' (1753-89) 190
Alchemy 26, 27, 33–4, 199, 259, 304
and *Die Zauberflöte* libretto 257–8, *257*
Aldgate, Priory, Masons' Hall at 4
Aldworth, Hon. Mrs Elizabeth (1693-1773) 115–16, *115*
Aldworth, Richard (d.1776) 115(n)
Alembert, Jean Le Rond d' (1717-83), *Preliminary Discourse* 141
Alexander I (1777-1825), from 1801 Tsar of Russia 214(n), 228
Alexander I, King of Scots (r.1107-24) 27
Alexander III, 'the Great' (356-323 BC), from 336 King of Macedon 75
Alexander VI (Rodrigo Borja y Borja [1431-1503]), from 1492 Pope 38
Alexander, Sir Anthony (d.1637), from 1629 Master of Works 32
Alexandria, Virginia 136
All-Seeing Eye 49, 52, 105, 106, *121*, 151, *151*, 242–3, ***308***
Alsace, sundials 59
Altar(s) 9, *93*, 94, 111, *114*, 242, ***308***
Herodian Temple 76, 78–9, 83
Solomon's Temple 72–4
Warning (Wörlitz) 211, *211*
Zerubbabel's Temple 75
Amenhotep III, Pharaoh (r.c.1391-c.1353 BC) 48
Amenhotep or Amenhotpe, son of Hapu, architect (c.1440-c.1350 BC) 48

Amiens, labyrinth 50
Ancient Knowledge 32, 39, 53–4, 88
Egypt as source of 19, 22, 26, 34, 38, 52–3, 62, 65, 155, 304
Freemasonry and 43, 60, 205
from Greece 22
Anderson, James (c.1679-1739) xviii, 18–19, **97**
Constitutions (1723) 63, 119
The New Book of the Constitutions of...Free and Accepted Masons (1738) 6, 41
Andreae, Johan(nes) Valentin(us) (1586-1654), *Fama* 43
Andrewes, Lancelot (1555-1626) 41
Androgynous Masonry 56(n), ***308***
Anglo-Irish Ascendancy 292
Anglo-Saxons 178, 180
Anhalt-Bernburg, Prince Franz of (b.1769) 212
Anhalt-Dessau, Johann Georg von (1748-1811) 207
Anhalt-Dessau, Leopold III Friedrich Franz (1740-1817), from 1751 r.Prince of 205–6, 212, 244
Anhalt-Dessau, Leopold IV Friedrich (1794-1871), from 1817 r.Duke of 280
Anhalt-Köthen, Duke Friedrich Ferdinand of (1769-1830) 212
Anhalt-Köthen, Duke Heinrich of (1778-1847) 212
Ankh 38, 48, *48*, 257, ***308***, *311*
Annan, Thomas (1829/30-87) 299
Anne (1665-1714), from 1702 Queen of Great Britain and Ireland 61, 63
Anne of Denmark (1574-1619), from 1589 Consort of James VI, from 1603 Queen of England, Scotland, and Ireland 24, 27-30, 53, 62
Annius (Annio) of Viterbo, Annius (1432-1502) 38
Anselmo da Campione (Anselmus) (*fl.*1171) 50
anti-clericalism 144, 145, 146
Belgium 134
France 16, 195, 196, 293
Germany 250
Poland 214
Schubert's 280
anti-Semitism 291
France 293
linked with Freemasonry 294–6, *294*, *295*, *296*
Antinoüs (c.110-30) 201–2, *233*
Antioch, pavement 159
Antiochus IV Epiphanes, Seleucid king (r.175-164 BC) 75
Antiquity
and origins of Christianity 49
rediscovery of 147, 305
see also Egypt; Greece; Rome, ancient
antis, in 131, *132*, 133, *233*, ***308***
Antonius, Marcus (Mark Antony) (c.83-30 BC) 75
Antwerp, *Les Amis du Commerce...* 134
Aphanism ***308***
Apianus, Petrus (1495-1552) 57–8
Apis-bull 35, 38, 47, *257*, *274*, ***308***
Apocrypha 65

Appiani, Giuseppe (c.1701-c.1786) *271*
Apprentices ('Entered Apprentice') 4, 5, 9, 11, 45, ***308***, ***312***
'Boaz' and 43
Degree of 6, 13, 60–1, 98, 101
instruction of 51
Reception of *99*, *112*, *114*
Aprons 61, 62, 106, *110*, *111*, 283, 298, ***308***
French Masonic *167*, *167*
Apuleius (c.125-c.175) 49
Metamorphoses 202
The Golden Ass 158, 206, ***314***
Arabi (*or* Orabi), Ahmed (1841-1911) 283(n)
Arcadia 211, 218, 220
landscape 184–6
see also Arkadia
Arch of Heaven ***308***
Arch of Masonry, motif 106
Archel(a)us, son of Herod the Great (reigned 4BC-AD6) 76
Architects
in French Freemasonry 148, 155, 160
and Masons' Company 5
Mediaeval masons as 16–17, 20
Architects' Club xvi
Architecture 12, 19–22, ***308***, ***317***
Egyptian 34, 133–5, *134*, *135*, 136–7, *137*, *139*, *139*, 301
Freemasonic motifs and allusions xxvi, xxvii, 105–7
French Order *91*, *92*, *92*
Gothic 3–4, 177
history of xvii
Islamic influences 136
links with Freemasonry xviii
Masonic Style 299–304
Scotland 24, 32
see also Classical Orders; columns; Neo-Classicism; Palladianism
Argenville, Antoine-Joseph Dézallier d' (1680-1765) 175(n)
Ariès, Philippe (1914-84) 290–1
Arithmetic 21, ***308***
Ark of the Covenant 71, 72, 73, 75, 93, ***308***
(*or* Noah's) 111
Ark of the Masonic Covenant 125–6, *125*
Arkadia, garden 215, 217–18
Amphitheatre 227–8
Chimaera fountain *220*
Circus 227, *227*, *228*, *228*
Classical Temple 223
Garden of Allusions 218–30
Gothic House 223, *223*, 225
'Greek Arch' 223–4, *224*
Grotto of the Sybil 223, *223*
High Priest's Sanctuary *220*, 221, *221*
Island of Poplars 224, *225*, *226*
Knight's Tent 224, 225
'Margrave's House' 224–5, *226*
Mythology in 220
plan *219*
'Roman Aqueduct' 224, *225*
Swiss Cottage and new village 229
Temple of Diana 221–2, *223*
Tomb of Illusions 226–7, *226*
Arms, grant of, Masons' Company (1472) 4
Arnold, Matthew (1822-88) 132
Arnold, Thomas (1823-1900) 291
Aron, Raymond (1905-83) **141**
Arouet, François-Marie *called* Voltaire (1694-1778) 14(n), 149, 183, 188
Candide 230
Olimpie 274
Arras, Matthias of (*fl.*1342-52) 50
Art, and Nature 198, 211
Art-Déco 267, 269
Artaria, Pasquale (d.1785) 249
artefacts, early Freemasonry in Scotland 55–9
Artleburgh (Attleborough), John (*fl.*1376) 3
Artemis/Diana of Ephesus 274–5, *275*
Articles of Religion, abolition of Purgatory 23
Artois, Charles-Philippe, Comte d' (1757-1836), r. 1824-30 as King Charles X of France 200

Ashlar, Rough and Perfect 105, *105*, **308–9**
Ashley, Henry Victor (1872-1945) 131, *131*, 302
Ashmole, Elias (1617-92) 5, 27, 43, 60
Assyrians 74
Astrology 37, ***309***
Astronomy 21, 24, 80, ***309***
Atlanta, Georgia 136
Aubrey, John (1626-97) 59–60
Auchinleck MS 3
Audi, Vide, Tace 121, 283, ***309***
Aufklärung (German Enlightenment) 155, 182, 211–12, 220, ***309***
Augustine, St (354-430) 21
Augustodunensis, Honorius (or Henricus) (d.c.1140) 21
Augustus, Emperor (r.27 BC-AD 14) 6
Augustus II 'The Strong' (1670-1733), r.from 1694 as Elector Friedrich August I of Saxony and 1697-1704/6 and 1709/10-33 as King of Poland 117, 230
Augustus III (1696-1763), r.from 1733 as Elector Friedrich August II of Saxony and King of Poland 117
Auschwitz-Birkenau concentration camp 94, *95*, 96, 294
Austen, Jane (1775-1817) 169
Austin, John C. (1870-1963) 136
Australia 135
Austria ***309***
Freemasonry in 143, 247–8, 249–52, 253–4, 280
National Anthems 252(n), 253
National Grand Lodge 247
see also Vienna
Babel, Tower of 8, *14*, ***309***
Babylon 6, 65, 74, 75
Bach, Johann Sebastian (1685-1750) 250
Bacon, Francis (1561-1626), *Instauratio Magna* 69
Bacon, Nathaniel (1593-1660) 178
Bagatelle, Bois de Boulogne, Paris 200
Bähr, Georg (1666-1738) 79
Baily, Edward Hodges (1788-1867) 132
Baird, John (1816-93) 298
Ballanche, Pierre-Simon (1776-1847) 161
Bankes, William John (1786-1838) 166
Barbara, St (d.235 or c.303) 31
Barbieri, Giovanni Francesco (*Il Guercino*) (1591-1666) 184
Barker, Christopher (1528/9-99) 44
Barnstaple, Devon 140, *140*
Baroque 68, 89, 92, 196, 304
and *Synthesis* 245
Barrow, Ernest Robert (1869-1948) 136
Barruel, Abbé Augustin (1741-1820) 292
Barry, Marie-Jeanne Bécu, Comtesse du (1746-93) 159
Bartolozzi, Francesco (1727-1815) xvi, 125
Bath, Somerset 84
Freemason's Hall 132–3, *133*
Batzko (Baczko), Ludwig von (1756-1823) 255
Baud, Benjamin (c.1807-75) 290
Baudard de Saint-James, Claude (1738-87) 235(n)
Bauhaus movement 96, 298
Bayle, Pierre (1647-1706) 144
Beardsley, Aubrey (1872-98) 255
Beattie, Reverend Alexander Ogilvie (1783-1858) 296(n)
Beaufort, Henry Somerset (1744-1803), from 1756 5th Duke of 121
Beaumont, Guillaume (*fl.*late 17th-early 18th century) 175(n)
Beauty 20, 262, 278, ***309***
see also Corinthian Order
Beauvais, Vincent de (d.1642) 42
Beckford, William Thomas (1760-1844) 150–1, 181
Fonthill Abbey 159–60
Bede, The Venerable (673/4-735) 81
bees and beehives 21, *121*, 271, ***309***
Beethoven, Ludwig van (1770-1827), *Fidelio* 255

347

Begemann, Georg Emil Wilhelm (1843-1914) 1–2, 7, 10
Bélanger, François-Joseph (1744-1818) 192, 200
Belgium
  'Cazin de Terlinden' at s'Gravensel 170
  Lodges 134–5, 155
Beloeil, Belgium, garden 200, 212, 244
Belzoni, Giovanni Battista (1778-1823) 129, 165–6
Bene, Adriana Ferrarese del (c.1744-after 1798) 249
Benedict XIV (1675-1758), from 1740 Pope 116-17, 150, 292
Benedict XV (1854-1922), from 1914 Pope 293
benefits 14, 60
Bérage, Chevalier de (fl.mid-18th century) 159
Berenhorst, Georg Heinrich (1733-1814) 207
Berk, Matheus Franciscus Maria (b.1938) 259
Berlin, production of *Die Zauberflöte* at 270
Berlin-Kreuzberg, Eben Mausoleum 301, *301*
Bernigeroth, Johann Martin (1713-67) 99, *100*, *101*, *104*
Bernini, Giovanni Lorenzo (1598-1680) 86, 91, 224
Besold, Christoph (1577-1649) 35
Beuther, Friedrich Christian (1777-1856) 278, *278*
Beveridge, William, Bishop of St Asaph (c.1637-1708) 7
Biberstein, Johannes Rogalla von (b.1940) 295
Bible 12, 93, **309**
  and origins of Freemasonry 8
  pillars in 65–6, 69–70
  raising of the dead 42
  references to Temple **71** 73
Binghamton, New York 136
Bischoff, Karl (1897-1950) 96
Bishopsden, Sir John (fl.14th century) 3
Bissy, Claude de Thyard, Comte de (1721-1810) 183
Bittner, Norbert (1786-1851) 277, *277*
Black 298, **309**
  Two Men in Black Armour 250, 260
Blaikie, Thomas (1750-1838) 192
Blair, Robert (1699-1746) 181–2
Blake, William (1757-1827) 51
Blazing Star 258, *271*, **309**
Blumauer, Aloys (1757-98) 251
'Boaz' 43, 48–9, 61, *112*, **309**
  Karlskirche 87–8
  pillar 67, *68*, 70
Boccaccio, Giovanni (1313-75), *Filocolo* 3
Bode, Johann Joachim Christoph (1730-93) 314
Boehmer, Charles-Auguste & Paul Bassenge, jewellers 159
Boethius, Anicius Manlius Severinus (c.480-c.524) 21
Boetzkes, Manfred 275
Böheim, Joseph Michael (1748-1811) *271*
Böhm, Johann(es) Heinrich (fl.1745-92) 247
Boisselier, Antoine-Félix (1790-1857) *197*, *198*
Boizot, Simon-Louis (1743-1809) 284
Bolívar, Simón (1783-1830) 304
Bomarzo, Viterbo, garden 202–3
Bonaparte, Joseph (1768-1844), Joint Grand Master of the Grand Orient (from 1804) 167, 192
Bonaparte, Louis (1778-1846) 167, *167*, 192
Bonaparte, Napoléon (1759-1821), Emperor (1804-14 and 1815) of the French 284, *285*
  and Duchy of Warsaw 217–18
  Egyptian Campaign (1798-1801) 163, 166, 284
Bond, Sir Edward Augustus (1815-98) 7
Bondoni, Giotto di (1267-1337) 50
bondsmen and bondage 11–12
Bonduelle, Paul (1877-1955) 134
Bone 41, **309**
  see also marrow-bone
Bonomi, Joseph, Jr. (1796-1878) 133–4, 290
Book of Constitutions (1723) xviii, **308**
Book of Constitutions (1784) 125

Book of the Law 106, **309**
Bordelon, Abbé Laurent (1653-1730), *La Coterie des Anti-Façonniers* 153
Born, Ignaz Edler von (1742-91) 247, 248, 251, 255
  'Egyptian Mysteries' 256
Borromeo, St Charles (1538-84) 87
Borromini, Francesco (1599-1667) 90
Boston, Lincolnshire, Freemasons' Hall 133–4, *134*
Böttger, Johann Friedrich (1682-1719) 117
Bouchard, Pierre-François-Xavier (1772-1832) 165(n)
Boullée, Étienne-Louis (1728-99) 152–3, 160, 305
Bourgeois, Constant (1767-1841) 192, *193*, *194*
Bourget, Paul-Charles-Joseph (1852-1935), *Le Démon du Midi* 305
'Bouville', 'Comte de' 169
Bovinet, Edmé (1767-1832) 153
Boyle, Richard (1694-1753), from 1704 3rd Earl of Burlington and 4th Earl of Cork 29, 143–4, 179
Boyle, Robert (1627-91) 61, 124
Bradshaw, Henry (d.1513), *The Holy Lyfe… of Saynt Werburge* 3
Brahe, Tycho (1546-1601) 27, 80
Bralle, François-Jean (1750-c.1832) 284, 285
Bretzner, Christoph Friedrich (1748-1807) 3(n)
Bridge, motif 106
Bridgeman, Charles (d.1738) 175, 176
Brifaut, Charles (1781-1857) 274
Brillat-Savarin, Jean-Anthelme (1755-1826) 169
Brodziński, Kazimierz (1791-1835) 215
Brongniart, Alexandre-Théodore (1739-1815) 191–2, *193*, 260
  and cemeteries 196
brooch *111*
Brown, Alexander Burnett (1867-1948) 131, 136
Brown, Lancelot 'Capability' (1716-83) xv, 144, 175
Browne, Sir Thomas (1605-82) **33**, **281**
Brugge, *Temple de la Flandre* 134
Brühl, Karl Friedrich Moritz Paul, Graf von (1772-1837) 267
Bruno, Giordano (1548-1600) 35, 38–9, 52, 143, 291
Brussels
  Grand Temple of the *Amis Philanthropes* Lodge 134
  Grote Temple 134
Bry, Johann Theodore De (1566-1623) 37
Bryce, David (1803-76) 298(n)
Buch, David Joseph (b.1950) 256, 259, 280(n)
Bunning, James Bunstone (1802-63) 290
Buondelmonte of Florence, Cristofero (c.1375-c.1435) 22
Büren, Nikolaus von (d.1445) 51
burials
  in gardens 186, 188–92, 209
  grave markers 43, 56
  at night 183–4
  see also cemeteries; Death
Burke, Edmund (1729-97) 153
Burlington, Lord *see* Boyle, Richard
Burn, William (1789-1870) 298(n)
Burns, Robert (1759-96) 254, *262*
Buscheto (Busketus, Boschetto) (fl.1063-1110), architect of Pisa 51
Busink, Th. A (1898-1980) 94(n)

Cabbala 35, 304, **309**
Cabiri 47, 48, 49, **309**
Cadogan, Charles Sloane (1728-1807), from 1800 1st Earl xv
Caduceus 37, 92, *261*, **309**
'Cagliostro' (Guiseppe Balsamo) (1743-95) 150, 170, 200, **309**
  'Egyptian Rite' 158–9
Cahill, Reverend Edward, SJ (1868-1941) 291–2
Cahusac, Jean-Louis de (1706-59) 265–6
Caithness, lighthouse 286
Calcidius (4th cent AD) 21
Callebout, Ernest (1887-1952) 134
Calvin, John (1509-64) 79
Calvinism
  and imagery 59–60
  in Scotland 16, 24, 53

Cambacérès, Jean-Jacques Régis, Duc de Parme (1753-1824), Joint Grand Master of the Grand Orient of France (1805-14) 167, 192
Cambridge, Prince George William Frederick Charles (1819-1904), from 1850 2nd Duke of 289
Camillo, Giulio (c.1480-1544) 41
Campbell, Colen (1676-1729) 29
  Vitruvius Britannicus 179
candles 98, 112
candlesticks 101, 112, 147
Canopus 159
  at Tivoli 201, 228
Canterbury Lodge 116, *116*
Capella, Martianus Minneus Felix (5th cent AD) 8(n), 21
Carabelli, Francesco (1737-98) 235
Carden, George Frederick (1798-1874) 288
Cardinal Virtues 100, 120, **310**
Carlisle, Charles Howard (1674-1738), from 1692 3rd Earl of 176
Carlone, Carl(o) Martin(o) (1616-79) 267(n)
Carmontelle *see* Carrogis
Carpenter's trade 9
Carrogis, Louis, known as 'Carmontelle' (1717-1806) 186
Carson, Sir Edward Henry (1854-1935) 292
Cary, John (1755-1835) 140
Cary, William (1759-1825) 140
Casanova de Seingalt, Giovanni Giacomo (1725-98) 159
Casley, David (1681/2-1754) 7
Cassiodorus, Magnus Aurelius (c.490-585) 21
Castle Howard, Yorkshire 176, *176*, 184
catacombs 195, *196*, 271, 290
cathedrals, Mediaeval xxiii, 12, 14, 16, 50
Catherine II, 'The Great' (1729-96), from 1762 Empress of Russia 214(n)
'Catholic Enlightenment', Vienna 251
Caus, Salomon de (1576-1626) 37, 38, 203
Cave, Walter Frederick (1863-1939) 131
Cecil, Sir Robert (1563-1612), from 1605 1st Earl of Salisbury 28
Celis, Marcel M. (b.1950) 136
cemeteries 288–90
  emergence of 195–7
  see also memorials
Cephas 69, **310**
certificates 119–20
  French *157*, *158*
Chailley, Jacques (1910-99) 255, 256, 259, 280
Chalgrin, Jean-François-Thérèse (1739-1811) 148
Chalk, Charcoal, Clay 46, 99, 104, **310**
Chamberlain, Houston Stewart (1855-1927) 94–5
Chambers, Ephraim (c.1680-1740) 19
  Cyclopaedia 144–5
Chambers, Sir William (1723-96) 239
Chamoust, Ribart de (fl.1776-83) 91, 92
Champollion, Jean-François (1790-1832) 165–6
  obelisk for 197
Chantrey, Sir Francis Leggatt (1781-1841) 132, 281, *282*
Chantries 16, 23
Chapiter 58, 66, 70, 73–4, 79, **310**
  'lily-work' 139, *139*, 140
Charges 4, 6–10, 12, 18, **310**
  Hermetic Rite in 39
  pillars 65, 66
  and ritual 61
  Scotland 26
Charity 45–6, **310**
Charlemagne (Karl der Grosse—742/3-814), from c.768 King of the Franks, and from 800 Emperor 88
Charles Edward Stuart, the 'Young Pretender' or 'Bonnie Prince Charlie' (1720-88), from 1766 styled Charles III 61, 145
Charles I (1600-49), from 1625 King of England, Scotland, and Ireland 28, 29
Charles II (1630-85), from 1660 King of England, Scotland, and Ireland 7
Charles V (1500-58), r.from 1518 as Charles I of Spain and 1519/20-1555/6 as Holy Roman Emperor 69, 88

Charles VI (1685-1740), from 1711 Holy Roman Emperor 87
Charles XII (1682-1718) from 1697 King of Sweden 117
Charney, Gaufrid (Geoffroi) de (d.1314) 56(n)
Charney, Melvin (b.1935) 94, *95*
Chartres, Cathedral 50, *50*, 149
Chasseboeuf, Constantin-François, Comte de Volney (1757-1820) 166
Châtillon, Gaspard de, Comte Coligny (1519-72) 144, 192, 209
Chatillon, Sébastien (1515-63) 80
Chaux
  church *161*
  Ledoux's designs 151–3, *151*, *152*, *153*, 160–2
  Oikéma 163
  Panarêthéon 162
  Temple of Memory 162
Chesterfield, Philip Dormer Stanhope (1694-1773), from 1726 4th Earl of 62
Chetwode Crawley, William John (1843-1916) 18–19
Chiarini, Luigi (1789-1832) 295(n)
chisel 14, *109*, **310**
Chiswick, St Nicholas church 160
Christian IV (1577-1648) from 1588 King of Denmark and Norway 28
Christianity 22
  and religion of Egyptians 38, 48–9
  see also Protestantism; Roman Catholic Church
Christie, James (1773-1831) 129
Christina (1629-89), Queen of Sweden (1632-54) 87
Chronicles of Jerameel, The 66
Church of Scotland, and Freemasonry 25
Churchill, Winston Leonard Spencer (1874-1965) 294, *295*
churchyards
  urban 195
  see also cemeteries
Cicero, Marcus Tullius (106-43 BC) **33**
Cincinnati, Ohio 136
Ciołek, Gerard Antoni (1909-66) 224
Cipriani, Giovanni Battista (1727-85) xvi, 122, 124
Circumambulation 199, **310**
City of London
  Common Council 2, 3
  London Letter-Books 3
  Plea and Memoranda Rolls 3
City Viewers, Master Masons as 4
Claremont House, Esher xvi
Clark, Peter (b.1944) xvii
Classical Orders 65, 105, 120, *120*, 149–53
  Composite 105(n), 127, **310**
  Corinthian 70, 105, 120, 126, 262, **310**
  Doric 65, 70, 262, **310**
  Ionic 70, 120, *315*, **315**
  Paestum Doric (Greek) 150, 302–3, *317*, **317**
  Tuscan *321*, **321**
Classicism, political significance of 177–8
Claudius, Matthias (1740-1815) 256(n)
Clemens, Titus Flavius (c.150-211/16) 22
Clement V (c.1260-1314), from 1305 Pope 55-6
Clement VIII (1536-1605), from 1592 Pope 52
Clement XII (1652-1740), from 1730 Pope 150
  attack on Freemasonry 116, 292
Clérisseau, Charles-Louis (1721-1820) 209, 216(n)
Clinton & Russell 136
Clochard, Pierre (1774-before 1855) 163, *198*, *300*
clocks and watches, Masonic 300, *301*
Closing 252, **310**
Coalbrookdale, Iron Bridge 206, *206*
Cobham, Richard Temple (1675-1749), from 1718 1st Viscount 176, 180
Cochin, Charles-Nicolas II (1715-90) 145
Cockerell, Charles Robert (1788-1863) 130
Cockerell, Frederick Pepys (1833-78) 130–1, *130*
coffin, as motif *100*, *107*, *113*, **310**
Cohn, Norman (1915-2007) 96, 296
Colchester, Essex xviii
Coldham, Gabriel, mason (fl.early 16th century) 3

Colman, George, the elder (c.1732-94) xxiii
Cologne Cathedral 51
Colonna, Francesco (1433-1527) 202
Colonna, Pompeo (1479-1532) 38
Colours 33, *310*
columns *310*
 broken xxvi, 149, *309*
 Classical Orders of Architecture 120, 120, 126
 definition 65–70
 djed 48, *48*, 135
 as emblem 69, 88
 Freemasons' Hall, Dublin 139
 in antis 131, *132*, 133, 233, *308*
 interpretations of 68
 in porticos *318*, *318*
 St Vincent Street Church, Glasgow 298
 in Solomon's Temple 73
 and spirals 68, 88, 91–2, *173*
 square 303
 Warden's 70
 see also Boaz; Jachin; Pillars
Columns, Two 65–70, 106, 152
Colvin, Sir Howard Montagu (1919-2007) 195(n)
Comacine School of masons 68
Comber, County Down 137
 Gillespie monument 281–2, *282*, *283*
Comenius (Johann Amos Komensky) (1592-1670) 35–6
Comestor, Peter (d.c.1185) 21
 Historia Scholastica 66
Commonwealth (1649-1660) 62–3
Como, City of, *Broletto* 68
Como, Lake 68
compass, points of 68, 107
compasses *105*, *109*, *283*, *310*
 motif 35, 51, 106, 107, 112, 300
Composite Order 105(n), 127, *310*
Compton, Charles (d.1755) 116
Connaught and Strathearn, Prince Arthur (1850-1942), from 1874 1st Duke of 131
Conroy, Sir John Ponsonby, Bt (1786-1854) 289
Constantine I 'The Great' (c.285/8-337), from 306 Augustus, and from 324 Emperor 76
Constantinople
 Hagia Sophia 90
 Sack of (1453) 22
Constitutiones Artis Geometrie Secundum Euclidem 6–7
Constitutions of Masonry *see* Old Charges
Cook, Captain James (1728-79) 192, *193*
Cooke, Matthew (d.1883) 6
 Cooke MS 6, 7, 18, 21, 66
Cooper, Robert Leslie Day (b.1952) 69
Cooper, Sir Thomas Edwin (1874-1942) 132(n)
Cope, Sir Arthur Stockdale (1857-1940) 132
Copernicus (Nicolaus Koppernigk) (1473-1543) 61
Copland, Robert (fl.1508-47) 40
Corbett, Harvey Wiley (1873-1954) 136
Corinthian Order 70, 105, 120, 126, 262, *310*
 Greek 105(n), *311*
 Roman 105(n), *311*
Corn, Ear of 106, *312*
Cornford, Stephen (*Editor*) 182
Cornucopia *121*, 258, *310*
Coudray, Clemens Wenzeslaus (1775-1845) 301(n)
Counter-Reformation 32, 38, 42
Court de Gébelin, Antoine (1725-84) 147, 148, 190, *191*
 Monde Primitif 129, 149, *316*
Coustos, John (1703-46) 116
Cóvens, Jean (Johannes) (1697-1774) 83
Cowans (non-Freemasons) xxiv, 46, *310*
 Scotland 2, 25
Cowley, Abraham (1618-67) 40, 184
Craft of Masonry xxiv, 4, 12, *310*
 mythology 6, 12, 60
 Scotland 2, 24–5
 craftsmanship 9
Craig, James (1871-1940) 292
Crispin and Crispianus, Sts (d.c.285) 30
Cromarty, lighthouse 286
Cross charged with Rose 42, *311*
Cross, Frank Moore (1921-97) 94(n)
crosses
 Templar 56

types *311*
Crossle, Francis Clements (1847-1910), Masonic Notes 281
Croxton, John (fl.1411-47), mason 3
Crusader Kingdom, collapse of 56
Cryer, Revd Neville Barker (b.1924) 140
crypts 237
cube 38, 124, *311*
cubits 66(n), 71–3, 155, *311*
Cumberland, Prince William Augustus (1721-65), from 1726 Duke of 122
Cynocephalus 35, *311*
Cyrus 'the Great', Pasargadian King, founder of the Persian Empire (r.c.559-529 BC) 75
Czartoryska, Princess Antonina (1728-46) 214(n)
Czartoryska, Princess Izabela (*née* Fleming) (1746-1835) 214, 215, 216, 222
Czartoryski, Prince Adam Jerzy (1770-1861) 215
Czartoryski, Prince Adam Kazimierz (1734-1823) 214(n)
Czartoryski family 216

Daedalus 49, 50
Daladier, Édouard, French Prime Minister (1884-1970) 294
Dalkeith, Francis Scott (1694-1751), from 1704/5 Earl of 119
Dampier, William (1652-1715) 112
Darius I, 'The Great', King of Persia (r.522-486 BC) 73, 74, 75
Darkness 47, 98, 216, 263, 280, 285, *312*
Darmstadt, Germany, *Herrengarten* 188
Darwin, Charles Robert (1809-82), *Origin of Species* 53
Dashwood, Sir Francis (1708-81) 119(n)
Davies, Malcolm (1952-2010) 285(n)
Davioud, Gabriel-Jean-Antoine (1824-81) 284
Dawkins, Peter (b.1945) 69
Dead, Cult of the 196
Dead, raising of 41–2, *101*, 106–7
Death
 concepts of xxvi–xxvii, 181–5
 as Eternal Rest 196
 iconography of 213–14, 286, 290
 Masonic symbolism of 52, 100, 149, 222, 264, 298
 representations of 149, *149*, *251*, *305*
 shrine of, Arkadia 221–2
 taming of/victory over 49, 196–7, 264, 265
 Temples of 160, 221–2
 see also burials
Debs, Eugene Victor (1855-1926) 142
Deconstructivism 20
Dee, John (1527-1609) 20, 27, 35
Degrees of Freemasonry 25–6, 43–4, 61, 97, 98, 105–7, *312*
Deism 25, 64, 142, 251
Dejaco, Walther (1909-78) 96
Delille, Jacques (1738-1813) *197*, *198*, 229
 Les Jardins 188–9, 215
Denon, Baron Dominique Vivant (1747-1825) 133, 163, 165
 Point de lendemain 217
 Voyage 217, 268, 273, 274, *274*
Dent, Edward Joseph (1876-1957) 279
Derrida, Jacques (1930-2004) 149
Desaguliers, John Theophilus (1683-1744) 6, 62, 64, 119, 145–6
Desanges, Louis William (1822-87) 305
Descartes, René (1596-1650) 188
Désert de Retz, France 199
Desprez, Louis-Jean (1743-1804) 250, *251*
Dessau, new cemetery 213–14, *213*, 301
Detroit, Michigan 136
Dézallier d'Argenville, Antoine-Joseph (1680-1765) 175(n)
Diamond Necklace, Affair of 159
Dickson, Alexander (1558-c.1604) 52, 53
Diderot, Denis (1713-84), *Encyclopédie* 79, 141–2, 145, 167
Diederichs, Eugen (1867-1930) 205
Dietrich, Friedrich Christoph (1779-1847) 268
Dietrichstein, Johann Baptist, Graf von (1728-1808) 247
Dieulafoy, Joseph-Marie Armand Michel (1762-1833) 274
Diocletian (c.240-c.312), Emperor (284-

305) 8
Diodorus Siculus (1st century BC) 22, 157
Djed columns 48, *48*, 135
Dods, Marcus (1834-1909) 21(n)
Dodsley, Robert (1703-64) 185
Domvile, Sir Barry Edward (1878-1971) 291
Donne, John (1572-1631) 41
Doric Order 65, 70, 262, *312*
 Greek Paestum 150, 302–3, *317*, *317*
Douai, Masonic Temple 135
Douglas, George Norman (1868-1952) 40, 185
Doyle, Sir Arthur Ignatius Conan (1859-1930) *307*
Dresden, *Frauenkirche* 79
Dreyfus, Alfred (1859-1935) 293
drinking 63
Duad 259, 282, *312*
Dublin
 Freemasons' Hall 139, *139*, *140*, 155
 Wellington Testimonial, Phoenix Park 283–4, *284*
Duboy, Philippe 169
Duchamp, Marcel (1887-1968) 169
Dugourc, Jean-Demosthène (1749-1825) 199–200
Dunfermline
 Abbey 36
 Palace and Abbey 27, 28, 29
Durie, John (1537-1600) 36
Durie, Robert (1556-1616) 36
Dury, John (1596-1680) 36

Eadwine (Edwin), the Æthling (d.993) 10
East 98, 107, 148, *312*
Eben, Franz Ephraim (1727-1804) 301
Eben, Johann Ephraim (1748-1805) 301
Ebert, Johann Arnold (1723-1804) 182
Eckert, Eduard Emil (1723-95) 96
eclecticism 143, 153, 190, 241
Edgehill, Warwickshire 180
 Gothick Tower 177, *177*
Edinburgh
 Holyrood Palace 27
 Masonic Hall, Queen Street 136, *137*, 155
Edward II (1284-1327), from 1307 King of England and Lord of Ireland 56
Edward IV (1442-83), from 1461 King of England and Lord of Ireland 8
Edward VII (1841-1910), from 1901 King of Great Britain and Ireland and Emperor of India 131
 as Grand Master 305, *306*
Egerton MS 3
Egmond aan Zee 285
Egypt 8, 9, 12, 21–2
 connections with Freemasonry xxv–xxvi, 8–9, 12, 25–6, 43, 159
 cults and religion 22, 34, 35, 46–9, 52, 157, 222, 304
 and Lost Wisdom (hidden knowledge of) 19, 22, 26, 34, 38, 52–3, 62, 65, 155, 304
 Napoléon's Campaign (1798-1801) 163, 166, 284
 and origins of Christianity 38, 48–9
 Renaissance interest in 22, 34–5
 see also 'Hermetic' tradition
Egyptian (Egyptianising) architecture 34, 133–5, *134*, 135, 136–7, *137*, 139, *139*, 301
 in *Die Zauberflöte* 247, 256–7, 267–80
 in gardens 159, 203, 222
 motifs 57, 155, 160, 167
 in Neo-Classical architecture 153–60
Egyptian Mysteries 35, 146, *312*
Egyptian Revival xxv, 155, 217
Egyptian Rite 158–9, 170, 200, 252, 286
Egyptology 90, 160, 163, 166–7
Egyptomania 283–4
Eleusinian Mysteries 147, 235–6, 263, *312*
Elisabeth Augusta (1721-94), Electress Palatine, Consort of Elector Karl Theodor 232
Elizabeth I (1533-1603), from 1558 Queen of England and Ireland 35
Elizabeth, Princess (1596-1662), from 1613 Electress Palatine and (1619-20) 'Winter' Queen of Bohemia 29, 36-7, 42
Ellingford, Herbert Frederick (1876-1966) 279

Elliott, Brent (b.1952) **175**
Elwes, Simon Vincent Edmund Paul (1902-75) 132
Élysée 186, 188, 192
Élysian Fields 176, 184, 185, 225–6, 301
emblems xxvi, 24, 34, 47, *312*
 as aid to memory 39, 40, 148
 All-Seeing Eye 151, 242
 in architecture 120, 122, 300
 Christian 52
 columns 69, 88, 148, *283*
 French 152–3, 271
 Harpocrates 42
 Masonic, on buildings 137
 on memorials 57, *283*
 and symbols 120
 on tracing boards 98–113
 see also imagery; motifs
Encyclopaedism 145
Engel, Johann Jakob (1741-1802) 255
Engel, Leopold (1858-1931) 264
England, origins of constitution 178
English Civil War 61, 62
Enlightenment, the xvii, 264, *312*
 'Catholic' (Vienna) 251
 in France 61, 96, 128, 171, 173, 199
 German (*Aufklärung*) 155, 182, 211–12, 220
 'Josephinian' 250, 253, 256
 and rediscovery of Antiquity 147, 305
 and science 124–5
 Scottish 144, 155
 and separation of theological and political theory 144–5, 171
 see also Diderot; *Philosophes*
Enoch 21, *312*
Entered *see* Apprentices
Enthüllte Welt-Freimaurerei 295, 296
Epstein, Wenzel Tobias (1758-1824) 249, 254, 261
Erdmannsdorff, Friedrich Wilhelm, Freiherr von (1736-1800) 205, 209, 212–13, 301
Erlach, Johann Bernhard Fischer von (1695-1742) 143
 Karlskirche, Vienna 152
 and Temple 85–7, *87*, *88*, 89
Erlach, Joseph Emanuel Fischer von (1656-1723) 91
Ermenonville, France 186, *187*, 188, *188*, 209
 Île des Peupliers 186, *187*, 188
Ertl, Friedrich Karl (1908-c.1990) 96
Este, Cardinal Ippolito d' (1509-72) 203
Esterházy family 267
Esterházy von Galántha, Count Franz (Ferenc) known as 'Quinquin' (1715-85) 249
Esterházy von Galántha, Count Franz Seraphim (Ferenc Szeráf, son of 'Quinquin') (1753-1815) 253
Esterházy von Galántha, Johann (János) Baptist ('Red John') (1748-1800) 253
Esterházy von Galántha, Count Johann Nepomuk (1754-1840) 253, 261
Esterházy von Galántha, Count Nikolaus Josef 'The Magnificent' (Miklós József—1714-90, styled 'Prince' from 1783) 253, 154, 261, 267(n)
Esterházy von Galántha, Prince Nikolaus (Miklós II—1765-1833) 267(n)
Esterházy von Galántha, Prince Nikolaus (Miklós III—1817-94) 267(n)
Estienne, Robert (c.1503-59) 79
Etlin, Richard (b.1947) 184
Étupes, France, garden 203
Euclid (c.325-250 BC) 6, 8, 12, 21
 47th Proposition (motif) 105, *106*, *313*
Eugen, Prince of Savoy (1662-1736) 61, 87, 143
Europe
 Freemasonry in xxvii–xxviii, 59, 61–2, 63, 142–9
 Scotland and 24
Eyserbeck, Johann Friedrich (1734-1818) 205
Ezekiel, prophet (fl.c.593-573 BC) 80, 241, 244
 and temple 74–5, 94

Faber, Pater Ignaz (fl.1790) 254, 261
fabriques (garden edifices) 190, 195, 199–201, 202–3
 at Arkadia 218, 228
 at Maupertuis 209
 at Puławy 215, 216

at Schwetzingen 232
façades, windowless 133
Faith 312
   Three Steps of 105
Falkirk, Palace of 24
Farnese, Giulia (d.1557) 202–3
Farquhar, George (1679-1707), *Harry Wildair* 184
Favart, Charles-Simon (1710-92) 246
Favart, Marie-Justine Benoîte (1727-72) 246
Fellow Craft 312
   Degree of 25–6, 43–4, 61, 97, 98, 105–7, 109, 312
Fénelon, François de Salignac de la Mothe (1651-1715) 145
Ferguson, James (1710-76) 142
feudalism 11
Ficino, Marsilio (1433-99) 22, 35
Fielding, Henry (1707-54) 1–2
Finch, Daniel (1647-1730), from 1682 2nd Earl of Nottingham and from 1729 7th Earl of Winchilsea 5
Fitler (Fittler), James (1758-1835) 125
Fitzgerald, Augustus Frederick (1791-1874), from 1804 3rd Duke of Leinster 64
Fitzgibbon, Gerald, Lord Justice (1837-1909) 64
Five Points of Fellowship 41, 43, 45, 60
Flanders, Guilds of stonemasons 64
Fleming, Count Jerzy Detloff (1699-1771) 214(n)
Flitcroft, Henry ('Burlington Harry') (1679-1769) 176
floor cloths 100, 104–5, 310
floor plans 113, 114, 312
   chalked or marked 98, 99
Florence Cathedral 50
Floris and Blancheflour 3
Fludd, Robert (c.1574-1637) 35
Fokke, Simon (1712-84) 101(n)
Fontana, Carlo (1638-1714) 86
Fonthill Abbey, Wiltshire 159
Förderer, Andreas Johannes (b.1971) 234
Forrest, Richard (fl.1820s-1840s) 289(n)
Forster, Harold Bagley (1913-85) 183
Fortrose, lighthouse 286
Foster, John (c.1787-1846) 289
Foucault, Michel (1926-84) 170
Fouquet, Jean (c.1415/20-c.1481) 91
Fouquier (Foucquier), Jacques (1590/1-1659) 37
Four Crowned Martyrs (Quatuor Coronati) 8, 31, 140, 241, 313
Fourier, François-Marie-Charles (1772-1837), *Phalanstère* 160–1, 305
Fourier, Joseph (1768-1830) 166
Fowler, William (1560/1-1612) 53
France 313
   attacks on Freemasonry 293
   burial of Protestants at night 183–4
   cemeteries 195–7
   Egyptian Rite 159
   Enlightenment in 61, 96, 128, 171, 173, 199
   'exposures' 101–3, 101, 102, 103, 104
   fascination with Egypt 153, 166–7
   Freemasonry 63, 146–9, 199
   government poster (1941) 294, 295
   Lodges 135, 135, 148–9
   masonic literature 100–1
   Ordre des Sophisiens 163
   Philosophes 61, 94–5, 141–2, 143, 250
   stonemasons (*Compagnonages*) 14, 15, 16, 64
   Vichy Government 294
   'Youngism' in 182, 183
   see also Ermenonville; Franconville; Maupertius; Paris
Francis, John (1780-1861) 132
Franconville-la-Garenne 189, 190–1, 190, 191, 192
Frankl, Paul (1878-1962) 51
Franklin, Benjamin (1706-90) 147, 148, 254
Franz I (1708-65), from 1729 Duke of Lorraine, from 1735 Grand Duke of Tuscany, from 1736 Consort of Maria Theresia, and from 1745 Holy Roman Emperor 61-2, 247
Franz II (1768-1835), Holy Roman Emperor 1792-1806, and 1804-35 Emperor of Austria 254
Frazer, John (fl.1838-93) 283(n)
Frederick II (1534-88), from 1536 King of Denmark and Norway 27
Frederick Lewis (1707-51), from 1729 Prince of Wales 64
Frederick V (1596-1632), Elector Palatine of the Rhine 1610-22, and (1619-20) 'Winter' King of Bohemia 29, 36–7, 42, 203, 230
Freemason 313
   first occurrence of word 3
   as 'free' of a Guild 4–11
   as itinerant craftsmen 11–16
   origins and definitions of word 1–17
   as specialist mason working with freestone 1–4
Freemasonry 313
   as Brotherhood 64, 309
   connection with Mediaeval stonemasons 64
   Craft of xxiv, 4, 12, 310
   degrees of 25–6, 43–4, 61, 97, 98, 109, 312
   early 'histories' of 6–8
   historians of xxiii–xxv, 7–8
   hostility to xxiv, xxviii, 290–6
   and Jews 95–6, 291, 294–6, 294, 295, 296
   and landscape gardens 198–9, 244, 300
   liberal Whig strand 142, 144, 146
   links with Templars 56–7
   and Neo-Classicism 149–53, 301
   as philosophy 25, 26
   religiosity of 143
   Republican strand 144
   Royalist Stuart strand 144
   secrecy of xxiv, xxvii
   as society of men 97
   as subversive in Europe 62
   see also 'Accepted' Masons; Operative Masons; Speculative Masonry
Freemasons' Hall, first (Queen Street) xvi, 120–32, 122, 125
   Council Chamber xxv, 126–8, 126, 127
Freemasons' Hall, new (Cockerell's) 130–2, 130, 131
   Library and Museum 300
   sculptures 132
Freemasons' halls
   Bath 132–3, 133
   Boston 133–4, 134
   Dublin 139, 139, 140, 155
   Edinburgh 136, 137, 155
   Ulster 137, 139
   see also Lodges
Freemasons' Tavern, London xvi, 121, 122, 123, 124, 288
   new 130–1, 131
freestone, definition 1–2, 10
French Army, Freemasonry in 284–5
French Revolution 170–1, 254
Frey, Jan Zachariasz (1769-1829) 224, 224
Friedrich August I 'The Strong' (1670-1733), from 1694 Elector of Saxony, 1697-1704/6 and 1709/10-33 King (Augustus II) of Poland 117
Friedrich August I (1750-1827), *see* Friedrich August III of Saxony
Friedrich August II (1696-1763), from 1733 Elector of Saxony and King (Augustus III) of Poland 117
Friedrich August III (1750-1827), from 1763 Elector of Saxony, in 1806 assumed title of King Friedrich August I of Saxony, created Duke of Warsaw (r.1807-14) by Napoléon 218
Friedrich I 'The Great' (1712-86), from 1740 King of Prussia 250-1
Friedrich Wilhelm II (1744-97), from 1786 King of Prussia 255
Friedrich, Caspar David (1774-1840) 182
Frochot, Nicolas-Thérèse-Benoît, Comte (1761-1828) 186, 195
Fuller, Thomas (1608-61) 55
Fulwood, William (fl.1560-93) 40
Fuzellier, Louis (1672-1752) 265

'G' motif 106, 258–9, 283, 283, 313
Gaitte, Antoine-Joseph (1752-c.1838) 155
Galle, Philipp (1537-1612) 89
Gallonio, Fr. Antonio (d.1605) 142(n)
Gandy, Joseph Michael (1771-1843) 126, 127, 127, 128
Garden of Allusions 40, 144, 200, 201, 202, 203, 300
   Arkadia (Poland) 218–30
   at Wörlitz 204, 205–14
Garden, Francis (1721-93), from 1764 Lord Gardenstone 183
gardens xxviii, 175–203
   burials in 186, 188–92
   English landscape 175–7, 180–1
   follies 179
   iconography of design 37–8
   mazes 50
   memorials in 184–5, 186, 188–92
   mysterious Paris 150, 150
   symbolism in 205, 300
   Tivoli 201–2
   see also Arkadia; *fabriques*; landscape; Puławy; Schwetzingen
Garfield, James Abram, US President (1831-81) 286, 287, 288
Garth, Major General Thomas (1744-1828) 289
Garway, Herefordshire 56
Gassmann, Florian (1729-74) 260(n)
gauge 109
Gaulle, General Charles de (1890-1970) 294–5, 295
Gaume, Monsignor Jean-Joseph (1802-79) 291
gavel 107, 109, 313
   see also mallet
Gazzaniga, Giuseppe (1743-1818), *Circe* 259
Geary, Stephen (1797-1854) 290
Gebler, Tobias Philipp, Freiherr von (1726-86), *Thamos: König in Ägypten* 246–7, 248, 256
Gellée, Claude (Le Lorrain(e)) (1600-82) 181
Gemmingen-Hornberg, Otto Heinrich, Freiherr von (1755-1836) 248, 251, 267
General Cemetery Company 288, 289
Geography 106
Geometry 6, 8–9, 12, 18, 20–2, 63, 106, 129, 155, 238, 313
   treatises on 60, 80, 147, 163
George I (1660-1727), from 1698 Elector Georg Ludwig of Hanover and from 1714 King of Great Britain and Ireland 61, 63, 119, 179
George II (1683-1760), from 1727 Elector of Hanover and King of Great Britain and Ireland 116
George IV (1762-1830), from 1762 Prince of Wales, and from 1820 King of Great Britain and Ireland and of Hanover xv, xvi, 70
Germany 313–14
   anti-Freemasonry views 96
   early Masons (*Steinmetzen*) in 13–14, 13, 64
   'English' gardens 188
   Freemasonry in 212, 247, 251
   landscape gardens 204–45
   Nazi propaganda leaflet (1943) 294–5, 295
   Roman Catholicism 230
   and Rome 177–8
   Schloss Pillnitz 143
   see also Schwetzingen; Weimar; Wörlitz
Gessner, Salomon (1730-88) 188
   Idyllen 185–6
Gibbs, James (1682-1754) 176, 176, 180
Gibraltar, Straits of, Pillars of Hercules 69, 70
Giesecke, Johann Georg Karl Ludwig (1761-1833), *otherwise* Johann Georg Metzler, *called* Sir Charles Lewis Giesecke xxvi, 252-3, 261
   and *Die Zauberflöte* 257
Gilbert, Walter (1871-1946) 292
Gillespie, Major-General Sir Robert Rollo (1766-1814) 281–3, 282, 283
Gilly, Friedrich (1772-1800) 288, 301
Girardin, René-Louis, Marquis de (1735-1808) 186, 209
Girardin, Stanislas-Cécile-Xavier-Louis, Comte de Girardin, Vicomte d'Ermenonville (1762-1827) 188
Glasgow
   Caledonia Road Church 296–7
   Necropolis 289, 297
   Queen's Park Church 296, 297
   St Vincent Street Church 132(n), 296–7, 298, 299
Globe 70, 105, 283, 314
   winged 133, 135, 303
Gluck, Christoph Willibald, Ritter von (1714-87) 247
Glyndbourne Festival Opera, Hockney's set for *Die Zauberflöte* 278, 279
Godde, Étienne-Hippolyte (1781-1869) 197
Godin, Jean-Baptiste-André (1817-88) 161
gods
   Egyptian 22, 33, 35, 47–8, 48
   see also Syncretism
Godwin, Joscelyn (b.1943) xix
Goethe, Johann Wolfgang von (1749-1832) 155, 182–3, 204, 204, 204, 211–12, 215(n), 301
   The Elective Affinities 215
Gogh, Vincent van (1853-90) 255
Goldoni, Carlo (1707-93) 255
Goodwin, Francis (1784-1835) 288, 290
Goose and Gridiron tavern 60, 120, 122
Gossé, Marcel (b.1922) 139–40
Gothein, Eberhard (1853-1923) 205
Gothein, Marie Luise Schroeter (1863-1931) 205
Gothic
   and 'Graveyard Poets' 181–2
   political interpretation of 177–81, 213
   style of Architecture 3–4, 177
Gothic Revival 179–81
Gothick, 'Georgian' ('Carpenters') 179, 239
Gould, Robert Freke (1836-1915) 7, 153
Gradidge, John Roderick Warlow (1929-2000) 23
Graeco-Roman world, and origins of Christianity 49
Graham MS 41
Grammar 8, 170, 314
Grand Lodge 314
   'Antient' 61
   first (1717) xviii, 63, 119
   formation 19, 60, 145
Grand Master 70, 159, 314
Le Grand Secret dévoilé des Francs-Maçons 294, 294
Grandidier, Abbé Philippe-André (1752-87) 150
Grass, Philippe (1801-76) 203
Gratarolo, Guglielmo (c.1516-c.1568) 40
graves, markers 43, 56
'Graveyard Poets' 181–2
Gray, Thomas (1716-71), *Elegy in a Country Churchyard* 181
Great Architect, concept of xxvii, 47–8, 142–4, 152, 162, 314
   God as 39, 49, 51–2, 61
Greece, ancient 160
   knowledge from 22
Greek-key pattern 49, 50, 92
Gregory I, St (c.540-604), from 590 Pope 81
Gregory XIII (1502-85), from 1572 Pope 81
Gregory XVI (1765-1846), from 1831 Pope 292
Gregory, David (1659-1708) 60
Gresset, Jean-Baptiste-Louis (1709-77) 145
Greuze, Jean-Baptiste (1725-1805) 148
Griffith, John (1796-1888) 289
Grosseteste, Robert, Bishop of Lincoln (c.1168-1253) 21
grottoes 184, 200, 233, 265
Grumbold, Robert, 'Freemason' (1639-1720) 2
Guedalla, Philip (1889-1944) xv
Guericke, Otto von (1602-86) 124(n)
Guerra, Giovanni (1544-1618) 242(n)
Guerville, Harny de (fl.1755-72) 246
Guilds of Masons, honorary members 5
Guilds, Mediaeval xxiii, 2–3
   'free' of 1, 4–11
   and Protestantism 23–4
   religious and charitable duties 9, 22–4
Guillaumot, Charles-Axel (1730-1807) 148
Guillotin, Dr Joseph-Ignace (1738-1814) 147
Gunnis, Rupert Forbes (1899-1965) 281-2
Gustavus III (1746-92), from 1771 King of Sweden 250(n), 251
Gwilt, Joseph (1784-1863) 10
Gwynne, Howell Arthur (1865-1950) 291(n)

'ha-ha', introduction 175
Haddington, East Lothian, sundial 58, 58

Index / 351

Hadrian (76-138), from 117 Roman Emperor 47
  Villa at Tivoli 201–2
Hafenreffer, Matthias (1561-1619) 95
  and Temple 79–80, *80*
Hagley Castle, Worcestershire 180
The Hague, first Lodge (1710) 143
Halfe Moone Tavern 5
Halicarnassus, Mausoleum 78
Hall, Manly Palmer (1901-90), *Freemasonry of the Ancient Egyptians* 159
Haller, Albrecht von (1708-77) 190–1, *191*
Hallett, Philip Edward (1884-1948) 291
Halliwell, James Orchard (1820-89), *Early History of Freemasonry in England* 6–7
Hamer, Douglas (1897-1981) xxiii
Hamill, John McKenzie (b.1947) **97**
Hamilton, David (1768-1843) 298(n)
Hamilton, Thomas (1784-1858) 298(n)
Hamilton, Sir William (1730-1803) 209
Hampton & Sons 136
Händel, Georg Friedrich (1685-1759) 260(n)
Hanke, Karl (1750-1803) 253(n)
Hanotte, Johann Lambert von (*fl*.1790) Augustinian Abbot of Huy, near Liège, 254, *261*
Haran, Menahem (b.1924) 94(n)
Hardwick, Philip (1792-1870) 130
Harington, James (1611-77) 178
Harland-Jacobs, Jessica (b.1970) xvii
Harpocrates (Horus) 42, 49, 157, 169, **314**
Hartlib, Samuel (*c*.1599-1662) 36
Harvey, John Hooper (1911-97) 19
Haschka, Lorenz Leopold (1749-1827) 252
Hasse, Jean-Laurent (1849-1925) 134
Hastings, Lady Flora Elizabeth (1806-39) 289(n)
Haunch, Terence Osborne (b.1919) xx–xxi, 46(n), 65(n), 92, 124(n), 155(n), 280(n)
Hawksmoor, Nicholas (*c*.1662-1736) 176, *176*
Hay & Henderson, architects 136
Haydn, Franz Josef (1732-1809) 252(n)
  Die Schöpfung (The Creation) 279
Haydn, Michael (1737-1806) 250
Heemskerck, Maarten van (1498-1574) 84, 88, *89*, 268
Heermann, Paul (1673-1732) 117
Hefele, Melchior (1716-94) 267(n)
Heidelberg 230, 233
  Hortus Palatinus 36–8, *36*, *37*, 203
Hellfire Club 119
Héloïse (d.1163), tomb 197
Henckel von Donnersmarck, Guido Georg Friedrich Erdmann Heinrich Adalbert, Graf (1830-1916) 288
Henckel von Donnersmarck, Wilhelm Ludwig Viktor, Graf (1775-1849) 288
Henckel-Donnersmarck, Counts of, tomb of 288, *288*
Henderson, George (1846-1905) 136
Henderson, Peter Lyle Barclay (1848-1912) 136, *137*
Henrietta Maria (1609-69), from 1625 Consort of Charles I 28
Henry IV (1366-1413), from 1399 King of England and Lord of Ireland 18
Henry Frederick (1594-1612), from 1610 Prince of Wales 29, 36
Henry V (1386/7-1422), from 1413 King of England and Lord of Ireland 18(n)
Hensler, Karl Friedrich (1759-1825) 264
Henwick, Robert (*fl*.late 14th century) 3
Heraclius (*c*.575-642), from 610 Roman Emperor 77
Heraldry, French 103
Herbert, Sir Thomas (1606-82), *Travels* 44
Herder, Johann Gottfried von (1744-1803) 153, 182, 211–12, 314
Herland, Hugh (*c*.1330-*c*.1411) 16
Hermes Trismegistus 22, 26, 35, 66, **314**
'Hermetic' tradition 22, 26, 51, 304, **314**
  and Art of Memory 51–3, 62
  and Egypt 33–9, 133, 155, 157, 192, 239
  and Rosicrucianism 42, 44
  and Speculative Freemasonry 62
  see also Egypt; Memory
Hermetic Vase 258
Herod Agrippa I (10 BC-AD 44), from AD 41 King of Judaea 76
Herod 'the Great' (*c*.79 or 73-4 BC), Tetrarch from 41 BC, King of Judaea

from 40 BC (confirmed by Octavian in 37 BC) 75-6
Herodotus of Halicarnassus (*c*.484-425 BC) 47
Herrera, Juan de (*c*.1530-97) 81–2
Hesekiel, Georg Christoph (1732-1818) 211, 213, *213*
Hess, Tobias (1568-1614) 35
Hesse-Darmstadt, Henrietta Caroline (1721-74), *Landgräfin* of 188
Heterotopias 170
hexalpha 258, 283, *283*, 288, 295, **314**
Hezekiah, King of Judah (*r.c*.705 or *c*.716- 687 BC) 74
hieroglyphs, Egyptian 22, 26, 34–5, 133, 134, **314**
  deciphered 165–6
Higden, Ranulf (d.1364), *Polychronicon* 66
High Twelve 297, **314**
Highgate, St James's Cemetery 290, *290*
Hildebrandt, Johann Lukas von (1668-1745) 143
Himmelfarb, Gertrude (b.1922) 170
Hiram Abif (Abiff), legend of 41–6, 44, 47, 70, 206
Hiram, King of Tyre 70, **314**
Hirschau, Abbot William of (1069-91) 14
Hirschfeld, Christian Cajus Lorenz (1742-92) 184, 217
historiography xvii, xxvii–xxviii
Hitler, Adolf (1889-1945) 96
  Mein Kampf 94
Hittorff, Jakob Ignaz (1792-1867) 133(n)
Hoare, Henry (1705-85), Stourhead 176
Hobbes, Thomas (1588-1679) 144
Hochmitternacht **314**
Hockney, David (b.1937), set for *Die Zauberflöte* 278, *279*
Hoffmann, Ernst Theodor Amadeus (formerly Wilhelm) (1776-1822) 267, 271
  Olimpia 274
Hoffmann von Fallersleben, August Heinrich (1798-1874) 252(n)
Hofmannstahl, Hugo von (1874-1929) 249(n)
Hohenheim, Philipp Theophrastus Bombast von (*c*.1490-1541) (Paracelsus) 42
Hohenzollern-Sigmaringen, Anton Alois, Fürst von (1762-1831) 253
Holbach, Paul Heinrich Dietrich, Baron von (1723-89) 145
Holland, Henry, Senior (1712-85) xv
Holland, Henry, the Younger (1745-1806) xv–xvi, 144
Holme, Randle (1627-1700), *Theatrum Chemicum Britannicum* 27
Holmes, Edward (1864-1921) 139
Holy Roman Empire 14
Holy Royal Arch, Degree of 98
Holzer, Johann (1753-1818) 253
Honnecourt, Villard de (*fl*.1175-*c*.1240) 14, 51
Hontheim, Johann Nikolaus von (1701-90) 250
Hope 105, 298, **314**
Hori Apollonis Hieroglyphia 22
Horn Tavern 121
Hosking, Prof. William (1800-61) 290
Hotman, François (1524-90), *Franco-Gallia* 178
Houdon, Jean-Antoine (1741-1828) 148
Hour-glass 70, 196, 257, 258, **314**
Howard, Thomas (1585-1646), from 1595 14th Earl of Arundel and 4th of Surrey, and from 1644 1st Earl of Norfolk 29
Hoyle, Edmond (1672-1769) 41
Hugh of St Cher (*c*.1200-63) 80
Hugh of St Victor (*c*.1096-1141) 9, 21
Hughan, William J. (1841-1911) 7
Humanism 38, 52
  Renaissance 22
Humboldt, Friedrich Heinrich Alexander, Freiherr von (1769-1859) 268
Hume, David (1711-76) 144
Hummel, Johann Nepomuk (1778-1830) 269
Hungary, sundials 59
Huntly, Henrietta Stewart, Countess of (1573-1642) 27
Huskisson, William, MP (1770-1830) 289
Hutchinson, William (1732-1814) 184(n)
Huxley, Thomas Henry (1825-95) 34

Hymmen, Bernhard (1731-87) 159
Hypnerotomachia Poliphili (Francesco Colonna) 202, 203, 286, *287*

Ibsen, Henrik (1828-1906) 142
Idelsohn, Abraham Zvi (1882-1938) 249
'Ideology of Reason' 170–1
Il Guercino see Barbieri
Illuminism and Illuminatists 161, 242–3, 264
  Society of Illuminati 170, 252, 264, **314**
imagery
  Masonic 58, 62, 153
  see also emblems; symbolism
Imhotep, Architect (*fl.c*.2600 BC) 47–8, 51
Inett, John (1647-1717) 178
Ingolstadt, Bavaria, *Torquetum* 57–8
initiation xxvii, 12, 19, 43, 60, 64, **100**, 265
  Continental ceremonies 199
  French rites 16, 147–9
  Lequeu's *Trials* 164, *165*, *166*
  Scottish 26, 59
Inquisition 38, 116
Inverness, Cecilia Letitia (1793-1873), from1840 Duchess of 289
Ionic Order 70, 120, 315, **315**
Ireland 61
  Roman Catholicism 292
  see also Dublin; Ulster
Irish Rebellion (1798) 292
Irminger, Johann Jacob (1635-1724) 117
Iron Bridge, Coalbrookdale, 206, *206*
Isiac Mysteries 47–9, 157–8, 159, 200, 304
Isidore, St, Bishop of Seville (*c*.560-636) 20–1
  Encyclopaedia 22
Isis 35, 49, **315**
  and Mary 39
Islam, spread of 55–6
Israel, kingdom of 72–3, 74, 93
  see also Solomon's Temple
Israel, State of, Grand Lodge 44
Israelites, in Egypt 71–2, 155
Italy **315**
  Freemasonry in 63, 64, 290
  see also Rome
Ittar, Henryk (1773-1850) 216, 218, 225

'Jachin' 43, 48–9, 61, *112*, **315**
  Karlskirche 87–8
  pillar 67, *68*, 70
Jachin and Boaz (1776), frontispiece 112–13, *112*
Jäck, Carl (d.1809) 271
Jackson, John, RA (1778-1831) xxv, 126
Jacob, Margaret C. (b.1943) xvii, xviii
Jacobite Rebellion (1715) 61, 63, 179, 306
Jacobite Rebellion (1745) 61, 116
Jacobites 142, 145
Jacob's Ladder 76, 105, 284, **315**
Jacquemart, Henri-Alfred-Marie (1824-96) 284
Jahn, Otto (1813-69) 247
James II and VII (1633-1701), King of England, Scotland, and Ireland (r.1685-1688/9) xviii, 63, 64, 178
James VI (1566-1625), from 1567 r. as King of Scotland, and from 1603 as James I of England and Ireland 24, 143
James Francis Edward Stuart (1688-1766), Prince, known as the 'Old Pretender', styled from 1701 King James III and VIII of England, Scotland, and Ireland 119
James, John (*c*.1673-1746), translator of Perrault's *Treatise...* xviii
Jane, William (1645-1707) 7
Jaszczołd, Wojciech (1763-1821) 218
Jeanneret, Charles-Édouard ('Le Corbusier') (1887-1965) 299
Jefferson, Thomas (1743-1826) 301
Jeffreys, Judge George (1645-89) 64
Jeremiah (*fl*.627-586 BC) 74
Jerome, St (*c*.341-420) 81
Jerusalem 93, **315**
  'Dome of the Rock' 76, 88, 210
  Temple 33, 55, 89
Jeshua, Temple 75
Jesuits 142, 230, 231
jewellery, Masonic 108, *111*, 300, *301*
Jewels **315**
Jewish Revolts

First (AD 66-70) 76
Second (AD 131-5) 76
Jewish Temple 33, 55, 71–4, *72*
  altar 94
  descriptions 237
  Fischer von Erlach and 85–7, *87*, *88*, *89*
  Herodian temple 75–7
  representations of 77–85
  Tabernacle 71, *72*
  Zerubbabel's Temple 75, **320**
  see also Solomon's Temple
Jews
  linked with Freemasonry 95–6, 291, 294–6, *294*, *295*, *296*
  persecution of 94–6
Jogand-Pagès, Marie-Joseph Gabriel Antoine ('Léo Taxil') (1854-1907) 293
Johann Georg III (1647-91), from 1680 Elector of Saxony 117
Johann Georg IV (1669-94), from 1691 Elector of Saxony 117
John III Sobieski (1624-96), from 1674 King of Poland 117
John of Northampton, mayor of London (1381/2) (*fl*.late 14th century) 2–3
John Paul II (1920-2005), from 1978 Pope 294
John, St, the Baptist (d.*c*.30) 30–1
John, St, the Evangelist (d.*c*.101) 30–1
John of Salisbury, Bishop of Chartres (d.1180), *Polycraticus* 66
Johnson, Ben (1572-1637) 28
Johnson (Johnston), James (1809-68) 281–2
Johnson, Matthew Wharton (*fl*.1820-60) 289(n)
Johnston, John (*fl*.1835-61) 283
Joly, Maurice (1831-78) 96(n)
Jomard, Edme François (1777-1862) 166
Jones, Bernard Edward (1879-1965) 4, **97**, 149
Jones, Gwilym Peredur (1982-1975) 6, 8
  see also Knoop
Jones, Inigo, Architect (1573-1652) xviii(n), 28–9, 143–4, 179
Jordanes, historian of Goths (*fl.c*.550) 177
Joseph II (1741-90), reigned jointly with his mother, Maria Theresia, 1765-80, and solely thereafter as Holy Roman Emperor 250, 251, 254
'Josephinian Enlightenment' 250, 253, 256
Josephus, Flavius (37-*c*.98) 75–6, 91, 237
  Jewish Antiquities 21, 67
Jouin, Monsignor Ernest (1844-1932), *Le Péril judéo-maçonnique* 293
Judah, kingdom of 74, 93
Judaism, Rabbinical law 76, 77–8
Judas Maccabeus (*c*.190-160 BC) 75
Jügel, Friedrich (d.1833) 268, *273*
Julianus Flavius Claudius, 'Julian the Apostate' (*c*.AD 331-63), from 361 Roman Emperor 33, 76-7
Justice 147, 171, **315**

Kamsetzer, Jan Chrystian (1753-95) 235(n)
Kändler, Johann Joachim (1706-75) 117, 118
Kant, Immanuel (1724-1804) 153
Karl August (1757-1828), from 1775 Duke and from 1815 Grand Duke of Saxe-Weimar 215(n)
Karl Philipp (1661-1742), from 1716 Elector Palatine 230
Karl Theodor (1724-99), from 1742 Elector Palatine, and from 1777 Elector of Bavaria 230, 231-2, 242–3, 247, 248, 252
Karpiński, Franciszek (1742-1825) 215, 216
Kayser, Christian Bernhard (1720-78) 182
Keats, John (1795-1821) 205
Keith, George, Earl Marischal (1549/50-1623) 27
Kemp, George Meikle (1795-1844) 298(n)
Kennedy, Charles Pratt (d.1875) 281(n)
Kennedy, Jane (fl.1569-89) 27
Kent, Prince George (1902-42), from 1934 Duke of 132
Kent, William (*c*.1685-1748) 175, 176, 185, 239
Kepler, Johann (1571-1630) 27, 80
Kerényi, Carl (1897-1973) 147
Key **315**
  to Lodge 105, *157*

Kielce, Poland, massacre (1946) 294
Kilmartin, Argyll 56
Kilmory Knap, Argyll 56
King's Arms Tavern 119
Kircher, Athanasius (1602-80) 34, 86
Kirk, Rev. Robert (c.1647-92) 43
Kirnberger, Johann Philipp (1721-83) 250
Kismarton, Esterházy seat at 267, 268
Kléber, Jean-Baptiste (1753-1800) 203
Klenze, Leo von (1784-1864) 227
Klopstock, Friedrich Gottlieb (1724-1803) 182
Kloss, Georg Franz Burckhard (1787-1854) xix
Knee 41, 101, **315**
Kniaźnin, Franciszek Dionizy (1749/50-1807) 215, 216
Knigge, Adolf, Freiherr von (1752-96) 264
Knights Hospitallers 31, 56
Knights Templar 16, 55–7, 77, 146
Knoop, Douglas (1883-1948) 10
and Gwilym Peredur Jones
An Introduction to Freemasonry xxiii–xxiv
The Genesis of Freemasonry **18**, 55
———, G.P.Jones, & D. Hamer (eds)
The Two Earliest Masonic MSS 6, 8
knowledge *see* Ancient Knowledge
Knowles, Harry Percy (1871-1923) 136
Koberger, Anton (c.1440-1513), and Temple 78–9, *78*
Koblenz 203
Köchel, Ludwig Alois Ferdinand, Ritter von (1800-77) 247(n)
Köppen, Carl Friedrich (1734-97) 159
Korngold, Erich Wolfgang (1897-1957) 38
Krafft, Johann Carl (Jean-Charles) (1764-1833) 169–70
Kraft, Adam (fl.1490-d.1509) 51
Krasicki, Ignacy (1735-1801) 216
Kuene, Konrad (d.1469) 51
Kuntz, Karl (1770-1830) *208*

La Chaux-de-Fonds, Switzerland 299
la Fontaine, Jean de (1621-95) 197, *197*
la Motte, Antoine-Nicolas de (1755-1831) 159
La Pérouse, Jean-François de Galaup, Comte de (1741-88) 192
la Rive, Abel Clarin de (1855-1914) 293
La Rochefoucauld, François VI, Duc de, Prince de Marcillac (1613-80) **xix**
Laborde, Alexandre-Louis-Joseph, Comte de (1773-1842) 192
Laborde, Jean-Joseph, Marquis de (1724-94) 192, 200
Labyrinths 36, 148, *186*, **315**
significance of 49–50, *50*, *51*
Wörlitz 206, *208*
Lacey, Arthur T. (fl.1923-59) 136
Lalande, Joseph-Jérome Lefrançais de (1732-1807) 147, 148, 149
Lamancha House, Peeblesshire, lectern-sundial 58
Lamy, Bernard (1640-1715), *De Tabernaculo Foederis* 84–5, *85*, *86*
Lancie, Franciszek Maria (1799-1831) 225
Landon, Howard Chandler Robbins (1926-2009) 254, 260–1, *261*
landownership 178, 179, 180
landscape
Arcadia 184–6
gardens and Freemasonry 198–9, 244, 300
as interpretation 177–81
see also gardens
Lange, Joseph (1751-1831) 248(n)
Langhans, Carl Gotthard (1732-1808) 276
Langley, Batty (1696-1751) 239, 303
Langley, Thomas (1702-c.1751) 239
Lansdowne, Henry Petty-Fitzmaurice (1780-1863), from 1809 3rd Marquess of 288
Lansdowne MS 7
Laout, Pierre-François (1825-1903) 134
Larudan, Abbé (fl. mid-18th century), *Les Francs-Maçons Écrasés* 101, 102–3, *102*
Latrobe, Benjamin Henry Boneval (1764-1820) 302
Laugier, Abbé Marc-Antoine (1713-69) 92, 149–50, 153
Laurence, St (d.258) 40, 81, 151

Laval, Pierre (1883-1945) 294(n)
Lavater, Johann Caspar (1741-1801) 248
Lavoisier, Antoine-Laurent (1743-94) 244
Law, Bernard Francis (b.1931), former RC Archbishop of Boston 293
Lawrence, Sir Thomas (1769-1830) 132
Le Camus de Mézières, Nicolas (1721-89) 129, 148
Le Clerc, Sébastian (1637-1714), *A Treatise of Architecture* 19
'Le Corbusier' *see* Jeanneret
Le Geay, Jean-Laurent (1710-c.1786) 258–9
Le Sueur, Jean-François (1760-1837) 259
Le Tourneur, Pierre Prime Félicien (1737-88) 183
Les Nuits de Young 182
Leasowes, The, Halesowen, Worcestershire 185, 209
Lebas, Louis-Hippolyte (1782-1867) 197, *198*
Ledoux, Claude-Nicolas (1736-1806) 46, 151, 160–70, 301, 305
designs for Chaux 151–3, *151*, *152*, *153*, 160–2, *161*, *162*, *163*
L'Architecture considerée 129
and Primitive Simplicity 150, *151*
Lee, Elizabeth (c.1718-36) 183
Leeds, Yorkshire, Temple Mills 134
Leibnitz, Gottfried Wilhelm (1646-1716) 86, 230
Leinster, Augustus Frederick Fitzgerald (1791-1874), from 1804 3rd Duke of 64
Lemere, Harry Bedford (1864-1944) 137
Lenoir, Alexandre-Marie (1761-1839) 197
La Franche-Maçonnerie 128–9
Leo III, Pope and Saint (r.795-816) 88(n)
Leo IV, Pope and Saint (r.847-55) 8
Leo X (1475-1521), from 1513 Pope 38
Leo XII (1760-1829), from 1823 Pope 292
Leo XIII (1810-1903), from 1878 Pope **281**
Leopold II (1747-92), from 1765 Grand Duke of Tuscany and from 1790 Holy Roman Emperor 254
Lepagelet, etcher (fl.1770-1807) 190
Lepsius, Carl Richard (1810-84) 133
Lequeu, Jean-Jacques (1757-1826) 66, 152, 161–3, *169*
'Architecture Civile' 167
Cool Room *174*
dwelling in Egyptian style *171*
Temple of Divination *172*
Temple of the Earth *173*
Temple of Silence 168, 169–70, *169*, *170*
Temple of Verdure of Ceres *171*
Temple of Wisdom *172*
Trials by Fire, Water and Air 164, 165, *166*
Victory Square Monument *173*
Lesnes, John (fl.late 14th century) 3
Lessing, Gotthold Ephraim (1729-81) 182
Lettsom, John Coakley (1744-1815) 306
level **315**
motif 107, *109*
Leveson-Gower, George Granville (1786-1861), from 1833 2nd Duke of Sutherland 3
Levick, Thomas Fisher (1864-1945) 135
Lewis (device) *109*, 124, **315**
Lewis, Matthew Gregory (1775-1818) 181
L'Hôte, Nestor (1804-42) 166
Liberal Arts, Seven 6, 8, 65–6, 146, **308**
Libergié (Libergier), Hue (Hugues) (d.1263) 51
Liddell, The Hon. Thomas (1800-56) 289(n)
Liebeskind, August Jakob (1758-93), *Lulu* 266
Liège (Luik), *La Parfait Intelligence* Lodge 134–5
Light 35, 49, 98, 112, 145, 253, **315–16**
lighthouses 285–6
Ligne, Charles-Joseph, Prince de (1735-1814) 200, 201, 212, 244
Ligorio, Pirro (1513/14-84) 203
lime-mortar **316**
preserve of freemasons 2, 25
as Symbol 45–6
Linck, Johann Konrad (1730-93) 236
Lindau-am-Bodensee, *Stiftskirche* 271
Lindsay, Sir David (1585-1641) 42–3
Lisbon, Inquisition in 116

Liverpool
Cemetery of St James 289
Low Hill Necropolis 289
Livery Companies 4–5
see also Masons' Company
Llandaff Cathedral 84
Locke, John (1632-1704) 144
Loddiges, George (1784-1846) 290
'Lodge Book' (Villard de Honnecourt) 51
Lodge of Harmony 121
Lodge of Unity, *Horn Tavern* 121
Lodges **309**, **316**
floor plans 98–113, *113*, *114*
layout 67, 108–9, 111, *111*
organisation of 97–8
origins of 12–13, *13*, *15*
as places 97–8
Prince of Wales xv, xvi
see also Grand Lodges
Lodges of Adoption 97(n), 116, 117, 162, 214(n)
Lodges, Belgium 134–5, 155
Lodges, France 135, *135*, 148–9
Lodges, Scotland 25, 298
Edinburgh 59, 136, *137*
Kilwinning Lodge 25, 108–9, *262*
Logic 8, **316**
London
Carlton House, Pall Mall xv
cemeteries 288–90
Company of Masons 3, 4–5
General Cemetery of All Souls, Kensal Green 289–90
Great Eastern Hotel, Liverpool Street, Masonic Temple in Abercorn Rooms 136, *138*
Hans Town, Chelsea xv
Primrose Hill cemetery 288
St Anne's churchyard, Limehouse 286, *286*
St James's Cemetery, Highgate 290, *290*
St Paul's Cathedral 281, *282*
Templar churches 58
see also City of London
London Assize of Wages (1212) 2
London Bridge, original building of 4
London, Great Fire of (1666) 3–4, *5*
Lorrain(e), Claude Gellée Le (c.1604/5–82), known as Claude 175
Los Angeles, California 136
loss, concept of 56–7
Lost Wisdom *see* Ancient Knowledge
Lothringen (Lorraine), Franz Stephan (1708-65), from 1729 Duke of, from 1735 Grand Duke of Tuscany, and from 1745 Holy Roman Emperor Franz 161–2, 247
Loudon, John Claudius (1783-1843) 290
Louis XIV (1638-1715), from 1643 King of France 38
Louis XV (1710-74), from 1715 King of France 117(n), 159, 230
Louth, Lincolnshire, Church of St James 211
Loutherbourg, Philippe-Jacques de (1740-1812) 159–60
Łowicz, Collegiate church and Primate's palace 221
Lubomirska, Izabela (1736-1816) 214
Lucca, Italy
Cathedral of San Martino 50
Church of San Michele 68
Ludlow, Shropshire, Church of St Laurence 23
Lull, Raimon (1232-1315) 81
Lussy (Lussi), F. Marie de (fl.1780s) 190
Luther, Martin (1483-1546) 42, 250
Lüthi, Urs (b.1947) 296
Lutyens, Sir Edwin Landseer (1869-1944) 131
Luyken, Jan (1649-1708) 83, *83*
Lydgate, John (c.1370-c.1449/50), *Everything to his Semblable* 6
Lyra, Nicolaus de (1270-1349), and Temple 78–9, *78*
Lyttelton, George (1709-73), from 1751 5th Baronet, and from 1756 1st Baron Lyttelton of Frankley 180

MacDonnell, Randal (1609-83), from 1620 Viscount Dunluce, from 1636 2nd Earl and from 1645 1st Marquess of Antrim 28(n)
McIntosh, Christopher (b.1943) 203, 205
Mackey, Albert Gallatin (1807-81) **281**
Mackintosh, Charles Rennie (1868-1928) 255
McLeod, Wallace Edmond (b.1931) 44
Maclot, Petra M. C. I. (b.1954) 136
Macpherson, James (1736-96), 'Ossian' 216
Macrobius, Ambrosius Theodosius (5th century) 21
Madden, Sir Frederick (1801-73) 6
Maderno, Stefano (1576-1636) 224
Madox, Thomas (1666-1723) 180
Madrid, Escorial Palace 81–2, *82*, 130
Maestlin, Michael (1550-1631) 80
Magus xxvi, 54, 65
mahabyn (M.B.) 43–6, *107*, **316**
mahoe, trees 46
Maier, Michael (1569-1622)
Arcana Arcanissima 35
Symbola Aureae 35
Maimonides (Moses Ben Maimon) (1135-1204), and Jewish Temple 77–8, *77*
Malevez, Jules (fl.1900-14) 135
mallet 107, 126, **316**
Malmesbury, William of (c.1090-c.1142) 8
Man, Perfectability of 155, 161, 231, 305
Manasseh, King of Judah (r.c.687-c.642/3) 74
Mandela, Nelson R. (b.1918) 65(n)
Manners, Francis (1578-1632), from 1616 6th Earl of Rutland 28(n)
Manners, Katherine (c.1603-1649), from 1620 Countess of and from 1623 Duchess of Buckingham, then (from 1645) Marchioness of Antrim 28(n)
Manners, Roger (1576-1612), from 1588 5th Earl of Rutland 28
Mannheim 230, 232, 248
Nationaltheater 267, *267*
School of musicians 247
Mansart, François (1598-1666) 90
Mansart, Jules Hardouin (1646-1708) 90
Mansfeld, Sebastian (fl.1751-1816) 249
Manutius, Aldus (1450-1515) 202
Marceau, General François-Severin-Desgraviers (1769-96) 203
Maria Clementina Sobieska (1702-35), Consort from 1719 of Prince James Francis Edward Stuart 144(n)
Maria Leszczyńska, (1703-68), from 1725 Queen of France 117(n)
Maria Theresia (1717-80), from 1741 Queen of Hungary, from 1743 Queen of Bohemia, and from 1745 Holy Roman Empress 247
Marie Antoinette (1755-93), from 1774 Queen of France 254
Mark Mason Degrees 98
Marks, Mason's 12–13, 25, 98, **316**
Marraccius, Hippolytus (1604-75) 52
marrow, bone, significance of 43–5
Marsden, Victor Emile (1866-1920) 95
Martin, Benjamin (1705-82) 142
Marwe, John (fl.1400-42) 3
Mary of Guise (1515-60), from 1538 Queen of Scots, from 1542 Queen Dowager, and from 1554 Queen Regent 30
Mary II (1662-94), Queen of England, Scotland, and Ireland, *r.* from 1689 jointly with William III and II 63
Mary, Queen of Scots (1542-87) 28, 30, 63
Mary the Virgin
and Isis 39
syncretism of cult 52
Marye, Alger & Vinour 136
Marye, P. Thornton (1872-1935) 136(n)
Mason Word 41, 43–4, 61–2, 100, 105, 107
use of 45
Masonic Peace Memorial 131–2, *131*, *132*, 297
masons, definitions 20–1
Masons' Company (London) 3, 4–5, 19, 59, **316**
acquisition of Hall 4
Charter (1677) 5
grant of arms 4, 18
as Livery Company (1481) 4, 60
Master Mason
Degree of 98
Reception of 99, *100*, *113*, *114*
Master-Builders 50–1
portraits of 50–1
Master-mason-cum-Architects 58–9
Master's Word 43, 45, 61
Mathematics 12, 22, 39

see also Geometry
Matthisson, Friedrich von (1761-1831), *Adelaide* 211
maul (mallet, gavel) 107, 126, **316**
Maupertuis, Manche, France 191–2, *193*, 203, 209, 260
Maurer, Carl (fl.1800-14) 267
  sets for *Die Zauberflöte* 268
Maurus, Hrabanus (Rabanus Magnentius Maurus [c.776-856]), from 847 Archbishop of Mainz, *De Universo* 70
mazes 49–50, 149
  see also Labyrinths
Mecklenburg-Strelitz, Sophia Charlotte (1744-1818), from 1761 Queen of Great Britain and Ireland, and Electress, later (from 1814) Queen of Hanover 249(n)
Mecklenburg-Strelitz, Georg August (1748-85), Duke of 249
Mederitsch-Gallus, Johann Georg Anton (1752-1835) 256
Mediaeval style 177
  see also Gothic
Medical Society of London, Coade Stone panel 306, *306*
Meissen porcelain factory 117–18, *118*
Melancholy, cult of 181–2
Melchiades or Miltiades, Saint (d.314), from 311 Pope 8
Membury, Simon (fl.1390-1400) 16
Memmo, Andrea (1729-93) 159
memorials
  emblems 57, 283
  in gardens 184–5, 186, 188–92
  obelisks 184, 188, 197, 283–4
  Templar 56
Memory 39–41
  Ancient 25–6
  Art of 52–3, 62, 162, 202, **316**
  Temples of *162*, 215, *215*, 300
  see also Hermetic tradition
Memphis, Reception of Initiates 166
Méréville, Essonne, France 192, *193*, 200
Merian the Elder, Matthaeus (Matthäus) (1593-1650), and Temple 37, 83, 84
Mesmer, Franz Anton (1734-1815) 170, 246
Messerschmidt, Franz Xaver (1736-83) 167
Metaphysical poetry 34
Metzler, Johann Georg *see* Giesecke
Meulenaer, Dowager of (fl.1780s) 170
Meurin, Monsignor Johann Gabriel Léon Louis (1825-95) 293
Meyer, Georg Friedrich (1735-79) 188
Meyer, Hannes (1889-1954) 96
Meyer, Professor Friedrich Ludwig Wilhelm (1758-1840) 129
Michałowicz, Jan (c.1530-c.1583) 221
Middle Ages xxiii, 4
Middleton, Reverend George Marshall (1826-66) 296(n)
Mies van der Rohe, Ludwig (1886-1969) 96
Milan, Porta Romana 50
Miller, Sanderson (1716-80) *176*, 177, 177, 180–1
Milton, John (1608-74) 181
Mirala, Petri (b.1965) xvii
Mirandola, Count Giovanni Pico della (1463-94) 35
Mirk, John (fl.c.1382-c.1414) 9
  Instructions for Parish Priests 7
Mishnah (Rabbinical texts) 76, 77–8
mnemonic techniques 39–41, 202
mnemonics, *fabriques* as 228
Modernism 20, 96, 298–9
Molay, Jacques de (c.1244/5-1314) 56(n)
Molesworth, Robert (1656-1725) 178, 179
Molière (Jean-Baptiste Poquelin) (1622-73) 197, *197*
Monge, Gaspard, Comte de Péluse (1746-1818) 163, 166, 197
  mausoleum 300
Mons, Belgium, Temple of Perfect Union 134
Monsigny, Pierre-Alexandre (1729-1817) 265
Montagu, John Montagu (1690-1749), from 1709 2nd Duke of 6, 119, *119*, 121
Montano (Montanus), Benedictus (Benito) Arias (1527-98) 80
  Exemplar 47

Montesquieu, Charles-Louis de Secondat (1689-1755), from 1718 Baron de la Brède et de 116-17, 188
Montesquiou-Fézensac, Anne-Pierre, Marquis de (1739-98) 191–2
Montgolfier, Jacques-Étienne (1745-99) 148
Montgolfier, Joseph-Michel (1740-1810) 148
Montmorency-Luxembourg, Anne-Charles-Sigismond de (1737-1803) 147
Montreuil, Pierre de (d.1267) 51
Monville, François-Nicolas-Henri Racine de (1734-97) 199(n)
Moon 107, 233, 257–8, 262–3, **316**
Moore, Thomas (1799-1852), *The Epicurean* 157
Mopses **316**
  Order of 113, 115, *115*, 117–18, *118*
  plan 229, *229*
  Society of the Order of 214, 214(n)
Moray, Sir Robert (1608/9-73) 26, 42, 60
Moreau, Jean-Michel (1741-1814) *166*, 187
Moréri, Louis (1643-80) 144
Morfontaine, Louis Le Peletier de, Marquis de Montmélian (1730-99) 192
Morfontaine, Oise, France 192, *194*
Morrison, William Vitruvius (1794-1838) 284, *284*
mortar 46, 216, 227, **316**
  see also lime-mortar
Mortier, Corneille (Cornelius/Cornelis) (1699-1783) 83
mosaic pavement 99–100, 105, 107, 316–17
Mossdorf, Friedrich (pseudonym of C. Lenning) (1757-1830) xx
Mosser, Monique (b.1947) 199, 200
Mossman, John (1817-90) 298
Moszyński, August Fryderyk (1731-86) 214, 217
motifs
  actual and imagined xxvi
  in antis 133
  Masonic 105–7
  Nilotic *120*
  see also emblems; imagery; symbolism
motto, *Vide, Audi, Tace* 121, 283, **309**
Mount Stuart, obelisk-sundial 57
Mountbatten of Burma, Louis (1900-79), from 1947 1st Earl 23
Mouret, Jean-Joseph (1682-1738) 265
Mowl, Timothy (b.1951) 150
Mozart, Constanze (née Weber) (1762-1842) 265
Mozart, (Johann Georg) Leopold (1719-87) 230, 231, 248
Mozart, Wolfgang Amadeus (1756-91) 231, 246–80, *261*, 300–1
  Bastien und Bastienne 246
  La Clemenza di Tito 249, 254
  Così fan tutte 305
  Credo Mass 279
  D Minor *Requiem* 250
  and Death 264
  death of 264–5
  Dir, Seele des Weltalls, O Sonne 252
  'Dissonance' String Quartet in C Major 279
  first associations with Freemasonry 247–51
  Ihr unsre neuen Leiter 252
  Kettenlied (Chain Song) 253
  last three symphonies 279–80
  later Masonic connections 251–4
  Le Nozze di Figaro 249, 305
  Lied der Freiheit 251
  Lied zur Gesellenreise 206
  'Little German Cantata' 252
  Die Maurerfreude Cantata 248, 254
  Maurerische Trauermusik 249, 250
  Missa Brevis in F 279
  O heiliges Band der Freundschaft... 47
  and Protestant music 250, 260–1
  Requiem 260(n)
  Singspiel xxvi, 206, 246
  Symphony No. 33 279
  Symphony No. 40 279
  Symphony No. 41 279
  and *Thamos* 246, 247
  Die Zauberflöte xxvi, 206, 212, 250, 254–9
  Zerfließet heut' geliebte Brüder 252

Zum Schluß der Freimaurerloge 252
  and *Zur Wohltätigkeit* Lodge 247
Müller, Ernst Max (fl.1899) 9
Müller, Johann H.F. (1738-1815) 246
Müller, Wenzel (1767-1835), *Singspiel Kaspar der Faggottist* 266
Müller, Wilhelm (1794-1827), *Winterreise* 280
Mumtaz-i Mahal, Arjumand Banu Begum (d.1631) 46
Munich
  English Garden 244
  Nationaltheater 276
Münster, Westphalia, Cathedral 51
Müntz, Johann Heinrich (1727-98) 239
music, E flat Major key 259
Musil, Robert (1880-1942) 94
Mylne, John (1611-67) 45
Mysteries 46–52
  of Antiquity xxvi
  Egyptian 35, 146, **312**
  Eleusinian 147, 235–6, 263, **312**
  Isiac 47–9, 157–8, 159, 200, 304
'Mystery', definition 2–3
Myth and Mythology 26, 155
  in Arkadia 220
  of masons 6, 12, 60
  Scots' creation of 60, 63

Namur, Belgium, Temple 135
Napoleonic Wars 97
Narcissa's burial 183–4
Nash, John (1752-1835) xx
National Socialist German Workers' Party (Nazism) xxiv, 38
Natural Philosophy 69
Nature
  Art and 198, 211
  Cult of 210, 221, 223, 235, 244, 248, 263–4, 268
  Enlightenment and 61, 147
  powers of 25, 160, 218
  Romanticism and 181, 188, 197
  Silence of 271
  tamed 37, 69
Nebuchadnezzar II (c.634-562 BC), from c.605 BC King of Babylon 6, 74
necromancy, in rituals 60–1
Nehmitz, Melchior (1670-1739) 117
Nelson, Horatio (1758-1805), from 1799 Duke of Bronté and from 1801 1st Viscount Nelson of the Nile and of Burnham Thorpe 65(n)
Nelson's Column 65
Neo-Classicism
  and Freemasonry 149–53, 301
  Freemasonry and Egyptian elements in 153–60
  Scotland 296–9
Neo-Platonism 21, 33–5
The Netherlands
  Freemasonry in 143, 201
  St-Jean de Montmorency-Luxembourg lodge 201
  sundials 59
Netherlands Lodges 143, 201
Nettl, Paul (1889-1972) 255, 256, 259
Neudeck, Schloß 288
Neumark, Johann Christian (1741-1811) 206
Neveu, Olimpe (fl.early-19th century) *194*
Neville, Richard 'The Kingmaker' (1428-71), from 1449 16th Earl of Warwick and from 1460 6th Earl of Salisbury 177
New York
  Brooklyn, Kismet Temple 136
  Mecca Temple 136
Newbattle Abbey, Midlothian 58, *59*
Newman, Francis Winton (1878-1953) 131, *131*, 302
Newton, Sir Isaac (1642-1727) 64, 83–4, 188, 251
  Boullée's cenotaph to 153, *154*
  Philosophiae Naturalis Principia Mathematica 61
Nicholas le Freemason (fl.1325) 3
Nicholl, William Grinsell (1796-1871) 130
Nicholson, Peter (1765-1844) *207*
Night Thoughts (Young) 182–3, 212
  Narcissa's burial 183–4
Nile, River 21–2
Nilotic motifs *120*
Nilus, Sergei Aleksandrovich (1862-1929) 95–6

Nine Muses xvi
Nissen, Nikolaus, Freiherr von (1761-1826) 265
Nizet, Charles (1841-1925) 135, *135*
Noah 41–2, 43, **317**
Norblin, Jan Piotr de la Gourdaine (1773-1830) 215, 221
  and Arkadia 218
Norden, Frederick Ludvig (1708-42), *Travels in Egypt and Nubia* 274
Normand, Louis-Marie the Younger (1789-1874) *197*, *198*, 300
Northumberland, Alan Ian Percy (1880-1930), from1918 8th Duke of 291
Norwich, Rosary Cemetery 289
Noss Head, lighthouse 286
Nostell Priory, Yorkshire 27
numbers 33, 37, **317**
  mystic 53
Nuremberg
  Church of St Lorenz 51
  Schreyer-Landauer monument 51

Oakley, Edward (fl.1721-d.1765) 19
obelisks 35, 303, **317**
  gardens 189–90, 201, 216, 228, 235
  memorials 184, 188, 197, 283–4
  and pyramids 153, 283, 286, *287*
  sundials 57–8, *57*
Oblong Square 98, **317**
occultism 199, 251
neo-Platonic 34
O'Connell, Daniel (1775-1847) 292
Octagon 57–8, 210, **317**
Olausson, Magnus (b.1956) 199
Old Charges (*Constitutions of Masonry*) 6–7, 10, 11
Oldmixon, John (1673-1742) 178
Operative Masons 4, 5, 16, 19(n), 22, **317**
  and Acception 16
  and sundials 58–9
Orabi *see* Arabi
Ordo ab Chao 135, **317**
Orel, Alfred (1889-1967) 247
Orléans, Louis-Philippe-Joseph, Duc d'Orléans (Égalité) (1747-93) 147, 186
Orłowski, Aleksander (1777-1832) 218, 223
Orpheus 263
Orrery 124
Orsini, Pier Francesco 'Vicino' (c.1513-84) 202–3
Orzelska, Countess Anna Karolina (1707-69) 230, *230*
Osiris 22, 35, 48–9, 51–2, 274, **317**
'Ossian' 158, 216
ossuaries, Paris 195
Ostrowski, Józéf (fl.1839-40) *219*
ouroboros 155, **317**, 319
owls, symbols 169
Oxford, Mediaeval masons 2

Pabst von Ohain, Gottfried (1656-1729) 117
Paestum Doric 150, 302–3, **317**, *317*
Paine, Thomas (1737-1809) 141–2
Pakenham family xv
Palestine, Foundation of Royal Order of the Free Masons 44
Palladianism 143–4
  First Revival 144, 179
  Second Revival 144(n)
Palladio, Andrea (1508-80) xviii(n)
  Quattro Libri 29
palm trees 265
Papal Bulls
  Ad Providam 56
  In eminenti (1738) 116, *117*, 142
  Pastoralis Praeminentiae 56
  Providas Romanorum Pontificum (1751) 116–17
Papworth, Wyatt Angelicus van Sandau (1822-94) 10
Paracelsus *see* Hohenheim
Paris
  Basilica of Saint-Denis 15
  Catacombs 195, *196*
  Churchyard of the Innocents 195
  Fontaine de la Victoire 284, *285*
  Grand Lodge (1725) 145
  Grand Orient Lodge 147, 149, 293
  Ledoux's *Barrières* 151–2, *152*
  Les Coeurs Simple d l'Étoile Polaire Lodge 148
  Lodge of the Nine Sisters 147–8
  Masons 13–14

Montmartre cemetery 299
Montparnasse cemetery 299
Montparnasse ossuary 195
Musée des Monuments Français 128
mysterious garden 150, *150*
Panthéon 195
Parc Monceau 186, *186*, *187*, 199
Père-Lachaise Cemetery 163, 166, 196–7, *197*, *198*
Rue de la Bourse/Rue des Colonnes 302–3, *303*
St Germain-des-Prés 51
Temple du Droit Humain 135, *135*
Parker, Edward (fl.1770-1780s) 122, *123*
Parler, Peter (1333/5-99) 50
Parsons, Eliza (1739-1811) 169(n)
Pastoret, Claude-Emmanuel-Joseph-Pierre (1756-1840), from 1817 Marquis de 148
Patron Saints, of guilds and fraternities 13–14, 22–3, 30–1
Paul II (1417-71), from 1464 Pope 10
Paul, Sir John Dean, Bt (1775-1852) 288
Paulze, Marie-Anne (1758-1836) 244
Payne, George, Grand Master (d.1757) 6
Peacock, Thomas Love (1785-1866) 157
pedestals 229, *318*
pediment **318**
  segmental 192
Pelt, Robert Jan van (b.1955) 94
pencil *109*
Penn, William (1644-1718) 188
Pentalpha 283, *283*, **318**
Pérau, Abbé Gabriel-Louis-Calabre (1700-67) 117, 229
  Les Secrets de L'Ordre des Francs-Maçons 112, 113, *113*, *114*, *115*
Père-Lachaise Cemetery 163, 166, 196–7, 281, 288, 299, 300, 301
Perinet, Joachim (1763-1816) 266
Perpendicular 113, 114, **318**
Perrault, Claude (1613-88) 85
  Temple in Jerusalem 90, *90*
  Treatise of the Five Orders of Architecture xviii
Perrin, François (d.1571) 79
Persepolis 66, 74
  palace temples 73
Perth, Scotland 29
Pertl, Anna Maria Walpurga (1720-78) 247(n)
Pesne, Antoine (1683-1757) 230, *230*
Pétain, Marshal Henri Philippe Benoni Omer Joseph (1856-1951) 249(n)
Petran, Franz Xaver (d.1811) 248
Petrarch, Francesco (1307-74) 222
Petre, Robert Edward (1742-1801), from 1742 9th Baron 121
Petri, Johann Ludwig (1714-94) 232
Petrus of Ravenna (c.1448-1508/9) 40
Pevsner, Sir Nikolaus (1902-83) 51
Phallus **318**
Philadelphia, Pennsylvania 136
Philip II (1527-98), from 1556 King of Spain 81, 82, 130
Philippe IV 'The Fair' (1268-1314), from 1285 King of France 55–6
Philippon, architect (fl. early 19th century) 197, *198*
Phillips, Ursula (translator) 216
Philo Judaeus (Philon) (c.30 BC-c.AD 40) 75
Philosophes 61, 94–5, 141–2, 143, 250
Philostorgius (c.368-c.440) 237
phoenix 40–1
Photius, Patriarch of Constantinople (c.810-c.893) 237
Pian, Antonio di (fl.late 18th-early 19th centuries) 277, *277*
Piccinni, Niccolò (1728-1800) 148
Pickaxe 258, **318**
'Picturesque' 175, 200
pier, definition 65
Pigage, Anselm de (d.1775) 232
Pigage, Nicolas de (1723-96) 232, *233*
Pike, Albert (1809-91) 293
Pilgram, Anton (c.1450-1515) 51
pilgrimage, ritual 50
Pillars **318**
  definition 65
  interpretations of 68
  Three 70
  Two 65–70, 88
  see also columns
Pillars of Hercules 69, 70, 152
Pine, John (1690-1756), *The Constitutions of the Freemasons* 119, *119*
Pingo, Lewis (1743-1830) 122, *123*
Pinto, Hector (d.1584) 80
Piranesi, Giovanni Battista (1720-78) 153, 160, 217, 258, 305
  fireplace design *269*
Pisa, Cathedral 51
Pisano, Andrea (c.1295-1348/9) 50
Pitcairn, Robert (1793-1855) 42
Pitt, Thomas (1737-93), from 1784 1st Baron Camelford 183
Pitzhanger Manor, Ealing 127
Pius VI (1717-99), from 1775 Pope 250
Pius VII (1742-1823), from 1800 Pope 292
Pius VIII (1761-1830), from 1829 Pope 292
Pius IX 'Pio Nono' (1792-1878), from 1846 Pope 292
Pius XI (1857-1939), from 1922 Pope 293
plaque *109*
Plat, Sir Hugh (1552-1608) 52
plate, Belleek *109*
Plato (c.429-347 BC) 21, 40
Platzer, Josef Ignác (1751-1810) 277, *277*
Playfair, William Henry (1790-1857) 298(n)
playing cards, Ackermann's 303–4, *304*
Plessis-Chamand, garden 192, *195*
Pliny the Elder (23-79) 78
Płoński, Michał (1778-1812) 218
Plot, Robert (1640-96) 59
Plotinus (205-269/70) 49
plumb-line 35, 106, 107, *109*, **318**
Plutarch (Mestrius Plutarchus) (before AD 50-after 120) 33
'Poem of Moral Duties' 6–7
Points of Fellowship, Five 41, 43, 45, 60–1, **318**
Poland
  folk traditions 229
  Freemasonry in 214, 216, 217–18
  partition of 223
  see also Arkadia; Puławy; Warsaw
pomegranate 58, 66, 140, **318**
Pompey (Gnaeus Pompeius Magnus) (106-48 BC) 75
Poncet, Pierre (fl.1734-1817?) 149
Poniatowski, Prince Józef Anton (1763-1813), created (1813) Marshal of France 218
Pope, Alexander (1688-1744) 181
  at Twickenham 126
Pope, John Russell (1873-1937) 136
Pöppelmann, Matthäus Daniel (1662-1736) 143
Poquelin, Jean-Baptiste *see* Molière
Porphyry (*also* Malchus) (234-c.305) 33
Portico 74, 76, 89, 133, 205, 318, **318**
Potocki, Ignacy (1738-94) 214
Potocki, Stanisław Kostka (1755-1821) 214
Poussin, Gaspard Dughet *called* (1615-75) 175
Poussin, Nicolas (1594-1665) 175, *180*, 181, 218
  et in Arcadia ego 180, *184*
Powązki, Czartoryska Garden 222
Poyet, Bernard (1742-1824) 148, 303
Pozzo, Andrea (1642-1709), *Rules and Examples of Perspective* xviii
Prades, Abbé Jean-Martin de (c.1720-82) 145
Prado, Hieronymo de (1547-95) 80
Prague
  cathedral 13
  St Vitus Cathedral 50
Prehistoric, as architectural influence 160
Preradovic, Paula von (1887-1951) 253
Prescott, Andrew John (b.1954) 9
Preston, William (1742-1818) **xxiii**, 127, 245
  Illustrations of Masonry xviii, 19, 45–6
Prévost, Benoît-Louis (c.1735-1809) 145
Price, Sir Uvedale (1747-1829), *Essay on the Picturesque* 175
'Primitive Hut' 150, 152
'Primitive' society 160
Primitivism 227, 228
  cult of 158
prisoners of war 97
Prisse d'Avennes, Achille-Constant-Théodore-Émile (1807-79) 136
Pritchard, Thomas Farnolls (1723-77) 206
  Masonry Dissected 41
Probst, Israel Salomon (fl.1780s) 206

Proclus (410/12-485) 33
Protestantism 23, 36, 79
  and cemeteries 288–9
  and Counter-Reformation 38
  and English Freemasonry 62
  and music of Mozart 250, 260–1, 260(n)
Prudence 298, **318**
Prüfer, Kurt (1891-1952) 96(n)
Prussia 213, 218, 223, **318**
  see also Osiris
Ptah (Egyptian Deity) 47–8, *48*, 51–2
Ptolemy I Soter (367/6-282 BC), from 305 Macedonian King of Egypt 75
Ptolemy V Epiphanes (c.210-180 BC), from 205 Macedonian King of Egypt 165
Puchot, Hector (1842-1920) 134
Pug-dogs (*Mops*) 115, 117, 118, *118*, 229, *230*
Puisieux, Jean-Baptiste de (d.1776) 148
Puławy, gardens 214–18
  Temple of Memory 215, *215*
Purchas, Samuel (c.1575-1626), *Pilgrimes* 44
Purgatory, abolition of 23
pyramids 151, 153, 158–9, 252
  in architecture 86, 155, 160, 205
  as monuments 286, *286*, *287*, 288, *288*
Pythagoras (c.569-500 BC) 21, 66, **318–19**

Quaglio, Angelo (1784-1815) 276
Quaglio, Domenico (c.1708-73) 267
Quaglio, Giulio (1764-1801) 267
Quaglio, Giuseppe (1747-1828) 267, *267*, 276
Quaglio, Simon (1795-1878) 275–6, *276*, 277
Quatremère de Quincy, Antoine-Chrysostôme (1755-1849) 155, *156*, 189
  and catacombs 195
Quatuor Coronati (early 4th century) (Four Crowned Martyrs) 8, 31, 140, 241
Queen's Tavern Arms 120

Radziwiłł family 216
Radziwiłł, Michał Gedeon (1778-1850) 223, 228
Radziwiłł, Michał Piotr (1853-1903) 228
Radziwiłł, Zygmunt (1822-92) 228
Radziwiłłowa, Aniela (1781-1808) 225
Radziwiłłowa, Róża (1788-1806) 225
Radziwiłłowa, Princess Helena (1753-1821) 215, 216, 244
  description of Arkadia 222–3
  as Freemason 214, 217
Radziwiłłowa, Krystyna Magdalena (1776-96) 222, 225
Raeburn, Henry (1756-1823) 253
Railton, William (c.1801-77) 65
Rainaldi, Carlo (1611-91) 90
Rainbow 254, **319**
Rameau, Jean-Philippe (1683-1764)
  Zaïs 265
  Zoroastre 265–6
Ramée, Daniel (1806-87) 153
Ramsay, Andrew Michael (1686-1743) 145–6
Ramsey, William de (fl.1323-d.1349) 12, 16
Raphael Sanzio (1483-1520) 91
  The Marriage of the Virgin 205
Raschdorff, Julius Karl (1823-1914) 288
Ratschky, Josef Franz von (1757-1810) 200(n), 248
Rawlinson, Richard (1690-1755) 60
Realms, of Physical World and Spirit 105
Reason 141–2
Red 144(n), 257, **319**
Reformation 61, 79
regalia, Freemasonic *xxv*, xxviii
Regensburg, cathedral 14
Le Régulateur du Maçon (1801) 271
Reid, William, Grand Secretary (fl.1727-33) 6
Reilly, Luke (fl.late 18th century) 121
Relativism 20
religion
  Enlightenment view of 144
  Secular 173
  see also Christianity; Egypt; Syncretism
religious ceremonies, Mysteries 47
religious observance, by guilds 22–4

religious toleration 25
Renaissance 34–5, 53, 79
  Humanism in 22
Rénard, Henryka (c.1685-after 1724) 230
Republicanism 144
  English 61
Restoration of the Monarchy (1660) 63
Rey, Marc-Michel (1720-80) 145
Reynolds, Dunstan (fl.1920s-30s) 135
Rheims Cathedral, labyrinth 50, *51*
Rhetoric 8, **319**
Richard II (1367-1400), r.1377-99 as King of England and Lord of Ireland 11
Richard of St Victor (d.1173) 78, 80
Richards, Franklin Thomas Grant (1872-1948) 291(n)
Right Angle 106, **319**
rituals xvii–xviii, 97–8
  Scotland 25
  secrecy of xxvii
Robaut, Félix (1799-1879) 135
Robert I 'The Bruce' (1274-1329), from 1306 King of Scots 56
Robert, Hubert (1733-1808) 148, 192, 198
Roberts, David (1796-1864) 133
Roberts, John (1928-2003) xvii
Robison, John (1739-1805), *Proofs of a Conspiracy* 292
Rochead, John Thomas (1814-78) 298(n)
Rode, August von (1751-1837) **204**, 206
Roe, Thomas (1581-1644) 36
Rohan-Guéménée, Louis-René-Édouard (1734-1803), Prince de, from 1778 Cardinal, and from 1779 Archbishop of Strasbourg 159
Roman Catholic Church
  in France 142
  in Germany 230
  hostility to Freemasonry xxiv, 143, 147
  Papal attacks on Freemasonry 116–17, 150, 292–3
  and religious observance in Middle Ages 22–3
  in Scotland 27–8, 53, 61, 63
Romantic Movement 181
Rome 8, 160, 227, 235
  Basilica of St Peter 68,76, 90, 91
  Church of *Santa Cecilia in Trastévere* 224
  Church of *Sant'Agnese in Agone* 90
  Church of *San Stefano Rotondo* 88
Romsey Abbey, Hampshire 23
Ronalds, Hugh (1759-1833) 289(n)
Roosevelt, Franklin Delano (1882-1945) 294, *295*
Roriczer (Roritzer) family 14
Roriczer (Roritzer), Matthäus *or* Mathes (c.1430/40-95) 14
Rosa, Salvator (1615-73) 175, 181
Rose **319**
  as symbol of silence 42
Rosellini, Ippolito (1800-43) 166
Rosenkreutz, Christian (allegedly 1378-1484), supposed founder of Rosicrucianism (sometimes identified with Johan Valentin Andreae 42, 43
roses, symbolism of 261–2
Rosicrucianism xxvii, 38, 42, 142, 304, **319**
  in Germany 251
Ross, Major-General Robert (1766-1814) 284, *284*
Ross, Thomas (1839-1930) 57
Rosslyn (Roslin)
  pillars/piers 68–9
  St Matthew's Chapel 31, 32
Rostrevor, County Down, Ross monument 284, *284*
round churches 88
Rousseau, Jean-Jacques (1712-78) 186, 188, 198–9, 230
  La Nouvelle Héloïse 209
  Le Devin du Village 246
Roussel, Raymond (1877-1933) 169
Royal Arch 98, **319**
Royal Institute of British Architects, Portland Place 302, *303*
Royal Institution, London 244
Royal Masonic Cyclopaedia 149
Royal patrons 10
  Scotland 27–32
Royal Society 64, 251
Rudolf I (1218-91), crowned German King 1273, *called* Emperor 17
Rudolf II (1552-1612), from 1576 Holy Roman Emperor 27, 35

Rule 31, 283, **319**
Rumford, Graf von *see* Thompson
Rykwert, Joseph (b.1926) 199

Sabran, Françoise Éléonore Dejean de Manville, Comtesse de (1749-1827) 291
Sachs, Hans (1494-1576) 30
Sacy, Baron Antoine-Isaac Silvestre de (1758-1838) 166
Saffron Walden, Essex 149
St Albans Cathedral, Hertfordshire 51
St Clair Charters 31–2
St Clair, William (1700-78) 32
St John the Almoner 31, 239, **319**
St John (Baptist & Evangelist) 30–1, 237, 239, **319**
St John's Masonry 30, 262, **319**
St Leger, Arthur (d.1727), from 1703 1st Viscount Doneraile 115
St Louis, Missouri 136
St Victor, Hugh of (c.1096-1141) 9, 21
St Victor, Richard of (d.1173) 78, 80
Saint-Léon, Étienne-Martin (1860-after 1900) 16
Saint-Meaux, Charles-François Viel de (1745-1819) 129
Saint-Pierre, Bernardin de (1737-1814) 189
Saints 13–14, 22–3, 30–1, 40
Sallengre, Albert-Henri de (1694-1723) 63
Saltmarsh, John (1908-74) xxiii
Salzburg 230
Samyn, Adolphe (1842-1903) 134
San Antonio, Texas 136
Sandby, Thomas (1721-98) xvi, 121–5, *123*
sandstones 2
Sarasin, Jacob (1742-1802) 200
Savary, Claude-Étienne (1750-88) 166
Saxe-Gotha-Altenburg, Ernst II (1745-1804), from 1772 Duke of 252
Saxe-Weimar, Karl August (1757-1828), from 1815 Grand Duke of 215(n)
Scalpay, Eilean Glas, lighthouse 286
Scamozzi, Vincenzo (1548-1616) 29
Scandinavia, Egyptianising iconography 135
Scanlan, Matthew D. J. (b.1964) 64
Scannell, Thomas Bartholomew (1854-1917) 291
Schachmann, Karl Adolf Gottlob, Freiherr von (1725-89) 302
Schachtner, Johann Andreas (1731-95) 246
Schaw Statutes, Scotland 13, 25, 53, **319**
Schaw, William (1549/50-1602) 25–6, 27–32, 29, 52
Schikaneder, Emanuel Johann Joseph Baptist (1751-1812) xxvi, 66, 254
Babylons Piramiden 256
Der Höllenberg 256
Das Labyrinth 256
Der Stein der Weisen 256
and *Die Zauberflöte* 246, 260, 263, 266
Schiller, Johann Christoph Friedrich von (1759-1805) 142, 264
Schinkel, Karl Friedrich (1781-1841) xxvi, 288, **301**
and 'Greek' Thomson 296
sets for *Die Zauberflöte* 267, *268*, *269*, *270*, *271*, *272*, *273*, *274*
sets for *Olimpia* 275, 276
Schittlersberg, Augustin Veith Edler von (1751-1817) **246**, 252
Schlotterbeck, Wilhelm Friedrich (1770-1819) 208
Schoch, Johann Georg (1758-1826) 205
Schoch, Johann Leopold Ludwig (1728-93) 205
Schoch, Leopoldine Luise (1767-1813) 213
Schönau, Abbey Church 13
Schrattenbach, Sigismund III Christoph, Graf von (1698-1771), from 1753 Prince-Archbishop of Salzburg 247(n)
Schreker, Franz (1878-1934) 38
Schubart, Christian Friedrich Daniel (1739-91) 259
Schubert, Franz Peter (1797-1828), *Winterreise* 280
Schwetzingen, garden 230–44, *232*, 245, 306
allusions to Minerva 233, 244
allusions to Sun and Moon 233
Bath House 233–4, *234*
Botanic Temple 235, *236*, 237
End of the World diorama 234–5, *234*
Freemasonic references 237–8, 242–3
Minerva Temple 237
'Mosque' 238, *239*, *239*, *240*, 241–2, *241*, *242*, *243*
Obelisk 235
plan *231*
'Roman Water Fort' 235
Ruined Aqueduct 235
Temple of Apollo 234, 235, *236*
Temple of Mercury 237–8, *238*
'Turkish Garden' 241–2, *241*, *242*
views from 244
Scientific Revolution 61, 63
Sckell, Friedrich Ludwig von (1759-1832) 232, 244
Scone, Abbey of 27
Scot, Reginald (c.1538-99) 42
Scotland **319**
'Cowans' 2
early Freemasonry 2, 24–7, 55–9
early Masons in 13, 16
influence on Freemasonry 63
Neo-Classicism 296–9
proof of memory 39
relations with England 63
rituals in 60–1
Royal patrons 27–32
sundials 57, 57, 58, 59, 304–5
see also Lodges
Scott, Robert, bookseller (c.1632-1709/10) 7
Scott, Sir Giles Gilbert (1880-1960) 128
Scottish Enlightenment 144, 155
Scottish Reformation 16
Scriptores Historiae Augustae 201
Seal of Solomon 295, **319**
Second World War 293
secret signs 5, 11
Secular Religion 173
Sellier, François-Noel (1737-c.1824) 161
Senex, John (c.1678-1740) xviii, 144
Sennacherib, Assyrian King (r.c.705-681 BC) 74
serfs and serfdom 12
Sering, John (fl.1590s) 28
Serlio, Sebastiano (1475-1554) 105(n)
serpents 233, **319**
twisted round columns 92
Séthos, Egyptian prince 157–8, 256
and *Thamos* 246
Seti (or Sethos) I, Pharaoh (r.c.1290-c.1279 BC) 129
Seton, Alexander (1556-1622), from 1605 1st Earl of Dunfermline 28
Seton, Alexander, Alchemist (d.1604) 28(n)
Seton family 29, 68–9
Seton, George (c.1530-86), from 1549 5th Lord Seton 28
Seton, Robert (c.1552-1603), from 1586 6th Lord Seton and, from 1600, 1st Earl of Winton 28
setting-maul 107, **319**
Seven **319**
steps *113*, *114*, 271
see also Liberal Arts
Seven Wonders of the World 19
Seville, Cathedral of Santa Maria de la Asunción 69
Seyler, Friederike Sophie (née Sparmann) (1738-89) 253(n)
Shaftesbury, Anthony Ashley Cooper (1671-1713), from 1699 3rd Earl of 179
Shenstone, William (1714-63) 181, 185, 188, 209
Shepherd, Henry (c.1783-1858) 289
Shepherd, John (c.1764-1836) 289
Sherar, Robert Forbes (fl.1880-1910) 136
Sheshbazzar, Prince of Judah (fl.c.530s BC) 75
Shibboleth 149, **319**
Shipwrights Company, play 9
Short, Richard Thomas (c.1870-after 1916) 136
Shotover Park, Oxfordshire 179, *179*
Shovel 257, **319**
Sidney, Algernon (1622-83), *Discourses* 178
Sierakowski, Józef (1765-1831) 215, 218
Sigüenza, Fray José de (c.1544-1606) 82
Silence 112
Silvestre, Louis de (1675-1760) 230
Simplicity 160
Neo-Classical 149–50
Sinclair (St Clair) of Roslin, family 31–2
Sinclair (St Clair) of Roslin, William (d.1602) 31
Sinclair (St Clair), William (c.1408-80), from 1434 3rd Earl of Orkney and from 1455 1st Earl of Caithness 31
Sinclair (St Clair), William (son) (d.1650) 31
Sippara, City of the Sun 65
skirret 109, **319–20**
skull and crossbones 107, **320**
Slade, Alexander (fl.1754) 110
Slave Trade, abolition 11–12
Slezer, John (d.1717) xviii
Sloane MS 45
Smirke, Robert (1780-1867) 284
Smith, Adam (1723-90) 144
Snoek, Johannes (Jan) Augustinus Maria (b.1946) 46, 60, 238(n)
snuff box 111
Snyers, Arthur (1865-1942) 135, *135*
Soane, Sir John (1752-1837) xvi, xxv, *xxv*, 125–30, *125*, 299–300
mausoleum 128, *128*
Museum 128, 133
Sobieska, Princess Maria Clementina of Poland (1702-35) 144(n)
social class, Freemasonry and 62, 63
Soissons, Louis-Emmanuel-Jean-Guy de Savoie-Carignan (1890-1962) 302
Solomon, King (r.c.970-c.928 BC) 16, 46–7, 66, 72–3, 74, 93
Solomon's Temple xvi, xvii, 12, 21, 55, 72–4, 93–6, 155, **320**
and circular Temples 205
destruction 74–5, 89
mnemonics of 297
pillars 66, 67
recreation of/myth of 26
see also Jewish Temple
song-book, Masonic 271
Sonnenfels, Joseph von (1733-1817) 250
Sonnleithner, Leopold von (1797-1873) 266
Sophia, Princess of Great Britain and Ireland (1777-1848) 289
Soufflot, Jacques-Germain (1713-80) 148, 150
Church of *Sainte-Geneviève* 195
South 253, **320**
Speculative Masonry 18, 22, **320**
evolution from 'Operative' Lodges 62
origin of term 19
and Scientific Revolution 63
tracing-boards 99–101
Speer, Albert (1905-81) 76, 160
Speijk, Jan Carel Josephus van (1802-31) 285
Spenser, Edmund (c.1552-99) 35, 181
Speth, George William (1847-1901) 18
sphere, as emblem 173
sphinx 155, 203, 306, **320**
Spinoza, Baruch (1632-77) 144
spirals **320**
on columns 68, 88, 91–2
vines as variant 92
Spontini, Gaspare (1774-1851), *Olimpia* 274, 275, 276
Spottiswoode, Andrew (1786-1866) 288
square 35, 106, 107, 109, **320**
and compasses 320
Stadler, Anton Paul (1753-1812) 249
Stadler, Johann Nepomuk Franz (1755-1804) 249
Staggi, Gioacchino (fl.1781-96) 221
Staggi, Pietro (fl.1780s) 224
Stalin, Joseph Vissarionovich (1879-1953) xxiv, 294–5, *295*
Stamp, Gavin Mark (b.1948) 296
Stanisław Antoni Poniatowski (1732-98), r.1764-95 as King Stanisław II Augustus of Poland 214, 216
Stanisław Leszczyński (1677-1766), r.1704-9 and again 1733-6 as King Stanisław I of Poland before becoming (1736) Duke of Lorraine and Bar 117
star **320**
blazing 233, 258, *271*, **309**
Stavisky, Serge Alexandre (1888-1934), *Affaire* of 294
Stecka, Aleksandra (1796-1864) 228
steps 102, **320**
seven *113*, *114*, 271

three 101, 105, 112, 261, 283
Stevenson, Alan (1807-65) 286
Stevenson, David (b.1942) xvii, xxiv, 12, 39, 106(n)
on Masonry in Scotland 24–5, 52–3
on sundials 59
Stewart, Alwen Trevor (b.1943) **97**
Stewart, Dugald (1753-1828) 288(n)
Stirling
Castle 27
Palace of 24
Stone, Nicholas (1587-1647) 60
Stow, John (1524/5-1605) 19
Stowe, Buckinghamshire 175, *176*, *176*, 177, 179–80
Elysian Fields 185
Strang, John (1795-1863) **175**, 289
Strassburg (Strasbourg)
cathedral 13, 14, 17
Place Kléber 203
Strauss, Richard (1864-1949) 249(n)
Strength 43, 67, 70, 105, 120, 136, 257, 262, **320**
Stroganov, Count Aleksandr Sergeyevich (1734-1811) 147
Stroud, Dorothy (1910-97) xv, xvi
Stukeley, William (1687-1765) 6
Sturt, John (1658-1730) 19
editions of Perrault's *Treatise...* xviii
Sublime, the 182
Sulzer, Johann Georg (1720-79) 188
Summerson, Sir John Newenham (1904-92) 195
Sun and Moon **316**
motifs/emblems 105, 235, 279
sundials
lectern 57–8, *58*
multi-faceted 58, *58*
obelisk 57, *57*
Supports 262, **320**
Surenhuis (Surenhusius), Guglielmus (Willem) (c.1664-1729) 83, *83*
Sussex, Prince Augustus Frederick (1773-1843), from 1801 Duke of xvi, 126, 129, 289-90
Sutherland, Gordon John (1891-1958) 135
Sweden, Norrköping, Lodge 135
Swieten, Freiherr Gottfried van (1733-1803) 251, 260(n), 265
Switzerland
allusions to 190
Loge L'Amitié, La Chaux-de-Fonds 299
symbolism xvi, 21, 34, 36
'Greek' Thomson's use of 296, 297
Syncretism 21, 36, 46–52, 67, 203
labyrinths 50
Synthesis 245

T∴G∴A∴O∴T∴U∴ **320**
Tablets of Cebes 244–5
Tablets (Ten Commandments) 107–8
Tacitus, Cornelius (c.56-c.118) 177
Taj Mahal 46
Talmon, Jacob Laib (1916-80) 250
Talmud 35, 75–6
Tasselled Cord (*Houpe Dentelée* or *Cordon de Veuve*) 100, 103, 271, **314**, **320**
Tau 297, *297*, 320, **320**
taverns 120
'Taxil' *see* Jogand-Pagès
Taylor, René 81, 82
TBC, for TuBal Cain 107, **321**
Telamones 260, *260*, **320**
Tell Tayinat, temple 66
Temperance 167, 235, 241, **320**
Tempesta, Antonio (1555-1630) 142(n)
temple
use for non-Roman church 210
use for Protestant church 79
see also Jewish Temple; Solomon's Temple
Temple, Henry (1672/3-1757), from 1723 1st Viscount Palmerston 183
Temple, Richard (1675-1749), from 1718 1st Viscount Cobham 176
Terrasson, Abbé Jean (1670-1750) 66
Séthos 155, 157–8, 217, 256, 260
Tesi, Mauro Antonio (1730-66) 247
Raccoltà di Disegni Originali 274
Tessellated Border 99, *271*, **320**
Tetragrammaton 224, **320**
Thatched House Tavern, London xvi
The Two Earliest Masonic MSS 6
Thebes, Egyptian temple 156
Themistius (c.317-c.388) 147
Theocritus, Greek poet (fl. 3rd century

BC) 184, 188
Theodosius I (c.346-395), from 379
  Roman Emperor 201(n)
Theological Virtues, Three 90, **320**
Theyer, Charles (b.1651) 7
Theyer, John (c.1598-1673) 7
Thibierge, Habert (fl.18th century) 302
Thiele, Carl Friedrich (c.1780-1836) 267-8
Thomae, Johann Benjamin (1682-1731) 117
Thomas the Apostle, St (1st cent AD) 31
Thomas, Walter (fl.late 19th-early 20th century) 184
Thompson, Sir Benjamin (1753-1814), from 1792 Count Rumford of the Holy Roman Empire 243-4
Thomson, Alexander 'Greek' (1817-75) 227, 296-9
Thomson, James (1700-48) 188
  The Castle of Indolence 181
  The Seasons 220-1
Thornton, Peter (1925-2007) xxi
Thoth, Egyptian deity 22
Three
  Globes **320**
  Steps 101, 105, 112, 261, 283, **320**
Thun, Franz Josef, Graf (1734-1800) 248
Thun, Maria Wilhelmine, Gräfin (1744-1800) 248(n)
Thury, Louis-Étienne-François Héricart-Ferrand (1776-1854), from 1825 Vicomte de 195
Thynne, Sir Thomas (1640-1714), from 1682 1st Viscount Weymouth 192(n)
Till, Nicholas (b.1955) 251
Titian (Tiziano Vecellio) (c.1485-1576) 175
Titus, Emperor (r.79-81 AD) 76
Tivoli, Italy 233
  Canopus 201, 228
  Hadrian's Villa at 201-2
toast rack 109
Tocqueville, Alexis Charles Henri Maurice Clérel, Comte de (1805-59) 141
Toledo, Juan Bautista (c.1515-67) 81
tolerance 64
tomb, Egyptian (Desprez) 251
Tongue, Sutherland, obelisk-sundial 57
Tools 109
  depictions of 106, *108*, *110*
  as motifs 108
torquetum 57-8, *58*
Tournes, Jean de (1539-1615) 79
Tower of Babel 14
tracing, use of term 98-9
tracing boards 98-113, *106*, **320**
  of First Degree 105-6, *107*
  of Second Degree 106, *107*
  of Third Degree 106-7, *107*
Traetta, Tommaso Michele Francesco Saverio (1727-79), *Armida* 259
Traherne, Thomas (c.1637-74) 34
Travenol, Louis-Antoine (1698 *or* 1708-83) 93, *93*
  Nouveau Cathéchisme 102-3, *103*, *104*, *105*
Trembecki, Stanisław (c.1739-1812) 215
Trevor-Roper, Hugh Redwald (1914-2003), from 1979 Baron Dacre of Glanton 35-6
triangle 35, 237, 242, 283, 295, **321**
  motif 90, 106
Tringham, William (fl.1760-91) 110
Trinity College, Dublin MS 43
Triple Tau within Triangle 283, *283*, **321**
Trithemius, Johannes (1462-1516) 14
trowel 45-6, **321**
Troy, John Thomas (1739-1823), from 1786 RC Archbishop of Dublin 292
Tschirnhaus, Ehrenfried Walther von (1651-1708) 117
TuBal Cain 107, **321**
Tübingen, University of 35
Tuft, Laced or Indented (*La Houpe Dentelée*) 100, 103, *271*
Tufton, Cecily (d.1653), from 1612 Countess of Rutland 28(n)
Tulla, Johann Gottfried (1770-1828) 237
Tuscan Order **321**, **321**
Tuscania, Italy, Church of Santa Maria Maggiore 68
Tyler, William (d.1801) 122, *124*
Tyminiecki, Konstanty (1767-1814) 216
Tyrrell, James (1642-1718) 178

Discourses 179

Ulster, Masonic Halls 137, *139*
United States
  Classical lodges 136
  Freemasons in xvi-xvii
  and Masonic Style 301-2
  Roman Catholic Church in 293
  see also New York; Washington
Unlawful Oaths (Ireland) Act (1823) 292
Unterberger, Ignaz (1742-97) 249, *249*, 251, *261*
Urbanitatis 8
Uvarov, Count (1786-1855) 129

Valenciennes, Masonic Temple 135
Valois, Jeanne de Saint-Rémy de (1756-91) 159
Vanbrugh, Sir John (1664-1726) 176
Vatablus, Franciscus (d.1547), and Temple 79-80, *79*
Vaudoyer, Antoine-Laurent-Thomas (1756-1846) 152, 195
Vaudoyer, Léon (1803-72) 152
Vaughan, Diana *see* Jogand-Pagès
Vaughan, Thomas (1622-66) 43
vaults 237
Veil, Louis Compiègne de (1637-c.1710) 90
  De Cultu Divino 77-8
Verbueeken, Henri (1848-1926) 134
Vernet, Claude-Joseph (1714-89) 148
Verrocosus, Quintus Fabius Maximus (d.203 BC) 10
Verstegan (*alias* Rowlands), Richard (fl.1565-1620) 178
Vestier, Archimède (1794-1859) 303
Vestier, Nicholas-Jacques-Antoine (1765-1816) 302-3
Vestier, Phidias (1796-1874) 303
Vézélay, Abbey of the Sainte-Madeleine 15
Victoria (1819-1901), from 1837 Queen of Great Britain and Ireland and, from 1877, Empress of India 289
Victoria, Australia
  Emulation Lodge 135
  Sandringham Masonic Centre 135
  Zetland Temple 135
Vidler, Anthony (b.1941) 155, 199
  on *fabriques* 209-10
Vienna 61
  Belvedere Palace 143
  Karlskirche 69, 87-91, *88*, *89*, 266
  Masonic Lodges 247-51, 253, 261
    reduction in numbers 252
    Zur wahren Eintracht 247-8, 251
    Zur Wohltätigkeit 247, 248, 251
Villa d'Este, Italy 203
Villalpando, Juan Bautista (1552-1608), and Temple 80-3, *81*, *82*
Villette, Charles-Michel de la, Marquis du Plessis (1736-93) 195
Villette, Rétaux de (fl. late-18th century) 159
Villiers, George (1592-1628), from 1623 1st Duke of Buckingham 28(n)
Vincent, Antoine (d.1568) 79
Virgil (Publius Vergilius Maro) (70-19 BC) 181, 184, 185, 188
Vitruvius Britannicus xviii, 84
Vitruvius (Marcus Vitruvius Pollio) (fl. later 1st century BC) 20(n)
Vogel, Zygmunt (1764-1826) 224
Voltaire *see* Arouet, François-Marie
Voragine, Jacobus de (c.1229-98) 8(n)

Wagner, Wilhelm Richard (1813-83) 30
Wailly, Charles de (1730-98) 149
Waite, Arthur Edward (1857-1942) 293
Walker, Sarah (1739-92) 244(n)
Walker, William (fl.19th century) 283
Walpole, Horatio (Horace) (1717-97), from 1791 4th Earl of Orford 176, 180
  and Gothic 'Gloomths' 181
Walpole, Sir Robert (1676-1745), from 1742 1st Earl of Orford 62, 144, 176
Warmenbol, Eugène L. C. (b.1956) 116(n),134(n), 136, 217(n)
Warren, Charles (fl.1760s) 108, *111*
Warsaw
  Duchy of 223
  Eden Adoption Lodge 217
  Grand Adoption Lodge 214
  Grand Charity Lodge of the Grand Orient 214, 217

Lodge of the Temple of Isis 218
  Mniejszy Palace 217, *217*
Warwick, 3 High Street 134
Was sceptre 48, *48*
Washington, DC xvi-xvii
  Capitol 302, *302*
  Scottish Rite lodge 136
Washington, George (1732-99) xvi, 254
Wastell, John (c.1460-c.1515) xxv
water
  in landscape gardens 206, 213, 235
  sacral connotations 202
Waterfall 106, **321**
Watkin, David John (b.1941) xv, xxv, 127
  on Cockerell 130
Watson, William Stewart (1800-70) 254, *262*
Watts, Isaac (1674-1748) 64(n)
Webber, Frederick (fl.early 20th century) 136
Weber, Eugen Joseph (1925-2007) 293
Webster, Nesta Helen (1876-1960) 291
Węgierski, Tomasz Kajetan (1756-87) 215
Weimar
  Fürstengruft 301
  gardens at 215(n)
  Hoftheater 278, *278*
Weishaupt, Johann Adam (1748-1830) 252
Weiskern, Friedrich Wilhelm (1710-68) 246
Wellesley, Richard (1760-1842), from 1781 2nd Earl of Mornington and from 1799 Marquess Wellesley 284
Wellington, Arthur Wellesley (1769-1852), from 1814 1st Duke of, 284
Wend, Christoph Gottlieb (d.1745) 246
West, Gilbert (1703-56) 177(n)
West India and American Lodge, *Queen's Tavern Arms* 120
Westminster, Church of St Mary, Bourne Street 23
Wharton, Philip James Wharton (1698-1731), from 1716 Jacobite Duke of Northumberland and from 1718 Duke of 119, *119*
Whigs and Whiggery
  Freemasonry associated with 61, 64, 119, 142, 144, 146
  landscape and 179, 181
Whiting, Charles (fl.1830s) 287
Wichtl, Friedrich (1872-1922) 295
Wiegand, Christian Friedrich (1752-1832) 213
Wieland, Christoph Martin (1733-1813) 211, 215(n), 246
  Dschinnistan oder Auserlesene Feen- und Geister-Mährchen 246
Wilde, Oscar (1854-1900) 255
Wilhelm II (1859-1941), r.1888-1918 as German Emperor and King of Prussia 288
Wilkins, William (1778-1839) 132-3
William III and II, Prince of Orange (1650-1702), from 1689 King of England, Scotland, and Ireland (Joint Monarch with Mary II until 1694) 63
William IV (1765-1837), from 1830 King of Great Britain, Ireland, and Hanover 289
William of Malmesbury (c.1090-c.1142), *Gesta Regum Anglorum* 8
Williams, William James (1864-1949) 3
Willson, Thomas (c.1814-*after* 1882) 286, *287*, 288
Willson, Thomas John (1824-1903) 286(n)
Wilmshurst, Walter Leslie (1867-1939) 108
Wilson, Edward 9
Winchester, cathedral 8(n), 23
Winckelmann, Johann Joachim (1717-68) 209
Winding Stair 106, **321**
Windrin, James Hamilton (1840-1919) 136
Wing, Rutland 149
Winter, Peter (1754-1825) 256
Wirtemberska, Maria Anna (1768-1854), *Malvina* 215, 216
Witt, Reginald Eldred (1903-80) 1
Wocher, Marquard (1758-1830) 182
Wolf-Ferrari, Ermanno (1876-1948) 255(n)
Wölfl, Joseph (1773-1812) 256

women
  as Freemasons 113-18, 214
  'Moll' at Canterbury Lodge 116, *116*
Wood, John, the Elder (1704-54), Architect 84, *84*
  The Origin of Building... xvi
Woodford, Adolphus Frederick Arthur (1821-87) 7
Woodford, James (1893-1976) 302
Woodhouselee, Penicuik, Midlothian, lectern-sundial 58
Word *see* Mason Word; Master's Word
Wordsworth, William (1770-1850) 205
Wörlitz in Anhalt, Germany 144, 204, 205-14, 300
  Adelaide (Matthisson) 211
  Der Stein (island) 206, *207*, *208*, 209
  Eiserne Brücke 206
  Elbewall 211
  Gothic House 213, *213*
  Gothic Revival Church 211, *211*
  Labyrinth 206
  La Nouvelle Héloïse 209
  Nymphaeum 210-11, *210*
  Rousseauinsel 209, *210*
  Synagogue 210, 211, *211*
  Temple of Memory 300
  Temple of Venus 212-13
  'Vesuvius' *208*, 209
  'Villa Hamilton' 209, *209*
  Wahlverwandtschaften, Die (Goethe) 204, 212
  Warning Altar 211, *211*
  way of the mystagogue 206-7, *208*
Wornum, George Grey (1888-1957) 302
Wotton, Sir Henry (1568-1639) 20
Wranitsky, Paul (1756-1808), *Oberon der Elfkönig* 253
Wrek, Thomas (fl.1354-93) 3
Wren, Christopher (1632-1723) 3, 20, 60, 87
Wright, Joseph, of Derby (1734-97) 124-5
Wright, Michael (1936-2006) xx
Wright, Thomas (1711-86) 239
Württemberg-Mömpelgard, Friedrich II Eugen (1732-97), Duke of 203
Würzburg, Cathedral 67-8, *68*
Wy, Henry (fl.c.1324-6) 51
Wynford, William de (fl.1360-d.1405) 16
Wynne, Justine, Countess Rosenberg-Orsini (1737-91) 159

yarn, symbolism of 49
Yates, Frances Amelia (1899-1981) **1**
  Giordano Bruno 39
  The Art of Memory 39, 52
Yeveley (Yevele), Henry (c.1320/30-1400) xxv, 4, 16
York Minster, Lodge at 12
Young, Edward (1683-1765) 181, 192
  Night Thoughts 182-4, 209
Young, Dr Thomas (1773-1829) 165
Yvelines, France 199
Yvon, Abbé Claude (1714-91) 145

Zanth, Karl Ludwig Wilhelm von (1796-1857) 133(n)
Zauberflöte, Die (Mozart) xxvi, 206, 212, 250, 254-9
  Egyptian architecture 267-80
  Egyptian influences 256, *257*, 260, 263
  garden scenes 266
  incidence of three 259-60, 263
  libretto 257-8, *257*, 259-66
  music of 259-66
  Orpheus connection 263
  Pamina 260, 262, 263
  Papagena 260
  Papageno 256, 260
  Queen of the Night 255, 262-3
  Sarastro 256-7, 260, 262
  stage sets 267-80
  Tamino 259-60, 262, 263-4
  Two Men in Black Armour 250, 260
Zerubbabel **321**
  Temple 75, **320**
Zetland, Thomas Dundas (1795-1873), from 1839 2nd Earl of 131
Ziegenhagen, Franz Heinrich (1753-1806) 252
Zocher, Jan David (1791-1870) 285
Zodiac 41, 53
Zoroaster (Zarathustra) 65-6
Zug, Simon Gottlieb (Szymon Bogumił) (1733-1807) 214, 216-17, 221-2
Zwingli, Ulrich (1484-1531) 79